T0332454

# Cross–Disciplinary Applications of Artificial Intelligence and Pattern Recognition:

## Advancing Technologies

Vijay Kumar Mago
*Simon Fraser University, Canada*

Nitin Bhatia
*DAV College, India*

A volume in the Advances in
Computational Intelligence and Robotics
(ACIR) Book Series

Information Science
**REFERENCE**

| | |
|---|---|
| Managing Director: | Lindsay Johnston |
| Senior Editorial Director: | Heather Probst |
| Book Production Manager: | Sean Woznicki |
| Development Manager: | Joel Gamon |
| Development Editor: | Mike Killian |
| Acquisitions Editor: | Erika Gallagher |
| Typesetters: | Lisandro Gonzalez |
| Cover Design: | Nick Newcomer, Lisandro Gonzalez |

Published in the United States of America by
Information Science Reference (an imprint of IGI Global)
701 E. Chocolate Avenue
Hershey PA 17033
Tel: 717-533-8845
Fax: 717-533-8661
E-mail: cust@igi-global.com
Web site: http://www.igi-global.com

Library of Congress Cataloging-in-Publication Data

Cross-disciplinary applications of artificial intelligence and pattern recognition : advancing technologies / Vijay Kumar Mago and Nitin Bhatia, editors.
   p. cm.
  Summary: "This book provides a common platform for researchers to present theoretical and applied research findings for enhancing and developing intelligent systems, discussing advances in and applications of pattern recognition technologies and artificial intelligence"-- Provided by publisher.
  Includes bibliographical references and index.
  ISBN 978-1-61350-429-1 (hardcover) -- ISBN 978-1-61350-430-7 (ebook) -- ISBN 978-1-61350-431-4 (print & perpetual access) 1. Pattern recognition systems. 2. Artificial intelligence. I. Mago, V. K. II. Bhatia, Nitin, 1978-
  TK7882.P3C66 2012
  006.3--dc23
                                     2011046541

This book is published in the IGI Global book series Advances in Computational Intelligence and Robotics (ACIR) Book Series (ISSN: 2327-0411; eISSN: 2327-042X)


British Cataloguing in Publication Data
A Cataloguing in Publication record for this book is available from the British Library.

# Advances in Computational Intelligence and Robotics (ACIR) Book Series

ISSN: 2327-0411
EISSN: 2327-042X

## MISSION

While intelligence is traditionally a term applied to humans and human cognition, technology has progressed in such a way to allow for the development of intelligent systems able to simulate many human traits. With this new era of simulated and artificial intelligence, much research is needed in order to continue to advance the field and also to evaluate the ethical and societal concerns of the existence of artificial life and machine learning.

The **Advances in Computational Intelligence and Robotics (ACIR) Book Series** encourages scholarly discourse on all topics pertaining to evolutionary computing, artificial life, computational intelligence, machine learning, and robotics. ACIR presents the latest research being conducted on diverse topics in intelligence technologies with the goal of advancing knowledge and applications in this rapidly evolving field.

## COVERAGE

- Adaptive & Complex Systems
- Agent Technologies
- Artificial Intelligence
- Cognitive Informatics
- Computational Intelligence
- Natural Language Processing
- Neural Networks
- Pattern Recognition
- Robotics
- Synthetic Emotions

IGI Global is currently accepting manuscripts for publication within this series. To submit a proposal for a volume in this series, please contact our Acquisition Editors at Acquisitions@igi-global.com or visit: http://www.igi-global.com/publish/.

# Titles in this Series

*For a list of additional titles in this series, please visit: www.igi-global.com*

*Intelligent Technologies and Techniques for Pervasive Computing*
Kostas Kolomvatsos (University of Athens, Greece) Christos Anagnostopoulos (Ionian University, Greece) and Stathes Hadjiefthymiades (University of Athens, Greece)
Information Science Reference • copyright 2013 • 349pp • H/C (ISBN: 9781466640382) • US $195.00 (our price)

*Mobile Ad Hoc Robots and Wireless Robotic Systems Design and Implementation*
Raul Aquino Santos (University of Colima, Mexico) Omar Lengerke (Universidad Autónoma de Bucaramanga, Colombia) and Arthur Edwards-Block (University of Colima, Mexico)
Information Science Reference • copyright 2013 • 347pp • H/C (ISBN: 9781466626584) • US $190.00 (our price)

*Intelligent Planning for Mobile Robotics Algorithmic Approaches*
Ritu Tiwari (ABV – Indian Institute of Information, India) Anupam Shukla (ABV – Indian Institute of Information, India) and Rahul Kala (School of Systems Engineering, University of Reading, UK)
Information Science Reference • copyright 2013 • 320pp • H/C (ISBN: 9781466620742) • US $195.00 (our price)

*Simultaneous Localization and Mapping for Mobile Robots Introduction and Methods*
Juan-Antonio Fernández-Madrigal (Universidad de Málaga, Spain) and José Luis Blanco Claraco (Universidad de Málaga, Spain)
Information Science Reference • copyright 2013 • 497pp • H/C (ISBN: 9781466621046) • US $195.00 (our price)

*Prototyping of Robotic Systems Applications of Design and Implementation*
Tarek Sobh (University of Bridgeport, USA) and Xingguo Xiong (University of Bridgeport, USA)
Information Science Reference • copyright 2012 • 321pp • H/C (ISBN: 9781466601765) • US $195.00 (our price)

*Cross-Disciplinary Applications of Artificial Intelligence and Pattern Recognition Advancing Technologies*
Vijay Kumar Mago (Simon Fraser University, Canada) and Nitin Bhatia (DAV College, India)
Information Science Reference • copyright 2012 • 784pp • H/C (ISBN: 9781613504291) • US $195.00 (our price)

*Handbook of Research on Ambient Intelligence and Smart Environments Trends and Perspectives*
Nak-Young Chong (Japan Advanced Institute of Science and Technology, Japan) and Fulvio Mastrogiovanni (University of Genova, Italy)
Information Science Reference • copyright 2011 • 770pp • H/C (ISBN: 9781616928575) • US $265.00 (our price)

*Particle Swarm Optimization and Intelligence Advances and Applications*
Konstantinos E. Parsopoulos (University of Ioannina, Greece) and Michael N. Vrahatis (University of Patras, Greece)
Information Science Reference • copyright 2010 • 328pp • H/C (ISBN: 9781615206667) • US $180.00 (our price)

www.igi-global.com

701 E. Chocolate Ave., Hershey, PA 17033
Order online at www.igi-global.com or call 717-533-8845 x100
To place a standing order for titles released in this series, contact: cust@igi-global.com
Mon-Fri 8:00 am - 5:00 pm (est) or fax 24 hours a day 717-533-8661

# Table of Contents

# Detailed Table of Contents

**Chapter 1**
*Rigas Kouskouridas, Democritus University of Thrace, Greece*
*Antonios Gasteratos, Democritus University of Thrace, Greece*

Recognizing objects in a scene is a fundamental task in image understanding. The recent advances in robotics and related technologies have placed more challenges and stricter requirements to this issue. In such applications, robots must be equipped with a sense of location and direction with a view to the efficient accomplishment of navigation or demanding pick and place tasks. In addition, spatial information is required in surveillance processes where recognized targets are located in the working space of the robot. Furthermore, accurate perception of depth is mandatory in driver assistance applications. This chapter presents several recently proposed methods capable of first recognizing objects and then providing their spatial information in cluttered environments.

**Chapter 2**
*Carlos Eduardo Thomaz, Centro Universitário da FEI, Brazil*
*Vagner do Amaral, Centro Universitário da FEI, Brazil*
*Gilson Antonio Giraldi, Laboratório Nacional de Computação Científica, Brazil*
*Edson Caoru Kitani, Universidade de São Paulo, Brazil*
*João Ricardo Sato, Universidade Federal do ABC, Brazil*
*Duncan Fyfe Gillies, Imperial College London, UK*

This chapter describes a multi-linear discriminant method of constructing and quantifying statistically significant changes on human identity photographs. The approach is based on a general multivariate two-stage linear framework that addresses the small sample size problem in high-dimensional spaces. Starting with a 2D data set of frontal face images, the authors determine a most characteristic direction of change by organizing the data according to the patterns of interest. These experiments on publicly available face image sets show that the multi-linear approach does produce visually plausible results for gender, facial expression and aging facial changes in a simple and efficient way. The authors believe that such approach could be widely applied for modeling and reconstruction in face recognition and possibly in identifying subjects after a lapse of time.

This chapter focuses on the usage of image orthogonal moments as discrimination features in pattern recognition applications and discusses their main properties. Initially, the ability of the moments to carry information of an image with minimum redundancy is studied, while their capability to enclose distinctive information that uniquely describes the image's content is also examined. Along these directions, the computational formulas of the most representative moment families will be defined analytically and the form of the corresponding moment invariants in each case will be derived. Appropriate experiments have taken place in order to investigate the description capabilities of each moment family, by applying them in several benchmark problems.

# Chapter 4

Triangulation is a fundamental problem in computer vision that consists of estimating the 3D position of a point of the scene from the estimates of its image projections on some cameras and from the estimates of the projection matrices of these cameras. This chapter addresses multiple view L2 triangulation, i.e. triangulation for vision systems with a generic number of cameras where the sought 3D point is searched by minimizing the L2 norm of the image reprojection error. The authors consider the standard case where estimates of all the image points are available (referring to such a case as certain triangulation), and consider also the case where some of such estimates are not available for example due to occlusions (referring to such a case as uncertain triangulation). In the latter case, it is supposed that the unknown image points belong to known regions such as line segments or ellipses. For these problems, the authors propose a unified methodology that exploits the fundamental matrices among the views and provides a candidate 3D point through the solution of a convex optimization problem based on linear matrix inequalities (LMIs). Moreover, the chapter provides a simple condition that allows one to immediately establish whether the found 3D point is optimal. Various examples with synthetic and real data illustrate the proposed technique, showing in particular that the obtained 3D point is almost always optimal in practice, and that its computational time is indeed small.

# Chapter 5

Camera calibration is a process that allows to fully understand how the camera forms the image. It is necessary especially when 3D information of the scene must be known. Calibration can be performed using a 1D pattern (points on a straight line). This kind of pattern has the advantage of being "visible" simultaneously even by cameras in opposite positions from each other. This makes the technique suitable for calibration of multiple cameras. Unfortunately, the calibration with 1D patterns often leads to poorly accurate results. In this work, the methods of single and multi-camera calibration are analyzed. It is shown that, in some cases, the accuracy of this type of algorithm can be significantly improved by simply performing a normalization of coordinates of the input points. Experiments on synthetic and real images are used to analyze the accuracy of the discussed methods.

## Chapter 6

 *Sang-Myoung Ye, Sogang University, Korea*
 *Rae-Hong Park, Sogang University, Korea*
 *Dong-Kyu Lee, Sogang University, Korea*

Object segmentation in video sequence is a basic and important task in video applications such as surveillance systems and video coding. Nonparametric snake algorithms for object segmentation have been proposed to overcome the drawback of conventional snake algorithms: the dependency on several parameters. In this chapter, a new object segmentation algorithm for video, based on a nonparametric snake model with motion prediction, is proposed. Object contour is initialized by using the mean absolute difference of intensity between input and previous frames. And in order to convert initial object contours into more exact object contours, the gradient vector flow snake is used. Finally object contour is predicted using a Kalman filter in successive frames. The proposed object segmentation method for video can provide more detailed and improved object segmentation results than the conventional methods. Various experimental results show the effectiveness of the proposed method in terms of the pixel-based quality measure and the computation time.

## Chapter 7

 *C.J. Prabhakar, Kuvempu University, India*

The major contribution of the research work presented in this chapter is the development of effective face recognition algorithm using analysis of face space in the interval-valued subspace. The analysis of face images is used for various purposes such as facial expression classification, gender determination, age estimation, emotion assessment, face recognition, et cetera. The research community of face image analysis has developed many techniques for face recognition; one of the successful techniques is based on subspace analysis. In the first part of the chapter, the authors present discussion of earliest face recognition techniques, which are considered as mile stones in the roadmap of subspace based face recognition techniques. The second part presents one of the efficient interval-valued subspace techniques, namely, symbolic Kernel Fisher Discriminant analysis (Symbolic KFD), in which the interval type features are extracted in contrast to classical subspace based techniques where single valued features are used for face representation and recognition.

## Chapter 8

 *Yuexing Han, National Institute of Advanced Industrial Science and Technology, Japan*
 *Bing Wang, University of Tokyo, Japan*
 *Hideki Koike, University of Electro-Communications, Japan*
 *Masanori Idesawa, University of Electro-Communications, Japan*

One of the main goals of image understanding and computer vision applications is to recognize an object from various images. Object recognition has been deeply developed for the last three decades, and a lot of approaches have been proposed. Generally, these methods of object recognition can successfully achieve their goal by relying on a large quantity of data. However, if the observed objects are shown to diverse configurations, it is difficult to recognize them with a limited database. One has to prepare enough data to exactly recognize one object with multi-configurations, and it is hard work to collect enough data only for a single object. In this chapter, the authors will introduce an approach to recognize objects with multi-configurations using the shape space theory. Firstly, two sets of landmarks are obtained from two objects in two-dimensional images. Secondly, the landmarks represented as two points are projected into a pre-shape space. Then, a series of new intermediate data can be obtained from data models in the pre-shape space. Finally, object recognition can be achieved in the shape space with the shape space theory.

# Chapter 9

In this chapter, the authors propose and implement an improved iris recognition method based on image enhancement and heuristics. They make major improvements in the iris segmentation phase. In particular, the authors implement the raised to power operation for more accurate detection of the pupil region. Additionally, with their technique they are able to considerably reduce the candidate limbic boundary search space; this leads to a significant increase in the accuracy and speed of the segmentation. Furthermore, the authors selectively detect the limbic circle having center within close range of the pupil center. The effectiveness of the proposed method is evaluated on a grand challenge, large scale database: the Iris Challenge Evaluation (ICE) dataset.

# Chapter 10

The study of medical image analysis encompasses the various techniques for acquisition of images of biological structures pertaining to human body using radiations in different frequency ranges. The advancements in medical imaging over the past decades are enabling physicians to non-invasively peer inside the human body for the purpose of diagnosis and therapy. In this chapter, the objective is to focus on the studies relating to the analysis of endoscopic images of lower esophagus for abnormal region detection and identification of cancerous growth. Several color image segmentation techniques have been developed for automatic detection of cancerous regions in endoscopic images, which assists the physician for faster, proper diagnosis and treatment of the disease. These segmentation methods are evaluated for comparing their performances in different color spaces, namely, RGB, HSI, YCbCr, HSV, and CIE Lab. The segmented images are expected to assist the medical expert in drawing the biopsy samples precisely from the detected pathological legions. Further, various methods have been proposed for segmentation and classification of squamous cell carcinoma (SCC) from color microscopic images of esophagus tissue during pathological investigation. The efficacy of these methods has been demonstrated experimentally with endoscopic and microscopic image set and compared with manual segmentation done by medical experts. It is envisaged that the research in this direction eventually leads to the design and production of efficient intelligent computer vision systems for assisting the medical experts in their task of speedy accurate diagnosis of diseases and prescription of appropriate treatment of the patients.

**Chapter 11**

*T. Ravindra Babu, Infosys Limited, India*
*Chethan S.A. Danivas, Infosys Limited, India*
*S.V. Subrahmanya, Infosys Limited, India*

Face Recognition is an active research area. In many practical scenarios, when faces are acquired without the cooperation or knowledge of the subject, they are likely to get occluded. Apart from image background, pose, illumination, and orientation of the faces, occlusion forms an additional challenge for face recognition. Recognizing faces that are partially visible is a challenging task. Most of the solutions to the problem focus on reconstruction or restoration of the occluded part before attempting to recognize the face. In the current chapter, the authors discuss various approaches to face recognition, challenges in face recognition of occluded images, and approaches to solve the problem. The authors propose an adaptive system that accepts the localized region of occlusion and recognizes the face adaptively. The chapter demonstrates through case studies that the proposed scheme recognizes the partially occluded faces as accurately as the un-occluded faces and in some cases outperforms the recognition using un-occluded face images.

**Chapter 12**

*Sridhar Arjunan, RMIT University, Australia*
*Dinesh Kumar, RMIT University, Australia*
*Hans Weghorn, Baden-Wuerttemberg Cooperative State University, Germany*
*Ganesh Naik, RMIT University, Australia*

The need for developing reliable and flexible human computer interface is increased and applications of HCI have been in each and every field. Human factors play an important role in these kinds of interfaces. Research and development of new human computer interaction (HCI) techniques that enhance the flexibility and reliability for the user are important. Research on new methods of computer control has focused on three types of body functions: speech, bioelectrical activity, and use of mechanical sensors. Speech operated systems have the advantage that these provide the user with flexibility. Such systems have the potential for making computer control effortless and natural. This chapter summarizes research conducted to investigate the use of facial muscle activity for a reliable interface to identify voiceless speech based commands without any audio signals. System performance and reliability have been tested to study inter-subject and inter-day variations and impact of the native language of the speaker. The experimental results indicate that such a system has high degree of inter-subject and inter-day variations. The results also indicate that the variations of the style of speaking in the native language are low but are high when the speaker speaks in a foreign language. The results also indicate that such a system is suitable for a very small vocabulary. The authors suggest that facial sEMG based speech recognition systems may only find limited applications.

An accurate Content Based Image Retrieval (CBIR) system is essential for the correct retrieval of desired images from the underlying database. Rotation invariance is very important for accurate Content Based Image Retrieval (CBIR). In this chapter, rotation invariance in Content Based Image Retrieval (CBIR) system is achieved by extracting Fourier features from images on which Dual Tree Complex Wavelets Transform (DT-CWT) has been applied. Before applying DT-CWT, the Fourier feature set is reduced by exploiting the symmetry property of Fourier transform. For an N x N image, feature set has been reduced from $N^2/2$ features to $N^2/4$ features. This reduction in feature set increases the speed of the system. Hence, this chapter proposes a method which makes the Content Based Image Retrieval (CBIR) system faster without comprising accuracy and rotation invariance.

# Chapter 14

Devnagari script is the most widely used script in India and its Optical Character Recognition (OCR) poses many challenges. Handwritten script has many variations, and existing methods used are discussed. The authors have also collected a database on which the techniques are tested. The techniques are based on structural methods as opposite to statistical methods. There are some special properties of Devnagari script like the topline, curves, and various types of connections that have been exploited in the methods discussed in this chapter.

# Chapter 15

Reliable corner detection is an important task in pattern recognition applications. In this chapter an approach based on fuzzy-rules to detect corners even under imprecise information is presented. The uncertainties arising due to various types of imaging defects such as blurring, illumination change, noise, et cetera. Fuzzy systems are well known for efficient handling of impreciseness. In order to handle the incompleteness arising due to imperfection of data, it is reasonable to model corner properties by a fuzzy rule-based system. The robustness of the proposed algorithm is compared with well known conventional detectors. The performance is tested on a number of benchmark test images to illustrate the efficiency of the algorithm in noise presence.

# Chapter 16

Eye detection is an important initial step in an automatic face recognition system. Though numerous eye detection methods have been proposed, many problems still exist, especially in the detection accuracy and efficiency under challenging image conditions. The authors present a novel eye detection method using color information, Haar features, and a new efficient Support Vector Machine (eSVM) in this chapter. In particular, this eye detection method consists of two stages: the eye candidate selection and validation. The selection stage picks up eye candidates over an image through color information, while the validation stage applies 2D Haar wavelet and the eSVM to detect the center of the eye among these candidates. The eSVM is defined on fewer support vectors than the standard SVM, which can achieve faster detection speed and higher or comparable detection accuracy. Experiments on Face Recognition Grand Challenge (FRGC) database show the improved performance over existing methods on both efficiency and accuracy.

## Chapter 17

*Amit Konar, Jadavpur University, India*
*Aruna Chakraborty, St. Thomas' College of Engineering & Technology, India*
*Pavel Bhowmik, Jadavpur University, India*
*Sauvik Das, Jadavpur University, India*
*Anisha Halder, Jadavpur University, India*

This chapter proposes new approaches to emotion recognition from facial expression and electroencephalogram signals. Subjects are excited with selective audio-visual stimulus, responsible for arousal of specific emotions. Manifestation of emotion which appears in facial expression and EEG are recorded. Subsequently the recorded information is analyzed for extraction of features, and a support vector machine classifier is used to classify the extracted features into emotion classes. An alternative scheme for emotion recognition directly from the electroencephalogram signals using Duffing Oscillator is also presented. Experimental results are given to compare the relative merits of the proposed schemes with existing works.

## Chapter 18

*Artem A. Lenskiy, Korea University of Technology and Education, Korea*
*Jong-Soo Lee, University of Ulsan, Korea*

In this chapter, the authors elaborate on the facial image segmentation and the detection of eyes and lips using two neural networks. The first neural network is applied to segment skin-colors and the second to detect facial features. As for input vectors, for the second network the authors apply speed-up robust features (SURF) that are not subject to scale and brightness variations. The authors carried out the detection of eyes and lips on two well-known facial feature databases, Caltech. and PICS. Caltech gave a success rate of 92.4% and 92.2% for left and right eyes and 85% for lips, whereas the PCIS database gave 96.9% and 95.3% for left and right eyes and 97.3% for lips. Using videos captured in real environment, among all videos, the authors achieved an average detection rate of 94.7% for the right eye and 95.5% for the left eye with a 86.9% rate for the lips.

This chapter presents a new method for binary classification that classifies input data into two regions separated by axis-aligned rectangular boundaries. Given the number of rectangular regions to use, this algorithm automatically finds the best boundaries that are determined concurrently. The formulation of the optimization problem involves minimizing the sum of minimum functions. To solve this problem, the author introduces underestimate of the minimum function with piecewise linear and convex envelope, which results in mixed integer and linear programming. The author shows several results of the algorithm and compare the effects of each term in the objective function. Finally, the chapter demonstrates that the method can be used in image capturing application to determine the optimal scheme that minimizes the total readout time of pixel data.

In recent times there is an urgent need for a simple yet robust system to identify natural hand actions and gestures for controlling prostheses and other computer assisted devices. Surface Electromyogram (sEMG) is a non-invasive measure of the muscle activities but is not reliable because there are multiple simultaneously active muscles. This research first establishes the conditions for the applicability of Independent Component Analysis (ICA) pattern recognition techniques for sEMG. Shortcomings related to order and magnitude ambiguity have been identified and a mitigation strategy has been developed by using a set of unmixing matrix and neural network weight matrix corresponding to the specific user. The experimental results demonstrate a marked improvement in the accuracy. The other advantages of this system are that it is suitable for real time operations and it is easy to train by a lay user.

# Chapter 21

This chapter describes a system of fuzzy methods designed to solve a broad range of problems in multiple-criteria evaluation, and also their software implementation, FuzzME. A feature common to all the presented methods is the type of evaluation, well suited to the paradigm of fuzzy set theory. All evaluations take on the form of fuzzy numbers, expressing the extent to which goals of evaluation are fulfilled. The system of fuzzy methods is conceived to allow for different types of interaction among criteria of evaluation. Under no interaction, the fuzzy weighted average, fuzzy OWA operator, or WOWA operator are used to aggregate partial evaluations (depending on the evaluator's requirements regarding type of evaluation). If interactions appear as redundancy or complementarity, the fuzzified discrete Choquet integral is the appropriate aggregation operator. Under more complex interactions, the aggregation function is defined through an expertly set base of fuzzy rules.

In this chapter, the authors have realized Interval Type-2 Fuzzy Logic Systems (IT2 FLSs) with the average of two Type-1 Fuzzy Logic Systems (T1 FLSs). The authors have presented two case studies by applying this realization methodology on (i) an arbitrary system, where an IT2 FLS is considered, in which its footprint of uncertainty (FOU) is expressed using Principal T1 FS+FOU approach, and the second (ii) the Mackey-Glass time-series forecasting. In the second case study, T1 FLS is evolved using Particle Swarm Optimization (PSO) algorithm for the Mackey-Glass time-series data with added noise, and is then upgraded to IT2 FLS by adding FOU. Further, four experiments are conducted in this case study for four different noise levels. For each case study, a comparative study of the results of the average of two T1 FLSs and the corresponding IT2 FLS, obtained through computer simulations in MATLAB environment, is presented to demonstrate the effectiveness of the realization approach. Very low values of Mean Square Error (MSE) and Root Mean Square Error (RMSE) demonstrate that IT2 FLS performance is equivalent to the average of two T1 FLSs. This approach is helpful in the absence of the availability of development tools for T2 FLSs or because of complexity and difficulty in understanding T2 FLSs that makes the implementation difficult. It provides an easy route to the simulation/realization of IT2 FLSs and by following this approach, all existing tools/methodologies for the design, simulation and realization of T1 FLSs can be directly extended to T2 FLSs.

There are available metrics for predicting fault prone classes, which may help software organizations for planning and performing testing activities. This may be possible due to proper allocation of resources on fault prone parts of the design and code of the software. Hence, importance and usefulness of such metrics is understandable, but empirical validation of these metrics is always a great challenge. Random Forest (RF) algorithm has been successfully applied for solving regression and classification problems in many applications. In this work, the authors predict faulty classes/modules using object oriented metrics and static code metrics. This chapter evaluates the capability of RF algorithm and compares its performance with nine statistical and machine learning methods in predicting fault prone software classes. The authors applied RF on six case studies based on open source, commercial software and NASA data sets. The results indicate that the prediction performance of RF is generally better than statistical and machine learning models. Further, the classification of faulty classes/modules using the RF method is better than the other methods in most of the data sets.

Artificial neural networks form a class of soft computing tools, which are made up of interconnected computational primitives for the analysis of numeric data. These are inspired by the functional behavior of the human nervous system comprising millions of nerve cells or neurons. Different artificial neural network architectures have been evolved over the years based on the storage, transmission, and processing characteristics of the human nervous system. These networks generally operate in two different modes, viz., supervised and unsupervised modes. The supervised mode of operation requires a supervisor to train the network with a training set of data. Networks operating in unsupervised mode apply topology preservation techniques so as to learn inputs. Representative examples of networks following either of these two modes are presented with reference to their topologies, configurations, types of input-output data and functional characteristics. Recent trends in this computing paradigm are also reported with due regards to the application perspectives.

### Chapter 25

This chapter presents a new optimization method for clustering fuzzy data to generate Type-2 fuzzy system models. For this purpose, first, a new distance measure for calculating the (dis)similarity between fuzzy data is proposed. Then, based on the proposed distance measure, Fuzzy c-Mean (FCM) clustering algorithm is modified. Next, Xie-Beni cluster validity index is modified to be able to valuate Type-2 fuzzy clustering approach. In this index, all operations are fuzzy and the minimization method is fuzzy ranking with Hamming distance. The proposed Type-2 fuzzy clustering method is used for development of indirect approach to Type-2 fuzzy modeling, where the rules are extracted from clustering fuzzy numbers (Zadeh, 1965). Then, the Type-2 fuzzy system is tuned by an inference algorithm for optimization of the main parameters of Type-2 parametric system. In this case, the parameters are: Schweizer and Sklar t-Norm and s-Norm, $\alpha$-cut of rule-bases, combination of FATI and FITA inference approaches, and Yager parametric defuzzification. Finally, the proposed Type-2 fuzzy system model is applied in prediction of the steel additives in steelmaking process. It is shown that, the proposed Type-2 fuzzy system model is superior in comparison with multiple regressions and Type-1 fuzzy system model, in terms of the minimization the effect of uncertainty in the rule-base fuzzy system models an error reduction.

### Chapter 26

Artificial Neural Network (ANN) is a non-parametric statistical tool which can be used for a host of pattern classification and prediction problems. It has excelled in diverse areas of application ranging from character recognition to financial problems. One of these areas, which have ample of scope of application of the ANN, is wireless communication. Especially, in segments like Multi-Input Multi-Output (MIMO) wireless channels ANNs have seldom been used for problems like channel estimation. Very few reported work exists in this regard. This work is related to the application of ANN for estimation of a MIMO channel of a wireless communication set-up. As Orthogonal Frequency Division Multiplexing (OFDM) is becoming an option to tackle increased demands of higher data rates by the modern generation mobile communication networks, a MIMO-OFDM system assisted by an ANN based channel estimation can offer better quality of service (QoS) and higher spectral efficiency.

**Chapter 27**

   *E. Grace Mary Kanaga, Karunya University, India*
   *M.L. Valarmathi, Government College of Technology, India*
   *Preethi S.H. Darius, Karunya University, India*

This chapter presents a novel 3D approach for patient scheduling (3D-PS) using multi-agents. Here the 3Ds refers to the Distributed, Dynamic and Decentralized nature of the patient scheduling. As in many other scheduling problems, in the hospital domain, a major problem is the efficient allocation of resources to the patients. The resources here mean the doctor, diagnosing equipments, lab tests, et cetera. Commonly, patient scheduling is performed manually by human schedulers with no automated support. Human scheduling is not efficient, because the nature of the problem is very complex; it is inherently distributed, dynamic, and decentralized. Since agents are known to represent distributed environment well and also being capable of handling dynamism, an agent based approach is chosen. The objectives are to reduce patient waiting times, minimize the patient stay in the hospital, and to improve resource utilization in hospitals. The comparison of several agent-based approaches is also reviewed, and the auction-based approach is chosen. The complete multi-agent framework given in literature is adapted to suit the patient scheduling scenario. The patient scheduling system is implemented in the JADE platform where patients and resources are represented as agents. The chief performance metric is the weighted tardiness which has to be minimized in order to obtain an effective schedule. The experiment is carried out using constant number of resources and varying number of patients. The simulation results are presented and analyzed. 3D-PS produces up to 30% reduction in total weighted tardiness in a distributed environment, as compared to other traditional algorithms. A further enhancement to this approach aims to reduce the communication overhead by reducing the number of messages passed and hence resulting in a better coordination mechanism. This auction based mechanism aims to provide the basic framework for future enhancements on patient scheduling.

**Chapter 28**

   *Jan Stoklasa, Palacky University in Olomouc, Czech Republic*

The decision making process of the Emergency Medical Rescue Services (EMRS) operations centre during disasters involves a significant amount of uncertainty. Decisions need to be made quickly, and no mistakes are tolerable, particularly in the case of disasters resulting in a large number of injured people. A multiphase linguistic fuzzy model is introduced to assist the operator during the initial phase of the medical disaster response. Based on uncertain input data, estimating the severity of the disaster, the number of injured people, and the amount of forces and resources needed to successfully deal with the situation is possible. The need for reinforcements is also considered. Fuzzy numbers, linguistic variables and fuzzy rule bases are applied to deal with the uncertainty. Outputs provided by the model (severity of the disaster, number of reinforcements needed etc.) are available both as fuzzy sets (for the purposes of disaster planning) and linguistic terms (for emergency call evaluation purposes).

**Chapter 29**

   *Elpiniki I. Papageorgiou, Technological Educational Institute of Lamia, Greece*

In this study, the fuzzy causal map inference mechanisms are analyzed for decision making tasks and a comparative analysis is performed to handle with the uncertainty in the problem of pulmonary risk prediction. Fuzzy Cognitive Mapping (FCM) is a causal graphical representation including nodes, determining the most relevant factors of a complex system, and links between these nodes determining the relationships between those factors. It represents knowledge in a symbolic manner and relates states, processes, policies, events, values, and inputs in an analogous manner. In the proposed work, a modified inference mechanism for FCM approach, which handles uncertainty and missing data, is presented and compared with the common fuzzy causal graph reasoning process for a medical diagnosis problem. Through this study, we overcome the problem of missing data and/or incomplete knowledge, especially for the cases where there is no any information about a concept-state or the knowledge of some concepts is insufficient. By this way, the rescaled inference process is proved more reliable, yielding more exact and natural inference results than traditional FCMs. A number of different scenarios for medical diagnosis concentrated on the pulmonary infections are elaborated to demonstrate the functioning of the rescaled FCM inference mechanism.

## Chapter 30

*Kostas Kolomvatsos, National and Kapodistrian University of Athens, Greece*
*Stathes Hadjiefthymiades, National and Kapodistrian University of Athens, Greece*

Today, there is a large number of product providers in the Web. Electronic Marketplaces (EMs) enable entities to negotiate and trade products. Usually, intelligent agents assume the responsibility of representing buyers or sellers in EMs. However, uncertainty about the characteristics and intentions of the negotiating entities is present in these scenarios. Fuzzy Logic (FL) theory presents a lot of advantages when used in environments where entities have limited or no knowledge about their peers. Hence, entities can rely on a FL knowledge base that determines the appropriate action on every possible state. FL can be used in offers, trust, or time constraints definition or when an agent should decide during the negotiation process. The autonomic nature of agents in combination with FL leads to more efficient systems. In this chapter, the authors provide a critical review on the adoption of FL in marketplace systems and present their proposal for the buyer side. Moreover, the authors describe techniques for building FL systems focusing on clustering techniques. The aim is to show the importance of FL adoption in such settings.

## Chapter 31

*Mohammad Hossein Fazel Zarandi, Amirkabir University of Technology, Iran*
*Milad Avazbeigi, European Centre for Soft Computing, Spain*
*Meysam Alizadeh, University of Maryland, USA*

In today's competitive markets, prediction of financial variables has become a critical issue. Especially in stock market analysis where a wrong prediction may result in a big loss in terms of time and money, having a robust prediction is a crucial issue. To model the chaotic, noisy, and evolving behavior of stock market data, new powerful methods should be developed. Soft Computing methods have shown a great confidence in such environments where there are many uncertain factors. Also it has been observed through many experiments that the hybridization of different soft computing techniques such as fuzzy logic, neural networks, and meta-heuristics usually results in better results than simply using one method. This chapter presents an adaptive neuro-fuzzy inference system (ANFIS), trained by the particle swarm optimization (PSO) algorithm for stock price prediction. Instead of previous works that have emphasized on gradient base or least square (LS) methods for training the neural network, four different strategies of PSO are implemented: gbest, lbest-a, lbest-b, and Euclidean. In the proposed fuzzy rule based system some technical and fundamental indexes are applied as input variables. In order to generate membership functions (MFs), a robust noise rejection clustering algorithm is developed. The proposed neuro-fuzzy model is applied for an automotive part-making manufactory in an Asia stock market. The results show the superiority of the proposed model in comparison with the available models in terms of error minimization, robustness, and flexibility.

## Chapter 32

*Koushik Bakshi, Jadavpur University, India*
*Sourav Chandra, Jadavpur University, India*
*Amit Konar, Jadavpur University, India.*
*D.N. Tibarewala, Jadavpur University, India*

This chapter provides a prototype design of a hand tremor compensator/controller to reduce the effect of the tremor to an external device/ apparatus, such as a magnetic pen for the patients suffering from Parkinson and similar diseases. It would also be effective for busy surgeons suffering from hand tremor due to muscle fatigue. Main emphasis in this chapter is given on the prediction of the tremor signal from the discrete samples of electromyogram data and tremor. The predicted signal is inverted in sign and added to the main tremor signal through a specially designed magnetic actuator carrying the external device, such as a magnetically driven pen or surgical instrument. Two different prediction algorithms, one based on neural nets and the other based on Kalman Filter have been designed, tested, and validated for the proposed application. A prototype model of the complete system was developed on an embedded platform. Further development on the basic model would be appropriate for field applications in controlling tremors of the subjects suffering from Parkinson and the like diseases.

# Preface

The aim of this book is to provide a common platform for the researchers from diverse backgrounds to present their theoretical and applied research findings in artificial intelligence and pattern recognition. This book may prove to be a building block for enhancing/developing intelligent systems as it highlights the core concepts as well as applicability in real world problems.

The need of intelligent machines in day to day activities such as medical diagnostics, biometric security systems, image processing, et cetera, motivates the researchers to develop and explore new techniques, algorithms, and their applications. The techniques of pattern recognition are evolving rapidly and boosting the research areas mentioned above. Also, the advances in fuzzy logic, neural networks and other decision making techniques have contributed immensely in the development of artificial intelligence and its usage. Most of the methods used in intelligent systems apply pattern recognition in artificial intelligence based systems and vice-versa. For instance, medical diagnostic systems, which are traditionally an AI task, get enhanced and provide better results using pattern recognition methods. Similarly, biometric imagery, feature recognition, document image analysis, and other pattern recognition tasks perform well with the induction of artificial intelligence techniques. This book provides a common platform to artificial intelligence and pattern recognition researchers to disseminate new ideas and techniques.

This book is organized in self-contained chapters to provide greatest reading flexibility. In response to the call for papers, the book received around 100 abstracts. Based on the suitability, the editors invited full chapters from 67 researchers of various disciplines (Pattern Analysis and Recognition, Image Processing, Artificial Intelligence and Soft Computing) and from 19 different countries. All submitted chapters have been reviewed on a double-blind review basis, by at least three reviewers. After an evaluation process by the EBM members, 32 chapters were selected. Acceptance was based on relevance, technical soundness, originality, and clarity of presentation.

This book is organized as follows:

Chapter 1: The recent advances in robotics and related technologies have placed more challenges and stricter requirements to the issue of recognizing objects in a scene. In such applications, robots must be equipped with a sense of location and direction with a view to the efficient accomplishment of navigation or demanding pick and place tasks. In addition, spatial information is required in surveillance processes where recognized targets are located in the working space of the robot. Furthermore, accurate perception of depth is mandatory in driver assistance applications. This chapter presents several recently proposed methods capable of first recognizing objects and then providing their spatial information in cluttered environments.

Chapter 2: This chapter describes a multi-linear discriminant method of constructing and quantifying statistically significant changes on human identity photographs. The approach is based on a general multivariate two-stage linear framework that addresses the small sample size problem in high-dimensional spaces. Starting with a 2D data set of frontal face images, the authors determine a most characteristic direction of change by organizing the data according to the patterns of interest. These experiments on publicly available face image sets show that the multi-linear approach does produce visually plausible results for gender, facial expression and aging facial changes in a simple and efficient way.

Chapter 3: This chapter focuses on the usage of image orthogonal moments as discrimination features in pattern recognition applications and discusses their main properties. Initially, the ability of the moments to carry information of an image with minimum redundancy is studied, while their capability to enclose distinctive information that uniquely describes the image's content is also examined. Along these directions, the computational formulas of the most representative moment families will be defined analytically and the form of the corresponding moment invariants in each case will be derived. Appropriate experiments have taken place in order to investigate the description capabilities of each moment family, by applying them in several benchmark problems.

Chapter 4: Triangulation is a fundamental problem in computer vision that consists of estimating the 3D position of a point of the scene from the estimates of its image projections on some cameras and from the estimates of the projection matrices of these cameras. This chapter addresses multiple view L2 triangulation, i.e. triangulation for vision systems with a generic number of cameras where the sought 3D point is searched by minimizing the L2 norm of the image reprojection error. The authors consider the standard case where estimates of all the image points are available, and consider also the case where some of such estimates are not available for example due to occlusions.

Chapter 5: Camera calibration is a process that allows to fully understand how the camera forms the image. It is necessary especially when 3D information of the scene must be known. Calibration can be performed using a 1D pattern (points on a straight line). This kind of pattern has the advantage of being "visible" simultaneously even by cameras in opposite positions from each other. This makes the technique suitable for calibration of multiple cameras. Unfortunately, the calibration with 1D patterns often leads to poorly accurate results. In this work, the methods of single and multi-camera calibration are analyzed. It is shown that, in some cases, the accuracy of this type of algorithm can be significantly improved by simply performing a normalization of coordinates of the input points. Experiments on synthetic and real images are used to analyze the accuracy of the discussed methods.

Chapter 6: Nonparametric snake algorithms for object segmentation have been proposed to overcome the drawback of conventional snake algorithms: the dependency on several parameters. In this chapter, a new object segmentation algorithm for video, based on a nonparametric snake model with motion prediction, is proposed. Object contour is initialized by using the mean absolute difference of intensity between input and previous frames. And in order to convert initial object contours into more exact object contours, the gradient vector flow snake is used. Finally object contour is predicted using a Kalman filter in successive frames. The proposed object segmentation method for video can provide more detailed and improved object segmentation results than the conventional methods. Various experimental results show the effectiveness of the proposed method in terms of the pixel-based quality measure and the computation time.

Chapter 7: The analysis of face images is used for various purposes such as facial expression classification, gender determination, age estimation, emotion assessment, face recognition, et cetera. The research community of face image analysis has developed many techniques for face recognition; one of the successful techniques is based on subspace analysis. In the first part of the chapter, the authors present discussion of earliest face recognition techniques, which are considered as mile stones in the roadmap of subspace based face recognition techniques. The second part presents one of the efficient interval-valued subspace techniques, namely, symbolic Kernel Fisher Discriminant analysis (Symbolic KFD), in which the interval type features are extracted in contrast to classical subspace based techniques where single valued features are used for face representation and recognition.

Chapter 8: The authors introduce an approach to recognize objects with multi-configurations using the shape space theory. Firstly, two sets of landmarks are obtained from two objects in two-dimensional images. Secondly, the landmarks represented as two points are projected into a pre-shape space. Then, a series of new intermediate data have been obtained from data models in the pre-shape space. Finally, object recognition has been achieved in the shape space with the shape space theory.

Chapter 9: In this chapter, the authors propose and implement an improved iris recognition method based on image enhancement and heuristics. They make major improvements in the iris segmentation phase. In particular, the authors implement the raised to power operation for more accurate detection of the pupil region. Additionally, with their technique they are able to considerably reduce the candidate limbic boundary search space; this leads to a significant increase in the accuracy and speed of the segmentation. Furthermore, the authors selectively detect the limbic circle having center within close range of the pupil center. The effectiveness of the proposed method is evaluated on a grand challenge, large scale database: the Iris Challenge Evaluation (ICE) dataset.

Chapter 10: This chapter focuses on the studies relating to the analysis of endoscopic images of lower esophagus for abnormal region detection and identification of cancerous growth. Several color image segmentation techniques have been developed for automatic detection of cancerous regions in endoscopic images, which assists the physician for faster, proper diagnosis and treatment of the disease. These segmentation methods are evaluated for comparing their performances in different color spaces, namely, RGB, HSI, $YC_bC_r$, HSV, and CIE Lab. The segmented images are expected to assist the medical expert in drawing the biopsy samples precisely from the detected pathological legions. Further, various methods have been proposed for segmentation and classification of squamous cell carcinoma (SCC) from color microscopic images of esophagus tissue during pathological investigation.

Chapter 11: Recognizing faces that are partially visible is a challenging task. Most of the solutions to the problem focus on reconstruction or restoration of the occluded part before attempting to recognize the face. In the current chapter, the authors discuss various approaches to face recognition, challenges in face recognition of occluded images, and approaches to solve the problem. The authors propose an adaptive system that accepts the localized region of occlusion and recognizes the face adaptively. The chapter demonstrates through case studies that the proposed scheme recognizes the partially occluded faces as accurately as the un-occluded faces and in some cases outperforms the recognition using un-occluded face images.

Chapter 12: Research and development of new human computer interaction (HCI) techniques that enhance the flexibility and reliability for the user are important. Research on new methods of computer control has focused on three types of body functions: speech, bioelectrical activity, and use of mechanical sensors. Speech operated systems have the advantage that these provide the user with flexibility. Such systems have the potential for making computer control effortless and natural. This chapter summarizes research conducted to investigate the use of facial muscle activity for a reliable interface to identify voiceless speech based commands without any audio signals. System performance and reliability have been tested to study inter-subject and inter-day variations and impact of the native language of the speaker.

Chapter 13: An accurate Content Based Image Retrieval (CBIR) system is essential for the correct retrieval of desired images from the underlying database. Rotation invariance is very important for accurate Content Based Image Retrieval (CBIR). In this chapter, rotation invariance in Content Based Image Retrieval (CBIR) system is achieved by extracting Fourier features from images on which Dual Tree Complex Wavelets Transform (DT-CWT) has been applied. Before applying DT-CWT, the Fourier feature set is reduced by exploiting the symmetry property of Fourier transform. For an N x N image, feature set has been reduced from $N^2/2$ features to $N^2/4$ features. This reduction in feature set increases the speed of the system. Hence, this chapter proposes a method which makes the Content Based Image Retrieval (CBIR) system faster without comprising accuracy and rotation invariance.

Chapter 14: Devnagari script is the most widely used script in India and its Optical Character Recognition (OCR) poses many challenges. Handwritten script has many variations, and existing methods used are discussed. The authors have also collected a database on which the techniques are tested. The techniques are based on structural methods as opposite to statistical methods. There are some special properties of Devnagari script like the topline, curves, and various types of connections that have been exploited in the methods discussed in this chapter.

Chapter 15: Reliable corner detection is an important task in pattern recognition applications. In this chapter an approach based on fuzzy-rules to detect corners even under imprecise information is presented. The uncertainties arising due to various types of imaging defects such as blurring, illumination change, noise, et cetera. Fuzzy systems are well known for efficient handling of impreciseness. In order to handle the incompleteness arising due to imperfection of data, it is reasonable to model corner properties by a fuzzy rule-based system. The robustness of the proposed algorithm is compared with well known conventional detectors.

Chapter 16: Eye detection is an important initial step in an automatic face recognition system. Though numerous eye detection methods have been proposed, many problems still exist, especially in the detection accuracy and efficiency under challenging image conditions. The authors present a novel eye detection method using color information, Haar features, and a new efficient Support Vector Machine (eSVM) in this chapter. In particular, this eye detection method consists of two stages: the eye candidate selection and validation. The selection stage picks up eye candidates over an image through color information, while the validation stage applies 2D Haar wavelet and the eSVM to detect the center of the eye among these candidates. The eSVM is defined on fewer support vectors than the standard SVM, which can achieve faster detection speed and higher or comparable detection accuracy.

Chapter 17: This chapter proposes new approaches to emotion recognition from facial expression and electroencephalogram signals. Subjects are excited with selective audio-visual stimulus, responsible for arousal of specific emotions. Manifestation of emotion which appears in facial expression and EEG are recorded. Subsequently the recorded information is analyzed for extraction of features, and a support vector machine classifier is used to classify the extracted features into emotion classes. An alternative scheme for emotion recognition directly from the electroencephalogram signals using Duffing Oscillator is also presented.

Chapter 18: In this chapter, the authors elaborate on the facial image segmentation and the detection of eyes and lips using two neural networks. The first neural network is applied to segment skin-colors and the second to detect facial features. As for input vectors, for the second network the authors apply speed-up robust features (SURF) that are not subject to scale and brightness variations. The authors carried out the detection of eyes and lips on two well-known facial feature databases, Caltech. and PICS.

Chapter 19: This chapter presents a new method for binary classification that classifies input data into two regions separated by axis-aligned rectangular boundaries. Given the number of rectangular regions to use, this algorithm automatically finds the best boundaries that are determined concurrently.

The formulation of the optimization problem involves minimizing the sum of minimum functions. To solve this problem, the author introduces underestimate of the minimum function with piecewise linear and convex envelope, which results in mixed integer and linear programming. The author shows several results of the algorithm and compares the effects of each term in the objective function.

Chapter 20: In recent times there is an urgent need for a simple yet robust system to identify natural hand actions and gestures for controlling prostheses and other computer assisted devices. Surface Electromyogram (sEMG) is a non-invasive measure of the muscle activities but is not reliable because there are multiple simultaneously active muscles. This research first establishes the conditions for the applicability of Independent Component Analysis (ICA) pattern recognition techniques for sEMG. Shortcomings related to order and magnitude ambiguity have been identified and a mitigation strategy has been developed by using a set of unmixing matrix and neural network weight matrix corresponding to the specific user. The experimental results demonstrate a marked improvement in the accuracy. The other advantages of this system are that it is suitable for real time operations and it is easy to train by a lay user.

Chapter 21: This chapter describes a system of fuzzy methods designed to solve a broad range of problems in multiple-criteria evaluation, and also their software implementation, FuzzME. A feature common to all the presented methods is the type of evaluation, well suited to the paradigm of fuzzy set theory. All evaluations take on the form of fuzzy numbers, expressing the extent to which goals of evaluation are fulfilled. The system of fuzzy methods is conceived to allow for different types of interaction among criteria of evaluation. Under no interaction, the fuzzy weighted average, fuzzy OWA operator, or WOWA operator are used to aggregate partial evaluations (depending on the evaluator's requirements regarding type of evaluation). If interactions appear as redundancy or complementarity, the fuzzified discrete Choquet integral is the appropriate aggregation operator. Under more complex interactions, the aggregation function is defined through an expertly set base of fuzzy rules.

Chapter 22: In this chapter, the authors have realized Interval Type-2 Fuzzy Logic Systems (IT2 FLSs) with the average of two Type-1 Fuzzy Logic Systems (T1 FLSs). The authors have presented two case studies by applying this realization methodology on (i) an arbitrary system, where an IT2 FLS is considered, in which its footprint of uncertainty (FOU) is expressed using Principal T1 FS+FOU approach, and the second (ii) the Mackey-Glass time-series forecasting. In the second case study, T1 FLS is evolved using Particle Swarm Optimization (PSO) algorithm for the Mackey-Glass time-series data with added noise, and is then upgraded to IT2 FLS by adding FOU. Further, four experiments are conducted in this case study for four different noise levels.

Chapter 23: There are available metrics for predicting fault prone classes, which may help software organizations for planning and performing testing activities. This may be possible due to proper allocation of resources on fault prone parts of the design and code of the software. Hence, importance and usefulness of such metrics is understandable, but empirical validation of these metrics is always a great challenge. Random Forest (RF) algorithm has been successfully applied for solving regression and classification problems in many applications. In this work, the authors predict faulty classes/modules using object oriented metrics and static code metrics. This chapter evaluates the capability of RF algorithm and compares its performance with nine statistical and machine learning methods in predicting fault prone software classes. The authors applied RF on six case studies based on open source, commercial software and NASA data sets.

Chapter 24: Artificial neural networks form a class of soft computing tools, which are made up of interconnected computational primitives for the analysis of numeric data. These are inspired by the functional behavior of the human nervous system comprising millions of nerve cells or neurons. Different artificial neural network architectures have been evolved over the years based on the storage, transmission, and processing characteristics of the human nervous system.

Chapter 25: This chapter presents a new optimization method for clustering fuzzy data to generate Type-2 fuzzy system models. For this purpose, first, a new distance measure for calculating the (dis) similarity between fuzzy data is proposed. Then, based on the proposed distance measure, Fuzzy c-Mean (FCM) clustering algorithm is modified. Next, Xie-Beni cluster validity index is modified to be able to valuate Type-2 fuzzy clustering approach. In this index, all operations are fuzzy and the minimization method is fuzzy ranking with Hamming distance.

Chapter 26: Artificial Neural Network (ANN) is a non-parametric statistical tool which can be used for a host of pattern classification and prediction problems. It has excelled in diverse areas of application ranging from character recognition to financial problems. One of these areas, which have ample of scope of application of the ANN, is wireless communication. Especially, in segments like Multi-Input Multi-Output (MIMO) wireless channels ANNs have seldom been used for problems like channel estimation. Very few reported work exists in this regard. This work is related to the application of ANN for estimation of a MIMO channel of a wireless communication set-up. As Orthogonal Frequency Division Multiplexing (OFDM) is becoming an option to tackle increased demands of higher data rates by the modern generation mobile communication networks, a MIMO-OFDM system assisted by an ANN based channel estimation can offer better quality of service and higher spectral efficiency.

Chapter 27: This chapter presents a novel 3D approach for patient scheduling (3D-PS) using multi-agents. Here the 3Ds refers to the Distributed, Dynamic and Decentralized nature of the patient scheduling. As in many other scheduling problems, in the hospital domain, a major problem is the efficient allocation of resources to the patients. The resources here mean the doctor, diagnosing equipments, lab tests, et cetera. Commonly, patient scheduling is performed manually by human schedulers with no automated support. Human scheduling is not efficient, because the nature of the problem is very complex; it is inherently distributed, dynamic, and decentralized. Since agents are known to represent distributed environment well and also being capable of handling dynamism, an agent based approach is chosen. The objectives are to reduce patient waiting times, minimize the patient stay in the hospital, and to improve resource utilization in hospitals.

Chapter 28: The decision making process of the Emergency Medical Rescue Services (EMRS) operations centre during disasters involves a significant amount of uncertainty. Decisions need to be made quickly, and no mistakes are tolerable, particularly in the case of disasters resulting in a large number of injured people. A multiphase linguistic fuzzy model is introduced to assist the operator during the initial phase of the medical disaster response. Based on uncertain input data, estimating the severity of the disaster, the number of injured people, and the amount of forces and resources needed to successfully deal with the situation is possible. The need for reinforcements is also considered. Fuzzy numbers, linguistic variables and fuzzy rule bases are applied to deal with the uncertainty.

Chapter 29: In this study, the fuzzy causal map inference mechanisms are analyzed for decision making tasks and a comparative analysis is performed to handle with the uncertainty in the problem of pulmonary risk prediction. Fuzzy Cognitive Mapping (FCM) is a causal graphical representation including nodes, determining the most relevant factors of a complex system, and links between these nodes determining the relationships between those factors. It represents knowledge in a symbolic manner and relates states, processes, policies, events, values, and inputs in an analogous manner. In the proposed work, a modified inference mechanism for FCM approach, which handles uncertainty and missing data, is presented and compared with the common fuzzy causal graph reasoning process for a medical diagnosis problem.

Chapter 30: Electronic Marketplaces (EMs) enable entities to negotiate and trade products. Usually, intelligent agents assume the responsibility of representing buyers or sellers in EMs. However, uncertainty about the characteristics and intentions of the negotiating entities is present in these scenarios. Fuzzy Logic (FL) theory presents a lot of advantages when used in environments where entities have limited or no knowledge about their peers. Hence, entities can rely on a FL knowledge base that determines the appropriate action on every possible state. FL can be used in offers, trust, or time constraints definition or when an agent should decide during the negotiation process. The autonomic nature of agents in combination with FL leads to more efficient systems. In this chapter, the authors provide a critical review on the adoption of FL in marketplace systems and present their proposal for the buyer side.

Chapter 31: In today's competitive markets, prediction of financial variables has become a critical issue. Especially in stock market analysis where a wrong prediction may result in a big loss in terms of time and money, having a robust prediction is a crucial issue. To model the chaotic, noisy, and evolving behavior of stock market data, new powerful methods should be developed. Soft Computing methods have shown a great confidence in such environments where there are many uncertain factors. Also it has been observed through many experiments that the hybridization of different soft computing techniques such as fuzzy logic, neural networks, and meta-heuristics usually results in better results than simply using one method. This chapter presents an adaptive neuro-fuzzy inference system (ANFIS), trained by the particle swarm optimization (PSO) algorithm for stock price prediction. Instead of previous works that have emphasized on gradient base or least square (LS) methods for training the neural network, four different strategies of PSO are implemented.

Chapter 32: This chapter provides a prototype design of a hand tremor compensator/controller to reduce the effect of the tremor to an external device/ apparatus, such as a magnetic pen for the patients suffering from Parkinson and similar diseases. It would also be effective for busy surgeons suffering from hand tremor due to muscle fatigue. Main emphasis in this chapter is given on the prediction of the tremor signal from the discrete samples of electromyogram data and tremor. The predicted signal is inverted in sign and added to the main tremor signal through a specially designed magnetic actuator carrying the external device, such as a magnetically driven pen or surgical instrument. Two different prediction algorithms, one based on neural nets and the other based on Kalman Filter have been designed, tested, and validated for the proposed application.

*Vijay Kumar Mago*
*Simon Fraser University, Canada*

*Nitin Bhatia*
*DAV College, India*

# Chapter 1
# From Object Recognition to Object Localization

**Rigas Kouskouridas**
*Democritus University of Thrace, Greece*

**Antonios Gasteratos**
*Democritus University of Thrace, Greece*

## ABSTRACT

*Recognizing objects in a scene is a fundamental task in image understanding. The recent advances in robotics and related technologies have placed more challenges and stricter requirements to this issue. In such applications, robots must be equipped with a sense of location and direction with a view to the efficient accomplishment of navigation or demanding pick and place tasks. In addition, spatial information is required in surveillance processes where recognized targets are located in the working space of the robot. Furthermore, accurate perception of depth is mandatory in driver assistance applications. This chapter presents several recently proposed methods capable of first recognizing objects and then providing their spatial information in cluttered environments.*

## INTRODUCTION

Computer vision generally interferes with recognizing patterns and targets. A wealth of research is devoted to the building of algorithms capable of either detecting simple blob-like structures or recognizing complicated patterns. Generally, the efficiency of a pattern recognition technique depends on its ability to decode, with as much accuracy as possible, vital visual information contained in the natural environment. During the past few years, remarkable efforts were made to build new algorithms for robust object recognition in difficult environments. To this end, researchers emphasized in developing recognition paradigms based on appearance features with local potency (Nister, D., & Stewenius H. 2006, Sivic, J., & Zisserman, A. 2003). Algorithms of this field extract features with local extent that are invariant to possible illumination, viewpoint, rotation and scale changes.

Another aspect that has received much attention in the literature is to exploit the data derived during recognition with a view to provide objects' spatial

DOI: 10.4018/978-1-61350-429-1.ch001

information. Apart from its identity, several other object-related characteristics, such as its distance to the camera or its pose (orientation relative to the camera's plane), could be obtained (Thomas, A., et al. 2009, Sandhu, R., et al. 2009, Ekvall, S., 2005). As a result, assigning spatial attributes to recognized objects provides solutions to numerous technical problems. In robotics applications robots must be equipped with a sense of location and direction with a view to the efficient accomplishment of navigation or demanding pick and place tasks (Kragic, D., et al. 2005, Wong, B., & Spetsakis, M. 2000). In addition, spatial information is required in surveillance processes, where recognized targets are located in the working space of the robot. Furthermore, accurate perception of depth is mandatory in driver assistance applications (Borges, A. P. et al. 2009). Quality control procedures of industrial production frameworks demand accurate acquisition of enhanced spatial information in order to reject faulty prototypes. To sum up, the ultimate challenge for computer vision society members is the building up of advanced vision systems capable of both recognizing objects and providing their spatial information in cluttered environments.

This chapter is mainly devoted to two major and heavily investigated aspects. Initially, the current trend in recognition algorithms suitable for spatial information retrieval is presented. Several recently proposed detectors and descriptors are analytically presented along with their merits and disadvantages. Their main building blocks are examined and their performance against possible image alterations is discussed. Furthermore, the most known techniques emphasizing in the estimation of pose and location of recognized targets are presented. The remainder of the chapter is structured as follows: In Section 2, we give an overview of the current trend in object recognition techniques. A review of recently proposed pose estimation and 3D position calculation algorithms is presented in Section 3. Furthermore, at the last part of the section a comparison study of the presented pose estimation schemes is illustrated. Finally, the chapter concludes with a discussion and an outlook to the future work.

## LOCAL APPEARANCE-BASED OBJECT RECOGNITION AND MULTI-CAMERA SYSTEMS

State-of-the-art object recognition frameworks rely on local appearance-based features extracted and organized by detectors and descriptors respectively. Generally, the main idea behind interest location detectors is the pursuit of points or regions containing exceptional information about an object or a scene. These spots or areas hold data that distinguish them from others in their local neighborhood. Thus, regions in a scene that enjoy solitary quality and quantity of information can be easily detected. It is apparent that, detector's efficiency is directly related to its ability to locate as many distinguishable areas as possible in an iterative process. Harris and Stephens (Harris, C., & Stephens M. 1988) were the first to implement an interest point detector, known as Harris Corner detector. Due to the fact that it provides significant repeatability, many recent proposed studies (Rothganger, F.et al.2006, Schmid, C., & Mohr, R. 2006) have adopted it in order to perform demanding object recognition tasks. Furthermore, several variations of Harris Corner detector, such as Harris-Laplace (Mikolajczyk, K., & Schmid, C. 2004) and Harris-affine (Mikolajczyk, K., et al. 2005), were presented due to the fact that they provide significant efficiency. In turn, another profitable detector, the Maximal Stable Extremal Regions Detector (MSER), was recently proposed in (Matas, J.et al. 2004). In short, regions darker or brighter than their surroundings are detected, while the efficiency of the algorithm relies on the trade-off between pixels' intensity value on the center of the mask and those on the local neighborhood. In turn, the "Features from Accelerated Segment Test (FAST)" feature detector constitutes the most recently interest point extractor and it was proposed in (Rosten, E., & Drummond, T. 2006). It incorporates the Bresenham's circle theory into a window-based interest point pursuit. Moreover, biological inspired vision systems aim at the human's visual cortex simulation and, as a result, to the development of human-based interest point detector. For this purpose Kadir's Salient Detector proposed in (Kadir, T., & Brady, M. 2001) extracts spots in an image that contain important information which distinguish them from others in their local neighborhood. The Salient Detector is based on the probability density function (PDF) of intensity values over an elliptical region, whilst for each pixel an entropy extremum is estimated.

On the other hand, a descriptor organizes the information collected from the detector in a discriminating manner. Thus, high dimensional feature vectors corresponding to locally sampled feature descriptions are produced. In other words, an object (or parts of it) located in a scene is represented by descriptors. Furthermore, the final object depiction is accomplished by stacking descriptors in a logical coherence. Generally, by organizing descriptors from multiple patterns into large databases demanding multiple-object recognition tasks can be achieved. These databases, that play essential role in all the recently proposed recognition approaches, are structured in a vocabulary-tree format. In (Lepetit, V., & Fua, P. 2006), simple real-time recognition of a single object that is based on multiple randomized trees is presented. One of the most profitable vocabulary-tree formats was presented in (Nister, D., & Stewenius H. 2006), where each descriptor from training set represents a single leaf of the tree. In (Lazebnik, S., & Ponce, J. 2005), a new invariant descriptor, called Spin Image, that outperforms Gabor filter was presented. The most important drawback of this detector is its inefficiency to directly transpose spin image descriptor to region-based information. On the contrary, complex filters that were proposed in (Schaffalitzky, F., & Zisserman, A. 2002) and (Baumberg, A. 2000),

were applied to the descriptor matching process since it composes the prerequisite for every object recognition method. Moreover, complex filters, that use either Gaussian or polynomial derivatives, generate kernels for the purposes of average intensity estimation of a region.

The complexity of the visual information contained in a scene is described by generalized moment invariants as it is proposed in (Van Gool, J., & Moons, T., & Ungureanu, D. 1996). These moments can be easily computed for arbitrary order and degree, whilst they also characterize the distribution of shape and intensity over a region in an image. In turn, local and gradient histograms were efficiently utilized as adequate feature descriptors. Local Energy based Shape Histogram (LESH), which was introduced in (Sarfraz, MS., et al. 2008), encodes the shape of an object by accumulating local energy of the underlying signal. Finally, this local energy is organized into 128-dimensional spatial histogram. Gradient Location and Orientation Histogram (GLOH) that was proposed in (Mikolajczyk, K., & Schmid, C. 2005), produces descriptor histograms that are calculated on a fine circular grid. The final outcome corresponds to 272-dimensional histogram that efficiently represents visual spatial information over a region in an image. Techniques comprising of a detector and a descriptor are referred in the literature as two-part approaches. Currently, the two most popular approaches that implement both a detector and descriptor are the Scale Invariant Feature Transform (SIFT) (Lowe, D.G. 2004) and Speeded up Robust Features (SURF) (Bay, H., et.al 2008).

## Scale Invariant Feature Transform (SIFT)

In order to detect interest point locations, that are invariant to scale change of the image, the usage of a scale space function is mandatory. In (Lindeberg, T. 1994), it has been shown that the only possible scale space mechanism, which can be used for interest point detection, is the Gaussian function. Thus, SIFT's detector requires that the image is convolved with the variable-scale Gaussian function for the production of the scale-space image:

$$L(x, y, \sigma) = G(x, y, \sigma) * I(x, y)$$

with

$$G(x, y, \sigma) = \frac{1}{2\pi\sigma^2} e^{-(x^2+y^2)/2\sigma^2}$$

L(x, y, σ) represents the function of scale space of an image, G(x, y, σ) the variable-scale Gaussian and I(x, y) the input image. Afterwards, stable key-point locations are detected by using scale-space extremum in the difference-of-Gaussian (DoG) function convolved with the image D(x, y, σ). The later is computed from the difference of two nearby scales separated by a constant multiplicative factor κ:

$$D(x, y, \sigma) = (G(x, y, \kappa\sigma) - G(x, y, \sigma)) * I(x, y)$$
$$= L(x, y, \kappa\sigma) - L(x, y, \sigma)$$

In (Lindeberg, T. 1994) it was shown that, the DoG function provides a close approximation to the scale-normalized Laplacian of Gaussian, $\sigma^2 \nabla^2 G$, needed for the true scale invariance of a key-point location. The local maxima and minima estimation of D(x, y, σ) is executed with the procedure shown in Figure 1. Each sample point is compared to its eight neighbors in the current image and nine in the scale above and below. Finally, it is selected only if it is greater than all these neighbors or smaller than all of them. After the efficient key-point location assignment by the detector, information around a feature point is exploited for the needs of the descriptor. Initially, a consistent orientation to each key-point based

on local image properties is estimated. For each image sample, L(x, y), the gradient magnitude m(x, y), and orientation, θ(x, y), is computed using pixels' intensity values differences:

$$m(x, y) = \sqrt{\begin{array}{l}(L(x+1, y) - L(x-1, y))^2 \\ +(L(x, y+1) - L(x, y-1))^2\end{array}}$$

$$\theta(x, y) = tan^{-1}((L(x, y+1) - L(x, y-1)) \\ /(L(x+1, y) - L(x-1, y)))$$

These gradient orientations of every sample point within a 16x16 region around the key-point are used to form an orientation histogram. The later contains 36 bins representing the 360 degree range of orientations, whilst each added sample is weighted by its gradient magnitude. Afterwards, a 4x4 descriptor matrix containing vectors with magnitude and orientation relative to the contents of the orientation histogram is produced. The final descriptor representation is a 4x4x8=128 element feature vector with magnitude and orientation derived from the algebraic sum of the

*Figure 1. The marked pixel (with X) is compared to its 26 neighbors in 3X3 regions at the current and adjacent scales*

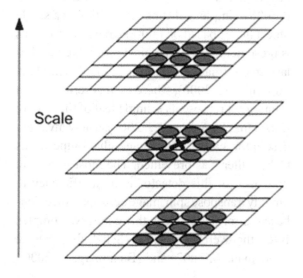

*Figure 2. The matching process of the SIFT algorithm along with the estimated feature correspondences*

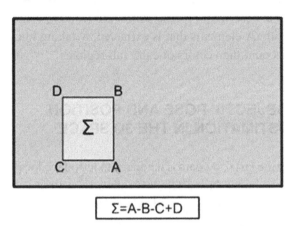

$$\Sigma = A - B - C + D$$

orientation histogram contents for every key-point. The matching process of SIFT is illustrated in Figure 2, where the feature correspondences are extracted over the surface of the object.

## Speeded Up Robust Features (SURF)

Interest point detection is performed by using the basic Hessian matrix approximation, and as a result, the usage of integral images, which were proposed in (Viola, P., & Jones, M. 2001), is mandatory. The most important advantage of integral images is that they reduce the computation time drastically by allowing box type convolution filters. The record of an integral image $I_\Sigma(\chi)$ at a location $\chi = (x, y)^T$ corresponds to the sum of all pixels' intensities of the input image I within a rectangular region formed by the origin and $\chi$.

$$I_\Sigma\left(\chi\right) = \sum_{i=0}^{i \leq x}\sum_{j=0}^{j \leq y} I(i, j)$$

The sum of the intensities over any upright, rectangular area is calculated after three additions and four memory accesses. Thus, the computation time is directly related to the size of the rectangular region. The main structure of an integral image is shown in Figure 3. For the needs of the

*Figure 3. The sum of intensities inside the rectangle area Σ is taken into account for the needs of integral images*

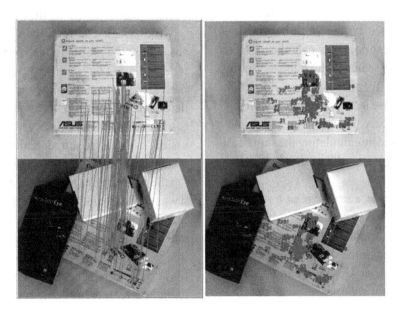

efficient detection of blob-like structures, SURF's detector is based on the Hessian matrix because of its good performance in accuracy. A key-point is found where the determinant of the Hessian matrix becomes maximum. Given a point $\chi = (x, y)$ in an image I, the Hessian Matrix $H(\chi, \sigma)$ in $\chi$ at scale $\sigma$ is defined as follows:

$$H\left(\chi,\sigma\right) = \begin{bmatrix} L_{xx}\left(\chi,\sigma\right) & L_{xy}\left(\chi,\sigma\right) \\ L_{yx}\left(\chi,\sigma\right) & L_{yy}\left(\chi,\sigma\right) \end{bmatrix}$$

where $L_{xx}(\chi, \sigma)$ represents the convolution of the Gaussian second order derivative with the image I at point $\chi$, and similarly for $L_{xy}(\chi, \sigma)$ and $L_{yy}(\chi, \sigma)$.

The accurate key-point localization in the image and over scales is accomplished by applying non-maximum suppression in a 3X3X3 neighborhood, as it was proposed in (Neubeck, A., & Van Gool, L. 2006). The final estimation of interest's point location is fulfilled by the interpolation of the maxima of the Hessian's matrix determinant in scale and image space. The construction process of SURF's descriptor is divided into two phases. In the first stage, and with a view to descriptor's invariance to a possible image rotation, a reproducible orientation of the interest points is estimated. Especially, the Haar wavelet responses in x and y direction within a circular neighborhood of radius 6s around the interest point are calculated. Here s corresponds to the scale at which the key-point was detected. Only six operations are needed to compute the response in x and y direction in any scale. Finally, for every interest point an orientation, that is estimated by calculating the sum of all Haar wavelet responses within a sliding window of size $\pi/3$, is assigned.

In the second phase, a square region with size of 20s, whilst centered around the key-point and oriented along the orientation extracted in the previous stage, is constructed. This region is split up regularly into smaller 4X4 square sub-regions, for each of them Haar wavelet responses at 5X5 sample points are computed. Afterwards, for each sub-region a vector, that is produced by the sum of Haar responses in x and y, is estimated. The final descriptor representation is a feature vector with 64 elements that is extracted by taking into account the vectors of each sub-region.

## OBJECTS' POSE AND POSITION ESTIMATION IN THE 3D SPACE

In the last few years, a tendency to introduce local appearance-based features into pose estimation procedures is discerned. Matched features from 2D images are combined in order to produce the 3D model of a pre-recognized object. In (Wu, C. et al. 2008) a method that is able to compute camera poses from single query images and to efficiently search for 3D models in a city-scale database is presented. It employs Viewpoint Invariant Patches (VIP) that are based on the creation of ortho-textures for the 3D models and on the detection of local features, e.g. SIFT or SURF, on them. In turn, Time-of-Flight (ToF) cameras can be used for the precise 3D environment mapping, as it was shown in (May, S., et al 2008). Camera's pose was estimated using visual odometry, whilst SIFT was employed, among other feature extraction mechanisms, during the registration process.

Additionally, in (Andreopoulos, A., & Tsotsos, J. 2009) a model for actively searching for a target in a 3D environment, which incorporates both multi-view and single view recognition and detections schemes, is presented. However, the results stand only in theory when sophisticated vision systems required realistic and practical measurements of targets' location in the 3D space. On the contrary, in (Husler, G., & Ritter, D. 1999) it was shown that it is possible to estimate objects' location in a scene by combining 3D-based target models with information derived by a single 2D image. The final 6 DOF localization is obtained by accumulating the correspondences between extracted features (edges, corners or centers of ellipses) and the 3D target on a Hough table. On the contrary, the main drawbacks of the method include both its deficiency to recognize and estimate the location in the 3D space of non-rigid objects and the extraction only low-level features.

Due to the large amount of pose estimation methods available in the literature, this chapter's section is devoted to the presentation of those techniques that exploit information derived through object recognition procedures based on local features. As a result, in the following paragraphs respective methods for objects' pose estimation or localization are presented. At the last part of the section, the merits and the disadvantages of the referred methods are noted.

## Objects' Depth Estimation Using Any Two-Part Recognition Technique (Kouskouridas, R., et al. 2010)

The main idea underlying this algorithm is the maintenance of any two-part approach's properties whilst it exploits spatial information to derive depth. The method initiates with the construction of a large database containing images from several objects. With a view to database's enrichment, these objects are photographed from different viewpoints and distances from the camera. Moreover, by taking into account SIFT's and SURF's matching sub-procedures an on-line scene search engine is built. Estimations derived from this engine are taken into consideration for the position estimation task.

The algorithm is divided into five discriminative stages, when during the first one the detector mechanism is applied to the scene's and object's image, in order to estimate the features position in both of them. This stage could be apprehended as the training session of the algorithm. In this phase, for each image in the database the key-point features are extracted using the detector mechanism. Images of each object are captured at different distances from the camera and the measured depth $d_O$ is stored. This process is performed while the

system remains off-line, thus, execution time is not taken into account. The results are stored for further use at the next phases.

During the second phase, the N matching features in the two images are obtained by applying the matching sub-procedure of the two-part algorithm. Define as $(X_{Si}, Y_{Si})$, i=1,…,N the positions of the N features in the scene image and $(X_{Oi}, Y_{Oi})$, i=1,…,N the positions of the N features in the object image. Specifically, in this stage the matching sub-procedure of the two-part algorithm is performed. Especially, descriptors that are common in both images (scene and object) are extracted. It is apparent that, one image representing the scene is compared with several others, representing the object from different viewpoints. Furthermore, the locations of the common features are stored for further use. Afterwards, define as $(X_{Sc}, Y_{Sc})$ and $(X_{Oc}, Y_{Oc})$ the features' centers of mass for both images. This is accomplished by estimating the mean values of the features positions in the two images:

$$X_{Sc} = \frac{1}{N}\sum_{i=1}^{N} X_{Si} \text{ and } Y_{Sc} = \frac{1}{N}\sum_{i=1}^{N} Y_{Si}$$

$$X_{Oc} = \frac{1}{N}\sum_{i=1}^{N} X_{Oi} \text{ and } Y_{Oc} = \frac{1}{N}\sum_{i=1}^{N} Y_{Oi}$$

During the third stage, the position estimation sub-procedure takes place till the conclusion of the algorithm. Moreover, at this phase the features' centers of mass in both images are calculated. The last are obtained by estimating the mean values of features locations in both representations. As a next step, calculate the mean Euclidean distance (in pixels) of each feature from the corresponding center of mass that is extracted in the previous stage. Set as $E_S$ and $E_O$ the mean Euclidean distances in the scene and object image, respectively. The following relations are used:

$$E_S = \frac{1}{N} \sum_{i=1}^{N} \sqrt{(X_{Si} - X_{Sc})^2 + (Y_{Si} - Y_{Sc})^2}$$

$$E_O = \frac{1}{N} \sum_{i=1}^{N} \sqrt{(X_{Oi} - X_{Oc})^2 + (Y_{Oi} - Y_{Oc})^2}$$

During this phase, the distance of each key-point from the centre of mass is calculated. This is measured in pixels with the use of Euclidean Distance. By the end of this sub-routine, significant spatial information of an object in a scene is collected. This is accomplished by simply estimating the distribution of trained features around their center of mass. Finally, estimate $d_S$ that correspond to the ratio of the two mean distances $E_S$ and $E_O$. Furthermore, the pre-computed depth $d_O$ is introduced, which is obtained during the training session and while the object is captured alone. The final object's distance (Z) from the camera is obtained by multiplying this ratio with the respective sought object's distance from the sensor ($d_O$):

$$Z = d_O \cdot d_S = d_O \cdot \frac{E_O}{E_S}$$

During the last phase of the algorithm, object's distance from the camera is computed. The pre-computed depth $d_O$, measured during the training session of the first phase, is taken into account. The ratio $d_S$ is used to measure the proportion of object's features to those found in the scene. Concluding, after the necessary training session and the database construction at the first stages of the method, an on-line search engine takes over. It is responsible for querying in the scene for objects contained in the trained database. After an object is found, the scene is compared to the image of the object, providing the majority of common matches. Finally, features' information from both images is interpolated with a view to object's position

allocation. This approach excels in simplicity and computational cost, whilst its database can be easily modified for the needs of multiple-object recognition and location assignment.

## Real-Time 3D Object Pose Estimation and Tracking for Natural Landmark Based Visual Servo (Choi, C., et al 2008)

This method combines scale invariant features matching with optical flow based tracking, KLT tracker, for real-time 3D pose tracking. SIFT matching process makes the system robustly estimate an initial pose of a target object due to the fact that it is invariant to scale, rotation, illumination, and partial change in 3D viewpoint. To overcome SIFT's computational burden this difficulty, this approach adopts KLT tracker to calculate 3D pose consecutively from initially estimated pose. This tracker is already well known method, whilst there are several implementations available (Bouguet, J.-Y. 2000). The advantages of the KLT tracker are in that it is free from prior knowledge and computationally cheap. On the other hand, possible illumination changes or occlusions directly affect the efficiency of the method. In addition, KLT tracking points are likely to drift due to the aperture problem of optical flow. The system excels in removing outliers to get accurate pose results.

The method is able to estimate objects' pose utilizing both mono images and stereo pairs, whilst the whole process is divided into two separate phases. The first one is devoted to the initial pose estimation of the object when the second emphasizes in calculating targets' orientation locally. The system initiates by taking several images of the target and calculating 3D points from a structured light system. This off-line data is taken into account and accompanied with the POSIT algorithm (Intel 2006) produce the initial pose hypothesis. As a next step, KLT tracking points are built around those of SIFT and 3D reference features are stored for further exploitation at the later stages. The most important issue that arises is that the tracked points are generated only inside the convex hull of a set of the matched SIFT features with the respective criteria proposed in (Jianbo, S., & Tomasi, C. 1994).

In turn, during the second phase, the correspondences between the 3D reference points and those of the KLT are taken into account. As a result, the system is able to both quickly track a possible target and estimate its pose. However, this process produces a large number of outliers that affect directly the efficiency of the algorithm. To this end, with a view to overcome this problem, the RANSAC algorithm is utilized and, as a result, the outliers are eliminated. The algorithm executes until the number of the remained tracking points are less than a threshold. In cases where the number of key-points available is not adequate, the system returns to the first phase in order to execute the initial pose estimation process, which in turn, restarts SIFT's matching procedure globally.

## Robust Pose Estimation with 3D Textured Models (Gall, R.B.J., & Seidel, H.P. 2006)

This method implies that assuming a prior knowledge of object's 3D model, the final pose estimation is mainly based in correspondences between some 2D features located in the images and their actual positions on the 3D model. Moreover, the system is enhanced by simply incorporating texture information over the targets' surface, which in turn, provides more accurate and reliable correspondences. The system initiates by assuming a prior knowledge of the object's pose for frame t-1, where a textured 3D model is generated. The latter is formed in the same world coordinate system used for the calibration of the cameras, where the calibration matrices are converted to the model-view and projection matrix representation

of OpenGL. It is important to keep in mind that image sequences are undistorted by hand and a number of initial views of the 3D model (by rotating and storing the respective extracted features) are rendered. This phase terminates by projecting the 3D model onto the image plane according the calculated calibration matrix.

During the second stage, at frame t, numerous features from both the objects' rendered images and those depicting the scene are extracted using PCA-SIFT (Ke, Y., & Sukthankar, R. 2004). Afterwards, the reliable correspondences needed for the accurate pose estimation are established by assuming that each 2D point lies inside or on the border of a projected triangle of the 3D mesh. Thus, considering an affine transformation, the respective triangle for a point is efficiently determined by a look-up table comprising of information concerning the color index and the vertices of each triangle.

The next phase is devoted to the accurate estimation of object's orientation relative to the one at frame t-1. The contour based philosophy of the method is mainly responsible to the large amount of outliers contained in the feature correspondences. The latter are minimized by adopting a least squares method, which involves the estimation of the object's motion. In cases where not enough feature correspondences are extracted by PCA-SIFT an auto-regression model is utilized for the adequate estimation of the target's pose.

Finally, an image segmentation technique that involves color and texture information (Brox, T., et al. 2003) is utilized for the extraction of the object's contour. Thus, by simply matching the latter with the projected contour of the model (using the closest point algorithm (Zhang, Z. 1994)) generates new feature correspondences between the 3D model and the 2D image. The latter correspondences accompanied with those extracted from the PCA-SIFT are used for the final object's pose estimation at frame t.

## Robot-Vision Architecture for Real-Time 6-DOF Object Localization (Sumi, Y., & Ishiyama, Y., & Tomita, F. 2007)

This method proposes a robot - vision architecture, called Hyper Frame Vision (HFV), which is able to both detect moving objects and estimate their 6-DOF motion. The recognition scheme is mainly dependent on a feature extractor based on information derived from edges. Practically, the presented detection framework implements the same procedure followed at the SIFT's detector. The system consists of calibrated stereo cameras for 3D sensing and stereo-vision-based identification (Sumi, Y., et al. 2002) and tracking algorithms. The latter require 3D edge segments (known to be robust against possible illumination changes) that are provided by the stereo cameras in terms of extracted features for object localization. Moreover, in order to achieve real time execution, both algorithms are implemented as independent software modules requiring stereo image sequences as input.

The stereo cameras used in the HFV system continuously capture a stereo image sequence, which is buffered into the large frame memory. In turn, the object recognition task is performed by the identification module, which chooses the latest frame of stereo images that includes the object. Furthermore, this module is responsible for the model matching procedures and the final 6-DOF localization of the object. Targets' tracking is adequately fulfilled by the respective algorithm that exhibits frame-by-frame operations, which, in turn, result in the accurate objects' motion estimations.

Generally, the method is divided into three discriminative steps. The first one is responsible for the object localization, which is accomplished by adopting the identification algorithm at frame $t_{st}$. During the task, all input stereo images are buffered in the frame memory. Define $p_{id}$ as the processing time of the identification task, whilst

$T(i)$ as a 3x4 transformation matrix representing the 6-DOF object's position in the $i^{th}$ frame. It is apparent that, the task terminates at time $t_{st} + p_{id}$, whilst an object is identified using the respective confidence value. The latest process of this first step involves the data transferring between the identification module and the tracking one.

During the second phase, the tracking module takes place that requires as input the buffered image sequence provided by the first stage. When the tracking module receives the identification result $T(i_0)$ as the initial position of the object, it starts a new tracking task from the frame $i_0+1$ to measure the object's motions $T(i = i_0+1, i_0+2,...)$ and to calculate the confidence values. Finally, the tracking frame catches up with the input frame (at frame k in the time diagram). It is important to keep in mind that the only restriction of the tracking module is the frame-by-frame period, $p_f$, which is mainly depended on the working computer.

The final step emphasizes in the real-time object motion tracking, where the tracking algorithm is made to wait for the latest images. As a result, if $p_{tr}$ is the average processing time per frame of the tracking process, then $p_{tr} < p_f$. In instances where the latter is not satisfied the HFV system repeats the process presented in step 2, which in turn invokes re-estimation of object's motion and confidence values. Furthermore, if a tracking failure is detected then the system terminates and returns to the initial step 1.

## Combination of Foveal and Peripheral Vision for Object Recognition and Pose Estimation (Bjorkman, M., & Kragic, D. 2004)

This method presents a biologically inspired one, capable of adequately accomplish object recognition and pose estimation tasks. A real-time vision system that integrates a series of algorithms for object recognition, tracking and pose estimation tasks is presented. Furthermore, both monocular and binocular cues are taken into account by using one set of stereo cameras for object recognition tasks and one camera responsible for object's tracking and pose estimation. SIFT is mainly used for the recognition purposes, although, its' spatial attributes are exploited during the pose estimation procedure. The most important and interesting issue constitute the fact that this method involves a stereo-head where the sensors are positioned respectively.

The system is divided into four individual modules that are responsible for specific tasks. The first sub-system is called Visual Front-End and is devoted to the figure-ground segmentation, in order to obtain constant flow of reliable data from the surrounding environment. Moreover, this part of the system extracts metric information, i.e. sizes and distances concerning objects and obstacles, by adopting a stereo-based philosophy. Since most efficient methods for dense disparity estimation assume the image planes to be parallel, rectification is performed using epipolar geometry's attributes. Fragmentally, this module could be apprehended as a three-step process, which includes epipolar geometry estimation, image rectification and calculation of dense disparity maps.

The second subsystem emphasizes in generating a number of hypotheses about the objects in the scene that may be relevant to the task in hand. Practically the purpose of this component is to derive qualified guesses of where a requested object might be located in the current scene. In turn, the third module corresponds to the object recognition framework. For the adequate accomplishment of this task, the system adopts the SIFT algorithm and an appearance based module that relies on color histograms. Co-occurrence Color Histograms are utilized in a classical learning framework that facilitates a winner-takes-all strategy across scales.

The last module of the system is referred as Action Generation and is responsible for triggering visual tracking and pose estimation. The last require input derived from the aforementioned modules, including recognition and hypotheses generation. As far as the tracking is concerned, it is based on the accumulation of several visual cues including motion, colors and gradients, whilst the framework incorporates a "voting" procedure. On the other hand, pose estimation is adequately accomplished by taking into account information derived through SIFT and by adopting the technique presented in (Kragic, D., & Christensen, H. I. 2003).

## Comparison

The following section is devoted to the qualitative and quantitative results that are extracted from both surveys, i.e. the one concerning the object recognition algorithms and the other over the pose estimation methods. In the first case, the amount of recognition algorithms available generates numerous applicable solutions to several target detection problems. The most accurate and reliable comparison studies available in the literature are presented in (Mikolajczyk, K., & Schmid, C. 2004, Mikolajczyk, K. et al. 2005, Mikolajczyk, K., & Schmid, C. 2005), where several detectors and descriptors are experimentally evaluated through numerous tests. Fragmentally, in general the SIFT algorithm outperforms almost any two-part approach when its disadvantages constitute its computational cost and its descriptors' complexity. On the other hand, and remaining at the two-part strategies, the SURF method can be adopted in procedures that require real time execution due to the fact that provides adequate feature correspondences accompanied with low computational burden. Moreover, SIFT extract features that are distributed more over the surface of the object in cases where SURF only detects points that mostly lay at the center of the image. As far as the non two-part approaches are concerned, several detectors have been proposed, whereas all of them provide adequate fulfillment of the feature extraction process. Depending on the task, a computer vision researcher is able to select several solutions from a large deposit of available ones.

In turn, the task of finding an object located in a scene only constitutes the first step of a larger scale framework that emphasize in providing more information concerning the object. Especially, computer vision researchers aim at providing a sense of location for any potential application, such as robotic platforms or automated driving vehicles. To this end, state of the art research is devoted to the accurate estimation of objects' – targets' orientation relative to a pre-defined coordinate system. Through this chapter several methods that produce effective solutions to this problem have been presented. Moreover, these methods and their main building blocks have been experimentally assessed, whilst numerous qualitative and quantitative results have been extracted. The latter are summed in Table 1. The estimation

error actually corresponds to each method's efficiency, whilst the "dealing with occlusions" topic examines algorithms' solutions to the respective problem. Furthermore, execution time refers to the computation time and it is, obviously, related to the computational burden of the framework. Finally, the pose estimation schemes are collated according to their feasibility. Despite the fact that an algorithm have been shown to provide remarkable results, it is possible that its implementation constitutes its adoption prohibitory.

## CONCLUSION AND FUTURE WORK

Throughout this chapter two major topics of the computer vision society were assessed, i.e. the

*Table 1. Accumulated qualitative and quantitative results concerning the pose estimation methods already presented in Section 3*

| Method | Estimation Error | Dealing with occlusions | Execution time | Implementation – feasibility |
|---|---|---|---|---|
| Kouskouridas, R. et al. 2010 | < 9% | Partial occlusions reduce algorithm's efficiency to 70% | ~ 2 seconds per object | Very easy to implement since it requires only a two-part recognition approach |
| Choi, C. et al 2008 | < 15% | Partial occlusions affect directly the efficiency of the algorithm (the system fails to estimate the object's pose) | Real-time | Requires either stereo or mono image sequences captured with Bumblebee camera. (use of KLT feature tracker) |
| Gall, R.B.J., & Seidel, H.P. 2006 | < 50% in cases where only the contour of the 3D model is taken into account | Partial occlusions affect directly the efficacy of the algorithm (failure to estimate 3D model's contour) | Very time demanding operation with high computational burden | Almost infeasible since it involves 3D object modeling in OpenGL and enough time devoted to the off-line training of the system |
| Sumi, Y., et al. 2007 | < 10% (The confidence value alters drastically depending on the constant rotational velocity) | The system fails to initially track and afterwards estimate target's 6-DOF location in cases where the latter is occluded spontaneously | Real-time | Feasible enough although it requires a stereo camera and a large amount of memory buffer available |
| Bjorkman, M., & Kragic, D. 2004 | < 25% (Possible object's rotation over 20 degrees leads to efficiency reduction) | This is the most heavily influenced by occlusions method, since information derived through SIFT are lost in such cases | ~ 6 sec per object | CCH's require large amount of time dedicated to off-line training of the system |

object recognition and pose estimation. As far as the recognition process is concerned, the current trend implies the usage of local appearance-based detection schemes that rely on locally sampled descriptions of the target. The detectors and descriptors constitute the two main mechanisms underlying any recently proposed recognition framework. Moreover, SIFT and SURF that are referred as two-part approaches, are constantly adapted to numerous of robotics applications providing remarkable solutions to several vision – based problems.

On the other hand, a pose estimation procedure aims at making one step further from a typical recognition scheme in terms of providing spatial information to the sought targets. All the presented methods are based on feature correspondences between 2D image features and the respective 3D ones located in the real world. Moreover, the frameworks presented utilize local appearance based recognition techniques (e.g. SIFT), whilst the pose estimation task is fulfilled by exploiting the extracted features' attributes. Generally, the overall estimation error mainly depends on general assumptions made during the first stages of the algorithms or, in the best case, on the re-projection error of the camera.

Finally, the ultimate goal of the chapter was to both present the state-off-the-art in the field of object recognition and pose estimation algorithms, and to actually, point out possible solutions in real problems. Towards this end, in this chapter the most important methods are analytically presented. During the last few years, a tendency to introduce autonomous vehicles into domestic environments is discerned. Thus, due to the fact that only the visual sense provides the majority of the information available, computer vision researchers have to outcome the challenge of making simple and easy to build solutions to everyday tasks.

# REFERENCES

Andreopoulos, A., & Tsotsos, J. (2009). A theory of active object localization. In *The Proceedings of the International Conference on Computer Vision, Poster Session.*

Baumberg, A. (2000). Reliable feature matching across widely separated views. In *Proceedings of the IEEE Computer Society Conference on Computer Vision and Pattern Recognition,* (pp. 774-781). Hilton Head, USA.

Bay, H., Ess, A., Tuytelaars, T., & Van Gool, L. (2008). Speeded-up robust features (surf). *International Journal of Computer Vision and Image Understanding, 110*(3), 346–359. doi:10.1016/j.cviu.2007.09.014

Bjorkman, M., & Kragic, D. (2004) Combination of foveal and peripheral vision for object recognition and pose estimation. In *Proceedings of the IEEE International Conference on Robotics and Automation,* (pp. 5135-5140).

Borges, A. P., Ribeiro, R., Avila, B. C., Enembreck, F., & Scalabrin, E. E. (2009). A learning agent to help drive vehicles. In *Proceedings of the International Conference on Computer Supported Cooperative Work in Design,* (pp. 282-287).

Bouguet, J.-Y. (2000) *Pyramidal implementation of the Lucas Kanade feature tracker: Description of the algorithm.* Technical Report, Intel Corporation, Microprocessor Research Labs, OpenCV documentation.

Bradski, G. R., & Kaehler, A. (2008). *Learning OpenCV* (1st ed.). Sebastopol, CA: O'Reilly Media, Inc.

Brox, T., Rousson, M., Deriche, R., & Weickert, J. (2003). Unsupervised segmentation incorporating colour, texture, and motion. In *Computer analysis of images and patterns,* (LNCS 2756, pp. 353-360).

Choi, C., Baek, S. M., & Lee, S. (2008). Real-time 3D object pose estimation and tracking for natural landmark based visual servo. In *Proceedings of the IEEE/RSJ International Conference on Intelligent Robots and Systems,* (pp. 3983-3989). Nice, France.

Ekvall, S., Kragic, D., & Hoffmann, F. (2005). Object recognition and pose estimation using color cooccurrence histograms and geometric modeling. *International Journal of Image and Vision Computing, 23*(11), 943–955. doi:10.1016/j.imavis.2005.05.006

Gall, R. B. J., & Seidel, H. P. (2006). *Robust pose estimation with 3D textured models.* Lecture Notes in Computer Science.

Harris, C., & Stephens, M. (1988). A combined corner and edge detection. In *Proceedings of the Fourth Alvey Vision Conference* (pp. 147-151). Manchester, UK.

Husler, G., & Ritter, D. (1999). Feature-based object recognition and localization in 3D-space, using a single video image. *International Journal of Computer Vision and Image Understanding, 73*(1), 64–81. doi:10.1006/cviu.1998.0704

Intel. (2006). *Open source computer vision library.* Retrieved from http://www.intel.com/research/mrl/research/opencv/

Jianbo, S., & Tomasi, C. (1994) Good features to track. In *Proceedings of the International Conference on Computer Vision and Pattern Recognition,* (pp. 593-600).

Kadir, T., & Brady, M. (2001). Saliency, scale and image description. *International Journal of Computer Vision, 45*(2), 83–105. doi:10.1023/A:1012460413855

Ke, Y., & Sukthankar, R. (2004). PCA-SIFT: A more distinctive representation for local image descriptors. In *Proceedings of the IEEE Conference on Computer Vision and Pattern Recognition,* (pp. 506-513).

Kouskouridas, R., Badekas, E., & Gasteratos, A. (2010). (in press). Evaluation of two-parts algorithms for objects' depth estimation. *IET Computer Vision.*

Kragic, D., Bjorkman, M., Christensen, H., & Eklundh, J. (2005). Vision for robotic object manipulation in domestic settings. *International Journal of Robotics and Autonomous Systems, 52*(1), 85–100. doi:10.1016/j.robot.2005.03.011

Kragic, D., & Christensen, H. I. (2003). Confluence of parameters in model-based tracking. In *Proceedings of the IEEE International Conference on Robotics and Automation,* Taipei, Taiwan.

Lazebnik, S., & Ponce, J. (2005). A sparse texture representation using local affine regions. *IEEE Transactions on Pattern Analysis and Machine Intelligence, 27*(8), 1265–1278. doi:10.1109/TPAMI.2005.151

Lepetit, V., & Fua, P. (2006). Keypoint recognition using randomized trees. *IEEE Transactions on Pattern Analysis and Machine Intelligence, 28*(9), 1465–1479. doi:10.1109/TPAMI.2006.188

Lindeberg, T. (1994). Scale-space theory: A basic tool for analyzing structures at different scales. *International Journal of Applied Statistics, 21*(2), 414–431.

Lowe, D. G. (2004). Distinctive image features from scale-invariant keypoints. *International Journal of Computer Vision, 60*(2), 91–110. doi:10.1023/B:VISI.0000029664.99615.94

Matas, J., Chum, O., Urban, M., & Pajdla, T. (2004). Robust wide-baseline stereo from maximally stable extremal regions. *International Journal of Image and Vision Computing, 22*(10), 761–767. doi:10.1016/j.imavis.2004.02.006

May, S., Droeschel, D., Holz, D., Wiesen, C., Birlinghoven, S., & Fuchs, S. (2008). 3D pose estimation and mapping with time-of-flight cameras. In *Proceedings of the International Conference on Intelligent Robots and Systems (IROS), 3D Mapping Workshop*, Nice, France.

Mikolajczyk, K., & Schmid, C. (2004). Scale & affine invariant interest point detectors. *International Journal of Computer Vision, 60*(1), 63–86. doi:10.1023/B:VISI.0000027790.02288.f2

Mikolajczyk, K., & Schmid, C. (2005). A performance evaluation of local descriptors. *IEEE Transactions on Pattern Analysis and Machine Intelligence, 27*(10), 1615–1630. doi:10.1109/TPAMI.2005.188

Mikolajczyk, K., Tuytelaars, T., Schmid, C., Zisserman, A., Matas, J., & Schaffalitzky, F. (2005). A comparison of affine region detectors. *International Journal of Computer Vision, 65*(1-2), 43–72. doi:10.1007/s11263-005-3848-x

Neubeck, A., & Van Gool, L. (2006). Efficient non-maximum suppression. In *Proceedings of the International Conference on Pattern Recognition*, (pp. 850-855).

Nister, D., & Stewenius, H. (2006). Scalable recognition with a vocabulary tree. In *Proceedings of the IEEE International Conference on Computer Vision and Pattern Recognition*. (pp. 2161-2168). New York, USA.

Rosten, E., & Drummond, T. (2006). *Machine learning for high-speed corner detection* (pp. 395–430). Lecture Notes in Computer Science.

Rothganger, F., Lazebnik, S., & Ponce, J. (2006). 3D object modeling and recognition from photographs and image sequences. In *Proceedings toward Category-Level Object Recognition* (pp. 105-126).

Sandhu, R., Dambreville, S., Yezzi, A., & Tannenbaum, A. (2009). Non-rigid 2D-3D pose estimation and 2D image segmentation. In *Proceedings of the IEEE Conference on Computer Vision and Pattern Recognition* (pp. 786-793). Miami, USA.

Sarfraz, M. S., Hellwich, O., Yilmaz, U., Bellmann, A., Rodehorst, V., & Erten, E. (2008). Head pose estimation in face recognition across pose scenarios. In *International Conference on Computer Vision Theory and Applications* (pp. 235-242). Funchal, Portugal.

Schaffalitzky, F., & Zisserman, A. (2002). *Multiview matching for unordered image sets, or How do I organize my holiday snaps?* (pp. 414–431). Lecture Notes in Computer Science.

Schmid, C., & Mohr, R. (1997). Local grayvalue invariants for image retrieval. *IEEE Transactions on Pattern Analysis and Machine Intelligence, 19*(5), 530–535. doi:10.1109/34.589215

Sivic, J., & Zisserman, A. (2003). Video Google: A text retrieval approach to object matching in videos. In *Proceedings of the Ninth IEEE International Conference on Computer Vision* (pp. 1470-1477). Nice, France.

Sumi, Y., Ishiyama, Y., & Tomita, F. (2007). Robot-vision architecture for real-time 6-dof object localization. *International Journal of Computer Vision and Image Understanding, 105*(3), 218–230. doi:10.1016/j.cviu.2006.11.003

Sumi, Y., Kawai, Y., Yoshimi, T., & Tomita, F. (2002). 3D object recognition in cluttered environments using segment-based stereo vision. *International Journal of Computer Vision, 46*(1), 5–23. doi:10.1023/A:1013240031067

Thomas, A., Ferrari, V., Leibe, B., Tuytelaars, T., & Van Gool, L. (2009). Shape-from-recognition: Recognition enables meta-data transfer. *International Journal of Computer Vision and Image Understanding, 113*(12), 1222–1234. doi:10.1016/j.cviu.2009.03.010

Vaish, V., Levoy, M., Szeliski, R., Zitnick, C., & Kang, S. (2006). Reconstructing occluded surfaces using synthetic apertures: Stereo, focus and robust measures. In *Proceedings of the International Conference on Pattern Recognition*.

Van Gool, J., Moons, T., & Ungureanu, D. (1996). Affine/photometric invariants for planar intensity patterns. In *Proceedings of the European Conference on Computer Vision* (pp. 642-651). Cambridge, UK.

Viola, P., & Jones, M. (2001). Rapid object detection using a boosted cascade of simple features. In *Proceedings of IEEE Computer Society Conference on Computer Vision and Pattern Recognition* (pp. 511-518).

Wong, B., & Spetsakis, M. (2000). Scene reconstruction and robot navigation using dynamic fields. *International Journal of Autonomous Robots, 8*(1), 71–86. doi:10.1023/A:1008992902895

Wu, C., Fraundorfer, F., Frahm, J., & Pollefeys, M. (2008). 3D model search and pose estimation from single images using VIP features. In *Proceedings of IEEE Computer Society Conference on Computer Vision and Pattern Recognition Workshops*, (pp. 1-8).

Zhang, J., McMillan, L., Yu, J., & Hill, U. (2006) Robust tracking and stereo matching under variable illumination. In *Proceedings of the International Conference on Pattern Recognition*.

Zhang, Z. (1994). Iterative point matching for registration of free-form curves and surfaces. *International Journal of Computer Vision, 7*(3), 119–152. doi:10.1007/BF01427149

Zwicker, M., Vetro, A., Yea, S., Matusik, W., Pfister, H., & Durand, F. (2007). Resampling, antialiasing, and compression in multiview 3-D displays. *IEEE Signal Processing Magazine, 24*(6), 88–96. doi:10.1109/MSP.2007.905708

## ADDITIONAL READING

Duda, R. O., Hart, P. E., & Stork, D. G. (2001). *Pattern classification*. Wiley-Interscience.

Forsyth, D. A., & Ponce, J. (2002). Computer vision: A modern approach (US ed.). Prentice Hall Professional Technical Reference

Hartley, R. I., & Zisserman, A. (2004). *Multiple view geometry in computer vision* (2nd ed.). Cambridge University Press. doi:10.1017/CBO9780511811685

Paragios, N., Chen, Y., & Faugeras, O. (2005). *Handbook of mathematical models in computer vision*. Secaucus, NJ, USA: Springer-Verlag New York, Inc.

Steger, C., Ulrich, M., & Wiedemann, C. (2008). *Machine vision algorithms and Applications*. Wiley VCH.

Treiber, M. A. (2010). *An introduction to object recognition: Selected algorithms for a wide variety of applications (Advances in pattern recognition)*. Springer.

## KEY TERMS AND DEFINITIONS

**3D Position Estimation:** The task of identifying and estimating the absolute position of an object in the 3D space. At least two different views are required, whilst multi-camera systems provide the majority of the information needed.

**Computer Vision:** The science devoted to the design and implementation of process that emphasize in making machines capable of sensing what is visually perceived. It is directly related to the extraction of information contained in images, whilst algorithms of this field try to decode vital visual information contained in natural environments.

**Depth Calculation:** The procedure of calculating a target's distance from the capturing device (camera). Stereo-vision algorithms have been proven to provide the most efficient solutions to this problem.

**Descriptor:** Organizes the information collected from the detector in a discriminating manner. Therefore, high dimensional feature vectors corresponding to locally sampled feature descriptions are produced. In other words, an object, or parts of it, located in a scene are represented by these vectors, namely the descriptors.

**Detector:** A mechanism contained in advanced object recognition algorithms. The main idea behind interest location detectors is the pursuit of points or regions in a scene containing unique information. These spots or areas hold data that distinguish them in their local neighborhood from any other.

**Object Manipulation:** The task of handling of objects usually via a robotic arm. In order to adequately accomplish manipulation tasks, computer vision algorithms emphasize in estimating the necessary spatial information of the target along with the accompanied grasping positions of the object.

**Object Recognition:** The process of querying an image for a specific target. Illumination circumstances (resulting in shadows) along with possible object occlusions affect directly the efficiency of the respective algorithms.

**Pose Estimation:** The task of estimating recognized object's orientation and position relative to a given coordinate system. Generally, the goal of this process is to calculate the 6 Degrees of Freedom (rotation and translation matrixes) of an object relative to a specific frame. Information extracted is utilized in either manipulation tasks or obstacle avoidance ones.

# Chapter 2
# A Multi-Linear Statistical Method for Discriminant Analysis of 2D Frontal Face Images

**Carlos Eduardo Thomaz**
*Centro Universitário da FEI (FEI), Brazil*

**Vagner do Amaral**
*Centro Universitário da FEI (FEI), Brazil*

**Gilson Antonio Giraldi**
*Laboratório Nacional de Computação Científica (LNCC), Brazil*

**Edson Caoru Kitani**
*Universidade de São Paulo (USP), Brazil*

**João Ricardo Sato**
*Universidade Federal do ABC (UFABC), Brazil*

**Duncan Fyfe Gillies**
*Imperial College London, UK*

## ABSTRACT

*This chapter describes a multi-linear discriminant method of constructing and quantifying statistically significant changes on human identity photographs. The approach is based on a general multivariate two-stage linear framework that addresses the small sample size problem in high-dimensional spaces. Starting with a 2D data set of frontal face images, the authors determine a most characteristic direction of change by organizing the data according to the patterns of interest. These experiments on publicly available face image sets show that the multi-linear approach does produce visually plausible results for gender, facial expression and aging facial changes in a simple and efficient way. The authors believe that such approach could be widely applied for modeling and reconstruction in face recognition and possibly in identifying subjects after a lapse of time.*

DOI: 10.4018/978-1-61350-429-1.ch002

## INTRODUCTION

Multivariate statistical approaches have played an important role of analyzing face images and characterizing their differences. The importance of using multivariate techniques to analyze face images is related to the well-known fact that face images are highly redundant not only owing to the evidence that the image intensities of adjacent pixels are often correlated but also because every individual has some common facial features such as mouth, nose, and eyes. As a consequence, an input image with *n* pixels can be projected onto a lower dimensional space without significant loss of information.

The most straightforward and successful statistical methods for visual interpretation of well-framed face images have been based on Principal Component Analysis (PCA). Since the pioneering works of Sirovich and Kirby (Sirovich & Kirby, 1987), and Turk and Pentland (Turk & Pentland, 1991), published approximately 20 years ago, several subsequent works have projected face images on a Principal Component Analysis (PCA) feature space to not only reduce the dimensionality of the original samples for further classification and analysis but also to interpret and reconstruct the most expressive components (Swets & Weng, 1996) described by all the training images. Impressive results on this latter goal have been achieved by the Active Appearance Model (AAM) proposed by Cootes et al. (Cootes et al., 1995; Cootes et al., 1998; Cootes et al., 2000; Cootes & Lanitis, 2004). Unfortunately, since the AAMs rely on PCA directions ranked by the principle of maximum variance, the first principal components with the largest eigenvalues do not necessarily represent important discriminant directions to separate sample groups.

Thus, in the last years, a number of novel multivariate statistical approaches inspired by AAM and its variants has been proposed to model human facial changes due not only to pose, lighting and expression, but also to aging on face

recognition problems. For instance, Ramanathan and Chellapa (Ramanathan & Chellapa, 2006) have proposed a craniofacial growth model that estimates the shape variations of frontal face images of subjects under 18 years of age. Using specific facial landmarks based on anthropometric studies (Farkas, 1994), their method can be used to predict a subject's appearance across years and to perform face recognition of young faces taking into account the unique age progression of each subject (Ramanathan & Chellapa, 2006). Another recent work related to automatic age estimation based on facial features has been proposed by Geng et al. (Geng et al., 2007). In this work, a method named AGES (Aging PattErn Subspace) combines the 2D facial landmarks extracted by AAM with the time information of each sequence of a particular individual's face images, building an aging pattern composed of personal characteristics sorted in temporal ascending order. The performance of their method on automatically estimating the age of face images has been shown to be comparable to that of the human observers (Geng et al., 2007). The degradation in accuracy of automatic face recognition systems owing to temporal variance has also been investigated using 3D models. In 2010, Park et al. (Park et al., 2010) has extended the shape and texture face modeling from 2D to 3D domain, modeling and simulating an age invariant face recognition system on three different publicly available databases with good practical results.

In this chapter, we describe a multi-linear discriminant method of constructing and quantifying statistically significant unseen views of human identity photographs. Given a single photograph of an unseen subject it is possible to construct new images with, for example, a range of different expressions or with different gender characteristics. The method could be widely applied for modeling and reconstruction in face recognition and possibly in identifying subjects after a lapse of time. It is based on the use of two-stage method focused on a separating hyper-plane strategy and called

Statistical Discriminant Method (SDM) (Kitani et al., 2006; Thomaz et al., 2009). Starting with a data set of well-framed frontal face images, we determine a most characteristic direction of change by organizing the data according to the patterns of interest. For example, we may identify one group where all the subjects are smiling, and a second group where all the subjects have a neutral expression. If we now find the best separating hyperplane of these two groups, for example by using a linear discriminant regularized method called Maximum uncertainty Linear Discriminant Analysis (MLDA) (Thomaz et al., 2006; Sato et al., 2008; Sato et al., 2009; Thomaz et al., 2009), we can use its normal vector to define the most characteristic direction of change. Given a new subject image we can adjust it by moving parallel to this direction in the image space. Thus, for instance, we can transform a face image with a neutral expression into a smiling one or vice versa. The constructed images represent the maximum likelihood estimate of the appearance of the subject given the data set that we start with. Our experiments on distinct publicly available face image sets show that the multi-linear statistical method does produce visually plausible results for gender, facial expression and some aging facial changes.

The chapter is divided as follows. In the next section, we provide some background definitions and briefly review the multivariate statistical techniques that form the basis of SDM. Firstly, we introduce PCA and highlight its importance as a multivariate statistical technique on reducing the high dimensionality of face images but without losing information, a computational efficient trick particularly useful in small sample size problems such as the one under investigation. Also, in the same section, we introduce the standard linear discriminant analysis (LDA) and state the reasons for using a maximum uncertainty version of this approach to perform the face experiments required. The main focus of the chapter is then presented in the section entitled Statistical Discriminant Method. In this section, we describe the two-stage SDM implementation and several experimental results using three publicly available face databases to demonstrate the SDM effectiveness on performing plausible multi-linear discriminant analyses on gender, facial expression and aging separation tasks. Next, in the section entitled Future Research Direction, we discuss some perspectives and applications of SDM towards an automatic framework to predict the age-progression in frontal face images using familiar features acquired under controlled conditions. Finally, in the last section of the chapter, we conclude this work, summarizing its main points and highlighting potential SDM real-world applications.

## BACKGROUND

Although PCA and LDA are well-known statistical techniques (Fukunaga, 1990; Devijver & Kittler, 1982; Johnson & Wichern, 1998) that have been used in several image recognition problems, we describe next some background definitions and particularities of both multivariate methods that are important for the problem under investigation owing to its small sample size singularities.

### Principal Component Analysis (PCA)

In any image analysis, and particularly in face image analysis, an input image with $n$ pixels can be treated as a point in an $n$-dimensional space called the image space. The coordinates of this point represent the values of each pixel of the image and form a vector $x^T = [x_1, x_2, \ldots, x_n]$ obtained by concatenating the rows (or columns) of the image matrix. It is well known that well-framed face images are highly redundant. As a consequence, an input image with $n$ pixels can be projected onto a lower dimensional space without significant loss of information by using few linear combinations of these $n$ pixels.

Thus, let an $N \times n$ training set matrix $X$ be composed of $N$ input face images with $n$ pixels. This means that each column of matrix $X$ represents the values of a particular pixel observed all over the $N$ images. Let this data matrix $X$ have covariance matrix $S$ with respectively $P$ and $\Lambda$ eigenvector and eigenvalue matrices, that is,

$$P^T S P = \Lambda. \tag{1}$$

It is a proven result that the set of $m$ ($m \leq n$) eigenvectors of $S$, which corresponds to the $m$ largest eigenvalues, minimizes the mean square reconstruction error over all choices of $m$ orthonormal basis vectors (Fukunaga, 1990). Such a set of eigenvectors that defines a new uncorrelated coordinate system for the training set matrix $X$ is known as the principal components. In the context of face recognition, those $P_{pca} = [p_1, p_2, \ldots, p_m]$ components are frequently called eigenfaces (Turk & Pentland, 1991) and represent the most expressive changes on $X$ (Swets & Weng, 1996).

In order to reproduce the total variability of the sample $X$, we have composed the PCA transformation matrix by selecting all principal components with non-zero eigenvalues. Since our application is a small sample size problem where the original variables (or pixels) are highly correlated and the number of training patterns (or images) is much smaller than the number of pixels, that is $N \ll n$, it is possible to transform data in a way that patterns occupy as compact regions in a lower dimensional feature space as possible with far fewer degrees of freedom to estimate. In other words, assuming that all the $N$ training patterns are linearly independent, the rank of the total scatter covariance matrix $S$ is $N - 1$ (Fukunaga, 1990) and the number of principal components selected is $m = N - 1$. This procedure will reduce dramatically the computational and storage requirements for the subsequent LDA-based covariance method, without losing information of the images when mapped back into the original image space because we have used not only the major principal components with large eigenvalues but also all

the principal components with some variance information, that is, with non-zero eigenvalues (Thomaz et al., 2007).

## Maximum Uncertainty LDA (MLDA)

The primary purpose of the Linear Discriminant Analysis, or simply LDA, is to separate samples of distinct groups by maximizing their between-class separability while minimizing their within-class variability. LDA assumes implicitly that the true covariance matrices of each class are equal because the same within-class scatter matrix is used for all the classes considered.

Let the between-class scatter matrix $S_b$ be defined as

$$S_b = \sum_{i=1}^{g} N_i (\bar{x}_i - \bar{x})(\bar{x}_i - \bar{x})^T \tag{2}$$

and the within-class scatter matrix $S_w$ be defined as

$$S_w = \sum_{i=1}^{g} (N_i - 1) S_i = \sum_{i=1}^{g} \sum_{j=1}^{N_i} (x_{i,j} - \bar{x}_i)(x_{i,j} - \bar{x}_i)^T \tag{3}$$

where $x_{i,j}$ is the $n$-dimensional pattern $j$ from class $\pi_i$, $N_i$ is the number of training patterns from class $\pi_i$, and $g$ is the total number of classes or groups. The vector $\bar{x}_i$ and matrix $S_i$ are respectively the unbiased sample mean and sample covariance matrix of class $\pi_i$ (Fukunaga, 1990). The grand mean vector $\bar{x}$ is given by

$$\bar{x} = \frac{1}{N} \sum_{i=1}^{g} N_i \bar{x}_i = \frac{1}{N} \sum_{i=1}^{g} \sum_{j=1}^{N_i} x_{i,j}, \tag{4}$$

where $N$ is, as described earlier, the total number of samples, that is, $N = N_1 + N_2 + \cdots + N_g$.

The main objective of LDA is to find a projection matrix $W_{lda}$ that maximizes the ratio of the determinant of the between-class scatter matrix to the determinant of the within-class scatter matrix (Fisher's criterion), that is,

$$W_{lda} = \arg\max_{W} \frac{\left| W^T S_b W \right|}{\left| W^T S_w W \right|}. \tag{5}$$

The Fisher's criterion described in equation (5) is maximized when the projection matrix $W_{lda}$ is composed of the eigenvectors of $S_w^{-1} S_b$ with at most $(g-1)$ nonzero corresponding eigenvalues (Fukunaga, 1990; Devijver & Kittler, 1982). In the case of a two-class problem, the LDA projection matrix is in fact the leading eigenvector $w_{lda}$ of $S_w^{-1} S_b$, assuming that $S_w$ is invertible.

However, in limited sample and high dimensional problems, such as in face images analysis, $S_w$ is either singular or mathematically unstable and the standard LDA cannot be used to perform the separating task. To avoid both critical issues, we have calculated $w_{lda}$ by using a maximum uncertainty LDA-based approach (MLDA) that considers the issue of stabilizing the $S_w$ estimate with a multiple of the identity matrix (Thomaz, 2004; Thomaz et al., 2004; Thomaz et al., 2006). In a study (Thomaz et al., 2006) with application to the face recognition problem, Thomaz et al. showed that the MLDA approach improved the LDA classification performance with or without a PCA intermediate step and using less linear discriminant features. The $w_{mlda}$ is calculated by replacing $S_w$ in the Fisher's criterion formula described in equation (5) with its regularization version. This regularization is based on the maximum entropy idea that in limited sample size and high dimensional problems where the within-class scatter matrix is singular or poorly estimated, the Fisher's linear basis found by minimizing a more difficult but appropriate *inflated* within-class scatter matrix would also minimize a less reliable *shriveled* within-class estimate (Thomaz, 2004).

## STATISTICAL DISCRIMINANT METHOD (SDM)

The Statistical Discriminant Method is a two-stage PCA+MLDA separating hyperplane that reduces the dimensionality of the original images and extracts discriminant information from images (Kitani et al., 2006; Thomaz et al., 2009).

In order to estimate the SDM separating hyper-plane, we use training examples and their corresponding labels to construct the classifier. First a training set is selected and the average image vector of all the training images is calculated and subtracted from each $n$-dimensional vector. Then the training matrix composed of zero mean image vectors is used as input to compute the $P_{pca}$ transformation matrix. The columns of this $n$ x $m$ transformation matrix are eigenvectors, not necessarily in eigenvalues descending order. We have retained all the PCA eigenvectors with non-zero eigenvalues, that is, $m = N - 1$, to reproduce the total variability of the samples with no loss of information. It is important to emphasize that this PCA intermediate step has been applied here because $N \ll n$, allowing the MLDA scatter matrices to be calculable in computers with a normal memory size. In situations where $N \gg n$, the SDM approach does not need such PCA step for dimensionality reduction and the maximum entropy regularization of the LDA Fisher's criterion.

Thus, the zero mean image vectors are projected on the principal components and reduced to $m$-dimensional vectors representing the most expressive features of each one of the $n$-dimensional image vector. Afterwards, this $N$ x $m$ data matrix is used as input to calculate the $W_{mlda}$ discriminant transformation matrix, as described in the previous section. Since in this work we have limited ourselves to two-group classification problems, there is only one $W_{mlda}$ discriminant eigenvector. The most discriminant feature of each one of the $m$-dimensional vectors is obtained by multiplying the $N$ x $m$ most expressive features matrix by the $m$ x 1 MLDA linear discriminant eigenvector. Hence, the initial training set of face images consisting of $N$ measurements on $n$ variables, is reduced to a data set consisting of $N$ measurements on only 1 most discriminant feature.

Once the two-stage SDM classifier has been constructed, we can move along its corresponding projection vector and extract the discriminant differences captured by the classifier. Any point on the discriminant feature space can be converted to its corresponding $n$-dimensional image vector by simply: (1) multiplying that particular point by the $w_{mlda}$ linear discriminant eigenvector previously computed; (2) multiplying its $m$ most expressive features by the $P_{pca}$ transformation matrix; and (3) adding the average image calculated in the training stage to the $n$-dimensional image vector. Therefore, assuming that the spreads of the classes follow a Gaussian distribution and applying limits to the variance of each group, such as $\pm 3\sigma_i$, where $\sigma_i$ is the standard deviation of each group $i \in \{1, 2\}$, we can move along the SDM most discriminant features and map the results back into the image domain.

Additionally, any face image $x$ that followed the same acquisition and spatial normalization protocols can incorporate the discriminant information captured by the two-stage linear classifier. More specifically, this procedure of transferring the most discriminant feature can be generated through the following expression (Thomaz et al., 2006; Giraldi et al., 2008; Sato et al., 2008; Sato et al., 2009):

$$y_i = x + k\sigma_i \cdot P_{pca} w_{mlda}, \qquad (6)$$

where $k \in \{-3, -2, -1, 0, 1, 2, 3\}$ and $i \in \{1, 2\}$. This operation is useful not only to transfer the most discriminant feature to any point on the original image space, but also, and most importantly, predict how the discriminant information can affect a particular sample that does not necessarily belong to the training set.

## Face Databases and Pre-Processing

We have used frontal images of three distinct face databases publicly available to carry out the experiments.

The first database is maintained by the Department of Electrical Engineering of FEI, São Paulo, Brazil. In this data set[1] the number of subjects is equal to 200 (100 men and 100 women) and each subject has two frontal images (one with a neutral or non-smiling expression and the other with a smiling facial expression), so there is a total of 400 images to perform gender, facial expression and aging experiments. In the aging experiments, we have composed the young training set of 354 images (a mixture of non-smiling and smiling face images of 177 subjects under 30 years of age) and the old training set of 46 images (a mixture of non-smiling and smiling face images of 23 subjects over 30 years of age).

Besides the FEI face database, we have used the well-known FERET (Philips et al., 1998) and Japanese Female Facial Expression (JAFFE) (Lyons et al., 1999) databases. In the FERET database, we have considered 200 subjects (107 men and 93 women) and each subject has two frontal images (one with a neutral or non-smiling expression and the other with a smiling facial expression), providing a total of 400 images to perform the gender and facial expression experiments. The JAFFE database is a facial expression data set composed of frontal face images of expressions posed by Japanese subjects only, all women. Each person posed three or four examples of each of six fundamental facial expressions: anger, disgust, fear, happiness, sadness and surprise. This database has at least 29 images for each fundamental facial expression. To perform the multi-linear discriminant analysis all the 182 frontal face images of the six facial expressions (anger, disgust, fear, happiness, sadness and surprise) have been analyzed on two-group classification tasks, where the training sets are composed of the facial expression of interest versus a mixture of the other

*Figure 1. Some samples of the FEI (first row), FERET (second row), and JAFFE (third row) frontal images after the pre-processing procedure that aligned, cropped and equalized all the original images to the size of 193x162 pixels for the SDM experiments.*

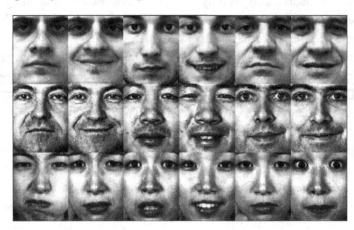

distinct five facial expressions. For example, for the anger experiment, we have discriminated a training set of 30 frontal female images composed only of the anger samples from a training set of 152 non-anger frontal female images composed of a mixture of disgust, fear, happiness, sadness and surprise facial expressions.

To minimize image variations that are not necessarily related to differences between the faces, we previously aligned all the frontal face images using affine transformations and the directions of the eyes as a measure of reference so that the pixel-wise features extracted from the images correspond roughly to the same location across all subjects. Also, in order to reduce the surrounding illumination and some image artifacts owing to distinct hairstyle and adornments, especially present on the FEI and FERET face images, all the frontal images were cropped to the size of 193x162 pixels, had their histograms equalized and were then converted to 8-bit gray scale. Figure 1 illustrates some samples of the FEI (first row), FERET (second row), and JAFFE (third row) frontal images used in the SDM experiments after this pre-processing procedure.

## Interpretation and Reconstruction of the PCA Most Expressive Components

Analogously to the works by Cootes et al. (Cootes et al., 1995; Cootes et al., 1998; Cootes et al., 2000; Cootes & Lanitis, 2004), we have reconstructed the average face images of each face databases by changing each principal component separately using the limits of $\pm 3\sqrt{\lambda_i}$, where $\lambda_i$ are the corresponding largest eigenvalues. As the average face image is an $n$-dimensional point ($n = 193 \times 162 = 31,266$) that retains all common features from the training sets, we could use this point to firstly interpret what happens visually when we move along the principal components and reconstruct the respective coordinates on the image space.

Figure 2 illustrates, as an example, the transformations on the first eight PCA most expressive components of the FERET database only. Since we have used the same training images for gender and facial expression experiments, the PCA most expressive components are equal in both the experiments. Looking at the Figure 2, it is important to note that because changes in either gender or facial expression are not major, PCA is unable to capture such variations in its first most expressive

*Figure 2. FERET database: Interpretation and reconstruction of the first eight, from top to bottom, PCA most expressive components. From left to right: [–3√λ$_i$, –2√λ$_i$, –1√λ$_i$, $\bar{x}$, +1√λ$_i$, +2√λ$_i$, +3√λ$_i$], where i = {1, 2, ..., 8}*

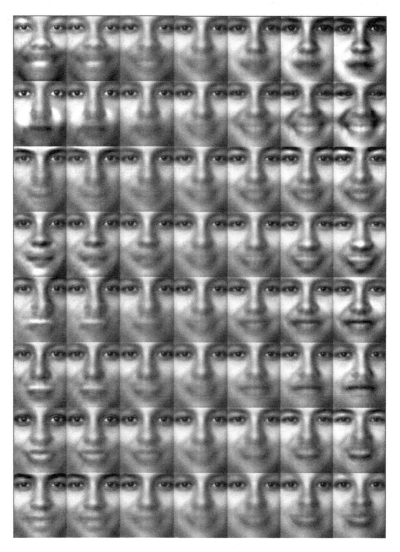

component. These results are expected because PCA tends to capture features that have a considerable variation between all training samples, like changes in the skin color in our FERET experiments. Therefore, if we need to identify specific changes such as the variation in gender, PCA has not proved to be a useful solution for this problem. In fact, when we consider a whole intensity-level model to perform the PCA analysis, there is no guarantee that a single principal component will capture a specific variation alone, no matter how discriminant that variation might be.

## Interpretation and Reconstruction of the SDM Hyper-Planes

To perform the multi-linear discriminant analysis on the face images, we have used the training sets previously selected and their respective labels to construct the linear classifiers corresponding to the aforementioned separation tasks of each face database. Since in all the experiments we have limited ourselves to two-group classification problems, there is only one SDM discriminant eigenvector per separation task.

Figures 3, 4 and 5 present the SDM most discriminant features for each one of the two-group separation tasks performed on the FEI, FERET and JAFFE pre-processed frontal face images. For instance, Figure 3 displays the image regions captured by the SDM approach that change when we move from the left side (group 1 of female, smiling and old labeled samples) of the dividing hyper-plane to the right one (corresponding group 2 of male, non-smiling and young labeled samples), following limits to the standard deviation and mean of each sample group.

As can be seen, for example in Figure 3, the SDM hyper-plane effectively extracts the group differences, showing separately the gender, facial expression and aging features that mainly distinguish the FEI sample groups, without enhancing other image artifacts. More specifically, in the first row of Figure 3, from top to bottom, there are some gender variations that are more significant and consequently predominant in the most

*Figure 3. FEI database: Interpretation and reconstruction, from top to bottom, of the most discriminant features captured by the SDM hyper-planes for the gender, facial expression and aging experiments. From left (group 1 of either female, smiling or old labeled samples) to right (group 2 of either male, non-smiling or young labeled samples): [$-3\sigma_1$, $\overline{x}_1$, $+1\sigma_1$, boundary, $-1\sigma_2$, $\overline{x}_2$, $+3\sigma_2$].*

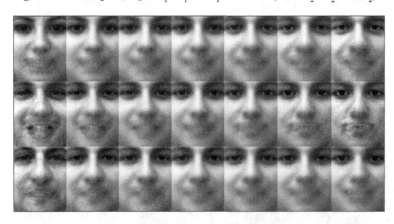

*Figure 4. FERET database: Interpretation and reconstruction, from top to bottom, of the most discriminant features captured by the SDM hyper-planes for the gender and facial expression experiments. From left (group 1 of either female or smiling labeled samples) to right (group 2 of either male or non-smiling labeled samples): [$-3\sigma_1$, $\overline{x}_1$, $+1\sigma_1$, boundary, $-1\sigma_2$, $\overline{x}_2$, $+3\sigma_2$].*

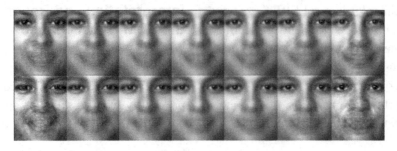

*Figure 5. JAFFE database: Interpretation and reconstruction, from top to bottom, of the most discriminant features captured by the SDM hyper-planes for the six facial expression experiments. From left (group 1 of either non-anger, non-disgust, non-fear, non-happiness, non-sadness, or non-surprise labeled samples) to right (group 2 of either anger, disgust, fear, happiness, sadness and surprise labeled samples): $[-3\sigma_1, \bar{x}_1, +1\sigma_1, boundary, -1\sigma_2, \bar{x}_2, +3\sigma_2]$.*

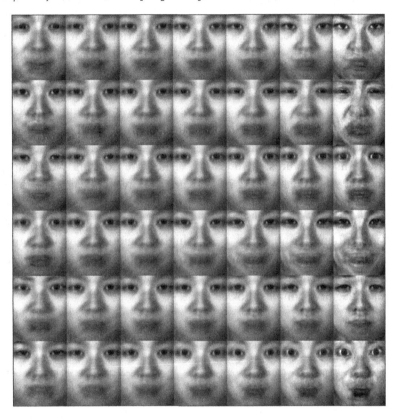

discriminant direction selected, such as the flatness and length of the nose, thickness of the eyebrows, and shape of the eyes. Analogously to the gender experiments, it is possible to see that the SDM hyper-plane has been able to capture the facial expression changes, showing what we should expect intuitively from a face image when someone changes their expression from smiling to non-smiling. In fact, looking at the Figure 4 that describes the SDM gender and facial expression changes using the FERET sample groups and comparing them to the ones described in the first and second rows of the Figure 3, we can see that similar multivariate changes have been described by SDM, no matter the face database used.

As another example, the third row of Figure 3, from top to bottom, displays the image regions captured by the SDM hyper-plane that change when we move from the group 2 of labeled samples under 30 years of age (right side) of the dividing hyper-plane to the group 1 of labeled samples over 30 years of age (left side). Despite the very different sample sizes of these groups of the FEI database, it is possible to see that the SDM hyper-plane captures a number of plausible changes owing to aging, such as thickness of the eyelids, growth of the nose, and a general reduction of the skin elasticity with the appearance of facial wrinkles. Also, looking at the Figure 5, it is important to note that SDM has been able to capture the minor variations related to the six facial expressions described in the JAFFE database, showing clearly and separately the anger, disgust, fear, happiness, sadness and surprise facial features that mainly distinguish linearly the sample groups, despite as well the unbalanced sample sizes used in the corresponding two-group classification tasks.

## Effect Size of the Multi-linear Discriminant Differences

In the previous sub-section, the detection of the differences has been based only on visual inspection of the most discriminant features. In this sub-section, we investigate the effectiveness of the separating hyper-planes on recognizing the group samples and the statistical significance of the discriminant changes found for all the two-group classification experiments. This two-group analysis where we organize the patterns of interest according to positive and negative samples allows

a better understanding of the distribution of the whole data set on the original image space.

We have adopted the leave-one-out method to evaluate the classification performance of the multi-linear classifiers. Throughout all the classification experiments, we have assumed that the prior probabilities and misclassification costs are equal for both groups of the two-group experiments. On the PCA+MLDA subspace, the mean of each class has been calculated from the corresponding training samples and the Euclidean distance from each class mean has been used to assign a test observation to either one of the classes of the corresponding two-group experiments. Figure 6 shows the leave-one-out recognition rates of the multi-linear classifiers. In all experiments and face databases, the SDM approach achieves high recognition rates, indicating that differences between the 2D frontal pre-processed face images can be linearly extracted by the SDM classifiers.

*Figure 6. Leave-one-out recognition rates of all the two-group experiments and face databases*

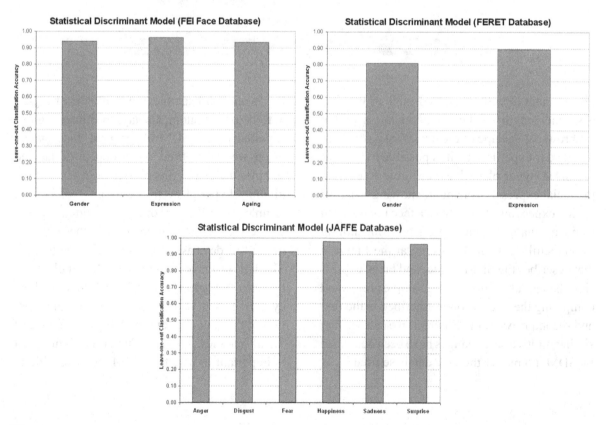

In order to determine and rank the statistical significance of the SDM changes and avoid the use of raw units that are quite arbitrary or lack meaning outside the investigation, we have calculated the effect size of the differences, that is,

$$e = \frac{x_1^* - x_2^*}{\sigma_p}, \tag{7}$$

where $x_1^*$ and $x_2^*$ denote, as shown in Figures 3-5, the transformed images for the statistical extremes points calculated at 3 standard deviations from each corresponding sample group on the SDM separating hyper-plane and projected back on the original image space. The parameter $\sigma_p$ corresponds to the pooled standard deviation of the sample images and is given by

$$\sigma_p = \sqrt{\frac{(N_1 - 1)\sigma_1^2 + (N_2 - 1)\sigma_2^2}{(N_1 + N_2 - 2)}}, \tag{8}$$

where $\sigma_1^2$ and $\sigma_2^2$ are the variances of each sample group and, as a reminder, $N_1$ and $N_2$ are the number of training samples of group 1 and group 2. We have used the pooled variance rather than the variance of each sample group in the $e$-values because the number of samples is limited and $N_1$ and $N_2$ might be different from each other.

Figure 7[2] illustrates the spatial distribution of the intensity $e$-changes superimposed on the average face image of each face database. In both pictures the color scales red-yellow and blue-green shows relative intensity changes as a range of the effect size. In red-yellow the tissues contained within the lines are brighter in the corresponding group 1 compared to the respective group 2. Analogously, the areas in blue-green show discriminant regions of relative tissue darkness in the group 1 compared to the corresponding group 2. Face regions contained within the lines and closer to the spectrum of yellow and green show areas of relatively larger statistical significance.

We can see clearly that by exploring the separating hyper-planes found by the multi-linear

*Figure 7. Statistical significance mapping of the SDM differences. From left to right: (top row) gender, facial expression and aging FEI two-group experiments; (middle row) gender and facial expression FERET two-group experiments; (bottom row) anger, disgust, fear, happiness, sadness and surprise JAFFE two-group experiments.*

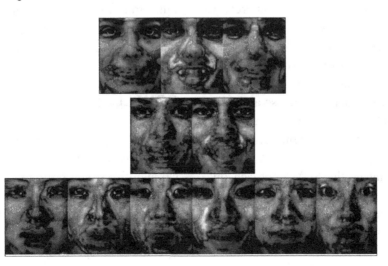

discriminant analysis and quantifying its most statistically significant changes with the *e*-values we are able to identify and highlight facial features that are most discriminant between the group samples, such as: forehead, eyebrow, eyes, nose and upper lip for both the FEI and FERET gender experiments; eyes, shadow, cheek, lips and mouth for both the FEI and FERET facial expression experiments; eyebrow, eyes, nose, and skin elasticity around the mouth for the FEI aging experiments; and forehead, eyebrow, eyelids, eyes, cheek and mouth for almost all the six JAFFE facial experiments.

## FUTURE RESEARCH DIRECTIONS

We believe that the importance of the SDM results for face interpretation and reconstruction, particularly on the aging experiments, is beyond the scope of capturing and extracting discriminant information. For instance, the proposed method can be seen as an automatic framework to predict the age-progression in frontal face images using familiar features acquired under controlled conditions. A number of pioneering researchers (Lanitis et al., 2002; Hutton et al., 2003; Scandrett et al., 2006a; Scandrett et al., 2006b) have modeled facial changes with age using either PCA on different models for texture and shape information (Lanitis et al., 2002; Scandrett et al., 2006a; Scandrett et al., 2006b) or 3D facial meshes in shape space only (Hutton et al., 2003). The reader is refereed to (Fu et al., 2010) for a recent survey on this topic. The main difference of SDM over these works is based on the fact that we use a classifier and all the pre-processed intensity features simultaneously to estimate the aging effects on the original image space.

In order to evaluate the SDM approach on the problem of estimating the age-progression in frontal face images using familiar features, we carried out some preliminary experiments by selecting two sets of pre-processed frontal images

(with at least one neutral and one smiling facial expression) of two distinct families composed respectively of a very small number of 6 and 3 subjects over 37 years of age. Figure 8 shows the frontal images used in this experiment, where the first 24 images, from top to bottom and left to right, are from the family 1 and the others 18 from family 2.

Figure 9 illustrates the transformed images for the family 1 and family 2, which are the statistical extreme points calculated at 3 standard deviations from each corresponding sample group on the SDM separating hyper-plane, and the spatial distribution of these *e*-changes superimposed on the average face image. Despite the small sizes of both sample groups, it is possible to see that the SDM hyper-plane captures a number of changes inherent to the families considered, such as the relative size of the forehead, thickness of the eyebrows, shape of the nose, and some significant differences on the shadows.

Figure 10 shows these most discriminant family features transferred to two example images, not included on the training set, when we move it to the statistical extremes using equation (6) and the direction defined by the SDM separating hyper-plane. Despite the appearance of some artifacts, due the lack of a non-rigid pre-processing step, we can note the main differences between the families captured by the SDM hyperplane and fairly translated to the example images, like the changes related to the size, position and shape of the eyebrows, eyes, nose, and shadows.

## CONCLUSION

In this chapter, we described a multi-linear method of constructing plausible and statistical significant unseen views of human identity photographs. Since the multi-linear statistical discriminant approach is not restricted to any particular set of samples and involves the same operations irrespective of the complexity of the

*Figure 8. Families face samples for some age-progression experiments using SDM*

*Figure 9. SDM statistical extremes and corresponding significance of the family e-changes superimposed on the average image: (left) family 1 model; (middle) family 2 model; (right) statistical significance mapping of the SDM differences.*

*Figure 10. SDM reconstruction when we move two example images (middle) in parallel to the statistical extremes of the family hyper-plane: (left) to family 1 model; and (right) to family 2 model.*

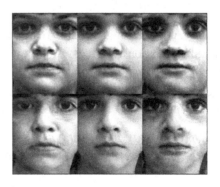

experiment, straightforward improvements can be made to this approach by using larger training sets with non-rigid spatially normalized images. We believe that the detailed discriminant mapping provided by the multi-linear analysis can

facilitate, for instance, forensic specialists on the task of recognizing missing children and adults, particularly in situations where ethnic, gender, and parental face image samples are available. Further work is being undertaken to investigate this possibility in practice.

# REFERENCES

Cootes, T. F., Edwards, G. J., & Taylor, C. J. (1998). Active appearance models. In *Proceedings of European Conference on Computer Vision (ECCV)*, vol. 2, (pp. 484-498). Springer Verlag.

Cootes, T. F., & Lanitis, A. (2004). *Statistical models of appearance for computer vision. Technical Report*. University of Manchester.

Cootes, T. F., Taylor, C. J., Cooper, D. H., & Graham, J. (1995). Active shape models - Their training and application. *Computer Vision and Image Understanding, 61*(1), 38–59. doi:10.1006/cviu.1995.1004

Cootes, T. F., Walker, K. N., & Taylor, C. J. (2000). View-based Active appearance models. In *Proceedings of International Conference on Automatic Face and Gesture Recognition (FG)*, (pp. 227-232). IEEE CS Press.

Devijver, P. A., & Kittler, J. (1982). *Pattern classification: A statistical approach*. Prentice-Hall.

Farkas, L. G. (1994). *Anthropometry of the head and face*. New York, NY: Raven Press.

Fu, Y., Guo, G., & Huang, T. S. (2010). Age synthesis and estimation via faces: A survey. *IEEE Transactions on Pattern Analysis and Machine Intelligence, 32*(11), 1955–1976. doi:10.1109/TPAMI.2010.36

Fukunaga, K. (1990). *Introduction to statistical pattern recognition*. New York, NY: Academic Press.

Geng, X., Zhou, Z., & Smith-Miles, K. (2007). Automatic age estimation based on facial aging patterns. *IEEE Transactions on Pattern Analysis and Machine Intelligence, 29*(12), 2234–2240. doi:10.1109/TPAMI.2007.70733

Giraldi, G. A., Rodrigues, P. S., Kitani, E. C., Sato, J. R., & Thomaz, C. E. (2008). Statistical learning approaches for discriminant features selection. *Journal of the Brazilian Computer Society, 14*(2), 7–22. doi:10.1007/BF03192556

Hutton, T. J., Buxton, B. F., Hammond, P., & Potts, H. W. W. (2003). Estimating average growth trajectories in shape-space using Kernel smoothing. *IEEE Transactions on Medical Imaging, 22*(6), 747–753. doi:10.1109/TMI.2003.814784

Johnson, R. A., & Wichern, D. W. (1998). *Applied multivariate statistical analysis*. New Jersey: Prentice Hall.

Kitani, E. C., Thomaz, C. E., & Gillies, D. F. (2006). A statistical discriminant model for face interpretation and reconstruction. In *Proceedings of Brazilian Symposium on Computer Graphics and Image Processing (SIBGRAPI)*, (pp. 247-254). IEEE CS Press.

Lanitis, A., Taylor, C. J., & Cootes, T. F. (2002). Toward automatic simulation of ageing effects on face images. *IEEE Transactions on Pattern Analysis and Machine Intelligence, 24*(4), 442–455. doi:10.1109/34.993553

Lyons, M. J., Budynek, J., & Akamatsu, S. (1999). Automatic classification of single facial images. *IEEE Transactions on Pattern Analysis and Machine Intelligence, 21*(12), 1357–1362. doi:10.1109/34.817413

Park, U., Tong, Y., & Jain, A. K. (2010). Age-invariant face recognition. *IEEE Transactions on Pattern Analysis and Machine Intelligence, 32*(5), 947–954. doi:10.1109/TPAMI.2010.14

Philips, P. J., Wechsler, H., Huang, J., & Rauss, P. (1998). The FERET database and evaluation procedure for face recognition algorithms. *Image and Vision Computing, 16*(5), 295–306. doi:10.1016/S0262-8856(97)00070-X

Ramanathan, N., & Chellapa, R. (2006). Modeling age progression in young faces. In *Proceedings of the Conference on Computer Vision and Pattern Recognition (CVPR)*, (pp. 387-394). IEEE CS Press.

Sato, J. R., Fujita, A., Thomaz, C. E., Morais-Martin, M. G., Mourao-Miranda, J., Brammer, M. J., & Junior, E. A. (2009). Evaluating SVM and MLDA in the extraction of discriminant regions for mental state prediction. *NeuroImage, 46*(1), 105–114. doi:10.1016/j.neuroimage.2009.01.032

Sato, J. R., Thomaz, C. E., Cardoso, E. F., Fujita, A., Morais-Martin, M. G., & Junior, E. A. (2008). Hyperplane navigation: A method to set individual scores in fMRI group datasets. *NeuroImage, 42*(4), 1473–1480. doi:10.1016/j.neuroimage.2008.06.024

Scandrett, C. M., Solomon, C. J., & Gibson, S. J. (2006a). Towards a semi-automatic method for the statistically rigorous ageing of the human face. *IEE Proceedings. Vision Image and Signal Processing, 153*(5), 639–649. doi:10.1049/ip-vis:20050027

Scandrett, C. M., Solomon, C. J., & Gibson, S. J. (2006b). A person-specific, rigorous aging model of the human face. *Pattern Recognition Letters, 27*, 1776–1787. doi:10.1016/j.patrec.2006.02.007

Sirovich, L., & Kirby, M. (1987). Low-dimensional procedure for the characterization of human faces. *Journal of the Optical Society of America, 4*, 519–524. doi:10.1364/JOSAA.4.000519

Swets, D., & Weng, J. (1996). Using discriminants eigenfeatures for image retrieval. *IEEE Transactions on Pattern Analysis and Machine Intelligence, 18*(8), 831–836. doi:10.1109/34.531802

Thomaz, C. E. (2004). *Maximum entropy covariance estimate for statistical pattern recognition*. Unpublished doctoral thesis, Department of Computing, Imperial College, London, UK.

Thomaz, C. E., Amaral, V., Giraldi, G. A., Kitani, E. C., Sato, J. R., & Gillies, D. F. (2009). A multi-linear discriminant analysis of 2D frontal face images. In *Proceedings of Brazilian Symposium on Computer Graphics and Image Processing (SIBGRAPI)*, (pp. 216-223). IEEE CS Press.

Thomaz, C. E., Boardman, J. P., Counsell, S., Hill, D. L. G., Hajnal, J. V., & Edwards, A. D. (2007). A multivariate statistical analysis of the developing human brain in preterm infants. *Image and Vision Computing, 25*(6), 981–994. doi:10.1016/j.imavis.2006.07.011

Thomaz, C. E., Gillies, D. F., & Feitosa, R. Q. (2004). A new covariance estimate for Bayesian classifiers in biometric recognition. *IEEE Transactions on Circuits and Systems for Video Technology, 14*(2), 214–223. doi:10.1109/TCSVT.2003.821984

Thomaz, C. E., Kitani, E. C., & Gillies, D. F. (2006). A maximum uncertainty LDA-based approach for limited sample size problems - With application to face recognition. *Journal of the Brazilian Computer Society, 12*(2), 7–18. doi:10.1007/BF03192391

Turk, M., & Pentland, A. (1991). Eigenfaces for recognition. *Journal of Cognitive Neuroscience, 3*, 71–86. doi:10.1162/jocn.1991.3.1.71

## ENDNOTES

[1]     The FEI face database is publicly available on the following web site: http://www.fei.edu.br/~cet/facedatabase.html

[2]     Please, for color images, see the online version of this chapter.

# Chapter 3
# Orthogonal Image Moment Invariants:
## Highly Discriminative Features for Pattern Recognition Applications

**G.A. Papakostas**
*Democritus University of Thrace, Greece*

**E.G. Karakasis**
*Democritus University of Thrace, Greece*

**D.E. Koulouriotis**
*Democritus University of Thrace, Greece*

## ABSTRACT

*This chapter focuses on the usage of image orthogonal moments as discrimination features in pattern recognition applications and discusses their main properties. Initially, the ability of the moments to carry information of an image with minimum redundancy is studied, while their capability to enclose distinctive information that uniquely describes the image's content is also examined. Along these directions, the computational formulas of the most representative moment families will be defined analytically and the form of the corresponding moment invariants in each case will be derived. Appropriate experiments have taken place in order to investigate the description capabilities of each moment family, by applying them in several benchmark problems.*

## 1. INTRODUCTION

A crucial part of a modern intelligent imaging system, which learns from its environment and interacts with it, is the pattern recognition procedure. In general, a pattern recognition process employs four stages: 1) image acquisition, 2) im-age pre-processing (denoising, filtering, etc.), 3) feature extraction and finally 4) classification. The third step is probably the most complicated and it affects the overall performance of the system. A Feature Extraction Method (FEM) can be termed successful if the resulted features (descriptors) describe uniquely the processed object in a scene. The more successful the FEM, the more efficient the classification.

DOI: 10.4018/978-1-61350-429-1.ch003

Image moments constitute an important FEM, which generates high discriminative features, able to capture the particular characteristics of the described pattern, which distinguish it among similar or totally different objects.

In the next sections the most representative moment families are described and their invariants are derived. Moreover, appropriate experimental scenarios for different pattern recognition applications will be arranged, in order to investigate the recognition capabilities of each moment family. For this reason, several benchmark datasets will be selected from the literature, by covering a wide spread of different applications such as face, facial expression, hand postures and object recognition of the artificial intelligence research field the general perspective of the chapter.

## 2. BACKGROUND IN IMAGE MOMENTS

Although the first usage of moments in image understanding and analysis was a long time ago, they still preserve scientists' interest. Image moments have been used successfully in image processing and pattern recognition after image normalization and proper selection, with Hu (Hu, 1962) being the pioneer in introducing a set of moment invariants for classification purposes. However, Hu invariants and geometric moments suffer from high information redundancy.

More precisely, geometric moments are the projection of the intensity function of an image onto specific monomials, which do not construct an orthogonal basis. Orthogonal moments came to overcome this disadvantage of the conventional moments used until then, since their kernels are orthogonal polynomials. This property of orthogonality gives to the corresponding moments the feature of minimum information redundancy, meaning that different moment orders describe different image parts of the image.

The first introduction of orthogonal moments in image analysis performed by Teague (Teague, 1980), who made use of Legendre (Papakostas et al., 2010a) and Zernike (Papakostas et al., 2010b, 2007a) moments in image processing. Other families of orthogonal moments were proposed through the years, such as Pseudo-Zernike (Papakostas et al., 2010b) and Fourier-Mellin (Papakostas et al., 2007b) moments, to better describe the image in process and to ensure robustness in noise presence. However, the above orthogonal moments used till the recent years, present some approximation errors due to the fact that the kernel polynomials are defined in the continuous space (Liao & Pawlak, 1996; Wee & Paramesran, 2007). Therefore, when the moments of a discrete intensity function are needed to be computed, some errors are generated which influence the final results.

Apart from some remarkable attempts that compute the theoretical image moment values (Liao & Pawlak, 1996; Wee & Paramesran, 2007), new moment families with discrete polynomial kernels, have been proposed, which permit the direct computation of the image moments in the discrete domain. Such discrete moment invariants are the Tchebichef (Mukundan et al., 2001), Krawtchouk (Yap et al., 2003), Hahn (Zhu et al., 2007a), and Racah ones (Zhu et al., 2007a), which present significant properties in describing an image in process.

Due to their high popularity, many works in different research directions have been published the last three decades regarding the computation, usage and enhancement of the image moments for pattern recognition purposes.

## 3. IMAGE MOMENTS

In this section, a detailed description of the computational formulas of the most representative orthogonal image moments is presented. Also, the main properties of each moment family are discussed and the ability of the families to describe the image's content is analysed through reconstruction experiments. Moreover, by comparing the reconstruction performance of the families, some useful conclusions are drawn.

## 3.1 A General Computational Form

The general computational form of a $(n+m)^{th}$ order moment of a $MxN$ image having intensity function $f(x,y)$, is defined as follows (Papakostas et al., 2010c):

$$M_{nm} = NF \times \sum_{x=0}^{M-1} \sum_{y=0}^{N-1} Kernel_{nm}(x,y) f(x,y) \tag{1}$$

where $Kernel_{nm}(\cdot)$ corresponds to the moment's kernel consisting of specific polynomials of order n and m, which constitute the orthogonal basis (in the case of geometric moments the kernel has the form of a monomial) and $NF$ is a normalization factor. The type of Kernel's polynomial gives the name to the moment family by resulting to a wide range of moment types.

## 3.2 Type I: Continuous Moments

The first type of image moments includes those moments defined in the continuous coordinate space and therefore their computation over the discrete domain of the image's pixels, generates some approximation errors (Liao & Pawlak, 1996; Wee & Paramesran, 2007). The most known moment families of this category are the Geometric, Legendre, Zernike and Pseudo-Zernike moments, which are defined as follows.

### 3.2.1 Geometric Moments (GMs)

Geometric moments are the simplest type of moments and chronologically are firstly introduced in image processing.

The geometric moment of $(n+m)^{th}$ order (Papakostas et al., 2008), of a continuous intensity function $f(x,y)$ is defined as:

$$GM_{nm} = \int_{-\infty}^{\infty} \int_{-\infty}^{\infty} x^n y^m f(x,y) \, dxdy \tag{2}$$

where $n,m = 0,1,2,....$.

The above Eq.(2) is a continuous form and is impractical for the computation of image moments, where the intensity function is a discrete function. For this reason, the geometric moment of a $MxN$ image $f(x,y)$, is defined in discrete form as follows:

$$GM_{nm} = \sum_{x=0}^{M-1} \sum_{y=0}^{N-1} x^n y^m f(x,y) \tag{3}$$

The geometric moments computed by using Eq.(3), are making use of the monomials $x^n y^m$, which do not constitute an orthogonal basis and therefore the geometric moments are redundant. Furthermore, the geometric moments cannot be used as image descriptors for pattern recognition applications, since they are not invariant under basic image transformations, such as translation, rotation and scaling.

For this reason, the so-called central and normalized moments, which are translation and scaling invariant respectively, have been introduced in the past (Mukundan & Ramakrishnan, 1998; Papakostas et al., 2010d).

### 3.2.2 Legendre Moments (LMs)

The $(n+m)^{th}$ Legendre moment (Papakostas et al., 2010a) of an intensity function $f(x,y)$, is defined as:

$$LM_{nm} = \frac{(2n+1)(2m+1)}{4} \int_{-1}^{1} \int_{-1}^{1} P_n(x) P_m(y) f(x,y) dxdy$$

$$(4)$$

where $P_n(x)$ is the $n^{th}$ order Legendre polynomial defined as:

$$P_n(x) = \sum_{k=0}^{n} a_{k,n} x^k = \frac{1}{2^n n!} \left(\frac{d}{dx}\right)^n \left[(x^2 - 1)^n\right]$$

$$(5)$$

where $x \in [-1, 1]$.

The above Legendre polynomials have the following properties:

$$P_0(x) = 1,$$ $$(6a)$$

$$P_1(x) = x,$$ $$(6b)$$

$$P_n(x) = \left[(2n-1)xP_{n-1}(x) - (n-1)P_{n-2}(x)\right] / n$$

$$(6c)$$

The recursive Eq.(6c), permits the fast computation of the Legendre polynomials by using polynomials of lower order.

In case of computing the Legendre moments of a *MxN* image, Eq.(4) cannot be applied since this holds in the continuous space. Instead a discrete form of Eq.(4) is used as follows:

$$LM_{nm} = \frac{(2n+1)(2m+1)}{(M-1)(N-1)} \sum_{x=0}^{M-1} \sum_{y=0}^{N-1} P_n(x) P_m(y) f(x,y)$$

$$(7)$$

The Legendre moments computed by using Eq.(7), differ from the theoretical values of Eq.(4), since approximation errors are generated during the transformation of the double integral to the double summation. Due to these approximation errors, the resulted Legendre moments do not carry the properties of the theoretical ones, by affecting their ability to describe the image in process. For this reason new algorithms, which ensure the accurate computation of the moments have been proposed (Hosny, 2007; Papakostas et al., 2010a).

### 3.2.3 Zernike Moments (ZMs)

Zernike moments (ZMs) are the most widely used family of orthogonal moments due to their extra inherent property of being invariant to an arbitrary rotation of the object they describe. They are used, after making them invariant to scale and translation, as object descriptors in pattern recognition applications (Kan & Srinath, 2002; Papakostas et al., 2005, 2007a).

The introduction of ZMs in image analysis was made by Teague (Teague, 1980), using a set of complex polynomials, which form a complete orthogonal set over the interior of the unit circle $x^2+y^2=1$.

These polynomials have the form:

$$V_{nm}(r,\theta) = R_{nm}(r) \exp(jm\theta)$$ $$(8)$$

where $n$ is a non-negative integer and $m$ is a non zero integer subject to the constraints $n-|m|$ even and $|m| \le n$, $r$ is the length of vector from the origin $(\bar{x}, \bar{y})$ to the pixel $(x,y)$ and $\theta$ the angle between vector $r$ and $x$ axis in counter-clockwise direction. $R_{nm}(r)$, are the Zernike radial polynomials (Zernike, 1934) in $(r,\theta)$ polar coordinates defined as:

$$R_{nm}(r) =$$

$$\sum_{s=0}^{\frac{n-|m|}{2}} (-1)^s \cdot \frac{(n-s)!}{s!\left(\dfrac{n+|m|}{2}-s\right)!\left(\dfrac{n-|m|}{2}-s\right)!} r^{n-2s}$$

(9)

Note that $R_{n,-m}(r) = R_{nm}(r)$.

The polynomials of Eq. (8) are orthogonal and satisfy the orthogonality principle:

$$\iint\limits_{x^2+y^2\leq1} V_{nm}^*(x,y) \cdot V_{pq}(x,y)dxdy = \frac{\pi}{n+1}\delta_{np}\delta_{mq}$$

(10)

where $\delta_{\alpha\beta}=1$ for $\alpha=\beta$ and $\delta_{\alpha\beta}=0$ otherwise, is the Kronecker symbol.

The Zernike moment of order n with repetition m for a continuous image function $f(x,y)$, that vanishes outside the unit disk is:

$$ZM_{nm} = \frac{n+1}{\pi}\iint\limits_{x^2+y^2\leq1} f(x,y)V_{nm}^*(r,\theta)dxdy$$

(11)

For a digital image, the integrals are replaced by summations to get:

$$ZM_{nm} = \frac{n+1}{\pi}\sum_{x=0}^{M-1}\sum_{y=0}^{N-1} f(x,y)V_{nm}^*(r,\theta), \quad x^2+y^2\leq1$$

(12)

As it can be seen from Eq.(9) there are a lot of factorial computations, operations that may consume too much computer time. For this reason, recursive algorithms for the computation of the radial polynomials of Eq.(9) have been developed (Chong et al. 2003; Papakostas et al. 2010b, 2010c).

## 3.2.4 Pseudo-Zernike Moments (PZMs)

Pseudo-Zernike moments (PZMs) are used in many pattern recognition (Haddadnia et al., 2003) and image processing applications (Teh & Chin, 1988) as alternatives to the traditional ZMs. It has been proved that they have better feature representation capabilities and are more robust to image noise (Teh & Chin, 1988) than Zernike moments.

The kernel of these moments is the orthogonal set of Pseudo-Zernike polynomials defined inside the unit circle. These polynomials have the form of Eq.(8) with the Zernike radial polynomials replaced by the Pseudo-Zernike radial polynomials:

$$S_{nm}(r) =$$

$$\sum_{s=0}^{n-|m|} (-1)^s \cdot \frac{(2n+1-s)!}{s!\left(n+|m|+1-s\right)!\left(n-|m|-s\right)!} r^{n-s}$$

(13)

with additional constraints:

$$0 \leq |m| \leq n, \quad n = 0,1,2,...\infty$$

(14)

The corresponding PZMs are computed using the same formulas Eq.(11) and Eq.(12) as in the case of ZMs, since the only difference is in the form of the polynomial being used.

Due to the above constraints (14), the set of Pseudo-Zernike polynomials of order $\leq n$, contain $(n+1)^2$ linearly independent polynomials of degree $\leq n$. On the other hand, the set of Zernike polynomials contain only $(n+1)(n+2)/2$ linearly independent polynomials of degree $\leq n$, due to the additional condition that $n-|m|$ is even.

Thus, PZMs offer more feature vectors than the Zernike moments of the same order. As it can be seen from Eq.(13) the computation of Pseudo-Zernike moments, involves the calculation of some factorial terms, an operation that adds an extra computational effort. Consequently, as in the case of Zernike moments, there is a demand for developing fast and numerical robust algorithms (Papakostas et al. 2010b), able to calculate accurate moments in a short time.

## 3.3 Type II: Discrete Moments

As it has already been mentioned in the introductory section, the main drawback of the continuous moments is the generation of approximation errors, which significantly affect their ability to describe the image's content. Apart from some remarkable attempts to compute the theoretical image moment values (Liao & Pawlak, 1996; Wee & Paramesran, 2007; Hosny, 2007; Papakostas et al., 2008), new moment families with discrete polynomial kernels, have been proposed, which permit the direct computation of the image moments in the discrete coordinate space. The most well known families of this category are the Tchebichef, Krawtchouk and dual Hahn moments.

### 3.3.1 Tchebichef Moments (TMs)

Tchebichef moments (TMs), were the first type of discrete orthogonal moments introduced in image analysis by Mukundan et.al. (Mukundan et al., 2001). These moments use as kernel, the Tchebichef orthogonal polynomials defined in the discrete domain having the following form:

$$t_n(x) = (1-N)_n \,_3F_2\left(-n,-x,1+n;1,1-N;1\right)$$
$$= \sum_{k=0}^{n}(-1)^{n-k}\binom{N-1-k}{n-k}\binom{n+k}{n}\binom{x}{k}$$

$$(15)$$

where $_3F_2$, is the generalized hypergeometric function, $n,x = 0,1,2,...,N-1$, and $N$ the image size.

For numerical stability purposes and limited dynamical range, the normalized Tchebichef polynomials are introduced (Mukundan et al., 2001), as follows:

$$\tilde{t}_n(x) = \frac{t_n(x)}{\beta(n,N)} \tag{16}$$

where $\beta(n,N)$ is a suitable constant independent of $x$ that serves as scaling factor, such as $N^n$.

The normalized Tchebichef moment of $(n+m)^{th}$ order, of a $MxN$ image having intensity function $f(x,y)$, has the following form:

$$TM_{nm} =$$
$$\frac{1}{\tilde{\rho}(n,M)\tilde{\rho}(m,N)}\sum_{x=0}^{M-1}\sum_{y=0}^{N-1}\tilde{t}_n(x)\tilde{t}_m(y)f(x,y)$$

$$(17)$$

where $\tilde{\rho}(n,N)$ is the normalized norm of the polynomials:

$$\tilde{\rho}(n,N) = \frac{\rho(n,N)}{\beta(n,N)^2} \tag{18}$$

and $\rho(n,N)$ is defined:

$$\rho(n,N) = (2n)!\binom{N+n}{2n+1}, \quad n = 0,1,...,N-1$$

$$(19)$$

The Tchebichef moments proved to be superior to Zernike and Legendre moments in describing objects, while their robustness in the presence of high noise levels makes them appropriate to real-time pattern classification and computer vision applications. Some very promising attempts to increase the computational rates of the Tchebichef moments have been presented in (Wang & Wang, 2006; Papakostas et al., 2009).

### 3.3.2 Krawtchouk Moments (KMs)

Krawtchouk moments (KMs) are the second type of discrete moments introduced in image analysis by Yap et al. (Yap et al., 2003). These moments make use of the discrete Krawtchouk polynomials, and have the following form:

$$K_n\left(x;p,N\right) = {}_2F_1\left(-n,-x;-N;\frac{1}{p}\right) = \sum_{k=0}^{N} a_{k,n,p} x^k$$

(20)

In the same way as the Tchebichef polynomials, the computation of the Krawtchouk polynomials using Eq.(20) presents numerical fluctuations; thus, a more suitable version of them, the weighted Krawtchouk polynomials, is used:

$$\bar{K}_n\left(x;p,N\right) = K_n\left(x;p,N\right)\sqrt{\frac{w\left(x;p,N\right)}{\rho\left(n;p,N\right)}}$$

(21)

where $\rho(n;p,N)$ is the norm of the Krawtchouk polynomials:

$$\rho\left(n;p,N\right) = \left(-1\right)^n\left(\frac{1-p}{p}\right)^n\frac{n!}{\left(-N\right)_n}, \quad n = 1,...,N$$

(22)

and $w(x;p,N)$ is the weight function of the Krawtchouk moments:

$$w\left(x;p,N\right) = \binom{N}{x}p^x\left(1-p\right)^{N-x}$$

(23)

In Eq.(22) the symbol $(\cdot)_n$ is the Pochhammer symbol, which for the general case is defined as $(a)_k = a(a+1)...(a+k+1)$.

The $(n+m)^{th}$ order orthogonal discrete Krawtchouk moment, of a *MxN* image function *f(x,y)* is defined as follows:

$$K_{nm} = \sum_{x=0}^{M-1}\sum_{y=0}^{N-1}\bar{K}_n\left(x;p_1,M-1\right)\bar{K}_m\left(y;p_2,N-1\right)f\left(x,y\right)$$

(24)

In practice, the computation of the weighted Krawtchouk polynomials is not performed through Eq.(24), since this is a very time consuming procedure; instead, a recursive algorithm (Yap et al., 2003) is usually applied.

The Krawtchouk moments prove to be effective local descriptors, since they can describe the local features of an image, unlike the other moment families, which capture only the global features of the objects they describe. This locality property is controlled by appropriate adjustment of the $p_1, p_2$ parameters (a common value is 0.5 for both parameters – describing the image from its center) of Eq.(24).

### 3.3.3 Dual Hahn Moments (DHMs)

The $n^{th}$ order dual Hahn polynomial (Zhu et al., 2007a) is defined as:

$$W_n^{(c)}\left(s,a,b\right) = \frac{\left(a-b+1\right)_n\left(a+c+1\right)_n}{n!}\\ {}_3F_2\left(-n,a-s,a+s+1;a-b+1,a+c+1;1\right)$$

(25)

for $n = 0, 1, ..., N-1$, $s = a, a+1, ..., b-1$, where ${}_3F_2$ is the generalized hypergeometric function given by:

$${}_3F_2\left(a_1,a_2,a_3,a_4;b_1,b_2,b_3;z\right) =\\ \sum_{k=0}^{\infty}\frac{\left(a_1\right)_k\left(a_2\right)_k\left(a_3\right)_k}{\left(b_1\right)_k\left(b_2\right)_k}\frac{z^k}{k!}$$

(26)

To avoid numerical instability, like the previous moment families, the weighted dual Hahn polynomials are defined as follows:

$$\hat{W}_n^{(c)}\left(s,a,b\right) = W_n^{(c)}\left(s,a,b\right)\sqrt{\frac{\rho\left(s\right)}{d_n^2}\left[\Delta x\left(s-\frac{1}{2}\right)\right]}$$

$$(27)$$

where $\rho(s)$ is the weighting function.

The $(n+m)^{th}$ order dual Hahn moment of a *MxN* image with intensity function *f(x,y)* has the following form:

$$W_{nm} = \sum_{x=a}^{b-1}\sum_{y=a}^{b-1} W_n^{(c)}\left(x,a,b\right)W_m^{(c)}\left(y,a,b\right) f\left(x,y\right),$$
$$n = 0,1,...,M-1, m = 0,1,...,N-1$$

$$(28)$$

It is obvious from the above equations that the computation of dual Hahn polynomials is a time-consuming task, so efficient recursive algorithms need to be used (Zhu et al., 2007a).

## 3.4 Image Reconstruction by the Method of Moments

A significant and useful property of the orthogonal moments is that they permit the reconstruction of the image they describe. The reconstruction of an image by a finite number of moments is described by the following formula:

$$f\left(x,y\right) = \sum_{n=0}^{n_{max}}\sum_{m=0}^{m_{max}} M_{nm} Kernel_{nm}\left(x,y\right) \qquad (29)$$

where $M_{nm}$ is the $(n+m)^{th}$ order moment and $Kernel_{nm}(\cdot)$ corresponds to the moment's kernel consisting of specific polynomials of order n and m, which constitute the orthogonal basis of the corresponding moment family.

## 3.5 Comparative Study I: Reconstruction Performance

Before studying the recognition capabilities of the moment families described in the previous

sections, it is useful to investigate their reconstruction performance as a measure of their ability to capture the information of the image's content they describe.

For this purpose, a well known benchmark image, the Lena image with 128x128 pixels size, is selected and the corresponding results are illustrated in the following Figure 1 and Figure 2.

In Figure 1, the reconstruction of the original image by using *Legendre, Zernike, Pseudo-Zernike, Tchebichef, Krawtchouk, dual Hahn* moments up to $5^{th}, 15^{th}, 25^{th}, 35^{th}, 45^{th}$ and $55^{th}$ order is depicted.

Furthermore, Figure 2 illustrates the normalized reconstruction error defined in Eq.(30) versus the moment order, up to which is used in each case.

*Figure 1. Original image (1ˢᵗ row) and reconstructed images using LMs (2ⁿᵈ row), ZMs (3ʳᵈ row), PZMs (4ᵗʰ row), TMs (5ᵗʰ row), KMs (6ᵗʰ row) and DHMs (7ᵗʰ row) for moment orders up to 5,15,25,35,45,55*

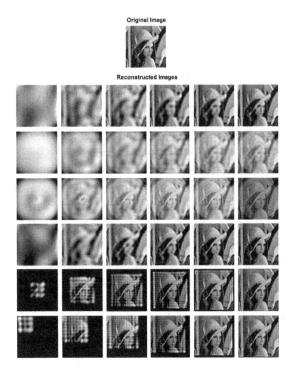

Original Image

Reconstructed Images

*Figure 2. Normalized error of all moment families in reconstructing Lena image by using several moment orders*

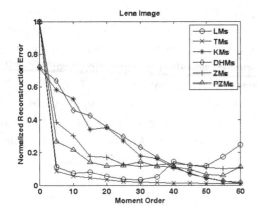

$$\bar{e}^2 = \frac{\sum\limits_{x=0}^{M-1}\sum\limits_{y=0}^{N-1}[f\left(x,y\right)-\hat{f}\left(x,y\right)]^2}{\sum\limits_{x=0}^{M-1}\sum\limits_{y=0}^{N-1}\left[f\left(x,y\right)\right]^2} \qquad (30)$$

where $f(x, y)$ is the intensity function of the original image and $\hat{f}\left(x, y\right)$ the intensity function of the reconstructed one.

From the above figures it is concluded that the Legendre moments perform better when compared to other continuous moments for low moment orders, due to two main reasons. Firstly, the number of moments that participate to the image reconstruction is bigger for the case of LMs, since both ZMs and PZMs have some constraints between m,n as mentioned in the previous sections. Moreover, the approximation errors in the case of LMs are increased as the moment order increases and are caused only by the transformation from the continuous to the discrete domain. The ZMs and PZMs, despite this error source, have the additional errors regarding the polar coordinates mapping, which is necessary in order to define the radial polynomials into the unit disc. However, the performance of the continuous moments can be significantly improved by using more exact

computation formulas, recently proposed (Wee et al., 2007; Hosny, 2007).

On the other hand, the discrete moments which are free from these approximation errors, work well with the Tchebichef ones being the most efficient. The limited performance of the Krawtchouk and dual Hahn moments is caused by their property to localize to specific image portion through the appropriate adjustment of some control parameters. This nature of KMs and DHMs restrict their reconstruction capabilities for low moment orders, while their performance is boosted as order approaches image size.

Conclusively, Tchebichef moments seem to be the most effective choice for reconstructing a gray-scale image, followed by Legendre ones. Moreover, Krawtchouk and dual Hahn moments are suitable to describe small portions of the image, while Zernike and Pseudo-Zernike moments can be useful in describing noisy images, where are more robust in comparison to the other moment families.

# 4. ORTHOGONAL IMAGE MOMENT INVARIANTS

Apart from the ability of the moments to describe the content of an image in a statistical fashion and to reconstruct it perfectly (orthogonal moments) according to Eq.(29), they can also be used to distinguish a set of patterns belonging to different categories (classes). This property makes them suitable for many artificial intelligence applications such as biometrics, visual inspection or surveillance, quality control, robotic vision and guidance, biomedical diagnosis, mechanical fault diagnosis etc. However, in order to use the moments to classify visual objects, they have to ensure high recognition rates for all possible object's orientations. This requirement constitutes a significant operational feature of each modern pattern recognition system and it can be satisfied during the feature extraction stage, where discriminative information of the objects is retrieved.

## 4.1 Invariants Derivation

Mainly, two methodologies used to ensure invariance under common geometric transformations such as rotation, scaling and translation, either by image coordinates normalization and description through the geometric moment invariants (Mukundan & Ramakrishnan, 1998; Zhu et al., 2007c) or by developing new computation formulas which incorporate these useful properties inherently (Zhu et al., 2007c). The former strategy is applied on the rest sections for deriving the moment invariants of each moment family, since it can be applied in each moment family in a similar way.

### 4.1.1 Geometric Moment Invariants (GMIs)

By applying coordinates normalization (Rothe et al., 1996) the GMs of Eq.(3) are transformed to invariant quantities called Geometric Moment Invariants (GMIs) having the following form:

$$
\begin{aligned}
GMI_{nm} = \\
GM_{00}^{-\gamma} \sum_{x=0}^{M-1} \sum_{y=0}^{N-1} \left[ (x - \bar{x}) \cos\theta + (y - \bar{y}) \sin\theta \right]^n \\
\left[ (y - \bar{y}) \cos\theta - (x - \bar{x}) \sin\theta \right]^m f(x, y)
\end{aligned}
$$

(31)

with:

$$
\begin{aligned}
\gamma &= \frac{n + m}{2} + 1 \\
\bar{x} &= \frac{GM_{10}}{GM_{00}} \\
\bar{y} &= \frac{GM_{01}}{GM_{00}} \\
\theta &= \frac{1}{2} \tan^{-1} \left( \frac{2\mu_{11}}{\mu_{20} - \mu_{02}} \right)
\end{aligned}
$$

(32)

where $(\bar{x}, \bar{y})$ are the coordinates of the image's centroid, $GM_{nm}$ are the geometric moments of Eq.(3) and $\mu_{nm}$ are the central moments defined as:

$$
\mu_{nm} = \sum_{x=0}^{M-1} \sum_{y=0}^{M-1} (x - \bar{x})^n (y - \bar{y})^m f(x, y)
$$

(33)

which are translation invariant. The value of angle $\theta$ is limited to $-45° \leq \theta \leq 45°$ and additional modifications (Mukundan & Ramakrishnan, 1998) have to be performed in order to extent $\theta$ into the range $0° \leq \theta \leq 360°$.

### 4.1.2 Legendre Moment Invariants (LMIs)

The LMIs can be constructed by describing the LMs in terms of GMs and substituting the GMs by their invariant version. Assuming that the Legendre polynomials have the following form:

$$
P_n(x) = \sum_{i=0}^{n} a_{n,i} x^i
$$

(34)

By applying simple mathematical operations, the LMs can be expressed in terms of GMs, according to the following formula.

$$
LM_{nm} = \frac{(2n + 1)(2m + 1)}{NM} \sum_{i=0}^{n} \sum_{j=0}^{m} a_{n,i} a_{m,j} GM_{ij}
$$

(35)

where:

$$
\begin{aligned}
a_{00} &= 1, a_{11} = 1 \\
a_{p+1,0} &= \frac{(-p) a_{p-1,0}}{p + 1} \quad, \quad p \geq 1 \\
a_{p+1,n} &= \frac{(-p) a_{p-1,n}}{p + 1} + \frac{(2p + 1) a_{p,n-1}}{p + 1} \quad, \\
p &\geq 1 \quad and \quad 1 \leq n \leq p + 1
\end{aligned}
$$

(36)

By substituting the GMs of Eq.(35) with the GMIs of Eq.(31), the computational form of the LMIs is derived, as follows:

$$LMI_{nm} = \frac{(2n+1)(2m+1)}{NM} \sum_{i=0}^{n} \sum_{j=0}^{m} a_{n,i} a_{m,j} GMI_{ij}$$

(37)

This equation produces translation, rotation and scaling invariant quantities able to describe uniquely different patterns.

### 4.1.3 Zernike Moment Invariants (ZMIs)

Zernike Moment Invariants (ZMIs) have been used successfully in pattern recognition applications (Kan & Srinath, 2002; Papakostas et al., 2005, 2007a), as alternative to the geometric and Hu moment invariants, discrimination feature vectors. Their main inherent property is that their magnitude remain unchanged under rotation of the image. In order to achieve invariance under translation and scaling, the ZMs are described in terms of GMs, according to the following formula (Wee & Paramesran, 2007).

$$ZM_{nm} =$$
$$\frac{n+1}{\pi} \sum_{k=m}^{n} B_{nmk} \sum_{i=0}^{s} \sum_{j=0}^{m} w^j \binom{s}{i}\binom{m}{j} GM_{k-2i-j,2i+j}$$

(38)

where $n$ is a non-negative integer and $m$ is a non zero integer subject to the constraints $n-|m|$ even and $|m| \leq n$ and:

$$w = \begin{cases} -i & , \ m > 0 \\ +i & , \ m \leq 0 \end{cases} \quad with \quad i = \sqrt{-1}$$

$$s = \frac{1}{2}(k - m)$$

$$B_{nmk} = \frac{(-1)^{\frac{(n-k)}{2}} \left(\frac{n+k}{2}\right)!}{\left(\frac{n-k}{2}\right)! \left(\frac{k+m}{2}\right)! \left(\frac{k-m}{2}\right)!}$$

(39)

By substituting the GMs of Eq.(38) with the GMIs of Eq.(31), the computational form of the ZMIs is derived, as follows:

$$ZMI_{nm} =$$
$$\frac{n+1}{\pi} \sum_{k=m}^{n} B_{nmk} \sum_{i=0}^{s} \sum_{j=0}^{m} w^j \binom{s}{i}\binom{m}{j} GMI_{k-2i-j,2i+j}$$

(40)

The above ZMIs are invariant under translation, rotation and scaling of the image and therefore are appropriate for invariant pattern recognition applications.

### 4.1.4 Pseudo-Zernike Moment Invariants (PZMIs)

Working in a similar way as in the previous cases, the Pseudo-Zernike moment invariants take the form shown in Box 1, where:

$$s = (n - m - k) / 2$$
$$d = (n - m - k - 1) / 2$$

(42)

and:

$$D_{nmk} = (-1)^k \cdot \frac{(2n+1-k)!}{k!\left(n+|m|+1-k\right)!\left(n-|m|-k\right)!}$$

(43)

*Box 1.*

$$
\begin{aligned}
PZMI_{nm} &= \frac{n+1}{\pi} \sum_{(n-m-k)even,k=0}^{n-|m|} D_{nmk} \sum_{a=0}^{s} \sum_{b=0}^{m} \binom{s}{a}\binom{m}{b}(-j)^{b} GMI_{2s+m-2a-b,2a+b} \\
&+ \frac{n+1}{\pi} \sum_{(n-m-k)odd,k=0}^{n-|m|} D_{nmk} \sum_{a=0}^{d} \sum_{b=0}^{m} \binom{d}{a}\binom{m}{b}(-j)^{b} RMI_{2s+m-2a-b,2a+b}
\end{aligned}
\tag{41}
$$

Moreover, $RMI_{nm}$ corresponds to the $(n+m)^{th}$ order, *radial geometric moment invariant* defined as shown in Box 2, where $(\bar{x}, \bar{y})$ are the coordinates of the image's centroid.

### 4.1.5 Tchebichef Moment Invariants (TMIs)

The corresponding invariants are constructed in a similar way with the previous moment families, by describing the Tchebichef moments through the GMs and by replacing the geometric moments with their invariant form (Zhu et al., 2007c), as shown in the following Eq.(51) (see Box 3), where:

$$
B_{n,k} = \frac{(n+k)!}{(n-k)! \cdot (k!)^2} \langle n - M \rangle_{n-k} \tag{46}
$$

with:

$$
\begin{aligned}
\langle a \rangle_k &= (-1)^k (-a)_k \\
&= a(a-1)(a-2)...(a-k+1) , \\
&\quad k \geq 1 \quad and \quad \langle a \rangle_0 = 1
\end{aligned}
\tag{47}
$$

and $(a)_k$ being the Pochhammer symbol given by:

$$
\begin{aligned}
(a)_k &= a(a+1)...(a+k-1) , \\
&\quad k \geq 1 \quad and \quad (a)_0 = 1
\end{aligned}
\tag{48}
$$

Moreover:

$$
\begin{aligned}
\beta(n, N) &= \sqrt{\rho(n, N)} \\
\rho(n, N) &= (2n)! \binom{N+n}{2n+1}
\end{aligned}
\tag{49}
$$

*Box 2.*

$$
RMI_{nm} = \frac{\sum_{x=0}^{M-1} \sum_{y=0}^{N-1} \sqrt{\left[(x-\bar{x})^2 + (y-\bar{y})^2\right]}(x-\bar{x})^n (y-\bar{y})^m f(x,y)}{GM_{00}^{(n+m+2)/2}}
\tag{44}
$$

*Box 3.*

$$
TM_{nm} = \frac{1}{\beta(n,M)\beta(m,N)} \sum_{k=0}^{n} \sum_{l=0}^{m} B_{n,k} B_{m,l} \sum_{i=0}^{k} \sum_{j=0}^{l} s(k,i) s(l,j) GM_{ij}
\tag{45}
$$

*Box 4.*

$$TMI_{nm} = \frac{1}{\beta(n,M)\beta(m,N)} \sum_{k=0}^{n} \sum_{l=0}^{m} B_{n,k} B_{m,l} \sum_{i=0}^{k} \sum_{j=0}^{l} s(k,i) s(l,j) GMI_{ij} \qquad (51)$$

is a normalization factor which reduces the dynamic range of the extracted invariants and the norm of the Tchebichef polynomials respectively.

Finally, *s(i,j)* are the *Stirling* numbers of the first kind satisfying the following recursive formula.

$$s(0,0) = 1$$
$$s(k,0) = s(0,i) = 0 \;, \;\; k,i \geq 1$$
$$s(k,i) = s(k-1,i-1) - (k-1)s(k-1,i),$$
$$\quad k,i \geq 1$$
$$(50)$$

By replacing the GMs with the corresponding GMIs of the same order in Eq.(45), the computational formula of the TMIs is derived (see Box 4).

The discrimination capabilities of the TMIs are expected to be significantly better than the previous moment families, due to the absence of any approximation error and therefore the fundamental mathematical properties concerning the polynomial base's orthogonality are hold exactly.

## 4.1.6 Krawtchouk Moment Invariants (KMIs)

Krawtchouk orthogonal moments constitute a high discriminative moment family in the discrete domain introduced in image analysis by Yap et al. (Yap et al., 2003).

The Krawtchouk Moment Invariants (KMIs) are constructed by firstly expanding the KMs in terms of GMs according to the following formula.

$$KM_{nm} =$$
$$\left[ \rho(n)\rho(m) \right]^{-\frac{1}{2}} \sum_{i=0}^{n} \sum_{j=0}^{m} \alpha_{i,n,p_1} \alpha_{j,m,p_2} GM_{ij} \qquad (52)$$

where $\rho(\cdot)$ is the norm of the Krawtchouk polynomials:

$$\rho(n;p,N) = (-1)^n \left( \frac{1-p}{p} \right)^n \frac{n!}{(-N)_n}, \quad n = 1,...,N$$
$$(53)$$

The symbol $(\cdot)_n$ corresponds to the Pochhammer symbol Eq.(48) and $\alpha_{k,n,p}$ are the coefficients relative to the definition of the Krawtchouk polynomial.

These coefficients can be evaluated by using the following equations:

$$a_{k,0,p} = 1$$
$$a_{k,n,p} = (-1)^n \sum_{i=n-1}^{k-1} B_{k,i+1,p} \times \left| s(i+1,n) \right| \;, \;\; n \geq 1$$
$$(54)$$

where:

$$B_{k,n,p} = \frac{(-k)_n}{(-N)_n \cdot p^n \cdot n!} \qquad (55)$$

and *s(i,j)* are the Stirling numbers described in Eq.(50).

By substituting the GMs of Eq.(52) with the corresponding GMIs of the same order, the Krawtchouk Moment Invariants (KMIs) are formed.

However, due to the fact that the GMIs have to fall inside the domain of $[0, M-1] \times [0, N-1]$, the GMIs of Eq.(31) have to be modified according to the formula shown in Box 5 (Yap et al., 2003).

Based on the above modification the KMIs can be defined correctly inside the image's coordinate system indirectly through the GMIs, as follows:

$$KMI_{nm} = \left[ \rho(n)\rho(m) \right]^{-\frac{1}{2}} \sum_{i=0}^{n} \sum_{j=0}^{m} \alpha_{i,n,p_1} \alpha_{j,m,p_2} v_{ij}$$

(57)

It has to be noted that KMs and therefore KMIs are proved to be effective local descriptors (Papakostas et al., 2010e), since they can describe the local features of an image, unlike the other moment families which capture the global features of the objects they describe.

## 4.1.7 Dual Hahn Moment Invariants (DHMIs)

Working in the same way as in the case of Krawtchouk moment invariants, the Dual Hahn moment invariants (DHMIs) are derived (Karakasis et al., submitted), according to the formula shown in Box 6, where:

$$d_n = \sqrt{\frac{\Gamma(a+c+n+1)}{n!(b-a-n-1)!\Gamma(b-c-n)}},$$
$$n = 0,1,...,N-1$$

(59)

$$R_n(a,b,c) = \frac{(a-b+1)_n(a+c+1)_n}{n!}$$

(60)

$$B_{nk}(a,b,c) = \frac{<n>_k}{(a-b+1)_k(a+c+1)_k \cdot k!}$$

(61)

$$a = (r_{alpha} + r_{beta})/2$$
$$b = a + N$$
$$c = (r_{beta} - r_{alpha})/2$$

(62)

where $r_{alpha}$ and $r_{beta}$ are some free parameters (Zhu et al., 2007a). In the following sections, the experiments with the DHMIs are executed for $a=c=0$ and $b=N$.

Moreover, parameters $C_{k,r}$ are defined as:

*Box 5.*

$$v_{nm} = \sum_{p=0}^{n} \sum_{q=0}^{m} \binom{n}{p}\binom{m}{q}\left(\frac{N \times M}{2}\right)^{\frac{p+q}{2}+1}\left(\frac{N}{2}\right)^{n-p}\left(\frac{M}{2}\right)^{m-q} GMI_{pq}$$

(56)

*Box 6.*

$$DHIM_{nm} = \frac{R_n(a,b,c)R_m(a,b,c)}{d_n d_m} \sum_{k=0}^{n} B_{nk}(a,b,c) \sum_{r_1=0}^{2k} C_{k,r_1} \sum_{t=0}^{m} B_{mt}(a,b,c) \sum_{r_2=0}^{2t} C_{t,r_2} m_{r_1,r_2}$$

(58)

$$C_{0,0} = 1$$
$$C_{k,0} = 0$$
$$C_{k,r} = A_{k,r} \cdot a_k + A_{k,r-1} \ ,$$
$$a_k = 2a + k \ , \ r = 1, 2, ..., 2k \ , \ \forall k \geq 1 \tag{63}$$

where

$$A_{0,0} = 1$$
$$A_{k,0} = 0$$
$$A_{k,2k} = 0$$
$$A_{k,r} = \sum_{t=1}^{r} s(k,t) \cdot L_{k-1,k-r+t-1} \quad , \ r = 1, 2, ..., k$$
$$A_{k,r} = \sum_{t=r-k+1}^{k} s(k,t) \cdot L_{k-1,k-r+t-1} \ ,$$
$$r = k + 1, k + 2, ..., 2k - 1 \tag{64}$$

$$L_{m,0} = 1$$
$$L_{m,n} = \sum_{z=1}^{m-n+1} D_{z,n-1} a_{z+n-1} \ , \ n = 1, 2, ..., m \tag{65}$$

and

$$D_{z,1} = \sum_{t=1}^{z} a_t$$
$$D_{z,n} = \sum_{t=1}^{z} D_{t,n-1} a_{t+n-1} \ , \ n > 1 \tag{66}$$

The DHMIs of $(n+m)^{th}$ order have recently been introduced by the authors (Karakasis et al., submitted) in order to investigate the discrimination capability of these orthogonal moment family, while a first attempt to use them in pattern recognition problems is presented in the next section.

## 4.2 Comparative Study II: Recognition Performance

In order to investigate the discrimination power of the moment invariants discussed in the previous sections, a set of pattern recognition experiments have been arranged by using some well-known benchmark datasets. Table 1 summarizes the main characteristics of the datasets being used, from different application fields (computer vision, face, facial expression and hand posture recognition). Moreover, Figure 3 illustrates six pattern samples from each dataset.

For each dataset, a set of moment invariants up to a specific order per moment family is computed, by resulting to several feature vectors of near the same lengths. These feature vectors are formed by computing the invariants up to a specific order so as the resulted vectors have nearly the same length. By selecting the length to be 64, the moment invariants are computed up to $14^{th}$ and $7^{th}$ for the case of ZMIs and GMIs, LMIs, TMIs, KMIs, DHMIs respectively. For the case of PZMIs, where extra conditions are hold (section 3.2.4), the invariants are computed up to $10^{th}$ order giving vectors of 66 length.

The extracted feature vectors are applied on the input layer of a feed-forward neural network (Multi-layer Perceptron) used as classifier. After some trial and error experiments, a structure of a neural network with one hidden layer of 80 neurons (the number of neurons of the output layer is equal to the number of classes in each dataset), is selected for all the cases. The training of the classifier is performed by using the back-propagation algorithm, while the algorithm works repeatedly for 1000 epochs, by using the 50% of the dataset. The rest 50% samples of each dataset are used to test the generalization ability of the classifier, measured by its Classification Rate: *Classification Rate = (number of correct classified/total number of samples)* × 100. The classification results are summarized in Table 2.

From Table 2, it is obvious that the performance of the orthogonal moment invariants are in some cases very high, with the PZMIs being the most discriminative ones, followed by the LMIs and GMIs.

*Table 1. Characteristics of the datasets*

| Dataset | | Type | Num. Classes | Instances / Class | Total Instances |
|---|---|---|---|---|---|
| ID | Name | | | | |
| D1 | COIL (Nene et al., 1996) | computer vision | 10 | 12 | 120 |
| D2 | ORL (Samaria & Harter, 1994) | face recognition | 40 | 10 | 400 |
| D3 | JAFFE (Lyons et al., 1998) | facial expression recognition | 7 | 30,29,32,31,30,31,30 | 213 |
| D4 | TRIESCH I (Triesch & von der Malsburg, 1996) | hand posture recognition | 10 | 24 (only the dark background) | 240 |

*Figure 3. Six pattern samples of the D1 (1ˢᵗ row), D2 (2ⁿᵈ row), D3 (3ʳᵈ row) and D4 (4ᵗʰ row) datasets*

The KMIs and DMIs are of limited discrimination power, due to the fact that they describe the images locally, through some free parameters ($p_1, p_2$ and $a, b, c$) of the polynomials and therefore more moments are needed in order to describe a bigger part of the image. These invariants can improve their performance by appropriately selecting these parameters in a way they describe the most discriminant part of the images.

The TMIs is surprisingly less efficient, although the corresponding moments can describe the images satisfactory, as shown by the reconstruction experiments of the previous section. However, the derivation of the TMIs through their description in terms of GMIs seems to have some problems, probably due several numerical instabilities and thus additional research on obtaining TMIs have to be performed in the future.

Moreover, it has to be noted that the classification results of the orthogonal moment invariants displayed in Table 2, can be significantly improved, by finding more optimum experimental configurations. Different moment invariant sets (from several moment orders) and more suitable structure of the neural classifier (more neurons, different activation functions, etc) can lead to improved results.

*Table 2. Classification results*

| Moment Invariants | Datasets | | | |
|---|---|---|---|---|
| | D1 | D2 | D3 | D4 |
| *GMIs* | 82.92% | 45.00% | 33.93% | 69.17% |
| *LMIs* | 80.42% | 47.00% | 41.07% | 79.17% |
| *ZMIs* | 79.44% | 33.00% | 30.36% | 57.50% |
| *PZMIs* | 90.00% | 65.50% | 41.07% | 70.83% |
| *TMIS* | 59.03% | 27.00% | 23.21% | 40.00% |
| *KMIs* | 55.56% | 25.50% | 25.00% | 42.50% |
| *DHMIs* | 51.53% | 18.50% | 30.36% | 33.33% |

## FUTURE RESEARCH DIRECTIONS

The useful properties of moments in describing an image and their invariants in discriminating patterns under common geometric transformations, impose a future research along three main directions: in developing 1) fast and accurate computational algorithms for the image moments and moment invariants, 2) more accurate and under several image transformations (blur, affine, etc.) moment invariants and in finding 3) new application areas where they can be applied to solve ill-posed cases.

## CONCLUSION

A detailed analysis of the main properties of the most representative orthogonal moment families and their corresponding invariants has been performed in the previous sections. Through this study the computational formulas of each moment family were presented and their behaviour in reconstructing and uniquely describing the image's contents were investigated through appropriate experimental configurations.

## REFERENCES

Chong, C. W., Raveendran, P., & Mukundan, R. (2003). A comparative analysis of algorithms for fast computation of Zernike moments. *Pattern Recognition, 36*(3), 731–742. doi:10.1016/S0031-3203(02)00091-2

Haddadnia, J., Ahmadi, M., & Faez, K. (2003). An efficient feature extraction method with Pseudo-Zernike moment in RBF neural network-based human face recognition system. *EURASIP Journal on Applied Signal Processing*, (9): 890–901. doi:10.1155/S1110865703305128

Hosny, K. M. (2007). Exact Legendre moment computation for gray level images. *Pattern Recognition, 40*(12), 3597–3705. doi:10.1016/j.patcog.2007.04.014

Hu, M. K. (1962). Visual pattern recognition by moment invariants. *I.R.E. Transactions on Information Theory, 8*, 179–187. doi:10.1109/TIT.1962.1057692

Kan, C., & Srinath, M. D. (2002). Invariant character recognition with Zernike and orthogonal Fourier-Mellin moments. *Pattern Recognition, 35*(1), 143–154. doi:10.1016/S0031-3203(00)00179-5

Karakasis, E. G., Papakostas, G. A., & Koulouriotis, D. E. (submitted). *Translation, scale and rotation dual Hahn moment invariants.*

Liao, S. X., & Pawlak, M. (1996). On image analysis by moments. *IEEE Transactions on Pattern Analysis and Machine Intelligence, 18*(3), 254–266. doi:10.1109/34.485554

Lyons, M. J., Akamatsu, S., Kamachi, M., & Gyoba, J. (1998). Coding facial expressions with Gabor wavelets. *Proceedings of the 3rd IEEE International Conference on Automatic Face and Gesture Recognition* (pp. 200-205). Nara, Japan.

Mukundan, R., Ong, S. H., & Lee, P. A. (2001). Image analysis by Tchebichef moments. *IEEE Transactions on Image Processing, 10*(9), 1357–1364. doi:10.1109/83.941859

Mukundan, R., & Ramakrishnan, K. R. (1998). *Moment functions in image analysis.* Singapore: World Scientific Publisher. doi:10.1142/9789812816092

Nene, S. A., Nayar, S. K., & Murase, H. (1996). *Columbia Object Image Library* (COIL-20). Technical Report No. CUCS-006-96.

Papakostas, G., Karras, D. A., Boutalis, Y., & Mertzios, B. G. (2010d). Efficient computation of moment descriptors. In Karras, D. A. (Ed.), *Recent advances in applied signals, systems and image processing (Series: Signals and communication technology)*. Springer.

Papakostas, G. A., Boutalis, Y. S., Karras, D. A., & Mertzios, B. G. (2007a). A new class of Zernike moments for computer vision applications. *Information Sciences, 177*(13), 2802–2819. doi:10.1016/j.ins.2007.01.010

Papakostas, G. A., Boutalis, Y. S., Karras, D. A., & Mertzios, B. G. (2007b). Fast numerically stable computation of orthogonal Fourier-Mellin moments. *IET Computer Vision, 1*(1), 11–16. doi:10.1049/iet-cvi:20060130

Papakostas, G. A., Boutalis, Y. S., Karras, D. A., & Mertzios, B. G. (2010b). Efficient computation of Zernike and Pseudo-Zernike moments for pattern classification applications. *Pattern Recognition and Image Analysis, 20*(1), 56–64. doi:10.1134/S1054661810010050

Papakostas, G. A., Karakasis, E. G., & Koulouriotis, D. E. (2008). Efficient and accurate computation of geometric moments on gray-scale images. *Pattern Recognition, 41*(6), 1895–1904. doi:10.1016/j.patcog.2007.11.015

Papakostas, G. A., Karakasis, E. G., & Koulouriotis, D. E. (2010a). Accurate and speedy computation of image Legendre moments for computer vision applications. *Image and Vision Computing, 28*(3), 414–423. doi:10.1016/j.imavis.2009.06.011

Papakostas, G. A., Karakasis, E. G., & Koulouriotis, D. E. (2010e). Novel moment invariants for improved classification performance in computer vision applications. *Pattern Recognition, 43*(1), 58–68. doi:10.1016/j.patcog.2009.05.008

Papakostas, G. A., Karras, D. A., Mertzios, B. G., & Boutalis, Y. S. (2005). An efficient feature extraction methodology for computer vision applications using wavelet compressed Zernike moments. *ICGST International Journal on Graphics, Vision and Image Processing. Special Issue: Wavelets and Their Applications, SI1*, 5–15.

Papakostas, G. A., Koulouriotis, D. E., & Karakasis, E. G. (2009). A unified methodology for efficient computation of discrete orthogonal image moments. *Information Sciences, 179*(20), 3619 3633. doi:10.1016/j.ins.2009.06.033

Papakostas, G. A., Koulouriotis, D. E., & Karakasis, E. G. (2010c). Computation strategies of orthogonal image moments: a comparative study. *Applied Mathematics and Computation, 216*(1), 1–17. doi:10.1016/j.amc.2010.01.051

Rothe, I., Susse, H., & Voss, K. (1996). The method of normalization to determine invariants. *IEEE Transactions on Pattern Analysis and Machine Intelligence, 18*(4), 366–376. doi:10.1109/34.491618

Samaria, F., & Harter, A. C. (1994). Parameterisation of a stochastic model for human face identification. In *Proceedings of the 2nd IEEE Workshop on Applications of Computer Vision* (pp. 138–142). Sarasota, FL, USA.

Teague, M. (1980). Image analysis via the general theory of moments. *Journal of the Optical Society of America, 70*, 920–930. doi:10.1364/JOSA.70.000920

Teh, C. H., & Chin, R. T. (1988). On image analysis by the methods of moments. *IEEE Transactions on Pattern Analysis and Machine Intelligence, 10*(4), 496–513. doi:10.1109/34.3913

Triesch, J., & von der Malsburg, C. (1996). Robust classification of hand postures against complex backgrounds. In *Proceedings of the 2nd International Conference on Automatic Face and Gesture Recognition* (pp. 170-175). Killington, Vermont, USA.

Wang, G., & Wang, S. (2006). Recursive computation of Tchebichef moment and its inverse transform. *Pattern Recognition, 39*(1), 47–56. doi:10.1016/j.patcog.2005.05.015

Wee, C. Y., & Paramesran, R. (2007). On the computational aspects of Zernike moments. *Image and Vision Computing, 25*(6), 967–980. doi:10.1016/j.imavis.2006.07.010

Yap, P. T., Paramesran, R., & Ong, S. H. (2003). Image analysis by Krawtchouk moments. *IEEE Transactions on Image Processing, 12*(11), 1367–1377. doi:10.1109/TIP.2003.818019

Zernike, F. (1934). Beugungstheorie des Schneidenverfahrens und seiner verbesserten Form, der Phasenkonstrastmethode. *Physica, 1,* 689–701. doi:10.1016/S0031-8914(34)80259-5

Zhu, H., Shu, H., Liang, J., Luo, L., & Coatrieux, J. L. (2007b). Image analysis by discrete orthogonal Racah moments. *Signal Processing, 87*(4), 687–708. doi:10.1016/j.sigpro.2006.07.007

Zhu, H., Shu, H., Xia, T., Luo, L., & Coatrieux, J. L. (2007c). Translation and scale invariants of Tchebichef moments. *Pattern Recognition, 40*(9), 2530–2542. doi:10.1016/j.patcog.2006.12.003

Zhu, H., Shu, H., Zhou, J., Luo, L., & Coatrieux, J. L. (2007a). Image analysis by discrete orthogonal dual Hahn moments. *Pattern Recognition Letters, 28*(13), 1688–1704. doi:10.1016/j.patrec.2007.04.013

# Chapter 4
# Certain and Uncertain Triangulation in Multiple Camera Vision Systems via LMIs

**Graziano Chesi**
*University of Hong Kong, Hong Kong*

**Yeung Sam Hung**
*University of Hong Kong, Hong Kong*

## ABSTRACT

*Triangulation is a fundamental problem in computer vision that consists of estimating the 3D position of a point of the scene from the estimates of its image projections on some cameras and from the estimates of the projection matrices of these cameras. This chapter addresses multiple view L2 triangulation, i.e. triangulation for vision systems with a generic number of cameras where the sought 3D point is searched by minimizing the L2 norm of the image reprojection error. The authors consider the standard case where estimates of all the image points are available (referring to such a case as certain triangulation), and consider also the case where some of such estimates are not available for example due to occlusions (referring to such a case as uncertain triangulation). In the latter case, it is supposed that the unknown image points belong to known regions such as line segments or ellipses. For these problems, the authors propose a unified methodology that exploits the fundamental matrices among the views and provides a candidate 3D point through the solution of a convex optimization problem based on linear matrix inequalities (LMIs). Moreover, the chapter provides a simple condition that allows one to immediately establish whether the found 3D point is optimal. Various examples with synthetic and real data illustrate the proposed technique, showing in particular that the obtained 3D point is almost always optimal in practice, and that its computational time is indeed small.*

DOI: 10.4018/978-1-61350-429-1.ch004

# INTRODUCTION

It is well-known that triangulation is a fundamental problem in computer vision. This problem consists of estimating the 3D position of a point of the scene from its image projections on some cameras and from the projection matrices of these cameras. Triangulation has numerous applications in various areas, for instance it is exploited in the construction of 3D models of real objects from a sequence of images of such objects, procedure known as 3D object reconstruction, see e.g. (Faugeras and Luong (2001), Hung and Tang (2006), Mai et al. (2010)) and references therein. Also, triangulation is exploited in visual servoing for determining the location of a camera mounted on a robot end-effector with respect to a reference object present in the scene: this is realized, firstly, by determining the camera pose between the current and the desired camera locations, and, secondly, by calculating the 3D points of the reference object with respect to the determined projection matrices, see e.g. (Chaumette and Hutchinson (2006), Chaumette and Hutchinson (2007), Chesi and Hashimoto (2010)) and references therein.

In the ideal case where the image projections and projection matrices are exactly known, the triangulation problem can be readily solved, specifically it amounts to solving a system of linear equations (deriving from the projective constraints) in three scalar unknowns, which are the three coordinates of the sought 3D point with respect to an absolute frame used to express the frames of the cameras. The number of equations in this system is equal to twice the number of views, which means that at least two views are required, and that the system is over-determined (i.e., there are more constraints than variables). However, image projections and projection matrices cannot be measured exactly due to image noise, image distortion, etc. This means that the image projections and projection matrices can be only estimated and are hence affected by measurement errors. As a result, the system of linear equations defining the sought 3D point turns out to be infeasible in the general case, i.e. the equations cannot be satisfied for any choice of the three scalar unknowns.

Hence, whenever the data is affected by measurement errors, the problem amounts to finding the 3D point that ``fits'' the projective constraints better than other 3D points. A possibility consists of looking for the 3D point that minimizes the equation errors, also known as algebraic error. This requires the solution of a linear least-squares minimization, which can be simply obtained either in closed-form or via singular value decomposition (SVD) techniques. However, this criterion may provide unsatisfactory results in some situations since it minimizes an algebraic error rather than a geometric one. In order to cope with this problem, it has been proposed to find the 3D point that minimizes the so-called 2D reprojection error, i.e. the distance between the image projections of the sought 3D point on the camera views and the available measurements.

The 2D reprojection error can be defined in various ways depending on the choice of the distance adopted in the image domain. Typically, this distance is chosen as the standard Euclidean distance since it is known to provide more satisfactory results, and the triangulation is referred to as L2 triangulation. There have been various contributions to the problem of L2 triangulation in the existing literature. In (Hartley and Sturm (1997), Hartley and Zisserman (2000)) the authors show how the exact solution of triangulation with two views can be obtained by computing the roots of a one-variable polynomial of degree six. For triangulation with three-views, the exact solution is obtained in (Stewenius et al. (2005)) by solving a system of polynomial equations through methods from computational commutative algebra, and in (Byrod et al. (2007)) through Groebner basis techniques. Multiple view triangulation is considered for example in (Lu and Hartley (2007)) via branch-and-bound algorithms. See also (Hartley and Seo (2008)) that addresses the problem of verifying global minima and (Bartoli and Lapreste (2008)) that considers the case of points on lines. It is also useful to note some contributions for triangulation with non-L2 norms, such as (Hartley and Schaffalitzky (2004), Ke and Kanade (2006)).

This chapter addresses multiple view L2 triangulation in two cases. The first is the standard case where estimates of all the image points and all projection matrices are available (we refer to such a case as certain triangulation). The second is the case where some estimates of the image points are not available for example due to occlusions (we refer to such a case as uncertain triangulation). In the latter case, it is supposed that the unknown image points belong to known regions such as line segments or ellipses. For these problems we propose a unified methodology that exploits the fundamental matrices among the views and provides a candidate 3D point through the solution of a convex optimization problem based on linear matrix inequalities (LMIs). Moreover, we provide a simple condition that allows one to immediately establish whether the found 3D point is optimal. This condition also provides a guaranteed lower bound and a guaranteed upper bound for the minimum cost of the triangulation problem in the case where the found 3D point is not optimal. The proposed technique is illustrated through various examples with synthetic and real data, which show in particular that the obtained 3D point is almost always optimal in practice, and that its computational time is indeed small.

The chapter is organized as follows. First, we introduce the notation and the problem formulation. Then, we describe the proposed technique for computing a candidate of the sought 3D point and for establishing its optimality. We hence present some examples with synthetic and real data. Lastly, we conclude the chapter with some final remarks.

## NOTATION AND PROBLEM FORMULATION

The notation adopted throughout the chapter is as follows:

- R: real number space;
- $M^T$: transpose of matrix M;
- $I_n$: identity matrix in $R^{n \times n}$;
- $0_n$: null vector in $R^{n \times 1}$;
- $e_i$: i-th column of the matrix $I_3$;
- SO(3): set of rotation matrices in $R^{3 \times 3}$;
- SE(3): Cartesian product of SO(3) and $R^3$;
- $\|v\|$: Euclidean norm of vector v, i.e. $(v^T v)^{1/2}$;
- $diag(M_1, M_2, ..., M_k)$: block diagonal matrix having the square matrices $M_1, M_2, ..., M_k$ on the main diagonal and zero elsewhere;
- s.t.: subject to.

Let us consider the situation where N cameras are observing a common 3D point of the scene. Let $F_i = (O_i, c_i)$ be in SE(3) and denote the coordinate frame of the i-th camera, where $O_i$ is in SO(3) and represents the orientation matrix, while $c_i$ is in $R^3$ and represents the translation vector, both expressed with respect to a common reference coordinate frame $F_{ref} = (O_{ref}, c_{ref})$. The observed 3D point in homogeneous coordinates is expressed as:

$$X = (x, y, z, 1)^T \qquad (1)$$

where the scalars x, y and z are expressed with respect to $F_{ref}$. The projection of X onto the image plane of the i-th camera is given by:

$$x_i = (u_i, v_i, 1)^T \qquad (2)$$

where the scalars $u_i$ and $v_i$ are the coordinates of $x_i$ along the horizontal and the vertical directions. The relation between X and $x_i$ is expressed by the projective law:

$$d_i x_i = P_i X \qquad (3)$$

where the scalar $d_i$ is the depth of the point with respect to the i-th camera, and $P_i$ is the projection matrix in $R^{3 \times 4}$ of the i-th camera, which is given by:

$$P_i = K_i (O_i \, c_i) \qquad (4)$$

where $K_i$ is the upper triangular matrix in $R^{3 \times 3}$ containing the intrinsic camera parameters of the i-th camera. The solution for $x_i$ is denoted by $prj(X, P_i)$ and has the expression:

$$prj(X, P_i) = (e_3^T \, P_i \, X)^{-1} P_i \, X . \qquad (5)$$

The standard triangulation problem is to compute an estimate $X^*$ of X from estimates $x_1^\#,...$ $,x_N^\#$ of the image points $x_1,...,x_N$ and estimates $P_1^\#,...,P_N^\#$ of the projection matrices $P_1,...,P_N$. Typically such an estimate of X is defined as the minimizer of the mean square re-projection error in L2 norm, i.e.

$$X^* = \arg \inf_X \Sigma_{i=1,...,N} \|prj(X, P_i^\#) - x_i^\#\|^2 . \qquad (6)$$

In this chapter we address a more general triangulation problem as follows:

$$X^* = \arg \inf_X \Sigma_{i=1,...,N} dist(prj(X, P_i^\#), A_i)^2 \qquad (7)$$

where $A_i$ is the region of admissible values for $x_i^\#$, and $dist(prj(X, P_i^\#), A_i)$ is the Euclidean distance from the projection $prj(X, P_i^\#)$ to the region $A_i$, i.e.

$$dist(prj(X, P_i^\#), A_i) = \inf_x \|prj(X, P_i^\#) - x\| \text{ s.t. } x \text{ in } A_i . \qquad (8)$$

This allows one to consider the case where the measurements $x_1^\#,...,x_N^\#$ are not exactly known (for instance, due to occlusions), and can vary inside the regions $A_1,...,A_N$. Some cases of interests are as follows.

First, one can consider the case where the measurement is known to be $x_i^\#$ simply according to:

$$A_i = \{x_i^\#\} . \qquad (9)$$

Then, one can consider the case where the measurement is known to lie on a line segment. In particular, let us denote the extremes of the line segment with $x_i^\# + y_i^- \, l_i$ and $x_i^\# + y_i^+ \, l_i$, where $y_i^-$ and $y_i^+$ are two scalars and $l_i$ is in $R^{3 \times 1}$. The set $A_i$ is hence given by:

$$A_i = \{x_i^\# + y_i \, l_i, \, y_i \text{ in } (y_i^-, y_i^+)\} . \qquad (10)$$

Also, one can consider the case where the measurement is known to lie on the border of an ellipse. In particular, let us denote the center of the ellipse with $x_i^\#$. The set $A_i$ is hence given by:

$$A_i = \{x: (x - x_i^\#)^T E_i (x - x_i^\#) = 1\} \qquad (11)$$

for some suitable symmetric matrix $E_i$ in $R^{3 \times 3}$. Lastly, one can consider the case where the measurement is known to lie inside such an ellipse, i.e. with $A_i$ given by:

$$A_i = \{x: (x - x_i^\#)^T E_i (x - x_i^\#) \leq 1\} . \qquad (12)$$

It is worth observing that:

- (9) is the typical case when the image point is available;
- (10)-(11) are cases when the image point is known to belong to the border of an object. In particular, (10) considers line segments (e.g., the edges of books, boxes, screens, rooms, etc) while (11) considers ellipses (e.g., the borders of cups, road signals, wheels, etc);
- (12) is the case when the image point is known to lie inside an ellipse.

## PROPOSED TECHNIQUE

First of all, let us define the optimal cost of the triangulation problem (7). This is given by:

$$m^* = (\Sigma_{i=1,\ldots,N} \text{ dist}(\text{prj}(X^*, P_i^{\#}), A_i)^2/(2N))^{1/2} . \tag{13}$$

The first step consists of rewriting $m^*$ by using variables in the image domain rather than in the 3D space. Let us gather the variables $x_1, \ldots, x_N$ into a new variable as $p = (x_1, \ldots, x_N)$. The optimization problem (13) can be equivalently rewritten as:

$$m^* = \inf_p (\Sigma_{i=1,\ldots,N} \text{ dist}(x_i, A_i)^2/(2N))^{1/2} \text{ s.t. } p \text{ in } J \tag{14}$$

where J is the set of admissible values for the variable p, which is given by:

$$J = \{(\text{prj}(X, P_1^{\#}),\ldots, \text{prj}(X, P_N^{\#})) \text{ for some 3D point X}\} . \tag{15}$$

The next step is to eliminate the regions $A_1, \ldots, A_N$ from the cost function. This can be done in the following way:

- for the values of the index i for which $A_i$ is a point, we explicitly write $\text{dist}(x_i^{\#}, A_i)^2$ as shown in (16).

- we introduce an additional variable $y_i$ in R for each value of the index i for which $A_i$ is a line segment as in (10) (we will explain in the sequel how to take into account the limits $y_i^-$ and $y_i^+$ for $y_i$). The term $\text{dist}(x_i, A_i)^2$ is hence given in (17).

- we introduce an additional variable $z_i = (u_i^@, v_i^@, 1)^T$ for each value of the index i for which $A_i$ is an ellipse, where $u_i^@$ and $v_i^@$ are scalars (we will explain in the sequel how to take into account the fact that $z_i$ belongs to an ellipse). The term $\text{dist}(x_i, A_i)^2$ can be written as seen in (18).

$$\|x_i - x_i^{\#}\|^2 ; \tag{16}$$

$$\|x_i - x_i^{\#} + y_i l_i\|^2 ; \tag{17}$$

$$\|x_i - z_i\|^2 . \tag{18}$$

Let us gather all the scalar unknowns of the variables $x_1, \ldots, x_N, \ldots, y_i, \ldots, z_i, \ldots$ into a vector together with the constant 1, in particular according to:

$$w = (u_1, v_1, \ldots, u_N, v_N, \ldots, y_i, \ldots, u_i^@, v_i^@, \ldots, 1)^T \tag{19}$$

Let us observe that the functions $\|x_i - x_i^{\#}\|^2$, $\|x_i - x_i^{\#} + y_i l_i\|^2$ and $\|x_i - z_i\|^2$ are quadratic in the variables of the problem, and hence can be rewritten as $w^T C_i w$ for some symmetric positive semidefinite matrices $C_i$ of suitable dimension. Therefore, it follows that (14) can be equivalently rewritten as:

$$m^* = (\inf_w w^T C w/(2N))^{1/2} \text{ s.t. } p \text{ in } J \, g_i(w) \geq 0 \text{ for all } i = 1, \ldots, N_1 \, h_i(w) = 0 \text{ for all } i = 1, \ldots, N_2 \tag{20}$$

where C is a symmetric positive semidefinite matrix of suitable dimension, $N_1$ and $N_2$ are integers, $g_1(w), g_2(w), \ldots$ describe inequality constraints on w (e.g., deriving from (10) or (12)), and $h_1(w)$, $h_2(w), \ldots$ describe equality constraints on w (e.g., deriving from (11)). In the sequel it will be assumed that the functions $g_1(w), g_2(w), \ldots$ and $h_1(w), h_2(w), \ldots$ are quadratic (including the cases of linear and constant functions as special cases).

In order to solve (20), we introduce the following modified optimization problem:

$$m_F^* = (\inf_w w^T C w/(2N))^{1/2} \text{ s.t. } p \text{ in } J_F \, g_i(w) \geq 0 \text{ for all } i = 1, \ldots, N_1 \, h_i(w) = 0 \text{ for all } i = 1, \ldots, N_2 \tag{21}$$

where the set $J_F$ is defined as:

$$J_F = \{(x_1, \ldots, x_N): x_i^T F_{i,j}^{\#} x_j = 0 \text{ for all } i = 1, \ldots, N-1, j = i+1, \ldots, N\} \tag{22}$$

and $F_{i,j}^{\#}$ in $R^{3 \times 3}$ is the estimate of the fundamental matrix between the i-th and the j-th view. This estimate can be simply computed from the estimates of the projection matrices $P_i^\#$ and $P_j^\#$ as described for example in (Hartley and Zisserman(2000)).

The optimization problem (21) is a relaxation of the optimization problem (20). In fact, one has that the feasible set of (20) is included in the feasible set of (21) since:

J is a subset of $J_F$ . (23)

This clearly implies that the solution of the optimization problem (21) is smaller than or equal to the solution of the optimization problem (20), i.e.

$m_F^* \leq m^*$. (24)

Therefore, the solution of the modified optimization problem (21) may be different from the solution of the optimization problem (20) since the variables are allowed to vary in a possibly larger set. Nevertheless, we will verify in the results section that such a case seldom occurs in practice.

Let us describe now the proposed strategy for solving the optimization problem (21). This can be rewritten as:

$m_F^* = (\inf_w w^T C w/(2N))^{1/2}$ s.t. $g_i(w) \geq 0$ for all i = 1, ..., $N_1$ $h_i(w) = 0$ for all i = 1, ..., $N_3$ (25)

where the constraints $x_i^T F_{i,j}^\# x_j = 0$ defining the set $J_F$ are included via additional equalities $h_i(w) = 0$ (the total number of equalities is now denoted by the integer $N_3$). Let $s_0$, $s_i^g$ and $s_j^h$ be scalar variables, for i= 1, ..., $N_1$ and for j = 1, ..., $N_3$, and let us define the vector:

$s = (s_0, s_1^g, s_2^g, ..., s_1^h, s_2^h, ...)^T$ . (26)

Let us define the function:

$q(w) = w^T C w - s_0 - \Sigma_{i=1,2,...} s_i^g g_i(w) - \Sigma_{i=1,2,...} s_i^h h_i(w)$ (27)

and the optimization problem:

$m_1 = (\sup_s s_0/(2N))^{1/2}$ (28) s.t. $q(w) \geq 0$ for all w $s_i^g \geq 0$ for all i = 1, ..., $N_1$.

It follows that:

$m_1 \leq m_F^*$ . (29)

In fact, let us observe that the first constraint, $q(w) \geq 0$ for all w, implies that:

$w^T C w \geq s_0 + \Sigma_{i=1,2,...} s_i^g g_i(w) + \Sigma_{i=1,2,...} s_i^h h_i(w)$ . (30)

Moreover, from the second constraint and for any w such that the constraints in (25) hold, one has:

$s_i^g g_i(w) \geq 0$ for all i = 1, ..., $N_1$ $s_i^h h_i(w) = 0$ for all i = 1, ..., $N_3$ (31)

Hence, it follows that:

$w^T C w \geq s_0$ (32)

which implies that $(s_0/(2N))^{1/2}$ is a lower bound of $m_F^*$ whenever the constraints in (28) hold. This relaxation procedure exploited in the optimization problem (28) is known as S-procedure, see for instance (Boyd et al.(1994)) and references therein. It is useful to observe that the constraints $g_i(w) \geq 0$ and $h_i(w) = 0$ in the optimization problem (25) are not present in the optimization problem (28), whose constraints are $q(w) \geq 0$ and $s_i^g \geq 0$ only (the variables $s_j^h$ are completely free).

It turns out that the optimization problem (28) is convex. Indeed, since q(w) is quadratic, it follows that the optimization problem (28) can be equivalently rewritten as:

$m_1 = (\sup_s s_0/(2N))^{1/2}$ s.t. $Q(s) \geq 0$ $s_i^g \geq 0$ for all i = 1, ..., $N_1$ (33)

where $Q(s)$ is the symmetric matrix function satisfying:

$$q(w) = w^T Q(s) w. \qquad (34)$$

Let us observe that $Q(s)$ is an affine linear function of $s$ from the definition of $q(w)$, and hence that the constraint $Q(s) \geq 0$ is a linear matrix inequality (LMI). The feasible set of an LMI is a convex set and, therefore, the optimization problem (33) is convex since its cost function is linear and since the feasible sets of its constraints are convex (clearly, the feasible set of each constraint $s_i^g \geq 0$ is convex as well). More specifically, the optimization problem (33) belongs to the class of eigenvalue problems (EVPs), which can be solved with powerful tools based for example on interior-point methods. See e.g. (Boyd et al. (1994)) for details on EVPs, and see e.g. (Chesi et al. (2002), Chesi and Hung (2007), Chesi (2009a), Chesi (2009b), Chesi et al. (2009)) for applications of EVPs in the estimation of the fundamental matrix, determination of worst-case errors in camera positioning, estimation of the camera pose, visual servoing path-planning, and robustness analysis of uncertainty dynamical systems.

Once the optimization problem (33) is solved, one builds a candidate solution $X^\#$ for the solution $X^*$ of the original triangulation problem (7) as follows. Let $w^\#$ be a vector with form as $w$ in (19) satisfying:

$$Q(s^\#) w^\# = \lambda_{min}(Q(s^\#)) w^\# \qquad (35)$$

where $s^\#$ is an optimal value of $s$ in (33), and $\lambda_{min}(Q(s^\#))$ denotes the smallest eigenvalue of the matrix $Q(s^\#)$ (in other words, $w^\#$ is an eigenvector with eigenvalue equal to $\lambda_{min}(Q(s^\#))$ and form as $w$ in (19)). Let us extract $x_1^\#, \ldots, x_N^\#$ from $w^\#$. The candidate solution $X^\#$ for the solution $X^*$ of the original triangulation problem (7) is computed as:

$$X^\# = \min_X \Sigma_{i=1,\ldots,N} \|P_i X - x_i^\#(e_3^T P_i X)\|^2 . \qquad (36)$$

Let us observe that the optimization problem (36) is a linear least-squares minimization, and hence can be readily solved, for example in closed-form or via SVD. Let us also observe that, in general, there is no guarantee that the so computed $X^\#$ lies in front of all the cameras. One can ensure this property by introducing the linear constraints $e_3^T P_i X > 0$ for all $i = 1, \ldots, N$ in (36): observe in fact that the new linear least-square problem is still convex and can be readily solved, for example via LMIs. It is worth mentioning, however, that these constraints are typically superfluous, see for instance the examples in the results section where the candidate $X^\#$ provided by (36) always lies in front of the cameras though these constraints are not imposed.

What can be said about the optimality of the found candidate $X^\#$? Let us define the scalar:

$$m_2 = (\Sigma_{i=1,\ldots,N} \text{dist}(\text{prj}(X^\#, P_i^\#), A_i)^2/(2N))^{1/2} . \qquad (37)$$

Clearly, $m_2$ is an upper bound of the solution of the original triangulation problem (7) since it is its cost function evaluated at a feasible point. It follows that, so far, we have found a lower bound and an upper bound of the optimal cost $m^*$ in (13): indeed, one has that:

$$m_1 \leq m^* \leq m_2 . \qquad (38)$$

From these bounds it is clearly possible to derive an immediate test for establishing whether $X^\#$ is the sought solution of (7). In fact, the condition:

$$m_1 = m_2 \qquad (39)$$

clearly implies that

$$m^* = m_1 \text{ and } X^\# \text{ is optimal} . \qquad (40)$$

Before proceeding it is worth observing that the method just described can be sub-optimal because the set of admissible image points $J_F$ in the optimization problem (21) can be larger than the set of admissible image points J in the optimization problem (20) according to (23). Nevertheless, the cases where $X^\#$ is not optimal are rare in practice, see the examples in the results section. Moreover, whenever $X^\#$ is not optimal, the proposed strategy provides a lower bound and an upper bound of the solution of the original triangulation problem (7) as expressed by (38).

## RESULTS

In this section we present some results obtained with the proposed technique. Specifically, we consider first an illustrative example with synthetic data in both cases of certain and uncertain triangulation. Then, we present the results obtained with real data for a well-known example in the case of certain triangulation. Lastly, we consider an example of uncertain triangulation with real data.

### Illustrative Example with Synthetic Data

Let us consider an illustrative example using randomly generated synthetic data with N = 3 cameras. The projection matrices are chosen as follows:

$$P_1^\# = \begin{pmatrix} 0 & 1 & -1 & 2 \\ 0 & 1 & 1 & 1 \\ 2 & 1 & 1 & 1 \end{pmatrix}, P_2^\# = \begin{pmatrix} 2 & 1 & 1 & 0 \\ 1 & 0 & 0 & 1 \\ 0 & 1 & 1 & 1 \end{pmatrix}, P_3^\# = \begin{pmatrix} 1 & 2 & 0 & 1 \\ -1 & 1 & 3 & 1 \\ 1 & 0 & 2 & 1 \end{pmatrix}$$

$$(41)$$

Firstly, we consider the case where estimates of the image projections of the sought 3D point are available in all the three views, in particular the sets $A_1$, $A_2$ and $A_3$ are given by:

$$A_1 = \{(0.5, 0.9, 1)^T\} \; A_2 = \{(-0.8, -0.1, 1)^T\} \; A_3 = \{(0.2, -0.6, 1)^T\} \,. \tag{42}$$

By solving the optimization problem (33) we find $m_1 = 0.866$. Then, from the vector $w^\#$ in (35) we extract the image points:

$$x_1^\# = (0.597, 1.146, 1)^T, \; x_2^\# = (-0.164, 0.972, 1)^T, \; x_3^\# = (-0.247, 1.037, 1)^T \,. \tag{43}$$

Hence, we compute the candidate solution $X^\#$ in (36), finding $X^\# = (-0.062, -0.766, 0.731, 1)^T$. The depths of $X^\#$ with respect to the cameras are given by 0.842, 0.965 and 2.401, and hence $X^\#$ remains in front of all the three cameras since these depths are positive. Then, we compute $m_2$ in (37), obtaining $m_2 = 0.866$. Therefore, from (39)-(40) we conclude that the found solution is optimal, and:

$$m^* = 0.866, \; X^* = (-0.062, -0.766, 0.731, 1)^T \,. \tag{44}$$

Secondly, we consider the case where an estimate of the image projection of the sought 3D point is available in the first view, while such an estimate is not available in the other views. Instead, we suppose that the unknown image projection in the second view is known to lie on a line segment, while the image projection in the third view is known to lie on an ellipse. Specifically, we consider the sets $A_1$, $A_2$ and $A_3$ given by:

$$A_1 = \{(0, 0, 1)^T\} \; A_2 = \{(0, 0, 1)^T + y_2(1, 2, 0)^T, \; y_2 \text{ in } (-0.1, 0.1)\} \; A_3 = \{x: \|x - (0, 0, 1)^T\|^2 \le 0.01\} \,. \tag{45}$$

By solving the optimization problem (33) we find $m_1 = 0.588$. Then, from the vector $w^\#$ in (35) we extract the image points:

$$x_1^\# = (0.055, 0.765, 1)^T, \; x_2^\# = (0.553, 0.908, 1)^T, \; x_3^\# = (-0.110, 0.977, 1)^T \,. \tag{46}$$

Hence, we compute the candidate solution $X^\#$ in (36), finding $X^\# = (0.203, -0.790, 1.116, 1)^T$. The depths of $X^\#$ with respect to the cameras are given by 1.733, 1.326 and 3.435, and hence $X^{\#}$ remains in front of all the three cameras since these depths are positive. Then, we compute $m_2$ in (37), obtaining $m_2 = 0.588$. Therefore, from (39)-(40) we conclude that the found solution is optimal, and:

$$m^* = 0.588, X^* = (0.203, -0.790, 1.116, 1)^T. \tag{47}$$

## Examples with Real Data

Let us consider first the well-known dinosaur example, which is a turntable sequence of 36 views of a toy dinosaur with 4983 3D points. We estimate each of these points by solving the triangulation problem (33) with all the available views. The number of such views is shown in Table 1. Figure 1 shows an image of the sequence and the estimated 3D points. The solution provided by the proposed technique is optimal for all the points. The average computational time per point ranges from 0.01 seconds (case of N = 2 views) to 1.10 seconds (case of N = 21 views). This time is relative to an implementation of the proposed method in Matlab on a standard personal computer with Intel Pentium 4, 3 GHz, 2 GB RAM, and Windows XP.

Next, we consider a situation with real data in the presence of occlusions as shown in Figure 2. The sequence consists of three views of a calendar showing Mona Lisa, see Figures 2a, 2c and 2e. The 3D point that we want to estimate is the extreme of the right index finger of Mona Lisa, see the corresponding zoom-in areas in Figures 2b, 2d and 2f. This point is visible in Figures 2c and 2e, but is occluded in Figure 2a. Nevertheless, a region where this point obviously lies in can be easily identified, for instance via an ellipse as

*Table 1. Dinosaur example: Number M of 3D points observed in N views*

| N | 2 | 3 | 4 | 5 | 6 | 7 | 8 | 9 | 10 | 11 | 12 | 13 | 14 | 21 |
|---|---|---|---|---|---|---|---|---|----|----|----|----|----|----|
| M | 2300 | 1167 | 584 | 375 | 221 | 141 | 88 | 44 | 26 | 15 | 14 | 5 | 2 | 1 |

*Figure 1. Dinosaur example: (a) an image of the sequence, and (b) the reconstructed model with the proposed technique by using for each 3D point all the available views shown in Table 1*

(a)          (b)

shown in Figure 2b. Hence, we estimate the 3D point by solving the triangulation problem (33) with two image points and an ellipse. We find $m_1$ = 2.228 and $X^{\#}$ = (0.071, -0.444, 2.725, 1)$^T$. Then, we compute $m_2$ in (37), obtaining $m_2$ = 2.228. Therefore, from (39)-(40) we conclude that the found solution is optimal, and:

$$m^* = 2.228, X^* = (0.071, -0.444, 2.725, 1)^T .$$
$$(48)$$

## FUTURE DIRECTIONS

The technique proposed in this chapter provides a new methodology for solving multiple view L2 triangulation in certain and uncertain cases. Numerous research directions can be explored in future works starting from this technique. For instance, it would be interesting to investigate the possibility of extending this methodology to multiple view triangulation with other norms but

*Figure 2. Mona Lisa example: The extreme of the right index finger is visible in the second and third views (c and e), but is occluded by an object in the first view (a). The figures b, d and f are zoom-in areas of the figures a, c and e, respectively.*

the L2. Also, one could try to exploit the particular structure of the LMI problem derived here in order to further decrease the computational time of the proposed technique.

## CONCLUSION

This chapter has addressed multiple view L2 triangulation, which is a fundamental problem in computer vision with numerous applications in various areas. Specifically, the problem has been considered in the standard case where estimates of all the image points are available (here referred to as certain triangulation) and in the more general case where some of such estimates are not available for example due to occlusions (here referred to as uncertain triangulation). In the latter case, it has been supposed that the unknown image points belong to known regions such as line segments or ellipses. A unified methodology has been proposed for these problems in this chapter. This methodology exploits the fundamental matrices among the views and provides a candidate 3D point through the solution of a convex optimization problem based on LMIs. Moreover, a simple condition that allows one to immediately establish whether the found 3D point is optimal has been provided. This condition also provides a guaranteed lower bound and a guaranteed upper bound for the minimum cost of the triangulation problem in the case where the found 3D point is not optimal. As shown by various examples with synthetic and real data, the proposed technique is almost always optimal in practice, moreover its computational time is indeed small.

## ACKNOWLEDGMENT

The work in this chapter was supported in part by the CRCG of the University of Hong Kong (Project 200907176048) and the Research Grants Council of Hong Kong (GRF Projects HKU 712808E and HKU 711208E).

## REFERENCES

Bartoli, A., & Lapreste, J.-T. (2008). Triangulation for points on lines. *Image and Vision Computing*, *26*(2), 315–324. doi:10.1016/j.imavis.2007.06.003

Boyd, S., El Ghaoui, L., Feron, E., & Balakrishnan, V. (1994). *Linear matrix inequalities in system and control theory*. SIAM. doi:10.1137/1.9781611970777

Byrod, M., Josephson, K., & Astrom, K. (2007). Fast optimal three view triangulation. In *Asian Conference on Computer Vision, LNCS 4844*, Tokyo, Japan, (pp. 549-559).

Chaumette, F., & Hutchinson, S. (2006). Visual servo control, part I: Basic approaches. *IEEE Robotics & Automation Magazine*, *13*(4), 82–90. doi:10.1109/MRA.2006.250573

Chaumette, F., & Hutchinson, S. (2007). Visual servo control, part II: Advanced approaches. *IEEE Robotics & Automation Magazine*, *14*(1), 109–118. doi:10.1109/MRA.2007.339609

Chesi, G. (2009a). Camera displacement via constrained minimization of the algebraic error. *IEEE Transactions on Pattern Analysis and Machine Intelligence*, *31*(2), 370–375. doi:10.1109/TPAMI.2008.198

Chesi, G. (2009b). Visual servoing path-planning via homogeneous forms and LMI optimizations. *IEEE Transactions on Robotics*, *25*(2), 281–291. doi:10.1109/TRO.2009.2014131

Chesi, G., Garulli, A., Tesi, A., & Vicino, A. (2009). *Homogeneous polynomial forms for robustness analysis of uncertain systems*. Springer.

Chesi, G., Garulli, A., Vicino, A., & Cipolla, R. (2002). Estimating the fundamental matrix via constrained least-squares: A convex approach. *IEEE Transactions on Pattern Analysis and Machine Intelligence, 24*(3), 397–401. doi:10.1109/34.990139

Chesi, G., & Hashimoto, K. (Eds.). (2010). *Visual serving via advanced numerical methods*. Springer.

Chesi, G., & Hung, Y. S. (2007). Image noise induced errors in camera positioning. *IEEE Transactions on Pattern Analysis and Machine Intelligence, 29*(8), 1476–1480. doi:10.1109/TPAMI.2007.70723

Faugeras, O., & Luong, Q.-T. (2001). *The geometry of multiple images*. Cambridge, MA: MIT Press.

Hartley, R., & Schaffalitzky, F. (2004). L-infinity minimization in geometric reconstruction problems. In *IEEE Conference on Computer Vision and Pattern Recognition*, Washington, USA, (pp. 504-509).

Hartley, R., & Seo, Y. (2008). Verifying global minima for L2 minimization problems. In *IEEE Conference on Computer Vision and Pattern Recognition*, Anchorage, USA, (pp. 1-8).

Hartley, R., & Sturm, P. (1997). Triangulation. *Computer Vision and Image Understanding, 68*(2), 146–157. doi:10.1006/cviu.1997.0547

Hartley, R., & Zisserman, A. (2000). *Multiple view in computer vision*. Cambridge University Press.

Hung, Y. S., & Tang, W. K. (2006). Projective reconstruction from multiple views with minimization of 2D reprojection error. *International Journal of Computer Vision, 66*(3), 305–317. doi:10.1007/s11263-005-3675-0

Ke, Q., & Kanade, T. (2006). Uncertainty models in quasiconvex optimization for geometric reconstruction. In *IEEE Conference on Computer Vision and Pattern Recognition*, New York, USA, (pp. 1199-1205).

Lu, F., & Hartley, R. (2007). A fast optimal algorithm for l2 triangulation. In *Asian Conference on Computer Vision. Tokyo, Japan, LNCS 4844*, (pp. 279-288).

Mai, F., Hung, Y. S., & Chesi, G. (2010). Projective reconstruction of ellipses from multiple images. *Pattern Recognition, 43*(3), 545–556. doi:10.1016/j.patcog.2009.07.003

Stewenius, H., Schaffalitzky, F., & Nister, D. (2005). How hard is 3-view triangulation really? In *International Conference on Computer Vision*, Beijing, China, (pp. 686-693).

## KEY TERMS AND DEFINITIONS

**Computer Vision:** automatic acquisition and elaboration of visual information from cameras by a computer.

**Convex Optimization:** class of minimization problems with convex cost function and cost feasible set.

**L2 Norm:** Euclidean norm.

**LMI:** linear matrix inequality.

**Stereo Vision:** a vision system composed of two cameras observing a common scene.

**Triangulation:** estimation of the 3D coordinates of a scene point from its image projections on some cameras.

**Uncertainty:** one or more parameters that are either partially or completely unknown.

# Chapter 5
# Camera Calibration with 1D Objects

**José Alexandre de França**
*Universidade Estadual de Londrina, Brazil*

**Marcelo Ricardo Stemmer**
*Universidade Federal de Santa Catarina, Brazil*

**Maria B. de Morais França**
*Universidade Estadual de Londrina, Brazil*

**Rodrigo H. Cunha Palácios**
*Universidade Tecnológica Federal do Paraná, Brazil*

## ABSTRACT

*Camera calibration is a process that allows to fully understand how the camera forms the image. It is necessary especially when 3D information of the scene must be known. Calibration can be performed using a 1D pattern (points on a straight line). This kind of pattern has the advantage of being "visible" simultaneously even by cameras in opposite positions from each other. This makes the technique suitable for calibration of multiple cameras. Unfortunately, the calibration with 1D patterns often leads to poorly accurate results. In this work, the methods of single and multi-camera calibration are analyzed. It is shown that, in some cases, the accuracy of this type of algorithm can be significantly improved by simply performing a normalization of coordinates of the input points. Experiments on synthetic and real images are used to analyze the accuracy of the discussed methods.*

## 1. INTRODUCTION

Mathematically, in the process of image creation, the camera accomplishes a mapping between a 3D space (the world environment) and a plane (the image plane). During this process, some informa-

tions are lost (e.g., angles, distances and volume). If these informations are needed, it becomes necessary to estimate the intrinsic and extrinsic camera parameters, i.e., matrices with special properties that represent the camera mapping, through a procedure known as calibration. Usually, during this procedure, the camera captures images from an object with well known dimensions and form

DOI: 10.4018/978-1-61350-429-1.ch005

(known as the calibration apparatus or calibration pattern). Afterwards, the relation between some points of the calibration pattern and their respective projections in the image plane is used to determine the camera parameters.

The first calibration algorithms to become widely used were based on 3D patterns (Lenz and Tsai, 1988; Tsai, 1987). Typically, such calibration objects are composed of two or more orthogonal planes with a well-known pattern on their faces. These methods have the advantage of performing the calibration with few images and have excellent accuracy. Over the years, new calibration methods have been proposed using 2D patterns (Sturm and Maybank, 1999; Zhang, 2000). In this case, the main advantages are the simplicity of the calibration apparatus (even a sheet of paper with a known pattern can be used) and the abundance of planes in man-made environments (which enables the use of some pre-existing pattern in the camera environment as a calibration apparatus). In fact, the abundance and ease of detection of planes in the environment led to the proposition of self-calibration algorithms based on planes (Triggs, 1998). In self-calibration, there is no need for a calibration apparatus. Instead, the camera performs some displacements while capturing images. Then, typically, it is enough to trace down a few points over these images to be able to perform the calibration. However, despite the convenience and abundance of already proposed self-calibration algorithms (Dornaika and Chung, 2001; Hartley, 1997b; Maybank and Faugeras, 1992; Mendonça and Cipolla, 1999), the self-calibration is still rarely used in practice. This is mainly due to the large number of variables that need to be estimated, which leads to inaccurate algorithms and high computational complexity.

More recently, Zhang (2004) proposed a calibration procedure using patterns of only one dimension (points in a straight line). Here, the 1D pattern has to execute unknown displacements while the camera captures images from it. The only restriction of this method is that one of the

pattern's points must remain stationary during the image acquisition. This method has been investigated and extended by several other authors (Hammarstedt et al., 2005; Qi et al., 2007a,b; Wu et al., 2005). Wu et al. (2005) equated the problem in a different form, showing that the 1D calibration object with a segment rotating around a stationary point in Zhang's setup is in essence equivalent to a 2D rectangular calibration object with unknown sides. Still, such change does not bring any gain in accuracy. In fact, the results from Wu et al. (2005) are comparable to the ones obtained by Zhang (2004). More recently, Qi et al. (2007a) extended the work from Wu, removing the need for one of the pattern points to be stationary. Instead, it is necessary that the trajectory of the calibration pattern's center of mass is a parable. Furthermore, Qi et al. (2007a) demonstrated that a significant part of the instability in the method of Wu et al. (2005) is due to movements that cause singularities, which can be detected and avoided. With this care, the accuracy of the method of Wu et al. (2005) is significantly improved. However, the movement that the calibration pattern has to execute in the method of Wu et al. (2005) is very difficult to accomplish in practice. Therefore, only with the work of de França, J. A. and Stemmer, M. R. and de M. França, M. B. and Alves, E. G. (2010) the calibration with 1D patterns became usable in practice and with an accuracy comparable to other traditional methods. This work has shown that the accuracy of the original method of Zhang (2004) can be significantly improved simply by analyzing the mathematical equating of the problem and that it is possible to improve the numerical conditioning by performing a simple data normalization.

If, instead of one camera, a set of two or more cameras is considered, the epipolar restriction increases the degree of freedom of the problem and allows the calibration pattern to perform unrestricted displacements. The main advantage of this approach is the possibility of calibrating more than one camera at the same time. This happens because the points of the 1D pattern can be captured simultaneously even by cameras with very distinctive points of view. However, only with the works of Kojima et al. (2005) and Zhao and Liu (2008) this aspect could be effectively explored. Nevertheless, in the work of Kojima et al. (2005), in spite of the pattern being free to perform unrestricted and unknown movements, it is necessary to know the intrinsic parameters of at least one of the cameras being calibrated. On the other hand, in the work of Zhao and Liu (2008), the parameters of all cameras can be estimated but the calibration pattern has to move with one of its points permanently stationary.

The first work that made possible the calibration of multiple cameras at the same time and using a 1D pattern that performs unrestricted movements was proposed by Wang et al. (2007). In this work, the procedure begins by computing the vanishing points of the 1D calibration objects. With These vanishing points, infinite homographies between cameras can be computed. Then the affine projection matrices and the metric projection matrices can be obtained. Unfortunately, the estimation of vanishing points is very susceptible to noise and, in practice, this reduces the accuracy of the estimated parameters.

In the next sections, we present the state of the art in camera calibration with patterns of a single dimension, making a critical analysis of the main articles on the topic and presenting results of practical experiments with real images. The text addresses the following topics: a) basic concepts of projective geometry and camera modeling; b) overview of the classical calibration methods; c) the principles of monocular calibration with 1D patterns; d) analysis of singularities and numerical conditioning, and e) calibration of multiple cameras with 1D patterns.

## 2. BACKGROUND

In this section, some important aspects necessary for understanding the theory of camera calibration with 1D patterns are presented in detail.

### 2.1. Camera Model

In the process of image formation, the camera makes a mapping of points in 3D space (the camera coordinate System) into points on a 2D plane (the image plane coordinate system). More specifically, as sketched in Figure 1, given a point $\mathbf{M}$ in the camera coordinate system, the camera performs a perspective projection of this point, through its optical center (the point $\mathbf{C}$) and focusing on the point $\mathbf{m}$ in the image plane. In figure 1, the camera coordinate system is orthogonal and has its origin in $\mathbf{C}$, while the origin of the image plane coordinate system is the point $\mathbf{c}$ (the perspective projection from the point $\mathbf{C}$, perpendicular to the image plane), called the image center. Thus, the relationship between the coordinates of the points $\mathbf{M} = [X_C, Y_C, Z_C]^{\mathrm{T}}$ and $\mathbf{m} = [x_C, y_C]^{\mathrm{T}}$ is given by:

$$x_C = -f\frac{X_C}{Z_C} \text{ and } y_C = -f\frac{Y_C}{Z_C},$$

here $f$ is the focal distance, i.e., the perpendicular distance from point $\mathbf{C}$ to the image plane.

Despite the previous relationship is nonlinear, it can be linearized if the points are expressed in homogeneous coordinates, $\tilde{\mathbf{M}} = \left[X_C, Y_C, Z_C, 1\right]^T$ and $\tilde{\mathbf{m}} = \left[x_C, y_C, 1\right]^T$, i.e.,

$$\begin{bmatrix} Z_C x_c \\ Z_C y_c \\ Z_C \end{bmatrix} = \begin{bmatrix} -f & 0 & 0 & 0 \\ 0 & -f & 0 & 0 \\ 0 & 0 & 1 & 0 \end{bmatrix} \begin{bmatrix} X_C \\ Y_C \\ Z_C \\ 1 \end{bmatrix}.$$

*Figure 1. Sketch of the pinhole camera model*

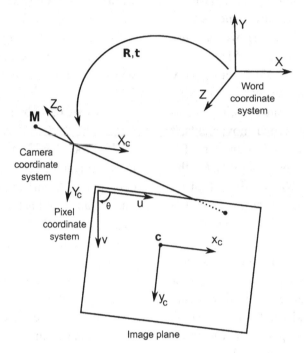

Furthermore, usually the previous equation is expressed as

$$
\begin{bmatrix} x_c \\ y_c \\ 1 \end{bmatrix} \simeq \begin{bmatrix} -f & 0 & 0 \\ 0 & -f & 0 \\ 0 & 0 & 1 \end{bmatrix} \begin{bmatrix} 1 & 0 & 0 & 0 \\ 0 & 1 & 0 & 0 \\ 0 & 0 & 1 & 0 \end{bmatrix} \begin{bmatrix} X_C \\ Y_C \\ Z_C \\ 1 \end{bmatrix},
$$

(1)

where the symbol "$\simeq$" indicates that both sides of the equation can differ by a non-zero constant.

The equation (1) is a simplification of what happens in practice. For instance, in some cases the world coordinate system may not coincide with the camera coordinate system. Moreover, the coordinates of the points in the image plane are usually given in pixel units and in relation to the upper left corner of the camera's sensor matrix. Because of this, the camera is better modeled by

$$\tilde{\mathbf{m}} \simeq \mathbf{A}[\mathbf{R}\,\mathbf{t}]\tilde{\mathbf{M}},$$ (2)

where

$$
\mathbf{A} = \begin{bmatrix} -\alpha & \alpha \cot \theta & u_0 \\ 0 & -\beta & v_0 \\ 0 & 0 & 1 \end{bmatrix},
$$

(3)

$\mathbf{R}$ is a rotation matrix $3 \times 3$ and $\mathbf{t}$ is a 3D translation vector. $\mathbf{R}$ and $\mathbf{t}$ are called extrinsic camera parameters and represent the displacement of the camera coordinate system in relation to the world coordinate system.

In equation (3), $f$ has been replaced by $\alpha$ and $\beta$, that provide the relation between length and pixels. Moreover $\mathbf{c} = [u_0, v_0]^T$ are the coordinates of the image center in relation to the pixel coordinate system (figure 1). Also, the angle $\theta$ models the non-orthogonality of the sensor matrix. However, in practice, $\theta$ is very near to $\pi/2$. Therefore, in the remaining text, we consider $\cot \theta = 0$, i.e., the matrix $\mathbf{A}$ has only four degrees of freedom, called the intrinsic camera parameters.

## 2.2. Epipolar Geometry

Figure 2 illustrates what happens when two cameras capture images of the same scene. In this case, without loss of generality, one can assume that one of the cameras is the origin of the world coordinate system. Then, considering the equation (2), we have

$$\tilde{\mathbf{m}}_0 \simeq \mathbf{A}_0[\mathbf{I}\,0]\tilde{\mathbf{M}} \text{ e } \tilde{\mathbf{m}}_1 \simeq \mathbf{A}_1[\mathbf{R}_1\,\mathbf{t}_1]\tilde{\mathbf{M}}, \qquad (4)$$

where $\mathbf{m}_i$ is the projection of the point $\mathbf{M}$ in the image plane $I_i$, $\mathbf{A}_i$ are the intrinsic camera parameters; $i$, $\mathbf{R}$ and $\mathbf{t}$ represent, respectively, the rotation and the translation of the second camera in relation to the reference camera. Furthermore, often the equation (4) is expressed in terms of projection matrices of the cameras, $\mathbf{P}_0$ and $\mathbf{P}_1$. In this case,

$$\mathbf{P}_0 = \mathbf{A}_0[\mathbf{I}\,0] \text{ e } \mathbf{P}_1 = \mathbf{A}_1[\mathbf{R}_1\,\mathbf{t}_1], \qquad (5)$$

In Figure 2, $\mathbf{C}_0$ and $\mathbf{C}_1$ are, respectively, the optical centers of the first and second cameras. Then, given a point $\mathbf{m}_0$ in the first image, $I_0$, the corresponding point, $\mathbf{m}_1$, in the second image, $I_1$, is restricted to a straight line, called the "epipolar line" of $\mathbf{m}_0$ and represented in the figure by $\mathbf{l}_1$. The line $\mathbf{l}_1$ is the intersection of the plane $\Pi$, defined by $\mathbf{M}$, $\mathbf{C}_0$ and $\mathbf{C}_1$ (called the epipolar plane), with the plane $\Pi$. That happens because the point $\mathbf{m}_0$ can match any point of the line $\overline{\mathbf{C}_0\mathbf{M}}$ and the projection of $\overline{\mathbf{C}_0\mathbf{M}}$ in $I_1$ is the line $\mathbf{l}_1$. Moreover, we observe that all epipolar lines of the points of $I_0$ pass through a common point, el, in $I_1$. This point is known as "epipole" and is defined by the intersection of the line $\overline{\mathbf{C}_0\mathbf{C}_1}$ with the plane $I_1$. Finally, one can easily observe the symmetry of the epipolar geometry. The correspondent of each point $\mathbf{m}_1 \in I_1$, on the line $\mathbf{l}_1$, must belong to the epipolar line $\mathbf{l}_0$, that is the intersection of the same plane $\Pi$ with the plane $I_0$. All the epipolar lines in $I_0$ intercept each other in the epipole $\mathbf{e}_0$, which is the intersection of the line $\overline{\mathbf{C}_0\mathbf{C}_1}$ with the plane $I_0$.

*Figure 2. Sketch of the epipolar geometry*

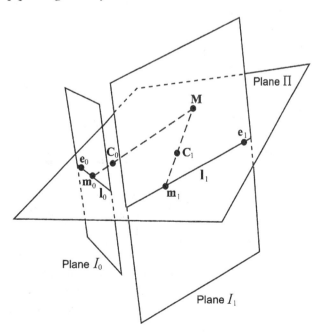

From Figure 2, we observe that the line $\mathbf{l}_1$ can be completely defined by the epipole $\mathbf{e}_1$ and any projection in $I_1$ of a point on $\overline{\mathbf{C}_0\mathbf{M}}$. In particular, a point on $\overline{\mathbf{C}_0\mathbf{M}}$ can be expressed by $\mathbf{P}_0^+\tilde{\mathbf{m}}_0$, whose projection in $I_1$ is given by $\mathbf{P}_1\mathbf{P}_0^+\tilde{\mathbf{m}}_0$, where $\mathbf{P}_0^+$ is the pseudoinverse of $\mathbf{P}_0$, i.e., $\mathbf{P}_0^+ = (\mathbf{P}_0^T\mathbf{P}_0)^{-1}\mathbf{P}_0^T$. Thus,

$$\mathbf{l}_1 = \tilde{\mathbf{e}}_1 \times \left(\mathbf{P}_1\mathbf{P}_0^+\tilde{\mathbf{m}}_0\right) = [\tilde{\mathbf{e}}_1]_\times \left(\mathbf{P}_1\mathbf{P}_0^+\right)\tilde{\mathbf{m}}_0, \qquad (6)$$

Where $[\tilde{\mathbf{e}}_1]_\times$ is the antisymmetric matrix of $\tilde{\mathbf{e}}_1$.

The previous equation relates $\mathbf{m}_0$ and $\mathbf{l}_1$ mathematically and, normally, the matrix

$$\mathbf{F} = [\tilde{\mathbf{e}}_1]_\times \left(\mathbf{P}_1\mathbf{P}_0^+\right) \qquad (7)$$

is called the "fundamental matrix" of the binocular set.

The equation (6) shows that, for each point $\mathbf{m}_0 \in I_0$, there is an epipolar line, $\mathbf{l}_1$, in the image $I_1$, i.e., there is a correspondence between points in the first image and epipolar lines in the second image. Furthermore, starting from the equation (7), the fundamental matrix can also be expressed in terms of the intrinsic and extrinsic parameters of the binocular set. This can be done considering the equation (4) and remembering that the epipole $\mathbf{e}_1$ is the projection of the point $\mathbf{C}_0$ in the image plane $I_1$, i.e.,

$$\tilde{\mathbf{e}}_1 = \mathbf{P}_1\tilde{\mathbf{C}}_0$$
$$= \mathbf{A}_1[\mathbf{R}_1 \ \mathbf{t}_1]\begin{bmatrix}\mathbf{0}\\1\end{bmatrix} = [\mathbf{A}_1\mathbf{R}_1 \ \mathbf{A}_1\mathbf{t}_1]\begin{bmatrix}\mathbf{0}\\1\end{bmatrix} = \mathbf{A}_1\mathbf{t}_1.$$

$$(8)$$

Moreover, as already discussed,

$$\mathbf{P}_0^+ = (\mathbf{P}_0^T\mathbf{P}_0)^{-1}\mathbf{P}_0^T, \text{ i.e.,}$$

$$\mathbf{P}_0^+ = \left(\begin{bmatrix}\mathbf{A}_0^T\\\mathbf{0}^T\end{bmatrix}[\mathbf{A}_0 \ \mathbf{0}]\right)^{-1}\begin{bmatrix}\mathbf{A}_0^T\\\mathbf{0}^T\end{bmatrix}$$
$$= \begin{bmatrix}\mathbf{A}_0^{-1}\mathbf{A}_0^{-T} & \mathbf{0}\\\mathbf{0}^T & 0\end{bmatrix}\begin{bmatrix}\mathbf{A}_0^T\\\mathbf{0}^T\end{bmatrix} = \begin{bmatrix}\mathbf{A}_0^{-1}\\\mathbf{0}^T\end{bmatrix}.$$

Thus,

$$\mathbf{P}_1\mathbf{P}_0^+ = \mathbf{A}_1[\mathbf{R}_1 \ \mathbf{t}_1]\begin{bmatrix}\mathbf{A}_0^{-1}\\\mathbf{0}^T\end{bmatrix}$$
$$= [\mathbf{A}_1\mathbf{R}_1 \ \mathbf{A}_1\mathbf{t}_1]\begin{bmatrix}\mathbf{A}_0^{-1}\\\mathbf{0}^T\end{bmatrix} = \mathbf{A}_1\mathbf{R}_1\mathbf{A}_0^{-1}, \qquad (9)$$

which is often refered as "the infinite homography", $\mathbf{H}_{1\infty}$, of the binocular set, since it relates vanishing points on the plane $I_0$ to their matching points on the plane $I_k$. Finally, replacing (8) and (9) in (7), we obtain the desired relation, i.e.[1],

$$\mathbf{F} = [\mathbf{A}_1\mathbf{t}_1]_\times \mathbf{A}_1\mathbf{R}_1\mathbf{A}_0^{-1} = \mathbf{A}_1^{-T}[\mathbf{t}_1]_\times \mathbf{A}_1^{-1}\mathbf{A}_1\mathbf{R}_1\mathbf{A}_0^{-1}$$
$$= \mathbf{A}_1^{-T}[\mathbf{t}_1]_\times \mathbf{R}_1\mathbf{A}_0^{-1}.$$

The point $\mathbf{m}_1$ is on the line $\mathbf{l}_1$, thus, from the equations (6) and (7), we derive

$$\tilde{\mathbf{m}}_1^T\mathbf{F}\tilde{\mathbf{m}}_0 = 0, \qquad (10)$$

which is a fundamental constraint behind any two images if they are perspective projections of the same scene.

## 2.3. Camera Calibration

From the previous section, it is known that a correspondence of points $(\mathbf{m}_1 \leftrightarrow \mathbf{m}_2)$ defines a single 3D point, $\mathbf{M}$ (figure 2). Then, using algorithms that allow to establish correspondence between points of two images of the same scene (taken from different points of view), it is possible to retrieve the 3D information lost during the formation of images through triangulation algorithms (Hartley and Sturm, 1997). This is useful, for example, for the navigation of autonomous mobile robots, which need to determine the location of obstacles, and for the reconstruction of parts to look for manufacturing defects. However, techniques based on triangulation are only possible if the process by which the cameras form the image is well known, i.e., the camera intrinsic and extrinsic parameters need to be estimated. For this, calibration algorithms are used, which will be discussed in detail.

Given a 3D point, $\mathbf{M}_i$, and its projection on the image plane, $\mathbf{m}_i$, the equation (2) can be expressed in terms of the cross product, i.e., $\tilde{\mathbf{m}}_i \times \mathbf{P}\tilde{\mathbf{M}}_i = 0$. Furthermore, if the $j$-th line of the matrix $\mathbf{P}$ is denoted by, $\mathbf{p}_j^T$ one can write

$$\mathbf{P}\tilde{\mathbf{M}}_i = [\mathbf{p}_1^T\tilde{\mathbf{M}}_i, \mathbf{p}_2^T\tilde{\mathbf{M}}_i, \mathbf{p}_3^T\tilde{\mathbf{M}}_i]^T.$$

Thus, considering, $\tilde{\mathbf{m}}_i = [u_i, v_i, t_i]^T$, we have

$$\tilde{\mathbf{m}}_i \times \mathbf{P}\tilde{\mathbf{M}}_i = \begin{bmatrix} v_i\mathbf{p}_3^T\tilde{\mathbf{M}}_i - t_i\mathbf{p}_2^T\tilde{\mathbf{M}}_i \\ t_i\mathbf{p}_1^T\tilde{\mathbf{M}}_i - u_i\mathbf{p}_3^T\tilde{\mathbf{M}}_i \\ u_i\mathbf{p}_2^T\tilde{\mathbf{M}}_i - v_i\mathbf{p}_1^T\tilde{\mathbf{M}}_i \end{bmatrix} = 0$$

However, since $\mathbf{p}_j^T\tilde{\mathbf{M}}_i = \tilde{\mathbf{M}}_i^T\mathbf{p}_j$, $j = 1, \dots, 3$, the previous equation can be written as

$$\mathbf{U}_i\mathbf{p} = 0,$$

Where $\mathbf{p} = [\mathbf{p}_1^T, \mathbf{p}_2^T, \mathbf{p}_3^T]^T$ and

$$\mathbf{U}_i = \begin{bmatrix} \mathbf{0}^T & -t_i\tilde{\mathbf{M}}_i^T & v_i\tilde{\mathbf{M}}_i^T \\ t_i\tilde{\mathbf{M}}_i^T & \mathbf{0}^T & -u_i\tilde{\mathbf{M}}_i^T \\ -v_i\tilde{\mathbf{M}}_i^T & u_i\tilde{\mathbf{M}}_i^T & \mathbf{0}^T \end{bmatrix}$$

The former equation set has only two independent equations and, because it is an homogeneous matrix, $\mathbf{P}$ has only eleven degrees of freedom.

Thus, we need at least six pairs ($\mathbf{M}_i$, $\mathbf{m}_i$) in order to univocally determine it. Furthermore, if $n > 6$ of these pairs are available, we can solve the system of equations

$$\begin{bmatrix} \mathbf{U}_1 \\ \mathbf{U}_2 \\ \vdots \\ \mathbf{U}_n \end{bmatrix} \mathbf{p} = 0 \qquad (11)$$

and determine $\mathbf{p}$ using redundancy, which significantly improves the robustness of the method with respect to noise.

The calibration of cameras by solving the system of equations (11), despite being a nonlinear method and iterative, is not ideal because it minimizes a criterion without any physical meaning. To circumvent this problem, one should take into consideration the following observation. Normally, the coordinates of 3D points, $\mathbf{M}_i$, are obtained with the help of a calibration pattern. In this case, two or three orthogonal planes, with patterns whose shape and size are well known, are used to form an "imaginary" coordinate system. Thus, the accuracy of the coordinates of the points $\mathbf{M}_i$ depends only on the manufacturing process of the calibration pattern and is, in general, known with extreme accuracy. Thus, it is reasonable to assume that the main source of calibration error using patterns comes from the determination of the coordinates of the points $\mathbf{m}_i$. Thus a better alternative to estimate $\mathbf{P}$ is to solve

$$\min_{\mathbf{P}} \sum_{i=1}^{n} d(\tilde{\mathbf{m}}_i, \mathbf{P}\tilde{\mathbf{M}}_i)^2,$$

where $d(\cdot, \cdot)^2$ denotes the square of the euclidean distance between two points.

The problem of the previous equation is to minimize the Euclidean distance between the measured point, $\mathbf{m}_i$, and the "real" point, $\mathbf{P}\tilde{\mathbf{M}}_i$, with respect to the entire set of *n* points. Evidently, this new technique requires the use of a non-linear minimizing algorithm which usually requires an initial estimate of **P** that can be obtained by solving the system of equations (11).

As seen in section 2.1, the camera model used in this work can be considered linear. However, some cameras have radial distortions. In this case, in order to take this characteristic into account, using a nonlinear model for the camera is required. Therefore, it is common to find classic works in the literature (see, for example, the method of Tsai (1987) and the works of Shih et al. (1996) and Salvi et al. (2002) for two critical analysis) or even some current work (e.g., the work of Heikkilä (2000)), which propose solutions to estimate also the radial distortion of the cameras. These solutions use approaches that differ from the methods discussed in this work. However, the current state of the art in camera construction allow the manufacture of lenses whose model is very close to linear. Thus, the radial distortion is neglected in this work.

In some special applications, cameras whose main feature is the radial distortion are used. One of these applications is the civilian surveillance, because in these cases fixed cameras with broad angle of vision are employed. Examples of works with such cameras are (Corrêa et al., 2003; Gaspar et al., 2002; Grassi Junior and Okamoto Junior, 2000). However, this type of application is out of the context of this work.

Calibration methods that rely on patterns similar to those of Figure 3 enable to find all parameters of the camera with extreme accuracy, capturing a few or even a single image of the pattern. However, the structure of these patterns requires a certain degree of caution in the confection process. This is because it is necessary to unite two or more planes orthogonally. Moreover, the distance between points of concurrent planes must also be known. In view of this, calibration algorithms based on planes were proposed. In this case, the calibration apparatus may simply be a

checkerboard pattern of well known dimensions, printed on a sheet of paper by a common laser printer. In addition, planes are very common in man-made environments. In some cases, this can allow to perform a calibration with objects of the environment in the visual field of the camera.

The calibration using planar devices appeared in the work of Triggs (1998) and was latter improved in independent form by Sturm and Maybank (1999) e Zhang (2000). Basically, the method requires that the camera captures *n* > 2 images of a pattern in the form of a plane in motion. Then, in all images, the coordinates of the pattern points should be extracted and used to estimate the homography of points along the *n* images. From these homographies, all camera parameters are estimated.

Recently, Zhang (2004) made more progress in the flexibilization of the calibration procedure, further reducing the complexity and size of the pattern to just a single dimension (points on a line). This technique, which greatly increases the flexibility of the calibration procedure (especially when it involves the calibration of multiple cameras), is described in detail in the following sections.

*Figure 3. Example of planar calibration apparatus*

## 3. SINGLE CAMERA CALIBRATION

In the calibration of cameras using 1D objects, the pattern used for calibration has to be something like a stick with several spheres (indexed by $j$) along its extension. The distance between consecutive spheres must be precisely known. In order to execute the calibration process, the pattern should move in the visual field of the camera. While the pattern moves, a sequence of images (indexed by $i$) is captured. In the method of Zhang (2004), the monocular calibration with this sort of pattern is executed using a stick with three or more points (spheres), where one of the points, $\mathbf{M}_1$, is fixed, as shown in Figure 4. This way, $\mathbf{m}_1$, the projection of the point $\mathbf{M}_1$, is the same in all images of the sequence.

In the draft shown in Figure 4, the length $L$ of the pattern is expressed by

$$\|\mathbf{M}_{2i} - \mathbf{M}_1\| = L. \tag{12}$$

Moreover, since the relative positions of the spheres are known, a point in the pattern located between $\mathbf{M}_1$ and $\mathbf{M}_{2i}$ can be expressed by

$$\mathbf{M}_{ji} = \lambda_{1j}\mathbf{M}_1 + \lambda_{2j}\mathbf{M}_{2i}, \tag{13}$$

where $\lambda_{1j}$ and $\lambda_{2j}$ are known constants that depend on the distances $\overline{\mathbf{M}_1\mathbf{M}_{ji}}$ and $\overline{\mathbf{M}_{2i}\mathbf{M}_{ji}}$.

From equation (2), considering the (unknown) depth of the point $\mathbf{M}_{ji}$ equal to $z_{ji}$, we have

$$\mathbf{M}_1 = z_1\mathbf{A}^{-1}\tilde{\mathbf{m}}_1, \tag{14}$$

$$\mathbf{M}_{2i} = z_{2i}\mathbf{A}^{-1}\tilde{\mathbf{m}}_{2i}, \tag{15}$$

$$\mathbf{M}_{ji} = z_{ji}\mathbf{A}^{-1}\tilde{\mathbf{m}}_{ji}, \tag{16}$$

Thus, replacing the former equations in (13), we obtain

$$z_{ji}\tilde{\mathbf{m}}_{ji} = z_1\lambda_{1j}\tilde{\mathbf{m}}_{1i} + z_{2i}\lambda_{2j}\tilde{\mathbf{m}}_{2i}$$

after eliminating $\mathbf{A}^{-1}$ from both sides.

Now, after some algebraic manipulation, the former equation can be expressed as

$$z_{2i} = -z_1\frac{\lambda_{1j}(\tilde{\mathbf{m}}_{1i} \times \tilde{\mathbf{m}}_{ji}).(\tilde{\mathbf{m}}_{2i} \times \tilde{\mathbf{m}}_{ji})}{\lambda_{2j}(\tilde{\mathbf{m}}_{2i} \times \tilde{\mathbf{m}}_{ji}).(\tilde{\mathbf{m}}_{2i} \times \tilde{\mathbf{m}}_{ji})}. \tag{17}$$

Replacing (14) and (15) in (12) and considering $z_{2i}$ given by (17), we obtain

$$z_1\|\mathbf{A}^{-1}\mathbf{h}_{ji}\| = L, \tag{18}$$

where

$$\mathbf{h}_{ji} = \tilde{\mathbf{m}}_1 + \frac{\lambda_{1j}(\tilde{\mathbf{m}}_1 \times \tilde{\mathbf{m}}_{ji}).(\tilde{\mathbf{m}}_{2i} \times \tilde{\mathbf{m}}_{ji})}{\lambda_{2j}(\tilde{\mathbf{m}}_{2i} \times \tilde{\mathbf{m}}_{ji}).(\tilde{\mathbf{m}}_{2i} \times \tilde{\mathbf{m}}_{ji})}\tilde{\mathbf{m}}_{2i}. \tag{19}$$

*Figure 4. Draft of the 1D calibration pattern*

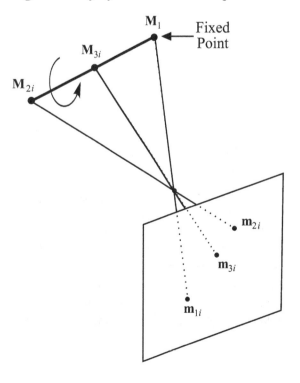

The equation (18) is equivalent to

$$\mathbf{h}_{ji}^T \mathbf{B} \mathbf{h}_{ji} = L^2, \qquad (20)$$

where, considering $\cot \theta = 0$,

$$\mathbf{B} = z_1^2 \mathbf{A}^{-1} \mathbf{A}^{-1} = \begin{bmatrix} B_{11} & 0 & B_{13} \\ 0 & B_{22} & B_{23} \\ B_{13} & B_{23} & B_{33} \end{bmatrix}. \qquad (21)$$

Moreover, taking into account that

$$\mathbf{h}_{ji}^T \mathbf{B} \mathbf{h}_{ji} = \left[ a_{ji}^2, b_{ji}^2, 2a_{ji}c_{ji}, 2b_{ji}c_{ji}, c_{ji}^2 \right]^T \mathbf{b} = \mathbf{u}_{ji} \mathbf{b}, \qquad (22)$$

with $\mathbf{h}_{ji} = [a_{ji}, b_{ji}, c_{ji}]^T$ and $\mathbf{b} = [B_{11}, B_{22}, B_{13}, B_{23}, B_{33}]^T$, the equation (20) can be rewritten as

$$\mathbf{u}_{ji}^T \mathbf{b} = L^2. \qquad (23)$$

With $n$ images, we have $\mathbf{U}_n = [\mathbf{u}_{j1}, \mathbf{u}_{j2}, ..., \mathbf{u}_{jn}]^T$. This way, considering $\mathbf{L} = [L^2, ..., L^2]^T$, one can find b solving

$$\mathbf{U}_n \mathbf{b} = \mathbf{L}, \qquad (24)$$

that is to say,

$$\mathbf{b} = \mathbf{U}_n^+ \mathbf{L}, \qquad (25)$$

where $\mathbf{U}_n^+ = \left( \mathbf{U}_n^T \mathbf{U}_n \right)^{-1} \mathbf{U}_n^T$ is the pseudoinverse from $\mathbf{U}_n$.

If we choose a pattern with more than three points, we obtain a bigger amount of vectors $\mathbf{h}_{ji}$. However, for each image, only one vector is linearly independent. Thus, since there are five unknowns (the four parameters from $\mathbf{A}$ and $z_1$),

we need at least five displacements of the pattern to solve the problem.

Once $\mathbf{B}$ is known, the matrix $z_1 \mathbf{A}^{-1}$ can be obtained from $\mathbf{B}$ through the Cholesky decomposition (Golub and Van Loan, 1996). With $z_1$ and $\mathbf{A}$ known, the point $\mathbf{M}_1$ can be obtained from (14) and the points $\mathbf{M}_{2i}$ from (17) and (15). Finally, we can use (13) in order to obtain $\mathbf{M}_{ji}$.

# 4. IMPROVEMENT OF THE METHOD

The solution of the problem (24) can also be given in terms of the singular value decomposition of the matrix $\mathbf{U}_n$, i.e.,

$$\mathbf{U}_n = \mathbf{U} \sum \mathbf{V}^T \qquad (26)$$

In that case, its pseudoinverse is given by $\mathbf{U}_n^+ = \mathbf{V} \sum^+ \mathbf{U}^T$, where $\sum^+$ is the transposed of $\sum$ with every element different from zero replaced by its reciprocal. Thus, the solution of (24) is expressed as

$$\mathbf{b} = \mathbf{V} \sum^+ \mathbf{U}^T \mathbf{L} \qquad (27)$$

Of what was discussed in the previous section, it is known that the matrix $\mathbf{U}_n$ depends entirely on the homogeneous coordinates of points in the image plane (the projections of the 1D pattern), e.g., $\tilde{\mathbf{m}} = [u, v, 1]$. In this case, assuming that a typical point has coordinates $\tilde{\mathbf{m}} = [100, 100, 1]$, one would have $\mathbf{h}_{ji}$ of the same order, i.e., $\mathbf{h}_{ji} = [100, 100, 1]$. Thus, the magnitude order of the elements of the vector $\mathbf{u}_{ji}$, in (22), can be expressed as being $\mathbf{u}_{ji} = [10^4, 10^4, 10^2, 10^2, 1]^T$. Of course, this makes the columns of the matrix $\mathbf{U}_n$ to be in that same proportion, making the matrix $\mathbf{U}_n$ bad-conditioned. Furthermore, one can see that even the addition of a noise with small RMS value causes a huge variation in the lines of $\mathbf{U}_n$ and, consequently, in the solution of the problem.

Fortunately, applying a projective transform $\mathbf{T}_2$ to the image points $\tilde{\mathbf{m}}$, we have $\tilde{\tilde{\mathbf{m}}} = \mathbf{T}_2 \tilde{\mathbf{m}}$. This way, from equation (2), we obtain $s\tilde{\tilde{\mathbf{m}}} = \mathbf{T}_2 \mathbf{A}[\mathbf{I}\ \mathbf{0}]\tilde{\mathbf{M}}$. This relation implies that $\hat{\mathbf{A}} = \mathbf{T}_2 \mathbf{A}$ represents the camera intrinsic parameters that correspond to the projections $\hat{\mathbf{m}}$. From the work of Hartley (1997a), applied to the calculation of the fundamental matrix (Armangué and Salvi, 2003), we know that, in order to significantly improve the numerical conditioning of, $\mathbf{U}_n$, $\mathbf{T}_2$ should be such that the centroid of the point set is in the origin and the average distance between a point and the origin should be $\sqrt{2}$.

As we empirically demonstrate in section 4.2, the transform $\mathbf{T}_2$ significantly improves the accuracy of the camera parameters estimated by the linear method of Zhang (2004). Besides that, the computational cost added to the problem due to that normalization is negligible.

Once the intrinsic parameters have been estimated in the coordinate system defined by $\mathbf{T}_2$, the matrix $\mathbf{A}$ (of the original coordinate system) can be obtained by doing

$$\mathbf{A} = \mathbf{T}_2^{-1}\hat{\mathbf{A}}. \tag{28}$$

## 4.1. Non-Linear Solution

The solution of the problem given by (24) minimizes a criterion with no geometric meaning. This is another reason why the original method does not give good results in the presence of noise. Thus, Zhang (2004) defined an optimization criterion that involves the projections of the points in the stick, that is,

$$\square(\mathbf{A}, \mathbf{M}_{ji}) = \sum_{i=1}^{n} \sum_{j=2}^{q} \left\| \mathbf{m}_{ji} - \hat{\mathbf{m}}_{ji}(\mathbf{A}, \mathbf{M}_{ji}) \right\|^2, \tag{29}$$

where n is the number of captured pattern images, $q$ is the number of points of the pattern and $\hat{\mathbf{m}}_{ji}(\mathbf{A}, \mathbf{M}_{ji})$ is the estimated projection of $\mathbf{M}_{ji}$ according to (2), (13) and

$$\mathbf{M}_{2i} = \mathbf{M}_1 + L[\text{sen},_i \cos\phi_i, \text{sen},_i \text{sen}\phi_i, \cos,_i]^T \tag{30}$$

where $\theta_i$ and $\square_i$ are angles that define the pattern orientation.

The minimization of equation (29) involves solving a nonlinear minimization problem. In computer vision, the Levenberg-Marquardt (Levenberg, 1944; Marquardt, 1963) is widely used to solve these kinds of problems. However, the computational complexity of this algorithm is $N^3$, where $N$ is the number of unknowns to be estimated. Unfortunately, the problem (29) has an excessive number of unknowns, i.e., the four intrinsic parameters of $\mathbf{A}$, the three coordinates of the point $\mathbf{M}_1$ and $2n$ angles, $\theta_i$ and $\phi_i$. Thus, the Levenberg-Marquardt algorithm is not suitable for the monocular calibration with 1D patterns. However, calibrating the camera by minimizing (29) is equivalent to finding the vector $\mathbf{Y}$ satisfying

$$\square(\mathbf{Y}) = \mathbf{X} \tag{31}$$

where $\mathbf{Y} = [\mathbf{e}^T, \mathbf{d}^T]^T$ is the vector of parameters to be estimated, i.e., $\mathbf{e} = [\alpha, \beta, u_0, v_0, \mathbf{M}_1^T]^T$ and $\mathbf{d} = [\mathbf{d}_1^T, \mathbf{d}_2^T, ..., \mathbf{d}_n^T]^T$, with $\mathbf{d}_i = [\theta_i, \phi_i]^T$, and $\mathbf{X} = [\mathbf{X}_1^T, \mathbf{X}_2^T, ..., \mathbf{X}_n^T]^T$ is a vector of observations, i. e., $\mathbf{X}_i = [\mathbf{m}_{2i}^T, \mathbf{m}_{3i}^T, ..., \mathbf{m}_{qi}^T]^T$. Furthermore, observing the equations (2), (13) and (30), it becomes clear that a change in the elements of $\mathbf{A}$ or $\mathbf{M}_1$ alters the coordinates of the points $\mathbf{m}_{ji}$ of all images, while a change in $\theta_i$ or $\phi_i$ reflects only in the points of the $i$-th image. Thus, each observation $\mathbf{X}_i$ depends on the vectors $\mathbf{e}$ and $\mathbf{d}_i$, but on no other $\mathbf{d}_k$. In this case, $\partial \mathbf{X}_i / \partial \mathbf{d}_k = 0$ for $i \neq k$, while no supposition can be made concerning

$\partial \mathbf{X}_i / \partial \mathbf{e}$. This causes the jacobian matrix, $\mathbf{J} = \partial \mathbf{X} / \partial \mathbf{Y}$, has a sparse structure. Fortunately, there is a derivation of the Levenberg-Marquardt algorithm, popularized by Hartley and Zisserman (2000) and refered as the Partitioned Levenberg-Marquardt algorithm, that takes advantage of the problem's structure to reduce significantly the complexity of the algorithm. This is an important result, since each step of the Partitioned Levenberg-Marquardt algorithm has linear complexity in $N$. Of course, this makes the monocular calibration problem much more suitable for practical use.

The Partitioned Levenberg-Marguardt algorithm requires an initial estimation of all unknowns to be refined. That estimation can be performed by doing: a) with the linear algorithm given by (24), $\mathbf{A}$ and $z_1$ are estimated; b) $\mathbf{m}_1$ is estimated by the method proposed by Zhang (2004); c) $\mathbf{M}_1$ is obtained through (14); d) the points $\mathbf{M}_{2i}$ are known through (15) and (17), and; e) the angles $\theta_i$ and $\Box_i$ are obtained from (30).

Equation (30) provides a non-iterative method to determine $\theta_i$ and $\Box_i$. However, it is based on a non-linear and redundant equation system. For that reason, in the presence of noise, the derivation of $\theta_i$ and $\Box_i$ from (30) is not satisfactory, since it can demand more iterations in the minimization of (29) or even lead the system to a local minimum. Thus, it is necessary to use the Levenberg-Marquardt algorithm to solve

$$\min_{\theta_i, \phi_i} \left\| \mathbf{M}_{2i} - \hat{\mathbf{M}}_{2i}(\theta_i, \phi_i) \right\|^2, \qquad (32)$$

where $\mathbf{M}_{2i}$ is the reconstruction of $\mathbf{m}_{2i}$ according to (15), while $\hat{\mathbf{M}}_{2i}(\theta_i, \phi_i)$ is the same reconstruction obtained from (30).

Equation (32) represents a quite simple minimization problem, with only two unknowns. Nevertheless, its solution is required for the convergence of the problem (29).

## 4.2. Experimental Results

In the present work, four methods were analyzed: a) the linear method with normalized data described in section 4 and called **LINEAR1**; b) the linear method proposed by Zhang (2004) and referred in this chapter as **LINEAR2**; c) the method that refines the estimation of **LINEAR1** through the Partitioned Levenberg-Marquardt algorithm (referred as **NOLIN1**), and; d) the method that refines the estimation of **LINEAR2** through the Partitioned Levenberg-Marquardt algorithm (referred as **NOLIN2**). In the solution of the iterative algorithms, the tolerance was always chosen as $10^{-7}$.

In order to acquire the real data, a pattern with five plastic spheres (one white and four black) with 2 cm diameter each was used. The spheres were fixed on a metal stick. The distance between the centroids of the neighbor spheres was measured with the help of a paquimeter. The calibration pattern was manually placed in different positions at a distance of approximately 50 cm from the camera. During the movement, 121 images were acquired (three images of that sequence are shown in figure 5). With the help of a "blob processing tool"[2], the coordinates of the centroid of the black spheres in each image were automatically estimated. The coordinates of the fixed point where estimated with the help of the linear algorithm proposed by Zhang (2004). Those coordinates were applied to the four tested algorithms and the camera parameters were estimated.

The intrinsic camera parameters used in the tests were also estimated by the method proposed by Zhang (2000). The calibration apparatus used in this method is a flat object with a checkered pattern on it. In the present work, we used a pattern with 156 points (figure 3). During the calibration, 22 camera displacements were executed and a sequence of 22 images was captured. After that, the implementation proposed by Bouguet (2008) of the algorithm of Zhang (2000) was used to estimate the intrinsic parameters. Those parameters were adopted as the real camera parameters.

The parameters estimated by the analyzed methods were compared to the real parameters obtained with the tool of Bouguet (2008). Again, the errors of all parameters are presented in relation to the parameter $\alpha$. The number n of images used in the calibration varied between 5 and 75. The $n$ images of the pattern were randomly chosen among the total available set. For each value of $n$ we executed 250 essays and, again, the median of each intrinsic parameter was retained and the relative error was calculated. The result is presented in Figure 6.

The experiment has some flaws. The main one is the rudimentary constructive form of the calibration apparatus, which lead to an inaccurate pattern point linearity, invalidating an important assumption of the adopted model. Another source of error is the tool used to extract the centroid of the pattern points. Due to illumination differences, the tool was unable to segment the spheres as perfect circles. Thus, the sphere centroids were imprecisely calculated. Finally, during the capture of the images sequence, the pattern point that should be fixed actually moved slightly from the original position.

Considering all the imperfections of the experiment, we concluded that the difference between the two results (real and synthetic data) is acceptable. Furthermore, for the **NOLIN1** method with $n \geq 70$ images, the error of the most important parameters ($\alpha$ and $\beta$) is in the order of $10^{-1}\%$. On the other hand, the parameters $u_0$ and $v_0$ are estimated with a smaller accuracy. However, it is well-know that those parameters are difficult to estimate even with traditional methods.

The **NOLIN2** method had a performance similar to the **NOLIN1** method, i.e., the accuracy obtained with both methods had the same magnitude order. However, as shown in figure 7, the **NOLIN2** method requires much more iterations to reach

*Figure 6. Accuracy of the analyzed methods concerning the number of real images used: a) linear method* **LINEAR1**; *b) linear method* **LINEAR2**; *c) non-linear method* **NOLIN1**, *and; d) non-linear method* **NOLIN2**.

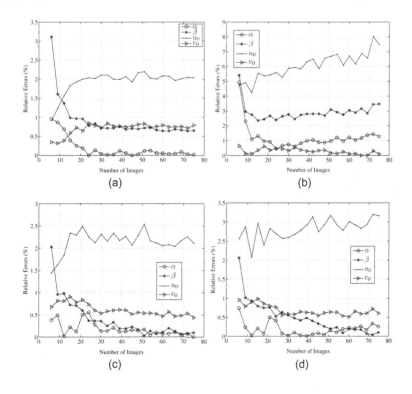

*Figure 7. Accuracy of the iterative methods concerning the number of real images used*

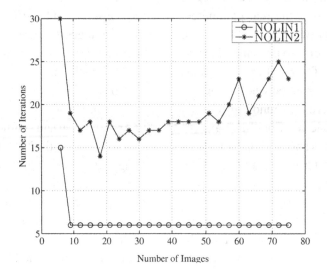

Number of Images

the same accuracy obtained with the **NOLIN1**. In some cases, the number of required iterations is almost five times bigger. It occurs in view of the fact that the algorithm **NOLIN1** is initialized from the result of the **LINEAR1** method, that is closer to the final result, compared to **LINEAR2**. Thus, a suitable initialization is as important as the cost function that is being minimized. Evidently this contributes directly to reduce the computational cost of the method.

## 5. MULTIPLE CAMERA CALIBRATION

The main advantage of using 1D patterns for the calibration is that it allows the calibration of multiple cameras simultaneously. This is because the points of a 1D pattern can be captured even from quite different points of view. In fact, the consideration of more than one camera inserts more restrictions to the problem. Thus, the calibration becomes possible even when the pattern moves freely, without the need for one of its points to be stationary.

The Figure 8 outlines a set of $K+1$ cameras that capture images from a 1D calibration pat-

tern with $q$ points, while it performs unrestricted displacements (indexed by $i$). Considering pairs of cameras always composed by the same reference camera and another camera $k$, in figure 8, there is a total of $K$ binocular sets (indexed by $k$). In this case, for each binocular set, there is a point matching $(\mathbf{m}_{0ji} \leftrightarrow \mathbf{m}_{kji})$ for each point $\mathbf{M}_{ji}$ belonging to the pattern, where $j = 1, 2,..., q$. Wang et al. (2007) observed that, from these correspondences, it is possible to completely calibrate all the $K+1$ cameras estimating the intrinsic and extrinsic parameters of each one. This is done as follows.

The cross ratio among four points $(\mathbf{p}_1, \mathbf{p}_2, \mathbf{p}_3$ and $\mathbf{p}_4)$ is defined as

$$\text{Cross}(\mathbf{p}_1, \mathbf{p}_2, \mathbf{p}_3, \mathbf{p}_4) = \frac{\|\mathbf{p}_4 - \mathbf{p}_2\| \|\mathbf{p}_1 - \mathbf{p}_3\|}{\|\mathbf{p}_4 - \mathbf{p}_3\| \|\mathbf{p}_1 - \mathbf{p}_2\|}. \quad (33)$$

Thus, considering $\mathbf{V}_i$ a 3D point at infinity and on the line defined by the 1D pattern, we have

$$\text{Cross}(\mathbf{M}_{1i}, \mathbf{M}_{2i}, \mathbf{M}_{ji}, \mathbf{V}_i) = \frac{1}{\lambda_{2j}}, \quad (34)$$

*Figure 8. Binocular calibration scheme using a pattern with three points, whose relative positions are known.*

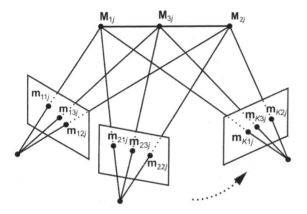

since

$$\frac{\left\| \mathbf{V}_i - \mathbf{M}_{2i} \right\|}{\left\| \mathbf{V}_i - \mathbf{M}_{ji} \right\|} = 1.$$

Thus, as the cross ratio is one of the few properties that are preserved after projective transformations, the previous equation also applies to the pattern points projections on the image plane $I_k$, i.e.,

$$\text{Cross}(\mathbf{m}_{01i}, \mathbf{m}_{02i}, \mathbf{m}_{0ji}, \mathbf{v}_{0i}) = \frac{1}{\lambda_{2j}}. \tag{35}$$

The previous equation allows to estimate $\mathbf{v}_{0i}$, the projection of $\mathbf{V}_i$ on the image plane of the reference camera. In a similar way, it is also possible to estimate $\mathbf{v}_{ki}$, the projection of $\mathbf{V}_i$ on the image plane of the camera $k$. Then, for each binocular set with $n \geq 8$ pairs of images from pattern displacements, it is possible to estimate $n$ matchings ($\mathbf{v}_{0i} \leftrightarrow \mathbf{v}_{ki}$) and hence the infinite homography,

$$\mathbf{H}_{k\infty} = \mathbf{A}_k \mathbf{R}_k \mathbf{A}_0^{-1}, \tag{36}$$

that satisfies the relation

$$\tilde{\mathbf{v}}_{ki} \simeq \mathbf{H}_{k\infty} \tilde{\mathbf{v}}_{0i}. \tag{37}$$

With all the homographies $\mathbf{H}_{k\infty}$ estimated, from the result of the equations (8) and (9), it is possible to obtain the affine camera matrices

$$\begin{cases} P_0 = [\mathbf{I} \mid \mathbf{0}], \\ P_1 = [\mathbf{H}_{1\infty} \mid \tilde{\mathbf{e}}_1], \\ \cdots \\ P_k = [\mathbf{H}_{k\infty} \mid \tilde{\mathbf{e}}_k]. \end{cases} \tag{38}$$

Evidently, this is only possible if all the epipoles $\mathbf{e}_k$ are estimated. For this, one can use the method proposed by Rother (2003). In it, considering the affine camera matrices, we have

$$\tilde{\mathbf{m}}_{kji} \simeq P_k \tilde{M}_{ji} = [\mathbf{H}_{k\infty} \quad \mathbf{e}_k]\tilde{M}_{ji} = \mathbf{H}_{k\infty} M_{ji} + \mathbf{e}_k.$$

The previous equation provides three linear equations in terms of the coordinates of the $K$ epipoles $\mathbf{e}_k$ and all the points $\mathbf{M}_{ji}$, i.e.,

$$\begin{aligned} u_{kji}(\mathbf{h}_{2k}M_{ji}^T + e_{vk}) - v_{kji}(\mathbf{h}_{1k}M_{ji}^T + e_{uk}) &= 0, \\ u_{kji}(\mathbf{h}_{3k}M_{ji}^T + e_{tk}) - t_{kji}(\mathbf{h}_{1k}M_{ji}^T + e_{uk}) &= 0, \\ u_{kji}(\mathbf{h}_{3k}M_{ji}^T + e_{tk}) - t_{kji}(\mathbf{h}_{2k}M_{ji}^T + e_{vk}) &= 0, \end{aligned} \tag{39}$$

where it was considered $\tilde{\mathbf{m}}_{kji} = [u_{kji}, v_{kji}, t_{kji}]^T$, $\tilde{\mathbf{e}}_k = [e_{uk}, e_{vk}, e_{tk}]^T$ and $\mathbf{H}_{k\infty} = [\mathbf{h}_{1k}, \mathbf{h}_{2k}, \mathbf{h}_{3k}]^T$, with $k = 1, ..., K$, $j = 1, ..., q$ and $i = 1, ..., n$.

The equations (39) provide an interesting solution, because, while finalizing the affine calibration (through the estimation of epipoles $\mathbf{e}_k$), they provide also an estimation of all the affine reconstructions $M_{ji}$.

Again, as in the case of monocular calibration (section 4), to make the problem better conditioned, for each image $I_k$, the projective transform,

$T_2$, has to be applied to all the points $\mathbf{m}_{kji}$. In this case, in the equations (39), the homography $\mathbf{H}_{k\infty}$ has to be replaced by $\hat{\mathbf{H}}_{k\infty} = \mathbf{T}_2\mathbf{H}_{k\infty}$. In this way, the solution of the system of equations (39) provides the same reconstructions, $M_{ji}$, but the obtained epipoles are in the form $\tilde{\hat{\mathbf{e}}}_k = \mathbf{T}_2\tilde{\mathbf{e}}_k$.

Comparing the equation (38) with (4), (8) and (9), it becomes clear that the relation between the affine and euclidean projections matrices is given by

$$\mathbf{P}_k = P_k \begin{bmatrix} \mathbf{A}_0 & \\ & 1 \end{bmatrix}, k = 0, 1, \ldots, K. \qquad (40)$$

Therefore, the relation between the affine and euclidean coordinates is given by

$$\mathbf{M}_{ji} = \mathbf{A}_0^{-1} M_{ji}. \qquad (41)$$

Thus, applying this relation to the equation (12), we obtain $\left\| \mathbf{A}_0^{-1}(M_{2i} - M_{1i}) \right\| = L$. From it we obtain

$$(M_{2i} - M_{1i})^T \mathbf{A}_0^{-T} \mathbf{A}_0^{-1}(M_{2i} - M_{1i}) = L^2. \qquad (42)$$

The previous equation is linear in terms of the six elements of the matrix $\omega_0 = \mathbf{A}_0^{-T}\mathbf{A}_0^{-1}$. Hence, considering $\cot \theta_k = 0$ (figure 1), after $n > 5$ displacements of the pattern, it is possible to estimate $\omega_0$ and, consequently, determine $\mathbf{A}_0$ through the decomposition of Cholesky. Then, from (40) and (41), it is possible to determine also the projection matrices of all the cameras and the 3D reconstruction of all pattern points, concluding the calibration.

In order to refine the matrices $\mathbf{P}_0$ to $\mathbf{P}_K$, a criterion that involves the projection of the points of the pattern on the image planes of all cameras should be used. An alternative is to find the matrices $\mathbf{P}_K$ and the points $\tilde{\mathbf{M}}_{ji}$ that minimize

$$\Box(\mathbf{P}_k, \tilde{\mathbf{M}}_{ji}) = \sum_{k=0}^{K}\sum_{i=1}^{N}\sum_{j=1}^{n} \left\| \tilde{\mathbf{m}}_{kji} - \tilde{\hat{\mathbf{m}}}_{kji}(\mathbf{P}_k, \tilde{\mathbf{M}}_{ji}) \right\|^2 \qquad (43)$$

where $\tilde{\hat{\mathbf{m}}}_{kji}(\mathbf{P}_k, \tilde{\mathbf{M}}_{ji})$ is the projection of $\tilde{\mathbf{M}}_{ji}$ in the image plane of the camera $k$, according to (4) and considering the equations (13) and (30).

The minimization of equation (43) involves the solution of a non-linear minimization problem with an excessive number of unknowns, i. e., the four elements of $\mathbf{P}_0$, the $10K$ elements of the set of matrices $\mathbf{P}_k$ (which depend on $\mathbf{A}_k$, $\mathbf{R}_k$ and $\mathbf{t}_k$), the $3N$ coordinates of the points $\mathbf{M}_{1i}$ and $2N$ angles ($\alpha_i$ and $\phi_i$). Again, an initial estimation of the unknowns is required. Of course, this can be obtained by estimating the vanishing points from (35), which makes it possible to execute the affine calibration (38) and determine $\mathbf{A}_0$ from (42). Finally, the reconstructions and euclidean projection matrices can be obtained from (40) and (41).

## 5.1. Experimental Results

The presented method was evaluated using synthetic data obtained from the simulation of five cameras. The intrinsic parameters of the simulated cameras are shown in Table 1 (Considering $\cos \theta = 0$ for all cameras). In the simulation, each camera was positioned at one of the vertices of a pentagon with a 252 cm width. Furthermore, all cameras were on the same plane, i.e., the matrices $\mathbf{R}_k$ model rotation just around the vertical axis. Finally, the image resolution was equal to 512×512 pixels and the pattern is supposed to have a length of 90 cm, with three collinear and equidistant points. Moreover, in the generation of synthetic data, the point $\mathbf{M}_{1i} = [X_i, Y_i, Z_i]$, with $\{X_i, Y_i, Z_i\} \in [-135, 135]$, and the angles of the equation (30), $\theta_i \in [\pi/6, 5\pi/6]$ and $\Box_i \in [\pi, 2\pi]$, varied randomly, but according to a uniform distribution.

As in section 4.2, gaussian noise with zero average and standard deviation $\sigma$ was added to

*Table 1. Intrinsic parameters of the five simulated cameras*

| Camera | $\alpha$ | $\beta$ | $u0$ | $v0$ |
|--------|----------|---------|------|------|
| 0 | 1,715 | 1,712 | 325 | 232 |
| 1 | 1,700 | 1,730 | 335 | 222 |
| 2 | 1,730 | 1,705 | 300 | 215 |
| 3 | 1,700 | 1,712 | 325 | 222 |
| 4 | 1,712 | 1,725 | 320 | 250 |

the points of the stick projected in the synthetic images. After that, the camera parameters were estimated using the close form solution and the method based on (43). Finally, the obtained parameters were compared to the simulated camera parameters. The errors of all parameters are presented in relation to the parameter $\alpha$, as proposed by Triggs (1998).

The synthetic data were used to evaluate the method's performance with respect to noise level. In this experiment, $N = 100$ pattern images were generated with the standard deviation $\sigma$ ranging from 0.1 to 2.0 pixels. For each noise level, 150 simulations were performed and, finally, the median of each intrinsic parameter was retained. These medians were compared with the parameters of the table 1. The comparison results are shown in Figures from 9(a) to 9(e).

The low precision of the method is mainly due to the poor estimation of the matrix $\mathbf{H}_\infty$. This is because the estimation of the correspondences ($\mathbf{v}_{0i} \leftrightarrow \mathbf{v}_{ki}$) from the cross-ratio is very susceptible to noise. For example, Figure 9(f) shows the residue depending on the level of noise present in the data. This residue is a good measure of the quality of estimated homography $\mathbf{H}_{k\infty}$. It is observed that the quality of this matrix decreases rapidly with increasing $\sigma$. Obviously, this influences negatively the quality of the obtained calibration.

$$\frac{1}{2N} = \sum_{i=1}^{N}\left(\left\|\tilde{\mathbf{v}}_{1i} - \mathbf{H}_{1\infty}\tilde{\mathbf{v}}_{0i}\right\|^2 + \left\|\tilde{\mathbf{v}}_{0i} - \mathbf{H}_{1\infty}^{-1}\tilde{\mathbf{v}}_{1i}\right\|^2\right)$$

## 6. FURTHER READING

In the same year in which the primary calibration algorithm with 1D patterns was proposed, Cao and Foroosh (2004) changed the method from Zhang (2004) in order to make dispensable the knowledge of the distance between the points of the pattern. However, in this case it is necessary to use a simplified model for the camera, more specifically, in the equation (3), $\alpha$ and $\beta$ must be equal. Of course, this is not always reasonable in practice. Another important research for the area was developed by Hammarstedt et al. (2005), which identified and equated the degenerate cases of the problem, making it easy to identify them and thus eliminate them. Moreover, in the same work, close-form solutions for simplified models are presented when several cameras are used. In the same year, Wu et al. (2005) showed that a 1D pattern that revolves around a central point is geometrically equivalent to a 2D calibration device with unknown sides. Thus, it was demonstrated that the calibration is also possible when the pattern makes a unknown displacement on the surface of a plane. However, in practice this does not bring more flexibility to the calibration problem, besides the convenience already obtained using 2D patterns. All methods mentioned previously and which address the calibration of a single camera assume special pattern movements. In fact, up today there are no methods for calibrating a single camera with 1D patterns that move freely. Instead, Qi et al. (2007a) extended the work of Wu et al. (2005) and proposed a necessary and

*Figure 9. Accuracy of the estimated intrinsic parameters versus the noise level for the: a) reference camera; b) camera 1; c) camera 2; camera 3; camera 4, and; f) quality of homography $\mathbf{H}_{k\infty}$, where k = 1,..., 4, concerning the noise level.*

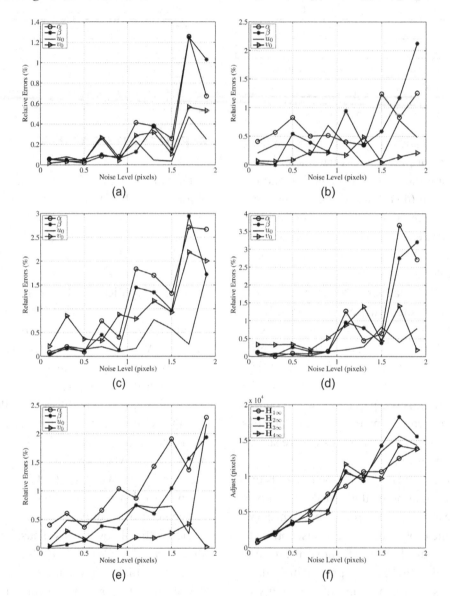

sufficient condition that specifies the constraints on general motions for calibration. Moreover, it was demonstrated that the solution can be achieved when a 1D pattern moves only under the action of gravity. Yet again, despite possible, the movement that the pattern must accomplish is difficult to be repeated in practical situations.

More recently, Peng and Li (2010) used 1D objects for calibration of cameras in uncontrolled environments, for example, in the case of a sequence of images taken from security cameras. In this case, it is easier to segment 1D objects of an uncontrolled scene than 2D or 3D structures suitable for calibration. The work of Peng and Li

(2010) deserves special attention mainly because 1D structures with only two points were used.

Although Zhang (2004) has highlighted the advantages of using 1D patterns for the calibration of multiple cameras, only after the work of Kojima et al. (2005) this became possible in fact. This is because, in the case of a set of cameras, the algorithm of Kojima also estimates the extrinsic parameters of all cameras. However, unfortunately it is necessary that at least one of the cameras, called "the reference camera", is already calibrated. This drawback could be eliminated only with the work of Zhao and Liu (2008) integrating the rank-4 factorization technique (Sturm and Triggs, 1996) with the 1D calibration theory into a factorization-based multi-camera calibration algorithm. According to the geometrical property of the 1D object, Zhao and Liu (2008) can estimate the projective depths in the simple analytical form instead of a recursive form as described by Sturm and Triggs (1996). For this, however, the pattern should rotate while fixed by its central point.

## 7. CONCLUSION

In the process of image formation, some informations are lost. Therefore, in certain applications, it is necessary to calibrate the camera before beginning the visual inspection. Although it is possible to perform calibration in a full automatic way using self calibration algorithms, classical calibration methods based on patterns are still used. This is due to the computational complexity and lack of accuracy of automatic techniques. In classical calibration methods, the camera captures images of an object with well defined dimensions. Then, through the relationship between points of the pattern and their projections in the image plane, the mathematical model of the camera is completely and accurately determined. Historically, the patterns used for calibration were always 2D or 3D objects. However, in the middle of this decade, the technique of camera calibration with 1D patterns (points on a line) was proposed. This kind of pattern has the advantage of being "visible" simultaneously even by cameras in opposite positions to each other. This makes the technique suitable for calibration of multiple cameras. In this study, the monocular and multiple camera calibration techniques were analyzed. It was demonstrated that, in the case of the monocular calibration, the accuracy of the method can be significantly improved simply by performing a normalization in the input data. For the calibration of multiple cameras, unlike the monocular calibration, the calibration pattern can move freely. However, the technique still needs further studies to increase its accuracy. This is because it is still very sensitive to noise present in the data, i.e., even the addition of a small value of RMS noise in the projections of the 1D pattern can cause a wide variation in the camera parameters.

## REFERENCES

Armangué, X., & Salvi, J. (2003). Overall view regarding fundamental matrix estimation. *Image and Vision Computing, 21*(2), 205–220. doi:10.1016/S0262-8856(02)00154-3

Bouguet, J. Y. (2008). *Camera calibration toolbox for Matlab*. Retrieved from http://www.vision.caltech.edu/bouguetj/calibdoc/

Cao, X., & Foroosh, H. (2004). Camera calibration without metric information using 1D objects. In *International Conference on Image Processing, 2,* (pp. 1349–1352).

Corrêa, F. R., Deccó, C. C. G., & Okamoto, J., Jr. (2003). *Obtaining range information with an omnidirectional vision system*. In XVII Congresso Brasileiro de Engenharia Mecânica.

de França, J. A., & Stemmer, M. R., de M. França, M. B., & Alves, E. G. (2010). Revisiting Zhang's 1D calibration algorithm. *Pattern Recognition, 43*(3), 1180–1187. doi:10.1016/j.patcog.2009.08.001

Dornaika, F., & Chung, R. (2001). An algebraic approach to camera self-calibration. *Computer Vision and Image Understanding, 83*(3), 195–215. doi:10.1006/cviu.2001.0925

Gaspar, J., Decc'o, C., Okamoto, J., Jr., & Santos-Victor, J. (2002). In *Constant resolution omnidirectional cameras*. In III Workshop on Omnidirectinal Vision.

Golub, G. H., & Van Loan, C. F. (1996). *Matrix computations*. The Johns University Press.

Grassi Junior, V., & Okamoto Junior, J. (2000). Development of an omnidirectional vision system. *Journal of the Brazilian Society of Mechanical Sciences and Engineering, 28*(1), 58–68. doi:10.1590/S1678-58782006000100007

Hammarstedt, P., Sturm, P., & Heyden, A. (2005). Closed-form solutions and degenerate cases for camera calibration with one-dimensional objects. In *Proceedings of X IEEE International Conference on Computer Vision*.

Hartley, R. (1997a). In defence of the eight point algorithm. *IEEE Transactions on Pattern Analysis and Machine Intelligence, 19*(6), 580–593. doi:10.1109/34.601246

Hartley, R. (1997b). Self-calibration of stationary cameras. *International Journal of Computer Vision, 22*(1), 5–23. doi:10.1023/A:1007957826135

Hartley, R., & Sturm, P. (1997). Triangulation. *Computer Vision and Image Understanding, 68*(2), 146–157. doi:10.1006/cviu.1997.0547

Hartley, R., & Zisserman, A. (2000). *Multiple view geometry in computer vision*. Cambridge University Press.

Heikkilä, J. (2000). Geometric camera calibration using circular control points. *IEEE Transactions on Pattern Analysis and Machine Intelligence, 22*(10), 1066–1076. doi:10.1109/34.879788

Kojima, Y., Fujii, T., & Tanimoto, M. (2005). New multiple camera calibration method for a large number of cameras. In *Proceedings of VIII Videometrics Conference*.

Lenz, R., & Tsai, R. (1988). Techniques for calibration of the scale factor and image center for high accuracy 3-d machine vision metrology. *IEEE Transactions on Pattern Analysis and Machine Intelligence, 10*(5), 713–720. doi:10.1109/34.6781

Levenberg, K. (1944). A method for the solution of certain non-linear problems in least squares. *Quarterly of Applied Mathematics*, 164–168.

Marquardt, D. W. (1963). An algorithm for least-squares estimation of nonlinear parameters. *Journal of the Society for Industrial and Applied Mathematics, 11*(2), 431–441. doi:10.1137/0111030

Maybank, S., & Faugeras, O. (1992). A theory of self-calibration of a moving camera. *International Journal of Computer Vision, 8*(2), 123–151. doi:10.1007/BF00127171

Mendon.ca, P. R. S., & Cipolla, R. (1999). A simple technique for self-calibration. In *IEEE Conference on Computer Vision and Pattern Recognition*, (pp. 1500–1505).

Peng, E., & Li, L. (2010). Camera calibration using one-dimensional information and its applications in both controlled and uncontrolled environments. *Pattern Recognition, 43*(3), 1188–1198. doi:10.1016/j.patcog.2009.08.003

Qi, F., Li, Q., Luo, Y., & Hu, D. (2007a). Camera calibration with one-dimensional objects moving under gravity. *Pattern Recognition, 40*(1), 343–345. doi:10.1016/j.patcog.2006.06.029

Qi, F., Li, Q., Luo, Y., & Hu, D. (2007b). Constraints on general motions for camera calibration with one-dimensional objects. *Pattern Recognition*, *40*(6), 1785–1792. doi:10.1016/j.patcog.2006.11.001

Rother, C. (2003). *Multi-view reconstruction and camera recovery using a real or virtual reference plane*. PhD thesis, Royal Institute of Technology, Stockholm, Sweden.

Salvi, J., Armangu'e, X., & Batlle, J. (2002). A comparative review of camera calibrating methods with accuracy evaluation. *Pattern Recognition*, *35*(7), 1617–1635. doi:10.1016/S0031-3203(01)00126-1

Shih, S., Hung, Y., & Lin, W. (1996). *Accuracy analysis on the estimation of camera parameters for active vision systems*. Technical Report TR-IIS-96-006, Institute of Information Science, Taipei, Taiwan.

Sturm, P. F., & Maybank, S. J. (1999). On plane-based camera calibration: A general algorithm, singularities, applications. In *IEEE Conference on Computer Vision and Pattern Recognition*, (pp. 432–437).

Sturm, P. F., & Triggs, B. (1996). A factorization based algorithm for multi-image projective structure and motion. In *IV European Conference on Computer Vision,* volume 2, (pp. 709–720). London, UK: Springer-Verlag.

Triggs, B. (1998). Autocalibration from planar scenes. In *V European Conference on Computer Vision*, (pp. 89–105).

Tsai, R. Y. (1987). A versatile camera calibration technique for high-accuracy 3D machine vision metrology using off-the-shelf cameras and lenses. *IEEE Journal on Robotics and Automation, RA-3*(4), 323–344. doi:10.1109/JRA.1987.1087109

Wang, L., Wu, F. C., & Hu, Z. Y. (2007). Multi-camera calibration with one-dimensional object under general motions. In *IEEE 11th International Conference on Computer Vision*, (pp. 1–7). Rio de Janeiro, Brazil.

Wu, F., Hu, Z., & Zhu, H. (2005). Camera calibration with moving one-dimensional objects. *Pattern Recognition*, *40*(1), 755–765. doi:10.1016/j.patcog.2004.11.005

Zhang, Z. (2000). A flexible new technique for camera calibration. *IEEE Transactions on Pattern Analysis and Machine Intelligence*, *22*(11), 1330–1334. doi:10.1109/34.888718

Zhang, Z. (2004). Camera calibration with one-dimensional objects. *IEEE Transactions on Pattern Analysis and Machine Intelligence*, *26*(7), 892–899. doi:10.1109/TPAMI.2004.21

Zhao, Z., & Liu, Y. (2008). New multi-camera calibration algorithm based on 1D objects. *Journal of Zhejiang University Science A*, *9*(6), 799–806. doi:10.1631/jzus.A071573

## ENDNOTES

[1] In this demonstration, we used the fact that, given a non-singular matrix $\mathbf{M}$ and a vector $\mathbf{v}$, $[\mathbf{Mv}]_\times = \mathbf{M}^{-T} [\mathbf{v}]_\times \mathbf{M}^{-1}$. See, e.g. (Hartley and Zisserman, 2000, page 555) for a proof.

[2] The blob tool is clearly not the most adequate way to extract the spheres centroids. However, this can be useful to know how the proposed method behaves in extreme noisy situations.

# Chapter 6
# Object Segmentation Based on a Nonparametric Snake with Motion Prediction in Video

**Sang-Myoung Ye**
*Sogang University, Korea*

**Rae-Hong Park**
*Sogang University, Korea*

**Dong-Kyu Lee**
*Sogang University, Korea*

## ABSTRACT

*Object segmentation in video sequence is a basic and important task in video applications such as surveillance systems and video coding. Nonparametric snake algorithms for object segmentation have been proposed to overcome the drawback of conventional snake algorithms: the dependency on several parameters. In this chapter, a new object segmentation algorithm for video, based on a nonparametric snake model with motion prediction, is proposed. Object contour is initialized by using the mean absolute difference of intensity between input and previous frames. And in order to convert initial object contours into more exact object contours, the gradient vector flow snake is used. Finally object contour is predicted using a Kalman filter in successive frames. The proposed object segmentation method for video can provide more detailed and improved object segmentation results than the conventional methods. Various experimental results show the effectiveness of the proposed method in terms of the pixel-based quality measure and the computation time.*

## INTRODUCTION

The goal of object segmentation is to identify meaningful components in an image or video and to group the pixels belonging to such components (Zhang & Lu, 2001). Object segmentation, espe-

cially in video, is more challenging, because it is necessary to consider motion information for segmenting moving objects. Object segmentation in video has been used for various multimedia applications. In surveillance systems, object segmentation plays an essential role, which is implemented for automatic monitoring, recogni-

DOI: 10.4018/978-1-61350-429-1.ch006

tion and prediction of human. It is also used to achieve high compression performance in video coding. In addition, it is used in the areas of robotics and medical imaging (Blake & Isard, 1998).

In general, segmentation of moving objects can be categorized into motion-based and spatio-temporal methods (Zhang & Lu, 2001). Motion-based segmentation methods can be based on either motion representations or clustering. Traditional motion-based segmentation methods use only temporal (motion) information to deal with the scenes with rigid motion. On the other hand, spatio-temporal segmentation methods use both spatial and temporal information embedded in the sequence. They can reduce the drawbacks of an over-segmentation problem in image segmentation and overcome the noise-sensitivity and inaccuracy problems in motion-based segmentation (Zhang & Lu, 2001).

The spatio-temporal segmentation methods can be classified into two different methods: region-based and contour-based methods. The region-based methods have the advantage of the low computational cost, however, their results are sensitive to the parameter values selected. Among the contour-based methods, edge-based methods detect and combine the edges of an image to produce object contours. These methods have an advantage that they give a good performance. Another approach that has evolved from contour-based segmentation algorithms is active contours, so called snake-based segmentation algorithms (Jin et al., 2006; Kim, Alattar, & Jang, 2006; Kang, Kim, & Kweon, 2001; Hon, Yunmei, Huafeng, & Pengsheng, 2005).

Active contour algorithms have been widely used for object segmentation. Kass, Witkin, and Terzopoulos (1987) presented the active contour algorithm, in which parameterized contours are defined in an image domain. The active contour or snake algorithm is a segmentation process that utilizes energy-minimizing splines in the image with the internal forces coming from the curve itself and with external forces computed

from image data. However, in the active contour algorithms, there are three major drawbacks: the dependency on many parameters, the very narrow capture range, and the difficulty in moving into boundary concavities.

A gradient vector flow (GVF) snake (Xu & Prince, 1998), with a high capability to deform contours into concave parts of the object, was addressed to reduce the sensitivity to contour initialization. Ozertem and Erdogmus (2007) proposed a nonparametric snake algorithm. They converted the problem of selecting unknown parameters of a snake into the problem of finding a good edge probability density estimate and removed the high dependency on parameter values of a snake model. Martin, Refregier, Galland, and Guerault (2006) presented the nonparametric statistical snake algorithm which is based on the minimum stochastic complexity. They minimized the energy of a snake based on the minimum stochastic complexity, in which they used a criterion that need not control any user-defined parameter. Abd-Almaged, Smith, and Ramadan (2003) and Rolfes and Rendas (2004) also proposed nonparametric snake algorithms. Abd-Almaged et al. (2003) presented a nonparametric technique to obtain statistical models based on the Bayesian decision. Rolfes and Rendas (2004) proposed a nonparametric snake algorithm based on mixtures of the probability distributions of the region nearby the contour.

In video, a number of snake algorithms have been widely used for contour extraction of moving objects. Park, Schoeflin, and Kim (2001) presented an object segmentation algorithm based on a snake using the gradient directional information. They included the gradient-directional information to the external image force in a snake using the gradient strength and direction of the image. Kim, Hong, and Lee (1999) proposed a segmentation algorithm for moving objects based on a snake using image flow. They presented a new contraction energy that is independent of the object shape and defined image flow as the velocity field over the points of an image. In (Sun, Haynor, & Kim, 2003), using VSnakes, a semiautomatic video object segmentation was proposed. The VSnakes is a process that includes selection of control points, contour relaxation, and connecting contour operation. Another approach based on active contours to object segmentation uses graph cuts (Chen, Sun, Heng, & Xia, 2008) and the matching degree image of object contour points (Xu, Ahuja, & Bansal, 2007).

The Kalman filter is an efficient recursive filter to estimate the state of a dynamic system using processes of prediction and correction (Grewal & Andrews, 2008). The Kalman filter is implemented in a dynamic system from a series of incomplete and noisy measurements. Generally, the performance of snake algorithms shows the high dependency on locations of initial object contours. Combining the Kalman filter and the snake algorithms can reduce the computational load, i.e., number of iterations. Peterfreund (1999) presented a Kalman filtering approach using optical flow measurements for a velocity snake model. He detected and rejected measurements which belong to other objects. Dambreville, Rathi, and Tannenbaum (2006) proposed an object tracking algorithm based on unscented Kalman filtering and geometric active contours in a computationally efficient manner. Lee, Kang, Shin, and Paik (2007) proposed a hierarchical active shape model using motion prediction. They used a block-matching algorithm to estimate initial snake points, in which a Kalman filter is employed to increase the accuracy of motion estimation. Betser, Vela, and Tannenbaum (2004) presented a tracking algorithm based on an active contour model for target extraction, in which a Kalman filter is used for relative pose estimation.

In this chapter, a new object segmentation algorithm for video is proposed based on a nonparametric snake using moving edges and a Kalman filter. The contribution of this chapter is to extend the existing nonparametric snake algorithm (Ozertem & Erdogmus, 2007) to video images and to improve the efficiency of the algorithm using motion prediction with a Kalman filter. In order to obtain the probability density estimate used in a nonparametric snake algorithm, moving edges derived from successive frames are used.

This chapter is organized as follows: in the second section, conventional snake algorithms, a spatio-temporal edge detection method, and a Kalman filter used in the proposed algorithm are reviewed. In the next section, a new object segmentation method for video based on a nonparametric snake with motion prediction using a Kalman filter is presented and performance comparisons of the proposed algorithm with previous works are presented. In the fourth section, future research directions are presented. The chapter is concluded in the final section.

## BACKGROUND

We review the conventional snake algorithms and then describe the nonparametric, GVF, and multi-scale GVF snake algorithms that overcome the drawbacks of conventional snake algorithms. Next, we review the spatio-temporal edge detection method and a Kalman filter that are used in the proposed algorithm.

### Snake Algorithm and its Improvements

Kass et al. (1987) first proposed an active contour algorithm. The total energy $E$ is defined as

$$E = \int_0^1 \{E_{\text{int}}(w(s)) + E_{\text{ext}}(w(s))\}ds \qquad (1)$$

where $s$ denotes the length parameter of arc in the range of 0 to 1, and $w(s) = [x(s), y(s)]$ represents the position of the curve in an image in parametric form. $E_{\text{int}}(w(s))$ signifies the internal energy derived from the physical characteristics of a snake and is defined as

$$E_{\text{int}} = \frac{\alpha \left| w'(s) \right| + \beta \left| w''(s) \right|}{2}, \ s \in \left[ 0, 1 \right] \qquad (2)$$

where $\alpha$ and $\beta$ represent weights for the elastic force and the bending force of the internal energy, respectively. $w'(s)$ is the first-order difference of $w(s)$ with respect to $s$ that controls the rate of curve length whereas $w''(s)$ signifies the second-order difference of $w(s)$ that determines the rate of curvature. $E_{\text{ext}}(x, y)$ signifies the external energy computed from image data and is defined as

$$E_{\text{ext}}(x, y) = - \left| \nabla (G_{\sigma}(x, y) * I(x, y)) \right|^2 \qquad (3)$$

where $I(x, y)$ is intensity derived from an image, $G_{\sigma}(x, y)$ is a two-dimensional (2-D) Gaussian function with the standard deviation $\sigma$, and $\nabla$ denotes the gradient operation.

A snake algorithm can be computed by solving the following Euler equation

$$\alpha w''(s) + \beta w''''(s) - \nabla E_{\text{ext}} = 0. \qquad (4)$$

Ozertem and Erdogmus (2007) proposed a nonparametric snake algorithm. They converted the problem of selecting unknown parameters of a snake into the problem of finding a good edge probability density estimate.

An external energy is computed from image data. In general, an external energy takes smaller values at the features of interest, such as at boundaries, than in the relatively uniform region. So, the binary edge map or gradient magnitude of intensity derived from an image is generally used to compute an external energy of an image. Ozertem and Erdogmus (2007) employed the probability density estimate of boundary pixels of an object using the 2-D Gaussian kernel function. They denoted the probability density estimate as a new external energy for a snake and removed parameters in the snake algorithm.

The nonparametric snake algorithm is employed by computing a kernel density estimate (KDE) of edges. A nonparametric snake uses edge distribution estimates which can be obtained using the KDE as a new external energy.

The GVF is a new external force for snakes, which is employed as a diffusion of the gradient vectors of a gray-level or binary edge map derived from the image (Xu & Prince, 1998). The field of GVF has a larger capture range and a more forceful external energy into concave regions than those of the conventional active contours. The GVF snake algorithm can be used for overcoming the drawbacks of conventional snake algorithms. Object contour movement in GVF is performed by minimizing an energy functional in a variational framework.

Jin et al. (2006) proposed a multi-scale GVF snake algorithm which can improve the GVF snake algorithm. They combined a GVF snake with a multi-scale Gaussian filter. The standard deviation $\sigma$ in a 2-D Gaussian kernel used for increasing the capture range of the snake is changed in order to extract accurate contours of a target object. Thus, the standard deviation $\sigma$ can control the capture range and determine the performance of the snake. If the larger $\sigma$ is used, the external energy derived from the image tends to be blurred more. And final smoothness of a curve computed from contour evolution of a snake may be larger and the capture range will be increased. In contrast, if the smaller $\sigma$ is used, the capture range of the GVF snake will be narrower, but then the more accurate contour of a target object will be obtained.

Park et al. (2001) proposed an active contour model with gradient directional information, named *directional snake*. They used both the gradient strength and direction of the image and introduced a new external force model in the active contour algorithm. They experimentally showed a significantly better final result than the conventional method (the edge-based segmentation method).

## Spatio-Temporal Edge Detection

Object segmentation and tracking algorithm in video for content-based applications were addressed in (Kim and Hwang, 2002). Kim and Hwang used the spatio-temporal edge detection method which contains the process of extracting shape information of moving objects using the difference of edges between previous and current frames. By using changes of the edge locations in successive frames, change detection was performed. The change detection using the inter-frame difference has been widely used because it enables automatic detection of moving objects. Using the spatial edge information, they extracted the moving edge points from moving edges of the current frame.

For change detection, a region of interest is roughly detected using the intensity difference between the current and previous frames. Let $D_k$ denote the inter-frame difference edge map, determined by

$$D_k(x, y) = \left| \nabla \left( G_\sigma(x, y) * \left( I_k(x, y) - I_{k-1}(x, y) \right) \right) \right|. \tag{5}$$

The Canny edge detector has been commonly used as the optimal edge detector (Canny, 1986; Sharifi, Fathy, & Mahmoudi, 2002). Canny edge detection is performed on $D_k$. $E_k^d$ is the changed region edge map, which can be expressed as

$$E_k^d(x, y) = Canny\left( D_k(x, y) \right) \tag{6}$$

where $Canny(\cdot)$ represents Canny edge detection and the superscript $d$ denotes the difference edge map.

For moving edge detection, the changed region edge map $E_k^d$ and edge map detected in the current frame $E_k$ are combined to produce moving edges. First, the background index $B_k$ is determined by accumulating over several previous frames.

Then, the changed moving edge map $M_k^c$ and the temporarily still moving edge map $M_k^s$ are computed. Finally, the moving edge map $M_k$ is obtained by combining these two types of edge maps. Each procedure is briefly described in the following.

The background index $B_k$ is denoted by:

$$B_k(x, y) = \begin{cases} B_{k-1}(x, y) + 1, & \text{if } E_k^d(x, y) = 1 \\ B_{k-1}(x, y), & \text{otherwise} \end{cases} \tag{7}$$

where $E_k^d$ denotes the changed region edge map. Using the background index $B_k$, $E_k^b$ is determined by

$$E_k^b(x, y) = E_k(x, y) \quad \text{if } B_k(x, y) > T_k^b \tag{8}$$

where $E_k$ denotes the edge map in the current frame and $T_k^b$ represents the threshold.

The moving edge map is obtained by combining two types of edge maps: changed moving edge map $M_k^c$ and the temporarily still moving edge map $M_k^s$. The changed moving edge map $M_k^c$ is constructed based on the Euclidean norm between edge points in the current frame, $E_k$ and inter-frame difference edge points $E_k^d$ with the distance threshold $T^e$. This map represents the edge points in the current frame and also includes changed region edge points in $E_k^d$. $M_k^c$ can be determined by edge points in the current frame, if they are near (within the neighborhood of the Euclidean distance $T^e$ the changed region edge points $E_k^d$. The moving edge map $M_k^c$ is determined by Box 1.

The other is the temporarily still moving edge map $M_k^s$. This map represents the edge points in the current frame but does not include background edge points in $E_k^b$. The temporarily still moving edge map $M_k^s$ can be determined by edge points in the current frame, if they are near (within the

*Box 1.*

$$M_k^c(x, y) = \begin{cases} 1, & \text{if } E_k(x, y) = 1 \text{ and } E_k^d(x', y') = 1 \text{ and } \sqrt{(x - x')^2 + (y - y')^2} \leq T^c \\ 0, & \text{otherwise.} \end{cases} \tag{9}$$

neighborhood of the Euclidean distance $T^S$) the background edge points which are detected as moving edges in the previous frame. The temporarily still moving edge map $M_k^s$ is determined by Box 2.where $M_{k-1}$ represents the moving edge map of $k - 1^{th}$ frame.

The moving edge map in the current frame $M_k$ is constructed by combining $M_k^c$ and $M_k^c$ which can be expressed as

$$M_k(x, y) = \begin{cases} 1, & \text{if } M_k^c(x, y) = 1 \text{ or } M_k^s(x, y) = 1 \\ 0, & \text{otherwise.} \end{cases} \tag{11}$$

Note that the set of moving edge points $M_k$ is detected using the spatio-temporal edge information through change detection and moving edge detection (Kim & Hwang, 2002).

## Kalman Filter

A Kalman filter is a recursive filter that estimates the state of a dynamic system in prediction and correction steps (Grewal & Andrews, 2008). Let $\hat{\mathbf{x}}_k$ be the estimated state vector consisting of location and velocity of snake elements (snaxels) with the subscript $k$ denoting the time index, and

$\mathbf{u}_k$ be the control vector. The state vector $\hat{\mathbf{x}}_k^-$ is defined as

$$\hat{\mathbf{x}}_k^- = A\hat{\mathbf{x}}_{k-1} + B\mathbf{u}_k \tag{12}$$

where $A$ denotes the state transition matrix, $B$ signifies a control input matrix, and the superscript symbol $^-$ indicates the measurements that are not updated yet.

In the prediction step, the covariance matrix $P_k^-$ is computed by

$$P_k^- = AP_{k-1}A^T + Q \tag{13}$$

using the state transition matrix $A$, previous measurement of the covariance matrix $P_{k-1}$, and the process noise covariance matrix $Q$. After the process noise covariance matrix $Q$ is determined, we obtain the Kalman gain $K_k$. It is used to update the global motion vector and covariance matrix.

In the correction step, the Kalman gain is estimated by

$$K_k = P_k^- H^T (HP_k^- H^T + R)^{-1} \tag{14}$$

*Box 2.*

$$M_k^s(x, y) = \begin{cases} 1, & \text{if } E_k(x, y) = 1 \text{ and } E_k^b(x', y') = 0 \text{ and } M_{k-1}(x', y') = 1 \text{ and } \sqrt{(x - x')^2 + (y - y')^2} \leq T^s \\ 0, & \text{otherwise} \end{cases} \tag{10}$$

where $H$ and $R$ denote the observation matrix and the measurement noise covariance matrix, respectively. The state vector $\hat{\mathbf{x}}_k$ is estimated by

$$\hat{\mathbf{x}}_k = \hat{\mathbf{x}}_k^- + K_k(\mathbf{z}_k - H\hat{\mathbf{x}}_k^-) \qquad (15)$$

where $\mathbf{z}_k$ denotes the global motion vector. Then, the covariance matrix $P_k$ is updated as

$$P_k = (I - K_k H)P_k^- \qquad (16)$$

using the initial parameter matrix $P$.

# A PROPOSED OBJECT SEGMENTATION METHOD IN VIDEO

## Issues and Problems

Generally, snake-based algorithms have three major drawbacks: the dependency on many parameters, the very narrow capture range, and the difficulty in moving into boundary concavities. In order to overcome these drawbacks, GVF snake algorithm (Xu & Prince, 1998) and nonparametric snake algorithm (Ozertem & Erdogmus, 2007) have been proposed. However, when these snake algorithms are applied to a moving object in video, it occurs that the segmented boundary information of a moving object in the current frame would stay far from the same moving object in the next frame, due to rapid motion of a moving object. So, it gives the wrong external force model and may cause initial object contour to converge to the wrong edges. Therefore, in the proposed object segmentation method in video, using motion prediction we extend the nonparametric snake algorithm with GVF snake and overcome drawbacks of previous algorithms for moving objects.

## Overview of the Proposed Object Segmentation Method in Video

We describe the proposed object segmentation algorithm for video. Our approach is based on an existing nonparametric snake algorithm (Ozertem & Erdogmus, 2007) and a Kalman filter (Grewal & Andrews, 2008). We extend the existing nonparametric snake algorithm to video images using the Kalman filter.

The proposed algorithm consists of three steps: contour initialization, contour evolution, and contour prediction. First, initial snaxel points are computed using the mean absolute difference (MAD). This step can be used for introduction of snaxel points of an object which suddenly appears in the current frame. In the contour evolution step, we employ the probability density estimate, which is computed using moving edges. The probability density estimate of moving edges, which indicates the probability of boundary location of a moving object, is a new external force model for the GVF snake. The probability density estimate indicates the probability of boundary location of a moving object. The computed probability density estimate is used for contour evolution that is performed using a new external force model by the GVF active contour algorithm. In successive frames, the locations of the next snaxels are predicted from the current snaxels in the current frame. The Kalman filter is used to estimate the state of a dynamic system and to reduce the cost of detecting the locations of initial object contours. Figure 1 shows the overall block diagram of the proposed object segmentation algorithm.

## Contour Initialization: Initialization of Snake Points

In this step, initialization of snake points is performed. Setting initial contours of a snake is important to effectively reduce the computational cost of a snake algorithm. To derive initial contours, we use the MAD of intensity between input and

*Figure 1. Overall block diagram of the proposed object segmentation algorithm*

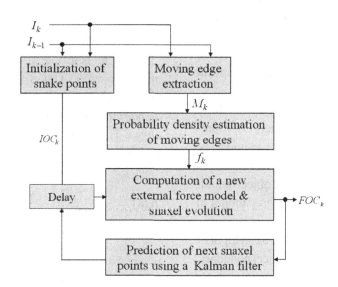

previous frames and then perform morphology operations.

Let $I_k(x, y)$ denote the intensity component with the subscript $k$ denoting the current frame. We employ the difference of intensity in gray-scale between the current and previous frames of the input sequence. The MAD $MAD_k(x, y)$ is computed by:

$$MAD_k(x, y) = \frac{1}{N_r N_c} \sum_{i=1}^{N_r} \sum_{j=1}^{N_c} \left| I_k(x, y) - I_{k-1}(x, y) \right|$$

(17)

where $I_k(x, y)$ and $I_{k-1}(x, y)$ represent the intensity of the current and previous frames of the input sequence, respectively. $N_r$ and $N_c$ denote the row and column sizes, respectively.

Then, using $MAD_k$, we formulate the primary motion mask (PMM) $PMM_k$, which is determined by:

$$PMM_k(x, y) = \begin{cases} 1, & \text{if } MAD_k(x, y) > T \\ 0, & \text{otherwise} \end{cases}$$

(18)

with $T$ representing the intensity threshold. To remove isolated pixels or noisy components in a PMM, we employ a morphological open operation followed by a close operation, in which pixels of a $3 \times 3$ structuring element are assigned to '1'.

Let $ERMM_k$ denote the expanded refined motion mask. To expand the PMM, a morphological dilation operator is applied to the PMM using a $15 \times 15$ structuring element, in which the size of the structuring element is experimentally selected. The primary effect of the dilation operation on a binary image is to gradually enlarge arbitrary regions.

Finally, boundary pixels of $ERMM_k$ are extracted as initial object contours $IOC_k$.

## Contour Evolution: Computation of a New External Force Model

In order to obtain an input of a nonparametric snake algorithm, i.e., the probability density estimate, the spatio-temporal edge detection step combines moving edges and edges detected in the current frame using the spatio-temporal information in successive frames.

Spatio-temporal edge detection for computing the probability density estimate is decomposed into two steps: change detection and moving edge detection. Using the difference image between the current and previous frames, change regions are detected. Then, using them, moving edge map $M_k$ is extracted from edges detected in the current frame (Kim & Hwang, 2002).

Using the moving edge map $M_k$, the probability density estimate is determined, where $M_k$ represents edge points in moving object boundaries. The probability density estimate of moving edges denotes the probability density of the object boundary that is used as a new external force model in a GVF snake algorithm.

The moving edge map $M_k$ is used as an input of the probability density estimate of object boundary. The coordinates in the probability density estimate of moving edges are formulated in vector form **s**. The coordinates in the moving edge map are 2-D location coordinates $(x, y)$ So, we convert the coordinates in the moving edge map $M_k$ to those in the moving edges of the probability density estimate $E_k(\mathbf{s}_i)$. $E_k(\mathbf{s}_i)$ denotes the moving edges obtained from spatio-temporal edge detection and can be determined by

$$E_k(\mathbf{s}_i) = \begin{cases} 1, & \text{if } \mathbf{s}_i \text{ is a moving edge pixel} \\ 0, & \text{otherwise} \end{cases}$$

$$(19)$$

where $\mathbf{s}_i = [x_i, y_i]^T$ is the vector of $i^{th}$ location. Using the binary edge map $E_k(\mathbf{s}_i)$ and the 2-D Gaussian kernel function $K$, the probability density estimate $f_{k, edge}(\mathbf{s})$ is defined by:

$$f_{k, edge}(\mathbf{s}) = \frac{1}{N_e} \sum_{i=1}^{N} E_k(\mathbf{s}_i) K \Sigma_i (\mathbf{s}_i - \mathbf{s}_i^{edge}) \qquad (20)$$

where $\mathbf{s}_i^{edge}$ denotes the location of $i^{th}$ edge in vector form, $\Sigma_i$ is the covariance matrix of $i^{th}$ pixel, $N$ represents the number of pixels, and $N_e$ is the number of moving edge pixels expressed as

$$N_e = \sum_{i=1}^{N} E_k(\mathbf{s}_i). \qquad (21)$$

$K$ is an isotropic (circularly symmetric) or anisotropic 2-D Gaussian kernel function. The Gaussian kernel function called the *normal distribution* is often described as a *bell-shaped curve*. The isotropic 2-D Gaussian kernel function is defined as

$$K(\mathbf{s}) = \frac{1}{2\pi\sigma^2} \exp\left(-\frac{\mathbf{s}^T \mathbf{s}}{2\sigma^2}\right) \qquad (22)$$

where $\sigma$ denotes the standard deviation of a Gaussian kernel function.

Next, a new external force model is determined using the probability density estimate of moving edges in the GVF snake, and contour evolution is performed by the GVF active contour algorithm. The GVF is a new external force for snakes, in which a diffusion of the gradient vectors of an image is used (Xu & Prince, 1998). The GVF field has an advantage of a large capture range and forces active contours into concave regions. The GVF field is defined as a vector field:

$$\mathbf{V}(x, y) = \big(p(x, y), q(x, y)\big). \qquad (23)$$

The total energy $E_{gvf}$ is defined as

$$E_{gvf} = \iint \left[ \mu(p_x^2 + p_y^2 + q_x^2 + q_y^2) + \left|\nabla f_{edge}\right|^2 \left|\mathbf{V} - \nabla f_{edge}\right|^2 \right] dx dy \qquad (24)$$

where $f_{edge}$ denotes the probability density estimate in the previous step computed from the moving edges, $\mu$ represents a regularization parameter of the GVF snake, and the subscripts $x$ and $y$ represent derivatives along the row and column directions, respectively.

The GVF snake algorithm can be determined by solving the following Euler equations using the calculus of variations (Xu & Prince, 1998)

$$\mu\nabla^2 p - (p - f_{edge,x})(f_{edge,x}^2 + f_{edge,y}^2) = 0 \tag{25}$$

$$\mu\nabla^2 q - (q - f_{edge,y})(f_{edge,x}^2 + f_{edge,y}^2) = 0 \tag{26}$$

where $\nabla^2$ denotes the Laplacian operator and the subscripts $x$ and $y$ represent derivatives along the row and column directions, respectively. We convert initial object contours into exact object contours using the GVF active contour algorithm.

## Contour Prediction: Prediction of the Next Snaxels

Snake algorithms conventionally have the high dependency on locations of initial object contours. Given snaxels which are converged to exact object contours in the current frame, the locations of the next snaxels are predicted using a Kalman filter. The predicted snaxels are used as the next initial object contours $IOC_{k+1}$ and efficiently reduce the number of iterations in the GVF snake algorithm.

Let $(x_k, y_k)$ and $(u_k, v_k)$ denote location and velocity of snaxel points in the current frame, respectively. The state equation can be represented using the state vector $\mathbf{x}_k = [x_k y_k u_k v_k]^T$ First, the state vector of $k^{th}$ frame is estimated using the state vector of $k-1^{th}$ frame and the state transition matrix $A$ which is defined as

$$A = \begin{bmatrix} 1 & 0 & \Delta t & 0 \\ 0 & 1 & 0 & \Delta t \\ 0 & 0 & 1 & 0 \\ 0 & 0 & 0 & 1 \end{bmatrix}. \tag{27}$$

The state transition matrix $A$ assumes that the relationship between snaxels in the current and next frames satisfies a uniform velocity model. We compute the state vector $\hat{\mathbf{x}}_k^-$ between the current and next snaxels and then, determine the covariance matrix.

In the prediction step, the covariance matrix $P_k^-$ is computed by Equation 13, where noise covariance matrix $Q$ is empirically given as

$$Q = \begin{bmatrix} 0.1 & 0 & 0 & 0 \\ 0 & 0.1 & 0 & 0 \\ 0 & 0 & 0.1 & 0 \\ 0 & 0 & 0 & 0.1 \end{bmatrix}, \tag{28}$$

and the initial parameter matrix $P$ is experimentally chosen as

$$P = \begin{bmatrix} 0.01 & 0 & 0 & 0 \\ 0 & 0.01 & 0 & 0 \end{bmatrix}. \tag{29}$$

In the correction step, the observation matrix $H$ and the measurement noise covariance matrix $R$ in Equation 14 are empirically given as

$$H = \begin{bmatrix} 1 & 0 & 0 & 0 \\ 0 & 1 & 0 & 0 \end{bmatrix} \text{ and } R = \begin{bmatrix} 1 & 0 \\ 0 & 1 \end{bmatrix}, \tag{30}$$

respectively. Next, using Equation 15, we estimate the state vector $\hat{\mathbf{x}}_k$ which contains the locations of the next initial object contours $IOC_{k+1}$. We use $IOC_{k+1}$ to reduce the cost in detecting the locations of initial object contours.

## Experimental Results and Discussions

In this section, experimental results show the effectiveness and performance of the proposed object segmentation algorithm compared with three conventional methods (Kass et al., 1987; Jin et al., 2006; Park et al., 2001). As test sequences, we use three types of video with moving objects: Hall Monitor and Viptraffic sequences as well as the Walk sequence from the CAVIAR database (CAVIAR, 2005). The Hall Monitor sequence is a surveillance video sequence containing a lot of noise whereas the Viptraffic sequence shows running cars on highway.

Figure 2 shows input images, results of each step, and final result of the proposed algorithm.

Figures 2(a) and (b) show two input frames. Figure 2(a) shows the current frame (Hall Monitor frame 69) whereas Figure 2(b) shows the previous frame (Hall Monitor frame 67). Figure 2(c) shows the initial object contours $IOC_k$ that are computed using the MAD of intensity between input and previous frames, and morphological operations. We use initial object contours $IOC_k$ for initial snaxels of the GVF snake algorithm. Figure 2(d)

*Figure 2. Input images, results of each step, and final result of the proposed algorithm (Hall Monitor frame 69). (a) current frame (frame 69), (b) previous frame (frame 67), (c) initial object contours $IOC_k$ (d) moving edge map $M_k$ (e) probability density estimate of $M_k$ (f) final result*

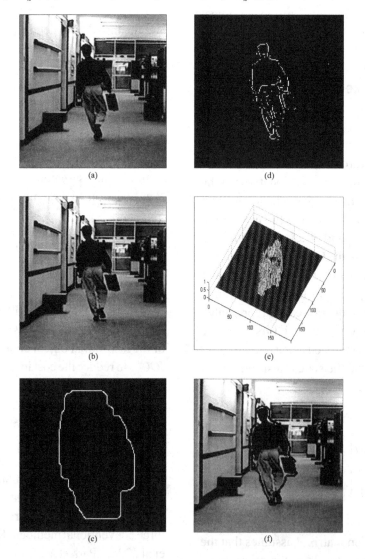

shows the moving edge map $M_k$, using which we determine the probability density estimate $f_{k,edge}$. Figure 2(e) shows the probability density estimate of $M_k$ with the 3 × 3 kernel of the 2-D Gaussian kernel function and the standard deviation of σ = 1. This probability density estimate $f_{k,edge}$ forms the fixed and stronger external energy than the energy of the conventional snake method. The probability density estimate has a shape like a castle wall around the object boundary and this sum of external energy can make the parameter

unnecessary in a snake algorithm. Final result of the proposed method is shown in Figure 2(f).

Figure 3 shows results of the proposed method for three test sequences from the CAVIAR database in which three frames are shown for each test sequence. Figures 3(a), (b), and (c) show the Hall Monitor frames 34, 69, and 278, respectively, in which a lot of noise is contained. Figures 3(d), (e), and (f) show the Viptraffic frames 12, 97, and 113, respectively, in which running cars on highway are shown. Figures 3(g), (h), and (i)

*Figure 3. Results of the proposed method for three test sequences. (a) Hall Monitor (frame 34), (b) Hall Monitor (frame 69), (c) Hall Monitor (frame 278), (d) Viptraffic (frame 12), (e) Viptraffic (frame 97), (f) Viptraffic (frame 113), (g) Walk (frame 276), (h) Walk (frame 318), (i) Walk (frame 335)*

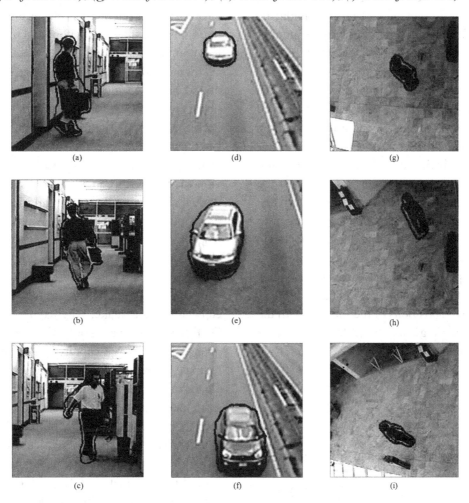

show the Walk frames 276, 318, and 335, respectively.

Results of the proposed method with the Walk frames, where the size of a moving object is smaller than those of the other test sequences, show good boundary convergence, in which a few false positives and negatives are shown. If a lot of boundary concavities exist and the amount of motion is large, the proposed method shows poor results (see Figures 3(a), (c), (e), and (f)).

Figure 4 shows comparison of experimental results of the proposed method with and without a Kalman filter, which shows the efficiency of the Kalman filter in the proposed algorithm, with experimental results as a function of the number of iterations $L$. Figure 4(a) shows the locations of initial snaxels in the Viptraffic frame 17. Figures 4(b) and (c) show segmentation results without the Kalman filter as a function of the iteration number $L$: $L=2$ and 12, respectively. In contrast, Figures 4(d), (e), and (f) show experimental results of the proposed method with a Kalman filter. Figure 4(d) shows the locations of the next snaxels predicted from the current snaxels using a Kalman filter. These predicted locations of snaxels are used as initial snaxels in the next frame. Figures 4(e) and (f) are segmentation results as a function of the number of iterations $L$: $L=2$ and 12, respectively. From Figure 4, it is noted that a Kalman filter reduces the number of iterations greatly when snaxels are converged to final object contours.

For a proper termination condition of iterations, we employ the squared error. Let $(x, y)_t$ and $(x', y')_{t-1}$ denote the positions of the snaxels, with the subscript $t$ denoting $t^{th}$ iteration. Then, the squared error $SE_t$ is denoted by

$$SE_t = \sum_{i=1}^{N_s} \left( (x_i - x_i')^2 + (y_i - y_i')^2 \right) \qquad (31)$$

where $N_s$ represents the number of snaxels. If $SE_t$ is smaller than an arbitrary constant, the iteration terminates (Ting, Yu, Tzeng, & Wang, 2006).

Figure 5 shows convergence comparison of the squared error as a function of the number of iterations for the Viptraffic frame 17, for two cases in which the next snaxels are estimated with and without a Kaman filter. First, without a Kalman filter, $SE_t$ becomes smaller than 5 when the number of iterations, $L$ is equal to 42. Whereas with a Kalman filter, when $L$ is equal to 12. The computation time per iteration is 0.16 (sec) and that of Kalman filtering is 0.12 (sec) on 3.2 GHz CPU processor (MATLAB 7.0). Thus, computation times for two cases can be obtained. Without a Kalman filter, the total computation time for the Viptraffic frame 17 is equal to $42 \times 0.16 = 6.72$ (sec). Whereas with a Kalman filter, the total computation time is equal to $12 \times 0.16 + 0.12 = 2.04$ (sec). It is noted that prediction of locations of the next snaxels using a Kalman filter efficiently reduces the number of iterations in a snake algorithm and thus requires less computational load.

Figure 6 shows the performance comparison of the proposed algorithm with three conventional methods (Kass et al., 1987; Jin et al., 2006; Park et al., 2001). Figures 6(a), (e), and (i) show final results of Kass et al.'s method and Figures 6(b), (f), and (j) show those of Jin et al.'s method whereas Figures 6(c), (g), and (k) show those of Park et al.'s method, for the Hall Monitor frame 69, Viptraffic frame 12, and Walk frame 335, respectively. The conventional active contour algorithm (Kass et al., 1987) and the directional snake algorithm (Park et al., 2001) have a low computational load, but are sensitive to parameter values in a snake, whereas the multi-scale GVF snake (Jin et al., 2006) shows good performances with a large capture range for concave regions, but requires a high computational load. On the other hand, the proposed algorithm shows good performance with respect to the above-mentioned aspects. First, the proposed algorithm is not sensitive to parameter values because it is based on the nonparametric snake model. Next, since the computational load of the proposed algorithm is reduced by motion prediction, its

*Figure 4. Comparison of results of the proposed method (without and with a Kalman filter) as a function of the number of iterations L (Viptraffic frame 17). (a) location of initial snaxels without the Kalman filter, (b) segmentation result without the Kalman filter (L=2), (c) segmentation result without the Kalman filter (L=12), (d) location of initial snaxels with the Kalman filter, (e) segmentation result with the Kalman filter (L=2), (f) segmentation result with the Kalman filter (L=12)*

computational load is lower than the conventional GVF snake algorithm (Jin et al., 2006), which is shown in Figure 5. Figures 6(d), (h), and (l) show the results of the proposed method with good boundary convergence, in which a few false positives and negatives are shown. Especially, the boundary of concave region such as person's head

in Figure 6(d) is converged well with few false positives and negatives. In contrast to the conventional methods, the proposed algorithm does not have a dependency on parameter values in the snake algorithm and produces more accurate segmentation results.

*Figure 5. Convergence comparison of the squared error as a function of the number of iterations L (Viptraffic frame 17)*

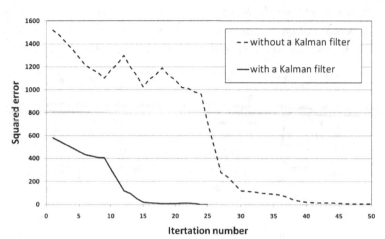

## Pixel-Based Quality Measure

The spatial distortion using the binary video object mask is measured in terms of a pixel-based quality measure, which is computed as follows. Let $O_{seg}$ represent the final segmentation result and $O_{ref}$ denote the reference ground truth model. Then, the pixel-based quality measure $d(O_{seg}, O_{ref})$ is defined by

$$d\left(O_{seg}, O_{ref}\right) = \frac{\sum_{(x,y)} O_{seg}(x, y) \oplus O_{ref}(x, y)}{\sum_{(x,y)} O_{ref}(x, y)}$$
(32)

where $\oplus$ represents the exclusive OR operation. The pixel-based quality measure $d(O_{seg}, O_{ref})$ is computed by the exclusive OR operation of the final segmentation result $\Sigma_{(x, y)} O_{seg}(x, y)$ and the reference ground truth model $\Sigma_{(x,y)} O_{seg}(x, y)$ in an image, and divided by $\Sigma_{(x, y)} O_{seg}(x, y)$ in order to normalize the measure. The reference ground truth model $O_{ref}$ is derived by manually drawing the moving object boundary in successive sequence frames. The more the final segmentation result $O_{seg}$ is similar to the reference ground truth model $O_{ref}$, the closer to zero the pixel-based quality measure $d(O_{seg}, O_{ref})$ is.

Table 1 shows the objective performance comparison of the proposed algorithm with three conventional methods (Kass et al., 1987; Park et al., 2001; Jin et al., 2006) for the Hall Monitor, Viptraffic, and Walk sequences. The objective performance is represented in terms of the average pixel-based quality measure (Correia & Pereira, 2002), where the average value is computed over all the frames of each sequence. The Hall Monitor, Viptraffic, and Walk sequences used in experiments consist of a total of 273, 118, and 200 frames, respectively.

Table 1 shows that the average pixel-based quality measure $d(O_{seg}, O_{ref})$ of the proposed method is smaller than those of three conventional methods, noting that the proposed segmentation method gives results more similar to the ground truth model than the conventional methods. The average pixel-based quality measure is computed by averaging the pixel-based quality measures over successive frames: Hall Monitor (frames 1~273), Viptraffic (frames 1~118), and Walk (frames 300~499).

Figure 7 shows the graphs of the pixel-based quality measure, as a function of the frame number, of the proposed algorithm along with three conventional methods. Figures 7(a), (b), and (c)

*Figure 6. Performance comparison of the proposed algorithm with three conventional methods (Hall Monitor frame 69, Viptraffic frame 12, and Walk frame 335). (a), (e), and (i) (Kass et al., 1987), (b), (f), and (j) (Jin et al., 2006), (c), (g), and (k) (Park et al., 2001), (d), (h), and (l) proposed method*

*Table 1. Performance comparison of four methods in terms of the average pixel-based quality measure (Correia & Pereira, 2002)*

| Images | Kass et al. (1987) | Jin et al. (2006) | Park et al. (2001) | Proposed Method |
|---|---|---|---|---|
| Hall monitor (1~273 frames) | 0.2155 | 0.2299 | 0.1993 | 0.1804 |
| Viptraffic (1~118 frames) | 0.1984 | 0.2095 | 0.1857 | 0.1682 |
| Walk (300~499 frames) | 0.2075 | 0.2135 | 0.1926 | 0.1740 |

show the pixel-based quality measure as a function of the frame number with the Hall Monitor, Viptraffic, and Walk sequences, respectively.

In case of the Hall Monitor and Viptraffic sequences, a moving object first appears in the middle of the sequence. At the start of the Hall Monitor and Viptraffic sequences, there exists no moving object and a moving object gradually appears in the middle of the sequence. Thus, the pixel-based quality measure is gradually increased. But in case of the Walk sequence, only 200 frames that contain a moving object are used in experiments and the pixel-based quality measure is not increased but fluctuated.

The pixel-based quality measures of the proposed method are smaller than those of the three conventional methods for all the three test sequences. Figure 7 shows that the proposed method gives more accurate segmentation results and that its segmentation results are more similar to the ground truth model, than the three conventional methods.

## FUTURE RESEARCH

A decade ago, commercial applications of object segmentation in video were limited, because of the lack of computing power of hardware available, etc. However, recent improvement of hardware ability with the development of efficient algorithms has made them used for a variety of commercial areas. In the areas of surveillance system, video coding, robotics, and medical imaging, object segmentation is an essential tool. Our future research will focus on the implementation of the proposed algorithm to construction of a surveillance system. In the surveillance system, the object segmentation in video enables automatic monitoring, recognition, and prediction of human activity. From surveillance cameras, we can get information about the state of people, e.g., the number or motion of people. The object segmentation algorithm is suitable for analysis of image sequences because outline of human is constrained and predictable. Thus, using the proposed algorithm, motion and behavior of people can be monitored using surveillance video cameras.

## CONCLUSION

This chapter proposes a new object segmentation algorithm based on a nonparametric snake with motion prediction in the GVF snake. It is a nonparametric snake algorithm using moving edges in order to extend the existing nonparametric snake algorithm to video images. It replaces the conventional external force model by the probability density estimate in a nonparametric snake and reduces the computational complexity using a Kalman filter. First, object contours are initialized by using MAD between input and previous frames, and then the initial object contours are converted into more exact object contours by using the GVF snake. Finally, object contour is predicted using a Kalman filter in successive frames. Various experimental results with three test sequences

*Figure 7. Pixel-based quality measure for four methods as a function of the frame number. (a) Hall Monitor (frames 1~273), (b) Viptraffic (frames 1~118), (c) Walk (frames 300~499)*

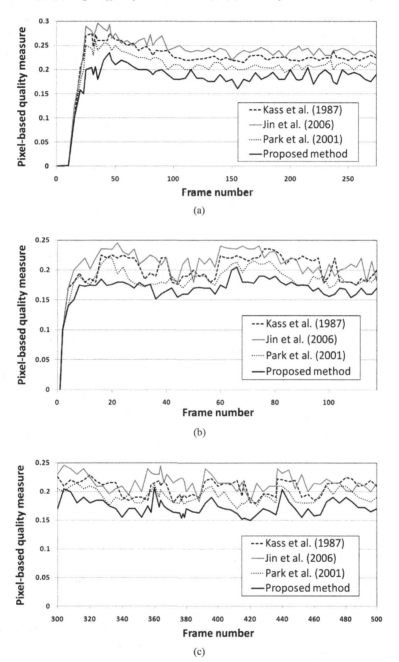

(a)

(b)

(c)

show the effectiveness of the proposed algorithm, in which the proposed algorithm is shown to be insensitive to parameter values. The proposed algorithm gives good performances with a large capture range for concave regions. Thus, the proposed algorithm provides more detailed and improved object segmentation results than three conventional methods compared in this chapter. Also it shows good performance in terms of the computational load, in which the computational load is reduced by using a Kalman filter.

The proposed algorithm can be used as a preprocessing for automatic monitoring, recognition, and prediction of human activity in video. It can also be applied to surveillance systems using a fixed camera and to reduction of the cost in content video coding using moving object extraction.

## ACKNOWLEDGMENT

This work was supported in part by the Second Brain Korea 21 Project.

## REFERENCES

Abd-Almaged, W., Smith, W., & Ramadan, S. (2003). Kernel snakes: Non-parametric active contour models. In *Proceedings of IEEE International Conference on Systems, Man, and Cybernetics* (vol. 1, pp. 240-244).

Betser, A., Vela, P., & Tannenbaum, A. (2004). Automatic tracking of flying vehicles using geodesic snakes and Kalman filtering. In *Proceedings of IEEE Conference on Decision and Control* (vol. 2, pp. 14-17).

Blake, A., & Isard, M. (1998). *Active contour*. Secausus, NJ: Springer-Verlag New York.

Canny, J. F. (1986). A computational approach to edge detection. *IEEE Transactions on Pattern Analysis and Machine Intelligence, 8*(6), 679–698. doi:10.1109/TPAMI.1986.4767851

CAVIAR. (2005). *CAVIAR: Context aware vision using image-based active recognition*. Retrieved from http://homepages.inf.ed.ac.uk/rbf/CAVIAR/

Chen, Q., Sun, Q.-S., Heng, P.-A., & Xia, D.-S. (2008). Parametric active contours for object tracking based on matching degree image of object contour points. *Pattern Recognition Letters, 29*(2), 126–141. doi:10.1016/j.patrec.2007.09.009

Correia, P. L., & Pereira, F. (2002). Objective evaluation of video segmentation quality. *IEEE Transactions on Image Processing, 12*(2), 186–200. doi:10.1109/TIP.2002.807355

Dambreville, S., Rathi, Y., & Tannenbaum, A. (2006). Tracking deformable objects with unscented Kalman filtering and geometric active contours. In *Proceedings of American Control Conference* (vol. 1, pp. 14-16).

Grewal, M. S., & Andrews, A. P. (2008). *Kalman filtering: Theory and practice using MATLAB*. Hoboken, NJ: Wiley & Sons.

Hon, H.-P., Yunmei, C., Huafeng, L., & Pengcheng, S. (2005). Level set active contours on unstructured point cloud. In *Proceedings of IEEE International Conference on Computer Vision and Pattern Recognition* (vol. 2, pp. 20-25).

Jin, L., Junhong, X., Wang, C., Lulu, Z., Hong, Y., & Hong, L. (2006). Contour segmentation algorithm of multi-scale GVF snake. In *Proceedings of IEEE International Conference on Mechatronics and Automation* (pp. 537-542).

Kang, D. J., Kim, J. Y., & Kweon, I. S. (2001). A stabilized snake constraint for tracking object boundaries. In *Proceedings of IEEE International Symposium on Industrial Electronics* (vol. 1, pp. 672-677).

Kass, M., Witkin, A., & Terzopoulos, D. (1987). Snakes: active contour models. *International Journal of Computer Vision, 1*(4), 321–331. doi:10.1007/BF00133570

Kim, C., & Hwang, J.-K. (2002). Fast and automatic video object segmentation and tracking for content-based applications. *IEEE Transactions on Circuits and Systems for Video Technology, 12*(2), 122–129. doi:10.1109/76.988659

Kim, S.-H., Alattar, A., & Jang, J. W. (2006). A snake-based segmentation algorithm for objects with boundary concavities in stereo images. In *Proceedings of International Conference on Computational Intelligence and Security* (vol. 1, pp. 645-650).

Kim, W., Hong, S.-G., & Lee, J.-J. (1999). An active contour model using image flow for tracking a moving object. In *Proceedings of IEEE/RSJ International Conference on Intelligent Robots and Systems* (vol. 1, pp. 216-221).

Lee, S.-W., Kang, J., Shin, J., & Paik, J. (2007). Hierarchical active shape model with motion prediction for real-time tracking of non-rigid objects. *IET Computer Vision, 1*(1), 17–24. doi:10.1049/iet-cvi:20045243

Martin, P., Refregier, Ph., Galland, F., & Guerault, F. (2006). Nonparametric statistical snake based on the minimum stochastic complexity. *IEEE Transactions on Image Processing, 15*(9), 2762–2770. doi:10.1109/TIP.2006.877317

Ozertem, U., & Erdogmus, D. (2007). Nonparametric snakes. *IEEE Transactions on Image Processing, 16*(9), 2361–2368. doi:10.1109/TIP.2007.902335

Park, H. W., Schoeflin, T., & Kim, Y. (2001). Active contour model with gradient directional information: Directional snake. *IEEE Transactions on Circuits and Systems for Video Technology, 11*(2), 252–256. doi:10.1109/76.905991

Peterfreund, N. (1999). Robust tracking of position and velocity with Kalman snakes. *IEEE Transactions on Pattern Analysis and Machine Intelligence, 21*(6), 564–569. doi:10.1109/34.771328

Rolfes, S., & Rendas, J. (2004). Statistical snakes: Robust tracking of benthic contours under varying background. In *Proceedings of IEEE/RSJ International Conference on Intelligent Robots and Systems* (vol. 3, pp. 3056-3061).

Sharifi, M., Fathy, M., & Mahmoudi, M. T. (2002). A classified and comparative study of edge detection algorithms. In *Proceedings of International Conference on Information Technology: Coding and Computing* (pp. 117-120).

Sun, S., Haynor, D.-R., & Kim, Y. (2003). Semiautomatic video object segmentation using VSnakes. *IEEE Transactions on Circuits and Systems for Video Technology, 13*(1), 75–82. doi:10.1109/TCSVT.2002.808089

Ting, C.-C., Yu, J.-S., Tzeng, J.-S., & Wang, J.-H. (2006). Improved snake model for fast image segmentation. In *Proceedings of International Joint Conference on Neural Networks* (pp. 3936-3941).

Xu, C., & Prince, J. L. (1998). Snakes, shape, and gradient vector flow. *IEEE Transactions on Image Processing, 7*(3), 359–369. doi:10.1109/83.661186

Xu, N., Ahuja, N., & Bansal, R. (2007). Object segmentation using graph cuts based active contours. *Computer Vision and Image Understanding, 107*(3), 210–224. doi:10.1016/j.cviu.2006.11.004

Zhang, D., & Lu, G. (2001). Segmentation of moving objects in image sequence: A review. *International Journal of Circuits, Systems, and Signal Processing, 20*(2), 143–189. doi:10.1007/BF01201137

## ADDITIONAL READING

Barat, C., & Lagadec, B. (2008). A corner tracker snake approach to segment irregular object shape in video image. In *Proceedings of IEEE International Conference on Acoustics, Speech and Signal Processing* (pp. 717-720).

Caselles, V., Kimmel, R., & Sapiro, G. (1997). Geodesic active contours. *International Journal of Computer Vision, 22*(1), 61–79. doi:10.1023/A:1007979827043

Chan, T. F., & Vese, L. A. (2001). Active contours without edges. *IEEE Transactions on Image Processing, 10*(2), 266–277. doi:10.1109/83.902291

Chen, Q., Sun, Q.-S., Heng, P. A., & Xia, D.-S. (2010). Two-stage object tracking method based on kernel and active contour. *IEEE Transactions on Circuits and Systems for Video Technology, 20*(4), 605–609. doi:10.1109/TCSVT.2010.2041819

Cheng, J., & Foo, S. W. (2006). Dynamic directional gradient vector flow for snakes. *IEEE Transactions on Image Processing, 15*(6), 1563–1571. doi:10.1109/TIP.2006.871140

DeCarlo, R. A. (1989). *Linear systems*. Englewood Cilffs, NJ: Prentice Hall.

Durikovic, R., Kaneda, K., & Yamashita, H. (1995). Dynamic contour: a texture approach and contour operations. *The Visual Computer, 11*(6), 277–289. doi:10.1007/BF01898405

Elagmmal, A., Harwood, D., & Davis, L. (2000). Non-parametric model for background subtraction. In *Proceedings of the Sixth European Conference on Computer Vision* (pp. 751-767).

Forsyth, D. A., & Ponce, J. (2003). *Computer vision: a modern approach*. Upper Saddle River, NJ: Prentice Hall.

Friedman, N., & Russell, S. (1997). Image segmentation in video sequence: a probabilistic approach. In *Proceedings of the Thirteenth Conference on Uncertainty in Artificial Intelligence* (pp. 175-181).

Gouet-Brunet, V., & Lameyre, B. (2008). Object recognition and segmentation in videos by connecting heterogeneous visual features. *Computer Vision and Image Understanding, 111*, 86–109. doi:10.1016/j.cviu.2007.10.004

Haykin, S. (1989). *Modern filters*. New York: Macmillan Publishing Company.

Jain, R., Kasturi, R., & Schunck, B. G. (1995). *Machine vision*. New York: McGraw-Hill.

Krinidis, S., & Chatzis, V. (2009). Fuzzy energy-based active contours. *IEEE Transactions on Image Processing, 18*(12), 2747–2755. doi:10.1109/TIP.2009.2030468

Leymarie, F., & Levine, M. D. (1993). Tracking deformable objects in the plane using an active contour model. *IEEE Transactions on Pattern Analysis and Machine Intelligence, 15*(6), 617–634. doi:10.1109/34.216733

Li, B., & Acton, S. T. (2007). Active contour external force using vector field convolution for image segmentation. *IEEE Transactions on Image Processing, 16*(8), 2096–2106. doi:10.1109/TIP.2007.899601

Lobregt, S., & Viergever, M. A. (1995). A discrete dynamic contour model. *IEEE Transactions on Medical Imaging, 14*(1), 12–24. doi:10.1109/42.370398

Roh, M.-C., Kim, T.-Y., Park, J., & Lee, S.-W. (2007). Accurate object contour tracking based on boundary edge selection. *Pattern Recognition, 40*(3), 931–943. doi:10.1016/j.patcog.2006.06.014

Stauffer, C., & Grimson, W. E. L. (1999). Adaptive background mixture models for real-time tracking. In *Proceedings of IEEE Computer Society Conference on Computer Vision and Pattern Recognition* (Vol. 2, pp. 246-252).

Terzopoulos, D., & Szeliski, R. (1992). Tracking with Kalman snakes. In Blake, A., & Yuille, A. (Eds.), *Active Vision* (pp. 3–20). Cambridge, MA: MIT Press.

Wang, Y., Ostermann, J., & Zang, Y.-Q. (2002). *Video processing and communications*. Upper Saddle River, NJ: Prentice Hall.

Xie, X., & Mirmehdi, M. (2008). MAC: magnetostatic active contour model. *IEEE Transactions on Pattern Analysis and Machine Intelligence*, *30*(4), 632–647. doi:10.1109/TPAMI.2007.70737

Xu, C., & Prince, J. L. (1998). Generalized gradient vector flow external forces for active contours. *Signal Processing*, *71*(2), 131–139. doi:10.1016/S0165-1684(98)00140-6

Yilmaz, A., Javed, O., & Shah, M. (2006). Object tracking: a survey. *ACM Computing Surveys*, *38*(13), 1–45.

Zhu, G., Zhang, S., Zeng, Q., & Wang, C. (2010). Gradient vector flow active contours with prior directional information. *Pattern Recognition Letters*, *31*(9), 845–856. doi:10.1016/j.patrec.2010.01.011

Zhu, S. C., & Yuille, A. (1996). Region competition: unifying snakes, region growing, energy/Bayes/MDL for multi-band image segmentation. *IEEE Transactions on Pattern Analysis and Machine Intelligence*, *18*(9), 884–900. doi:10.1109/34.537343

## KEY TERMS AND DEFINITIONS

**Active Contour Model:** A model for delineating an object outline from an image, which is computed by minimizing a sum of an internal and external energy at the current contour.

**Dynamic System:** A mathematical system that is influenced by past input as well as current input.

**Gradient Vector Flow (GVF):** An external force which is computed by a diffusion of the gradient vectors of a specific map derived from the image. It is used for snake.

**Kalman Filter:** A recursive filter that estimates the latent state with measurement in prediction and correction steps.

**Pixel-Based Quality Measure:** Quality measure that is computed by the exclusive OR operation of the final segmentation result and the reference ground truth model in an image and is normalized.

**Segmentation:** Subdividing an image into the meaningful components, regions, or objects.

**Snake Algorithm:** An algorithm that segments an image into a meaningful foreground and background using various energies in the image.

# Chapter 7
# Analysis of Face Space for Recognition using Interval– Valued Subspace Technique

**C.J. Prabhakar**
*Kuvempu University, India*

## ABSTRACT

*The major contribution of the research work presented in this chapter is the development of effective face recognition algorithm using analysis of face space in the interval-valued subspace. The analysis of face images is used for various purposes such as facial expression classification, gender determination, age estimation, emotion assessment, face recognition, et cetera. The research community of face image analysis has developed many techniques for face recognition; one of the successful techniques is based on subspace analysis. In the first part of the chapter, the authors present discussion of earliest face recognition techniques, which are considered as mile stones in the roadmap of subspace based face recognition techniques. The second part presents one of the efficient interval-valued subspace techniques, namely, symbolic Kernel Fisher Discriminant analysis (Symbolic KFD), in which the interval type features are extracted in contrast to classical subspace based techniques where single valued features are used for face representation and recognition.*

## INTRODUCTION

Biometric access control is a set of automated methods of verifying or recognizing the identity of a living person on the basis of some physiological characteristics, such as fingerprints or facial features, or some aspects of the person's behavior, like his/her handwriting style or keystroke pat-

terns. Biometric access controls have emerged as the most promising technology for recognizing individuals in recent years. Since, instead of authenticating people and granting them access to physical and virtual domains based on passwords, PINs, smart cards, plastic cards, tokens, keys and so forth, these methods examine an individual's physiological and/or behavioral characteristics in order to determine and/or ascertain his identity. Since biometric systems identify a person by bio-

DOI: 10.4018/978-1-61350-429-1.ch007

logical characteristics, they are difficult to forge. Among the various biometric ID methods, the physiological methods (fingerprint, face, DNA) are more stable than the methods in behavioral category (keystroke, voice print). The reason is that physiological features are often non-alterable except by severe injury. The behavioral patterns, on the other hand, may fluctuate due to stress, fatigue, or illness. However, behavioral IDs have the advantage of being non intrusive. Face recognition is one of the few biometric methods that possess the merits of both high accuracy and low intrusiveness.

Iris and retina identification require expensive equipment and are much too sensitive to any body motion. Voice recognition is susceptible to background noises in public places and auditory fluctuations on a phone line or tape recording. Signatures can be modified or forged. However, facial images can be easily obtained with a couple of inexpensive fixed cameras. Good face recognition algorithms and appropriate preprocessing of the images can compensate for noise and slight variations in orientation, scale and illumination. Finally, technologies that require multiple individuals to use the same equipment to capture their biological characteristics potentially expose the user to the transmission of germs and impurities from other users. However, face recognition is totally non-intrusive and does not carry any such health risks. For this reason, since the early 70's, face recognition has drawn the attention of researchers in fields from security, psychology, and image processing, to computer vision. Face recognition is used for two primary tasks:

1. Verification (one-to-one matching): When presented with a face image of an unknown individual along with a claim of identity, ascertaining whether the individual is who he/she claims to be.
2. Identification (one-to-many matching): Given an image of an unknown individual,

determining that person's identity by comparing (possibly after encoding) that image with a database of (possibly encoded) images of known individuals.

## CHALLENGES IN FACE RECOGNITION

Although great deal of effort has been devoted to 2D intensity image based face recognition task, it still remains a challenging problem in a general setting. Successful 2D face recognition systems have been deployed only under constrained situations (Zhao et al., 2003). There are numerous factors that cause the appearance of the face to vary. The sources of variation in the facial appearance can be categorized into two groups: intrinsic factors and extrinsic ones. Intrinsic factors are based on physical nature of the face and are independent of the observer. Some examples are age, facial expression, facial hair, glasses, cosmetics, etc. Intrinsic factors are also responsible for the differences in the facial appearance of different people, some examples being ethnicity and gender. Extrinsic factors cause the appearance of the face to alter via the interaction of light with the face and the observer. These factors include illumination, pose, scale and imaging parameters (e.g., resolution, focus, imaging, noise, etc.).

## APPLICATIONS OF FACE RECOGNITION

There are numerous application areas in which face recognition can be exploited, a few of which are outlined below:

1. Security (access control to buildings, airports/seaports, ATM machines and border checkpoints; computer/network secu-

rity; email authentication on multimedia workstations);

2.  Surveillance (a large number of close circuit televisions can be monitored to look for known criminals, drug offenders, etc. and authorities can be notified when one is located);

3.  General identity verification (electoral registration, banking, electronic commerce, identifying newborns, national IDs, passports, drivers' licenses, employee IDs);

4.  Criminal justice systems (mug-shot/booking systems, post-event analysis, forensics);

5.  Image database investigations (searching image databases of licensed drivers, benefit recipients, missing children, immigrants and police bookings);

6.  "Smart Card" applications (in lieu of maintaining a database of facial images, the faceprint can be stored in a smart card, bar code or magnetic stripe, authentication of which is performed by matching the live image and the stored template);

7.  Multi-media environments with adaptive human computer interfaces (part of ubiquitous or context aware systems, behavior monitoring at childcare or old people's centers, recognizing a customer and assessing his needs);

8.  Video indexing (labeling faces in video);

9.  Witness faces reconstruction;

In addition to these applications, face recognition technology has also been used for gender classification, expression recognition, facial feature recognition and tracking. Face recognition is also being used in conjunction with other biometrics such as speech, iris, fingerprint, ear and gait recognition in order to enhance the recognition performance of these methods.

## APPEARANCE-BASED FACE RECOGNITION TECHNIQUES

The method for acquiring face images depends upon the underlying application. For instance, surveillance applications may best be served by capturing face images by means of a video camera while image database investigations may require static intensity images taken by a standard camera. Some other applications, such as access to top security domains, may even necessitate the forgoing of the nonintrusive quality of face recognition by requiring the user to stand in front of a 3D scanner or an infra-red sensor. Therefore, depending on the face data acquisition methodology, face recognition techniques can be broadly divided into three categories: methods that operate on intensity images, those that deal with video sequences, and those that require other sensory data such as 3D information or infra-red imagery.

Face recognition methods for intensity images fall into two main categories: feature-based and appearance-based techniques. Feature-based approaches first process the input image to identify and extract (and measure) distinctive facial features such as the eyes, mouth, nose, etc., as well as other fiducial marks, and then compute the geometric relationships among those facial points, thus reducing the input facial image to a vector of geometric features. Standard statistical pattern recognition techniques are then employed to match faces using these measurements. Whereas, the appearance-based (View based) approaches attempt to identify faces using global representations, i.e., descriptions based on the entire image rather than on local features of the face. In these techniques, no explicit feature extraction takes place and each face view is stored as a vector of image intensities. The face image representation is largely based on direct representations of image intensity (i.e., learn the appearance characteristics of an object from training imagery). Many appearance-based approaches use statistical techniques to analyze the distribution of the object image vectors in the vector space and derive an efficient and effective representation (feature space) according to different applications. Given a test image, the similarity between the stored prototypes and the test view is then carried out in the feature space. The following discussion sheds some light on the appearance-based methods that operate on intensity images. An overview of some of the well-known methods in these categories is given below.

## Linear Subspaces

The classical linear appearance-based classifiers are commonly applied on face images for face recognition. Each classifier has its own representation (basis vectors) of a high dimensional face vector space based on different statistical viewpoints. By projecting the face vector to the basis vectors, the projection coefficients are used as the feature representation of each face image. The matching score between the test face image and the training prototype is calculated between their coefficients vectors. The larger the matching score, the better the match. All the linear classifiers representations can be considered as a linear transformation from the original image vector to a projection feature vector:

$$Y = W^T X, \tag{1}$$

where $Y = d \times N$ feature vector matrix, $d$ is the dimension of the feature vector, and $W$ is the transformation matrix.

The first successful linear classifier for face recognition is based on Principal Component Analysis (PCA) projection (Kirby and Sirovich, 1990). PCA based face recognition method proposed by Kirby and Sirovich was suffering from computational inefficiency due to larger dimensionality of face space. To overcome the drawbacks of PCA for face recognition, Turk and Pentland (1991) has extended PCA as eigenfaces and it was the first really successful demonstration of ma-

chine recognition of faces. Sample vectors $x$ can be expressed as linear combinations of the orthogonal basis $\phi_i : x = \sum_{i=1}^{n} a_i \phi_i \approx \sum_{i=1}^{m} a_i \phi_i$ by solving the eigen problem

$$C\phi = \phi \Lambda, \tag{2}$$

where $C$ is the covariance matrix for the input $x$. The PCA reconstructed images are much better than the original distorted images in terms of their global appearance (Turk and Pentland, 1991).

The role of PCA in the original eigenfaces was largely confined to dimensionality reduction. The similarity between images $I_1, I_2$ ($I_1, I_2$ represents the column vector representation of the face images) was measured in terms of the Euclidean norm of the difference $\Delta = I_1 - I_2$ projected to the subspace, essentially ignoring the variation modes both within the subspace and outside of it. This was improved in the extension of eigenfaces proposed by Moghaddam and Pentland (1997) and it uses a probabilistic similarity measure, based on a parametric estimate of the probability density $p(\Delta \mid \Omega)$. The PCA is adopted to divide the vector space $R^N$ into two subspaces. The principal subspace $F$, obtained by $\Phi_k$ and its orthogonal complement $\bar{F}$ spanned by the remaining columns of $\Phi$. The probability density can be decomposed into two orthogonal components:

$$P(\Delta \mid \Omega) = P_F(\Delta \mid \Omega) \cdot P_{\bar{F}}(\Delta \mid \Omega). \tag{3}$$

In Probabilistic PCA (PPCA) proposed by Tipping and Bishop (1997), the complete likelihood estimate can be written as the product of two independent marginal Gaussian densities. A large performance improvement of this probabilistic matching technique over standard nearest-neighbor eigenspace matching was reported using large face datasets including the FERET database (Phillips et al., 2000). In (Moghaddam and Pentland,

1997), experimental results have been reported using different subspace dimensionalities $M_I$ and $M_E$ for $\Omega_I$ and $\Omega_E$. For example, $M_I = 10$ and $M_E = 30$ were used for internal tests, while $M_I = M_E = 125$ were used for the FERET test. A similar idea was explored in (Sung and Poggio, 1997).

The PCA and probabilistic based PCA techniques essentially select a subspace which retains most of the variation, and consequently the similarity in the face space is not necessarily determined by the identity. When substantial changes in illumination and expression are present, much of the variation in the data is due to these changes. A commonly used measure for quantifying discriminatory power is the ratio of the determinant of the between-class scatter matrix of the projected samples to the determinant of the within-class scatter matrix. In (Belhumeur et al., 1997), it is proposed to solve this problem with "Fisherfaces" - an application of Fisher's Linear Discriminant (FLD). The FLD selects the linear subspace $\Phi$ which maximizes the ratio:

$$\frac{\Phi^T S_b \Phi}{\Phi^T S_w \Phi}, \tag{4}$$

where $S_b = \sum_{i=1}^{m} N_i(\bar{x}_i - \bar{x})(\bar{x}_i - \bar{x})^T$, is the between-class scatter matrix and

$$S_w = \sum_{i=1}^{m} \sum_{x \in X_i} (x - \bar{x}_i)(x - \bar{x}_i)^T, \tag{5}$$

is the within-class scatter matrix; $m$ is the number of subjects (classes) in the database. Intuitively, FLD finds the projection of the data in which the classes are most linearly separable. It can be shown that the dimension of $\Phi$ is at most $m - 1$ (Belhumeur et al., 1997).

Face recognition systems using Linear Discriminant Analysis (LDA)/FLD have been very successful (Belhumeur et al., 1997; Etemad and Chellappa, 1997; Swets and Weng, 1996; Zhao et al., 1998; Zhao et al., 1999). In (Swets and Weng, 1996), discriminant analysis of eigenfeatures is applied in an image retrieval system to determine not only class (human face vs. nonface objects) but also individuals within the face class. Experiments have been carried out using a set of 800 images of 42 classes for training. The proposed algorithm achieves 87% recognition rate using 78 test images of disjoint set and 87% for 38 nonface images based on the top choice.

Since, in practice, $S_w$ is usually singular, the Fisherfaces algorithm first reduces the dimensionality of the data with PCA, and then applies FLD to further reduce the dimensionality to $m - 1$. The recognition is then accomplished by a Nearest Neighbor (NN) classifier in this final subspace. The experiments reported in (Belhumer et al., 1997) were performed on data sets containing frontal face images of 5 people with drastic lighting variations and another set with faces of 16 people with varying expressions and again drastic illumination changes. The results of the experiments showed that the Fisherface method performed significantly better than the other three methods. However, no claim was made about the relative performance of these algorithms on larger databases.

To improve the performance of LDA based systems, a regularized subspace LDA system that unifies PCA and LDA was proposed in (Zhao, 1999) and (Zhao et al., 1998). The fixed PCA subspace of dimensionality 300 was trained from a large number of samples. An augmented set of 4056 mostly frontal-view images constructed from the original 1078 FERET images of 444 individuals by adding noise and mirroring was used in (Zhao et al., 1998). Zhao et al., have selected the dimensionality of the universal face subspace based on the characteristics of the eigenvectors (face-like or not) instead of the eigenvalues, as is commonly done. Later it was concluded in (Penev and Sirovich, 2000) that the global face subspace dimensionality is of the order of 400 for large databases of 5,000 images. A weighted distance metric in the projection space $z$ was used to improve performance (Zhao, 1999). Finally, the LDA training was regularized by modifying the $S_w$ matrix to $S_w + \delta I$, where $\delta I$ is a relatively small positive numbered matrix. Doing this solves a numerical problem when $S_w$ is close to being singular.

In the extreme case where only one sample per class is available, this regularization transforms the LDA problem into a standard PCA problem with $S_b$ being the covariance matrix $C$. Applying this approach, without retraining the LDA basis, to a testing/probe set of 46 individuals of which 24 were trained and 22 were not trained (a total of 115 images including 19 untrained images of non frontal views), the authors reported the following performance (in percentage) based on a front-view-only gallery database of 738 images: 85.2 for all images and 95.1 for frontal views. An evolution pursuit (EP) based adaptive representation and its application to face recognition was presented in (Liu and Wechsler, 2000). The feasibility of this method has been demonstrated for face recognition, where the large number of possible bases requires a greedy search algorithm. The particular face recognition task involves 1107 FERET frontal face images of 369 subjects; there were three frontal images for each subject, two for training and the remaining one for testing. The authors reported improved face recognition performance as compared to eigenfaces, and better generalization capability than Fisherfaces (Belhumeur et al., 1997).

Based on the argument that for tasks such as face recognition much of the important information is contained in high-order statistics, it has been proposed in (Bartlett et al., 1998) to use Independent Component Analysis (ICA) to extract features for face recognition. The ICA is a generalization of PCA, which decorrelates the high-order moments of the input in addition to the second-order moments. Like PCA, the ICA

also yields a linear projection $R^N \rightarrow R^M$ but with different properties:

$$x \approx Ay, A^T A \neq I, P(y) \approx \Pi p(y_i), \qquad (6)$$

that is, approximate reconstruction, non-orthogonality of the basis $A$ and the near factorization of the joint distribution $P(y)$ into marginal distributions of the ICs. ICA is intimately related to the blind source separation problem: decomposition of the input signal (image) $x$ into a linear combination (mixture) of independent source signals. Formally, the assumption is that $x^T = As^T$, with $A$ the unknown mixing matrix. The ICA algorithms try to find $A$ or the separating matrix $W$ such that $u^T = Wx^T = WAs^T$ when the data consist of $M$ observations with $N$ variables, the input to ICA is arranged in an $N \times M$ matrix $X$. ICA is performed on the first 200 eigenvectors in the first architecture, and is carried out on the first 200 PCA projection coefficients in the second architecture. The authors reported performance improvement of both architectures over eigenfaces in the following scenario: a FERET subset consisting of 425 individuals was used; all the frontal views (one per class) were used for training and the remaining (up to three) frontal views for testing. In (Bartlett et al., 1998), it is shown that ICA representation outperforms PCA representation in face recognition, using a subset of frontal FERET face images. However, Moghaddam (1999) showed that ICA representation does not provide significant advantage over PCA. The experimental results suggest that seeking non-Gaussian and independent components may not necessarily yield better representation for face recognition.

The linear analysis methods discussed above have been shown to be suitable when pose, illumination or expressions are fixed across the face database. When any of these parameters is allowed to vary, the linear subspace representation does not capture this variation well. The Multi-linear approach, called Tensorfaces, has been proposed by Vasilescu and Terzopoulos (2003). The notion of tensor can be applied to a face image ensemble in the following way (Vasilescu and Terzopoulous, 2003): consider a set of $N$ pixel images of $N_p$ people's faces, each photographed in $N_v$ viewpoints, with $N_i$ illuminations and $N_e$ expressions. The entire set may be arranged in a $N_p \times N_v \times N_i \times N_e \times N$ tensor of order 5. In this context, the face image tensor can be decomposed into:

$$A = Z \times_1 U_p \times_2 U_v \times_3 U_i \times_4 U_e \times_5 U_{Pixels}. \tag{7}$$

Each mode matrix represents a parameter of the object appearance. For example, the columns of the $N_e \times N_e$ matrix $U_e$ span the space of expression parameters. The columns of $U_{Pixels}$ span the image space; these are exactly the eigenfaces which would be obtained by direct PCA on the entire data set. Every person in the database can be represented by a single $N_p$ vector, which contains coefficient with respect to the bases comprising the tensor

$$B = X \times_2 U_v \times_3 U_i \times_4 U_e \times_5 U_{Pixels}.$$

For a given viewpoint $v$, illumination $i$ and expression $e$, an $N_p \times N$ matrix $B_{v,i,e}$ can be obtained by indexing into $B$ for $v, i, e$ and attending the resulting $N_p \times 1 \times 1 \times 1 \times N$ sub-tensor along the identity (people) mode. Now a training image $X_{p,v,i,e}$ of a person $j$ under the given conditions can be written as

$$X_{p,v,i,e} = B_{v,i,e}^T c_p, \tag{8}$$

where $c_j$ is the $j$-th row vector of $U_p$. Given an input image $X$, a candidate coefficient vector $c_{v,i,e}$ is computed for all combinations of viewpoint, expression and illumination, by solving the equation. The recognition is carried out by finding the value of $j$ that yields the minimum distance

between $c$ and the vector $c_j$ across all illuminations, expressions and viewpoints.

## Non Linear Subspaces

Non linear subspace techniques overcome many limitations of its linear counterpart by nonlinearly mapping the input space to a high dimensional feature space. The linear subspace techniques like PCA, a powerful technique for reducing a large set of correlated variables to a smaller number of uncorrelated components, has been applied extensively for both face representation and recognition. The PCA technique, however, encodes only for second order statistics, i.e., pixel wise covariance among the pixels, and which insensitive to the dependencies of multiple (more than two) pixels in the patterns. As these second order statistics provide only partial information on the statistics of both natural images and human faces, it might become necessary to incorporate higher order statistics as well. Higher order dependencies in an image include nonlinear relations among the pixel intensity values, such as the relationships among three or more pixels in an edge or a curve, which can capture important information for recognition. PCA is extended to a nonlinear form by mapping nonlinearly the input space to a feature space, where PCA is ultimately implemented. Applying different mappings, nonlinear PCA can encode arbitrary higher order correlations among the input variables. Kernel PCA applies kernel functions (Scholkopf et al., 1998) for nonlinear mapping between the input space and the feature space. The dot products in the high dimensional feature space are replaced by those in the input space, while computation is related to the number of training examples rather than the dimension of the feature space.

The kernel PCA is to apply a nonlinear mapping from the input space $R^M$ to the feature space $R^L$, denoted by $\psi(x)$, where $L$ is larger than $M$. This mapping is made implicit by the use of kernel functions satisfying the Mercer's theorem:

$$k(X_i, X_j) = (\psi(X_i) \cdot \psi(X_j)), \qquad (9)$$

where kernel function $k(X_i, X_j)$ in the input space correspond to inner-product in the higher dimensional feature space. Because computing covariance is based on inner products, performing a PCA in the feature space can be formulated with kernels in the input space without the explicit computation of $\psi(x)$. Suppose the covariance in the feature space is calculated as

$$\sum\nolimits_{K} = < \psi(X_i), \psi(X_i)^T > . \qquad (10)$$

The corresponding eigen-problem is $\lambda V = \Sigma_K V$. It can be proved that $V$ can be expressed as

$$V = \sum_{i=1}^{N} w_i \psi(X_i), \qquad (11)$$

where $N$ is the total number of training samples. The equivalent eigenvalue problem can be formulated in terms of kernels in the input space

$$N\lambda W = KW, \qquad (12)$$

where $W = (w_1, ..., w_T)^T$ is the vector of expansion of coefficients of a given eigenvector $V$. The kernel matrix $K_{ij} = k(X_i, X_j)$ is a $N \times N$ matrix. The KPCA principal components of any input vector can be efficiently computed with simple kernel evaluations against the dataset. The $n^{th}$ principal components $y_n$ of $X$ can be calculated by

$$y_n = (V_n \cdot \psi(X)) = \sum_{i=1}^{N} w_i^n k(X, X_i), \qquad (13)$$

where $V_n$ is the $n^{th}$ eigenvector of the feature space defined by $\psi$. As with PCA, the eigenvectors $V_n$ can be ranked by decreasing order of their eigenvalues $\lambda_n$ and an $d$-dimensional manifold projection of $X$ is $y = (y_1, ..., y_d)^T$, with individual components.

Three classes of kernel functions widely used in kernel classifiers, neural networks and support vector machines are polynomial kernels, Gaussian kernels, and sigmoid kernels.

Polynomial kernels:

$$k(x, y) = (x \cdot y)^d, \qquad (14)$$

Gaussian kernels:

$$k(x, y) = \exp\left(\frac{- \| x - y \|^2}{\sigma^2}\right), \qquad (15)$$

Sigmoid kernels:

$$k(x, y) = \tanh(k(x \cdot y) + v), \qquad (16)$$

where $d \in N$, $\sigma > 0$, $k > 0$, and $v < 0$.

In (Scholkopf et al., 1998), the conventional PCA is extended to Kernel Principal Component Analysis (KPCA). Empirical results on digit recognition using MNIST dataset and object recognition using a database of rendered chair images showed that kernel PCA is able to extract non linear features and thus provided better recognition results. Similar to the derivation of KPCA, one may extend the Fisherfaces method by applying the FLD in the feature space. M.H. Yang et al. (2000) compared face recognition performance using kernel PCA and the eigenfaces method. Yang et al.(2002) derives the Kernel Fisherfaces algorithm, that maximizes the between-scatter to within-scatter ratio in the feature space through the use of the kernel matrix K. This algorithm has shown performance clearly superior to that of ICA, PCA and KPCA and better than that of the standard Fisherfaces. Moghaddam (2002) demonstrated that kernel PCA performed better than PCA for face Recognition. Chengjun Liu (2004) extended kernel PCA method to include fractional power polynomial models for enhanced face recognition performance.

The classical Fisher linear discriminant analysis (FLDA) is a commonly used and efficient method for multiclass classification because of its simplicity. Motivated from the active development of statistical learning theory (Vapnik, 1998) and the popular and successful usage of various kernel machines (Scholkopf and Smola, 2002), there has emerged a hybrid approach which combines the idea of feature map in SVM with the classical FLDA (Mika et al., 1999; Baudat and Anouar, 2000; Mika, Ratsch and Muller, 2001; Van Gestel, Suykens and De Brabanter, 2001). Mika et al. (1999), Baudat and Anouar (2000) and others have used the term kernel Fisher discriminant analysis (KFDA) for the hybrid method of FLDA and kernel machine. In all the above-mentioned articles, the KFDA is based on performing the FLDA in a kernel-spectrum-based feature space.

## SYMBOLIC KFD METHOD FOR FACE RECOGNITION

The defining characteristic of the classical appearance based algorithms is that they directly use the pixel intensity values in a face image as the features on which to base the recognition decision. The pixel intensities that are used as features are represented using single valued variables. However, in many situations, same face is captured in different orientation, lighting, expression and background, which lead to image variations. The pixel intensities do change because of image variations. The use of single valued variables may not be able to capture the variation of feature values of the images of the same subject. In such a case, we need to consider the symbolic data analysis (SDA) (Bock and Diday, 2000), in which the interval-valued data are analyzed. We have extended the classical subspace analysis techniques for face recognition as interval-valued subspace techniques to extract interval-type features in the framework of symbolic data analysis. In (Hiremath P.S. and Prabhakar C.J., 2006), The

kernel PCA is extended to symbolic data analysis as symbolic kernel PCA for face recognition and the experimental results show improved recognition rate. Polynomial kernel of degree three with symbolic KDA is used to extract non linear interval type features in (Hiremath P.S. and Prabhakar C.J., 2008b). The symbolic Factorial Discriminant Analysis (symbolic FDA) is developed for face recognition under variable lighting (Hiremath P.S. and Prabhakar C.J., 2008a). In all these techniques, the face space is analyzed in interval-valued subspace contrast to classical single-valued subspace. The face is represented in the form of interval-valued features to capture the variations of images within the same face class.

In this section, we have presented one of the efficient interval-valued subspace techniques, namely, symbolic Kernal Fisher Discriminant Analysis (symbolic KFD) method with new RBF kernel function for face recognition (Hiremath P.S. and Prabhakar C.J., 2009), which is an extension of classical KFD in the framework of Symbolic Data Analysis (SDA). In the first step, we represent the face images as symbolic objects (symbolic faces) of interval type variables. The representation of face images as symbolic faces accounts for image variations of human faces under different lighting conditions, orientation and facial expression. It also drastically reduces the dimension of the image space without losing a significant amount of information. Each symbolic face summarizing the variation of feature values through the different images of the same subject. In the second step, we apply new RBF kernel function to map input data into highly non linear data in a high dimensional space. Then we extract interval type non linear discriminating features, which are robust to variations due to illumination, orientation and facial expression. Finally, minimum distance classifier with squared Euclidean distance is employed for classification.

## RBF Kernel Function for Interval Data

The RBF kernel formula in (17) of two data vectors $x$ and $y$ of continuous type is based on the Euclidean distance between these vectors, $d_E(x, y) = \| x - y \|$.

$$K \langle x, y \rangle = \exp \left( - \frac{\| x - y \|^2}{\sigma} \right), \qquad (17)$$

where $\sigma > 0$ is width of the RBF kernel. For dealing with interval data, we only need to measure the distance between two vectors of interval type, then we substitute this distance measure for the Euclidean distance into RBF kernel formula. Thus the new RBF kernel can deal with interval data. The dissimilarity measure between two vectors of interval type is the Hausdorff distance. Let us consider two data vectors $u, v \in \Omega$ having $p$ dimensions of interval type:

$$u = ([u_{1, low}, u_{1, high}], [u_{2, low}, u_{2, high}], \ldots, [u_{p, low}, u_{p, high}])$$

$$v = ([v_{1, low}, v_{1, high}], [v_{2, low}, v_{2, high}], \ldots, [v_{p, low}, v_{p, high}])$$

The Hausdorff distance between two vectors $u$ and $v$ is defined by:

$$d_H(u, v) = \sqrt{\sum_{i=1}^{p} \max \left( \left| u_{i, low} - v_{i, low} \right|^2, \left| u_{i, high} - v_{i, high} \right|^2 \right)} \qquad (18)$$

By substituting the Hausdorff distance measure $d_H$ into RBF kernel formula (17), we obtain a new RBF kernel for dealing with interval data.

## Symbolic Faces

Consider the face images $\Gamma_1, \Gamma_2, \ldots, \Gamma_n$, each of size $N \times M$, from a face image database. Let $\Omega = \{\Gamma_1, \ldots, \Gamma_n\}$ be the collection of $n$ face images of the database, which are first order objects. Each object $\Gamma_l \in \Omega, l = 1, \ldots, n$, is described by a feature vector $\left( \tilde{Y}_1, \ldots, \tilde{Y}_p \right)$, of length $p = NM$, where each component $\tilde{Y}_j, \ j = 1, \ldots, p,$ is a single valued variable representing the intensity values of the face image $\Gamma_l$. An image set is a collection of face images of $m$ different subjects (face classes). Thus, there are $m$ number of second order objects (face classes) denoted by $E = \{c_1, c_2, \ldots, c_m\}$, each consisting of different individual images, $\Gamma_l \in \Omega$, of a subject. The view range of each face class is partitioned into q sub face classes and each sub face class contains r number of images. The feature vector of $k^{th}$ sub face class $c_i^k$ of $i^{th}$ face class $c_i$, where $k = 1\ 2, \ldots, q$, is described by a vector of $p$ interval variables $Y_1, \ldots, Y_p$, and is of length $p = NM$. The interval variable $Y_j$ of $k^{th}$ sub face class $c_i^k$ of $i^{th}$ face class is described as

$$Y_j(c_i^k) = [\underline{x}_{ij}^k, \overline{x}_{ij}^k], \qquad (19)$$

where $\underline{x}_{ij}^k$ and $\overline{x}_{ij}^k$ are minimum and maximum intensity values, respectively, among $j^{th}$ pixels of all the images of sub face class $c_i^k$. This interval incorporates variability of $j^{th}$ feature inside the $k^{th}$ sub face class $c_i^k$. We denote:

$$X_i^k = \left( Y_1\left( c_i^k \right), \ldots, Y_p\left( c_i^k \right) \right). \qquad (20)$$

The vector $X_i^k$ of interval variables is recorded for $k^{th}$ sub face class $c_i^k$ of $i^{th}$ face class. This vector is called as *symbolic face* and is represented as:

$$X_i^k = \left( \alpha_{i1}^k, \ldots, \alpha_{ip}^k \right), \qquad (21)$$

where $\alpha_{ij}^k = Y_j(c_i^k) = [\underline{x}_{ij}^k, \overline{x}_{ij}^{-k}], \quad j = 1, \ldots, p$ and $k = 1, \ldots, q$; $i = 1, 2, \ldots, m$. We represent the $qm$ symbolic faces by a $(qm \times p)$ matrix.

## Symbolic KFD

Let us consider the matrix $\underline{X}$ containing $qm$ symbolic faces pertaining to the given set $\Omega$ of images belonging to $m$ face classes. For a given non linear mapping $\Phi$, the input data space $R^p$ can be mapped into the feature space $H$ by using the proposed RBF kernel function:

$$\Phi : R^p \rightarrow H, X_i^k \rightarrow \Phi(X_i^k), \qquad (22)$$

As a result, a pattern in the original input space $R^p$ is mapped into a potentially much higher dimensional feature vector in the feature space $H$. Since the feature space $H$ is possibly infinite dimensional, it is reasonable to view $H$ as a Hilbert space. The covariance operator on the feature space $H$ can be constructed by:

$$S_t^\Phi = \frac{1}{qm} \sum_{j=1}^{qm} (\Phi(X_i^k) - m_o^\Phi)(\Phi(X_i^k) - m_o^\Phi)^T, \qquad (23)$$

where $m_o^\Phi = \frac{1}{qm} \sum_{i=1}^{m} \sum_{k=1}^{q} \Phi(X_i^k)$. It is easy to show that every eigenvector of $S_t^\Phi$, $\beta$ can be linearly expanded by

$$\beta = \sum_{i=1}^{m} \sum_{k=1}^{q} a_i^k \Phi(X_i^k). \qquad (24)$$

To obtain the expansion coefficients, let us denote:

$$Q = \left[ \Phi(X_1^1), \ldots, \Phi(X_1^q), \ldots, \Phi(X_m^1), \ldots, \Phi(X_m^q) \right]$$

and form a $qm \times qm$ Gram matrix $\tilde{R} = Q^T Q$, whose elements can be determined by virtue of kernel tricks.

$$\tilde{R} = \Phi(X_i^k)^T \Phi(X_j^k)$$
$$= (\Phi(X_i^k) \cdot \Phi(X_j^k)) = k(X_i^k, X_j^k).$$

Centralize $\tilde{R}$ and calculate the orthonormal eigenvectors $V_1, V_2, \ldots, V_S$ corresponding to the $S$ largest positive eigenvalues $\lambda_1 \geq \lambda_2 \geq \ldots \geq \lambda_S$. The orthonormal eigenvectors $\beta_1, \beta_2, \ldots, \beta_S$ of $S_t^\Phi$ corresponding to the $S$ largest positive eigenvalues are:

$$\beta_j = \frac{1}{\sqrt{\lambda_j}} Q V_j, \qquad j = 1, \ldots, S. \qquad (25)$$

After the projection of the mapped symbolic face $\Phi(X_i^k)$ onto the eigenvector system $\beta_1, \beta_2, \ldots, \beta_S$, we can obtain the symbolic KPCA transformed feature vector $y = (y_1, y_2, \ldots, y_S)^T$ by

$$y = P^T \Phi(X_i^k), \qquad (26)$$

where $P = (\beta_1, \beta_2, \ldots, \beta_S)$. Specifically, the $j^{th}$ symbolic KPCA component $y_j$ is obtained by

$$y_j = \beta_j^T \Phi(X_i^k) = \frac{1}{\sqrt{\lambda_j}} V_j^T Q^T \Phi(X_i^k) \qquad (27)$$

$$= \frac{1}{\lambda_j} V_j^T [K(X_1^1, X_i^k), \ldots, K(X_1^q, X_i^k), \ldots, K(X_m^1, X_i^k), \ldots, K(X_m^q, X_i^k)] \qquad (28)$$

Let us define the two matrices $S_b$ and $S_w$, which are between and within class scatter matrices in $R^S$. We can construct them directly by

$$S_b = \frac{1}{qm} \sum_{i=1}^{m} q_i (m_i - m_0)(m_i - m_0)^T, \qquad (29)$$

$$S_w = \frac{1}{qm} \sum_{i=1}^{m} \sum_{k=1}^{q_i} (X_i^k - m_i)(X_i^k - m_i)^T, \qquad (30)$$

where $X_i^k$ denotes the $k^{th}$ symbolic face of $i^{th}$ face class, $q_i$ is the number of symbolic faces in face class $i$, $m_i$ is the mean of the symbolic faces belong to face class $i$, $m_0$ is the mean across all $qm$ symbolic faces. Since $\beta_1, \beta_2, ..., \beta_S$ are eigenvectors of $S_t^{\Phi}$ corresponding to positive eigenvalues, this transformation maps the input space $R^p$ into $R^S$ Now let us view the issues in the symbolic KPCA transformed space $R^S$. Since $S_b$ and $S_w$ are between class and within class scatter matrices in the Fisher criterion function can be defined by

$$J(\eta) = \frac{\eta^T S_b \eta}{\eta^T S_w \eta} (\eta \neq 0), \qquad (31)$$

where $\eta_1, \eta_2, ..., \eta_d$ are the associated Fisher optimal discriminant vectors. Since, each symbolic face $X_i^k$ is located between the lower bound symbolic face $\underline{X}_i^k$ and upper bound symbolic face $\bar{X}_i^k$, so it is possible to obtain the Fisher linear discriminating interval type features $[\underline{B}_i^k, \bar{B}_i^k]$ in the KPCA transformed space $R^S$, by using the following transformation: The lower bound features of each symbolic face $X_i^k$ is given by

$$\underline{B}_i^k = G^T y, \qquad (32)$$

where $G = (\eta_1, \eta_2, ..., \eta_d)$ and $y = P^T \Phi(\underline{X}_i^k)$, $P = (\beta_1, \beta_2, ..., \beta_S)$. Similarly the upper bound features of each symbolic face $X_i^k$ is given by

$$\bar{B}_i^k = G^T y, \qquad (33)$$

where $G = (\eta_1, \eta_2, ..., \eta_d)$ and $y = P^T \Phi(\bar{X}_i^k)$, $P = (\beta_1, \beta_2, ..., \beta_S)$ Let $c_{test} = [\Gamma_1, \Gamma_2, ..., \Gamma_l]$ be the test face class that contains face images of same subject with different expression, lighting condition and orientation. The test symbolic face $X_{test}$ is constructed for test face class $c_{test}$ as explained in the previous section. The lower bound test symbolic face of test symbolic face $X_{test}$ is described as:

$$\underline{X}_{test} = \left( \underline{x}_1^{test}, \underline{x}_2^{test}, ..., \underline{x}_p^{test} \right).$$

Similarly, the upper bound test symbolic face is described as:

$$\bar{X}_{test} = \left( \bar{x}_1^{test}, \bar{x}_2^{test}, ..., \bar{x}_p^{test} \right).$$

The interval type features $[\underline{B}^{test}, \bar{B}^{test}]$ of test symbolic face $X_{test}$ are computed as:

$$\underline{B}^{test} = G^T y, \qquad (34)$$

where $G = (\eta_1, \eta_2, ..., \eta_d)$ and $y = P^T \Phi(\underline{X}_{test})$, $P = (\beta_1, \beta_2, ..., \beta_S)$.

$$\bar{B}^{test} = G^T y, \qquad (35)$$

where $G = (\eta_1, \eta_2, ..., \eta_d)$ and $y = P^T \Phi(\bar{X}_{test})$, $P = (\beta_1, \beta_2, ..., \beta_S)$.

## Face Recognition Based on a Minimum Distance Classifier

When test face class $c_{test}$ is presented to the symbolic KFD classifier, low dimensional interval features $[\underline{B}^{test}, \overline{B}^{test}]$ are derived. Let, $[\underline{B}_i^k, \overline{B}_i^k]$, $i = 1, ..., m; k = 1, ..., q$ be the interval type features of $qm$ symbolic faces. The classifier applies the minimum distance rule for classification using squared Euclidean distance $\delta$:

$$\delta\left([\underline{B}^{test}, \overline{B}^{test}], [\underline{B}_i^k, \overline{B}_i^k]\right) =$$

$$\min_i \delta\left([\underline{B}^{test}, \overline{B}^{test}], [\underline{B}_i^k, \overline{B}_i^k]\right) \rightarrow c_{test} \in c_i. \tag{36}$$

The symbolic KFD interval feature vector $[\underline{B}^{test}, \overline{B}^{test}]$ is classified as belonging to the face class $c_i$, using squared Euclidean distance, which is defined as follows:

$$d([\underline{B}^{test}, \overline{B}^{test}], [\underline{B}_i^k, \overline{B}_i^k]) =$$

$$\sum_{j=1}^p \left[\left(\underline{x}_{ij}^k - \underline{x}_j^{test}\right)^2 + \left(\overline{x}_{ij}^k - \overline{x}_j^{test}\right)^2\right]. \tag{37}$$

## Experimental Results

The experiments are conducted to evaluate the performance of the proposed algorithm using ORL and Yale face database. The ORL database is used to evaluate the proposed method under variable orientation and expression. Yale Face database is selected to test the performance of the proposed method using face images with different facial expressions. The minimum distance classifier with squared Euclidean distance is employed in all the experiments. Since there are many factors which affect face recognition, such as different image resolutions, different face sizes, face skew, different backgrounds and illuminations. The face images in the databases need to be preprocessed before they are used. The normalized face images will have d × d pixels, uniform image mean and variance, and no face skew. The preprocessing includes the location of the positions of the two eyes in the face image, and rotation of the image inversely by an angle specified in the line through the two eyes. Then, clip out the face part from the face image and finally, normalize the luminance mean and variance of the resized face image. All the pre-processed face images have the same size, the same image mean, and the same image standard deviation.

In the training phase for each database, the first step is construction of symbolic faces. If the database images (for example ORL database) contain faces with orientation then training images of each face class are manually arranged from left side view to right view. Otherwise such an arrangement is not required. The face class is partitioned into Q subface classes and each sub face class contains R number of images. Suppose the image size is $P \times P$, then $P^2Q$ - dimensional vectors (symbolic faces) are obtained, and the elements of vectors are the intervals.

To verify an efficiency of dimensionality reduction of proposed method, we display each symbolic face by taking center of the intervals. Suppose displayed image looks like face without loss of information and misalignment then R value will be optimal parameter. Otherwise we need to refine the R value by considering a large number of images in the class. If the faces have more orientation (>10°) in the images then the optimal number of images per symbolic face will be more than two. Therefore, optimal number of images per symbolic face is depends on the characteristics of images such as face orientations of the particular face database. The dimension of feature space for proposed method is depends on the number of symbolic faces constructed.

## Experiments on the ORL Database

The ORL face database (developed at the Olivetti Research Laboratory, Cambridge, U.K.) is composed of 400 images with ten different facial views that represent various expressions and orientations for each of the 40 distinct subjects. All the images were taken against a dark homogeneous background with the subjects in an upright, frontal position, with tolerance for some tilting and rotation of up to about 200. There is some variation in scale of up to about 10%. The spatial and gray level resolutions of the images are $92 \times 112$ and 256, respectively.

In our experiments, based on the eye positions, all these images are preprocessed into the $80 \times 80$ closely cropped face images. Eight images are randomly chosen from the ten images available for each subject for training, while the remaining images are used for testing. In the phase of model selection, our goal is to determine optimal kernel parameters (i.e., the width of the RBF kernel) and optimal dimension of the projection subspace for proposed method. Since it is very difficult to determine these parameters at the same time, a stepwise strategy is adopted here. First we try to find optimal kernel parameter, and then based on the chosen kernel parameter, the selection of the subspace sizes is performed. The Experimental results show that the width of the RBF kernel should be four for proposed symbolic KFD with respect to a minimum distance classifier. After determining the optimal kernel parameter, we set out to select the optimal subspace dimension for proposed method. The optimal subspace size is 28 for symbolic KFD method. Thus, we can conclude that symbolic KFD achieves more dimensionality reduction than other popular methods.

After selection of optimal parameters and optimal subspace for proposed method with respect to new RBF kernel, we apply cross validation testing strategy to evaluate the proposed method.

In the first set of experiments, the above described experiment is repeated in 10 times. Each time, the images are selected in such a way that training sample set and testing set are disjoint. The careful selection strategy was adopted to avoid the repetition of face images in every test. The average recognition rate is shown in Table 1. The maximum and minimum recognition rate is 99.15 and 97.15 respectively. The standard deviation is 0.724396. In the second set of experiments, we have repeated the above experiment 10 times. Each time, we considered some of the training images of first set of experiments as test images and some test images of first set of experiments as training images. The training sample set and testing set are disjoint. The average recognition rate is shown in the Table 1. The maximum and minimum recognition rate is 99.15 and 97.75 respectively. The standard deviation is 0.5385.

We have compared our algorithm with DCT based (Hafed Z.M. and Levine M.D., 2001) face Recognition method, eigenface (Turk and Pentland, 1991), Fisherface (Belhumeur et al., 1997) and classical KFD (Mika et al., 1997). The comparison of classification performance of symbolic KFD is shown in Table 2. We note that the symbolic KFD method outperforms other face recognition methods in the sense of using small number of features. This is due to the fact that first few eigenvectors of symbolic KFD method account for highest variance of training samples and these few eigenvectors are enough to represent image for recognition purposes. Thus, fewer eigenvectors of symbolic KFD are required as compared to the large number of eigenvectors of other face recognition methods necessary to contain the same amount of information, which implies the dimensionality reduction. Hence, improved recognition results can be achieved at less computational cost by using symbolic KFD method, by virtue of its low dimensionality.

*Table 1. Recognition rate (%) of symbolic KFD method using ORL database*

| | 1 | 2 | 3 | 4 | 5 | 6 | 7 | 8 | 9 | 10 | Average |
|---|---|---|---|---|---|---|---|---|---|---|---|
| First set of Experiments | 97.15 | 97.85 | 99.00 | 99.15 | 98.15 | 98.00 | 97.75 | 98.45 | 97.45 | 99.10 | 98.20 |
| Second set of Experiments | 99.15 | 97.75 | 99.00 | 97.75 | 98.45 | 98.25 | 98.65 | 98.50 | 97.75 | 97.75 | 98.30 |

*Table 2. Comparison of classification performance using ORL database*

| Method | Recognition Rate (%) | Feature Dimension |
|---|---|---|
| Eigenface (Liu and Wechsler, 2000) | 89.00 | 138 |
| Fisherface (Yang M.H, 2002) | 80.94 | 39 |
| DCT based method (Liu et al., 2000) | 92.00 | 49 (DCT coefficients) |
| KFD (Yu and Yang, 2001) | 97.25 | 38 |
| Proposed Symbolic KFD | 98.25 | 28 |

## Experiments on the Yale Face Database

The Yale Face database (Belhumeur et al., 1997) consists of a total 165 images obtained from 15 different people, with 11 images from each person. The images contain variations in the following facial expressions or configurations: center-light, with glasses, happy, left light, without glasses, normal, right light, sad, sleepy, surprised and wink.

As described earlier, we have preprocessed these images by aligning and scaling them so that the distances between the eyes were the same for all images and also ensuring that the eyes occurred in the same co-ordinates of the image. The resulting image was then cropped. The final image was 128 × 128 The model selection process is performed using the same method as in previous section. The experimental results show that the width of the RBF kernel is three and optimal dimension of the projection subspace for proposed method is 14 with respect to a minimum distance classifier. We have adopted cross validation testing strategy to evaluate the proposed method. In our experiments, 9 images are randomly chosen from each class for training, while the remaining two images

are used for testing. The ten-fold experiments are conducted by changing the training and testing images. The average recognition rate is shown in Table 3. The maximum and minimum recognition rate is 97.85 and 94.65 respectively. The standard deviation is 0.9749.

We have compared our proposed algorithm with eigenface (Turk and Pentland, 1991) and Fisherface (Belhumeur et al., 1997). The recognition rates and optimal subspace dimension are listed in Table 4. It is observed that symbolic KFD achieves improved recognition rates.

## FUTURE RESEARCH DIRECTIONS

The most effective face recognition algorithm presented in this chapter is the resultant combination of appearance-based face recognition technique with symbolic data analysis using statistical technique. There is still a great deal of development that may be done in this area. Firstly, one can extend the multi-linear approach, called Tensorfaces, proposed by Vasilescu and Terzopoulos (2003) to symbolic data analysis. The combination of SDA with Tensorfaces could

*Table 3. Recognition rate (%) of symbolic KFD method using Yale face database*

| Experiment # | 1 | 2 | 3 | 4 | 5 | 6 | 7 | 8 | 9 | 10 | Average |
|---|---|---|---|---|---|---|---|---|---|---|---|
| Symbolic KFD | 96.15 | 97.85 | 95.45 | 94.65 | 96.15 | 95.50 | 95.50 | 94.75 | 96.00 | 97.00 | 95.90 |

*Table 4. Comparison of classification performance using Yale face database*

| Methods | Recognition Rates (%) | Feature dimension |
|---|---|---|
| Eigenface (Belhumeur et al., 1997) | 84.07 | 30 |
| Fisherfaces (Belhumeur et al., 1997) | 92.07 | 15 |
| Proposed Symbolic KFD | 95.90 | 14 |

perform better for face images with larger variations in pose, expressions and lighting conditions. Secondly, the proposed approach of combining appearance-based method with SDA can be applied to 2D/3D object recognition in still/video images. Thirdly, the proposed algorithm can be employed more effectively in CBIR techniques for face image retrieval from face image databases, which is a very significant problem in criminal investigation. Thus, the present research work does open up new avenues of research in the area of Computer Vision.

## CONCLUSION

In this chapter, we have presented the symbolic KFD method with RBF kernel function for face recognition. The analysis of face space is carried out using interval-valued subspace in which interval type features are extracted. This modification tremendously changes the performance of symbolic KFD compared to classical subspace techniques and it has been evaluated successfully using standard databases, namely, ORL database and Yale face database. The experimental results show that the symbolic KFD achieves improved recognition rates as compared to other popular face recognition methods. The experimental results demonstrate the efficacy of the proposed method.

The robustness of the algorithm is primarily due to the interval type features which capture the face image variability of the same person owing to pose, illumination and facial expression variations. Furthermore, the symbolic KFD has low computational cost, require little memory space, and can overcome retraining problem. Based on these results, the symbolic KFD is useful in the design of real-time face recognition systems.

## REFERENCES

Bartlett, H., Lades, M., & Sejnowski, T. J. (1998). Independent component representations for face recognition. In . *Proceedings of the SPIE: Conference on Human Vision and Electronic Imaging, 3299,* 528–539.

Baudat, B., & Anouar, A. (2000). Generalized discriminant analysis using kernel approach. *Neural Computation,* 2385–2404. doi:10.1162/089976600300014980

Belhumeur, P., Hespanha, J., & Kriegman, D. (1997). Eigenfaces vs. Fisherfaces: Recognition using class specific linear projection. *IEEE Transactions on Pattern Analysis and Machine Intelligence, 19*(7), 711–720. doi:10.1109/34.598228

Bock, H. H., & Diday, E. (2000). *Analysis of symbolic data*. Springer Verlag.

Chengjun, L. (2004). Gabor based kernel PCA with fractional power polynomial models for face recognition. *IEEE Transactions on Pattern Recognition and Machine Intelligence, 26*(5), 572–581. doi:10.1109/TPAMI.2004.1273927

Etemad, K., & Chellappa, R. (1997). Discriminant analysis for recognition of human face images . *Journal of the Optical Society of America, 14*, 1724–1733. doi:10.1364/JOSAA.14.001724

Hafed, Z. M., & Levine, M. D. (2001). Face recognition using the discrete cosine transforms. *International Journal of Computer Vision, 43*(3), 167–188. doi:10.1023/A:1011183429707

Hiremath, P. S., & Prabhakar, C. J. (2006). Acquiring non linear subspace for face recognition using symbolic kernel PCA method. *Journal of Symbolic Data Analysis, 4*, 15–26.

Hiremath, P. S., & Prabhakar, C. J. (2008a). Extraction and recognition of non linear interval type features using symbolic KDA algorithm with application to face recognition. *Research Letters in Signal Processing, 2*, 1–5.

Hiremath, P. S., & Prabhakar, C. J. (2008b). Symbolic factorial discriminant analysis for illumination invariant face recognition. *International Journal of Pattern Recognition and Artificial Intelligence, 22*(3), 371–387. doi:10.1142/S021800140800634X

Hiremath, P. S., & Prabhakar, C. J. (2009). Symbolic kernel Fisher discriminant method with a new RBF kernel function for face recognition. *International Journal of Machine Graphics and Vision, 18*(4), 383–404.

Kirby, M., & Sirovich, L. (1990). Application of the Karhunen-Loeve procedure for the characterization of human faces. *IEEE Transactions on Pattern Analysis and Machine Intelligence, 12*(1), 103–108. doi:10.1109/34.41390

Liu, C., & Wechsler, H. (2000). Robust coding schemes for indexing and retrieval from large face databases. *IEEE Transactions on Image Processing, 9*(1), 132–137. doi:10.1109/83.817604

Liu, C., & Wechsler, H. (2000). Evolutionary pursuit and its appliction to face recognition. *IEEE Transactions on Pattern Analysis and Machine Intelligence, 22*(6), 570–582. doi:10.1109/34.862196

Mika, S., Ratsch, G., & Muller, K. R. (2001). A mathematical programming approach to the kernel Fisher Algorithm. *Advances in Neural Information Processing Systems, 13*, 591–597.

Mika, S., Ratsch, G., Weston, J., Scholkopf, B., & Mullers, K. R. (1999). Fisher discriminant analysis with kernels. *Proceedings of IEEE International Workshop on Neural Networks for Signal Processing*, (pp. 41-48).

Moghaddam, B. (1999). Principal manifolds and probabilistic subspaces for visual recognition. In *Proceedings of International Conference on Computer Vision*, (pp. 1131-1136).

Moghaddam, B. (2002). Principal manifolds and probabilistic subspaces for visual recognition. *IEEE Transactions on Pattern Analysis and Machine Intelligence, 24*(6), 780–788. doi:10.1109/TPAMI.2002.1008384

Moghaddam, B., & Pentland, A. (1997). Probabilistic visual learning for object representation. *IEEE Transactions on Pattern Analysis and Machine Intelligence, 19*(7), 696–710. doi:10.1109/34.598227

Penev, P. S., & Sirovich, L. (2000). The global dimensionality of face space. In *Proceedings of IEEE International Conference on Face and Gesture Recognition,* (pp. 264-270), Grenoble, France.

Phillips, P. J., Moon, H., Rizvi, S. A., & Rauss, P. J. (2000). The FERET evaluation methodology for face recognition algorithms. *IEEE Transactions on Pattern Analysis and Machine Intelligence,* *22*(10), 1090–1104. doi:10.1109/34.879790

Scholkopf, B., Smola, A., & Muller, K. (1998). Nonlinear component analysis as a kernel Eigenvalue problem. *Neural Computation,* *10,* 1299–1319. doi:10.1162/089976698300017467

Scholkopf, B., & Smola, A. J. (2002). *Learning with kernels: Support vector machines, regularization, optimization, and beyond.* Cambridge, MA: MIT Press.

Sirovich, L., & Kirby, M. (1987). Low-dimensional procedure for the characterization of human face. *Journal of the Optical Society of America,* *4,* 519–524. doi:10.1364/JOSAA.4.000519

Sung, K. K., & Poggio, T. (1997). Example-based learning for view-based human face detection. *IEEE Transactions on Pattern Analysis and Machine Intelligence,* *20*(1), 39–51. doi:10.1109/34.655648

Swets, D. L., & Weng, J. J. (1996). Using discriminant eigenfeatures for image retrieval. *IEEE Transactions on Pattern Analysis and Machine Intelligence,* *18*(8), 831–836. doi:10.1109/34.531802

Tipping, M. E., & Bishop, C. M. (1997). *Probabilistic principal component analysis.* Technical Report NCRG/97/010, Aston University.

Turk, M., & Pentland, A. (1991). Eigenfaces for recognition. *Journal of Cognitive Neuroscience,* *3*(1), 71–86. doi:10.1162/jocn.1991.3.1.71

Van Gestel, T., Suykens, J. A. K., De Brabanter, J., De Moor, B., & Vandewalle, J. (2001). Least squares support vector machine regression for discriminant analysis. *Proc. International Joint INNS-IEEE Conf. Neural Networks (INNS2001),* (pp. 2445-2450). New York, NY: Wiley.

Vapnik, V. N. (1998). *Statistical learning theory.* New York, NY: Wiley.

Vasilescu, M. A. O., & Terzopoulos, D. (2003). Multilinear subspace analysis of image ensembles. In *Proceedings of IEEE Computer Vision and Pattern Recognition,* (pp. 93-99). Madison, WI.

Yang, M. H. (2002). Kernel eigenfaces vs. kernel fisherfaces: Face recognition using kernel methods. *Proceedings of the Fifth IEEE International Conference on Automatic Face and Gesture Recognition,* (pp. 215-220).

Yang, M. H., Ahuja, N., & Kriegman, D. (2000). Face recognition using kernel eigenfaces. *Proceedings of IEEE International Conference on Image Processing,* *1,* (pp. 37-40).

Yu, H., & Yang, J. (2001). A Direct LDA algorithm for high dimensional data with application to face recognition. *Pattern Recognition,* *34*(7), 2067–2070. doi:10.1016/S0031-3203(00)00162-X

Zhao, L., & Yang, Y. H. (1999). Theoretical analysis of illumination in PCA based vision systems. *Pattern Recognition,* *32,* 547–564. doi:10.1016/S0031-3203(98)00119-8

Zhao, W., Chellappa, R., & Krishnaswamy, A. (1998). Discriminant analysis of principal components for face recognition. In *Proceedings of International Conference on Automatic Face and Gesture Recognition,* (pp. 336-341).

Zhao, W., Chellappa, R., & Phillips, P. (1999). *Subspace linear discriminant analysis for face recognition. Technical Report, CS-TR4009.* University of Maryland.

Zhao, W., Chellappa, R., Phillips, P. J., & Rosenfeld, A. (2003). Face recognition: A literature survey. *ACM Computing Surveys, 35*(4), 399–458. doi:10.1145/954339.954342

## ADDITIONAL READING

Bartelett, M. S., Movellan, J. R., & Sejnowski, T. J. (2002). Face recognition by Independent component analysis. *IEEE Transactions on Neural Networks, 13*, 1450–1464. doi:10.1109/TNN.2002.804287

Bell, A. J., & Sejnowski, T. J. (1995). An information maximization approach to blind separation and blind deconvolution. *Neural Computation, 7*, 1129–1159. doi:10.1162/neco.1995.7.6.1129

Boser, B. E., Guyon, I. M., & Vapnik, V. N. (1992). A training algorithm for optimal margin classifiers. *In Proceedings of workshop on Computational Learning Theory,* (pp. 144-152).

Brunelli, R., & Poggio, T. (1993). Face recognition: Features vs. templates. *IEEE Transactions on Pattern Analysis and Machine Intelligence, 15*(10), 1042–1052. doi:10.1109/34.254061

Chen, H. F., Belhumeur, P. N., & Jacobs, D. W. (2000). In search of Illumination Invariants. *In Proceedings of IEEE CVPR 2000,* (pp. 254-261).

Chen, L. F., Liao, H. Y. M., Ko, M. T., Lin, J. C., & Yu, G. J. (2000). A new LDA based face recognition system which can solve the small sample size problem. *Pattern Recognition, 33*, 1713–1726. doi:10.1016/S0031-3203(99)00139-9

Chen, W. S., Yuen, P. C., Huang, J., & Dai, D. Q. (2005). Kernel machine-based one parameter regularized Fisher discriminant method for face recognition. *IEEE Transactions on System, Man, and Cybernatics - Part B, 35*(4), 659–669. doi:10.1109/TSMCB.2005.844596

Draper, B. A., Baek, K., Bartlett, M. S., & Beveridge, J. R. (2003). Recognizing faces with PCA and ICA. *Computer Vision and Image Understanding, 91*(12), 115–137. doi:10.1016/S1077-3142(03)00077-8

Hallinan (1995). *A Deformable Model for Face Recognition Under Arbitrary Lighting Conditions.* PhD thesis, Harvard University.

Lee, K. C., Ho, J., & Kriegman, D. (2005). Acquiring Linear Subspaces for Face Recognition under Variable Lighting. *IEEE Transactions on Pattern Analysis and Machine Intelligence, 27*(5), 1–15.

Lin, S. H., Kung, S. Y., & Lin, L. J. (1997). Face recognition/Detection by Probabilistic Decision Based Neural Network. *IEEE Transactions on Neural Networks, 8*(1), 114–132. doi:10.1109/72.554196

Liu, C., & Wechsler, H. (2003). Independent Component Analysis of Gobor Features for Face Recognition. *IEEE Transactions on Neural Networks, 14*(4), 919–928. doi:10.1109/TNN.2003.813829

Lu, J., Plataniotis, K. N., & Venetsanopoulos, A. N. (2003). Face Recognition using LDA based algorithms. *IEEE Transactions on Neural Networks, 14*(1), 195–200. doi:10.1109/TNN.2002.806647

Lu, J., Plataniotis, K. N., & Venetsanopoulos, A. N. (2003). Face recognition using kernel direct discriminant analysis algorithms. *IEEE Transactions on Neural Networks, 14*(1), 117–126. doi:10.1109/TNN.2002.806629

Lu, X., & Jain, A. K. (2005). *Multimodal Facial Feature Extraction for automatic 3D Face Recognition. Technical Report.* Department of Computer Science, Michigan State University.

Moon, H., & Phillips, P. J. (2001). Computational and performance aspects of PCA-based face recognition algorithms. *Perception, 30*, 303–321. doi:10.1068/p2896

Muller, K. R., Mika, S., Ratsch, G., Tsuda, K., & Scholkopf, B. (2001). An Introduction to kernel based Learning Algorithms. *IEEE Transactions on Neural Networks, 12*(2), 181–201. doi:10.1109/72.914517

Murase, H., & Nayar, S. K. (1995). Visual learning and recognition of 3D objects from appearance. *International Journal of Computer Vision, 14*(1), 5–24. doi:10.1007/BF01421486

Yang, J., Frangi, A. F., Yang, J. Y., Zhang, D., & Jin, Z. (2005). KPCA Plus LDA: A Complete Kernel Fisher Discriminant Framework for Feature Extraction and Recognition. *IEEE Transactions on Pattern Analysis and Machine Intelligence, 27*(2), 230–244. doi:10.1109/TPAMI.2005.33

Zhang, L., & Samaras, D. (2003). Face recognition under variable lighting using harmonic image exemplars. *IEEE Conference on Computer Vision and Pattern Recognition*, (pp. 19-25).

## KEY TERMS AND DEFINITIONS

**Face Image Analysis:** Face images consist of large information and the analysis on these images can be useful for various purposes. The face image analysis concerns the extraction of information from an image. In a general sense, an image yields data, which can be used for various purposes. In the case of face image analysis, the extracted data can be the measurement results associated with specific face image properties or the representative symbols of face attributes.

**Face Space:** The face images are represented by high-dimensional pixel arrays, which forms manifold of low dimension.

**Kernel Fischer Discriminant Analysis (KFDA):** KFDA finds the direction in a feature space, defined implicitly by a kernel, onto which the projections of positive and negative classes are well separated in terms of Fisher discriminant ratio (FDR). KFDA combines the kernel trick with FLDA. Firstly the kernel trick is used to project the input data into an implicit feature space through nonlinear kernel mapping, then FLDA is performed in this feature space, thus a nonlinear discriminant can be yielded in the input data.

**Kernel Function:** In support vector machines, the kernel function is a generalization of the distance metric; it measures the distance between two expression vectors as the data are projected into higher-dimensional space. The kernel trick transforms any algorithm that solely depends on the dot product between two vectors. Wherever a dot product is used, it is replaced with the kernel function.

**Subspace:** Let K be a field (such as the field of real numbers), and let V be a vector space over K. As usual, we call elements of V vectors and call elements of K scalars. Suppose that W is a subset of V. If W is a vector space itself, with the same vector space operations as V has, then it is a subspace of V.

**Symbolic Data Analysis (SDA):** Data analysis using statistical methods have been developed for the analysis of single valued variables. There are many cases in which more complete information can be surely achieved by describing a set of statistical units in terms of interval data. Symbolic data analysis deals with such interval data. The gist of symbolic approach in pattern classification is to extend problems and methods on classical data to interval data, which is adapted to represent knowledge.

# Chapter 8
# Object Recognition with a Limited Database Using Shape Space Theory

**Yuexing Han**
*National Institute of Advanced Industrial Science and Technology, Japan*

**Bing Wang**
*University of Tokyo, Japan*

**Hideki Koike**
*University of Electro-Communications, Japan*

**Masanori Idesawa**
*University of Electro-Communications, Japan*

## ABSTRACT

*One of the main goals of image understanding and computer vision applications is to recognize an object from various images. Object recognition has been deeply developed for the last three decades, and a lot of approaches have been proposed. Generally, these methods of object recognition can successfully achieve their goal by relying on a large quantity of data. However, if the observed objects are shown to diverse configurations, it is difficult to recognize them with a limited database. One has to prepare enough data to exactly recognize one object with multi-configurations, and it is hard work to collect enough data only for a single object. In this chapter, the authors will introduce an approach to recognize objects with multi-configurations using the shape space theory. Firstly, two sets of landmarks are obtained from two objects in two-dimensional images. Secondly, the landmarks represented as two points are projected into a pre-shape space. Then, a series of new intermediate data can be obtained from data models in the pre-shape space. Finally, object recognition can be achieved in the shape space with the shape space theory.*

DOI: 10.4018/978-1-61350-429-1.ch008

# 1. INTRODUCTION

In the area of computer vision, object recognition has been considered as the most important research subject. One of the main goals of image understanding and computer vision applications is to recognize objects from various images. The goal of object recognition is to build computer-based vision systems which perform the same functions as the human vision system. Object recognition has been applied in a lot of domains such as industrial machine vision, computer-assisted medical image analysis and treatment, exploiting handwritten digits, information management systems, image processing, process control, multiphase screening and analysis, content-based image retrieval. Many approaches have been proposed for object recognition, and we will describe the basic idea of object recognition and some important approaches in Section 2.

In general terms, a shape of an object can be defined as the total of all information that includes invariance under translations, rotations, and rescaling. If two shapes of two objects are similar in the sense of some geometry, e.g., Euclidean geometry, the two objects can be considered to have the same shape. Not only Euclidean geometry theory, but also some other theories have been used in the area of object recognition, e.g. the shape space theory. The shape space concept has been introduced by Kendall for describing the shape formed by a set of random points, and it has been used subsequently in shape-related statistical problems in archaeology and astronomy (Kendall, 1984) and object recognition (Zhang, 1998; Zhang, 2003; Glover, 2006; Glover, 2008; Han, 2010). Since the approaches of object recognition in this chapter are based on this theory, we will introduce the basic knowledge of the shape space theory and its pre-shape spaces in detail in Section 3.

Current object recognition systems are generally limited to the recognition of objects which are presented in their database and any deviation from these objects renders the object in the scene as unrecognizable and unmatched. Generally, data in the database corresponds to an observed object. But some objects may possess many configurations, e.g., scissors and pliers with various opening degrees. Recognizing the sort of objects with many configurations is defined as *the Recognition of Multiple Configurations of Objects* (RMCO) (Han, 2010). Humans can easily recognize various configurations of an object, since our brain has a highly efficient system for self-learning including object recognition. But for machines or robots, it is very difficult to achieve RMCO. Generally, to recognize objects with many alterable configurations, multiple data are needed in the database. However it is hard to collect a large amount of data to recognize such objects. Since recognition systems ultimately need to be designed for operation in the real world, it is reasonable to require that the system has the ability to learn about new objects that it may encounter and add them to its database. So it is emergent and necessary to be able to build new data based on the original data in the database to match more observed objects. In this chapter, we will describe an approach to augment a database by obtaining new data from a continuous curve between any two pre-shapes in a pre-shape space without calculating any orthogonal geodesics. We will introduce the work in detail in Section 4.

After augmenting database, we can use the new data to match the observed objects. We will describe a series of algorithms of object recognition based on the shape space theory, and give some examples in Section 5, where the objects are differentiated in static state and in dynamic state. We will also extend the works in the future in Section 6 and give a brief conclusion in Section 7.

# 2. BACKGROUND

The problem in object recognition is to determine what the observed objects are, if a given set of data objects includes analogues of the observed objects. Current understanding of the recognition process divides recognition into three phases (Grimson, 1990):

1. **Selection:** what subset of the data corresponds to the object?
2. **Indexing:** which object model corresponds to the data subset?
3. **Correspondence:** which individual model features correspond to each data feature?

Thus, object recognition is a process of hypothesizing an object-to-model correspondence and then verifying if the hypothesis is correct. On one hand, if an error between the projected model features and its corresponding object features is below a threshold, the hypothesis is considered correct; on the other hand, if the error is larger than the threshold, the hypothesis is considered incorrect.

In the following, some of the theories that have been proposed for object recognition over the past 40 years are described (Pal, 2002). Some of them are models of human vision, and others are possible schemes for machine vision. Some of the proposed schemes are general in nature and other groups of them were developed for specific application domains (Besl, 1985; Binford, 1981). Various approaches to object recognition are based on different methods of extracting features from images, whether the process relies primarily on two or three-dimensional information. Furthermore, they are dependent on the objects variability and the observed places.

These kinds of theories are described as follows.

1. **The Manifold Approach:** This is a common approach for object recognition which assumed that objects have certain invariant properties that are common to all of their views (Pitts, 1947). If there are $n$ different properties, mostly landmarks, extracted from an object, the object can be represented by a point made up of the $n$ properties. Then, the point can be projected into a $n$-dimensional space or its subspace. The space or the subspace is a manifold surface. This representation is very useful to identify and classify objects with some criteria, e.g. a sort of distance. In the shape space theory, a shape space is a manifold space.

2. **The Statistical (Probability) Approach:** Statistics and probability theory are realized as ideal tools when pattern recognition which includes object recognition was beginning to develop as a distinct subject. The statistical approach can help us to model the inherent variability of objects via multivariate probability distributions. The approach provides a consistent framework for the quantification and manipulation of uncertainty, and it becomes one of the central foundations for pattern recognition. Fisher (1936) has firstly proposed the classical approach, and Rao (1948) has extended it later. Over the years, a multitude of alternative techniques have been developed for two-dimensional and three-dimensional object recognition.

3. **The Syntactic Approach:** In the area of pattern recognition, various approaches beside the statistical approach, the structural information that describes objects are also important. However, a significant shortcoming of the statistical approach and most of the other subsequent approaches for object recognition is the fact that it is difficult to use them to handle contextual or structural information from objects. We can use the syntactic approach to overcome the shortcoming to recognize objects. An object can be decomposed into simpler sub-shapes, and each one can be decomposed into even simpler sub-shapes again, and so on. It is no longer looked upon as arrays of numbers, and it can be described in terms of very simple sub-elements. Using these sub-elements, the syntactic approach works very well for idealized patterns.

4. **The ANNs Approach:** The "Artificial Neural Networks" (ANNs) simulates the architecture and processing mechanism of the human nervous system. ANNs, which is based on the actual biology, are mathematical inventions inspired by observations made in the study of biological systems. An ANN is described as mapping an input space to an output space. Generally, there are three broad paradigms of learning: supervised, unsupervised and reinforcement. In the area of pattern recognition, it has been established that ANNs are natural classifiers to resist to noise and tolerate distorted images. ANNs have the superior ability to recognize partially occluded or degraded images or to discriminate among overlapping pattern classes.

5. **The Data Mining and Knowledge Discovery Approach:** The approach of data mining and knowledge discovery can deal with the process of identifying valid, novel, potentially useful, and ultimately understandable patterns in data. They can be applied to object recognition and machine learning principles in the context of voluminous, heterogeneous data sets.

6. **The Genetic Algorithms Approach:** Genetic algorithms (GAs) are a type of parallel heuristic randomized search and optimization techniques. They are regulated by the laws of genetics since the techniques are inspired by the principle of survival of the fittest governing evolution and selection in natural populations. Technique of GAs has become an appropriate and a natural choice to achieve many of problems including object recognition. Many researchers have developed object recognition based on GAs during the past twenty years.

7. **The Fuzzy Set Theoretic Approach:** The approach has been proposed by Zadeh (1965), which can be used in knowledge-based approaches to achieve pattern recognition problems. With the knowledge-based approaches, classes are described by rules and recognition tasks are accomplished through automated reasoning or inference procedures. These describing rules can be solved with fuzzy logic.

8. **The Geometric Approach:** Generally, the most reliable information of an object in an image is geometric information. So a library of geometric models is built in an object recognition system, containing the geometric information about the shapes of the known objects. Usually, recognition is considered successful if the geometric configuration of an object can correspond with a geometric model of the object.

9. **The Hybrid Approach:** In the context of object recognition, based on other approaches, various hybrid methods have been developed by taking into account the merits of the constituent technologies. A combination of some methods and techniques are more robust.

The above mentioned approaches are basic ones for object recognition. In the chapter, we will introduce how to achieve RMCO using geometric invariants of objects in two-dimensional images and knowledge of manifold learning, i.e., the shape space theory. David Kendall published a brief note (Kendall, 1977) in which a representation of shapes was introduced as elements of complex projective spaces in 1977. Following a sequence of conferences around the world, David Kendall continued to introduce his theory and some applications to problems in archeology. These talks in the conferences gradually generated wider interest after presented with great clarity and with excellent graphics (Small, 1996). It was not until 1984 that the full details of the theory were published (Kendall, 1984). At that point it became clear that Kendall's shape theory, i.e., the shape space theory, was developed greatly and contained some interesting research areas for object recognition, the archeological, astronomical sciences, three-dimensional animation, and studying the shapes of random sets of points such as the points in a Poisson scattering.

A key step of using the shape space theory is that the induced distribution of shape is obtained, i.e., extracting landmarks from shape. Landmarks are feature points of objects, and they can determine what the observed object is. There are three basic types of landmarks in the applications of object recognition: *anatomical, mathematical and pseudo-landmarks*. In the literature there have been various synonyms words for landmarks, including vertices, anchor points, control points, sites, profile points, sampling points, design points, key points, facets, node, model points, markers, fiducial markers, etc (Dryden, 1998). Humans can recognize objects or navigate them by recognizing reference points. Sometimes, computers and machines more rely on landmarks than humans, which landmarks may be on contours or contexts of objects, because features points are generally characteristic local image structures with some meaningful information. Obtaining landmarks is an important step of some methods of object recognition including the method using the shape space theory. Landmarks extraction process is composed of interesting point detection, invariant neighborhood extraction and description. Many approaches of obtaining landmarks from objects have been proposed and discussed (Hoffman, 1984; Forstner, 1987; Bookstein, 1996; Bookstein, 1997; Fatemizadeh, 2003; Zhang, 2003; Saeng-deejing, 2003; Han, 2010; Han(IPTA), 2010). We will not describe the methods of obtaining landmarks in this chapter. For more detail of obtaining landmarks, please refer to the above mentioned papers.

# 3. THE SHAPE SPACE THEORY

A shape space is used to describe an object and all its variations by an equivalent class, which can be represented as a point in the non-Euclidean space. In shape spaces, we don't need to consider the shapes' position, scaling, and orientation. Then object recognition can then be achieved with the shape space analysis, i.e., the shortest distance, which is called the Procrustean distance or the Procrustean metric in shape spaces. Recently, the theories and applications of the shape spaces have been developed rapidly, and more and more researchers have explored two-dimensional graphs and three-dimensional graphs by using the theory. In this section, we will introduce shape spaces of two-dimensional shapes.

## 3.1 Pre-Shape Space and Shape Space for Shapes in Two-Dimensional Euclidean Space

A two-dimensional shape can be represented by a set of points of two-dimensional space, called landmarks of the shape. Let the landmarks be represented by a feature point in Euclidean space,

$$P = \left\{ p_1\left(x_1, y_1\right), p_2\left(x_2, y_2\right), \cdots, p_n\left(x_n, y_n\right)\right\} \tag{3.1}$$

where $n$ is the total number of landmarks, and $p_i(x_i, y_i)$ is the position of the $i^{th}$ landmark, which can be represented as a point in $R^{2n}$, the $2n$-dimensional real space, or in $C^n$, the $n$-dimensional complex space. One of virtues in shape space is that the effects associated with translation, scaling and rotation are filtered away. To exclude the effect of position, the means in $x$ and $y$ can be removed simply with the following formula:

$$P' = \left\{ p_i' = \left(x_i - \overline{x}, y_i - \overline{y}\right)\right\} i = 1, \cdots, n \tag{3.2}$$

$\overline{x}$ and $\overline{y}$ are the means and the centroid of $\{x_i\}$ and $\{y_i\}$, respectively, and satisfy the conditions:

$$\overline{x} = \frac{1}{n}\sum_{i=1}^{n} x_i \quad \text{and} \quad \overline{y} = \frac{1}{n}\sum_{i=1}^{n} y_i \, .$$

Now $P'$ satisfies:

$$\sum_{i=1}^{n} p_i' = 0 \tag{3.3}$$

Hence, $P'$ is a point in a $2n-2$-dimensional real hyperplane (isometric to $R^{2n-2}$) passing through the origin of $R^{2n}$; or in a $n-1$ complex hyperline (isometric to $C^{n-1}$) passing through the origin of $C^n$.

After removing the effect of translation, two degrees of freedom are taken away from the feature point. Similarly, we can exclude scaling and denote the resulting point $\tau$ as a *pre-shape* of $P'$:

$$\tau = \frac{P'}{\|P'\|} \tag{3.4}$$

where $\|\cdot\|$ denotes the Euclidean norm, and it is assumed that $\|\cdot\| > 0$. Clearly, the space of all possible pre-shapes of feature points with $n$ landmarks is on a surface of an unit hyper-sphere embedded in a $(2n-2)$-dimensional linear sub-space of $R^{2n}$ or in a $(n-1)$-dimensional linear sub-space of $C^n$.

In the following content, we will describe pre-shape space and shape space. Firstly, we consider that objects are in real space. Since $\|\tau\| = 1$ for all $\tau$, it has $2n-3$ degrees of freedom and we denote the surface of the hyper-sphere as $S_*^{2n-3}$ in $R^{2n}$. This is a smooth and curved non-Euclidean space, i.e., a differentiable manifold, which we call it *pre-shape space*. A pre-shape is a point on the hyper-sphere $S_*^{2n-3}$, and all rotations, translations, scaling of the shape lie on an orbit, denoted by $O(\tau)$. The appropriate set for representing shapes is an orbit space $\sum_2^n$ of a sphere $S_*^{2n-3}$ and the space $\sum_2^n$ is a *shape space*, described as:

$$\sum_2^n = \left\{ O(\tau) : \tau \in S_*^{2n-3} \right\} \tag{3.5}$$

The space $S_*^{2n-3}$ of such pre-shapes is known as the *pre-shape space* of configurations of $n$ labeled vertices in $R^2$ and is the unit sphere of dimension $2(n-1) - 1$ (Kendall, 1999; Small, 1996; Dryden, 1998). We use some polygons with different position, scaling and rotation in Euclidean space to illustrate pre-shape space and shape space. In Figure 1, pre-shapes of the same polygons are on a great circle on $S_*^{2n-3}$, or a pre-shape space, see (A); all the same polygons on the great circle are a point in a shape space as shown in (B).

Now, let us introduce pre-shape space and shape space when the objects are in complex space. In complex space, the representations of the objects are similar to that in real space because the differential manifold $C^n$ have $n$ complex dimensions and it is equivalent to $2n$ real dimensions.

*Figure 1. The sphere in (A) is denoted by $S_*^{2n-3}$, i.e., pre-shape space. Pre-shapes of the same polygons, which are not in same position, scaling and rotation in Euclidean space, are on a great circle (dotted line) of $S_*^{2n-3}$. In (B), all polygons on the great circle are a point in the shape space and different points represent different great circles in pre-shape space.*

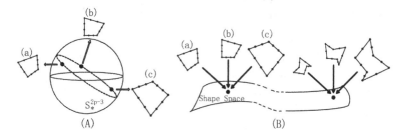

It can be regarded as a collection of complex lines through the origin in $C^n$ as a collection of planes through the origin in $R^{2n}$. In complex space, after removing the effect of translation, we can remove the effect of rotation and scaling by associating $P'$ with an equivalence class and a set:

$$\tau^* = \left\{ \lambda P', \ \lambda \in C \ and \ |\lambda| = 1 \right\} \qquad (3.6)$$

where $C$ is the set of complex numbers; $\tau^*$ covers all possible scaling and rotations of $P'$ as $\lambda$ varies over $C$. Now $\tau^*$ is a point in shape space and it is same as above mentioned $O(\tau)$. In this chapter, point in shape space is marked as $O(\tau)$. The use of the symbol $O$ reflects the fact that these great circles are *orbits*, or equivalent classes, in the terminology of differential geometry.

Because $\tau^*$ represents a complex line passing through origin and on the $n-1$ dimensional complex hyperline defined by Eq. (3.3), $\tau^*$ is a point in a space isometric to $CP^{n-2}$, the $n-2$ dimensional complex projective space.

## 3.2 Distances in Pre-Shape Space and Shape Space

The shape space theory can be used to achieve object recognition. Similarity of two objects is determined by the distance between the two shapes in the shape space $\sum_2^n$. So we will introduce the distance in shape space in this section.

Since we have defined shapes as orbits of a hyper-sphere, it is natural to define the distance between two shapes in shape space as the shortest distance between the pre-shape orbits in pre-shape space. On a hyper-sphere or in a pre-shape space, the Geodesic distance rather than Euclidean distance is necessary between two points and pre-shapes.

We define $\tau_1$ and $\tau_2$ as two pre-shapes in pre-shape space, then the great circle distance, i.e., the Geodesic distance between $\tau_1$ and $\tau_2$, is given by

$$d(\tau_1, \tau_2) = \cos^{-1}(< \tau_1, \tau_2 >) \qquad (3.7)$$

where $<\tau_1, \tau_2>$ is the inner product between $\tau_1$ and $\tau_2$. $d(\tau_1, \tau_2)$ is the shortest distance between them in pre-shape space. Now we can naturally obtain the distance in shape space $\sum_2^n$, by looking for the shortest distance between $O(\tau_1)$ and $O(\tau_2)$ in pre-shape space, and the induced metric in shape space $\sum_2^n$ can be expressed as (Ref. (Small, 1996; Kendall, 1984)):

$$d_p[O(\tau_1), O(\tau_2)] = \inf[d(A, B) : \ A \in O(\tau_1), \ B \in O(\tau_2)] \qquad (3.8)$$

then

$$d_p[O(\tau_1), O(\tau_2)] =$$
$$\inf[\cos^{-1}(< A, B >) : \ A \in O(\tau_1), \ B \in O(\tau_2)] \qquad (3.9)$$

We can intuitively understand this formula that it means that the distance from one great circle to another one is the shortest gap between them, see Figure 2. The minimum can be achieved at every value of $A$ by minimizing over $B$, or correspondingly, at every value of $B$ by minimizing over $A$. $d_p$ is called as the *Procrustean distance*, or the *Procrustean metric*.

The above mentioned formula is used in real coordinates. Now, the manifold that we shall consider next will be in complex coordinates, which can be achieved through the identification of $R^2$ with the complex plane $C$. We have denoted the complex projective space as $CP^n$. The inner product in complex space can be written as the Hermitian inner product on $S_*^{2n-3}$ embedded in $C^n$, represented as:

$$< a, b >= \Re\left(\left\langle\left\langle a, b \right\rangle\right\rangle\right) = \Re\left(\sum_j a_j b_j^*\right) \qquad (3.10)$$

*Figure 2. $O(\tau_1)$ and $O(\tau_2)$ are two great circles on $S_*^{2n-3}$. There are a variety of geodesics from a given point on $O(\tau_1)$ to $O(\tau_2)$. Among these geodesics, a horizontal geodesic has the shortest length and meet the two great circles $O(\tau_1)$ and $O(\tau_2)$ at right angles, i.e., the Geodesic between "M" and "N". "Horizontal Geodesic" is the shortest great circle path from $O(\tau_1)$ and $O(\tau_2)$ and its distance is the Procrustean distance.*

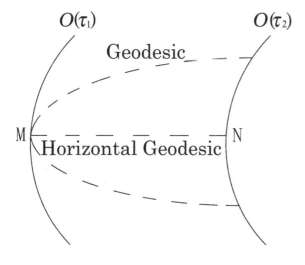

where $a_j$ and $b_j$ are the $j^{th}$ complex coordinates of $a$ and $b$ respectively. Thus the formula of the Procrustean distance can be expressed as:

$$d_p[O(\tau_1), O(\tau_2)] = \cos^{-1}\left(\left\|\sum_{j=1}^{n} \tau_{1j}\tau_{2j}^*\right\|\right) \quad (3.11)$$

where $\tau_{1j}$ and $\tau_{2j}$ are the $j^{th}$ complex coordinates of $\tau_1$ and $\tau_2$, respectively. $\tau_{2j}^*$ is the complex conjugate of $\tau_{2j}$. This is the famous Fubini-Study metric in $CP^n$, which does not depend on the specific choice of $\tau_1$ and $\tau_2$ within the great circles $O(\tau_1)$ and $O(\tau_2)$. See Ref. (Small, 1996) in detail.

With formula (3.11), we can obtain the shortest distance, i.e., the Procrustean distance, between two shapes in the shape space. The shorter the distance between two objects is, the higher the similarity between them will be. So formula (3.11)

is very important to achieve object recognition using the shape space theory.

The shape space theory has been developed greatly since 1984. In this section, we have only introduced some basic knowledge of the shape space theory of the two-dimensional shapes. The basic knowledge can be used to deal with two-dimensional images. We have not introduced the shape space based on higher-dimensional shapes because only two-dimensional shapes are recognized with this theory here. More knowledge about the shape space theory can be found in Refs. (Kendall, 1999; Small, 1996).

## 4. AUGMENTING DATABASE CONTENT

In this section, we will introduce how to augment database content by using some data models in the database. The work of enlarging database is done in pre-shape space, and we have introduced pre-shape spaces and shape spaces in above section. We will use the pre-shape space theory to augment database. Here, we will create a continuous curve between any two pre-shapes in pre-shape spaces without calculating any orthogonal geodesics. Then the database size can be augmented by generating more data along the curve.

### 4.1 The Shortest Path between two Points in Pre-Shape Space

To recognize objects with many alterable configurations, multiple data has to be included in database. However, it is hard to collect a large amount of data to recognize such objects. It is emergent and necessary to build new data based on the original data in the database. As introduced in the above section, the pre-shape space $S_*^{2n-3}$ may be considered as a surface of a super ball, i.e., a surface of a high-dimensional ball. So, in pre-shape space, the distance which is not the

*Figure 3. (A) An illustration of formula (4.1). $\tau_1$ and $\tau_2$ are two pre-shapes in the pre-shape space. $\theta_{(\tau_1,\tau_2)}$ is Geodesic distance between them. s is the Geodesic distance from $\tau_1$ to $\tau$. $\tau$ is a new obtained data. (B) $\tau_1$, $\tau_2$ and $\tau_3$ are three pre-shapes of three configurations of one object in the pre-shape space. $\alpha$ and $\beta$ are the pre-shapes which will be used to adjust the paths to approach the real paths.*

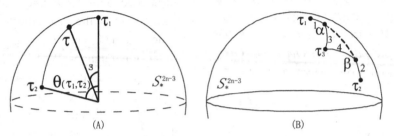

(A)  (B)

Euclidean distance but the Geodesic distance is considered, and the shortest path is the Geodesic distance path in the pre-shape space.

Two landmarks sets of two configurations of one object can be projected into a pre-shape space as two points and pre-shapes. Here, the two pre-shapes are denoted as $\tau_1$ and $\tau_2$. The shortest path, i.e. the Geodesic distance between them can be obtained by the following formula:

$$P_{(\tau_1,\tau_2)}(s) = (\cos s)\tau_1 + (\sin s)\frac{\tau_2 - \tau_1\cos\theta_{(\tau_1,\tau_2)}}{\sin\theta_{(\tau_1,\tau_2)}}$$

$$\left(0 \leq s \leq \theta_{(\tau_1,\tau_2)}\right)$$

(4.1)

where $\theta_{(\tau_1,\tau_2)}$ is the Geodesic distance between $\tau_1$ and $\tau_2$ in pre-shape space. Angle $s$ represents the Geodesic distance between the new point $\tau$ and $\tau_2$, and it is varied from 0 to $\theta_{(\tau_1,\tau_2)}$. If $s$ equals 0, $\tau$ equals $\tau_1$; and if $s$ equals $\theta_{(\tau_1,\tau_2)}$, $\tau$ equals $\tau_2$. Following the shortest path $P_{(\tau_1,\tau_2)}(s)$ in the pre-shape space, a series of new data and pre-shapes between $\tau_1$ and $\tau_2$ can be obtained, i.e. we can enlarge a database with two basic data in the database, see Figure 3 (A).

## 4.2 The Shortest Path among More than two Points in Pre-Shape Spaces

The shortest path between two points and pre-shapes in pre-shape spaces has been introduced in Sec. 4.1. The obtained data on the path will be considered as a new data shape to match observed objects. In fact, to make the generated path curve approach to the real path, more number of basic data is needed to adjust the generated path. Hence, the above mentioned method can be extended to multiple configurations of objects. Here, three configurations of one object are taken as three basic data to obtain path in pre-shape space as an example, see Figure 3 (B).

From formula (4.1), the following formulas can be easily obtained (Han, 2010):

$$P_1(s_1(t)) =$$

$$(\cos s_1(t))\tau_1 + (\sin s_1(t))\frac{\tau_2 - \tau_1\cos\theta_{(\tau_1,\tau_2)}}{\sin\theta_{(\tau_1,\tau_2)}},$$

$$(0 \leq t \leq t_1 < t_2 < t_3 < 1)$$

(4.2)

$$P_3(s_3(t)) =$$

$$(\cos s_3(t))P_1(s_1(t_1)) + (\sin s_3(t))\frac{\tau_3 - P_1(s_1(t_1))\cos\theta_{(P_1(s_1(t_1)),\tau_3)}}{\sin\theta_{(P_1(s_1(t_1)),\tau_3)}},$$

$$(t_1 < t \leq t_2)$$

(4.3)

$$P_4(s_4(t)) =$$

$$(\cos s_4(t))\tau_3 + (\sin s_4(t)) \frac{P_2(s_2(t_2)) - \tau_3 \cos \theta_{(\tau_3, P_2(s_2(t_2)))}}{\sin \theta_{(\tau_3, P_2(s_2(t_2)))}},$$

$$(t_2 < t \leq t_3)$$

$$(4.4)$$

$$P_2(s_2(t)) =$$

$$(\cos s_2(t))\tau_1 + (\sin s_2(t)) \frac{\tau_2 - \tau_1 \cos \theta_{(\tau_1, \tau_2)}}{\sin \theta_{(\tau_1, \tau_2)}},$$

$$(0 < t_1 < t_2 < t_3 < t \leq 1)$$

$$(4.5)$$

where $\theta(*, *)$ is the Geodesic distance between two relevant points. $\tau_1$, $\tau_2$ and $\tau_3$ are three points of three configurations of one object in pre-shape space. $t$ is a time scale, and $s_*(t)$ are Geodesic distances on super-ball $S_*^{2n-3}$. $P_1(s_1(t))$, $P_3(s_3(t))$, $P_4(s_4(t))$ and $P_2(s_2(t))$ represent formulas of paths 1, 3, 4, 2 as shown in Figure 3 (B), respectively. Specifically, $P_1(s_1(0))$ equals $\tau_1$; $P_1(s_1(t_1))$ equals point $\alpha$; $P_3(s_3(t_2))$ is point $\tau_3$; $P_4(s_4(t_3))$ is point $\beta$; $P_2(s_2(1))$ is $\tau_2$. We can adjust the generated paths to approach the real path curve by adjusting the parameters $s_1(t_1)$ and $s_4(t_3)$, i.e., $\alpha$ and $\beta$.

If more data configurations are used to adjust the Geodesic path in pre-shape space, a more precisely fitted path can be obtained. In addition to using the configurations of the object to adjust paths, we can adjust points $\alpha$, $\beta$, ..., to obtain a more precise path. However, it will become very difficult to find the middle points with the increase of the fitted points.

## 4.3 One Example

An example of obtaining new data from two airplanes is shown in Figure 4, where the airplane includes two basic configurations. Firstly, landmarks of outer contours can be extracted from two configurations of one object in input image. Then the two sets of landmarks are projected into pre-shape space as two points respectively. With the above mentioned method, the shortest path between the two points can be obtained in the pre-shape space. New pre-shapes or points can be computed following the path in the pre-shape space, which are shown by many contours points, see Figure 4. Following the arrows, we can observe the change of the airplane in pre-shape space.

## 5. OBJECT RECOGNITION BASED ON THE SHAPE SPACE THEORY

In section 4, we have introduced the method to augment the database with a limited number of data in pre-shape space. With the augmented database, we may recognize more objects.

Generally, objects can be classified as rigid and non-rigid. If the objects are non-rigid, for example, some biological objects, they are hardly forecasted their movement changes with limited data. In this chapter, we are only concerned with rigid objects recognitions.

Many object recognition algorithms rely on feature spaces where features include some quantities. Among these object recognition algorithms,

*Figure 4. (a) and (d) are two original figures of "Tu160". (b) and (c) are their outer contours and 20 landmarks respectively. Between (b) and (c), other shapes as pre-shapes are generated in the pre-shape space.*

shape is perhaps the most common and dominant one. With shape methods, a type of important methods of object recognition is based on spatial configurations of landmarks. The basic subroutine in objects matching takes the input image as an unknown object and compares it with a model (data) object in database. We have to solve the correspondence problem between the model object and the observed object, and then use the correspondence to estimate and compute a similarity based on the information of landmarks of both objects. Although shape space is manifold space, the method based on its theory is one of shape methods to achieve object recognition.

In the chapter, we mainly focus on two-dimensional object recognition with the shape space theory. This is motivated by three factors (Zhang, 2003). Firstly, the shape space theory has been more developed for two-dimensional object recognition. During the last forty years, a lot of researchers have studied the recognitions of two-dimensional shapes with the theory. Secondly, two-dimensional object recognition is not a purely academic problem. In many real-world images, for example, the objects of interested in aerial photographs can be viewed approximately in two-dimensional space. Thirdly, several two-dimensional implementation issues of object recognition need to be resolved and studied, such as landmarks selection and extraction, and how to deal with occlusion, also occur in $n$-dimensional object recognition ($n \geq 3$). So, in this section, we will introduce the algorithms of two-dimensional object recognition with the shape space theory and give some examples to show the validity of the algorithms.

According to the change states of objects, the states of object recognition are divided into *static state* and *dynamic state*. Object recognition in *static state* means that objects do not own multiple configurations. Most methods of object recognition are achieved in static state. Object recognition in *dynamic state* means that objects own multiple configurations, i.e., RMCO.

In this section, firstly, we will introduce the method of recognizing objects in static state with the shape space theory. Then, we will extend the method to recognize objects in dynamic state.

## 5.1 Object Recognition in Static State

Generally, most algorithms of object recognition are achieved in static state. Shape space theory can also be used to recognize objects in static state, and now let us introduce the approach.

After obtaining the landmarks from outer contours of two-dimensional shapes, they will be projected into an optimal dimension of shape space and pre-shape space.

Suppose we have obtained two sets of data from different contours landmarks representing two objects. If the numbers of elements of the two sets are different, or although the numbers are same, but only part of landmarks of the two sets represent same position, we have to consider how to choose part of landmarks from the sets and project them into pre-shape space and shape space.

Given $n$ landmarks for an object, there are $n \cdot (n-1) \ldots 1 = n!$ sets to be obtained. Generally, it is not easy to find a consistent set of landmarks of observed object to correspond a set of data object. To illustrate the approach of object recognition with the shape space theory, we suppose the numbers of two sets of landmarks are same as $n$. Double recursions will be used to match two shapes here.

The order of the landmarks is preserved, such as counter clockwise. Thus, given two sets of $n$ landmarks of outer contours $L_1$ and $L_2$, the number of valid matching is $n^2$. It is so big to cost the computing time, for example, if the number of landmarks is 15, the number of valid matching is 225. However, many of these matching are redundant, since the result of matching objects is not changed with the start points of the two set of landmarks changing. For example, the result of the set $\{l_{1,1}, l_{1,2}, l_{1,3}\}$ matching $\{l_{2,1}, l_{2,2}, l_{2,3}\}$ is same as the one of $\{l_{1,2}, l_{1,3}, l_{1,1}\}$ matching $\{l_{2,2}, l_{2,3}, l_{2,1}\}$.

Thus the number of matching objects is $n$. In other words, the landmarks' order is counter-clockwise and continuous and there will be only $n$ possible arrays which depend on the landmarks' number $n$. The order and the number of the landmarks of the first object are fixed, and the order and the number of the landmarks of the others' objects are changed to all $n$ possible points irrespectively. During recognition, we need to consider all these circular shifts, and compare the results of their matching. Only one result, e.g., the minimum value with the shape space theory, is considered to be correct one.

One of the classical approaches to pattern recognition is to minimize the probability of error, i.e., maximize the posteriori probability of the object class with the given observed objects. The idea can also be extended to object recognition with the shape space theory. Although some researchers have achieved object recognition by the methods of combining the shape space theory and probability theory, such as (Glover, 2006; Glover, 2008), we can consider a simpler idea that the result of object recognition is only determined by some kinds of metric without requiring these probability densities and distributions. Here, we use the minimum distance as the metric, i.e., the Procrustean distance in shape space. As Small (1996) mentioned, the similarity of two shapes in two-dimensional space depends on the Procrustean distance between two points in shape spaces. The shorter their Procrustean distance is, the higher the similarity of the two shapes will be.

Considering the order of $n$ landmarks, $n$ Procrustean distances can be computed. The minimum Procrustean distance is taken as the final value to determine the result of object recognition. The formula is shown as follows:

$$d_{p\_\min} = \min_n d_p(O(\tau_1), O(\tau_2)) = \min_n d_p(O(C^n L_1), O(\tau_2)) \quad (5.1)$$

where $d_{p\_\min}$ is the minimum one among the $n$ Procrustean distances with formulas (3.9) and (3.11); $\tau_1$ and $\tau_2$ are pre-shapes in the pre-shape space; $L_1$ is one shape which is represented as a set of landmarks in the Euclidean space; the operator $C^n$ represents all the circular shift operators to change the order of landmarks, for example, $C^0 L_1 = (l_1, l_2, ..., l_n)$, $C^1 L_1 = (l_2, l_3, ..., l_1)$, ..., $C^{n-1} L_1 = (l_n, l_1, ..., l_{n-1})$ (Zhang, 2003).

With the formula, we can obtain the minimum Procrustean distance to achieve object recognition in static state. We will give an example to show its validity later. Object recognition in static state is one foundation of that in dynamic state. Now, let us introduce the method of object recognition in dynamic state.

## 5.2 Object Recognition in Dynamic State

Object recognition in *dynamic state* means that the objects own multiple configurations, i.e., RMCO. There are some approaches to recognize objects in dynamic state. Some approaches are that the database owns enough data to include all similar shapes of multiple configurations of objects. It is difficult to obtain so many models as data. Some approaches are to forecast the change of the observed objects and enlarge the original database. Following this idea, we can recognize objects in dynamic state with a limited database. We have introduced how to enlarge and augment database in pre-shape space in section 4 in detail.

Augment database is the first step of recognizing objects in dynamic state. The second step is to match objects with the obtained data in static state. We have proposed the method of object recognition in static state as above mentioned. Now, we will demonstrate how to achieve object recognition in dynamic state in detail.

First of all, we obtain landmarks from two configurations of an object. Here, the numbers of two sets of landmarks are set to $n$ and we only match the two sets of $n$ landmarks instead of $p$

$< n$ landmarks. Then the two sets of landmarks are projected into a pre-shape space as two pre-shapes. We use $\tau_1$ and $\tau_2$ to represent the two pre-shapes of the two different configurations in the pre-shape space.

From formula (4.1), a series of new data can be obtained which include the two configurations of the same object. Among the new generated data and an observed object, we can compute a lot of the Procrustean distances in shape spaces by computing double recursions: one visits the generated data; the other is changing the orders of two sets of landmarks. For example, if the number of steps from $\tau_1$ to $\tau_2$ following the shortest path in pre-shape space is 20, and the number of landmarks is 12, we can obtain $20 \times 12 = 240$ Procrustean distances. From these distances, the minimum value is the final Procrustean distance, i.e., after these Procrustean distances are computed and compared, the minimum one is recoded in a temp file.

Now, we assume that there are $m$ data objects in database, and all of them have multi-configurations. The number of steps from $\tau_1$ to $\tau_2$ (the two end configurations) is set to 20. So the number of all Procrustean distances of the observed object and the $m$ data objects is $n \times m \times 20$. Then all the Procrustean distances are compared, and the observed object is similar to the data object corresponding the shortest Procrustean distance.

The algorithm of two points of two sets of landmarks with fixed orders is shown in Figure 5 (A). The two points $\tau_1$ and $\tau_2$ represent two different configurations of a data object in the pre-shape space. By using Formula (4.1), the data of the shortest path between $\tau_1$ and $\tau_2$ can be obtained, which will be used to match other $k$ shapes whose orbits are denoted as $O(S_1)$, ..., $O(S_k)$ in the pre-shape space.

It is worth noting that the shortest path is not the one between $O(\tau_1)$ and $O(\tau_2)$ in shape space, but the one between $\tau_1$ and $\tau_2$ in the pre-shape space. There are two reasons for it. First reason is that, it is hard to find two shapes whose distance is the shortest path between their circles in pre-shape space; and second one is that, if only a small rotation angle of $\tau_3$ and $\tau_2$ is different, the path between $\tau_1$ and $\tau_2$ is close to the path between $\tau_1$ and $\tau_3$. If $\tau_3$ is very different from $\tau_2$, for instance, $\tau_3$ is the one by rotating $\tau_2$ 90 degree, the two paths are very different. Since we can control the data in database, we can also adjust the two configurations data of one shape to the appropriate positions and rotation angles, making the path between the two configurations near the shortest path. For example, if one airplane can change its wings, its views of its two configurations are adjusted to be the same direction, i.e., their aeroplane noses toward same orientation. After obtaining the path in the pre-shape space, the process of RMCO can be achieved, as shown in Figure 5.

Another point that we should note is that sometimes the path curve between two pre-shapes is too different from the real path curve to describe it. In this case, we need to use more configurations data to represent the path curve in pre-shape space. More discussions have been introduced in detail in Section 4.2.

## 5.3 Experimental Results

The first experiment of object recognition is performed in static state by using an airplanes database. See Figure 6 (C). There are 21 data which represent 21 airplanes in the database. Figure 6 (A) shows an observed airplane, and its landmarks of the outer contour are shown in (B). On one hand, if the number of the landmarks is too many, it costs much time to compute the Procrustean distance between the observed object and the data objects; on the other hand, if the number is too few, the landmarks can not accurately represent the objects. The number of the obtained landmarks is determined by the object's shape. Here, 12 landmarks are extracted from the airplanes data and the observed airplane since we need to project them as points into the same dimensional pre-shape space and shape space.

*Figure 5. (A) and (B) are the process of RMCO. $\tau_1$ and $\tau_2$ are two configuration points of an object in pre-shape space. $O(\tau_1)$ and $O(\tau_2)$ are the great circles of $\tau_1$ and $\tau_2$, and $O(S_1)$, ..., $O(S_k)$ are the great circles of other k observed objects which will be recognized in the same pre-shape space. Along the path (bold curve in (A)) from $\tau_1$ to $\tau_2$, many points (in the chapter, the number is 20) can be obtained to recognize these shapes whose orbits are denoted as $O(S_1)$, ..., $O(S_k)$ in the shape space.*

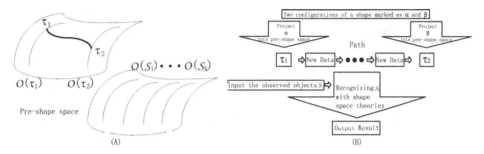

With the above mentioned approach in static state, the Procrustean distances between the observed airplane and every data airplane are computed, and shown in Figure 6 (C). The shortest Procrustean distance among them is found and recorded with an underline after the Procrustean distances have been compared. The smallest value shows the observed object is "F16".

Another example is achieved in dynamic state as shown in Figure 7. Two outer contours and landmarks of two tools are shown in Figure 7 (A), including slip joint pliers and mini pliers which are taken orthogonally. The numbers of the landmarks are 10 respectively. Here, we only use slip joint pliers and mini pliers to show how to recognize objects in dynamic state. Figure 7 (B) contains two configurations of the mini pliers as data object. Firstly, we extract outer contours and landmarks from the two data models. Although the numbers of the landmarks are different, we can determine that the one star point in (II) corresponds to the three star points in (I) of (B) because we can control the two data models (Han, 2010).

The two sets of landmarks of the two data objects are projected into a pre-shape space. With the approach described in section 5.3, we can obtain 30 new pre-shapes including the two basis pre-shapes (suppose the number of steps between the two end configurations is 30). The Procrus-

tean distances among the generated data and the observed objects are computed. Among them, the smallest value determines the result of recognition. In Table 1, the smallest one is shown with an underline.

## 6. FUTURE RESEARCH DIRECTIONS

In this chapter, we have introduced the theories and methods that can recognize more objects with a limited database. The theories and methods are used to recognize objects from two-dimensional images based on the shape space theory. With the theory developed, it is possible to extend the present work to high dimensional shape spaces. In fact, some researchers are studying geometric modeling in three-dimensional spaces with the shape space theory (Kilian, 2007). Thus, we can recognize three-dimensional objects from two-dimensional images in future work based on the previous works.

Objects can be classified as rigid and non-rigid as introduced in Section 5. In the chapter, the method is based upon rigid objects. In future work, it is possible to extend the method to recognize non-rigid objects. Some non-rigid objects, such as snake, can change and move themselves to many shapes, and it is very hard to forecast

*Figure 6. (A): an observed airplane; (B): landmarks of the outer contour of the airplane; (C): data airplanes and results of object recognition. Firstly, 12 landmarks are extracted from the observed airplane and the data airplanes; then, the Procrustean distances of the every observed one and the data are computed. The shortest one is represented with underlines and it shows the observed object is "F16".*

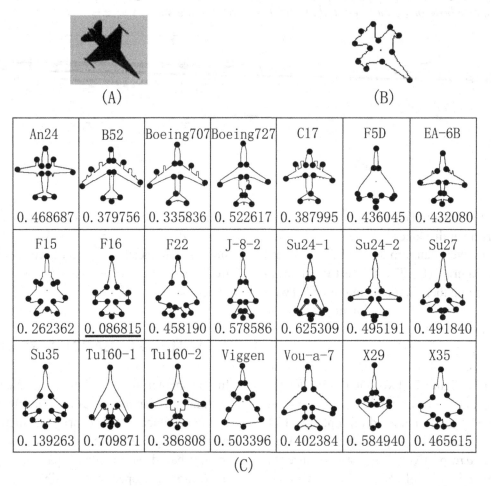

(A)                                      (B)

| An24 | B52 | Boeing707 | Boeing727 | C17 | F5D | EA-6B |
|------|-----|-----------|-----------|-----|-----|-------|
| 0. 468687 | 0. 379756 | 0. 335836 | 0. 522617 | 0. 387995 | 0. 436045 | 0. 432080 |
| F15 | F16 | F22 | J-8-2 | Su24-1 | Su24-2 | Su27 |
| 0. 262362 | 0. 086815 | 0. 458190 | 0. 578586 | 0. 625309 | 0. 495191 | 0. 491840 |
| Su35 | Tu160-1 | Tu160-2 | Viggen | Vou-a-7 | X29 | X35 |
| 0. 139263 | 0. 709871 | 0. 386808 | 0. 503396 | 0. 402384 | 0. 584940 | 0. 465615 |

(C)

*Figure 7. (A): observed tools and 10 landmarks of the outer contour of the slip joint pliers and the mini pliers; (B): two configurations of one tool, and their landmarks. Here, there are two data models in database.*

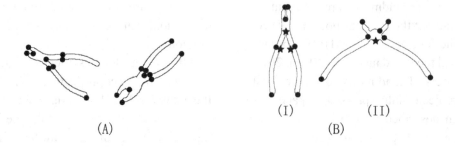

(A)                     (I)        (II)
                              (B)

*Table 1. The data in database is the mini pliers, and the observed objects are shown in Figure 7 (A) where the slip joint pliers and the mini pliers are used to compute the Procrustean distances. 'Step' represents 30 new pre-shapes obtained from the first pre-shape and the last pre-shape. Two sets of 30 Procrustean distances are computed among two observed objects and the new pre-shapes respectively, shown in column "m-p" and "s-p". "m-p" and "s-p" mean the Procrustean distances of the mini pliers and slip joint pliers respectively. Shortest Procrustean distances is 0.072 recoded with an under line and it represents the observed object is mini pliers.*

| Step | m-p | s-p |
|---|---|---|
| 0 | 0.649 | 0.801 |
| 0.026 | 0.623 | 0.776 |
| 0.052 | 0.597 | 0.751 |
| 0.078 | 0.571 | 0.725 |
| 0.104 | 0.545 | 0.700 |
| 0.131 | 0.519 | 0.675 |
| 0.157 | 0.493 | 0.650 |
| 0.183 | 0.467 | 0.625 |
| 0.209 | 0.442 | 0.600 |
| 0.235 | 0.416 | 0.575 |
| 0.262 | 0.390 | 0.550 |
| 0.288 | 0.364 | 0.525 |
| 0.314 | 0.339 | 0.501 |
| 0.340 | 0.313 | 0.476 |
| 0.366 | 0.288 | 0.452 |
| 0.393 | 0.263 | 0.428 |
| 0.419 | 0.237 | 0.405 |
| 0.445 | 0.213 | 0.381 |
| 0.471 | 0.188 | 0.358 |
| 0.497 | 0.164 | 0.336 |
| 0.524 | 0.141 | 0.314 |
| 0.550 | 0.119 | 0.292 |
| 0.576 | 0.100 | 0.272 |
| 0.602 | 0.084 | 0.252 |
| 0.628 | 0.073 | 0.234 |
| 0.655 | 0.072 | 0.217 |
| 0.681 | 0.079 | 0.203 |
| 0.707 | 0.094 | 0.190 |
| 0.733 | 0.112 | 0.181 |
| 0.759 | 0.134 | 0.175 |

their movement changes. Therefore, the kind of non-rigid objects are difficultly recognized with a limited database. However, movement of some non-rigid objects under given conditions can be forecasted. For example, a dog is running without gazing around. The kind of non-rigid objects can be recognized with some data objects. To achieve the kind of object recognition, two important steps are how to select "good" data configurations and how to optimize the path in pre-shape space respectively.

We have omitted the introduction of the approaches of obtaining landmarks from objects. However, it does not mean that the step is not important. As a matter of fact, half work will be finished if we can extract a set of appropriate landmarks. For two data objects, how to obtain two sets of corresponding landmarks from objects, especially non-rigid objects, is still a difficult and interesting study. In this chapter, the approach of augment database is based on landmarks on outer contour of object. Although the outer contour possesses much information for object recognition, the information inside the object ought not to be ignored. Therefore, the fact that the present approaches will be extended to considering the landmarks inside the objects is one of the possible future woks.

## 7. CONCLUSION

The topic of the chapter is to recognize more objects by augmenting the database content. Firstly, we have introduced the basic knowledge of object recognition briefly. Then we have introduced the shape space theory in detail, including its history, development, basic knowledge, applications, and so on. Since the theory includes too much knowledge, we have only introduced some of the important contents which influence the two-dimensional object recognition. Then the method has been described to augment the database content in pre-shape space. After two groups of landmarks are extracted from two basic data objects and projected into a pre-shape space as two feature points, a shortest path can be built between the two feature points in the pre-shape space. With the approach, we can obtain a lot of new data from two or more data objects, i.e., we can augment the database. Next, we have described the approaches of object recognition in two states with the shape space theory. One is to recognize

objects in static state, i.e., we do not augment database to recognize this kind of objects. The other is to recognize objects in dynamic state, i.e., the objects are with multiple configurations and we need to augment database to recognize the sort of objects. We have also shown the efficiencies of the algorithms with some examples. Finally, we have given some possible extending works and studies in future.

## REFERENCES

Besl, P. J., & Jain, R. C. (1985). Three-dimensional object recognition. *Computing Surveys*, *17*(1), 75–145. doi:10.1145/4078.4081

Binford, T. O. (1981). Inferring surfaces from images. *Artificial Intelligence*, *17*, 205–244. doi:10.1016/0004-3702(81)90025-4

Bookstein, L. (1996). Landmark methods for forms without landmarks: Morphometrics of group differences in outline shape. *Medical Image Analysis*, *1*(3), 225–243. doi:10.1016/S1361-8415(97)85012-8

Bookstein, L. (1997). *Morphometric tools for landmark data: Geometry and biology*. Cambridge, UK: Cambridge Univ. Press.

Dryden, I. L., & Mardia, K. V. (1998). *Statistical shape analysis*. John Wiley and Sons.

Fatemizadeh, E., Lucas, C., & Soltanian-Zadeh, H. (2003). Automatic landmark extraction from image data using modified growing neural gas network. *IEEE Transactions on Information Technology in Biomedicine*, *7*, 77–85. doi:10.1109/TITB.2003.808501

Fisher, R. A. (1936). The use of multiple measurements in taxonomic problems. *Annals of Eugenics*, *7*, 179–188. doi:10.1111/j.1469-1809.1936.tb02137.x

Förstner, W., & Gülch, E. (1987). A fast operator for detection and precise location of istinct points, corners and centers of circular features. In *Proc. Intercommission Conf. Photogrammetric Data*, Interlaken, Switzerland, (pp. 281-305).

Glover, J., Rus, D., & Roy, N. (2008). Probabilistic models of object geometry for grasp planning. *Robotics: Science and Systems IV Conference*, held in 2008 at the Swiss Federal Institute of Technology in Zurich, (pp. 278-285).

Glover, J., Rus, D., Roy, N., & Gordon, G. (2006). Robust models of object geometry. In *Proceedings of the IROS Workshop on From Sensors to Human Spatial Concepts*, Beijing, China.

Grimson, W. E. L. (1990). *Object recognition by computer: The role of geometric constraints* (p. 33). Cambridge, MA: MIT Press.

Han, Y., Koike, H., Wang, B., & Idesawa, M. (2010). Recognition of objects in various situations from two dimensional images. *IEEE International Conference on Image Processing Theory, Tool and Applications* (IPTA'10), (pp. 405-410).

Han, Y., Wang, B., Idesawa, M., & Shimai, H. (2010). Recognition of multiple configurations of objects with limited data. *Pattern Recognition*, *43*, 1467–1475. doi:10.1016/j.patcog.2009.09.028

Hoffman, D. D., & Richards, W. A. (1984). Parts of recognition. *Cognition*, *18*, 65–96. doi:10.1016/0010-0277(84)90022-2

Kendall, D. G. (1984). Shape manifolds, Procrustean metrics, and complex projectivespaces. *Bulletin of the London Mathematical Society*, *16*, 81–121. doi:10.1112/blms/16.2.81

Kendall, D. G., Barden, D., Carne, T. K., & Le, H. (1999). *Shape and shape theory*. John Wiley and Sons Inc.

Kilian, M., Mitra, N., & Pottmann H. (2007). *Geometric modeling in shape space*. ACM SIGGRAPH 2007.

Pal, S. K., & Pal, A. (2002). *Pattern recognition: From classical to modern approaches*. World Scientific Pub Co Inc.

Pitts, W., & McCulloch, W. S. (1949). How we know universals: The perception of auditory and visual forms. *The Bulletin of Mathematical Biophysics*, *9*, 127–147. doi:10.1007/BF02478291

Rao, C. R. (1948). The utilization of multiple measurements in problems of biological classification. *Journal of the Royal Statistical Society. Series B. Methodological*, *10*, 159–203.

Saengdeejing, A., Qu, Z. H., Chaeroenlap, N., & Jin, Y. F. (2003). 2-D shape recognition using recursive landmark determination and fuzzy ART network learning. *Neural Processing Letters*, *18*, 81–95. doi:10.1023/A:1026261202044

Small, C. G. (1996). *The statistical theory of shape. Springer series in statistics*. New York, NY: Springer-Verlag Inc.

Ullman, S. (1996). *High-level vision*. Cambridge, MA: MIT Press.

Zhang, J., Zhang, X., & Krim, H. (1998). Invariant object recognition by shape space analysis. ICIP 98, (vol.3 pp. 581-585).

Zhang, J., Zhang, X., Krim, H., & Walter, G. G. (2003). Object representation and recognition in shape spaces. *Pattern Recognition*, *36*, 1143–1154. doi:10.1016/S0031-3203(02)00226-1

## ADDITIONAL READING

Aytekin, A. M., Terzo, M., Rasmont, P., & Cagatay, N. (2007). Landmark based geometric morphometric analysis of wing shape in Sibiricobombus Vogt (Hymenoptera: Apidae: Bombus Latreille). *Annales de la Société Entomologique de France*, *43*, 95–102.

Balan, V., & Patrangenaru, V. (2006). *Geometry of Shape Spaces*. The Fifth Conference of Balkan Society of Geometers, MangaliaRomania, pp. 28-33.

Bishop, C. M. (2006). *Pattern recognition and machine learning*. Springer.

Dryden, L. L., & Mardia, K. V, (1998). *Statistical shape analysis*. J. Wiley.

Evans, K., Dryden, I. L., & Le, H. (2010). Shape curves and geodesic modeling. *Biometrika, 97*, 1–17.

Fletcher, P. T., Lu, C., & Joshi, S. (2003). *Statistics of shape via principal geodesic analysis on Lie groups*. Computer Vision and Pattern Recognition Conference (CVPR2003), vol. 1, pp. 95-101.

Gill, D., Ritov, Y., & Dror, G. (2007). Is Pinocchio's Nose Long or His Head Small? *Learning Shape Distances for Classification.*, ISCV2007, 652–661.

Heo, G., & Small, C. G. (2006). Form representions and means for landmarks: A survey and comparative study. *Computer Vision and Image Understanding, 102*, 188–203. doi:10.1016/j.cviu.2006.01.003

Kenobi, K. (2010). Shape curves and geodesic modeling. *Biometrika, 97*, 567–584. doi:10.1093/biomet/asq027

Kent, J. T. (1994). The complex Bingham distribution and shape analysis. *J. R. Statist, 56*, 285–299.

Kent, J. T. (1995). *Current issues for statistical inference in shape analysis*. In Proceedings in Current Issues in Statistical Shape Anaysis, pp. 167-175.

Kent, J. T., & Mardia, K. V. (2001). Shape, Procrustes tangent projections and bilateral symmetry. *Biometrika, 88*, 469–485. doi:10.1093/biomet/88.2.469

Kubota, T. (2009). A Shape Representation with Elastic Quadratic Polynomials—Preservation of High Curvature Points under Noisy Conditions. *International Journal of Computer Vision, 82*, 133–155. doi:10.1007/s11263-008-0192-y

Kume, A., Dryden, I. L., & Le, H. (2007). Shape-space smoothing splines for planar landmark data. *Biometrika, 94*, 513–528. doi:10.1093/biomet/asm047

Le, H. (1991). On geodesics in Euclidian shape spaces. *Journal of the London Mathematical Society, 44*, 360–372. doi:10.1112/jlms/s2-44.2.360

Le, H. (1998). On consistency of procrustean mean shapes. *Advances in Applied Probability, 30*, 53–63. doi:10.1239/aap/1035227991

Le, H., & Kume, A. (2000). The Frechet Mean Shape and the Shape of the Means. *Advances in Applied Probability, 32*, 101–113. doi:10.1239/aap/1013540025

Li, W., Bebis, G., & Bourbakis, N. G. (2008). 3-D Object Recognition Using 2-D views. *IEEE Transactions on Image Processing, 17*, 2236–2255. doi:10.1109/TIP.2008.2003404

Rohlf, F. J. (1999). Shape Statistics: Procrustes Superimpositions and Tangent Spaces. *Journal of Classification, 16*, 197–223. doi:10.1007/s003579900054

Roy-Chowdhury, A. K. (2005). *A Measure of Deformability of Shapes, with applications to Human Motion Analysis*. Proceedings of the 2005 IEEE Computer Society Conference on Computer Vision and Pattern Recognition (CVPR'05).

Slice, D. E. (2001). Landmark Coordinates Aligned by Procrustes Analysis Do Not Lie in Kendall's Shape Space. *Systematic Biology, 50*, 141–149. doi:10.1080/10635150119110

Small, C. G. (2007). *Functional equations and how to solve them (Problem Books in Mathematics)*. Springer.

Small, C. G., & McLeish, D. L. (1994). *Hilbert space methods in probability and statistical inference*. Wiley.

Theodoridis, S., & Koutroumbas, K. (2006). *Patter recognition*. Academic Press.

Ullman, S. (2000). *High-level vision: object recognition and visual cognition*. MIT Press.

Wuhrer, S., Bose, P., Shu, C., O'Rourke, J., & Brunton, A. (2008). *Morphing of Triangular Meshes in Shape Space*. Computational Geometry, June 2, 2008, from http://arxiv.org/PS_cache/arxiv/pdf/0805/0805.0162v2.pdf.

## KEY TERMS AND DEFINITIONS

**Augment Database:** Augmenting database with a limited data.

**Dynamic State:** Recognizing objects in dynamic state.

**Object Configurations:** One object may have some different configurations.

**Object Recognition:** Recognizing objects.

**Pre-Shape Space:** A non-Euclidean space.

**Procrustean Distance:** It is used to decide the result of object recognition.

**Shape Space:** A non-Euclidean space.

**Shortest Path:** New data can be obtained from the path in pre-shape space.

# Chapter 9
# Efficient Iris Identification with Improved Segmentation Techniques

**Abhishek Verma**
*New Jersey Institute of Technology, USA*

**Chengjun Liu**
*New Jersey Institute of Technology, USA*

## ABSTRACT

*In this chapter, the authors propose and implement an improved iris recognition method based on image enhancement and heuristics. They make major improvements in the iris segmentation phase. In particular, the authors implement the raised to power operation for more accurate detection of the pupil region. Additionally, with their technique they are able to considerably reduce the candidate limbic boundary search space; this leads to a significant increase in the accuracy and speed of the segmentation. Furthermore, the authors selectively detect the limbic circle having center within close range of the pupil center. The effectiveness of the proposed method is evaluated on a grand challenge, large scale database: the Iris Challenge Evaluation (ICE) dataset.*

## 1. INTRODUCTION

Over the past decade biometric authentication has become a very active area of research due to the increasing demands in automated personal identification. More recently several new notable techniques and methods with applications to face recognition (Liu & Yang, 2009), (Liu, 2007), (Yang, Liu, & Zhang, 2010), eye detection (Shuo

DOI: 10.4018/978-1-61350-429-1.ch009

& Liu, 2010) and iris (Verma, Liu, & Jia, 2011) biometrics have been proposed. Among many biometric techniques, iris recognition is one of the most promising approaches due to its high reliability for person identification (Ma, Tan, Wang, & Zhang, 2004).

The iris is a thin circular diaphragm, which lies between the lens and cornea of the human eye. Figure 1 shows the iris region between the sclera and the pupil. The formation of the unique patterns of the iris is random and not related to

*Figure 1. Front view of the human eye. The various parts labeled are important to iris segmentation and recognition*

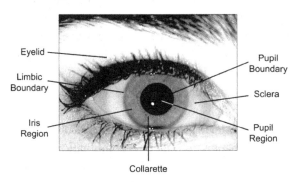

any genetic factors (Wildes, 1997), and the iris patterns remain stable throughout the adult life. Thus, the patterns within the iris are unique to each person and two eyes of an individual have independent iris patterns. Some research shows that when compared with other biometric features such as face and fingerprint, iris patterns are more stable and reliable (Du, Ives, & Etter, 2004).

A general approach to iris recognition consists of four stages: 1) image acquisition, 2) iris segmentation, 3) feature encoding, and 4) decision making. Recent work focuses on handling eye gaze and eyelash exclusion (Daugman, 2007). Bayesian approach to matching of warped iris patterns is discussed by Thornton, Savvides, and Vijayakumar (2007). Beacon guided search for faster iris matching is discussed by Hao, Daugman, and Zielinski (2008) and use of short-length iris codes from the most descriptive regions of the iris for fast iris matching is proposed by Gentile, Ratha, and Connell (2009).

In this paper, we propose and implement an improved iris recognition method based on image enhancement and heuristics. We make major improvements in the iris segmentation phase. In particular, we implement the raised to power operation for more accurate detection of the pupil region. Additionally, with our technique we are able to considerably reduce the candidate limbic boundary search space, this leads to a significant increase in the accuracy and speed of the segmen-

tation. The segmentation performance is further increased with the application of the thresholding. Furthermore, for higher accuracy and speed, we selectively detect the limbic circle having center within close range of the pupil center. The effectiveness of the proposed method is evaluated on a grand challenge, large scale database: the Iris Challenge Evaluation (ICE) (Phillips, 2006) dataset. The pupil is correctly segmented for 99.8% of the images in the dataset. Iris region detection is 98.5% for the right eye and 98.8% for the left eye. The rank-one recognition rate for our method is 3.5% and 2.7% higher than that of the ICE method for the right eye and the left eye respectively. Furthermore, we improve upon the ND_IRIS (Liu, Bowyer, & Flynn, 2005) by a significant 2% for the rank-one recognition rate of the left eye. The verification rate is about 10% higher than the ICE method for each eye at a much lower equal error rate; this emphasizes the higher accuracy of our system.

The rest of the paper is structured as follows: In Section 2, we briefly overview several representative works on image acquisition, segmentation, feature encoding and matching. Section 3 describes the dataset used in our experiments along with the implementation details of our improved recognition system. We evaluate the performance of our method and present a detailed analysis of the experimental results in Section 4. Future research directions are discussed in Section 5 and conclusions are drawn in Section 6.

## 2. RELATED WORK

Various algorithms have been proposed for iris recognition, one of the earlier systems proposed by Flom and Safir (1987) operates under highly controlled conditions: (i) a headrest is used; (ii) the subject is asked to look at an image in order to stabilize the gaze, and (iii) the process is supervised by an operator. The pupil region is detected by finding large connected regions of pixels with intensity values below a given threshold. In order to extract iris descriptors, the difference operator, edge detection algorithms, and the Hough transform are used.

Most commercial systems implement an algorithm using the iriscodes proposed by Daugman (2004, 2006, & 2007). The system first assesses the focus of the image in real time by looking at the power in the middle and upper frequency bands of the two-dimensional Fourier spectrum. The next step is to segment the iris region in an image, and the early work is based on the assumption that the inner and outer iris boundaries can be modeled as a circle. The more recent work on segmentation relaxes this assumption (Daugman, 2009). After the segmentation of the iris region, the next step describes the features of the iris in a way that facilitates the matching of the two irises. In order to account for variable iris sizes from pupil dilation caused by changes in illumination and camera distance the iris region is mapped into a normalized coordinate system. The rotation of the iris due to the head tilt is accounted for at the stage of matching. The normalized iris image is convolved with the 2D Gabor filters to extract the texture information. After the texture in the image is analyzed and represented, it is matched against the stored representation of other irises. In order to speed up the matching, from the texture features, the phase response of each filter is quantized into a pair of bits. Each complex coefficient is transformed into a two-bit code: the first bit is equal to one if the real part of the coefficient is positive, and the second bit is equal to one if the imaginary part of the coefficient is positive. Thus, after the quantization the texture of the iris image is summarized in a compact 256 byte binary code. The binary "iriscodes" can be compared efficiently using bitwise operations with a metric called the normalized Hamming distance, which measures the fraction of bits for which the two iriscodes differ. A small Hamming distance suggests strong similarity of the iriscodes.

The Wildes (1997) system uses low light level camera along with diffuse source and polarization for image acquisition. Such a light source is less-intrusive and designed to eliminate specular reflections. The system involves computing the binary edge map followed by the Hough transform to localize the iris boundary. The detection of eyelid is also incorporated into the system. For matching, it applies the Laplacian of Gaussian filter at multiple scales to produce a template and computes the normalized correlation as a similarity measure.

Tisse, Martin, Torres, & Robert (2002) construct the analytic image (a combination of the original image and its Hilbert transform) to demodulate the iris texture. Huang, Luo, & Chen (2002) perform localization of iris by canny edge detection and integro-differential operator, and encoding was done using Independent Component Analysis (ICA). Masek (2003) performs localization of iris by canny edge detection and circular Hough transform. Encoding was performed by 1D Log-Gabor wavelets and matching was based on hamming distance. Cui et al. (2004) propose a method of iris image synthesis based on the Principal Component Analysis (PCA) and super-resolution. The synthesized image was verified using Daugman's algorithm. Ives, Guidry, & Etter (2004) use histogram based technique to perform encoding. It is a computationally less intensive method when compared with other methods. Experiments were conducted on the CASIA eye image dataset. Liu, Bowyer, & Flynn (2005) propose the ND_IRIS method based on Masek's implementation. This method uses hamming distance to compare two iris templates.

## 3. NEW AND IMPROVED IRIS RECOGNITION METHOD AND ITS MAJOR COMPONENTS

We propose and implement an improved iris recognition method and show the improvement in iris recognition performance using the Iris Challenge Evaluation (ICE) (Phillips, 2006) dataset. First we give details of the ICE dataset in Section 3.1. Next we discuss the major components

*Figure 2. An overview of our iris recognition system*

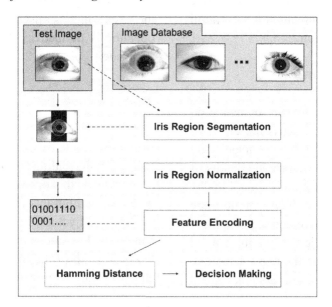

of our improved iris recognition method. These include iris segmentation, iris encoding, and iris matching. See Figure 2 for an overview of the iris recognition system.

We focus our efforts mainly on improving the segmentation stage of the system. This allows us to compare the performance of the segmentation stage with that implemented by the ICE method. The segmentation step performs the localization of the iris region by detecting the pupil and the limbic boundary along with the eyelids. The iris encoding and iris matching stage are similar to that implemented by the ICE method in the Biometric Experimentation Environment (BEE) system. Compared to the ICE method our proposed method leads to a significant increase in the accuracy of the iris region segmentation with a much higher overall recognition performance at a lower error rate. Furthermore, our method outperforms the rank-one recognition performance achieved by the ND_IRIS (Liu, Bowyer, & Flynn, 2005) method.

## 3.1. The ICE Dataset

The ICE dataset consists of 1425 right eye images of 124 different subjects and 1528 left eye images of 120 different subjects. Eye images belong to 132 total subjects with 112 overlapping subjects between the left eye and the right eye images. The iris images are intensity images with a resolution of 640 x 480 in the TIFF format. The average diameter of an iris is 228 pixels. The images vary in quality due to the percent of the iris area occluded, the degree of blur in the image, off angle image, and images with subject wearing the contact lens. Figure 3(a) shows some example images of the right eye and Figure 3(b) shows some images

*Figure 3. Example images of the (a) right eye and (b) left eye from the ICE dataset, under varying illumination levels, pupil dilation, angle and occlusion*

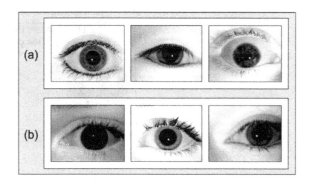

from the left eye from the ICE dataset. Notice the varying degree of illumination levels, pupil dilation, angle and occlusion.

## 3.2. Iris Segmentation

Here we give the details of our segmentation method. In particular, we discuss the effect of raised to power operation on an eye image along with its advantages. Next we provide details of efficiently determining the pupil region. Finally, we discuss the method to effectively determine the limbic boundary and the iris region segmentation. See Figure 4 for an overview of the three main stages in iris segmentation: the pupil detection, the limbic boundary detection, and the eyelid detection.

### 3.2.1. Performing the Raised to Power Operation on an Eye Image

The raised to power operator when applied to a grayscale image changes its dynamic range. The

pixel intensity values in the input image act as the basis which is raised to a (fixed) power. The operator is defined by the following formula (Gonzalez & Woods, 2001):

$$R(p) = c * I^{1/p} \tag{1}$$

where $I$ is the intensity value of a pixel in the input image, $c$ is the scaling factor and $1/p$ is the power.

For $p < 1$, this operation increases the bandwidth of the high intensity values at the cost of the low pixel values. For $p > 1$, this process enhances the low intensity value while decreasing the bandwidth of the high intensity values, i.e., enhances the contrast in the dark regions. For $p = 1$ the above transformation linearly scales the intensity value.

In Figure 5 the plot shows the result of the raised to power operation on the image intensity values at four different values of $p$. The output pixel value is scaled back to the intensity between 0 and 255. This operation when applied on the

*Figure 4. An overview of the three main stages in iris segmentation: the pupil detection, the limbic boundary detection, and the eyelid detection*

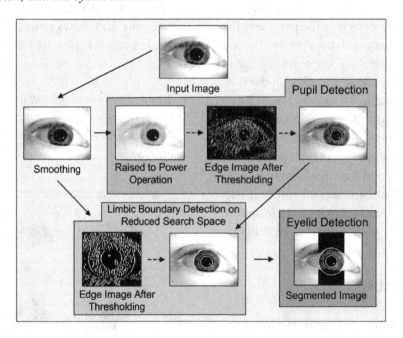

*Figure 5. The plot that shows the result of the raised to power operation on the image intensity values at four different p values*

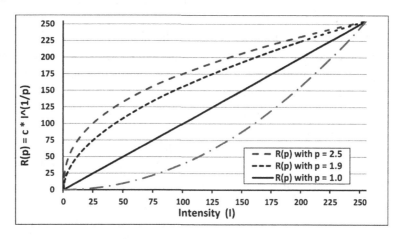

input pixel intensity with $p = 1$ and $c = 1$ does not have any effect on the output intensity. This can be seen in the plot for $R(p)$ at $p = 1$. For $p = 1.9$ and 2.5 the lower intensity values gain more than the higher intensity values. At $p = 0.5$ the intensity values get pulled down and the lower values tend to get mapped to a narrower range.

We assess the impact of the raised to power operation on an eye image in terms of the pixel intensity frequency in Figure 6. The original eye image is shown in Figure 6(a), transformed im-

*Figure 6. Results of the raised to power operation on (a) input eye image for p = 0.5, 1.9 and 2.5 shown in (b), (c) and (d) respectively. (e) Plot of the frequency of intensity of the input image at various p values. Plot at p = 1.0 corresponds to the input image in (a).*

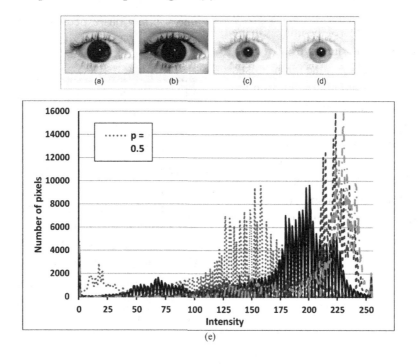

ages with $p$ values as 0.5, 1.9 and 2.5 can be seen in Figure 6(b), (c) and (d) respectively. The corresponding pixel intensity frequency plot for the four images is presented in Figure 6(e). For $p > 1$ many more pixels get mapped into a narrower brighter intensity range as seen in Figure 6(e). Also, this effect can be observed from the eye images in Figure 6(c) and (d) where the contrast between the pupil and the iris becomes more significant.

## 3.2.2. Efficient Determination of the Pupil Region

Our new iris segmentation method first applies the raised to power operation on an eye image and then detects the pupil boundary. We first detect the pupil boundary and then detect the outer iris boundary. The reason for this approach lies in the observation that the contrast between the iris and the pupil is usually larger than that between the iris and the sclera (Liu, Bowyer, & Flynn, 2005). The contrast is further enhanced from the application of the raised to power operation, this makes it easier to detect the pupil region and thereby increases the accuracy of the pupil segmentation. Our method results in the accurate detection of the pupil boundary for 99.8% of the images in the dataset, this includes all the right eye and the left eye images. The appropriate $p$ value for the raised to power operator is selected after analyzing the contrast between the iris and the pupil on a large number of eye images.

In Figure 4 we present the details of the pupil detection. In order to get rid of the noise, as a first step we apply the Gaussian filter to smooth the input image. The Gaussian smoothing filter is defined by the following formula (Forsyth & Ponce, 2003):

$$G(x, y) = \frac{1}{2\pi\sigma^2} e^{-\frac{x^2+y^2}{2\sigma^2}} \tag{2}$$

where $x$ is the distance from the origin in the horizontal axis, $y$ is the distance from the origin in the vertical axis, and $\sigma$ is the standard deviation of the Gaussian distribution. In the next stage, we apply the raised to power operation followed by the canny edge detector to detect edges in the image. Thresholding is performed to get rid of the weak edges.

Finally, we apply the circular Hough transform on the edge image to detect the pupil boundary. In order to make the pupil search more accurate and fast, we search for a candidate pupil having radius within a narrow range. This range is computed from a validation set chosen from the ICE dataset. See Figure 7(a) image on the left for the range of the radius and on the right the edge image space to be searched for candidate pupil circles. The circular Hough transform can be described as a transformation of a point in the $x$, $y$-plane to the circle parameter space. The parametric representation of the circle is given as:

$$x = a + r\cos(\theta)$$
$$y = b + r\sin(\theta) \tag{3}$$

where $a$ and $b$ are the center of the circle in the $x$ and $y$ direction respectively and where $r$ is the radius and $\theta$ is the angle between 0 and $2\pi$.

## 3.2.3. Efficient Determination of the Limbic Boundary and the Iris Region

We observe that when detecting the limbic boundary, the Hough transform often makes incorrect detections. Our research reveals that those incorrect detections are due to the presence of a large number of weak edges. Therefore, we apply a thresholding technique on the edge image produced by the Canny edge detector to get rid of the insignificant edge points. This has shown to improve the percentage of the correctly segmented iris region by close to 3% for both the right eye and the left eye images. See Figure 4 for details.

*Figure 7. Efficient determination of (a) determining the pupil region radius, (b) determining the iris region radius and search space, and (c) determining the limbic boundary center*

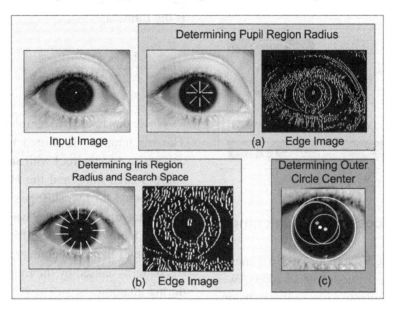

In order to further improve the accuracy of the Hough transform for detecting the limbic boundary, we search for the circle within a specific region around the detected pupil boundary. Furthermore, we search for a candidate limbic boundary having radius within a narrow range. The range for the radius is estimated on the validation set taken from the ICE dataset. The reduced search space and the narrow radius range thus considerably increase the speed of the circle detection. See Figure 7(b) left image for the range of the radius and on the right the reduced edge image space that will be searched for candidate limbic circles.

Additionally, we apply another efficient technique to detect the limbic boundary. The Hough transform implemented by the ICE method searches the maximum in the parameter space to detect the circle. We implement a technique based on the Hough transform that increases the accuracy of the correct limbic boundary detection by 1.3% for the right eye and by 1.4% for the left eye images. Specifically, when the center

of the detected circle is farther from the center of the detected pupil by a predefined threshold value, then the detected circle is rejected. Out of all the non-rejected circles we select the one that corresponds to the maximum in the parameter space of the Hough transform and has center coordinates within a predefined threshold value from the pupil center. As a result, our heuristic method considerably increases the accuracy of the Hough transform. In Figure 7(c) the center for the pupil is pointed in yellow, the incorrect limbic boundary circle with center in green is rejected as it is farther from the pupil center when compared to the correct limbic detection with center displayed in white.

We then model each eyelid as two straight lines. The eyelid detection is implemented by splitting the iris region horizontally and vertically resulting in four equal windows (Liu, Bowyer, & Flynn, 2005). We detect the eyelid in each of these four windows, and connect the results together. Figure 4 shows the result of the eyelid detection.

*Figure 8. (a) Segmented iris region and (b) its normalized iris region*

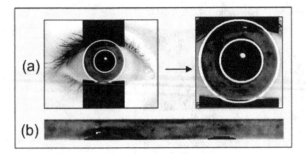

## 3.3. Feature Encoding and Matching

The feature encoding stage encodes the iris image texture patterns into iriscodes using filters. We normalize the iris region to a constant dimension before encoding. Denoising of the noise regions in the normalized pattern is implemented by means of averaging. This results in a bitwise template which contains iris information and a noise mask for corrupt areas within the iris pattern. Figure 8 shows the result of the normalization of the iris region.

Encoding is implemented by convolving the normalized iris pattern with the 1D Log-Gabor wavelets. The frequency response of a Log-Gabor filter is given as:

$$G(f) = \exp\left(\frac{-(\log(f / f_0))^2}{2(\log(\sigma / f_0))^2}\right) \qquad (4)$$

where $f_0$ represents the centre frequency, and $\sigma$ gives the bandwidth of the filter. Details of the Log-Gabor filter are given by Field, (1987).

We use the Hamming distance to measure the similarity of the two iris templates. The Hamming distance defines the similarity between two iriscodes, and the two iriscodes are a match when their Hamming distance is close to each other. In comparing the bit patterns X and Y, the Hamming distance (HD) is defined as the sum of disagreeing bits (sum of the XOR between X and Y) over N, the total number of bits in the bit pattern. Below is the formula:

$$HD = \frac{1}{N} \sum_{j=1}^{N} X_j \oplus Y_j \qquad (5)$$

Noise bits in the two templates are discarded. The iris template is shifted bit-wise from -15 degrees to +15 degrees with an increment of 1.5 degrees each time, and the Hamming distance is computed for two shift positions. The lowest Hamming distance is the best match between the two templates. Such shifting is necessary to take care of the misalignment in the normalized iris patterns caused by the rotational differences during imaging.

## 4. EXPERIMENTAL RESULTS

Here we present the details of the experimental evaluation of our proposed method on the ICE dataset. In order for us to make a through comparative assessment of the performance of our method with other methods, we conduct three sets of experiments for the right eye and the left eye. First we assess the correctness of iris segmentation, next we assess the rank-one recognition performance and finally we assess the verification performance for the right eye and the left eye according to the experimental setup proposed by the ICE system. The rank-one recognition criterion and the verification criterion evaluate the performance of our method for recognition from different viewpoints, we provide more details later in this Section. For all our experiments we scale the input image to 0.4 of its original size, this significantly cuts down the processing time without compromising the correctness of the results.

## 4.1. Assessing the Correctness of Segmentation

The first set of experiments is designed to assess the correctness of segmentation for the pupil region, the limbic boundary and the iris region on the right eye and the left eye. Considering the nature of the ICE dataset, we now define the correctness of segmentation based on the assumption that the pupil and iris can be modeled as a circle. The pupil region is said to be correctly segmented when the circle fully encloses the pupil region and does not include any area other than the dark pupil. Incorrect pupil segmentation may cover parts of the iris region and or only enclose the pupil region partially. Refer to Section 3.2.2 for the discussion on the method and Figure 9(c) and (d) for the results. The limbic boundary is said to be correctly segmented when the circle fully bounds the iris region from outside and does not include any area outside of the iris region other than the pupil or the eyelids that may sometimes occlude the iris. Incorrect limbic boundary segmentation may cover parts of the sclera region and or only enclose the iris region partially. Refer to Section 3.2.3 for the discussion on the method and Figure 10(a) and (b) for the results. The iris region is said to be correctly segmented when for any given eye image both the pupil and the limbic boundary are correctly detected.

In Table 1 we give the results of the correctness of the pupil and iris region segmentation. The raised to power operation is performed for pupil detection on the right and left eye image at different values of $p$. At $p = 1$ and $c = 1$ the raised to power operation leaves the intensity values of the pixels in the input image unchanged. For values of $p > 1$, the raised to power operation enhances the contrast in the dark regions and thereby makes the pupil boundary easier to detect. This is confirmed by the percentage of correct pupil detection as $p$ goes higher. Also, for $p < 1$, the contrast between the pupil and the surrounding region decreases making it harder to detect the pupil. We obtain best pupil detection results at $p = 1.9$ with close to 100% correct pupil detection for the left eye and 99.7% for the right eye. For the $p$ values higher than 1.9, we do not notice

*Figure 9. Comparison of the pupil segmentation performance of our improved method with the ICE method. (a) Input eye images, (b) images after the raised to power operation, (c) examples of correct segmentation of the pupil and iris region by our method. (d) Incorrect segmentation by the ICE method.*

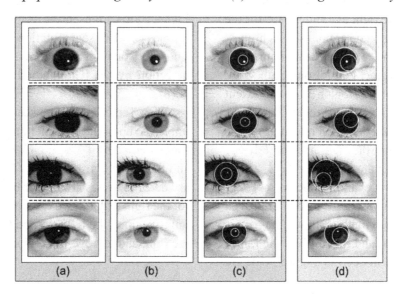

*Figure 10. Comparison of the limbic boundary segmentation performance of our improved method with the ICE method. (a) Examples of correct segmentation by our method. (b) Incorrect segmentation by the ICE method.*

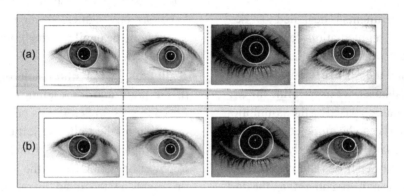

*Table 1. Correctness of segmentation for the pupil and iris region at different values of p*

| p | Right Eye | | Left Eye | |
|---|---|---|---|---|
| | **Pupil Region** | **Iris Region** | **Pupil Region** | **Iris Region** |
| 0.7 | 96.3% | 95.5% | 96.8% | 96.0% |
| 1.0 | 98.3% | 97.4% | 98.6% | 97.7% |
| 1.3 | 98.9% | 98.0% | 99.2% | 98.1% |
| 1.6 | 99.2% | 98.2% | 99.5% | 98.4% |
| **1.9** | **99.7%** | **98.5%** | **99.9%** | **98.8%** |
| 2.2 | 99.6% | 98.4% | 99.9% | 98.8% |
| 2.5 | 99.6% | 98.4% | 99.8% | 98.7% |

any significant change in the segmentation performance. The best result for the iris region detection is 98.5% for the right eye and 98.8% for the left eye. The iris region detection is at its highest when the pupil region detection is maximum; this is largely due to the fact that for our method the correct detection of iris region is to an extent dependent on the correct pupil region detection. Finally, the iris region detection rate at $p = 1.9$ is 1.1% higher for both the right and the left eye when compared with the rate at $p = 1$.

Figure 9(c) shows examples the correct segmentation of the pupil based on our improved pupil region detection method. Input images are shown in Figure 9(a) and the result of the raised to power operation in seen in Figure 9(b). We

compare our results with the incorrect segmentation results by the ICE method in Figure 9(d). In Figure 10(a) we present the results of our improved limbic boundary segmentation method and make a comparison with the incorrect limbic boundary detection by the ICE method shown in Figure 10(b).

From Table 2 it can be seen that our method improves upon the ICE method for pupil region segmentation by 4.3% and 4.2% for the right eye and the left eye respectively. Our limbic boundary detection rates are higher by 5.3% and 5.4% for the right and left eye respectively. Finally, we improve upon the ICE method by 8.3% for both the right and left eye iris region detection.

*Table 2. Comparison with the results from the ICE method of the correctness of segmentation for the pupil region, limbic boundary and iris region*

| | Our Method | | ICE Method | |
|---|---|---|---|---|
| | **Right Eye** | **Left Eye** | **Right Eye** | **Left Eye** |
| **Pupil Region** | 99.7% | 99.9% | 95.4% | 95.7% |
| **Limbic Boundary** | 98.7% | 99.0% | 93.4% | 93.6% |
| **Iris Region** | 98.5% | 98.8% | 90.2% | 90.5% |

## 4.2. Assessment of the Rank-One Recognition Performance

Here we evaluate the effectiveness of our method based on the rank-one recognition rate. This is a popular evaluation criterion for iris recognition. To obtain the recognition rate, we need to first calculate the Hamming distance between every pair of a query image and a target image, and then use the nearest-neighbor classifier for classifying all query images. If the query image and the target image belong to the same subject or class, it is a correct match. The recognition rate is the ratio of the number of correctly classified query images to the total number of query images. The rank-one recognition rate underlines the similarity of the samples that are close to one another within a class.

From Table 3 it can be seen that the best recognition rate is 99% for both the right eye and the left eye at $p = 1.9$, when compared to the rate at $p = 1$, this is higher by 1.4% for the right eye and by 0.9% for the left eye. We do not notice any significant change in the recognition performance for $p > 1.9$.

The rank-one recognition rate for our method as shown in Table 4 is 3.5% and 2.7% higher than that of the ICE method for the right eye and the left eye respectively. Furthermore, we improve upon the ND_IRIS by a significant 2% for the left eye. Please note that the authors in (Liu, Bowyer, & Flynn, 2005) do not report the recognition rate on the right eye.

## 4.3. Assessment of the Verification Performance and Equal Error Rate (EER)

In our final set of experiments we evaluate the verification performance and compare our results with the ICE method. The ICE protocol recommends using the receiver operating characteristic (ROC) curves, which plot the iris verification rate, i.e., the true accept rate versus the false accept rate (FAR), to report the iris recognition performance. The verification rate is the rate at which a matching algorithm correctly determines that a genuine sample matches an enrolled sample. The equal error rate (EER) is obtained when the FAR

*Table 3. Rank-one recognition performance at different values of p*

| $p$ | **Right Eye** | **Left Eye** |
|---|---|---|
| 0.7 | 95.4% | 95.9% |
| 1.0 | 97.6% | 98.1% |
| 1.3 | 98.3% | 98.5% |
| 1.6 | 98.7% | 98.8% |
| **1.9** | **99.0%** | **99.0%** |
| 2.2 | 98.9% | 99.0% |
| 2.5 | 98.9% | 98.9% |

*Table 4. Comparison of the rank-one recognition performance with the other methods*

|  | Right Eye | Left Eye |
|---|---|---|
| **Our Method** | **99.0%** | **99.0%** |
| **ND_IRIS** | - | 97.08% |
| **ICE Method** | 95.5% | 96.3% |

*Table 5. Iris verification performance at 0.1% false accept rate and EER at different values of p*

| *p* | Right Eye | | Left Eye | |
|---|---|---|---|---|
|  | VR | EER | VR | EER |
| 0.7 | 85.1% | 8.3% | 84.7% | 7.7% |
| 1.0 | 91.3% | 5.2% | 90.9% | 4.6% |
| 1.3 | 92.8% | 4.9% | 92.2% | 4.2% |
| 1.6 | 94.2% | 3.9% | 93.3% | 3.1% |
| **1.9** | **95.1%** | **2.8%** | **94.4%** | **2.3%** |
| 2.2 | 95.1% | 2.8% | 94.4% | 2.3% |
| 2.5 | 95.0% | 2.8% | 94.3% | 2.3% |

VR is the verification rate and EER is the equal error rate.

equals the false reject rate (FRR). Generally, the lower the EER value the higher is the accuracy of the biometric system.

The ROC curves are automatically generated by the BEE system when a similarity matrix is input to the system. In particular, the BEE system generates two ROC curves, corresponding to the Experiment 1 for the right eye and Experiment 2 for the left eye images. The iris verification rate at the false accept rate of 0.1% is generally used as a standard for performance comparison (Yang, Liu, & Zhang, 2010).

It should be pointed out that the verification rate in the ICE Experiment 1 and 2 emphasizes the similarity of samples that are relatively distant from one another within a class because it needs to measure all similarity between samples, whereas the recognition rate discussed in Section 4.2 emphasizes the similarity of samples that are close to one another within a class since it applies a nearest-neighbor classifier. Therefore, these two criteria evaluate the performance of our method for recognition from two different viewpoints.

From Table 5 it can be seen that the best verification rate and the lowest EER is achieved at *p* = 1.9. When compared to the performance at *p* = 1, the VR is higher by 3.8% at a low EER of 2.8% for the right eye and the VR is higher by 3.5% at the EER of 2.3% for the left eye. We do not notice any significant change in the verification performance for *p* > 1.9.

We compare in Figure 11 and Figure 12 the performance of our method with that of the ICE method in terms of the ROC curves. Figure 11 and Figure 12 show the ROC curves for the right eye experiment and the left eye experiment respectively. It can be observed that our proposed method improves the iris recognition performance significantly in comparison with the ICE method.

From Table 6 it can be seen that our method improves upon the ICE method notably. For the right eye, our proposed method has a verification rate of 95.1%, which is about 10% higher than the ICE method. The EER is 2.8%, which is much lower than the 8.5% for the ICE method. For the left eye, our proposed method has a VR of 94.4%,

*Figure 11. Comparison of the iris verification performance (ROC curve for the right eye) of the ICE method with our proposed method*

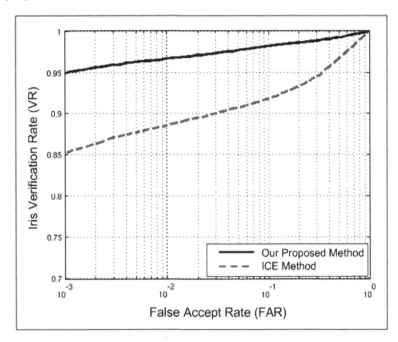

*Figure 12. Comparison of the Iris verification performance (ROC curve for the left eye) of the ICE method with our proposed method*

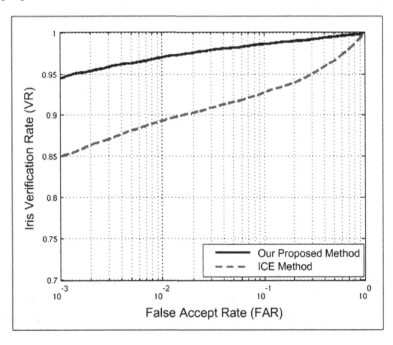

*Table 6. Comparison with the ICE method on the iris verification performance at 0.1% false accept rate and EER*

| | Right Eye | | Left Eye | |
|---|---|---|---|---|
| | **VR** | **EER** | **VR** | **EER** |
| **Our Method** | 95.1% | 2.8% | 94.4% | 2.3% |
| **ICE Method** | 85.2% | 8.5% | 84.9% | 7.8% |

VR is the verification rate and EER is the equal error rate.

which is again about 10% higher than the ICE method. The EER is 2.3%, which is much lower than the 7.8% for the ICE method; this emphasizes the higher accuracy of our system.

## FUTURE RESEARCH DIRECTIONS

The system presented here was able to perform accurately, however there are still several issues that need to be addressed. In order to make the iris recognition more practical in less-controlled conditions, we need to look at the segmentation of off-angle iris images, images with contacts and blurred images. Our experimental results also suggest that more work is needed on segmentation of the limbic boundary, especially for the iris images with relatively lower quality. In order to make the system for real-time recognition more robust, an indexing scheme based on the color of the iris can be performed, this would allow for faster search and matching.

## CONCLUSION

In this paper we presented an improved method for iris recognition with enhanced performance on the ICE dataset. In particular, we implement the raised to power operation for more accurate detection of the pupil region. Additionally, with our technique we are able to considerably reduce the candidate limbic boundary search space, this leads to a significant increase in the accuracy

and speed of the segmentation. The segmentation performance is further increased with the application of the thresholding. Furthermore, for higher accuracy and speed, we selectively detect the limbic circle having center within close range of the pupil center. The pupil is correctly segmented for 99.8% of the images in the dataset. Iris region detection is 98.5% for the right eye and 98.8% for the left eye. The rank-one recognition rate for our method is 3.5% and 2.7% higher than that of the ICE method for the right eye and the left eye respectively. Furthermore, we improve upon the ND_IRIS by a significant 2% on the rank-one recognition rate of the left eye. The verification rate is about 10% higher than the ICE method for each eye at a much lower equal error rate.

## REFERENCES

Cui, J., et al. (2004). An iris image synthesis method based on PCA and super-resolution. *Int. Conf. on Pattern Recognition*, (pp. 471-474).

Daugman, J. (2004). How iris recognition works. *IEEE Trans. on Circuits and Systems for Video Technology, 14*(1), 21–30. doi:10.1109/TCSVT.2003.818350

Daugman, J. (2006). Probing the uniqueness and randomness of iris codes: Results from 200 billion iris pair comparisons. *Proceedings of the IEEE, 94*(11), 1927–1935. doi:10.1109/JPROC.2006.884092

Daugman, J. (2007). New methods in iris recognition. *IEEE Trans. on Systems. Man and Cybernetics B*, *37*(5), 1167–1175. doi:10.1109/TSMCB.2007.903540

Du, Y., Ives, R. W., & Etter, D. M. (2004). Iris recognition: A chapter on biometrics. In *The electrical engineering handbook*. Boca Raton, FL: CRC Press.

Field, D. J. (1987). Relations between the statistics of natural images and the response properties of cortical cells. *Journal of the Optical Society of America*, *4*(12), 2379–2394. doi:10.1364/JOSAA.4.002379

Flom, L., & Safir, A. (1987). *Iris recognition system*. (U.S. Patent 4,641,349).

Forsyth, D., & Ponce, J. (2003). *Computer vision: A modern approach*. Upper Saddle River, NJ: Prentice Hall.

Gentile, J. E., Ratha, N., & Connell, J. (2009, September). *SLIC: Short length iris code*. International Conference on Biometrics: Theory, Applications and Systems, Washington, DC.

Gonzalez, C. G., & Woods, R. E. (2001). *Digital image processing*. Upper Saddle River, NJ: Prentice Hall.

Hao, F., Daugman, J., & Zielinski, P. (2008). A fast search algorithm for a large fuzzy database. *IEEE Transactions on Information Forensics and Security*, *3*(2), 203–212. doi:10.1109/TIFS.2008.920726

Huang, Y., Luo, S., & Chen, E. (2002). *An efficient iris recognition system* (pp. 450–454). Machine Learning and Cybernetics.

Ives, R. W., Guidry, A. J., & Etter, D. M. (2004). *Iris recognition using histogram analysis* (pp. 562–566). Signals, Systems and Computers.

Liu, C. (2007). The Bayes decision rule induced similarity measures. *IEEE Transactions on Pattern Analysis and Machine Intelligence*, *29*(6), 1116–1117. doi:10.1109/TPAMI.2007.1063

Liu, C., & Yang, J. (2009). ICA color space for pattern recognition. *IEEE Transactions on Neural Networks*, *20*(2), 248–257. doi:10.1109/TNN.2008.2005495

Liu, X., Bowyer, K. W., & Flynn, P. J. (2005). Experiments with an Improved Iris Segmentation Algorithm. *Workshop on Automatic Identification Advanced Technologies*, (pp. 118-123).

Ma, L., Tan, T., Wang, Y., & Zhang, D. (2004). Efficient iris recognition by characterizing key local variations. *IEEE Transactions on Image Processing*, *13*(6), 739–750. doi:10.1109/TIP.2004.827237

Masek, L. (2003). *Recognition of human iris patterns for biometric identification*. The University of Western Australia. Retrieved from www.csse.uwa.edu.au/~pk/studentprojects/libor

Phillips, P. J. (2006). *FRGC and ICE Workshop*. Tech. Report. National Institute of Standards and Technology.

Shuo, C., & Liu, C. (2010, September). *Eye detection using color information and a new efficient SVM*. International Conference on Biometrics Theory, Applications and Systems, Washington, DC.

Thornton, J., Savvides, M., & Vijayakumar, B. V. K. (2007). A Bayesian approach to deformed pattern matching of iris images. *Transactions on Pattern Analysis and Machine Intelligence*, *29*(4), 596–606. doi:10.1109/TPAMI.2007.1006

Tisse, C., Martin, L., Torres, L., & Robert, M. (2002). *Person identification technique using human iris recognition* (pp. 294–299). Proc. Vision Interface.

Verma, A., Liu, C., & Jia, J. (2011). New color SIFT descriptors for image classification with applications to biometrics. *International Journal of Biometrics*, *3*(1), 56–75. doi:10.1504/IJBM.2011.037714

Wildes, R. (1997). Iris recognition: An emerging biometric technology. *Proceedings of the IEEE*, *85*(9), 1348–1363. doi:10.1109/5.628669

Yang, J., Liu, C., & Zhang, L. (2010). Color space normalization: Enhancing the discriminating power of color spaces for face recognition. *Pattern Recognition*, *43*(4), 1454–1466. doi:10.1016/j.patcog.2009.11.014

## ADDITIONAL READING

Castleman, K. R. (1996). *Digital image processing*. Upper Saddle River, NJ: Prentice Hall.

Jähne, B. (1997). *Digital image processing – concepts, algorithms and scientific applications*. Berlin, BE: Springer.

Marion, A. (1991). *An introduction to image processing*. New York, NY: Chapman and Hall.

Marr, D. (1982). *Vision: a computational investigation into the human representation and processing of visual information*. San Francisco, CA: W. H. Freeman.

Trucco, E., & Verri, A. (1998). *Introductory techniques for 3D computer vision*. Upper Saddle River, NJ: Prentice Hall.

Vapnik, V. N. (2000). *The nature of statistical learning theory*. New York, NY: Springer-Verlag.

## KEY TERMS AND DEFINITIONS

**Biometrics:** Methods for uniquely recognizing humans based upon one or more inherent physical or behavioral traits.

**Heuristics:** Set of exploratory problem-solving methods that utilizes learning techniques by the 'discovery method' to improve performance.

**ICE:** Iris Challenge Evaluation.

**Image Enhancement:** Improving the interpretability or perception of information in images for human viewers or as an input for automated image processing techniques.

**Image Segmentation:** Changing the representation of a digital image by partitioning the image into multiple segments for simpler and easier analysis.

**Iris Recognition:** Method of biometric authentication that uses pattern-recognition techniques based on high-resolution images of the irises of an individual's eyes.

**Raised to Power Operation:** Transforming the intensity of an image through power operation.

# Chapter 10
# Color Image Segmentation of Endoscopic and Microscopic Images for Abnormality Detection in Esophagus

**P. S. Hiremath**
*Gulbarga University, India*

**Iranna Y. Humnabad**
*Gulbarga University, India*

## ABSTRACT

*The study of medical image analysis encompasses the various techniques for acquisition of images of biological structures pertaining to human body using radiations in different frequency ranges. The advancements in medical imaging over the past decades are enabling physicians to non-invasively peer inside the human body for the purpose of diagnosis and therapy. In this chapter, the objective is to focus on the studies relating to the analysis of endoscopic images of lower esophagus for abnormal region detection and identification of cancerous growth. Several color image segmentation techniques have been developed for automatic detection of cancerous regions in endoscopic images, which assists the physician for faster, proper diagnosis and treatment of the disease. These segmentation methods are evaluated for comparing their performances in different color spaces, namely, RGB, HSI, $YC_bC_r$, HSV, and CIE Lab. The segmented images are expected to assist the medical expert in drawing the biopsy samples precisely from the detected pathological legions. Further, various methods have been proposed for segmentation and classification of squamous cell carcinoma (SCC) from color microscopic images of esophagus tissue during pathological investigation. The efficacy of these methods has been demonstrated experimentally with endoscopic and microscopic image set and compared with manual segmentation done by medical experts. It is envisaged that the research in this direction eventually leads to the design and production of efficient intelligent computer vision systems for assisting the medical experts in their task of speedy accurate diagnosis of diseases and prescription of appropriate treatment of the patients.*

DOI: 10.4018/978-1-61350-429-1.ch010

# 1. INTRODUCTION

## 1.1 Medical Imaging

The study of medical image analysis encompasses the various techniques for acquisition of images of biological structures pertaining to human body using radiations in different frequency ranges. The image analysis is primarily influenced by the resolution and quality of the acquired images. The digital image processing techniques are employed to render such images amenable to more accurate and meaningful image analysis. In recent years, the improvement and the development of many image acquisition techniques, the enhancement of the general quality of the acquired images, advances in image processing and development of large computational capacities, have considerably eased this task. The acquisition of medical images in two (2D), three (3D), or higher dimensions, has become a routine task for clinical and research applications. The image acquisition techniques include magnetic resonance imaging (MRI), magneto encephalography (MEG), 3D ultra sound imaging, computed tomography (CT), positron emission tomography (PET), endoscopy imaging, single photon emission computed tomography (SPECT), functional MRI (fMRI), and diffusion weighted imaging (DWI).

## 1.1.1 Medical Image Analysis

Medical imaging is an important mode of capture of anatomical and functional information and is helpful for the accurate diagnosis and treatment of diseases. Medical images are the basis for a large number of clinical tasks in the daily routine of healthcare. The sustained developments in the field of acquisition technology enable capturing the increasing amounts of high-resolution images that reveal different aspects of the human body's structure and function with unprecedented detail. In the clinical routine, such large amounts of data pose not only storage problems but also challenges for image analysis. Medical images, for example,

are analyzed for examining relationships between structural abnormalities and deformations and certain functional abnormalities and diseases. Adopting computational aid for medical image analysis is no longer an option, but a necessity (Silvia D. Olabariaga et al. 2007). Among the primary tasks of medical image analysis are image segmentation, registration, and matching.

## 1.1.2 Medical Image Segmentation

Segmentation of the object of interest is a difficult step in the analysis of digital images. Fully automatic methods sometimes fail, producing incorrect results and requiring the intervention of a human operator. This is often true in medical applications, where image segmentation is particularly difficult due to restrictions imposed by image acquisition, pathology and biological variation. Segmenting an anatomical structure in a medical image amounts to identifying the region or boundary in the image corresponding to the desired structure. In the classical approach of segmentation by image labeling, image features are extracted and used to obtain a sparse collection of locations and data, which are then interpolated to form a representation and possible segmentation. Desired regions are identified by labeling each volume element (voxel) in a 3D scan, or picture elements (pixel) in 2D, based on the anatomical structure to which it corresponds. In more recent approaches, an initial curve or surface estimate of the structure boundary is provided and optimization methods are used to refine the initial estimate based on image data. A fully segmented scan allows surgeons to both visualize the shapes and relative positions of internal structures better qualitatively and measure their volumes and distances quantitatively more accurately.

The output of manual segmentation of medical images, by knowledgeable medical experts, can sometimes be considered optimal. Unfortunately, expert segmentation is far from recommended in many clinical situations.

## 1.2 Endoscopic Imaging

Electronic Videoendoscopy is commonly performed for a wide variety of diagnostic and therapeutic procedures due to the advent of miniature charge-coupled device (CCD) cameras and associated microelectronics. In minimally invasive surgical procedures, endoscopes that are inserted through natural orifices of the body, or small incisions, illuminate the surgical region of interest and transmit camera images to a video monitor. Minimally invasive procedures, such as resections and ablation, can reduce morbidity relative to traditional open procedures, because the smaller incisions minimize the damage to healthy tissues and reduce patient pain and convalescence time. Computerized image comprehension of endoscopic images offers a powerful tool for enhancing images and rendering them easier for the physician to point out abnormality. Computerized image processing techniques are gaining popularity to assist the clinician in diagnosing the related disease conditions.

### 1.2.1 Why is Endoscopy Performed?

Endoscopy can be used to diagnose various conditions by close examination of internal organs and body structures. Endoscopy can also guide therapy and repair, such as the removal of torn cartilage from the bearing surfaces of a joint. Biopsy (tissue sampling for pathologic testing) may also be performed under endoscopic guidance. Local or general anesthetic may be used during endoscopy, depending upon the type of procedure being performed. Internal abnormalities revealed through endoscopy include, abscesses, biliary (liver) cirrhosis, bleeding, bronchitis, cancer, cysts, degenerative disease, gallbladder stones, hernia, inflammation, metastatic cancer, polyps, tumors, ulcers, and other diseases and conditions. Endoscopy is a minimally invasive procedure and carries with it certain minor risks depending upon the type of procedure being performed.

### 1.2.2 The Esophagus

The esophagus is a hollow, highly distensible muscular tube that extends from the pharynx to the gastroeshphageal junction (Figure 1) measuring between 10 to 11 cm in the newborn, it grows to a length of about 23 to 25 cm in the adult. Several points of luminal narrowing can be identified along its course – proximally at the cricoid cartilage, midway in its course alongside the aortic arch and at the anterior crossing of the left main bronchus and left atrium, and distally where it pierces the diaphragm. Manometric recordings of intraluminal pressures in the esophagus have identified two higher-pressure areas that remain relatively contracted in the resting phase. A 3 cm segment in the proximal esophagus at the level of the cricopharyngeus muscle is referred to as the upper esophageal sphincter. The 2 to 4 cm segment just proximal to the anatomic esophagogastric junction, at the level of the diaphragm, is referred to as the lower esophageal sphincter (LES). The wall of the esophagus consists of a mucosa, submucosa, muscularis propria, and adventitia, reflecting the general structural organization of the gastrointestinal tract.

*Figure 1. The esophagus and stomach*

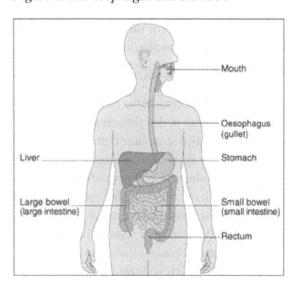

The functions of the esophagus are to conduct food and fluids from the pharynx to the stomach and to prevent reflux of gastric contents into the esophagus. These functions require motor activity coordinated with swallowing a wave of peristaltic contraction, relaxation of the LES in anticipation of the peristaltic wave, and closure of the LES after the swallowing reflex. The mechanisms governing this motor function are strikingly complex, involving both extrinsic and intrinsic innervation, humoral regulation and properties of the muscle wall itself. Cancer can occur anywhere along the length of esophagus.

Cancer is a disease that affects cells, the body's basic unit of life. To understand any type of cancer, it is helpful to know about normal cells and what happens when they become cancerous. The body is made up of many types of cells. Normally, cells grow, divide, and produce more cells when they are needed. This process keeps the body healthy and functioning properly. Sometimes, however, cells keep dividing when new cells are not needed. The mass of extra cells forms a growth or tumor. Tumor can be benign or malignant. Cancer that begins in the esophagus (also called esophageal cancer) is classified into two major types, squamous cell carcinoma and adenocarcinoma, depending on the type of cells that are malignant. Squamous cell carcinomas arise in squamous cells that line the esophagus. These cancers usually occur in the upper and middle part of the esophagus. Adenocarcinomas usually develop in the glandular tissue in the lower part of the esophagus. The treatment is similar for both type of esophageal cancer. If the cancer spreads outside the esophagus, it often goes to the lymph nodes first (lymph nodes are small, bean-shaped structures that are part of the body's immune system). Esophageal cancer can also spread to almost any other part of the body, including the liver, lungs, brain, and bones. The exact causes of cancer of the esophagus are not known. However, the studies show that any of the following factors, besides others, can increase the risk of developing esophageal cancer:

- **Age:** Esophageal cancer is more likely to occur as people get older; most people who develop esophageal cancer are over the age 60.
- **Sex:** Cancer of the esophagus is more common in men than in women.
- **Tobacco use:** Smoking cigarettes or using smokeless tobacco is one of the major risk factors for esophageal cancer.

## 1.2.3 Diagnosing Esophageal Cancer

In order to find the cause of symptoms, the doctor evaluates a person's medical history and performs a physical examination. The doctor usually orders a chest x-ray and other diagnostic tests. These tests may include the following:

- **A barium swallow (also called an esophagram):** is a series of x-rays of the esophagus. The patient drinks a liquid containing bariums, which coats the inside of the esophagus. If the barium makes any changes in the shape of the esophagus, it shows upon the x-rays.
- **Esophagoscopy (also called endoscopy):** is an examination of the inside of the esophagus using a thin lighted tube called an endoscope. An anesthetic (substance that causes loss of feeling or awareness) is usually used during this procedure. If an abnormal area is found, the doctor can collect cells and tissue through the endoscope for examination under a microscope. This is called a biopsy. A biopsy can show cancer, tissue changes that may lead to cancer, or other conditions.

## 1.2.4 Staging the Disease

If the diagnosis is esophageal cancer, the doctor needs to learn the stage (or extent) of disease. Staging is a careful attempt to find out whether the cancer has spread and, if so, to what parts of the body. Knowing the stage of the disease helps the doctor to plan for treatment. Listed below are descriptions of the four stages of esophageal cancer.

- **Stage 1:** The cancer is found only in the top layers of cells lining the esophagus.
- **Stage 2:** The cancer involves deeper layers of the lining of the esophagus, or it has spread to nearly lymph nodes. The cancer has not spread to other parts of the body.
- **Stage 3:** The cancer has invaded more deeply into the wall of the esophagus or has spread to tissues or lymph nodes near the esophagus. It has not spread to other parts of the body.
- **Stage 4:** The cancer has spread to other parts of the body. Esophageal cancer can spread almost anywhere in the body, including the liver, lump, brain and bones.

Endoscopically, the affected area is red and velvety. Medical experts detect the cancerous region based on the color information obtained from the endoscopic images, as discernible to their eyes and helps them in drawing the biopsy samples precisely from the detected pathological legions. These biopsy samples are sent to pathologists for microscopic analysis.

## 1.3 Microscopic Imaging

In pathology, diagnoses of disease are based on the recognition by a highly trained observer of visual clues or diagnostic criteria from various tissue specimens. Although many of these criteria have been clearly defined for each disease, they are often interpreted differently by each pathologist confronted with a specific specimen. With the hope of introducing more objective and accurate diagnostic criteria to the practice of pathology, many quantitative techniques have been developed. In quantitative pathology, the most important and, in fact, the most difficult task in image

morphometry is the recognition or segmentation of cells. Although the interactive manual tracing method is still the most reliable approach for the segmentation of cells, it involves considerable user participation and is very time-consuming. To simplify the tracing process, more efficient approaches are employed, which make use of a priori knowledge of medical cells, require less work from the user in tracing and are effective in practice.

Cell segmentation is a fundamental subject of quantitative analysis of cytological and histological images. Among various types of cell images, the ones obtained from biopsy are more difficult to segment, because of the diversity of the structures contained in the images, the intense variation of background caused by uneven staining, and overlapped cell clusters. As most of the malignant characteristics of cell are contained in cell nucleus, the isolation of cell nucleus is an important part of segmentation for this kind of cell images (Min Hu et al. 2004).

Many works have been reported in the literature as the area of cell segmentation. The major part of cell segmentation work is based on histogram techniques, region techniques and boundary techniques. (Yongming Chen et al. 1999) used spatial adaptive filter, watershed. (Dwi Anoraganingrum 1999) used a combination of median filter and mathematical morphology operation. (Hazem Refai et al. 2003) used similar approach as of (Dwi Anoraganingrum 1999) for cell segmentation. None of the above approaches are concerned with color textures. Texture is one of the important characteristics used in identifying an object or a region of interest in an image. Robust segmentation results generally require both the gray scale/color and textural information simultaneously. The statistical image segmentation technique is a feature based classification method which operates on a feature vector field resulting from the application of a vector operator on an input image. Statistical analysis based segmentation can be seen as a two step process identifying an appropriate feature vector set for mapping the patterns and, further, obtaining a classifier which can classify pixels of the image by using feature vectors. Feature extraction is one of the important steps of an image segmentation algorithm. Several feature extraction strategies are proposed in the literature. Textures may be regular or randomly structured and various structural, statistical, and spectral approaches have been proposed toward segmenting them (Haralick R.M. 1979), (L.V. Gool et al. 1985), (T.R. Reed and J. du Buf 1993). In general, most color texture representation schemes either use a combination of gray level texture features together with pure color features or they derive texture features computed separately in each of the three color spectral channels.

In (Timothy J. Muldoon et al. 2008), a novel, low-cost, high-resolution endoscopic microscope for obtaining fluorescent images of the cellular morphology of the epithelium of regions of the esophagus with Barrett's metaplasia has been described. This noninvasive point imaging system offers a method for obtaining real-time histologic information during endoscopy. In (Stavros A. Karkanis et al. 2003), an approach to the detection of tumors in colonoscopic video has been investigated. It is based on a new color feature extraction scheme to represent the different regions in the frame sequence. This scheme is built on the wavelet decomposition.

## 1.3.1 Pathological Features of Benign and Malignant Cells

This section deals with the basic concepts of pathology related to the present work. Majority of neoplasms can be categorized morphologically into benign and malignant on the basis of certain characteristics, the most important being degree of differentiation of the tumour cells. Differentiation is defined as the extent of morphological and functional resemblance of parenchymal tumour cells to corresponding normal cells. If the deviation of neoplastic cell in structure and function is

minimal as compared to normal cell, the tumour is described as well-differentiated such as most benign and low-grade malignant tumours. Poorly differentiated or undifferentiated are synonymous terms for poor structural and functional resemblance to corresponding normal cell. In other words, lack of differentiation is termed as anaplasia which is a characteristic feature of most malignant tumours. As a result of anaplasia, noticeable morphological and functional alterations in the neoplastic cells are observed. These are stated below (Harsh Mohan 1994):

1. **Pleomorphism:** The term pleomorphism means variation in size and shape of the tumour cells. The extent of cellular pleomorphism generally correlates with the degree of anaplasia. Tumour cells are often bigger than normal but they can be of normal size or smaller than normal.

2. **Nucleocytoplasmic (NC) changes:** The nuclei of tumour cells show most conspicuous changes compared to normal cells: (a) Generally, the nuclei of malignant tumour cells are enlarged, disproportionate to the cell size so that the NC ratio (the ratio of nuclei and cytoplasm areas) is increased. (b) Just like cellular pleomorphism, the nuclei, too, show variation in size (anisonucleosis) and shape in malignant tumour cells. (c) Characteristically, the nuclear chromatin of the malignant cell is increased and coarsely clumped. This is due to increase in the amount of nucleoprotein resulting in dark-staining nuclei, referred to as hyperchromatism. Besides, a prominent nucleolus or nucleoli may be present in these nuclei reflecting increased nucleoprotein synthesis. (d) The cytoplasm of tumour cells in better-differentiated cancers and in benign tumours may show the normal constituents from which the tumour is derived, e.g. the presence of mucus, keratin, cross striations etc.

## 1.3.2 Squamous Cell Carcinoma

This is the most commonly occurring malignant tumor of the esophagus. It is usually graded as well, moderately, or poorly differentiated. Well-differentiated tumours are those with abundant amounts of keratin, easily demonstrated intercellular bridges, and minimal nuclear and cellular pleomorphism. Poorly differentiated tumours are those with no or virtually no keratin and intercellular bridges or with marked celluar and nuclear plemorphism. Moderately differentiated tumours are those intermediate between well and poorly differentiated tumours (K.Oota and L.H. Sobin 1977).

## 1.4 Color Spaces

The use of color in image processing is motivated by two principal factors. First, color is a powerful descriptor that often simplifies object identification and extraction from a scene. Second, humans can discern thousands of color shades and intensities, compared to few shades of gray. This second factor is particularly important in manual image analysis. Color image processing is divided into two major areas: full-color and pseudo-color processing. In the first category, the images in question typically are acquired with a full-color sensor, such as a color TV camera or color scanner. In the second category, the problem is one of assigning a color to a particular monochrome intensity or range of intensities. Until recently, most digital color image processing was done at the pseudocolor level. However, in the past decade, color sensors and hardware for processing color images have become available at reasonable prices. The result is that full-color image processing techniques are now used in a broad range of applications, including publishing, visualization, and the internet (Rafael C. Gonzalez 2002).

A color space is a geometrical and mathematical representation of color. In the past, most of the color spaces have been proposed to define the colors with the similar way that the human perceives them. However, it is well known that no general method is applicable to all domains. In other words, the selection of suitable color space is application-specific and a complete theoretical analysis for the problem at hand is not feasible. Since the choice of a suitable color space is the first step toward a solution, several color spaces are investigated and described briefly as below.

## 1.4.1 The RGB Color Model

In this model, each color appears in its primary spectral components of red, green, and blue. This model is based on Cartesian coordinate system.

## 1.4.2 The HSI Color Model

When humans view a color object, the object is described by its hue, saturation and brightness. Hue (H) is a color attribute that describes a pure color (pure yellow, orange or red), whereas saturation (S) gives a measure of the degree to which a pure color is diluted by white light. The intensity (gray level) (I) is a most useful descriptor of monochromatic images. This quantity definitely is measurable, and easily interpretable. The RGB color space can be transformed to the HSI color space using the following equations (Rafael C. Gonzalez 2002):

$$H = \begin{cases} \theta & \text{if } B \leq G \\ 360 - \theta & \text{if } B \succ G \end{cases}$$

$$\theta = \cos^{-1} \left\{ \frac{\frac{1}{2}\left[(R-G)+(R-B)\right]}{\left[(R-G)^2+(R-B)(G-B)\right]^{\frac{1}{2}}} \right\} \quad (1)$$

The saturation component is given by

$$S = 1 - \frac{3}{(R + G + B)} \Big[\min\big(R, G, B\big)\Big].$$

$$(2)$$

Finally, the intensity component is given by

$$I = \frac{1}{3}\big(R + G + B\big). \tag{3}$$

## 1.4.3 The HSV Color Model

The HSV (hue, saturation, value) corresponds better to how people experience color than the RGB color space does: hue (H) represents the wavelength of a color if it would be monochromatic. Hue varies from 0 to 1 when color goes from red to green then to blue and back to red. H is then defined modulo 1. As color is seldom monochromatic, saturation (S) represents the amount of white color mixed with the monochromatic color. Value (V) does not depend on the color, but represent the brightness. So H and S are chrominance values and V is intensity. The following equations transform RGB color space to HSV color space (Vincent Arvis et al. 2004):

$$V = \max\big(R, G, B\big), \tag{4}$$

$$S = \frac{V - \min\big(R, G, B\big)}{V}, \tag{5}$$

$$H = \frac{G - B}{6S}, \text{ if V=R}, \tag{6}$$

$$H = \frac{1}{3} + \frac{B - R}{6S}, \text{ if V=G}, \tag{7}$$

$$H = \frac{2}{3} + \frac{R - G}{6S}, \text{ if V=B} \tag{8}$$

## 1.4.4 The YCbCr Color Model

The $YC_bC_r$ color space is sometimes referred to as the CCIR 601 color space (CCIR stands for International Consultative Committee on Broadcasting and the specification of $YC_bC_r$ is spelled out in the CCIR Recommendation 601-2 document). This color space was defined in response to increasing demands for digital approaches in handling video information, and has since become a widely used model in digital video. It belongs to the family of television transmission color spaces. The family includes others such as YUV and YIQ. The $YC_bC_r$ is a digital color system, while YUV and YIQ are analog spaces for the respective PAL and NTSC systems (PAL stands for Phase Alternation Line and NTSC stands for National Television System Committee) (Douglas Chai and Abdesselam Bouzardoum 2000). These color spaces separate RGB (Red, Green, Blue) into luminance and chrominance information and are useful in compression applications; however, the specification of colors is somewhat unintuitive. RGB values can be transformed to $YC_bC_r$ color space using equation:

$$\begin{bmatrix} Y \\ C_b \\ C_r \end{bmatrix} = \begin{bmatrix} 16 \\ 128 \\ 128 \end{bmatrix} + \begin{bmatrix} 65.481 & 128.553 & 24.966 \\ -37.797 & -74.203 & 112 \\ 122 & -93.786 & -18.214 \end{bmatrix} \begin{bmatrix} R \\ G \\ B \end{bmatrix}$$

$$(9)$$

where Y is the luminance component and, $C_b$ and $C_r$ are the chrominance blue and red components, respectively. (Victor J.D. Tsai 2006) has used various color models for the detection and compensation of shadow regions with shape information preserved in complex urban color aerial images for solving problems caused by cast shadows in digital image mapping.

## 1.4.5 The CIE Lab Color Model

The CIE Lab color space is based on a color vision model. The RGB space is transformed into CIE Lab tri-stimulus values and then into an achromatic lightness value L* and two chromatic values a* and b* using the transformation given by equations (10)-(13), where $X_n$, $Y_n$, and $Z_n$ are the tri-stimulus values of the reference (neutral) white point, and g(t) is defined in equation (14) (Iranna, September 2007):

$$\begin{bmatrix} X \\ Y \\ Z \end{bmatrix} = \begin{bmatrix} 0.412453 & 0.357580 & 0.180423 \\ 0.212671 & 0.715160 & 0.072169 \\ 0.019334 & 0.119193 & 0.950227 \end{bmatrix} \begin{bmatrix} R \\ G \\ B \end{bmatrix},$$

$$(10)$$

$$L^* = 116 \; g\left(\frac{Y}{Y_n}\right) - 16, \tag{11}$$

$$a^* = 500\left(g\left(\frac{X}{X_n}\right) - g\left(\frac{Y}{Y_n}\right)\right), \tag{12}$$

$$b^* = 200\left(g\left(\frac{Y}{Y_n}\right) - g\left(\frac{Z}{Z_n}\right)\right), \tag{13}$$

$$g(t) = \begin{cases} t^{1/3} & , \quad t > 0.008856 \\ 7.787\, t + \dfrac{16}{116} & , \quad t \le 0.008856 \end{cases}$$

$$(14)$$

The inherent properties of CIE Lab color space are that radial distance and angular position represent the chroma and hue of the color, respectively. It is much easier to handle color consistency and brightness in CIE Lab color space than in the other types of color spaces.

## 1.4.6 Pseudocolor Image Processing

Pseudocolor (also called false color) image processing consists of assigning colors to gray values based on the specified criterion. The term pseudo or false color is used to differentiate the process of assigning colors to monochrome images from the processes associated with true color images. The principal use of pseudocolor is for human visualization and interpretation of gray-scale events in an image or sequence of images. As noted in the section 1.4, one of the principal motivations for using color is the fact that humans can discern thousands of color shades and intensities, compared to few shades of gray.

## 1.4.7 Full-Color Image Processing

Full-color image processing approaches fall into two major categories. In the first category, each component image is processed individually and then a composite processed color image is formed from the individually processed components. In the second category, color pixels are processed directly. Because full-color images have at least three components, color pixels really are vectors. For example, in the RGB system, each color point can be interpreted as a vector extending from the origin to that point in the RGB coordinate system

## 2. DETECTION OF ABNORMAL REGION IN ENDOSCOPIC IMAGE

Conventional diagnosis of cancer based on endoscopic images employs visual interpretation of the images by the medical experts. For an automatic visual system to "understand a scene", it is necessary to extract regions of special interest by proper segmentation (P. Wang et al. 2001). Computerized image comprehension of endoscopic images offers a powerful tool for enhancing images and rendering them easier for the physician to point out abnormality. A wide variety of image segmentation techniques have been developed, viz., edge detection, region growing, histogram threshold and clustering. Among them, the methods of clustering and histogram threshold are extensively used for color image segmentation. For color image segmentation, there exist two basic problems. The first is uncertainty that most segmentation results are not always crisp or correct due to the grayness ambiguity and spatial ambiguity in an image. The second is that the definition of efficient quality measure is difficult and the segmentation methods using various parameters rely on image characteristic and environment. Therefore, the technique developed may not be applicable to other applications. Another difficulty is due to the lumen region which is the area of lowest intensity in an endoscopic image. As the endoscope uses several light sources at its tip and the illuminating distances of these sources are limited, the surface lying near the light source will be brighter than that lying further away. (Hiremath and Iranna, July 2003) have studied the detection of abnormal regions (esophageal cancer) in endoscopic images of esophagus using color image segmentation and proposed various techniques, which are discussed in the subsequent sections.

## 2.1 Feature Extraction and Segmentation using the Statistical Moments

The Figure 2 depicts the different stages of image processing for detection of the levels of esophageal cancer growth.

### 2.1.1 Pre-Processing and Feature Extraction

The endoscopic images of the lower section of esophagus obtained from the endoscopy instrument OLYMPUS CV-70 are considered as input images which are of size 128x128 pixels and are assumed to be free from lumen region and are preprocessed. The preprocessing involves smoothening of color images using average filter (Rafael C. Gonzalez 2002). The RGB color image contains three times more data than a gray-scale image. However, the three maps should not be processed independently because it appears that strong spatial and chromatic correlations exist. We have considered average filter for smoothening on the multi image (R(x,y), G(x,y), B(x,y)). Let $P_{xy}$ denote the set of coordinates defining a neighborhood centered at (x,y) in RGB color image. The average $\bar{c}(x, y)$ of the RGB component vectors in this neighborhood is given by

*Figure 2. Processing of images for detection of the levels of cancerous growth*

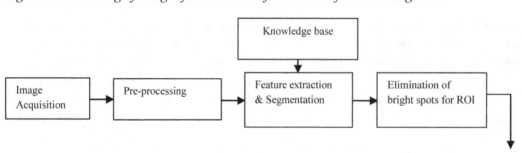

$$\bar{c}(x, y) =$$

$$\frac{1}{K} \left[ \sum_{(x,y) \in P_{xy}} R(x, y), \sum_{(x,y) \in P_{xy}} G(x, y), \sum_{(x,y) \in P_{xy}} B(x, y) \right]^T$$

$$(15)$$

where K is total number of pixels in $P_{xy}$. We recognize the components of this vector as the scale images that would be obtained by independently smoothing each plane of the starting RGB image using conventional gray-scale neighborhood processing. Thus, the smoothing by neighborhood averaging can be carried out on a per-color-plane basis.

From 25 sample images, the mean, standard deviation, skewness and kurtosis of RGB values, for the regions classified as initial stage or advanced stage of cancer, are determined using the statistical moments given below (Iranna, September 2007).

$$\bar{V}_j = \frac{1}{N} \sum_{(x,y) \in C} V_j(x, y) \quad \text{(Mean)} \qquad (16)$$

where $V_j(x, y)$ is the value of $j^{th}$ color component of the pixel at (x,y) in the cancerous region C.

$$\mu_{2j} = \frac{1}{N} \sum_{(x,y) \in C} \left[ V_j(x, y) - \bar{V}_j \right]^2 \quad \text{(Second moment}$$

about the mean) $\qquad (17)$

$$\mu_{3j} = \frac{1}{N} \sum_{(x,y) \in C} \left[ V_j(x, y) - \bar{V}_j \right]^3 \quad \text{(Third moment}$$

about the mean) $\qquad (18)$

$$\mu_{4j} = \frac{1}{N} \sum_{(x,y) \in C} \left[ V_j(x, y) - \bar{V}_j \right]^4 \quad \text{(Fourth moment}$$

about the mean) $\qquad (19)$

Standard deviation $\sigma_j = \sqrt{\mu_{2j}}$ (Measure of dispersion) $\qquad (20)$

Skewness $S_j = \dfrac{\mu_{3j}}{\sigma_j^3}$ (Measure of asymmetry)

$$(21)$$

Kurtosis $K_j = \dfrac{\mu_{4j}}{\mu_{2j}^2}$ (Measure of peakedness)

$$(22)$$

This information is stored as the knowledge base for automatic segmentation of any given input image. The Table 1 shows the estimated mean, standard deviation, skewness and kurtosis of RGB values of regions of interest, namely, regions showing initial and advanced stage of cancer growth.

Histograms of one sample endoscopic image containing initial stage cancerous region and that containing advanced stage cancerous region are shown in Figure 3 and Figure 4, respectively. The skewness (loss of symmetry) and kurtosis (peakedness) of histograms are evident from these figures.

Surface plots of one sample endoscopic image containing initial stage cancerous region and that containing advanced stage cancerous region are shown in Figure 5 and Figure 6, respectively.

## 2.1.2 Segmentation Using 3σ–Intervals

For a given input image, the segmentation is carried out using the 3σ–intervals (Willam W. Hines 1990) around mean RGB values stored in the knowledge base. The pixels of the input image are classified as belonging to initial stage or advanced stage cancer growth and thus the detection of different stages of esophageal cancer in endoscopic images is achieved.

These images may contain the bright spots which are due to the reflection from the light source. The RGB values of the pixels belonging to these bright spots are replaced by the mean RGB values. This process eliminates the bright spots

*Table 1. The statistical moments of RGB values for the two disease classes: Initial and advanced stages*

| Disease Class | Initial stage | | | Advanced stage | | |
|---|---|---|---|---|---|---|
| Variables | R | G | B | R | G | B |
| Mean | 177.12 | 56.45 | 45.47 | 120.63 | 60.28 | 56.90 |
| Standard deviation | 17.43 | 12.48 | 15.13 | 16.97 | 15.43 | 17.77 |
| Skewness | 0.05 | 0.93 | 0.74 | 0.31 | 0.55 | 0.48 |
| Kurtosis | 3.02 | 5.35 | 4.84 | 3.30 | 3.78 | 3.59 |

*Figure 3. (a) Sample endoscopic image containing initial stage cancerous region; (b), (c) and (d) Red, Green and Blue components of sample image (a), respectively; (e), (f) and (g) Histograms of Red, Green and Blue components in (b), (c) and (d), respectively.*

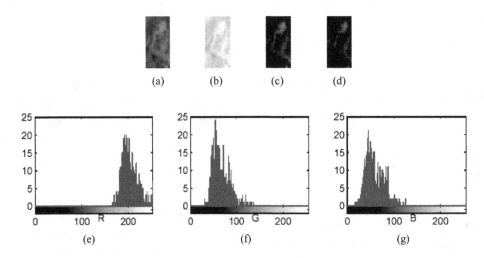

*Figure 4. (a) Sample endoscopic image containing advanced stage cancerous region; (b), (c) and (d) Red, Green and Blue components of sample image (a), respectively; (e), (f) and (g) Histograms of Red, Green and Blue components in (b), (c) and (d), respectively.*

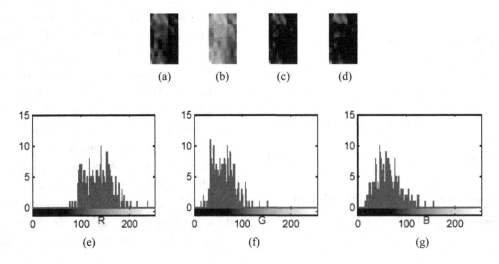

*Figure 5. (a) Sample endoscopic image containing initial stage cancerous region; (b), (c) and (d) Red, Green and Blue components of sample image (a), respectively; (e), (f) and (g) Surface plot of Red, Green and Blue components in (b), (c) and (d), respectively; (h) Surface plot of gray image of (a).*

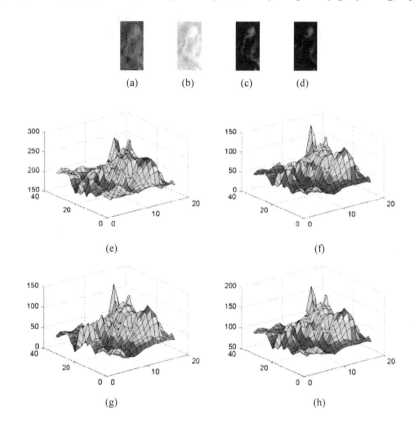

and thus minimizes the misdetection of cancerous region as normal region. The Figure 7 shows the different stages of processing of an endoscopic image. For experimentation, the 160 color endoscopic test images of size 128x128 pixels obtained from a medical expert are subjected to the segmentation process. The resulting images are shown in Figure 8 for five test images and compared with manual segmentation done by medical expert. The results are in good agreement with the manual segmentation (Hiremath and Iranna, July 2003).

### 2.1.3 Other Segmentation Methods

The other segmentation methods proposed for detection of abnormal regions in esophageal endoscopic images are based on the CG-transformation (Hiremath and Iranna, December 2003), the HSI color space, the K-means clustering (Hiremath and Iranna, August, 2005), and RGB textural features (Hiremath and Iranna, December 2006c), and their comparative performance analysis has been done.

## 2.2 Segmentation Using Non-Linear Skin Color Model

The non-linear skin color model is proposed in (Hiremath and Iranna, December 2006b). We have used $YC_bC_r$ color space and nonlinearly transformed it to make the skin cluster luma-independent. This is done by fitting polynomial boundaries to the skin cluster based on skin patches of abnormal regions collected from endsocopic images of esophagus (Figure 9). The transformed

*Figure 6. (a) Sample endoscopic image containing advanced stage cancerous region; (b), (c) and (d) Red, Green and Blue components of sample image (a), respectively; (e), (f) and (g) Surface plot of Red, Green and Blue components in (b), (c) and (d), respectively; (h) Surface plot of gray image of (a).*

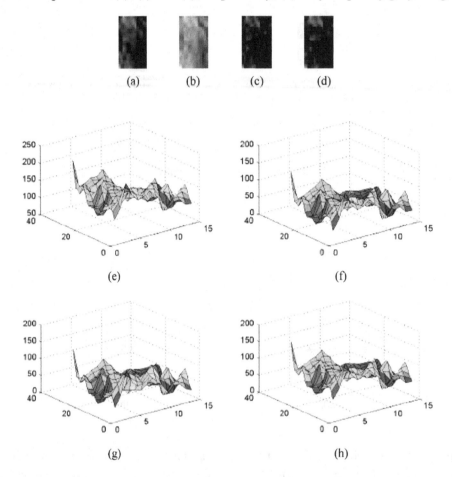

*Figure 7. (a) A color endoscopic image, (b) Image obtained after smoothing, (c) Image showing initial stage of cancer, (d) Image showing advanced stage of cancer, (e) and (f) Images with bright spots, (g) and (h) Images after filling bright spots.*

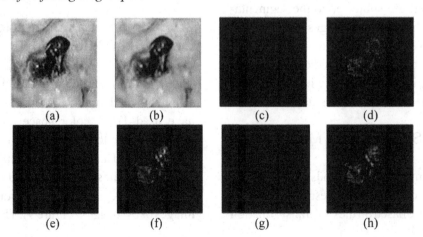

*Figure 8. (a) Original color endoscopic image, (b) Initial stage cancerous region and (c) Advanced stage cancerous region (d) Manual segmentation done by medical expert for initial stage cancerous region and (e) Manual segmentation done by medical expert for advanced stage cancerous region*

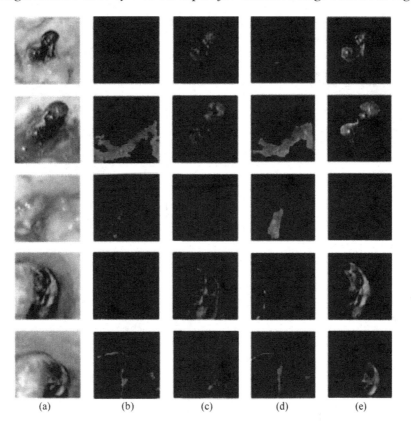

| (a) | (b) | (c) | (d) | (e) |

space (Figure 10) enables a robust detection of skin-tone colors. The skin-tone pixels are detected using an elliptical skin model in the transformed space, which is described below:

The smoothed RGB image is converted into $YC_bC_r$ color representation. The transformation from RGB space to $YC_bC_r$ space is defined by the equation (9). In the $YC_bC_r$ color space, we can regard the chroma ($C_b$ and $C_r$) as the functions of the luma (Y): $C_b(Y)$ and $C_r(Y)$. Let the transformed chroma be $C_b'(Y)$ and $C_r'(Y)$. The skin color model is specified by three polynomial curves upper, lower and centre (denoted by $C_b^u(Y)$, $C_b^l(Y)$ and $\bar{C}_b(Y)$) and by the spread of the cluster (denoted by $W_{C_b}(Y_p)$ and $W_{C_r}(Y_p)$). The transformed chroma $C_i'$ are given by:

$$C_i'(Y) = \left[ C_i(Y) - \bar{C}_i(Y) \right] \frac{W_{C_i}(Y_p)}{W_{C_i}(Y)} + \bar{C}_i(Y_p),$$

$$\text{for } Y \in \left[ Y_{\min}, Y_{\max} \right] \tag{23}$$

$$W_{C_i}(Y) = WL_{C_i} + \left( 2\tilde{a}Y_p + \tilde{b} \right)\left( Y - Y_{\min} \right),$$
$$\text{for } Y \in \left[ Y_{\min}, Y_p \right]$$
$$= WH_{C_i} + \left( 2\tilde{a}Y_p + \tilde{b} \right)\left( Y_{\max} - Y \right),$$
$$\text{for } Y \in \left[ Y_p, Y_{\max} \right] \tag{24}$$

$$W_{C_i}(Y_p) = C_i^u(Y_p) - C_i^l(Y_p), \tag{25}$$

*Figure 9. Nonlinear transformation of the $YC_bC_r$ color space: (a) the skin tone cluster of $YC_b$ subspace, (b) the skin tone cluster of $YC_r$ subspace. The polynomials $C_i^u$, $C_i^l$ and $\bar{C}_i$ are shown by continuous curves*

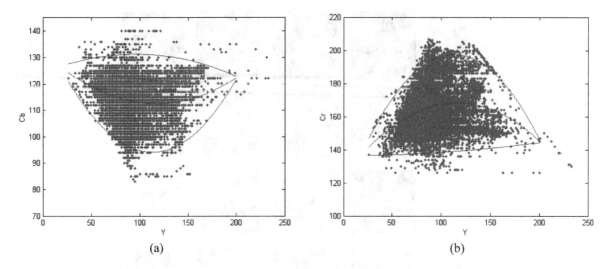

(a)                                        (b)

*Figure 10. Transformed $YC_bC_r$ color space (2D projection) in which the elliptical skin model is overlaid on the skin cluster.*

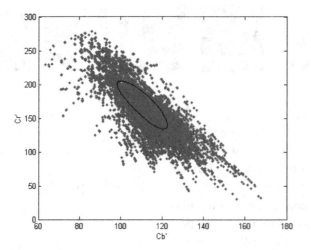

$$Y_p = -\frac{b}{2a} \quad if \;\; ab < 0,$$
$$= \frac{b}{2a} \quad otherwise, \tag{26}$$

$$C_i^u(Y) = a_u Y^2 + b_u Y + c_u,$$
$$C_i^l(Y) = a_l Y^2 + b_l Y + c_l, \tag{27}$$
$$\bar{C}_i(Y) = \bar{a} Y^2 + \bar{b} Y + \bar{c}$$

$$\tilde{a} = a_u - a_l, \tilde{b} = b_u - b_l \tag{28}$$

where $C_i$ in (6.2) to (6.6) is either $C_b$ or $C_r$, $Y_{min} = 26$, $Y_{max} = 233$, $Y_p = 114.5287$. In $YC_b$ plane, the parametric values are $a_u = -0.0008$, $b_u = 0.1474$, $c_u = 124.1446$, $a_l = 0.0036$, $b_l = -0.08045$, $\underline{c}l = 139.5016$, $\bar{a} = 0.0014$, $\bar{b} = -0.3285$, $\bar{c} = 131.8231$, $WL_{C_b} = 26$, and $WH_{C_b} = 233$. In $YC_r$

plane, the parametric values are $a_u = -0.0067$, $b_u = 1.5178$, $c_u = 111.7585$, $a_l = 0.0002$, $b_l = 0.0015$, $cl = 136.3597$, $\bar{a} = -0.0033$, $\bar{b} = 0.7597$, $\bar{c} = 124.05941$, $WL_{C_r} = 26$, and $WH_{C_r} = 233$. These parametric values are estimated from the training samples of skin patches of abnormal regions, which are known to be cancerous, drawn from the endoscopic images of esophagus and are used as the knowledge base for automatic segmentation process. The elliptical model for the skin tones of abnormal regions in the transformed $C_b' C_r'$ space (Figure 10) is:

$$\frac{\left(x - ec_x\right)^2}{a^2} + \frac{\left(y - ec_y\right)^2}{b^2} = 1, \tag{29}$$

$$\begin{bmatrix} x \\ y \end{bmatrix} = \begin{bmatrix} \cos\theta & \sin\theta \\ -\sin\theta & \cos\theta \end{bmatrix} \begin{bmatrix} C_b' - c_x \\ C_r' - c_y \end{bmatrix}, \tag{30}$$

where $c_x = 112.6679$, $c_y = 172.5544$, $\theta = 1.8$ (in radian), $ec_x = 111$, $ec_y = 170$, $a = 7.0$ and $b = 1.2$ are computed from the skin cluster in the $C_b' C_r'$ space.

## 2.2.1 Segmentation Using Piecewise Linear Skin-Color Model

The smoothed RGB image is converted into $YC_b C_r$ color representation. In the $YC_b C_r$ color space, we can regard the chroma ($C_b$ and $C_r$) as the functions of the luma (Y): $C_b(Y)$ and $C_r(Y)$. Let the transformed chroma be $C_b'(Y)$ and $C_r'(Y)$. The skin color model is specified by the centres (denoted as $\bar{C}_b(Y)$ and $\bar{C}_r(Y)$) and spread of the cluster (denoted as $W_{C_b}(Y)$ and $W_{C_r}(Y)$) and is used for computing the transformed chroma (Hiremath and Iranna, December 2005) (see Box 1), where $C_i$ in (6.10) and (6.11) is either $C_b$ or $C_r$, and the parameters have the values $W_{C_b} = 46.97$, $W_{LC_b} = 23$, $W_{HC_b} = 14$, $W_{C_r} = 38.76$, $W_{LC_r} = 20$, $W_{HC_r} = $

$10$, $K_l = 30$, $K_h = 85$, $Y_{min} = 16$, $Y_{max} = 235$. These parameter values are estimated from training samples of skin patches of abnormal region, which are known to be cancerous, drawn from the endoscopic images of esophagus and are used as the knowledge base for automatic segmentation.

The elliptical model for the skin tones in the transformed $C_b' C_r'$ space is described in (35) and (36).

$$\frac{\left(x - ec_x\right)^2}{a^2} + \frac{\left(y - ec_y\right)^2}{b^2} = 1 \tag{35}$$

$$\begin{bmatrix} x \\ y \end{bmatrix} = \begin{bmatrix} \cos\theta & \sin\theta \\ -\sin\theta & \cos\theta \end{bmatrix} \begin{bmatrix} C_b' - c_x \\ C_r' - c_y \end{bmatrix} \tag{36}$$

where $c_x = 125$, $c_y = 150$, $\theta = 2.53$ (in radian), $ec_x = 1.6$, $ec_y = 2.41$, $a = 25.39$ and $b = 14.03$ are computed from the skin cluster in the $C_b' C_r'$ space.

## 2.2.2 Experimental Results

In order to evaluate the performance of the non-linear skin color model, a series of experiments are performed by considering endoscopic images of cancerous esophagus wall obtained from the endoscopy instrument. The 160 images of size 128x128 pixels containing the cancerous region of the esophagus wall are considered, which are assumed to be free from lumen region and are pre-processed. The preprocessing involves smoothening of color images using average filter (Rafael C. Gonzalez 2002). The experimental results of segmentation of abnormal regions detected in the five test images using the non-linear skin color model and their comparison with those of 3σ-interval method, piecewise linear skin-color model and manual segmentation are shown in the Figure 11. The percentage of image pixels constituting the segmented region of interest (abnormal region) in all the five test cases are given in the Table 2.

*Box 1.*

$$C'_i(Y) = \begin{cases} \left(C_i(Y) - \bar{C}_i(Y)\right)\dfrac{W_{C_i}}{W_{C_i}(Y)} + \bar{C}_i\left(K_h\right) & \text{If } Y < K_l \text{ or } K_h < Y, \\[4mm] C_i(Y) & \text{If } Y \in \left[K_l, K_h\right] \end{cases} \tag{31}$$

$$W_{C_i}(Y) = \begin{cases} W_{LC_i} + \dfrac{\left(Y - Y_{\min}\right)\left(W_{C_i} - W_{LC_i}\right)}{K_l - Y_{\min}} & ; Y < K_l \\[4mm] W_{HC_i} + \dfrac{\left(Y_{\max} - Y\right)\left(W_{C_i} - W_{HC_i}\right)}{Y_{\max} - K_h} & ; K_h < Y \end{cases} \tag{32}$$

$$\bar{C}_b(Y) = \begin{cases} 168 + \dfrac{10\left(K_l - Y\right)}{K_l - Y_{\min}} & ; Y < K_l \\[4mm] 168 + \dfrac{10\left(Y - K_h\right)}{Y_{\max} - K_h} & ; K_h < Y \end{cases} \tag{33}$$

$$\bar{C}_r(Y) = \begin{cases} 184 + \dfrac{10\left(K_l - Y\right)}{K_l - Y_{\min}} & ; Y < K_l \\[4mm] 184 + \dfrac{22\left(Y - K_h\right)}{Y_{\max} - K_h} & ; K_h < Y \end{cases} \tag{34}$$

It is observed that the results of the non-linear skin color model based on a non-linear skin-tone color model are comparable with the $3\sigma$-interval segmentation method, piecewise linear skin-color model and the manual segmentation done by the medical expert.

The percentage differences between the non-linear skin color model and the $3\sigma$-interval method for the images 1,2,3,4 and 5 are 11.37, 32.72, 5664.51, 35.17 and 113.35 respectively. The very large differences observed for the image number 2, 3 and 5 can be attributed to the fact that, in the non-linear skin color model, luminance dependence of chromatic components is removed by using a skin-tone color model in $YC_bC_r$ color space, whereas the $3\sigma$-interval method is applied

in RGB color space in which chromatic components depend on luminance. The image number 2 has poor illumination, which is possible when endoscopic light source is far from the esophagus skin surface. The image number 3 and 5 have bright illumination, which is possible when the skin surface is nearer to the light source. Thus, the non-linear skin color model has detected larger area of abnormal region than the $3\sigma$-interval method, piecewise linear skin-color model and also accounts for the variations in the illumination conditions due to the varying distances of the skin surface and endoscopic light source while capturing the images. Especially, in the case of image number 3, the abnormal region identified by the medical expert is detected by piecewise linear

*Figure 11. (a) Original endoscopic color image of esophagus containing cancerous region, (b) Segmentation using non-linear skin-color model (c) Segmentation using 3σ-interval method, (d) Segmentation using piecewise linear model, (e) Manual segmentation done by medical expert and (f) Binary image of (b), (g) Binary image of (c), (h) Binary image of (d).*

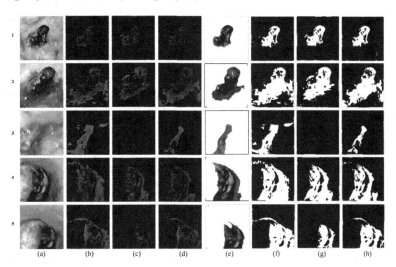

*Table 2. Comparison of segmentation results obtained by non-linear skin-color model, 3σ-interval method, piecewise linear skin-color model and manual segmentation*

| Image | Percentage of image pixels in the segmented region | | | |
|---|---|---|---|---|
| | Non-linear skin-color model (Hiremath and Iranna, December 2006b) | 3σ-interval Method (Hiremath and Iranna, August 2005) | Piecewise linear skin-color model (Hiremath and Iranna, December 2005) | Manual Segmentation |
| 1 | 10.91 | 12.31 | 10.63 | 19.97 |
| 2 | 39.02 | 29.40 | 39.87 | 37.76 |
| 3 | 17.87 | 00.31 | 12.05 | 12.09 |
| 4 | 41.58 | 30.76 | 28.93 | 46.89 |
| 5 | 28.59 | 13.40 | 24.56 | 28.30 |

skin-color model and is well detected by the non-linear skin color model in $YC_bC_r$ color space, whereas it has not been detected by the 3σ-interval method in RGB color space. This demonstrates the robustness of the non-linear skin color model to the illumination variations.

The percentage differences between the non-linear skin color model and the piecewise linear skin-color model for the images 1, 2, 3, 4 and 5 are 2.63, 2.13, 48.29, 43.72 and 16.40 respectively. These results imply significant improvement of

segmentation due to the non-linear skin color model.

The non-linear skin color model can be applied to any unknown sample image obtained by endoscopy of eshophagus in order to detect the abnormal regions, if any, present in the image. Further diagnostic tests can be conducted by taking tissue samples from the detected abnormal region for possible cancer detection. The segmented images assist the medical expert in drawing the biopsy samples precisely from the pathological legion.

# 3. CELL NUCLEI SEGMENTATION IN MICROSCOPIC IMAGES OF SQUAMOUS CELL CARCINOMA

## 3.1 Segmentation and Classification Using Statistical Textural Features

The histological material used in this study has been collected from Gulbarga Diagnostic and Research Laboratory, Gulbarga. The image data set comprised 120 image samples from H and E (Haematoxylin and Eosin) stained tissue sections of esophagus. The digital images of stained tissue slides are captured by using a light microscopy imaging system (Olympus BX51 with DP12 camera) at a magnification of x40. For experimentation 120 color microscopic images of size 256x256 pixels are used.

## 3.1.1 Segmentation of Nuclei

As indicated above, the major feature of malignancy related with the nuclei of the cells is nucleocytoplasmic ratio, which is the ratio of nuclei region to cytoplasm region for a cell in the image sample. In order to evaluate this ratio, we perform the segmentation of the image sample into three regions: nuclei, cytoplasm and background, using the fuzzy c-means clustering technique. The Figure 12 depicts the different stages of image processing for segmentation and classification of squamous cell carcinoma (SCC) in microscopic

image of esophagus tissue (Hiremath and Iranna, December 2006a).

The input image consists of three spectral channels i.e. R, G, and B. In each channel, the image is divided into 3x3 non overlapping blocks. For each block, the statistical features, namely, mean and standard deviation are computed. The feature vector consists of mean and standard deviation of a block in the three channels R, G, and B. The data set of these feature vectors is classified into three classes pertaining to three regions, namely, nuclei, cytoplasm and background, using fuzzy c-means clustering.

To build the knowledge base, we consider known sample images of squamous cell carcinoma in consultation with the medical expert. Let N be the number of pixels in the cell nuclei region C in an image. If $V_j(x, y)$ denote the value of the $j^{th}$ color component of the pixel at $(x, y)$ in the cell nuclei region, then the mean $\bar{V}_j$ and standard deviation $\sigma_j$ are computed by the formulas:

$$\bar{V}_j = \frac{1}{N} \sum_{(x,y)\in C} V_j(x, y), \sigma_j$$
$$= \sqrt{\frac{\sum_{(x,y)\in C} \left[ V_j(x, y) - \bar{V}_j \right]^2}{N}} \tag{37}$$

This procedure is repeated for several sample images. From the training images, the mean and standard deviation of RGB values for the cell

*Figure 12. Block diagram for segmentation and classification of SCC*

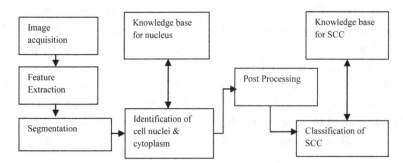

*Table 3. Statistical features for cell nuclei region of squamous cell carcinoma in RGB color space*

| Statistical features | RGB values $f_i$(knowledge) | | |
|---|---|---|---|
| | **R** | **G** | **B** |
| Mean | 72.69 | 46.71 | 144.98 |
| Standard Deviation | 15.44 | 13.22 | 12.59 |

nuclei region are determined using the statistical sampling technique (William W. Hines and D.C. Montgomery 1990), which are given in the Table 3. This information is stored as the knowledge base for automatic identification of cell nuclei of squamous cell carcinoma in a given input image.

We consider a test sample image. It is segmented into three classes as described above. For each class, the mean and standard deviation are computed. These values are compared with the corresponding values stored in the knowledge base using the distance vector formula

$$D(test\ class) = \sqrt{\sum_{i=1}^{6} \left[ f_i(knowledge) - f_i(test\ class) \right]^2} \quad (38)$$

where $f_i$(knowledge) are the components of knowledge base vector of features for cell nuclei region, $f_i$(test class) are the components of feature vector of a test class of the test image, and $D$(test class) is the Euclidean distance between the feature vectors of knowledge base and test classes. Then the test class for which $D$(test class) is minimum is identified as the cell nuclei region. The morphological operations are applied on this classified image to remove the squaring effect observed on the boundary of cell nuclei region (Rafael C. Gonzalez and Richard E. Woods 2002).

A cell comprises nucleus, and cytoplasm around it, enclosed in cell membrane. Thus, the region around the nuclei region but distinct from the background region is identified as the cytoplasm. This enables the evaluation of nucleocytoplasmic ratio in the input sample image. The cell nuclei

segmentation and identification is given in the form of an algorithm as shown below:

Algorithm: *Cell nuclei segmentation and identification*

**Step 1.** Input color cell image of size 256x256 as test image.

*Segmentation Phase:*

**Step 2.** For each non-overlapping 3x3 block of input image, calculate statistical textural features, namely mean and standard deviation, in each color plane. This yields 86x86 feature vectors, each of 6 components (2 for each plane).

**Step 3.** Use fuzzy c-means clustering method to classify the data set of feature vectors obtained in Step2 into three classes, namely, nuclei, cytoplasm and background.

*Identification Phase:*

**Step 4.** Compute average of the data vectors for each class.

**Step 5.** Compute Euclidean distance between the average feature vectors of the three classes obtained in Step4 and the feature vector of the knowledge base. The Euclidean distance is given by equation (38).

**Step 6.** The test class for which $D$(test class) is minimum is identified as cell nuclei region.

**Step 7.** Use morphological operations on the cell nuclei region obtained in Step6 to remove the squaring effect on the nuclei boundary.

*Table 4. Distribution parameters of nc ratio for well, moderately and poorly differentiated SCC*

| Statistical features | Squamous Cell Carcinoma | | |
|---|---|---|---|
| | Well differentiated | Moderately differentiated | Poorly differentiated |
| Mean $(\bar{n}_c)$ | 0.4103 | 0.3876 | 0.1838 |
| Standard deviation $(\sigma_{n_c})$ | 0.0704 | 0.0657 | 0.0361 |
| Skewness $(K_{n_c})$ | 0.0691 | -0.2468 | 0.1059 |

**Step 8.** The region surrounding the cell nuclei but distinct from background region is identified as cytoplasm.

## 3.1.2 Classification of Squamous Cell Carcinoma

The squamous cell carcinoma is classified as well differentiated, moderately differentiated or poorly differentiated, depending on the nucleo-cytoplasmic ratio, which is the ratio of nuclei and cytoplasm areas. We consider a set of training sample images for each class of squamous cell carcinoma. For each of the sample training images, which are known as belonging to a class of squamous cell carcinoma, the nuclei and cytoplasmic regions are identified using the algorithm given in the section 3.1.3. The average value $n_c$ of nucleocytoplasmic ratio for a cell is computed for each training image. Using statistical sampling technique, the mean $\bar{n}_c$, standard deviation $\sigma_{n_c}$ and skewness $K_{n_c}$ of the sampling distribution of nuleocytoplasmic (NC) ratio values are determined, for the training set of images in each class of squamous cell carcinoma. This information is stored as the knowledge base as shown in the Table 4, for the automatic classification of squamous cell carcinoma as well differentiated, moderately differentiated or poorly differentiated squamous cell carcinoma.

For a given test sample image, we compute the average value $n_c(test)$ of nucleocytoplasmic ratio for a cell. If $n_c(test)$ lies in the $2\sigma$-intervals of the $\bar{n}_c$ value of poorly differentiated class, then the test sample image is classified as poorly differentiated squamous cell carcinoma. Otherwise, the test image may be classified as either well differentiated or moderately differentiated squamous cell carcinoma, since the $2\sigma$-intervals around $\bar{n}_c$ for these classes overlap considerably. This classification requires a set of test sample images (of the same biopsy of a patient) for which mean $\bar{n}_c(test)$, standard deviation $\sigma_{n_c(test)}$ and skewness $K_{n_c(test)}$ are computed. If $\bar{n}_c(test)$ lies in the $2\sigma$-intervals of the $\bar{n}_c$ value of well differentiated squamous cell carcinoma and skewness value $K_{n_c(test)}$ is positive, then the test images are classified as well differentiated squamous cell carcinoma. Otherwise, the test images will be classified as moderately differentiated squamous cell carcinoma.

## 3.1.3 Experimental Results

In order to evaluate the performance of the algorithm, a series of experiments are performed and the 120 sample images of squamous cell carcinoma of esophagus are used, 40 images of each category: well differentiated, moderately differentiated and poorly differentiated squamous cell carcinoma. The three regions namely nucleus, cytoplasm and background in an image obtained by using fuzzy c-means clustering are shown in Figure 13.

*Figure 13. (a) Original microscopic color image, (b) Nuclei region, (c) Cytoplasm region, and (d) background region.*

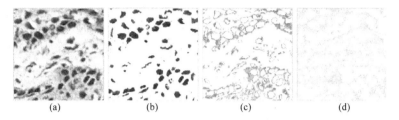

The nuclei region is identified using minimum distance classifier and then the morphological operations are applied on this segmented image to remove the squaring effect around the cell nuclei (Figure 14(a) and 14(b)).The results are compared with the manually segmented nuclei image shown in Figure 14(c). The sample images of well differentiated, moderately differentiated and poorly differentiated squamous cell carcinoma are shown in Figure 15.

The classification accuracy is 100% for poorly differentiated squamous cell carcinoma. The classification accuracy of 75% and 62.5% for well differentiated and moderately differenti-

ated squamous cell carcinoma, respectively, are obtained using five test sample images. However, higher classification accuracy could be obtained by using large test sample images pertaining to the same biopsy of a patient (Hiremath and Iranna, December 2006a).

## 3.2 Segmentation and Classification Using Color and Textural Features

In (Hiremath and Iranna, 2007), the color texture analysis of images based on Haralick features extracted from each of the spectral components has been investigated. The features are homogeneity

*Figure 14. (a) Identified cell nuclei image in Figure 2(b), (b) Cell nuclei image after applying the morphological operations, and (c) Manual Segmentation of nuclei done by the medical expert.*

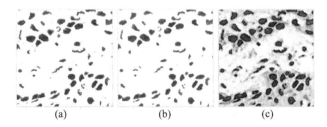

*Figure 15. The sample images of squamous cell carcinoma: (a) Well differentiated, (b) Moderately differentiated, and (c) Poorly differentiated.*

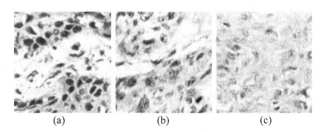

(E), contrast (C), correlation (Cor), entropy (H) and local homogeneity (LH), defined by:

$$E = \sum_i \sum_j \left( M(i,j) \right)^2 \quad (39)$$

$$C = \sum_{k=0}^{m-1} k^2 \sum_{|i-j|=k} M(i,j) \quad (40)$$

$$Cor = \frac{1}{\sigma_i \sigma_j} \sum_i \sum_j (i - \mu_i)(j - \mu_j) M(i,j) \quad (41)$$

where $\mu_i$ and $\sigma_i$ are the horizontal mean and variance and $\mu_j$ and $\sigma_j$ are the vertical statistics and $M(i,j)$ is the cooccurrence matrix,

$$H = \sum_i \sum_j M(i,j) \log \left( M(i,j) \right) \quad (42)$$

$$LH = \sum_i \sum_j \frac{M(i,j)}{1 + (i-j)^2} \quad (43)$$

## 3.2.1 Fusion of Color and Texture Features

The microscopic images of esophagus tissue samples are in RGB color space. The method consists of a change in the color space of the images, in order to obtain one channel containing the luminance information and two others containing chrominance information. Texture features are then computed from the luminance channel and other features, namely, color features are computed from the chrominance (intensity) channel. On the intensity channel, Haralick features are extracted as described in section 3.2. The cooccurrence matrix is computed on images with different gray tones by uniform quatization. The aim of this is to obtain an indication of the loss of texture information due to a reduction of gray

tones resolution. On the chromaticity channels, color features are extracted, consisting of the mean and standard deviation of each channel. Thus a total of 9 features characterize one image sample. The formula for mean and standard deviation are:

$$Mean(m) = \frac{1}{N^2} \sum_{i,j=1}^{N} p(i,j) \quad (44)$$

$$Standard\ deviation(sd) =$$
$$\sqrt{\frac{1}{N^2} \sum_{i,j=1}^{N} \left[ p(i,j) - m \right]^2} \quad (45)$$

Firstly, the HSV (hue, saturation, value) color space is used. It corresponds better to how people experience color than the RGB color space does: hue (H) represents the wavelength of a color if it would be monochromatic. Hue varies from 0 to 1 when color goes from red to green then to blue and back to red. H is then defined modulo 1. as color is seldom monochromatic, saturation (S) represents the amount of white color mixed with the monochromatic color. Value (V) does not depend on the color, but represent the brightness. So H and S are chrominance and V is intensity. The transformation from RGB to HSV color space is described in 1.4.3.

Secondly, the $YC_bC_r$ color space is used. This color space is widely used for digital video. In this format, luminance information is stored as a single component (Y), and chrominance information is stored as two color-difference components ($C_b$ and $C_r$). The $C_b$ represents the difference between the blue component and a reference value. The $C_r$ represents the difference between the red component and a reference value. These features are defined for video processing purposes and so are not meaningful concerning human experience. The transformation from RGB to $YC_bC_r$ color space is described in 1.4.4.

Thirdly, Lab color space is used. The CIE Lab color space is based on a color vision model. This space is transformed from CIE Lab tri-stimulus values into an achromatic lightness values L* and two chromatic values a* and b* using the transformation given in 1.4.5. The inherent properties of CIE Lab color space are that radial distance and angular position represent the chroma and hue of the color, respectively. It is much easier to handle color consistency and brightness in CIE Lab color space than in the other types of color spaces.

Algorithm: *Feature extraction for the three categories of SCC*

**Step 1.** Input the RGB microscopic image I of esophagus tissue
**Step 2.** Transform the RGB color space of I to $YC_bC_r$ / HSV/Lab and choose quantization level q.
**Step 3.** Compute the cooccurrence matrix for luminance channel in the color space chosen in Step 2 and extract Haralick features (as described in 3.2)
**Step 4.** Extract the color textural features for chrominance channels (as described in 3.2.1)
**Step 5.** Fuse the color and Haralick textural features to yield a feature vector with 9 features (i.e. 5 Haralick features + 2 statistical moment features x 2 chrominance channels, as shown in Figure 15) and store in feature library for the three categories of SCC.
**Step 6.** Repeat Step 1 through Step 5 for all the training images and build the feature library completely for the three categories of SCC.

## 3.2.2 Training and Classification

For experimentation, the data set consists of 40 microscopic images of esophagus tissue obtained from the abnormal regions of human esophagus detected through endoscopy of each category namely, poorly differentiated, moderately differentiated, and well differentiated Squamous Cell Carcinoma (SCC) of size 256x256. The entire image is used for feature computation. Thus, the dataset contains 120 images.

In the training phase, the color and texture features are extracted (as described in section 3.2) from t randomly selected sample images of each category, namely, poorly differentiated, moderately differentiated, and well differentiated SCC. These features are stored in the feature library, which are further used for classification of SCC images.

In the classification phase, the remaining 40-t images of each category (out of total 40 images of each category, t images of each category have been used for training) are used. The color and texture features are extracted for each test image as described in 3.2 and then compared with the features of all the images from the feature library. The Canberra distance measure is used for computing the distance between image features. This distance measure allows the feature set to be in unnormalized form. The Canberra distance is given by

$$CanbDist\left(x, y\right) = \sum_{i=1}^{d} \frac{\left|x_i - y_i\right|}{\left|x_i\right| + \left|y_i\right|} \qquad (46)$$

where x and y are the feature vectors of training and testing database, respectively, of dimension d. The K nearest neighbors (K-NN) classifier is used for classification. In the K-NN classifier, the class of the test sample is decided by the majority class among the K nearest neighbors. A neighbor is deemed nearest if it has the smallest distance in the feature space. In order to avoid a tied vote, it is preferable to choose K to be an odd number. The experiments are performed choosing K=3, K=5, and K=7.

## 3.2.3 Experimental Results

The experimentation has been done choosing a small training sample and also for a large training sample of images in different color spaces: $YC_bC_r$, HSV and Lab, with varying quantization levels. The experimental results are presented in Table 5 and Table 6, which show the percentage classifications for three different image classes, namely, poorly differentiated, moderately differentiated, and well differentiated SCC of esophagus tissue. The analysis of the experimental results shows that the classification accuracy of 100% is obtained using $YC_bC_r$ color space.

### Small Training Sample

The Table 5 shows that, for small training sample, the classification rate of 100% is achieved in all the three color spaces with varying quantization levels for poorly differentiated SCC. However, the overall classification rate is better in $YC_bC_r$ color space than in other color spaces.

### Large Training Sample

The Table 6 shows that, for large training samples, the classification rate is 100% in all the three color spaces with varying quantization levels for all the three disease classes of SCC. However, only in case of well differentiated SCC, the classification rate is 80-90% in HSV and Lab spaces. But, in $YC_bC_r$ space, the classification rate is 100% for all the three disease classes of SCC upto K=7 (except quantization level 128 at K=7).

Thus, in general, the classification rate is 100% in $YC_bC_r$ space. Further, the method is robust enough to yield classification rate of 100% even with small training/ testing sample of images in case of poorly differentiated SCC in all the three color spaces. These results are significant in view of the fact that in most cases of medical images of patients, the number of images available for training/ testing would be small (Hiremath and Iranna, 2007).

## 4. CONCLUSION AND FUTURE RESEARCH DIRECTIONS

### 4.1 Conclusion

In this Chapter we have dealt with the studies relating to the analysis of endoscopic images of lower esophagus for abnormal regions detection and identification of cancerous growth. Several color image segmentation techniques have been developed for automatic detection of cancerous regions in endoscopic images, which assists the physician for faster, proper diagnosis and treatment of the disease. These segmentation methods

*Table 5. Classification results (in %) with small training sample (10 training images and 30 test images of each class)*

| Value of k | Disease Class of SCC | Color Space | | | | | | | | |
|---|---|---|---|---|---|---|---|---|---|---|
| | | YCbCr | | | HSV | | | Lab | | |
| | | Quantization | | | Quantization | | | Quantization | | |
| | | 32 | 64 | 128 | 32 | 64 | 128 | 25 | 50 | 100 |
| 3 | PD | 100.00 | 100.00 | 100.00 | 100.00 | 100.00 | 100.00 | 100.00 | 100.00 | 100.00 |
| | MD | 96.66 | 96.66 | 96.66 | 80.00 | 83.33 | 80.00 | 96.66 | 96.66 | 100.00 |
| | WD | 76.66 | 80.00 | 73.33 | 73.33 | 73.33 | 73.33 | 76.66 | 73.33 | 70.00 |
| 5 | PD | 100.00 | 100.00 | 100.00 | 100.00 | 100.00 | 100.00 | 100.00 | 100.00 | 100.00 |
| | MD | 90.00 | 96.66 | 96.66 | 70.00 | 66.66 | 66.66 | 86.66 | 86.66 | 86.66 |
| | WD | 70.00 | 70.00 | 70.00 | 53.33 | 56.66 | 56.66 | 76.66 | 66.66 | 60.00 |
| 7 | PD | 100.00 | 100.00 | 100.00 | 100.00 | 100.00 | 100.00 | 100.00 | 100.00 | 100.00 |
| | MD | 90.00 | 90.00 | 90.00 | 70.00 | 73.33 | 70.00 | 86.66 | 86.66 | 86.66 |
| | WD | 93.33 | 66.66 | 63.33 | 60.00 | 63.33 | 63.33 | 63.33 | 63.33 | 60.00 |

PD: Poorly differentiated, MD: Moderately differentiated, and WD: Well differentiated

*Table 6. Classification results (in %) with large training sample (30 training images and 10 test images of each class)*

| Value of K | Disease Class of SCC | Color Space | | | | | | | | |
|---|---|---|---|---|---|---|---|---|---|---|
| | | YCbCr | | | HSV | | | Lab | | |
| | | Quantization | | | Quantization | | | Quantization | | |
| | | 32 | 64 | 128 | 32 | 64 | 128 | 25 | 50 | 100 |
| 3 | PD | 100.00 | 100.00 | 100.00 | 100.00 | 100.00 | 100.00 | 100.00 | 100.00 | 100.00 |
| | MD | 100.00 | 100.00 | 100.00 | 100.00 | 100.00 | 100.00 | 100.00 | 100.00 | 100.00 |
| | WD | 100.00 | 100.00 | 100.00 | 80.00 | 90.00 | 90.00 | 90.00 | 100.00 | 90.00 |
| 5 | PD | 100.00 | 100.00 | 100.00 | 100.00 | 100.00 | 100.00 | 100.00 | 100.00 | 100.00 |
| | MD | 100.00 | 100.00 | 100.00 | 100.00 | 100.00 | 100.00 | 100.00 | 100.00 | 100.00 |
| | WD | 100.00 | 100.00 | 100.00 | 90.00 | 90.00 | 90.00 | 90.00 | 90.00 | 90.00 |
| 7 | PD | 100.00 | 100.00 | 100.00 | 100.00 | 100.00 | 100.00 | 100.00 | 100.00 | 100.00 |
| | MD | 100.00 | 100.00 | 100.00 | 100.00 | 100.00 | 100.00 | 100.00 | 100.00 | 100.00 |
| | WD | 100.00 | 100.00 | 90.00 | 90.00 | 90.00 | 90.00 | 100.00 | 100.00 | 80.00 |

PD: Poorly differentiated, MD: Moderately differentiated, and WD: Well differentiated

are evaluated for comparing their performances in different color spaces, namely, RGB, HSI, $YC_bC_r$, HSV and CIE Lab. The segmentation methods are: statistical moments (3σ- interval method), color and texture features (statistical moments, Haralicks), model based method (skin color model), and clustering methods (fuzzy c-means, k-means) combined with moment features for classification.

The efficacy of these methods has been demonstrated experimentally with endoscopic image set and compared with manual segmentation done by medical expert. The segmented images are expected to assist the medical expert in drawing the biopsy samples precisely from the detected pathological legions.

Further, various methods have been proposed for segmentation and classification of squamous cell carcinoma (SCC) from color microscopic images of esophagus tissue obtained from the abnormal regions of esophagus through endoscopy. The efficacy of these methods has been demonstrated experimentally with microscopic image set and compared with manual segmentation done by medical expert

## 4.2 Future Research Directions

The development of computer vision systems for a fully automatic detection of abnormal regions in endoscopic images of esophagus and classification of squamous cell carcinoma (SCC) in microscopic images of tissue samples of pathological legions is a challenging task. The research work reported in this Book Chapter points to several future directions in which research work can progress. They are: (i) The building up of suitable effective feature space library as knowledge base for both endoscopic images and microscopic images. (ii) The design of efficient feature extraction algorithms, which are computationally inexpensive and yet yield good segmentation results. (iii) The efficient algorithms for classification of microscopic images of biopsy samples for each category of SCC. (iv) The design of efficient and intelligent computer vision systems which accept video sequence from endoscope and output quantitative and qualitative results. (v) The development of appropriate mathematical models to design intelligent systems interfaced with the endoscopy system to aid the physician and also with microscopes to aid the pathologist.

It is envisaged that the research in this direction eventually leads to the design and production of efficient intelligent computer vision systems for assisting the medical experts in their task of speedy accurate diagnosis of diseases and prescribing appropriate treatment of the patients.

## REFERENCES

Anoraganingrum, D. (1999). Cell segmentation with median filter and mathematical morphology operations. In *Proceedings of International Conference on Image Analysis and Processing*, (pp. 1043-1046).

Arvis, V., Debain, C., Berducat, M., & Benassi, A. (2004). Generalization of the cooccurrence matrix for colour image: Application to colour texture classification. *Image Analysis & Stereology, 23*, 63–72. doi:10.5566/ias.v23.p63-72

Chai, D., & Bouzerdoum, A. (2000). A Bayesian approach to skin color classification in YCbCr color space. *Proceedings, TENCON, 2*, 421–424.

Chen, Y., Biddeli, K., Sun, A., Relue, P. A., & Johonson, D. J. (1999). An automatic cell counting method for optical images. In *Proceedings of the First Joint BMES/EMBS Conference, Atlantic*, (p. 819).

Gonzalez, R. C., & Woods, R. E. (2002). *Digital image processing* (2nd ed.). Pearson Education.

Gool, L. V., Dewaele, P., & Oosterlinck, A. (1985). Texture analysis anno 1983. *Computer Vision Graphics and Image Processing, 29*, 336–357. doi:10.1016/0734-189X(85)90130-6

Haralick, R. M. (1979). Statistical and structural approaches to texture. *Proceedings of the IEEE, 67*(5), 786–804. doi:10.1109/PROC.1979.11328

Hines, W. W., & Montgomery, D. C. (1990). *Probability and statistics in engineering and management science* (3rd ed.). John Wiley and Sons.

Hiremath, P. S., & Humnabad Iranna, Y. (December 2006a). Automated cell nuclei segmentation and classification of squamous cell carcinoma from microscopic images of esophagus tissue. In *Proceedings of IEEE 14th International Conference on Advanced Computing and Communication (ADCOM-2006)*, NITK, Surathkal, Karnataka, India, IEEE, (pp. 211-216).

Hiremath, P. S., Dhandra, B. V., Humnabad Iranna, Y., Hegadi, R., & Rajput, G. G. (2003). Detection of esophageal cancer (necrosis) in endoscopic images using color image segmentation. In *Proceedings of the Second National Conference on Document Analysis and Recognition (NCDAR-2003)*, PES, Mandya, Karnataka, India, (pp. 417-422).

Hiremath, P. S., & Humnabad Iranna, Y. (December 2005). Color image segmentation based on clustering method for esophageal cancer detection in endoscopic images. In *Proceedings of the International Conference on Cognition and Recognition (ICCR-2005)*, Mysore, Karnataka, India, (pp. 705-710). Allied Publishers Pvt. Ltd.

Hiremath, P. S., & Humnabad Iranna, Y. (2005, August). Automated detection of esophageal cancer (necrosis) in endoscopic images using color image segmentation. *Global Engineering, Science, and Technology Society. International Transactions on Computer Science and Engineering, 16*(1), 107–118.

Hiremath, P. S., & Humnabad Iranna, Y. (2006b, December). Automatic detection of abnormal regions in endoscopic images of esophagus using a skin color model. *ICGST International Journal on Artificial Intelligence and Machine Learning, 6*(4), 53–57.

Hiremath, P. S., & Humnabad Iranna, Y. (December 2006c). Automatic identification of abnormal region (esophageal cancer) of esophagus from endoscopic images using textural features. In *Proceedings of the IEEE 1st International Conference on Signal and Image Processing (ICSIP-2006)*, BVB, Hubli, Karnataka, India, (pp. 295-299). Macmillan India Ltd.

Hiremath, P. S., Humnabad Iranna, Y., Dhandra, B. V., & Rajput, G. G. (December 2003). On the comparison of color image segmentation algorithms with reference to the detection of esophagus cancer (necrosis). In *Proceedings of the Fifth International Conference on Advances in Pattern Recognition (ICAPR-2003)*, ISI, Kolkata, India, (pp. 223-226). Allied Publishers Pvt. Ltd.

Hiremath, P. S., Humnabad Iranna, Y., & Pujari, J. D. (2007). Classification of squamous cell carcinoma based on color and textural features in microscopic images of esophagus tissues. *International Journal of Computer Science, 3*(7), 566–573.

Hu, M., Ping, X., & Ding, Y. (2004). *Automated cell nucleus segmentation using improved snake* (pp. 2737–2740). ICIP.

Humnabad, I. (September 2007). *A study on the medical image analysis using digital image processing techniques.* Gulbarga University, Gulbarga, Karnataka State, India.

Karkanis, S. A., Iakovidis, D. K., Maroulis, D. E., Karras, D. A., & Tzivars, M. (2003, September). Computer-aided tumor detection in endoscopic video using color wavelet features. *IEEE Transactions on Information Technology in Biomedicine, 7*(3), 141–152. doi:10.1109/TITB.2003.813794

Mohan, H. (1994). *Textbook of pathology* (2nd ed., pp. 148–151). Delhi, India: P.L. Printers, Rana Pratap Bagh.

Muldoon, T. J., Anandasabapathy, S., Maru, D. D., & Richards-Kortum, R. (2008, October). High-resolution imaging in Barrett's Esophagus: A novel, low-cost endoscopic microscope. *Gastrointestinal Endoscopy, 68*(4), 737–744. doi:10.1016/j.gie.2008.05.018

Olabarriaga, S. D., Snel, J. G., Botha, C. P., & Belleman, R. G. (2007, January). Intergrated support for medical image analysis methods: From development to clinical application. *IEEE Transactions on Information Technology in Biomedicine, 11*(1), 47–57. doi:10.1109/TITB.2006.874929

Oota, K., & Sobin, L. H. (1977). *Histological typing of gastric and oeophageal tumours* (pp. 33–35). Geneva, Switzerland: World Health Organization.

Reed, T. R., & du Buf, J. (1993). A review of recent texture segmentation and feature extraction techniques. *Computer Vision. Graphics and Image Processing: Image Understanding, 57*, 359–372. doi:10.1006/cviu.1993.1024

Refai, H., Li, L., Kent Teague, T., & Naukam, R. (September 2003). Automatic count of hepatocytes in microscopic images. In *Proceedings of International Conference on Image Processing, ICIP-2003*, (pp. 1101-1104).

Tsai, V. J. D. (2006, June). A comparative study on shadow compensation of color aerial images in invariant color models. *IEEE Transactions on Geoscience and Remote Sensing, 24*(6), 1661–1671. doi:10.1109/TGRS.2006.869980

Wang, P., Krishnan, S. M., Kugean, C., & Tjoa, M. P. (October 2001). Classification of endoscopic images based on texture and neural network. In *Proceedings of the 23rd Annual EMBS International Conference*, (pp. 3691-3695).

# Chapter 11
# Adaptive Face Recognition of Partially Visible Faces

**T. Ravindra Babu**
*Infosys Limited, India*

**Chethan S.A. Danivas**
*Infosys Limited, India*

**S.V. Subrahmanya**
*Infosys Limited, India*

## ABSTRACT

*Face Recognition is an active research area. In many practical scenarios, when faces are acquired without the cooperation or knowledge of the subject, they are likely to get occluded. Apart from image background, pose, illumination, and orientation of the faces, occlusion forms an additional challenge for face recognition. Recognizing faces that are partially visible is a challenging task. Most of the solutions to the problem focus on reconstruction or restoration of the occluded part before attempting to recognize the face. In the current chapter, the authors discuss various approaches to face recognition, challenges in face recognition of occluded images, and approaches to solve the problem. The authors propose an adaptive system that accepts the localized region of occlusion and recognizes the face adaptively. The chapter demonstrates through case studies that the proposed scheme recognizes the partially occluded faces as accurately as the un-occluded faces and in some cases outperforms the recognition using un-occluded face images.*

## 1. INTRODUCTION

With increasing need for surveillance, use of smart cards, and applications related to information security, Face Recognition has remained active research area in the last few years. The number of applications that involve recognizing faces is continuously on the increase. The main advantage of face recognition as biometric emanates from the ability of acquiring of subjects in non-intrusive manner.

Recognizing faces in a controlled environment is relatively a straight forward problem, albeit it has a number of challenges such as variation in

DOI: 10.4018/978-1-61350-429-1.ch011

illumination, pose and scale. The face recognition system is a typical pattern recognition system where learning takes place based on training set of images. The model is validated against validation dataset before it can predict a label or identity of a test image. Practically, when the images are acquired without the cooperation of the subject, often, they result in partial images with obstructions caused by multiple sources.

Often one encounters situations like a previously known person in a crowd needs to be identified whose face could be non-frontal, non-uniformly illuminated, oriented in some direction, and partially visible. Each of them is an important issue in recognizing the face. Depending on the *a priori* information on the subject that is available at our disposal, solutions based on mathematical and image processing techniques exist. In the current Chapter, however, we focus the issue of recognizing partially visible faces. Some indicative examples of common causes for partial visibility are the following.

1. Eyes covered with large, dark spectacles
2. Facial hair
3. Occlusion by a raised tea-cup, newspaper, cap, scarf or similar artifacts.

In addition to ability to detect partial faces, the methods discussed have applications in detecting a person in disguise where some part of the face is covered. The proposed scheme shall be able to handle (a) Occlusion at various regions within face region and (b) Variation in facial expression.

In the current Chapter, we propose an efficient and adaptive scheme, where occlusion of the face is not assumed as one among *a priori* known regions. The scheme makes a data dependent inference of the occluded region, synthesize the training data accordingly and identify the test face image with good classification accuracy. Hence it forms an adaptive scheme.

The solution integrates the following domains.

- Face Recognition
- Pattern Classification
- Pattern Clustering
- Image Processing Techniques
- Support Vector Machines

We conduct experiments by synthetically occluding various parts of the face and demonstrate the applicability of the proposed scheme to various test scenarios on an internally generated face database.

The Chapter is organized in the following manner. Section-2 contains a brief discussion on motivation in taking up the current work. Section-3 contains background details such as literature review, alternate schemes adapted earlier to solve the problem and a brief discussion of terminology that is used further in describing the scheme and some terms related to the topic. Section-4 discusses the proposed scheme in detail including experimentation and presentation of results. In Section-5, we present future research directions. We provide concluding remarks in Section-6. In the end we provide references and additional reading section.

In summary, the contributions of the Chapter are the following.

- Brief discussion on Face Recognition Systems
- Various approaches to handle face recognition with occlusions
- Proposed adaptive approach to handle occlusions by training data synthesis
- Demonstration of the approach through experimentation
- Research Trends

## 2. MOTIVATION

Recognition of partially visible faces is a challenging problem. Often when face images are collected without the knowledge and/or cooperation from the subjects, apart from many other challenges such as illumination, pose, and rotation in any of the three directions viz., Roll, Pitch and Yaw, *occlusion due to some obstruction* forms an important one.

Face Recognition systems with user cooperation is relatively straight forward problem with challenges related to appropriate preprocessing, methods of statistical estimation, image processing and pattern recognition methods. Recognizing the faces with partial information is an interesting problem. A good amount of work in this direction was done earlier by many researchers which we discuss in Section 3. When we can recognize the faces with occlusion with a fair amount of accuracy, a number of applications arise requiring to recognize faces with multiple causes of occlusions such as incidental obstruction to deliberate disguise.

Majority of methods focuses on reconstruction of occluded parts. It is interesting to explore whether we can avoid reconstructing the occluded region by accepting it as such and still be able to recognize the faces with good accuracy. Albeit some work was earlier carried out in this direction, for example by Lanitis (Lanitis, A., 2004), we propose a novel, adaptive way to handle such scenarios.

With this motivation we present our strategy in detecting the occlusion and recognizing occluded faces. In Section 3, we provide the background material, important work done so far in this direction. Also we briefly discuss various terms that are in use in the literature as well as that are referred to in the current work.

# 3. BACKGROUND

Face Recognition (Zhao, et al., 2003) refers to the activity of recognizing one or more persons in the given still or video image using *a priori* stored database of images. The challenges in achieving good accuracy are many, such as, face detection from the image that often contains distracting background, feature extraction from face region, classification, issues related to large image database, clustering, recognition and verification. Additional yet important challenges include orientation of face when taken without the knowledge of the persons, pose when the person may not exactly be looking into the camera, low or non-uniform illumination of the persons, overlapping nature of background with the persons in terms of color spaces, texture, features, etc. Over the years, many of the challenges to a large extent are being successfully handled. There is continued research in this direction resulting in improved alternate formulations. However, when the image of the person is incompletely available because of some obstruction, recognition of such faces offers additional challenge.

In Section 3.1 we discuss various approaches that are studied by researchers in this direction.

## 3.1 Literature Review

The problem of face recognition under occlusion is well studied. Recognition of occluded faces is achieved through 2D modeling (Jia and Martinez, 2009; Oh, Lee, Lee, Yim, 2008; Park, Oh, Ahn, Lee, 2005; Lanitis, 2004; Hwang and Lee, 2002; Martinez, 2002) as well as 3D modeling (DeSmet, Franses, Rik, Gool; 2006; Colombo, Cusano, Sehetini; 2006, 2009 ;). Predominantly, the approaches have focused on *reconstruction* or *restoration* of the occluded region. We discuss some related work by researchers.

Park et al (Park et al., 2005) demonstrated successful removal of occlusion on the face due to glasses and their reflection. A given face image is encoded and subsequently *reconstructed*. The method involves, face extraction, glass frame detection, approximate reconstruction of face image by example-based procedure, followed by recursive Principal Component Analysis (PCA) (Duda, Hart and Stork, 2002; Turk and Pentland, 1991) based reconstruction and error compensation until convergence. The method is extendable to other occlusions as well.

Martinez (Martinez, 2002) adapts a variant of PCA. The method suggests dividing a given occluded face into 6 mutually exclusive, local regions. PCA is applied to each local part. During recognition contribution of each part is weighted such that contribution from the occluded region for recognition is minimized.

Hwang and Lee (Hwang and Lee, 2002) suggest *restoration* of occluded image. For a given occluded image, initially the occlusion is localized. The proposed method makes use of least squares method to arrive at weights. The weights are used for decomposing the appearance of the non-occluded part of the image as a weighted sum of basis images. Together, the basis images and weights help *restoring* the occluded part of the image.

Lanitis (Lanitis, A, 2004) defines variations that inhibit the process of face recognition as systematic and non-systematic components. Systematic variations are referred to as those that are caused by changes in illumination, expression, view and age. He terms artificial or natural obstructions on a face image as non-systematic components. He proposes to detect occlusion and restore using PCA approach. The given image is subdivided into multiple small regions. Appearance of the image is coded, then reconstructed and residual intensity is computed. Based on normalized distance computation and comparison with sample statistics, occlusion is detected. For recognition, the detected occlusion is masked across all the images. Only face model representing un-occluded images is trained. Masked training images are encoded into model parameters of obtained model. Given a test image, its model based parametric distribution is extracted and comparison is made with the help of parametric description and Mahalonobis distance (Duda, et al., 2002).

Oh et al (Oh, et al, 2008) divide a given face into multiple disjoint regions, represent each of them by PCA from occlusion free training images, and for recognition adapt occlusion invariant local non-negative matrix factorization method [10].

Jia and Martinez (Jia and Martinez, 2009) describe a model that proposes to construct a model from occluded images using Support Vector Machines (SVM). In order to account for occluded portion of the image, the work proposes a concept known as Partial Support Vector Machines (PSVM). PSVM treats missing values in training samples due to occlusion as affine space in the feature space, which minimizes probability of overlap between affine space and separating hyperplane. Working of the method is demonstrated through experimentation.

Apart from above holistic methods of face recognition of partially occluded images, feature based methods for the same are also successful. Kapenikci et al (Kapenikci et al, 2002) use Gabor wavelets as variant of Elastic Bunch Graph methods to recognize occluded images.

Alessandro et al (Alesandro et al., 2006) use 3D modeling to detect and restore occlusions. Occlusions are considered as local deformations of the face and are restored from non-occluded faces using a procedure known as Gappy Principal Component Analysis (GCPA).

In the proposed method, we localize occlusions of the test image and mark the corresponding region across all training and test images for recognizing the occluded face. Thus the scheme adapts to the given occlusion of a face.

## 3.2 Discussion on Related Terms

In this Section, we provide definition and a brief discussion on some frequently used terms in the literature and some of the terms that are used subsequently in the Chapter. We briefly dwell on two holistic face recognition approaches and one feature-based approach.

### Occlusion

When face images are inhibited by obstructions caused by a number of factors, such inhibition is referred to as occlusion. Lanitis (Lanitis; 2004) differentiates such variations as those caused by systematic and non-systematic variations. The variations such as illumination, expression, view, and aging are referred to as systematic and those obstructions that inhibit part of face are referred to as non-systematic.

## Preprocessing

The activity in the current context of the Chapter refers to series of steps taken with the help of image processing techniques, mathematics and statistics that transforms a given image to uniform size, shape, direction and illumination. This enables the given set of images amenable for further processing. In the current Chapter, we carry out a number of preprocessing steps prior to application of methods suggested, which are not elaborated as it is out of scope of the Chapter.

## Eigenfaces

Eigenfaces (Turk and Pentland; 1991, Zhao et al; 2003) is an appearance based holistic face recognition approach and it is the first successful realization of machine based face recognition. It is based on application of Principal Component Analysis. The method efficiently handles computation of eigenvectors of covariance matrix of mean subtracted images. We make use of this method in the current Chapter. The method requires accurate location of various components of face such as eyes, nose, etc. Multiple variations of eigenfaces (Zhao et al; 2003) have been developed over the years. We elaborate the method in some more detail. Our proposed method makes use of the approach.

Eigenfaces approach (Turk and Pentland, 1991) is arguably the most celebrated method for face recognition. We briefly explain the method for the sake of completeness. Consider a set of face images, $F_k$, of 'k' persons. Each person has say, 'p' samples of images. Thus the total set of images is 'kp=k*p'. The data set is divided into training, validation and test datasets of t, v and s images respectively, such that kp=t+v+s. Each face image of N X N size is represented as a vector of $N^2X1$. Face Recognition by using Eigenfaces approach can be summarized as below.

1.  Compute average of t images, $F_1, F_2, ... F_t$ as illustrated in equation (1).
2.  Compute deviation of each image from its average, as $\xi_i$ (see equation (2))
3.  The set of vectors are subjected to Principal Component Analysis. Consider a matrix $B$ containing $\xi_i$ column vectors, $i=1,2,..t$. Form covariance matrix using $BB^T$. As it can be seen the matrix size is $N^2XN^2$. Important contribution of the work at this stage is to compute eigen values and eigen vectors in an efficient manner by exploiting the sample size, where $t<<N^2$, by solving for $tXt$ matrix first by pre-multiplying both sides of the characteristic equation by $B$ and by subsequent simplification. $Bx_i$ form the eigen vectors of $BB^T$ where $x_i$ determines linear combination of $t$ images $\xi_i$. It leads to computation of $t$ eigenfaces, $e_i, i=1,2...,t$. Following equations summarize the procedure. (see equations (3) & (4))
4.  Given a test image, $G_j$, compute its deviation from the mean image, $C$. Compute projection of this vector on each of the eigenfaces to obtain eigenface components. Together, eigenface components form a weight vector, $\Omega$. Assign the test image to that class for which the dissimilarity of the weight vector with the class is minimum, or as determined by pattern classification approaches.

$$C = \frac{1}{t}\sum_{i=1}^{t} F_i \qquad (1)$$

$$\xi_i = F_i - C, \qquad i = 1, 2, \cdots t \qquad (2)$$

$$B^TB \; x_i = \upsilon_i \, x_i \qquad (3)$$

$$BB^TB \; x_i = \upsilon_i \, Bx_i \qquad (4)$$

Classification of a test face can be made using multiple classification methods like Nearest Neighbourhood Classifier, Support Vector Machines. We make use of both the methods in the current work. We describe each of them in the following sections.

## Leader Clustering Algorithm

Leader clustering algorithm (Spath; 1980) has the advantage of generating abstraction of large data with single database scan. The algorithm considers a distance threshold for clustering, of say, $\varepsilon$. Value of $\varepsilon$ computed based on a preliminary analysis on sample dataset. Number of clusters depends on the value of the threshold. The algorithm is initiated by considering any arbitrary pattern of the input data as first leader. It considers subsequent pattern and assigns the pattern to cluster represented by first leader, if dissimilarity remains within given threshold; else it terms the current pattern a next leader. The procedure continues till all patterns are assigned to one of the leaders. Leaders form representative patterns of corresponding clusters.

## Fisherfaces

Fishersfaces is a successful face recognition method. It is based on Fisher's linear discriminant (Belhumeur, et al., 1997, Zhao, et al., 1998). The method represents total scatter matrix as sum of inter-class and intra-class scatter matrices. Optimal projection matrix is computed by solving for the eigen value problem that maximizes the ratio of determinant of inter-class projection matrix of samples to determinant of intra-class projection matrix. There are many successful variants of Fisherfaces in the literature (Zhao et al., 2003).

## Elastic Bunch Graph Matching

Elastic Bunch Graph Matching methods form feature based methods. The methods have the advantage over holistic methods in terms of less sensitivity (Zhao, et al; 2003) to variations to illumination, pose and location within the image. Elastic bunch graph matching (EBGM) (Wiskott, et al; 1999) and many of its variants and extensions have demonstrated successful application of wavelets to Face Recognition systems. EBGM represents face as a face graph. The features of feature land mark are represented as a set of Gabor wavelet features, known as jets. A new face is represented as face graph and it is fitted into the face by means of iterative face graph matching procedure.

## k- Nearest Neighbourhood Classifier (k-NNC)

Consider 'k' labeled training patterns. k-NNC (Duda, et al; 2002) is the method of assigning that label to a test pattern which is label of majority of its k-neighbours among the training patterns. The proximity measure is problem dependent. A number of dissimilarity measures exist in the literature. Value of k is a trade-off between reliability of estimate and equality of a posteriori probabilities of the training and test samples. When k=1, it is known as NNC.

## Support Vector Machines (SVM)

The essence of the method is to classify given set of patterns by non-linearly mapping them into a sufficiently high dimension such that the two categories are separated by hyperplane (Duda, et al; 2002). The objective of training SVM is to find a hyperplane with largest margin which is the distance from the decision hyperplane. Support vectors are those training patterns which are close to hyperplane and help classifying the patterns.

## Face Database

We consider internally acquired and preprocessed database for experimentation in the current work, viz., ExtendedEmpDB. The database contains 279 images. Of the images, 150 are considered for training and 129 as test images. As part of preprocessing, each of the acquired images are centered with reference to image area, scaled and vertically oriented. Some examples of the collected images are provided in Figure 1 and 3. The images contain multiple expressions, limited variation in illumination and uniform background.

## 4. PROPOSED SYSTEM

In the current section, we briefly deal with the need aspect of the system. Through various subsections, we present the proposed system, discussing various background material and concepts used at different stages of its working.

*Figure 1. Proposed face recognition system with occluded image*

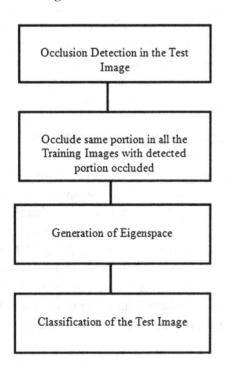

## 4.1 Need Aspect

Most face recognition methods with occluded images focus on reconstruction of occluded part from the normal images. Occlusions can occur at any part of the face. Some of the occlusions can be reconstructed from single frontal image, by exploiting the symmetric nature of a frontal face when they occur on one side of the face such as left or right part of face when placed vertical. Some parts cannot be reconstructed or replaced from single image. Another aspect is to understand mandatory nature of parts of face that help in recognizing the face. Equivalently, analysis of absence of which of the parts of the face do not impact classification of the occluded faces. For example, image with large dark glasses the eye information is completely unavailable. While detecting the occlusion, we occlude immediate superscribing rectangle. Consider another contrasting case, where a test image has large beard covering the lower part of the face. Having known that database does not contain any image with a beard, it would be prudent to conceal the entire part of face containing beard leading to synthetic occlusion.

We demonstrate through our experiments such synthetic occlusion provides equally good classification accuracy in labeling the face images as provided un-occluded images.

We provide outline of the method in the following Subsection.

## 4.2 Outline of the Method

We consider a scenario where normal training images are available and the test image is occluded either by design such as disguise or by accident such as covered by some artifact. It is interesting to explore to see whether such an occlusion really impacts recognition of the test image. We explore ways to ignore such unavailable portion, make use of the remaining image and recognize the given face image. With this consideration, we propose a method using which a given image is recognized with good classification accuracy. Interestingly, we show that on most scenarios such a scheme provides better classification accuracy than non-occluded test image. Further such proposed logic opens up a number of applications.

The proposed method can be outlined as provided in Figure 1 and through the following steps.

1.  Consider database of normal images without occlusion.
    - The images are preprocessed for normalizing pose, illumination, orientation and size. We refer to the activity as normalizing the images.
    - Given a test image containing occlusion, normalize the image.
    - Detect and localize the occluded region in the test image
2.  Consider entire training data set of images and occlude the equivalent portion across all the training images
3.  Generate Eigenfaces and set of projected coefficients as detailed in the Section 3.2.
4.  Classify the test image using different classifiers, viz., NNC and SVM.

## 4.3 Synthetic Occlusion

In order to demonstrate the concept, the test images are synthetically occluded. They are done in such a way that one of basic features in the face such as eyes, nose, or mouth is occluded in each of 14 such scenarios. During experimentation we can find out relative importance of those features while labeling a given test image accurately.

The scheme proposes to ignore the occluded portion across all the training images instead of reconstructing the missing portion; and still makes an attempt to recognize the image on the strength of remaining portion of the image.

We consider following fourteen different occlusion possibilities.

1.  Nose Occluded
2.  Both Eyes Occluded
3.  Mouth Occluded
4.  Below Nose Occluded
5.  Bottom Right Quarter of image occluded
6.  Top Right Quarter of image occluded
7.  Bottom Left Quarter of image occluded
8.  Top Left Quarter of image occluded
9.  Only Eye portion Visible
10. Top Half of Image Occluded
11. Bottom Half of Image Occluded
12. Left Half of Image Occluded
13. Right Half of Image Occluded
14. Left Eye Occluded

Further, combinations of the above possibilities lead to more such scenarios. We consider test images with each of the above simulated occlusions and make use of the proposed scheme to demonstrate recognition of the corresponding label accurately.

Figure 2 provides some such examples of one of the training images. However, each of the above scenarios is realistic.

## Reference Cell Structure

Each image is equally divided into 'c' cells. In the current implementation, we choose c as 16. Let the total number of training images be 't'. All the training images are in un-occluded form and the remaining images are occluded. Any one or more of the 16 cells could be occluded. For the current implementation, we generate 16 sets of synthetically occluded images where only one cell is occluded in each of the 16 sets. Correspondingly each training image is sub-divided into 16 cells taking number of training datasets to 16t. We call each part of such image where one of the cells is occluded as mask. We refer to the cells in (row and column) form, numbering from $(1,1)$ to $(4,4)$. We will make use of this definition later in the paper. We refer to this structure as *'reference cell structure'*.

*Figure 2. Examples of synthetically occluded face images*

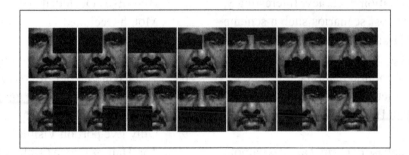

*Figure 3. Occlusion around nose region is in Test Image. Nearly the same region is synthetically occluded across all the training images. Notice near-uniform, normalized representation as an output of preprocessing step. The proposed method also successfully handles change in the facial expression*

## 4.4 Face Recognition of Occluded Images

We discuss each of the steps in detail in the current Subsection.

### 4.4.1 Preprocessing

Given a set of training and test data of face images, we preprocess the face images to *normalize* the representation so they are amenable for implementation of proposed scheme. Preprocessing involves following steps.

- Face Detection
- Orientation detection and normalization
- Placing the face image in uniform fashion such as head to chin longitudinally and ear to ear horizontally. This helps the *reference structure* to localize similar regions of face.
- Scale the images so as to bring all images to common scale.

- Illumination normalization, as it affects the accuracy of face recognition while using Eigenfaces approach.
- Detection of occlusion in test images using image processing methods. The output of this stage is face image with occluded region filled with *chosen pigment*

The steps are not elaborated further as they are beyond the scope of the current topic.

### 4.4.2 Occlusion Localization

Often when images are captured in uncontrolled environment, one encounters occlusion of a part of the face due to artifacts such as dark spectacles, scarves, sun-caps, etc. Before embarking on to recognizing the face, we need to localize occlusion. This is achieved in two stages.

- **Stage 1:** Identify the artifact using image processing method as well as connected component analysis and mark it with pre-chosen unique color / gray. Hereafter we refer to this gray as *chosen pigment*.

- **Stage 2:** Localize the occlusion cell by cell by computing availability of the specific colorgray in the image.
- **Stage 3:** Generate occluded region based on Stage-2.

In the current Subsection, we focus on Stage-2. The algorithm to achieve localizing the occlusion can be summarized below.

- Divide the image into multiple cells, similar to the work by Oh et al (Oh et al; 2008). The number of such divisions considered here is 4x4=16, as described earlier in the subsection 4.4.1. An occlusion may span one or more of the cells.
- Consider a structure where one cell at a time is occluded and all other 15 cells are un-occluded.
- Compute percentage availability of '*chosen pigment*'. If the percentage exceeds a chosen threshold, $\psi$, we declare that the corresponding cell as occluded.
- We repeat the procedure for each cell independently and mark all those cells exceeding $\psi$ as occluded. This identifies the occluded region in the given image, which hereafter refer to as '*reference occlusion*'.

The *reference occlusion* is made use in training data preparation for Face Recognition of Occluded images.

### Discussion on Reference Cell Size

When part of face is occluded, often it does not form a rectangular structure. Even if such structure exists *it need not exactly fit into the cell structure defined above*. With this uncertainty, we try to identify the cells that best represent the occlusion in a given face image. Depending on $\psi$, it can result into either over or under representation of

actual occlusion. However, for finer identification of occluded area, the cell division can be reduced to smaller cells. For example, the given image can be divided into 64X64 cells. Each cell is considered and tested to identify the occluded region with some value of $\psi$. The scheme represents occlusion to closer to reality. Alternatively, by choosing larger cells for occlusion, computation requirement is reduced and it might end up in showing larger region than reality as occluded. In essence, choice of cell size is basically a trade-off between additional computation requirement and representation inaccuracy. Eventually, it should be weighed against Face Recognition Accuracy.

### 4.4.3 Synthetic Occlusion of Training Images

We propose to occlude the identified cells at the Occlusion Localization stage for all the training images. Since during the preprocessing step, the images are normalized, when mask is applied across the images the corresponding cells nearly represent same region of a face across all the training and test images. With this approach, we synthetically occlude the corresponding portion on all the training images by considering identified cells as *mask*. Thus it covers all sample images spanning across all classes. This forms *synthetically regenerated training images*.

With the approach of synthetic occlusion, average image represents occlusion across all the training images. Consider an example of occlusion of nostril region in a test image. We localize the occlusion in terms of cells and synthetically occlude same region across all the images as depicted in Figure 3.

### 4.4.4 Eigenspace Generation

The occlusion in the test image forms the reference. The occlusion is detected and localized by forming *reference structure*. This results in *synthetic occlusion of all the training images* on the basis of reference structure. The synthetically occluded training images are used for eigenspace generation. The average face and eigenfaces will have the corresponding occluded portion clearly marked. Each of the training images is projected against chosen set of eigenfaces and the corresponding coefficients are computed.

## 4.4.5 Classification Using NNC And SVM

The test image is projected onto eigenfaces to obtain the projection coefficients. We classify the test image using both nearest neighbor classifier and support vector machines. Another interesting case is to deal with large image data. In order to deal with this, we adapt clustering of similar images in terms of the coefficients. The cluster representatives are used to classify the test image instead of entire training dataset. We use leader clustering algorithm as described in Section 3.2.

## 4.5 Experimentation and Results

A number of exercises have been carried out to validate the proposed algorithms on occlusion localization and face recognition. The experimentation required simulations, variation of threshold, $\psi$, occlusion localization using connected component analysis, face recognition for varying occlusion conditions.

## 4.5.1 Experiments on Localization of Occlusion

The localization of occlusion is carried out using the procedure as discussed in Section 4.2. We carried out experiments making use of multiple types of occlusions as detailed in Section 4. Different occlusions pose different types of challenges both to preprocessing as well as occlusion localization. In case of preprocessing, face detection and occlusion detection, for example, using color spaces poses multiple challenges. In case of localization of occlusion, identification of additional cells because of partial occupancy in the cells results into major cause of low classification accuracy. Similarly because of low value of $\psi$, occlusion may not get detected resulting into additional occlusion area in Test images as compared to training images.

The chosen pigment to represent the occlusion is blue. The image is partitioned into 4X4=16 cells or tiles. Each cell is considered checked for possible presence of occlusion. We present the results of exercises on occlusion localization in Table 1. Column-1 of the table contains description of part of the face occluded. Column-2 indicates value of '$\psi$', the threshold to identify occlusion. Column-3 indicates the list of cells out of 16 that are occluded. Notice the reduction in the number of occluded cells as a function of threshold, as '$\psi$' increases.

Prior to occlusion localization, occlusion detection is achieved through connected component analysis. It is identified through pre-chosen pigment. The pigment forms reference for occlusion

*Table 1. Occlusion detection (synthetic occlusion of mouth) using connected components*

| Occlusion Type of Original Test Image | Threshold (% area occluded) '$\psi$' | Tiles detected as Occluded |
|---|---|---|
| 1 | 2 | 3 |
| Mouth Occluded | 15 | 9,10,11,12,13,14,15,16 |
| Mouth Occluded | 20 | 10,11,12,13,14,15,16 |

*Table 2. Recognition (for synthetic occlusion of mouth)*

| Occlusion Type of Original Test Image | Occlusion Portion (Cells Occluded in Training and Test images) | Classification Accuracy (%) |
|---|---|---|
| 1 | 2 | 2 |
| Mouth Occluded | 10,11,12,13,14,15,16 | 95 |
| Mouth Occluded | 9,10,11,12,13,14,15,16 | 96 |
| No Occlusion | NONE | 89 |

localization. In declaring a cell as occluded, an aggressive approach is adapted where even 15-20% of occlusion of a cell is inferred as entire cell occluded. The results are provided in Table 1 and Table 2.

Choice of '$\psi$' has impact on classification accuracy of the Face Recognition system. We carry out experiments with different thresholds and provide the results. It can be observed from Table 1 that the number of cells declared as occluded depends on the value of '$\psi$'.

In Table 2, we demonstrate the impact of number of cells on Face Recognition Accuracy. Number of images for training and test are 150 and 129 respectively. Number of classes considered is 25. Number of image per class for training is 6 per class. Column-1 of the table contains list of part occluded. Column-2 contains list of cells that are occluded. The classification accuracy using eigenfaces and NNC is provided in Column-3.

By combining the results in Table 1 and 2, it can be concluded that the best classification accuracy of 96% is obtained with cells mentioned in Column-2 with $\psi$=15. Interestingly with full face, the classification accuracy obtained is 89%.

## 4.5.2 Experiments on Face Recognition

Accuracy of Face Recognition depends on accuracy of occlusion localization, sufficiency of the available remaining information which is discriminative enough, cell referencing, and accuracy of face detection. All the cells identified as occluded are marked across all the training images,

thus leading to generation of synthetic training images. Inaccuracy of occlusion in synthetic training images occurs due to natural size variation among the input images. This also is likely to cause inaccuracy in classification accuracy of Faces. The experiments on face recognition include multiple face occlusion scenarios, which are conducted as per the discussion in Section 4.3.

Table 3 provides the results of such exercises. Classification accuracy of face images under different occlusion conditions are presented in the Table.

As discussed previously, the training data is synthesized to exclude occluded region after its detection. The experiments conducted can be summarized in the following manner.

1. Classification using Nearest Neighbour Classifier(NNC)
2. Cluster the training images in the eigenspace using Leader Clustering Algorithm followed by Classification using NNC considering only cluster representatives.
3. Classification using Support Vector Machines (SVMs) using *libsvm* (Chang and Lin, 2001)

In case of (b) above, Clustering is carried out based on projected coefficients. Dissimilarity threshold, $\varepsilon$, is chosen dynamically and cluster representatives using Leader Clustering algorithm are computed. Now, the cluster representatives are used to assign label to test image. The distance threshold, $\varepsilon$, computed for the current image is

*Table 3. Experimental results of recognizing occluded images with different pattern classifiers*

| Sl. No. | Occlusion | NNC | SVM with C and gamma optimized | | |
|---|---|---|---|---|---|
| | | CA (%) | C | Gamma | CA(%) |
| 1 | **No occlusion** | **89.9225** | | | |
| 2 | Both Eyes occluded | 89.1473 | 8 | 0.125 | 93.7984 |
| 3 | Bottom Half of Image occluded | **96.124** | 2 | 0.5 | **97.6744** |
| 4 | Bottom left quarter of Image occluded | 93.0233 | 512 | 0.007813 | 97.6744 |
| 5 | Bottom right quarter of image occluded | 94.5736 | 32 | 0.03125 | 96.124 |
| 6 | Left eye occluded | 89.1473 | 32 | 0.125 | 95.3488 |
| 7 | Left half Face occluded | 91.4729 | 128 | 0.007813 | 94.5736 |
| 8 | Mouth and below occluded | **96.124** | 128 | 0.007813 | **97.6744** |
| 9 | Mouth occluded | 95.3488 | 128 | 0.007813 | 97.6744 |
| 10 | Only eyes visible | 92.2481 | 32 | 0.007813 | 95.3488 |
| 11 | Right eye occluded | 89.1473 | 32 | 0.125 | 91.4729 |
| 12 | Right half face occluded | 89.1473 | 2 | 0.125 | 93.7984 |
| 13 | Top half image occluded | 85.2713 | 32 | 0.03125 | 88.3721 |
| 14 | Top left quarter of image occluded | 88.3721 | 512 | 0.007813 | 90.6977 |
| 15 | Top right quarter of image occluded | 89.9225 | 32 | 0.125 | 93.7984 |

1100. Variation in number of clusters as a function of threshold value is provided in Figure 4. The optimal set of cluster representatives is obtained as a trade-off between representability and computation cost. The trade-off is arrived at based on classification accuracy on test dataset of images.

The experiments have been conducted on internally generated ExtEmpDatabase. As discussed previously, the number of training images and test images were 150 and 129 respectively. Number of eigenfaces considered is 20. The dimension of all images in number of pixels are 70

*Figure 4. Leader clustering - Variation in number of clusters as a function of threshold value, ε*

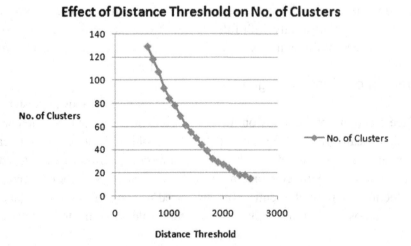

**Effect of Distance Threshold on No. of Clusters**

*Figure 5. Effect of no. of Eigenfaces on classification accuracy*

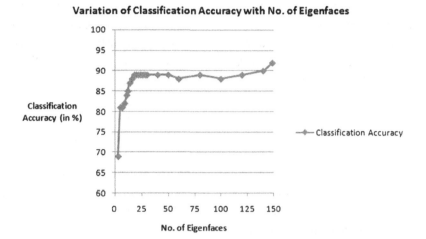

(Height) X 70 (Width). The results of the experiments are provided in Table 3.

It can be seen from the Table 3 that the best classification accuracy obtained using NNC is 96.124% for the case of occlusion of (a) bottom half of the image below nose and (b) mouth and below. Least classification accuracy of 85.2713% is obtained with NNC when the portion above nose is occluded. And for all the other cases classification accuracy remained between above two cases.

In case of SVM best classification accuracy of 97.67% has occurred for the cases when bottom half of face image is occluded, bottom left quarter of image occluded, mouth and below occluded, and mouth occluded. Worst accuracy of 88.37% has occurred when top half image is occluded. Impact of occluded region on classification accuracy for NNC and SVM is similar.

With NNC based on cluster representatives, classification accuracy is same as that obtained with original data. The advantage remains because of less number of comparisons, when we work with cluster representatives.

Interestingly, classification accuracy of face images when no occlusion is made is 89.92% and in many cases *occlusion has improved classification accuracy*.

Figure 5 contains effect of number of eigenfaces on classification accuracy for the case of both-eyes occluded. It can be noticed from the figure beyond certain number the classification accuracy does not improve significantly.

Validation is done in two ways: (a) by indentifying validation and test data sets separately and training is validated against validation dataset and results with test data are alone reported and (b) by drawing simple random sample without replacement to make training and test data sets separately and computing the classification accuracy with each test dataset. The classification accuracy in case of (b) is consistent for different disjoint training and test datasets.

## 5. FUTURE RESEARCH DIRECTIONS

An interesting aspect of our proposed work on Face Recognition with Occlusion is that in situations where a part of image is blurred or deliberately concealed we prefer ignoring the lack of data in the region and still be able to recognize the faces. Secondly, the work helps one to identify the region that either helps or hinders accurate classification of images. For example, experimentally, we find that concealing lower part of the face either from nose or below mouth consistently provided better accuracy than full face of 89.92%.

Further directions of research include use of singe or limited sample size of images per class, and kernel based methods for classification.

## 6. CONCLUSION

Face Recognition of Occluded faces is an active research area. Occlusions can occur due to multiple causes. Many of them are realistic. Some scenarios can be visualized such as those due to direction of light source, certain portion of the face could be invisible or result into a saturated reflective region. Another example is that the light source from top could occlude eyes for some individuals who have protruding forehead. This can be seen as a case of occlusion and can be handled as a new scenario. Similarly, individuals who deliberately resort to disguise like adding facial hair can be handled by synthetically occluding corresponding portion and subject to face recognition.

Many methods handling occlusion attempt to reconstruct the occluded region by multiple approaches. There is good amount of literature in this direction. In the current Chapter, we attempt to solve the problem by ignoring the occluded region across all the images under consideration. This is carried out in two stages, first by localizing the region of occlusion and secondly by occluding the region across all the training images as synthetic occlusion. Thus the proposed scheme adapts to a given occlusion condition.

The advantage of the proposed approach is its applicability for variety of occlusion conditions. One need not reconstruct the missing data. It does not require additional computation to reconstruct thereby reducing the computational requirement. The method involves localizing the occlusion, block the same region across all the images and re-training. The training is of O (N), where N is the number of training images. In order to further improve efficiency, we can resort to approaches

such as (a) converting occlusion to a template, (b) a priori computation of average image, (c) in-memory operations of avoiding computations related to template region thus resulting in reduced i/o operations of reading each image, and (d) appropriate sizing of the computer system the proposed system can be realized as a real time system.

We discuss different approaches of occlusion detection, face recognition and face detection. We present the algorithms to achieve good classification accuracy. We carried out experiments to demonstrate working of the proposed method in both the stages and presented the results.

## REFERENCES

Aluz, N., Gokberk, B., & Akarun, L. (2008). 3D face recognition system for expression and occlusion invariance. *2nd Intl. Conf. on Biometrics: Theory, Applications, and Systems,* (pp. 1-7).

Belhumeur, P., Hespanha, J., & Kriegman, D. (1997). Eigen Faces vs. Fisherfaces: Recognition using class specific linear projection. *IEEE Trans. on PAMI, 19*(7), 711–720. doi:10.1109/34.598228

Brunelli, R., & Poggio, T. (1993). Face recognition features versus templates. *IEEE Transactions on Pattern Analysis and Machine Intelligence, 15*(10), 1042–1052. doi:10.1109/34.254061

Chang, C. C., & Lin, C. J. (2001). *LIBSVM – A library for support vector machines*. Retrieved from http://www.cse.ntu.edu.tw/~cjlin/libsvm/

Colombo, A., Cusano, C., & Schettini, R. (2006). Detection and restoration of occlusions for 3D face recognition. *Proc. of IEEE Intl. Conf. on Multimedia & Expo (ICME),* (pp. 1541-1546).

Colombo, A., Cusano, C., & Schettini, R. (2009). Gappy PCA classification for occlusion tolerant 3D face detection. *Journal of Mathematical Imaging and Vision, 35*(5), 193–207. doi:10.1007/s10851-009-0165-y

DeSmet, M., Franses, R., & Gool, L. V. (2006). A generalized EM approach for 3D model based face recognition under occlusions. *CVPR, 2,* 1423–1430.

Duda, R. O., Hart, P. E., & Stork, D. G. (2002). *Pattern classification.* New York, NY: John Wiley and Sons.

Hwang, B. W., & Lee, S. W. (2003). Reconstruction of partially damaged face images based on a morphable face model. *IEEE Transactions on Pattern Analysis and Machine Intelligence, 25*(3), 365–372. doi:10.1109/TPAMI.2003.1182099

Jia, H., & Martinez, A. M. (2009). Support vector machines in face recognition with occlusions. *IEEE Conf. on Computer Vision and Pattern Recognition,* (pp. 136-141).

Kepenekci, B., Tek, F. B., & Akar, G. B. (2002). Occluded face recognition based on Gabor wavelets. *Proc. of Intl. Conf. on Image Processing,* vol. 1, (pp. 293-296).

Lanitis, A. (2004). Person identification from heavily occluded face images. *Proc. of the 2004 ACM Symposium on Applied Computing* (pp. 5-9).

Martinez, A. M. (2002). Recognizing imprecisely localized, partially occluded, and expression variant faces from a single sample per class. *IEEE Transactions on Pattern Analysis and Machine Intelligence, 24*(6), 748–763. doi:10.1109/TPAMI.2002.1008382

Oh, H. J., Lee, K. M., & Lee, S. U. (2008). Occlusion invariant face recognition using selective local non-negative matrix factorization basis images. *Image and Vision Computing, 26*(11), 1515–1523. doi:10.1016/j.imavis.2008.04.016

Park, J. S., Oh, Y. H., Ahn, S. C., & Lee, S. W. (2005). Glasses removal from facial image using recursive error compensation. *IEEE Transactions on Pattern Analysis and Machine Intelligence, 27*(5), 805–811. doi:10.1109/TPAMI.2005.103

Spath, H. (1980). *Cluster analysis – Algorithms for data reduction and classification of objects.* West Sussex, UK: Ellis Horwood Limited.

Tarres, F., Rama, A., & Torres, L. (2005). A novel method for face recognition under partial occlusion or facial expression variations. In *Proc. ELMAR,* (pp. 163-166).

Turk, M., & Pentland, A. (1991). Eigenfaces for recognition. *Journal of Cognitive Neuroscience, 3*(1), 71–86. doi:10.1162/jocn.1991.3.1.71

Wiskott, L., Fellous, J. M., Kruger, N., & Malsburg, C. V. D. (1999). Face recognition by elastic bunch graph matching. In Jain, L. C. (Eds.), *Intelligent biometric techniques in fingerprint and face recognition* (pp. 355–396). CRC Press. doi:10.1109/34.598235

Zhao, W., Chellappa, R., & Krishnaswamy, A. (1998). Discriminant analysis of principal components for face recognition. *Proc. of International Conference on Automatic Face and Gesture Recognition,* (pp. 336-341).

Zhao, W., Chellappa, R., Phillips, P. J., & Rosenfeld, A. (2003). Face recognition: A literature survey. *ACM Computing Surveys, 35,* 399–458. doi:10.1145/954339.954342

## ADDITIONAL READING

Blanz, V., & Vetter, T. (1999) A morphable model for the synthesis of 3D faces. *Proc. SIGGRAPH '99.* 187–194.

Blanz, V., & Vetter, T. (2003). Face recognition based on fitting a 3D morphable model. *IEEE Trans. On PAMI, 25*(9), 1063–1074. doi:10.1109/TPAMI.2003.1227983

Cootes, T. F., Edwards, G. J., & Taylor, C. J. (2001). Active Appearance Models. *IEEE Transactions on Pattern Analysis and Machine Intelligence, 23*(6), 681–685. doi:10.1109/34.927467

Cristianini, N., & Taylor, J. S. (2000). *An Introduction toSupport Vector Machines*. Cambridge University Press.

Duc, B., Fisher, S. and J. Bigün, J. (1999). Face Authentication with Gabor Information on Deformable Graphs. *IEEE Trans. On Image Proc., vol.8, no.4,* 504-515.

Edwards, G. J., Lanitis, A., Taylor, C. J., & Cootes, T. F. (1998). Statistical Face Models: Improving Specificity. *Image and Vision Computing, 16*(3), 203–211. doi:10.1016/S0262-8856(97)00069-3

Gross, R., Matthews, I., & Baker, S. (2004). Constructing and fitting active appearance models with occlusion. IEEE Workshop on Face Processing in Video (FPiV).

Hotta, K. (2004). Support Vector Machine with Local Summation Kernel for Robust Face Recognition. *Proc. Of 17ᵗʰ Intl. Conf. on Pattern Recognition (ICPR04, Vol.3.* 482-485.

Hu,. Y. Jiang, D., Yan, S., Zhang, L. & Zhang, H. (2004). Automatic 3D reconstruction for face recognition. *Proc. Face and Gesture Recognition.* 843–848.

Hwang, B. W., Roh, M. C., & Lee, S. W. (2004). Performance Evaluation of Face Recognition algorithms on Asian Face Recognition. *Proc. Sixth IEEE Int'l Conf. Automatic Face and Gesture Recognition*, 278-283.

Jia, H., & Martinez, A. M. (2008). Face recognition with occlusions in the training and testing sets. *Proc. IEEE Conf. Automatic Face and Gesture Recognition.* 1-6.

Krüger, N., Pötzsch, M., & Malsburg, C. V. (1997). Determining of Face Position and Pose with a learned Representation Based on Labeled Graphs. *Image and Vision Computing, 15,* 665–673. doi:10.1016/S0262-8856(97)00012-7

Lee, D.D., & Seung, H.S., H.S. (1999). Learning the parts of objects by non-negative matrix factorization. *Nature, 401,* 788–791. doi:10.1038/44565

Li, S. Z., Hou, X. W., Zhang, H. J., & Cheng, Q. S. (2001) Learning spatially localized, part based representation. *Proc. IEEE Conf. Computer Vision and Pattern Recognition*, 207-212.

Lyons, M. J., Budynek, J., & Akamatsu, S. (1999). Automatic Classification of Single Facial Images. *IEEE Trans. on PAMI, 21*(12), 1357–1362. doi:10.1109/34.817413

Moghaddam, B., Wahid, B. W., & Pentland, A. (1998). Beyond EigenFaces: Probabilistic Matching for Face Recognition. *3rd IEEE Int.l Conference on Automatic Face and Gesture Recognition*, (pp 30-35), Nara, Japan.

Oh, H. J., Lee, K. M., Lee, S. U., & Yim, C.-H. (2006). Occlusion Invariant Face Recognition using Selective Lnmf Basis Images. ACCV 2006 [Springer-Verlag.]. *LNCS, 3851,* pp120–pp129.

Ohba, K., & Ikeuchi, K. (1997). Detectability, Uniqueness, and Reliability of Eigen Windows for Stable Verification of Partially Occluded Objects. *IEEE Transactions on Pattern Analysis and Machine Intelligence, 19*(9), 1043–1048. doi:10.1109/34.615453

Pentland, A., Moghaddam, B., & Starner, T. (1994) View-based and Modular Eigenspaces for Face Recognition. *IEEE Conf. on Computer Vision and Pattern Recognition.* 84-91.

Samaria, F., & Harter, A. (1994). Parameterisation of a stochastic model for human face identification. *Proc. 2nd IEEE Workshop on Applications of Computer Vision*, 138–142.

Smet, M. D., Fransens, R., & Gool, L. V. (2006) A Generalized EM Approach for 3D Model Based Face Recognition under Occlusions, *IEEE Comp. Society Conf. on Computer Vision and Pattern Recognition. 1423-1430.*

Vapnik, V. N. (1998). *Statistical Learning Theory.* New York: John Wiley & Sons.

Vel, O. D., & Aeberhard, S. (1999). Line-Based Face Recognition Under Varying Pose. *IEEE Trans. on PAMI, 21*(10), 1081–1088. doi:10.1109/34.799912

Wiskott, L., Fellous, J. M., Krüger, N., & Malsburg, C. V. (1995). Face Recognition and Gender Determination. *Intl. Workshop on Automatic Face Recognition and Gesture Recognition.* (pp.92-97)

Wright, J., Ganesh, A., Yang, A., & Ma, Y. (2007). Robust Face Recognition via Sparse Representation, *IEEE. Trans. on PAMI., 31*(Issue 2), 210–227. doi:10.1109/TPAMI.2008.79

Xiao, Y., & Yan, H. (2004). Extraction of Glasses in Human Face Image. *Proc. First Int'l Conf. Biometric Authentication,* 214-220.

Yang, M. H. (2002). Face recognition using kernel methods. *Advances in Neural Information Processing Systems, 14,* 215–220.

Zhang, J. Yan, Y., and Lades, M. Face Recognition (1997). Eigenface, Elastic Matching, and Neural Nets. *Proc. IEEE, vol. 85.* 1423-1435.

# Chapter 12
# Facial Muscle Activity Patterns for Recognition of Utterances in Native and Foreign Language:
## Testing for its Reliability and Flexibility

**Sridhar Arjunan**
*RMIT University, Australia*

**Dinesh Kumar**
*RMIT University, Australia*

**Hans Weghorn**
*Baden-Wuerttemberg Cooperative State University, Germany*

**Ganesh Naik**
*RMIT University, Australia*

## ABSTRACT

*The need for developing reliable and flexible human computer interface is increased and applications of HCI have been in each and every field. Human factors play an important role in these kinds of interfaces. Research and development of new human computer interaction (HCI) techniques that enhance the flexibility and reliability for the user are important. Research on new methods of computer control has focused on three types of body functions: speech, bioelectrical activity, and use of mechanical sensors. Speech operated systems have the advantage that these provide the user with flexibility. Such systems have the potential for making computer control effortless and natural. This chapter summarizes research conducted to investigate the use of facial muscle activity for a reliable interface to identify voiceless speech based commands without any audio signals. System performance and reliability have been tested to study inter-subject and inter-day variations and impact of the native language of the speaker. The experimental results indicate that such a system has high degree of inter-subject and inter-day variations. The results also indicate that the variations of the style of speaking in the native language are low but are high when the speaker speaks in a foreign language. The results also indicate that such a system is suitable for a very small vocabulary. The authors suggest that facial sEMG based speech recognition systems may only find limited applications.*

DOI: 10.4018/978-1-61350-429-1.ch012

## 1. INTRODUCTION

One bottleneck in our technological advancements is the interface between the computer and the user. While till recently, Human computer interface (HCI) was largely restricted to the keyboard and the mouse, in the recent past the advancements have lead to systems that are voice, biosignals and gesture operated. Speech operated systems have the advantage that these provide the user with flexibility and time tested natural ability. Such systems provide a potential for natural and seamless interface that have the potential for making computer control almost effortless. Such HCI systems can provide richness comparable to human to human interaction. The success of such systems is based on the robustness of the speech recognition system which is a complex multidisciplinary research area including speech and language processing.

In recent years, significant progress has been achieved in advancing speech recognition technology, making speech an effective modality in both telephony and multimodal human-machine interaction. The technology has become increasingly usable and useful. However, currently speech recognition is largely audio based and suffers from three major shortcomings; (i) it is not suitable in noisy environments such as a vehicle or a factory, (ii) it is not suitable for people with speech impairment disability, such as people after a stroke attack, and (iii) it is not suitable for giving discrete commands or when there may be other people talking loudly in the vicinity.

Work conducted by Chen (Chen, 2001) has demonstrated that speech based human to human communication is multimodal where along with audio signal the listener also observes the facial and body gestures. When we speak in noisy environments, or with people with hearing loss, the lip and facial movements often compensate the lack of quality audio (Simpson et al. 1990; Stone et al 1992). The identification of the speech with lip movement can be achieved using visual sens-

ing, or sensing of the movement and shape using mechanical sensors (Manabe et.al., 2003) or by relating the movement and shape to the muscle activity (Chan et al. 2002; Kumar et al. 2004). To improve the speech classification systems, numbers of researchers have proposed the use of facial movements and gestures (Dimberg et al. 1997; Edward et al. 2006; Francis et.al., 2002). Proposed systems are based on vision, biosignals and mechanical sensor. The proposed systems are generally used along with audio speech recognition systems.

Each of these techniques has strengths and limitations. The video based technique is computationally expensive, requires a camera monitoring the lips that is fixed to the user's head, and is sensitive to lighting conditions. The sensor based technique has the obvious disadvantage that it requires the user to have sensors fixed to the face, making the system not user friendly. The muscle monitoring systems have limitations of low reliability. There are two possible reasons; (i) people use different muscles even when they make the same sound and (ii) cross talk due to different muscles makes the signal quality difficult to classify. These reasons were extensively studied by Harris (Harris, 1970) and reported that the suitable problems for EMG research will be divided into three classes: first, 'which muscle' problems; second, 'which mechanism' problems; and third, a more vaguely defined class of problems having to do with the general organization of the speech mechanism. The other difficulty of each of these systems is that these systems are user dependent and not suitable for different users. In this chapter we report the use of recording muscle activity of the facial muscles to determine the unspoken command from the user. Even the Myoelectric Signals (MES) based systems are heavily influenced by user dependencies, such as style of speaking, rate of speaking, and variation in pronunciation.

This chapter reports the usability, reliability and robustness of a stand-alone Surface Electromyogram (SEMG) to identify speech without audio speech recognition systems. The authors have identified the ability and limitations for such a system and tested it to identify intra-subject, inter-subject, inter-day variations and variations between native and non-native speakers of a language. The robustness of the system has been tested using different classification tools including cluster analysis, Bayesian classifier and neural networks.

The advantages of the SEMG systems are that these are simple to use and are non-invasive. As was expected, these systems are not sensitive to ambient audio noise. The results indicate that there are large inter-subject variations. The results also indicate that the system can be useful for individual users when the vocabulary is small and vowel based. The system may find limited use with people with speech impairment, who have lost their ability to use their vocal cords. By having an automated system that can recognize their facial muscle activity, they would be able to perform simple tasks of controlling devices such as light and power switches. It is also envisaged that this system may find applications for normal telephony purposes to identify the silent periods for data compression. This chapter has been divided into different sections explaining the methodology, analysis of data, and results determining the reliability of the SEMG based speech recognition system.

## 2. BACKGROUND

Numbers of researchers have attempted to use SEMG to identify speech commands. In 1991, Morse et al. (1991) worked on speech recognition using Myoelectric signals with neural network. Chan et al. (2002) demonstrated the use of myoelectric signals in conventional speech recognition. In their study, they attempted to classify words 'zero' to 'nine' using only the information contained in the five facial Myoelectric signals. These signals are indicator of the muscle activ-

ity and gives information about force of muscle contraction. Based on the force of contraction, the associated movement and posture information can be obtained from the myoelectric signals. Manabe et al. (2003) proposed a system called 'Mime Speech recognition'. They tried to classify five Japanese vowels using their system. They demonstrated that it can be advantageous to mobile communication system. Kumar et al. (2004) worked on the outcomes of preliminary study in using artificial neural network (ANN) to recognize and classify human speech based on EMG. One inherent shortcoming in the above works, often not acknowledged by the authors, is that such systems have not been tested for robustness. Further, these systems have been tested under laboratory conditions with number of factors such as inter-subject and inter-day variations having been ignored. The systems appear to have been tested for limited vocabulary without explanations of the choice of the vocabulary.

This chapter has identified factors that would determine the reliability and robustness of such a system. The authors have also attempted to identify factors that would influence the usability of such a system. Towards this aim, this chapter reports the study of impact of variations between people (inter-subject), between different experiments (inter-day) and also the impact of demographics. The chapter also reports techniques that will improve the reliability and robustness of the system. For analyzing the factors that influence a SEMG based speech recognition system, the various factors that are important include: (i) choice of phones to be identified, (ii) signal features, (iii) choice of classifier. This chapter has studied each of these factors below.

### 2.1 Articulatory Phonetics

The face can communicate a variety of information including subjective emotion, communitive intent, and cognitive appraisal (Lapatki et. al., 2003). The facial musculature is a three dimensional assembly of small, pseudo-independently controlled muscular slips (Wohlert and Goffman, 1994) performing a variety of complex orfacial functions such as speech, mastication, swallowing and mediation of motion (Lapatki et. al., 2003). Both speech and emotions need a higher level specification of the controlling parameters of the facial muscles. The parameterization used in speech is usually in terms of phonemes. A phoneme is a set of phones that are cognitively equivalent [reference] and based on the articulator model of speech this generally corresponds to particular position of the mouth during a sound emission. These phonemes in turn control the lower level parameters for the actual deformations. The required shape of the mouth and lips for the utterance of the phonemes is achieved by the controlled contraction of the facial muscles that is a result of the activity from the nervous system (Parsons, 1986).

The difficulty with speech identification using facial movement and shape is the temporal variation when the user is speaking complex time varying sounds. With the intra and inter subject variation in the speed of speaking, and the length of each sound, it is difficult to determine a suitable window, and when the properties of the signal are time varying, this makes identifying suitable features for classification less robust. An example of different facial movements during some facial gestures is shown in Figure 1.

The other difficulties also arise from the need for segmentation and the identification of the start and end of movement if the movement is complex. The selection of the phones that the system would be able to classify is based on the difference in

*Figure 1. Different facial movements while speaking some phonemes*

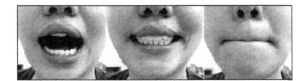

the way these phones are generated. Phones that may sound different but are not a result of difference in the facial movement cannot be differentiated based on the facial muscle activation (Jiang et al., 2002).

Articulatory phonetics considers the anatomical detail of the production speech sounds. This requires the description of speech sounds in terms of the position of the vocal organs. For this purpose, it is convenient to divide the speech sounds into vowels and consonants. The consonants are relatively easy to define in terms of the shape and position of the vocal organs, but the vowels are less well defined and this may be explained because the tongue typically never touches another organ when making a vowel (Parsons, 1986). While the movements and shape of the mouth when producing different sounds is important in visual analysis, the most common sources of visual speech parameters are text driven models of speech articulation. When considering the speech articulation, the shapes of the mouth during middle section of the utterance of vowels remain stationary while during consonants the shapes of the mouth changes.

In the presence of background noise, it is difficult to segment SEMG to identify activity (Basmajian & DeLuca, 1985). If the muscle activity within a phone is allowed to vary, there will be lack of information regarding the start and end of an articulation for robust segmentation of the signal. It is important that the phones be selected where the muscle activity is not varying during the utterance. For this reason, the authors have narrowed the phones to be the suitable phones for classification using SEMG to only vowels during the utterance of which the activity of the facial muscles is not changing.

With limited information that can be obtained from SEMG, such a system would have limited vocabulary, and would not be very natural, but would be reliable (Chan et al. (2002) and be an important step in the evolution. In such a system, using moving root mean square (RMS) threshold, the temporal location of each activity can be identified. By having a stationary set of parameters defining the muscle activity for each spoken event, this also makes the system have very compact set of features, making it suitable for real time classification.

## 2.2 Features of Surface Electromyogram (SEMG)

Surface electromyogram (SEMG) is the non-invasive recording of the muscle activity. It can be recorded from the surface using electrodes that are stuck to the skin and located close to the muscle to be studied. SEMG is a gross indicator of the muscle activity and is used to identify force of muscle contraction, associated movement and posture (Basmajian & DeLuca, 1985). There are number of challenges associated with the classification of muscle activity with respect to the associated movement and posture, such as the sensitivity of the location of electrodes, inter user variations, sensitivity of the system to variations in intrinsic factors such as skin conductance, and to external factors such as temperature, and electrode conditions. Veldhuizen et al. (2003) demonstrated the variation of facial EMG during a single day and has shown facial SEMG activity decreased during the workday and increased again in the evening.

SEMG is a complex and non-stationary signal. The strength of SEMG is a good measure of the strength of contraction of the muscle, and can be related to the movement and posture of the corresponding part of the body. The most commonly used feature to identify the strength of contraction of a muscle is the root mean square (RMS) of SEMG. RMS of SEMG is related to the number of active muscle fibres and the rate of activation, and is a good measure of the strength of the muscle activation, and thus the strength of the force of muscle contraction.

The preliminary study by Chan et al. (2003) has demonstrated the presence of speech information in facial EMG. Kumar et al (2004) have demonstrated the use of SEMG to identify the unspoken

sounds under controlled conditions. The unspoken sound refers to the when the person makes the required movement for uttering the sound but the sound is not audible. The timing of the activation of different groups of muscles is a central issue to identify the movement and shape of the mouth and lips. The issue regarding the use of SEMG to identify speech is the large variability of SEMG activity pattern associated with a phoneme of speech. A difference in the amount of motor unit activity was observed in one and the same muscle when different utterances like p, b were spoken in the same context (Basmajian & DeLuca, 1985).

The vowels correspond to stationary muscle activity, the muscle activity pre and post the vowel is non-stationary. The other issue is the variation in the inter-subject because of variation in the speed and style of utterance of the vowel. While it is relatively simple to identify the start and the end of the muscle activity related to the vowel, the muscle activity at the start and the end may often be much larger than the activity during the section when the mouth cavity shape is being kept constant, corresponding to the vowel. To overcome this issue, this research recommends the use of the integration of the RMS of SEMG from the start till the end of the utterance of the vowel. The temporal location of the start and the end of the activity is identifiable using moving window RMS.

Another shortcoming of the use of strength of SEMG is that it is dependent on the absolute of the magnitude of the recording, which can have large inter experimental variation. To overcome this shortcoming, this research reports the use of ratios of the area under the curve of SEMG from the different muscles. By taking the ratio rather than the absolute value, the difficulty due the variation of the magnitude of SEMG between different experiments and between different individuals can overcome. The normalization technique was used in this method to determine the robustness of the phoneme recognition using facial muscle activity signals.

## 2.3 Facial Muscles for Speech

When using facial SEMG to determine the shape of the lips and the mouth, there is the issue of the choice of the muscles and the corresponding location of the electrodes. Face structure is more complex than the limbs, with large number of muscles with overlaps. There is also the need to make the system easy to use, and for the electrodes be placed such that these can become an integral part of communication devices such as a hand-held telephone.

The complexity of the facial muscles makes it difficult to identify the specific muscles that are responsible for specific facial actions and shapes. There is also the difficulty of cross talk due to the overlap between the different muscles. This is made more complex due to the temporal variation in the activation and deactivation of the different muscles. The use of integral of the RMS of SEMG is useful in overcoming the issues of cross talk and the temporal difference between the activation of the different muscles that may be close to one set of electrodes. Due to the unknown aspect of the muscle groups that are activated to produce a sound, statistical distance based cluster analysis and back-propagation neural network has been used for classifying the integral of the RMS of the real time SEMG recordings.

It is impractical to consider the entire facial muscles and record their electrical activity. In this study, only the following four facial muscles have been selected: *(i) Zygomaticus Major* arises from the front surface of the zygomatic bone and merges with the muscles at the corner of the mouth, *(ii) Depressor anguli oris* originates from the mandible and inserts skin at an angle of mouth and pulls corner of mouth downward, *(iii) Masseter* originates from maxilla and zygomatic arch and inserts to ramus of mandible to elevate and protrude, assists in side-to-side movements mandible, *(iv) Mentalis* originates from the mandible and inserts into the skin of the chin to elevate and protrude lower lip, pull skin into a pout (Fridlund & Cacioppo, 1986).

## 2.4 Statistical Analysis in Classification of the Data Points Using Cross-Validation

To determine the robustness of the system, the choice of classifier and statistical methods is important. The works reported in literature have used different classifiers such as neural networks and hidden Markov models (HMM) to show the recognition accuracy. This may affect the performance of the system and makes comparison between systems difficult. This chapter reports the use of statistical analysis and clustering techniques to identify the fundamental properties of the data. To test and compare the system performance with similar systems reported in literature, neural networks have been used as the classifier to determine the performance of this vowel recognition using facial muscle activity signals.

Cross-validation is the statistical practice of partitioning a sample of data into subsets such that the analysis is initially performed on a single subset, while the other subset(s) are retained for subsequent use in confirming and validating the initial analysis. The initial subset of data is called the *training set*; the other subset(s) are called *validation or testing sets* (Gutierrez-Osuna, 2001). The *holdout* method is the simplest kind of cross validation. The data set is separated into two sets, called the training set and the testing set. The function approximator fits a function using the training set only. Then the function approximator is asked to predict the output values for the data in the testing set (it has never seen these output values before). The obtained errors are accumulated as before to give the mean absolute test set error, which is used to evaluate the model. To have a random selection of training and testing data sets, *Random Sub-sampling Cross-validation* method was used. Random Sub-sampling performs k data splits of the dataset. Each split randomly selects a (fixed) number of examples without replacement. For each data split we retrain the classifier from scratch with the training examples and estimate with the test examples. The true classification accuracy is obtained as the average of the separate estimates (Gutierrez-Osuna, 2001).

The classification accuracy of the data points can be computed statistically using cross-validation. The training and testing in the artificial neural network architecture was performed with equal number data sets selected randomly for each user. Thus for a total number of data being $n$, $m$ sets of data were randomly selected for training and $k$ data were taken randomly for testing, where $m$ and $k$ are both equal. Each $n$ data with three normalised features for every single vowel was specified to a target vector in Neural Network. In this analysis, the total number of data points (training and testing) was

$$n = s \times p \tag{1}$$

where s = number of vowels recorded from each user p = number of repetitions in experiment.

This process was repeated for all random values for training and testing for $N$ times for calculating the statistical mean of classification accuracy, the total number of data points considered for each participant was

$$X = N \times n \tag{2}$$

The total data vectors used for classification of y number of participants were

$$Y = X \times y \tag{3}$$

The statistical mean $M$ of the process (Eqn.4) was calculated and considered as the final recognition rate.

$$M = \frac{1}{N} \sum_{i=1}^{6} z_i \Big/ t \tag{4}$$

where: $z$ = *Number of correctly classified data;* t = Total number of data used for testing; and N = Number of times performing training and testing.

## 3. METHODOLOGY

The aim of this research study was to determine the reliability and robustness of vowel recognition using facial SEMG signals. Experiments were devised and conducted to evaluate the performance of the proposed speech recognition from facial EMG and validate the impact of variations like inter-subject, inter-day and between different languages. The experiments were approved by the Human Experiments Ethics Committee of RMIT University. Experiments were conducted where electromyography (EMG) activity of suitable facial muscles was acquired from the subjects speaking vowels of two different languages. As the muscle contraction is stationary during the utterance, root mean square values of each of the signals windowed for the duration of the utterance was computed and used for further analysis. The experimental protocols have been explained in the following sections.

### 3.1 EMG Recording and Processing

The experiment used 4 channel EMG configurations as per the recommended recording guidelines (Fridlund & Cacioppo, 1986). A four channel, portable, continuous recording MEGAWIN equipment (from MEGA Electronics, Finland) was used for this purpose. Raw signal sampled at 2000 samples/ second was recorded. Prior to the recording, the participants were requested to shave their facial hair. if necessary. The target sites were cleaned with alcohol wet swabs. Ag/AgCl electrodes (AMBU Blue sensors from MEDICOTEST, Denmark) were mounted on appropriate locations close to the selected facial muscles. The muscles selected were *the right side Zygomaticus Major, Masseter & Mentalis and left side Depressor anguli oris.* The inter electrode distance was kept constant at 1cm for all the channels and the experiments. Figure 2. shows a sample photograph of the participant during experiment. The permission was obtained from the participant to publish this

*Figure 2. A sample photo during the experiment*

photograph. The experimental procedures were designed to study the inter-day, inter-subject and demographics variations.

### 3.1.1 Experiment 1

The aim of the first experiment was to study the performance of sEMG system to classify simple English vowels and to study the inter-subject variations. Three male native English speakers participated in the experiment. Controlled experiments were conducted where the subjects were asked to speak. During this utterance, facial SEMG from the muscles was recorded. SEMG from Four channels were recorded simultaneously. The recordings were visually observed, and the recordings with any artefacts - typically due to loose electrodes or movement, were discarded. During the recordings, the subjects spoke the English vowels (/a/, /e/, /i/, /o/, /u/). Each vowel was spoken separately such that there was a clear start and end of the utterance. The experiment was repeated for ten times. A suitable resting time was given between each experiment. The participants were asked to vary their speaking speed and style to get a wide based training set. In order to collect a wide based training set, the participants were asked to utter the same vowel with short length and long length i.e. with high speed and low speed.

### 3.1.2 Experiment 2

In the second experiment, the aim was to determine the performance of the system to the variation in SEMG for different days. A male native speaker of English participated in the experiment. The subject was asked to speak the English vowels (/a/, /e/, /i/, /o/, /u/) and was also asked to vary the speed and style of speaking. The experiment was repeated for 10 - 15 times at different periods for 3 days.

### 3.1.3 Experiment 3

The aim of the third experiment was to determine the impact of the variations in the native language of the speaker on sEMG based vowel speech recognition. Two male and one female speaker participated in the experiment. All the participants in the experiment here were native speakers of German with English as their second language. Controlled experiments were conducted where the subjects were asked to speak English vowels (/a/, /e/, /i/, /o/, /u/) and German vowels (/a/, /o/, /i/, /e/, /u/). During this utterance, facial SEMG from the muscles was recorded for English and German vowels separately. The experiment procedure was repeated as in previous experiments. Figure 3 shows the general block diagram of process used in the methodology.

### 3.2 Data Analysis

The first step in the analysis of the data required identifying the temporal location of the muscle activity. Moving root mean square (MRMS) of the recorded signal was computed and thresholded against 1 sigma of the signal (Freedman et al., 1997). The MRMS was computed using a moving window of 20 samples over the whole signal. After identifying the start and the end of the muscle activity based on 1 sigma, these were confirmed visually. The variation in length of speech due to variation in speed and style has been visualised

*Figure 3. General block diagram of the methodology used in this analysis*

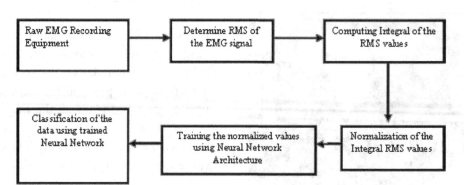

by change in time period in the EMG signal and its plot RMS as shown in Figure 4.

On the assumption that during the utterance of a vowel, the muscle activity would remain unchanged, the RMS of the SEMG between the start and the end of the muscle activity was integrated for each of the channels. This resulted in one number representing the muscle activity for each channel for each vowel utterance. These were tabulated and all the channels were normalised with respect to channel 1 by taking a ratio of the respective integral with channel 1.

This ratio is indicative of the relative strength of contraction of the different muscles and reduces the impact of inter-experiment variations.

Durand's rule (Weisstein, 2006) was used for computing the integral of RMS of SEMG because it produces simple and accurate approximations and a straightforward family of numerical integration techniques. The RMS values between the start and end of the muscle contraction was considered as $x_1$ to $x_n$, where h is the sample interval i.e., $x_{i+1} - x_i$.

*Figure 4. Raw SEMG signal and its RMS plot a) when subject speaking naturally b) when subject speaking by varying length, speed and style of the speech (X axis in Samples in secs and Y axis in millivolts)*

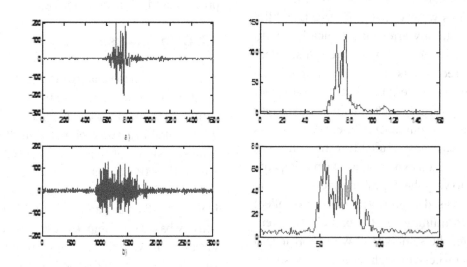

*Figure 5. a) 3D plot showing the normalized values of all vowels as per Experiment 1 b) Silhouette plot showing the silhouette values of the clusters c) 3D plot showing the normalized values of reduced 3 vowels*

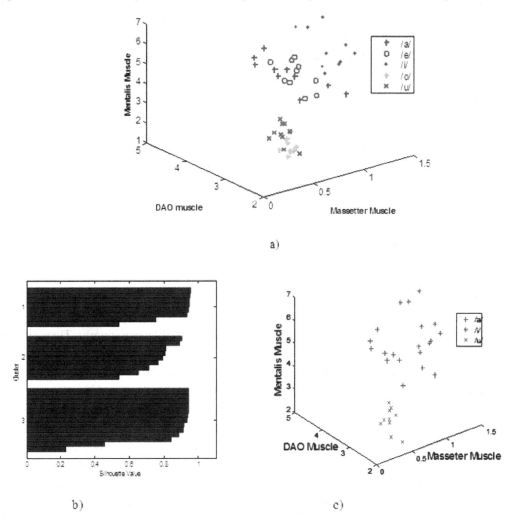

## 3.3 Classification of Data

Statistical description of the data and cluster analysis were used to identify the classification properties of the data and artificial neural network (ANN) were used to demonstrate the classification accuracy of the system for comparing with other reports. ANNs are simple to implement, can provide non-linear classification and have been used by number of other researchers making these suitable for comparison purposes.

## 3.3.1 Using Cluster Analysis

For each utterance of each vowel there were four numbers generated representing the total muscle activity of the four muscles. After normalisation with respect to the channel 1, this resulted in vector of length three for each utterance. As a first step, this data for each subject was plotted to generate a three-dimensional scatter plot. Data point from each of the vowels were given a distinct symbol and colour for ease of visual observation (Figure 5).

The data points in each plot forms a cluster, which is predominated by three clusters in every plot. This shows the linear separation of data into three distinct clusters. From these plots, it was clear that the normalised relative muscle activity values can be *linearly separated*, if three vowels were used for the classification. The cluster plot was done to show that the relative muscle activity can be used as a feature to classify the vowel utterance.

This is also verified using *k-means* Silhouette plot: it is clear that most data points have a large silhouette value, indicating that the clusters are separated from each other, and it suggests that there exists linear separation of the data. The average silhouette value for English vowels in experiment 1 is 0.8271 and for English vowels and German vowels in experiment 2 are 0.7634 and 0.8441 respectively. This result shows that the linear separation of data is stronger in German vowels (native language of the speaker) than for English vowels (foreign language). It may be attributed to the naturalness of speaking in ones own language making it more repeatable. This study could not be conducted for people (volunteers) whose native language was English due to their lack of knowledge of another language.

Artificial neural network architecture was used for its non-linear separability to classify the data points. To have better classification of these features, only three vowels from each experiment as per the linear separable property. From the experiment 1, the three distinct linear separable data for English vowels /a/, /i/, /u/ was considered for the better classification. From experiment 2, the three distinct linear separable data for English vowels /a/, /e/, /u/ and the German vowels /a/, /i/, /u/ was considered for the better classification. The linearly separability of these chosen vowels are shown in the Figure 6 and Figure 7.

### 3.3.2 Classification by Artificial Neural Networks

The classification of the data was performed using the designed ANN backpropogation network architecture. Supervised artificial neural network (ANN) approach lends itself for identifying the separability of data even when the statistical properties and the types of separability (linear or nonlinear) are not known. Other advantages of ANN are its fault tolerance and high computation rate due to the massive parallelism of its structure (Kulkarni, 1994). A feedforward Multi-layer ANN classifier with back propagation (BP) learning algorithm is used in the proposed approach. Due to the multilayer construction, such a network can be used to approximate any continuous functional mapping (Bishop, 1995).

Standard backpropagation is a gradient descent algorithm, as is the Widrow-Hoff learning rule, in which the network weights are moved along the negative of the gradient of the performance function. The term backpropagation refers to the manner in which the gradient is computed for nonlinear multilayer networks. There are a number of variations on the basic algorithm that are based on other standard optimization techniques, such as conjugate gradient and Newton methods. The architecture of the ANN consisted of two hidden layers and the 20 nodes for the two hidden layers were optimized iteratively during the training of the ANN. Sigmoid function was the threshold function and the type of training algorithm for the ANN was gradient descent and adaptive learning with momentum with a learning rate of 0.05 to reduce chances of local minima. The general steps in training the ANN is as follows:

- Set up the network with *'ni'* input units fully connected to *'nh'* non-linear hidden units via connections with weights $w_{jk}^{(1)}$, which in turn are fully connected to *'np'* output units via connections with weights $w_{jk}^{(2)}$
- Generate random initial weights, e.g. from the range *[–wt, +wt]*
- Select an appropriate error function $E(w_{jk}^{(n)})$ and learning rate $\eta$

*Figure 6. a) 3D plot showing the normalized values of all English vowels as per Experiment 3 b) Silhouette plot showing the silhouette values of the clusters c) 3D plot showing the normalized values of reduced 3 vowels*

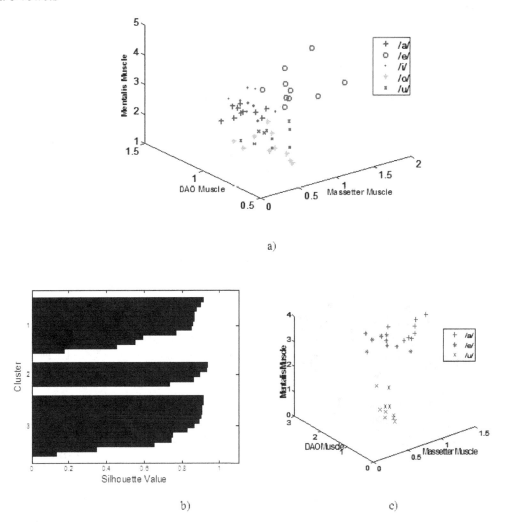

- Apply the weight update $\Delta w_{jk}^{(n)} = -\eta \partial E(w_{jk}^{(n)}) / \partial w_{jk}^{(n)}$ to each weight $w_{jk}^{(n)}$ for each training pattern $p$. One set of updates of all the weights for all the training patterns is called *one epoch* of training.
- Repeat the previous step until the network error function is minimal.

The designed ANN was used for training and testing. The training and testing was performed using data generated randomly. This was repeated for randomly for six times and the final classification accuracy was computed by taking mean of all the classification accuracies from this process.

### 3.3.3 Inter-Subject Variation

To determine the variability between subjects the data set of one subject was used to train the ANN and tested for the same subject to confirm that the system was functioning for the individual subject. After this, the ANN was tested for all the other

*Figure 7. a) 3D plot showing the normalized values of all German vowels as per Experiment 3 b) Silhouette plot showing the silhouette values of the clusters c) 3D plot showing the normalized values of reduced 3 vowels*

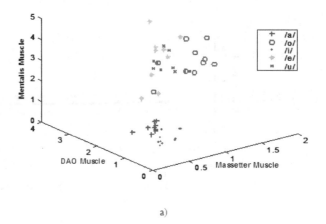

a)

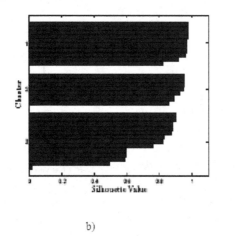

b)

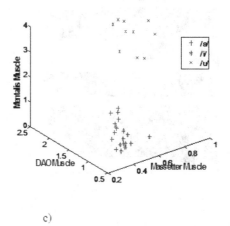

c)

subjects. The normalized integral RMS values of 5 recordings (for each vowel) for individual subject were used to train the ANN classifier with back propagation learning algorithm.

In the testing section, for the first part, the trained ANNs were used to classify the integral RMS values of 5 recordings of each vowel that were not used in the training of the ANN to test the performance of the proposed approach. This process was repeated for all the subjects. The data from subjects other than used for training was used for testing. The performance of these integral

RMS values was evaluated in this experiment by comparing the accuracy in the classification during testing.

### 3.3.4 Inter–Day Variation

The performance of the system was tested for its reliability between different days. The data from the second experiment was divided into two separate sections; the training section and the test section. In the training section, for the first part of the analysis, normalised integral RMS values of

5 recordings (for each vowel) for each single day was used to train the ANN classifier with back propagation learning algorithm. For the second part of the analysis, the neural network was trained with mixed data of 15 recordings (for each vowel) from different days and tested with other mixed data from different days. In the third part of the experiment, the neural network was trained using the data from the single day and tested with the data from other days.

### 3.3.5 Bilingual Variation

The variation in pronunciation of different languages by the same speaker was analyzed for the performance of the system. The data from the ten repetitions from experiment three for each subject speaking the vowels of two languages English and German was divided into two separate sections. In the first part of the training section, the normalised integral RMS values of 5 recordings (for each vowel) for individual subject speaking English vowels were used to train the ANN classifier with back propagation learning algorithm. In the second part of the training section, the normalised integral RMS values of 5 recordings (for each vowel) for individual subject speaking German vowels were used to train the ANN classifier with back propagation learning algorithm. The performance of these integral RMS values was evaluated in this experiment by comparing the accuracy of both the languages in the classification during testing.

## 3.4 Statistical Analysis in Classification of Data

The statistical descriptors were computed for the classification accuracy. The training and testing was performed with equal number of random data for each. Consider $n$ number of data, in which $m$ data were used for testing and $k$ data were used testing randomly. Each of the $n$ data points is a three dimensional normalized vector for each vowel utterance. This is the input while the vowel descriptor, the target for the ANN. For calculating the statistical descriptor of classification accuracy, this process was repeated six times with random selection of the training and testing data. Six was found to be sufficient, as the process began to repeat itself. The total data vectors used for classification of all subjects were $540 * 6 = 3240$. The statistical mean of the all process was considered as the final recognition rate.

## 4. RESULTS AND OBSERVATIONS

The results were analyzed to determine the performance of the system for its variations like inter-subject, inter-day and bilingual variation which are discussed in the following topics.

## 4.1 Inter-Subject Variation

The results of the experiment one report the performance of different subjects in classifying the integral RMS values of the 3 vowels. The three dimensional plot between the normalised area of the different muscle for different vowels is shown in Figure 5. The plot shows the different normalised values of vowels being separated from each other as clusters. It is evident from the plot that three different class of vowels form clusters that appear to be separate and distinct for each of the vowels. This is a clear indication that the three vowels are easy to separate using this technique.

The result of the use of these normalised values to train the ANN using data from individual subjects demonstrated easy convergence. The results of testing the ANN to correctly classify the test data based on the weight matrix generated using the training data is tabulated in Table 1. The accuracy was computed based on the percentage of correct classified data points to the total number of data points. The results indicate an overall average accuracy of 80%, where it is noted that the overall classification of the integral RMS values

*Table 1. Classification results for different subjects, when trained and tested individually*

| Vowels | No of Utterances used for testing | Correctly Classified Vowels | | |
|--------|-----------------------------------|------------------|------------------|------------------|
| | | Subject 1 | Subject 2 | Subject 3 |
| /a/ | 15 | (80%) | (60%) | (60%) |
| /i/ | 15 | (60%) | (80%) | (80%) |
| /u/ | 15 | (100%) | (100%) | (100%) |

of the EMG signal yields better recognition rate of vowels for 3 different subjects when it is trained individually.

The classification results for each subject when trained individually were analysed to determine the inter-subject variation. It is observed that

- the classification accuracy for vowel /a/ for subject 1 (80%) is marginally high when compared with the other subjects.
- the classification accuracy for vowel /i/ for subjects 2&3 (80%) is equal and marginally high when compared with the subject 1.
- the classification accuracy for vowel /u/ is equal for the all subjects (100%).

The mean classification accuracies of different vowels for different subjects are tabulated in Table 2.

The classification results for the subjects when using the training for all the subjects is tabulated in Table 3. The results indicate that the overall accuracy is *poor*. On closer observations, it is observed that while the system is able to accurately identify the utterance of '/u/' (accuracy 80%); the error for separating between '/a/' and '/i/' is poor. This suggests that while the system is able to identify the differences between the styles of speaking of different people at different times, the inter-subject variation is high. This suggests that the system would be functional if trained for individual subjects. Since its high variation between different subjects, it may affect the robustness of the system. This can be consid-

*Table 2. Mean classification accuracy for different participants*

| Vowels | Mean Classification accuracy | | |
|--------|------------------|------------------|------------------|
| | Subject 1 | Subject 2 | Subject 3 |
| /a/ | 83.333% | 66.667% | 66.667% |
| /i/ | 66.667% | 83.333% | 83.333% |
| /u/ | 100% | 100% | 100% |

*Table 3. Classification results for different subjects when trained with a subject and tested for other subjects*

| Vowels | No of Utterances for testing | Correctly Classified Vowels | | | |
|--------|------------------------------|-------|-------|-------|----------|
| | | Sub 1 | Sub2 | Sub 3 | Total |
| /a/ | 25 | 4 | 1 | 1 | 6(24%) |
| /i/ | 25 | 3 | 2 | 1 | 6(24%) |
| /u/ | 25 | 5 | 9 | 6 | 20(80%) |

*Table 4. Classification results when trained with data from different days and tested with other data*

| Vowels | No. of Utterances used for testing from different days | Correctly Classified Vowels | Recognition Rate (%) |
|--------|------------------------------------------------------|----------------------------|----------------------|
| /a/ | 20 | 14 | 70 |
| /i/ | 20 | 18 | 90 |
| /u/ | 20 | 20 | 100 |

ered as a limitation in using facial muscle activity, as the muscle activity pattern differs between individuals. The authors would like to mention that this study has a small sample size, and while it proves the principle, detailed studies need to be undertaken to optimize such a system and test the reliability for a larger cohort.

## 4.2 Inter-Day Variation

The analysis was also performed to check for reliability of muscle activity during different days. The training and testing was done using the values form different days. This normalised relative muscle activity feature gave a better classification even if there is variation in muscle activity during different days.

The classification results of experiment in the training section for the different days when trained using the data from different days and tested with other data are tabulated in Table 4. The results indicate that the classification accuracy for vowel /a/ (70%) is low when compared with other vowels and the system is able to accurately identify the utterance of /i/ (accuracy 90%) and /u/ (accuracy 100%). The classification accuracy when trained with data from Day 1 and tested with other days

is tabulated in Table 5 shows a small variation in the muscle activity during different days.

## 4.3 Bilingual Variation

The results of testing the ANN on the test data using weight matrix generated during training are tabulated in Table 6 for English Vowels and Table 8 for German Vowels. The overall classification of the integral RMS values of the EMG signal shows a better recognition rate of vowels for 3 different participants when it is trained individually. The mean classification accuracies of the English and German vowels are tabulated in Table 7 and Table 9 respectively.

The results indicate that this technique can be used under limited conditions for the classification of vowels for the native and foreign language, in this case- English and German. The results indicate that when people speak their native language, they repeat themselves, while when they speak in a foreign language, there appears to be a greater amount of variation. It is also observed that this change is observable using facial SEMG.

The results indicate that there is large inter-subject variation and the proposed method provides better results for identifying silently spoken

*Table 5. Classification results when trained with data from Day 1 and tested with data from other days*

| Vowels | No. of Utterances used for testing from different days | Correctly Classified Vowels | Recognition Rate (%) |
|--------|------------------------------------------------------|----------------------------|----------------------|
| /a/ | 20 | 12 | 60 |
| /i/ | 20 | 17 | 85 |
| /u/ | 20 | 20 | 100 |

*Table 6. Classification results for different participants uttering English vowels*

| Vowels | No of Utterances used for testing | Correctly Classified Vowels | | |
|---|---|---|---|---|
| | | Participant 1 | Participant 2 | Participant 3 |
| /a/ | 15 | (60%) | (80%) | (80%) |
| /e/ | 15 | (80%) | (80%) | (80%) |
| /u/ | 15 | (100%) | (100%) | (100%) |

*Table 7. Mean classification accuracy for different participants uttering English vowels*

| Vowels | Mean Classification accuracy | | |
|---|---|---|---|
| | Participant 1 | Participant 2 | Participant 3 |
| /a/ | 73.333% | 83.333% | 80% |
| /e/ | 76.667% | 76.667% | 83.333% |
| /u/ | 100% | 100% | 100% |

*Table 8. Classification results for different participants uttering German vowels*

| Vowels | No of Utterances for testing | Correctly Classified Vowels | | |
|---|---|---|---|---|
| | | Participant 1 | Participant 2 | Participant 3 |
| /a/ | 15 | 80% | 80% | 80% |
| /i/ | 15 | 100% | 80% | 80% |
| /u/ | 15 | 100% | 100% | 100% |

*Table 9. Mean classification accuracy for different participants uttering German vowels*

| Vowels | Mean Classification accuracy | | |
|---|---|---|---|
| | Participant 1 | Participant 2 | Participant 3 |
| /a/ | 86.667% | 83.333% | 83.333% |
| /i/ | 96.667% | 80% | 76.667% |
| /u/ | 100% | 100% | 100% |

vowels by measuring the movements of facial when it is trained and tested for an individual. The work has demonstrated that the performance of the speech recognition system using facial muscle activity signals is varied and unreliable because of its inter-subject, inter-day variations but is tolerant to intra-subject variations such as speed of utterance. This may be attributable to the low signal to noise ratio due to the overlapping of number of active muscles and low level of muscle activity.

## 5. CONCLUSION

This research describes a voiceless speech recognition approach that is based on evaluation of facial muscle contraction. The experiments indicate that the system is easy to train for a new user. Speech generated facial electromyography signals could assist HCI by disambiguating the acoustic noise from multiple speakers and background noise. The presented investigation focused on the reliability and robustness of the system using facial SEMG.

The experimental results suggest that the performance of the proposed approach is unreliable because of its inter-subject, inter-day and bilingual variation. The experiments indicate that the system is easy to train for a new user and is suitable for users of different native languages such as English and German. It is insensitive to variations in the speed of speaking. The applications of this include removal of any disambiguating caused by the acoustic noise for human computer interface or computer based speech analysis. The normalised integral RMS values of the facial EMG signals are used for analysis, and classification of these values is performed by ANN. The results indicate that the system is reliable for three vowels only and only when trained for the individual user, while the inter-subject variation is large. The authors believe that such a system will have limited applications due to the very small possible vocabulary, large inter-subject and inter-day variations and need for four set of electrodes. One possible application for such a system is for disabled user to give simple commands to a machine in specific conditions.

## FUTURE RESEARCH DIRECTIONS

The future research should involve in the need for developing reliable and flexible speech recognition system using facial muscle activity. The reliability of the system has to be tested. Speech recognition base on facial SEMG has its own application, where it can be sue for disabled people to give some discrete commands. But in order to develop these kinds of systems, the flexibility of the user has to be validated. This chapter has provided some insights into the reliability and robustness of these speech recognition systems. This chapter has also summarized research conducted to investigate the use of facial muscle activity for a reliable interface to identify voiceless speech based commands without any audio signals. In future, the research on speech recognition using facial muscle activity signals has to be focused on developing the algorithms for better system performance and reliability to study inter-subject and inter-day variations and impact of the native language of the speaker. This research will be helpful in developing a better speech recognition based on the facial muscle activity signals and it will be an application to speech impaired people.

## REFERENCES

Basmajian, J. V., & Deluca, C. J. (1985). *Muscles alive: Their functions revealed by electromyography* (5th ed.). Baltimore, MD: Williams & Wilkins.

Beyer, W. H. (1987). *CRC standard mathematical tables* (28th ed., p. 127). Boca Raton, FL: CRC Press.

Bickmore, T. W., & Picard, R. W. (2005). Establishing and maintaining long-term human-computer relationships. *ACM Transactions on Computer-Human Interaction*, *12*(2), 293–327. doi:10.1145/1067860.1067867

Bishop, C. M. (1995). *Neural networks for pattern recognition*. Oxford University Press.

Chan, A. D. C., Englehart, K., Hudgins, B., & Lovely, D. F. (2002). A multi-expert speech recognition system using acoustic and myoelectric signals. *24th Annual Conference and the Annual Fall Meeting of the Biomedical Engineering Society. Ottawa, Canada,* (vol. 1, pp. 72-73).

Chen, T. (2001). Audiovisual speech processing. *IEEE Signal Processing Magazine*, *18*(9).

Dimberg, U., & Karlsson, B. (1997). Facial reactions to different emotionally relevant stimuli. *Scandinavian Journal of Psychology*, 38.

Freedman, D., Pisani, R., & Purves, R. (1997). *Statistics* (3rd ed.). New York, NY: Norton College Books.

Fridlund, A. J., & Cacioppo, J. T. (1986). Guidelines for human electromyographic research. *Journal of Psychophysiology, 23*(4), 567–589.

Gutierrez-Osuna, R. (2001). *Lecture 13: Validation.* Wright State University. Retrieved September 2007 from http://research.cs.tamu.edu/prism/lectures

Harris, K. S. (1970). Physiological measures of speech movements: EMG and fiberoptic studies. *ASHA Reports, 5,* 271–282.

Jiang, J., Alwan, A., Keating, P., Auer, E. T., Jr., & Bernstein, L. E. (2002). On the relationship between face movements, tongue movements, and speech acoustics. *EURASIP Journal on Applied Signal Processing: Special Issue on Joint Audio-Visual Speech Processing,* 1174-1188.

Kulkarni, A. D. (1994). *Artificial neural network for image understanding.* Van Nostrand Reinhold.

Kumar, S., Kumar, D. K., Alemu, M., & Burry, M. (2004). EMG based voice recognition. *Intelligent Sensors, Sensor Networks and Information Processing Conference,* (pp. 593-597).

Lapatki, B. G., Stegeman, D. F., & Jonas, I. E. (2003). A surface EMG electrode for the simultaneous observation of multiple facial muscles. *Journal of Neuroscience Methods, 123*(2), 117–128. doi:10.1016/S0165-0270(02)00323-0

Lutz, J., Joachim, V., Frauke, M., Kai, L., & Karl, T. K. (1996). Facial EMG responses to auditory stimuli. *International Journal of Psychophysiology,* 22.

Manabe, H., Hiraiwa, A., & Sugimura, T. (2003). Unvoiced speech recognition using EMG - Mime speech recognition. *ACM Conference on Human Factors in Computing Systems,* Ft. Lauderdale, Florida, USA, (pp. 794-795).

Morse, S., & Wrightpp, M. (1991). Speech recognition using myoelectric signals with neural network. *Annual International Conference of the IEEE Engineering in Medicine and Biology Society,* (vol. 13, no. 4, pp. 1977-178).

Parsons, T. W. (1986). *Voice and speech processing* (1st ed.). New York, NY: McGraw-Hill.

Quek, F., Mcneill, D., Bryll, R., Duncan, S., Ma, X.-F., & Kirbas, C. (2002). Multimodal human discourse: Gesture and speech. *ACM Transactions on Computer-Human Interaction, 9*(3), 171–193. doi:10.1145/568513.568514

Simpson, A. M., Stone, M. A., & Glasberg, B. R. (1990). Spectral enhancement to improve the intelligibility of speech in noise for hearing-impaired listeners. *Acta Oto-Laryngologica. Supplementum, 469,* 101–107.

Stone, M. A., & Moore, B. C. (1992). Spectral feature enhancement for people with sensorineural hearing impairment: effects on speech intelligibility and quality. *Journal of Rehabilitation Research and Development, 29*(2), 39–56. doi:10.1682/JRRD.1992.04.0039

Tse, E., Shen, S., Greenberg, S., & Forlines, C. (2006). Enabling interaction with single user applications through speech and gestures on a multi-user tabletop. *AVI '06,* May 23-26, 2006, Venezia, Italy, (pp. 336-343).

Ursula, H., Pierre, P., & Sylvie, B. (1998). Facial reactions to emotional facial expressions: Affect or cognition? *Cognition and Emotion, 12*(4).

Veldhuizen, I. J., Gaillard, A. W., & de Vries, J. (2003). The influence of mental fatigue on facial EMG activity during a simulated workday. *Journal of Biological Psychology, 63*(1), 59–78. doi:10.1016/S0301-0511(03)00025-5

Wohlert, A. B., & Goffman, L. (1994). Human perioral muscle activation patterns. *Journal of Speech and Hearing Research, 37,* 1032–1040.

## ADDITIONAL READING

Freeman, A., & Skapura, M. (1991). *Neural Networks: Algorithms, Applications, and Programming Techniques*. Mass: Addison-Wesley.

Goldschen, A. J., Garcia, O. N., & Petajan, E. (1994). Continuous optical automatic speech recognition by lip-reading. presented at 28th Annual Asilomar Conf on Signal Systems and Computer.

Graupe, D., Salahi, J., & Kohn, K. H. (1982). Multifunction prosthesis and orthosis control via microcomputer identification of temporal pattern differences in singlesite myoelectric signals. *Journal of Biomedical Engineering*, 4, 17–22. doi:10.1016/0141-5425(82)90021-8

Haung, K.Y., (2001) Neural networks for robust recognition of seismic patterns. *IEEE Transactions on Geoscience and Remote sensing*.

Hazen, T. J. (2006). Visual model structures and synchrony constraints for audio-visual speech recognition. In *IEEE Transactions on Speech and Audio Processing*.

Hudgins, B., Parker, P. A., & Scott, R. N. (1993). A new strategy for multifunction myoelectric control. *IEEE Transactions on Bio-Medical Engineering*, 40(1), 82–94. doi:10.1109/10.204774

Kaynak, M. N., Qi, Z., Cheok, A. D., Sengupta, K., & Chi Chung, K. (2001). Audio-visual modeling for bimodal speech recognition. In *IEEE Transactions on Systems, Man and Cybernetics. Part A*, vol. 34, p. 564.

Leonard J. Trejo, K.R.W., Charles C. Jorgensen, S.T.C. Roman Rosipal, Bryan Matthews, & Andrew D. Hibbs, (2002) Multimodal Neuroelectric Interface Development. *IEEE Transactions on Neural Systems and Rehabilitation Engineering*, (Special Issue on BCI).

Liang, L., Liu, X., Zhao, Y., Pi, X., & Nefian, A. V. (2002). Speaker independent audio-visual continuous speech recognition. presented at ICME '02.

McGurk, H., & MacDonald, J. (1976). Hearing Lips and Seeing Voices. *Nature*, 264, 746. doi:10.1038/264746a0

Paul, A. Lynn, (1993). Signal Processing of Speech. *Macmillan New Electronics S Publisher: Palgrave Macmillan* ISBN: 033351921

Perez, J. F. G., Frangi, A. F., Solano, E. L., & Lukas, K. (2005).Lip Reading for Robust Speech Recognition on Embedded Devices. presented at ICASSP '05.

Petajan, E. D. (1984). Automatic lip-reading to enhance speech recognition. presented at GLOBECOM' 84.

Potamianos, G., Neti, C., Gravier, G., Huang, J., Connell, J. H., Chu, S., et al. (2004). Towards Practical Deployment of Audio-Visual Speech Recognition, In *IEEE Int. Conf. on Acoustics, Speech, and Signal Processing*. vol. 3,p. 777-780.

Rabiner, L. B. H. J. (1993). Fundamentals of speech recognition. *Fundamentals of speech recognition*. Englewood Cliffs, NJ.

Sugie, K. T. (1985). A speech prosthesis employing a speech synthesizer. *IEEE Transactions on Bio-Medical Engineering*, 32(7), 485–490. doi:10.1109/TBME.1985.325564

# Chapter 13
# Feature Set Reduction in Rotation Invariant CBIR Using Dual-Tree Complex Wavelet Transform

**Deepak Sharma**
*Maharishi Markandeshwar University, India*

**Ekta Walia**
*Maharishi Markandeshwar University, India*

**H.P. Sinha**
*Maharishi Markandeshwar University, India*

## ABSTRACT

*An accurate Content Based Image Retrieval (CBIR) system is essential for the correct retrieval of desired images from the underlying database. Rotation invariance is very important for accurate Content Based Image Retrieval (CBIR). In this chapter, rotation invariance in Content Based Image Retrieval (CBIR) system is achieved by extracting Fourier features from images on which Dual Tree Complex Wavelets Transform (DT-CWT) has been applied. Before applying DT-CWT, the Fourier feature set is reduced by exploiting the symmetry property of Fourier transform. For an N x N image, feature set has been reduced from $N^2/2$ features to $N^2/4$ features. This reduction in feature set increases the speed of the system. Hence, this chapter proposes a method which makes the Content Based Image Retrieval (CBIR) system faster without comprising accuracy and rotation invariance.*

DOI: 10.4018/978-1-61350-429-1.ch013

# 1. CONTENT BASED IMAGE RETRIEVAL (CBIR) SYSTEM: AN OVERVIEW

The term CBIR has been widely used to describe the process of retrieving desired images from a large collection of data on the basis of features that can be automatically selected from the images. CBIR uses many methods for image processing and is regarded by researchers as subset of this field.

## 1.1 Need of CBIR

The need of content based image retrieval (CBIR) system is increasing day by day because the interest in the digital images has increased enormously. There are various reasons which enhance the demand of CBIR system. Some of the reasons are given as follows:

- **Rapid Growth in Digital Image Database:** In today's world, the more and more image data is stored in data book. There is a need of a way to search an image quickly. The way should be fully automatic search tool to save time because the process of manual categorization of images is time consuming, expensive and tedious.
- **Professional Needs:** In many professional fields, users are getting the opportunities to access and manipulate remotely stored images in all kind of ways. The other professional need for the CBIR system is "Logo Search". The professionals are also dependent on system which gives an efficient and quick retrieval of images. In medicine, it is very useful for doctors who want to retrieve MRI, ultrasound, CT scan images matching the query image for diagnostic purposes.
- **Locating Images on the Web:** The interest in the potential of digital images has fuelled at least in part by the rapid growth

of imaging on the World Wide Web. As the collection of images in the web is increased there is a requirement of a system which has quick and efficient retrieval characteristics. The solution for these issues is "content based image retrieval" system, which provides quick and efficient retrieval of image in huge collection. The image retrieval problems are becoming widely recognized and search for solution is an increasingly active area of research and development. A number of critical areas were identified where research was needed including feature extraction and indexing, image query matching and presentation of images.

## 1.2 Basic Block Diagram of CBIR

In a CBIR system, the feature vectors from images stored in database are to be extracted and when a query image is given, its feature vectors are also computed. If the distance between feature vectors of the query image and image in the database is small enough, the corresponding image in the database is to be considered as a match to the query. The search is usually based on similarity rather than on exact match. The retrieval results are then compared according to the similarity index.

The basic block diagram of content based image retrieval system is given in Figure 1.

The basic blocks of the CBIR system are given as shown in the following sections.

### 1.2.1 Query Techniques

The implementation of CBIR in different fields makes use of different type of user queries. The various types of user queries are given as:

- **Query by Example:** It is a technique of user query that involves providing the CBIR system with an example image on which the search is based upon. The search algorithm may vary depending upon the

*Figure 1. Basic block diagram of content based image retrieval (CBIR)*

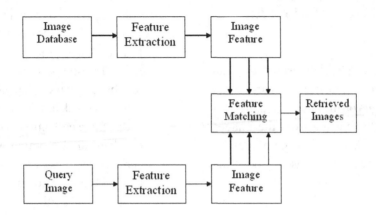

application, but result images should all share common elements with the provided example. The example should be provided in two ways:

- A pre-existing image may be supplied by the user or chosen from random set.
- The user draws rough approximation of the image they are looking for.
- **Other Query Method:** There are some more methods for user query which are given as:
  - Querying by image region
  - Querying by multiple images
  - Querying by visual sketch
  - Querying by direct specification of image features.

## 1.2.2 Feature Extraction

The most important segment of CBIR system is feature extraction because the CBIR operates on the principle of retrieving stored images from a collection by comparing features extracted from images. The feature vector is extracted for each image stored in the database. When a query image is submitted, the same work is done to get the query feature vector. The features extracted from the image can be categorized in two ways:

- **Primitive Features:** The primitive features which are used to characterize the image content. These features are given as:
  - **Color:** In image retrieval systems, color histogram is the most commonly used feature. The main reason is that it is independent of image size and orientation. Also it is one of the most straight-forward features utilized by human for visual recognition and discrimination. The retrieval systems are based on color similarity which is achieved by comparing the computed color histogram.
  - **Texture:** Texture is another important property of images but there is no precise definition for texture. However, one can define texture as the visual patterns that have properties of homogeneity that do not result from the presence of only a single color or intensity. Texture determination is ideally suited for medical image retrievals.
  - **Shape:** Shape is not referred to the shape of an image but to the shape of a particular region. Shape features are usually described after images have been segmented into regions

or objects. The use of shape filters to identify given shapes of an image is another method. For more accurate shape detection, human intervention will be required because methods like segmentation are very difficult to completely automate.

- **Semantic Features:** The ideal CBIR system, from a user perspective would involve what is referred to as semantic retrieval, where the user makes a request like "find pictures of cats". In Semantic features such as the type of object present in the image are harder to extract, though this remains an active research topic.

## 1.3 Practical Applications of CBIR

A wide range of possible applications for CBIR technology has been identified. Potentially fruitful areas include:

- **Crime Prevention:** Law enforcement agencies typically maintain large archives of visual evidence, including past suspects' facial photographs fingerprints, tyre threads and shoeprints. Whenever a serious crime is committed, they can compare evidence from the scene of the crime for its similarity to records in their archives.

- **The Military:** Military applications of Imaging Technology are probably the best-developed, though least publicized. Recognition of enemy aircraft from radar screens, identification of targets from satellite photographs, and provision of guidance systems for cruise missiles are known examples – though these almost certainly represent only the tip of the iceberg.

- **Intellectual Property:** Trademark image registration, where a new candidate mark is compared with existing marks to ensure that there is no risk of confusion, has long been recognized as a prime applica-

tion area for CBIR. Copyright protection is also a potentially important application area. Enforcing image copyright when electronic versions of the images can easily be transmitted over the Internet in a variety of formats is an increasingly difficult task. There is a growing need for copyright owners to be able to seek out and identify unauthorized copies of images, particularly if they have been altered in some way.

- **Architectural and Engineering Design:** Architectural and engineering design share a number of common features – the use of stylized 2- and 3-D models to represent design objects, the need to visualize designs for the benefit of non-technical clients, and the need to work within externally-imposed constraints, often financial. Such constraints mean that the designer needs to be aware of previous designs, particularly if these can be adapted to the problem at hand. Hence the ability to search design archives for previous examples which are in some way similar, or meet specified suitability criteria, can be valuable.

- **Fashion and Interior Design:** Similarities can also be observed in the design process in other fields, including fashion and interior design. Here again, the designer has to work within externally-imposed constraints, such as choice of materials. The ability to search a collection of fabrics to find a particular combination of color or texture is increasingly being recognized as a useful aid to the design process.

- **Journalism and Advertising:** Both newspapers and stock shot agencies maintain archives of still photographs to illustrate articles or advertising copy. These archives can often be extremely large (running into millions of images), and dauntingly expensive to maintain if detailed keyword indexing is provided. Broadcasting corporations are faced with an even bigger problem, having to deal with millions of hours of archive video footage, which are almost impossible to annotate without some degree of automatic assistance.

- **Medical Diagnosis:** The increasing reliance of modern medicine on diagnostic techniques such as radiology, histopathology, and computerized tomography has resulted in an explosion in the number and importance of medical images now stored by most hospitals. While the prime requirement for medical imaging systems is to be able to display images relating to a named patient, there is increasing interest in the use of CBIR techniques to aid diagnosis by identifying similar past cases.

- **Geographical Information Systems (GIS) and Remote Sensing:** Although not strictly a case of image retrieval, managers responsible for planning marketing and distribution in large corporations need to be able to search by spatial attribute. And the military are not the only group interested in analyzing satellite images. Agriculturalists and physical geographers use such images extensively, both in research and for more practical purposes, such as identifying areas where crops are diseased or lacking in nutrients – or alerting governments to farmers growing crops on land they have been paid to leave lying fallow.

- **Cultural Heritage:** Museums and art galleries deal in inherently visual objects. The ability to identify objects sharing some aspect of visual similarity can be useful both to researchers trying to trace historical influences, and to art lovers looking for further examples of paintings or sculptures appealing to their taste.

- **Education and Training:** It is often difficult to identify good teaching material to illustrate key points in a lecture or self-study module. The availability of searchable collections of video clips providing examples

of avalanches for a lecture on mountain safety, or traffic congestion for a course on urban planning, could reduce preparation time and lead to improved teaching quality. In some cases such videos might even replace a human tutor.

- **Home Entertainment:** Much home entertainment is image or video-based, including holiday snapshots, home videos and scenes from favorite TV programmes or films. This is one of the few areas where a mass market for CBIR technology could develop. Possible applications could include management of family photo albums or clips from commercial films.

- **Web Searching:** Cutting across many of the above application areas is the need for effective location of both text and images on the Web, which has developed over the last five years into an indispensable source of both information and entertainment. Text-based search engines have grown rapidly in usage as the Web has expanded; the well-publicized difficulty of locating images on the Web indicates that there is a clear need for image search tools of similar power.

## 1.4 Main Challenges to CBIR Systems

Many advances have been made in various directions including visual feature extraction, multidimensional indexing and system design. But there are still many open research issues or challenges that need to be solved.

1. Personalization of the search and image interpretation is part of big challenge that may lead to big success of CBIR. This approach is under the development in text retrieval systems and still subject to intense studies by the Google Inc. and Yahoo Inc (Niblack & Barber, 1994).

2. Unlike text retrieval where one notice the emergence of Text REtrieval Conference (TREC) like competition, which had a lot in the development of the field of text retrieval system, the development of coherent database that will help in enhancing the performance of CBIR systems (Chang & Fu, 1980).

3. High dimensionality is one of the important challenges in CBIR due to possible size of feature space and images. Therefore dimension reduction is important.

4. Several researchers encompassed the need for enhanced user interface as it often argued that the interfacing plays central role in CBIR systems that customizing the interface to fit user's specific query is not an easy task.

5. The ultimate end user of an image retrieval system is human, so aiming at exploring how humans perceive image content and how we can integrate such a human model into the image retrieval systems. The early research was conducted independently by the MIT team and NEC team and UIUC team (Dutta, 2005). Most recent study of human perception focuses on the psychological aspects of human perception.

6. In reality, most database community systems are non image databases, while the computer visions are image databases. A successful image database system requires an interdisciplinary research effort. Some successful examples of such research effort include the adaptation of Boolean retrieval model in image retrieval (Smith & Chang, 1996).

7. The development of automated indexing schemes is still an open issue. Indeed, while text indexing is widely accepted, there is an open debate on current indexing practice in CBIR (Chang, Eleftheriadis, & McClintock, 1998).

## 2. REVIEW OF EXISTING WORKS

Content Based Image Retrieval (CBIR) ((Lamard et al., 2007)-(Smeulders et al., 2000)) is the application of computer vision to the image retrieval problems, i.e. the problem of searching images in large database based on their contents. Content based means that the search will analyze the actual contents of the image. The term content might refer to colors, shape, texture or any other information.

Lamard et. al (Lamard et al., 2007) proposed a Content Based Image Retrieval (CBIR) method in which they computed signature distances between the query & database images. The signature distances may be of several types, but they used wavelet co-efficient distribution.

Bouguila et. al (Bougila & Ziou, 2004) stated that the performance of a statistical signal processing system depends in large part on the accuracy of the probabilistic model used. They presented a robust probabilistic mixture model based on the multinomial and the Dirichlet distributions.

Banerjee et. al (Banerjee & Kundu, 2006) proposed a region based approach for image retrieval. They develop an algorithm to segment an image into fuzzy regions based on coefficients of multi-scale wavelet packet transform. There is another region –based image retrieval method proposed by

Suematsu et. al (Suematsu et al., 2004) which performs image segmentation and indexing using texture features computed from wavelet coefficients. This method has advantages in texture feature extraction and hierarchical image segmentation over the previous region based techniques using wavelet transform.

Pabboju et. al (Pabboju & Reddy, 2009) identified that digital content has become a significant and inevitable asset for any enterprise and the need for visual content management is on the rise as well. There has been an increase in attention towards the automated management and retrieval of digital images owing to the drastic development in the number and size of image databases.

Smeulders et. al (Smeulders et al., 2000) presented a review of 200 references in content-based image retrieval. They have discussed the working conditions of content-based retrieval: patterns of use, types of pictures, the role of semantics, and the sensory gap. Similarity of pictures and objects in pictures is reviewed for each of the feature types, in close connection to the types and means of feedback the user of the systems is capable of giving by interaction. The authors stated that Wavelet transform has proved to be very popular & effective in Content Based Image Retrieval (CBIR).

Chen and Bui (Chen & Bui, 1999) invented an invariant descriptor by using a combination of Fourier transform and wavelet transform. They have used 1-D Fourier transform in angular direction and 1-D wavelet transform in radial direction.

Kingsbury (Kingsbury, 2005) has introduced a new kind of wavelet transform, called dual tree complex wavelet transform, which has approximate shift invariance property and improved angular resolution. A Support Vector Machine (SVM) with the auto-correlation of a compactly supported wavelet as a kernel is proposed in this paper. Kingsbury (Kingsbury, 2000) proved that this kernel is an admissible support vector kernel. The main advantage of the auto-correlation of a compactly supported wavelet is that it satisfies the translation invariance property. Kingsbury (Kingsbury, 1999) discussed the shift invariant properties of a new implementation of the discrete wavelet transform, which employs a dual-tree of wavelet filters to obtain the real and imaginary parts of complex wavelet coefficients. The transform uses filters in two trees $a$ and $b$. A simple delay of one sample between the level-1 filters in each tree and the use of alternate odd length and even length linear phase filter. There are some problems in even/odd filter method, due to which the author proposed a new approach named Q-shifted dual tree where all the filters beyond level-1 are even

length. In the both trees, the filters are time reversed of each other as the analysis and reconstruction filter. This introduces limited redundancy and allows the transform to provide approximate shift invariance and directionally selective filters while preserving the usual properties of perfect reconstruction and computational efficiency with good well-balanced frequency responses.

Multiresolution signal and image models based on the orthogonal wavelet transform suffer from shift-variance, making them less accurate and realistic (Romberg et al., 2000). Romberg et. al have extended the modeling framework to the complex wavelet transform, which features near shift-invariance and improved angular resolution compared to the standard wavelet transform.

Trier et. al (Trier, Jain, & Taxt, 1996) presented an overview of feature extraction methods for off-line recognition of segmented (isolated) characters. Selection of a feature extraction method is probably the single most important factor in achieving high recognition performance in character recognition systems. Different feature extraction methods are designed for different representations of the characters, such as solid binary characters, character contours, skeletons (thinned characters) or gray-level subimages of each individual character.

Wang et. al (Wang, Chen, & Lin, 1994) proposed a new shape descriptor, called moment Fourier descriptor, which can describe a complex object composed by a set of closed regions. This descriptor is shown to be independent of object's translation, rotation and scaling. The essential advantage of moment Fourier descriptor is that it can be used to recognize more complex patterns than the traditional Fourier descriptors. The accuracy of the CBIR system is a very crucial part of CBIR. The accuracy of CBIR system is affected by the rotation invariance of CBIR. Invariant descriptor is very essential part in rotation invariant CBIR. The dual tree complex wavelets can be successfully used in rotation invariant feature extraction for Content Based Image Retrieval (CBIR).

## 3. FEATURE EXTRACTION METHOD

Several invariant descriptors use the Fourier Transform and the Wavelet Transform to extract features.

### 3.1 Fourier Transform

In invariant features extraction, the Fourier Transform ((Trier, Jain, & Taxt, 1996)-(Wang, Chen, & Lin, 1994)) has been an effective tool due to which a shift in the time domain causes no change in the magnitude spectrum. The translation invariance can be optional by taking magnitude spectrum of the 2-D Fourier Transform. But the concept of interest is rotation invariance that is obtained by taking 1-D Fourier Transform in the direction of polar co-ordinates because due to circular shift property of Fourier transform, the spectrum of Fourier transform of circularly shifted signals are same. This circular shift property has been explained in the following section.

### 3.2 Circular Shift

Multiplying $x_n$ by a linear phase $e^{\frac{2\pi i}{N}nm}$ for some integer m corresponds to a circular shift of the output $X_k$. $X_k$ is replaced by $X_{k-m}$, where the subscript is interpreted modulo N (i.e., periodically). Similarly, a circular shift of the input $x_n$ corresponds to multiplying the output $X_k$ by a linear phase. Mathematically, if $\{x_n\}$ represents the vector **x** (Prokis & Manolakis, 2009), then

$$\text{if } F\left(\left\{x_n\right\}\right)_k = X_k \qquad (1)$$

$$\text{then } F\left(\left\{x_n . e^{\frac{2\pi i}{N}nm}\right\}\right)_k = X_{k-m} \qquad (2)$$

$$\text{and } F\left(\left\{x_{n-m}\right\}\right)_k = X_k . e^{\frac{-2\pi i}{N}km} \qquad (3)$$

### 3.3 Complex Wavelet Transform

One effective approach for implementing an analytic wavelet transform, first introduced by Kingsbury (Kingsbury, 2005) (Kingsbury, 2000) (Kingsbury, 1999), is called the dual-tree CWT. Like the idea of positive/negative post-filtering of real sub-band signals, the idea behind the dual-tree approach is quite simple. The dual-tree CWT employs two real DWTs; the first DWT gives the real part of the transform while the second DWT gives the imaginary part. The analysis and synthesis FBs used to implement the dual-tree CWT and its inverse are illustrated in Figure 2 and 3. The two real wavelet transforms use two different sets of filters, with each satisfying the PR conditions. The two sets of filters are jointly designed so that the overall transform is approximately analytic. Let $h_0(n), h_1(n)$ denote the low-pass/high-pass filter pair for the upper FB, and let $g_0(n)$, $g_1(n)$ denote the low-pass/high-pass filter pair for the lower FB. We will denote the two real wavelets associated with each of the two real wavelet transforms as $\psi_h(x)$ and $\psi_g(x)$. In addition to satisfy the Perfect Reconstruction (PR) conditions, the filters are designed so that the complex wavelet $\psi(x)$ is approximately analytic. The complex wavelet $\psi(x)$ is given as:

$$\psi\left(x\right) = \psi_h\left(x\right) + j\psi_g\left(x\right) \qquad (4)$$

Equivalently, they are designed so that $\psi_g(x)$ is approximately the Hilbert transform of $\psi_h(x)$ which is denoted as:

$$\psi_g\left(x\right) \approx H\left\{\psi_h\left(x\right)\right\} \qquad (5)$$

We follow the approach of Chan and Kegl (Chen & Kegl, 2005) for feature extraction using a combination of Fourier Transform and dual tree complex Wavelet Transform as shown in Figure1 for rotation invariant retrieval of images in CBIR.

*Figure 2. Analysis FB for the dual-tree discrete CWT*

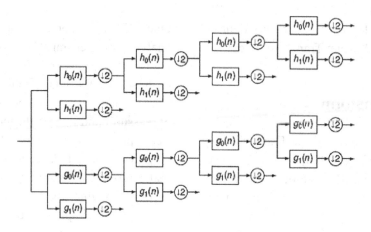

*Figure 3. Synthesis FB for the dual-tree CWT*

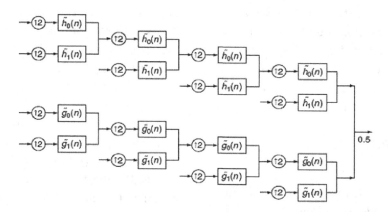

Firstly, the centroid is moved to centre of image and the image is polarized by taking polar transform of the image. Then 1-D Fourier Transform is obtained on polarized image $g(r, \theta)$ along axis of polar angle '$\theta$' and its spectrum magnitude is obtained.

$$G(r,\varphi) = \left| FT\big(g(r,\theta)\big) \right| \qquad (6)$$

Then 1-D dual tree complex Wavelet Transform is applied on $G(r, \varphi)$ along the radial axis '$r$'. The feature extracted by this method is rotation invariant descriptor.

$$WF(r,\varphi) = DTWT\big(G(r,\varphi)\big) \qquad (7)$$

This method is 100% rotation invariant, since it retrieves an image rotated by an angle between $0\,°$ to $360°$.

## 4. PROPOSED REDUCTION IN FEATURE SET

For an $N \times N$ image $f(x,y)$, the rotation invariant features can be extracted by applying 1-D Fourier Transform along the axis of the polar angle '$\theta$' of $g(r, \theta)$ to obtain its spectrum. The spectrum

*Figure 4. Block diagram of Feature Extraction*

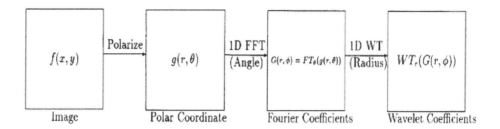

of Fourier Transform of circularly shifted signal are the same, therefore rotation invariant features are obtained. Since the spectrum of 1-D Fourier Transform is symmetric (Chen & Bui, 1999), only half co-efficients of the Fourier spectrum are used. The symmetry conditions of Fourier spectrum are given as follows.

## 4.1 Symmetry Conditions

When we take the Fourier Transform of a *real* function, for example a one-dimensional sound signal or a two-dimensional image we obtain a *complex* Fourier Transform. This Fourier Transform has special symmetry properties that are essential when calculating and/or manipulating Fourier Transforms. This is mainly aimed at the digital image analysis and theory of image processing that make extensive use of these symmetry conditions (Prokis & Manolakis, 2009).

## 4.2 One-Dimensional Symmetry

Firstly consider the case of a one dimensional real function $f(x)$, with a Fourier transform of $F(u)$. Since $f(x)$ is real then from previous we can write

$$F(u) = F_r(u) + iF_i(u) \qquad (8)$$

where the real and imaginary parts are given by the cosine and sine transforms to be

$$F_r(u) = \int f(x)\cos(2\pi ux)\,dx \qquad (9)$$

$$F_i(u) = -\int f(x)\sin(2\pi ux)\,dx \qquad (10)$$

now cos() is a symmetric function and sin() is an anti-symmetric function, as shown in Figure 5, so that:

$F_r(u)$ is Symmetric

$F_i(u)$ is Anti-symmetric

which can be written out explicitly as,

$$F_r(u) = F_r(-u) \qquad (11)$$

$$F_i(u) = -F_i(-u) \qquad (12)$$

The power spectrum is given by

$$\left|F(u)\right|^2 = \left|F_r(u)\right|^2 + \left|F_i(u)\right|^2 \qquad (13)$$

So that if the real and imaginary parts obey the symmetry property, then clearly the power spectrum is also symmetric with

$$\left|F(u)\right|^2 = \left|F(-u)\right|^2 \qquad (14)$$

*Figure 5. Symmetry properties of cos() and sin() functions*

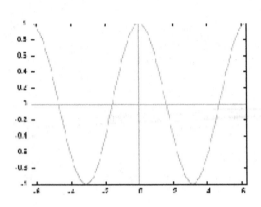
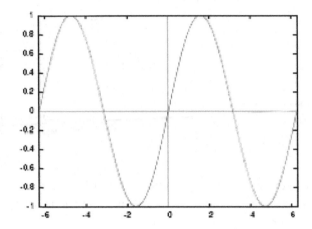

So when the power spectrum of a signal is calculated it is normal to display the signal from $0 \rightarrow u_{max}$ and ignore the negative components.

Suppose the image is of size *64×64*, the set of Fourier features is of size *64×64*. After applying the dual complex wavelets, the set of invariant features is of size *32 ×64*. On the other hand, when only half spectrum of Fourier Co-efficient are used, the set of Fourier Features is of size *64×32*. After using dual tree complex Wavelets, the set of invariant features is of size *32×32*. Hence, by using the concept of symmetry of Fourier spectrum the set of invariant features is reduced to half. In general, for *N* x *N* image, feature set is reduced from $N^2/2$ features to $N^2/4$ features. The symmetry

of Fourier spectra is shown in Figure6 and Fourier spectrum with reduced set is shown in Figure7.

## 5. INDEXING AND RETRIEVAL

### 5.1 Distance Measure

The feature vector is constructed from images and stored in the feature database. When a query image is submitted by the user, its features are extracted and put in a feature vector. For similarity comparison between the query image and the database image, the distance method is used. In this technique, Euclidean distance is measured be-

*Figure 6. Fourier spectrum with symmetry*

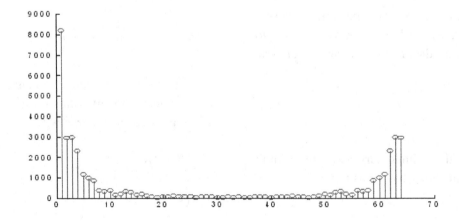

*Figure 7. Fourier spectrum with reduced set*

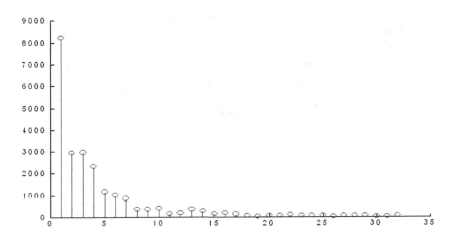

tween the features of Query Image and the images in the database. Using an appropriate threshold, images that are semantically closer are retrieved from the database and displayed as a thumbnail. The Euclidean distance $d(x, y)$ is given by:

$$d\left(x, y\right) = \left\| x - y \right\| = \left\| y - x \right\| \qquad (15)$$

where x & y are the feature sets of query image and image in the database respectively.

## 5.2 Evaluation Measures

For finding the retrieval efficiency of a CBIR system, the most common evaluation measures are precision and recall. The Standard formulas that are used to compute the precision and recall are given as:

$$\text{Precision} = \frac{\text{no. of relevant items retrieved}}{\text{no. of items retrieved}} \qquad (16)$$

$$\text{Recall} = \frac{\text{no. of relevant items retrieved}}{\text{no. of relevant items}} \qquad (17)$$

## 6. EXPERIMENTAL RESULTS

The proposed method is implemented by using MATLAB version 7.0. (Gonzalez & Woods, 2002) The implementation results of the described method may be given in following three ways:-

## 6.1 Effect on Speed

As the size of the invariant feature set is reduced, the time taken by the CBIR system to extract and match the features is reduced. Hence, it increases the speed of the CBIR system. A set of 52 trademark images was taken and experiments were performed. A sample of these images is shown in Figure 8. Reduction in average execution time of CBIR system for images of different sizes is given in Table 1.

The graphical representation of effect on speed on in terms of percentage reduction in execution time for different size of images is given in Figure 9.

## 6.2 Effect on Rotation

The final feature set extracted using this method is 100% rotation invariant. CBIR system retrieves correct image even when the query image is ro-

*Figure 8. A sample set of images*

*Table 1. Reduction in execution time for images of different sizes*

| SR No. | Image | Reduction in Execution Time (%) |
|--------|-------|----------------------------------|
| 1 | 64 × 64 | 6.55 |
| 2 | 128 × 128 | 7.23 |
| 3 | 256 × 256 | 9.62 |

tated by an angle between 0 ° to 360 ° as shown in Table 2.

## 6.3 Effect on Recall and Precision

The reduced invariant feature set maintains the degree of recall and precision of CBIR system. The recall and precision of CBIR system remains same as in the case of invariant feature set (without reduction). The average value of precision and recall for reduced and complete feature set is given Table 3.

The graphical representation of Effect on Recall and Precision for Complete and Reduced feature set is given in Figure 10. Figure 11(a) and 11(b) shows the query image and set of top ten retrieved images out of a database 52 images.

## 7. COMPARISON OF PERFORMANCE WITH EXISTING METHODS

The rotation invariance achieved by Hee-Jun You et al (You et al., 2003) is not for all angles but our

*Figure 9. Reduction in execution time for different image sizes*

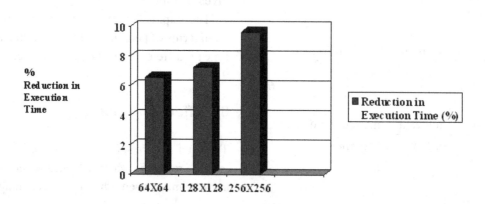

*Table 2. Rotation invariance for image rotated at different angles*

| Angle (θ) (in degrees) | Rotated Query Image by an Angle 'θ' | Retrieved Image |
|---|---|---|
| 0° | | |
| 60° | | |
| 120° | | |
| 180° | | |
| 240° | | |
| 300° | | |
| 360° | | |

*Table 3. Effect on recall and precision for complete and reduced feature set*

| Complete Feature Set | | Reduced Feature Set | |
|---|---|---|---|
| Precision | Recall | Precision | Recall |
| 0.34 | 0.25 | 0.37 | 0.27 |

method shows rotation invariance for all angles from 0° to 360°. The 100% rotation invariance is also achieved by G. Chen et al (Chen & Bui, 1999) but at some particular scaling factor. In our work, no scaling factor is required for achieving 100% rotation invariance. Although method proposed by G. Chen et al (Chen & Kegl, 2005) is similar to our proposed method our method is fast due

to reduced feature set and still achieves 100% rotation invariance.

## 8. CONCLUSION

This chapter proposes a method which increases the speed of the CBIR system keeping the accuracy of rotation invariant system intact. It can retrieve

*Figure 10. Comparison of precision and recall for complete and reduced feature set*

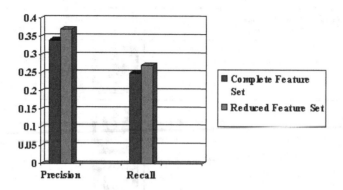

*Figure 11. (a) Query image (b) Retrieved Images*

(a)

(b)

the images rotated between angles 0° to 360° even with reduced feature set, which indicates that no compromise is made in accuracy of CBIR with reduction in feature set. The recall and precision are not affected by the use of reduced feature set.

## REFERENCES

Banerjee, M., & Kundu, M. K. (2006). Content-based image retrieval using wavelet packets and fuzzy spatial relations. *ICVGIP 2006. LNCS, 4338*, 861–871.

Bouguila, N., & Ziou, D. (2004). *Improving content based image retrieval systems using finite multinomial dirichlet mixture*. In IEEE Workshop on Machine Learning for Signal Processing, 2004.

Chang, N. S., & Fu, K. S. (1980). *Image query by pictorial–example*. IEEE Trans Software.

Chang, S. F., Eleftheriadis, A., & Mcclintock, R. (1998). Next generation content representation, creation and searching for new media and application in education. *IEEE Proc.*, 1998.

Chen, G. Y., & Bui, T. D. (1999). Invariant Fourier wavelet descriptor for pattern recognition. *Pattern Recognition, 32*(7), 1083–1088. doi:10.1016/S0031-3203(98)00148-4

Chen, G. Y., & Kegl, B. (2005). *Invariant pattern recognition using dual-tree complex wavelets and Fourier features*. IVCNZ 2005, Image and Vision Computing, New Zealand, 28-29 Nov. 2005.

Dutta, R., Joshi, D., Lee, J., & Nang, J. (2005). Image retrieval: Ideas, influences and trends of new age. *Proceedings of 7ᵗʰ ACM SIGMM International Workshop on Multimedia Retrieval Information*, November 10-11, 2005, Singapure.

Gonzalez, R. C., & Woods, R. E. (2002). *Digital image processing* (2nd ed.).

Kingsbury, N. G. (1999). Shift invariant properties of the dual-tree complex wavelet transform. *Proc. IEEE ICASSP '99*, Phoenix, AZ, March 1999.

Kingsbury, N. G. (2000). A dual-tree complex wavelet transform with improved orthogonality and symmetry properties. *Proc. IEEE ICIP*, Vancouver, Sept.11-13, 2000.

Kingsbury, N. G. (2005). The dual-tree complex wavelet transform- A coherent framework for multiscale signal and image processing. *IEEE Signal Processing Magazine*, (Nov): 2005.

Lamard, M., Cazuguel, G., Quelled, G., Bekri, L., Roux, C., & Cochener, B. (2007). Content based image retrieval based on wavelet transform coefficients distribution. In *Proceedings of the 29th Annual International Conference of the IEEE EMBS Cité International*, Lyon, France August 23-26, 2007.

Niblack, W., & Barber, R. (1994). The QBIC project: Querying images by content using color, texture, shape. In *Proc. SPIE Storage & Retrieval for Images & Video Database*, Feb 1994.

Pabboju, S., & Reddy, A. V. G. (2009). A novel approach for content-based image indexing and retrieval system using global and region features. *International Journal of Computer Science and Network Security, 9*(2).

Prokis, J. G., & Manolakis, D. G. (2009). Digital signal processing: Principles, algorithms & applications, 4ᵗʰ ed.

Romberg, J., Choi, H., Baraniuk, R., & Kingsbury, N. G. (2000). Multiscale classification using complex wavelets. *Proc. IEEE ICIP*, Vancouver, Sept. 11-13, 2000.

Smeulders, A. W. M., Worring, M., Santini, S., Gupta, A., & Jain, R. (2000). Content-based image retrieval at the end of the early years. *IEEE Transactions on Pattern Analysis and Machine Intelligence, 22*(12), 1349–1380. doi:10.1109/34.895972

Smith, J. R., & Chang, S. F. (1996). Tools and techniques for image color retrieval. In *Proc. IEEE Int. Conf. Acoust, Speech and Signal Proc.*, May 1996.

Suematsu, N., Ishida, Y., Hayashi, A., & Kanbara, T. (2004). Region-based image retrieval using wavelet transform. In *Transactions on Image Processing*, 2004.

Trier, O. D., Jain, A. K., & Taxt, T. (1996). Feature extraction methods for character recognition: A survey. *Pattern Recognition, 29*(4), 641–662. doi:10.1016/0031-3203(95)00118-2

Wang, S. S., Chen, P. C., & Lin, W. G. (1994). Invariant pattern recognition by moment Fourier descriptor. *Pattern Recognition, 27*(12), 1735–1742. doi:10.1016/0031-3203(94)90090-6

You, H.-J., Shin, D.-K., Kim, D.-H., Kim, H.-S., & Park, S.-H. (2003). A rotation invariant image retrieval with local features. *International Journal of Control, Automation, and Systems, 1*(3), 332–338.

## ADDITIONAL READING

Lee, K.-M., & Street, W. N. (2004). Cluster-driven refinement for content based digital image retrieval. *IEEE Transactions on Multimedia, 6*(6), 817–827. doi:10.1109/TMM.2004.837235

Manjunath, B. S., & Ma, W. Y. (1996). Texture features for browsing and retrieval of image data. *IEEE Transactions on Pattern Analysis and Machine Intelligence, 18,* 837–842. doi:10.1109/34.531803

Tieng, Q. M., & Boles, W. W. (1995). An application of wavelet based affine-invariant representation. *Pattern Recognition Letters, 16*(12), 1287–1296. doi:10.1016/0167-8655(95)00079-1

Tieng, Q. T., & Boles, W. W. (1997). Recognition of 2-D object contours using wavelet transform zero-crossing representation. *IEEE Transactions on Pattern Analysis and Machine Intelligence, 19*(8), 910–916. doi:10.1109/34.608294

Wouwer, G., Scheunders, P., & Dyck, D. (1999). Statistical texture characterization from discrete wavelet representations. *IEEE Transactions on Image Processing, 8,* 592–598. doi:10.1109/83.753747

# Chapter 14
# Devnagari Script Recognition:
## Techniques and Challenges

**P. Mukherji**
*University of Pune, India*

**P.P. Rege**
*College of Engineering Pune, India*

## ABSTRACT

*Devnagari script is the most widely used script in India and its Optical Character Recognition (OCR) poses many challenges. Handwritten script has many variations, and existing methods used are discussed. The authors have also collected a database on which the techniques are tested. The techniques are based on structural methods as opposite to statistical methods. There are some special properties of Devnagari script like the topline, curves, and various types of connections that have been exploited in the methods discussed in this chapter.*

## INTRODUCTION

In this chapter, techniques for Devnagari Handwritten Script Recognition are discussed. To accommodate the variations in handwritten characters Adaptive Zoning (AZ) method is proposed, where first a few features are examined and then, the region of interest of the character is isolated. Devnagari characters are analyzed on the basis of shape descriptions of provided by Devnagari script writers. A novel algorithm of segmenting a character in strokes and encoding the strokes into meaningful entities by Average Compressed Direction Coding (ACDC) algorithm is explained in Stroke Analysis method. Distribution of statistical and location features of strokes are compared with the stored model. Fuzzy location and stroke features are also used to include t he variations in handwriting. Inter-stroke properties of Devnagari characters are studied by generating Hierarchical Attributed Relational Graphs (HARG) method. There are two levels in this scheme in which first the sub-graphs are identified and then the graph is matched by converting it into a vectorial signature. Concept of segments and complement segments is introduced and their interconnections give the segment adjacency. The recognition accuracy achieved is comparable to recent published works.

DOI: 10.4018/978-1-61350-429-1.ch014

## BACKGROUND

Optical Character Recognition (OCR) is the study of teaching machines to observe the environment and learn to read characters and make decisions. Character and pattern recognition are basic requirements in Artificial Intelligence. A character also comes in the general category of a pattern. In Jain A. K., Duin R. P. W. & Mao J. (2000), pattern is defined "as opposite to chaos; it is an entity and could be given a name".

### OCR Basic Principles

Handwritten or typed data is converted to digital form either by scanning the writing on paper or by writing with a special pen on an electronic surface such as a digitizer combined with a liquid crystal display. The two approaches are distinguished as off-line and on-line OCR Plamondon R. & Srihari S. N. (2000), respectively.

Prior to feature extraction, preprocessing improves recognition efficiency. Preprocessing includes noise removal, machine and handwritten character segmentation, script identification, graphic and text segmentation and all such techniques that lead to improved recognition accuracy.

Feature extraction based methods work on extracting a set of invariant features from the test pattern and the classification is done in feature space.

Character classification can be achieved in two stages: coarse classification and fine classification. Coarse classification is accomplished by class set partitioning or dynamic character selection Duda R. O., Hart P. E. & Stork D.G. (2001). A tree classifier Gonzalez R. C. & Woods R. E.(2003) is used to selectively examine presence or absence of certain feature at each node thereby reducing the search.

### The Devnagari Script

Devnagari script is the most widely used script in India. Just as Kanji is used in Japanese and Chinese language, Devnagari is used in over forty languages including Sanskrit, Hindi, and Marathi etc.

The basic character set of Devnagari script is of 48 characters and Shivaji 01 font is shown in Figure 1(a). The character set of Devnagari script with 45 characters is shown in Figure 1(b).

Every individual word has a horizontal header line or the 'shirorekha'. This line serves as a reference to divide the character into two distinct portions: Head and Body, if the top modifier is present. Devnagari word may be divided in three zones. Zone 1 is the region of top-modifier; Zone 2 is the body of the word and Zone 3 is the lower modifier region. Another feature is the inter-character gap in a word that facilitates character segmentation and isolation.

*Figure 1. Devnagari character set*

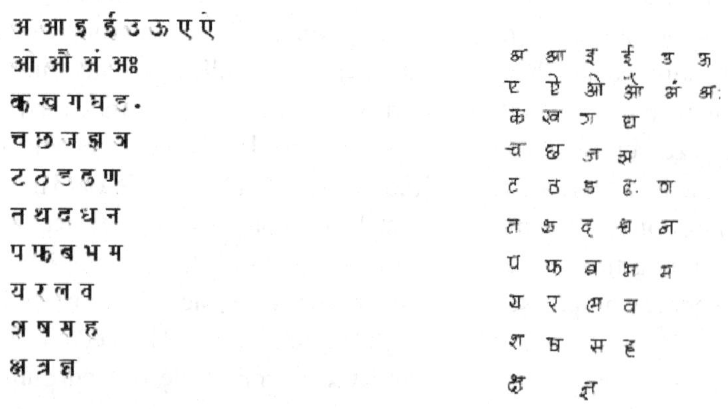

(a) Devnagari Character Set(Printed)  (b) Devnagari Character Set (Handwritten)

## LITERATURE SURVEY AND RELATED REFERENCES OF EXISTING TECHNIQUES FOR OCR

In this section existing techniques for feature extraction for OCR of other scripts used all over the world and Devnagari in particular are discussed.

## Feature Extraction Methods

Feature extraction can be divided into four basic approaches: template matching, statistical classification, structural approach and neural network based approach. Recognition based on graph matching uses a combination of statistical and structural features.

In Statistical approach each pattern is represented in terms of 'd' features or measurements and is viewed as a point in d-dimensional feature space. Y. Fujisawa et al. Fujisawa Y., Meng S., Wakabayashi T. & Kimura F. (2002) use edge and gradient features of gray scale images to achieve an accuracy of 99% on English numerals.

Zoning is a very popular technique used for OCR. This approach is used for Tamil characters in Hewavitharana S. & Fernando H. C. (2002), where each image is divided into equal number of horizontal and vertical strips, producing a grid with square shaped zones. Zoning for handwritten Devnagari characters has been used by Naik A. M. & Rege P. P. (2006).

Transform based approaches have been used extensively for Chinese and Japanese scripts. Gabor filter-based feature extraction method for handwritten numeral character recognition is widely reported. Majumdar A. (2007) addresses the problem of multi-font Bangla basic character recognition using Curvelet Transform.

Discrete orthogonal moment based features have been used to identify printed and handwritten Chinese words in Wang X., Yang Y. & Huang K. (2006). Hidden Markov Models (HMMs) are stochastic models Nishimura H. & Tsutsumi M. (2001) used extensively for off-line handwritten character recognition.

## Structural Approach

Recognition problems involving complex pattern adopt hierarchical perspective where a pattern is composed of simple sub-patterns. The simplest elementary sub-patterns are called primitives. A shape analysis model for recognition of multi-font printed Chinese character is given in Rocha J. & Pavlidis T. (1994). Stroke analysis is an important component in structural features method based techniques. In Joe.M. & Joo L. H. (1995) separated segments are connected together to make complete strokes. A stroke-guided pixel-matching algorithm is proposed for Chinese characters by Kim I., Liu C. & Kim J. (1997). This method has been used for handwritten Chinese characters and a result of 96.1% without explicit neighborhood information shows that it can be very promising. Srihari S. N., Hong T. & Srikantan G. (1997) use Local Stroke Direction (LSD) feature by scanning individual character from 8-directions. A structural method with local refining is presented in Congedo G., Dimauro G., Impedovo S. & Pirlo G.(1995). The experiments are performed on the Center for Excellence for Document Analysis and Research (CEDAR) database. Hybrid approach combines statistical and structural methods. Kim I. & Kim J. (2003) propose a statistical character structure modeling method. A combination of gradient, structural and concavity (GSC) feature is used by Favata J.T., Srikantan G. & Srihari S. N. (1994) for analysis of Roman and Japanese hand-printed scripts.

Neural Networks (NN) can be viewed as massively parallel computing systems consisting of an extremely large number of simple processors with many interconnections Ganis M. D., Wilson C. L., Blue J. L. (1998). In Sural S. & Das P.K. (2001), recognition of printed Bangla script using NN and Fuzzy features as input is presented. Overall efficiency achieved is 98.5% on printed documents of different sources.

## Inexact Graph Matching

Attributed and labeled graphs are used in pattern recognition and various other domains of computer science. They have been used to represent Chinese characters Cesar R. M., Bengoetzea E., Bloch I. & Larranaga P. (2005), hand-drawn symbols Bengoetzea E., Larranaga P., Bloch I., Perchant A. & Boeres C. (2002), word recognition Lopresti D. & Wilfong G. (2001) and others.

When graphs are used for representing structured objects, then the problem of measuring object similarity turns into the problem of computing similarity between graphs, which is generally referred to as graph matching Papadopoulos A.N. & Manolopoulos Y. (1999). The graph matching methods can be broadly divided into two main categories: exact and in-exact graph matching techniques. Exact graph matching methods Qiu H. & Hancock E.R. (2006) require strict correspondence between the two graphic objects being matched or at least among their subparts. The exact graph matching methods include graph isomorphism, sub-graph isomorphism, maximum common sub-graph etc.

The second approach defines inexact matching methods i.e., error-tolerant sub-graph isomorphism Auwatanamongkol S.(2007) or error-correcting sub-graph isomorphism detection Luo B. & Hancock E. R. (2001), where a matching can occur even if the two graphs being compared are structurally different to some extent.

## Status of Devnagari OCR

One of the first attempts for constrained hand-printed Devnagari characters is by Sethi I. K. & Chatterjee B.(1977). Pioneering work for typed Devnagari script is reported by Sinha R. M. K. & Mahabala H.N.(1979).

Sinha R. M. K. & Mahabala H.N (1979) divided the typed word in three strips and separated it in top strip, core strip and bottom strip and achieved 93% performance on individual characters. OCR for two scripts, Bangla and Devnagari have been attempted in Chaudhuri B.B. & Pal U. (1997). Recognition of Devnagari numerals using multiple connectionist scheme is reported in Joshi N. (2005) with 94% accuracy. Machine recognition of online handwritten Devnagari characters is reported in Connel(2000) with 82-85% accuracy and in Malik(2006), with 86.5% accuracy.

In Sharma(2006), use Quadratic classifier with direction feature based statistical parameters and achieved an accuracy of 81% for characters without top modifiers. More recently in Pal(2007), a 400 feature vector based on Roberts filter on isolated normalized characters is extracted and recognition accuracy of 94% is achieved. There are many challenges in Devnagari script Kompalli(2005), Mukherji(2006) which need to be addressed in the development of OCR system for Devnagari script.

## PREPROCESSING AND FEATURE EXTRACTION: EXISTING METHODOLOGIES

### Preprocessing

Preprocessing is required to filter the variability and noise from the documents. Different steps encompassing pre-processing are discussed in this section.

A variety of filters like Median filter, Gaussian filter etc. can be used and are given in Gonzalez R. C. & Woods R. E.(2003) in two dimensions. where D(u,v) is the distance from the origin and D0 is the cut-off frequency.

Binarization is the simplest method of image segmentation. Thresholding can be described as global thresholding and local thresholding. Otsu's method Gonzalez R. C. & Woods R. E. (2003) is used in this work.

Various skew detection techniques have been proposed. Hough transform is used to find and link line segments in an image Gonzalez R. C. &

Woods R. E. (2003). The algorithm is based on Martelli Gonzalez R. C. & Woods R. E. (2003).

The character segmentation from words is an important task in OCR. The segmented character is skeletonised by applying Median Axis Transformation (MAT) Gonzalez R. C. & Woods R. E. (2003). The skeletonization algorithm gives rise to extraneous spurs. These are removed using the spur removal algorithm Gonzalez R. C. & Woods R. E. (2003).

## Feature Extraction

A feature is a point of human interest in an image, a place where something happens. It could be an intersection between two lines, or it could be a corner, or it could be just a dot surrounded by space. These relationships are used for character identification, and hence the feature points are exploited for the task of character recognition.

The Horizontal Projection Histogram(HPH) Sinha R. M. K. & Mahabala H.N.(1979) is calculated for black pixels in each row. It indicates features such as the presence of the topline, presence of pixels above topline, etc. Consider that the value of the element in the mth row and nth column of the character matrix is given by a function f(m, n) where

$$f(m,n) = \alpha(m,n)$$

and $\alpha(m,n)$ takes binary values (i.e., 0 for white pixels and 1 for black pixels).

The HPH H(m) of the character matrix is the sum of black pixels in each row as given as H(m) = sum(f(m,n) for all n. Vertical Projection Histogram (VPH) Sinha R. M. K. & Mahabala H.N.(1979) is calculated as follows. The black pixels in each column are added and the total value as well as normalized value is stored. The peak in VPH, determines the presence and the position of the vertibar. A dip in the value indicates the presence of gaps and broken characters.

As the characters are varying in size, shadows Mukherji P., Rege P.P. & Pradhan L.K. (2006) and their relative values are studied. Increase and decrease of the shadow is coded as +1 or −1.

In Zoning, image is divided into a number of zones and statistical and structural features are extracted in each zone. As character size is variable, the row index and column index is normalized resetting M and N to one and dividing the remaining indices by these numbers. Character is divided in three horizontal and three vertical zone. Peak values in VPH and HPH in these zones are examined. A peak value above a threshold in Zone HZ1 indicates topline and also the presence or absence of top-modifier.

The VPH helps to classify vertibar and non-vertibar characters. Peak value above a set threshold in VZ2 indicates a character with central vertibar and peak in VZ3 indicates character with endbar.

Various transform-based techniques are suggested in literature. Binary Wavelet Transform (BWT) is applied to Devnagari characters Mukherji P., Gapchup V. B. & Rege P. P.(2006) and Gabor Transform to Devnagari numerals Mukherji P., Gapchup V. B. & Rege P. P.(2006). The results are not very encouraging.

## Graph Theory Basics

A graph G = (V,E) in its basic form is composed of vertices and edges. V is the set of vertices (also called nodes or points) and E ⊂ V × V, (also defined as E ⊂ [V]2) is the set of edges (also known as arcs or lines) of graph G. An attributed relational graph can be defined as G = (V, E, u, v) where u is the vector of nodal attributes and v is the vector of edge attributes. Although the terms, attributes and labels are used interchangeably in literature, a small distinction is made here in this work. Attributes refer to quantitative values and labels are primitive and relational descriptions.

## PRE-PROCESSING AND FEATURE EXTRACTION: MODIFICATIONS AND NEW ALGORITHMS FOR OCR

### Composition of Devnagari characters

Basic shapes of strokes in Devnagari characters are:

**Lines:** vertical, horizontal, slant, short and long lines.

**Arcs:** curves opening to left side, right side, u-curves, multiple curves shaped like 'S' of different sizes and shapes.

**Loops:** fully or partially closed, small and big.

The shapes are shown in Table 1. A character is made up of these shapes joined together in a number of ways. The connectivity between these shapes and the region where the connectivity is situated plays an important role in distinguishing similar characters.

### Character Level Preprocessing

Existing methods of HPH and VPH are sufficient for topline and top modifier detection when characters are written carefully. These methods fail when deviations occur from such ideally written characters. These errors are enlisted below

1. Some characters have incomplete toplines. Peak in HPH gives false point for topline detection.

2. Toplines that protrude from right side and / or left side of the character change the actual size of the character. Such extending toplines have to be removed to reduce variability in character size and it may be detected wrongly as top modifier.

3. A Small topline on the right side and character starting point well below the topline may lead to false detection of topline as top modifier.

4. A small part of the character merges with the topline and changes the shape of the character if topline is removed.

## FEATURE EXTRACTION AND CLASSIFICATION MODULE FOR DEVNAGARI OCR

This is the main module where the features are extracted, models are developed and unknown character is classified based on its feature vector.

*Table 1. Shapes of basic strokes*

| Shape | Description |
|---|---|
| Lines | |
| Arcs | |
| U curves | |
| Loops and circles | |

## Structure Based Methods

Structure based methods examine the structure of Devnagari methods. They are Adaptive Zoning, Stroke Analysis, Fuzzy Stroke Location Analysis, Fuzzy Stroke Analysis and Hierarchical Attributed Relational Graph method.

## Adaptive Zoning

The purpose of developing Adaptive Zoning[ Mukherji P. & Rege P. P. (2008)] technique is the requirement of extracting features for high accuracy OCR of handwritten data. Adaptive zoning concept is based on examining a few features first and then deciding the size and number of zones. It narrows the search of characters by partitioning the feature space.

Basic features like mean pixel density, number of endpoints, crosspoints have high variations in number and location in the fixed zones for handwritten data. In Adaptive Zoning presence of a few features like the topline and top modifier are marked first and then transitions below the topline are checked. Zoning is then dependent on the location of these features. Thus Adaptive Zoning is more suitable for handwritten Devnagari OCR.

Three new algorithms are developed in this method. They are

- Adaptive Zoning Algorithm
- Pixel Alignment Algorithm
- Modified direction coding algorithm.

The adaptive zones for different characters are shown in Figure 2.

## Stroke Analysis

In this technique given in Mukherji P. & Rege P.P. (2007), shape descriptions of Devnagari characters provided by discussions with people using Devnagari script are used. Different basic

*Figure 2. AZ in characters with two or more than two transitions*

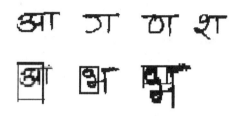

shapes are identified and then used to represent a Devnagari character.

First requirement of this scheme is to segment the character in its constituent strokes (segments), such that each stroke has exactly two neighbors. This is useful to identify neighboring pixels and code the strokes. Stroke segmentation is achieved by mapping the complete neighborhood pixels of the thinned character, modifying the map and thresholding to remove extra pixels.

Strokes have to be classified as curves, straight lines etc. For this, Average Compressed Direction Codes (ACDC) is developed by the authors. This algorithm codes the strokes and suppresses the variability in shapes observed in handwritten data and preserves approximate temporal information of the character. This algorithm has four main steps. The first one is labeling of segmented strokes, second one is coding of strokes, third step is averaging of the code obtained and fourth step is compression of the average code.

In the first step, segmented strokes are labeled using component labeling algorithm. Components are labeled left to right.

The second step of coding the strokes is based on Freeman's chain codes. Normally, Freeman chain codes define a closed boundary. They are used here to code the shape of the strokes only one pixel thick. Each pixel has only two neighbors except the two endpoints that have only one neighbor. Coding begins from the higher endpoint, i.e. endpoint with lower row index. If row indices are same, coding begins from the left endpoint, i.e. the endpoint with lesser column index. This is done to follow the intuitive left to right and top to bottom construction of Devnagari script.

The third step of averaging the direction codes obtained is required to average the changes in direction and helps in assigning different length strokes with similar shapes codes that have similar code sequences. This also reduces the code length. Depending upon the length of the stroke, code is averaged. Code lengths of 1 and 2 are treated separately. Code length obtained is divided by 3 and remainder is stored as it is. The value 3 is useful for the character strokes in the database used in this work. A higher value than 3 suppresses the changes and averaging leads to the loss of direction information. Every section of code length 3 of the stroke is converted into its angular contribution and then averaged. Each code is multiplied by 45 deg as in Freeman chain codes; the difference between two directions is 45 deg, with anticlockwise angle representation. These angles are quantized and coded according to values in Table 1. While considering the angular contribution care has to be taken for combinations of code 8 and 7 with 1 and 2 as direct averaging gives a wrong result. The reason behind this is the fact that angle 360 deg is same as 0 deg and angle 315 (code 7) is actually close to 0 deg though the difference between numbers 1 and 7 or 2 and 7 is large.

Stroke codes for long strokes may have redundancy and to further reduce the storage, the average codes are run length encoded. Only the compressed codes are used, not the positional information.

Six stroke features are extracted on each stroke. The stroke row and column index is the average of all row pixels and column pixels respectively. This average row value is further divided by the maximum row index M to bring the row-size of all characters between zero and one. Similarly, the average column value is divided by the maximum column index, N. This gives an indication of the location of the stroke. The circularity feature is extremely important as it is an indicator of the depth of the curve. The length of the stroke is useful to calculate the relative length feature which indicates prominent strokes. Area of the stroke indicates the extent of area occupied by individual strokes.

The stroke classification is model dependent where the presence of a particular stroke is first ascertained and then the model is built. The vector for characters is formed on the basis of stored model consisting of stroke type and the range of their six stroke features.

## Algorithm for Stroke Features

For all strokes find the length of the stroke k as per equation (1)

$$Lk = \sum s(i,j) \tag{1}$$

Find mean of row indices the stroke k. as given in equation (2)

$$Rk = (\sum i)/M, \tag{2}$$

Find mean of column indices the stroke k, given in equation (3)

$$Ck = (\sum j)/N, \tag{3}$$

Find relative Length of stroke Lk, given in equation (4)

$$RELk = Lk / Max(Lk), \tag{4}$$

Find circularity feature CIR k given in equation (5)

$$CIRk = sqrt[(R1k - R2k)2 + (C1k - C2k)2] / Lk, \tag{5}$$

Find RE2k and RE1k which are the row indices of top most row and lower most row and CE2k

*Figure 3. Examples of ACDC*

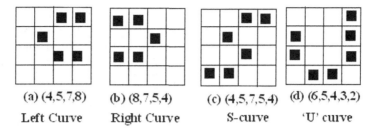

| (a) (4,5,7,8) | (b) (8,7,5,4) | (c) (4,5,7,5,4) | (d) (6,5,4,3,2) |
| Left Curve | Right Curve | S-curve | 'U' curve |

and CE1k which are the leftmost and rightmost column indices of the stroke.

Find Area of the stroke k, given in equation (6)

$$AREAk = | (RE2k - RE1k)| * | (CE2k - CE1k)|, \quad (6)$$

## Algorithm for Stroke Classification

Check the combinations of codes obtained.

Classify stroke as left curve, right curve, u curve, s- curve, straight line, and slanted line depending upon ACDC codes, as shown in Figure 3.

The right curve is coded as 8754, The S-curve is coded as 45754 and U-curve as 65432.

## Fuzzy Stroke Location Analysis

In Stroke Analysis the average row index and average column index decide the location of the stroke in the image frame. Sometimes this leads to wrong classification of strokes. For example, the average row index of a circular stroke is around the centre of the curve that may fall in the right side of the frame whereas the stroke may actually be towards the left side of the frame. Fuzzy Stroke Location Analysis (Mukherji P. & Rege P.P. (2009)) is used to classify the strokes in left, right upper or lower side of the image frame. The vector and its stroke description remain same. This helps to reduce the error in location of the strokes.

The fuzzy membership equations are based on finding the degree of stroke location from left, right, top and bottom of the image with the help of shadows of the strokes. This helps in eliminating the effect of averaging of row and column co-ordinates of strokes used with Stroke Analysis.

The algorithms developed in Stroke Analysis like the ACDC and segmentation algorithm are used here to first segment the character in its constituent strokes. To find fuzzy memberships four additional features are extracted on each stroke. They are given as:

$$D_{leftk} = (\textstyle\sum j) / AREA_k \quad (7)$$

$$D_{rightk} = (\textstyle\sum N-j)/ AREA_k \quad (8)$$

$$D_{upperk} = (\textstyle\sum i)/AREA_k \quad (9)$$

$$D_{lowerk} = (\textstyle\sum M-i)/AREA_k \quad (10)$$

Here k varies from 1 to Num, the value obtained in Stroke Analysis. Other variables i and j represent row and column indices of the stroke k. These fuzzy memberships given in classify the stroke as left, right, upper or lower stroke.

The fuzzy membership equations are given in equations (11)-(14). The value 4 in the equation is a modification carried out in the original equation given in Chaudhary B.B. & Majumdar D.D.(1993), as it has to be applied to thinned strokes. The value of $\beta$ is a number greater than 1. Value of $\beta$ is fixed to 2 after experimentation as it gives satisfactory result for stroke classification.

If $D_{leftk} <= N/2,$

$$\mu_{left}(S_k) = [1-(4*D_{leftk} / N)]^\beta \qquad (11)$$

Else $\mu_{left}(S_k) = 0$

If $D_{rightk} >= N/2,$

$$\mu_{right}(S_k) = [1-(4*D_{rightk} / N)]^\beta \qquad (12)$$

Else $\mu_{right}(S_k) = 0$

If $D_{upperk} <= M/2,$

$$\mu_{upper}(S_k) = [1-(4*D_{upperk} / M)]^\beta \qquad (13)$$

Else $\mu_{upper}(S_k) = 0$

If $D_{lowerk} >= M/2,$

$$\mu_{lower}(S_k) = [1-(4*D_{lowerk} / M)]^\beta \qquad (14)$$

Else $\mu_{lower}(S_k) = 0$

## Fuzzy Stroke Analysis

In the previous two methods, strokes are classified according to the codes obtained for a particular character. To improve the stroke classification and to bring all the strokes under a single classification scheme this method is developed by Mukherji P. & Rege P.P. (2008) & (2009).

Average Compressed Direction codes (ACDC) codes are classified as one of the 15 primitive types given in Table 2. Primitives are labeled as PL1 to PL15. The Stroke Analysis performed earlier on Devnagari characters and ACDC codes have been used to decide the primitives.

Fuzzy Stroke Analysis is different from Fuzzy Stroke Location Analysis as in this technique fuzzy membership is used to correctly identify the stroke type not its location.

Some strokes are misclassified if treated only on the basis of stroke codes. Stroke classification is achieved by using fuzzy membership on stroke circularity feature.

To avoid this ambiguity, fuzzy membership is found with the help of equation (15). Fixed weights $\mu_{fix}$ are decided according to the similarity between strokes and given in Table 3.

Circularity feature $CIR_k$ is found earlier. This membership function is useful in deciding the correct primitive type.

$$\mu = (1/ CIR_k)* \mu_{fix} \qquad (15)$$

## Algorithm for Feature Extraction

- The character is divided in 9 zones.
- Character size is normalized to 0-1 range on both X and Y-axis.
- The zones are marked as Z1 - Z9.
- The zone boundaries are 0-0.33, 0.33-0.67 and 0.67 -1 in both X and Y axis.
- Find occurrence of stroke in zones Z1 - Z9 from $R_k$ and $C_k$, given in equation (2) and (3).
- Divide the number of strokes in each zone by the total number of strokes This constitutes the Zonal Stroke Frequency (ZSF) feature.
- Combined strokes in zones in four ways to find Region Stroke frequencies (RSF) as given in equations 16-19.

$$REGION\ 1 = Z1 +Z2 \qquad (16)$$

$$REGION\ 2 = Z1+Z2+Z4+Z5 \qquad (17)$$

$$REGION\ 3 = Z4+Z5+Z7 +Z8 \qquad (18)$$

$$REGION\ 4 = Z3+ Z6+Z9 \qquad (19)$$

## Hierarchical Attributed Relational Graph (HARG) Method

While representing Devnagari characters with primitive labels in Fuzzy Stroke Analysis, Fuzzy Stroke Location Analysis and basic Stroke Analysis, it is observed that many characters that have

*Table 2. Stroke and its code*

| Stroke Type & Label | Segment | ACDC Codes |
|---|---|---|
| Straight Line (PL1) | | 6, 67, 76, 56, 65 |
| Slant Line 1(PL2) | | 7, 76, 67 |
| Slant Line2 (PL3) | | 5, 65, 56 |
| Left Curve (PL4) | | 468, 567, 5745678, 478 |
| Right curve (PL5) | | 864, 765, 7587654, 854 |
| Circular (PL6) | | 12345678, 2468 |
| Corners (PL7-PL10) | | 46, 86, 68, 64 |
| 'U' curve (PL11, PL12) | | 67812, 12876 |
| 'S' curve (PL13, (PL14) | | 457685487654658 |
| Horizontal Line (PL15) | | 8, 4 |

similar strokes in similar location are confused with each other. However, it is noted though that their connection points convey information regarding the type of character. An innovative approach is developed to study their connections and improve recognition accuracy. Devnagari characters are represented by means of Hierarchical Attributed Relational Graphs (HARG) having invariant attributes and labels associated to nodes and edges as given in Mukherji P. & Rege P.P. (2010).

Character image after stroke segmentation is subtracted from the original image. This gives rise to regions, also termed as complement segment regions (CR) that may possibly be connected to two or more strokes. These regions are the nodes of the graph. These regions occupy the higher level in the hierarchical representation of the character. Segments connected to these regions occupy the lower level and are found by Segment Adjacency algorithm.

The number of Primitive Labels (PL1-PL15) of segments connected to these nodes is found and forms the sub-graph. This is useful in identifying sub-structures of the character. The labels of sub-

*Table 3. Stroke fixed weight*

| Stroke | $\mid$ | $\backslash$ | $/$ | $\subset$ | $\supset$ | $-$ | $\llcorner$ |
|---|---|---|---|---|---|---|---|
| $\mid$ | 1 | .5 | .5 | .33 | .33 | 0 | .5 |
| $\backslash$ | .5 | 1 | .5 | .33 | .33 | 0 | 0 |
| $/$ | .5 | .5 | 1 | .33 | .33 | 0 | 0 |
| $\subset$ | .33 | .33 | .33 | 1 | 0 | .33 | .67 |
| $\supset$ | .33 | .33 | .33 | 0 | 1 | .33 | 0 |
| $-$ | 0 | 0 | 0 | .33 | .33 | 1 | .5 |
| $\llcorner$ | .5 | 0 | 0 | .67 | 0 | .5 | 1 |

graph are L, T, SU or SL as shown in Figure 4. The study of the symbolic attributes associated with edges and considering these informative labels as features also play an important role in clustering graphs corresponding to characters having similar shapes. The six stroke features discussed earlier, form the attributes of the nodes of these sub-graphs.

The graph node attributes are the average row and column index of regions. The connectivity between two regions is found and stored as edge label. This gives information about connected sub-structures. The graph labels are Primitive Label and the Relative Angle (RA). This helps in determining the relative location of the regions.

The relative length, $REL_k$ is found as shown in Figure 5 for every region. The value is normal-

*Figure 4. Topological relations*

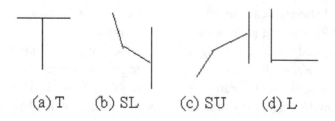

(a) T    (b) SL    (c) SU    (d) L

ized between 0 and 1, is discretized into 4 classes of interval 0.25 to allow inexact matching of the instances of the same class having minor distortion. Similarly, RA between regions is always between 0 and 180 and is divided into 4 classes of interval 45°. These features include number of edges having RA in specific interval.

Feature vectors are extracted from the HARG. The basic idea behind structural signature or the vectorial representation is to transform the graph representation of a graphic symbol into 1-dimensional feature vector containing a set of discriminating features, which is rather easy to store and manipulate. Range features are the major decisive features, which discriminate the two characters present in the same cluster. Though the graphs of more than one character may have same number of nodes or same number of symbolic features, it is certain that all of them cannot have same relative length as nodal attribute.

A distance metric is computed between the query graphs and the model graphs stored in the database, followed by utilization of a non-parametric minimum distance classifier like nearest neighbour rule (NNR) for the classification purpose.

## EXPERIMENTATION, RESULTS AND OBSERVATIONS

Experimentation is carried out for evaluation of various algorithms developed. The complete experimental procedure is illustrated in Figure 6.

## Collection and Preparation of Database

Three databases are prepared at different stages in the course of this work. The details of the number of persons and methodology adopted to collect data is given in this section.

### Database I

Database I is collected from 270 persons. The writers are given one sheet of handwritten Devnagari basic characters, modifiers and conjuncts and one sheet of unconstrained Devnagari script for reference. The reference sheet is specially prepared for the work such that it contains maximum possible characters, modifiers and conjuncts. Writers are instructed to write neatly and as close to as given in the sheet. A sheet with square blocks for isolated characters and a blank sheet of ruled paper is also provided for reference. Each person has written the characters three times and unconstrained script, once. About 40 sheets are selected and scanned to create Database I of isolated characters that are written neatly and correctly. The points for selection are as follows:

The characters are straight, without slant. The characters have a topline covering the entire character. The shapes of the characters are according to the rules of the script.

*Figure 5. Relative length (REL) of connected segments*

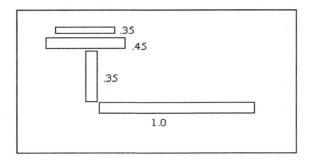

*Figure 6. Experimental procedure from start to finish*

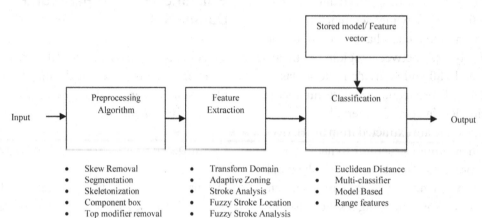

## Database II

Database II is collected from 20 persons for characters and 20 persons for Devnagari numerals. 25 postcards where the address is written in Devnagari are also collected and scanned. The writers are given a sheet for reference but no instructions. Every writer has written each character two or three times. The writers for Devnagari numeral database are instructed to write each numeral 10 times. Thus a total database of 2000 Devnagari numerals is available for feature extraction and testing. Seven sheets of isolated characters are considered for testing. 84 characters from each sheet total to 588 characters tested in this database.

## Database III

Database III is collected from 50 writers writing three to five times. Around 150 samples are available for each character. The writers are given no reference sheet and instructed orally to write the character. Writers are from different social, educational and linguistic backgrounds. One sheet contains only one type of character. This facilitates testing. These sheets are scanned and used for feature extraction and testing. A part sample of sheet for character 'KSHA' is shown in Figure 7.

## Results of Feature Extraction

Different techniques for feature extraction and their feature vector formation are explained along with method, features and model formation. The results of Adaptive Zoning, Stroke Analysis, Fuzzy Stroke Location Analysis, Fuzzy Stroke Analysis and HARG based feature extraction and classification are discussed in the following sections.

## Results of Adaptive Zoning

Ten representative characters from Database I of each class are selected for preliminary study. Samples of each character from the remaining database are used for validation. The method uses modified coding algorithm to code the character edges. The primitives are matched for recognizing the character. The system rejects 2.1% of the characters that are broken or do not match with any of the primitives.

## Observations of Adaptive Zoning Method

- Recognition accuracy for characters with top modifier is lesser than the characters without top modifier. Overall recognition accuracy is 88.3%.

*Figure 7. A sample sheet of Database III (grey image character 'Ksha')*

- Similar characters are confused with each other.
- Errors are noticed when top modifier characters are wrongly pre- classified as those without top modifier and vice-versa.
- Failure in pre-classification also results due to the disconnections from topline. Some tests on basic properties like the vertical and horizontal transitions fail.
- The results of this scheme failed on database II, due to high variability in shapes, which could not be described using modified direction coding.
- Modified direction coding is implemented with preferences to directions and for this reason the it could not code the edges where there were turning points or control points(CP).
- System not robust against slant and skew variations.
- Recognition is person dependent as the accuracy varied from 35% to 65% giving an average of 50% on Database II.
- This required a major change in algorithm to accommodate maximum shape variation and code the character without ambiguity. This led to the evolution of modified coding algorithm into ACDC algorithm.

## Results of Stroke Analysis

Isolated pre-processed Devnagari character is segmented in its constituent strokes. Various shape based and statistical features are extracted on the strokes, main being their classification on the basis of ACDC codes for shape analysis.

In this experiment, 100 characters from database II and III are used for feature extraction and testing. Improved segmentation module is used to preprocess the characters.

## Observations of Stroke Analysis Method

- Recognition accuracy is improved from 50% to 85% in this method.
- The highest accuracy is for characters that are gap characters and characters with unique strokes.
- In general, characters having simple structure categorized by less number of strokes have higher accuracy.
- The system is tolerant to slant and skew as ACDC codes are averaging codes extract the basic shape information.
- Multi-modeling also helps in this case, though it increases the space required to store the model.
- As the mean row and column indices are a part of the feature vector, the size variations are also nullified.

- When there are structural variations such that the extracted features are not in the range as designed in the model, characters are misclassified.
- Errors are observed when there is over-writing in the samples as it leads to over segmentation of the character and the basic shape defining curves are not identified.
- In some cases skeletonization algorithm removes some important strokes, which differentiate similar characters.
- Characters are confused when similar strokes are present in similar regions in the image frame.

## Results of Fuzzy Stroke Location Analysis Method

Fuzzy location features are included along with the fore-mentioned crisp stroke features. These fuzzy features roughly classify the strokes with the help of μleft, μright, μupper, and μlower as right left upper or lower stroke. The other classification is same. For this experimentation characters from both database II and III are used.

### Observations of Fuzzy Stroke Location Analysis Method

- Recognition accuracy varies from 63% to 100%.
- Average recognition accuracy is 86.4%.
- The overall accuracy is slightly better than using stroke features without using fuzzy memberships for location information.
- The minimum accuracy is for characters O and Au.
- The reason is due to extreme variation in their topline position leading to poor segmentation accuracy.
- It is observed that this method is useful for judging the location of the strokes in the image frame.

- Complexity and space required are both increased to store the models.
- Most confusing characters are Bha and Dha, Ya and Tha, Na and T, Da and Va, Ae and Pa.
- They are confused with each other as their shapes are similar, their strokes are similar. They get classified into wrong nodes in the pre-classification tree.

## Results of Fuzzy Stroke Analysis Method

In this method strokes are classified in fifteen primitives. Strokes are assigned weights on and then the fuzzy membership function is calculated. Samples from Database I and II are used for testing this method. Two new features the Zonal Stoke Frequency (ZSF) and Region Stroke Frequency (RSF) are used to preclassify the character.

### Observations of Fuzzy Stroke Analysis Method

- Recognition accuracy varies from 69% to 100%.
- Average recognition accuracy is 92%.
- The overall accuracy is slightly better than using Stroke Analysis and Fuzzy Stroke Location Analysis methods.
- The minimum accuracy is for character Au.
- The reason is due to extreme variation in their topline position leading to poor segmentation accuracy.
- It is observed that this method is useful for clustering characters with similar stroke distribution.
- Fuzzy stroke feature helps in better classification of strokes into their primitive type.
- Stroke Classification as one of fifteen primitives reduces storage space as in previous two cases character dependent stroke description was used.

- Most confusing characters are the same as in previous technique.

## Results of Hierarchical Attributed Relational Graph (HARG) Method

Due to their representational power, attributed graphs are widely used in various domains of computer science. Particularly in computer vision and pattern recognition, they have been used to represent hand drawn symbols, characters drawings etc. In this work statistical and structural signature has been developed to represent Devnagari Characters.

The nodes are classified as graph nodes from complement-segment region and sub-graph nodes represent the segments, as explained previoiusly. The segmented image and complement segment region (CR) images are shown in Figure 8(b) for line database shown in Figure 8(a).

### Observations of HARG Method

- Recognition accuracy varies from 69% to 100%.

- Average recognition accuracy is 95%.
- The overall accuracy is slightly better than using Stroke Analysis, Fuzzy Stroke Location Analysis and Fuzzy Stroke Analysis methods.
- The minimum accuracy is for character Au.
- The reason is due to extreme variation in their topline position leading to poor segmentation accuracy.
- It is observed that this method is useful for confusing characters.
- This is due to the extra but concise information regarding the connections between structures.
- Stroke classification as one of fifteen primitives is used to maximum advantage in forming the vector for the character.

The conclusions drawn from the results of these methods are discussed in the next section.

*Figure 8. Database and complement segment*

(a) Unconstrained database of 'KSHA'          (b) Segment and complement segment

## CONCLUSION AND FUTURE DIRECTIONS

In the absence of a standard database, a huge database has been prepared in three phases namely: Database I, II and III. The three databases have been collected at different times in the course of this research work and are of increasing complexity. The database is representative of a large section of users of Devnagari script. Persons from different age groups, linguistic and educational backgrounds have contributed in this database.

Shape analysis is carried out in Adaptive Zoning method based on modified coding algorithm developed in this work. This algorithm is applied to Database I with 88% recognition accuracy. The results fell down to 50% for Database II. The high error is due to more variation in shapes and skews and slant in the characters.

This failure and the idea to describe Devnagari characters on the basis of shape descriptions provided by ten children and ten adults, led to the development of Stroke Analysis method. It is based on stroke segmentation and ACDC algorithm developed in this work. Stroke Analysis result gives 85% accuracy. Multi-modeling has to be used to accommodate variations in handwritten database. As ACDC codes are based on averaging the system tolerated a slant of 10 deg and a skew of 5 deg. The major drawbacks of this scheme is the fact that many characters have similar shapes and features.

ACDC based algorithm is further modified to classify all codes into fifteen primitives. This is achieved by further compressing the long codes and identifying the basic primitive. Fuzzy stroke Analysis removes the ambiguity in stroke classification as all strokes are assigned weight based on their similarity to other standard primitives. This improved the accuracy to 92%.

In all the above stroke based schemes, many characters are confused with each other. This is primarily due to similar ACDC codes and stroke features. To overcome this drawback relative distribution of strokes is studied with the help of HARG method developed in this work. This improves the accuracy of the characters to 95%. As more data has to be stored and computed, complexity of this algorithm is maximum.

### Future Directions

The improvement in preprocessing methods will lead to higher accuracy. Skeletonization, top line detection and top modifier segmentation pose a challenging problem in the field of handwritten Devnagari OCR. The specific properties of Devnagari script like the top, bottom and side modifier segmentation and recognition will lead towards unconstrained script recognition.

Conjuncts in Devnagari script pose another challenging problem not yet attempted for handwritten OCR. Recognition by segmentation or holistic paradigm may be used. The study may be undertaken for a few conjuncts and then can be expanded.

Contextual processing is also an untouched problem not yet undertaken for Devnagari character recognition may prove useful in Devnagari bank cheque processing, postal automation systems, vehicle number plate recognition etc.

## REFERENCES

Auwatanamongkol, S. (2007). Inexact graph matching using a genetic algorithm for image recognition. *Pattern Recognition Letters*, *28*, 1428–1437. doi:10.1016/j.patrec.2007.02.013

Bengoetzea, E., Larranaga, P., Bloch, I., Perchant, A., & Boeres, C. (2002). Inexact graph matching by means of estimation of distribution algorithms. *Pattern Recognition*, *35*(12), 2867–2880. doi:10.1016/S0031-3203(01)00232-1

Cesar, R. M., Bengoetzea, E., Bloch, I., & Larranaga, P. (2005). Inexact graph matching for model-based recognition: Evaluation and comparison of optimization problems. *Pattern Recognition*, *38*(11), 2099–2113. doi:10.1016/j.patcog.2005.05.007

Chaudhary, B. B., & Majumdar, D. D. (1993). *Two tone image processing and recognition*. India: Wiley Eastern Ltd.

Chaudhuri, B. B., & Pal, U. (1997). An OCR system to read two Indian language scripts: Bangla and Devnagari (Hindi). In *International Conference on Document Analysis and Recognition*, (pp. 1011-1015). Ulm, Germany.

Congedo, G., Dimauro, G., Impedovo, S., & Pirlo, G. (1995). A structural method with local refining for handwritten character recognition. In *International Conference on Document Analysis and Recognition*, (pp. 853-856). Montreal, Canada.

Connel, S. D., Sinha, R. M. K., & Jain, A. K. (2000). Recognition of un-constrained on-line Devnagari characters. In *International Conference on Pattern Recognition ICPR*, (pp. 2368-2371). Barcelona, Spain.

Duda, R. O., Hart, P. E., & Stork, D. G. (2001). *Pattern classification*. Singapore: Wiley International.

Favata, J. T., Srikantan, G., & Srihari, S. N. (1994). Hand-printed character/digit recognition using a multiple feature/resolution philosophy. In *International Workshop in Frontiers of Handwriting Recognition*, (pp. 57-66), Taipei, Taiwan.

Fujisawa, Y., Meng, S., Wakabayashi, T., & Kimura, F. (2002). Handwritten numeral recognition using gradient and curvature of gray images. *Pattern Recognition*, *5*(10), 2051–2059.

Ganis, M. D., Wilson, C. L., & Blue, J. L. (1998). Neural network based systems for hand-print OCR applications. *Transactions on Image Processing*, *7*(8), 1097–1112. doi:10.1109/83.704304

Gonzalez, R. C., & Woods, R. E. (2003). *Digital image processing*. India: Pearson Education.

Hewavitharana, S., & Fernando, H. C. (2002). A two stage classification approach to Tamil handwriting recognition. *Tamil Internet*, 118–124.

Jain, A. K., Duin, R. P. W., & Mao, J. (2000). Statistical pattern recognition: A review. *Transactions on Pattern Analysis and Machine Intelligence*, *2*(1), 4–35. doi:10.1109/34.824819

Joshi, N., Sita, G., Ramakrishnan, G., Deepu, V., & Madhavnath, S. (2005). Machine recognition of online handwritten Devnagari characters. In *International Conference on Document Analysis and Recognition*, (pp. 1156-1160). Seoul, South Korea.

Kim, I., & Kim, J. (2003). Statistical character structure modeling and its application to handwritten Chinese character recognition. *Transactions on Pattern Analysis and Machine Intelligence*, *25*(11), 1422–1436. doi:10.1109/TPAMI.2003.1240117

Kim, I., Liu, C., & Kim, J. (1997). Stroke-guided pixel matching for handwritten Chinese character recognition, *In International Conference on Document Analysis and Recognition,* (pp.665-686). Bangalore, India.

Kompalli, S., Nayak, S., Setlur, S., & Govindaraju, V. (2005). Challenges in OCR of Devnagari documents. In *International Conference on Document Analysis and Recognition*, (pp. 327-331). Seoul, South Korea.

Lopresti, D., & Wilfong, G. (2001). Applications of graph probing to Web document analysis. In *International Workshop on Web Document Analysis, (*pp. 51-54). Seattle, USA.

Luo, B., & Hancock, E. R. (2001). Structural graph matching using the EM algorithm and singular value decomposition. *Transactions on Pattern Analysis and Machine Intelligence*, *23*(10), 1120–1136. doi:10.1109/34.954602

Majumdar, A. (2007). Bangla basic character recognition using digital curvelet transform. *Journal of Pattern Recognition Research, 2*(1), 99–107.

Malik, L., Deshpande, P. S., & Bhagat, S. (2006). Character recognition using relationship between connected segments and neural network. *Transaction on Computers, 5*(1), 229–234.

Moon, J. M., & Joo, L. H. (1995). A combined method on the handwritten character recognition. In *International Conference on Document Analysis and Recognition* (pp. 112–115). Montreal, Canada.

Mukherji, P., Gapchup, V. B., & Rege, P. P. (2006). Feature extraction of 'Devnagari' characters using sub-bands of binary wavelet transform. In *Proceedings of Recent Trends in Information Systems,* (pp. 176-179). Kolkata, India.

Mukherji, P., & Rege, P. P. (2006). A survey of techniques for optical character recognition of handwritten documents with reference to Devnagari script. In *International Conference on Signal and Image Processing* (pp. 178-184). Hubli, India.

Mukherji, P., & Rege, P. P. (2007). Stroke analysis of handwritten Devnagari characters. In *Proceedings of International Conference on circuit, System, Electronics, Control and Signal Processing,* (pp. 843 - 848). Cairo, Egypt.

Mukherji, P., & Rege, P. P. (2008). Feature dependent adaptive zoning based "Devnagari" handwritten character recognition. In *International Conference on Cognition and Recognition,* (pp. 141-146). Mandya, India.

Mukherji, P., & Rege, P. P. (2008). Fuzzy stroke analysis of 'Devnagari' handwritten characters. *World Scientific Engineering Academy and Society (WSEAS)'s Trans. on Computers, 7*(5), 351–362.

Mukherji, P., & Rege, P. P. (2009). Shape feature and fuzzy logic based offline 'Devnagari' handwritten optical character recognition. *Journal of Pattern Recognition Research, 4,* 52–68.

Mukherji, P., & Rege, P. P. (2010). Hierarchical attributed relational graph based 'Devnagari' character recognition. *International Journal of Information Processing, 4*(3), 22–33.

Mukherji, P., Rege, P. P., & Pradhan, L. K. (2006). Analytical verification system for handwritten 'Devnagari' script. In *International Conference on Visualization, Imaging and Image Processing,* (pp. 237-242). Palma de Mallorca, Spain.

Mukherji, P., Thipsay, A., & Sethuraman, S. (2008). Multi-discriminant analysis of 'Devanagri' numerals for postal automation. In *International Conference on Signal Processing, Communications and Networking,* (pp. 482 - 487). Chennai, India.

Naik, A. M., & Rege, P. P. (2006). Structural approach in recognition of handwritten Devnagari script. In *Symposium at Government College of Engineering,* (pp. 177-180). Aurangabad, India.

Nishimura, H., & Tsutsumi, M. (2001). Off-line handwritten character recognition using integrated 1-D HMMs based on feature extraction filters. In *International Conference on Document Analysis and Recognition* (pp. 417-421). Seattle, USA.

Pal, U., Sharma, N., Wakabayashi, T., & Kimura, F. (2007). Off- line handwritten character recognition of Devnagari script. In *International Conference on Document Analysis and Recognition,* (pp. 496-500). Brazil.

Papadopoulos, A. N., & Manolopoulos, Y. (1999). Structure-based similarity search with graph histograms. In *International Workshop on Database & Expert System Application,* (pp. 174–178).

Plamondon, R., & Srihari, S. N. (2000). On-line and off-line handwriting recognition: A comprehensive survey. *Transactions on Pattern Analysis and Machine Intelligence, 22*(1), 63–84. doi:10.1109/34.824821

Qiu, H., & Hancock, E. R. (2006). Graph matching and clustering using spectral partitions. *Pattern Recognition, 39*(1), 22–34. doi:10.1016/j.patcog.2005.06.014

Rocha, J., & Pavlidis, T. (1994). A shape analysis model with application to character recognition system. *Transactions on Pattern Analysis and Machine Intelligence, 16*(4), 393–404. doi:10.1109/34.277592

Sethi, I. K., & Chatterjee, B. (1977). Machine recognition of constrained hand-printed Devnagari. *Pattern Recognition, 9*(2), 69–75. doi:10.1016/0031-3203(77)90017-6

Sharma, N., Pal, U., Kimura, F., & Pal, S. (2006). Recognition of off-line handwritten Devnagari Characters using quadratic classifier. In *Indian Conference on Computer Vision Graphics and Image Processing,* (pp. 805-816). Madurai, India.

Sinha, R. M. K., & Mahabala, H. N. (1979). A complete OCR for printed Hindi text in Devnagari script. In *International Conference on Document Analysis and Recognition,* (pp. 800-804). Seattle, US.

Sinha, R. M. K., & Mahabala, H. N. (1979). Machine recognition of Devnagari script. *Transactions on Systems. Man and Cybernetics, 9*(8), 435–441. doi:10.1109/TSMC.1979.4310256

Srihari, S. N., Hong, T., & Srikantan, G. (1997). Machine-printed Japanese document recognition. *Pattern Recognition, 30*(8), 1301–1313. doi:10.1016/S0031-3203(96)00168-9

Sural, S., & Das, P. K. (2001). Recognition of an Indian script using multilayer perceptrons and fuzzy features. In *International Conference on Document Analysis and Recognition,* (pp. 1120-1124). Seattle, USA.

Wang, X., Yang, Y., & Huang, K. (2006). Combining discrete orthogonal moments and DHMMS for off-line handwritten Chinese character recognition. In *International Conference on Cognitive Informatics* (pp. 788-793). Beijing, China.

# Chapter 15
# Corner Detection Using Fuzzy Principles

**Erik Cuevas**
*Universidad de Guadalajara, Mexico*

**Daniel Zaldivar**
*Universidad de Guadalajara, Mexico*

**Marco Perez-Cisneros**
*Universidad de Guadalajara, Mexico*

## ABSTRACT

*Reliable corner detection is an important task in pattern recognition applications. In this chapter an approach based on fuzzy-rules to detect corners even under imprecise information is presented. The uncertainties arising due to various types of imaging defects such as blurring, illumination change, noise, et cetera. Fuzzy systems are well known for efficient handling of impreciseness. In order to handle the incompleteness arising due to imperfection of data, it is reasonable to model corner properties by a fuzzy rule-based system. The robustness of the proposed algorithm is compared with well known conventional detectors. The performance is tested on a number of benchmark test images to illustrate the efficiency of the algorithm in noise presence.*

## 1 INTRODUCTION

The human visual system has a highly developed capability for detecting many classes of patterns including visually significant arrangements of image elements. From the psychovisual aspect, points representing high curvature are one of the dominant classes of patterns that play an important role in almost all real life image analysis ap-

DOI: 10.4018/978-1-61350-429-1.ch015

plications (Lowe, 1985; Loupias & Sebe, 2000; Fischler & Wolf, 1994). These points encode a significant amount of shape information. Corners are generally formed at the junction of different edge segments which may be the meeting (or crossing) of two edges. Cornerness of an edge segment depends solely on the curvature formed at the meeting point of two line segments. Corner detection is one of the fundamental tasks in computer vision and it can be regarded as a special type of feature segmentation. Extracted corners can be used for measurement and/or recognition purposes. A large number of algorithms already exist in the literature. In particular, corner detection on gray level images can be classified into two main approaches. In the first approach, the gray level image is first converted into its binary version for extraction of boundaries using some thresholding technique. After a successful extraction of boundaries, the corners or the high curvature points are detected using directional codes or other polygonal approximation techniques (Freeman & Davis, 1977). In the second approach, the gray level image is taken directly as an input for corner detection. In this chapter, the discussion is restricted to the second approach only. Most of the general-purpose detectors based on gray level, use either a topology-based or an auto-correlation- based approach and most recently machine learning strategies (Rosten et al., 2010). Topology based corner detectors, mainly use gradients and surface curvature to define the measure of cornerness. Points are marked as corners, if the value of cornerness exceeds some predefined threshold condition. Alternatively a measure of curvature can be obtained using auto-correlation (Kitchen &Rosenfeld, 1982; Zheng et al., 1999; Rattarangsi & Chin, 1999; Teh & Chin, 1989; Rosenfeld & Johnston, 1973).

There exits several classical corner detection algorithms for estimating corner points. Such detectors are based on a local structure matrix which consists on the first partial derivatives of the intensity function. An clear example is the Harris feature point detector (Harris & Stephens, 1988), which is based on a comparison: the measure of the corner strength - which is defined by the method and is based on a local structure matrix - is compared to an appropriately chosen concrete threshold. Another well known corner detector is the SUSAN (Smallest Univalue Segment Assimilating Nucleus) detector which is based on brightness comparison (Smith & Brady, 1997). It does not depend on image derivatives. The SUSAN area will reach a minimum while the nucleus lies on a corner point. The effectiveness of the above mentioned algorithms is acceptable. Recent studies such as (Zou et al., 2008) demonstrate that the Harris corner detector performs better for several circumstances in comparison to the SUSAN algorithm.

Data from natural images are always imprecise and noisy due to inherent uncertainties that may arise from the imaging process (such as defocusing, wide variations of illuminations, etc.). As a result, precise localization and detection of corners become difficult under such imperfect situations. On the other hand, Fuzzy systems are well known for efficiently handling of impreciseness and incompleteness (Zadeh, 1965; Pal et al., 2000; Yua et al., 2007) due to imperfection of data. Therefore it may result reasonable to model corner properties using a fuzzy rule-based system as they have been successfully applied to image processing in a wide variety of applications (Karmakar & Dooley, 2002; Basak & Pal, 2005; Jacquey et al., 2008). This chapter seeks to contribute to enhance the application of fuzzy logic to image processing, just as it has been proposed in (Russo, 1999). The method adopts a template-based rule-driven procedure and has been specifically developed to deal with topics related to image processing purposes. This method is able to address many different processing tasks (Tizhoosh, 2003; Liang & Looney, 2003; Kim, 2004) and to produce better results than classical methods when applied to some critical issues such as noise (Tizhoosh, 2003; Russo, 2004; Yüksel, 2007).

Only few fuzzy approaches have specifically addressed the problem of corner detection for general purposes, one of the first works is reported in (Li, 1999). Banerjee & Kundu have proposed in (Banerjee & Kundu, 2008) an algorithm to extract significant gray level corner points. The measure of cornerness in each point is computed by means of the fuzzy edge strength and the gradient direction. Different corner fuzzy-sets are obtained by considering different threshold values from the fuzzy edge map. However, the algorithm's main drawback is that it uses several feature detectors which operate at different stages, yielding a high computational load.

On the other hand, Várkonyi-Kóczy have proposed in (Várkonyi-Kóczy, 2008), a fuzzy corner detector that employs a local structure matrix. It builds a continuous transient between the localized and not localized corner points. The algorithm uses a fuzzy pre-filter that improve the quality of the image under process. Despite both fuzzy approaches show a good performance, they demand an expensive computing load in comparison to other classical algorithms such as the Harris method or SUSAN.

This chapter presents a new robust approach to extract significant gray level corner points. The method is derived from a fuzzy-rule approach which aims to detect corners even under complex conditions. In the proposed approach, the measure of "cornerness" for each pixel in the image is computed by fuzzy rules (represented as templates) which are applied to a set of pixels belonging to a rectangular window. As the algorithm scans each pixel of the image at a time, a new pixel of the resulting image is generated by fuzzy reasoning. Hence, the possible uncertainty contained in the window-neighborhood is handled by using an appropriate rule base (template set). Experimental evidence shows the effectiveness of such method for detecting corners under several conditions. A comparison between one state-of-the-art Fuzzy-based method (Banerjee & Kundu, 2008) and the Harris algorithm (Harris & Stephens, 1988) demonstrates the performance of the proposed method.

The chapter is organized as follows: Section 2 briefly describes the mathematical approach and the fuzzy model used in this work. Section 3 describes the features extraction process while Section 4 describes the fuzzy corner extraction process. On the other hand, Section 5 describes the experimental results while Section 6 offers some conclusions about the development and performance of this technique.

## 2 FUZZY RULE-BASED SYSTEM

### 2.1 Fuzzy System

Most of the approaches for corner detection are easy to implement and demand a low computational load. However, their effective operation largely relies on the fact that noisiness must be limited. In this section, a more robust technique is proposed. The new procedure is set to deliver a better performance for noisy environments. The fuzzy system is simple to implement and still fast in computation if it is compared to some existing fuzzy methods (Banerjee & Kundu, 2008; Várkonyi-Kóczy, 2008). Also, it can be easily extended to detect other features. In the proposed approach, the fuzzy rules are applied to a set of pixels belonging to a rectangular $N \times N$ window (usually 3x3 pixels), where the gray-level differences between the center pixel $p_{m,n}$ and its surrounding pixels are computed and stored within matrix $E$ as follows:

$$E = \begin{bmatrix} p_{m,n} - p_{m-1,n-1} & p_{m,n} - p_{m-1,n} & p_{m,n} - p_{m-1,n+1} \\ p_{m,n} - p_{m,n-1} & 0 & p_{m,n} - p_{m,n+1} \\ p_{m,n} - p_{m+1,n-1} & p_{m,n} - p_{m+1,n} & p_{m,n} - p_{m+1,n+1} \end{bmatrix}$$

$$(1)$$

where $m$ and $n$ represent the coordinates of the central pixel. If the neighborhood is a homogenous region, then $E$ contains values near zero. In the case of corners, the matrix $E$ possesses a specific configuration depending on the corner type. These divide $E$ in two connected regions, one with positive (pixel type $A$) and another with negative (pixel type $B$) difference values (see Figure 1). The reasoning structure uses two different types of rules: the **THEN-rules** and the **ELSE-rules** (don't care conditions) respectively. Each THEN-rule includes a determined pixel configuration as antecedent and only one pixel as consequent. Antecedents are related to a corner existence test and the consequent to its presence

*Figure 1. Region shaping with respect to gray level differences: (a) the resulting template and (b) the real corner that originates the template*

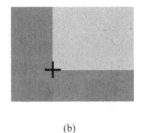

(a)                                        (b)

or absence. The rule-base gathers many fuzzy rules (THEN-rules) and only one ELSE-rule (i.e. do-not-care rule). Therefore only relevant rules (i.e. configurations) are formulated as THEN-rules while other not important configurations may be handled as a group of ELSE-rules.

The set of THEN-rules lies on the very core of the algorithm. The rules must deliver successful structure detection, i.e. corners in this case, while still cancelling other inconsistencies such as noise. Such tradeoff may be solved by using a reduced set of rules (configurations) which in turn represent the minimum number in order to coherently detect the structure as it is required by a given application. Such procedure allows dealing with noisy pixels or imprecision.

The proposed corner detector considers twelve THEN-rules that represent the same number of possible corner configurations and only one ELSE-rule as it is graphically explained by Figure 2. It may be also possible to consider some other corner configurations. However it may reduce the algorithm's ability to deal with noise or uncertainty (Russo, 1999; Tizhoosh, 2003; Yüksel, 2007).

Despite using a reduced rule base, the performance in the detection process can be considered acceptable when it is compared to other algorithms solving the same task. The rule base (THEN-rules and ELSE-rule) supporting the detector algorithm is shown in Table 1.

Each rule has the following form:

**If** the corner structure in $E$ possesses positive

elements

**and** the opposite region possesses negative

elements,

**then** the pixel represent a corner, ■

**else** the pixel does not represent a corner □

(2)

The principle can be explained as follows: If one region of the neighborhood, according to any of the twelve cases, contains positive/negative differences with respect to the center pixel, and if any other region contains the opposite (negative/positive) differences with respect to the center pixel, then the center pixel is a corner (see Figure 2). The procedure can be considered as the evaluation of each one of the 12 different THEN-rules (configurations), yielding two auxiliary matrices $E^p$ and $E^n$ as follows:

$$E^p(i, j) = \begin{cases} 1 & \text{if } E(i, j) \geq 0 \\ 0 & \text{else} \end{cases} \tag{3}$$

$$E^n(i, j) = \begin{cases} 1 & \text{if } E(i, j) < 0 \\ 0 & \text{else} \end{cases} \tag{4}$$

*Figure 2. Different corner cases to be considered for building the fuzzy rules. The image region containing the corner is shown in the upper section while the resulting 3x3 template is shown below each case.*

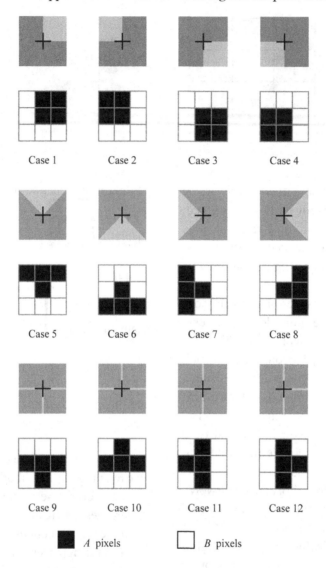

where $i,j$ represents de row and column of the matrix $E$ ($i, j \in (1, 2, 3)$), Eq. 1.

For the case that all elements of $E^p$ / $E^n$ are ones (meaning all elements of $E(i,j)$ are positives or negatives), it is possible to construct regions $A$ and $B$ within the window-neighbourhood according to the existing relative differences. Thus the values of $E^p$ and $E^n$ can be recalculated as follows:

$$E^p(i,j) = \begin{cases} 1 & \text{if } E(i,j) \leq t_h \\ 0 & \text{else} \end{cases}$$

$$E^n(i,j) = \begin{cases} 1 & \text{if } E(i,j) > t_h \\ 0 & \text{else} \end{cases} \tag{5}$$

For all the elements of $E^p$ being ones, and

$$E^p(i,j) = \begin{cases} 1 & \text{if } E(i,j) \geq -t_h \\ 0 & \text{else} \end{cases}$$

$$E^n(i,j) = \begin{cases} 1 & \text{if } E(i,j) < -t_h \\ 0 & \text{else} \end{cases} \tag{6}$$

*Table 1. The rule base (THEN-rules and ELSE-rule) supporting the corner detector algorithm*

For all the elements of $E^n$ being ones, $t_h$ is a threshold that controls the sensitivity of the considered differences. Typical values for $t_h$ normally fall into the interval (5-35). The lowest value of 5 would yield a higher detector's sensitivity which may detect a great number of corners corresponding to noisy intensity changes which are commonly found in images.

On the other hand, a maximum value of 35 would detect corners matching to a significant difference between several objects in the structure, i.e. object whose pixels may be considered as being connected. Although the selection of the best value for $t_h$ clearly depends on the particular application, a good compromise can be obtained

by taking a value on approximately half the overall interval, i.e. $t_h = 20$.

The membership values $\mu_c(m, n)$ (where $c = 1$, 2, ..., 12) are computed depending on the corner types (see Figure 2). According to (Russo, 1999) such values represent the antecedents of each employed THEN-rule. They can be calculated as shown in equation 7 (see Exhibit 1).

Expression (7) considers a normalization factor equal to 20 which represents the maximum possible value, i.e. the highest product of the multiplication among the pixels between $E^p$ and $E^n$. Hence, the membership value $\mu_c(m, n)$ falls between 0 and 1. Equation (7) can be considered as the numerical implementation of the generic

*Exhibit 1.*

$$\mu_c(m,n) = \frac{1}{20} \max \left[ \left( \sum_{ij \in A} E^p(i,j) \right) \cdot \left( \sum_{ij \in B} E^n(i,j) \right), \left( \sum_{ij \in B} E^p(i,j) \right) \cdot \left( \sum_{ij \in A} E^n(i,j) \right) \right] \qquad (7)$$

rule previously defined by Eq. 2. If Rule 1 (case 1) is considered as an example, the expressions corresponding to expression (7) would thus be:

$$\sum_{ij \in A} E^p(i,j) =$$
$$E^p(1,2) + E^p(1,3) + E^p(2,2) + E^p(2,3)$$

$$\sum_{ij \in B} E^n(i,j) =$$
$$E^n(1,1) + E^n(2,1) + E^n(3,1) + E^n(3,2) + E^n(3,3)$$

$$\sum_{ij \in B} E^p(i,j) =$$
$$E^p(1,1) + E^p(2,1) + E^p(3,1) + E^p(3,2) + E^p(3,3)$$

$$\sum_{ij \in A} E^n(i,j) = \qquad (8)$$
$$E^n(1,2) + E^n(1,3) + E^n(2,2) + E^n(2,3)$$

Analogously to (8), membership values $\mu_2(i,j)$, ..., $\mu_{12}(i,j)$ for other rules (cases) can be calculated. Finally, the 12 fuzzy rules can be added into a single fuzzy value using the ***max*** (maximum) operator. The final fuzzy value represents the linguistic meaning of cornerness yielding:

$$\mu_{cornerness}(m,n) = \qquad (9)$$
$$\max(\mu_1(m,n), \mu_2(m,n), ..., \mu_{12}(m,n))$$

The pixels whose value $\mu_{cornerness}(m,n)$ are near to one, belong to a feature similar to a corner, while values near to zero would represent any other feature.

## 2.2 Robustness

This kind of corner detection clearly differs from other classical procedures in several ways. Conventional corner detectors look usually for the explicit corner location by means of detecting the zero-crossing of derivatives in different directions. On the contrary the proposed approach detects the entire area where the corner could lie.

In particular, gradient-based methods are normally highly sensitive to the noise in real images and being mainly affected by the impulsive noise. Also, most of the corner detection algorithms incorporate several pre-filters (Moravec, 1997; Harris & Stephens, 1988; Smith & Brady, 1997; Lowe, 1985), which allow attenuation but do not eliminate impulsive noise.

On the other hand, fuzzy detectors allow corner marking despite noisy environments either by implementing fuzzy pre-filtering that eliminates uncertainty on the image or by incorporating fuzzy sets for modeling imprecision (Banerjee & Kundu, 2008). The method presented in this chapter considers vagueness due to noise and grayness ambiguity to be handled by the fuzzy rules introduced in expression (2). Considering the image in Figure 3, a pixel holding a different

*Figure 3. The effect of the impulsive noise in matrices $E^+$ and $E^-$. Matrices $E^+$ and $E^-$ would contain only ones or zeros depending on the gray-level difference*

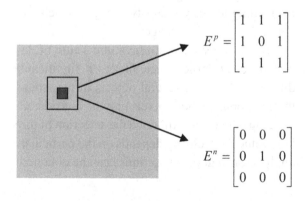

*Table 2. Parameter setup for the proposed corner detector*

| $t_h$ | $t_c$ | $H$ |
|---|---|---|
| 20 | 0.7 | 10 |

gray value from its neighbors is located within a homogeneous region. This situation can be considered as impulsive noise.

Under these circumstances, matrices $E^p$ and $E^p$ would contain only ones or zeros depending on the gray-level difference. Therefore, the values used to calculate the membership functions in expression (7), for any of the twelve cases, would yield

$$\left( \sum_{ij \in Rp} E^p(i,j) \right) \cdot \left( \sum_{ij \in Rn} E^p(i,j) \right) \approx 0 \qquad (10)$$

$$\left( \sum_{ij \in Rn} E^p(i,j) \right) \cdot \left( \sum_{ij \in Rp} E^n(i,j) \right) \approx 0 \qquad (11)$$

Now, considering the values from expressions (10) and (11) and a noisy pixel, the resulting value of its cornerness can be calculated by expression (9) as $\mu_{cornerness}(i,j) \approx 0$. The impulsive noise is thus classified by the fuzzy system as a homogeneous region. In the same way, the central pixel would not be marked as corner for cases not considered

in Table 2 which normally represent noisy configurations. It is mainly because the inference system works with ELSE-rules.

## 2.3 Corner Selection

In order to detect corners, it would be enough to choose an appropriate threshold $t_c$. If $\mu_{cornerness}(m, n) \geq t_c$, then the pixel $p_{m,n}$ can be assumed as such. Under these assumptions, the value $t_c$ must be selected as close to 1 as it is likely to assure that pixel $p_{m,n}$ may be a corner. However, a more convenient approach is to choose a small threshold value $t_c$ whose value allows detecting a wider number of corners despite a higher uncertainty. The corner selection process can therefore be explained as follows: For each pixel, if $\mu_{cornerness}(m, n) \geq t_c$, a neighborhood of $H \times H$ dimension is established around it (commonly $H > N$). The pixel $p_{m,n}$ is thus selected as a corner if its value $\mu_{cornerness}(m, n)$ is maximum within the neighborhood $H \times H$, otherwise it does not represent a corner point.

Figure 4 shows a selection example, where $\mu_{cornerness}(m, n)$ represents the cornerness of the

*Figure 4. Neighborhood method for corner selection*

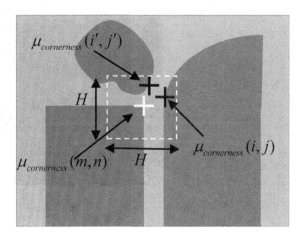

pixel currently under evaluation, by assuming $\mu_{cornerness}(m, n) \geq t_c$. Inside the window $H \times H$ that has been established around it, there exist other two pixels $p_{i,j}$ and $p_{i',j'}$, whose values $\mu_{cornerness}(m, n)$ and $\mu_{cornerness}(i', j')$ are lower than $\mu_{cornerness}(m, n)$. Therefore, a point $p_{m,n}$ can thus be considered as a corner within the image.

## 3 EXPERIMENTAL RESULTS

Different sorts of images have been tested in order to analyze the performance of the method for corner detection. Such benchmark set includes image alterations such as blurring, illumination change, impulsive noise etc. Table 2 presents the parameters of the proposed algorithm used in this chapter. Once they have been determined experimentally, they are kept for all the test images through all experiments.

First, Figure 5b shows the value of $\mu_{cornerness}(m, n)$, as it is computed by the fuzzy system according to Eq. (9) to detect corners in a real image. In Figure 5a, the blue crosses represent the corners obtained using the corner selection procedure explained in sub-section 2.3.

Figure 6 shows the algorithm's performance on different image conditions such as the case with variable illumination and blurring. Figures 6(a)-(b) present the performance of the fuzzy corner detector as it is applied to over-exposed

and over-illuminated images. The effect of high illumination on the images was made by applying a linear transformation of the form $I(i, j) + 80$. On the other hand, Figures 6(c)-(d) show the effectiveness of the proposed detector using low-illuminated or sub-exposed images. Such effect was made by another linear transformation: $I(i, j) - 40$. The images in Figures 6(e)-(f) illustrate the sensitivity of the fuzzy detector to blurring.

Such steamed up effect was made by applying a low-pass filter to the original images, with a 5x5 kernel as follows:

$$h(i, j) = \frac{1}{25} \begin{vmatrix} 1 & 1 & 1 & 1 & 1 \\ 1 & 1 & 1 & 1 & 1 \\ 1 & 1 & 1 & 1 & 1 \\ 1 & 1 & 1 & 1 & 1 \\ 1 & 1 & 1 & 1 & 1 \end{vmatrix} \tag{12}$$

From results shown in Figure 6, it can be observed as the fuzzy detector exhibits immunity to changes in illumination, see for instance Figures 6(a)-(b) and 6(c)-(d). However, it also shows sensitivity to blurring in Figures 6(e)-(f). For the case of blurring images, the detector is able to find all the corners over the simulated image in 6(e). The latter figure exhibits low distortion in the homogeneous gray levels within the image as a consequence of the filter operation. On the other hand, some sensitivity may be lost while applying the detector to the real image shown in

*Figure 5. (a) Detected corners using the proposed approach, and (b) values of $\mu_{cornerness}(m, n)$*

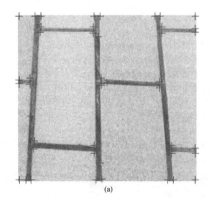
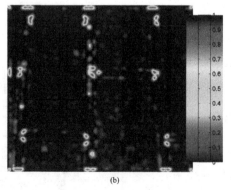

(a)  (b)

*Figure 6. Performance of the fuzzy corner detector over different conditions on the image: (a)-(b) over-exposition or high illumination, (c)-(d) sub-exposition or low illumination and (e)-(f) blurring.*

(a)      (b)

(c)      (d)

(e)      (f)

Figure 6(f). Moreover, after applying distortion to the image, several points that do not belong to a corner as such have been wrongly marked as corners. Despite all previous comments, the fuzzy detector was able to detect in Figure 6(f) the corners which delimit the object´s shape. This is not a common feature of other corner detectors (Rosenfeld & Johnston, 1973; Harris & Stephens, 1988; Smith & Brady, 1997; Zou et al., 2008).

## 4 PERFORMANCE COMPARISON

A variety of quantitative evaluation methods for corner detection algorithms have been proposed in the literature (Zou el al., 2008; Cordelia et al., 2000; Mokhtarian & Mohanna, 2006). Following the criteria in (Mokhtarian & Mohanna, 2006), the performance analysis considers the Harris algorithm (Harris & Stephens, 1988), the fuzzy method presented by Banerjee & Kundu (Banerjee

& Kundu, 2008) and the approach proposed in this chapter. A quantitative comparison over three criteria is presented: stability, noise immunity and computational effort. The study aims analyze the performance objectively.

The parameters for each detector algorithm are set as follows: For the Harris algorithm, the gradient operators [-2 -1 0 1 2] and [-2 -1 0 1 2]$^T$ are set in directions $u$ and $v$ separately. The Gaussian smoothing filter employs a Gaussian window function of size 7×7 and a standard deviation of 2 with $k$=0.06. The parametric setup appears as the best set following data in (Zou et al., 2008) and considering lots of hand tuning experiments. For the fuzzy method proposed by Banerjee & Kundu, the parameter are set following guidelines from (Banerjee & Kundu, 2008), with a Gaussian window function of size 3×3 and a standard deviation of 2, $\mu_d(P) \geq 0.9$ and $T_h = 0.2$. Finally the parameters of the proposed approach are set according to the Table 2.

## 4.1 Stability Criterion

Two frames in an image sequence are processed by the algorithm to detect corners. If the corner's positions are unchanged from one frame to the next one, the algorithm can be regarded as stable. However, the gray-level value of each pixel would normally vary in actual images because of several factors affecting the image. If the algorithm is applied to a given image, then it cannot be assured the number and position of all detected corners would be exactly the same. Therefore, absolute stability is almost non-existent. A factor $\eta$ to measure the stability of a corner algorithm can be defined as follows:

$$\eta = \frac{A_1 \cap A_2}{\min\left(|A_1|, |A_2|\right)} \times 100\%, \qquad (13)$$

where $A_1$ and $A_2$ representing the corner sets for the first and the second frame respectively (the intersection operator ∩ stands for common corners); $|A_i|$ represents the number of elements in $A_i$ set and the overall numerator holds the number of corresponding corners in two frames. From expression (8), it can be concluded that a greater $\eta$ yields a more stable corner detection algorithm. Fifty pairs of images holding different contrast and brightness levels are gathered in order to compare the proposed fuzzy detector and other classic methods. Figure 7a shows the comparison with respect to the stability factor, where the

*Figure 7. Performance comparison among corner detectors. (a) Stability factor and (b) noisy immunity factor.*

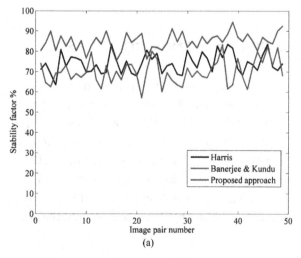

(a)

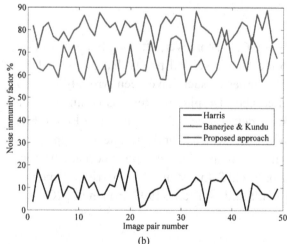

(b)

horizontal axis represents the image pair number and the vertical axis represents the value of such stability factor. The average stability factor of Harris detector is 75%, while the fuzzy method Banerjee & Kundu holds 70% and the proposed fuzzy detector shows 83%.

## 4.2 Noise Immunity

Noise immunity is measured by factor $\rho$ which it can be defined as follows:

$$\rho = \frac{B_1 \cap B_2}{\max\left(|B_1|, |B_2|\right)} \times 100\%, \qquad (14)$$

where $B_1$ is the corner set of the original image and $B_2$ is the corner set of the image with added noise. In this case, the maximum operator seeks to consider that false corners have been added as a result of additive noise. As $\rho$ increases, it can be assumed that the algorithm's ability to avoid noisy corners is stronger.

One experiment is focus on comparing such noise immunity among methods. Fifty images with 10% of added impulsive noise are considered. Figure 7b shows the noise immunity factor, with the Harris detector showing 9%, the fuzzy method Banerjee & Kundu holding 65% and the proposed fuzzy detector showing 80%.

## 4.3 Computational Effort

The speed and computational effort of a corner detector algorithm must meet demands for real-time tasks, regarding speed and required process-

ing time. The runtime of an algorithm can be a reference to its overall computational effort. In order to compare the three algorithms, fifty pairs of images are considered in order to register the algorithm's runtime for testing images holding 320×240 pixels. The average runtime for the Harris method, the fuzzy Banerjee & Kundu algorithm and the proposed corner detectors is 1.8686s, 6.2125s and 0.878s respectively, as all are tested under the MatLab© R2008b environment.

## 4.3 Comparison Results

Table 3 shows a final comparison between all the methods. The proposed fuzzy detector can be considered as equally stable as the Harris method. It also shows stronger noise immunity being slightly superior to the fuzzy detector proposed by Banerjee & Kundu. The proposed corner detector can also be regarded as the algorithm showing the best computational performance.

Figures 8, 9 and 10 shows the performance of the detector algorithms considered in the study while analyzing a number of benchmark images.

## 5 CONCLUSION

This chapter has presented a corner detection algorithm which models the structure of a potential corner in an images based on a fuzzy rule set. The method is able to tolerate implicit imprecision and impulsive noise.

Experimental evidence suggests that the fuzzy proposed algorithm produces better results than

*Table 3. Performance comparison among the three corner detectors considered by the study.*

| Corner Detector | Stability± Standard deviation(%) | Noise± Standard deviation(%) | Time± Standard deviation(s) |
|---|---|---|---|
| Harris | 75± 5.5 | 9± 4.4 | 1.8686± 0.3 |
| Fuzzy Banerjee & Kundu | 70± 7.8 | 65± 7.1 | 6.2125± 0.21 |
| The proposed detector | 83± 4.1 | 80± 4.6 | 0.878± 0.11 |

*Figure 8. House: (a) Original image and the output after applying (b) the Harris algorithm, (c) the fuzzy Banerjee & Kundu method and (d) the proposed detector.*

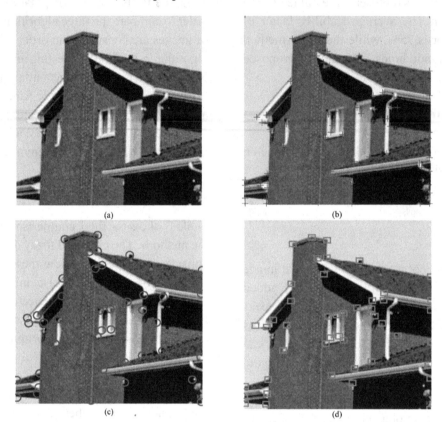

other common methods such as the Harris detector (Harris & Stephens, 1988) and the fuzzy approach proposed by Banerjee & Kundu (Banerjee & Kundu, 2008). The proposed algorithm is able to successfully identify corners on images holding different uncertainty conditions. However it is also sensitive to blurring in particular when a steaming up effect is produced by considering neighborhood window wider than the one previously considered for building the fuzzy model of corners (templates). Such fact shall not be considered as inconvenient because the fuzzy-based algorithm is still capable of identifying corners over similar blurring levels than those of conventional algorithms.

The proposed detector is stable and has shown robustness to impulsive noise which in turn represents its major advantage over the Harris method considering that impulsive noise is commonly found in real-time images. Although the algorithm exhibits a tolerance to imprecision that matches the performance of the Banerjee & Kundu fuzzy method, the presented approach requires a lighter computational cost for analyzing benchmark images.

## REFERENCES

Banerjee, M., & Kundu, M. K. (2008). Handling of impreciseness in gray level corner detection using fuzzy set theoretic approach. *Applied Soft Computing*, *8*(4), 1680–1691. doi:10.1016/j. asoc.2007.09.001

*Figure 9. Circle: (a) Original image and the output after applying (b) the Harris algorithm, (c) the fuzzy Banerjee & Kundu method and (d) the proposed detector.*

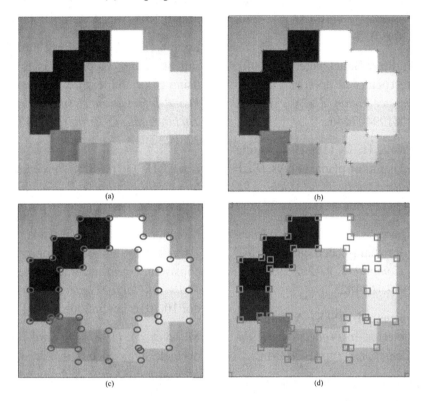

*Figure 10. Noisy chessboard image: (a) Original image and the output after applying (b) the Harris algorithm, (c) the fuzzy Banerjee & Kundu method and (d) the proposed detector.*

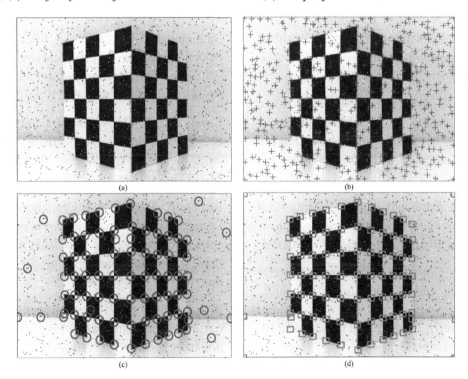

Basak, J., & Pal, S. (2005). Theoretical quantification of shape distortion in fuzzy Hough transform. *Fuzzy Sets and Systems, 154,* 227–250. doi:10.1016/j.fss.2005.02.014

Cordelia, S., Mohr, R., & Bauckhage, C. (2000). Evaluation of interest point detectors. *International Journal of Computer Vision, 37*(2), 151–172. doi:10.1023/A:1008199403446

Fischler, M., & Wolf, H. C. (1994). Locating perceptually salient points on planar curves. *IEEE Transactions on Pattern Analysis and Machine Intelligence, 16*(2), 113–129. doi:10.1109/34.273737

Freeman, H., & Davis, L. S. (1977). A corner-finding algorithm for chain-coded curves. *IEEE Transactions on Computers, C-26,* 297–303. doi:10.1109/TC.1977.1674825

Harris, C., & Stephens, M. (1988). A combined corner and edge detector. In *Proceedings of the 4th Alvey Vision Conference,* (pp. 147–151).

Jacquey, F., Comby, F., & Strauss, O. (2008). Fuzzy Edge detection for omnidirectional images. *Fuzzy Sets and Systems, 159,* 1991–2010. doi:10.1016/j.fss.2008.02.022

Karmakar, G., & Dooley, L. (2002). A generic fuzzy rule based in image segmentation algorithm. *Pattern Recognition Letters, 23,* 1215–1227. doi:10.1016/S0167-8655(02)00069-7

Kim, D., Lee, W., & Kweon, I. (2004). Automatic edge detection using 3x3 ideal binary pixel patterns and fuzzy-based edge thresholding. *Pattern Recognition Letters, 25,* 101–106. doi:10.1016/j.patrec.2003.09.010

Kitchen, L., & Rosenfeld, A. (1982). Gray-level corner detection. *Pattern Recognition Letters, 1,* 95–102. doi:10.1016/0167-8655(82)90020-4

Li, L. (1999). Corner detection and interpretation on planar curves using fuzzy reasoning. *IEEE Transactions on Pattern Analysis and Machine Intelligence, 21*(11), 1204–1210. doi:10.1109/34.809113

Liang, L., & Looney, C. (2003). Competitive edge detection. *Applied Soft Computing, 3,* 123–137. doi:10.1016/S1568-4946(03)00008-5

Loupias, E., & Sebe, E. (2000). Wavelet-based salient points: Applications to image retrieval using color and texture features. In *Advances in Visual Information Systems, Proceedings of the 4th International Conference, VISUAL 2000,* (pp. 223–232).

Lowe, D. G. (1985). *Perceptual organization and visual recognition.* USA: Kluwer Academic Publishers.

Mokhtarian, F., & Mohanna, F. (2006). Performance evaluation of corner detectors using consistency and accuracy measures. *Computer Vision and Image Understanding, 102*(1), 81–94. doi:10.1016/j.cviu.2005.11.001

Moravec, H. (1997). Towards automatic visual obstacle avoidance. In *Proceedings of the 5th International Joint Conference on Artificial Intelligence,* (p. 584).

Pal, S. K., Ghosh, A., & Kundu, M. K. (2000). *Soft computing for image processing* (pp. 44–78). Physica-Verlag.

Rattarangsi, A., & Chin, R. T. (1992). Scale-based detection of corners of planar curves. *IEEE Transactions on Pattern Analysis and Machine Intelligence, 14*(4), 430–449. doi:10.1109/34.126805

Rosenfeld, A., & Johnston, E. (1973). Angle detection on digital curves. *IEEE Transactions on Computers, C-22,* 858–875. doi:10.1109/TC.1973.5009188

Rosten, E., Porter, R., & Drummond, T. (2010). Faster and better: A machine learning approach to corner detection. *IEEE Transactions on Pattern Analysis and Machine Learning, 32*(1), 105–119. doi:10.1109/TPAMI.2008.275

Russo, F. (1999). FIRE operators for image processing. *Fuzzy Sets and Systems, 103,* 265–275. doi:10.1016/S0165-0114(98)00226-7

Russo, F. (2004). Impulse noise cancellation in image data using a two-output nonlinear filter. *Measurement*, *36*(3-4), 205–213. doi:10.1016/j.measurement.2004.09.002

Smith, S., & Brady, M. (1997). A new approach to low level image processing. *International Journal of Computer Vision*, *23*(1), 45–78. doi:10.1023/A:1007963824710

Teh, C., & Chin, R. T. (1989). On the detection of dominant points on digital curves. *IEEE Transactions on Pattern Analysis and Machine Intelligence*, *11*(8), 859–872. doi:10.1109/34.31447

Tizhoosh, H. (2003). Fast and robust fuzzy edge detection. In Nachtegael, M. (Ed.), *Fuzzy filters for image processing*. Berlin, Germany: Springer.

Várkonyi-Kóczy, A. (2008). Fuzzy logic supported corner detection. *Journal of Intelligent & Fuzzy Systems*, *19*, 41–50.

Yua, D., Hu, Q., & Wua, C. (2007). Uncertainty measures for fuzzy relations and their applications. *Applied Soft Computing*, *7*(3), 1135–1143. doi:10.1016/j.asoc.2006.10.004

Yüksel, M. (2007). Edge detection in noisy images by fuzzy processing. *International Journal of Electronics and Communications*, *61*, 82–89. doi:10.1016/j.aeue.2006.02.006

Zadeh, L. A. (1965). Fuzzy sets. *Information and Control*, *8*, 338–353. doi:10.1016/S0019-9958(65)90241-X

Zheng, Z., Wang, H., & Teoh, E. (1999). Analysis of gray level corner detection. *Pattern Recognition Letters*, *20*(2), 149–162. doi:10.1016/S0167-8655(98)00134-2

Zou, L., Chen, J., Zhang, J., & Dou, L. (2008). The comparison of two typical corner detection algorithms. *Second International Symposium on Intelligent Information Technology Application.* ISBN 978-0-7695-3497

# Chapter 16
# Eye Detection Using Color, Haar Features, and Efficient Support Vector Machine

**Shuo Chen**
*New Jersey Institute of Technology, USA*

**Chengjun Liu**
*New Jersey Institute of Technology, USA*

## ABSTRACT

*Eye detection is an important initial step in an automatic face recognition system. Though numerous eye detection methods have been proposed, many problems still exist, especially in the detection accuracy and efficiency under challenging image conditions. The authors present a novel eye detection method using color information, Haar features, and a new efficient Support Vector Machine (eSVM) in this chapter. In particular, this eye detection method consists of two stages: the eye candidate selection and validation. The selection stage picks up eye candidates over an image through color information, while the validation stage applies 2D Haar wavelet and the eSVM to detect the center of the eye among these candidates. The eSVM is defined on fewer support vectors than the standard SVM, which can achieve faster detection speed and higher or comparable detection accuracy. Experiments on Face Recognition Grand Challenge (FRGC) database show the improved performance over existing methods on both efficiency and accuracy.*

## 1. INTRODUCTION

Being an important initial step in an automatic face recognition system, eye detection has become a popular research topic in the last decade. Since face alignment for recognition is usually conducted according to eye positions, incorrect eye location would corrupt the face alignment in both spatial scale and rotation, and thus lead to the extremely poor performance of face recognition.

DOI: 10.4018/978-1-61350-429-1.ch016

Wang et al (2005) did experiments on FRGC 1.0 database to evaluate the impact of eye detection error on face recognition accuracy. It is shown that only 1% eye location error reduces the face recognition accuracy by over 10% while about 5% error reduces the accuracy by 50%. Phillips et al. (2000) did experiments on FERET database and similar conclusion was also reached. The "partial automatic face recognition algorithm", in which manual eye locations are given to align the face image, performs much better than the "fully automatic recognition algorithm".

Generally speaking, current eye detection methods can be classified into three categories (Zhu & Ji, 2005): template based methods, feature based methods and appearance based methods. For the template based methods, a sliding window is moved over the whole image to match with a pre-designed generic eye model in order to detect the eye position (Lam & Yan, 1996; Xie et. al., 1994). Feature based methods focus on the characteristic of eyes, such as the shape, color distribution, and intensity gradient information around eye regions (Kawaguchi & Rizon, 2004; Feng and Yuan, 1998; Zhou & Geng, 2004). Appearance based methods detect eyes based on their photometric appearance. These methods always need to train a classifier at first by collecting a large amount of training data and then detection is achieved via two-fold classification (Nguyen et. al., 2008; Zhang & Zhan, 2006; Wang et. al., 2005; Wang & Ji, 2007). Usually, feature based methods have much faster detection speed since they always only involve some image processing operations while appearance based methods have much higher detection accuracy since statistical learning technology is applied. We will further discuss these methods in details in the following section.

Though numerous eye detection methods have been proposed (Zhou & Geng, 2004; Khairosfaizal & Noraini, 2009), many problems still exist, especially in detection accuracy and efficiency under challenging image conditions. In this chapter, we present an accurate and efficient eye-center detection method, which combines the advantages of both feature and appearance based methods. In particular, this method consists of two stages: the features based eye candidate selection and appearance based validation. In the candidate selection stage, 99% non-eye pixels are rejected through eye color distribution analysis in the YCbCr color space. Only up to 1% pixels in an image as eye candidates enter the validation stage. In the validation stage, 2D Haar wavelet (Viola & Jones, 2001) is used for image representation in multi-scales and PCA (Stork, 2000) is applied for dimensionality reduction. Several popular and effective image representation methods for object detection, like HOG (Dalal & Triggs, 2005), Gabor (Liu & Wechsler, 2002), and LBP (Ahonen et. al., 2006), are assessed and the 2D Haar wavelet is chosen as the best for eye representation. Finally, a new efficient Support Vector Machine (eSVM) is proposed as the classifier. SVM has been widely applied in solving recognition and object detection problems in the last decade (Nguyen et. al., 2008; Jia & Martinez, 2009). Although the standard SVM exhibits many theoretical and practical advantages such as good generalization performance, when applied to complicated large-scale classification tasks, its classification speed is slower than other approaches due to its complex decision function. The eSVM, based on the idea of minimizing the maximum margin of misclassified samples, is defined on fewer support vectors than the conventional SVM, which can achieve faster detection speed and comparable or even higher detection accuracy.

To evaluate the effectiveness of our proposed method, we conduct experiments on the whole training dataset of FRGC version 2 experiment 4, which contains 12,776 controlled and uncontrolled images (Phillips et. al., 2005). Experiment results show that (i) our proposed method has higher detection accuracy compared with other state of the art approaches and (ii) eSVM greatly improves the efficiency and the detection system meets the real-time requirement. In particular, our method can processes 6.25 images with the size of 128*128 per second in average and achieves 94.92% eye detection accuracy.

## 2. BACKGROUND

An automatic face recognition system starts with the detection of faces and eyes in sometimes cluttered scenes. Much research has been carried out to accurately localize the eye-centers in the past decades. As we mentioned in the first section, these methods can be classified into three categories (Zhu & Ji, 2005): template based methods, feature based methods and appearance based methods. In this section, we will briefly review these state of the art techniques.

### 2.1 Template Based Methods

For the template based methods, a sliding window is moved over the whole image to match with a pre-designed generic eye model in order to detect the eye position. The detection performance highly depends on the design of eye model. Generally, the eye model is built upon some prior knowledge or a large eye database. Jorge et. al. (2007) applied the deformable template for eye detection. A novel eye template was proposed, which is represented by two distinct geometrical entities: a circumference, that defines the iris contour; and two parabolas, one concave and other convex, that define respectively, the above and below contours of the eye. The geometry shape of the eye model is controlled by a set of eleven parameters that allow its change in scale, position and orientation. Rurainsky & Eisert (2004) proposed a simplified deformable template, which is controlled by only 4 position parameters. This small number of parameters limits the range of changes and therefore the number of possible template shapes. Besides these artificial eye templates, natural eye templates taken from real persons are also used

(Moriyama et. al., 2006). These templates are commonly designed on a large eye database and thus in various orientations, sizes and illuminations. A preprocessing step is necessary to align and normalize the templates.

Obviously, template based methods are very time consuming since they have to match the whole face with an eye template pixel by pixel. This greatly restricts its application in real applications. Moreover, no matter what kind of templates are, they have different limitations in scale, comprehensiveness, and illumination variations. When facing a great challenge database in which faces expose to different scale, facial expressions, illumination conditions, and even cluttered scenes, the performance of template based methods will be hard to be satisfied. The deformable template approaches is more or less adaptive to the variety of image conditions and facial expressions. However, the weight factors for energy terms are determined manually. Improper selection of these terms will result in unexpected performance.

### 2.2 Feature Based Methods

Feature based methods focus on the characteristic of eyes, such as the shape, color distribution, and intensity gradient information around eye regions. Among these techniques (Kawaguchi, 2004; Khairosfaizal, 2009; Zhou, 2004) are Circle Hough Transform (CHT) and Projection Functions (PF).

### 2.2.1 Circle Hough Transform (CHT)

The circle formation of the iris is the most salient characteristic of eyes. Many approaches have been proposed to detect circular formation in an image by using CHT in order to localize eyes (Kawaguchi & Rizon, 2004; Khairosfaizal & Noraini, 2009). These approaches always start with applying an edge detector, like Sobel and Canny, to the original intensity image. Then CHT searches circular patterns over the edge image by a technique that is equivalent to a convolution between the edge image and a circle operator (Orazio et. al., 2004). Each edge point contributes a circle of radius R to an output accumulator space. The peak in the output accumulator space is detected where these contributed circles overlap at the center of the original circle. A number of modifications of CHT have been widely implemented in order to reduce the computational burden and the number of false positives. Kerbyson & Atherton (1995) used edge orientation information to limit the possible positions of the center for each edge point. In this way only an arc needs to be plotted perpendicular to the edge orientation at a distance R from the edge point, which reduces the computation requirements by plotting arcs in the accumulator space.

## 2.2.2 Projection Functions (PF)

Based on the observation that the eye regions, such as the boundary points between sclera and eyeball, have relatively higher change in intensity gradient than other face regions, PF, which is effective for capturing the intensity variation, attracts a lot of researcher's attention (Feng, 1998; Zhou & Geng, 2004).

Integral PF (IPF) is the one of the most popular PFs. Given a pixel at location $(x,y)$, the IPF between the intervals $[y_1,y_2]$ and $[x_1,x_2]$ in the horizontal and vertical directions are defined as follows:

$$
\begin{aligned}
IPF_v(x) &= \frac{1}{y_2 - y_1} \int_{y1}^{y2} I(x,y)dy \\
IPF_h(y) &= \frac{1}{x_2 - x_1} \int_{x1}^{x2} I(x,y)dx
\end{aligned}
\tag{1}
$$

where $I(x,y)$ is the intensity value at $(x,y)$. Although IPF is the most commonly used PF, it sometimes can not well reflect the intensity variation of an image. Feng and Yuen (1998) proposed the Variance PF (VPF), which is more sensitive to the

intensity variation. The VPF in the horizontal and vertical directions are defined as follows:

$$
\begin{aligned}
VPF_v(x) &= \frac{1}{y_2 - y_1} \sum_{y=y_1}^{y_2} \left\{ I(x,y) - IPF_v(x) \right\} \\
VPF_h(y) &= \frac{1}{x_2 - x_1} \sum_{x=x_1}^{x_2} \left\{ I(x,y) - IPF_h(y) \right\}
\end{aligned}
\tag{2}
$$

It is straightforward to find that IPF and VPF can be complementary with each other. IPF focuses on the mean of intensity while VPF focuses on the variance of intensity. Zhou and Geng (2004) proposed Generalized PF (GPF), which combines the advantage of both IPF and VPF. A parameter $0 \le \alpha \le 1$ was introduced to control the relative contribution of IPF and VPF. The GPF in the horizontal and vertical directions are defined as follows:

$$
\begin{aligned}
GPF_v(x) &= (1-\alpha)IPF_v(x) + \alpha VPF_v(x) \\
GPF_h(y) &= (1-\alpha)IPF_h(y) + \alpha VPF_h(y)
\end{aligned}
\tag{3}
$$

PFs are most effective to roughly locate the boundary of the eye regions. However, it is hard to localize the eye-center only using PFs. In addition, illumination variations have great effect on the performance of PFs.

## 2.3 Appearance Based Methods

Appearance based methods detect eyes based on their photometric appearance. These methods always need to train a classifier at first by collecting a large amount of training data and then detection is achieved via two-fold classification. Currently, Adaboost (Wang et. al., 2005; Wang & Ji, 2007) and Support Vector Machine (SVM) (Nguyen et. al., 2008; Zhang & Zhan, 2006) are two dominant learning methods in this category.

*Table 1. The Adaboost algorithm for classifier learning procedure*

- Given example images $(x_1, y_1), \ldots, (x_n, y_n)$ where $y_i = 0,1$ for negative and positive examples.

- Initialize weights $\omega_{1,i} = \dfrac{1}{2m}, \dfrac{1}{2l}$ for $y_i = 0,1$ respectively, where $m$ and $l$ are the number of negatives and positives respectively

- For $t = 1, \ldots, T$ :

  1. Normalize the weights $\omega_{t,i} \leftarrow \dfrac{\omega_{t,i}}{\sum_{j=1}^{n} \omega_{t,j}}$

  2. Select the best weak classifier with respect to the weight error
  $$\varepsilon_t = \min_{f,p,\theta} \sum_i \omega_i \left| h(x_i, f, p, \theta) - y_i \right|$$

  3. Define $h_t(x) = h(x, f_t, p_t, \theta_t)$ where $f_t$, $p_t$, and $\theta_t$ are the minimizers of $\varepsilon_t$

  4. Update the weights $\omega_{t+1,i} = \omega_{t,i} \beta_t^{1-e^i}$ where $e^i = 0$ if example $x_i$ is classified correctly, $e^i = 1$ otherwise, and $\beta_t = \dfrac{\varepsilon_t}{1-\varepsilon_t}$

- The final strong classifier is $C(x) = \begin{cases} 1 & \sum_{t=1}^{T} \alpha_t h_t(x) \geq \dfrac{1}{2} \sum_{t=1}^{T} \alpha_t \\ 0 & otherwise \end{cases}$ where $\alpha_t = \log \dfrac{1}{\beta_t}$

## 2.3.1 Adaboost

The Adaboost learning algorithm was first proposed by Freund and Schapire (1995) and is then widely used in Object Detection (Viola & Jones, 2001), Pedestrian Detection (Hou et. al., 2007) and face detection (Jones & Viola, 2003). Adaboost is able to boost the performance of simple classifier. It proceeds in rounds. On each round a week classifier that performs a little bit better than random guessing is chosen. A final strong classifier is built by combining a collection of weak classifiers in several rounds. Table 1 shows the learning procedure of Adaboost algorithm in detail.

However, Adaboost has some disadvantages when applied to real applications. First, it can not deal with large-scale training set because of its great time and space requirement; second, in some cases, especially when the characteristics of train-

ing samples vary in a large range, the convergence of the training procedure can not be guaranteed; finally, the speed of both training and testing procedure is very slow, which can not meet the real-time requirement.

## 2.3.2 Support Vector Machine (SVM)

Support Vector Machine (SVM), based on Statistical Learning Theory (SLT) (Vapnik, 1995), has been widely applied in solving recognition and object detection problems since it was proposed. Osuna et al. (1997) pioneered the research of face detection using SVM and demonstrated its generalization capability for face detection. Papageorgiou et al. (1998) developed a wavelet-based SVM method for pedestrian detection. Recently, Nguyen et al. (Nguyen et. al., 2008) presented a facial feature detection using optimal pixel reduction SVM, and Jia. et al. (2009) applied SVM to face recognition with interference of occlusions.

Given a set of training samples $x_i \in R^n$ and labels $y_i \in \{-1, 1\}, i = 1, 2, \ldots l$, the standard SVM builds up the optimal separating hyperplane $\omega^t \varphi(x) + b = 0$ by maximizing the geometric margin:

$$\max_{\omega, b} \frac{1}{\omega^t \omega} \quad (4)$$
$$subject\ to\ y_i(\omega^t \varphi(x_i) + b) \geq 1$$

where $\varphi(x)$ maps $x$ into a higher dimensional space.

Typically, the original training set will not be linearly separable. To address this problem, it is common to define a soft margin by including the slack variables $\xi_i \geq 0$ and a regularizing parameter $C > 0$,

$$\max_{\omega, b} \frac{1}{\omega^t \omega} + C \sum_{i=1}^{l} \xi_i$$
$$subject\ to\ y_i(\omega^t \varphi(x_i) + b) \geq 1 - \xi_i \quad (5)$$
$$\xi_i \geq 0,\ i = 1, 2, \ldots, l$$

Using a Largrangian, the optimization problem of (5) is solved by means of its dual, a quadratic convex programming (QP) problem:

$$\max_{\alpha} \sum_{i=1}^{l} \alpha_i - \frac{1}{2} \sum_{i,j=1}^{l} \alpha_i \alpha_j y_i y_j K(x_i, x_j)$$
$$subject\ to\ \sum_{i=1}^{l} y_i \alpha_i = 0 \quad (6)$$
$$0 \leq \alpha_i \leq C,\ i = 1, 2, \ldots, l$$

where $K(x_i, x_j) = \varphi(x_i)^t \varphi(x_j)$ is the kernel function. In order to solve the large QP problem of (6), a special optimizing algorithm, Sequential Minimization Optimization Algorithm (SMO), was proposed in (Keerthi & Shevade, 2003).

The decision function of SVM is defined as follows:

$$f(x) = \text{sgn}(\sum_{i \in SV} y_i \alpha_i K(x_i, x_j) + b) \quad (7)$$

where *SV* is the subscript set of support vectors.

Although the standard SVM exhibits many theoretical and practical advantages such as good generalization performance, when applied to complicated large scale classification problems, the decision function of SVM is over-complex, which leads to low computational efficiency and slower classification speed than other approaches. Much research has been carried out to simplify the SVM. We will discuss this issue in section 6 and propose a new efficient SVM (eSVM). To the best of our knowledge, eSVM, compared with currently existing simplified SVMs, has the best performance both in efficiency and accuracy when solving complicated large-scale classification problems.

## 3. OVERVIEW OF PROPOSED METHOD

In this chapter, we present a novel eye detection method using color information, 2D Haar wavelet, and eSVM. The proposed method combines both the feature and appearance based method so that it has the property of real-time and high accuracy. Figure 1 illustrates the system architecture of our proposed method. In particular, this method consists of two stages: feature based eye candidate selection and appearance based validation. In the candidate selection stage, 99% non-eye pixels are rejected through eye color distribution analysis in the YCbCr color space (Chamberlin, 1980). Only up to 1% pixels in an image as eye candidates enter the validation stage. Compared with the tradition appearance methods (Everingham & Zisserman, 2006) which move a sliding window

*Figure 1. System architecture of proposed eye detection method*

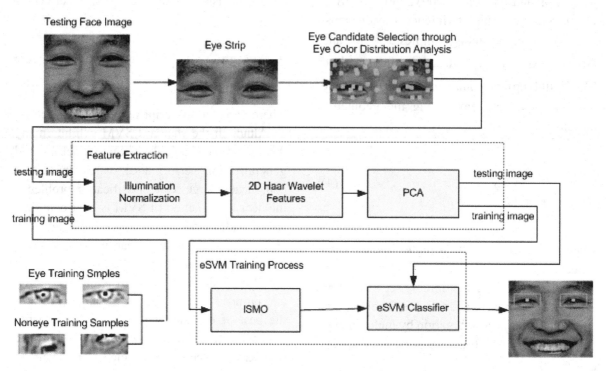

pixel by pixel over the whole image, the selection would greatly improve the validation efficiency and make the real-time possible. In the validation stage, 2D Haar wavelet (Viola & Jones, 2001) is used for multi-scale image representation and PCA (Stork et. al., 2000) is applied to extract the best features for representation while reducing their dimensionality. Previous research has proved that various effective image representations can provide more information for detection and recognition than just pixel-by-pixel intensity values. In section 5, several popular and effective image representation methods for object detection, like HOG (Dalal & Triggs, 2005), Gabor (Liu & Wechsler, 2002), and LBP (Ahonen et. al., 2006), are analyzed and compared with each other and the 2D Haar wavelet was chosen as the best for eye detection. Finally, a new efficient Support Vector Machine (eSVM) is proposed as the classifier. As we mentioned in Section 2.3.2, the classification speed of the standard SVM is slower than other approaches due to its complex

decision function. The eSVM, based on the idea of minimizing the maximum margin of misclassified samples, is defined on fewer support vectors than the standard SVM, which can achieve faster detection speed and comparable or even higher detection accuracy.

## 4. EYE CANDIDATE SELECTION

Conventional appearance based eye detection methods move a sliding window pixel by pixel over the whole image and each detection window is tested by a pre-trained classifier. Suppose the size of searched eye strip is 55*128 (the size used in our experiments). Totally, there are 7,040 classification operations for each image. This is very time-consuming due to the computation complexity of the statistical learning based classifier. In our method, we expect to first select a small amount of eye candidates per image according to

*Figure 2. The eye-tone distribution in the YCbCr color space. Blue dots represent skin pixels, green the eye region pixels, and red the pupil-center pixels.*

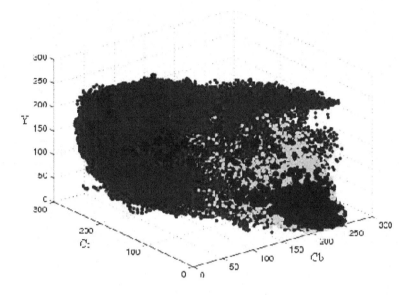

the characteristic of eyes before using classifier detecting them in the validation step.

In our method, the eye candidates are chosen through an eye color distribution analysis in the YCbCr color space. YCbCr color space is recently widely used in the face detection and recognition (Hsu et. al., 2002). In the YCbCr color space, the RGB components are separated into luminance (Y), chrominance blue (Cb), and chrominance (Cr). Previous researches show that the chrominance components of the skin-tone and eye-tone are independent of the luminance component. For the eye regions, especially for the pupil center, more pixels are with higher chrominance blue (Cb) and lower chrominance red (Cr) compared with the skin area. In addition, like in the gray-scale image, the luminance (Y) of eye region is much darker than other areas. In Figure 2, we manually collected random skin patches (4,078,800 pixels), eye regions (145,200 pixels), and pupil centers (1,200 pixels) from 600 face images of 128*128 to show our findings. Figure 2 reveals that the eye-centers, which are represented by red dots, are clustered in the right bottom corner with higher Cb value but lower Cr and Y values. Figure

3 shows some eye strip samples if the Y, Cb, and Cr channels are represented in RGB color space. We can find that the eye regions always have higher green values and lower blue value, which correspond to the Cb and Cr channel respectively. Therefore, we define a weight for each pixel in (8) and consider the first $K$ pixels with maximum weights as eye candidates.

$$weight(i,j) = \sum_{i-2,j-2}^{i+2,j+2} \begin{Bmatrix} Cb(i,j) \\ +(255 - Cr(i,j)) \\ +(255 - Y(i,j)) \end{Bmatrix}$$

(8)

In Figure 4, we compare the effectiveness and efficiency of our eye color distribution analysis method with other widely used feature based methods: one is GPF mentioned in section 2.3.1 (Zhou & Geng, 2004) and the other is a simple and effective intensity filter (IF) method proposed in (Wu & Zhou, 2003). IF is based on the observation that the eye region is usually much darker than other area of the face. Therefore, IF searches the lowest grayscale intensity over the whole

*Figure 3. Y, Cb, and Cr channels are presented in RGB color space*

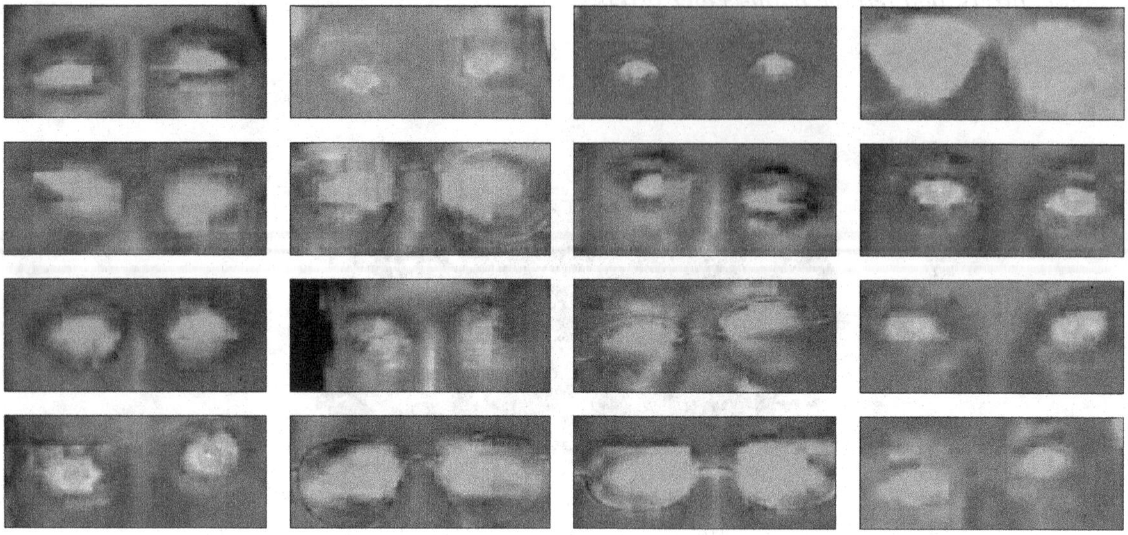

image. A threshold can be set up and pixels with lower intensity than the threshold can be considered eye candidates. Figure 4 shows that our method derives fewer candidates with better representation of the real eye locations: only 60 candidates per image, which account for only 0.85% of the whole image pixels, represent over 99% of the real eye locations, compared with 400 candidates representing 98% of the real eye locations by Wu & Zhou (2003) and 80% of the real eye locations by Zhou & Geng (2004), respectively.

## 5. DISCRIMINATORY IMAGE REPRESENTATIONS FOR EYES

Previous research (Liu, 2003) has proved that various image representations can provide more information for detection and recognition than just pixel by pixel intensity values. In this section, we analyze several state of the art image representation methods for eye detection, including Gabor Wavelet (Liu & Wechsler, 2002), HOG (Dalal & Triggs, 2005), LBP (Ahonen et. al., 2006), and 2D Haar Wavelet (Viola & Jones, 2001). In section 7, we do experiment to compare the performance among these representation methods, which proves that 2D Haar wavelet is most suitable for eye detection. Principal Component Analysis (PCA) used in our method is also presented in this section.

### 5.1 Gabor Wavelets

Gabor wavelets were introduced to image representation due to their biological relevance and computational properties (Daugman, 1988; Jones & Palmer, 1987). It is able to capture the local structure corresponding to spatial frequency (scale), spatial localization, and orientation selectivity. The Gabor wavelet can be defined as follows:

$$\psi_{\mu,\nu}(z) = \frac{\left\|k_{\mu,\nu}\right\|^2}{\sigma^2} e^{\left(-\left\|k_{\mu,\nu}\right\|^2\|z\|^2/2\sigma^2\right)} \left[e^{ik_{\mu,\nu}z} - e^{-\sigma^2/2}\right]$$

$$(9)$$

where the wave vector $k_{\mu,\nu} = k_\nu e^{i\varphi_\mu}$, $k_\nu = k_{max} / f^\nu$ ($k_{max}$ is the maximum frequency and $f$ is the spacing factor between kernels in the frequency domain), $\varphi_\mu = \pi\mu / 8$, $\mu$ and $\nu$ define the orientation and scale of the Gabor kernels, $z = (x,y)$, and $\|\cdot\|$

*Figure 4. Comparison among different eye candidate selection methods*

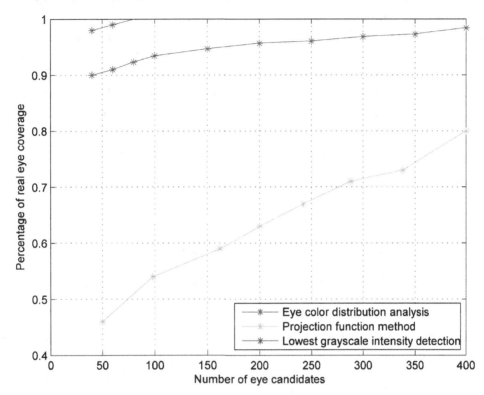

denotes the norm operator. In our experiment, we use Gabor wavelets of five different scales, $\nu \in \{0, \ldots 4\}$, and eight orientations, $\mu \in \{0, \ldots, 7\}$.

After the Gabor wavelets were built up, an image is convolution with a family of Gabor kernels as defined by (9). Given an image $I(x,y)$, its Gabor representation $S$ can be defined as follows:

$$O_{\mu,\nu}(z) = I(z) * \psi_{\mu,\nu}(z)$$
$$S = \{O_{\mu,\nu}(z), \ \mu \in \{0, \ldots, 7\}, \ \nu \in \{0, \ldots, 4\}\}$$

(10)

where $z = (x,y)$, * denotes the convolution operator.

## 5.2 Histogram of Oriented Gradient (HOG)

Histogram of Oriented Gradient (HOG) was first proposed by (Dalal & Triggers, 2005) for human

detection and shown that it can provide excellent performance relative to other existing feature representations including wavelets. Soon HOG was widely applied in general object and face detection (Zhu et. al., 2006).

HOG starts with gradient computation. Given an image $I(x,y)$, the gradient image is computed in the horizontal and vertical directions as follows:

$$G_h(x,y) = [-1 \quad 0 \quad 1] * I(x,y)$$
$$G_v(x,y) = [-1 \quad 0 \quad 1]^T * I(x,y)$$

(11)

The norm and orientation of the gradient in the location $(x,y)$ is defined as follows:

$$N_G(x,y) = \sqrt{G_h(x,y)^2 + G_v(x,y)^2}$$
$$\sigma_G(x,y) = \arctan\left(\frac{G_h(x,y)}{G_v(x,y)}\right)$$

(12)

Then the whole image is split into blocks and each block is further split into cells. For each cell, a histogram in terms of the gradient orientation is computed. The orientation values are evenly divided into $K$ bins in the range of $\left[-\dfrac{\pi}{2}, \dfrac{\pi}{2}\right]$. The histogram value for $k_{th}$ bin in a cell $C$ is computed as follows:

$$h_k(x,y) = \left\{ \sum_{(x,y) \in C} N_G(x,y), \ \sigma_G \in bin_k \right\} \qquad (13)$$

The final descriptor is obtained by normalizing all histograms within each block of cells and grouping all normalized histograms into a single vector.

## 5.3 Local Binary Pattern (LBP)

The LBP operator is one of the best textures performing descriptor (Ahonen et. al., 2004; Ahonen et. al., 2006). It has been proven to be highly discriminative. Its key advantage, namely, its invariance to monotonic gray scale changes and computational efficiency, makes it suitable for image analysis tasks.

LBP considers a local neighborhood around each pixel, thresholds the pixels of the neighborhood in terms of the central pixel intensity, and generates an image patch with binary values as image descriptor. It converts every 3*3 neighborhood of an image to an 8-bit-codes based binary value. Formally, given the central pixel $(x_c,y_c)$ and its surrounding pixels $(x_s,y_s)$,$s$=0,...,7, the LBP can be defined as follows:

$$LBP(x_c, y_c) = \sum_{s-0}^{7} 2^s \varphi(I(x_c,y_c) - I(x_s,y_s))$$
$$\varphi(u) = \begin{cases} 1 & if \ u \geq 0 \\ 0 & otherwise \end{cases}$$

$$(14)$$

where $I(\cdot)$ denotes the intensity value.

Two extensions of the basic LBP were further developed (Ahonen et. al., 2006). The first extension allows LBP to define on any size of neighborhood by using circular neighborhoods and bilinear interpolating the pixel values. The second extension defined the so-called *uniform patterns*. An LBP, when viewed as a circular bit string, is considered uniform if there are at most one transmission from 0 to 1 and one from 1 to 0. Combined with both above two extensions, LBP is commonly described as $LBP_{P,R}^{u2}$, where $u2$ represents using only uniform patterns and $P$ and $R$ represent $P$ sampling points on a circle of radius $R$.

## 5.4 2D Haar Wavelet

The Haar wavelet (Viola & Jones, 2001) is a natural set basis functions which encode the differences in average intensities between different regions in different scales. It has three kinds of representations in two dimension space as shown in Figure 5: (i) a two horizontal neighboring rectangular regions, which computes the difference between the sum of pixels within each of them, (ii) a two vertical neighboring rectangular regions, which computes the difference as (i) does, and (iii) a four neighboring rectangular regions, which computes the difference between diagonal pairs of rectangles. Please note that 2D Haar wavelet can be computed very rapidly using Integral Image proposed by Viola & Jones (2001).

In (Papageorgiou, 1998), an extension of 2D Haar wavelet based on overcomplete set of basis functions is proposed for pedestrian detection. It works not well on eye detection since eyes don't contain as much information as pedestrian and thus overcomplete features would capture more noise that leads to the decrease of the performance.

Compared with above mentioned representation methods, 2D Haar wavelet is more suitable to capture the structure characteristic of eyes in different scales: centered dark pupil is surrounded

*Figure 5. Examples of 2D Haar wavelet in different scale and locations*

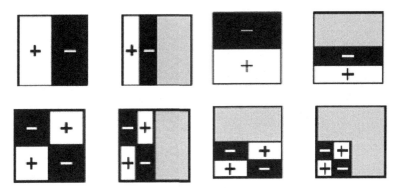

by a relatively white sclera. The comparison on detection accuracy among these features is shown in section 7.

## 5.5 Principal Component Analysis (PCA)

After the representing features are extracted, PCA is applied for dimensionality reduction. PCA is known as the best data representation in the least-square sense for classical recognition (Stork, 2000}. Let $Y \in R^N$ represents the extracted features. The covariance matrix of $Y$ is defined as follows:

$$\sum_Y = \varepsilon \left\{ \left[ Y - \varepsilon(Y) \right] \left[ Y - \varepsilon(Y) \right]^t \right\} \tag{15}$$

where $\varepsilon(\cdot)$ is the expectation operator and $\sum_Y \in R^{N*N}$. The PCA of a random vector Y factorizes the covariance matrix $\sum_Y$ into the following form:

$$\sum_Y = \Phi \Lambda \Phi \text{ with } \Phi = \left[ \varphi_1 \ \varphi_2 \cdots \varphi_N \right]$$
$$\Lambda = diag\{\lambda_1, \ \lambda_2, \ \cdots, \ \lambda_N\} \tag{16}$$

where $\Phi \in R^{N*N}$ is an orthogonal eigenvector matrix and $\Lambda \in R^{N*N}$ a diagonal eigenvalue matrix with diagonal elements in decreasing order ( $\lambda_1 \geq \lambda_2 \geq \ldots \geq \lambda_N$ ). An important application of PCA is dimensionality reduction:

$$Z = P^t Y \tag{17}$$

where $P = \left[ \varphi_1 \ \varphi_2 \cdots \varphi_m \right]$, $m < N$, and $P \in R^{N*m}$. In PCA, the eigenvectors corresponding to big eigenvalues always contains the most representing features of the original data. Therefore, the lower dimensional vector $Z \in R^m$ captures the most expressive information of the original data $Y$.

There exists an unsolved issue in PCA. Until now there is no standard criteria to determine how many principal component ($m$) should be used in (17). In one side, if $m$ is too small, the vector $Z$ can only present limited information in the original data and much information is lost after the dimension reduction. In the other side, if $m$ is too big, the vector $Z$ is likely to capture noise and thus affect the performance of the classifier. So it is needed to determine a proper $m$ to balance between the insufficient and overfull representation of original data in the PCA space. It is discussed above that the representing ability of eigenvectors depends on its corresponding eigenvalues. So we choose $m$ according to the distribution of eigenvalues. The selected eigenvalues should keep a proper balance in which it is big enough to account for most of the spectral energy of the raw data while

*Figure 6. The distribution of eigenvalues*

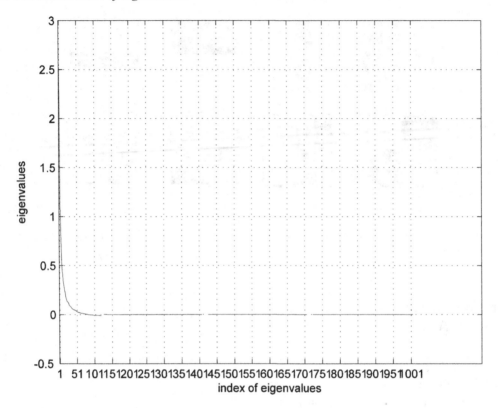

avoid to capture noise. In Figure 6, we take 2D Haar wavelet features as an example to show the distribution of eigenvalues since it was adopt in our detection system. The length of the original feature is 1,024. We can observe that the first 80 eigenvalues capture most of the energy and that the eigenvalues whose indices are greater than 100 are fairly small and most likely capture noise. So we set $m = 80$ in our experiments. Figure 9 in the experiment section shows the comparative performance of eye detection under different numbers of principal components.

## 6 EFFICIENT SUPPORT VECTION MACHINE (ESVM)

As we mentioned in Section 2.3.2, although the standard SVM exhibits many theoretical and practical advantages such as good generaliza-

tion performance, when applied to complicated large scale classification problems, the decision function of SVM is complex, which leads to low computational efficiency and slower classification speed than other approaches.

Much research has been carried out to simplify the SVM classification model and some simplified SVMs have been presented. Burges (Burges, 1996) proposed a method computing an approximation to the decision function in terms of a reduced set of vectors and decreasing the computation complexity of decision function by a factor of ten. Soon it was applied to handwritten digits recognition in (Scholkopf et. al., 1999) and face detection in (Romdhani et. al., 2001). However, this method does not only decrease the classification accuracy but also increased the computation cost to build up decision function since the computation of the optimal approximation costs much. Then a Reduced Support Vector Machine (RSVM) as an alternative of the standard SVM was proposed in (Lee & Mangasarian, 2001) and developed in (Lin & Lin, 2003). The authors generated a nonlinear kernel based separating surface (decision function) by solving a smaller optimization problem using a subset of training samples. RSVM works well when facing small classification problems but fails for large scale and complicated problems, since support vectors count great percentage of the whole training samples. In (Chen et. al., 2005), a new SVM, named $v-SVM$, was proposed. The relationship among the parameter $v$, the number of support vectors, and the classification error was analyzed. One disadvantage of this method is that it would reduce the generalization performance when the parameter $v$ is too small. Recently, Jayadeva & Khemchandani (2007) proposed a TWIN SVM for binary data classification. Although TWIN SVM is able to improve both the training speed and generalization performance, it can't do anything on improving testing speed and thus has same real-time trouble when applied to large-scale classification tasks.

In this section, we first analyze the key factor leading to the low efficiency of standard SVM. Then a new efficient SVM (eSVM) based on the idea of minimizing the maximum margin of misclassified samples is proposed. It is defined on fewer support vectors through a two step optimization procedure and thus can greatly improve the classification speed while maintaining comparable or even higher accuracy than standard SVM. To the best of our knowledge, eSVM, compared with currently existing simplified SVMs, has the best performance both in efficiency and accuracy when solving complicated large-scale classification problems.

## 6.1 Curse of the SV's Size

From (7), it is observed that the computation complexity of the decision function depends on the size of the support vectors (SV). The large size of SVs will greatly reduce the classification speed of SVM. SVs are defined as a subset of training samples whose corresponding $\alpha_i$ in (7) is not equal to zero.

According to Karush-Kuhn-Tucker (KKT) conditions in the optimization theory, the optimization problem of standard SVM defined in (6) should satisfy following equation:

$$\alpha_i \left[ y_i(\omega^t \varphi(x) + b) - 1 + \xi_i \right] = 0, \ i = 1, 2, \dots, l$$

$$(18)$$

where $\alpha_{i \neq} 0$ when $y_i(\omega^t \varphi(x) + b) - 1 + \xi_i = 0$. Because of the flexibility of the parameter $\xi_i$, the probability that $y_i(\omega^t \varphi(x) + b) - 1 + \xi_i = 0$ holds is very high, and thus $\alpha_i$ is more likely to get a nonzero value, which leads to the large size of SVs. More specifically, in (18), SVs are those samples between and on the two separating hyperplanes $\omega^t \varphi(x) + b = -1$ and $\omega^t \varphi(x) + b = 1$ (Figure 7). For complicated classification problem, since many misclassified samples exist between these two hyperplanes during the training procedure, the size of SVs will be very large.

Another potential harm of the large size of SVs is the possibility to reduce the classifier's generalization performance. It is known that previous classifiers like Neural Network mainly focused on the minimization of Empirical Risk, which emphasizes on minimizing the error rate on training samples. Therefore, the designed classifiers are easy to overfit on the training samples and thus may have poor generalization performance. SVM is developed based on the Structural Risk Theory (Vapnik, 1995), which is designed to keep a balance between seeking the best classifier on training samples and avoiding overfitting on them. However, large size of SVs may break this balance. Equation (7) indicates that large-sized SV will built up an overcomplex SVM model, which increases the possibility of overfitting and thus probably reduce its generalization performance.

*Figure 7. SVM in 2D space (red circles represent support vectors)*

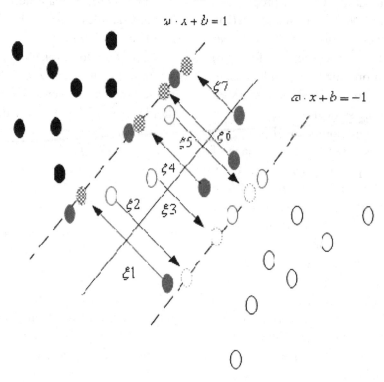

## 6.2 Efficient Support Vector Machine (ESVM)

Based on the idea of minimizing the maximum margin of misclassified samples, eSVM is built upon fewer support vectors while keeping the generalization performance of standard SVM.

Motivated by above analysis that it is the flexibility of the parameter $\xi_i$ that leads to the large size of support vectors, we propose our eSVM by executing second optimization of (5) as follows:

$$\max_{\omega,b} \frac{1}{\omega^t \omega} + C\xi$$

$$subject \ to \ y_i(\omega^t \varphi(x_i) + b) \geq 1, \ i \in V - MV$$

$$y_i(\omega^t \varphi(x_i) + b) \geq 1 - \xi, \ i \in MV, \ \xi \geq 0 \tag{19}$$

where $MV$ is the subscript set of the misclassified samples in standard SVM and $V$ is the subscript set of all training samples. Its dual quadratic convex programming problem is:

$$\max_{\alpha} \sum_{i=1}^{l} \alpha_i - \frac{1}{2} \sum_{i,j=1}^{l} \alpha_i \alpha_j y_i y_j K(x_i, x_j)$$

$$subject \ to \ \sum_{i \in V} y_i \alpha_i = 0 \ and \ \left( \sum_{i \in MV} \alpha_i \right) \leq C$$

$$0 \leq \alpha_i \leq C, \ i = 1, 2, \dots, l \tag{20}$$

Note that instead of the flexibility of the slack variables in (5), we set these slack variables to a fixed value in (19). Now the new KKT conditions of (19) become:

$$\alpha_i \Big[ y_i(\omega^t \varphi(x) + b) - 1 \Big] = 0, \ i \in V - MV$$

$$\alpha_i \Big[ y_i(\omega^t \varphi(x) + b) - 1 + \xi \Big] = 0, \ i \in MV \tag{21}$$

According to (21), $\alpha_i \neq 0$ when

$$y_i(\omega^t \varphi(x) + b) - 1 = 0, \quad i \in V - MV$$

or $y_i(\omega^t \varphi(x) + b) - 1 + \xi = 0, \quad i \in MV$ .

The support vectors are those samples on the two separating hyperplanes $\omega^t \varphi(x) + b = -1$ and $\omega^t \varphi(x) + b = 1$ and the misclassified samples farthest away from the hyperplanes (Figure 8). Therefore, the support vectors are much less than those defined by (7).

Compared with the standard SVM, which is defined on the compromise of least number of misclassified samples ($\min\limits_{\xi_i} C \sum\limits_{i=1}^{l} \xi_i$) and generalization performance ($\min\limits_{\omega,b} \frac{1}{2}\omega^t\omega$), the eSVM is defined on the compromise of the minimum margin of misclassified samples ($\min\limits_{\xi} C\xi$) and generalization performance ($\min\limits_{\omega,b} \frac{1}{2}\omega^t\omega$). The

eSVM pursues the minimal margin of misclassified samples and thus its decision function is more concise. Therefore, eSVM can be expected to achieve a little bit higher generalization performance than standard SVM. Experiments on eye detection in section 7 show that eSVM can achieve much faster detection speed and comparable or even higher detection accuracy than standard SVM.

We proposed an Improved Sequential Minimal Optimization algorithm (ISMO) to solve (20). ISMO breaks the large quadratic programming (QP) problem into a series of the smallest QP problems with size of two. These small QP problems are solved analytically, which avoids using a time-consuming numerical QP optimization. There are two key steps of ISMO: an analytic approach to solve the smallest QP problem with two Lagrange multipliers, and a heuristic approach to choose which two multipliers to optimize. For detailed

*Figure 8. eSVM in 2D space (red circles represent support vectors)*

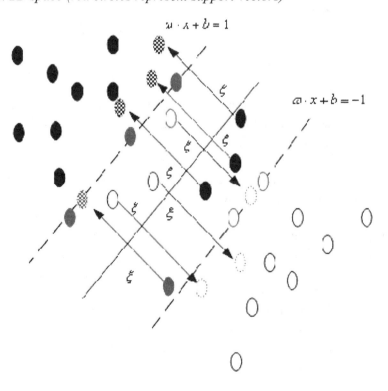

procedure of ISMO and complete assessment of eSVM, please refer to (Fang & Chen, 2006)

## 7. EXPERIMENTS

We verify our eye detection method on the Face Recognition Grand Challenge (FRGC) version 2 experiment 4, which contains both controlled and uncontrolled images (Phillips et. al., 2005). Note that while the faces in the controlled images have good image resolution and illumination, the faces in the uncontrolled images have lower image resolution and large illumination variations. In addition, facial expression changes are in a wide range from open eyes to closed eyes, from without glasses to with various glasses, from black pupils to red and blue pupils, from white skin to black skin, and from long hair to wearing a hat. All these factors increase the difficulty of accurate eye-center detection. In our experiments, we do the test on the whole training data set of FRGC 2.0, which contains 12,776 images. So there are 25,552 eyes totally to be detected. In order to train a robust eye detector, 3,000 pairs of eyes and 12,000 non-eye patches are collected as training samples from different sources.

As shown in Figure 1, a face is firstly detected using the Bayesian Discriminating Features method (BDF) in (Liu, 2003) and normalized to the size of 128*128. Then Geometric constraints are applied to localize the eyes, which means eyes are only searched in the top half (within the size of 55*128 in our experiment) of the detected face. The effect of illumination variations are alleviated by applying an illumination normalization procedure combining of the Gamma Correction, Difference of Guassian (DoG) filtering, and Contrast Equalization.

The first experiment we did is to prove our selection schema of principal component numbers ($m$) discussed in Section 5.5. Here, we only show the experiment results based on 2D Haar wavelets and SVM classifier. Other image representation

methods we mentioned in Section 5 have similar results. The length of original 2D Haar wavelet feature for each image is 1,024 in our experiment. In Section 5.5, we claimed that the optimal number of principal components should be around 80 since such amount of eigenvalues are able to capture most of the spectral energy of the raw data while avoid noise. In order to prove our claim, we did the experiment based on principal components with the size of 20, 40, 80, 200, and 400 respectively. The detection performance is shown in Figure 9. It indicates that when $m$ sets to 20, the detection accuracy is the lowest since lots of information is lost. As the $m$ increases, the detection accuracy goes up and reach the peak when $m$ is equal to 80. After 80, the detection rate goes down again since lots of noise is captured in the PCA space.

Then we evaluate the performance of eye detection among different image representing methods (2D Haar, HOG, Gabor, and LBP) and classifier (SVM and eSVM). According to our analysis on the selection of principal components, we set 80 out of 1024 principal components for 2D Haar wavelet, 400 of 10240 for Gabor, 80 of 1296 for HOG, and 59 of 59 for LBP. Please note that for HOG, we set 4*4 cells, 3*3 and 2/3 overlapping blocks, and 6 bin histogram for best performance. Figure 10 lists the comparison on performance through different localization error among different combination of representation methods and classifiers. From Figure 9, we can observe that 2D Haar wavelet is the most suitable representation for eye detection. Its average detection accuracy through different localization errors is higher than HOG by 1.76%, Gabor by 3.58%, and LBP by 40.25%, respectively. Figure 9 also indicates that the eSVM classifier has comparable or even higher detection accuracy no matter what representation method is applied. If we consider the eye is localized correctly when the Euclidean distance between the detected point and groundtruth is within 5 pixels, Table 2 lists the specific comparison on detection accuracy

*Figure 9. Performance comparison under different number of principal components based on 2D Haar*

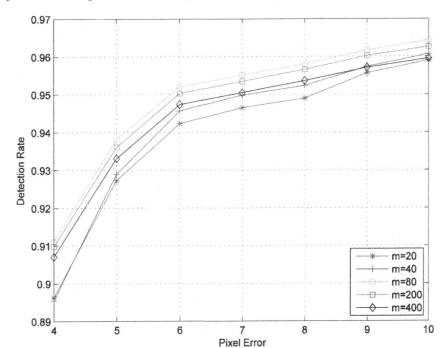

*Figure 10. Performance comparison among different methods*

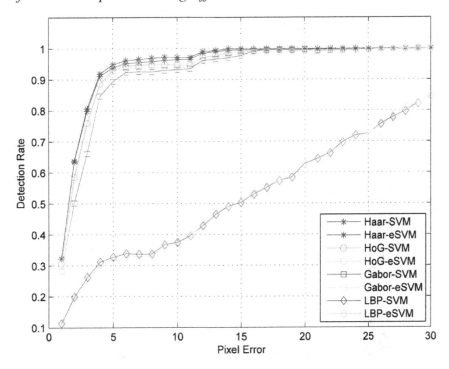

*Table 2. Performance comparison among different features and classifiers*

| Method \ Performance | # SVs | time (s) | time/image (s) | accuracy |
|---|---|---|---|---|
| 2D Haar + SVM | 9,615 | 112,729 | 3.04 | 93.82% |
| 2D Haar + eSVM | 267 | 5,991 | 0.16 | 94.92% |
| HOG + SVM | 4,898 | 56,025 | 1.51 | 92.91% |
| HOG + eSVM | 249 | 4,756 | 0.13 | 91.91% |
| Gabor + SVM | 11,086 | 632,093 | 17.06 | 89.41% |
| Gabor + eSVM | 514 | 34,902 | 0.94 | 89.16% |
| LBP + SVM | 11,844 | 112,854 | 3.05 | 32.78% |
| LBP + eSVM | 305 | 4,449 | 0.12 | 32.10% |

between SVM and eSVM under different representation methods.

Regarding the efficiency, eSVM performs much better than SVM under no matter what kind of representation method is applied. From Table 2, the size of support vectors of eSVM gets 97.23% reduced of SVM under 2D Haar Wavelet, 94.92% reduced under HoG, 95.36% reduced under Gabor, and 97.42% reduced under LBP. Because of the large size of support vectors, the computation complexity of standard SVM is very huge and real-time application is very hard to reach. Take the 2D Haar wavelet, which achieves the best detection accuracy, as an example, it takes 3.04 seconds (0.32 images per second) in average to process each image. However, by applying eSVM, the efficiency gets great improved and real-time becomes possible. It only takes 0.16 seconds (6.25 images per second) in average to process each

*Figure 11. Distribution of eye localization pixel errors*

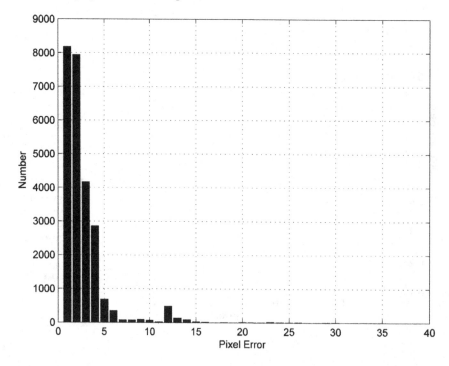

*Figure 12. Examples of detected eyes under various conditions. First two rows: blurred images; third row: various illumination conditions; fourth row: different races and skin colors; fifth and sixth rows: various facial expressions and poses; seventh and eighth rows: eyes with occlusions such as glasses and hair; ninth and tenth rows: closed eyes.*

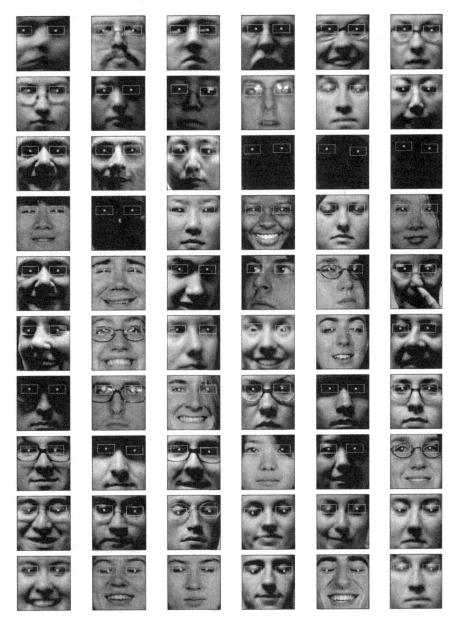

image under 2D Haar wavelet, which is 19 times faster than SVM.

In Figure 11, the distribution of the Euclidean distance of detected eyes compared to the ground truth is listed. The results are based on the 2D Haar wavelet + eSVM method that is proved to be the best in both performance and efficiency. The average Euclidean distance error is about 2.71 pixels. It is hard to make a quantitative comparison with other methods due to the different datasets

*Table 3. Comparison of eye localization error on x and y coordinates (ED stands for the Euclidean distance)*

| Method | Database | mean(x) | std(x) | mean(y) | std(y) | ED(mean) |
|---|---|---|---|---|---|---|
| Wang & Ji | FERET | 1.27 | 2.66 | 1.36 | 2.46 | N/A |
| Wang & Ji | FRGC 1.0 | 4.99 | 4.58 | 3.17 | 2.69 | 6.40 |
| Everingham | FERET | 1.29 | 1.28 | 1.04 | 1.29 | 2.04 |
| 2D Haar + eSVM | FRGC 2.0 | 2.39 | 2.43 | 1.41 | 1.42 | 2.71 |

used. Table 3 lists a typical comparison, with the boosting based method of Wang and Ji (2005), who report results on 400 images of FERET database and on 3000 images of FRGC 1.0 database, and with the Bayesian method of Everingham and Zisserman (Everingham, 2006), who report results on 1000 images of FERET database. Please note that the detection performance would decrease to some extent when the experiments do on large-scale and complicated dataset. This is can be seen from the Wang and Ji's report. When the same detection method is applied to the 3000 images of FRGC 1.0 database, the performance is worse than that on 400 images of FERET. Considering the FRGC 2.0 database we used has the huge size (12,776 images) and great compliancy (various illumination, pose and expression), our method indicates better and reliable performance. Finally, Figure 12 List some examples of the detection results.

## 8 CONCLUSION AND FUTURE WORK

In this chapter, we present a real-time accurate eye-center detection method in color images. First, the selection stage selects a small amount of eye candidates through an eye color distribution analysis in YCbCr color space. Then the validation stage applies 2D Haar wavelet for multi-scale image representation, PCA for dimension reduction, and eSVM for classification to detect the center of an eye. 2D Haar wavelet is proved to be the most suitable representation to capture the structure characteristic of eyes. eSVM is proposed to meet the real-time requirement while maintaining comparable or even higher accuracy than standard SVM. Experiments on FRGC database show the improved performance over existing methods on both efficiency and accuracy. Future work will focus on applying our eye detection method to an automatic face recognition system.

## REFERENCES

Ahonen, T., Hadid, A., & Pietikainen, M. (2004). Face recognition with local binary patterns. European Conference on Computer Vision, (pp. 469-481).

Ahonen, T., Hadid, A., & Pietikainen, M. (2006). Face descriptor with local binary patterns: Application to face recognition. *IEEE Transactions on Pattern Analysis and Machine Intelligence, 28*(12), 2037–2041. doi:10.1109/TPAMI.2006.244

Burges, C. J. C. (1996). *Simplified support vector decision rule*. IEEE International Conference on Machine Learning.

Chamberlin, G. J., & Chamberlin, D. G. (1980). *Colour: Its measurement, computation and application*. London, UK: Heyden & Son.

Chen, P. H., Lin, C. J., & Scholkopf, B. (2005). A tutorial on v-support vector machines. *Applied Stochastic Models in Business and Industry, 21*, 111–136. doi:10.1002/asmb.537

Dalal, N., & Triggs, B. (2005). Histograms of oriented gradients for human detection. *IEEE Int. Conf. on Computer Vision and Pattern Recognition,* (pp. 886-893).

Daugman, J. G. (1988). Complete discrete 2-D Gabor transforms by neural networks for image analysis and compression. *IEEE Transactions on Pattern Analysis and Machine Intelligence, 36,* 1169–1179.

Everingham, M., & Zisserman, A. (2006). *Regression and classification approaches to eye localization in face images.* Int. Conf. on Automatic Face and Gesture Recognition.

Fang, J. L., & Chen, S. (2006). A simplification to support vector machine for the second training. IEEE *International Conference on Artificial Reality and Telexistence,* (pp. 73-78).

Feng, G. C., & Yuan, P. C. (1998). Various projection function and its application to eye detection for human face recognition. *Pattern Recognition Letters, 19*(9), 899–906. doi:10.1016/S0167-8655(98)00065-8

Freund, Y., & Schapire, R. E. (1995). Experiments with a new boosting algorithm. The Thirteenth International Conference on Machine Learning, (pp. 148-156).

Hou, C., Ai, H. Z., & Lao, S. H. (2007). Multiview pedestrian detection based on vector boosting. *The 8th Asian Conference on Computer Vision,* (pp. 210-219).

Hsu, R. L., Abdel-Mottaleb, M., & Jain, A. K. (2002). Face detection in color images. *IEEE Transactions on Pattern Analysis and Machine Intelligence, 24*(5), 696–706. doi:10.1109/34.1000242

Jayadeva, R. K., & Khemchandani, R. (2007). TWIN support vector machines for pattern classification. *IEEE Transactions on Pattern Analysis and Machine Intelligence, 29*(5), 905–910. doi:10.1109/TPAMI.2007.1068

Jia, H. J., & Martinez, A. M. (2009). *Support vector machines in face recognition with occlusion.* IEEE International Conference on Computer Vision and Pattern Recognition.

Jones, J., & Palmer, L. (1987). An evaluation of the two dimensional gabor filter model of simple receptive fields in cat striate cortex. *Journal of Neural Networks, 58*(6), 1233–1258.

Jones, M. J., & Viola, P. (2003). *Face recognition using boosted local features.* IEEE International Conference on Computer Vision.

Jorge, F., Carvalho, S., Manuel, J., & Tavares, R. S. (2007). Eye detection using a deformable template in static images. *VIPimage - IECCOMAS Thematic Conference on Computational Vision and Medical Image Processing,* (pp. 209-215).

Kawaguchi, T., & Rizon, M. (2004). *An algorithm for real time eye detection in face images.* IEEE International Conference on Pattern Recognition.

Keerthi, S. S., & Shevade, S. K. (2003). SMO algorithm for least squares SVM. *IEEE International Joint Conference on Neural Networks, 3,* 2088–2093.

Kerbyson, D. J., & Atherton, T. J. (1995). *Circle detection using hough transform filter.* International Conference on Image Processing and Its Application.

Khairosfaizal, W. M. K. W. M., & Nor'aini, A. J. (2009). Eyes detection in facial images using circular hough transform. *IEEE Conference on Signal Processing and Its Application,* (pp. 238-242).

Lam, K. M., & Yan, H. (1996). Locating and extracting the eye in human face images. *Pattern Recognition, 29*(5), 771–779. doi:10.1016/0031-3203(95)00119-0

Lee, Y. J., & Mangasarian, O. L. (2001). *RSVM: Reduced support vector machines*. The First SIAM International Conference on Data Mining.

Lin, K. M., & Lin, C. J. (2003). A study on reduced support vector machine. *IEEE Transactions on Neural Networks, 14*(6), 1449–1559. doi:10.1109/TNN.2003.820828

Liu, C., & Wechsler, H. (2002). Gabor feature based classification using the enhanced \textsc{F} isher linear discriminant model for face recognition. *IEEE Transactions on Image Processing, 11*(4), 467–476. doi:10.1109/TIP.2002.999679

Liu, C. J. (2003). A Bayesian discriminating features method for face detection. *IEEE Transactions on Pattern Analysis and Machine Intelligence, 25*(6), 725–740. doi:10.1109/TPAMI.2003.1201822

Moriyama, T., Kanade, T., Xiao, J., & Cohn, J. F. (2006). Meticulously detailed eye region model and its application to analysis of facial images. *IEEE Transactions on Pattern Analysis and Machine Intelligence, 28*(5), 738–752. doi:10.1109/TPAMI.2006.98

Nguyen, M. H., Perez, J., & Frade, F. D. L. T. (2008). *Facial feature detection with optimal pixel reduction SVM*. IEEE International Conference on Automatic Face and Gesture.

Orazio, T. D., Guaragnellab, C., Leoa, M., & Distantea, A. (2004). A new algorithm for ball recognition using circle Hough transform and neural classifier. *Pattern Recognition, 37*, 393–408. doi:10.1016/S0031-3203(03)00228-0

Osuna, E., Freund, R., & Girosi, F. (1997). *Training support vector machines: An application to face detection*. IEEE International Conference on Computer Vision and Pattern Recognition.

Papageorgiou, C. P., Oren, M., & Poggio, T. (1998). *A general framework for object detection*. IEEE International Conference on Computer Vision.

Phillips, P. J., Flynn, P. J., & Scruggs, T. (2005). *Overview of the face recognition grand challenge*. IEEE Int. Conf. on Computer Vision and Pattern Recognition.

Phillips, P. J., Moon, H., Rizvi, S. A., & Rauss, P. J. (2000). The FERET evaluation methodology for face recognition algorithms. *IEEE Transactions on Pattern Analysis and Machine Intelligence, 22*(10), 1090–1104. doi:10.1109/34.879790

Romdhani, S., Torr, B., Scholkopf, B., & Blake, A. (2001). *Computationally efficient face detection*. IEEE International Conference on Computer Vision.

Rurainsky, J., & Eisert, P. (2004). *Eye center localization using adaptive templates*. IEEE Conference on Computer Vision and Pattern Recognition.

Scholkopf, B. (1999). Input space versus feature space in kernel-based methods. *IEEE Transactions on Neural Networks, 10*(5), 1000–1017. doi:10.1109/72.788641

Stork, D. G., Duda, R. O., & Hart, P. E. (2000). *Pattern classification*. Wiley, John, and Sons.

Vapnik, V. (1995). *The nature of statistical learning theory*. New York, NY: Springer-Verlag.

Viola, P., & Jones, M. (2001). *Rapid object detection using a boosted cascade of simple features*. IEEE Int. Conf. on Computer Vision and Pattern Recognition.

Wang, P., Green, M. B., Ji, Q., & Wayman, J. (2005). *Automatic eye detection and its validation*. IEEE International Conference on Computer Vision and Pattern Recognition.

Wang, P., Green, M. B., Ji, Q., & Wayman, J. (2005). Automatic eye detection and its validation. *IEEE International Conference on Computer Vision and Pattern Recognition*, (pp. 164–172).

Wang, P., & Ji, Q. (2005). *Learning discriminating features for multi-view face and eye detection*. IEEE Int. Conf. on Computer Vision and Pattern Recognition.

Wang, P., & Ji, Q. (2007). Multi-view face and eye detection using discriminant features. *Computer Vision and Image Understanding*, *105*(2), 99–111. doi:10.1016/j.cviu.2006.08.008

Wu, J. X., & Zhou, Z. H. (2003). Efficient face candidates selector for face recognition. *Pattern Recognition*, *36*(5), 1175–1186. doi:10.1016/S0031-3203(02)00165-6

Xie, X., Sudhakar, R., & Zhuang, H. (1994). On improving eye feature extraction using deformable templates. *Pattern Recognition*, *27*(8), 791–799. doi:10.1016/0031-3203(94)90164-3

Zhang, X. M., & Zhan, H. Y. (2006). *An illumination independent eye detection algorithm*. IEEE International Conference on Pattern Recognition.

Zhou, Z. H., & Geng, X. (2004). Projection function for eye detection. *Pattern Recognition*, *37*(5), 1049–1056. doi:10.1016/j.patcog.2003.09.006

Zhu, Q., Avidan, S., Yeh, M. C., & Cheng, K. T. (2006). *Fast human detection using a cascaded of histogram of oriented gradients*. IEEE International Conference on Computer Vision and Pattern Recognition.

Zhu, Z. W., & Ji, Q. (2005). Robust real-time eye detection and tracking under variable lighting conditions and various face orientations. *Computer Vision and Image Understanding*, *98*(1), 124–154. doi:10.1016/j.cviu.2004.07.012

## KEY TERMS AND DEFINITIONS

**Eye Detection:** Given an image, detect all eyes in it and locate their exact positions.

**Face Recognition:** A biometric technique that enables computer to recognize people by their facial characteristic.

**Face Recognition Grand Challenge (FRGC):** FRGC is a large-scale face database, which contains 12,776 training images, 16,028 target images, and 8,014 query images. It is conducted in an effort to promote and advance face recognition technology. FRGC has been a standard database to evaluate the performance of all kinds of face recognition technologies.

**Haar Wavelet:** The Haar wavelet is a natural set basis functions which encode the differences in average intensities between different regions in different scales.

**Principle Component Analysis (PCA):** PCA is the optimal method for dimensionality reduction in the sense of mean-square error. Its primary goal is to project the high dimensional data into a low dimensional space.

**Support Vector Machine (SVM):** SVM is a particular implementation of statistical learning theory, which describes an approach known as structural risk minimization by minimizing the risk functional in terms of both the empirical risk and the confidence interval.

**YCbCr Color Space:** YCbCr color space is defined by means of transformation from the original RGB color space. In YCbCr, the RGB components are separated into luminance (Y), chrominance blue (Cb) and chrominance red (Cr).

# Chapter 17
# Emotion Recognition from Facial Expression and Electroencephalogram Signals

**Amit Konar**
*Jadavpur University, India*

**Aruna Chakraborty**
*St. Thomas' College of Engineering & Technology, India*

**Pavel Bhowmik**
*Jadavpur University, India*

**Sauvik Das**
*Jadavpur University, India*

**Anisha Halder**
*Jadavpur University, India*

## ABSTRACT

*This chapter proposes new approaches to emotion recognition from facial expression and electroencephalogram signals. Subjects are excited with selective audio-visual stimulus, responsible for arousal of specific emotions. Manifestation of emotion which appears in facial expression and EEG are recorded. Subsequently the recorded information is analyzed for extraction of features, and a support vector machine classifier is used to classify the extracted features into emotion classes. An alternative scheme for emotion recognition directly from the electroencephalogram signals using Duffing Oscillator is also presented. Experimental results are given to compare the relative merits of the proposed schemes with existing works.*

## INTRODUCTION

Emotions represent internal psychological states of the human mind (Gordon, 1990). Recognition of human emotion from its external manifestations, such as facial expressions, voice, and physiological signals is a complex decision making problem. Several approaches to solve this problem have been attempted, but no satisfactory solution is known until this time. Usually, emotion recognition is regarded as a pattern classification/ clustering problem. So, like classical pattern classification, here too, we extract representative

DOI: 10.4018/978-1-61350-429-1.ch017

features from the external manifestation of the subject, pre-process them, and then feed them to a classifier to classify the manifestation into one of many possible emotion classes, such as anger, fear, happiness and the like. The main hurdles in emotion recognition lie in identification of the features, designing appropriate pre-processing/ filtering algorithms to segregate the emotive components from the natural ambiance, and selection of the most appropriate classification/clustering algorithm to classify the emotions from their measured attributes.

Although there is a vast literature on each of the above sub-problems, emotion recognition is still a hard problem for the following reasons. First, the level of ambience of individuals differs significantly. For example, the physiological conditions including blood pressure, body temperature, electrocardiogram (ECG), electromyogram (EMG) and electroencephalogram (EEG) of individual subjects in presence and absence of a specific emotive experience widely vary, and thus finding a generic consensus for the ambience is not always easy. Further, a subject experiencing similar emotions at different time often is found to have significant differences in his/her external manifestations. Naturally, accurately identifying one's correct emotional state from the measurements of his/her physiological conditions is also difficult. Moreover, subjects excited with stimulus responsible for arousal of a specific emotion, sometimes have a manifestation for mixed emotions. Recognition of emotion becomes more complex, when the subjects arouse mixed emotions.

The early research on emotion recognition was mainly confined in facial expression analysis (Ekman and Friesen, 1975; Fernandez-Dols et al. 1991; Black and Yacoob, 1997; Essa and Pentland, 1997; Donato et al. 1999; Zeng et al., 2006). This period continued for around two decades. The primary aim of emotion research at this period was to study the performance of the recognition algorithms. As a sequel, several

classification algorithms involving neural nets (Kobayashi and Hara, 1993; 1993a; 1993b; Ueki et al. 1994; Kawakami et al. 1994, Rosenblum et al. 1996; Uwechue and Pandya, 1997; Chakraborty, 2009b), fuzzy sets (Izumitani, 1984), and optic flow (Mase, 1991; Yacoob and Dadvis, 1996; Sprengelmeyer, 1998) have been attempted to solve the emotion recognition problem. Since the beginning of the millennium, researchers took active interest in designing algorithms for emotion recognition from multiple sources, including facial expression, voice and physiological signals, such as pulse rate, body temperature and ECG (Takahashi, 2004; Kollias and Karpouzis, 2005; Castellano et al. 2007). Almost at the same period, a small fraction of emotion researchers attempted to develop a new firmware for emotion recognition/synthesis for possible integration in the next generation human-computer interactive (HCI) systems (Lisetti and Schiano, 2000; Cowie et al., 2001; Brave and Nass, 2002). The next generation computers are thus expected to be smarter than the traditional ones, as they would have the potential to recognize the emotion of the users, and synthesize its emotional reaction to the user input. Bashyal and Venayagamoorthy (2008) employed Gabor wavelet and learning vector quantization for recognition of facial expression.

In 1997 Picard, coined the name: affective computing (Picard, 1997) for the subject dealing with emotions. According to her, the role of affective computing in HCI systems is to monitor the affective states of people, and provide them necessary support in critical/accident-prone environment. One interesting work in this regard is due to Li and Ji (2005), where the authors proposed a probabilistic framework to dynamically model and recognize the users' affective states for timely and efficient services to those people. Picard et al. (2001) also stressed the importance of emotions on our respective affective psychological states. Among others, the works of Scheirer et al. (2002), Conati (2002), Krammer et al. (1987), and Rani et al. (2004; 2007) also deserve special applause in the fields of affective computing.

Besides affective computing, the study of emotions and emotional intelligence (Goleman, 1995) has important applications in psychological counseling, detection of anti-socials, digital movie making with artificial agents, and many others. Details of this are available in Chakraborty and Konar (2009).

Cohen et al. considered variations in facial expressions, displayed in a live video to recognize emotions (2000; 2000a; 2003). She came up with a new architecture of hidden Markov models. It automatically segments and recognizes facial expressions, thus helping in emotion recognition. Gao et al. (2003) attempted to interpret facial expression from a single facial image using line-based caricatures. Lanitis et al. (1997) proposed a novel technique for automatic recognition and coding of face images using flexible models. Chakraborty et al. (2009) employed fuzzy relational algebra for recognition of emotion from facial expression of subjects with a good recognition accuracy of around 96%.

McGilloway et al. (2000) proposed a method for recognition of emotion from voice of the subjects with the help of discriminant analysis that uses linear combinations of variables to separate samples that belong to different categories using neural net classifiers. Petrushin (2000) proposed an approach of emotion recognition from voice data. He used a part of a corpus for extracting the features and for training computer-based emotion recognizers. He then took some of the features and fed them as inputs to different types of recognizers, ultimately concluding that the neural network based recognizers work best. Fellenz et al. (2000) and Busso and Narayanan (2007) considered both facial expression and voice for emotion recognition.

Among the well known schemes for emotion recognition from biopotential signals, the work by Haag et al. (2004) needs special mention. They obtained a very high recognition accuracy of 96%

using a large number of multi-sensory data, including electromyograms (EMG), skin-conductivity, skin temperature, blood volume pulse, electrocardiogram (ECG) (Rippon, 2006) and respiration rate. Li and Chen (2006) too designed a scheme for emotion recognition using physiological signals, including ECG, skin temperature, skin conductance and respiration rate with an accuracy of 85.3%. Dolan et al. considers conditioning of faces using magnetoencephalogram (MEG).

Recently Zhang and Lee (2009) employed brain imaging techniques, such as functional Magnetic Resonance Imaging (fMRI) and electroencephalogram (EEG) to recognize emotion of subjects excited by natural scenes. Murugappan et al. (2009) considered EEG based emotion recognition, using audio-visual stimulus with a reported recognition accuracy of around 66%. There exists a vast literature on emotion recognition, all of which cannot be included here for lack of space.

In this chapter, we present two different approaches for emotion recognition. Section II provides a scheme for bimodal emotion recognition from facial expression and EEG signal. In section III, we present a scheme for multimodal emotion recognition using facial expression and voice as input. Section IV presents a novel scheme for emotion recognition from EEG data only using Duffing oscillator. Conclusions are listed in section V.

## MULTIMODAL EMOTION RECOGNITION

Facial expression based emotion recognition is most popular for its simplicity in data collection. However, facial expression does not always carry sufficient information for emotion recognition. We in this section, consider facial expression and EEG of the subjects for emotion recognition. The process of emotion recognition from multiple data sources is usually referred to as multimodal in the literature (Chakraborty and Konar, 2009).

The multimodal emotion recognition has a fundamental advantage of having more information about the subject's mental state. On occasions, however, the modal data do not have a good parity. For example, the elicited emotion in facial expression may represent happiness, whereas the EEG data may vote for anger. A confusion matrix (Busso et al., 2004) is often used to determine the degree of similarity/dissimilarity in multimodal information content.

In this chapter, we however address the multimodal emotion recognition from a different angle. We use the same facial features as used in face recognition, and additional features from EEG, and use Principal Component Analysis (PCA) (Konar, 2005) technique to reduce the number of features. A linear Support Vector Machine (SVM) Classifier is then used to classify the reduced feature set into emotions.

## The Experimental Set-Up

A small research team at Artificial Intelligence Laboratory of Jadavpur University started working on multi-modal emotion recognition from EEG and facial expression of the subjects

(Chakraborty and Konar, 2009). The experimental set-up includes a PC-based stimulator, capable of presenting audio-visual stimulus to the subjects to excite different emotions. A 10-20 EEG system (Murugappan, 2009a) is used to record EEG signal at F3 (or F4) electrode position, and a high resolution pan-tilt type camera is used to capture the facial expression of the subjects during the period of the audio-visual presentation (Figure 1). The experiment was conducted with 7 subjects. Six snapshots were taken to determine the significant changes in the facial expression conveying emotion. For each facial expression, the features extracted include mouth-opening, eye-opening, and the length of eyebrow-constriction. Thus, for 6 frames, altogether 3×6=18 features were obtained. Further, during the same period of time, 162 EEG features are extracted. Now, the experiment was undertaken for 5 different emotions: anger, disgust, fear, happiness, and sadness, over 7 different individuals. Consequently, 5×7=35 distinct feature vectors of 162+18=180 dimension were obtained to describe 5 distinct emotions of 7 subjects. Figure 6 represents sample facial expression for 5 distinct emotions of a subject.

*Figure 1. Experimental set-up*

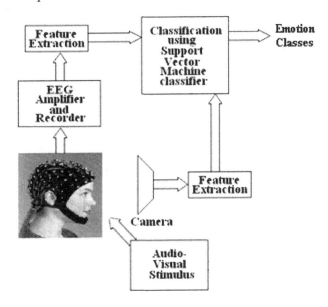

## Stimulus Selection

Prior experiments were undertaken over the last two years to identify the appropriate audio-visual movie clips that cause arousal of five different emotions: anxiety, disgusting, fear, happiness, and sadness.. A questionnaire was prepared to determine the consensus of the observers about the arousal of the above five emotions using a given set of audio-visual clips. It includes questions to a given observer on the percentage level of excitation of different emotions by a set of sixty audio-visual movie clips. The independent response of 50 observers from different students, faculties, non-teaching staff and family members of the staff of Jadavpur University were taken, and the results obtained from the questionnaire is summarized in the format of Table I. It is apparent from Table I that row- sum assigned to the emotions by a subject should be hundred (Chakraborty, A., 2009c).

To identify the right movie clip capable of exciting specific emotion, we now need to define a few parameters with respect to Table I, which would clearly indicate a consensus of the observers about an arousal of the emotion.

Let

$O_{ij,k}$ = percentage level of excitation of emotion j by an observer k using audio-visual clip i,

$E_{ji}$ = Average percentage score of excitation assigned to emotion j by n-no. of observers using clip i,

$\sigma_{ji}$ = standard deviation of the percentage score assigned to emotion j by all the subjects using clip i,

n = total no. of subjects, assessing emotion arousal.

Then $E_{ji}$ and $\sigma_{ji}$ are evaluated using the following expressions.

$$E_{ji} = \sum_{k=1}^{n} O_{ij,k} / n \qquad (1)$$

*Table 1. Assessment of the arousal potential of selected audio-visual movie clips in exciting different emotions*

| Subjects used to access the emotion aroused by the audio-visual clips | Title of audio-visual clips | Percentage arousals of different emotions by a clip | | | | |
|---|---|---|---|---|---|---|
| | | Anger | Relax | Joy | Sad | Fear |
| Subject 1 | Clip 1 | 0 | 20 | 80 | 0 | 0 |
| Subject 2 | Clip 1 | 0 | 25 | 75 | 0 | 0 |
| ... | | | | | | |
| Subject 50 | Clip 1 | 0 | 12 | 88 | 0 | 0 |
| Subject 1 | Clip 2 | 0 | 82 | 0 | 9 | 9 |
| Subject 2 | Clip 2 | 0 | 80 | 0 | 12 | 8 |
| ... | | | | | | |
| Subject 50 | Clip 2 | 0 | 84 | 0 | 10 | 6 |
| ... | | | | | | |
| Subject 1 | Clip 60 | 78 | 10 | 0 | 0 | 12 |
| Subject 2 | Clip 60 | 80 | 16 | 0 | 0 | 4 |
| Subject 50 | Clip 60 | 84 | 8 | 0 | 0 | 8 |

$$\sigma_{ji} = \sqrt{\sum_{k=1}^{n} \left(O_{ji,k} - E_{ji}\right)^2 / n} \qquad (2)$$

Now, to determine $E_{wi}$, i.e. the largest percentage average assigned to an emotion using audio-visual clip i, we compare $E_{ji}$s, and identify $E_{wi}$, such that $E_{wi} \geq E_{ji}$ for all j. Consequently, the emotion w, for which $E_{wi} \geq E_{ji}$ for all j, is the most likely aroused emotion due to excitation by audio-visual clip i. The above process is then repeated for 60 audio-visual clips, used as stimulators for the proposed experiments.

We next select only six audio-visual movies from the pool of 60 movie samples, such that the selected movies best excite six specific emotions. The selection was performed from the measure of average to standard deviation ratio for competitive audio-visual clips used for exciting the same emotion. The audio-visual clip for which the average to standard deviation ratio is the largest is considered to be the most significant sample to excite a desired emotion. We formalize this as follows.

For a specific emotion m, we determine $E_{mi}/\sigma_{mi}$ where the audio-visual clip i best excites emotion m, i.e., $E_{mi} \geq E_{ji}$, for any emotion j. Now, to identify the clip k that receives the best consensus from all the subjects, we evaluate $E_{mi}/\sigma_{mi}$ for all possible clips i that best excites emotion m. Let S be the set of possible samples, all of which best excite emotion m. Let k be a sample in S, such that $E_{ki}/\sigma_{ki} \geq E_{mi}/\sigma_{mi}$ for i$\in$S. Then we consider the k-th audio-visual movie sample to be the right choice to excite emotion m. This process is repeated to identify the most significant audio-visual movie sample for the stimulation of individual emotions. The facial expressions of the subjects recorded for the various stimuli are given in Figure 8 for one lady in the age group 22-25 years.

## Feature Extraction

Identification of facial expressions by pixel-wise analysis of images is both tedious and time consuming. This chapter attempts to extract significant components of facial expressions through segmentation of the image. Because of the differences in the regional profiles on an image, simple segmentation algorithms, such as histogram-based thresholding techniques, do not always yield good results. After conducting several experiments, we concluded that for the segmentation of the mouth region, a color-sensitive segmentation algorithm is most appropriate. Further, because of apparent non-uniformity in the lip color profile, a fuzzy segmentation algorithm is preferred. A color-sensitive fuzzy C-means clustering algorithm has therefore been selected for the segmentation of the mouth region.

Segmentation of eye-regions, however, in most images has been performed successfully by the traditional thresholding method. The hair region in human face can also be easily segmented by the thresholding technique. Segmentation of the mouth and the eye regions is required for subsequent determination of mouth-opening and eye-opening respectively. Segmentation of the eyebrow region is equally useful in determining the length of eyebrow constriction. The details of the segmentation techniques of different regions are presented below.

## Segmentation of the Mouth Region

Before segmenting the mouth region, we first represent the image in the L*a*b space from its conventional RGB space. The L*a*b system has the additional benefit of representing a perceptually uniform color space. It defines a uniform matrix space representation of color so that a perceptual color difference is represented by the Euclidean distance. The color information, however, is not adequate to identify the lip region. The position information of pixels together with their color would be a good feature to segment the lip region from the face. The fuzzy-C means (FCM) clustering algorithm that we employ to detect the lip region is supplied with both color and pixel-position information of the image.

The FCM clustering algorithm is a well-known technique for pattern classification. But its use in image segmentation in general and lip region segmentation in particular is a virgin area of research. A description of the FCM clustering algorithm can be found in books and papers on fuzzy pattern recognition (Bezdek, 1973; Klir and Yuan, 1995; Yamada, 1993; Pedrycz and Oliveria, 2008). Here, we just demonstrate how to use FCM clustering in the present application.

A pixel Here is denoted by five attributes: three attributes of color information (L*a*b) and two attributes of position information (x, y). The objective of the clustering algorithm is to classify the set of 5-dimensional data points into two classes/partitions - the lip region and the non-lip region. Initial membership values are assigned to each 5-dimensional pixel, such that the sum of the memberships in the two regions is equal to one. That is, for the $k^{th}$ pixel $x_k$,

$$\mu_L(x_k) + \mu_{NL}(x_k) = 1 \tag{3}$$

where $\mu_L(x_k)$ and $\mu_{NL}(x_k)$ denote the membership of $x_k$ to fall in the lip and the non-lip regions, respectively.

Given the initial membership values of $\mu_L(x_k)$ and $\mu_{NL}(x_k)$ for k = 1 to $n^2$ (assuming that the image is of size n × n), we use the FCM algorithm to determine the cluster centers, $V_L$ and $V_{NL}$, of the lip and the non-lip regions:

$$V_L = \sum_{k=1}^{n^2} [\mu_L(x_k)]^m x_k \Big/ \sum_{k=1}^{n^2} [\mu_L(x_k)]^m \tag{4}$$

And

$$V_{NL} = \sum_{k=1}^{n^2} [\mu_{NL}(x_k)]^m x_k \Big/ \sum_{k=1}^{n^2} [\mu_{NL}(x_k)]^m \tag{5}$$

Expressions (4) and (5) provide centroidal measures of the lip and non-lip clusters, evaluated over all data points xk for k=1 to n2. The parameter m (>1) is any real number that affects the membership grade. The membership values of pixel $x_k$ in the image for the lip and the non-lip regions are obtained from the following formulae:

$$L(x_k) = \left( \sum_{j=1}^{2} \left\{ \frac{|| x_k - v_L ||^2}{|| x_k - v_J ||^2} \right\}^{1/(M-1)} \right)^{-1} \tag{6}$$

$$NL(x_k) = \left( \sum_{j=1}^{2} \left\{ \frac{|| x_k - v_{NL} ||^2}{|| x_k - v_J ||^2} \right\}^{1/(M-1)} \right)^{-1} \tag{7}$$

where $V_j$ denotes the j-th cluster center for j∈{L, NL}.

Determination of the cluster centers (by (4) and (5)) and membership evaluation (by (6) and (7) are repeated several times following the FCM algorithm until the positions of the cluster centers do not change further (Chakraborty, 2005).

Figure 2 presents a section of a facial image with a large mouth opening. This image is passed through a median filter and the resulting image is shown in Figure 3. Application of the FCM algorithm to the image in Figure 3 yields the image in Figure 4. Figure 5 demonstrates the computation of mouth opening.

## Segmentation of the Eye-Region

The eye-region in a monochrome image has a sharp contrast to the rest of the face. Consequently, the thresholding method can be employed to segment the eye-region from the image. Images grabbed at poor illumination conditions have a very low average intensity value. Segmentation of the eye

*Figure 2. The original face image*

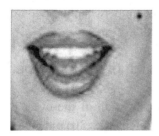

*Figure 3. The median-filtered image*

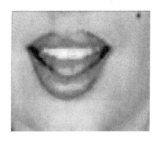

*Figure 4. The image after applying fuzzy C-means clustering*

region in these cases is difficult because of the presence of dark eyebrows in the neighborhood of the eye region. To overcome this problem, we consider images grabbed under good illuminating conditions. After segmentation in the image is over, we need to localize the left and the right eyes on the image. In this chapter, we use a template-matching scheme to localize the eyes. The eye template we used looks like Figure 6. The template-matching scheme, taken from our previous works (Biswas et al. 1995; Konar, 2005), attempts to minimize the Euclidean distance between a fuzzy descriptor of the template and the fuzzy descriptor of the part of the image where the template is located. Even when the template is not a part of the image, the nearest matched location of the template in the image can be traced.

## Localization of Eyebrow-Constriction Region

In a facial image, eyebrows are the second darkest region after the hair region. The hair region is easily segmented by setting a very low threshold in the histogram-based thresholding algorithm. The eye regions are also segmented by thresholding. A search for a dark narrow template can easily localize the eyebrows. Note that the localization

*Figure 5. Measurement of mouth opening from the dips in average intensity plot*

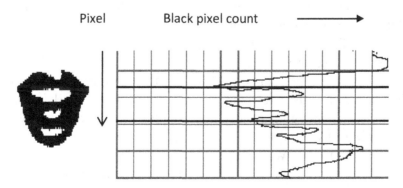

*Figure 6. A synthetic eye template*

of the eyebrow is essential for determining its length. This will be undertaken in the next section.

# EXTRACTION OF FACIAL ATTRIBUTES

In this section, we present a scheme for measurements of facial extracts such as mouth-opening (MO), eye-opening (EO) and the length of eyebrow-constriction (EBC).

## Determination of the Mouth-Opening

After segmentation of the mouth region, we plot the average intensity profile against the mouth opening. The dark region in the segmented image represents the lip profile, whereas the white regions embedded in the dark region indicate the teeth. Noisy images, however, may include false white patches. Figure 4, for instance, includes a white patch on the lip region. Determination of MO in a black and white image is easier because of the presence of the white teeth. A plot of the average intensity profile against the MO reveals that the curve has several minima, out of which the first and the third correspond to the inner region of the top lip and the inner region of the bottom lip, respectively. The difference between the above two measurements along the Y-axis gives a measure of the MO. An experimental instance of MO is shown in Figure 5 where the pixel count between the thick horizontal lines gives a measure of MO. When no white band is detected in the mouth region, MO is set to zero. When only two minima are observed in the plot of average intensity, the gap between the two minima is the measure of MO.

## Determination of the Eye-Opening

After the localization of the eyes, the count of dark pixels (intensity < 30) plus the count of the white pixels (intensity > 225) is plotted against the x-position. If the peak of this plot occurs at x = a, then the ordinate at x = a provides a measure of the eye-opening the details of which is given in (Chakroborty, 2009a).

## Determination of the Length of Eyebrow-Constriction

Constriction in the forehead region can be explained as a collection of white and dark patches called hilly and valley regions, respectively. The valley regions are usually darker than the hilly regions. Usually the width of the patches is around 10-15 pixels for a given facial image of $512 \times 512$ pixels.

Let $I_{av}$ be the average intensity in a selected rectangular profile on the forehead and $I_{ij}$ the intensity of pixel (i, j). To determine the length of eyebrow constriction on the forehead region, we scan for variation in intensity along the x-axis of the selected rectangular region. The maximum x-width that includes variation in intensity is defined as the length of *eyebrow-constriction*. The length of the eyebrow constriction has been measured in Figure 7 by using the above principle. An algorithm for eyebrow-constriction is presented below.

1. Take a narrow strip over the eyebrow region with thickness two-thirds the width of the forehead, determined by the maximum count of pixels along the length of projections from the hairline edge to the top edges of the eyebrows.
2. The length $l$ of the strip is determined by identifying its intersection with the hair

*Figure 7. Eyebrow constriction*

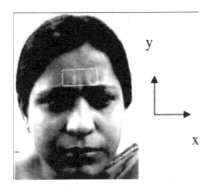

regions at both ends. Determine the center of the strip, and select a window of x-length $2l/3$ symmetric with respect to the center.

3. For x-positions central to window-right-end do

*Figure 8. Arousal of anxiety, disgust, fear, happiness, and sadness (row-wise) by audio-visual stimulus*

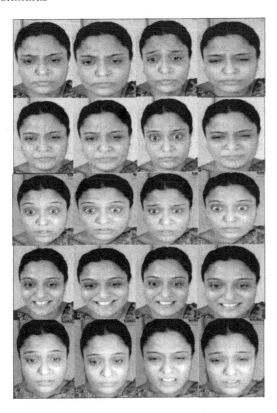

Select 9 vertical lines in the window and compute average intensity on each line;

Calculate the variance of the 9 average intensity values;

If the variance is below a threshold, stop;

Else shift one pixel right;

4. Determine the total right shift;
5. Following a procedure similar to step 3, determine the total left shift.
6. Compute length of eyebrow-constriction = total left shift + total right shift.

## Extraction of EEG Features

Both time- and frequency- domain features are extracted from the EEG signal. The frequency-domain features include peak power and average powers of $\delta$ (0-4 Hz), $\theta$ (4-8Hz), lower $\alpha$ (8-10Hz), upper $\alpha$ (10-12Hz), $\beta 1$ (12-16Hz), $\beta 2$ (16-24Hz), $\gamma$ (24-32 Hz) bands (Murugappan, 2009; 2009a), while the time-domain features include 16 Kalman filters coefficients, and spatio-temporal features include 132 wavelet coefficients (Bhowmik, 2009). Thus the total number of EEG features is 162. The details of EEG feature extraction are available in (Chakraborty, 2009).

## EMOTION CLASSIFICATION BY SUPPORT VECTOR MACHINE

### Support Vector Machine (SVM)

An SVM has been successfully used for both linear and non-linear classification. However, as non-linear classification yields results with relatively lower accuracy, in this chapter, we focus on the linear operation only. To understand the basic operation of SVM (Haykin, 1999; Taylor, 2000; Soman, 2009) let us consider X to be the input vector and y to be the desired scalar output which can take +1 or -1 values, indicating linear separation of the pattern vector X.

The function $f(X,W,b)$ can be represented as follows:

$$f(X, W, b) = \text{sign } (WX + b) \qquad (8)$$

where

$W = [w_1 \ w_2 .........w_n]$ is the weight vector

$X = [x_1 \ x_2 .........x_n]^T$ represents the input vector

$b =$ the bias

The function f classifies the input vector X into two classes denoted by +1 or -1. The straight line that segregates the two pattern classes is usually called a hyperplane. Further, the data points that are situated at the margins of the two boundaries of the linear classifier are called support vectors. Figure 9 describes support vectors for a linear SVM.

Let us now select two points $X^+$ and $X^-$ as two support vectors. Thus by definition

$$WX^+ + b = +1$$
$$\text{and } WX^- + b = -1 \qquad (9)$$

which jointly yields

$$W(X^+ - X^-) = 2$$

The separation between the two support vectors lying in the class +1 and class -1, called *marginal width* is given by

$$M = \{(WX^+ + b) - (WX^- + b)\}\big/\| W \|$$
$$= 2\big/\| W \| \qquad (10)$$

The main objective in a linear Support Vector Machine is to maximize M, i.e., to minimize $\|W\|$, which is same as minimizing $\frac{1}{2} W^T W$. Thus, the linear SVM can be mathematically described by:

$$Minimize \ \varphi(W) = \frac{1}{2} W^T W$$
$$subject \ to \ y_i(WX_i + b) > 1$$

for all i, where $y_i$ is either 1 or -1 depending on the class which $X_i$ belongs to.

Here, the objective is to solve W and b that satisfies the above equation. Here, we are not presenting the solution to the optimization problem, referred to above. This is available in any standard text in neural network (Haykins, 1999). One important aspect of SVM is the kernel function selection. For linear SVM, the kernel K for two data points $X_i$ and $X_j$ is defined by

$$K(X_i, X_j) = X_i^T X_j \qquad (11)$$

*Figure 9. Defining support vector for a linear SVM system*

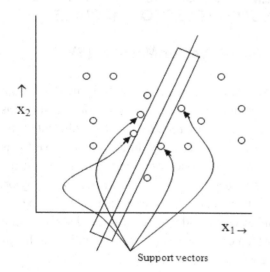

Support vectors

*Table 2. Accuracy of classification of both facial expression and eeg data using linear SVM*

| | | $k_1$ | | | | | |
|---|---|---|---|---|---|---|---|
| | | **0** | **0.2** | **0.4** | **0.6** | **0.8** | **1** |
| | **0** | 100 | 100 | 99.17 | 95.74 | 90.8 | 87.23 |
| | **0.1** | 100 | 100 | 99 | 95.2 | 90.74 | 86.46 |
| | **0.2** | 100 | 100 | 98.6 | 94.29 | 89.74 | 84.71 |
| | **0.3** | 100 | 99.94 | 97.29 | 92.63 | 89.46 | 85.23 |
| | **0.4** | 100 | 99.83 | 96.57 | 90.94 | 86.4 | 83.29 |
| $k_2$ | **0.5** | 100 | 99.66 | 94.69 | 88.37 | 85.69 | 81.6 |
| | **0.6** | 100 | 98.2 | 91.37 | 85.46 | 81.89 | 79.69 |
| | **0.7** | 100 | 95.89 | 86.29 | 82.14 | 79.03 | 76.94 |
| | **0.8** | 100 | 85.49 | 79.8 | 76.57 | 75.74 | 74.46 |
| | **0.9** | 77.14 | 72.34 | 72.6 | 72.14 | 72.43 | 71.4 |
| | **1** | 62.86 | 67.4 | 68.46 | 68.74 | 69 | 68.66 |

## Classification by SVM

After the feature extraction is complete, we constructed training instances using both facial and EEG, and used svmtrain code of MATLAB to train the support vector machine with the training instances. The classification of features into one of 5 classes is then studied with MATLAB code svmclassify. Performance of the classifier is studied in two ways: first by a leave-one-out cross validation, and sensitivity of the classifier to noise. The leave-one-out classification (Oweiss, 2010) yields 96% accuracy for facial expression-EEG based classification and 91% and 88% respectively to classify emotions from EEG and facial expressions independently.

Next we studied the effect of Gaussian noise on emotion classification (Das, 2009;2009 a;2010). We added Gaussian noise of specific mean and standard deviation over the mean and variance of individual components of the feature vector, and the classification was performed using MATLAB code svmclassify. The percentage classification of noisy feature vectors into emotion classes is then studied with varied ratio of noise mean ($k_1$) to data mean and noise variance ($k_2$) to data variance as in Table 2.

The classification accuracy obtained in Table 1 is plotted in Figure 10 for the sake of convenience. It is clear from Figure 10 that larger is the ratio of mean noise to mean data, and standard deviation of noise to standard deviation of data, the larger is the fall-off in percentage classification accuracy. It is clear from Figure 9 that for a 10% ratio of mean noise to data noise and 1% ratio of standard deviation of noise to standard deviation of data, the percentage accuracy in emotion classification is as high as 90.14%. This proves the robustness of the SVM classification.

## Classification with Only Facial and Only EEG Features

To study the significance of both EEG and facial features, we study the classification with only facial and only voice features, and plot the classification accuracy with varied ratio of mean noise to mean data, and standard deviation of noise to standard deviation of data. The results are tabulated in Table 3 and 4. Figure 11 and 12 present the classification accuracy surfaces for only facial and only EEG feature sets.

It is apparent from Figure 10 and 11 that the fall-off in percentage classification in only facial

*Figure 10. Accuracy plot for classification of facial expression and EEG data using linear SVM*

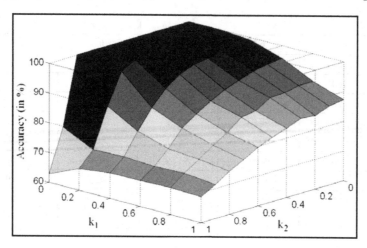

*Figure 11. Accuracy plot for classification of facial expression data using linear SVM*

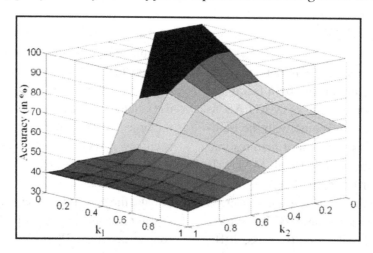

*Figure 12. Accuracy plot for classification of EEG data using linear SVM*

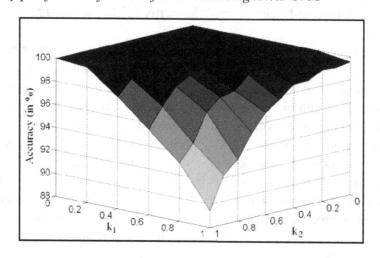

*Table 3. Accuracy of classification of facial expression data using linear SVM*

| | | $k_1$ | | | | | |
|---|---|---|---|---|---|---|---|
| | | **0** | **0.2** | **0.4** | **0.6** | **0.8** | **1** |
| | **0** | 100 | 89.83 | 78.37 | 72.29 | 68.57 | 65.69 |
| | **0.1** | 100 | 89.8 | 78.11 | 71.77 | 69.51 | 65.6 |
| | **0.2** | 100 | 86.51 | 77.17 | 71.06 | 66.91 | 63.49 |
| | **0.3** | 100 | 80.74 | 74.34 | 68.34 | 64 | 61.49 |
| | **0.4** | 68.57 | 74.71 | 69.69 | 64.06 | 59.77 | 57.31 |
| $k_2$ | **0.5** | 62.86 | 60.71 | 59.77 | 57.74 | 55.51 | 51.71 |
| | **0.6** | 42.86 | 49.43 | 50.43 | 50.49 | 49.06 | 47.23 |
| | **0.7** | 42.86 | 43.46 | 45.89 | 45.83 | 44.94 | 44.77 |
| | **0.8** | 42.86 | 42.29 | 42.91 | 42.97 | 41.34 | 41.29 |
| | **0.9** | 40 | 40.86 | 41.37 | 41.31 | 41.11 | 39.54 |
| | **1** | 40 | 40.11 | 40.57 | 39.83 | 38.86 | 37.89 |

*Table 4. Accuracy of classification of EEG data using Linear SVM*

| | | $k_1$ | | | | | |
|---|---|---|---|---|---|---|---|
| | | **0** | **0.2** | **0.4** | **0.6** | **0.8** | **1** |
| | **0** | 100 | 100 | 100 | 100 | 99.94 | 99.54 |
| | **0.1** | 100 | 100 | 100 | 100 | 99.91 | 99.31 |
| | **0.2** | 100 | 100 | 100 | 99.94 | 99.86 | 99.4 |
| | **0.3** | 100 | 100 | 100 | 99.97 | 99.69 | 98.77 |
| | **0.4** | 100 | 100 | 100 | 100 | 99.57 | 98.71 |
| $k_2$ | **0.5** | 100 | 100 | 100 | 99.86 | 99.31 | 97.69 |
| | **0.6** | 100 | 100 | 99.97 | 99.57 | 98.2 | 96.83 |
| | **0.7** | 100 | 100 | 99.91 | 99.29 | 97.91 | 95.37 |
| | **0.8** | 100 | 100 | 99.69 | 98.63 | 96.91 | 93.34 |
| | **0.9** | 100 | 99.97 | 99 | 97.14 | 94.49 | 92.26 |
| | **1** | 100 | 99.77 | 97.71 | 95.43 | 93.06 | 89.43 |

expression is much steeper than both facial expression and EEG based classification. Further, in either case the classification is poorer than only EEG based classification.

# EEG BASED EMOTION RECOGNITION

This section provides a novel scheme for emotion recognition from the stimulated EEG signals of the subjects. The proposed scheme does not require feature extraction. The EEG signal is directly fed to a non-linear dynamics called Duffing oscillator, the phase trajectory of which yields unique pattern for EEG signals associated with different emotions.

# THE DUFFING OSCILLATOR DYNAMICS

Duffing oscillator has a proven chaotic behavior (Bonatto, 2008), (Nakano, 2004) in its temporal response. The dynamics of Duffing Oscillator has a similarity with typical spring-mass load system of a conventional mechanical process (Kuo, 1985), (Ogata, 1990). However, the spring in the present context, being a non-linear device, has a restoration force proportional to its cubic linear displacement. Naturally, the restoration force of ideal spring that obeys Hooke's Law is also maintained in the Duffing Oscillator dynamics. Consequently, the restoration force has two components, one following Hooke's Law, while the other is due to a high stiffness condition of the spring, represented by a cubic displacement term. The dynamics of Duffing Oscillator is given in equation (12).

$$\frac{d^2x}{dt^2} + \delta\frac{dx}{dt} + \beta x + \alpha x^3 = \gamma\cos(\omega t) + e(t)$$

(12)

where, x represents the linear displacement, $\frac{dx}{dt}$ represents the velocity of a unit mass connected in spring-mass load system, $\beta x$ and $\alpha x^3$ are due to spring restoration force, $\gamma\cos(\omega t)$ is a fixed excitation input to maintain certain level of oscillation in the response of the dynamics, and e(t) is the disturbance input to the oscillator.

In this present context, we use the EEG signal as the disturbance input e(t). We took $\alpha=1$, $\beta=-1$, $\gamma=0.826$, $\delta=0.5$ and the gain of the EEG signal to be 5. The basic Duffing Oscillator dynamics (1) can equivalently be represented by (13) and (14).

$$\dot{x} = y$$

(13)

$$\dot{y} = \gamma\cos(\omega t) + e(t) - \delta\frac{dx}{dt} - \beta x - \alpha x^3$$

(14)

At first, the EEG signal, which was obtained in sampled version, was passed through a First-Order-Hold circuit, whose transfer function is given by:

$$G_h(s) = \left[\frac{1 + Ts}{T}\right] \times [\frac{1 - e^{-Ts}}{s}]^2$$

(15)

where

T= sampling time,

s= Laplace-domain operator.

The hold-circuit is used to get a continuous version of discrete EEG signal. A Runge-Kutta algorithm is used to solve the coupled-differential equations (13) and (14), and phase portraits for x against y at different time slots are plotted.. Since Duffing Oscillator has a non-linear dynamics, as shown in the block diagram in Figure 13, it is apparent that for varying initial conditions, the phase portraits could have different shapes. However, experimental instances reveal that a chaotic response of the dynamics prevails even for redefining new initial conditions. Figure 14 illustrates this behavior with different initial conditions.

*Figure 13. Block diagram of a Duffing Oscillator*

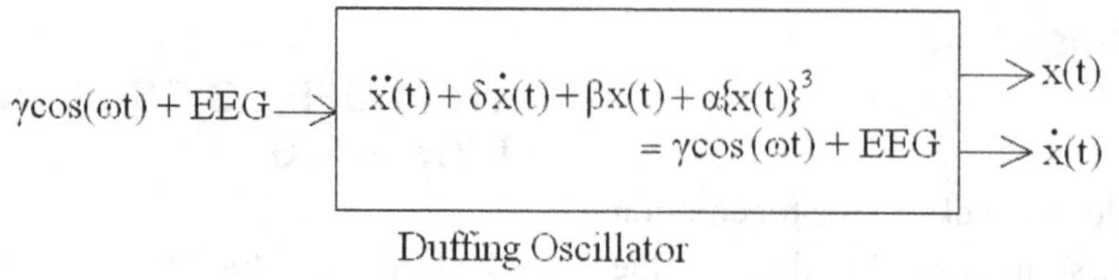

$$\gamma\cos(\omega t) + EEG \longrightarrow \boxed{\ddot{x}(t) + \delta\dot{x}(t) + \beta x(t) + \alpha\{x(t)\}^3 = \gamma\cos(\omega t) + EEG} \longrightarrow x(t), \dot{x}(t)$$

Duffing Oscillator

*Figure 14. A: Phase trajectory of emotion joy with initial condition (at x(0)= 2 and y(0)= 20) B: Phase trajectory of emotion joy with initial condition at x(0)= -2 and y(0)= 20. C: Phase trajectory of emotion joy with initial condition at x(0)= -2 and y(0)= -20.*

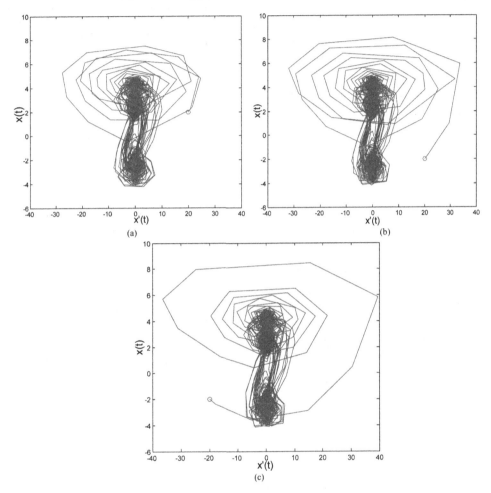

## EMOTION CLUSTERING USING DUFFING OSCILLATOR

In this section, we briefly outline the emotion classification technique using Duffing oscillator (Ott, 2002), (Yuan, 2008), (Bhowmik, 2010; 2010a). We perform two different experiments for clustering of emotions in the EEG space (Table 5). First, different audio-visual stimuli are used to excite a specific emotion of a subject. Response of the Oscillator with initial condition x= 0 and y= 0 is evaluated. We note that for three audio-visual stimuli responsible for exciting the same emotion, the phase trajectories look almost similar, supporting the intuitive assumption that similar excitations to brain results in similar brain-activities arousing similar EEGs. These EEG, when fed to a Duffing Oscillator, thus maintains similarity in the phase portraits of the oscillator state variables. Experiments with EEG of 50 subjects confirm that misclassification of emotion guided by shape-based information of phase portraits is as low as 6.8%. Consequently, the proposed mode of emotion recognition by EEG outperforms all classical modes including voice and facial expression.

*Table 5. Experimental results on the cluster-shapes*

| Emotions | Experimentally obtained cluster shapes (without noise) | Remarks |
|----------|-------------------------------------------------------|---------|
| Anger | | The phase trajectory covers the least area and width, confined within $\dot{x} = -8$ to $\dot{x} = 8$ |
| Fear | | An extension is visible to the right side of the main phase trajectory |
| Happiness | | The upper lobe is highly dispersed, less dense, thus covering the maximum area |
| Relaxation | | Above the upper lobe, a thick lobe is formed. An extension is formed nearer to the left side of the original upper lobe. |
| Sadness | | Below the lower lobe, another lobe is formed, which is sparse in nature. |

## Effect of Noise on Emotion Clustering from Duffing Oscillator Response

In this section, we experiment by adding Additive White Gaussian Noise to the original signal corresponding to a specific emotion, and note the changes in the phase portrait obtained from the Duffing Oscillator response. The additive white Gaussian noise (AWGN) channel model is one in which the only impairment is a linear addition of widcband or white noise with a constant spectral density (expressed as watts per hertz of bandwidth) and a Gaussian distribution of amplitude. It is interesting to note that when Signal-to-Noise Ratio of the EEG signal is maintained to a level of 25 dB, the phase portraits maintains similarity, indicating robustness in emotion clustering. Signal-to-noise ratio (often abbreviated SNR or S/N) is defined as the ratio of a signal power to the noise power corrupting the signal. A ratio higher than 1:1 indicates more signal than noise. In less technical terms, signal-to-noise ratio compares the level of a desired signal, in this case, the obtained EEG signals, to the level of added noise. The higher the ratio, the less obtrusive the background noise is. The value of SNR is given by the following equation:

$$\text{SNR}\,(dB) = 10 \log_{10}(\frac{P_{signal}}{P_{noise}})$$
$$= 20 \log_{10}(\frac{A_{signal}}{A_{noise}}) = P_{signal,\,dB} - P_{noise,\,dB}$$

(16)

Figure 15 demonstrates the behavior in the phase portrait for different level of Signal-to-Noise Ratio as indicated in the figure caption. It is also noteworthy that when the Signal-to-Noise Ratio goes below a threshold, misclassification starts, by noting differences in the phase portraits for a given emotion.

Classifications of obtained phase trajectories into different emotions were based on several features of the phase portrait. Those features include-

1. presence of any 3rd lobe (a value of +1 is taken for an extra upper lobe, a -1 is taken for an extra lower lobe, and a 0 is considered for absence of any extra lobe),
2. position of the centroid of the extra lobe (coordinates of the centroid is taken.(a value of (0,0) is taken if there is no extra lobe),
3. the maximum and the minimum values of x and dx/dt.

The features extracted from the phase portraits without noise were used to train support vector

*Figure 15. Phase trajectories for sadness when the EEG signal is corrupted with noise of SNR (a) 30dB, (b) 25dB, (c) 20 dB*

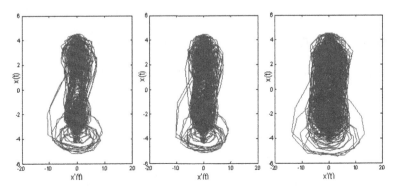

machine. The features of the phase portraits obtained from noisy EEG data were classified using the linear one-against-one SVM classifier. Intuitively, a good separation is achieved by the hyperplane that has the largest distance to the nearest training data points of any class (so-called functional margin), since in general the larger the margin the lower the generalization error of the classifier. The one-against-one approach of classification is done by a max-wins voting strategy, in which every classifier assigns the instance to one of the two classes, then the vote for the assigned class is increased by one vote, and finally the class with most votes determines the instance classification.

The accuracy of classification for different signal to noise ratios is tabulated in Table 6. Figure 16 gives a pictorial representation of the same.

It is evident from Table 6 that misclassification starts at 25dB. Misclassification percentage is 0.3% at SNR=25dB.

The leave-one-out classification is also used to study the performance of Duffing oscillator based emotion recognition. This is realized by first leaving one sample data from the overall training set for classification, and the former is used for testing the classifier performance. This process is repeated for all the training samples, and the average classification accuracy thus obtained is 92%.

*Table 6. Percentage of classification accuracy at decreasing values of SNR*

| Signal to Noise Ratio | Accuracy |
| --- | --- |
| 55 dB | 100% |
| 50 dB | 100% |
| 45 dB | 100% |
| 40 dB | 100% |
| 35 dB | 100% |
| 30 dB | 100% |
| 25 dB | 99.7% |
| 20 dB | 98.3% |
| 15 dB | 92.6% |
| 10 dB | 84.4% |

## RELATIVE PERFORMANCE OF THE PROPOSED SCHEMES

This section briefly compares the relative performance of the proposed emotion classifiers. The Duffing Oscillator acts as a non-linear mapping to map the stimulated EEG signal corresponding to a specific emotive stimulus onto its phase-space, and one can easily identify the emotion class from the shape of the phase trajectory. The SVM classifier used in the present context is just for the sake of automation, whereas in the multimodal emotion recognition introduced in section II SVM is essentially required as the high dimensional data can hardly be compared manually for classification. This is a favorable issue for Duffing oscillator based emotion classification. The feature-based classifiers are often over-sensitive to features

*Figure 16. Variation of classification accuracy with various amount of noise*

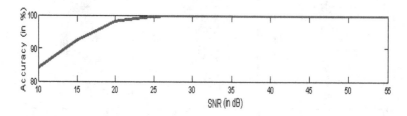

extracted. In Duffing Oscillator, we need no features for the non-linear mapping from EEG to emotion classes.

The leave-one-out classification when used to feature based classifier, yields an accuracy of 96%, 91% and 88% for multimodal, only EEG and only facial expression based classification. The Duffing Oscillator based classifier has an accuracy of 92%, better than only EEG based classification introduced in section III. The noise sensitivity analysis of classifier for both the methods cannot be directly compared as the methodologies of introducing noise in both the systems are different. In Duffing Oscillator based scheme, noise has been introduced over the stimulated EEG samples, whereas in the former method noise is introduced on individual features of the classifier input. Further, in Duffing Oscillator based scheme, the EEG is contaminated with a Gaussian noise of zero mean, but the effect of both mean and variance of Gaussian noise is examined in the former feature based classifier.

## CONCLUSION

The chapter introduced two novel schemes for emotion recognition. In both the schemes, audio-visual stimulus is used for excitation of emotion. The first scheme considers facial expression and EEG signals of the subjects for recognition of their emotions. A 162-dimensional feature vector is extracted by using several signal and image processing techniques on the received sensory data and images. An SVM classifier is then employed to classify emotions of the subjects from the extracted feature vectors. The leave-one-out cross validation offers a classification accuracy of 96% for the multimodal scheme for emotion recognition. it is indeed important to note here that proposed scheme outperforms the reported works on emotion recognition using facial expressions (Petrantonakis, 2010) and EEG (Gomathi, 2010), (Lin, 2010), (Murugappan, 2010; 2009a).

The second scheme proposed an alternative solution to the problem of emotion recognition by a non-linear mapping of stimulated EEG signal to emotions using Duffing Oscillator. The proposed scheme is better than the previous one as it does not require computations of EEG features. The leave-one-out cross validation yields an appreciably good classification accuracy of 92%, and outperforms all the reported works on EEG based emotion recognition (Gomathi, 2010), (Murugappan, 2010), (Lin, 2010).

Often the EEG signals and images containing facial expression are contaminated with noise. The chapter exhaustively studied the effect of noise on classification accuracy. Experimental results reveal that even with small signal-to-noise ration up to 10dB, the recognition accuracy of emotion by the Duffing Oscillator is as high as 84%. The effect of variation of $k_1$ and $k_2$ on the classification accuracy of the first scheme is also studied. When $k_1$=0.1 and $k_2$=0.01, the classification accuracy is as high as 90.14%.

## ADDITIONAL READING

The pioneering contribution in emotion recognition perhaps is due to Ekman and Friesen (1975). This is a first book to start with research on emotion recognition. The book Affective Computing by Picard (1997) is the most modern resource for emotion recognition. The edited volume by Cipolla and Pentland (1998) introduces several methods for emotion recognition with a special emphasis in human-machine interactions. The most attractive part of the book is on wearable hardwires for anytime-anywhere communications and computing, also called ubiquitous computing. A detailed discussion on ubiquitous computing is further found in Vasilakos and Pedrycz (2006). This has much relevance for online signal processing and sharing of emotions between any two people, such as a patient residing in a hospital, and a doctor far away on the outskirts of the city through high speed cellular network. The first text in emotion recognition and control is due to Chakraborty and Konar (2009 a). Besides the fundamentals on recognition algorithms, the book in addition examines the personality (stable/unstable/chaotic) of a subject from the temporal variations in facial expressions due to excitation by selective audio-visual stimulus. More rigorous analysis of human personality from temporal variations in facial expression is available in (Chakraborty et al., 2009 b).

The implementation of an automatic and an artificial emotion recognition system is found in (Datcu and Rothkrantz, 2008a; Xu et al., 2004). Horlings et al. (2008) emphasized the importance of brain activity in emotion recognition. Chen et al., (1998) studied joint processing of audio-visual information for the recognition of emotional expression in human-computer-interaction. Sebe and Lew (2002) projected a new technique for emotion recognition using Cauchy naïve based classifier. Cohen et al. (2000) proposed a new architecture of hidden Markov models to automatically segment and recognize facial expressions.

Zhang and Lee (2009), Johnstone et al. (2006), and Schneider et al. (1997) introduced novel methods for emotion recognition by brain imaging. Greene et al. (2001) employed fMRI experiments to study emotional engagement in moral judgement. Streit et al. (2003) considered EEG brain mapping in both schizophrenic patients and healthy subjects during facial emotion recognition. Yuan and Li (2008) in their recent work emphasized the study on EEG time series based on Duffing Equation. Kim and Andre (2008) considered the potential of physiological signals as reliable channels for emotion recognition. In order to collect a physiological data set from multiple subjects they used a musical induction method that would instinctively lead the arousal of real emotional states in the subjects. They used the four-channel biosensors to measure the electromyogram, electrocardiogram, skin conductivity, and respiration changes. Emotion recognition

based on a speech signal is one of the intensively studied research topics of this era. It is increasingly gaining importance in the domains of human-computer interaction and affective computing. Kim (2007) considered speech and physiological changes for bimodal emotion recognition. Cichosz and Slot (2007) proposed an emotion recognition procedure that involves new categories of speech signal features namely the emotional speech descriptors and a binary tree based recognition strategy. Datcu and Rothkrantz (2008b) described a novel technique to determine the most probable emotion of a subject. They combined the results from facial expression recognition and from the emotion recognition from speech using a bi-modal semantic data fusion model. Datcu and Rothkrantz (2006) further employed segmentation methods and performance of Gentle Boost Classifier on emotion recognition from speech.

Terzopoulus and Waters (1993) analyzed and set forth a novel approach to synthesize facial image sequences from physical and anatomical models. Vanger et al. (1995) discussed the various applications of synergetic in decoding various facial expressions of emotions.

Ekman and Friesen (1978) developed the Facial Action Coding System (FACS) for easily describing facial expressions by action units (AUs). Tian et al. (2001) further developed an Automatic Face Analysis (AFA) system to analyze facial expressions based on both permanent facial features (brows, eyes, mouth) and transient facial features (deepening of facial furrows) in a nearly frontal-view face image sequence.

Goleman (1995) first demonstrated the scope of emotional intelligence in business. This is a very useful book for those interested in emotion research for trading/business applications. Jamshidnejad and Jamshidneid (2009) in their paper present a facial expression recognition model using fuzzy techniques in order to further detect human behaviors in the e-business. Fuzzy C Means clustering algorithm is used to deal with the inconsistency between human perception and the machine recognition. Researchers have also developed a facial recognition system required for driver vigilance monitoring as in Dikkers et al., (2004).

# REFERENCES

Bashyal, S., & Venayagamoorthy, G. K. (2008). Recognition of facial expressions using Gabor wavelets and learning vector quantization. *International Journal of Engineering applications of Artificial Intelligence, 21*, 1056-1064.

Bezdek, J. C. (1973). *Fuzzy mathematics in pattern classification*, Ph.D. Thesis, Unpublished doctoral dissertation, Applied Mathematics Center, Cornell University, Ithaca.

Bhowmik, P., Das, S., Halder, A., Chakraborty, A., Konar, A., & Janarthanan, R. (2009). *Emotion classifier from stimulated EEG signals by support vector machine.* 5th National Conference on Innovation in Information and Communication Technology", NCIICT, 2009, September 25 - 26, Coimbatore, India.

Bhowmik, P., Das, S., Nandi, D., Chakraborty, A., Konar, A., & Nagar, A. K. (2010). *Electroencephalographic signal based clustering of stimulated emotion using Duffing Oscillator.* The 3rd International Multi-Conference on Engineering and Technological Innovation", IMETI 2010, June 29th - July 2nd, Orlando, Florida, USA.

Bhowmik, P., Das, S., Nandi, D., Chakraborty, A., Konar, A., & Nagar, A. K. (2010a). Emotion clustering from stimulated electroencephalographic signals using Duffing Oscillator. *The International Journal of Computers in Healthcare, 1*(1), 66–85. doi:10.1504/IJCIH.2010.034131

Biswas, B., Mukherjee, A. K., & Konar, A. (1995). Matching of digital images using fuzzy logic. *AMSE Publication, 35*(2), 7–11.

Black, M. T., & Yacoob, Y. (1997). Recognizing facial expressions in image sequences using local parameterized models of image motion. *International Journal of Computer Vision, 25*, 23–48. doi:10.1023/A:1007977618277

Bonatto, C., Gallas, J. A. C., & Ueda, Y. (2008). Chaotic phase similarities and recurrences in a damped-driven Duffing oscillator. *Physical Review E: Statistical, Nonlinear, and Soft Matter Physics, 77*, 026217.doi:10.1103/PhysRevE.77.026217

Brave, S., & Nass, C. (2002). Emotion in human–computer interaction. In Sears, A., & Jacko, J. A. (Eds.), *The human computer interaction handbook: Fundamentals, evolving technologies and emerging applications* (pp. 81–96). Hillsdale, NJ: L. Erlbaum Associates Inc.

Busso, C., Deng, Z., Yildirim, S., Bulut, M., Lee, C. M., & Kazemzadeh, A. … Narayanan, S. (2004). *Analysis of emotion recognition using facial expressions, speech and multimodal information.* ICMI'04, State College, Pennsylvania, USA.

Busso, C., & Narayanan, S. (2007). Interaction between speech and facial gestures in emotional utterances: A single subject study. *IEEE Trans. Audio. Speech and Language Processing, 15*(8), 2331–2347.doi:10.1109/TASL.2007.905145

Castellano, G., Kessous, L., & Caridakis, G. (2007). Multimodal emotion recognition from expressive faces, body gestures and speech. In F. de Rosis, & R. Cowie (Eds.), *Proc. of the Doctoral Consortium of 2nd International Conference on Affective Computing and Intelligent Interaction*, Lisbon.

Chakraborty, A., Bhowmik, P., Das, S., Halder, A., Konar, A., & Nagar, A. K. (2009c). *Correlation between stimulated emotion extracted from EEG.* 2009 IEEE International Conference on Systems, Man, and Cybernetics, IEEE SMC 2009, October 11 - 14, San Antonio, Texas, USA.

Chakraborty, A., Ghosh, M., Acharya, A., Konar, A., & Nagar, A. (2009b). A recurrent neural dynamics for parameter estimation of mixed emotions from facial expressions of the subject. *Proc. of the Int. Joint Conf. on Neural Networks*, Atlanta.

Chakraborty, A., & Konar, A. (2009). *Emotional intelligence: A cybernetic approach*. Heidelberg, Germany: Springer.

Chakraborty, A., Konar, A., Chakraborty, U. K., & Chatterjee, A. (2009a). Emotion recognition from facial expressions and its control using fuzzy logic. *IEEE Transactions on Systems, Man, and Cybernetics. Part A, Systems and Humans, 39*(4), 726–743. doi:10.1109/TSMCA.2009.2014645

Chakroborty, A. (2005). *Cognitive cybernetics – A study of the behavioral models of human interaction*. Unpublished doctoral dissertation, Jadavpur University, India.

Chen, L. S., Tao, H., Huang, T. S., Miyasato, T., & Natakatsu, R. (1998). Emotion recognition from audiovisual information. In *Proc. IEEE Workshop on Multimedia Signal Processing*, (pp. 83-88).

Cichosz1, J., & Ślot, K. (2007). Emotion recognition in speech signal using emotion extracting binary decision trees. In R. Cowie & F. Rosis (Chairs), *Affective Computing and Intelligent Interfaces-ACII*. Doctoral Consortium.

Cipolla, R., & Pentland, A. P. (1998). *Computer vision for human-machine interaction*. Cambridge, UK: Cambridge University Press.

Cohen, I. (2000). *Facial expression recognition from video sequences*. MS Thesis, Unpublished doctoral dissertation, Dept. of Electrical Engg., Univ. of Illinois at Urbana-Champaign.

Cohen, I., Garg, A., & Huang, T. S. (2000a). Emotion recognition using facial multilevel HMM. In *Proc. Of NIPS Workshop on Affective Computing*, Colorado.

Cohen, I., Sebe, N., Garg, A., Chen, L. S., & Huang, T. S. (2003). Facial expression recognition from video sequences: Temporal and static modeling. *Computer Vision and Image Understanding, 91*(1-2), 160–187. doi:10.1016/S1077-3142(03)00081-X

Conati, C. (2002). Probabilistic assessment of user's emotions in educational games. *J. of Applied Artificial Intelligence. Special Issue on Merging Cognition and Affect in HCT, 16*(7-8), 555–575.

Cowie, R., Douglas-Cowie, E., Tsapatsoulis, N., Votsis, G., Kollias, S., Fellenz, W., & Taylor, J. G. (2001). Emotion recognition in human-computer interaction. *IEEE Signal Processing Magazine, 18*(1), 32–80. doi:10.1109/79.911197

Das, S., Bhowmik, P., Halder, A., & Chakraborty, A. Konar, & A., Nagar, A. K. (2010). *Emotion recognition from facial expression and electroencephalographic signals using vector quantization and support vector machines*. 2010 World Congress in Computer Science, Computer Engineering, and Applied Computing, WORLDCOMP 2010, July 12 - 15, Las Vegas, Nevada, USA.

Das, S., Halder, A., Bhowmik, P., & Chakraborty, A. Konar, & Janarthanan, R. (2009a). *A support vector machine classifier of emotion from voice and facial expression data*. World Congress on Nature & Biologically Inspired Computing, NaBIC 2009, December 09-11, Coimbatore, India.

Das, S., Halder, A., Bhowmik, P., Chakraborty, A., Konar, A., & Nagar, A. K. (2009). *Voice and facial expression based classification of emotion using linear support vector machine*. Development in eSystems Engineering Conference, DeSE '09, December 14 - 16, Abu Dhabi, UAE.

Datcu, D., & Rothkrantz, L. (2008a). Semantic audiovisual data fusion for automatic emotion recognition. *Euromedia, 2008*, 58–65.

Datcu, D., & Rothkrantz, L. (2008b). Automatic bimodal emotion recognition system based on fusion of facial expressions and emotion extraction from speech. *Proceedings of the IEEE Face and Gesture Conference FG2008.*

Dikkers, H. J., Spaans, M. A., Datcu, D., Novak, M., & Rothkrantz, L. (2004). Facial recognition system for driver vigilance monitoring. In *Proceedings of the IEEE International Conference on System, Man and Cybernetics,* (pp. 3787-3792).

Donato, G., Bartlett, M. S., Hager, J. C., Ekman, P., & Sejnowski, T. J. (1999). Classifying facial action. *IEEE Transactions on Pattern Analysis and Machine Intelligence, 21,* 974–989. doi:10.1109/34.799905

Ekman, P., & Friesen, W. V. (1975). *Unmasking the face: A guide to recognizing emotions from facial clues.* Englewood Cliffs, NJ: Prentice-Hall.

Ekman, P., & Friesen, W. V. (1978). *The facial action coding system: A technique for the measurement of facial movement.* San Francisco, CA: Consulting Psychologists Press.

Essa, I. A., & Pentland, A. P. (1997). Coding, analysis, interpretation and recognition of facial expressions. *IEEE Transactions on Pattern Analysis and Machine Intelligence, 19,* 757–763. doi:10.1109/34.598232

Fellenz, W. A., Taylor, J. G., Cowie, R., Douglas-Cowie, E., Piat, F., & Kollias, S. … Apolloni, B. (2000). On emotion recognition of faces and of speech using neural networks, fuzzy logic and the ASSESS systems. In *Proc. IEEE-INNS-ENNS Int. Joint Conf. Neural Netw,* (pp. 93–98).

Fernandez-Dols, J. M., Wallbotl, H., & Sanchez, F. (1991). Emotion category accessibility and the decoding of emotion from facial expression and context. *Journal of Nonverbal Behavior, 15,* 107–123. doi:10.1007/BF00998266

Gao, Y., Leung, M. K. H., Hui, S. C., & Tananda, M. W. (2003). Facial expression recognition from line-based caricatures. *IEEE Transactions on Systems, Man, and Cybernetics. Part A, Systems and Humans, 33*(3), 407–412. doi:10.1109/TSMCA.2003.817057

Goleman, D. (1995). *Emotional intelligence.* New York, NY: Bantam.

Gomathi, V., Ramar, K., & Jeevakumar, A. Santhiyaku. (2010). A neuro fuzzy approach for facial expression recognition using LBP histograms. *International Journal of Computer Theory and Engineering, 2*(2), 1793–8201.

Gordon, R. N. (1990). *The structure of emotions: Investigations in cognitive philosophy.* Cambridge, UK: Cambridge Studies in Philosophy, Cambridge University Press.

Greene, J. D., Sommerville, R. B., Nystrom, L. E., Darley, J. M., & Cohen, J. D. (2001). An fMRI investigation of emotional engagement in moral judgment. *Science, 293*(5537), 2105–2108. doi:10.1126/science.1062872

Haag, A., Goronzy, S., Schaich, P., & Williams, J. (2004). *Emotion recognition using bio-sensors: First steps towards an automatic system, (LNCS 3068).* Berlin, Germany: Springer.

Haykins, S. (1999). *Neural networks and learning machines.* Upper Saddle River, NJ: Prentice-Hall.

Horlings, R., Datcu, D., & Othkrantz, I. J. M. (2008). Emotion recognition using brain activity. In *Proc. of Int. Conf. on Computer Systems and Technologies – CompSysTech,* (pp. 1-6).

Izumitani, K., Mikami, T., & Inoue, K. (1984). A model of expression grade for face graphs using fuzzy integral. *Syst. Control, 28*(10), 590–596.

Jamshidnejad, A., & Jamshidined, A. (2009). *Facial emotion recognition for human computer interaction using a fuzzy model in the e-business.* IEEE Conference on Innovative Technologies in Intelligent Systems and Industrial Applications (CITISIA 2009) Monash University, Sunway campus, Malaysia.

Johnstone, T., van Reekum, C. M., Oakes, T. R., & Davidson, R. J. (2006). The voice of emotion: An FMRI study of neural responses to angry and happy vocal expressions. *Social Cognitive and Affective Neuroscience, 1*(3), 242–249. doi:10.1093/scan/nsl027

Kawakami, F., Morishima, S., Yamada, H., & Harashima, H. (1994). Construction of 3-D emotion space using neural network. *Proc. of the 3rd International Conference on Fuzzy Logic, Neural Nets and Soft Computing,* Iizuka, (pp. 309-310).

Kim, J. (2007). Bimodal emotion recognition using speech and physiological changes. In Grimm, M., & Kroschel, K. (Eds.), *Robust speech recognition and understanding* (p. 460). Vienna, Austria.

Kim, J., & Andre, E. (2008). Emotion recognition based on physiological changes in music listening. *IEEE Transactions on Pattern Analysis and Machine Intelligence, 30*(12), 2067–2083. doi:10.1109/TPAMI.2008.26

Klir, G. J., & Yuan, B. (1995). *Fuzzy sets and fuzzy logic: Theory and applications.* NJ: Prentice-Hall.

Kobayashi H., & Hara, F. (1993). The recognition of basic facial expressions by neural network. *Trans. on the society of Instrument and Control Engineers, 29*(1), 112-118.

Kobayashi, H., & Hara, F. (1993a). Recognition of mixed facial expressions by neural network. *Trans. Jpn. Soc. Mech. Eng. (C), 59*(567), 184–189.

Kobayashi, H., & Hara, F. (1993b). Measurement of the strength of six basic facial expressions by neural network. *Trans. Jpn. Soc. Mech. Eng. (C), 59*(567), 177–183.

Kollias, S., & Karpouzis, K. (2005). Multimodal emotion recognition and expressivity analysis. *IEEE International Conference on Multimedia and Expo, ICME,* (pp. 779–783).

Konar, A. (2005). *Computational intelligence: Principles, techniques and applications.* Heidelberg, Germany: Springer.

Kramer, A. F., Sirevaag, E. J., & Braune, R. (1987). A psycho-physiological assessment of operator workload during simulated flight missions. *Human Factors, 29*(2), 145–160.

Kuo, B. C. (1985). *Automatic control systems.* John Wiley & Sons Inc.

Lanitis, A., Taylor, C. J., & Cootes, T. F. (1997). Automatic interpretation and coding of face images using flexible models. *IEEE Transactions on Pattern Analysis and Machine Intelligence, 19*(7), 743–756. doi:10.1109/34.598231

Li, L., & Chen, J. (2006). Emotion recognition using physiological signals. In Pan, Z. (Eds.), *ICAT 2006, LNCS 4282* (pp. 437–446). Berlin, Germany: Springer-Verlag.

Li, X., & Ji, Q. (2005). Active affective state detection and user assistance with dynamic Bayesian networks. *IEEE Transactions on Systems, Man, and Cybernetics. Part A, Systems and Humans, 35*(1), 93–105. doi:10.1109/TSMCA.2004.838454

Lin, Y. P., Wang, C.-H., Jung, T.-P., Wu, T. L., Jeng, S. K., Duann, J.-R., & Chen, J. H. (2010). EEG based emotion recognition in music listening. *IEEE Trans. on Biomedical Engg., 57*(7).

Lisetti, C. L., & Schiano, D. J. (2000). Automatic facial expression interpretation: Where human-computer interaction, artificial intelligence and cognitive science intersect. *Pragmatics and Cognition. (Special Issue on Facial Information Processing: A Multidisciplinary Perspective), 8*(1), 185-235.

Mase, K. (1991). Recognition of facial expression from optical flow. *Proc. IEICE Trans., Special Issue Coput. Vis. And Its Applications, 74*(10), 3474-3483.

McGilloway, S., Cowie, R., Cowie, E. D., Gielen, S., Westerdijk, M., & Stroeve, S. (2000). Approaching automatic recognition of emotion from voice: A rough benchmark. In *Speech and Emotion*, (pp. 207-212).

Murugappan, M., Juhari, M. R. B. M., Nagarajan, R., & Yaacob, S. (2009). An investigation on visual and audiovisual stimulus based emotion recognition using EEG. *International Journal of Medical Engineering and Informatics, 1*(3), 342–356.doi:10.1504/IJMEI.2009.022645

Murugappan, M., Nagarjana, R., & Sazali, Y. (2009a). *Appraising human emotions using time frequency analysis based EEG alpha band features*. 2009 Conference on Innovative Technologies in Intelligent Systems and Industrial Applications (CITISIA 2009), Monash University, Sunway campus, Malaysia, 25th & 26th July 2009.

Murugappan, M., Nagarjana, R., & Sazali, Y. (2010). Classification of human emotion from EEG using discrete wavelet transform. *Journal of Biomedical Science and Engineering, 3*(4), 390–396.doi:10.4236/jbise.2010.34054

Nakano, H., & Saito, T. (2004). Grouping synchronization in a pulse-coupled network of chaotic spiking oscillators. *IEEE Transactions on Neural Networks, 15*(5), 1018–1026.doi:10.1109/TNN.2004.832807

Ogata, K. (1990). *Modern control engineering*. Englewood Cliffs, NJ: Prentice-Hall.

Ott, E. (2002). *Chaos in dynamical systems* (2nd ed.). Cambridge University Press.

Oweiss, K. G. (2010). *Statistical signal processing for neuro- science and neurotechnology*. Burlington, VT: Academic Press, Elsevier.

Pedrycx, W., & de Oliveria, J. V. (2008). A development of fuzzy encoding and decoding through fuzzy clustering. *IEEE Trans. Instrumentation and Measurements, 57*(4), 829–837.doi:10.1109/TIM.2007.913809

Petrantonakis, P. C., & Hadjileontiadis, L. J. (2010). Emotion recognition from brain signals using hybrid adaptive filtering and higher order crossings analysis. *IEEE Transactions on Affective Computing*. IEEE computer Society Digital Library. Retrieved from http://doi.ieeecomputersociety.org/10.1109/T-AFFC.2010.7

Petrushin, V. A. (2000). *Emotion recognition in speech signal: experimental study, development, and application* (*Vol. 2*, pp. 222–225). ICSLP.

Picard, R. (1997). *Affective computing*. Cambridge, MA: MIT Press.

Picard, R. W., Vyzas, E., & Healy, J. (2001). Toward machine emotional intelligence: Analysis of affective psychological states. *IEEE Transactions on Pattern Analysis and Machine Intelligence, 23*(10), 1175–1191.doi:10.1109/34.954607

Rani, P., Sarkar, N., & Adams, J. (2007). Anxiety-based affective communication for implicit human-machine interaction. *Advanced Engineering Informatics, 21*(3), 323–334.doi:10.1016/j.aei.2006.11.009

Rani, P., Sarkar, N., Smith, C., & Kirby, L. (2004). Anxiety detecting robotic systems— Towards implicit human–robot collaboration. *Robotica, 22*(1), 83–93.doi:10.1017/S0263574703005319

Rippon, G. (2006). Electroencephalography. In Senior, C., Russell, T., & Gazzaniga, M. S. (Eds.), *Methods in mind*. Cambridge, MA: MIT Press.

Rosenblum, M., Yacoob, Y., & Davis, L. (1996). Human expression recognition from motion using a radial basis function network architecture. *IEEE Transactions on Neural Networks, 7*, 1121–1138. doi:10.1109/72.536309

Scheirer, J., Fernadez, R., Klein, J., & Picard, R. (2002). Frustrating the user on purpose: A step toward building an affective computer. *Interacting with Computers, 14*(2), 93–118.

Schneider, F., Grodd, W., Gur, R. E., Klose, U., Alavi, A., & Gur, R. C. (1997). PET and fMRI in the study of emotion. *Psychiatry Research: Neuroimaging, 68*(2-3), 174–175. doi:10.1016/S0925-4927(97)81569-7

Sebe, N., & Lew, M. S. (2002). Emotion recognition using a Cauchy naïve Bayes classifier. In. *Proc. Int. Conf. Pattern Recognition* (pp. 17-20).

Soman, K. P., Loganathan, R., & Ajay, V. (2009). *Machine learning with SVM and other kernel methods*. New Delhi, India: PHI Learning Private Limited, Connaught Circus.

Sprengelmeyer, R., Rausch, M., Eysel, U. T., & Przuntek, H. (1998). *Neural structures associated with recognition of facial expressions of basic emotions*. The Royal Society.

Streit, M., Brinkmever, J., Wolwer, W., & Gaebel, W. (2003). EEG brain mapping in Schizophrenic patients and healthy subjects during facial emotion recognition. *Schizophrenia Research, 61*(1), 121. doi:10.1016/S0920-9964(02)00301-8

Takahashi, K. (2004). *Remarks on emotion recognition from bio-potential signals*. 2nd International Conference on Autonomous Robots and Agents. December 13-15, Palmerston North, New Zealand.

Taylor, J. S., & Cristianini, N. (2000). *Support vector machines and other kernel-based learning methods*. Cambridge University Press.

Terzopoulus, D., & Waters, K. (1993). Analysis and synthesis of facial image sequences using physical and anatomical models. *IEEE Transactions on Pattern Analysis and Machine Intelligence, 15*, 569–579. doi:10.1109/34.216726

Tian, Y., Kanade, & T., Cohn, J. (2001). Recognizing action units for facial expression analysis. *IEEE Transactions on Pattern Analysis and Machine Intelligence, 23*(2), 97–116. doi:10.1109/34.908962

Ueki, N., Morishima, S., & Harashima, H. (1994). Expression analysis/synthesis system based on emotion space constructed by multilayered neural network. *Systems and Computers in Japan, 25*(13), 95–103.

Uwechue, O. A., & Pandya, S. A. (1997). *Human face recognition using third-order synthetic neural networks*. Boston, MA: Kluwer Academic publishers.

Vanger, P., Honlinger, R., & Haykin, H. (1995). Applications of synergetic in decoding facial expressions of emotions. *Proc. of Int. Workshop on Automatic face and Gesture recognition*, Zurich, (pp. 24-29).

Vasilakos, A., & Pedrycz, W. (2006). *Ambient intelligence, wireless networking and ubiquitous computing*. Norwood, MA: Artech House.

Xu, L. Zhuge, & Z., Yang, J. (2004). Artificial emotion and its recognition, modeling and applications: An overview. In. *Proc. of the 5th World Congress on Intelligent Control and Automation*, Hangzhou. P.R. China.

Yacoob, Y., & Davis, L. (1996). Recognizing human facial expression from long image sequences using optical flow. *IEEE Transactions on Pattern Analysis and Machine Intelligence*, *16*, 636–642. doi:10.1109/34.506414

Yamada, H. (1993). Visual information for categorizing facial expression of emotion. *Applied Cognitive Psychology*, *7*, 257–270.doi:10.1002/acp.2350070309

Yuan, Y., & Li, Y. (2008). Study on EEG time series based on Duffing equation. *International Conference on BioMedical Engineering and Informatics, BMEI*, vol. 2, (pp. 516-519).

Zeng, Z., Fu, Y., Roisman, G. I., Wen, Z., Hu, Y., & Huang, T. S. (2006). Spontaneous emotional facial expression detection. *J. of Multimedia*, *1*(5), 1–8.

Zhang, Q., & Lee, M. (2009). Analysis of positive and negative emotions in natural scene using brain activity and GIST. *Neurocomputing*, *72*, 1302–1306.doi:10.1016/j.neucom.2008.11.007

## KEY TERMS AND DEFINITIONS

**Duffing Oscillator:** An example of a periodically forced oscillator with a nonlinear elasticity, written as $\ddot{x} + \delta\dot{x} + \beta x + \alpha x^3 = \gamma\cos\omega t$, where the damping constant obeys $\delta > 0$, and it is also known as a simple model which yields chaos.

**Electroencephalography (EEG):** The recording of electrical activity along the scalp produced by the firing of neurons within the brain.

**K-Fold Cross-Validation:** The original sample is randomly partitioned into $K$ subsamples. Of the $K$ subsamples, a single subsample is retained as the validation data for testing the model, and the remaining $K - 1$ subsamples are used as training data. The cross-validation process is then repeated $K$ times (the *folds*), with each of the $K$ subsamples used exactly once as the validation data. The $K$ results from the folds then can be averaged (or otherwise combined) to produce a single estimation.

**Segmentation:** The process of partitioning a digital image into multiple segments (sets of pixels, also known as superpixels). The goal of segmentation is to simplify and/or change the representation of an image into something that is more meaningful and easier to analyze. Image segmentation is typically used to locate objects and boundaries (lines, curves, etc.) in images. More precisely, image segmentation is the process of assigning a label to every pixel in an image such that pixels with the same label share certain visual characteristics.

**Support Vector Machines (SVMs):** Are a set of related supervised learning methods that analyze data and recognize patterns, used for classification and regression analysis. It constructs a hyperplane or set of hyperplanes in a high or infinite dimensional space, which can be used for classification, regression or other tasks. Intuitively, a good separation is achieved by the hyperplane that has the largest distance to the nearest training data points of any class (so-called functional margin), since in general the larger the margin the lower the generalization error of the classifier.

# Chapter 18
# Detecting Eyes and Lips Using Neural Networks and SURF Features

**Artem A. Lenskiy**
*Korea University of Technology and Education, Korea*

**Jong-Soo Lee**
*University of Ulsan, Korea*

## ABSTRACT

*In this chapter, the authors elaborate on the facial image segmentation and the detection of eyes and lips using two neural networks. The first neural network is applied to segment skin-colors and the second to detect facial features. As for input vectors, for the second network the authors apply speed-up robust features (SURF) that are not subject to scale and brightness variations. The authors carried out the detection of eyes and lips on two well-known facial feature databases, Caltech. and PICS. Caltech gave a success rate of 92.4% and 92.2% for left and right eyes and 85% for lips, whereas the PCIS database gave 96.9% and 95.3% for left and right eyes and 97.3% for lips. Using videos captured in real environment, among all videos, the authors achieved an average detection rate of 94.7% for the right eye and 95.5% for the left eye with a 86.9% rate for the lips*

## INTRODUCTION

A number of approaches have been proposed to detect facial features. Among all facial features, eyes have become a maverick for their variety of applications and implications. In the case of car driver eye detection, color cameras and cameras with IR illumination have been widely used as

DOI: 10.4018/978-1-61350-429-1.ch018

a video capturing device. The use of cameras with IR illumination significantly simplifies the problem of eye detection. When an infrared led is located at the camera axis, the eye irises appear as two bright spots caused by the reflection of the blood-rich retina. Thus, IR illumination based approaches gained high popularity in eye detection (Zhao & Grigat, 2006) and consequently driver attention monitoring tasks. In (Ji & Yang, 2002) a system for monitoring driver vigilance is proposed. The main idea is to place two cameras at different angles. The camera axis coincides with two coplanar concentric rings where along their circumferences a number of IR LEDs are evenly and symmetrically distributed. One camera has a wide range view for head tracking, and the other has a narrow view for eye detection. A similar hardware setup was applied by Batista et al. (Batista, 2005), the difference from (Ji & Yang, 2002) consists in face and eye detection algorithms. Hammoud et al. (Hammoud, Witt, Dufour, Wilhelm, & Newman, 2008) proposed a complete driver drowsiness detection system that detects irises in the near infrared spectrum. Although IR based approaches perform reasonably at night time, it was noted (Hartley, Horberry, & Mabbott, 2000) that those methods often malfunctioned during daytime under the presence of sunlight. Moreover, when eyes are closed the reflection in IR range disappears, making eye detection a difficult task. Another disadvantage of IR based approaches is the necessity of installing an IR LEDs setup.

In comparison with IR cameras, CMOS and CCD cameras are passive, meaning there is no IR radiation. The effect of long term IR radiation should be studied to guarantee that there is no danger to eye health (Pitts, Cullen, & Dayhew-Barker, 1980). CMOS cameras are relatively inexpensive and ergonomic. Furthermore, according to (Hartley, et al., 2000) 52% of drivers nodded off while driving between the times of 6:00 a.m. and 9:00 p.m. comprising of the majority of bright daylight on any given day. As a consequence, using IR cameras during those hours is impractical since IR cameras inefficacious under direct sunlight.

In the case of a color camera, there is a possibility to take color information into account for skin-color segmentation purposes (Rong-ben, Ke-you, Shu-ming, & Jiang-wei, 2003). The skin-color segmentation process is commonly done in RGB, HSI or YCbCr color spaces. Some authors have heuristically found an RGB to 2-dimensional color space transform and then approximated the skin color domain in 2D space (Butler, Sridharan,

& Chandran, 2002; Hamdy, Elmahdy, & Elsabrouty, 2007; Naseem & Deriche, 2005; Phil & Christos, 2005; Tariq, Jamal, Shahid, & Malik, 2004).These color spaces along with manual skin-domain approximation methods(Hernandez & Kleiman, 2005; Rong-ben, et al., 2003) are not capable of finding complex boundaries of skin-color domains. One approach to define complex boundaries of skin-color domains is to train an artificial neural network to separate skin and non-skin colors. Several applications based on neural networks have been proposed for skin color filtering. A two layer multi-layer perceptron (MLP) with two inputs and three hidden neurons was applied by Chen et al. (Chen & Chiang, 1997). In their work the RGB color space was transformed into normalized CIE XYZ color space, then the values of X and Y coordinates served as inputs for MLP. Another attempt using the MLP skin-color filter was proposed by Seow (Seow, Valaparla, & Asari, 2003), where one additional neural network was used at the learning stage to interpolate spatial skin region in each of the training images. The two hidden layers MLP then learns to distinguish skin-colors obtained from interpolated regions and non-skin colors from the rest of the image. Sahbi and Boujemaa (Sahbi & Boujemaa, 2000) applied a two layer MLP with two hidden neurons and three inputs and outputs. This structure allowed them to extract principle skin color components. Lenskiy and Lee(A. Lenskiy & J.-S. Lee, 2010) applied one layer feed forward neural network to segment skin-colors. They suggest an interesting and simple approach to train the network with negative samples uniformly distributed in the color space. As soon as the segmentation process is over, the remaining skin-color segments are analyzed to select a face candidate. For this purpose facial proportions and morphological operators are usually applied.

For the detection of eyes and lips a number methods have been suggested. Some approaches are based on raw eye images which are fed into a classifier, such as support vector machines (Jee,

Lee, & Pan, 2004) or neural networks (Motwani, Motwani, & Harris, 2004; Rong-ben, et al., 2003; Rowley, Baluja, & Kanade, 2004). Other authors prior to classification extracted robust and compact features. The most popular features are based on wavelet transform (He, Zhou, Song, & Qiao, 2004; Motwani, et al., 2004), particularly on Gabor transform (Cheung, You, Kong, & D., 2004; Rong-ben, et al., 2003) or secondary derivatives of a Gaussian kernel(Gourier, Hall, & Crowley, 2004). There are other methods which utilize, the geometrical properties of eyes, for instance, by calculating generalized projection function (Zhou & Geng, 2004). One more approach to localizing eye regions is to consider the average intensity in the running window. Usually, the intensity of the eye region is lower compared to the rest of the face. This concept was applied in (Daw-Tung & Chen-Ming, 2004) and (H.-J. Kim & Kim, 2008). In the latter work the invariance to rotations is achieved with the use of Zernike Moments.

The contribution of our work consists in the following:

- We propose a novel eye and lips detection algorithm based on SURF features and conditional probability density functions that are estimated using a trained multi-layer neural network;
- We suggest facial features candidate selection based on utilizing facial proportions;

The robustness of the proposed algorithm relies on SURF features' invariance to projective transformations and on the capability of the neural network to capture most relevant information in the SURF feature space.

In the next section, we elaborate on the face detection algorithm followed by facial features detection scheme. In the two subsequent sections we show the experimental results and conclude with future work discussion.

## FACE DETECTION

The proposed system prior to facial features detection localizes the facial region thus minimizing the area for a facial features search. The face detection step relies on skin-color information. The skin color segmentation is performed to filter non-skin colors. Among the remaining skin-color segments, the one conforming to facial proportions is selected as a facial candidate.

### Skin-Color Segmentation

Several color spaces have been suggested, providing a convenient method for separating the skin-color domain from the rest of the color space. As mentioned earlier, most of these methods apply heuristic approaches to customize boundaries of skin-color domains. We suggest a unified method based on an adjustable model obtained through the training process. Our skin-color model utilizes a feed-forward neural network with two hidden layers. In (A. Lenskiy & J.-S. Lee, 2010) one hidden layer network was applied. Although theoretically one hidden layer is enough to approximate any function to any precision(Cybenko, 1989), we experimentally found that a two-layer network requires less neurons to achieve the same accuracy. The number of input neurons corresponds to the number of color components in RGB space i.e. red, green, and blue. The number of neurons in the hidden layers is not restricted. Using a trial and error method, we set up the number of neurons in the first hidden layer to 20 and in the second to 10 neurons.

The training process is summarized as follows:

1. A cumulative color histogram (Figure 1 c) is constructed:

$$H_k(\mathbf{x}) = \frac{1}{\|H\|} \sum_k^{N_I} \sum_j^{hight} \sum_i^{width} \delta\left(I_k(j,i) \cdot M_k(j,i) - \mathbf{x}\right),$$

(1)

*Figure 1. (a) Hand segmented masks, the skin-color are only extracted from regions marked with blue, (b) training images, (c) skin-color histogram with negative samples marked with red*

$$\|H\| = \sum_{\mathbf{x}} H(\mathbf{x}),$$

where $\mathbf{x} = \begin{bmatrix} r & g & b \end{bmatrix}^T$ is a color vector, $I_k$ is the image from the training set (Figure 1 b), $M_k$ is the hand segmented version of $I_k$ (Figure 1 a), $\delta$ is a delta function, $k = 1$. $N_I$ and $N_I$ is the number of training images.

2.  Divide the training set into two subset with positive i.e. skin-color samples and negative, non-skin-color samples.
3.  Train the neural network approximator by minimizing the following criteria:

$$e(\mathbf{w}) = \sum_{\mathbf{x}} \left( f(\mathbf{w}, \mathbf{x}) - H(\mathbf{x}) \right)^2 \longrightarrow \min$$

(2)

where $f$ is the two-layer feed forward neural network described as follows:

$$f(\mathbf{w}, \mathbf{x}) = \sum_{i=0}^{N3} w_{m,i}^{(3)} \sigma \left( \sum_{j=0}^{N2} w_{i,j}^{(2)} \sigma \left( \sum_{k=0}^{N1} w_{j,k}^{(1)} x_k \right) \right),$$

(3)

$\sigma(x) = \dfrac{2}{(1 + e^{-2x})} - 1$. $N_1, N_2$ are the number of neurons in first and second hidden layers and $N_3$ is a number of output neurons.

We experimented with Levenberg-Marquardt (LM) and 'resilient propagation' (RPROP) to analyze the influence of the training algorithms on the network performance. The idea behind RPROP algorithm (Riedmiller & Braun, 1993) is to introduce for each weight its individual update-value $\Delta_{i,j}$ which determines the size of the weight-update. Every time the partial derivative of the corresponding weight $w_{i,j}$ changes its sign, which indicates that the last update was too big and the algorithm has jumped over a local minimum, the update-value $\Delta_{i,j}$ is decreased by the factor $\mu$-. If the derivative retains its sign, $\Delta_{i,j}$ is slightly increased in order to accelerate convergence in shallow regions.

Probably, the most successful and widely used learning algorithm is the LM algorithm (Marquardt, 1963). The Quasi-Newton methods are considered to be more efficient than gradient decent methods, but their storage and computational requirements go up as the square of the size of the network. LM algorithm is taking advantages of both Gauss–Newton algorithm and the method of gradient descent. By applying both of these algorithms we did not notice any difference in the segmentation results, although LM algorithm converged in a smaller number of iterations than RPROP. Therefore, we chose LM algorithm as our main training algorithm.

Our trained neural network approximates the skin-color histogram. This approach differs from the previously proposed approaches by taking into account the statistical probability of skin-color appearance. We noticed that the skin-color domain fills only about 10 percent of RGB color space. Therefore, in the case if all colors with zero occurrences are considered in the training process, the proportion of positive training samples to negative training samples is one to ten. This ratio negatively reflects on the quality of histogram approximation as it is 'easier' for the network to reach smaller errors by minimizing the deviations on the flat areas filled with zeros which constitutes around 90% of the training set. Moreover, a great number of negative samples slows down the training process. Instead of taking into account all colors beyond the skin-color domain, we only consider the colors that are located close to the domain, plus colors regularly spaced through the whole color space (Figure 1 c). Instead of zeros we used a small negative value to make the density function decline quicker. Thus the number of negative samples is customized as so, that the ratio of the number of negative to positive samples is approximately 1.

Although we used a high number of training images, there is always a possibility that some skin-colors are not within the training set, thus to minimize this probability the original color space of 256x256x256 colors is reduced to 64x64x64 colors. The remaining empty regions are smoothed by the neural network.

The segmentation process simply utilizes the trained neural network to decide whether the pixel belongs to skin-colors or not. The desicion rule $\Gamma$ is set as

$$\Gamma(I(i,j)) = \begin{bmatrix} f\left(\mathbf{w}, I(i,j)\right), & 0 < f\left(\mathbf{w}, I(i,j)\right) \\ 0, & f\left(\mathbf{w}, I(i,j)\right) \le 0 \end{bmatrix}$$

(4)

Depending on the resolution, the segmentation process(4) may demand high computational resources. For the purpose of minimizing computational time the input image is decomposed into a pyramid, where higher levels contain lower resolution versions of the original image. The segmenation process starts from the top layer and the results from the higher levels are interpolated on lower levels. This allows us to skip those regions that have been marked as non-skin colors in previous lower resolution versions of the image. An example of the skin-color segmentation result is shown in Figure 2 b).

## Face Candidate Selection

The segmention process usually detects more than one skin-color segment. Among all extracted skin-color regions, we select the one that coform to the following criteria. Let $S = \{S_i, i = 1..N_s\}$ be a set of $N_s$ remain connected components (Figure 2 c), then

1.  Drop the segments with areas less than $\tau$:

$$\mathbf{S} = \left\{ S_i, \tau < \sum_{\mathbf{x} \in S_i} h\left(S_i\left(\mathbf{x}\right)\right) = \#(S_i) \right\},$$

(5)

we use the same notation for the filtered set as for the original set $\mathbf{S}$, $h$ is a step function with zero value at zero argument.

2.  Calculate the facial ratio for each segment:
    a.   Find covariance matrix:

$$\Sigma_i = \mathbf{M}\left[\left(\mathbf{x}^i - \mathbf{M}\left[\mathbf{x}^i\right]\right)\left(\mathbf{x}^i - \mathbf{M}\left[\mathbf{x}^i\right]\right)\right], \mathbf{x} \in S_i$$

(6)

where $\mathbf{M}$ is mean.

   b.   Find eigenvectors $\lambda = \begin{bmatrix} \lambda_1 & 0 \\ 0 & \lambda_2 \end{bmatrix}$ and eigenvalues $R$ for (6). Where $R$ is also a rotation matrix $R(\varphi) = \begin{bmatrix} \cos\varphi & -\sin\varphi \\ \sin\varphi & \cos\varphi \end{bmatrix}$

*Figure 2. (a) An input image, (b) The result of skin segmentation, (c) connected components (b) probability map, (c) the largest remain component rounded by the ellipse, (d) detected facial region*

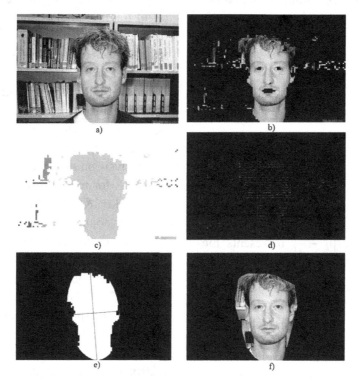

and $\varphi$ is a rotation angle, $\lambda_1$, $\lambda_2$ are major and minor radii.

c. The proportion between the major and minor axes of the segment $S_i$ is calculated as

$$\eta_i = \frac{\sqrt{\min(\lambda_1, \lambda_2)}}{\sqrt{\max(\lambda_1, \lambda_2)}} \qquad (7)$$

3. Calculate the ratio between the area of elipse fitted around the facial candidate and the number of skin-color pixes within the elipse:

$$\nu_i = \frac{\sum_x h\left(S_i(\mathbf{x})\right) \cdot \widehat{\mathbf{S}}\left(\mathbf{x} \in S_i\right)}{4\pi\sqrt{\lambda_1^{(i)}\lambda_2^{(i)}}}, \qquad (8)$$

where

$$\widehat{\mathbf{S}}(\mathbf{x}) = \begin{cases} 1 & \left[\mathbf{x} - \mathbf{M}(\mathbf{x})\right]\Sigma_i^{-1}\left[\mathbf{x} - \mathbf{M}(\mathbf{x})\right]^T \leq 1 \\ 0 & otherwise \end{cases}$$

$$(9)$$

is an ellipse filled with ones, centered at $\mathbf{M[x]}$ (Figure 2 e).

4. Calculate the average skin-color probability per component (Figure 2d)

$$\bar{p}_i = \frac{1}{\#(S_i^I)}\sum_x f^+\left(\mathbf{w}, I(\mathbf{x})\right), \mathbf{x} \in S_i, \qquad (10)$$

5. superscript + idicates that only positive values are added up.

343

Using the above described factors, the index of the most suitable facial region is selected according to the following criterion:

$$n = \arg\min \left( v_i - \left| \eta_i - \frac{3}{4} \right| - \frac{\overline{p_i}}{\max_i(\overline{p_i})} \right) \quad (11)$$

This criterion takes into account three quantities. The quantity $v$ reflects the ratio between the number of skin-color pixels within the elliptical region and the area of the ellipse. When $v = 1$, the elliptical region perfectly matches the facial candidate. The difference $\left| \eta_i - \frac{3}{4} \right|$ represents the deviation from the ideal facial proportions $\frac{3}{4}$, ideally $\left| \eta_i - \frac{3}{4} \right| = 0$. Where the numerator is face width and the denominator is its height. The last quantity calculates the average skin-color probability and normalizes it by the maximal average probability among all extracted facial candidates.

An example of the detected facial candidate $S_n$ is shown on (Figure 2 f).

## FACIAL FEATURES DETECTION

### Facial Features Segmentation

In this section we elaborate on the facial region detection segmenting the region into the meaningful facial regions like eyes, lips, etc. We treat facial regions as textures. Although eyes or lips of one person do not completely replicate the appearance of eyes and lips of another person, they look very similar. The proposed facial segmentation method is based on supervised learning to distinguish salient features extracted from different facial regions. The first step in the learning process is to obtain training pairs.

Each pair contains a feature descriptor and its class label. The features are extracted from the set of training images and their class labels are obtained from the corresponding hand segmented images. Each of the training images is processed to extract speeded-up robust features (SURF). We chose SURF features because of their robustness to changes in brightness, fast computation and comparably, to other feature detectors (SIFT (Lowe, 1999)), short descriptor vectors. The detail analysis on the quality of different versions of SURF for texture segmentation purposes(A. A. Lenskiy & J.-S. Lee, 2010), showed that 36-dimensional rotational dependent SURF (U-SURF36) vectors show better separability among tested variations of SURF. For these reasons in our further implementation we apply U-SURF36 features. The SURF algorithm consists of three stages. In the first stage, interest points and their scales are localized in scale-space by finding the maxima of the determinant of the Fast-Hessian matrix. In the second stage, orientation is found for each of features prior to computing the feature descriptor. We use rotation dependent SURF, thus we omit this step. Finally a descriptor based on sampled Haar responses is extracted. Extracted features are arranged into five groups depending on their class labels on hand segmented images. We considered five classes of facial features, eyes, eyebrows, lips, nose and the rest of the face.

A neural network classifier is trained to estimate a class membership value for a single SURF descriptor. The structure of the neural network is similar to the two hidden layer network we applied for skin-color segmentation (3). The difference consists in the numbers of inputs, outputs, and the numbers of neurons in each hidden layer. The number of inputs is equal to the number of dimensions in U-SURF36 descriptor. The number of outputs is limited to the number of classes. Thus the number of outputs equals to five. The component of an output vector that corresponds to the descriptor's class is set to one, others set to zeros. When choosing the number of neurons in

*Figure 3. (a) SURF feature space reduced to three dimensions. Only 25% of all features are shown. Among them features representing lips(red), eyes(green) and the rest of the facial region (blue) are shown. (b) A structure of two-layer feed-forward neural network applied for class membership values $\hat{p}_k^m$ estimation.*

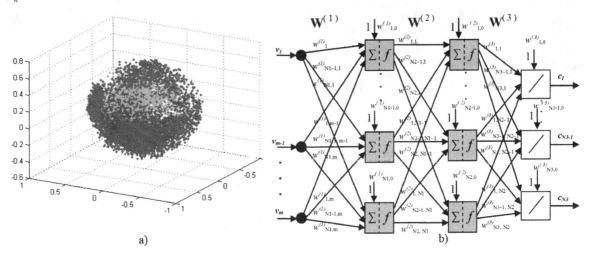

a)                                                                  b)

each layer we kept in mind two points. The first is the, relatively small for 36 dimensional space, number of features in the training set. Total 31293 features were extracted. The second, absents of the precise boundary between classes. Figure 3 a) shows a dimensionally reduced feature space, where the clustering property of features from different class can be seen, although the intersection of classes is clearly visible too. Therefore, the number of neurons in the network should be selected in a way that it allows the network to generalize the features form each class but at the same time avoid overfitting. For this purpose we experimented with the following structures: 36-80-60-5, 36-60-40-5 and 36-40-20-5. The whole set of pairs extracted from training images was split into training set, test set and validation set. The training set contains 80% of all training pairs and the test and validation sets contains 10% each. As is expected the mean square error (MSE) for the training samples is the highest for 36-40-20-5 and the lowest for 32-80-60-5. However, the minimum of the MSE on the testing and the validation sets among three structures is reached with 36-60-40-5 structures.

The trained neural network is then used in facial features segmentation procedure. The segmentation procedure consists of two steps. First U-SURF36 features are extracted from the input image (Figure 5 a). Descriptors of each extracted facial feature are processed with the neural network classifier, resulting in a 5-dimensional vector $p$. The vector's components represent how likely the descriptor belongs to the corresponding class. These values along with features spatial positions $l_k = (x_k, y_k)$ are utilized by the segmentation algorithm. The algorithm for labeling pixel $q_i$ is summarized in the following list of steps:

1.  Select indexes of extracted features that reside within radius $r$ around the pixel $q_i = (x_i, y_i)$:

$$\mathrm{T}\left(q_i\right) = \left\{ j \big| \left\| q_i - l_j \right\| < r, j = 1..N_e \right\} \qquad (12)$$

where $N_e$ is the number of extracted features.

*Figure 5. (a) Magenta points represent detected SURF features, (b) estimated membership functions for lip(red), eye(green), nose(cyan) and eyebrows (yellow) regions, (c) the vertexes of the black triangle connect detected eyes and lips, d) the detected facial features.*

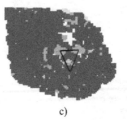
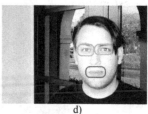

a)            b)                     c)              d)

2. For selected features $k \in T(q_i)$ estimate classes membership values

$$\hat{p}_k^m = \hat{p}(d_k \mid m), m = \{1..M\},$$

using the training neural network. $d$ is a 36 dimensional SURF descriptor.

3. Using $\hat{p}_k^m$ and position of pixel $q_i$ relative to features residing within radius $r$ (12) estimate class membership value for each pixel (Figure 5b) in the image:

$$\mathbf{p}^{1..M}\left(q_i\right) = \frac{1}{\#(\mathrm{T}(q_i))} \sum_{k=1}^{\#(\mathrm{T}(q_i))} \hat{p}_k^m$$

$$\cdot \frac{1}{\sigma_2 \sqrt{2\pi}} e^{-\frac{\|q_i - c_k\|^2}{2\tilde{A}_2}} \qquad (13)$$

4. Choose the class with the highest membership

$$label(q_i) = \arg\left(\max\left(\mathbf{p}^{1..M}\left(q_i\right)\right)\right) \qquad (14)$$

If the maximum of estimated **p** is lower than a predefined threshold, then the pixel's class is marked as unknown.

## Facial Features Selection

The result of facial segmentation process is usually a number of scattered segments. Among these segments only those that conform to facial proportions are selected. The following description of the facial feature selection process takes into account geometrical proportions of human face (Figure 4).

Let $L = \{L_i, i = 1..N_l\}$ be a set of detected lip segments and $E = \{E_i, i = 1..N_e\}$ is a set of detected eye segments. First, segments are filtered on the bases of their size $L = \{L_i, \tau < \#(L_i)\}$, $E = \{E_i, \tau < \#(E_i)\}$, where $\tau$ is a predfied threshold that depends on the image size. The remain segments are used to find a bundle of two eyes and one lip regions conforming to facial proportions. First each possible pair of eye regions is checked to reside within a distance $\rho$ and that the angle of the connecting line is within $|\pi / 6|$:

1.
$$\hat{\mathbf{E}} = \left\{\{E_i, E_j\} \left\| \arctan\left[\frac{\mathbf{M}_y\left(E_i\right) - \mathbf{M}_y\left(E_j\right)}{\mathbf{M}_x\left(E_i\right) - \mathbf{M}_x\left(E_j\right)}\right]\right\| \right.$$
$$\left. < |\pi / 6|, i \neq j \right\}$$
$$\cap \left\{E_i \left\|\mathbf{M}\left(E_i\right) - \mathbf{M}\left(E_j\right)\right\| < \rho, i \neq j\right\} \qquad (15)$$

The distance $\rho$ set proportionally to the input image size. We assume that faces width and height are larger than one half of a minimum dimension of the input image. If $\hat{E} = \{\varnothing\}$ then no eyes are detected, otherwise a suitable lip regions is searched:

*Figure 4. Facial proportions and the angular ranges that are use to search for facial features*

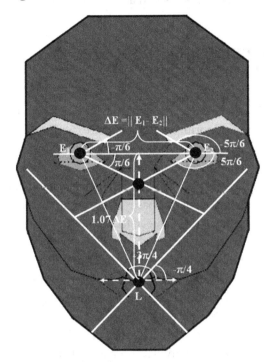

$$\varphi = \arctan\left[\frac{\mathbf{M}_y\left(E_1\right) - \mathbf{M}_y\left(E_2\right)}{\mathbf{M}_x\left(E_1\right) - \mathbf{M}_x\left(E_2\right)}\right], \left\{E_1, E_2\right\} \in \mathbf{T} \tag{18}$$

b. Calculate the center of the lip $\overset{\cup}{L}$ and the second eye $\overset{\cup}{E_2}$ region in new basis, where the center of the first eye is a new origin:

$$\mathbf{M}\left(\breve{L}\right) = R(\varphi)\left[\mathbf{M}\left(L\right) - \mathbf{M}\left(E_1\right)\right], \left\{L, E_1\right\} \in \mathbf{T} \tag{19}$$

$$\mathbf{M}\left(\breve{E}_2\right) = R(\varphi)\left[\mathbf{M}\left(E_2\right) - \mathbf{M}\left(E_1\right)\right], \left\{E_1, E_2\right\} \in \mathbf{T} \tag{20}$$

c. Calculate the error between the predicted, according to facial proportions, lip position and the detected lips:

$$e = \sqrt{\left(\frac{1}{2}\mathbf{M}_x\left(\breve{E}_2\right) - \mathbf{M}_x\left(\breve{L}\right)\right)^2 + \left(1.07 \cdot \mathbf{M}_x\left(\breve{E}_2\right) - \mathbf{M}_y\left(\breve{L}\right)\right)^2}, \tag{21}$$

$$\left\{E_1, E_2, L\right\} \in \mathbf{T}$$

The multiplier 1.07 corresponds to the ideal ratio between the distance between eyes and the shortest distance from the eye line to the lip center.

d. Select the triple with minimum error:

$$n = \arg \min_{i=1..\#\mathbf{T}}\left(e_i\right), \tag{22}$$

where #$\mathbf{T}$ is the number of triples.

Index $n$ defines the triple of two eye regions and the lip region that are detected as eyes and lips (figure 5 c,d).

$$2.\ \hat{\mathbf{L}} = \left\{\left\{L_i, E_j\right\} \left| -\frac{3}{4}\pi < \left|\arctan\left[\frac{\mathbf{M}_y\left(L_i\right) - \mathbf{M}_y\left(E_j\right)}{\mathbf{M}_x\left(L_i\right) - \mathbf{M}_x\left(E_j\right)}\right]\right|\right. \right. \\ \left. < -\frac{1}{4}\pi, E_j \in \hat{\mathbf{E}}\right\} \\ \left. \cap\left\{E_i \left\|\mathbf{M}\left(L_i\right) - \mathbf{M}\left(E_j\right)\right\| < \rho, E_j \in \hat{\mathbf{E}}\right\}\right. \tag{16}$$

If $\hat{L} = \{\varnothing\}$ then no lip region is detected, otherwise each triple

$$\mathbf{T} = \left\{\left\{L, E_j\right\}, E_j \cap \hat{\mathbf{E}}\right\}, \tag{17}$$

is processed to select the one which proportions are closer to facial proportions.

3. Select the triple that is close to facial proportions:

   a. Estimate angle of the line connecting two eye regions:

4.  In the case when $\overset{\cap}{L} = \{\varnothing\}$ i.e. no lip regions are detected, the eye pair is selected as follows:

    a.  Calculate the filling factors:

$$\eta_1^i = \frac{\#\left(E_1^i\right)}{\left[\max_x\left(E_1^i\right) - \min_x\left(E_1^i\right)\right]\cdot\left[\max_y\left(E_1^i\right) - \min_y\left(E_1^i\right)\right]}$$

$$\eta_2^i = \frac{\#\left(E_2^i\right)}{\left[\max_x\left(E_2^i\right) - \min_x\left(E_2^i\right)\right]\cdot\left[\max_y\left(E_2^i\right) - \min_y\left(E_2^i\right)\right]}$$

where $\left\{E_1^i, E_2^i\right\} \in \widehat{\mathbf{E}}, i = 1..\#\widehat{\mathbf{E}}$.

    b.  Calculate the proportion of eye region area relative to the maximum eye region area:

$$\nu^i = \frac{\#\left(E_1^i\right) + \#\left(E_2^i\right)}{\max_i(\nu^i)}, \left\{E_1^i, E_2^i\right\} \in \widehat{\mathbf{E}}, i = 1..\#\widehat{\mathbf{E}}$$

    c.  Select the eye pair with the maximum of the following criterion:

$$n = \arg\max_{i=1..\#\widehat{\mathbf{E}}}\left(\eta_1^i + \eta_2^i + \nu^i\right), \qquad (23)$$

where $\#\overset{\cap}{E}$ is the number of eye pairs.

Index $n$ defines the pair of eye regions that are detected as eyes.

5.  If only one eye region satisfies (16), i.e. $E_j \cap \overset{\cap}{E} = \varnothing$ in (17), then the following criterion is applied to select the best sutible eye/lip pair:

$$n = \arg\max_{i=1..\#T}\left(\#\left(E^i\right) + \#\left(L^i\right)\right) \qquad (24)$$

Index $n$ defines the pair of an eye and a lip regions that are detected as an eye and lips.

## EXPERIMENTAL RESULTS AND DISCUSSION

To measure the performance of our facial features detection algorithm we conducted experiments on two well known facial databases obtained from the Internet and on the video sequences we captured while drivers were driving in the real environment.

Among facial databases obtained on the Web, the first one is call Caltech face database (Weber). It contains 450 images of 27 unique people under different lighting and with different facial expressions and backgrounds. The image resolution is 896 x 592. To check generalization properties of our algorithm we selected two sets of images for the training purpose. The first one contained 20 images and the second 25 images that is 4.5% and 5.5% of the original data set. The images were selected in a way to cover the variety of face appearances including images or different people and with different lighting conditions. The recognition results are shown in Table 1 and Table 2. The numbers in true positive column indicate how many of facial features, were correctly detected, while the numbers in false positive shows how many facial features were incorrectly detected. The column true negative indicates that absence of a facial feature was correctly recognized. On the other hand the false negative column shows the number of false rejections of a facial feature. The detection rate is calculated as the sum of true positives and true negatives divided by the total number of images in the data set. The detection rate is shown in the last column of the table. It can be seen from the Table 1 that only 4.5% of the image set is enough to reach a high detection accuracy. Moreover, adding 5 more images in the training set increased the detection rate by about 5%.

*Table 1. The detection results when 4.5% (20 images) of the Caltech image set is used for training*

|  | True positive | True negative | False positive | False negative | Detection rate |
|---|---|---|---|---|---|
| Left eye | 391 | 3 | 14 | 42 | 87.5% |
| Right eye | 390 | 4 | 10 | 46 | 87.5% |
| Lips | 382 | 3 | 5 | 60 | 85.5% |

*Table 2. The detection results when 5.5% (25 images) of the Caltech image set is used for training*

|  | True positive | True negative | False positive | False negative | Detection rate |
|---|---|---|---|---|---|
| Left eye | 413 | 3 | 11 | 23 | 92.4% |
| Right eye | 412 | 3 | 13 | 22 | 92.2% |
| Lips | 402 | 3 | 11 | 31 | 90.0% |

The second data set is named PICS (PICS) contains 690 images of frontal and profile faces of around 100 unique people. The resolution of images in the database is 432x528. All faces are presented on the plain background. In this experiment we only used 2.1% (15 images) of the image set for training. The detection rate is presented in Table 3. The high detection rate supports high generalization properties of the proposed system. Some examples of detected facial features are shown in Figure 6.

In (Khac, Park, & Jung, 2009) variance based Haar-like features were extracted from an image and then classified with SVM to localize the face. The detection rate on a Caltech database reached 79.08%. The paper (An, Ma, & Li, 2009) focuses on face detection and recognition. They applied skin-color detection scheme to segment a facial candidate and fit an ellipse to extract the face. Then 64 dimensional SURF features were extracted for recognition purposes. They reached

96% face detection rate, it is comparable to our rates of eye detections. (D. Kim & Dahyot, 2008) also proposed to use SURF features for facial features detection. Although, in their paper they did not solve the problem of facial features detection rather a problem of SURF features classification was proposed. In the paper they state 97% rate for left and right eye detection and 93% for mouth for only 100 images from Caltech database. Moreover, they did not present the results in the form of detected positions of bounding boxes, but showed only positions of classified SURF features.

Although the described image sets contains faces of many unique people and with different expressions, the majority of faces are frontal. That may be a reason for high detection rate achieved on small training sets. To verify that the proposed algorithm is able to accurately detect facial features under head rotations in the real environment, we recorded three video sequences of a driver while driving a car under different illuminations. A CCD

*Table 3. The detection results when 2.1% (15 images) of the PICS image set is used for training*

|  | True positive | True negative | False positive | False negative | Detection rate |
|---|---|---|---|---|---|
| Left eye | 643 | 0 | 46 | 1 | 93.2% |
| Right eye | 637 | 0 | 50 | 3 | 92.3% |
| Lips | 587 | 0 | 8 | 95 | 85.0% |

*Figure 6. Examples of detected facial features from (a) Caltech database, (b) PICS database*

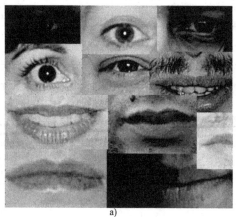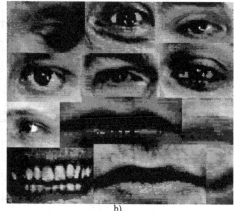

a)                    b)

color camera was placed on the car dashboard. Each video was recorded for a unique person. First, second and third video contains 1192, 1006 and 901 frames correspondingly. Overall, 100 images were selected for the training process that is about 3% of the total number of frames in all three videos. The images were selected in a way to diversify facial appearance i.e. illumination and pose. The detection results are presented in Table 4, 5 and 6 for the first(Figure 7), second(Figure 8) and third(Figure 9) video sequences correspondingly.

## CONCLUSION

The chapter elaborates on the segmentation of facial images and the detection of eyes and lip. We tested the proposed system on the well-known facial image databases as well as on the video sequences we captured in car driver environment. The experiment results show that the proposed system is able to detect facial features precisely from the images with complex backgrounds, variations in lighting and skin-color.

The advantage of the proposed system is based on two factors. The first is robustness of SURF features under illumination and scale variations.

*Table 4. The detection results of the first driving video sequence*

|  | True positive | True negative | False positive | False negative | Detection rate |
|---|---|---|---|---|---|
| **Left eye** | 1157 | 0 | 36 | 1 | 96.9% |
| **Right eye** | 1162 | 0 | 32 | 0 | 97.3% |
| **Lips** | 1037 | 0 | 26 | 131 | 86.8% |

*Table 5. The detection results of the second driving video sequence*

|  | True positive | True negative | False positive | False negative | Detection rate |
|---|---|---|---|---|---|
| **Left eye** | 921 | 1 | 85 | 0 | 91.5% |
| **Right eye** | 947 | 0 | 57 | 3 | 94.0% |
| **Lips** | 929 | 0 | 33 | 45 | 92.2% |

*Table 6. The detection results of the third driving video sequence*

|  | True positive | True negative | False positive | False negative | Detection rate |
|---|---|---|---|---|---|
| Left eye | 863 | 0 | 38 | 0 | 95.8% |
| Right eye | 859 | 0 | 36 | 6 | 95.3% |
| Lips | 736 | 0 | 20 | 145 | 81.7% |

*Figure 7. Examples of detected facial features while driver is driving a car during the first video sequence*

*Figure 8. Examples of detected facial features while driver is driving a car during the second video sequence*

*Figure 9. Examples of detected facial features while driver is driving a car during the third video sequence*

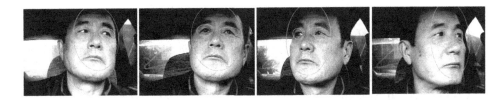

The second is the generalization capabilities of the neural networks that allow the system to extract the most important information from SURF feature space and use it in the segmentation process. The required time for the training directly depends on the size of the training set, but the performance stage depends on the number of neurons in the neural network classifier.

For the future work we analyze the detected eye regions to extract iris positions, and lip regions to find lips corners. That will allow us to reconstruct head orientations and monitors driver's attention.

## REFERENCES

An, S., Ma, X., & Li, R. S. Y. (2009). *Face detection and recognition with SURF for human-robot interaction.* Paper presented at the International Conference on Automation and Logistics, Shenyang, China.

Batista, J. P. (2005). A real-time driver visual attention monitoring system. *Iberian Conference on Pattern Recognition and Image Analysis, 3522,* (pp. 200-208).

Butler, D., Sridharan, S., & Chandran, V. (2002). Chromatic colour spaces for skin detection using GMMs. *Inter. Conf. on Acoustics, Speech, and Signal Processing, 4,* (pp. 3620-3623).

Chen, C., & Chiang, S.-P. (1997). Detection of human faces in colour images. *IEE Proceedings. Vision Image and Signal Processing, 144,* 384–388. doi:10.1049/ip-vis:19971414

Cheung, K.-H., You, J., Kong, W.-K., & D., Z. (2004). A study of aggregated 2D Gabor features on appearance-based face recognition. *Proceedings of Image and Graphics,* (pp. 310-313).

Cybenko, G. (1989). Approximation by superposition of a sigmoidal function. *Mathematics of Control, Signals, and Systems, 2,* 303–314. doi:10.1007/BF02551274

Daw-Tung, L., & Chen-Ming, Y. (2004). Real-time eye detection using face circle fitting and dark-pixel filtering. *IEEE International Conference on Multimedia and Expo, 2,* (pp. 1167-1170).

Gourier, N., Hall, D., & Crowley, J. L. (2004). *Facial features detection robust to pose, illumination and identity.* Paper presented at the IEEE International Conference on Systems, Man and Cybernetics.

Hamdy, A., Elmahdy, M., & Elsabrouty, M. (2007). Face detection using PCA and skin-tone extraction for drowsy driver application. *5th International Conference on Information & Communications Technology,* (pp. 135-137).

Hammoud, R. I., Witt, G., Dufour, R., Wilhelm, A., & Newman, T. (2008). On driver eye closure recognition for commercial vehicles. *Proceedings of SAE Commercial Vehicles Engineering Congress and Exhibition,* Chicago, IL, USA.

Hartley, L., Horberry, T., & Mabbott, N. (2000). *Review of fatigue detection and prediction technologies:* Institute for Research in Safety and Transport, Murdoch University, Western Australia and Gerald Krueger - Krueger Ergonomics Consultants, Virginia, USA.

He, K., Zhou, J., Song, Y., & Qiao, Q. (2004). Multiresolution eye location from image. *Proceedings of Signal Processing, 2,* 901–905.

Hernandez, O. J., & Kleiman, M. S. (2005). Face recognition using multispectral random field texture models, color content, and biometric features. *Proceedings of Applied Imagery and Pattern Recognition Workshop,* (p. 209).

Jee, H., Lee, K., & Pan, S. (2004). Eye and face detection using SVM. *Conference on Intelligent Sensors, Sensor Networks and Information,* (pp. 577-580).

Ji, Q., & Yang, X. (2002). Real-time eye, gaze, and face pose tracking for monitoring driver vigilance. *Real-Time Imaging, 8,* 357–377. doi:10.1006/rtim.2002.0279

Khac, C. N., Park, J. H., & Jung, H.-Y. (2009). Face detection using variance based Haar-Like features and SVM. *World Academy of Science. Engineering and Technology, 60,* 165–168.

Kim, D., & Dahyot, R. (2008). *Face components detection using SURF descriptors and SVMs.* Paper presented at the International Machine Vision and Image Processing Conferenc.

Kim, H.-J., & Kim, W.-Y. (2008). Eye detection in facial images using Zernike moments with SVM. *ETRI Journal, 30*(2), 335–337. doi:10.4218/etrij.08.0207.0150

Lenskiy, A., & Lee, J.-S. (2010). Face and iris detection algorithm based on SURF and circular Hough transform. *Signal Processing, The institute of Electronics Engineers of Korea, 47*(5).

Lenskiy, A. A., & Lee, J.-S. (2010). Machine learning algorithms for visual navigation of unmanned ground vehicles. In Igelnik, B. (Ed.), *Computational modeling and simulation of intellect: Current state and future perspectives.* Hershey, PA: IGI Global.

Lowe, D. G. (1999). Object recognition from local scale-invariant features. *Proceedings of the International Conference on Computer Vision, 1,* (pp. 1150-1157).

Marquardt, D. (1963). *Ab algorithm for least squares estimation of nonlinear paramteres.* Paper presented at the SIAM.

Motwani, R., Motwani, M., & Harris, F. (2004). Eye detection using wavelets and ANN. *Proceedings of GSPx.*

Naseem, I., & Deriche, M. (2005). Robust human face detection in complex color images. *IEEE International Conference on Image Processing, 2,* (pp. 338-341).

Phil, C., & Christos, G. (2005). *A fast skin region detector.* ESC Division Research.

PICS. (n.d.). *The psychological image collection at Stirling.* Retrieved from http://pics.psych.stir.ac.uk/

Pitts, D., Cullen, A., & Dayhew-Barker, P. (1980). *Determination of ocular threshold levels for infrared radiation cataractogenesis.* (NIOSH research report, DHHS publication; no. (NIOSH) 80-121, DHHS publication - no. (NIOSH) 80-121).

Riedmiller, M., & Braun, H. (1993). *A direct adaptive method for faster backpropagation learning the RPROP algorithm.* Paper presented at the IEEE International Conference on Neural Networks (ICNN).

Rong-Ben, W., Ke-You, G., Shu-Ming, S., & Jiang-Wei, C. (2003). A monitoring method of driver fatigue behavior based on machine vision. *Intelligent Vehicles Symposium,* (pp. 110-113).

Rowley, H. A., Baluja, S., & Kanade, T. (2004). Neural network-based face detection. *IEEE Transactions on Pattern Analysis and Machine Intelligence, 20,* 23–38. doi:10.1109/34.655647

Sahbi, H., & Boujemaa, N. (2000). *From coarse to fine skin and face detection.* Paper presented at the Proceedings of 8th ACM International Conference on Multimedia.

Seow, M.-J., Valaparla, D., & Asari, V. K. (2003). Neural network based skin color model for face detection. *Proceedings of Applied Imagery Pattern Recognition Workshop,* (pp. 141-145).

Tariq, U., Jamal, H., Shahid, M. Z. J., & Malik, M. U. (2004). Face detection in color images, a robust and fast statistical approach. *Proceedings of INMIC,* (pp. 73-78).

Weber, M. (n.d.). *Caltech face database.* Retrieved from http://www.vision.caltech.edu/html-files/archive.html

Zhao, S., & Grigat, R.-R. (2006). Robust eye detection under active infrared illumination. *In Proceedings of the 18th International Conference on Pattern Recognition (ICPR 2006),* (pp. 481-484).

Zhou, Z.-H., & Geng, X. (2004). Projection functions for eye detection. *Pattern Recognition, 37*(5), 1049–1056. doi:10.1016/j.patcog.2003.09.006

## KEY TERMS AND DEFINITIONS

**Face Detection:** The face detection is an algorithm finding position of a bounding box encompassing a face in an image. The algorithm considers factors like variations in illumination, changes in head orientation and in distance between the camera and the person.

**Facial Features Detection:** A technique finding positions of eyes, lips, nose, eye brows and other facial features. The detected facial features are usually further analyzed for emotion recognition and attention monitoring.

**Feature Extraction:** Feature extraction is a process of finding robust under various deformation vectors, by applying various transforms to image patches.

**Image Segmentation:** A process partitioning an image into segments based on specified criteria. The purpose of segmentation is to obtain a meaningful segmented map that simplifies an image for the further analysis. The criteria for combining pixels into segments are based on color, texture or structural information in the input image.

**Multilayer Perceptron:** A network connecting simple neural models with the interconnecting weights. The network is structured into multiple layers and neurons of each layer are connected to those of the next layer sequentially from the first (input) to the last(output) layer.

**Salient Features:** In computer vision, salient features are the distinctive patches of an image that are used for image matching, object recognition and 3D reconstruction.

# Chapter 19
# Classification with Axis–Aligned Rectangular Boundaries

**Sung Hee Park**
*Stanford University, USA*

## ABSTRACT

*This chapter presents a new method for binary classification that classifies input data into two regions separated by axis-aligned rectangular boundaries. Given the number of rectangular regions to use, this algorithm automatically finds the best boundaries that are determined concurrently. The formulation of the optimization problem involves minimizing the sum of minimum functions. To solve this problem, the author introduces underestimate of the minimum function with piecewise linear and convex envelope, which results in mixed integer and linear programming. The author shows several results of the algorithm and compare the effects of each term in the objective function. Finally, the chapter demonstrates that the method can be used in image capturing application to determine the optimal scheme that minimizes the total readout time of pixel data.*

## INTRODUCTION

The main goal of a classification problem is to figure out an efficient algorithm to come up with good decision classifiers to categorize random input data into several groups. The classified results give better representation of underlying structure of input data and make it easier to handle them in more complex processing stage afterwards. Each classification algorithm is designed to handle data in a systematic way, based on the assumptions it makes on its input data and how it will be used.

Many applications involving image data usually make an assumption that image data is given as a rectangular shape rather than an arbitrary form. Thus, if you want to apply classification methods to image data and feed the results to other image processing or computer vision algorithms, the classified regions must be reformulated into rectangular shape. Also, treating the object of interest as a bounding box is a common technique to make it easier to handle multiple complicated objects at the same time. Both cases require a separate method to transform a specific region or data points to a rectangular box and using a simple straightforward method may not give the best results.

DOI: 10.4018/978-1-61350-429-1.ch019

In this chapter, we would like to propose a classification method that does the two tasks at the same time, data classification and determining rectangular boundaries. The classification method will automatically choose multiple rectangular regions to separate data. Each rectangular region is axis-aligned, which means that its sides are aligned to the axes of orthogonal coordinate system and it is not allowed to rotate to arbitrary angles.

In the following sections, we will present several properties that good classification methods should have. Then, we will explain details about our algorithm and demonstrate it satisfies the properties stated. Also, we will show the application for image capturing that utilizes our classification method. Finally, further research topics and conclusion are given.

## BACKGROUND

Classification has been intensively studied in machine learning and pattern recognition (Jain, Duin & Mao, 2000). Researchers have developed tons of methods to tackle their problems and various approaches have evolved to handle specific applications. Here, we would like to mainly focus on the characteristics of the resulting decision boundaries that each classification technique provides. In some real world applications, users might have very specific constraints on the geometry of decision boundaries they will get in the end. Even more, users sometimes want to construct their boundaries to have certain shapes, such as circles, ellipses or polygons. However, most of classifiers do not explicitly focus on the geometry of results they provide. One main approach in classification is based on similarity matching. Popular methods such as template matching, the minimum distance classifier and k-nearest neighbor algorithm fall into this category. Although these methods usually results in piece-wise linear decision boundaries, the classifiers are implicitly determined and no control on the boundaries is provided to users.

Another main approach is the probabilistic approach. The Bayes decision rule (Fukunaga, 1990) and a logistic classifier (Anderson, 1982) try to maximize a likelihood function to construct decision rules. Depending on which assumption they make on the distribution of data, they result in linear or quadratic decision boundaries, which we don't have any control on as the previous cases. The third category of classifiers is to explicitly determine decision boundaries by optimizing classification error costs. These methods allow direct handling of the geometry of the decision rules. However, many approaches such as Fisher's linear discriminant and the perceptron are limited to a linear case. Another popular approach in machine learning is to use support vector machines (Cortex & Vapnik, 1995). This class of methods is based on optimizing classification errors while maximizing the geometric margin to provide a maximum-margin hyperplane that separates the data. Even though this approach is effective for various applications, extension to nonlinear classification is not trivial. The kernel trick is applied to achieve nonlinear decision boundaries, but they are no longer explicitly handled in the original input space.

The goal of this work is to find a good classifier that is suitable for the specific application: finding multiple axis-aligned rectangular decision boundaries for binary input data. Before going into the details of our approach, we propose four desirable characteristics that our classification algorithm should have so that it can be easily applied to real world applications.

### Automatic Classification

Once the algorithm gets all labeled input data, it is desired to work by itself. Users can not always guide or train classification process if the size of input data is large or clustering should be done many times iteratively.

## Optimality

Rather than using heuristic methods, solving the optimization problem guarantees to give the best results. Also, it can be served as a standard reference case to evaluate other variant methods.

## Robustness to Outliers

The real data tend to be noisy and include many outliers. The algorithm should be robust enough to handle outliers efficiently. Also, it is very common to get non-separable input data and error terms should be handled properly.

## Adjustable Objective Function

The method should be easily modified so that it can fit into various applications with different constraints. In addition, having explicit trade-off parameters will help users to tweak the algorithm to work well on the problem.

One straightforward way to classify with rectangular boundary regions is finding a smallest bounding box that contains every point with a certain label. This method is simple and intuitive, but you can only find one big rectangle that may not compactly match the distribution of desired data points. Also, it is very susceptible to noisy data because a single data point can drastically change the rectangular boundaries.

One may try to apply some existing classification methods, such as finding an ellipse classifier using quadratic discriminant analysis, and then fit a rectangle that contains the resulting decision boundaries. However, it does not guarantee anything about how the rectangular region is good for the classification since the optimization process is done on the boundaries obtained in the first step. Also, extending linear discriminant method such as the Fisher's method or simple support vector machine to solve this problem is not trivial. These methods can not be easily applied for the case

of finding rectangular boundaries since multiple classifiers have to be determined concurrently.

Ryoo (2006) presented a sophisticated pattern classification method that concurrently determines a convex region with piecewise linear boundaries. This method gives optimal results that are robust to outliers and suitable to be used in our task. Thus, our proposed algorithm uses the method as a basic framework with additional constraints since determining rectangular boundaries becomes a special case of finding piecewise linear convex boundaries. We can also extend the idea to determine multiple convex boundaries at the same time, which can adaptively give the boundaries that fit better. In the next section, we will explain details about our proposed method and show it is able to give tight and robust classifiers with flexible controls.

## A PROPOSED CLASSIFICATION METHOD

### Classification as an Optimization Problem

Input data is given with binary labels on the two-dimensional (2-D) plane. We want to formulate an optimization problem to classify binary labeled data with axis-aligned rectangles efficiently. Figure 1 shows one example when three rectangles are used to classify the given input data. In general, input data may not be separable with rectangular classification as in Figure 1. Therefore, our goal is to maximize the number of interesting points classified in the rectangles, while keeping the number of unwanted points as small as possible in them. In the following sections, we will define several penalty functions for misclassification and formulate an optimization problem for the case with one rectangular boundary. Then, we will extend our framework to handle multiple rectangles at the same time.

*Figure 1. An example of input and output of our classification method. (a) input data, (b) classification with three rectangular regions.*

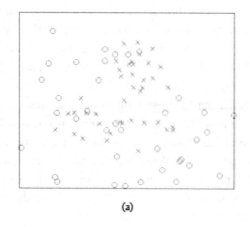

(a)

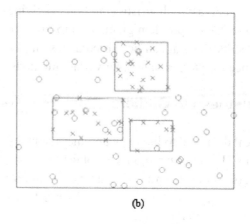

(b)

## Classification Error for one Rectangular Region

We would like to define two types of classification error. Type A error quantifies the amount of violation when unwanted points are located inside the rectangle. Similarly, type B error is incurred when our target points are not included in the rectangle. In Figure 2, $y_i$ is type A error of $i^{th}$ data point with label A and $z_j$ represents type B error

*Figure 2. Classification error for one rectangular region*

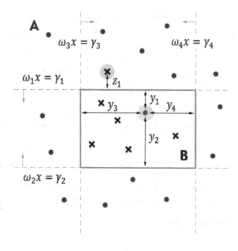

of $j^{th}$ point with label B. Let a rectangle be defined as a hyperplane set $\{\omega_k x = \gamma_k, 1 \le k \le K = 4\}$, where $x$ represents coordinates in 2-D plane, $\omega_k$ and $\gamma_k$ are constants for representation of a rectangle with $K$ denoting the total number of sides of a rectangle which is equal to 4 in 2-D case. Then, type A and B errors can be formulated as

$$y_{ik} = \max\{\omega_k A_i - \gamma_k, 0\},$$

$$z_{jk} = \max\{-\omega_k B_j + \gamma_k, 0\},$$

$$1 \le i \le m_a, 1 \le j \le m_b, 1 \le k \le K = 4$$

where $A_i$ is $i^{th}$ input coordinate data with label A, $B_j$ is $j^{th}$ input coordinate data with label B, $m_a$ is the number of input data with label A, $m_b$ is the number of input data with label B, and

$$\omega = \begin{pmatrix} 0 & 0 & -1 & 1 \\ -1 & 1 & 0 & 0 \end{pmatrix}$$ is used to represent four

sides of an axis-aligned rectangle. Note that $y_{ik}$ is an error incurred by $i^{th}$ data from $k^{th}$ side of the axis-aligned rectangle and $z_{jk}$ is an error by $j^{th}$ data from $k^{th}$ side of the rectangle.

When a type A point is in the rectangle, then all the $y_{ik}$ are positive. Thus, we define type A error of $i^{th}$ point as $y_i = \min_k y_{ik}$. On the contrary, type B error occurs when type B points have at least one positive value of $z_{ik}$. Type B error can be set as $z_j = \sum_{k=1}^{4} z_{jk}$. Then, our goal is to minimize the sum of two error terms over all input points. However, we have the sum of minimum functions involved in our objective, which are concave. This term prevents us to directly apply convex optimization techniques. Thus, we use some trick to formulate the problem as a *mixed integer and linear programming (MILP)* which will be described in the next section.

## Classification Error for Multiple Rectangular Regions

Let $L$ be the number of rectangles. Then, every term we defined in the previous section can be used with index $l$ to represent that they are the terms regarding $l^{th}$ rectangular region. Thus, we can write $y_{ik}^l$ and $z_{jk}^l$ as

$$y_{ik}^l = \max\{\omega_k^l A_i - \gamma_k^l, 0\},$$

$$z_{jk}^l = \max\{-\omega_k^l B_i + \gamma_k^l, 0\},$$

from which we define type A error and type B error of $l^{th}$ rectangular region, respectively, as

$$y_i^l = \min_k y_{ik}^l,$$

$$z_j^l = \sum_{k=1}^{4} z_{jk}^l.$$

If we consider all $L$ rectangles, then we have non-zero type A error when $A_i$ point is enclosed by any rectangular boundary. So, we can represent type A error as $y_i = \max_l y_i^l$ as shown in Figure 3. Likewise, type B points are located outside of all rectangles to have non-zero misclassification. Therefore, we can formulate it as $z_j = \min_l z_j^l$. Figure 3 shows type A and B errors when we use two rectangles. As a result, for the case with $L$ rectangular boundaries, our optimization problem becomes

$$\min_{\gamma, y, z} \left\{ \sum_{i=1}^{m_a} \max_l \min_k \left( y_{ik}^l \right) + \sum_{j=1}^{m_b} \min_l \left( \sum_{k=1}^{K} z_{jk}^l \right) \right\}$$

subject to inequalities for classification errors

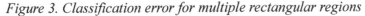

*Figure 3. Classification error for multiple rectangular regions*

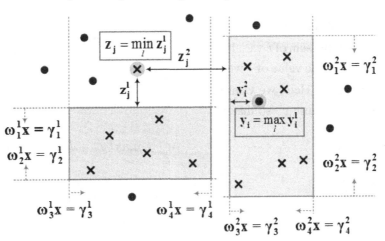

$$y_{ik}^l \geq \omega_k^l A_i - \gamma_k^l, \quad 1 \leq i \leq m_a, \forall l, \forall k$$

$$z_{jk}^l \geq -\omega_k^l B_j + \gamma_k^l, \quad 1 \leq j \leq m_b, \forall l, \forall k$$

$$y_{ik}^l \geq 0, \quad 1 \leq i \leq m_a, \forall l, \forall k$$

$$z_{jk}^l \geq 0, \quad 1 \leq j \leq m_b, \forall l, \forall k$$

where $K = 4$ and $\omega^l = \begin{pmatrix} 0 & 0 & -1 & 1 \\ -1 & 1 & 0 & 0 \end{pmatrix}$.

## MILP Formulation Using Integer Variables

As noted at the beginning of this section, our objective function is not a convex function. To reformulate the problem as a convex form, we introduce new variables. Let's consider type B error term first. We can write

$$v_j^l = z_j^l t_j^l$$

with the constraint for integer variables

$$\sum_{l=1}^{L} t_j^l = 1$$

where $t_j^l$ are integer variables that can have values either 0 or 1. Also, since the sum of $L$ variables is one, only one $t_j^l$ will have the value of 1 while the other $L-1$ terms are zero. Here, we want to make $t_j^{l'} = 1$ where $l' = \operatorname{argmin}_l z_j^l$ so that we have

$$\sum_{l=1}^{L} v_j^l = \min_l z_j^l = \min_l \left( \sum_{k=1}^{4} z_{jk}^l \right).$$

To enforce the relation, we introduce the underestimate of the minimum function by piecewise linear and convex envelope as done in Ryoo and Sahinidis (2001) and Ryoo (2006), which is expressed as

$$v_j^l \geq \max\{z_j^l + Mt_j^l - M, 0\},$$
$$1 \leq j \leq m_b, \forall l$$

where $M$ is an arbitrary positive number that is greater than the maximum value of $z_j^l$. We can see that $v_j^l$ will have non-zero value only when $t_j^l = 1$ and the optimization process will minimize $v_j^l$ to have the minimum of $z_j^l$ for each $j$. As a result, the terms relevant to $z_{jk}^l$ in the objective function can be formulated into

$$\sum_{j=1}^{m_b} \min_l \left( \sum_{k=1}^{4} z_{jk}^l \right) = \sum_{j}^{m_b} \sum_{l}^{L} v_j^l.$$

Now the objective function becomes linear. We can apply the same linearization trick to type A error $y_{ik}^l$. Let the variable $u_i$ be defined as

$$u_i^l = \min_k \{y_{ik}^l\}$$

$$u_i = \max_l u_i^l = \max_l \min_k \{y_{ik}^l\}.$$

Then, we can redefine $u_i$ using integer variables and the underestimate as follows

$$u_{ik}^l = y_{ik}^l s_{ik}^l$$

$$u_{ik}^l \geq \max\{y_{ik}^l + Ms_{ik}^l - M, 0\}$$

$$u_i \geq u_i^l = \sum_{k=1}^{4} u_{ik}^l, \sum_{k} s_{ik}^l = 1, \quad 1 \leq i \leq m_a, \forall l$$

where $s_{ik}^l$ are integer variables that can have values either 0 or 1. Consequently, our objective function for $y_{ik}^l$ becomes

$$\sum_{i=1}^{m_a} \max_l \min_k \{y_{ik}^l\} = \sum_{i=1}^{m_a} u_i.$$

Combining all together, our final convex optimization problem using integer variables can be reformulated as

$$\min_{u,v,y,z,t,s} \left\{ C_1 \sum_{i=1}^{m_a} u_i + C_2 \sum_{j=1}^{m_b} \sum_{l=1}^{L} v_j^l \right\}$$

subject to inequalities for classification errors

$$y_{ik}^l \geq \omega_k^l A_i - \gamma_k^l, \quad 1 \leq i \leq m_a, \forall l, \forall k$$

$$z_{jk}^l \geq -\omega_k^l B_j + \gamma_k^l, \quad 1 \leq j \leq m_b, \forall l, \forall k$$

$$y_{ik}^l \geq 0, \quad 1 \leq i \leq m_a, \forall l, \forall k$$

$$z_{jk}^l \geq 0, \quad 1 \leq j \leq m_b, \forall l, \forall k$$

and underestimate constraints

$$v_j^l \geq z_j^l + M t_j^l - M, \quad 1 \leq j \leq m_b, \forall l$$

$$u_{ik}^l \geq y_{ik}^l + M s_{ik}^l - M, \quad 1 \leq i \leq m_a, \forall l, \forall k$$

$$v_j^l \geq 0, \quad 1 \leq j \leq m_b, \forall l$$

$$u_{ik}^l \geq 0, \quad 1 \leq i \leq m_a, \forall l, \forall k$$

$$u_i \geq \sum_{k=1}^{4} u_{ik}^l, \quad 1 \leq i \leq m_a, \forall l$$

and equalities for integer variables

$$\sum_{l=1}^{L} t_j^l = 1, \quad 1 \leq j \leq m_b, t_j^l \in \{0,1\}$$

$$\sum_{k=1}^{4} s_{ik}^l = 1, \quad 1 \leq i \leq m_a, s_{ik}^l \in \{0,1\}, \forall l$$

where $C_1$ and $C_2$ are weighting parameters. If we increase $C_2$ weight by fixing $C_1$, then we consider type B errors are more important and optimization will try more to reduce type B classification error. On the contrary, if $C_1$ is increasing while $C_2$ is fixed, then optimization will focus more on trying to exclude $B_j$ points.

## Applying Additional Geometry Constraints

Since our problem formulation involves only linear constraints, it is straightforward to add additional geometry constraints to determine the shape of rectangular regions. First, we can add quadratic terms in the objective function to control the dimensions of the rectangles, which is expressed as

$$\min_{u,v,y,z,t,s} \left\{ \begin{array}{l} C_1 \sum_{i=1}^{m_a} u_i + C_2 \sum_{j=1}^{m_b} \sum_{l=1}^{L} v_j^l \\ + C_3 \sum_{l=1}^{L} \left( (w_l)^2 + (h_l)^2 \right) \end{array} \right\}$$

where $h_l = \gamma_1^l + \gamma_2^l$ and $w_l = \gamma_3^l + \gamma_4^l$ correspond to the height and width of $l^{th}$ rectangle respectively. Thus, the third term will give tighter rectangular bounds and user can control $C_3$ to change the strength of the effect. This term also has the effect of minimizing the area of the rectangles because it minimizes the upper bound of the area. This relation comes from the following inequality

$$h_l w_l \leq 0.5(h_l^2 + w_l^2).$$

Moreover, we can specify the aspect ratio of the rectangle or exactly fix the dimension of the rectangles by adding the following constraints

$$w_l = \alpha h_l$$

Where $\alpha$ denotes the aspect ratio, or

$$w_l = \alpha_1, h_l = \alpha_2$$

where $\alpha_1$ and $\alpha_2$ are constants.

## Classification Results

We applied our algorithm to a test data set with 64 type A points and 40 type B points. We used $C_1=1$, $C_2 = 10$, and $C_3 = 0.1$ as weighting terms. AMPL/CPLEX is used to solve MILP (Fourer, Gay & Kernighan, 2002; ILOG, 1998). Figure 4 shows the visualization of the results we obtained. When no additional constraint is applied, the optimizer finds arbitrary axis-aligned rectangles to minimize the objective function. This case gives the tightest rectangles that fit input data as shown in Figure 4(a). If we give fixed aspect ratio constraints, 4:3 in this example, all boundaries has the same shape but different scales. For $L=2$ case in Figure 4(b), we can see that rectangular regions are less tight than the case for arbitrary rectangles, but it still tries to find the best ones with the same aspect ratio. Figure 4(c) is obtained by locating fixed size rectangles to reduce error terms. Since the area of each rectangle is the same, the third term in the objective function is not taken into account. The solver places fixed-size rectangles in the best locations. The result looks quite compelling, which confirms the correctness of our problem formulation.

## The Effects of the Weighting Terms

Here, we briefly show how the results will change depending on the weighting terms in the objective function. First, we compare the effect of first two terms of the objective function. We set $C_1=1$ and use $C_2=0.1$, 1, and 10. The brightest rectangle in Figure 5(a) corresponds to $C_2=10$ case which has the largest area among three. It tries to minimize misclassification of type B data and the rectangular region includes all type B points. On the other hands, the dark color rectangle, when $C_2=0.1$, makes correct decision for all type A points, forcing them to be located outside the rectangle. Figure 5(b) shows the effect of the third term in the objective function. Let $C_1=1$, $C_2=10$, and $C_3=0.1$, 1, 10, and 100. As $C_3$ gets bigger, the resulting rectangular region becomes smaller. Bigger $C_3$ is represented as brighter gray level in Figure 5(b). This experiment shows that each term in the objective function plays an important role in deciding the best classification result and users can tweak the weighting parameters to obtain the boundaries they want.

## Image Capturing Application

In this section, we will present a novel way of capturing image data using our algorithm. The readout speed of imaging system is often bandwidth-limited and it becomes a bottleneck for increasing capturing frame rates. For the limited amount of pixel budget you have at a certain amount of time, it will be better if we can only capture image data that we are more interested in, rather than capturing every pixel from the whole scene. Thus, we can adaptively design an efficient image readout scheme by determining which information is more interesting and how to capture that data efficiently. Since most image sensors are restricted to readout only rectangular windows from sensor plane, determining how to capture data becomes a problem of deciding

*Figure 4. Classification results of rectangles with different constraints for L=1, 2, and 3 ($C_1$=1, $C_2$=10, and $C_3$=0.1). (a) classification with arbitrary size rectangles, (b) classification with 4:3 aspect ratio, (c) classification with fixed size rectangles*

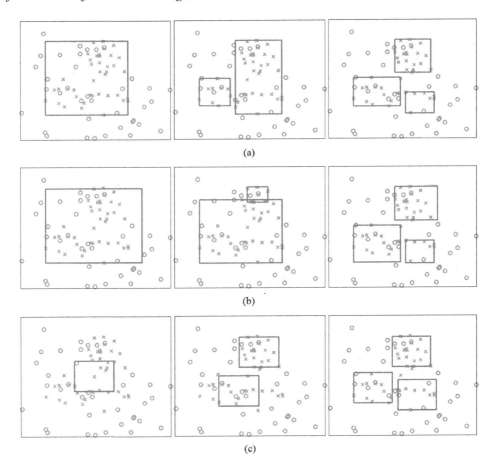

*Figure 5. The effects of changing weighting terms in the objective function. (a) weights on type A and B misclassification, (b) weights on the dimensions of a rectangle*

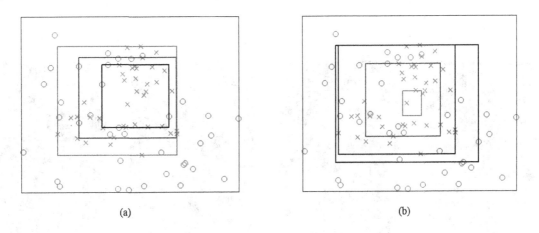

rectangular regions that efficiently incorporate important pixel data. Thus, once you determined which regions are more important, the next step can be solved by applying the algorithm discussed in this chapter.

For instance, you cycle through multiple exposure levels by changing parameter settings every frame to capture high dynamic range video (Debevec & Malik, 1997; Mitsunaga & Nayar, 2000; Kang, Uyttendaele, Winder & Szeliski, 2003). If over-exposed or under-exposed regions are clumped in small regions, you will want to capture only badly exposed regions again since most parts of image are already well-captured by mid-exposure frames and you don't want to waste your pixel budget to capture them again. In this case, badly exposed pixels are points you want to put inside rectangular regions in next capture, while the rest of the area is supposed to be outside of rectangles. This case is shown in Figure 6. Here, we want to set the regions so that we can capture most of over-exposed area while minimizing total readout time. We defined interesting pixels as the ones with value higher than the threshold, which means that they are saturated. A mask is generated to use them as an input data set for the algorithm. Figure 6(b) through 6(d) show the results applied on 86 x 128 image for the cases of one, two, and three rectangular regions respectively. The total readout time for each case will be determined by actual image sensor characteristics, where

the total readout time is the sum of pixel readout time and overhead time. Pixel readout time is proportional to the sum of area of all rectangular regions and overhead time grows as the number of rectangles increases. Thus, if the sensor has very small overhead time, then having more number of rectangular regions will result in less total readout time. However, if overhead time is big relative to pixel readout time, using one or two rectangles will be desirable.

## FUTURE RESEARCH

In this chapter, we come up with a new image capturing scheme as an example of practical applications that use our proposed algorithm. We believe that tons of applications, mostly the ones using image data, will be able to take advantage of using our method and it will be worth to explore various other possibilities that the proposed method is useful in different data sets of multidimensional signal processing.

Also, it will be very useful to extend this method to be applied on larger data sets. Rather than using all input data samples, finding a better feature representation of data by pre-clustering (feature selection or dimensionality reduction) can help reducing the amount of computation required. Using hierarchical approach with some heuristics may give reasonable results in much less time.

*Figure 6. Results of classification applied on real image data. (a) original, (b) L=1, (c) L=2, (d) L=3*

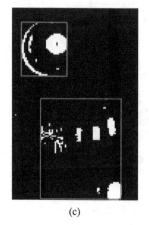
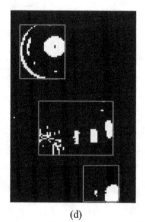

(a)    (b)    (c)    (d)

Some variants of this method will make them more applicable to various real world situations.

## CONCLUSION

In this chapter, we have proposed an automatic classification algorithm that classifies binary labeled data into two regions separated by multiple axis-aligned rectangles. By formulating the problem as a mixed integer and linear programming, we arc able to determine the boundaries of multiple rectangles at the same time. It gives satisfactory results and is easily extended to problems with additional constraints such as enforcing rectangles to have specific aspect ratio or fixed sizes. We also demonstrated that this method can be applied to real image data to come up with an optimal image capturing scheme. We believe that there are various kinds of algorithms and other multidimensional applications in image processing and computer vision field that will benefit from using this work.

## REFERENCES

Anderson, A. J. (1982). *Handbook of statistics*. Amsterdam, The Netherlands: North Holland.

Cortes, C., & Vapnik, V. (1995). Support-vector networks. *Machine Learning*, 273–297. doi:10.1007/BF00994018

Debevec, P. E., & Malik, J. (1997). Recovering high dynamic range radiance maps from photographs. In *Proceedings of the 24th Annual Conference on Computer Graphics and Interactive Techniques* (pp. 369-378).

Fourer, R., Gray, D. M., & Kernighan, B. W. (2002). *AMPL: A modeling language for mathematical programming*. Duxbury Press.

Fukunaga, K. (1990). *Introduction to statistical pattern recognition*. New York, NY: Academic Press.

ILOG, Inc. (1998). *CPLEX 6.0 documentation supplement*.

Jain, A. K., Duin, R. P. W., & Mao, J. (2000). Statistical pattern recognition: A review. *IEEE Transactions on Pattern Analysis and Machine Intelligence, 22*(1), 4–37. doi:10.1109/34.824819

Kang, S. B., Uyttendaele, M., Winder, S., & Szeliski, R. (2003). High dynamic range video. *ACM Transactions on Graphics, 22*(3), 319–325. doi:10.1145/882262.882270

Mitsunaga, T., & Nayar, S. K. (2000). High dynamic range imaging: Spatially varying pixel exposures. In *Proceedings of the IEEE Computer Vision and Pattern Recognition, 1*, 472–479. doi:10.1109/CVPR.2000.855857

Ryoo, H. S. (2006). Pattern classification by concurrently determined piecewise linear and convex discriminant functions. *Computers & Industrial Engineering, 51*(1), 79–89. doi:10.1016/j.cie.2006.06.015

Ryoo, H. S., & Sahinidis, N. V. (2001). Analysis of bounds for multilinear functions. *Journal of Global Optimization, 19*(4), 403–424. doi:10.1023/A:1011295715398

## ADDITIONAL READING

Bishop, C. M. (2006). *Pattern recognition and machine learning*. New York: Springer.

Boyd, S., & Vandenberghe, L. (2004). *Convex optimization*. Cambridge University Press.

Breuel, T. M. (2003). An algorithm for finding maximal whitespace rectangles at arbitrary orientations for document layout analysis. In *Proceedings of Seventh International Conference on Document Analysis and Recognition* (pp. 66-70).

Burges, C. J. C. (1998). A tutorial on support vector machines for pattern recognition. *Data Mining and Knowledge Discovery*, *2*, 121–167. doi:10.1023/A:1009715923555

Das, G. K., & Nickerson, B. G. (2010). I/O-efficient rectangular segment search. In *Proceedings of 2010 International Conference on Computational Science and Its Applications* (pp. 61-67).

Duda, R. O., Hart, P. E., & Stork, D. G. (2001). *Pattern classification* (2nd ed.). New York: Wiley.

Jain, A. K. (2010). Data clustering: 50 years beyond K-means. *Pattern Recognition Letters*, *31*(8), 651–666. doi:10.1016/j.patrec.2009.09.011

Montgomery, E. B. Jr, Huang, H., & Assadi, A. (2005). Unsupervised clustering algorithm for N-dimensional data. *Journal of Neuroscience Models*, *144*(1), 19–24. doi:10.1016/j.jneumeth.2004.10.015

Rikun, A. D. (1997). A convex envelope formula for multilinear functions. *Journal of Global Optimization*, *10*(4), 425–437. doi:10.1023/A:1008217604285

Syeda-Mahmood, T., & Wang, F. (2007). Unsupervised clustering using multi-resolution perceptual grouping. In *Proceedings of the IEEE Computer Vision and Pattern Recognition* (pp. 1-8).

## KEY TERMS AND DEFINITIONS

**Classification:** Supervised learning procedure in which each input data is given a label or class based on quantitative evaluation of one or more decision criteria constructed using training data.

**Clustering:** An example of unsupervised learning in which a set of observations or measurements is assigned into subclasses or clusters.

**Convex Programming:** The object function or cost function is convex and the constraints form a convex set.

**Integer Programming:** A type of nonconvex programming in which some or all variables are forced to take on integer values.

**Linear Programming:** A type of convex programming in which the objective function or cost function is linear with the constraints of linear equalities or inequalities.

**Minimum Bounding Box:** A box with the smallest quantitative measure (eg., number of pixels or area, volume, or hypervolume in higher dimensions) that contains all the data points given.

**Optimization:** Finding the best solution from some sets of candidates based on the quantitative measures (objective functions, cost function, or penalty function).

**Region of Interest (ROI):** A selected subset of observations or samples within a given dataset identified for a specific goal.

**Support Vector Machine:** A supervised classifier that consists of a set of learning methods for data analysis and pattern recognition, with a hyperplane or a set of hyperplanes in a multidimensional feature space.

**Type A Error:** False positive, the error of rejecting a null hypothesis when it is actually true, e.g., unwanted points are located inside the rectangle.

**Type B Error:** False negative, the error of failing to reject a null hypothesis when it is in fact not true, e.g., target points are not included in the rectangle.

**Unsupervised Learning:** A class of machine learning where one finds to determine how the given data or examples are organized without information of a desired output.

Chapter 20

# ICA as Pattern Recognition Technique for Gesture Identification:
## A Study Using Bio–Signal

**Ganesh R Naik**
*RMIT University, Australia*

**Dinesh Kumar**
*RMIT University, Australia*

**Sridhar Arjunan**
*RMIT University, Australia*

## ABSTRACT

*In recent times there is an urgent need for a simple yet robust system to identify natural hand actions and gestures for controlling prostheses and other computer assisted devices. Surface Electromyogram (sEMG) is a non-invasive measure of the muscle activities but is not reliable because there are multiple simultaneously active muscles. This research first establishes the conditions for the applicability of Independent Component Analysis (ICA) pattern recognition techniques for sEMG. Shortcomings related to order and magnitude ambiguity have been identified and a mitigation strategy has been developed by using a set of unmixing matrix and neural network weight matrix corresponding to the specific user. The experimental results demonstrate a marked improvement in the accuracy. The other advantages of this system are that it is suitable for real time operations and it is easy to train by a lay user.*

## INTRODUCTION

Hand actions and maintained gestures are a result of complex combination of contraction of multiple muscles in the forearm. There are numerous possible applications that are based on reliable

DOI: 10.4018/978-1-61350-429-1.ch020

identification of hand gestures including prosthesis control, human computer interface and games. There are three major modes of identification of the hand gestures;

1. mechanical sensors e.g. - sensor gloves. Pavlovic et al (1997) noted that, ideally, naturalness of the interface requires that

any and every gesture performed by the user should be interpretable. The use of glove requires an external device and it also needs the user to noticeably move their limbs in a way that may not be convenient, especially in case of amputees. For amputees, the control commands should be based on the intent of the movement rather than the mechanical movement.

2. vision data with video analysis (Rehg & Kanade, 1993; Schlenzig, Hunter, & Jain, 1994). The state of the art in vision-based gesture recognition is far from providing a satisfactory solution to this problem. A major reason obviously is the complexity associated with the analysis and recognition of gestures. The video sensing is dependent on lighting conditions and unsuitable for very small gestures.

3. muscle electrical activity (Cheron, Draye, Bourgeios, & Libert, 1996; Koike & Kawato, 1996). Surface Electromyography (sEMG) is the electrical recording of the muscle activity from the surface. It is closely related to the strength of muscle contraction and an obvious choice for control of the prosthesis and other similar applications.

Many attempts have been made to use sEMG signal as the command to control the prosthesis (Doerschuk, Gustafon, & Willsky, 1983; Wheeler & Jorgensen, 2003), but to obtain a reliable command signal, the muscle needs to have high level of contraction and with only one primary muscle being active. These techniques are not suitable for gestures where the muscle activity is small and there are multiple muscles active simultaneously such as during maintained hand gestures. This is largely attributable to the high level of cross-talk and low signal to noise ratio, both of which are more significant when the muscle activation level is low. To reliably identify the small movements and gesture of the hand, there is a need to decompose sEMG into muscle activity originating from the different muscles. Spectral and temporal filtering is not suitable for this because of overlapping spectrum and simultaneously active muscles. Blind source separation (BSS) techniques have recently been developed and these provide a solution for such a situation.

BSS techniques such as Independent Component Analysis (ICA) have found numerous applications in audio and biosignal processing disciplines. ICA of sEMG has been proposed for cortical activation of arm, which is outer portion related to arm-movement combinations in 2000 (M. McKeown, 2000). Mckewon and Radtke (2001) demonstrated a method for Phasic and Tonic Coupling between Electroencephalogram (EEG) and sEMG using ICA. Decomposition of sEMG into motor unit action potentials (MUAP) originating from different muscles and motor units has been reported in 2004 (Nakamura, Yoshida, Kotani, Akazawa, & Moritani, 2004). The authors have demonstrated the separation of sEMG using ICA into individual muscle activity for the hand gesture identification (Naik, Kumar, & Palaniswami, 2008; Naik, Kumar, Singh, & Palaniswami, 2006; Naik, Kumar, Weghorn, & Palaniswami, 2007). Other researchers have also demonstrated the use of ICA for separation of other biosignals such as EEG (T.-P. Jung et al., 2000; T. P. Jung et al., 2000). The approaches of Jung et al (T.-P. Jung, et al., 2000; T. P. Jung, et al., 2000) and (Djuwari, Kumar, Naik, Arjunan, & Palaniswami, 2006) are based on using the mixing matrix as an indicator of the relative location of the active sources and these remain unchanged for an individual. This overcomes the magnitude and order ambiguity associated with ICA. One difficulty associated with ICA is that it is an iterative process and the initialisation is random in nature. Most of the ICA algorithms use machine learning based approach in estimating the sources. Because of this reason, the outcome of the separation has a randomness associated with it and the overall performance is not optimum. This results in reduced reliability when the separated signals are classified.

This research reports overcoming limitations of ICA based sEMG decomposition technique. The chapter reports a pattern recognition technique that has substantial improvement in the accuracy of identification of hand gesture based on sEMG. It is a combination of model based approach with blind source separation technique. The proposed technique overcomes the randomness associated with ICA by multiple repetition of estimation of the un-mixing matrix and selecting the best un-mixing matrix based on the highest Signal to Interference Ratio (SIR). This selected matrix is used to decompose the sEMG and the decomposed sEMG is then classified to identify the hand gestures. The results show that, with raw sEMG classification accuracy is 60%, which is significantly improved (up to 99% accuracy) using Multi run ICA (MICA).

## RELATED WORK

There are two broad approaches that have been used for classification of the sEMG to obtain command signals for controlling a prosthetic device. The first approach is to use the amplitude of the *steady state* sEMG signal where the subject exerts constant force with a chosen muscle. A single recording site or channel on this muscle is then used to control in a manner proportional to the amplitude. Many commercially available prosthetics fall into this category, but generally afford the use of only a single degree of freedom such as a gripper for grasping and releasing objects due to the inability of such a system to identify small changes in muscle activity. The second approach uses the initiation of an action as a trigger, coding of which produces functional movements.

Graupe & Cline (1975) were one of the pioneers to classify sEMG signals for prosthetic control. They obtained 85% accuracy in classifying magnitude data from a single channel with autoregressive coefficients as features. While their work is impressive, it is neither suitable for automation nor for identifying number of complex actions. (Englehart & Hudgins, 2003) identified four discrete elbow and forearm movements using the transient structure in the signal by using time-frequency representations of the signal. They achieved accuracy up to 93.7% with four channels of sEMG data from the biceps and triceps. Such a scheme is suitable when there are single prime movers but not for hand gestures, where there are number of multiple active muscles. Nishikawa et al (1999) classified ten discrete movements of the wrist and fingers using four electrodes placed on the forearm. They proposed an online learning scheme, and obtained an average accuracy of 85.1%. The shortcoming in this approach is the large inter-group variations with accuracy of identifying the correct action ranging from 75.2% to 91.7%. Ju, Kaelbling, & Singe (2000) report finger action identification for consumer electronics applications and their technique achieved 85% accuracy in classifying four finger movements with the aid of two pair of electrodes placed close to the wrist. Such accuracy may be suitable for consumer electronics but is unsuitable for rehabilitation and aged care applications. Further, this system has the inter-subject and intra-subject variations and requires the user to train the system for each experiment limiting the suitability of this approach.

Numerous approaches have been applied to solve the problem of visual interpretation of gestures. Many of these approaches have been chosen and implemented to focus on a particular aspect of gestures: Hand tracking, pose classification, or hand posture interpretations (Rehg & Kanade, 1993; Schlenzig, et al., 1994). Farry & Walker (1993) presented myoelectric control of NASM Johnson Space Center's sixteen degree-of-freedom Utah/MIT Dextrous Hand for two grasping (key and chuck) options and three thumb motions (abduction, extension, and flexion). Their work discussed myoelectric signal processing approaches, data collection apparatus, and a real-time teleoperation implementation. They also demonstrated results in real-time discrimination of key and chuck grasps and offline discrimination of thumb motions. Their research outcome included a 90% correct grasp selection rate and an 87% correct thumb motion selection, both using the myoelectric spectrum. Peleg et al (2002) used a combination of a K-nearest neighbour (KNN) classifier and a Genetic Algorithm (GA) for feature selection which results in an average error rate of approximately 2%, thereby making it feasible to operate a robotic replacement arm with relatively few errors using only two pairs of electrodes. Four subjects were participated in the experiment.

Most recent work includes the investigation of hand gestures for six distinct actions (Chan & Englehart, 2005) and a framework where myoelectric signals from natural hand and finger movements can be decoded with a high accuracy. Chan & Englehar (2005) presented the work related to prosthetic applications. Their work includes the investigation of twelve normally limbed subjects (eight males and four females) for six distinct limb motions: *wrist flexion, wrist extension, supination, pronation, hand open*, and *hand close*. Each subject underwent four 60-s sessions, producing continuous contractions. They used short time Fourier transform and a Linear Discriminant Analysis (LDA) classifier to classify the data. Tenore et al., (2007) presented a hand gesture identification device using 32 sEMG electrodes were placed on the forearm of an able-bodied subject while performing individual finger movements. Using time-domain feature extraction methods as inputs to a neural network classifier, they showed that 12 individuated flexion and extension movements of the fingers can be decoded with accuracy higher than 98%. While this approach has the merits of reliability, the difficulty with this approach is that it requires multiple actions, leading to an unnatural and slow system. There is a need for systems that can recognize a range of hand actions that are more subtle and that are a result of multiple active muscles. Such a technique will allow the user to give natural control commands and would not require learning to make a series of actions for a specific command. To reliably identify actions that are based on contraction of multiple muscles requires identifying the level of muscle activity of the different muscles. In this research a model based approach to identify six different hand gestures accurately is presented. The system uses the multi run ICA model with fixed unmixing matrix, which addresses the ambiguity associated with ICA. The extracted features are classified using simple neural network classifier. The system is easy to train and simple to use for gesture recognition.

## BACKGROUND

### Surface Electromyography

sEMG is the recording of the electrical activity of skeletal muscle from the skin surface. It is a result of the superposition of a large number of transients (muscle action potentials) that have temporal and spatial separation that is pseudo-random. The origin of each of the Motor Unit Action Potentials (MUAP) is inherently random and the electrical characteristics of the surrounding tissues are non-linear. Due to the nature of this signal the amplitude of the EMG signal is pseudo-random and the shape of the probability distribution function (PDF) resembles a Gaussian function. sEMG is a non-invasive recording of muscle activity. It requires relatively simple equipment, and is suitable for numerous control applications (Basmajian & Deluca, 1985; Fridlund & Cacioppo, 1986). The close relationship of sEMG with the force of contraction of the muscle is useful for number of applications such as sports training, urinary incontinence and for machine control. The relationship of sEMG spectrum with muscle fatigue is also very useful for occupational health and sports training. While there are numerous applications for sEMG, some are limited due to reliability issues arising due to the complexity of the signal. sEMG may be affected by various factors such as.

- The muscle anatomy (number of active motor units, size of the motor units, the spatial distribution of motor units).
- Muscle physiology (trained or untrained, disorder, fatigue).
- Nerve factors (disorder, neuromuscular junction).
- Contraction (level of contraction, speed of contraction, isometric/non-isometric, force generated).
- Artefacts (crosstalk between muscles, ECG interference).
- Recording apparatus factors (recording-method, noise, electrode's properties and recording sites).

The anatomical/ physiological processes such as properties and dimensions of tissues, and force and duration of contraction of the muscle are known to influence the signal. Peripheral factors such as spacing, type and size of electrodes may also have an influence on the signal (Basmajian & Deluca, 1985), and to obtain reliable information, considering such factors is critical. Some of these factors may be handled through careful skin preparation, and by selecting proper anatomical landmarks for the placement of electrodes. While these factors influence sEMG in general, these factors are more apparent when the sEMG signal strength is very small, such as during static posture.

The complexity of the human body along with the high level of environmental noise results in the bioelectric signal recordings getting corrupted. Environmental noise and electrical activity from parts of the body other than the target muscles gets super-imposed on the recordings. There are number of techniques that are employed to reduce the environmental noise and artefacts from other organs such as by careful selection of the electrode location and with suitably designed acquiring

equipment. But there are number of conditions where the artefacts may be very strong and prevent the useful interpretation of the desired signals. Examples of such situations include sEMG recordings from the back and thorax region that have ECG and breathing artefacts, and the artefacts maybe of much greater magnitude than the signal. The other example is during the sEMG recordings of the digitas muscles to identify the hand gestures where the cross talk due to the different muscles can result in unreliable recordings. One property of the sEMG is that the signal originating from one muscle can generally be considered to be independent of other bioelectric signals such as electrocardiogram (ECG), electro-oculargram (EOG), and signals from neighbouring muscles. This opens an opportunity of the use of ICA for this application.

## Basic Principles of ICA

Signals from different sources can get mixed during recording. Often it is required to separate the original signals, and there is little information available of the original signals. An example is the cocktail party problem (Bell & Sejnowski, 1995; Hyvärinen, Karhunen, & Oja, 2001). Even if there is no (limited) information available of the original signals or the mixing matrix, it is possible to separate the original signals using ICA under certain conditions. ICA is an iterative technique that estimates the statistically independent source signals from a given set of their linear combinations. The process involves determining the mixing matrix. The independent sources could be audio signals such as speech, voice, music, or signals such as bioelectric signals (Bell & Sejnowski, 1995; Hyvärinen, Karhunen, & Oja, 2001).

ICA is a new statistical technique that aims at transforming an input vector into a signal space in which the signals are statistically in-dependent. The drawback of ICA, namely the need of high order statistics in order to determine ICA expansion, is counterbalanced by its performances, which are more meaningful compared with other methods like Principal Component Analysis (PCA)

ICA assumes the mixing process as linear, so it can be expressed as:

$$X = As \qquad (1)$$

Where $x = [x_1(t), x_2(t), ..., x_n(t)]$ are the recordings, $s = [s_1(t), s_2(t), ..., s_n(t)]$ the original signals and $A$ is the $n \times n$ mixing matrix of real numbers. This mixing matrix and each of the original signals are unknown. To separate the recordings to the original signals (estimated original signals, $u$), the task is to estimate an un-mixing matrix $W$ ($W = A^{-1}$) so that:

$$u = Wx = A^{-1}As \qquad (2)$$

For this purpose, ICA relies strongly on the statistical independence of the sources $s$.

The ICA technique iteratively estimates the un-mixing matrix using the maximisation of independence of the unmixed signals as the cost function. Signals $s = [s_1(t), s_2(t), ..., s_n(t)]$ are statistically independent if the joint probability density of those components can be expressed as a multiplication of their marginal probability density. It is important to observe the distinction between independence and uncorrelatedness, since decorrelation can always be performed by transforming the signals with a whitening matrix $V$ to get the identity covariance matrix $I$. Independent signals are always uncorrelated but uncorrelated signals are not always independent. But in case of Gaussian signals, uncorrelatedness implies independence. Transforming of a Gaussian signal with any orthogonal un-mixing matrix or transform results in another Gaussian signal, and thus the original signals cannot be separated. Hence Gaussian signals are forbidden for ICA. Thus the key of independent component estimation is measuring the non-Gaussianity of the signals (Bell & Sejnowski, 1995, 1997; Comon, 1994;

Hyvärinen, et al., 2001; Lee, 1998). Numerous ICA algorithms have been developed for signal processing research. An efficient algorithm is Fast ICA that is based on the Gaussianity as the cost function and has been used in this research. This has been found to be suitable for near Gaussian signals such as sEMG.

## FastICA

The ICA technique iteratively estimates the unmixing matrix using the maximisation of independence of the unmixed signals as the cost function. Substantial research has been conducted on algorithms using higher order statistics for estimation of ICA. One of the widely used techniques among these is FastICA. FastICA is a fixed point algorithm that employs higher order statistics for the recovery of independent sources (Hyvärinen, Karhunen, & Oja, 2001). Separation is performed to obtain uncorrelated and independent sources whose amplitude distributions are as non-Gaussian as possible are obtained. The non-Gaussianity is measured with the differential entropy $J$, called negentropy, which is defined as the difference between the entropy of a Gaussian random variable $y\_gauss$ (having the same mean and variance of the observed random variable $y$) and the entropy $y$.

$$J(y) = H(y_{gauss}) - H(y) \qquad (3)$$

Where the entropy $H$ is given by

$$H(y) = -\int f(y) \log(f(y)) \, dy \qquad (4)$$

Since Gaussian random variables have the largest entropy H among all random variables having equal variance, maximizing the negantropy, $J(y)$ leads to the separation of independent source signals. FastICA can estimate Independent Components (ICs) one by one (deflation approach) or simultaneously (symmetric approach), and the extracted number of ICs can be lower than the number of mixtures so that the unmixing matrix W can be rectangular. FastICA uses simple estimates of negentropy based on the maximum entropy principle (Hyvärinen, Karhunen, & Oja, 2001).

The successful separation of the original signals is dependent on the fulfilment of the following conditions;

- The source signals s(t) are at each time instant statistically independent
- The source signals must have non Gaussian distributions
- The number sensors (recordings) must be greater than or equal to the number of sources
- The recorded signals must be (approximately) linear combinations of the independent sources and
- There should be no (little) noise common to the sources

While ICA has demonstrated success in the ability to separate signals, the output of ICA suffers from the following ambiguities:

- The order of the independent components cannot be fixed and this may change for each estimate.
- The amplitude and sign of the independent components cannot be determined.

In most applications such as the cocktail party problem, these are not serious problems. The supervisor is able to identify the different sources and determine the quality of the separation by listening to the sounds. When dealing with signals such as sEMG signals, the order of signals and the relative value of the signal magnitude are very important to estimate the correct action. To summarise from the above, the signals that can be separated need to be non-Gaussian and independent. For the purpose of applying ICA to sEMG recordings, there is a need to determine the conditions under which these signals can be considered as independent and non-Gaussian, and the mixing matrix can be considered to be stationary and linear. The following section verifies the suitability of ICA for sEMG decomposition.

## Suitability of ICA for Decomposing sEMG

The suitability of ICA to separate the signals originating from different sources is based on the following assumptions:

- The sources are independent.
- The sources are stationary (relative to the recorder),
- The signals are non-Gaussian, and
- Signal propagation delay is negligible.

Below are the arguments demonstrating that muscle electrical activity at low level of muscle contraction satisfies each of the above criteria.

Each muscle is a set of motor units that is well separated from the other muscles and hence each muscle can be assumed to be an independent source.

- At low level of contraction, the muscle activity can be assumed to be made of independent motor unit action potentials (MUAP) that are individual pulses and thus the finite sum of these is non-Gaussian.
- At low level of muscle contraction, the length and position of the muscles with respect to the skin and other muscles remains stationary and hence with respect to the recording electrodes.
- Volume conduction in tissue is essentially instantaneous (T. P. Jung, et al., 2000; Makeig, Bell, Jung, & Sejnowski, 1996).

Based on the above, the authors have developed and reported the technique where the un-mixing

*Table 1. Overall average results for hand gestures using ICA*

| Number of gestures | Type of gestures recognized | Accuracy of Classification % |
|---|---|---|
| Three | G1, G2 and G5 <br> G2, G2 and G6 <br> G1, G3 and G5 | 100 <br> 99.8 <br> 99.7 |
| Four | G1, G2, G5 and G6 <br> G1,G3, G4 and G5 <br> G2,G4, G5 and G6 | 85 <br> 84.5 <br> 84 |
| Five | G1, G2, G4, G5 and G6 <br> G1,G3, G4,G5 and G6 | 73 <br> 72.4 |
| Six | G1, G2, G3,G4, G5 and G6 | 65 |

matrix is estimated using ICA (Naik, et al., 2008). Using this un-mixing matrix, sEMG recordings can be decomposed on an ongoing basis for a given electrode position. The vector consisting of Root Mean Square (RMS) values averaged over the duration of the action are representative features of the action. Other researchers have reported success in the use of this approach to decompose EEG data (T. P. Jung, et al., 2000; Makeig, et al., 1996).

The preliminary work (Table 1) by the authors demonstrates that the reliability of this technique becomes very low when the number of complex gestures is greater than 3. This can be attributable to one major shortcoming of this approach which is the randomness associated with the iterative process. There are two major techniques proposed in literature for improving the outcome of an iterative learning method;

1. by reducing the tolerable error, and
2. changing the cost-function.

Choice of the cost-function has an impact but did not make any large impact of the final outcome. Our preliminary work demonstrated that reduction of the tolerable error during training beyond did not have an impact on reduction of the error. From the above, it is evident that, choice of cost function and reduction of error during training are not able to overcome the shortcoming and there is

a need for identifying a technique that can be used to obtain the best estimate of the unmixing matrix.

## Multi-Run ICA

The pseudo-random initialization and iterative process of estimating the un-mixing matrix can be modeled as a viscosity based stochastic process modeled using Langevin equation. The repetition of the ICA iteration would lead to a converging number of un-mixing matrices. ICA is an iterative technique and provides different un-mixing matrix for each ICA computation. This also suggests that if the order ambiguity associated with ICA was to be ignored, a set of finite repetition of ICA (such as fastICA) would result in the estimation of all possible un-mixing matrices. This indicates that choice of un-mixing matrix is highly important for best possible source estimation. Based on this principle, the authors estimated all possible un-mixing matrices for a given set of mixture of source signals and using a quality of separation as the criteria, to compute the best estimate. While there are number of measures of quality, the most suitable measure for quality of separation of biosignals is SIR.

### Signal to Interference Ratio

SIR as a cost factor is a very efficient criteria for reducing the effect of co-channel interference (Cichocki & Amari, 2002). SIR is the ratio of the power of the wanted signal to the total residue power of the unwanted signals. This performance index could be used for full-rank or non-full rank analysis. To determine the efficacy of using SIR for an application, the authors have demonstrated the quality of separation on synthetically mixed data and experimentally tested this for real data, where the original source signals $s_j$ $(j = 1,...,N)$, the mixing matrix $A$, the observations $x_i$ $(i = 1,...,M)$, the estimated separation matrix $W$, and the estimated source signals $y_j$ $(j = 1,...,N)$ are all available. For real world problems, there is no access to the original signals $s_j$ and the mixing matrix $A$. In this scenario the computation of the $SIR_{estimate}$ would be the SIR for real world data.

In view of the problem of one component estimation, we have

$$y_i = w_i^T X = \left( w_i^T A \right) S = g_i S = \sum_{j=1}^{N} g_{ij} s_j \qquad (5)$$

where $y_i$ and $s_j$ are the estimated component and the $j$-th source, respectively; $w_i^T$ is a row vector of un-mixing matrix $W$, $g_i$ is a normalized row vector $[\,0\ 0\ g_{ij}\ 0\ 0\,]$. Because $y_i$ is the estimation of $s_j$, the ideal normalized vector $g_i$ is the unit vector $u_j = [0\ 0\ ...1\ ...0]$. Therefore, one analysis is successful if and only if its vector $g_i$ is similar to one unit vector $u_j$. Actually, vector $g_i$ is one row of matrix $G$. So, the quality of each estimated component just depends on one row of matrix $G$. The more different each row of $G$ is to each corresponding unit vector of $R^{NxN}$, the less quality of output we have. The SIR of each mixing matrix was computed using the following expression which evaluates the success of one component separation (Cichocki & Amari, 2002).

$$SIR\_g = -10\log \left( \left\| g_i - u_j \right\|_2^2 \right) \qquad (6)$$

The above equation explains the SIR computation for individual matrix components. The SIR of the whole matrix can be computed using equation (5) which is explained below.

Taking into account that the global transfer function of the mixing-separating system can be defined as $G = A*W$, one can formulate the SIR for the matrix as (Cichocki & Amari, 2002)

$$SIR = SIR\_estimate$$
$$= -10\log \frac{E\left\{ \left( g_{jj} * s_j \right)^2 \right\}}{E\left\{ \left[ \sum_{\substack{k=1 \\ k \neq j}}^{N} g_{jk} * s_k \right]^2 \right\}}, \qquad j = 1,...,N$$
$$(7)$$

The best un-mixing matrix is selected based on the computation of the highest SIR of the repeated mixing matrices. Once the best un-mixing matrix is identified, this is then representing the model of sEMG recording at the site and is to be maintained for the specific electrode location. The output of this un-mixing matrix is an estimate of activity of the different muscles associated with the action or gestures. RMS values of these estimated muscle activity are indicator of the relative strength of contraction of the muscles and can be used to identify the action that is corresponding to the recorded sEMG using a suitable supervised classifier.

Based on the above, the authors propose - a sEMG based action identification system that is suitable when muscle activity is low and there are multiple muscles that are simultaneously active for that action. The system is based on MICA that identifies a suitable un-mixing matrix based on SIR, and classifies the RMS of the separated muscle activity using a Back propagation Neural Network (BPN).

*Figure 1. Hand gesture experimental set up with four bipolar electrodes*

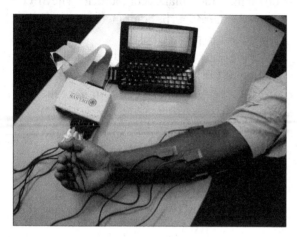

## MATERIALS AND METHODS

Experiments were conducted to evaluate the performance of the proposed system to identify finger and wrist flexion from sEMG recorded on the forearm. The RMIT University human experiments ethics committee approved the experimental protocol. Seven volunteers, aged between 21 and 32 years, participated in the experiments.

## Data Acquisition

sEMG recordings were obtained using a proprietary sEMG acquisition system by DELSYS (Boston, MA, USA). The parallel-bar sEMG sensor was used for recording. Each channel consists of a pair of differential electrodes with a fixed inter-electrode distance of 10mm and a gain of 1000 (Figure 1). The signal was band-pass filtered between 20-450Hz. Prior to placing the electrode, skin of the participant was prepared by shaving (if required) and exfoliation to remove dead skin. Skin was cleaned with 70% v/v alcohol swab to remove any oil or dust from the skin surface (Basmajian & Deluca, 1985). The skin impedance between the electrodes was measured and in all cases was less than 60 Kilo Ohm. Standard isometric manual muscle testing was performed to verify

electrode placement (Basmajian & Deluca, 1985; Fridlund & Cacioppo, 1986; Hermens, 1999). Four muscle groups in forearm were chosen for this study: *Brachioradialis, Flexor Carpi Radialis (FCR), Flexor Carpi Ulnaris (FCU)* and *Flexor Digitorum Superficialis (FDS)*. These muscles play an important role in wrist and finger flexion movements (Basmajian & Deluca, 1985).

Subjects were asked to keep the forearm resting on the table with elbow at an angle of 90 degree (approximately) and in a comfortable position. Six subtle (low level contraction) actions involving finger and wrist flexion were performed and repeated 12 times (refer Figure 2). Raw sEMG was sampled at 1024 samples/second and recorded. Markers were manually inserted to obtain the start and completion of each action. The actions were chosen such that these corresponded to simultaneous contraction by multiple muscles to test the ability of the system to decompose muscle activity when multiple muscles are simultaneously active. The six actions and the short names are given below:

- G1 - Wrist flexion- basal
- G2 - Finger flexion -ring finger and the middle finger together
- G3 - Wrist flexion towards little finger.
- G4 - Wrist flexion towards thumb.
- G5 - Finger and wrist flexion together.
- G6 - Finger and wrist flexion towards little finger.

## Preliminary Analysis Using Scatter Plot

Prior to classification of the hand gesture data, the preliminary analysis was performed, where the patterns of both the raw sEMG Hand gesture data and the multi run ICA data was plotted. The raw sEMG and multi run ICA separated sEMG data are shown in the Figures 3 and 4 respectively. From the preliminary data analysis, it is evident that MICA is able to separate the different classes.

*Figure 2. Six gestures performed during the experiment*

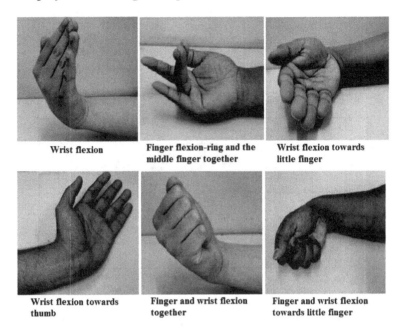

| | | |
|---|---|---|
| **Wrist flexion** | **Finger flexion-ring and the middle finger together** | **Wrist flexion towards little finger** |
| **Wrist flexion towards thumb** | **Finger and wrist flexion together** | **Finger and wrist flexion towards little finger** |

This analysis also shows that MICA is able to extract the best features for further classification.

## Data Analysis

The data was analyzed to compare the performance of MICA based un-mixing matrix that has been optimized using SIR with the performance of general ICA based sEMG separation and that of unseparated sEMG for identifying finger and wrist flexion. The length of each sEMG segment was approximately 2500 samples (2.5 seconds) and this corresponded to the duration of each action. To

*Figure 3. Scatter plot of 2 channel raw sEMG data*

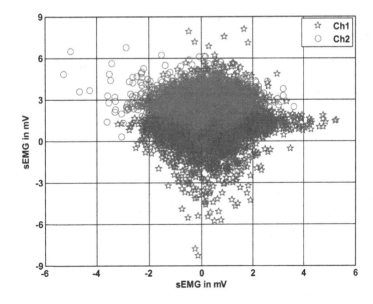

*Figure 4. Scatter plot of 2 channel MICA separated sEMG data*

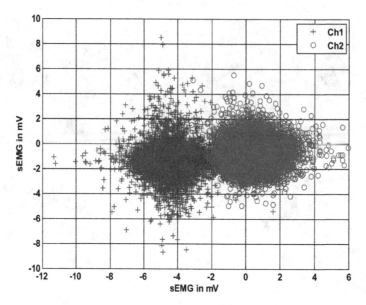

determine the efficacy of MICA, sEMG recordings were analyzed under the three conditions;

1. when sEMG was not separated,
2. when sEMG was separated using ICA and
3. when sEMG was separated using MICA.

These are described below:

- RMS of the unseparated sEMG was computed for each action, and 4 randomly selected examples out of the 12 were used to train the BPN. This was then tested using the balance 8 examples and the results were recorded. The training and testing was done for each subject.

- sEMG was separated using fastICA (one of the example is show in Figure 5) and computing RMS for the separated muscle

*Figure 5. One of the examples of estimated four channel source signals s(t) from a four channel recording x(t)-1024 sampling rate using fast ICA*

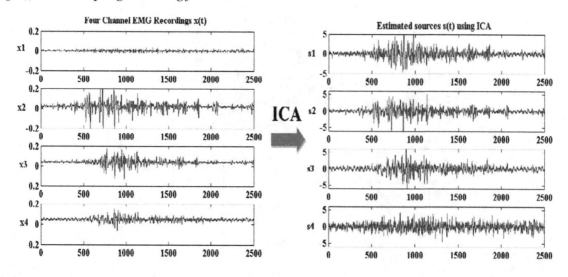

activity for each of the actions. Similar to earlier, 4 examples were randomly selected for the purpose of training, and the balance 8 was used for testing. This was repeated for each subject.

- sEMG was separated using MICA by repeating the estimation of un-mixing matrix using the same signals and the system initialized randomly each time prior to computing the ICA. Preliminary experiments revealed that after 10 repetitions, the mixing matrices begin to repeat and hence the MICA was performed for 10 runs. FastICA was used for these experiments, but it should be mentioned that this is a general approach and is suitable for other similar ICA algorithms as well. Example of the SIR values for the MICA for hand gesture experiments are shown in Table 2. Similar to earlier, four examples were randomly selected for the purpose of training, and the balances eight were used for testing. This was repeated for each subject.

## Pattern Classification Using Neural Network

Gesture recognition requires the classification of features of EMG recordings. One of the widely used techniques to classify the EMG features includes Artificial Neural Networks (ANN) and fuzzy clustering techniques. Hudgins' identification of non random structure in the myoelectric signal at the onset of a muscle contraction suggests that pattern-recognition techniques may be beneficially applied to the myoelectric control problem (Hudgins, Parker, & Scott, 1993). If the myoelectric signal patterns caused by a variety of voluntary muscle motions can be reliably identified, they can be used to control prosthetic devices. Fundamental process of pattern recognition is some form of classification decision in which input data are assigned to a limited number of distinct classes. Data samples within the same class are assumed to have one or more specific features in common which would cause them to be placed in the same class. This basic classification-process model is used in several approaches which have been developed to analyze the structure of the sEMG signal. Of significance to the current work are approaches which take advantage of the unique computational abilities of ANN to perform the classification task. ANN-based classifiers are able to classify input data into distinct classes by "learning" the optimum set of boundary definitions given the desired class membership of each input case. This adaptive behaviour makes the neural network a powerful idea for classification applications where the relationship between the inputs and the respective desired output classes is complex or difficult to resolve.

This work reports the use of BPN for identifying the gestures from EMG features. BPN is a supervised ANN that gives the user the flexibility of choosing the parameters. The data was classified using BPN that consisted of two hidden layers with a total of 20 nodes. This was determined by trial and error approach. Back propagation gradient descent ANN training algorithm with sigmoid threshold was used for training and testing. After training, the weight matrix was saved and used during testing to classify the input data not used for training.

The input to the BPN was the vector of four values of RMS corresponding to each action and the output was a number 1 to 6 corresponding to the action number. The RMS was computed for 2.5 seconds long windows which corresponds to the speeds of the commonly available motor based robotic hands. Preliminary experiments were also conducted with window size corresponding to 500 milliseconds with no change in the overall outcomes of the results indicating the system is suitable for 500 milliseconds window size. The output of the BPN during testing was recorded and compared with the known action. Error was measured by adding zero when the output was same as known action and one when the output was different and thus corresponding to the output being erroneous. Performance was measured by determining the average error (percentage) during the testing.

The data was classified using BPN that consisted of two hidden layers with a total of 20 nodes. This was determined by trial and error approach. Back propagation gradient descent ANN training algorithm with sigmoid threshold was used for training and testing. After training, the weight matrix was saved and used during testing to classify the input data not used for training. The input to the BPN was the vector of four values of RMS corresponding to each action and the output was a number 1 to 4 corresponding to the action number. The output of the BPN during testing was recorded and compared with the known action. Error was measured by adding zero when the output was same as known action and one when the output was different and thus corresponding to the output being erroneous. Performance was measured by determining the average error (percentage) during the testing.

## RESULTS

From the preliminary analysis it is clear that the raw sEMG is unable to separate the different gestures, as it has more overlapping patterns (Figure 3). Whereas, the MICA separated pattern (Figure 4) shows that, the source separation technique, such as MICA is suitable for the gesture identification task.

The experimental results corresponding to hand gesture identification using single run ICA for different gesture combinations are tabulated in Table 1. From the table it can be seen that traditional ICA is able to classify various 3 gesture combinations near 100% accuracy. This decreases to 84.5% (average) for four combinations. For five and six gesture combinations the ICA accuracy drops to 72.7% and 65% respectively. The results

indicate that traditional ICA method is good for simple gestures, while for complex gestures it shows poor performance. This could be attributable to the randomness associated with traditional ICA methods.

An example of the variations in the values of SIR when using the same signal files and using the same ICA algorithm is shown in Table 2.

From Table 2 it is observed that there is a very large variation (in this example) ranging from 11.4dB to 44.3dB and this indicates that if the unmixing matrix was chosen without considering SIR, the quality of the output may have a high level of variability.

The average results (seven subjects) of identifying all the six hand gestures using sEMG based on three methods for experiments conducted on two different days are shown in Table 3. The three methods used are:

- Method 1 - Classification results for hand gestures using Raw sEMG (without using ICA)
- Method 2 - Classification results for hand gestures using traditional ICA
- Method 3 - Classification results for hand gestures using MICA

*Table 2. SIR values for multi run ICA. Trial 3 has the lowest and trial 9 has the highest value of SIR in this example.*

| Multi run ICA trials | SIR values (dB) |
|:---:|:---:|
| 1 | 17.7088 |
| 2 | 18.0703 |
| 3 | **11.4211** |
| 4 | 25.7227 |
| 5 | 18.4163 |
| 6 | 24.6118 |
| 7 | 31.9806 |
| 8 | 29.8952 |
| 9 | **44.3187** |
| 10 | 21.8637 |

*Table 3. Average classification accuracy to identify hand gesture for RMS of (i) raw sEMG, (ii) sEMG separated using ICA and (iii) sEMG separated using MICA*

| Method 1 | | Method 2 | | Method 3 | |
|---|---|---|---|---|---|
| Day 1 | Day 2 | Day 1 | Day 2 | Day 1 | Day 2 |
| 60% | 60% | 65% | 65% | 99% | 99% |

From this table it is observed that the raw sEMG results (Method 1) show an overall efficiency of 60%. The accuracy of classification after sEMG was separated using ICA (Method 2) is 65% (average). The accuracy of classification using MICA (Method 3) is 99% (average). From this table, it is also observed that the average accuracy remained unchanged for the two days trials for all the three methods. The same results on two days show that there is no inter-subject or intra-subject variation associated with the proposed techniques. The results indicate that using raw sEMG has the poorest results and there was only a small improvement when sEMG is separated prior to classification using ICA, but with the use of MICA, there is a dramatic improvement of the accuracy from 65% to 99%.

The presented work has demonstrated that use of the RMS of sEMG recorded from four channels from the forearm and ICA methods are not suitable to accurately identify finger and wrist flexions. Using MICA, there is a substantial improvement and the accuracy of the system increases to 99%.

## Confusion Matrix for Gestures

To measure the performance of the classifiers for both datasets, a confusion matrix is used. This matrix illustrates the result of the classification. It has as many rows and columns as classes of gestures. The element placed in the row $i$ and column $j$ indicates the percentage of gestures of type $j$ that are classified as gestures of type $i$. Therefore, correctly classified gestures will be in the diagonal of the matrix. In the following results each element of the tables has two num-

bers. The first and second numbers indicate the classification accuracy of the training and testing set respectively.

Table 4 shows the confusion matrix of the gesture recognition system based on MICA and neural networks. The overall performance of this classifier is 99.0%. The recognition accuracy ranges from 99.2% to 98.7%, and the order of the recognition is: G4 (99.2%), G2 (99.1%), G3 and G6 (98.9%) and G1 and G5 (98.7%). G1 (wrist flexion) is misclassified partly with G5 (finger and wrist flexion) (1.3%), while G2 is misclassified partly with G6 (0.9%). From this list, it can be observed that there is little difference between the misclassification of the different gestures.

## DISCUSSIONS AND CONCLUSION

From the results it is evident that classifying sEMG against 6 different finger and wrist flexion actions without any separation gives poor results of only 60%, while after separation using ICA, there is only a small improvement to 65%. Using MICA, there is a substantial improvement and the accuracy of the system increases to 99%. The reason for this is due to randomness associated with the estimation of un-mixing matrix using ICA, and the variation in the quality of separation measured with SIR is very large varying from a low of 11.4 to a high value of 44.3. A result of this large variation is that the resultant classification has a high level of variation and results in an overall poor accuracy in the classification. This research has compared the outcomes of using sEMG without separation, using sEMG after separating using ICA, and sEMG

*Table 4. Confusion matrix for 6 gestures*

| Gestures | G1 | G2 | G3 | G4 | G5 | G6 |
|---|---|---|---|---|---|---|
| G1 | **100.0/98.7** | 0.0/0.0 | 0.0/0.7 | 0.0/0.0 | 0.0/0.4 | 0.0/0.0 |
| G2 | 0.0/0.0 | **100.0/99.1** | 0.0/0.4 | 0.0/0.0 | 0.0/0.0 | 0.0/0.0 |
| G3 | 0.0/0.0 | 0.0/0.0 | **100.0/98.9** | 0.0/0.0 | 0.0/0.0 | 0.0/0.6 |
| G4 | 0.0/0.0 | 0.0/0.0 | 0.0/0.0 | **100.0/99.2** | 0.0/0.9 | 0.0/0.5 |
| G5 | 0.0/1.3 | 0.0/0.0 | 0.0/0.0 | 0.0/0.3 | **100.0/98.7** | 0.0/0.0 |
| G6 | 0.0/0.0 | 0.0/0.9 | 0.0/0,0 | 0.0/0.5 | 0.0/0.0 | **100.0/98.9** |

separated using MICA. The results indicate the very poor accuracy using unseparated sEMG and sEMG after ICA, and this is attributable to the high level of cross-talk, noise and low signal strength. The poor accuracy using ICA is also indicated from Table 1 which demonstrates that the quality of separation using ICA can be highly variable. MICA overcomes this shortcoming of ICA and the results clearly show that there is a marked improvement from 65% to 99%.

Overall, the purpose of this project is to develop new perceptual interfaces for human-computer-interaction based on hand gesture identification, and to investigate how such interfaces can complement or replace traditional interfaces based on keyboards, mice, remote controls, data gloves or speech. Applications fields for hand gestures analysis include control of consumer electronics, interaction with visualization systems, control of mechanical systems, and computer games.

One important benefit of such a Human Computer Interface (HCI) approach is that visual information makes it possible to communicate with computerized equipment at a distance, without a need for physical contact to the controlled target. Compared to speech commands, hand gestures are especially advantageous in noisy environments – particularly in situations where speech commands would be disturbed – as well as for communicating quantitative information and spatial relationships. Furthermore, the human user shall be enabled to control electronic systems in a quite natural manner, without requiring specialized external equipment.

MICA based system requires only 4 set of electrodes that can be easily mounted by the user and trained using 4 examples of the actions. Such a system is easy to train and use, making it suitable for being used by an individual without expert assistance. There are number of possible applications of such a system including human computer interface for the elderly, the weak and people with special needs. The small number of electrodes makes it also suitable for prosthetic control where the electrodes may be easily placed above the amputation point. Such a system gives a natural and seamless means of giving commands or controlling devices.

One of the possible shortcomings of such the proposed technique is that even after separation, background noise can make the segmentation difficult to automate and hence there is need for identifying a non-linear feature set that can replace RMS of the signal. The other shortcoming of such a technique is that while it has made a set of unmixing and classification matrices, there is the randomness associated with genetic algorithms and this set is not optimized. There is a need for optimizing such a system.

## FUTURE DIRECTIONS

While this chapter reports experiments conducted for finger and wrist flexion, this technique is suitable for the analysis of other actions and postures where cross-talk due to overlapping muscles is an issue such as when studying muscles of the lower back. Future research based on this pattern recognition includes the control of sEMG based prosthetic or robotic hands, that can perform more humanlike and inherent movements is desired in rehabilitation engineering and welfare work, especially by amputee patients. Prosthetic hand controlled by sEMG has the ability to control more joints than other conventional prosthetic hands, such as functional upper extremity prostheses, which can control no more than two joints. The visual feedback for these kinds of systems requires training based on the control of a virtual hand. The reported pattern recognition technique can be extended to identification for various hand and finger movements based on the user input, which can be used to control the virtual hand. This will be useful for training the amputee before the use of the actual prosthetic hand, where the feedback is provided based on the user intentions.

# REFERENCES

Basmajian, & Deluca, C. (1985). *Muscles alive: Their functions revealed by electromyography*. Williams & Wilkins.

Bell, A. J., & Sejnowski, T. J. (1995). An information-maximization approach to blind separation and blind deconvolution. *Neural Computation*, 7(6), 1129–1159. doi:10.1162/neco.1995.7.6.1129

Bell, A. J., & Sejnowski, T. J. (1997). The independent components of natural scenes are edge filters. *Vision Research*, 37(23), 3327–3338. doi:10.1016/S0042-6989(97)00121-1

Chan, A. D. C., & Englehart, K. B. (2005). Continuous myoelectric control for powered prostheses using hidden Markov models. *IEEE Transactions on Bio-Medical Engineering*, 52(1), 121–124. doi:10.1109/TBME.2004.836492

Cheron, G., Draye, J. P., Bourgeios, M., & Libert, G. (1996). A dynamic neural network identification of electromyography and arm trajectory relationship during complex movements. *IEEE Transactions on Bio-Medical Engineering*, 43(5), 552–558. doi:10.1109/10.488803

Cichocki, A., & Amari, S.-I. (2002). *Adaptive blind signal and image processing: Learning algorithms and applications*. John Wiley \& Sons, Inc.

Comon, P. (1994). Independent component analysis: A new concept? *Signal Processing*, 36(3), 287–314. doi:10.1016/0165-1684(94)90029-9

Djuwari, D., Kumar, D. K., Naik, G. R., Arjunan, S. P., & Palaniswami, M. (2006). Limitations and applications of ICA for surface electromyogram. *Electromyography and Clinical Neurophysiology*, 46(5), 295–309.

Doerschuk, P., Gustafon, D., & Willsky, A. (1983). Upper extremity limb function discrimination using EMG signal analysis. *IEEE Transactions onBiomedical Engineering*, BME-30(1), 18-29.

Englehart, K., & Hudgins, B. (2003). A robust, real-time control scheme for multifunction myoelectric control. *IEEE Transactions onBiomedical Engineering*, 50(7), 848-854.

Farry, K. A., & Walker, I. D. (1993). *Myoelectric teleoperation of a complex robotic hand*. Paper presented at the IEEE International Conference on Robotics and Automation.

Fridlund, A. J., & Cacioppo, J. T. (1986). Guidelines for human electromyographic research. *Psychophysiology*, 23(5), 567–589. doi:10.1111/j.1469-8986.1986.tb00676.x

Graupe, D., & Cline, W. (1975). Functional separation of EMG signals via ARMA identification methods for prosthesis control purposes. *IEEE Transactions on Systems, Man, and Cybernetics*, 5, 252–259.

Hermens, H. (1999). *European recommendations for surface electromyography: Results of the Seniam Project (SENIAM)*. Roessingh Research and Development.

Hudgins, B., Parker, P., & Scott, R. N. (1993). A new strategy for multifunction myoelectric control. *IEEE Transactions on Bio-Medical Engineering, 40*(1), 82–94. doi:10.1109/10.204774

Hyvärinen, A., Karhunen, J., & Oja, E. (2001). *Independent component analysis*. Wiley-Interscience. doi:10.1002/0471221317

Ju, P., Kaelbling, L. P., & Singer, Y. (2000). *State-based classification of finger gestures from electromyographic signals*. Paper presented at the Seventeenth International Conference on Machine Learning.

Jung, T. P., Makeig, S., Humphries, C., Lee, T. W., McKeown, M. J., & Iragui, V. (2000). Removing electroencephalographic artifacts by blind source separation. *Psychophysiology, 37*(2), 163–178. doi:10.1111/1469-8986.3720163

Jung, T.-P., Makeig, S., Lee, T.-W., McKeown, M., Brown, G., Bell, A., et al. (2000). *Independent component analysis of biomedical signals*. Paper presented at the International Workshop on Independent Component Analysis and Signal Separation.

Koike, Y., & Kawato, M. (1996). Human interface using surface electromyography signals. *Electronics and Communications in Japan (Part III Fundamental Electronic Science), 79*(9), 15–22. doi:10.1002/ecjc.4430790902

Lee, T.-W. (1998). *Independent component analysis: Theory and applications*. Kluwer Academic Publishers.

Makeig, S., Bell, A., Jung, T., & Sejnowski, T. (1996). *Independent component analysis of electroencephalographic data*. Paper presented at the Advances in Neural Information Processing Systems.

McKeown, M. (2000). Cortical activation related to arm-movement combinations. *Muscle & Nerve, 23*(S9), S19–S25. doi:10.1002/1097-4598(2000)999:9<::AID-MUS5>3.0.CO;2-L

McKeown, M. J., & Radtke, R. (2001). Phasic and tonic coupling between EEG and EMG demonstrated with independent component analysis. *Journal of Clinical Neurophysiology: Official Publication of the American Electroencephalographic Society, 18*(1), 45–57. doi:10.1097/00004691-200101000-00009

Naik, G., Kumar, D., & Palaniswami, M. (2008). *Multi run ICA and surface EMG based signal processing system for recognising hand gestures*. Paper presented at the Computer and Information Technology, 2008. CIT 2008. 8th IEEE International Conference on.

Naik, G., Kumar, D., Singh, V., & Palaniswami, M. (2006). *Hand gestures for HCI using ICA of EMG*. Paper presented at the VisHCI '06: The HCSNet workshop on Use of Vision in Human-Computer Interaction.

Naik, G., Kumar, D., Weghorn, H., & Palaniswami, M. (2007). *Subtle hand gesture identification for HCI using temporal decorrelation source separation BSS of surface EMG*. Paper presented at the 9th Biennial Conference of the Australian Pattern Recognition Society on Digital Image Computing Techniques and Applications (DICTA 2007), Glenelg, Australia.

Nakamura, H., Yoshida, M., Kotani, M., Akazawa, K., & Moritani, T. (2004). The application of independent component analysis to the multichannel surface electromyographic signals for separation of motor unit action potential trains: Part I-Measuring techniques. *Journal of Electromyography and Kinesiology: Official Journal of the International Society of Electrophysiological Kinesiology, 14*(4), 423–432.

Nishikawa, D., Yu, W., Yokoi, H., & Kakazu, Y. (1999). *Emg prosthetic hand controller discriminating ten motions using real time learning method*. Paper presented at the IEEE/RSJ international conference on intelligent robots and systems.

Pavlovic, V., Sharma, R., & Huang, T. (1997). Visual interpretation of hand gestures for human-computer interaction: A review. *IEEE Transactions on Pattern Analysis and Machine Intelligence, 19*(7), 677–695. doi:10.1109/34.598226

Peleg, D., Braiman, E., Yom-Tov, E., & Inbar, G. (2002). Classification of finger activation for use in a robotic prosthesis arm. *IEEE Transactions on Neural Systems and Rehabilitation Engineering: A Publication of the IEEE Engineering in Medicine and Biology Society, 10*(4), 290-293.

Rehg, J., & Kanade, T. (1993). *DigitEyes: Vision-based human hand tracking*.

Schlenzig, J., Hunter, E., & Jain, R. (1994). *Vision based hand gesture interpretation using recursive estimation*. Paper presented at the 1994 Conference Record of the Twenty-Eighth Asilomar Conference on Signals, Systems and Computers.

Tenore, F., Ramos, A., Fahmy, A., Acharya, S., Etienne-Cummings, R., & Thakor, N. (2007). *Towards the control of individual fingers of a prosthetic hand using surface EMG signals*. Paper presented at the IEEE Engineering in Medicine and Biology Society. IEEE Engineering in Medicine and Biology Society.

Wheeler, K. R., & Jorgensen, C. C. (2003). Gestures as input: Neuroelectric joysticks and keyboards. *Pervasive Computing, IEEE, 2*(2), 56–61. doi:10.1109/MPRV.2003.1203754

## ADDITIONAL READING

Ajiboye, A. B., & Weir, R. F. (2009). Muscle synergies as a predictive framework for the EMG patterns of new hand postures. *Journal of Neural Engineering, 6*(3), 036004. doi:10.1088/1741-2560/6/3/036004

Baker, Scheme, Englehart, K., Hutcinson, & Greger. (2010). Continuous Detection and Decoding of Dexterous Finger Flexions with Implantable MyoElectric Sensors. *IEEE Transactions on Neural Systems and Rehabilitation Engineering.*

Bretzner, L., Laptev, I., & Lindeberg, T. (2002). *Hand gesture recognition using multi-scale colour features, hierarchical models and particle filtering*. Paper presented at the Automatic Face and Gesture Recognition, 2002. Proceedings. Fifth IEEE International Conference on.

Calinon, S., & Billard, A. (2005). *Recognition and reproduction of gestures using a probabilistic framework combining PCA, ICA and HMM*. Paper presented at the ICML '05: Proceedings of the 22nd international conference on Machine learning.

Castellini, C., & van der Smagt, P. (2009). Surface EMG in advanced hand prosthetics. *Biological Cybernetics, 100*(1), 35–47. doi:10.1007/s00422-008-0278-1

Coogan, T., Awad, G., Han, J., & Sutherland, A. (2006). *Real Time Hand Gesture Recognition Including Hand Segmentation and Tracking* (pp. 495–504).

Englehart, K., & Hudgins, B. (2003). A robust, real-time control scheme for multifunction myoelectric control. *50*(7), 848-854.

Erol, A., Bebis, G., Nicolescu, M., Boyle, R., & Twombly, X. (2007). Vision-based hand pose estimation: A review. *Special Issue on Vision for Human-Computer Interaction, 108*(1-2), 52–73.

Ishibuchi, K., Takemura, H., & Kishino, F. (1993). *Real time hand gesture recognition using 3D prediction model.* Paper presented at the Systems, Man and Cybernetics, 1993. 'Systems Engineering in the Service of Humans', Conference Proceedings., International Conference on.

Kato, M., Chen, Y.-W., & Xu, G. (2006). *Articulated Hand Tracking by PCA-ICA Approach.* Paper presented at the FGR '06: Proceedings of the 7th International Conference on Automatic Face and Gesture Recognition.

Kawashima, H., Tsujiuchi, N., & Koizumi, T. (2008). Hand motion discrimination by EMG signals without incorrect discriminations that elbow motions cause. *Conference Proceedings;... Annual International Conference of the IEEE Engineering in Medicine and Biology Society. IEEE Engineering in Medicine and Biology Society. Conference, 2008,* 2103–2107.

Kosmidou, V. E., Hadjileontiadis, L. J., & Panas, S. M. (2006). Evaluation of surface EMG features for the recognition of American Sign Language gestures. *Conference Proceedings;... Annual International Conference of the IEEE Engineering in Medicine and Biology Society. IEEE Engineering in Medicine and Biology Society. Conference, 1,* 6197–6200. doi:10.1109/IEMBS.2006.259428

Kurisu, N., Tsujiuchi, N., & Koizumi, T. (2009). Prosthetic hand control using motion discrimination from EMG signals. *Conference Proceedings;... Annual International Conference of the IEEE Engineering in Medicine and Biology Society. IEEE Engineering in Medicine and Biology Society. Conference, 2009,* 6922–6925.

Kurzynski, M., & Wolczowski, A. (2009). Control of dexterous bio-prosthetic hand via sequential recognition of EMG signals using fuzzy relations. *Studies in Health Technology and Informatics, 150,* 799–803.

Lee, H.-J., & Chung, J.-H. (1999). *Hand gesture recognition using orientation histogram.* Paper presented at the TENCON 99. Proceedings of the IEEE Region 10 Conference.

Liu, X., & Fujimura, K. (2004). *Hand gesture recognition using depth data.* Paper presented at the Automatic Face and Gesture Recognition, 2004. Proceedings. Sixth IEEE International Conference on.

Meilink, A., Hemmen, B., Seelen, H. A., & Kwakkel, G. (2008). Impact of EMG-triggered neuromuscular stimulation of the wrist and finger extensors of the paretic hand after stroke: a systematic review of the literature. *Clinical Rehabilitation, 22*(4), 291–305. doi:10.1177/0269215507083368

Min, B.-W., Yoon, H.-S., Soh, J., Yang, Y.-M., & Ejima, T. (2002). *Hand gesture recognition using hidden Markov models.* Paper presented at the Systems, Man, and Cybernetics, 1997. 'Computational Cybernetics and Simulation'., 1997 IEEE International Conference on.

Naik, G. R., Kumar, D. K., & Palaniswami, M. (2008). Surface EMG based hand gesture identification using semi blind ICA: validation of ICA matrix analysis. *Electromyography and Clinical Neurophysiology, 48*(3-4), 169–180.

Nakano, T., Nagata, K., Yamada, M., & Magatani, K. (2009). Application of least square method for muscular strength estimation in hand motion recognition using surface EMG. *Conference Proceedings;... Annual International Conference of the IEEE Engineering in Medicine and Biology Society. IEEE Engineering in Medicine and Biology Society. Conference, 2009,* 2655–2658.

Nolker, C., & Ritter, H. (2002). Visual recognition of continuous hand postures. *Neural Networks. IEEE Transactions on, 13*(4), 983–994.

Rekimoto, J. (2001). GestureWrist and Gesture-Pad: Unobtrusive Wearable Interaction Devices. *Wearable Computers, 2001. Proceedings. Fifth International Symposium on, 0*, 21-27.

Ryait, H. S., Arora, A. S., & Agarwal, R. (2009). Study of issues in the development of surface EMG controlled human hand. *Journal of Materials Science. Materials in Medicine, 20*(Suppl 1), S107–S114. doi:10.1007/s10856-008-3492-4

Su, M.-C., Jean, W.-F., & Chang, H.-T. (1996). *A static hand gesture recognition system using a composite neural network.* Paper presented at the Fuzzy Systems, 1996., Proceedings of the Fifth IEEE International Conference on.

Sudderth, E., Mandel, M., Freeman, W., & Willsky, A. (2004). *Visual Hand Tracking Using Nonparametric Belief Propagation.* Paper presented at the CVPRW '04: Proceedings of the 2004 Conference on Computer Vision and Pattern Recognition Workshop (CVPRW'04) Volume 12.

Trejo, L. J., Wheeler, K. R., Jorgensen, C. C., Rosipal, R., Clanton, S. T., Matthews, B., et al. (2003). Multimodal neuroelectric interface development. *Neural Systems and Rehabilitation Engineering, IEEE Transactions on [see also IEEE Trans. on Rehabilitation Engineering], 11*(2), 199-203.

Wheeler, K. R., & Jorgensen, C. C. (2003). Gestures as input: neuroelectric joysticks and keyboards. *Pervasive Computing, IEEE, 2*(2), 56–61. doi:10.1109/MPRV.2003.1203754

Yang, M.-H., Ahuja, N., & Tabb, M. (2002). Extraction of 2D motion trajectories and its application to hand gesture recognition. *Pattern Analysis and Machine Intelligence. IEEE Transactions on, 24*(8), 1061–1074.

Zhou, H., Lin, D. J., & Huang, T. S. (2004). *Static Hand Gesture Recognition based on Local Orientation Histogram Feature Distribution Model.* Paper presented at the Computer Vision and Pattern Recognition Workshop, 2004 Conference on.

# Chapter 21
# Fuzzy Methods of Multiple–Criteria Evaluation and Their Software Implementation

**Pavel Holeček**
*Palacký University Olomouc, Czech Republic*

**Jana Talašová**
*Palacký University Olomouc, Czech Republic*

**Ivo Müller**
*Palacký University Olomouc, Czech Republic*

## ABSTRACT

*This chapter describes a system of fuzzy methods designed to solve a broad range of problems in multiple-criteria evaluation, and also their software implementation, FuzzME. A feature common to all the presented methods is the type of evaluation, well suited to the paradigm of fuzzy set theory. All evaluations take on the form of fuzzy numbers, expressing the extent to which goals of evaluation are fulfilled. The system of fuzzy methods is conceived to allow for different types of interaction among criteria of evaluation. Under no interaction, the fuzzy weighted average, fuzzy OWA operator, or WOWA operator are used to aggregate partial evaluations (depending on the evaluator's requirements regarding type of evaluation). If interactions appear as redundancy or complementarity, the fuzzified discrete Choquet integral is the appropriate aggregation operator. Under more complex interactions, the aggregation function is defined through an expertly set base of fuzzy rules.*

## INTRODUCTION

This chapter intends, in an easy-to-read style, to introduce a broad reading public (experts on theory and practice of multiple-criteria evaluation and decision making, readers interested in applications of the fuzzy set theory, and students) to a system of fuzzy methods for multiple-criteria evaluation which can be used to solve a wide range of real-life problems. Within an allotted space, we will try to comprehensively cover this topic. The theoretical approach to evaluation is common to all the presented methods, with the leading idea that the evaluation of an alternative can be viewed as a (fuzzy) degree of fulfillment of a pursued

DOI: 10.4018/978-1-61350-429-1.ch021

goal. We will explain how this evaluation is carried out in case of both quantitative and qualitative criteria. The basic hierarchical structure of evaluation model can comprise various methods for consecutive aggregation of partial evaluations into an overall evaluation. Next, we will turn our attention to a detailed analysis of particular aggregation methods. We specify the conditions under which a given aggregation method is appropriate, and give illustrative examples. We will describe the FuzzME tool, which is a software implementation of the presented methods. A reader can use the demo version of FuzzME, freely available at www, to experiment with these methods on his/her own, thus reaching deeper appreciation of their behavior. Real-world applications of using FuzzME will be described. They are from banking industry (soft-fact rating of bank clients) and from the area of human resource management.

## BACKGROUND

Worldwide, one can witness an ever-increasing interest in high-quality mathematical models of multiple-criteria evaluation (e.g. rating of clients in banks, assessment of universities, comparison of alternative solutions to ecological problems). For the tasks of building evaluation models, setting some of their inputs, and interpreting their outputs, expert knowledge is needed (e.g. evaluations of alternatives according to qualitative criteria, partial evaluating functions for quantitative criteria, choice of a suitable aggregation operator, weights of partial evaluations, rule bases describing multiple-criteria evaluating functions, verbal interpretation of obtained results). With uncertainty being a characteristic feature of any expert information, a suitable mathematical tool for creating such models is the fuzzy set theory (Zadeh, 1965; Dubois & Prade 2000). For practical use of the fuzzy models of multiple-criteria evalu-

ation, their user-friendly software implementation is necessary.

Out of numerous papers and books covering the theory and methods of multiple-criteria evaluation, a large number make use of fuzzy approach (e.g. Bellman & Zadeh, 1970; Yager, 1988; Rommelfanger, 1988; Lai & Hwang, 1994; Carlsson & Fullér, 1996; Talašová, 2003; Ramík & Perzina, 2010). Multiple-criteria evaluation (as a basis for decision making) was even one of the earliest applications of fuzzy sets (Bellman & Zadeh, 1970). In more than 40 years of existence of the fuzzy set theory, several software products for multiple-criteria decision making have been developed that utilize fuzzy modeling principles to different degrees and in different ways, e.g. FuzzyTECH (Von Altrock 1995, 1996; http://www.fuzzytech.com/) and NEFRIT (Talašová, 2000).

The fuzzy methods of multiple-criteria evaluation and the FuzzME software (Fuzzy models of Multiple-criteria Evaluation), presented in this chapter, are based primarily on the theory and methods of multiple-criteria evaluation that were published in Talašová (2000) and Talašová (2003). The theory of normalized fuzzy weights, the definition of fuzzy weighted average, and the algorithm for its calculation were taken from Pavlačka & Talašová (2006, 2007) and Pavlačka (2007). The fuzzified OWA operator and the algorithm for its calculation were published in Talašová & Bebčáková (2008). The theory of fuzzy Choquet integral and the method of its computation were taken from Bebčáková, Talašová & Pavlačka (2010). This chapter also focuses on the relationship between the nature of a problem to be solved (interaction among criteria, evaluator's requirements on the behavior of evaluating function) and the choice of appropriate mathematical model (type of aggregation operator, or perhaps an expert system). As of yet, these results have not been published in such a comprehensive form.

# FUZZY MODELS OF MULTIPLE-CRITERIA EVALUATION

## Basics of Fuzzy- and Linguistic Fuzzy Modeling

Fundamentals of the fuzzy set theory (introduced in Zadeh (1965)) are described in detail, e.g., in Dubois & Prade (2000). A fuzzy set $A$ on a universal set $X$ is characterized by its membership function $A: X \rightarrow [0,1]$. $Ker A$ denotes a kernel of $A$, i.e. $Ker A = \{x \in X | A(x) = 1\}$. For any $\alpha \in [0,1]$, $A_\alpha$ denotes an $\alpha$-cut of $A$, i.e. $A_\alpha = \{x \in X \mid A(x) \geq \alpha\}$. A support of $A$ is defined as $Supp A = \{x \in X \mid A(x) > 0\}$. The symbol $hgt A$ denotes a height of the fuzzy set $A$, that is $hgt A = \sup\{A(x) | x \in X\}$. An intersection and a union of fuzzy sets $A$ and $B$ on $X$ are defined for all $x \in X$ by formulas:

$$(A \cap B)(x) = \min\left\{A(x), B(x)\right\},$$

$$(A \cup B)(x) = \max\left\{A(x), B(x)\right\}.$$

A fuzzy number is a fuzzy set $C$ on the set of all real numbers $\Re$ which satisfies the following conditions: (1) the kernel of $C$, $Ker C$, is non-empty; (2) the $\alpha$-cuts of $C$, $C_\alpha$'s, are closed intervals for all $\alpha \in (0,1]$; (3) the support of $C$, $Supp C$, is bounded. A fuzzy number $C$ is said to be defined on $[a,b]$ if $Supp C \subseteq [a,b]$. In the following text, $\mathcal{F}_N([a,b])$ denotes all fuzzy numbers on $[a,b]$. Real numbers $c^1 \leq c^2 \leq c^3 \leq c^4$ are called significant values of the fuzzy number C if the following holds: $[c^1,c^4]=Cl(SuppC), [c^2,c^3]=KerC$, where $Cl(Supp\ C)$ denotes a closure of $Supp\ C$.

Any fuzzy number $C$ can be characterized by a pair of functions $\underline{c}: [0,1] \rightarrow \Re$, $\overline{c}: [0,1] \rightarrow \Re$ which are defined as follows: $C_\alpha = [\underline{c}(\alpha), \overline{c}(\alpha)]$ for all $\alpha \in (0,1]$ and $Cl(Supp\ C) = [\underline{c}(0), \overline{c}(0)]$. Therefore, a fuzzy number can also be written as $C = \{[\underline{c}(\alpha), \overline{c}(\alpha)], \alpha \in [0,1]\}$.

The fuzzy number $C$ is said to be linear if its membership function is of the following form: if $c^1 \neq c^2$, $c^3 \neq c^4$, then

$$C(x) = \begin{cases} 0, & \text{for } x < c^1; \\ \dfrac{x - c^1}{c^2 - c^1}, & \text{for } c^1 \leq x \leq c^2; \\ 1, & \text{for } c^2 < x < c^3; \\ \dfrac{c^4 - x}{c^4 - c^3}, & \text{for } c^3 \leq x \leq c^4; \\ 0, & \text{for } c^4 < x; \end{cases}$$

if $c^1 = c^2$, then $C(c^1) = C(c^2) = 1$; similarly, if $c^3 = c^4$, then $C(c^3) = C(c^4) = 1$, with the rest of the formula remaining unchanged. Real numbers and closed intervals can be represented by linear fuzzy numbers with $c^1=c^2=c^3=c^4$, or $c^1 = c^2 < c^3=c^4$, respectively. A linear fuzzy number $C$ is called triangular if $c^2 = c^3$, otherwise it is called trapezoidal. Because any linear fuzzy number is fully determined by its significant values, we will use the simplified notation $C = (c^1, c^2, c^3, c^4)$. For triangular fuzzy numbers we can write $C = (c^1, c^2, c^4)$, since $c^2 = c^3$. This notation will be used primarily in examples. Besides linear fuzzy numbers, there exist other special types of fuzzy numbers; for example, piecewise linear fuzzy numbers (Talašová, 2003) are convenient for calculations.

An ordering of fuzzy numbers is defined as follows: a fuzzy number $C$ is greater than or equal to a fuzzy number $D$ if $C_\alpha \geq D_\alpha$ for all $\alpha \in (0,1]$. The inequality of the $\alpha$-cuts $C_\alpha \geq D_\alpha$ is the inequality of intervals

$$C_\alpha = [\underline{c}(\alpha), \overline{c}(\alpha)], \ D_\alpha = [\underline{d}(\alpha), \overline{d}(\alpha)]$$

which is defined as $[\underline{c}(\alpha), \overline{c}(\alpha)] \geq [\underline{d}(\alpha), \overline{d}(\alpha)]$ if, and only if, $\underline{c}(\alpha) \geq \underline{d}(\alpha)$ and $\overline{c}(\alpha) \geq \overline{d}(\alpha)$. The disadvantage is that many fuzzy numbers are not comparable in this manner (the above relation is only a partial ordering). But all fuzzy numbers

*Box 1.*

$$D\left(y\right) = \begin{cases} \max\left\{ \min\left\{ C_1\left(x_1\right), ..., C_n\left(x_n\right)\right\} \mid y = f\left(x_1, ..., x_n\right), \ x_i \in \left[0,1\right], \ i = 1, 2, ..., n \right\} & \text{if } f^{-1}\left(y\right) \neq \varnothing \\ 0 & \text{otherwise.} \end{cases}$$

can be compared according to their centers of gravity (Dubois & Prade, 2000).

Any real continuous function $f$ of $n$ real arguments can be extended to a FNV-function (a fuzzy-number-valued function) of $n$ FNV-arguments. This is done by the so-called extension principle. For example, let $f$: $[0,1]^n \rightarrow [0,1]$ be a real continuous function of $n$ variables. Then its fuzzy extension is a mapping

$$F: \ \mathcal{F}_N\left(\left[0,1\right]\right)^n \rightarrow \mathcal{F}_N\left(\left[0,1\right]\right)$$

assigning to any $n$-tuple of fuzzy numbers $C_1,..., C_n$ on $[0,1]$ a fuzzy number $D = F(C_1,..., C_n)$ on $[0,1]$, such that for any y Î $[0,1]$ the equation in Box 1 holds.

A linguistic variable (Zadeh, 1975) is defined as a quintuple $(X, \mathcal{T}(X), U, G, M)$, where $X$ is a name of the variable, $\mathcal{T}(X)$ is a set of its linguistic values (linguistic terms), $U$ is an universe on which the mathematical meanings of the linguistic terms are modeled, $G$ is a syntactic rule for generating linguistic terms from $\mathcal{T}(X)$, and $M$ is a semantic rule which to every linguistic term $\mathcal{A} \in \mathcal{T}(X)$ assigns its meaning A$= M(\mathcal{A})$ which is a fuzzy set on $U$. In this chapter, the linguistic term $\mathcal{A}$ will be distinguished from its mathematical meaning A, which is a fuzzy set, by means of a different font. In real-life applications, the universe $U$ is usually an interval of real numbers, i.e. $U = [a,b]$, and meanings of linguistic terms are fuzzy numbers on $U$.

A linguistic scale (Talašová, 2003) is a special case of a linguistic variable. A linguistic scale offers simplified description of a continuous real variable with values on $[a,b]$ by specifying a finite number of linguistic values modeled by fuzzy numbers on $[a,b]$. We say that a linguistic variable $(X, \mathcal{T}(X), [a,b], M, G)$, where $\mathcal{T}(X) = \left\{\mathcal{T}_1, \mathcal{T}_2, ..., \mathcal{T}_s\right\}$, is a linguistic scale on $[a,b]$ if the fuzzy numbers $T_1, T_2, ..., T_s$, representing meanings of its linguistic values, form a fuzzy scale on $[a,b]$. A fuzzy scale on $[a,b]$ is defined as a set of fuzzy numbers $T_1, T_2, ..., T_s$ on this interval that form a fuzzy partition on the interval, i.e., for all $x \in [a,b]$ it holds that $\sum_{i=1}^{s} T_i(x) = 1$, and the $T$'s are indexed according to their ordering.

Other structures have also been derived from the linguistic scale (Talašová, 2000 and 2003). For example, an *extended linguistic scale* contains, besides the basic terms of linguistic scale, also derived terms of the form $\mathcal{A}$ *to* $\mathcal{B}$, where $\mathcal{A}$ and $\mathcal{B}$ are basic terms. Another structure is a *linguistic scale with intermediate values* that includes also terms in the form *between $\mathcal{A}$ and $\mathcal{B}$*.

A linguistic approximation to a fuzzy number $C$ by means of linguistic scale is a linguistic value from this scale whose meaning is closest to the fuzzy number $C$ in terms of a metric defined on fuzzy numbers (Talašová, 2000 and 2003).

## Definition of the Multiple-Criteria Evaluation Problem

The problem we have set out to tackle can be described as follows. It is necessary to build a mathematical model for evaluating a certain type of alternatives with respect to a given goal, the fulfillment of which can be measured by a set of criteria. The set of evaluated alternatives is not supposed to be known in advance; it is of interest to set up an evaluation procedure applicable also to individual incoming alternatives. What we consider here is the case of complex multiple-criteria evaluation, i.e., such an evaluation where a large number of criteria must be taken into account, complex interactions among these criteria are not excluded, and various requirements of the evaluator on behavior of evaluating function should be met. The proposed model of multiple-criteria evaluation must be able to process uncertain, expertly-defined data and utilize expert knowledge related to the evaluation process. Output from the model will often serve as a support to decision making, and therefore it must take on a form as much intelligible to a human decision maker as possible.

## Type of Evaluation Used

Because, with respect to the problem specification given above, we not only compare alternatives within a pre-specified set but we also need to assess – against multiple criteria – alternatives entering into the system one by one, we cannot work with evaluation of a relative type. We must consider such an evaluation that is of absolute type with respect to a given goal. Instead of simply comparing two alternatives as to which one is better with respect to a pursued goal (relative evaluation on an ordinal scale), or comparing how many times larger is the difference in evaluation with one pair of alternatives in contrast to this difference with another pair (relative evaluation on a cardinal, interval scale), we need to assess the goodness of an alternative in terms of its fulfilling a given goal, i.e., how much it meets a pursued goal. Assessment of a bank client requesting a credit can serve as an example.

An appropriate scale of evaluation for this kind of assessment is the interval [0,1], where, on the one hand, 0 means that the alternative does not meet the goal at all, and, on the other hand, 1 means that the alternative fully satisfies the goal; evaluation inside the interval [0,1] then denotes the degree

to which the goal has been fulfilled (for example, evaluation of 0.8 can be interpreted as reaching the goal at 80%). To applied mathematicians who are familiar with tools of the fuzzy set theory, this approach to evaluation naturally evokes the idea that the evaluation of an alternative can be conceived of as a degree of membership of an alternative to a fuzzy set of alternatives fulfilling a given goal. It is in this manner that Bellman and Zadeh (1970) interpret the evaluation of alternatives in their classic article. The notion that the goal of evaluation can be viewed as a fuzzy set will be encountered several times in this chapter.

In the evaluation models described further in the text the evaluation will take on the form of not only real numbers from [0,1] but also fuzzy numbers defined on this interval. These fuzzy numbers then express uncertain extent of fulfillment of a given goal by respective alternatives (see Talašová, 2000, 2003), and goals can be viewed as type-2 fuzzy sets (see Dubois & Prade, 2000). Fuzzy evaluations expressing uncertain extent of goal fulfillment will be implemented in the presented models on all levels of evaluation. This feature will pertain to partial evaluations with respect to goals linked to particular criteria (both qualitative and quantitative), as well as to evaluations with respect to an overall goal. The choice of aggregation methods will preserve this feature in overall evaluation.

## The Basic Structure of Evaluation Model

The basic structure of the fuzzy model of multiple-criteria evaluation will be expressed by a goals tree (Figure 1). The root of the tree represents the overall goal of evaluation and every other node corresponds to a partial goal. The goals at the ends of branches are connected with either quantitative or qualitative criteria.

When an alternative is evaluated, evaluations with respect to criteria connected with the terminal branches are calculated first. Independently

*Figure 1. Partial goals tree*

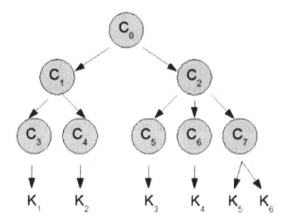

of the criterion type, each evaluation is described by a fuzzy number defined on [0,1].

According to qualitative criteria, alternatives are evaluated verbally, by means of values of linguistic variables of special types. Mathematical meanings of linguistic values are modeled by fuzzy numbers on [0,1], as mentioned above. The evaluation of an alternative with respect to a quantitative criterion is calculated from the measured value of the criterion by means of an evaluating function expertly defined for this criterion. The evaluating function is the membership function of the fuzzy set that represents the corresponding partial goal. Both crisp and fuzzy values of quantitative criteria are admitted.

The partial fuzzy evaluations are then consecutively aggregated according to the structure of the goals tree. The aggregation of partial fuzzy evaluations is done either by one of fuzzified aggregation operators or by a fuzzy expert system. The choice of the appropriate mode of aggregation depends on interactions among criteria.

In case of independent criteria, the evaluator can choose from three types of aggregation operators – Fuzzy Weighted Average (FuzzyWA, see Pavlačka & Talašová, 2007), Ordered Fuzzy Weighted Average (FuzzyOWA, see Talašová & Bebčáková, 2008; for crisp OWA operator see Yager, 1988), and the fuzzified WOWA operator

(for crisp WOWA operator see Torra & Narukawa, 2007). A particular choice of aggregation operator is determined by the evaluator's requirements on properties of aggregated evaluation.

If relationships of redundancy or complementarity are present among criteria, the fuzzified discrete Choquet integral is used for aggregating partial evaluations (for fuzzy Choquet integral see Bebčáková *et al.* (2010); for crisp Choquet integral see Choquet (1953), Grabisch & Labreuche (2010), Torra & Narukawa (2007)).

Generally, it holds that any continuous (even any Borel-measurable) function can be approximated to arbitrary precision by a fuzzy rule base with a final number of rules and a suitable inference algorithm (e.g. Kosko, 1993). For that reason, fuzzy expert systems with alternative approximate-reasoning algorithms (Mamdani, Sugeno) can be used to aggregate partial evaluations under complex interactions. Fuzzy expert systems make it possible to utilize expert knowledge for modeling complex evaluating functions. In order to obtain required properties of evaluating functions, it is possible to modify usual fuzzy-inference algorithms by employing less common aggregation operators (Sugeno-WA, Sugeno-WOWA, see Holeček, 2010).

The final result of consecutive aggregation of partial fuzzy evaluations is the overall fuzzy evaluation of a given alternative. The obtained overall fuzzy evaluation is again a fuzzy number on [0,1]. It expresses uncertain degree of fulfillment of the main goal by a particular alternative. By means of a linguistic approximation algorithm, the verbal description of final results is obtained.

## The Goals Tree

The considered fuzzy model of multiple-criteria evaluation has a hierarchical structure. A goals tree is constructed in such a way that, first, for the overall goal a set of lower-level partial goals is specified with the property that the extent of their fulfillment suggests the extent of fulfillment of the overall goal, i.e. the higher-level goal. This process of attributing sets of lower-level goals to higher-level goals keeps repeating until such goals are reached whose fulfillment can be assessed by means of some known characteristics of alternatives (i.e. quantitative or qualitative criteria).

The type of each node in the tree must be specified. For the nodes at the ends of branches the expert makes explicit if the node is connected with a quantitative or qualitative criterion. For the other nodes he/she sets the type of aggregation – FuzzyWA, FuzzyOWA, fuzzified WOWA, fuzzified Choquet integral or a fuzzy expert system. (Of course, non-fuzzified versions of all these aggregation operators can be used as well, as special cases of their respective fuzzy versions.)

## Evaluation Criteria

In the evaluation models, two types of criteria can be used – qualitative and quantitative. Both types can be combined arbitrarily within the same goals tree.

Qualitative criteria are those criteria of evaluation whose values cannot be measured and should be evaluated expertly. According to qualitative criteria, alternatives are evaluated verbally, by means of values of linguistic variables of special kinds – linguistic scales, extended linguistic scales, and linguistic scales with intermediate values. When an alternative is evaluated according to a qualitative criterion, the expert chooses the best fitting term from the set of terms of a linguistic variable. For example, the linguistic scale *Quality of Product* can contain linguistic values *poor, substandard, standard, above standard,* and *excellent*. When an alternative is evaluated the expert chooses one of those verbal values. With an extended linguistic scale, the expert has more options to choose from because the terms of the form $A$ to $B$ are also included. The expert can thus say that the *Quality of Product* is *standard to excellent*. In the linguistic scale with intermediate values, terms of the form *between $A$ and $B$* are

added. In such a scale the expert can rate *Quality of Product* as *between substandard and standard*. These three structures of linguistic values are also applied when resulting fuzzy evaluations are approximated verbally.

The evaluation of an alternative with respect to a quantitative criterion is calculated from the measured value of the criterion by means of an evaluating function expertly defined for this criterion. When the model is created the expert specifies a domain $D$ for each quantitative criterion and an evaluating function $u: D \rightarrow [0,1]$ on this domain. The evaluating function is the membership function of the fuzzy set representing the corresponding partial goal. It says which values of the criterion are desirable and which are not. For any $x$ from the criterion domain, $u(x) = 0$ means that if the criterion value is $x$, then the corresponding partial goal is not fulfilled at all. Conversely, $u(x) = 1$ means that the value $x$ is considered fully appropriate by the expert.

Both crisp and fuzzy values of quantitative criteria are admissible. Fuzzy values represent inaccurate measurements or expert estimates of criteria values. The degree of goal fulfillment is calculated from the values of criteria for a particular alternative. If the value is crisp, it can be inserted into the evaluating function directly. If the measured value is a fuzzy number, then the degree of fulfillment of the corresponding goal is calculated by the extension principle.

## Methods of Aggregation of Partial Evaluations

Now we have calculated partial evaluations of alternatives with respect to individual criteria. From these partial evaluations, it is necessary to come to an overall evaluation. Aggregation is performed in accordance with the structure of the goals tree. For each node of the tree, a proper mode of aggregation is determined by both the evaluator's preferences and existing interactions among criteria of evaluation, if there are any. The key requirement is that the evaluation at each level of aggregation should express (uncertain) extent of fulfillment of the corresponding goal. The reason for choosing fuzzy aggregation models is to utilize expert knowledge to the full.

Next, five different aggregation methods will be discussed – FuzzyWA, FuzzyOWA, fuzzified WOWA operator, fuzzified Choquet integral, and a fuzzy expert system.

## Aggregation by Fuzzy Weighted Average (FuzzyWA)

The FuzzyWA is the simplest of fuzzy methods discussed in this text. Despite its relative simplicity, most of fuzzy MCDM problems can be solved satisfactorily with FuzzyWA. The method can be used if the goal corresponding to the node of interest is fully decomposed into disjunctive goals of the lower level. In other words, significance defined on a system of subsets of these goals represents a standard additive normalized measure (probability measure) on the set of partial goals, the evaluations of which are to be aggregated.

This aggregation method is a fuzzification of the standard weighted average. In order to aggregate partial evaluations $u_i$, $u_i \in [0,1]$, $i = 1,\ldots, m$, by means of weighted average, normalized weights of partial goals must be set. The normalized weights express the shares of partial goals in a superior goal.

In a crisp case, Weighted Average is defined as follows

$$u = \sum_{i=1}^{m} v_i \cdot u_i,$$

where the real numbers $v_i$, $i = 1,\ldots, m$, are normalized weights, i.e. $\sum_{i=1}^{m} v_i = 1$ and $v_i \in [0,1]$ for all $i = 1, \ldots, m$.

In reality, the weights are seldom known exactly because they usually represent expertly-set parameters to a model, which is why the fuzzy weighted average is appropriate here. In our case, both the weights and the partial evaluations will be represented by fuzzy numbers. To define uncertain weights consistently, a special structure – normalized fuzzy weights – must be used.

Fuzzy numbers $V_1,\ldots, V_m$ defined on $[0,1]$ are normalized fuzzy weights if for any $i \in \{1,\ldots,m\}$ and any $\alpha \in (0,1]$ it holds that for any $v_i \in V_{i\alpha}$ there exist $v_j \in V_{j\alpha}, j = 1,\ldots, m, j \neq i$, such that

$$v_i + \sum_{j=1,j\neq i}^{m} v_j = 1.$$

Fuzzy Weighted Average of fuzzy numbers $U_1,\ldots,U_m$ defined on $[0,1]$, with the normalized fuzzy weights $V_1,\ldots,V_m$, is a fuzzy number $U$ on $[0,1]$ whose membership function is defined for any $u \in [0,1]$ in Box 2.

Two problems arise if we want to use Fuzzy-WA for aggregating partial evaluations: (1) it is difficult to set normalized fuzzy weights that satisfy the above-mentioned condition; and (2) an effective algorithm for FuzzyWA calculation is necessary. Both problems were solved in Pavlačka (2007), Pavlačka & Talašová (2006, 2007), and this solution will be now briefly described.

It can be quite difficult for the expert to set normalized fuzzy weights without breaching the above condition. It was proved in Pavlačka (2007)

*Box 2.*

$$U(u) = \max \left\{ \begin{array}{l} \min \left\{ V_1(v_1),\ldots, V_m(v_m), U_1(u_1),\ldots, U_m(u_m) \right\} \\ \mid \sum_{i=1}^{m} v_i \cdot u_i = u, \sum_{i=1}^{m} v = 1, v_i, u_i \in [0,1], i = 1,\ldots m \end{array} \right\}$$

that symmetric triangular fuzzy numbers with the same spans form normalized fuzzy weights if elements of their kernels form normalized weights. For example, let the following normalized weights represent crisp estimates of significance of three partial goals: $v_1 = 0.2$, $v_2 = 0.5$ and $v_3 = 0.3$. Then the following triangular fuzzy numbers can form normalized fuzzy weights: $V_1 = (0.1, 0.2, 0.3)$, $V_2 = (0.4, 0.5, 0.6)$ and $V_3 = (0.2, 0.3, 0.4)$. This is a very simple way of setting normalized fuzzy weights.

In more complex cases, it is possible to set rough estimates of uncertain weights and then to transform these into normalized fuzzy weights, removing only inconsistencies in the expert's formulation without losing any information (Pavlačka & Talašová, 2007). First, the expert gives estimates of weights by means of fuzzy numbers $W_1,\dots,W_m$,

$$W_i = \{[\underline{w}_i(\alpha), \overline{w}_i(\alpha)], \alpha \in [0,1]\}, \; i=1,\dots,m$$

Regardless of the condition mentioned above, these estimates are only required to satisfy the following weaker condition:

$$\exists w_1, \dots w_m, \; w_i \in \mathrm{Ker}(W_i), \; i = 1, \dots, m : \sum_{i=1}^{m} w_i = 1.$$

In the next step, normalized fuzzy weights $V_1,\dots,V_m$, $V_i = \{[\underline{v}_i(\alpha), \overline{v}_i(\alpha)], \alpha \in [0,1]\}$, $i=1,\dots,m$ are calculated by the formula

$$\underline{v}_i(\alpha) = \max\left\{\underline{w}_i(\alpha), 1 - \sum_{j=1, j\neq i}^{m} \overline{w}_j(\alpha)\right\},$$

$$\overline{v}_i(\alpha) = \min\left\{\overline{w}_i(\alpha), 1 - \sum_{j=1, j\neq i}^{m} \underline{w}_j(\alpha)\right\}.$$

This method is also implemented in FuzzME and it makes it very easy to set normalized weights.

Another obstacle in using FuzzyWA is that its definition is not very handy for computation. That is why FuzzME utilizes the algorithm described in Pavlačka & Talašová (2007) which is very time efficient.

Evaluation with FuzzyWA is appropriate in many situations. As an example, suppose we want to evaluate members of academic staff according to their performance in two areas – *Research* and *Teaching*. Each area can have a different significance. First, we set the crisp weights $v_{research} = 0.4$, $v_{teaching} = 0.6$. Because we do not know the significance precisely we add some uncertainty. The normalized fuzzy weights can be, e.g., $V_{research} = (0.3, 0.4, 0.5)$ and $V_{teaching} = (0.5, 0.6, 0.7)$.

An interesting feature of FuzzyWA is how the dispersion of evaluations with respect to individual partial goals is reflected into the uncertainty of the resulting fuzzy evaluation. In crisp case, if the weights were the same, then an academic staff member who is excellent in one area and unsatisfying in the other would have the same evaluation as his/her colleague who is average in both. In case of FuzzyWA, the resulting fuzzy evaluations would have the same center of gravity, but the former would contain more uncertainty. Let us note that the fuzzy average of linear fuzzy numbers with normalized fuzzy weights expressed by linear fuzzy numbers need not be a linear fuzzy number.

The structure of normalized fuzzy weights and the FuzzyWA operator are studied in more detail in Pavlačka (2007) and Pavlačka & Talašová (2006, 2007).

## Aggregation by Fuzzy Ordered Weighted Average (FuzzyOWA)

FuzzyOWA is a fuzzification of the OWA operator (see Yager, 1988). Similarly to the FuzzyWA operator, FuzzyOWA also uses the structure of normalized fuzzy weights. Contrary to FuzzyWA, the weights are not related to particular partial goals. They express the evaluator's requirements concerning the structure of partial evaluation. In particular, the $i$-th weight is linked to the $i$-th largest evaluation of partial goals. With OWA, various preferences can be modeled by weights of special form as it will be shown on the examples later.

The following notation will be used to define the OWA operator. If $(u_1,...,u_m)$ is a vector of real numbers, then $(u^{(1)},...,u^{(m)})$ is a vector where, for all $j \in \{1,...,m\}$, $u^{(j)}$ is the $j$-th largest number of $u_1,...,u_m$.

For the crisp case, Ordered Weighted Average is defined as

$$u = \sum_{i=1}^{m} v_i \cdot u^{(i)}.$$

FuzzyOWA represents a fuzzification of the crisp OWA operator according to the extension principle where the condition of normalized weights is respected. Uncertain weights are modeled by normalized fuzzy weights, as with FuzzyWA. Again, partial evaluations are modeled by fuzzy numbers on [0,1].

Fuzzy Ordered Weighted Average of fuzzy numbers $U_1,...,U_m$ defined on [0,1], with normalized fuzzy weights $V_1,...,V_m$, is a fuzzy number $U$ on [0,1] whose membership function is defined for any $u \in [0,1]$ in Box 3.

Unfortunately, this definition is not well suited for computation. However, an effective algorithm exists (Talašová & Bebčáková, 2008) and can be used. The algorithm is analogous to the one used for FuzzyWA. The procedures of setting normalized fuzzy weights are the same as with FuzzyWA. The use of FuzzyOWA will be demonstrated in the following two examples.

First, imagine an evaluator who does not want any of partial goals to be satisfied poorly. Then

the weight of the minimum partial evaluation of any alternative equals 1, and the weights of all other partial evaluations equal 0. The aggregated fuzzy evaluation then represents the guaranteed fuzzy degree of fulfillment of all the partial goals (the fuzzy MINIMAX method).

Second, in many sports, contestants are rated by several judges. In disciplines such as figure skating, the final rating is based on the following principle. The biggest and the lowest ratings are discarded and the rest are simply aggregated by arithmetic mean. The OWA operator with the weights $(0, \dfrac{1}{m-2}, \dfrac{1}{m-2}, ... \dfrac{1}{m-2}, 0)$ leads exactly to this type of aggregation.

Fuzzification of the OWA operator is described in detail in Talašová & Bebčáková (2008).

## Aggregation by the Fuzzified WOWA Operator

In many situations, the weighted average and the OWA operator are sufficient. As already mentioned, weighted average is used when significancies of partial goals are known. On the other hand, OWA is used when preferences of evaluations of partial goals according to their ordering is known. But what if the expert needs to take into account both? The answer to this question is the WOWA (weighted OWA) operator that is described e.g. in Torra & Narukawa (2007). WOWA uses two sets of normalized weights – the first set of weights, $\{w_1, w_2,..., w_m\}$, is connected to individual partial goals; the second one, $\{p_1, p_2,..., p_m\}$, is related to the decreasing order of partial evaluations.

*Box 3.*

$$U(u) = \max \left\{ \begin{array}{l} \min \left\{ V_1(v_1),...,V_m(v_m), U_1(u_1),...,U_m(u_m) \right\} \\ | \sum_{i=1}^{m} v_i \cdot u^{(i)} = u, \sum_{i=1}^{m} v_i = 1, v_i, u_i \in [0,1], i = 1,...,m \end{array} \right\}$$

Weighted Ordered Weighted Average (WOWA) operator is defined as

$$u = \sum_{i=1}^{m} \omega_i \cdot u^{(i)},$$

where the permutation $(1), \ldots, (m)$ is the same as with OWA, i.e., $u^{(i)}$ is the $i$-the largest among the numbers $u^{(1)}, \ldots, u^{(m)}$. The weight $\omega_i$ is defined as

$$\omega_i = z\left(\sum_{j \leq i} w^{(j)}\right) - z\left(\sum_{j < i} w^{(j)}\right),$$

for $i = 1, \ldots, m$, and $z$ is a non-decreasing function interpolating the set of points

$$\{(0,0)\} \cup \{(\frac{i}{m}, \sum_{j \leq i} p_j)\}_{i=1,\ldots,m}.$$

It can be easily shown that WOWA is a generalization of both weighted average and OWA. If the weights $p_i$, $i = 1, \ldots, m$, are uniform, the result will be the same as aggregation with weighted average with the weights $w_i$, $i = 1, \ldots, m$. Vice versa, using uniform weights $w_i$, $i = 1, \ldots, m$, is equivalent to aggregation by OWA with the weights $p_i$, $i = 1, \ldots, m$.

The fuzzified WOWA operator (first-level fuzzification) accepts fuzzy partial evaluations $U_i = \{[\underline{u}_i(\alpha), \overline{u}_i(\alpha)], \alpha \in [0,1]\}, i=1,\ldots,m$, but the weights $w_1, w_2, \ldots, w_m$ and $p_1, p_2, \ldots, p_m$ are crisp. The result of aggregation by means of fuzzified WOWA, a fuzzy number

$$U = \{[\underline{u}(\alpha), \overline{u}(\alpha)], \alpha \in [0,1]\},$$

is defined for any $\alpha \in [0,1]$ as follows

$$\underline{u}(\alpha) = \sum_{i=1}^{m} \omega_i \cdot \underline{u}^{(i)}(\alpha),$$

$$\overline{u}(\alpha) = \sum_{i=1}^{m} \omega_i \cdot \overline{u}^{(i)}(\alpha),$$

where the definition of $\omega_i$ is the same as in the crisp case, $\underline{u}^{(i)}(\alpha)$ denotes the $i$-th largest number of $\underline{u}_1(\alpha), \ldots, \underline{u}_m(\alpha)$ and $\overline{u}^{(i)}(\alpha)$ denotes the $i$-th largest number of $\overline{u}_1(\alpha), \ldots, \overline{u}_m(\alpha)$. Correctness of this definition is ensured by the extension principle applied to the WOWA operator and by the fact that the aggregation operator is a non-decreasing function of its arguments (Talašová, 2003; Pavlačka, 2007).

To demonstrate capabilities of the fuzzified WOWA operator, we will take up the example of evaluating academic staff. We have used weighted average with the following weights for the two partial goals: $w_{research} = 0.4$, $w_{teaching} = 0.6$. These weights are set by an executive. On the other hand, the executive also allows a member of academic staff to partly specialize in either teaching or research. That is why another pair of weights, $p_1 = 0.7$, $p_2 = 0.3$, is set. These weights express significancies of partial evaluations according to their ordering. The weight $p_1$ corresponds to the area where the subject performs better, $p_2$ where he/she performs poorer. The evaluations of an employee in the areas of interest can be modeled by fuzzy numbers on $[0,1]$. Partial evaluations can then be aggregated with the fuzzified WOWA operator.

The crisp WOWA operator is studied in detail in Torra & Narukawa (2007).

## Aggregation by the Fuzzified Choquet Integral

If there are interactions among criteria (or among corresponding partial goals), the fuzzified discrete Choquet integral should be considered for aggregation of partial evaluations. Generally, the Choquet integral can be used for such interactions among criteria that are stable over the whole domain of criteria. There are two types of interaction among criteria (or partial goals) that can be modeled by the Choquet integral – redundancy and comple-mentarity.

In case of redundancy, partial goals are overlap-ping – they have something in common. Therefore, the significance of this set of overlapping goals is lower than the sum of weights of individual goals. Therefore, weighted average cannot be used for aggregation of partial evaluations because the evaluation of the overlapping part would be included several times.

The opposite type of interaction is comple-mentarity (also called a support between criteria or partial goals (Torra & Narukawa, 2007)). The occurrences when all the partial goals are fulfilled are especially valuable for the evaluator. We can say that fulfilling all these partial goals brings some "additional value". The total significance of a considered group of partial goals is then greater than the sum of weights of the individual goals. Again, the weighted average is not suitable for this case because this "additional value" would not be incorporated at all.

If the Choquet integral is used for aggrega-tion, significance is no longer a standard additive normalized measure (probability measure) defined on a set of partial goals whose evaluations are to be aggregated. A more general normalized measure (fuzzy measure) must be used here to express significancies of all subsets in this set of partial goals.

A fuzzy measure on a finite nonempty set $G$ is a set function $\mu : \wp(G) \to [0,1]$ satisfying the following axioms:

- $\mu(\varnothing) = 0$, $\mu(G) = 1$,
- $C \subseteq D$ implies $\mu(C) \leq \mu(D)$ for any $C, D \in \wp(G)$.

Let $G = \{G_1,..,G_m\}$ be a nonempty finite set, $\mu$ be a fuzzy measure on $G$, and $f : G \to [0,1]$, $f(G_i) = u_i, i = 1,...,m$. Then the Choquet integral of $f$ is defined as

$$(C)\int_G f \, d\mu = \sum_{i=1}^{m} \left[ u_{(i)} - u_{(i-1)} \right] \cdot \mu\left( B_{(i)} \right),$$

where $(1),...,(m)$ is a permutation of indices $1,...,$ $m$ such that $u_{(1)} \leq u_{(2)} \leq ... \leq u_{(m)}$, $B_{(i)} = \left\{ G_{(i)}, G_{(i+1)},..., G_{(m)} \right\}$, and $u_{(0)}=0$ by con-vention.

In fuzzy case, the weights of subsets of par-tial goals are defined by a FNV-fuzzy measure (fuzzy-number-valued fuzzy measure). The fuzzy measure itself generalizes a standard measure, with additivity replaced by monotonicity; in case of a FNV-fuzzy measure, values of the fuzzy measure are modeled by fuzzy numbers.

A FNV-fuzzy measure on a finite set $G$ is a set function $\tilde{\mu} : \wp(G) \to F_N\left([0,1]\right)$ satisfying the following axioms:

- $\tilde{\mu}(\varnothing) = 0$, $\tilde{\mu}(G) = 1$,
- $C \subseteq D$ implies $\tilde{\mu}(C) \leq \tilde{\mu}(D)$ for any $C, D \in \wp(G)$.

Let $G = \{G_1, G_2,...,G_m\}$ be a nonempty finite set, $\wp(G)$ be the family of all its subsets, $\tilde{\mu}$ be a FNV-fuzzy measure on $G$, and $F : G \to \mathcal{F}_N([0,1])$, $F(G_i) = U_i, i = 1,..., m$, be a FNV-function. The Choquet integral of the FNV-function $F$ with respect to the FNV-fuzzy measure $\tilde{\mu}$ is defined as a fuzzy number $U$ with a member-ship function given for any $u \in [0,1]$ by the equa-tion in Box 4.

Calculation of the fuzzified Choquet integral according to its definition tends to be very com-plicated. Fortunately, an effective algorithm was found (Bebčáková, Talašová & Pavlačka, 2010). Let us introduce the following notation: for a FNV-function $F$, $F : G \to \mathcal{F}_N([0,1])$, $F(G_i) = U_i$, $i=1,...,m$, let us denote

$$U_i = \{[\underline{u}_i(\alpha), \overline{u}_i(\alpha)], \alpha \in [0,1]\}, i = 1,..., m.$$

*Box 4.*

$$U(u) = \max \left\{ \begin{array}{l} \min \left\{ U_1(u_1),...,U_m(u_m), \tilde{\mu}(B_{(1)})(\mu_1),...,\tilde{\mu}(B_{(m)})(\mu_m) \right\} \mid \\ u = (C)\int_G f d\mu, \text{ where } f : G \rightarrow [0,1] \text{ such that } f(G_i) = u_i,\ i = 1,...,m, \\ \mu \text{ is a fuzzy measure on G such that } \mu(B_{(i)}) = \mu_i,\ i = 1,...,m, \\ B_{(i)} = \{G_{(i)},...,G_{(m)}\},\ i = 1,...,m, \\ \text{and } (1),...,(m) \text{ is such a permutation of } 1,...,m \text{ that } u_{(1)} \leq ... \leq u_{(m)} \end{array} \right\}$$

For a FNV-fuzzy measure $\tilde{\mu}$ on $G$, $G = \{G_1, G_2,...,G_m\}$, and for any permutation $(1),...,(m)$ of indices $1,..., m$ let us denote

$$\tilde{\mu}(B_{(i)}) = \{[\underline{\mu}_{B(i)}(\alpha), \bar{\mu}_{B(i)}(\alpha)], \alpha \in [0,1]\},$$

where $B_{(i)} = \{G_{(i)},...,G_{(m)}\}$. Then the fuzzy value $U$ of the fuzzified Choquet integral, $U = \{[\underline{u}(\alpha), \bar{u}(\alpha)], \alpha \in [0,1]\}$, can be calculated for any $\alpha \in [0,1]$ as follows:

$$\underline{u}(\alpha) = \sum_{i=1}^{m} \left[ \underline{u}_{(i)}(\alpha) - \underline{u}_{(i-1)}(\alpha) \right] \cdot \underline{\mu}_{B(i)}(\alpha),$$

where $\underline{u}_{(0)}(\alpha) = 0$ by definition and $(1),..., (m)$ is such a permutation of indices $1,..., m$ that $\underline{u}_{(1)}(\alpha) \leq ... \leq \underline{u}_{(m)}(\alpha)$;

$$\bar{u}(\alpha) = \sum_{i=1}^{m} \left[ \bar{u}_{(i)}(\alpha) - \bar{u}_{(i-1)}(\alpha) \right] \cdot \bar{\mu}_{B(i)}(\alpha),$$

where $\bar{u}_{(0)}(\alpha) = 0$ by definition and $(1),..., (m)$ is such a permutation of indices $1,..., m$ that $\bar{u}_{(1)}(\alpha) \leq ... \leq \bar{u}_{(m)}(\alpha)$.

As already mentioned, the Choquet integral can be used when there is redundancy or complementarity among partial goals. Both cases will be demonstrated in examples.

First, the case of redundancy, i.e., when partial goals are overlapping, can be clearly identified in the situation where we want to evaluate high school students' aptitude for study of Science. The evaluation will be based on the students' test results in *Mathematics*, *Physics*, and *Chemistry*. For the sake of simplicity, we use crisp numbers as values of a fuzzy measure. The measure of the partial goals will be $\mu(Mathematics) = 0.5$, $\mu(Physics) = 0.4$ and $\mu(Chemistry) = 0.3$. Students who are good at Math are usually also good at Physics. The reason is that these two subjects have a lot in common. Therefore, we set the measure $\mu(Mathematics, Physics) = 0.7$, which is less than $\mu(Mathematics) + \mu(Physics)$. Similarly, $\mu(Mathematics, Chemistry) = 0.6$ and $\mu(Physics, Chemistry) = 0.6$. The measure $\mu(Mathematics, Physics, Chemistry) = 1$, and $\mu(\emptyset) = 0$.

Second, the opposite type of criteria interaction is complementarity. Let us consider the following example. We would like to evaluate career perspective of young mathematicians according to three criteria – *Mathematical Ability*, *English Proficiency* and *Communication Skills*. The knowledge of Math is the most important for them but without the other skills they will not be able to publish, which is a necessity in science. The significances of partial evaluations can be expressed by a fuzzy measure, say: $\mu(\emptyset) = 0$, $\mu(Math) = 0.6$, $\mu(English) = 0.1$, $\mu(Communication) = 0.05$, $\mu(Math, English) = 0.8$, $\mu(Math, Communication)$

= 0.7, $\mu$(*English, Communication*) = 0.2, $\mu$(*Math, English, Communication*) = 1.

For more information on the fuzzified Choquet integral, see Pavlačka (2010) and Bebčáková *et al.* (2010). Besides the FuzzME software, a simple software tool called CHOQUET (http://FuzzME.wz.cz/) can be used to perform evaluation by means of the fuzzy Choquet. The tool is freeware and because of its simple user interface is convenient for first experiments with this type of aggregation.

## Aggregation by a Fuzzy Expert System

A fuzzy expert system is used if the relationship between partial evaluations and the overall evaluation is complicated. Theoretically, it is possible to model, with an arbitrary precision, any Borel-measurable function by means of a fuzzy rule base (properties of the Mamdani and Sugeno fuzzy controllers, see e.g. Kosko (2003)). In reality, the quality of approximation is limited by the expert's knowledge of the relationship. If the relationship between fulfillment of lower-level goals and fulfillment of the goal directly superior is modeled by a fuzzy rule base, then the evaluating function is of the form in Box 5.

- $\left(\mathcal{E}_j, \mathcal{T}\left(\mathcal{E}_j\right), [0,1], M_j, G_j\right)$ are linguistic scales representing partial evaluations,

- $\mathcal{U}_{ij} \in \mathcal{T}\left(\mathcal{E}_j\right)$ are their linguistic values, and $U_{ij} = M_j(\mathcal{U}_{ij})$ are fuzzy numbers representing their meanings,

- $\left(\mathcal{E}, \mathcal{T}\left(\mathcal{E}\right), [0,1], M, G\right)$ is a linguistic scale representing the overall evaluation,

- $\mathcal{U}_i \in \mathcal{T}\left(\mathcal{E}\right)$ are its linguistic values, and $U_i = M(\mathcal{U}_i)$ are fuzzy numbers representing their meanings.

For given values of partial evaluations, the resulting fuzzy evaluation is calculated by the Mamdani, Sugeno-WA, or Sugeno-WOWA fuzzy inference algorithms.

In case of the Mamdani fuzzy inference (Mamdani & Assilian, 1975; Talašová, 2003), calculation proceeds in three steps.

First, the degree $h_i$ of correspondence between the given *m*-tuple of fuzzy values $\left(U_1', U_2', ..., U_m'\right)$ of partial evaluations and the mathematical meaning of the left-hand side of the *i*-th rule is calculated for any $i = 1, ..., n$ in the following way

$$h_i = \min \left\{ hgt(U_1' \cap U_{i,1}), ..., hgt(U_m' \cap U_{i,m}) \right\}.$$

For each of the rules, the output fuzzy value $U_i''$, $i = 1, ..., n$, corresponding to the given input fuzzy values, is calculated as follows

$$\forall y \in [0,1] : U_i''(y) = \min \left\{ h_i, U_i(y) \right\}.$$

*Box 5.*

```
If  𝓔₁ is  𝒰₁₁ and ... and  𝓔ₘ is  𝒰₁ₘ, then  𝓔  is  𝒰₁.
If  𝓔₁ is  𝒰₂₁ and ... and  𝓔ₘ is  𝒰₂ₘ, then  𝓔  is  𝒰₂.
............................................................
If  𝓔₁ is  𝒰ₙ₁ and ... and  𝓔ₘ is  𝒰ₙₘ, then  𝓔  is  𝒰ₙ,
where for  i = 1,..., n,   j = 1,..., m,
```

The final fuzzy evaluation of the alternative is given as a union of all the fuzzy evaluations that were calculated for the particular rules in the previous step, i.e.,

$$U = \bigcup_{i=1}^{n} U_i''.$$

Generally, the result obtained by the Mamdani inference algorithm need not be a fuzzy number (in fact, in most cases it is *not*). So, for further calculations within the fuzzy model, it must be approximated by a fuzzy number.

On the other hand, the advantage of the Sugeno-WA and Sugeno-WOWA algorithms (Holeček & Talašová, 2010) is that their output is always a fuzzy number. The Sugeno-WA inference algorithm is a generalization of the classic Sugeno algorithm (Sugeno, 1985; Talašová, 2003) where real numbers on right-hand sides of the rules are replaced by fuzzy numbers. These fuzzy numbers can represent meanings of linguistic terms, and therefore this inference algorithm can be also used with the rule base mentioned above.

The result of the Sugeno-WA inference is obtained as follows.

1. In its first step, the degrees of correspondence $h_i$, $i = 1, ..., n$, are calculated in the same way as in the Mamdani fuzzy inference algorithm.
2. The resulting fuzzy evaluation $U$ is then computed as a weighted average of the fuzzy evaluations $U_i$, $i = 1, ..., n$, which model mathematical meanings of linguistic evaluations on the right-hand sides of the rules, with the weights $h_i$. This is done by the formula

$$U = \frac{\sum_{i=1}^{n} h_i \cdot U_i}{\sum_{i=1}^{n} h_i}.$$

For more complex cases, the Sugeno-WOWA inference can be used (Holeček & Talašová, 2010). This method requires, besides a fuzzy rule base, normalized weights $p_1, p_2, ..., p_k$. These normalized weights are assigned to individual values of the linguistic scale representing the output variable $\mathcal{E}$. By these weights, the expert can express his/her optimism or pessimism (a pessimist assigns larger weights to bad evaluations, while an optimist to good evaluations). This can be utilized, for example, when the risk of a bank client is evaluated by a fuzzy expert system. The scale for the resulting evaluations can consist of the following terms – *very high risk, high risk, medium risk,* and *no risk recognized.* The expert can assign, for example, a weight 0.45 to the term *very high risk*, 0.35 o *high risk*, 0.15 to *medium risk*, and 0.05 to *no risk recognized.*

Any of these inference algorithms can be applied in evaluation models. The Mamdani inference algorithm is the best-known. The Sugeno-WA algorithm is preferred for its simplicity and the fact that it always results in a fuzzy number. The last algorithm, Sugeno-WOWA, can be used when the expert has additional requirements on the evaluation (Holeček & Talašová, 2010).

## The FuzzME Software

In the previous text, a theoretical framework for fuzzy methods of multiple-criteria evaluation was described. Each new method calls for its software implementation so that it could be applied in practice. For this reason, software called FuzzME was developed. This software includes all the methods described in this chapter. Its intuitive user interface (Figures 2 and 3) makes the whole evaluation process very easy to carry out.

When a model is being built in FuzzME, the goals tree is designed first. The user creates the structure of the tree and then determines the type of each node. For nodes at the ends of branches, the user selects between qualitative and quantitative criteria. For the rest of the nodes, he/she

*Figure 2. Main window of the program*

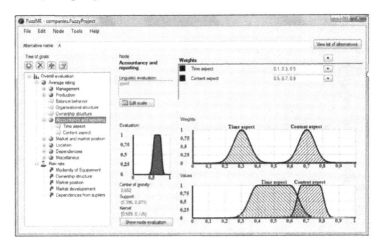

*Figure 3. Scale editing window*

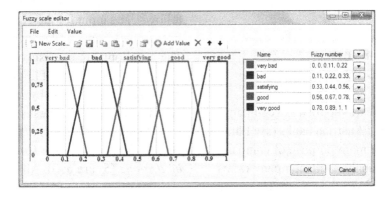

chooses an appropriate aggregation method. All the aggregation methods can be arbitrarily integrated within the frame of one goals tree.

FuzzME takes maximum advantage of linguistic approximation. The user can design a linguistic fuzzy scale for each node. This step is not necessary but is recommended. If the scale is created, the user can also see the linguistic evaluation of a particular partial goal.

The next step is to fill in necessary information as to the selected aggregation method. For FuzzyWA and FuzzyOWA, normalized fuzzy weights are defined. For the fuzzified WOWA operator, two sets of normalized (crisp) weights are set. The fuzzified Choquet integral requires a FNV-fuzzy measure to be defined. And finally, a

fuzzy rule base must be designed if aggregation by a fuzzy expert system is required. As far as criteria are concerned, for each quantitative criterion the user must specify its domain and define the evaluating function. For qualitative criteria, it suffices to define the linguistic evaluating scales.

All these steps having been completed, the model is finished and ready for the evaluation process. The alternatives (Figure 4) can be inserted manually by the user, but import from outside sources, such as Microsoft Excel, is also supported. The resulting evaluations can be exported, e.g. to Excel, for further analysis and processing.

FuzzME requires Windows XP (or newer) and .NET framework 2.0 (or newer). The demo version

*Figure 4. A list of alternatives*

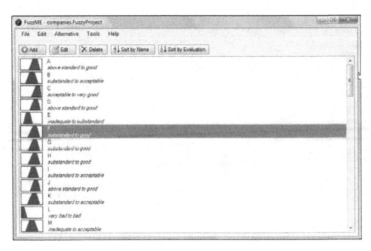

of FuzzME can be downloaded from http://FuzzME.wz.cz.

## Example 1: Soft-Fact Rating of Bank Clients

The FuzzME software was applied as a company-rating model in one of Austrian banks (see Fürst, 2010). Generally, the main purpose of company rating systems is to analyze the company ratios and calculate a rating score from them. This score is a measure of financial status and rigidity of the company.

The rating system currently used by the bank utilizes self-organizing maps and neural networks to analyze hard-fact data from the company's balance sheet and to calculate 17 ratios from them. These ratios are then analyzed by four expert systems and the result is the hard-fact rating of the company. The applied rating system makes it possible to include also soft-fact rating to calculate the overall evaluation. The weights assigned to hard- and soft-fact ratings are 80% and 20%, respectively. In cooperation with colleagues from the Technical University in Vienna, we have focused on soft-fact rating procedures and tried to enhance them by means of instruments of the fuzzy set theory.

The original soft-fact rating system works as follows: The input for the given company comes from a questionnaire filled in by the bank experts. The questionnaire consists of 28 questions. The answers take the form of linguistic terms, whose meanings are modeled by integers 1 to 5. For instance, one of the questions could be: "*How would you rate the company's experience?*" To answer, linguistic terms from *very good* (1) to *inadequate* (5) are used. All the questions in the questionnaire are grouped into 10 sections: *quality of management, accounting and reporting, balancing behavior, organizational structure, ownership structure, production, market and market position, dependencies, location,* and *miscellaneous.* A crisp weight is assigned to each section and to each question within the section. The rating score for every section is calculated as a weighted average of questions' scores. Again, the final soft-fact rating score is obtained from section scores by the weighted average operator. Finally, the hard-fact and soft-fact rating scores are aggregated and the system yields the final rating.

The original model was fuzzified by means of FuzzME. First, the items on the original discrete scales were replaced by fuzzy numbers. Here it turned out that in some cases the correspondence between the linguistic and numerical values of the original scales was not ideal. Therefore, two alternative mathematical structures (equal fuzzy scales and unequal fuzzy scales) were employed in modeling the expert evaluation. The equal fuzzy scales represent a natural fuzzification of the original numeric scales. The unequal fuzzy scales work with fuzzy values that strive to model, as closely as possible, the linguistic values used in the original evaluation model. As a next step, the normalized crisp weights were replaced by the normalized fuzzy weights. This is more suitable in situations when the criteria weights are set expertly.

The newly formed soft-fact rating fuzzy model was tested on real data from 62 companies. Four alternatives of the soft-fact rating model were tested and compared – they differed in using either crisp or fuzzy weights, and in two possible mathematical interpretations of the linguistically defined values in the questionnaire (equal or unequal fuzzy scales). The alternative of the model with fuzzy weights and unequal fuzzy scales was evaluated as the most promising. The reason was that the fuzzy weights correspond better to the vague, expertly defined information and the unequal scales model better the real meaning of used linguistic terms.

The results of the proposed fuzzy model were analyzed and compared to the original results. The main difference concerns the uncertainty of the calculated evaluations. For instance, let us suppose that the weights of two criteria of interest are the same. In the original model, a company with one criterion graded as 1 (*excellent*) and the

other as 5 (*very bad*) would get the same overall evaluation as a company with both criteria graded as 3 (*average*). In reality, the former company is considered more risky as regards loan granting. With the new fuzzy model, the evaluations of both companies would have the same centers of gravity but their uncertainties would differ. For the former company, worse values of overall evaluation are possible, denoting the company as more risky.

However, as became apparent through testing and discussion of the results, the condition of independent criteria, which is necessary for the weighted average, was not fully met in all cases. Thus it was proposed that, besides the above evaluation based on the fuzzy weighted average (*average rating*), another rating should be obtained by a fuzzy expert system (*a risk rate of the company*). This new rating indicates dangerous combinations of criteria values. Both these ratings were then aggregated with the FuzzyMin aggregation operator (Figure 5) (a special case of FuzzyOWA).

Fuzzy rules of the fuzzy expert system for the *risk rate* calculation are e.g. of the following form: "If *equipment is outdated and market position is bad, then risk rate is very high*". The linguistic scale for the company's *risk rate* contains the following terms: *very high risk, high risk, medium risk*, and *no risk recognized*. Their meanings are modeled by fuzzy numbers on [0, 1], where 0 means the completely unsatisfactory rating and 1 means fully satisfactory rating of a company from this point of view. To each of these terms, a

*Figure 5. Aggregation – A simplified diagram*

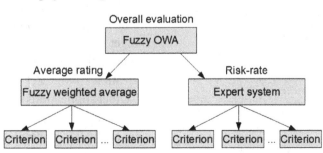

weight is attached (the bigger the risk, the greater the weight). To calculate the risk rate, the Sugeno-WOWA inference algorithm was used. The result of the algorithm (*risk rate*) is calculated by means of WOWA operator applied to the *risk rate* fuzzy scale. Two sets of weights are employed. In the first set, the weight is given as the maximum degree in which the rules leading to each of the values are met; the weights are then normalized. In the other set, normalized weights are assigned to individual values of the *risk rate* fuzzy scale as explained earlier.

Fürst (2010) summarizes the results of testing from the bank's point of view, and concludes that the instruments of fuzzy set theory in the soft-fact rating model are a step in the right direction. In particular, the ability to visualize the uncertainty of ratings (Figure 6) gives a better idea of the company's status.

## Example 2: Human Resource Management Applications

The FuzzME software is a part of the Academic Staff Performance Evaluation model which is currently being launched at Palacky University in Olomouc (see Talašová and Stoklasa, 2010).

The performance of each member of academic staff is evaluated in both pedagogical, and research and development (R&D) areas of activities. Input data are acquired from a form filled in by the staff where particular activities are assigned a score according to their importance and time-consumption. Three areas are taken into consideration for pedagogical performance evaluation: (a) lecturing, (b) supervising students, and (c) work associated with the development of fields of study. The evaluation of research and development activities is based on the R&D methodology of evaluation valid in the Czech Republic. Both pedagogical and R&D areas are assigned standard scores – different for senior assistant professors, associate professors, and professors. The number representing a partial evaluation of a member of academic staff in a certain area is determined as a multiple of the respective standard for his or her position. For better clarity and easier interpretation, these numbers are transformed into verbal evaluation using linguistic scales.

A linguistic fuzzy expert system is then used to aggregate both partial evaluations – for pedagogical and R&D areas of activities. The main advantage of this type of aggregation is that it allows setting the shape of the aggregation function completely in line with the evaluator's requirements (e.g. to appreciate excellence achieved in one of the areas). This type of aggregation is transparent and comprehensible even to a layman, as it is described in linguistic terms. The overall aggregated evaluation is also available as a linguistic expression.

The development and piloting is subsidized from the Structural Funds of EU and the state budget of the Czech Republic under the project "Maintaining and assessing quality in tertiary education" (No. CZ.1.07/4.1.00/22.0001).

Other applications of FuzzME in HR management could be mentioned here, for example, periodic evaluation of employees in the IT company

*Figure 6. The partial goals tree for this example*

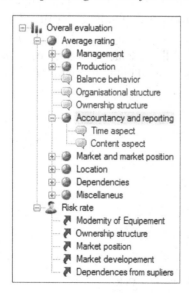

AXIOM SW Ltd; see Zemková and Talašová (2010). The evaluation is based on both qualitative and quantitative criteria and the fuzzy weighted average is used for aggregation. Also, this company is planning to use FuzzME to determine the optimal working role for a given worker.

## FUTURE RESEARCH DIRECTIONS

At present our research team focus on applications of the Choquet and fuzzy Choquet integral in multiple-criteria decision making. In the center of our attention there is a search for efficient methods and procedures for setting FNV-fuzzy measures that express significance of sets of partial goals. Several inroads are suggested in Bebčáková & Talašová (2010).

At the same time we investigate possibilities of using even more general mathematical tools for defining uncertain weights of criteria for the fuzzified WA and OWA operators. In view of real-life applications it shows that under certain circumstances it is reasonable to use a so-called fuzzy vector of normalized weights instead of an *n*-tuple of normalized fuzzy weights (Pavlačka & Talašová, 2010).

Another topic worth attention is derivation of evaluating functions from actual data (datasets containing both values of criteria and objective evaluation of alternatives – for example, characteristics of a bank client and information on his/her paying back a debt). For such data, it seems promising to use neural networks to create verbally expressed fuzzy rule bases of evaluation (Von Altrock, 1995, 1996). Also, it would be interesting to build models of multiple-criteria evaluation that combine information from real data with expert knowledge about behavior of evaluating function.

As regards the type of evaluation used in our models, further generalization is possible in the sense that besides the extent of fulfillment of a goal by a given alternative, also the extent of non-fulfillment of a goal by the alternative could be considered (Atanassov, 1999), i.e., to switch from Zadehian fuzzy sets to intuitionistic fuzzy sets where the sum of these two values need not equal one. Similarly to the models described in this chapter, the real membership degrees can be replaced by fuzzy membership degrees and type-2 intuitionistic fuzzy sets can be utilized e.g. in decision-making model proposed by Tan and Chen (2010). Moreover, the FNV-fuzzy measure could replace the fuzzy measure used in the model based on intuitionistic fuzzy Choquet integral.

## CONCLUSION

In this chapter we introduced a new type of evaluation – evaluation expressed by fuzzy numbers defined on the interval [0,1] that represent uncertain extent of fulfillment of partial goals. Fuzzified versions of aggregation operators were described (WA, OWA, WOWA) that were used to aggregate partial evaluations of this type. We outlined a structure of fuzzy numbers suitable for modeling uncertain normalized weights that, in case of the fuzzy WA and fuzzy OWA operators, express uncertain shares of partial evaluations in the overall evaluation. In connection with the Choquet integral, a FNV-fuzzy measure was introduced that, by way of analogy, expresses for each subset of partial goals their share in the overall evaluation. Together with definitions of these fuzzified aggregation operators, newly invented computational algorithm was described in the text. New inference algorithms (Sugeno-WA and Sugeno-WOWA) were mentioned also in the case when the evaluating function was modeled by a fuzzy expert system. Our own results were employed in the general field of fuzzy modeling and linguistic fuzzy modeling – special types and structures of fuzzy numbers (normalized fuzzy weights, fuzzy numbers defining a FNV-fuzzy measure on a given set), special structures of values of a linguistic variable (linguistic scales, extended linguistic scales and linguistic scales with intermediate values) and the algorithm of linguistic approximation based on a metrics defined for fuzzy numbers.

## REFERENCES

Atanassov, K. (1999). *Intuitionistic fuzzy sets: Theory and applications*. Berlin, Germany: Springer Physica-Verlag.

Bebčáková, I., & Talašová, J. (2010). Fuzzified Choquet integral: A way to model interacting criteria in decision making. *Proceedings of the 28th International Conference on Mathematical Methods in Economics*, (vol. 1, pp. 30–35). ISBN 978-80-7394-218-2

Bebčáková, I., Talašová, J., & Pavlačka, O. (2010). Fuzzification of Choquet integral and its application in multiple criteria decision making. *Neural Network World*, 20, 125–137.

Bellman, R. E., & Zadeh, L. A. (1970). Decision-making in fuzzy environment. *Management Science*, 17(4), 141–164. doi:10.1287/mnsc.17.4.B141

Carlsson, C., & Fullér, R. (1996). Fuzzy multiple criteria decision making: recent developments. *Fuzzy Sets and Systems - Special Issue on Fuzzy Multiple Criteria Decision Making*, 78(2), 139-153.

Choquet, G. (1953). Theory of capacities. *Ann. Inst. Fourier*, 5, 131–295. doi:10.5802/aif.53

Dubois, D., & Prade, H. (Eds.). (2000). *Fundamentals of fuzzy sets. The handbook of fuzzy sets series*. Boston, MA: Kluwer Academic Publishers.

Fürst, K. (2010). Applying fuzzy models in rating systems. *Neural Network World*, 20, 113–124.

Grabisch, M., & Labreuche, C. (2010). A decade of application of the Choquet and Sugeno integrals in multicriteria decision making. *Annals of Operations Research*, 175, 247–286. doi:10.1007/s10479-009-0655-8

Holeček, P., & Talašová, J. (2010). FuzzME: A new software for multiple-criteria fuzzy evaluation. *Acta Universitatis Matthiae Belii, series Mathematics*, 16(2010), 35–51

Kosko, B. (1993). *Fuzzy thinking: The new science of fuzzy logic*. New York, NY: Hyperion.

Lai, Y. J., & Hwang, C. L. (1994). *Multiple objective decision making*. Berlin, Germany: Springer - Verlag.

Mamdani, E. H., & Assilian, S. (1975). An experiment in linguistic synthesis with a fuzzy logic controller. *International Journal of Man-Machine Studies*, 7, 1–13. doi:10.1016/S0020-7373(75)80002-2

Pavlačka, O. (2007). *Fuzzy methods of decision making (in Czech)*. PhD thesis, Faculty of Science, Palacký Univerzity, Olomouc

Pavlačka, O. (2010) *Definition of the Choquet integral with respect to fuzzified fuzzy measure*. Retrieved August 15, 2010, from http://aix-slx.upol.cz/~pavlacka/fuzzy_choquet.pdf

Pavlačka, O., & Talašová, J. (2006). The fuzzy weighted average operation in decision making models. In L. Lukáš (Ed.), *Proceedings of the 24th International Conference Mathematical Methods in Economics*, 13th - 15th September 2006, Plzeň (pp. 419–426).

Pavlačka, O., & Talašová, J. (2007). Application of the fuzzy weighted average of fuzzy numbers in decision-making models. In M. Štěpnička, V. Novák, & U. Bodenhofer (Eds.), *New Dimensions in Fuzzy Logic and related technologies, Proceedings of the 5th EUSFLAT Conference*, Ostrava, Czech Republic, September 11-14 2007 (pp. 455–462)

Pavlačka, O., & Talašová, J. (2010). Fuzzy vectors as a tool for modeling uncertain multidimensional quantities. *Fuzzy Sets and Systems*, 161, 1585–1603. doi:10.1016/j.fss.2009.12.008

Ramík, J., & Perzina, R. (2010). A method for solving fuzzy multicriteria decision problems with dependent criteria. *Fuzzy Optimization and Decision Making, 9*(2), 123–141. doi:10.1007/s10700-010-9078-x

Rommelfanger, H. (1988). *Fuzzy decision support system*. Berlin, Germany: Springer - Verlag.

Sugeno, M. (1985). An introductory survey on fuzzy control. *Information Sciences, 36*, 59–83. doi:10.1016/0020-0255(85)90026-X

Talašová, J. (2000). NEFRIT - Multicriteria decision making based on fuzzy approach. *Central European Journal of Operations Research, 8*(4), 297–319.

Talašová, J. (2003). *Fuzzy methods of multiple-criteria evaluation and decision making*. Olomouc: VUP. (in Czech)

Talašová, J., & Bebčáková, I. (2008). Fuzzification of aggregation operators based on Choquet integral. *Aplimat - Journal of Applied Mathematics, 1*(1), 463–474. ISSN 1337-6365

Talašová, J., & Stoklasa, J. (2010). Fuzzy approach to academic staff performance evaluation. *Proceedings of the 28th International Conference on Mathematical Methods in Economics 2010*, September 2010, České Budějovice, Czech Republic, (pp. 621-626). ISBN 978-80-7394-218-2

Tan, C.-Q., & Chen, X.-H. (2010). Intuitionistic fuzzy Choquet integral operator for multicriteria decision making. *Expert Systems with Applications, 37*(1), 149–157. doi:10.1016/j.eswa.2009.05.005

Torra, V., & Narukawa, Y. (2007). *Modelling decisions*. Berlin, Germany: Springer-Verlag. doi:10.1007/978-3-540-73729-2

Von Altrock, C. (1995). *Fuzzy logic and neurofuzzy applications explained*. New Jersey: Prentice Hall.

Von Altrock, C. (1996). *Fuzzy logic and neurofuzzy applications in business and finance*. New Jersey: Prentice Hall.

Yager, R. R. (1988). On ordered weighted averaging aggregation operators in multicriteria decision making. *IEEE Transactions on Systems, Man, and Cybernetics, 3*(1), 183–190. doi:10.1109/21.87068

Zadeh, L. A. (1965). Fuzzy sets. *Information and Control, 8*, 338–353. doi:10.1016/S0019-9958(65)90241-X

Zadeh, L. A. (1975). The concept of linguistic variable and its application to approximate reasoning. *Information Sciences, 8*, 199–249. doi:10.1016/0020-0255(75)90036-5

Zemková, B., & Talašová, J. (2010). Application of fuzzy sets in human resources management. *Proceedings of the 28th International Conference Mathematical Methods in Economics*, 8th – 10th September 2010, České Budějovice, (pp. 682 – 687). ISBN 978-80-7394-218-2

## ADDITIONAL READING

Dong, W. M., & Wong, F. S. (1987). Fuzzy weighted averages and implementation of the extension principle. *Fuzzy Sets and Systems, 21*, 183–199. doi:10.1016/0165-0114(87)90163-1

Dubios, D., & Prade, H. (1979). The use of fuzzy numbers in decision analysis, in: M. M. Gupta, E. Sanchez (Eds.), *Fuzzy Information and Decision Processes*, North-Holland, Amsterodam, pp. 309-321.

Fishburn, P. C. (1970). *Utility Theory for Decision Making. J.* New York: Willey.

Fodor, J., De Beates, B., & Perny, P. (2000). *Preference and Decision under Incomplete Knowledge*. Heidelberg, New York: Physica-Verlag.

Geweke, J. (Ed.). (1992). *Decision Making under Risk and Uncertainty*. Dordrecht: Kluwer Academic Publishers. doi:10.1007/978-94-011-2838-4

Grabisch, M. (1995). Fuzzy integral in multicriteria decision making. *Fuzzy Sets and Systems*, *69*, 279–298. doi:10.1016/0165-0114(94)00174-6

Grabisch, M. (1996). The application of fuzzy integrals in multicriteria decision making. *European Journal of Operational Research*, *89*, 445–456. doi:10.1016/0377-2217(95)00176-X

Grabisch, M., Murofushi, T., & Sugeno, M. (Eds.). (2000). *Fuzzy measures and integrals: theory and applications*. Heidelberg, New York: Physica Verlag.

Grabisch, M., & Roubens, M. (2000). *Application of the Choquet integral in multicriteria decision making, Fuzzy measures and integrals-theory and applications* (pp. 348–374). Göttingen: Physica Verlag.

Guh, Y. Y., Hon, Ch. Ch., & Lee, E. S. (2001). Fuzzy weighted average: The linear programming approach via Charness and Cooper's rule. *Fuzzy Sets and Systems*, *117*, 157–160. doi:10.1016/S0165-0114(98)00333-9

Guo, C., & Zhang, D. (2007) On Choquet integrals of fuzzy-valued functions with respect to fuzzy-valued fuzzy measures. *Proceedings of the Sixth international conference on machine learning and cybernetics*, pp. 3180-3183.

Guo, C., Zhang, D., & Wu, C. (1998). Fuzzy-valued fuzzy measures and generalized fuzzy integrals. *Fuzzy Sets and Systems*, *97*, 255–260. doi:10.1016/S0165-0114(96)00276-X

Holeček, P., & Talašová, J. (2010). *A New Software for Multiple-Criteria Fuzzy Evaluation*. Fuzz, ME.

Hwang, C. L & Yoon, K. (1980). *Multiple Attribute Decision Making*. Springer - Verlag, Berlin, Heidelberg, New York.

Klir, G. J., & Cooper, J. A. (1996). On constrained fuzzy arithmetic. In: *Proc 5th Int IEEE Conf on Fuzzy Systéme*. New Orleans, 1285–1290.

Klir, G. J., & Pan, Y. (1998). Constrained fuzzy arithmetic: Basic questions and some answers. *Soft Computing*, *2*, 100–108. doi:10.1007/s005000050038

Klir, G. J., & Yuan, B. (1996). *Fuzzy Sets and Fuzzy Logic: Theory and Applications*. New Jersey: Prentice Hall.

Liou, T. S., Wang, M. J. J., & Elton, D. J. (1992). Fuzzy weighted average: An improved algorithm. *Fuzzy Sets and Systems*, *49*, 307–315. doi:10.1016/0165-0114(92)90282-9

Meyer, P., & Roubens, M. (2006). On the use of the Choquet integral with fuzzy numbers in multiple criteria decision support. *Fuzzy Sets and Systems*, *157*, 927–938. doi:10.1016/j.fss.2005.11.014

Pavlačka, O., & Talašová, J. (2008). Fuzzy Vectors of Normalized Weights and their Application in Decision Making Models. *Aplimat -. Journal of Applied Mathematics*, *1*(1), 451–462.

Pavlačka, O., & Talašová, J. (2009). Application of Fuzzy Vectors of Normalized Weights in Decision Making Models, in: J. P. Carvalho, D. Dubois, U. Kaymak and J. M. C. Sousa (Eds.), *Proceedings of the Joint 2009 International Fuzzy Systems Association World Congress and 2009 European Society of Fuzzy Logic and Technology Conference*, Lisbon, Portugal, July 20-24, 2009, pp. 495-500.

Talašová, J. (2005). Fuzzy sets in decision-making under risk. (In Czech), in: M. Kováčová (Eds.), *Proceedings of the 4th Conference Aplimat*. EX, Bratislava 2005, pp. 532-544

Talašová, J. (2006). Fuzzy approach to evaluation and decision making. In *Proceedings of Aplimat 2006* (pp. 221–236). Bratislava: SUT. (in Czech)

Talašová, J., & Pavlačka, O. (2006). Fuzzy probability spaces and their applications in decision making. *Austrian Journal of Statistics, 35,* 347–356.

Wang, Y. M., & Elhag, T. M. S. (2006). On the normalization of interval and fuzzy weights. *Fuzzy Sets and Systems, 157,* 2456–2471. doi:10.1016/j.fss.2006.06.008

Yager, R. R. (1981). A new methodology for ordinal multiobjective decisions based on fuzzy sets. *Decision Sciences, 12,* 589–600. doi:10.1111/j.1540-5915.1981.tb00111.x

Yang, R., Wang, Z., Heng, P., & Lejny, K. (2005). Fuzzy numbers and fuzzification of the Choquet integral. *Fuzzy Sets and Systems, 153,* 95–113. doi:10.1016/j.fss.2004.12.009

## KEY TERMS AND DEFINITIONS

**Aggregation:** Calculation of overall evaluation from partial evaluations; the WA, OWA, and WOWA aggregation operators, or Choquet's integral are used, depending on existing ties among partial goals and on the evaluator's requirements on behavior of evaluating function. Fuzzy expert system can be used for aggregation under complicated ties.

**FuzzME:** Software for solving a broad range of real-life problems of multiple-criteria fuzzy evaluation.

**Fuzzy Methods of Multiple-Criteria Evaluation:** Models where evaluations are described by fuzzy numbers which express uncertain extent of fulfillment of particular goals; fuzzy numbers are used to describe significance of partial goals; and fuzzy rule base can describe the relationship between partial evaluations and overall evaluation. Tools of linguistic fuzzy modeling are used (linguistic scales, linguistically defined rule bases, linguistic approximations to output values).

**Goals Tree:** A diagram depicting the structure of evaluation model; criteria are attached to terminal nodes; for every other node, a type of aggregation is set.

**Multiple-Criteria Evaluation:** Evaluation of alternatives where the extent of fulfillment of a given goal can be deduced from values of quantitative or qualitative characteristics, i.e. criteria, pertaining to these alternatives. The majority of utilized models have a partial goal linked to each criterion, and overall evaluation of an alternative is calculated from its evaluations with respect to these partial goals.

**Significance:** Partial goals can differ in their significance, i.e., in their share in the overall goal of evaluation. Significance is usually defined through normalized weights of partial goals (criteria). If partial goals are linked through relationships of redundancy or complementarity, significance for all subsets of partial goals should be given by a fuzzy measure.

# Chapter 22
# Realizing Interval Type-2 Fuzzy Systems with Type-1 Fuzzy Systems

**Mamta Khosla**
*NIT Jalandhar, India*

**R K Sarin**
*NIT Jalandhar, India*

**Moin Uddin**
*Delhi Technological University, India*

**Satvir Singh**
*Shaheed Bhagat Singh College of Engineering & Technology, India*

**Arun Khosla**
*NIT Jalandhar, India*

## ABSTRACT

*In this chapter, the authors have realized Interval Type-2 Fuzzy Logic Systems (IT2 FLSs) with the average of two Type-1 Fuzzy Logic Systems (T1 FLSs). The authors have presented two case studies by applying this realization methodology on (i) an arbitrary system, where an IT2 FLS is considered, in which its footprint of uncertainty (FOU) is expressed using Principal T1 FS+FOU approach, and the second (ii) the Mackey-Glass time-series forecasting. In the second case study, T1 FLS is evolved using Particle Swarm Optimization (PSO) algorithm for the Mackey-Glass time-series data with added noise, and is then upgraded to IT2 FLS by adding FOU. Further, four experiments are conducted in this case study for four different noise levels. For each case study, a comparative study of the results of the average of two T1 FLSs and the corresponding IT2 FLS, obtained through computer simulations in MATLAB environment, is presented to demonstrate the effectiveness of the realization approach.*

DOI: 10.4018/978-1-61350-429-1.ch022

*Very low values of Mean Square Error (MSE) and Root Mean Square Error (RMSE) demonstrate that IT2 FLS performance is equivalent to the average of two T1 FLSs. This approach is helpful in the absence of the availability of development tools for T2 FLSs or because of complexity and difficulty in understanding T2 FLSs that makes the implementation difficult. It provides an easy route to the simulation/realization of IT2 FLSs and by following this approach, all existing tools/methodologies for the design, simulation and realization of T1 FLSs can be directly extended to T2 FLSs.*

## INTRODUCTION

Zadeh in 1965 (Zadeh, 1965) gave the concept of Type-1 Fuzzy Sets (T1 FSs) for modeling uncertainty, vagueness and imprecision. T1 FLSs that use T1 FSs have been successfully used in various domains. However, there are various sources of uncertainties facing T1 FLSs in most of the real world applications. In a broad sense, these uncertainties can be classified in four groups (Mendel and John, 2002):

1.  The words that are used in antecedents and consequents of rules can mean different things to different people.
2.  Consequents obtained by polling a group of experts will often be different for the same rule because the experts will not necessarily be in agreement.
3.  Measurements that activate a T1 FLS may be noisy and therefore uncertain.
4.  The data that are used to tune the parameters of a T1 FLS may also be noisy.

T1 FLSs, cannot fully handle these uncertainties because they use precise and crisp T1 FSs. However, T2 FLSs, which use Type-2 FSs (T2 FSs) characterized by fuzzy membership functions (MFs), have an additional third dimension. This third dimension and FOU provide an additional degree of freedom for T2 FLSs to directly model and handle uncertainties (Mendel and John, 2002). Thus, T2 FLSs are expected to perform better than their traditional counter parts. Although T2 FLSs have been used successfully in a number of applications (Hagras, 2004, Liang and Mendel,

2000a, 2001), generally they are difficult to understand and use. T2 FLSs are computationally hard and difficult to visualize and many a times, due to the non availability of suitable software tools, the designer cannot ripe the benefits of T2 FLSs. Whereas, T1 FLSs are much simpler to design, simulate and realize, and their popularity has been greatly aided by the Graphical User Interface (GUI) based software tools like Fuzzy Logic Toolbox (FLT) for MATLAB. The objective of this chapter is to validate that a T2 FLS can approximated by the average of two T1 FLSs so that all the existing realization methods for T1 FLSs can be directly used for realizing T2 FLSs. Hameed (Hameed, 2009) gave a simplified architecture of a T2 FLS using four embedded T1 FLSs and used it in greenhouse climate control system. In 2010, Castillo *et al.* (Castillo et al., 2010) evolved an IT2 FLS using Human Evolutionary algorithm. They realized their evolved IT2 FLS through average of two T1 FLSs with an objective to show that IT2 fuzzy controllers obtained with the evolutionary algorithm outperform T1 fuzzy controllers.

In this chapter, the realization methodology of approximating an IT2 with the average of two T1 FLSs is applied to two different case studies with a viewpoint to show that the results obtained through this averaging approach are comparable to the results of an IT2 FLS. For quantifying the error, we utilized two widely used performance criteria, these are: value of the mean square error (MSE), and the root mean square error (RMSE). In the first case study, an arbitrary IT2 FLS is considered and in the second case study, an IT2 is obtained by upgrading a genetically evolved T1 FLS. This T1 FLS is evolved from the Mackey-

Glass time-series data with added noise. Further, in this study, four sets of experiments are conducted under different Signal to Noise Ratios (SNRs) i.e. 15dB, 20dB, 25dB, and 30dB. In both the case studies, the IT2 FLS is simulated with the Generalised Fuzzy Systems Toolbox developed by two of the authors and is hosted on SourceForge. net as an open-source software.

The chapter is organized as follows. The next two sections present an introductory description of generalized T2 and IT2 fuzzy sets and the working flow of an IT2 FLS. After that, we describe the realization methodology followed here for an IT2 FLS. Subsequent section is devoted to two case studies upon which this realization is applied; the Mackey-Glass time-series forecasting, that is a benchmark problem used for the validation of fuzzy models, is described under case study II in this section; we are presenting simulation results from several experiments using SNR values; and we are including a performance comparison between the used realization approach i.e. the average of two T1 FLSs and IT2 FLS. Finally, conclusions are drawn in the last section.

## GENERAL T2 FSS

Before starting with a detailed description of general T2 FSs, it is important to define T1 and T2 FSs, and Representation Theorem. This theorem is one of the most useful results in T2 FS theory as it can be used to derive many associations with both old and new theories of FLSs in a simple and straightforward manner.

If membership value for a particular FS is crisp (certain) for some crisp input over the Universe of Discourse (UOD), the FS is called T1 FS as shown in Figure 1 and denoted as $A$. It may be expressed in two different mathematical formats as in (1) and (2):

$$A = \{(x, \mu_A(x) \mid x \in X)\} \tag{1}$$

*Figure 1. Gaussian shaped T1 FS*

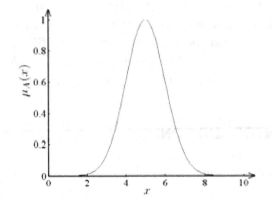

and

$$A = \int_X \mu_A(x) / x; \quad x \in X \tag{2}$$

However, if the membership value for a particular FS is not one crisp value for a crisp input but is another single FS or multiple FSs (called secondary Membership Functions (MFs)) of any shape, then such an FS is called generalized T2 FS. Such a T2 FS is denoted by $\tilde{A}$, and is characterized by a T2 MF, $\mu_{\tilde{A}}(x, u)$, where $x \in X$ and $u \in U \subseteq [0\ 1]$. $\tilde{A}$ can be expressed mathematically in either of the following forms as in (3) and (4):

$$\tilde{A} = \{(x, u), \mu_{\tilde{A}}(x, u) \mid \forall x \in X, J_x \subseteq [0\ 1]\} \tag{3}$$

and

$$\tilde{A} = \int_{x \in X} \mu_{\tilde{A}}(x, u) / x$$

$$\tilde{A} = \int_{x \in X} \left[ \int_{u \in J_x} f_x(u) / u \right] / x; \quad J_x \subseteq [0\ 1] \tag{4}$$

where / denotes a tuple rather than a division and $\int$ denotes continuous union over all admissible $x \in X$ rather than mathematical integration. In case UOD is discrete, then $\sum$ replaces the $\int$ .

## Representation Theorem for a Generalized T2 FS

Mendel and John (Mendel and John, 2002) introduced the following new representation for a T2 FS.

### Theorem (Representation Theorem)

Assume that primary variable $x$, is sampled at $N$ values, $x_1, x_2, \ldots x_N$ , and at each of these values its primary memberships, $u_i$, are sampled at $M_i$ values, $u_{i1}; u_{i2}; \ldots u_{iM_i}$ (See Figure 2). Let $\tilde{A}_e^j$ denote the $j$th embedded set (only one primary membership at each $x_i$, also called a wavy slice) for T2 FS, $\tilde{A}$ , i.e.,

*Figure 2. Typical T2 FS over discrete UODs. Vertical Slices (i.e., Secondary MFs) and Wavy Slice (i.e., Embedded FSs) are represented with same colored vertical lines and red colored bottom line, respectively.*

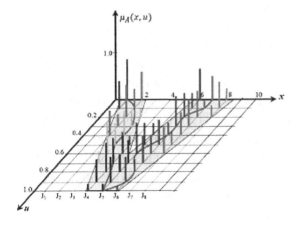

$$\tilde{A}_e^j = \{(x_i, (u_i^j, f(u_i^j))), \{u_i^j \in u_{ik}, k = 1, 2, \ldots, M_i\}, i = 1, 2, \ldots, N\} \tag{5}$$

$\tilde{A}$ can also be expressed as (6),

$$\tilde{A}_e^j = \sum_{i=1}^{N} [f_{x_i}(u_i^j) / u_i^j] / x_i ; \qquad u_i^j \in \{u_{ik}, k = 1, 2, \ldots, M_i\} \tag{6}$$

Then $\tilde{A}$ can be represented as the union of its T1 embedded sets as in (7)

$$\tilde{A} = \sum_{j=1}^{n_A} \tilde{A}_e^j \ where \ n_A = \prod_{i=1}^{N} M_i \tag{7}$$

This representation of a T2 FS, in terms of embedded T1 FSs is very useful for deriving theoretical results, however, it is not recommended for computational purposes, as it would require an explicit enumeration of the $n_A$ embedded T1 FSs and $n_A$ can be astronomical.

## IT2 FSS AND IT2 FLSS

In this section, we begin by specializing the Representation Theorem for IT2 FSs, because it has been and continues to be widely used for such FSs.

## Representation Theorem for an IT2 FS

An IT2 FS, $\tilde{A}$ , is completely described by its Lower Membership Function (LMF) and Upper Membership function (UMF), $\underline{\mu}_{\tilde{A}}(x)$ and $\overline{\mu}_{\tilde{A}}(x)$ , respectively. The FOU of an IT2 FS is described in terms of these MFs, as in (8)

$$FOU(\tilde{A}) = \bigcup_{x \in X} [\underline{\mu}_{\tilde{A}}(x), \overline{\mu}_{\tilde{A}}(x)] \tag{8}$$

If $X$ is discrete, then (8) is modified to (9)

$$FOU(\tilde{A}) = \bigcup_{x \in X} \{\underline{\mu}_{\tilde{A}}(x), \dots\dots, \overline{\mu}_{\tilde{A}}(x)\} \qquad (9)$$

In (9), the ',....,' notation denotes all of the embedded T1 FSs between the LMF and UMF. Frequently, (8) and (9) are used interchangeably without any confusion. The particularization of Representation Theorem for T2 FS to an IT2 FS follows.

## Corollary (Representation for an IT2 FS (Mendel et. al., 2006))

For an IT2 FS, for which $X$ and $U$ are discrete, the domain of $\tilde{A}$ is equal to the union of all of its embedded T1 FSs, so that $\tilde{A}$ can be expressed as (10)

$$\tilde{A} = 1/FOU(\tilde{A}) = 1 \Big/ \bigcup_{j=1}^{n_A} A_e^j \qquad (10)$$

where $n_A$ is given by (7) and $A_e^j$ is an embedded T1 FS (that acts as the domain for $A_e^j$, $j = 1,2,\dots,n_A$), given by (11):

$$A_e^j = \bigcup_{i=1}^{N} (u_i^j, x_i) \quad u_i^j \in \{\underline{\mu}_{\tilde{A}}(x), \dots.\overline{\mu}_{\tilde{A}}(x)\}$$

$$(11)$$

In (8), it is understood that the notation $1/FOU(\tilde{A})$ means putting a secondary membership of 1 at all elements in the $FOU(\tilde{A})$, as shown in Figure 3.

## Interpretations of an IT2 FS

The IT2 FS has always been considered to be a special case of a general T2 FS, consequently, issues that were developed for the latter were then specialized to the former. Embedded T2 FSs, Representation Theorem, type-reduction and

*Figure 3. Typical IT2 FS over discrete UODs with secondary membership of 1 at all elements in the FOU*

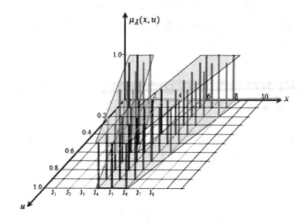

centroid, all originated for a general T2 FS and were then particularized to an IT2 FS.

For a general T2 FS (refer Figure 4), the new third dimension of its secondary MFs is very important, as it provides additional knowledge about the FS. When all of these grades are the same, as in an IT2 FS, then they convey no new information at that level, and so for such a T2 FS, the third dimension is superfluous. This is why an IT2 FS can be completely described by its two-dimensional FOU, as in (8) and graphically in Figure 5.

To-date, because of involved computational complexity in using general T2 FSs, in an FLS, most people use only IT2 FSs; the result being an IT2 FLS (Liang and Mendel, 2000b). Unfortunately, there is a heavy educational burden on the practitioner even in using an IT2 FLS. This burden has to do with first learning general T2 FS mathematics, and then specializing it to an IT2 FS. Mendel *et al.* (Mendel et al., 2006) demonstrate that it is unnecessary to take the route from general T2 FS to IT2 FS, and all of the results that are needed to implement an IT2 FLS can be obtained using T1 FS mathematics. Their paper is a simple door way for the novices to the field of IT2 FLSs to get into it quickly.

*Figure 4. Typical 3D views of generalized T2 and IT2 FSs over continuous X and U*

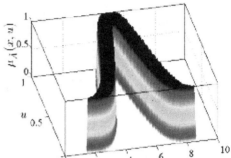

## Working of an IT2 FLS

A general block diagram for a T2 FLS is depicted in Figure 6 (Mendel, 2007) (bold solid line represents the path from crisp inputs to crisp outputs). It is very similar to a T1 FLS, the major structural difference being that the defuzzifier block of a T1 FLS is replaced by the Output Processing block in a T2 FLS. This block consists of a Type-Reduction sub-module followed by a Defuzzifier.

An IT2 FLS, is an FLS, where all of the consequent and antecedent T2 FSs are IT2 FSs. Hence, the working of an IT2 FLS is also similar to that of a general T2 FLS, as depicted in Figure 6. The

IT2 FLS works as follows: the crisp inputs are first fuzzified into IT2 FSs, which then activate the inference engine and the rule base to produce output IT2 FSs. These IT2 FSs are then processed by a type-reducer. Type-reduction basically represents mapping of T2 FS into a T1 FS that combines all fired-rule output sets in some way (just like a T1 defuzzifier combines the T1 rule output sets), which leads to a T1 FS that is called a type-reduced set. A defuzzifier then defuzzifies the type-reduced set to produce crisp outputs (Karnik and Mendel, 2001).

## REALIZATION METHODOLOGY FOR IT2 FLS WITH T1 FLSS

The realization methodology uses two T1 FLSs to emulate an IT2 FLS. The first T1 FLS is constructed using LMFs and the second one with the UMFs so as to emulate the FOU in an IT2 FLS. The fuzzification, fuzzy inference and defuzzification are done as traditionally for two T1 FLSs and the outputs are averaged as shown in Figure 7. The benefit of following this realization approach is that all the existing T1 design approaches can be adopted to realize an IT2 FLS. Moreover, this methodology reduces the computational burden while preserving the advantages of IT2 FLSs as it eliminates the requirement of type-reduction.

*Figure 5. Typical 2D representations of an IT2 FS and its Embedded FSs over continuous UODs*

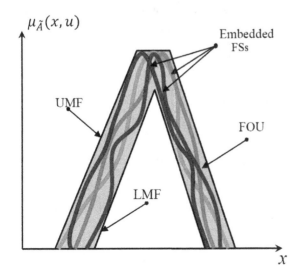

*Figure 6. A T2 FLS block diagram*

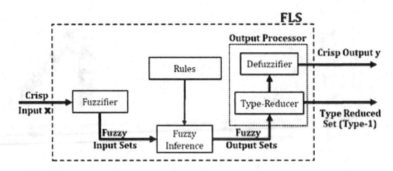

## EXPERIMENTS AND SIMULATION RESULTS

### Case Study I: An Arbitrary System

An arbitrary system with two inputs and single output was taken. Firstly, IT2 FLS was considered and simulated with the Generalised Fuzzy Systems (GFS) Toolbox developed by two of the authors (Satvir Singh and Arun Khosla). This MATLAB based toolbox has been released under General Public License and is hosted on SourceForge.net[1]. It supports the design and simulation of both T1 and T2 FLSs. The various modules of GFS toolbox are viz. GFS Set Editor, GFS Rule Editor, GFS Rule Analyzer and GFS Surface Analyzer (Singh et. al., 2010). GFS Rule Analyzer is similar to MATLAB FLT Rule Viewer but is capable of simulating rule firing with both T1 and T2 FSs.

GFS Surface Analyzer of GFS toolbox is similar to Surface Viewer module of MATLAB FLT for the overall evaluation of FLSs. There are many ways to express FOU and hence approaches to describe IT2 FLS (Mendel, 2001, Mendel et al., 2006, Zadeh, 1975) and most of the popular approaches have been implemented in GFS toolbox. For the arbitrary IT2 FLS considered in this chapter, *Principal T1 FS+FOU* approach is used for expressing FOU. For example, an arbitrary Gaussian shaped T1 FS with mean $m$ and standard deviation $\sigma$ can be upgraded to T2 FS by blurring the T1 FS towards the left and right uniformly if the noise is considered to be uniform, i.e., $m$ may range from $m-r$ to $m+r$, where $r$ is the measure of FOU.

All the information for a given FLS is provided in GFS structure that can be thought of as a hierarchy of structures. Various fields of GFS struc-

*Figure 7. Realization methodology for IT2 FLS with T1 FLSs*

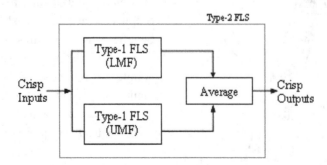

*Figure 8. GFS structure variable fields*

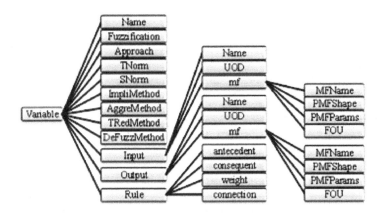

ture variable for a typical fuzzification, *Interval Type-2*, and the corresponding approach, *Principal MF+FOU* are shown in Figure **8** (Singh, 2010).

For some arbitrarily selected input values [0.5 0.7], snap shot of the GFS Rule Analyzer for IT2 FLS is shown in Figure 9. Then two T1 fuzzy models were considered, where the first T1 FLS was constructed using LMFs and the second one

with UMFs so as to emulate the FOU in an IT2 FS. Snap shots of the GFS Rule Analyzer for T1 FLS (LMF) and T1 FLS (UMF) are shown in Figure 10 and Figure 11 respectively corresponding to earlier selected input values [0.5 0.7] and rulebase. All the model parameters of IT2 FLS, T1 FLS (LMF) and T1 FLS (UMF) are listed in Table 1.

*Figure 9. Snap shot of the GFS rule analyzer for IT2 FLS*

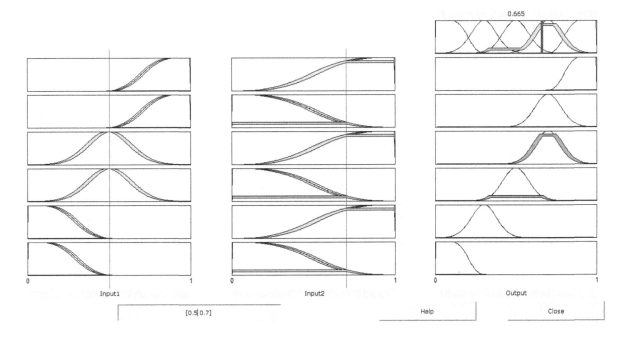

*Figure 10. Snap shot of the GFS rule analyzer for T1 FLS (LMF)*

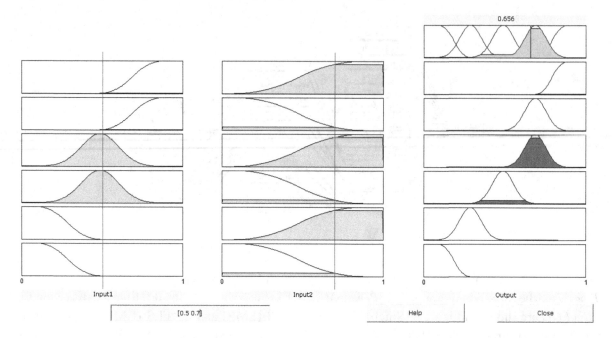

The simulation results are summarized in Table 2.

For the overall evaluation of the various fuzzy systems under consideration, GFS Analyzer of the GFS Toolbox was used to plot surfaces in 3-D in which two inputs are shown along x-axis and y-axis and single output is plotted along z-axis. Overlapped GFS Surface Analyzer plots for IT2 and the average of T1 FLS (LMF) and T1 FLS (UMF) are shown in Figure 12. MSE and RMSE

*Figure 11. Snap shot of the GFS rule analyzer for T1 FLS (UMF)*

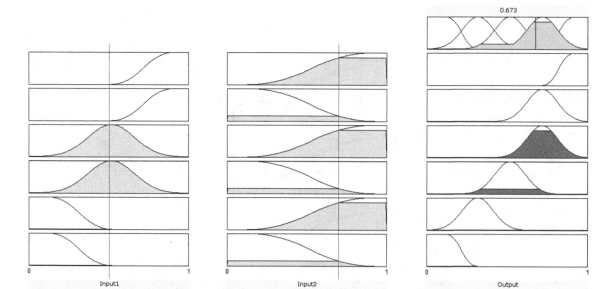

*Table 1. Model parameters of IT2 FLS, T1 FLS (LMF) and T1 FLS (UMF)*

| Fuzzy Model | IT2 FLS | T1 FLS (LMF) | T1 FLS (UMF) |
|---|---|---|---|
| Fuzzification | Internal Type-2 | Simple Type-1 | Simple Type-1 |
| Approach | Principal MF+FOU | T1 FS | T1 FS |
| t-norm | Minimum | Minimum | Minimum |
| s-norm | Maximum | Maximum | Maximum |
| Implication | Minimum | Minimum | Minimum |
| Aggregation | Maximum | Maximum | Maximum |
| Type Reduction | Centroid | Centroid | Centroid |
| Defuzzification | Centroid | Centroid | Centroid |
| Number of Inputs | 2 | 2 | 2 |
| Number of Outputs | 1 | 1 | 1 |
| Number of Rules | 6 | 6 | 6 |
| Input1 | UOD = [0 1]<br>Number of mfs = 3<br>MF1 = Z-Shaped [0.1 0.5], 0.03<br>MF2 = Gaussian, [0.13 0.5], 0.03<br>MF3 = S-Shaped, [0.5 0.9], 0.03 | UOD = [0 1]<br>Number of mfs = 3<br>MF1 = Z-Shaped [0.085 0.485]<br>MF2 = Gaussian, [0.115 0.485]<br>MF3 = S-Shaped, [0.485 0.885] | UOD = [0 1]<br>Number of mfs = 3<br>MF1 = Z-Shaped, [0.115 0.515]<br>MF2 = Gaussian, [0.145 0.515]<br>MF3 = S-Shaped, [0.515 0.915] |
| Input2 | UOD = [0 1]<br>Number of mfs = 2<br>MF1 = Z-Shaped, [0.1 0.9],0.05<br>MF2 = S-Shaped, [0.1 0.9],0.05 | UOD = [0 1]<br>Number of mfs = 2<br>MF1 = Z-Shaped,[0.075 0.875]<br>MF2 = S-Shaped',[0.075 0.875] | UOD = [0 1]<br>Number of mfs = 2<br>MF1 = Z-Shaped, [0.125 0.925]<br>MF2 = S-Shaped,[0.125 0.925] |
| Output | UOD = [0 1]<br>Number of mfs = 5<br>MF1 = Z-Shaped, [0.1 0.3],0.03<br>MF2 =Gaussian, [0.08 0.3],0.03<br>MF3 =Gaussian, [0.08 0.5],0.03<br>MF4 =Gaussian, [0.08 0.7],0.03<br>MF5 =S-Shaped, [0.7 0.9],0.03 | UOD = [0 1]<br>Number of mfs = 5<br>MF1 = Z-Shaped, [0.085 0.285]<br>MF2 =Gaussian, [0.065 0.285]<br>MF3 =Gaussian, [0.065 0.485]<br>MF4 =Gaussian, [0.065 0.685]<br>MF5 =S-Shaped, [0.685 0.885] | UOD = [0 1]<br>Number of mfs = 5<br>MF1 = Z-Shaped, [0.115 0.315]<br>MF2 =Gaussian, [0.095 0.315]<br>MF3 =Gaussian, [0.095 0.515]<br>MF4 =Gaussian, [0.095 0.715]<br>MF5 =S-Shaped, 0.715 0.915] |
| Rulebase | 1 1,1<br>1 2,2<br>2 1,3<br>2 2,4<br>3 1,4<br>3 2,5 | 1 1,1<br>1 2,2<br>2 1,3<br>2 2,4<br>3 1,4<br>3 2,5 | 1 1,1<br>1 2,2<br>2 1,3<br>2 2,4<br>3 1,4<br>3 2,5 |

*Table 2. Simulation results (case study I)*

| Fuzzy Model | Output for input [0.5 0.7] | Error |
|---|---|---|
| IT2 | 0.665 | - |
| T1 (LMF) | 0.656 | - |
| T1 (UMF) | 0.673 | - |
| Average of T1 (LMF) and T1 (UMF) | 0.664 | 0.15% |

*Figure 12. GFS surface analyzer plots for IT2 FLS and average of two T1 FLSs*

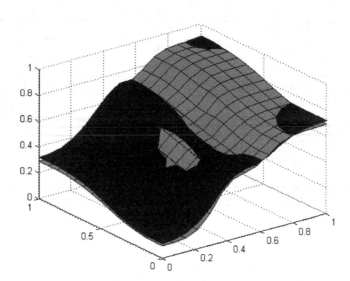

values have been used as fitness functions to numerically compare the effectiveness of realization methodology for IT2 FLS by using T1 FLSs. Mathematically,

$$MSE = \frac{1}{N} \sum_{i=1}^{N} (c_i - t_i)^2 \qquad (12)$$

$$RMSE = \sqrt{\frac{1}{N} \sum_{i=1}^{N} (c_i - t_i)^2} \qquad (13)$$

where, $c_i$ and $t_i$ are the $i$th computed and target values respectively from total $N$ training data points.

The values of MSE and RMSE between the outputs of IT2 FLS and the output obtained through the averaging of two T1 FLSs have been worked out to be 0.00001 and 0.0032 respectively. The error surface plot shown in Figure 13 has been obtained from the difference of two overlapping plots in Figure 12. An almost flat surface, a very small error for some arbitrary inputs as listed in Table 2 and small values of fitness functions (MSE and RMSE) validate the realization approach.

## Case Study II: Mackey-Glass Time-Series Forecasting

Time series forecasting is the use of a model to forecast future events based on known past events and to predict data points before they are measured. An example of time-series forecasting is predicting the opening price of a stock based on its past performance. FLSs designing for forecasting of Mackey-Glass time-series (Mackey and Glass, 1977) is a benchmark problem used for the validation of fuzzy models. In this case study, the process of designing T1 FLS from the noisy data and its upgradation to IT2 FLS to contain uncertainties is presented. Such experiments have been reported in the literature (Karnik and Mendel, 1999, Singh, 2010) to compare the performance of T1 and T2 fuzzy models. However, here we have presented this case study with a viewpoint to demonstrate that IT2 FLS performance is equivalent to the average of two T1 FLSs.

Mackey-Glass chaotic time-series can be represented mathematically as in (14)

*Figure 13. Error surface plot*

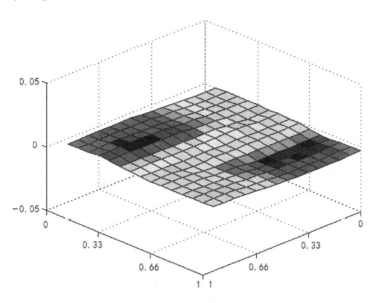

$$\frac{ds(t)}{dt} = \frac{0.2s(t-\tau)}{1+s^{10}(t-\tau)} - 0.1s(t) \qquad (14)$$

Such a system with $\tau \leq 17$ known to demonstrate deterministic/periodic behavior that turns chaotic with $\tau > 17$. For the purpose of simulation of (14), it is required to be converted to discrete-time system through Euler method (Quinney, 1985) represented in (15).

$$f(s,n) = \frac{0.2s(n-t)}{1+s^{10}(n-t)} - 0.1s(n) \qquad (15)$$

$$s(n+1) = s(n) + hf(s,n)$$

where $h$ is a small number and the initial values of $s(n) \; \forall \; n \leq \tau$ are set randomly.

A typical noise-less Mackey-Glass time-series data using $h=1$ and $\tau=30$ is shown graphically in Figure 14. The data set consists of 200 training points (blue line) and the next 200 data points (red line) are used for testing. The data has been generated through MATLAB code implementing

(15) created by one of the authors (Satvir Singh) and is available on MATLAB Central[2].

The flow followed for validating the IT2 realization approach through this case study is shown in Figure 15. Firstly, the Mackey-Glass time-series data is deliberately corrupted with noise. In this case study, four different experiments were performed, each with differently corrupted data sets. This is followed by the evolution of T1 FLS for the given Mackey-Glass time-series data that uses Particle Swarm Optimization (PSO) algorithm as an optimization engine. In other words, PSO is used for the identification of parameters of T1 FLS. We considered a 4 input, 1 output, single-stage T1 FLS based forecaster. If $x(k)$ ($k=1, 2, 3...$) is the time series, given $x(k-3)$, $x(k-2)$, $x(k-1)$ and $x(k)$, we have to predict $x(k+1)$. The design of T1 FLS can be formulated as a search and optimization problem in high-dimensional space where each point corresponds to a fuzzy system i.e. represents membership functions, rule-base and hence the corresponding system behaviour. Given some objective/fitness function, the system performance forms a hypersurface and designing the optimal fuzzy system is equivalent to finding

*Figure 14. Mackey-Glass time-series data sets for training (blue) and testing (red) of FLSs*

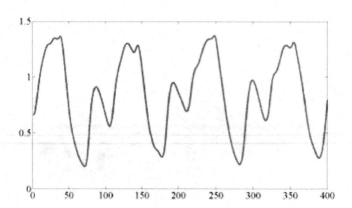

the optimal location on the hypersurface. The hypersurface is generally found to be infinitely large, nondifferentiable, complex, noisy, multimodal and deceptive (Shi et. al., 1999). These characteristics make evolutionary algorithms good candidates for searching than the traditional gradient-based methods. PSO algorithm has the capability to find the optimal or near optimal solution in a given complex search space and can

be used to modify/learn the parameters of fuzzy models.

All four T1 FLSs, with all triangular FSs evolved from differently corrupted data sets, which correspond to four experiments, are tabulated in Figure 16 (Singh, 2010).

Karnik and Mendel (Karnik and Mendel, 1999), also developed T1 FLSs for single-stage forecasting of Mackey-Glass time-series using noisy

*Figure 15. Flow corresponding to case study II*

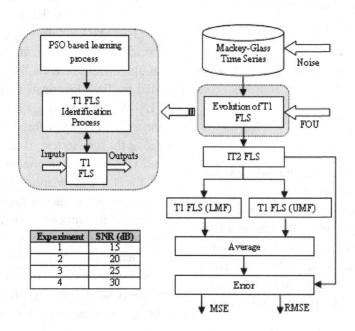

*Figure 16. Evolved T1 FLSs from noisy data with SNR= 15dB, 20dB, 25dB and 30 dB*

| Variables | Names | FLS Parameters (SNR= 15dB) | FLS Parameters (SNR= 20dB) | FLS Parameters (SNR= 25dB) | FLS Parameters (SNR= 30dB) |
|---|---|---|---|---|---|
| Input1 | mf1 | [1.1 1.775 2.45] | [1.1, 1.86, 2.62] | [0.2, 1.6, 3] | [-0.16, 0.88, 1.92] |
|  | mf2 | [-0.23 1.3 2.83] | [1.05, 2.025, 3] | [0.05, 1.41, 2.77] | [1.07, 2.03, 2.99] |
|  | mf3 | [0.58 1.465 2.35] | [-1.13, 0.935, 3] | [-1.52, 0.485, 2.49] | [2.12, 2.19, 2.26] |
|  | mf4 | [0.11 1.555 3] | [1.19, 2.095, 3] | [2.44, 2.57, 2.7] | [-0.54, 1.23, 3] |
|  | mf5 | [-1.25 0.73 2.71] | [2.15, 2.575, 3] | [2.85, 2.925, 3] | [-0.46, -0.24, -0.02] |
| Input2 | mf1 | [-0.24 0.58 1.4] | [1.73, 2.005, 2.28] | [1.89, 2.445, 3] | [1.65, 2.195, 2.74] |
|  | mf2 | [1 1.92 2.84] | [-0.14, 0.52, 1.18] | [0.91, 1.6, 2.29] | [-1.2, 0.165, 1.53] |
|  | mf3 | [-0.15 1.325 2.8] | [0.09, 1.535, 2.98] | [0.79, 1.475, 2.16] | [1.07, 2.035, 3] |
|  | mf4 | [1.03 2.015 3] | [-0.51, 0.71, 1.93] | [0.41, 0.975, 1.54] | [-1.18, 0.91, 3] |
|  | mf5 | [0.39 1.66 2.93] | [-0.61, 0.865, 2.34] | [-0.63, 0.815, 2.26] | [0.11, 1.435, 2.76] |
| Input3 | mf1 | [0.25 0.765 1.28] | [1.63, 2.24, 2.85] | [2.28, 2.64, 3] | [1.76, 2.015, 2.27] |
|  | mf2 | [0.44 1.705 2.97] | [-0.55, 0.785, 2.12] | [-0.43, 1.285, 3] | [-0.51, -0.165, 0.18] |
|  | mf3 | [-0.62 0.6 1.82] | [0.33, 1.1, 1.87] | [0.03, 0.85, 1.67] | [-1.22, 0.89, 3] |
|  | mf4 | [-1.03 0.985 3] | [0.43, 1.715, 3] | [-0.79, 0.895, 2.58] | [-1.06, 0.52, 2.1] |
|  | mf5 | [0.1 1.55 3] | [-0.57, 0.785, 2.14] | [0.13, 1.565, 3] | [-0.78, 0.285, 1.35] |
| Input4 | mf1 | [1 312.155 3] | [-0.88, 0.18, 1.24] | [-1.4, -0.32, 0.76] | [1.45, 2.225, 3] |
|  | mf2 | [-0.97 0.31 1.59] | [0.39, 1.11, 1.83] | [-0.21, 1.01, 2.23] | [-1.26, 0.15, 1.56] |
|  | mf3 | [-1.26 0.87 3] | [1.23, 2.115, 3] | [2.51, 2.755, 3] | [0.25, 1.625, 3] |
|  | mf4 | [-0.78 0.505 1.79] | [-0.38, 0.58, 1.54] | [-0.03, 1.485, 3] | [-2, 0.045, 2.09] |
|  | mf5 | [1 2 2.13] | [0.08, 0.93, 1.78] | [-0.45, 0.455, 1.36] | [-1.6, 0.285, 2.17] |
| Output | mf1 | [-0.62 0.6 1.82] | [0.33, 1.1, 1.87] | [0.03, 0.85, 1.67] | [-1.22, 0.89, 3] |
|  | mf2 | [-1.03 0.985 3] | [0.43, 1.715, 3] | [-0.79, 0.895, 2.58] | [-1.06, 0.52, 2.1] |
|  | mf3 | [0.1 1.55 3] | [-0.57, 0.785, 2.14] | [0.13, 1.565, 3] | [-0.78, 0.285, 1.35] |
|  | mf4 | [1 312.155 3] | [-0.88, 0.18, 1.24] | [-1.4, -0.32, 0.76] | [1.45, 2.225, 3] |
|  | mf5 | [-0.97 0.31 1.59] | [0.39, 1.11, 1.83] | [-0.21, 1.01, 2.23] | [-1.26, 0.15, 1.56] |
| Rulebase | | *(numeric rule matrices — not clearly legible)* | *(numeric rule matrices — not clearly legible)* | *(numeric rule matrices — not clearly legible)* | *(numeric rule matrices — not clearly legible)* |

training data, however, they did not evolve the FLS with any evolutionary algorithms and, therefore, total number of FSs and fuzzy rules in their case are quite large. For grading the performance of each candidate solution during the process of evolution, the minimization of MSE/RMSE was taken as the fitness function. For the current case study, four T1 FLSs were evolved with all triangular FSs from noisy data corresponding to the four experiments. These evolved T1 FLSs were then upgraded to IT2 FLS by adding FOU equal to 0.25. This value of FOU has been obtained through some additional experiments with an objective to optimize the performance of T2 FLSs with reference to T1 FLSs (Singh, 2010).

From the IT2 FLS thus created corresponding to each experiment, two T1 FLSs viz. T1 FLS (LMF) and T1 FLS (UMF) were obtained. The performances of these two T1 FLSs were evaluated separately and averaged to compare it with the output of IT2 FLS. The fitness functions values corresponding to the four experiments are listed in Table 3.

*Table 3. Fitness functions values for different experiments*

| Experiment | MSE | RMSE |
|---|---|---|
| **1** | **0.001182** | **0.034381** |
| 2 | 0.001849 | 0.043001 |
| 3 | 0.000485 | 0.020008 |
| 4 | 0.000400 | 0.020008 |

## CONCLUSION AND FUTURE WORK

We have presented the use of two T1 FLSs for realizing an IT2 FLS. For validating the realization methodology, we applied it on two case studies: an arbitrary IT2 FLS, and also on the Mackey-Glass time-series data. The simulation results and the low values of MSE and RMSE obtained for different sets of experiments carried out under different SNR levels validate that IT2 can be approximated very closely by the average of two T1 FLSs. This approach provides an easy route to the simulation/realization of IT2 FLSs. This is specifically advantageous when the designer wishes to exploit the advantages of T2 FLSs in the absence of availability of GUI based tools for design and simulation and/or because of inadequate understanding due to complexity and difficulty in visualization of T2 FLSs. The future work could be following this methodology for other applications.

## REFERENCES

Castillo, O., Melin, P., Alanis, A., Montiel, O., & Sepulveda, R. (2010). Optimization of interval type-2 fuzzy logic controllers using evolutionary algorithms. *Soft Computing-A Fusion of Foundations. Methodologies and Applications*, *1*, 1–16.

Hagras, H. (2004). A type-2 fuzzy logic controller for autonomous mobile robots. In *Proceeding of IEEE FUZZ Conference*, Budapest, Hungary.

Hameed, I. A. (2009). Simplified architecture of a type-2 fuzzy controller using embedded type-1 fuzzy controllers and its application to a greenhouse climate control system. *Proceedings of the Institution of Mechanical Engineers. Part I, Journal of Systems and Control Engineering*, *233*(5), 619–631. doi:10.1243/09596518JSCE708

Karnik, N. N., & Mendel, J. M. (1999). Applications of type-2 fuzzy logic systems to forecasting of time-series. *Information Sciences*, *120*, 89–111. doi:10.1016/S0020-0255(99)00067-5

Karnik, N. N., & Mendel, J. M. (2001). Centroid of a type-2 fuzzy set. *Information Sciences*, *132*(6), 195–220. doi:10.1016/S0020-0255(01)00069-X

Liang, Q., & Mendel, J. M. (2000a). Equalization of nonlinear time-varying channels using type-2 fuzzy adaptive filters. *IEEE Transactions on Fuzzy Systems*, *8*, 551–563. doi:10.1109/91.873578

Liang, Q., & Mendel, J. M. (2000b). Interval type-2 fuzzy logic systems: Theory and design. *IEEE Transactions on Fuzzy Systems*, *8*(5), 535–550. doi:10.1109/91.873577

Liang, Q., & Mendel, J. M. (2001). MPEG VBR video traffic modeling and classification using fuzzy techniques. *IEEE Transactions on Fuzzy Systems*, *9*(1), 183–193. doi:10.1109/91.917124

Mackey, M. C., & Glass, L. (1977). Oscillation and chaos in physiological control systems. *Science*, *197*, 287–289. doi:10.1126/science.267326

Mendel, J. (2007). Type-2 fuzzy sets and systems: An overview. *Computational Intelligence Magazine, IEEE, 2*(1), 20–29. doi:10.1109/MCI.2007.380672

Mendel, J. M. (2001). *Uncertain rule-based fuzzy logic systems: Introduction and new directions*. Upper Saddle River, NJ: Prentice-Hall.

Mendel, J. M., & John, R. I. (2002). Type-2 fuzzy sets made simple. *IEEE Transactions on Fuzzy Systems, 10*(2), 117–127. doi:10.1109/91.995115

Mendel, J. M., John, R. I., & Liu, F. (2006). Interval type-2 fuzzy logic systems made simple. *IEEE Transactions on Fuzzy Systems, 14*(6), 808–821. doi:10.1109/TFUZZ.2006.879986

Quinney, D. (1985). *An introduction to the numerical solution of differential equation*. Hertforshire, UK: Research Studies.

Shi, Y., Eberhart, R., & Chen, Y. (1999). Implementation of evolutionary fuzzy systems. *IEEE Transactions on Fuzzy Systems, 7*(5), 109–119. doi:10.1109/91.755393

Singh, S. (2010). *Investigations in evolution of type-1 and type-2 fuzzy systems*. Unpublished doctoral dissertation, Maharshi Dayanand University, Rohtak, India.

Singh, S., Saini, J. S., Khosla, A. (2010). A MATLAB based versatile toolbox for generalized fuzzy system design automation. *Applied Soft Computing* (Elsevier).

Zadeh, L. A. (1965). Fuzzy SETS. *Information Sciences, 8*, 338–353.

Zadeh, L. A. (1975). The concept of a linguistic variable and its application to approximate reasoning - 1. *Information Sciences, 8*, 199–249. doi:10.1016/0020-0255(75)90036-5

## ENDNOTES

[1] http://sourceforge.net/projects/gfstool
[2] http://www.mathworks.com/MATLABcentral/fileexchange/30232

Chapter 23

# Comparative Analysis of Random Forests with Statistical and Machine Learning Methods in Predicting Fault-Prone Classes

**Ruchika Malhotra**
*Delhi Technological University, India*

**Arvinder Kaur**
*GGS Indraprastha University, India*

**Yogesh Singh**
*GGS Indraprastha University, India*

## ABSTRACT

*There are available metrics for predicting fault prone classes, which may help software organizations for planning and performing testing activities. This may be possible due to proper allocation of resources on fault prone parts of the design and code of the software. Hence, importance and usefulness of such metrics is understandable, but empirical validation of these metrics is always a great challenge. Random Forest (RF) algorithm has been successfully applied for solving regression and classification problems in many applications. In this work, the authors predict faulty classes/modules using object oriented metrics and static code metrics. This chapter evaluates the capability of RF algorithm and compares its performance with nine statistical and machine learning methods in predicting fault prone software classes. The authors applied RF on six case studies based on open source, commercial software and NASA data sets. The results indicate that the prediction performance of RF is generally better than statistical and machine learning models. Further, the classification of faulty classes/modules using the RF method is better than the other methods in most of the data sets.*

DOI: 10.4018/978-1-61350-429-1.ch023

# 1 INTRODUCTION

As the complexity and the constraints under which the software is developed are increasing, it is difficult to produce software without faults. Such faulty software classes may increase development and maintenance costs due to software failures, and decrease customer's satisfaction (Khoshgoftaar, 2002). Effective prediction of fault-prone software classes/modules may enable software organizations for planning and performing testing by focusing resources on fault-prone parts of the design and code. This may result in significant improvement in software quality (Koru, 2005).

Identification of fault prone classes is commonly achieved through binary prediction models by classifying a class/module as fault-prone or not fault-prone. These prediction models can be built using design metrics, which can be related with faults as independent variables.

RF algorithm is being successfully applied for solving both classification and regression problems. It is therefore important to investigate the capabilities of RF algorithm in predicting software quality. In this work, we investigate the capability of RF algorithm in predicting faulty classes and compare its result with nine other statistical and machine learning methods using WEKA tool (Weka). We investigate the accuracy of the fault proneness predictions using Object-Oriented (OO) design metrics suite given by (Chidamber, 1994) and static code metrics given by Halstead (Halstead, 1977) and McCabe (McCabe, 1976) metrics. In order to perform the analysis we validate the performance of the 10 well known statistical and machine learning methods. We applied RF on two open source software Jedit and Sakura, one NASA data set KC1 (NASA, 2004) and three commercial software (AR1, AR3, AR5) (Promise). The Jedit, sakura and KC1 were developed using OO languages whereas AR1, AR3 and AR5 were developed using procedural language C. The compared models are a) one statistical classifier:

Logistic Regression (LR); b) two neural networks: (i) Multi-layer Perceptrons (MLP) and (ii) Radial Basis Function (RBF); c) two Bayesian methods: (i) Bayesian Belief Networks (BBN) and (ii) Naïve Bayes (NB); d) two tree classifiers (i) Random Forest (RF) and (ii) Decision Tree (J48); e) others include (i) Support Vector Machine (SVM), NNage and LogitBoost (LB)..

The contributions of the chapter are summarized as follows: First, both open source software systems and proprietary software are analyzed. Hence we have applied RF on six OO and procedural systems. In previous studies mostly proprietary software were analyzed. Since our analysis is based on six data sets, we will be able to generalize the findings. Second, comparative study of ten different algorithms has been performed to find which algorithm performs the best to predict the fault proneness of the code. The results showed that RF method predict faulty classes with better accuracy.

# 2 AN OVERVIEW OF RANDOM FOREST (RF) ALGORITHMS

RF combines the advantages of two machine learning methods bagging and random selection. Bagging makes predictions by majority vote of trees by training each tree on bootstrap sample of the training data. Random feature selection (Amit, 1997; Breiman, 2001) searches at each node for the best split over a random subset of the features. Random features and inputs produce good results (Breiman, 2001).

RF uses randomly selected subset of features in order to split at each node while growing a tree. The main characteristics of RF are (Breiman, 2001):

- RF performs faster than boosting and bagging.
- RF is robust to outliers and noise.

- RF comparatively reported to be accurate than currently available algorithms for classification.
- RF is efficient for large data sets.
- RF is an efficient method for estimating missing data (Guo, 2004).
- RF gives better internal estimate of error, correlation, strength, and variable importance.
- RF is simple and can be easily parallelized.

Breiman formalized the concept of RF with A trees as an estimator consisting of a collection of tree structured classifiers $\{h(x, \Theta_A), A = 1, ......\}$ where the $\{\Theta_A\}$ are independent identically distributed random vectors. At input x, each tree casts a unit vote for the most popular class.

RF constructs a randomized tree without pruning. Breiman (Breiman, 2001) proved that RFs do not overfit as the number of trees increases, but produce a limiting value of the generalization error. Breiman showed that strength of the classifiers and correlation between them are involved in generalization error. The framework given by (Breiman, 2001) gives insight into the ability of the RF to predict. The strength and correlation are made concrete by using out-of-bag estimation.

The following steps are followed in growing each tree in the forest (Bernard, 2007):

- For M cases in the training set, sample M cases at random (with replacement). The result will be the training set of the tree.
- For N input features a number K is taken (K<<N) such that at each node a subset of K features is randomly drawn, and best split is selected among these features. The value of K is constant during the forest growing.
- Trees are grown to their maximum size (unlimited) and there is no pruning.
- Vote the trees in order to get the predictions.

## 3 EMPIRICAL EVALUATION

This section presents the goal and hypothesis of the study (section 3.1), empirical data collection (section 3.2), Independent variables (section 3.3) and dependent variables (section 3.4).

### 3.1 Goal and Hypothesis

The goal of this study is to compare the performance of RF against the prediction performance of other statistical and machine learning methods. The performance is evaluated using OO metrics, Halstead and Mc Cabe metrics for predicting faulty classes using six data sets.

**RF Hypothesis:** *RF outperforms the nine compared methods (LR, MLP, RBF, SVM, BBF, NB, LB, J48, and, NNage) in predicting fault-prone software classes/modules (Null Hypothesis: RF does not outperforms the nine compared methods (LR, MLP, RBF, SVM, BBF, NB, LB, J48, and, NNage) in predicting fault-prone software classes/modules).*

### 3.2 Empirical Data Collection

In this work, we used six data sets in order to analyze and compare the performance of RF with other machine learning methods. The summary statistics of the data sets are provided in Table 1.

### 3.2.1 Data Set Jedit and Sakura

We used Jedit and Sakura open source software in this study (Promise). JEdit is a programmer's text editor developed using Java language where as sakura is also a text editor written in C++. JEdit combines the functionality of Window, Unix, and MacOS text editors. It was released as free software and the source code is available on www.sourceforge.net/projects/jedit. The LOC of JEdit is 169,107 including 274 classes. The number of developers involved in this project was 144. The

*Table 1. Data sets used in this study*

| Data Set | Language | Type | Lines of Code | Total classes/modules |
|---|---|---|---|---|
| JEdit | Java | Open Source Software | 169,107 | 274 |
| Sakura | C++ | Open Source Software | 131,275 | 80 |
| KC1 | C++ | Store Management for ground data | 42965 | 145 |
| AR1 | C | Embedded controller for white goods | - | 121 |
| AR3 | C | Embedded controller for white goods | 5624 | 63 |
| AR5 | C | Embedded controller for white goods | 2732 | 36 |

project was started in 1999. Similarly, the LOC of Sakura editor is 131,275 with 80 classes.

The metric data was computed using metric tool, Understand for Java (Scitools). The metrics proposed by (Chidamber, 1994) were computed using this tool. The number of bugs were computed using SVC repositories. The release point for both the projects was identified in 2002. The log data from that point to 2007 was collected. The header files in C++ were excluded in data collection.

## 3.2.2 Data Set KC1

This study makes use of the public domain data set KC1 from the NASA Metrics Data Program (NASA, 2004). The NASA data repository stores the data, which is collected and validated by the Metrics Data Program (MDP, 2006). The data in KC1 was collected from a storage management system for receiving/processing ground data, which was implemented in the C++ programming language. This system consists of 145 classes that comprises 2107 methods, with 40K lines of code. KC1 provides both class-level and method-level static metrics. At the method level, 21 software product metrics based on product's complexity, size and vocabulary are given. At the class level, values of 10 metrics are computed including six metrics given by Chidamber and Kemerer (Chidamber, 1994). The 7 OO metrics are taken in our study (see section 2.1) for analyses.

## 3.2.3 Data Sets AR1, AR3, and AR5

This study makes use of the public domain data sets AR1, AR3 and AR5 from the Promise data repository (Promise) and donated by Software Research Laboratory (Softlab), Bogazici University, Istanbul, Turkey. The data in AR1, AR3 and AR5 are collected from embedded software in a white-goods product. The data was collected and validated by the Prest Metrics Extraction and Analysis Tool available at http://softlab.boun. edu.tr/?q=resources&i=tools. The AR1, AR3 and AR5 were implemented in the C programming language. Both the data sets were collected in 2008 and donated by Softlab in 2009. The AR1 system consists of 121 modules (9 faulty / 112 non faulty). The AR3 system consists of 63 modules (12.7% faulty). Similarly, the AR5 system consists of 36 modules out of which 22.22% are faulty. All the data sets comprise of 29 static code attributes (McCabe, Halstead and LOC measures) and 1 fault information (false/true).

## 3.3 Independent Variables

The software metrics can be used in predicting the quality attributes. In this study, we empirically validated metrics given by (Chidamber, 1994) (see Table 2).

To incorporate the correlation of independent variables, a correlation based feature selection

*Table 2. OO metrics studied*

| Metric | Definition |
|---|---|
| Coupling between Objects (CBO) | CBO for a class is count of the number of other classes to which it is coupled and vice versa. |
| Lack of Cohesion (LCOM) | It measures the dissimilarity of methods in a class by looking at the instance variable or attributes used by methods. Consider a class $C_1$ with n methods $M_1, M_2 ..., M_n$. Let $(I_j)$ = set of all instance variables used by method $M_i$. There are n such sets $\{I_1\}, ....... \{I_n\}$. Let P $= \{(I_i, I_j) \mid I_i \cap I_j = 0\}$ and $Q = \{((I_i, I_j) \mid I_i \cap I_j \neq 0\}$. If all n sets $\{(I_1), ......... (I_n)\}$ are 0 then P=0 $$LCOM = |P|-|Q|, \text{ if } |P| > |Q|$$ $$= 0 \text{ otherwise}$$ |
| Number of Children (NOC) | The NOC is the number of immediate subclasses of a class in a hierarchy. |
| Depth of Inheritance (DIT) | The depth of a class within the inheritance hierarchy is the maximum number of steps from the class node to the root of the tree and is measured by the number of ancestor classes. |
| Weighted Methods per Class (WMC) | The WMC is a count of sum of complexities of all methods in a class. Consider a class K1, with methods M1,........ Mn that are defined in the class. Let C1,..........Cn be the complexity of the methods. $$WMC = \sum_{i=1}^{n} C_i$$ If all method complexities are considered to be unity, then WMC = $n$, the number of methods in the class. |
| Response for a Class (RFC) | The response set of a class (RFC) is defined as set of methods that can be potentially executed in response to a message received by an object of that class. It is given by RFC=\|RS\|, where RS, the response set of the class, is given by $RS = M_i \cup_{all\ j} \{R_{ij}\}$ |
| Number of Public Methods (NPM) | It is the count of number of public methods in a class. |
| Lines Of Code (LOC) | It is the count of lines in the text of the source code excluding comment lines |

technique (CFS) is applied to select the best predictors out of independent variables in the datasets (Hall, 2000). The best combinations of independent variable were searched through all possible combinations of variables. CFS evaluates the best of a subset of variables (OO metrics and static code metrics in our case) by considering the individual predictive ability of each feature along with the degree of redundancy between them.

Table 3 provides the summary of the static code metrics selected in this study.

## 3.4 Dependent Variable

This study focuses on predicting whether a class/module is faulty or not, rather than how many faulty classes/modules it contains. We use ten statistical and machine learning algorithms to predict the faulty or non faulty classes/modules.

## 4 RESEARCH METHODOLOGY

This section presents the research methodology followed in this study.

## 4.1 Descriptive Statistics, Outlier Analysis, and Correlation Analysis

The role of statistics is to function as a tool in analyzing research data and drawing conclusions from it. The research data must be suitably reduced so that the same can be read easily and

*Table 3. Static code metrics*

| McCabe (McCabe, 1976) | Cyclomatic_Complexity |
|---|---|
| | Design_Complexity |
| | Essential_Complexity |
| Halstead (Halstead, 1977) | Num Operands (N1) |
| | Num Operators (N2) |
| | Num Unique Operands (n1) |
| | Num Unique Operators (n2) |
| | Error Estimate |
| | Length: $N = N_1 + N_2$ |
| | Level: $L = V^*/V$ <br> $V^* = (2+n_1{}^*)\log_2(2+n_2{}^*)$ |
| | Volume: $V = N^*\log_2(n_1+n_2)$ |
| | Content: $I = \overline{L} * V$ , $\overline{L} = \dfrac{2}{n_1} * \dfrac{n_1}{N_2}$ |
| | Difficulty: D=1/L |
| | Effort: $E = V \,/\, \overline{L}$ |
| | Program Time: $T = E\,/\,\beta$ |
| Lines of Code (LOC) | Blank |
| | Code_and_Comments |
| | Comments |
| | Executable |
| | Total |
| Miscellaneous | Branch_Count |
| | Call_Pairs |
| | Condition_Count |
| | Cyclomatic_Density |
| | Decision_Count |
| | Decision_Density |
| | Design_Density |
| | Edge_Count |
| | Essential_Density |
| | Maintenance_Severity |
| | Modified_Condition_Count |
| | Multiple_Condition_Count |
| | Node_Count |
| | Normalized_Cylomatic_Complexity |
| | Parameter_Count |
| | Percent_Comments |

can be used for further analysis. Descriptive statistics concern development of certain indices or measures to summarize data. The important statistics measures used for comparing different case studies include mean, median, and standard deviation. Data points, which are located in an empty part of the sample space, are called outliers. Outlier analysis is done to find data points that are over influential and removing them is essential. Univariate and multivariate outliers are found in our study. To identify multivariate outliers, we calculate for each data point the Mahalanobis Jackknife distance. Mahalanobis Jackknife is a measure of the distance in multidimensional space of each observation from the mean center of the observations (Aggarwal, 2008; Hair, 2006).

The influence of univariate and multivariate outliers were tested. If by removing a univariate outlier the significance (see Section 3.4) of metric changes i.e., the effect of that metric on fault proneness changes then the outlier is to be removed. Similarly, if the significance of one or more independent variables in the model depends on the presence or absence of the outlier, then that outlier is to be removed.

Correlation analysis studies the variation of two or more variables for determining the amount of correlation between them. In order to analyze the relationship among the software metrics we use Spearman's Rho coefficient of correlation. We preferred to use a non-parametric technique (Spearman's Rho) for measuring relationship among software metrics as we usually observe the skewed distribution of the design measures. The results of the analysis are not shown due to space constraint in this chapter.

## 4.2 Performance Evaluation Measures

The performance of binary prediction models is typically evaluated using confusion matrix (see Table 4). In this study, we used the commonly used evaluation measures described in (Witten, 2005). These measures include Accuracy, Precision, Recall, Specificity, F measure, and ROC analysis.

### 4.2.1 Accuracy

It is defined as the ratio of number of classes correctly predicted to the total number of classes.

$$Accuracy = \frac{TFP + TNFP}{TFP + FNFP + FFP + TNFP}$$

### 4.2.2 Precision

Precision or also called correctness is defined as the ratio of the number of classes correctly predicted as fault prone to the number of classes predicted as fault-prone.

$$\Pr esicion = \frac{TFP}{TFP + FFP}$$

### 4.2.3 Recall

Recall is also known as Sensitivity. It is defined as the ratio of the number of classes correctly predicted as fault prone to the total number of classes that are actually fault prone.

*Table 4. Confusion matrix*

| Observed | Predicted | |
|---|---|---|
| | 1.00 (Fault-Prone) | 0.00 (Not Fault-Prone) |
| 1.00 (Fault-Prone) | True Fault Prone (TFP) | False Not Fault Prone (FNFP) |
| 0.00 (Not Fault-Prone) | False Fault Prone (FFP) | True Not Fault Prone (TNFP) |

$$\mathrm{Re}\,call = \frac{TFP}{TFP + FNFP}$$

Precision and recall are important measures for evaluating the performance of predicted fault proneness models. Higher value of precision implies less effort wasted in testing and inspection, higher value of recall implies that fewer fault prone classes go undetected (Koru, 2003).

There is a tradeoff between precision and recall measures (Koru, 2003; Witten, 2005). For example, if a proposed model predicts a class to be faulty and this class is actually faulty then the precision will be one but recall will be low if there are other classes that are fault-prone. In another example if a fault proneness model predicts all classes as faulty then the recall will be one but the precision of the predicted model will be low. Hence, there is a need for another measure, which combines both precision and recall, known as F-measure.

### 4.2.4 F Measure

It takes the harmonic mean of the measures precision and recall.

$$Fmeasure = \frac{2 * \mathrm{Pr}\,ecision * \mathrm{Re}\,call}{\mathrm{Pr}\,ecision + \mathrm{Re}\,call}$$

### 4.2.5 Receiver Operating Characteristics (ROC) Curve

The performance of the predicted models was evaluated using ROC analysis. ROC curve, which is defined as a plot of sensitivity on the y-coordinate versus its 1-specificity (it is defined as the ratio of predicted non faulty classes to the number of classes actually non faulty) on the x coordinate, is an effective method of evaluating the quality or performance of predicted models (Hanley, 1982). While constructing ROC curves, one selects many cutoff points between 0 and 1 in our case, and calculates sensitivity and specificity at each cut off point.

Area Under the ROC Curve (AUC) is a combined measure of sensitivity and specificity. In order to compute the accuracy of the predicted models, we use the area under ROC curve.

### 4.3 Machine Learning Parameter Initialization

The following machine learning algorithms were passed as parameters in order to predict fault proneness models (mostly with the default settings) in WEKA tool (Weka):

- Random Forests (RF): The number of trees to be generated was set to 10. The randomly selected number of input variables at each node was set to 2. The maximum depth of a tree was set to 0 which implies unlimited.

- Logistic Regression (LR): LR is used to predict the dependent variable (fault proneness) from a set of independent variables (OO metrics) to determine the percent of variance in the dependent variable explained by the independent variable.

- Multi-layer Perceptrons (MLP): The network used in this work belongs to Multilayer Feed Forward networks and is referred to as M-H-Q network with M source nodes, H nodes in hidden layer and Q nodes in the output layer (Aggarwal, 2007). The input nodes are connected to every node of the hidden layer but are not directly connected to the output node. Thus, the network does not have any lateral or shortcut connection. The network learns by finding a vector of connection weights that minimizes the sum of squared errors on the training data set. The learning rate was set to of 0.005. We used sigmoid transfer function. We used one hidden layer as what can be achieved in function approximation with more than one hidden layer can also be achieved by one hidden layer (Jun, 2007).

- Radial Basis Function (RBF) Network: RBF implements a guassian radial basis function network. The centers and widths of hidden units are derived using m-means and the outputs are combined from the hidden layer using LR. The value of m was set to 2.

- Support Vector Machine (SVM): SVM constructs an N-dimensional hyperplane that optimally separates the data set into two categories. The purpose of SVM modeling is to find the optimal hyperplane that separates clusters of vector in such a way that cases with one category of the dependent variable on one side of the plane and the cases with the other category on the other side of the plane (Sherrod, 2003). The regularization parameter (c) was set to 1. The kernel function used was Polykernel (We also used radial basis function but the results obtained were not good).

- Bayesian Belief Network (BBN): BBN uses algorithm for estimating the conditional probability tables of the network. K2 algorithm was used for performing search.

- Naïve Bayes (NB): NB uses a probalistic classifier based on applying bayes theorem with strong interdependent assumptions. No parameters are required to be passed to this method.

- Logit Boost (LB): It is a type of boosting algorithm that performs additive LR. The number of iterations was set to 10. The shrinkage parameter was set to 1. Reweighing was used instead of resampling.

- Decision Tree (J48): J48 reimplements C4.5 algorithm. The confidence factor for pruning was set to 0.25 and the minimum number of instances permissible in a leaf was set to 2.

- NNage: NNage is a nearest-neighbor-like technique for generating rules using non-nested generalized algorithms. The number of attempts for generalization was set to 5. The number of folder for mutual information was set to 5.

## 4.4 Cross Validation

In order to predict accuracy of model it should be applied on different data sets. We therefore performed k-cross validation of models (Stone, 1974). The data set is randomly divided into k subsets. Each time one of the k subsets is used as the test set and the other k-1 subsets are used to form a training set. Therefore, we get the fault proneness for all the k classes.

## 4.5 Significance Test

We performed the corrected resampled t-test for comparing the result of RF method with other nine methods. The standard t-test can generate too many significant differences caused due to dependencies in the estimates especially when one run of k-fold method of cross validation is used (Dietterich, 1998). The resampled t-test was performed at 0.05 significance level.

## 5. ANALYSIS RESULTS

This section presents the analysis results, following the procedure described in Section 3. Descriptive statistics (Section 5.1), Summary of Results (Section 5.2), Discussion of Results (Section 5.3) results are presented.

## 5.1 Summary of Results

In this section, the comparative results of 10 methods chosen in this work are summarized on the six data sets. The criteria of comparision are the performance measures given in section 4. Table 5, Table 6, Table 7, Table 8, and Table 9 show the accuracy, precision, recall, F-measure and AUC for each method across six data sets. The results of t-test (see Section 4.5) are reported in the Sig. column of Tables 5-9. The "SIG(+)" value means that there is a significant performance difference between RF and the compared models and RF outperforms the compared models. The "NS(+)" means that the RF model does not significantly outperform the compared model. The "SIG(-)" means that the compared model significantly outperforms the RF model. The "NS(-)" means that the compared model does not significantly outperform the RF model. Tables 5-9 show the results by each prediction models. The standard deviation (Std. Dev.) and significance (Sig.) of accuracy, precision, recall, F-measure, and AUC measures are shown in Tables 5-9. The models were applied to six data sets.

## 5.1.1 Jedit Data Set Results

JEdit data set is the largest data set taken for analysis in this work. It consists of 169,107 lines of code. The subset of attributes was selected using CFS method described in Section 3.3. DIT, CBO, RFC, NPM, and LOC were selected from the set of eight metrics. The results of t-test (see Section 4.5) are reported in the Sig. column of Tables 5-9. Tables 5-9 show the results by each prediction models. The standard deviation (Std. Dev.) and significance (Sig.) of accuracy, precision, recall, F-measure, and AUC measures are shown in Tables 5-9. The models were applied to 274 classes.

In Table 5, the accuracy of RF is higher than all the other nine prediction models. The precision of RF model is higher than three other methods (J48, NNage, and MLP), but is not significantly higher for rest of the models. However, RF achieves higher recall then all the other predicted models and this is significant for six predicted models (LR, RBF, SVM, BBN, NB, and LB) out of nine models. As explained in section 4.2.3, there is a tradeoff between precision and recall measures, hence, F-measure is taken. F-measure calculates the harmonic mean of both precision and recall

measures. The results presented in Table 8, show that RF model achieves higher F-measure than all the other proposed models. Moreover, the value of F-measure is significantly higher than the three compared models.

It can be observed in Table 9, that AUC of RF is higher than all the models in comparison. The AUC of RF is significantly higher than three models out of the nine models.

Thus, the model predicted using RF method achieves highest accuracy (74.24 percent), highest recall (79 percent), highest F-measure (75 percent), and highest AUC (0.81). However, NB achieves the highest precision (78 percent) but precision of NB is not significantly higher than the precision of RF. It is of great practical relevance that the RF model correctly predicts 6.48-45.37% of classes higher than the compared nine models. The RF model has 42.59-45.39% higher fault detection rate as compared to SVM and NB models. The RF model correctly classifies 49 classes more than the compared NB model. Hence, this data set clearly shows the fault prediction capability of the RF model.

## 5.1.2 Sakura Data Set Results

In Sakura data set, WMC, DIT, LCOM, NPM, and LOC metrics were selected from the set of eight metrics. The accuracy and the precision of the RF model is higher than the three other models (BBN, LB, J48), however it is not higher than the compared models. The recall of RF model is higher as compared to other seven models (MLP, RBF, BBN, NB, LB, and J48). Moreover, the recall of the RF model is significantly higher than NB model. The F-measure of the RF model is higher than six other models (MLP, RBF, BBN, NB, LB, and J48) and significantly higher than the NB model. The results of AUC found using ROC analysis show that the RF model outperforms the compared four models out of 9 models (SVM, BBN, LB, and J48). The AUC of LR is significantly higher than the AUC of the RF model.

*Table 5. Accuracy measure*

| Method | Jedit | Sig. | Sakura | Sig. | KC1 | Sig. | AR1 | Sig. | AR3 | Sig. | AR5 | Sig. |
|---|---|---|---|---|---|---|---|---|---|---|---|---|
| RF | 74.24 (6.99) | | 57.88 (16.73) | | 68.61 (12.22) | | 91.08 (7.11) | | 90.48 (11.04) | | 86.75 (18.08) | |
| LR | 71.74 (7.87) | NS(+) | 65.63 (16.22) | NS(-) | 72.17 (11.32) | NS(-) | 91.15 (4.16) | NS(-) | 91.33 (10.64) | NS(-) | 87.50 (18.18) | NS(-) |
| MLP | 72.21 (8.30) | NS(+) | 59.63 (15.06) | NS(+) | 68.49 (10.62) | NS(+) | 91.48 (5.85) | NS(-) | 89.60 (11.21) | NS(+) | 86.67 (17.45) | NS(+) |
| RBF | 71.76 (7.74) | NS(+) | 59.88 (16.02) | NS(-) | 69.59 (11.10) | NS(-) | 91.31 (4.78) | NS(-) | 89.10 (11.60) | NS(+) | 86.00 (18.11) | NS(+) |
| SVM | 65.66 (7.93) | NS(+) | 61.75 (14.08) | NS(-) | 69.66 (10.34) | NS(-) | 92.56 (2.50) | NS(-) | 89.02 (7.29) | NS(+) | 78.00 (15.24) | NS(+) |
| BBN | 71.59 (7.50) | NS(+) | 54.13 (11.24) | NS(+) | 71.52 (10.03) | NS(-) | 91.73 (4.59) | NS(-) | 91.93 (11.07) | NS(-) | 89.58 (15.32) | NS(-) |
| NB | 66.76 (8.19) | NS(+) | 58.13 (14.58) | NS(-) | 71.64 (10.28) | NS(-) | 90.24 (7.78) | NS(+) | 91.93 (10.88) | NS(-) | 89.08 (16.57) | NS(-) |
| LB | 72.01 (8.15) | NS(+) | 54.00 (15.37) | NS(+) | 71.40 (11.02) | NS(-) | 91.81 (6.21) | NS(-) | 90.81 (11.26) | NS(-) | 87.17 (16.85) | NS(-) |
| J48 | 70.52 (7.04) | NS(+) | 51.25 (15.34) | NS(+) | 70.20 (10.24) | NS(-) | 90.74 (5.20) | NS(+) | 91.10 (10.75) | NS(-) | 81.50 (20.71) | NS(+) |
| NNage | 69.77 (7.14) | NS(+) | 60.75 (17.04) | NS(-) | 68.65 (11.21) | NS(-) | 88.68 (7.31) | NS(+) | 90.52 (11.57) | NS(+) | 84.75 (19.21) | NS(+) |

*Table 6. Precision measure*

| Method | Jedit | Sig. | Sakura | Sig. | KC1 | Sig. | AR1 | Sig. | AR3 | Sig. | AR5 | Sig. |
|---|---|---|---|---|---|---|---|---|---|---|---|---|
| RF | 72.14 (0.08) | | 62.37 (0.15) | | 62.37 (0.18) | | 94.90 (0.04) | | 93.57 (0.08) | | 92.25 (0.14) | |
| LR | 74.02 (0.10) | NS(-) | 70.89 (0.16) | NS(-) | 70.27 (0.19) | NS(-) | 92.62 (0.03) | NS(+) | 93.39 (0.08) | NS(+) | 94.17 (0.13) | NS(-) |
| MLP | 71.58 (0.10) | NS(+) | 65.24 (0.20) | NS(-) | 64.12 (0.18) | NS(-) | 93.39 (0.04) | NS(+) | 92.70 (0.08) | NS(+) | 91.75 (0.14) | NS(+) |
| RBF | 76.68 (0.12) | NS(-) | 67.05 (0.20) | NS(-) | 63.74 (0.15) | NS(-) | 92.76 (0.03) | NS(+) | 92.43 (0.08) | NS(+) | 93.75 (0.12) | NS(-) |
| SVM | 76.88 (0.15) | NS(-) | 64.47 (0.12) | NS(-) | 65.61 (0.16) | NS(-) | 92.56 (0.02) | NS(+) | 89.02 (0.07) | NS(+) | 82.42 (0.14) | NS(+) |
| BBN | 74.63 (0.10) | NS(-) | 53.79 (0.20) | NS(+) | 60.83 (0.10) | NS(+) | 92.48 (0.03) | NS(+) | 95.09 (0.08) | NS(-) | 97.25 (0.08) | NS(-) |
| NB | 77.76 (0.14) | NS(-) | 75.30 (0.37) | NS(-) | 75.55 (0.20) | NS(-) | 94.80 (0.04) | NS(+) | 96.71 (0.07) | NS(-) | 96.92 (0.09) | NS(-) |
| LB | 73.69 (0.10) | NS(-) | 62.05 (0.17) | NS(+) | 66.43 (0.16) | NS(+) | 93.72 (0.04) | NS(+) | 93.45 (0.08) | NS(+) | 91.58 (0.13) | NS(+) |
| J48 | 70.73 (0.09) | NS(+) | 55.57 (0.17) | NS(+) | 59.57 (0.10) | NS(-) | 92.65 (0.03) | NS(+) | 93.87 (0.08) | NS(-) | 89.67 (0.19) | NS(+) |
| NNage | 68.68 (0.08) | NS(+) | 66.14 (0.17) | NS(-) | 62.59 (0.18) | NS(-) | 93.44 (0.04) | NS(+) | 93.50 (0.08) | NS(+) | 92.17 (0.16) | NS(+) |

*Table 7. Recall measure*

| Method | Jedit | Sig. | Sakura | Sig. | KC1 | Sig. | AR1 | Sig. | AR3 | Sig. | AR5 | Sig. |
|--------|-------|------|--------|------|-----|------|-----|------|-----|------|-----|------|
| RF | 79.16 (0.10) | | 72.15 (0.21) | | 64.30 (0.19) | | 95.63 (0.06) | | 96.10 (0.08) | | 91.83 (0.17) | |
| LR | 66.87 (0.12) | SIG(+) | 73.95 (0.19) | NS(-) | 59.20 (0.21) | NS(+) | 98.30 (0.04) | NS(-) | 97.37 (0.07) | NS(-) | 90.50 (0.19) | NS(+) |
| MLP | 74.63 (0.15) | NS(+) | 66.30 (0.26) | NS(+) | 62.33 (0.26) | NS(+) | 97.74 (0.05) | NS(-) | 96.03 (0.09) | NS(+) | 92.50 (0.16) | NS(-) |
| RBF | 62.87 (0.14) | SIG(+) | 65.05 (0.24) | NS(+) | 64.30 (0.22) | NS(+) | 98.28 (0.04) | NS(-) | 95.73 (0.09) | NS(+) | 89.17 (0.20) | NS(+) |
| SVM | 43.74 (0.13) | SIG(+) | 79.60 (0.18) | NS(-) | 58.97 (0.19) | NS(+) | 100 (0.00) | NS(-) | 100 (0.00) | NS(-) | 93.50 (0.15) | NS(-) |
| BBN | 66.09 (0.15) | SIG(+) | 67.25 (0.36) | NS(+) | 90.77 (0.12) | SIG(-) | 99.09 (0.04) | NS(-) | 96.03 (0.09) | NS(+) | 90.00 (0.18) | NS(+) |
| NB | 45.83 (0.14) | SIG(+) | 35.40 (0.23) | SIG(+) | 46.37 (0.21) | SIG(+) | 94.72 (0.07) | NS(+) | 94.27 (0.10) | NS(+) | 89.33 (0.18) | NS(+) |
| LB | 68.62 (0.16) | SIG(+) | 61.10 (0.21) | NS(+) | 65.63 (0.21) | NS(-) | 97.73 (0.05) | NS(-) | 96.67 (0.08) | NS(-) | 93.67 (0.15) | NS(-) |
| J48 | 70.32 (0.15) | NS(+) | 64.85 (0.29) | NS(+) | 89.93 (0.14) | SIG(-) | 97.74 (0.05) | NS(-) | 96.43 (0.07) | NS(-) | 85.67 (0.23) | NS(+) |
| NNage | 71.84 (0.13) | NS(+) | 70.70 (0.23) | NS(+) | 62.17 (0.22) | NS(+) | 94.47 (0.07) | NS(+) | 96.13 (0.09) | NS(+) | 88.50 (0.21) | NS(+) |

*Table 8. F measure*

| Method | Jedit | Sig. | Sakura | Sig. | KC1 | Sig. | AR1 | Sig. | AR3 | Sig. | AR5 | Sig. |
|--------|-------|------|--------|------|-----|------|-----|------|-----|------|-----|------|
| RF | 74.95 (0.07) | | 65.85 (0.16) | | 61.97 (0.16) | | 95.11 (0.04) | | 94.52 (0.07) | | 90.92 (0.13) | |
| LR | 69.56 (0.09) | NS(+) | 70.94 (0.15) | NS(-) | 62.28 (0.16) | NS(-) | 95.31 (0.02) | NS(-) | 94.12 (0.06) | NS(+) | 90.90 (0.14) | NS(+) |
| MLP | 72.06 (0.09) | NS(+) | 63.32 (0.19) | NS(+) | 59.58 (0.17) | NS(+) | 95.44 (0.03) | NS(-) | 93.98 (0.07) | NS(+) | 90.90 (0.12) | NS(+) |
| RBF | 67.95 (0.10) | NS(+) | 63.72 (0.19) | NS(+) | 61.67 (0.15) | NS(+) | 95.39 (0.03) | NS(-) | 93.69 (0.07) | NS(+) | 89.70 (0.14) | NS(+) |
| SVM | 54.60 (0.13) | SIG(+) | 70.33 (0.12) | NS(-) | 60.41 (0.14) | NS(+) | 96.12 (0.01) | NS(-) | 94.04 (0.04) | NS(+) | 86.10 (0.11) | NS(+) |
| BBN | 68.89 (0.09) | NS(+) | 57.03 (0.25) | NS(+) | 72.33 (0.09) | SIG(-) | 95.62 (0.03) | NS(-) | 94.24 (0.07) | NS(+) | 92.03 (0.13) | NS(-) |
| NB | 56.50 (0.13) | SIG(+) | 46.03 (0.26) | SIG(+) | 55.19 (0.19) | NS(+) | 94.63 (0.04) | NS(+) | 94.11 (0.07) | NS(+) | 91.77 (0.13) | NS(-) |
| LB | 69.85 (0.10) | NS(+) | 59.78 (0.15) | NS(+) | 64.10 (0.15) | NS(-) | 95.60 (0.03) | NS(-) | 94.71 (0.07) | NS(+) | 91.43 (0.12) | NS(-) |
| J48 | 69.45 (0.09) | NS(+) | 57.91 (0.20) | NS(+) | 71.00 (0.10) | NS(-) | 95.05 (0.03) | NS(+) | 94.50 (0.06) | NS(+) | 86.02 (0.19) | NS(+) |
| NNage | 69.51 (0.08) | NS(+) | 66.63 (0.17) | NS(-) | 60.40 (0.17) | NS(+) | 93.78 (0.04) | NS(+) | 94.48 (0.07) | NS(+) | 88.65 (0.17) | NS(+) |

*Table 9. AUC measure*

| Method | Jedit | Sig. | Sakura | Sig. | KC1 | Sig. | AR1 | Sig. | AR3 | Sig. | AR5 | Sig. |
|---|---|---|---|---|---|---|---|---|---|---|---|---|
| RF | 0.81 (0.07) | | 0.59 (0.19) | | 0.76 (0.11) | | 0.83 (0.22) | | 0.80 (0.26) | | 0.87 (0.24) | |
| LR | 0.79 (0.07) | NS(+) | 0.73 (0.18) | SIG(-) | 0.81 (0.11) | NS(-) | 0.84 (0.20) | NS(-) | 0.83 (0.26) | NS(-) | 0.86 (0.24) | NS(+) |
| MLP | 0.80 (0.08) | NS(+) | 0.69 (0.20) | NS(-) | 0.81 (0.10) | NS(-) | 0.79 (0.21) | NS(+) | 0.83 (0.27) | NS(-) | 0.92 (0.17) | NS(-) |
| RBF | 0.79 (0.08) | NS(+) | 0.66 (0.20) | NS(-) | 0.81 (0.11) | NS(-) | 0.70 (0.29) | NS(+) | 0.77 (0.33) | NS(+) | 0.86 (0.26) | NS(+) |
| SVM | 0.65 (0.08) | NS(+) | 0.58 (0.14) | NS(+) | 0.68 (0.11) | NS(+) | 0.50 (0.00) | SIG(+) | 0.56 (0.17) | SIG(+) | 0.58 (0.19) | SIG(+) |
| BBN | 0.79 (0.07) | NS(+) | 0.49 (0.09) | NS(+) | 0.76 (0.09) | NS(-) | 0.49 (0.02) | SIG(+) | 0.85 (0.23) | NS(-) | 0.95 (0.13) | NS(-) |
| NB | 0.76 (0.10) | NS(+) | 0.71 (0.17) | SIG(-) | 0.81 (0.11) | NS(-) | 0.78 (0.22) | NS(+) | 0.84 (0.26) | NS(-) | 0.93 (0.15) | NS(-) |
| LB | 0.80 (0.07) | NS(+) | 0.57 (0.20) | NS(+) | 0.81 (0.12) | NS(-) | 0.88 (0.13) | NS(-) | 0.74 (0.31) | NS(+) | 0.86 (0.24) | NS(+) |
| J48 | 0.75 (0.08) | SIG(+) | 0.49 (0.16) | NS(+) | 0.73 (0.10) | NS(+) | 0.53 (0.23) | SIG(+) | 0.75 (0.26) | NS(+) | 0.76 (0.26) | NS(+) |
| NNage | 0.70 (0.07) | SIG(+) | 0.59 (0.17) | | 0.68 (0.12) | SIG(+) | 0.56 (0.19) | SIG(+) | 0.74 (0.26) | NS(+) | 0.80 (0.25) | NS(+) |

The RF model correctly classifies 17 classes more than the compared NB model i.e. about one-half of the classes are correctly predicted by the RF model as compared to the NB model.

### 5.1.3 NASA Data Set KC1 Results

In this data set, WMC, DIT, LCOM, NPM, and LOC metrics were selected from the set of eight metrics. The accuracy of eight other models is higher than the KC1 data set. However, the accuracy of these compared models is not significantly higher than the accuracy of the RF model. The precision of the RF model is higher than the three other compared models (BBN, LB, and J48). The recall of RF model is higher than the recall of five models under comparision (LR, MLP, SVM, NB, and NNage).and significantly higher than the NB model. The F-measure of the RF model is higher than the F-measure of five models (MLP, RBF, SVM, NB, NNage). The F-measure of the BBN model is significantly higher then the F-measure of the RF model. The results of AUC show that the AUC of the RF model is higher than the three other compared models (SVM, J48, and NNage).

### 5.1.4 AR1 Data Set Results

In this data set, unique_operators, halstead_error, and multiple_condition_count metrics were selected using CFS method. The accuracy of the RF model is higher than the accuracy of three other models (NB, J48, and NNage). The recall of the RF model is higher than the recall of the NB and NNage models. The F-measure of the RF model is higher than the F-measure of the NB, J48, NNage models. The AUC of the RF model is higher than seven compared models and out of these models the AUC of the four models (SVM, BBN, J48, and NNage) is significantly higher.

### 5.1.5 AR3 Data Set Results

In AR3 data set, comment_loc, code_and_comment_loc, halstead_volume, and halstead_error metrics were selected using CFS method. The accuracy of the RF model is higher than the accuracy of the three RF models (MLP, RBF, and SVM). The precision of the RF model is higher than the precision of the six compared models (LR, MLP, RBF, SVM, LB, and NNage). The recall of the RF model is higher than the four out of nine compared models (MLP, RBF, BBN, and NB). The RF model achieves highest F-measure (94.52%). The AUC of the RF model is higher than the AUC of five compared models and is significantly higher than the SVM model.

### 5.1.6 AR5 Data Set Results

In AR5 data set, unique_operands, unique_operators, halstead_vocabulary, halstead_level, and multiple_condition_count metrics were selected using CFS method. The RF model outperforms five compared models in terms of accuracy (MLP, RBF, SVM, J48, NNage). The precision of the RF model is also high than the other five compared models. The recall of RF model is higher than the recall of six compared models. The F-measure of the RF model is higher in six models out of nine compared models. Similarly, the AUC of the RF model is higher than the AUC of the six compared model and out of these six models the AUC of the RF model is significantly higher than the SVM model. See Table 5, Table 6, Figure 1, Table 7, Table 8, Figure 2, Table 9, and Figure 3 for depictions of the data.

## 5.2 Discussion of the Results

1. The RF model achieves higher accuracy than at least three out of nine models in five out of six data sets. In addition, the RF model significantly outperforms two other models in JEdit data set.

2.  The RF model achieves higher precision than at least three models out of nine compared models in all the data sets. In AR1 data set the precision of the RF model is higher than all the compared models.

3.  The recall of the RF model is higher than the recall of at least four models in the five data sets. Moreover the recall of the RF model is significantly higher than the recall of the three models in JEdit data set, one model in Sakura data set, and one model in KC1 data set.

4.  The F-measure of the RF model is higher than the F-measure of five compared models in five out of six data sets. The F-measure of the RF model is significantly higher than the F-measure of two compared model in JEdit data set and one compared model in the Sakura data set. Moreover, the F-measure of the RF model is highest in the AR3 data set.

5.  The RF model achieves higher AUC than at least six compared models in five data sets. Thus, the F-measure of the RF model is higher than five out of nine compared models in five data sets. In addition, the AUC of the RF model is higher than the AUC of six out of nine compared models in five data sets.

## 5.3 Guidelines for using RF

1.  RF can be used for predicting faulty classes/modules with higher accuracy as compared to other methods.

*Figure 1. Compared accuracy and precision*

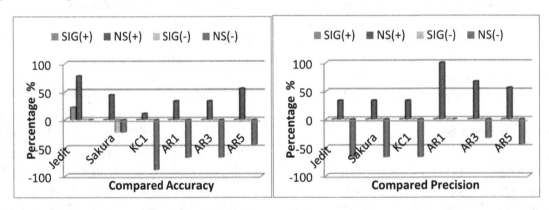

*Figure 2. Compared recall and f-measure*

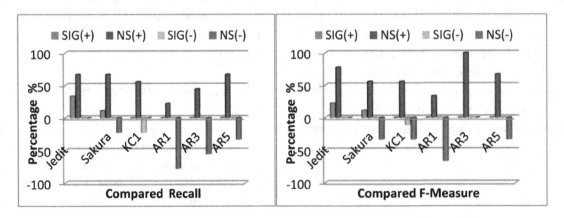

*Figure 3. Compared AUC*

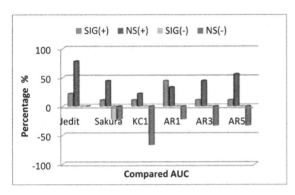

2.  The results of RF show that it has performed very well on the large sized data set Jedit. The results shown in (Guo, 2004) also proved that RF performs efficiently on large data sets and further takes few seconds to generate the trees on Windows XP machine, with a Pentium 4 processor and RAM 250 MB.

3.  RF is more robust to outliers and noise as compared to other methods. It is already shown that RF can classify 42.59-45.39% higher faulty classes as compare to SVM and NB methods on JEdit data set.

Table 10, table 11, and table 12 summarize the results of hypothesis stated in section 3.1.

## 6 CONCLUSION

This chapter empirically evaluates the performance of RF in predicting fault-prone classes. We compared the prediction performance of RF against nine statistical and machine learning models using six data sets. The statistical and machine learning methods were evaluated using OO metrics proposed by Chidamber and Kemerer and static code metrics proposed by Halstead and Mc Cabe. The results indicate that RF is generally better than, or at least competitive against the other statistical and machine learning models.

The overall accuracy of RF models is within 57.88-91.08%. The correct detection of faulty classes/modules is up to 96.10% in our data sets. The F-measure is up to 95.11 percent in the six data sets. The AUC of the RF model is within 0.59-0.87 in all the data sets. The results show that the RF method generally achieves higher fault detection, F-measure and AUC on all data sets.

An important contribution of this work is that we have compared results of various machine learning methods on several OO and procedural as well as open source, NASA and proprietary systems. Hence, our results form a *"generalisable and repeatable ground"* for future empirical studies.

This study confirms that construction of RF model is feasible, adaptable to OO and procedural systems, and useful in predicting fault prone classes/modules. While research continues, practitioners and researchers may apply RF for constructing the model to predict faulty classes. The prediction performance of RF particularly in recall measure, can help in improving software quality in the context of software testing by reducing risks of faulty classes go undetected.

## REFERENCES

Aggarwal, K. K., Singh, Y., Kaur, A., & Malhotra, R. (2007). *Application of artificial neural network for predicting fault proneness models.* International Conference on Information Systems, Technology and. Management (ICISTM 2007), March 12-13, New Delhi, India.

Aggarwal, K. K., Singh, Y., Kaur, A., & Malhotra, R. (2008). *Empirical analysis for investigating the effect of object-oriented metrics on fault proneness: A replicated case study. Software Process Improvement and Practice.* Wiley.

Amit, Y., & Geman, D. (1997). Shape quantization and recognition with randomized trees. *Neural Computation, 9,* 1545–1588. doi:10.1162/neco.1997.9.7.1545

*Table 10. Summary of hypothesis*

| Method | Jedit | | | | | Sakura | | | | |
|---|---|---|---|---|---|---|---|---|---|---|
| | Accuracy | Precision | Recall | F-measure | AUC | Accuracy | Precision | Recall | F-measure | AUC |
| LR | √ | × | √* | √ | √ | × | × | × | × | × |
| MLP | √ | √ | √ | √ | √ | × | √ | √ | √ | × |
| RBF | √ | × | √* | √* | √ | × | × | √ | √ | × |
| SVM | √* | × | √* | √* | √* | | √ | × | × | √ |
| BBN | √ | × | √* | √ | √ | √ | × | √ | × | √ |
| NB | √* | × | √* | √* | √ | × | × | √* | √* | ×* |
| LB | √ | × | √* | √ | √ | √ | × | √ | √ | √ |
| J48 | √ | √ | √ | √ | √* | √ | √ | √ | √ | √ |
| NNage | √ | √ | √ | √ | √* | × | √ | √ | × | √ |

√ implies that RF model outperforms the compared model. × implies that the compared model outperforms the RF model. * implies that the results are significant at 0.05 significance level.

*Table 11. Summary of hypothesis*

| Method | KC1 | | | | | AR1 | | | | |
|---|---|---|---|---|---|---|---|---|---|---|
| | Accuracy | Precision | Recall | F-measure | AUC | Accuracy | Precision | Recall | F-measure | AUC |
| LR | × | × | √ | × | × | × | √ | × | × | × |
| MLP | √ | × | √ | √ | × | × | √ | × | × | √ |
| RBF | × | × | √ | √ | × | × | √ | × | × | √ |
| SVM | × | × | √ | √ | √ | × | √ | × | × | √* |
| BBN | × | √ | ×* | ×* | × | × | √ | × | × | √* |
| NB | × | × | √* | √ | × | √ | √ | √ | √ | √ |
| LB | × | √ | × | × | × | × | √ | × | × | × |
| J48 | × | √ | ×* | × | √ | √ | √ | × | √ | √* |
| NNage | × | × | √ | √ | √* | √ | √ | √ | √ | √* |

√ implies that RF model outperforms the compared model. × implies that the compared model outperforms the RF model. * implies that the results are significant at 0.05 significance level.

*Table 12. Summary of hypothesis*

| Method | AR3 | | | | | AR5 | | | | |
|---|---|---|---|---|---|---|---|---|---|---|
| | Accuracy | Precision | Recall | F-measure | AUC | Accuracy | Precision | Recall | F-measure | AUC |
| LR | × | √ | × | √ | × | × | × | √ | √ | √ |
| MLP | √ | √ | √ | √ | × | × | √ | × | √ | × |
| RBF | √ | √ | √ | √ | √ | × | × | √ | √ | √ |
| SVM | √ | √ | × | √ | √* | × | √ | × | √ | √* |
| BBN | × | × | √ | √ | × | × | × | √ | × | × |
| NB | × | × | √ | √ | × | × | √ | × | × | × |
| LB | × | √ | × | √ | √ | × | √ | × | × | √ |
| J48 | × | × | × | √ | √ | √ | √ | √ | √ | √ |
| NNage | × | √ | × | √ | √ | √ | √ | √ | √ | √ |

√ implies that RF model outperforms the compared model. × implies that the compared model outperforms the RF model. * implies that the results are significant at 0.05 significance level.

Bernard, S., Heutte, L., & Adam, S. (2007). Using random forests for handwritten digit recognition. *Ninth International Conference on Document Analysis and Recognition*, 23-26 September, (pp. 1043-1047).

Breiman, L. (2001). Random forests. *Machine Learning*, *45*, 5–32. doi:10.1023/A:1010933404324

Chidamber, S., & Kamerer, C. (1994). A metrics suite for object-oriented design. *IEEE Transactions on Software Engineering*, *20*(6), 476–493. doi:10.1109/32.295895

Dietterich, T. (1998). Approximate statistical tests for comparing supervised classification learning algorithms. *Neural Computation*, *10*, 1895–1924. doi:10.1162/089976698300017197

Guo, L., Ma, Y., Cukic, B., & Singh, H. (2004). Robust prediction of fault proneness by random forests. In *Proceedings of the 15th International Symposium on Software Reliability Engineering* (ISSRE'04), (pp. 417–428).

Hair, J., Anderson, R., & Tatham, W. (2006). *Black multivariate data analysis*. Pearson Education.

Hall, M. (2000). Correlation-based feature selection for discrete and numeric class machine learning. In *Proceedings of the 17th International Conference on Machine Learning*, (pp. 359–366).

Halstead, M. (1977). *Elements of software science*. Elsevier.

Hanley, J., & McNeil, B. J. (1982). The meaning and use of the area under a receiver operating characteristic (ROC) curve. *Radiology*, *143*, 29–36.

Harrison, R., Counsell, S. J., & Nithi, R. V. (1998). An evaluation of MOOD set of object-oriented software metrics. *IEEE Transactions on Software Engineering*, *24*(6), 491–496. doi:10.1109/32.689404 jedit. (n.d.). *Website*. Retrieved from http://source-forge.net/projects/jedit/

Jun, L., Shunyi, Z., Ye, X., & Yanfei, S. (2007), Identifying Skype traffic by random forest. *International Conference on Wireless Communications, Networking and Mobile Computing*, 21-25 September, (pp. 2841–2844).

Khoshgaftaar, T. M., Allen, E. D., Hudepohl, J. P., & Aud, S. J. (1997). Application of neural networks to software quality modeling of a very large telecommunications system. *IEEE Transactions on Neural Networks*, 8(4), 902–909. doi:10.1109/72.595888

Khoshgoftaar, T., Allen, E., & Deng, J. (2002). Using regression trees to classify fault-prone software modules. *IEEE Transactions on Reliability*, 51(4), 455–462. doi:10.1109/TR.2002.804488

Koru, A., & Liu, H. (2005). Building effective defect-prediction models in practice. *IEEE Software*, 23–29. doi:10.1109/MS.2005.149

Koru, A., & Tian, J. (2003). An empirical comparison and characterization of high defect and high complexity modules. *Journal of Systems and Software*, 67, 153–163. doi:10.1016/S0164-1212(02)00126-7

McCabe, T. A. (1976). Complexity measure. *IEEE Transactions on Software Engineering*, 2(4), 308–320. doi:10.1109/TSE.1976.233837

MDP. (2006). *Website*. Retrieved from http://sarpresults.ivv.nasa.gov/ViewResearch/107.jsp

NASA. (2004). *Metrics data repository*. Retrieved from www.mdp.ivv.nasa.gov

Promise. (n.d.). *Promise data repository*. Retrieved from http://promisedata.org/repository/

Scitools. (n.d.). *Website*. Retrieved from http://www.scitools.com/index.php

Sherrod, P. (2003). *DTreg predictive modeling software*.

Stone, M. (1974). Cross-validatory choice and assessment of statistical predictions. *Journal of the Royal Statistical Society. Series A (General)*, 36, 111–147.

Weka. (n.d.). *Website*. Retrieved from http://www.cs.waikato.ac.nz/ml/weka/

Witten, I., & Frank, E. (2005). *Data mining: Practical machine learning tools and techniques* (2nd ed.). San Francisco, CA: Morgan Kaufmann.

## ADDITIONAL READING

A detailed discussion on machine learning methods used in this chapter may be obtained from:

Basili, V., Briand, L., & Melo, W. (1996). A validation of object-oriented design metrics as quality indicators. *IEEE Transactions on Software Engineering*, 22(10), 751–761. doi:10.1109/32.544352

Briand, L., Daly, W., & Wust, J. (2000). Exploring the relationships between design measures and software quality. *Journal of Systems and Software*, 51(3), 245–273. doi:10.1016/S0164-1212(99)00102-8

Briand, L., Wüst, J., & Lounis, H. (2001). Replicated Case Studies for Investigating Quality Factors in Object-Oriented Designs, Empirical Software Engineering. *International Journal (Toronto, Ont.)*, 6(1), 11–58.

Chidamber, S., & Kamerer, C. (1991) Towards a metrics suite for object oriented design. In Proceedings of the Conference on Object-Oriented Programming: Systems, Languages and Applications (OOPSLA'91). SIGPLAN Notices, 26(11): 197-211.

Chidamber, S., & Kamerer, C. (1994). A metrics suite for object-oriented design. *IEEE Transactions on Software Engineering*, 20(6), 476–493. doi:10.1109/32.295895

Gyimothy, T., Ferenc, R., & Siket, I. (2005). Empirical validation of object-oriented metrics on open source software for fault prediction. *IEEE Transactions on Software Engineering, 31*(10), 897–910. doi:10.1109/TSE.2005.112

Han, J., & Kamber, M. (2001). *Data Mining: Concepts and Techniques*. Harchort India Private Limited.

Henderson-Sellers, B. (1996). *Object-oriented metrics, measures of complexity*. Englewood Cliffs, N.J.: Prentice Hall.

Kothari, C. R. (2004). *Research Methodology. Methods and Techniques*. New Delhi: New Age International Limited.

Lake, A., & Cook, C. (1994) Use of factor analysis to develop OOP software complexity metrics. In Proceedings of the 6th Annual Oregon Workshop on Software Metrics, Silver Falls, Oregon.

Lee, Y., Liang, B., Wu, S., & Wang, F. (1995) Measuring the coupling and cohesion of an object-oriented program based on information flow. In *Proceedings of the International Conference on Software Quality*, Maribor, Slovenia.

Li, W., & Henry, S. (1993). Object-oriented metrics that predict maintainability. *Journal of Systems and Software, 23*(2), 111–122. doi:10.1016/0164-1212(93)90077-B

Lorenz, M., & Kidd, J. (1994). *Object-oriented software metrics*. Englewood Cliffs, N.J.: Prentice-Hall.

Olague, H., Etzkorn, L., Gholston, S., & Quattlebaum, S. (2007). Empirical Validation of Three Software Metrics Suites to Predict Fault-Proneness of Object-Oriented Classes Developed Using Highly Iterative or Agile Software Development Processes. *IEEE Transactions on Software Engineering, 33*(8), 402–419. doi:10.1109/TSE.2007.1015

Pai, G. (2007). Empirical analysis of Software Fault Content and Fault Proneness Using Bayesian Methods. *IEEE Transactions on Software Engineering, 33*(10), 675–686. doi:10.1109/TSE.2007.70722

Porter, A., & Selly, R. (1990). Empirically guided Software Development using Metric-Based Classification Trees. *IEEE Software, 7*(2), 46–54. doi:10.1109/52.50773

Tang, M.H, Kao,, M.H., and Chen, M.H. (1999) An Empirical Study on Object-Oriented Metrics, In *Proceedings of Metrics*, 242-249.

Watanabe, S., Kaiya, H., & Kaijiri, K. (2008). Adapting a Fault Prediction Model to Allow Inter Language Reuse. *PROMISE, 08*(May), 12–13.

Yuming, Z., & Hareton, L. (2006). Empirical analysis of Object-Oriented Design Metrics for predicting high severity faults. *IEEE Transactions on Software Engineering, 32*(10), 771–784. doi:10.1109/TSE.2006.102

# Chapter 24
# Neural Networks:
## Evolution, Topologies, Learning Algorithms and Applications

**Siddhartha Bhattacharyya**
*RCC Institute of Information Technology, India*

## ABSTRACT

*Artificial neural networks form a class of soft computing tools, which are made up of interconnected computational primitives for the analysis of numeric data. These are inspired by the functional behavior of the human nervous system comprising millions of nerve cells or neurons. Different artificial neural network architectures have been evolved over the years based on the storage, transmission, and processing characteristics of the human nervous system.*

*These networks generally operate in two different modes, viz., supervised and unsupervised modes. The supervised mode of operation requires a supervisor to train the network with a training set of data. Networks operating in unsupervised mode apply topology preservation techniques so as to learn inputs. Representative examples of networks following either of these two modes are presented with reference to their topologies, configurations, types of input-output data and functional characteristics. Recent trends in this computing paradigm are also reported with due regards to the application perspectives.*

## INTRODUCTION

A neural network is a powerful data-modeling tool that is able to capture and represent complex input-output relationships (Haykin, 1999; Kumar, 2004). The motivation for the development of neural network technology stemmed from the desire to develop an artificial system that could perform intelligent tasks similar to those performed by the human brain. These tasks include understanding, cognition, perception, control of human body parts etc. Above all, the brain being the pivotal organ of the human body is also entrusted with the synchronization of these actions to avoid functional disorders with the help of the central nervous system, which by itself is an information

DOI: 10.4018/978-1-61350-429-1.ch024

processing entity. This multifaceted functionality of the human brain is attributed to the inherent massively parallel computing structure gifted by a highly dense structure of interconnected computing units referred to as *neurons* (approximately more than 10 billion in number), which evoke appropriate responses to external world signals (Rojas, 1996). These neurons or neuronal cells, which form the human nervous system, imbibe a series of biochemical reactions for the purpose of reception, storage, processing and transmission of information incident from the real world.

The neural cell body or *soma* houses the nucleus and is connected to treelike networks of nerve fibers called *dendrites* (Rojas, 1996). A single long fiber referred to as the *axon* extends from the soma. This axon eventually branches into strands and substrands to connect other neurons through junctions referred to as *synapses*. Complex biochemical reactions enable the transmission of signals from one neuron to another via the intermediate synapses when some transmitter compounds are released from the sending end of the junction. These compounds either raise or lower the electrical potential inside the body of the connected receiving soma. When the electric potential reaches above a threshold value, the signal pulse is sent from the sending soma to the receiving soma via the axon. At this point, the receiving cell is activated or fired. Thus, it is evident that the functioning of the nervous system is mainly carried out by the neurons (Rojas, 1996).

Artificial neural networks are targeted to model the information processing capabilities of the nervous system. The initial steps in this direction were envisaged by the introduction of the simplified neuron by McCulloch and Pitts in 1943 (McCulloch 1943). An artificial neural network comprises several computing primitives interconnected together in different topologies for processing and propagation of information. In analogy with the human nervous system, these primitives are referred to as neurons or *nodes*. The synapses or junctions between these neurons are

represented by connection strengths (or *weights*), which weight or modulate the incident input signals. The nonlinear processing power of these neurons is guided by a characteristic *activation/ transfer* function. To be precise, the impinging weighted signals from the anterior neurons sum up to generate a neuronal impulse by means of a transformation in the posterior neuron. In this way incident input information gets processed and propagated from the preceding neurons to the following ones. Eventually, relevant features of the information are learnt by the individual neurons by means of an application specific learning algorithm, which entails the adjusting of the interconnection weights until the desired precision is attained (Haykin 1999; Kumar, 2004). This learning of information content by the neurons of an artificial neural network is referred to as the training of the neural network. So much so forth, this trained information is manifested in the adjusted weights in a neural network.

A plethora of literature (Egmont-Petersen, 2002; Huang, 2009) is available on the possible incarnations of the artificial neural network models, which have evolved through the ages. These models differ in their structures, topological connectivities, operational modes, learning algorithms, activation characterizations etc. Since the functioning of the nervous system inspires these models, a proper understanding of the biological mechanisms involved inside the nervous system is a prerequisite for designing artificial neural network models appropriate for a specific task.

The proposed chapter is targeted at providing an understanding of the essence of the neural networking paradigm with reference to the biological processes involved in the nervous system. The following section discusses the mechanisms of transmission, storage and cognition of information in the nervous system. A detailed analysis of the artificial neural networking paradigm is presented in the subsequent section with reference to the basic neuronal model, its mathematical formalism, constituent components, structure and topology.

The different operational modes of artificial neural networks are also discussed in this section with due regards to the learning algorithms employed. The next section introduces the basic model of an artificial neural network due to McCulloch and Pitts (McCulloch, 1943). The architecture and operational dynamics of five different artificial neural network models are illustrated in the next section. These include the multilayer perceptron (MLP) (Haykin, 1999), Hopfield network (Hopfield, 1982), Kohonen's self-organizing feature map (SOFM) (Kohonen, 1982), the radial basis function network (RBFN) (Buhmann, 2003) and the adaptive resonance theory (ART) (Carpenter, 1987a). Highlights of the recent advances clinched in the neural networking paradigm as well as the paradigm shift towards the *neuro-fuzzy*, *neuro-genetic*, *neuro-fuzzy-genetic*, *rough set* theoretic and *quantum* domains are discussed in the subsequent section. The application perspectives of the neural networking paradigm with reference to scientific, engineering and financial applications are touched upon in the penultimate section. Finally, the chapter concludes with a summary of the topics elucidated in this chapter.

## THE BIOLOGICAL NEURON: STRUCTURE AND OPERATION

As stated earlier, the neural networking paradigm is based upon the brain metaphor in that the operations of the neural networks mimic the behavior of human brain in as much as intelligent reasoning and decision-making are concerned. Hence there exists a strong analogy between the operations of the biological nervous system and the artificial neural networking paradigm. This section deals with an in-depth discussion regarding the cellular structure of biological neurons formed of selective permeable membranes, the guiding Nernst formulations (Matthews, 1991) for measurement of membrane potentials and the chemical action

potentials at neuronal synapses which facilitate the storage, processing and subsequent transmission of signals.

## Structure of Biological Neurons

The human nervous system is composed of similar neuronal cells or neurons, which otherwise vary in terms of functionalities and organizational complexities. Basically, there are two different kinds of nerves, viz., (i) motor nerves and (ii) sensory nerves. The motor nerves act as generators of signals/impulses to be propagated to the other nerves. The sensory nerves are the recipient nerves, which elicit responses to the signals received from the motor nerves. The neurons in the human cortex are organized in a hierarchical structure of six different layers differing in functionalities (Matthews, 1991; Brown, 1991). These layers carry out the tasks of processing and transmission of input signals. Figure 1a shows the structure of a biological neuron comprising the cell body or soma, dendrites, axon and synapses. Dendrites are the pathways for the incoming signals received from the neighboring cells via the synapses, which serve as the storehouse of information. There are three types of synapses in the nervous system, viz., (i) axon-to-axon synapses, (ii) axon-to-dendrite synapses and (iii) dendrite-to-dendrite synapses. The number of the axon-to-dendrite synapses is larger than the other two types of synapses with the axon-to-axon synapses being the smallest in number. Similar to the nerve cells, the axons are classified as afferent axons, which generate the outgoing signals and efferent axons, which receive the incoming signals. The *mitochondria* in the cell body supply energy to the cell elements and sustain the operation of the cell structure with the help of internal biochemical reactions. The myelin sheath membrane covers the axon protruding from the cell body. The uncovered parts of the axon are referred to as the nodes of Ranvier. Figure 1a also shows the *axon hillock* (the part of the axon

*Figure 1. The biological neuron (a) structure and components (b) information transmission via synaptic cleft*

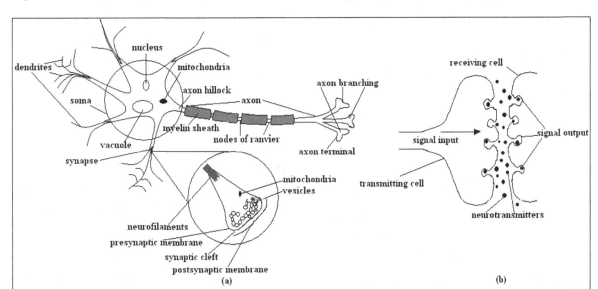

(a)

(b)

nearest to the cell body) and the branching of the axon to transmit information to the following cells. On reception of a signal, the neurons produce an output signal or response, which is transmitted to another neighboring cell through the axon.

## Transmission of Information in Biological Neurons

A cell encloses protoplasm and other cell components inside a selective permeable cell membrane composed of a double layer of molecules (Rojas, 1996). Negative and positive ions are formed in the intracellular and extra-cellular fluids in the human body out of dissociation of the dissolved salts and minerals therein. Salts like sodium chloride (NaCl) and potassium chloride (KCl) dissociate into positive ions $Na^+$, $K^+$ respectively and the negative ion $Cl^-$ is produced in the process. The degree of permeability of the cell membrane depends among various factors on the number and size of pores in the membrane as well as on the types of these ions (Rojas, 1996). By virtue of the varying degrees of permeability, the cell

membranes behave as ionic channels of varying diffusivity and act as diffusion barriers. Since the cell membranes/ionic channels are selectively permeable to the sodium, potassium or calcium ions, the specific permeability of a membrane leads to different ionic distributions in the interior and the exterior of the cells by means of diffusion of ions. The potential difference thus developed between the cell interior and exterior is referred to as the *diffusion potential*. This process of diffusion of ions occurs until a thermodynamic equilibrium is attained (Rojas, 1996). As an example, if the initial concentration of $K^+$ ions in the cell interior is greater than in its exterior, positive $K^+$ ions will diffuse out through the open potassium-selective channels in the cell. These channels would however, prevent any negative ion to diffuse out through the cell membrane, which would make the cell interior to become negatively charged with respect to the exterior. Thus, a potential difference is created between both the sides of the cell membrane. This balances the aforestated diffusion potential, thereby mitigating further diffusion of potassium ions through the cell membrane. Eventually, the net flow of the positive potassium ions from the interior to the exterior of the cell falls to zero. At this point, the biological system is said to attain a steady state (Rojas, 1996).

The potential difference *E* for a particular ion is given by the Nernst formula (Matthews, 1991; Rojas, 1996) as

$$E = \kappa\left(\ln \eta_o - \ln \eta_i\right) \tag{1}$$

where, $\eta_i$ is the ionic concentration inside the cell, $\eta_o$ is the ionic concentration in the extracellular fluid and $\kappa$ is a proportionality constant (Matthews, 1991; Rojas, 1996). The equilibrium potential has been measured to be −80 mV for $K^+$ ions (Rojas, 1996).

However, the exact potential in the interior of a cell depends on the mixture of ionic concentrations. The cell's equilibrium potential lies closer to a value measured for potassium, due to the fact that the cell membrane's permeability is greater for potassium as compared to that for sodium (Rojas, 1996). This potential value leads to a net outflow of $K^+$ ions out of the cells and a net inflow of $Na^+$ ions into the cells. A self-sustained sodium ion pump inside the cell maintains the concentrations of the potassium and sodium ions on both sides of the cell membrane, thereby ensuring a polarization potential of −70 mV. This ion pump gets the requisite operational energy from a compound viz. adenosine triphosphate (ATP) produced by the mitochondria.

Neural signal information in the form of depolarization waves/spikes are transmitted into and out of a human cell by means of the diffusion of these dissociated ions across the cell membranes. These waves are also referred to as *action potentials*. These action potentials, as the name suggests, are generated by means of the formation of a potential out of a depolarization of the cell membrane (Rojas, 1996). The starting polarization potential rises from −70 mV up to

+40 mV dipping to as low as −80 mV in the process (Rojas, 1996). After a switching time of 2.4 ms, the cell membrane returns back to the initial potential of −70 mV, which is referred to as the *resting potential* (Rojas, 1996).

These action potentials are responsible for producing small perturbations in the cell membrane thereby opening sodium-selective channels therein (Rojas, 1996). This phenomenon leads to the inflow of $Na^+$ ions into the cell. After a short interval of time, potassium-selective channels are opened enabling the outflow of $K^+$ ions out of the cell and preventing further inflow of $Na^+$ ions. This biological mechanism of opening of sodium and potassium-selective channels is propagated through the cell membrane in the form of impulses. These impulses, however, remain active as far as to perturb the next channel onwards. In this way, neural signals get transmitted across a cell modulated by these impulses (Rojas, 1996).

## Storage and Processing of Signals in Biological Neurons

A synapse houses small *vacuoles* and generates the synaptic vesicles (shown in the magnified view of the synapse in Figure 1a), which contain some chemical transmitters. A small gap referred to as the synaptic cleft/gap, lies between a cell and its attached synapse. In the event of an arrival of an electric impulse these synaptic vesicles fuse with the cell membrane. Subsequently, the chemical transmitters flow into the synaptic gap and open the ionic channels as shown in Figure 1b. This allows ions to flow from the exterior to the interior of the cell thereby altering the cell's potential (Rojas, 1996). An action potential is generated if the potential in the interior of the cell raises and the synapse is then referred to as an excitatory synapse. An inhibitory synapse results if the cell's potential reduces, which prevents the generation of any action potential.

The synapses operate as the storehouse of information in neural networks. The storage mechanism can be appreciated by studying the role of NMDA (*N*-methyl *D*-aspartate) receptors (Brown, 1991; wikiNMDA; Li, 2009) in the cell membrane. The NMDA receptors (NMDAR) are ionotropic glutamate receptors, which control synaptic plasticity and memory functions of the human brain (wikiNMDA; Li, 2009). An interesting feature of these receptors is that the activations of these receptors are voltage dependent. On activation, these receptors allow specific ionic channels, which are nonselective to $Na^+$, $Ca^{2+}$, or $K^+$ ions, to be opened (Li, 2009; Dingledine, 1999). However, when an $Mg^{2+}$ ion is received by these receptors, these channels get blocked preventing further diffusion of $Na^+$ or $Ca^{2+}$ ions. On the contrary, the NMDA receptors lose the $Mg^{2+}$ ion and switch from the blocked state to an unblocked one when the cell is excited above a threshold level. Henceforth, ions with greater permeability flow into the cell effecting a change in the threshold level of the cell (Steward, 1989; Reichert, 1990).

Thus, it can be surmised that neurons do not transmit information only by electrical perturbations but also through chemical signaling (Rojas, 1996). Signal processing is effected in the nervous system by means of an integration of the electrical transmission of action potential induced perturbations inside the cell and the chemical transmission at the synaptic gaps between cells. Neural cells process signals by integrating several incoming signals, which are able to excite attached cells to open sufficient ionic channels. If enough channels are opened above a requisite threshold, an action potential is generated at the axon hillock. This is because the number of ionic channels is larger and the cell's threshold is lower at the axon-hillock (Thompson, 1990). Interested readers may refer to (Rojas, 1996; Matthews, 1991; Brown, 1991) for details regarding the storage, transmission and processing of information in the biological nervous system.

# ARTIFICIAL NEURAL NETWORKS

Human intelligence is represented artificially by means of the artificial neural networks (ANNs) (Fausett, 1994; Haykin, 1999; Rojas, 1996), which are artificial counterparts of the biological neurons. This form of intelligence, also referred to as artificial intelligence, provides a means for representation of diverse kinds of knowledge in a knowledge base. It also forms a framework for reasoning of the underlying rules of the knowledge base and therefore induces a mechanism of learning of environmental (Hebb, 1949) data on which such an intelligent system operates. The basis of an artificial neural network would be dealt with in this section with due regards to the basic structure and components of an artificial neural network supported by a mathematical modeling and the different modes of operation.

## Components, Structure and Topology

Any computational paradigm should entail basic primitives for implementing the fundamental set of functions characteristic of the paradigm and artificial neural networks are no exceptions in this regard (Rojas, 1996). Similar to the biological paradigm, the neurons/nodes act as elementary computational primitives in the neural networking paradigm. According to Kohonen (Kohonen, 1982):

*Artificial neural networks are massively parallel adaptive networks of simple nonlinear computing elements called neurons, which are intended to abstract and model some of the functionality of the human nervous system in an attempt to partially capture some of its computational strengths.*

The corresponding flow of information in a neural network is achieved by the interconnection topology of the neurons. The distributed representation of the interconnections of the networks induces massive parallelism therein. Moreover, the generalization capabilities of the networks make them amenable to graceful degradation and failsafe. These network structures differ from one to another in the topology of the interconnection structure and the real life problems they are used for (Haykin, 1999; Kumar, 2004). Since the essence of neural network operation is based on the behavior of human brain, these networks require a form of training so as to acquire the learning ability of the human brain. Once these networks are trained with the different aspects of the problem at hand, viz. the input-output data relationships and distributions, they can be used to replicate the learnt relationships, given the immense generalization capabilities embedded therein. Thus the functionality of a neural network architecture depends on the nature of the characteristic functions performed by the primitive neurons, the interconnection topology and the methodology of transfer of information. A neural network generally comprises the following components (Haykin, 1999; Kumar, 2004)

- *Neurons:* As stated earlier, neurons are the basic computational elements of a neural network (Rojas, 1996; Kumar, 2004; Bhattacharyya, in press). Generally, there are three types of neurons in a neural network architecture, viz. input, hidden and output neurons. The input neurons accept real world data. The hidden neurons lie in the form of layers between the input and output neurons. These neurons operate on and process the data fed by the input neurons. The output neurons finally generate the network output responses based on the data processed by the hidden neurons.
- *Neuron activation state vector:* As stated earlier, the transmission of information through the different neurons of a human nervous system depends on the excitation/activation levels of the nerve cells or neurons. The same reasoning applies to

the artificial neural networking paradigm as well. A neuron activation state vector determines the activation levels of the neurons. If there are $n$ number of neurons, $x_i$, $i$=1, 2, …, $n$, the activation state vector $X \in R^n$ is represented as (Kumar, 2004; Bhattacharyya, in press).

$$X = \begin{bmatrix} x_1 \\ x_2 \\ . \\ . \\ x_n \end{bmatrix} \qquad (2)$$

- *Activation/transfer function:* This function represents the transfer characteristics of the individual neurons in a neural network in that it determines the activation behavior of the neurons to incident inputs (Kumar, 2004). The function responds to the range of incident input signals and transforms them by using a suitable learning algorithm. Though different constituent neurons may exhibit different transfer characteristics, yet most of the existing neural network architectures are field-homogeneous (Bhattacharyya, in press) with all the neurons in a layer characterized by the same activation. Commonly used activation functions include the binary threshold, sigmoid, linear threshold, or probabilistic activation functions. Figure 2 shows some of the widely used neural network activation functions and their mathematical forms.
- *Interconnection topology:* This refers to the mode of interconnections of the neurons in different layers of a neural network architecture similar to (but not so exactly complex) to the axon interconnections in biological nervous system. These interconnections act as the storage junctions/mem-

*Figure 2. Commonly used neural network activation functions (a) Binary threshold (b) Bipolar threshold (c) Linear (d) Linear threshold (e) Sigmoid (f) Hyperbolic tangent (g) Gaussian*

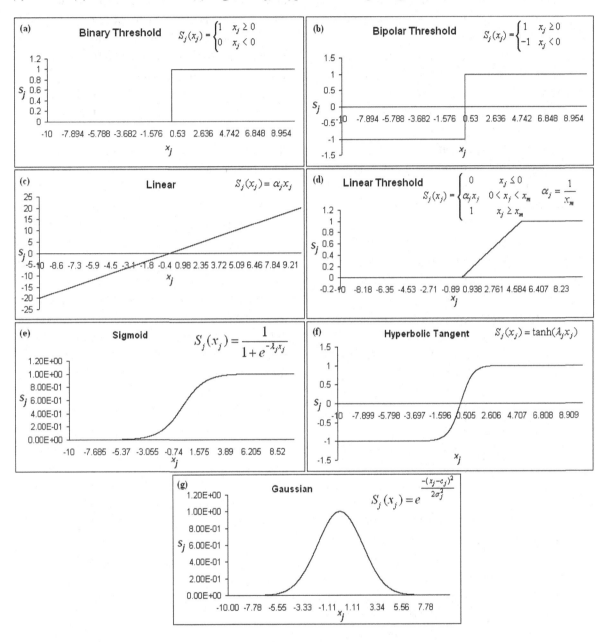

ory of the artificial neural network. Similar to the synapses of biological neurons, these interconnections are also characterized by a weight value, which ascertains their excitation/activation levels (Egmont-Petersen, 2002; Kumar, 2004; Bhattacharyya, in press).

• *Neuron firing behavior:* This component determines the processing capabilities of the neurons in a given layer given the characteristic activation functions employed therein (Kumar, 2004; Bhattacharyya, in press). The constituent neurons aggregate the incoming input signals by applying an inner product of the input vector and the neuron fan-in interconnection strength (weight) vector and impress the embedded activation function.

- *Learning algorithm:* The learning rule provides a mechanism for training a neural network with a training set of input-output pairs of data relationships (Kumar, 2004; Bhattacharyya, in press). The objective of the algorithm is to compensate the network system error by modifying the interconnection weights and to enable the network to arrive at the desired end result.

Common neural network architectures can be categorized in the following two main categories depending on the interconnection topologies.

- A *feedforward* manner where the network does not possess any loops. Representative examples include the single layer/multilayer perceptron (McCulloch, 1943; Haykin, 1999), support vector machines (SVM) (Vapnik, 1995; Vapnik, 1997; Burges, 1998), radial basis function networks (RBFN) (Buhmann, 2003) to name a few.
- A *feedback* (recurrent) manner where there exist loops due to feedback connections. Typical examples include the Hopfield network (Hopfield, 1982), brain-in-a-state-box (BSB) model (Anderson, 1977), Boltzmann machine (Ackley, 1985), bi-directional associative memories (BAM) (Kosko, 1988), adaptive resonance theory (ART) (Carpenter, 1987a), Kohonen's self-organizing feature maps (SOFM) (Kohonen, 1982) to name a few.

## Mathematical Formalism

One important aspect of understanding the structure and operations of the artificial neural

networks is to get an insight into the formalism and application perspectives of these networks. This section is devoted to providing a simple mathematical formalism of the neural networking paradigm so that both the structural and operational characteristics clearly stand out.

The constituent neurons in an artificial neural network are entrusted with the dual functions of accepting real world numeric inputs and processing them to yield a desired output depending on either an *a priori* knowledge base or some prototypic information regarding the system at hand. Put in simple terms, a neuron receives inputs from its preceding activated neuron/neurons, sums them up and applies a characteristic activation to generate an impulse. The summing mechanism is controlled by the interconnection weights between the receiving neuron and its preceding ones in as much they decide the activation state of the preceding neurons. The operational dynamics of any neural network architecture can thus be represented by the following mathematical formalism.

Let the $n$ inputs $\{q_1, q_2, q_3, ..., q_n\}$ arriving at a receiving neuron from $n$ preceding neurons, lie in a vector space $Q^n$. If the interconnection weight matrix from $m$ such receiving neurons to their $n$ preceding neurons is represented by $W_{m \times n} = \{w_{ij}, i=1, 2, 3, ..., n; j=1, 2, 3, ..., m\}$, then the summing mechanism in a neuron simplifies to a matrix-vector multiplication only, i.e.,

$$O = \begin{bmatrix} w_{11} & w_{12} & w_{13} & \cdot & \cdot & w_{1n} \\ w_{21} & w_{22} & w_{23} & \cdot & \cdot & w_{2n} \\ w_{31} & w_{32} & w_{33} & \cdot & \cdot & w_{3n} \\ \cdot & \cdot & \cdot & \cdot & \cdot & \cdot \\ \cdot & \cdot & \cdot & \cdot & \cdot & \cdot \\ w_{m1} & w_{m2} & w_{m3} & \cdot & \cdot & w_{mn} \end{bmatrix} \times \begin{bmatrix} q_1 \\ q_2 \\ q_3 \\ \cdot \\ \cdot \\ q_n \end{bmatrix}$$

(3)

which is simply a vector given by

$$O = \begin{bmatrix} o_1 \\ o_2 \\ o_3 \\ . \\ . \\ . \\ o_m \end{bmatrix} \quad (4)$$

Thus, each $j^{th}$, $j$=1, 2, 3, ..., $m$, neuron is fed with an element of the vector $[o_1 o_2 o_3 \cdot \cdot o_m]^T$ resulting out of the summing mechanism. As a part of the processing task, each such $j^{th}$, $j$=1, 2, 3, ..., $m$, neuron then applies the corresponding activation/transfer function ($f$) to the elements of this vector to yield the corresponding output response $Y_j$, $j$=1, 2, 3, ..., $m$, as

$$Y_j = f\left(\begin{bmatrix} o_1 & o_2 & o_3 & \cdot & \cdot & o_m \end{bmatrix}^T\right) \quad (5)$$

Thus, given a set of inputs in $Q^n$, the interconnection weight matrix $W_{m \times n} = \{w_{ij}, i$=1, 2, 3, ..., $n$; $j$=1, 2, 3, ..., $m\}$ along with the characteristic activation function $f$ decide the output responses of the neurons. Any variations in $W_{m \times n} = \{w_{ij}, i$=1, 2, 3, ..., $n$; $j$=1, 2, 3, ..., $m\}$ would yield different responses subject to the same characteristic neuronal activation $f$. Looking from the biological perspective, the interconnection weight matrix $W_{m \times n} = \{w_{ij}, i$=1, 2, 3, ..., $n$; $j$=1, 2, 3, ..., $m\}$ thus serves similar to the synaptic weights of a biological neuron and house the memory of an artificial neural network. Furthermore, for achieving a stable memory, which can be effective in recalling/recognizing test inputs, the interconnection weight matrix must be adapted in tune with the neuronal activation state vectors through a proper learning algorithm. Once the matrix achieves a stable configuration, a neural network is able to successfully recognize test inputs in the testing phase of the network learning procedure. The output responses $Y_j'$, $j$=1, 2, 3, ..., $m$, thus

obtained corresponding to the test patterns, can also be represented in matrix-vector product formalism as

$$Y_j' = f\left(\begin{bmatrix} w'_{11} & w'_{12} & w'_{13} & \cdot & \cdot & w'_{1n} \\ w'_{21} & w'_{22} & w'_{23} & \cdot & \cdot & w'_{2n} \\ w'_{31} & w'_{32} & w'_{33} & \cdot & \cdot & w'_{3n} \\ . & . & . & . & . & . \\ . & . & . & . & . & . \\ w'_{m1} & w'_{m2} & w'_{m3} & \cdot & \cdot & w'_{mn} \end{bmatrix} \times \begin{bmatrix} t_1 \\ t_2 \\ t_3 \\ . \\ . \\ t_n \end{bmatrix}\right) \quad (6)$$

where, $T = \{t_1, t_2, t_3, ..., t_n\}^T$ is the test input vector and $W'_{m \times n} = \{w'_{ij}, i$=1, 2, 3, ..., $n$; $j$=1, 2, 3, ..., $m\}$ is the stabilized interconnection weight matrix.

## Operational Modes

The dynamics and operation of a neural network architecture depends among other factors on the nature of the learning mechanism employed (Haykin, 1999; Kumar, 2004; Bhattacharyya, in press). The operational modes of neural network architectures can be classified into two main categories viz., *supervised* mode and *unsupervised* mode.

- *Supervised mode of operation*: As the name suggests, the supervised mode of operation of a neural network architecture implies the use of some *a priori* knowledge base to guide the learning phase. This knowledge base puts forward to the neural network a training set of input-output patterns and an input-output relationship. The neural network is then supervised to embed an approximation function in its operational behavior, which replicates the relationship of the input-output training data vector presented to the network (Haykin, 1999). If an input vector $X_k \in R^n$ is related to an output vector $D_k \in R^p$ by means of a relationship $D_k = T\{X_k,\}$, the basic philosophy behind the supervised learning algorithm is to yield a mapping of the form $f: R^n \Rightarrow R^p$, in consonance with $T$ such that the input-output data relationship is aptly replicated in the process (Kumar, 2004; Bhattacharyya, in press). To achieve this, the supervised algorithm aims to reduce the error ($E=D_k-S_k$), where $S_k$ is the output response generated by $X_k$. This error reduction mechanism is effected by a technique referred to as the *gradient descent* method (Kumar, 2004; Bhattacharyya, in press; Snyman, 2005). Obviously, when the error $E$ gets reduced to an acceptable limit, if the network is fed with an input similar to $X_k$, it would generate a response similar to $D_k$ (Kumar, 2004; Bhattacharyya, in press). A network behaving in this fashion is said to be operating in a supervised mode.

- *Unsupervised mode of operation*: There are different schools of thoughts regarding this mode of operation of neural networks. According to one theory, this is an adaptive learning paradigm, which presents the neural network with an input $X_k$ and allows it to self-organize the topological configuration depending on the distribution of input data by means of generation of exemplars/prototypes of input vectors presented. Thus, the algorithm stores the exemplars/prototypes of the input data set into different number of predefined categories/classes (Haykin, 1999; Kumar, 2004; Bhattacharyya, in press). When an unknown input data is presented to the network, it matches it to the stored prototypes and associates it to one of the stored categories. However, if the input data belongs to a completely new category/class, the storage states of the network are updated to incorporate the new class encountered. Another school of thought however, differs on the definition of the term "unsuper-

vised" in the sense that suitable classical and soft computing approaches are employed to determine the number of classes to be assigned the network rather than using a predefined number of classes.

Apart from these two modes of operation, neural network architectures also employ the reinforcement learning mode (Kaelbling, 1996), semi-supervised mode (Chapelle, 2006) and transduction mode (Vapnik, 1998) of operation.

## The Basic Neuron

As stated earlier, a neuron in a neural network architecture receives inputs from some other neurons, or the external world via coupling of synaptic weights. The neuron adds up its inputs and produces an output after comparing the sum to a threshold value (Bhattacharyya, in press). Based upon this basic functionality, Frank Rosenblatt (Bhattacharyya, in press, Rosenblatt, 1958) proposed the *single layer perceptron* model with the following features:

- The output of the neuron depends on its inputs and the synaptic weights which couple the inputs to the network neurons. This output would remain either on (activated or fired) or off (deactivated) depending on the activation level, which again depends on the strengths of the impinging inputs and weights (Bhattacharyya, in press, Rosenblatt, 1958).
- A certain number of inputs to a particular neuron must be high at any point of time in order to make that neuron fire. The coupling efficiency of the synapses is aptly represented by a multiplicative factor on each of the inputs to the neuron. This multiplicative factor often referred to as the interconnection weight $w$, can be modified so as to model synaptic learning (Bhattacharyya, in press, Rosenblatt,

1958). A more efficient synapse having a larger weight transmits more of the signal, while a weak synapse has a smaller weight. The output of a neuron, in turn, serves as an input to other units. This process of propagation of incident information to the network continues hierarchically through the different interconnected neurons of the network structure.

McCulloch and Pitts (McCulloch, 1943) devised the first model of the basic neuron as shown in Figure 3. It comprises an input layer and an output layer. Processed information propagates from the input layer to the output layer via the unidirectional interconnections between the input and output layer neurons. Each of these interconnections possesses a weight $w$, which indicates its strength. However, there is no interconnection from the output layer back to the input layer the other way round as is evident from the figure.

If $m$ such input layer neurons are connected to $n$ output layer neurons, then the input-output layer interconnections are represented by

$$W_{m \times n} = \begin{bmatrix} w_{11} & w_{12} & w_{13} & \cdot & \cdot & w_{1n} \\ w_{21} & w_{22} & w_{23} & \cdot & \cdot & w_{2n} \\ w_{31} & w_{32} & w_{33} & \cdot & \cdot & w_{3n} \\ \cdot & \cdot & \cdot & \cdot & \cdot & \cdot \\ \cdot & \cdot & \cdot & \cdot & \cdot & \cdot \\ w_{m1} & w_{m2} & w_{m3} & \cdot & \cdot & w_{mn} \end{bmatrix} \quad (7)$$

Apart from the $m$ input layer neurons, an additional input of 1 (encircled) is also shown in Figure 3. This is referred to as the bias input to the neural network. The corresponding interconnection weight is $-k$, the bias/offset to the network. Hence, there are actually $m+1$ input lines, i.e., $j=1$, 2, 3, …, $m+1$. Though this bias input is generally not shown in neural network diagrams, it has been shown in Figure 3 for the sake of self-sufficiency.

*Figure 3. McCulloch and Pitts model of a basic neuron*

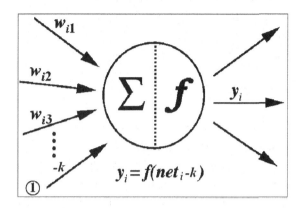

$$y_i = f(net_i - k)$$

The $i^{th}$ output neuron first computes the weighted sum of the $m$ number of inputs (excluding the bias/offset) arriving from $m$ interconnected input layer neurons as (Bhattacharyya, in press; McCulloch, 1943).

$$y_i = \sum_{j=1}^{n} w_{ji} y_j = net_i \quad (8)$$

where $w_{ji}$ refers to the interconnection weight from $j^{th}$ input layer neuron to the $i^{th}$ output layer neuron. Taking the bias term $-k$ into consideration the output becomes (Bhattacharyya, in press; McCulloch, 1943).

$$y_i = \sum_{j=1}^{n} w_{ji} y_j - k = net_i - k \quad (9)$$

Subsequently, the neuron applies its activation function $f$, which performs a thresholding operation on the computed sum in equation 9. The output $y_i$ of the $i^{th}$ neuron can then be written as (Bhattacharyya, in press; McCulloch, 1943)

$$y_i = f(\sum_{j=1}^{n} w_{ji} y_j - k) = f(net_i - k) \quad (10)$$

The thresholding process ensures that if the sum is greater than a threshold value defined by the function (*f*), then the neuron produces 1 else it produces 0. This output value signifies the status of the neuron, i.e. whether it is fired or not.

## Learning Algorithm of the Network

The single layer perceptron operates in a supervised mode. Hence, it requires learning/training by means of some *a priori* knowledge base for its operation. This learning mechanism for the single layer perceptron comprises the following phases (Bhattacharyya, in press; McCulloch, 1943).

- *Input phase*: In this phase, the training set inputs are presented to the input layer of the network. The input-to-output layer interconnection weights are set to small random values. The activation threshold for the transfer function employed in the output layer neuron is also set randomly.
- *Input propagation phase*: The inputs to the input layer neurons are multiplied by the corresponding interconnection weights and the resultant products are summed up to obtain the input to the lone neuron in the output layer of the network.
- *Output generation phase*: The characteristic activation function (*f*) is applied by the output layer neuron to the input information to obtain its output response (*y*).
- *Error estimation phase*: In this phase, the output response (*y*) obtained in the previous phase is compared to the desired output (*d*) to estimate the network error (*E*).
- *Weight adjustment phase*: The computed error (*E*) is used to iteratively adjust the initially set random input-to-output layer interconnection weights so as to reduce the gradient of the error with time, i.e. to minimize the computed error. This process is referred to as *gradient descent* (Haykin, 1999; Snyman, 2005), whereby the net-

work is forced to take correct decisions and abandon incorrect decisions.

Since $E$ is obtained by the assimilation of all the individual error terms at the output layer neurons through the interconnection weights $w_{ji}$, $j=1, 2, 3, ..., m$; $i=1, 2, 3, ..., n$, the gradient $\nabla E$ of the error term is given by

$$\nabla E = \frac{\partial E}{\partial w_{ji}} \qquad (11)$$

The weight adjustment term is then given by (Haykin, 1999; Snyman, 2005; Kumar, 2004; Rojas, 1996)

$$\Delta w_{ji} = -\mu \frac{\partial E}{\partial w_{ji}} \qquad (12)$$

where, $\mu$ is the learning rate. $\mu$ defines the step length of weight adjustment in the gradient descent algorithm. This learning algorithm is repeated with the adjusted interconnection weights and training set inputs until the network converges, i.e. the network error falls down under a tolerable limit specified by the supervisor.

## Computation of the Error Gradient

As stated earlier, the error minimization procedure during the training of a neural network involves the computation of the gradient of the error function with time (Haykin, 1999; Snyman, 2005). In fact, the gradient $G_E$ of the network error $E$ is computed with respect to each interconnection weight $w_{ji}$ so as to decipher the contribution of the initially set random interconnection weights towards the overall $E$. The network error is represented as

$$E = \frac{1}{2} \sum_{j=1}^{N} (y_j - d_j)^2 \qquad (13)$$

where, $N$ is the number of neurons in the output layer of the network. The square of the error term is taken since it will always be positive. Moreover, it will be greater if the difference $(y - d)$ is large and lesser if it is small.

For the $i^{th}$ output layer neuron, the error becomes (Haykin, 1999; Bhattacharyya, in press; Snyman, 2005).

$$E_i = \frac{1}{2}(y_i - d_i)^2 \tag{14}$$

Now, the gradient $G_{E_i}$ is given by

$$G_{E_i} = \frac{\partial E_i}{\partial w_{ji}} \tag{15}$$

Using chain rule, one gets

$$\frac{\partial E_i}{\partial w_{ji}} = \frac{\partial E_i}{\partial y_i}\frac{\partial y_i}{\partial w_{ji}} \tag{16}$$

Since $E_i = \frac{1}{2}(y_i - d_i)^2$ (from equation 14), the first term of equation 16 is given by

$$\frac{\partial E_i}{\partial y_i} = (y_i - d_i) \tag{17}$$

Using $y_i = \sum_j w_{ji}y_j$, the second term of equation 16 becomes

$$\frac{\partial y_i}{\partial w_{ji}} = \frac{\partial}{\partial w_{ji}}\sum_j w_{ji}y_j = y_i \tag{18}$$

Hence, equation 16 becomes

$$\frac{\partial E_i}{\partial w_{ji}} = (y_i - d_i)y_i \tag{19}$$

Therefore, using equation 12, the interconnection weight $w_{ji}$ between the $j^{th}$ input layer neuron and the $i^{th}$ output layer neuron is adjusted as (Haykin, 1999; Bhattacharyya, in press; Snyman, 2005).

$$\begin{aligned} w_{ji} &= w_{ji} - \Delta w_{ji} = w_{ji} - (-\mu\frac{\partial E_i}{\partial w_{ji}}) \\ &= w_{ji} + \mu(y_i - d_i)y_i \end{aligned} \tag{20}$$

It may be noted that if $\mu$ is too small, the algorithm takes a longer time to converge, while for a larger value of $\mu$, the algorithm diverges.

The single layer perceptron is efficient in classifying linearly separable data sets (Haykin, 1999; Kumar, 2004). However, it suffers from several limitations. It is not a good approximator. Moreover, it fails to classify in situations where the divisions between the classes are nonlinear and complex.

## ARTIFICIAL NEURAL NETWORK ARCHITECTURES

Researchers and scientists have proposed several neural network architectures (Rojas, 1996; Egmont-Peterson, 2002; Kumar, 2004) differing in topology and operational characteristics so as to capture the essence of neural computation. These architectures have been evolved keeping in mind the operational behavior of the human brain. This section would introduce some of the important artificial neural network models, which are efficient in classification and recognition problems. The architectures discussed here fall into either of the two categories of network models, viz. supervised and unsupervised depending on the learning methodology adopted.

*Figure 4. A three-layer neural network architecture*

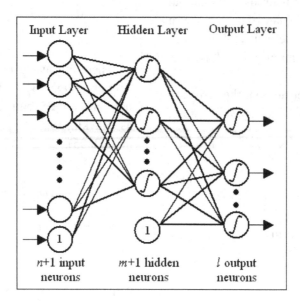

## Multilayer Perceptron

As mentioned before, a single layer perceptron can only classify/discriminate linearly separable data (Haykin, 1999; Kumar, 2004). This limitation can be attributed to its solo output layer, which cannot incorporate nonlinearity prevalent in real life data. This limitation can be addressed by introducing additional layers (also referred to as hidden layers) between the input and output layers of the perceptron so as to incorporate some information regarding nonlinearly separable inputs. These multilayer neural network architectures therefore comprise several hidden layers between the input and output layers. The most commonly used multilayer perceptron architecture (Haykin, 1999) comprises three layers of nodes, viz., input, hidden and output layers. Such a three-layer architecture is shown in Figure 4 comprising $n+1$ ($n$ real world data input layer neurons and one bias input neuron of 1 [encircled in the figure]) input neurons, $m+1$ ($m$ hidden layer neurons for accepting inputs from $n+1$ input layer neurons and one bias input neuron of 1 [encircled in the figure]) hidden neurons and $l$ output neurons. All the $n+1$ input layer neurons are connected to $m$ hidden layer neurons (excluding the hidden neuron for providing the bias input) by means of input-to-hidden layer interconnections $w_{ij}$, $i=1, 2, 3, ..., n+1; j=1, 2, 3, ..., m$. Similarly, all the $m+1$ hidden layer neurons are connected to $l$ output layer neurons by means of hidden-to-output layer interconnections $w_{jk}, j=1, 2, 3, ..., m+1; k=1, 2, 3, ..., l$. It may be noted that since the $(n+1)^{th}$ input layer neuron and the $(m+1)^{th}$ hidden layer neuron serve as biases/offsets for the respective layers, the respective interconnection weights $w_{n+1j}, j=1, 2, 3, ..., m$ and $w_{m+1k}, k=1, 2, 3, ..., l$, are both equal to a threshold value of $-\theta$.

It is evident from the architecture of Figure 4 that all the hidden layer neurons excepting the $(m+1)^{th}$ neuron and all the output layer neurons exhibit nonlinear transfer characteristics shown by the nonlinear functions inside each neuron. Moreover, since the hidden layer neurons contribute to the inputs for the output layer neurons, it is not possible to know the target values for the hidden layers. Hence, the gradient descent algorithm (Snyman, 2005), which depends on the estimation of errors at the output layer neurons only, is not sufficient to train these types of networks with hidden layers. This is because of the fact that only a computation of the partial derivative of the error function at the output layer (as carried out in the gradient descent algorithm) with respect to each weight does not enable one to derive the errors at the hidden layers. Moreover, one cannot anticipate the direction of change of the network error in the gradient descent method as well. But, it is required to estimate the errors and their derivatives at each network layer. On the contrary, if the negatives of these derivatives are computed and added to the weights, then the overall system error would decrease until it reaches a local minimum. This method would also ascertain as to whether the errors are increasing when the weights are increasing, since then it would yield positive values for the derivatives. In case of a multilayer architecture with multiple hidden layers, this process of computing the partial derivatives and applying them to each of the weights can be initiated with the hidden-output layer weights and then proceeding to the preceding hidden layers to carry out the computation for the remaining hidden-hidden layer weights (for more than one hidden layers) and finally ending up with the input-hidden layer weights. This also implies that a change in a particular layer-to-layer set of weights requires that the partial derivatives in the preceding layer are also known at place. This algorithm of adjusting the weights of the different network layers (Rumelhart, 1986; Chauvin, 1995) starting from the output layer and proceeding downstream is referred to as the backpropagation algorithm (Rumelhart, 1986; Haykin, 1999; Rojas, 1996). It is readily used for overcoming the shortcomings of the gradient descent algorithm in dealing with the error compensation and weight adjustment procedure in higher layered neural network architectures.

## Backpropagation Algorithm

In the backpropagation algorithm (Rumelhart, 1986; Haykin, 1999; Rojas, 1996), the outputs are computed in a multilayer neural network architecture after the inputs are presented to it. Subsequently, the network system error is calculated using supervised learning by comparing the obtained outputs with the expected ones. This training of the network with the expected outputs starts with random weights assigned to the network layer interconnections. The backpropagation algorithm aims to adjust the interconnection weights until the system error is minimized.

A good treatise on the backpropagation algorithm is provided in (Rojas, 1996). In the treatment, Rojas elucidated the computation of weight adjustments for a multilayer feedforward neural network architecture comprising any number of hidden layers with the neurons activated with sigmoidal activation functions by presenting an in-depth analysis of the functional primitives at each constituent neuron of the network. A summary of the concepts presented by Rojas in (Rojas, 1996) is presented below with reference to an example three-layer neural network architecture for a better understanding and analysis of the algorithm.

As stated earlier, each neuron, considered as an intelligent computational primitive (Rojas, 1996), essentially carries out the dual tasks of summation of incoming inputs and the application of the transfer function, thereby producing the output. Moreover, each neuron also computes two other quantities considered essential for the operation of the network, viz., (i) an error term due to the difference between the expected and obtained outputs and (ii) the derivative of the error term. The error term and its derivative are required for the computation of the overall network system error and the adjustment of the interconnection weights between the different network layers by the backpropagation algorithm.

Figure 5 shows the computational, storage and propagation characteristics of the individual neurons of the example three-layer neural network architecture, redrawn with the concepts presented in (Rojas, 1996).

Figure 5a illustrates the forward propagation of inputs from the input layer to the output layer

*Figure 5. Computational, storage and propagation characteristics of a three-layer neural network architecture*

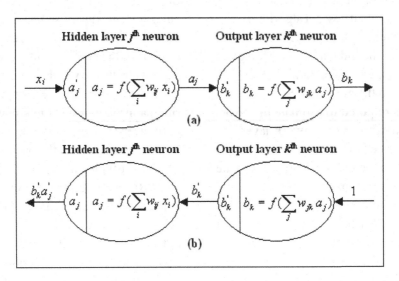

of the network via its hidden layer neurons. Only a single hidden layer and a single output layer neuron are shown for the sake of simplicity. The $j^{th}$ hidden layer neuron receives inputs $x_i$, $i=1, 2, 3, ..., n$ from the input layer neurons connected to it through the input-to-hidden layer interconnection weights $w_{ij}$, $i=1, 2, 3, ..., n; j=1, 2, 3, ..., m$. It also receives another constant input of 1 via an interconnection weight of $-\theta$ (the bias/offset) as shown in Figure 4. The $j^{th}$ hidden layer neuron computes the sum of the weighted inputs and applies the characteristic activation function $f$ to yield the output $a_j$. In addition, the $j^{th}$ hidden layer neuron computes the derivative of the obtained output $a_j$, i.e. $a_j'$ (Rojas, 1996). Finally, the neuron stores both $a_j$ and $a_j'$ (Rojas, 1996). $a_j$ is propagated to the following output layer neurons by means of the hidden-to-output interconnection weights $w_{jk}$, $j=1, 2, 3, ..., m$, $k=1, 2, 3, ..., l$ in the feedforward step along with an additional constant bias input of 1 with an interconnection weight of $-\theta$ (the bias/offset) as shown in Figure 4. Similarly, the $k^{th}$ output layer neuron computes the weighted summation of $a_j$, $j=1, 2, 3, ..., m$ and the bias/offset and applies the same activation

function $f$ (considering the architecture to be field homogeneous) to yield the output $b_k$ (Rojas, 1996). Subsequently, the $k^{th}$ output layer neuron computes $b_k'$ from $b_k$ and stores both $b_k$ and $b_k'$ (Rojas, 1996). Each such $b_k$, $k=1, 2, 3, ..., l$ forms the outputs at the output layer neurons of the three-layer neural network architecture.

As stated earlier, the essence of the back-propagation algorithm lies in the adjustments of interconnection weights in the backward direction starting from the output layer backwards until the input layer is reached. This is similar to propagating information in the backward direction through the neural network architecture.

Rojas (Rojas, 1996) also illustrated the transfer characteristics of the computational primitives when information is fed into the neurons in the backward direction as well. Figure 5b shows the mechanism of transfer of information from the output layer backward to the input layer of the network. Taking 1 (the neuron status when it is fired or activated) as the backward input to the $k^{th}$ output layer neuron, the backward direction output of this output layer neuron is simply the product of this backward input of 1 and the previously stored derivative of $b_k$, i.e. $1 \times b_k' = b_k'$ (Rojas, 1996). Similarly, the backward direction output of the $j^{th}$ hidden layer neuron is its backward input $b_k'$ multiplied by the stored derivative term $a_j'$, i.e. $b_k' \times a_j'$ (Rojas, 1996). With these computational and propagation characteristics of the individual neurons of the example three-layer architecture in the background, the network system error $E$ can be evaluated and corresponding weight adjustments can be carried out using the backpropagation algorithm.

In general, the output $b_k$ of a particular $k^{th}$ output layer neuron due to the forward inputs $a_j$, $j$=1, 2, 3, …, $m$ and the bias/offset from the $m$+1 interconnected neurons of the preceding hidden layer depends on $a_j$, $w_{jk}$ and the impressed activation function $f$. With a sigmoidal activation function, the output produced by each such neuron is given by

$$b_k = \frac{1}{1 + e^{-\lambda(\sum\limits_{j=1}^{m} a_j w_{jk} - \theta)}} \qquad (21)$$

where, $\lambda$ controls the slope of the function. The obvious advantages offered by the use of a sigmoidal activation function are its continuity, asymptotic behavior and differentiability. Moreover, the sigmoidal activation function generates a response closer to 1 for larger positive numbers, a response of 0.5 at zero, and a response closer to zero for larger negative numbers. This feature sharply demarcates the lower and higher states of a neuron. Hence, the derivative of this output is given by

$$b_k' = \frac{db_k}{da_j} = \frac{d\left[\dfrac{1}{1 + e^{-\lambda(\sum\limits_{i=1}^{m} a_j w_{jk} - \theta)}}\right]}{da_j} = b_k(1 - b_k) \qquad (22)$$

The error function $E_k$ at the $k^{th}$ output layer neuron with an expected output $d_k$ for a particular pattern presented to the network is then given by equation 14 as

$$E_k = \frac{1}{2}[b_k - d_k]^2 \qquad (23)$$

The error of the network will simply be the sum of the errors of all the neurons in the output layer taken over all the $p$ patterns presented to the network. It is thus given by

$$E = \frac{1}{2}\sum_p \sum_{k=1}^{l} E_k^p = \frac{1}{2}\sum_p \sum_{k=1}^{l} (b_k - d_k)^2 \qquad (24)$$

Once the network system error is calculated, the adjustment of the interconnection weight $w_{jk}$ between the $k^{th}$ neuron of the output layer and the $j^{th}$ connected neuron of the preceding hidden layer can be obtained through the gradient descent algorithm using equation 12. Subsequently the backpropagation algorithm can be used to determine the errors at the hidden layer neurons and adjust the intermediate layer interconnection weights.

The computational, storage and backpropagation characteristics of the individual neurons of the architecture of Figure 5 are redrawn in Figure 6 with regards to the network system error and all other information stored therein. The storage characteristics of the neurons have been generalized to incorporate the error and its derivative components as well. Moreover, Figure 6 also extends the simple architecture of Figure 5 by showing more than one output layer neuron along with their interconnection weights with the $j^{th}$ hidden layer neuron.

From Figure 6 it is seen that the $k^{th}$ output layer neuron (shown by dotted lines) can be regarded as a collection of two connected computational/storage parts, with one part housing the output $b_k$ and its derivative $b_k' = b_k(1 - b_k)$ while

*Figure 6. Computational, storage and backpropagation characteristics of a three-layer neural network architecture with error components (the arrowheads are for representative purposes only)*

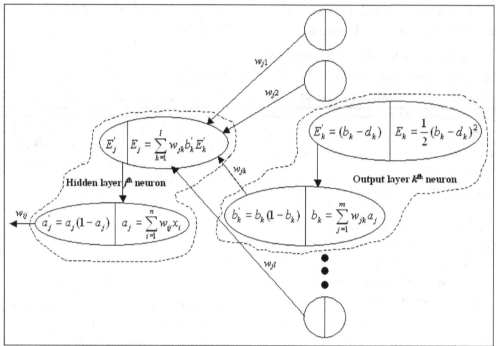

the other part houses the error term $E_k$, its derivative $E_k^{'} = (b_k - d_k)$. Similar reasoning applies for all other output and hidden layer neurons. Following the propagation characteristics of the neurons as depicted in Figure 5, $E_k^{'}$ from one part of the $k^{th}$ output layer neuron is propagated to its other part containing $b_k$ and $b_k^{'}$ (Rojas, 1996). Hence this $k^{th}$ output layer neuron computes the product of $E_k^{'}$ and $b_k^{'}$, i.e.,

$$\delta_k = E_k^{'} \times b_k^{'} = b_k(1 - b_k)(b_k - d_k),$$

which represents the $k^{th}$ component of the error to be backpropagated to the connected hidden layer neurons. This backpropagated error term arises from the summed up product of two components (i) the forward direction propagated outputs $a_j$, $j$=1, 2, 3, ..., $m$ and the bias/offset of connected hidden layer neurons and (ii) the hidden-to-output layer interconnection weights $w_{jk}$. Hence, the back-

propagated error $(\delta_k)$ is given by the gradient of $E$ with respect to both $a_j$ and $w_{jk}$, i.e. (Rojas, 1996)

$$\delta_k = \frac{\partial E}{\partial a_j w_{jk}} \qquad (25)$$

Since, $a_j$ is a processed training set input, it may be treated as a constant for all practical purposes. Hence,

$$\frac{\partial E}{\partial w_{jk}} = a_j \frac{\partial E}{\partial a_j w_{jk}} = a_j \delta_k \\ = a_j b_k (1 - b_k)(b_k - d_k) \qquad (26)$$

What remains now is to compute the back-propagated error terms at the hidden layer neurons. From Figure 6, it is seen that the $j^{th}$ hidden layer neuron is connected to $l$ output layer neurons by means of interconnection weights $w_{jk}$, $k$=1, 2, 3,

..., *l*. According to the propagation characteristics of the neurons, the backpropagation error $\delta_j$ at the $j^{\text{th}}$ hidden layer neuron is thus composed of a product of the collection of *l* number of error terms $\delta_k$, *k*=1, 2, 3, ..., *l* backpropagated from *l* output layer neurons multiplied by the corresponding hidden-to-output layer interconnections and the derivative of its forward direction output $a_j' = a_j(1 - a_j)$ (from equation 22). It is given by (Rojas, 1996)

$$
\begin{aligned}
\delta_j &= a_j(1 - a_j)\sum_{k=1}^{l} w_{jk}\delta_k \\
&= a_j(1 - a_j)\sum_{k=1}^{l} w_{jk}b_k(1 - b_k)(b_k - d_k)
\end{aligned}
\tag{27}
$$

Therefore the gradient of *E* with respect to the input-to-hidden layer interconnection weights $w_{ij}$ is given by (Rojas, 1996)

$$
\begin{aligned}
\frac{\partial E}{\partial w_{ij}} &= x_i\delta_j \\
&= x_i a_j(1 - a_j)\sum_{k=1}^{l} w_{jk}b_k(1 - b_k)(b_k - d_k)
\end{aligned}
\tag{28}
$$

where, $x_i$ is the input propagated from the $i^{\text{th}}$ input layer neuron to the $j^{\text{th}}$ hidden layer neuron.

These gradients of *E* are finally used to adjust the hidden-to-output layer interconnection weights $w_{jk}$ and the input-to-hidden interconnection weights $w_{ij}$ using equation 20. The respective weight adjustment expressions are given by (Rojas, 1996)

$$
\begin{aligned}
w_{jk} &= w_{jk} + \mu a_{jk}b_k(1 - b_k)(b_k - d_k); \\
j &= 1,2,3,...,m + 1; k = 1,2,3,...,l
\end{aligned}
\tag{29}
$$

and

$$
\begin{aligned}
w_{ij} &= w_{ij} + \mu x_i a_j(1 - a_j)\sum_{k=1}^{l} w_{jk}b_k(1 - b_k)(b_k - d_k), \\
i &= 1,2,3,...,n + 1; j = 1,2,3,...,m
\end{aligned}
\tag{30}
$$

These updated weights are used to compute the outputs of the network in the next epoch with fresh sets of input-output pairs and the network system error is again determined. The computed errors in the next epoch are similarly used to adjust the hidden-to-output and input-to-hidden layer interconnection weights using the backpropagation algorithm (Rumelhart, 1986; Haykin, 1999; Rojas, 1996). This procedure is continued until the network converges or the system error gets reduced to below some tolerable limits set by the supervisor. At this point, the network can be used for recognition/classification tasks on incomplete, corrupted or unknown inputs.

For another additional hidden layer, the same calculation would proceed to yield the error for the corresponding layer. However, it may be noted that the backpropagation algorithm is a time-complex procedure since the time for training a network grows exponentially for each additional layer.

Of late, several refinement strategies to the backpropagation algorithm have been proposed, to achieve a faster learning rate. Suitable choices of the initial weight selection mechanism, maximization of derivatives and the backpropagated errors at the neurons and avoidance of the computation of the nonlinear activation functions at the different network layers by use of look-up tables are few of the refinements, which can speed up the convergence of the backpropagation algorithm. Another significant approach in this direction is the data preconditioning technique by Silva and Almeida (Almeida, 1991). The proposed adaptive data decorrelation method (Almeida, 1991) brings about an acceleration of the convergence speed of the backpropagation algorithm. A variant backpropagation algorithm through time has been proposed for time lag recurrent networks (TLRN) (Mandic, 2001), which has lesser time complexity. Silva and Almeida (Silva, 1990) also proposed an adaptive step algorithm, which runs with different learning rates for each weight in a network thereby bringing about an exponential increase in the convergence rate. The delta-bar-delta algorithm (Jacobs, 1988) is another adaptive step algorithm to speed up the backpropagation algorithm. In (Gerke, 1997), Gerke and Hoyer applied fuzzy set (Zadeh, 1965) theoretic concepts to accelerate the speed of convergence of the backpropagation algorithm. Since the backpropagation algorithm often gets stuck to a local minimum, efforts (Wang, 2004; Bi, 2005) have been made to address this problem as well. Other contributions in this direction include the gradient descent with momentum and variable learning rate (GDMV) (Hagan, 1996), resilient backpropagation (RPROP) (Riedmiller, 1993) by Riedmiller and Braun, the conjugate gradient (CG) algorithm (Charalambous, 1992), Levenberg–Marquadrt (LM) method (Hagan, 1994), the adaptive momentum algorithm (Yu, 1993) and the dynamic adaption algorithm (Salomon, 1992), which relies on a global learning rate. Higher order algorithms have also been devised to reach a faster convergence. These include the QuickProp (Pfister, 1993; Pfister, 1995), QRPROP (a hybrid of RPROP and QuickProp), and second order backpropagation (Leonard, 1990) to name a few.

## Associative Memory and Hopfield Network

Associative memory (Kosko, 1988; Rojas, 1996) forms a class of systems intended to associate a known set of input vectors with a given set of output vectors. In addition, the concept of association also implies that the neighborhood of an input vector should also be mapped to the image to which it has been mapped. The selection of the mapping neighborhood depends on the distance of the neighbors from the input vector under consideration. Thus, even noisy input vectors can be associated with noise-free output vectors

if a proper neighborhood selection mechanism is employed (Kosko, 1988). Associative memories find wide application in machine vision due to their capability of recalling a mapping already associated. Associative memories can be implemented with a feedback network, where the output is fed back repeatedly for every new input until the mapping process converges. The following three different kind of associative memories are in vogue (Kosko, 1988; Rojas, 1996).

- *Heteroassociative memories*, where $n$ number of input vectors in an $m$ dimensional vector space are mapped to $n$ number of output vectors in an $l$ dimensional space.
- *Autoassociative memories*, where a vector is associated to itself.
- *Pattern recognition memories*, where a vector is associated with a scalar.

The bidirectional associative memory (BAM) (Kosko, 1988) is a synchronous associative model with bidirectional interconnections/edges. It comprises two layers, viz., (i) an input layer and (ii) an output layer. Processed information is propagated recursively between these layers until the network operation converges. The input layer accepts inputs and sends the processed input information to the output layer via the bidirectional edges. The output layer operates on the incoming processed input information from the input layer and in turn sends the processed output information back to the input layer for further processing.

The Hopfield network (Hopfield, 1982) due to the American physicist John Hopfield is a recurrent asynchronous neural network architecture, which serves as a content-addressable memory (Rojas, 1996). A Hopfield network (shown in Figure 7) is a fully connected neural network architecture in that each neuron is connected to all other neurons except to itself. Moreover, the interconnections are symmetric (Rojas, 1996) such that the interconnection weight $w_{ij}$ from the $i^{th}$ neuron to the $j^{th}$ neuron is equal to the interconnection

*Figure 7. Schematic of Hopfield network comprising eight interconnected neurons*

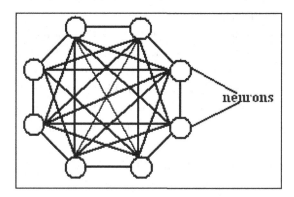

or [wikiHop]

$$t_i = \begin{cases} +1 & \text{if} \quad \sum_{j=1}^{N} w_{ij} s_j(t) > \theta_i \\ -1 & \text{otherwise} \end{cases} \quad (32)$$

where, $w_{ij}$ represents the interconnection weight from the $i^{th}$ neuron to the $j^{th}$ neuron, $s_j(t)$ is the state of the $j^{th}$ neuron at time $t$ and $\theta_i$ is the activation threshold of the $i^{th}$ neuron.

## Activation Update Mechanism

The fully interconnected topology of the Hopfield network indicates that the network possesses a finite energy arising out of the activation states $s_i(t)$ and $s_j(t)$ of the neurons at any instant of time $t$. This energy is given by the Lyapunov function (Hahn, 1963) as

$$E(t) = -\frac{1}{2} \sum_{i,j} w_{ij} s_i(t) s_j(t) + \sum_i \theta_i s_i(t) \quad (33)$$

As the states $s_i(t)$ or $s_j(t)$ of the neurons are updated to newer states $s_i(t+1)$ or $s_j(t+1)$ of lower energy, the Hopfield network switches to an overall lower energy state $E(t+1)$. Subsequently, the network converges at a minimum of the energy state. However, until the current states of the neurons are updated, the neurons preserve their individual states.

One of the important applications of the Hopfield network is its ability to serve as an associative memory, where the interconnection weights are ultimately set in such a fashion so as to replicate the stable patterns already stored in the network. In other words, if a noisy or incomplete pattern is presented to the network, the network automatically converges to a stable state, which replicates a pattern similar to that presented. Details regarding

weight $w_{ji}$ the other way round, i.e. from the $j^{th}$ neuron to the $i^{th}$ neuron. Due to this symmetric bidirectional interconnection topology, it forms a class of bidirectional associative memory (BAM) (Kosko, 1988).

In general, a Hopfield network comprises a set of $N$ binary thresholded neurons connected following the topology as shown in Figure 7. There is no sharp delineation between the input and output neurons in this network. All the neurons act as both input and output neurons so that the inputs presented to the network retain their states until they are updated. The activation state of each neuron is updated asynchronously irrespective of the activation states of the other neurons.

Since the neurons in a Hopfield network are binary in nature, they exhibit binary/bipolar behavior. Hence, they can exist with activation values of either 1(+1) [or 0(-1)] depending on whether the activation values exceed [or do not exceed] the corresponding thresholds $\theta_i$. Thus, the activation value $t_i$ of the $i^{th}$ neuron in a Hopfield network can be expressed as either [wikiHop]

$$t_i = \begin{cases} 1 & \text{if} \quad \sum_{j=1}^{N} w_{ij} s_j(t) > \theta_i \\ 0 & \text{otherwise} \end{cases} \quad (31)$$

the different incarnations of the Hopfield network are available in (Hopfield, 1982; Rojas, 1996).

## Kohonen's Self-Organizing Feature Map (SOFM)

As mentioned in previous sections, neural networks can also be put to use in situations where there are neither target outputs nor class labels i.e. they can operate in an unsupervised manner as well in the absence of any supervisor. The main objective of such a learning paradigm is to either discover the underlying structure of data followed by the encoding, compression and transformation of data.

Kohonen's self-organizing feature map (SOFM) (Kohonen, 1982; Kohonen, 1988) is a good example of the unsupervised learning model. Kohonen's self-organizing feature map is centered on preserving the topology in the data presented to the network thereby discovering the underlying structure of data by means of reducing the dimensions of data through self-organization. The topological map of input data reflects its structure by means of a mapping that preserves the neighborhood relations therein. This is brought about by subjecting the output data units to certain neighborhood constraints so that more neurons are allocated to recognize those parts of the input space where there are larger number of input vectors and fewer neurons are allocated to the other parts where fewer input vectors occur. Hence, the topology preservation procedure ensures that the neighboring neurons respond to similar vectors and the network learns the categorization, topology, and distribution of input vectors in the process (Kohonen, 1982).

Kohonen's SOFM (Kohonen, 1982; Kohonen, 1988) differs from the perceptrons or other networks in terms of its architectural makeup. While in other network architectures, it is assumed that each neuron in a given layer is identical with respect to its connection to all the other nodes in the preceding and/or following layer, in SOFM,

the physical arrangement of these neurons are also taken into consideration. Neurons tend to group together around a winning neuron, which bears the greatest similarity with an input pattern. Moreover, neurons that are closer together interact differently than those that are further apart from each other. A network that performs this kind of mapping is called a feature map (Kohonen, 1982; Kohonen, 1988). Figure 8 shows the topological structure of a SOFM comprising two layers, viz., (i) input layer and (ii) computational/output layer. Each computational layer neuron is connected to all the input layer neurons. Only fewer interconnections are shown in Figure 8 for the sake of clarity.

## SOFM Self-Organizing Algorithm

The SOFM operates in a self-supervised manner. It organizes data into output responses based upon the correlations in the input data. The concept of grouping of similarly behaved neurons around a winning neuron enables the generation of localized output responses from these neurons. SOFM adaptively transforms an incoming signal pattern of arbitrary dimensions into a one or a two-dimensional discrete map in a topologically ordered fashion. The output layer of the SOFM therefore comprises neurons placed in either a one or a two-dimensional lattice. A competitive learning process between the neurons of the computational layer helps them to become selectively tuned to various input patterns. The winning neurons therefore, group together so as to replicate the features of the input patterns. The self-organizing process in a SOFM comprises the following phases (Kohonen, 1982; Kohonen, 1988).

1. *Initialization*: All the interconnection weights are initialized with small random values in this phase.
2. *Competitive learning*: In this phase, each computational layer neuron computes its value of a discriminant function for each input pattern presented, which provides the

*Figure 8. Schematic of Kohonen's SOFM*

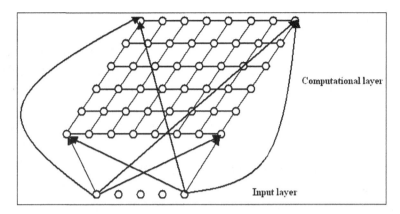

basis for its selection as a winning neuron. The discriminant function generally employed is the squared Euclidean distance between the input vector $\mathbf{x}=\{x_1, x_2, x_3, \ldots, x_n\}$ ($n$ being the input vector dimension) and the interconnection weight vector $\mathbf{w_j}=\{w_{j1}, w_{j2}, w_{j3}, \ldots, w_{jn}\}$ for each $j^{\text{th}}$ neuron in the computational layer. It is given by (Kohonen, 1982; Kohonen, 1988)

$$D_j(\mathbf{x}) = \sum_{i=1}^{n}(x_i - w_{ji})^2 \qquad (34)$$

As a part of this competitive process, the neuron having the smallest value of the discriminant function is declared as the winner.

3. *Cooperative process*: This phase ensures the firing of the closest neighbors of the constituent neurons due to the lateral interaction between the excited neurons. It also ascertains that the topological features of the input patterns are preserved. Thus, the winning neuron determines the spatial location of a topological neighborhood of similarly excited neurons, thereby forming the so-called feature map. However, the degree of excitation decays with the distance from the firing neuron. The rate of decay is

decided by a neighborhood function of the form (Kohonen, 1982; Kohonen, 1988)

$$U_{j,x_w} = \exp(-\frac{S_{j,x_w}^2}{2\sigma^2}) \qquad (35)$$

where, $S_{j,x_w}$ is the lateral distance between the $j^{\text{th}}$ computational layer neuron and the winning neuron $x_w$ and $\sigma$ is the size of the neighborhood. As the cooperative process in SOFM proceeds, the size $\sigma$ is decreased with time according to the following equation (Kohonen, 1982; Kohonen, 1988).

$$\sigma(t) = \sigma_0 \exp(-\frac{t}{\tau_\sigma}) \qquad (36)$$

Here, $\sigma_0$ is the initial neighborhood size and $\tau_\sigma$ is a time constant.

4. *Adaptation*: Once the topological feature map is constructed, it should be preserved. This phase ensures the stability of the topological feature map by allowing the excited neurons to decrease the values of their discriminant functions with time by means of suitable adjustments of the associated

interconnection weights $w_{ji}$ by the following equation (Kohonen, 1982; Kohonen, 1988).

$$w_{ji}(t+1)$$
$$= w_{ji}(t) - \eta(t)U_{j,x_w}(t)[x_i - w_{ji}(t)] \qquad (37)$$

where, $\eta(t) = \eta_0 \exp(-\dfrac{t}{\tau_\eta})$ is a time dependent learning rate. As a consequence, when an input pattern similar to the learnt pattern is presented to the network, the winning neurons elicit similar responses in consonance with the structure in the presented pattern.

SOFM finds wide applications in feature extraction from multidimensional datasets due to its capabilities of dimensionality reduction and approximation. In addition, SOFM is widely used in classification/recognition problems in computer vision.

## Radial Basis Function Networks (RBFN)

The evolution of the Radial Basis Function Network (RBFN) (Buhmann, 2003; Haykin, 1999; Paul, 2001) is motivated by the fields of statistical pattern classification and clustering, function approximation, spline interpolation techniques (Abraham, 2004; Bishop, 1995; Box, 1970; Poggio, 1990; Jones, 1990). The RBFN is a three-layer feed-forward network architecture comprising an input layer, a hidden layer and an output layer. The input layer simply propagates the input information to the hidden layer. Hence, there is no processing at the input layer. Nonlinear radial activation functions (normally Gaussian) are employed for the hidden layer neurons (Chen, 1991) while the output layer neurons use linear activations. The output layer neurons simply carry out a weighted sum of the outputs of the hidden layer neurons. Thus, the RBFN accepts nonlinear inputs and maps them to linear outputs. A typical RBFN is shown in Figure 9.

Due to this approximation capability, a RBFN is best suited for modeling complex mappings by resorting to only a single hidden layer (Buhmann, 2003; Haykin, 1999; Paul, 2001). The input-to-hidden layer interconnection weights are decided by taking into cognizance the clustered behavior of the input dataset. Given a training set of input-output pairs, the network parameters can be trained to establish a sought input-output relationship.

*Figure 9. Schematic of a RBF network*

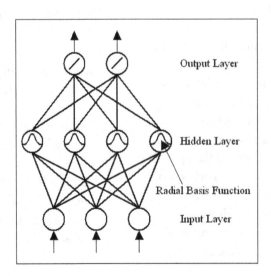

Once a RBFN is trained, it can be used to map any data with statistical distributions and properties similar to those used to form the training set (Buhmann, 2003; Haykin, 1999; Paul, 2001). The dynamics of a RBFN varies from one application to another.

## RBFN Activation Functions

Several types of nonlinear activation functions are used for the hidden layer (Buhmann, 2003; Lukaszyk, 2004) in a RBFN. These functions form a family of functions referred to as radial basis functions (RBFs) [wikiRadial1, wikiRadial2]. Some commonly used activation functions include (i) the Gaussian function $\psi(x) = e^{-\beta(\|x-c\|)^2}$; $\beta > 0$, where $\beta$ is the RBF width parameter [wikiRadial1], (ii) the thin-plate spline function $\psi(x) = \| x - c \|^2 \ln \| x - c \|$ [wikiRadial1] (iii) the polyharmonic spline function $\psi(x) = \| x - c \|^k$; $k = 1, 3, 5, \dots, 2n\text{-}1$ or $\psi(x) = \| x - c \|^k \ln \| x - c \|^k$; $k = 2, 4, 6, \dots, 2n$ [wikiRadial1] and (iv) the multiquadric function $\psi(x) = \sqrt{(\| x - c \|) + \beta^2}$; $\beta > 0$ [wikiRadial1].

The general form of the Gaussian function for the $i^{th}$ hidden layer neuron in a RBFN is given by (Broomhead, 1988; Casdagli, 1989; Cha, 1996)

$$\psi_i(x) = e^{-\frac{(\|x-c_i\|)^T}{\sigma_i(\|x-c_i\|)}} \qquad (38)$$

where, $i = 1, 2, 3, \dots, H$ (the number of hidden layer neurons). $c_i$ and $\sigma_i$ are the mean/center and covariance of the $i^{th}$ Gaussian function, respectively. $c_i$ determines the position and $\sigma_i$ controls the shape of the function.

As already stated, the output layer of a RBFN yields a linear combination of the weighted hidden layer neurons' outputs given by (Buhmann, 2003; Adrian, n.d.)

$$\varepsilon_k(x) = \sum_{i=1}^{H} w_{ik} \psi_i(x) \qquad (39)$$

where, $w_{ik}$ are the hidden-to-output layer weights and $k = 1, 2, 3, \dots, O$ (the number of output layer neurons). Since $\varepsilon_k$ can have a wide range of values, $\varepsilon_k$ is often squashed in the interval [0, 1] by the standard sigmoidal function in specific applications.

## Training of RBF Networks

RBFN operates in both supervised and unsupervised modes of operation (Buhmann, 2003; Haykin, 1999; Paul, 2001). In the supervised mode of operation, a training set of input-output pairs is used to train the network so as to adapt the RBF width parameter $\beta$, the center $c$ and the interconnection weight $w$ such that an objective/cost function involving the expected outputs $o$ and the input feature vector $x$ is minimized. The most widely used cost function is given by (Adrian, n.d.)

$$F_t(w) = [o(t) - \varepsilon(x(t), w)]^2 \qquad (40)$$

Since $F_t(w)$ depends on the interconnection weights, an optimal set of weights is needed to achieve the desired minimum of the cost function. Hence, the training procedure of a RBFN boils down to an optimization procedure. It may be noted this optimization procedure also enables the incorporation of multiple cost functions in specific applications. In those situations, the cost function may be carved out of an additive combination of the individual cost functions.

Similar to the multilayer perceptron, the gradient descent algorithm (Snyman, 2005) is used in RBFN to adaptively minimize the cost function. In addition, the standard backpropagation algorithm (Rumelhart, 1986; Haykin, 1999; Rojas, 1996) is also used for iteratively adapting the interconnection weights by computing the derivatives of the cost function with respect to the weights. Other notable algorithms employed for training of RBF networks include the Gram-Schmidt orthogonalization (Golub, 1996), learning vector quantization (Somervuo, 2004), the *k*-means clustering algorithm (MacQueen, 1967) etc.

RBF networks find wide applications in data interpolation (Davies, 1995), chaotic time-series modeling (Lukaszyk, 2004), speech recognition (Niranjan, 1990), image processing (Cha, 1996), motion estimation (Bors, 1998) to name a few.

## Adaptive Resonance Theory (ART)

Among the early cognitive models, the exemplar model (Grossberg, n.d.; Medin, 1978; Murphy, 1985) and the prototype model (Smith, 1998; Minda, 1997) deserve special mention. The exemplar models rely on the storage of exemplars of each new event/pattern encountered during the learning phase for the purpose of eliciting cognitive responses. In the recognition phase, these models resort to comparing the test items to each of the exemplars of events/patterns stored in the learning phase. This comparison process finally assigns the test items presented, to a particular class of exemplars, which bears the greatest resemblance with the test items. Thus, it is evident that the cognitive capabilities of the exemplar models rest on the generation of suitable exemplars from events/patterns and subsequent searching for the nearest match with the test items.

On the contrary, the prototype models insist on storing only abstractions/prototypes of multiple exemplars generated from new events/patterns encountered (Grossberg, n.d.). During the recognition phase, the prototype models compare the test items to each stored prototype and assign the class of the test items to the one, which contains a prototype bearing a strong resemblance with the test items. Hence, both the storage and search complexity are lower in the prototype models as compared to the exemplar counterparts. However, both these models require a *bottom-up learning* mechanism in which exemplars/prototypes are generated and learnt followed by a *top-down learning* phase, where the similarity of the test items presented to the stored exemplars/prototypes is derived. Moreover, both these models suffer from the problems of generation of suitable abstractions and complexities arising out of the search procedures adopted (Grossberg, n.d.).

As a consequence, the rules-plus-exceptions cognitive model (Grossberg, n.d.; Nosofsky, 1998; Nosofsky, 2002) was introduced to overcome the shortcomings of the exemplar and prototype models. It is a hybrid model comprising a mixture of the exemplar and prototype models. The rules-plus-exceptions cognitive model learns both specific (exemplars) patterns, which form the guiding recognition rules and generic (prototypes) patterns, which incorporate out-of-rules exceptions for patterns, which deserve special attention, thereby keeping all avenues open for newer patterns without allowing the learnt ones to be destroyed. This is in sharp contrast to the competitive learning methodology adopted in feed-forward neural networks, where the trained synaptic weights tend to alter as newer events/patterns are learnt leading to a possible loss of older knowledge with time. Thus, to sustain the older knowledge, the synaptic weights have to be accommodative of the newer knowledge vis-à-vis the older ones. This paradox is referred to as the famous *stability-plasticity dilemma* (Grossberg, n.d.; Grossberg, 1976).

Carpenter and Grossberg introduced the Adaptive Resonance Theory (ART) (Grossberg, 1976; Carpenter, 1987a) during 1976-1986 as an effort to imbibe a dynamic balance in the so-called *stability-plasticity dilemma* by self-organizing newer input patterns in addition to those originally stored. The primary motivation behind the ART model lies in the postulate that humans possess cognitive capabilities due to an interaction between *top-down expectations*, which involve a learning of prototypes for selection of consistent bottom-up signals followed by suppression of inconsistent bottom-up signals (also referred to as attentional focusing) and *bottom-up sensory activation*, which involves automatic activation of target prototypes during the learning process. To be precise, the *top-down expectations* form the basis for a *bottom-up sensory activation* based comparison of newer patterns with the exemplars/prototype generated in the learning phase leading to a class assignment. Moreover, a threshold value referred to as the *vigilance parameter* ($\chi$) ensures an expected class assignment as long as the differences between the expectations and the sensation do not exceed the threshold value. As such, the ART model is suited as both a supervised and an unsupervised neural network model.

The ART model essentially comprises an *attentional subsystem* and an *orienting subsystem* (Grossberg, 1976; Carpenter, 1987a). The attentional subsystem carries out the stabilization of learning and activation procedures by means of matching of *bottom-up input activation* and *top-down expectations*. The orienting subsystem detects any mismatch, which may occur in the attentional subsystem during learning. Hence, it controls the attentional subsystem. An ART model possesses the following properties (Ekrafft, 2001; Carpenter, 1987a; Carpenter, 2003).

- *Self-scaling computational units:* The attentional subsystem functions using the principles of competitive learning, which ensures learning of patterns with features of importance. Moreover, it also ensures immunity to noisy patterns (Ekrafft, 2001).
- *Self-adjusting memory search:* This property enables an adaptive and parallel search of memory of stored patterns (Ekrafft, 2001).
- *Direct category access:* This feature enables the stored patterns to directly access their corresponding categories (Ekrafft, 2001).
- *Adaptive modulation of attentional vigilance:* As mentioned earlier, a vigilance parameter ($\chi$) acts as a threshold in the categorization process. ART possesses the ability to adaptively tune the attentional vigilance parameter in accordance with the operating environment (Ekrafft, 2001).

Several versions of the ART model are in vogue (Carpenter, 1987a; Carpenter, 2003). The basic ART model (ART1) (Carpenter, 1987a; Carpenter, 2003) is an unsupervised model for learning and recognition of binary input patterns. ART2 (Carpenter, 1987b; Carpenter, 1991a; Carpenter, 2003) is efficient in categorizing both analog and binary input patterns. ART3 (Carpenter, 1990; Carpenter, 2003), ARTMAP (Carpenter, 1991b; Carpenter, 2003), fuzzy ART (Carpenter, 1991c; Carpenter, 2003), fuzzy ARTMAP (Carpenter, 1992; Carpenter, 2003) are complex and distributed incarnations of the basic ART model, which are suitable for distributed recognition tasks. The following subsections discuss the architectures and operations of ART1 and ART2 models.

## ART1

An extended version of the diagram (Carpenter, 1987a; Carpenter, 2003; art, n.d.) illustrating the basic components of the ART1 model (Carpenter, 1987a; Carpenter, 2003) is shown in Figure 10. The attentional subsystem (shown in the dotted right box) comprises two competitive network layers (i) the comparison layer $C$ (consisting of $N$ number of neurons) and (ii) the recognition layer $R$ (consisting of $M$ number of neurons) along with respective control gains $G_C$ and $G_R$ (Carpenter, 1987a; Carpenter, 2003; art, n.d.). The orienting subsystem (shown in the dotted right box) comprises a reset layer ($S$) to control the operational dynamics of the attentional subsystem.

Each neuron in $C$ is connected to all the neurons in $R$ by the continuous-valued forward long-term memory (LTM) gates/weights $W_f$. Only a single $W_f$ weight is shown for the sake of clarity. On the other hand, each neuron in $R$ is connected to all the neurons in $C$ by the binary-valued back-

*Figure 10. Schematic of ART1 model*

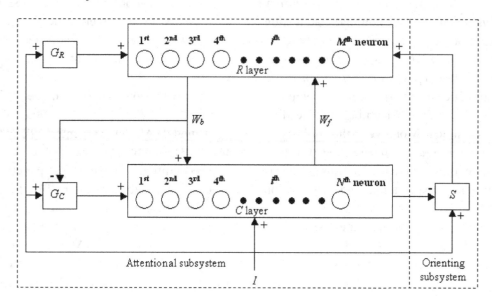

ward LTM gates/weights $W_b$. Similarly, a single $W_b$ weight is shown for the sake of clarity of the schematic. Both $C$ and $R$ generate short term memory (STM) activations/activity patterns when fed with inputs. Given this topology, each neuron in $C$ receives three input signals, one each from (i) the external input vector $I$, (ii) the control gain $G_C$ and (iii) internal network inputs corresponding to the STM activity pattern outputs of $R$ ($O_{R_j}$ $j$=1, 2, 3, ..., $M$) multiplied by corresponding weights $W_{b_{ji}}$, $j$=1, 2, 3, ..., $M$; $i$=1, 2, 3, ..., $N$. The output ($O_{C_i}$, $i$=1, 2, 3, ..., $N$) from each neuron in $C$ is propagated forward to $R$ and fed to the orienting subsystem as shown in Figure 10 (Carpenter, 1987a; Carpenter, 2003; art, n.d.). Similarly, each neuron in $R$ receives three signals, one each from (i) the reset layer ($S$) of the orienting subsystem, (ii) the control gain $G_R$ and (iii) internal network inputs corresponding to the outputs of $C$ ($O_{C_i}$, $i$=1, 2, 3, ..., $N$) multiplied by corresponding weights $W_{f_{ij}}$, $i$=1, 2, 3, ..., $N$; $j$=1, 2, 3, ..., $M$. The output ($O_{R_j}$, $j$=1, 2, 3, ..., $M$) of each of these neurons is fed back to $C$ and propagated to $G_C$

simultaneously. It may be noted that in the ART1 model, the neurons in both $C$ and $R$ follow the *two-thirds rule* to fire, i.e., they output a 1 if and only if at least two of their three inputs are high (Carpenter, 1987a; Carpenter, 2003; Alfredo, n.d.).

## ART1 Operation

On reception of a binary input vector $I$, the comparison layer propagates it forward to the recognition layer for matching with a stored class template. The selected class is passed back to the comparison layer for verification with the input vector. If the verification process yields favorable results, a new input vector is read and the operations are repeated for the new vector. However, in case of a mismatch, the orienting subsystem comes into play. It inhibits the selected class and pushes the recognition layer to searches for a new class for the input vector.

The entire processing task carried out by ART1 can be summarized as follows (Carpenter, 1987a; Carpenter, 2003; Alfredo, n.d.).

- *Recognition phase/bottom-up activation*: In this phase, no input vector is applied to

$C$ thereby disabling any recognition in $R$ and making $G_C$=0; $G_R$=0. This sets all the neurons of $R$ to zero, deeming them equally fit to win any subsequent recognition. However, when an input vector $I$ arrives, one or more neurons are reset to 1 thereby setting $G_C$=1; $G_R$=1 (Carpenter, 1987a; Carpenter, 2003; Alfredo, n.d.).

Thus,

$$G_C - \begin{cases} 1 & \text{if} \quad I \neq 0 \quad \text{and} \quad O_{R_i} = 0 \\ 0 & \text{otherwise} \end{cases}$$

(41)

i.e., even if $R$ does not produce any output, $G_C$ is set to 1 if there is an input vector and

$$G_R = \begin{cases} 1 & \text{if} \quad I \neq 0 \\ 0 & \text{otherwise} \end{cases}$$

(42)

implying that $R$ is activated by $G_R$ when there is an input vector.

Since, both $C$ and $R$ layers represent the short-term memory (STM) of the ART1 model, each $C$ layer neuron excites a positive nonzero ($G_C$=1) STM activity pattern which results in the generation of an output which is an exact replica of the input vector $I$ i.e., $O_C = I$. The $C$ layer neurons whose activity is greater than a threshold excite the $R$ layer neurons by their outputs. Thus, each $j^{th}R$ layer neuron receives an input $I_{Rj}$ given by (Carpenter, 1987a; Carpenter, 2003; Alfredo, n.d.)

$$I_{R_j} = \sum_{i=1}^{N} O_{C_i} W_{f_{ij}}$$

(43)

Since the $R$ layer acts as a winner-take-all layer, the neuron in $R$ that receives the largest of all $O_{C_i}$, $i$=1, 2, 3, ..., $N$ in its input $I_{R_j}$, matches the input vector best and fires leaving all other neurons in $R$ to be set to 0 by means of lateral inhibition.

*Comparison phase/top-down expectation:* In this phase, the outputs $O_{R_j}$, $j$=1, 2, 3, ..., $M$ generate a top-down template given by (Carpenter, 1987a; Carpenter, 2003; Alfredo, n.d.)

$$I_{C_i} = \sum_{j=1}^{M} O_{R_j} W_{b_{ji}}$$

(44)

This is fed back to the $C$ layer for comparison with the input vector $I$. Meanwhile, $G_C$ is inhibited in the process and set to 0. The reset layer ($S$) in the orienting subsystem is responsible for adjudging the measure of similarity between $I$ and $I_C$. This measure of similarity is determined by the vigilance parameter $\chi$, $0 < \chi \leq 1$. After comparison, if a match is found, the system is ready to learn. On the other hand, mismatch occurs if $I$ and $I_C$ differ by a value greater than $\chi$. At this point, a reset signal generated by $S$ inhibits $R$ from further recognition. A larger value of $\chi$ allows the system to learn newer categories. On the other hand, a smaller value of $\chi$ ensures that more input patterns are classified into the same category (Carpenter, 1987a; Carpenter, 2003; Alfredo, n.d.).

Once $R$ has been disabled, both $O_R$ and $I_C$ are discarded and the STM activity pattern of $C$ is generated again. This cancels the reset signal and the recognition phase starts afresh. If no further mismatch occurs, the classification is said to have been completed (Carpenter, 1987a; Carpenter, 2003; Alfredo, n.d.).

## ART2

ART2 (Carpenter, 1987b; Carpenter, 1991a; Carpenter, 2003; Alfredo, n.d.) operates on continuous valued inputs. In this model, the comparison layer $C$ accepts $n$ number of six types of units, viz.,

$W$, $X$, $U$, $V$, $P$ and $Q$, where $n$ is the input vector dimension. The recognition layer $R$ is a competitive layer. The connection patterns in $C$ follow: $P \rightarrow Q \rightarrow V \rightarrow U \rightarrow P$ and $W \rightarrow X \rightarrow V \rightarrow U \rightarrow W$ (Alfredo, n.d.). The top-down and bottom-up connections between the different units of $C$ and $R$ preserve the prototypes already learnt. Initially, the activations of all the six units are set to zero. Computation starts at $U$, which holds the normalized value of the activation at $V$. This computation result is forwarded to both $W$ and $P$. $W$ receives the input vector from the external world and sums it up with the result received from $U$. Similarly, $P$ sums up the result from $U$ and the top-down activations from $R$ when $R$ is active. $X$ and $Q$ hold the normalized values of the activations at $W$ and $P$, respectively. $V$ sums up the values received concurrently from $X$ and $Q$. When the $C$ layer activations have stabilized, $P$ sends its activation for recognition to the $R$ layer. The reset unit $S$ sums up the reset signals it receives from both $P$ and $U$ and sends the result to the vigilance parameter $\chi$. $\chi$ determines as to whether $R$ is to be deactivated or not. Control gains $G_C$ and $G_R$ are responsible for the normalization of the activity patterns in the different units (Alfredo, n.d.).

The ART networks are efficient in fast category learning and category recognition/classification of binary/analog patterns. The networks also find wide use in incremental supervised learning of multidimensional data and feature spaces.

## ADVANCES IN NEURAL NETWORKING PARADIGM

Over the years, several novel neural network models suitable for different applications have been evolved. The task of listing each and every one of them would mean a book and is beyond the scope of this chapter. Moreover, it may be noted that the plethora of models evolved from time to time has been motivated by different fields of engineering and science. Notable among these fields are the machine vision, image processing, pattern recognition, data clustering and mining. This section throws some light on some of the important neural network architectures, which have been developed for different applications with due regards to the fields of image processing and pattern recognition.

One of the important breakthroughs in this direction is the evolution of modular and recurrent neural networks. Modular networks (Gallinari, 1995) are formed by the admixture of different neural network models discussed in the previous sections, thereby incorporating the features of several networks together. The advantages offered by such networks include (i) reduced time complexity, (ii) heterogeneous knowledge base, (iii) flexibility in learning strategies and (iv) scalability. Typical examples include the counterpropagation networks due to Hecht-Nielsen (Hecht, 1987) and the spline networks (Walter, 1995). Among the recurrent models proposed, significant are the Elman and Jordan recurrent networks (Elman, 1990). The Hidden Markov Models (HMM) (Huang, 1990) is another recurrent network model, which is capable of existing in either of different possible states at any instant of time. The change of state in a HMM is governed by some probabilistic dynamics. Chua and Yang (Chua, 1988a; Chua, 1988b; Nossek, 1993) proposed the cellular neural network (CNN) architecture. A CNN comprises neurons locally connected in a cellular structure. Though the CNN architecture is faster in operation, it requires user specified parameters to control its operation, which limits its use in real time applications. Convolutional networks (CN) (Cun, 1995) have been proposed for feature detection and character recognition. The central idea behind the operation of a CN lies in the concept of local receptive fields, which decide the interconnections between the different layers of the network. The network also incorporates the concept of shared weights and spatial subsampling, which result in shift and deformation invariance with reduced number of parameters. Phung and

Bouzerdoum (Phung, 2007) proposed a new neural architecture motivated by the concepts of image pyramids and local receptive fields. The proposed architecture, referred to as the pyramidal neural network (PyraNet), is efficient for classification of visual patterns. The architecture has a hierarchical structure of neural layers. A subset of the constituent layers of the network is organized in form of a pyramid and the remaining layers are simply one-dimensional layers. The PyraNet operates in a supervised mode and is capable of classifying two-dimensional patterns. An exhaustive survey of the advances in the neural networking paradigm can be found in (Egmont-Petersen, 2002; Huang, 2009).

So much so forth, the proposed neural network models are able to classify/recognize patterns after they are suitably trained with real world inputs. However, real world data exhibit varying degrees of uncertainty and vagueness. Traditional neural network models are unable to handle the uncertainty in knowledge base. Moreover, the complexity of the models increases with the number of model parameters as well as with the volume of the knowledge base. Hence, researchers have incorporated other soft computing tools viz., fuzzy sets, genetic algorithms, wavelets and rough sets to evolve more robust neural network models, which can effectively handle the vagueness in data as well as operate with an optimum set of parameters. These models, which have resulted out from the synergism of the neural networking paradigm with the other tenets of the soft computing paradigm are referred to as the neuro-fuzzy-genetic models.

Models (Kasabov, 2000; Russo, 1999; Russo, 2000; Pal, 1996; Estevez, 2005; Villmann, 2005; Muhammed, 2002; Martinetz, 1993; Hammer, 2005) based on the neuro-fuzzy paradigm have been successfully used to deal with imprecise knowledge bases. Fuzzy neural networks are used in (Horikawa, 1992) to automatically identify the fuzzified model of a nonlinear system. Simpson (Simpson, 1993) proposed a fuzzy min-max neural network, which is efficient for image segmentation and clustering. In (Lin, 1996), Lin *et al.* incorporated fuzzy clustering into a Hopfield network so as to avoid the problems of finding weighting factors in the energy function, thereby resulting in more efficient neural network architecture. The proposed fuzzy Hopfield neural network converges faster than its conventional counterpart. Tzeng and Chen (Tzeng, 1998) proposed a fuzzy neural network and applied it to SAR image classification. Jang (Jang, 1993) introduced the ANFIS (Adaptive-Network-based Fuzzy Inference System) framework useful in modeling real world systems. Ghosh *et al.* (Ghosh, 1993) proposed a multilayer self-organizing neural network (MLSONN) architecture based on a fuzzy measure driven estimation of the system errors. The architecture comprises an input layer, one or more hidden layers and an output layer of neurons. The novelty of the architecture lies in the use of indices of fuzziness at the output layer of the network to determine the system errors. The network is efficient in extracting binary objects from a noisy/blurred perspective. However, the use of the standard backpropagation algorithm for the adjustment of interconnection weights limits its use in real time applications. In addition, the use of the bilevel sigmoidal activation function also restricts its usage to the binary domain. The limitations of the MLSONN (Ghosh, 1993) architecture as regards to its inability to deal with multilevel/color inputs as well its high time complexity have led to the evolution of more efficient network architectures and activation functions. Bhattacharyya *et al.* (Bhattacharyya, 2008a; Bhattacharyya, 2010) introduced a multilevel version of the sigmoidal activation function, which is capable of handling multilevel inputs. Hence, the MLSONN (Ghosh, 1993) architecture guided by the proposed multilevel sigmoidal (MUSIG) activation function (Bhattacharyya, 2008a; Bhattacharyya, 2010) is able to deal with the extraction and segmentation tasks of multilevel input data. Bhattacharyya *et al.* (Bhattacharyya, 2007a; Bhattacharyya, 2007b) also devised a parallel version of the MLSONN architecture to process multiple featured inputs. The proposed parallel self-organizing neural network (PSONN) architecture is capable of extracting/segmenting pure and true color images. Bhattacharyya *et al.* (Bhattacharyya, 2006a; Bhattacharyya, 2007c) alleviated the usage of the backpropagation algorithm, which is used for the adjustment of interconnection weights in most of the traditional neural network architectures, by proposing a bi-directional self-organizing neural network (BDSONN) architecture. The proposed architecture comprises three interconnected fuzzy layers of neurons, viz., an input layer, an intermediate layer and an output layer. The input layer as usual accepts fuzzy inputs from the real world. The remaining two layers viz. the intermediate and the output layers are counterpropagating in nature. The neurons in all the layers are connected in a cellular fashion. In addition, the neurons in the different network layers are connected to each other using a neighborhood-based topology. The architecture uses fuzzy membership based weight assignment and subsequent updating procedure, thereby obviating the use of the time-complex backpropagation algorithm based weight adjustment mechanism. The network architecture uses a dynamic context sensitive thresholding mechanism and self organizes the input information by counter-propagation of the fuzzy network states between the intermediate and the output layers of the network.

*Genetic algorithms* (Goldberg, 1989) are heuristic search techniques, which use a feature space to arrive at an optimal solution space by means of application of several genetic operators. Significant contributions in the neuro-genetic domain are available in the literature (Zamparelli, 1997; Sklansky, 1996; Estevez, 2003). De *et al.* (De, 2009; De, 2010) applied a genetic algorithm based approach to determine the optimum transition levels of the MUSIG activation function (Bhattacharyya, 2008a; Bhattacharyya, 2010).

The resultant neuro-fuzzy-genetic architecture is efficient in image processing applications.

A *wavelet* transform (Goswami, 1999; Daubechies, 1988; Mallat, 1989; Meyer, 1993) is an efficient tool for data approximation, compression, and noise removal. The decomposition and approximation powers of wavelets have been used to develop wavelet-based neural network architectures (Cristea, 2000; Shashidhara, 2000; Ho, 2001), which possess more noise immunity and generalization capabilities than the conventional neural network architectures. Applications of wavelet-based models also appear in the literature (Desch^enes, 1998; Iftekharuddin, 1995).

Rough sets (Pawlak, 1982) are extensions of the classical set theory for describing imprecision and vagueness in real world data. Rough sets do not require any *a priori* information regarding the system at hand. Moreover, imprecision is defined in rough sets in terms of the boundary region of a set. The approximating capabilities of rough set theory have been put to use to evolve robust neural network architectures as well (Pan, 2003; Peters, 2000; Peters, 2001).

Support vector machines (SVMs) (Vapnik, 1995; Vapnik, 1997; Burges, 1998; Cristianini, 2000) fall into the recent advances in the neural networking paradigm as far as classification is concerned. SVMs are based on the principles of structural risk minimization. These are a set of supervised generalized linear classifiers more efficient than the traditional neural network based classifiers. In fact, a SVM model using a sigmoid kernel function is equivalent to a two-layer perceptron. A SVM performs classification using support vector methods. Input vectors are first mapped onto a higher-dimensional space in order to widen the separation between the data samples. Subsequently it constructs a hyperplane, which forms an optimal separator/discriminator of these vectors. Thus, it does not suffer from being stuck to a local minimum.

Most of the conventional neural network architectures discussed so far, inclusive of those resorting to a neighborhood-based topology, employ a large number of interconnected neurons. Larger the number of neurons, larger is the number of interconnections between them. A larger network implies larger network complexity and more processing time. Moreover, redundancy in the network interconnections also leads to the problem of false classification and recognition. Researchers have tried out several methods for arriving at an optimized neural network topology, which would sever the redundant interconnections in the architecture, thereby evolving space and time-efficient topologies (de Kruif, 2003; White, 1993; Whitley, 1990; Castellano, 1997; Zhou, 1999; Weymaere, 1994; Reed, 1993; Zeng, 2005). Several attempts (Ghosh, 2002) have been made to optimize the Hopfield network architecture, thereby reducing the network complexity. Methods are also reported (Harp, 1989) where the network structure is represented as a bit string and optimized using genetic algorithms. In (Miller, 1990), Miller *et al.* used a connectivity constraint matrix so as to optimize a layered feed-forward network of $N$ units. Genetic algorithm based optimization techniques have been combined with backpropagation for speeding up the convergence of neural networks (Kitano, 1990). The optimization algorithm is used to determine the starting weights of the network, which are subsequently refined using backpropagation. Some methods (Miller, 1989; Oliker, 1992), which aim at encoding each network connections, are found to perform well for smaller sized networks. Larger sized networks have been optimized effectively (Harp, 1989; Dodd, 1990) by encoding only a subset of the network features. Opitz and Shavlik (Opitz, 1994) introduced a refining algorithm (REGENT) for arriving at an optimized neural network topology generated from a knowledge base using the genetic algorithm. Bhattacharyya *et al.* (Bhattacharyya, 2006b; Bhattacharyya, 2008b) proposed a fuzzy-set theoretic method to design pruned neighborhood neural network architectures. The resultant pruned architectures have

been efficient compared to their fully connected counterparts both in terms of network complexity and extraction efficiency. Other notable contributions in this direction are the intuitive pruning methods based on weight and unit activation values (Hagiwara, 1993) or the magnitude-based pruning (MBP) method (Sietsma, 1991), which assumes that small weights are irrelevant.

Statistical analysis of the network parameters has often been used for pruning neural network architectures. Steppe *et al.* (Steppe, 1996) used the likelihood-ratio test statistics of the interconnection weights to refine the network topology. They pruned those hidden units having weights statistically different from zero. Belue and Bauer (Belue, 1995) injected a noisy input parameter into a neural network model and decided upon the relative significance of the original network parameters with the injected noisy parameter. Parameters with lower significance than the noisy parameter are pruned. Prechelt (Prechelt, 1997) developed methods to determine the number of weights to be pruned.

Sensitivity analysis pruning techniques (Ruck, 1990; Karnin, 1990; Mozer, 1989), which model the network parameters as small perturbations to the network sensitivity, have been widely used for evolving pruned network topologies. Zurada et al. (Zurada, 1994; Zurada, 1997) removed redundant network input units by means of the sensitivity analysis of the network output function with respect to perturbations of input units. This approach was further extended in (Engelbrecht, 2001). Ponnapalli *et al.* (Ponnapalli, 1999) devised a formal selection and pruning technique based on the concept of sensitivity index proposed by Karnin (Karnin, 1990). The approach is efficient in reducing redundancy in feedforward neural network architectures without requiring any *a priori* knowledge about the system. In the optimal brain damage (OBD) (Cun, 90), optimal brain surgeon (OBS) (Hassibi, 1993) and optimal cell damage (OCD) (Cibas, 1996), sensitivity analysis is performed with regard to the training error.

The field of *quantum computing* (Steane, 2000; Shor, 1997; Grover, 1998; Williams, 1998; Berman, 1998) entails the applications of the concepts of quantum mechanics/physics in the development of a computing paradigm much faster as compared to the conventional computing paradigm. The increase in the computing speed is obtained by means of utilizing the inherent parallelism observed in the *qubits*, the building blocks of a quantum computer. Researchers are actively involved in the design and implementation of neural network architectures inspired by the features offered by the quantum computing paradigm. Oliveira (de Oliveira, 2009) proposed a quantum RAM based neural network, which enables a direct realization of the architecture in quantum circuits. Liu *et al*. (Liu, 2007) developed an image segmentation method based on the discrete Tchebichef moments and quantum neural networks using multilevel transfer functions. A score of quantum neural network models exist in the literature (Faber, 1989; Menneer, 1995; Ventura, 1998; Goertzel, n.d.; deOliveira, 2008; Gopathy, 1997).

## APPLICATION PERSPECTIVES

Artificial neural networks (ANNs) find wide applications to a broad spectrum of different data-intensive application areas in science, engineering and finance. These can be classified into following.

- Cognitive science and machine learning (Egmont-Petersen, 2002), where ANNs have been widely used to mimic the behavior of human brain.
- Process modeling and control (Agarwal, 1997; Balakrishnan, 1996; Hunt, 1992; Kerr, 1998; Sanner, 1992), where ANNs have been used for modeling higher and lower levels of reasoning in the form of (i) language, (ii) problem solving, (iii) vision,

(iv) speech recognition for generating the best process control settings.

- Optimization (Chen, 1994; Scales, 1985; Shanno, 1990), where ANNs have been used to find out an optimal solution of a problem for a particular set of constraints and a cost function.
- Classification (Egmont-Petersen, 2002), which is one of the most important application areas where ANNs have been put to use. This involves grouping of data based patterns into classes for proper understanding and analysis of the same.
- Signal processing applications (Zaknich, 2003) for suppressing line noise and blind source separation.
- Pattern recognition (Phung, 2007; Egmont-Petersen, 2002), for faithful analysis of corresponding datasets.
- Associative memory (Kosko, 88), where ANNs are used to recall memory based on a partial match of previously trained patterns.
- Regression analysis (Sengupta, 1995), where ANNs are used for mapping of functions and time series predictions.

Apart from the aforestated application areas, other applications involving artificial neural networks include portfolio management (Zimmermann, 2001; Freitas, 2009), robotics (Kwan, 2000; Sanger, 1994; Kim, 1999; Barambones, 2002), target recognition (Egmont-Petersen, 2002), medical diagnosis (Moein, 2008), quality control (Bahlmann, 1999; Benvenuto, 2000) to name a few.

## DISCUSSIONS AND CONCLUSION

An overview of artificial neural networks has been presented with due regards to the evolution, topologies, learning algorithms and applications. The structure and functions of the human nervous system, which remains the motivation behind the evolution of the neural networking paradigm, is elucidated. A detailed analysis of the different components that make up this computing paradigm is also presented with due regards to the possible variations thereby. The topology, structure, operational characteristics and applications of some of the important neural network models are illustrated with emphasis on the learning methodologies adopted by these networks. The latest trends in researches in this direction are also discussed with reference to the significant breakthroughs achieved over the years. Finally, the application areas that these neural networks are put to are mentioned for a proper understanding of the relevance of the computing paradigm.

## ACKNOWLEDGMENT

The author would like to take this opportunity to render his reverence to Prof. (Dr.) Asit Kumar Datta, Retired Professor of the Department of Applied Optics and Photonics, University College of Science and Technology, University of Calcutta, Kolkata and presently Head of the Department of Electronics & Communication Engineering, Aliah University, Kolkata for being a constant source of inspiration in his endeavors. The author feels highly privileged to have a professor and a mentor in Prof. (Dr.) A. K. Datta in the early days of his enlightenment of the topic under consideration.

## REFERENCES

Abraham, A. (2004). Meta-learning evolutionary artificial neural networks. *Neurocomputing, 56c*, 1–38. doi:10.1016/S0925-2312(03)00369-2

Ackley, D. H., Hinton, G. E., & Sejnowski, T. J. (1985). A learning algorithm for Boltzmann machines. *Cognitive Science, 9*, 147–169. doi:10.1207/s15516709cog0901_7

Adrian. (n.d.). *Paper*. Retrieved from www-users. cs.york.ac.uk/~adrian/Papers/Others/OSEE01. pdf

Agarwal, A. (1997). A systematic classification of neural-network-based control. *IEEE Control Systems Magazine, 17*(2), 75–93. doi:10.1109/37.581297

Alfredo. (n.d.). *Website*. Retrieved from www. cannes.itam.mx/Alfredo/English/Nslbook/Mit-Press/Publications/157_170.CH08.pdf

Almeida, L. B., & Silva, F. (1991). Speeding-up backpropagation by data orthonormalization. *Artificial Neural Networks, 2*, 56–149.

Anderson, J. A., Silverstein, J. W., Ritz, S. A., & Jones, R. S. (1977). Distinctive features, categorical perception, probability learning: Some applications of a neural model. *Psychological Review, 84*, 413–451. doi:10.1037/0033-295X.84.5.413

ART. (n.d.). *Website*. Retrieved from http://www. learnartificialneuralnetworks.com/art.html

Bahlmann, C., Heidemann, G., & Ritter, H. (1999). Artificial neural networks for automated quality control of textile seams. *Pattern Recognition, 32*(6), 1049–1060. doi:10.1016/S0031-3203(98)00128-9

Balakrishnan, S. N., & Weil, R. D. (1996). Neurocontrol: A literature survey. *Mathematical Modeling and Computing, 23*, 101–117. doi:10.1016/0895-7177(95)00221-9

Barambones, O., & Etxebarria, V. (2002). Robust neural control for robotic manipulators. *Automatica, 38*, 235–242. doi:10.1016/S0005-1098(01)00191-1

Belue, L. M., & Bauer, K. W. (1995). Determining input features for multilayer perceptrons. *Neurocomputing, 7*, 111–121. doi:10.1016/0925-2312(94)E0053-T

Benvenuto, F., & Marani, A. (2000). Neural networks for environmental problems: Data quality control and air pollution nowcasting. *International Journal of Global Nest.*, *2*(3), 281–292.

Berman, G. P., Doolen, G. D., Mainieri, R., & Tsifrinovich, V. I. (1998). *Introduction to quantum computers*. London, U. K.: World Scientific. doi:10.1142/9789812384775

Bhattacharyya, S., & Dutta, P. (2006b). Designing pruned neighborhood neural networks for object extraction from noisy background. *International Journal of Foundations of Computing and Decision Sciences*, *31*(2), 105–134.

Bhattacharyya, S., Dutta, P., & DuttaMajumder, D. (2007b). A parallel self-organizing neural network (SONN) based color object extractor using MUSIG activation function with CONSENT. In D. Chakraborty, S. Nanda, & D. DuttaMajumder (Eds.), *Fuzzy logic and its application in technology and management* (pp. 206-213). New Delhi, India: Narosa Publishing House.

Bhattacharyya, S., Dutta, P., & Maulik, U. (2007c). Binary object extraction using bi-directional self-organizing neural network (BDSONN) architecture with fuzzy context sensitive thresholding. *International Journal of Pattern Analysis and Applications,* 345-360.

Bhattacharyya, S., Dutta, P., & Maulik, U. (2008a). Self organizing neural network (SONN) based gray scale object extractor with a Multilevel Sigmoidal (MUSIG) activation function. *International Journal of Foundations of Computing and Decision Sciences*, *33*(2), 46–50.

Bhattacharyya, S., Dutta, P., Maulik, U., & Nandi, P. K. (2006a). A self supervised bi-directional neural network (BDSONN) architecture for object extraction guided by beta activation function and adaptive fuzzy context sensitive thresholding. *International Journal of Intelligent Systems and Technologies*, *1*(4), 345–365.

Bhattacharyya, S., Dutta, P., Maulik, U., & Nandi, P. K. (2007a). Multilevel activation functions for true color image segmentation using a self supervised parallel self organizing neural network (PSONN) architecture: A comparative study. *International Journal of Computer Science, 2*(1), 09-21.

Bhattacharyya, S., Maulik, U., & Bandyopadhyay, S. (in press). Soft computing and its applications. In Dai, Y., Chakraborty, B., & Shi, M. (Eds.), *Kansei engineering and soft computing: Theory and practice*. Hershey, PA: IGI Global.

Bhattacharyya, S., Maulik, U., & Dutta, P. (2008b). A pruning algorithm for efficient image segmentation with neighborhood neural networks. *IAENG International Journal of Computer Science*, *35*(2), 191–200.

Bhattacharyya, S., Maulik, U., & Dutta, P. (2010). Multilevel image segmentation with adaptive image context based thresholding. *International Journal of Applied Soft Computing*, *11*, 946–962. doi:10.1016/j.asoc.2010.01.015

Bi, W., Wang, X. G., Tang, Z., & Tamura, H. (2005). Avoiding the local minima problem in backpropagation algorithm with modified error function. *IEICE Trans. Fundam. Electron. Commun. Comput. Sci. E (Norwalk, Conn.)*, *88-A*, 3645–3653.

Bishop, C. M. (1995). *Neural networks for pattern recognition*. Oxford, UK: Oxford University Press.

Bors, A. G., & Pitas, I. (1998). Optical flow estimation and moving object segmentation based on median radial basis function network. *IEEE Transactions on Image Processing*, *7*(5), 693–702. doi:10.1109/83.668026

Box, G. E. P., & Jenkins, G. M. (1970). *Time series analysis, forecasting and control*. CA: Holden Day.

Broomhead, D. S., & Lowe, D. (1988). Multivariable functional interpolation and adaptive networks. *Complex Systems*, *2*, 321–355.

Brown, A. (1991). *Nerve cells and nervous systems*. Berlin, Germany: Springer-Verlag.

Buhmann, M. D. (2003). *Radial basis functions: Theory and implementations*. Cambridge University Press. doi:10.1017/CBO9780511543241

Burges, C. J. C. (1998). A tutorial on support vector machines for pattern recognition. *Data Mining and Knowledge Discovery*, *2*, 121–167. doi:10.1023/A:1009715923555

Carpenter, G. A., & Grossberg, S. (1987a). A massively parallel architecture for a self-organizing neural pattern recognition machine. *Computer Vision Graphics and Image Processing*, *37*, 54–115. doi:10.1016/S0734-189X(87)80014-2

Carpenter, G. A., & Grossberg, S. (1987b). ART2: Self-organization of stable category recognition codes for analog input patterns. *Applied Optics*, *26*, 4919–4930. doi:10.1364/AO.26.004919

Carpenter, G. A., & Grossberg, S. (1990). ART 3: Hierarchical search using chemical transmitters in self-organizing pattern recognition architectures. *Neural Networks*, *3*, 129–152. doi:10.1016/0893-6080(90)90085-Y

Carpenter, G. A., & Grossberg, S. (2003). Adaptive resonance theory (ART). In Arbib, M. A. (Ed.), *The handbook of brain theory and neural networks* (pp. 79–82). Cambridge, MA: MIT Press.

Carpenter, G. A., Grossberg, S., Markuzon, N., Reynolds, J. H., & Rosen, D. B. (1992). Fuzzy ARTMAP: A neural network architecture for incremental supervised learning of analog multidimensional maps. *IEEE Transactions on Neural Networks*, *3*, 698–713. doi:10.1109/72.159059

Carpenter, G. A., Grossberg, S., & Reynolds, J. H. (1991b). ARTMAP: Supervised real-time learning and classification of nonstationary data by a self-organizing neural network. *Neural Networks*, *4*, 565–588. doi:10.1016/0893-6080(91)90012-T

Carpenter, G. A., Grossberg, S., & Rosen, D. B. (1991a). ART 2-A: An adaptive resonance algorithm for rapid category learning and recognition. *Neural Networks*, *4*, 493–504. doi:10.1016/0893-6080(91)90045-7

Carpenter, G. A., Grossberg, S., & Rosen, D. B. (1991c). Fuzzy ART: Fast stable learning and categorization of analog patterns by an adaptive resonance system. *Neural Networks*, *4*, 759–771. doi:10.1016/0893-6080(91)90056-B

Casdagli, M. (1989). Nonlinear prediction of chaotic time series. *Physica D. Nonlinear Phenomena*, *35*, 335–356. doi:10.1016/0167-2789(89)90074-2

Castellano, G. (1997). An iterative pruning algorithm for feedforward neural networks. *IEEE Transactions on Neural Networks*, *8*(3), 519–537. doi:10.1109/72.572092

Cha, I., & Kassam, S. A. (1996). RBFN restoration of nonlinearly degraded images. *IEEE Transactions on Image Processing*, *5*(6), 964–975. doi:10.1109/83.503912

Chapelle, O., Schölkopf, B., & Zien, A. (2006). *Semi-supervised learning*. Cambridge, MA: MIT Press.

Charalambous, C. (1992). Conjugate gradient algorithm for efficient training of artificial neural networks. *Proceedings of the IEEE*, *139*(3), 301–310.

Chauvin, Y., & Rumelhart, D. E. (1995). *Backpropagation: Theory, architectures, and applications*. Hillsdale, NJ: L. Erlbaum Associates Inc.

Chen, Q., & Weigand, W. A. (1994). Dynamic optimization of nonlinear processes by combining neural net model with UDMC. *AIChE Journal. American Institute of Chemical Engineers*, *40*, 1488–1497. doi:10.1002/aic.690400908

Chen, S., Cowan, C. F. N., & Grant, P. M. (1991). Orthogonal least squares learning algorithm for radial basis function networks. *IEEE Transactions on Neural Networks*, *2*(2), 302–309. doi:10.1109/72.80341

Chua, W., & Yang, L. (1988a). Cellular networks: Theory. *IEEE Transactions on Circuits and Systems*, *35*(10), 1257–1272. doi:10.1109/31.7600

Chua, W., & Yang, L. (1988b). Cellular networks: Applications. *IEEE Transactions on Circuits and Systems*, *35*(10), 1273–1290. doi:10.1109/31.7601

Cibas, T., Souli, F. F., Gallinari, P., & Raudys, S. (1996). Variable selection with neural networks. *Neurocomputing*, *12*, 223–248. doi:10.1016/0925-2312(95)00121-2

Correction Neural Networks*Modeling and forecasting financial data, techniques of nonlinear dynamics* (Soofi, A., & Cao, L., Eds.). Kluwer Academic Press.

Cristea, P., Tuduce, R., & Cristea, A. (2000). Time series prediction with wavelet neural networks. In *Proceedings of IEEE Neural Network Applications in Electrical Engineering*, *25-27*, 5–10.

Cristianini, N., & Taylor, J. S. (2000). *An introduction to support vector machines and other kernel-based learning methods*. New York, NY: Cambridge University Press.

Cun, Y. L., & Bengio, Y. (1995). Convolutional networks for images, speech, and time series. In Arbib, M. A. (Ed.), *The handbook of brain theory and neural networks* (pp. 255–258). Cambridge, MA: MIT Press.

Cun, Y. L., Denker, J. S., & Solla, S. A. (1990). Optimal brain damage. In Touretzky, D. S. (Ed.), *Advances in neural information processing systems*, *2* (pp. 598–605). San Mateo, CA: Morgan Kaufmann.

Daubechies, I. (1988). Orthonormal bases of compactly supported wavelets. *Communications on Pure and Applied Mathematics*, *41*, 909–996. doi:10.1002/cpa.3160410705

Davies, J. R., Coggeshall, S. V., Jones, R. D., & Schutzer, D. (1995). Intelligent security systems. In Freedman, S. R., Flein, A. R., & Lederma, J. (Eds.), *Artificial intelligence in the capital markets*. Chicago, IL: Irwin.

De, S., Bhattacharyya, S., & Dutta, P. (2009). Multilevel image segmentation using OptiMUSIG activation function with fixed and variable thresholding: A comparative study. In Mehnen, J., Koppen, M., Saad, A., & Tiwari, A. (Eds.), *Applications of soft computing: From theory to praxis, advances in intelligent and soft computing* (pp. 53–62). Berlin: Springer-Verlag. doi:10.1007/978-3-540-89619-7_6

De, S., Bhattacharyya, S., & Dutta, P. (2010). Efficient gray level image segmentation using an optimized MUSIG (OptiMUSIG) activation function. *International Journal of Parallel, Emergent and Distributed Systems*, 1-39.

Deschenes, S., Sheng, Y., & Chevrette, P. C. (1998). Three-dimensional object recognition from two-dimensional images using wavelet transforms and neural networks. *Optical Engineering (Redondo Beach, Calif.)*, *37*(3), 763–770.

de Kruif, B. J., & de Vries, T. J. (2003). Pruning error minimization in least squares support vector machines. *IEEE Transactions on Neural Networks*, *14*(3), 696–702. doi:10.1109/TNN.2003.810597

de Oliveira, W. R. (2009). Quantum RAM based neural networks. In *Proceedings of European Symposium on Artificial Neural Networks - Advances in Computational Intelligence and Learning* (pp. 331-336).

de Oliveira, W. R., et al. (2008). Quantum logical neural networks. In *Proceedings of 10th Brazilian Symposium on Neural Networks SBRN '08* (pp. 147-152).

Dingledine, R., Borges, K., Bowie, D., & Traynelis, S. F. (1999). The glutamate receptor ion channels. *Pharmacological Reviews, 51*(1), 7–61.

Dodd, N. (1990). Optimization of network structure using genetic techniques. In *Proceedings of IEEE International Joint Conference on Neural Networks, 3*, 965-970.

Egmont-Petersen, M., de Ridder, D., & Handels, H. (2002). Image processing with neural networks—A review. *Pattern Recognition, 35*, 2279–2301. doi:10.1016/S0031-3203(01)00178-9

Ekrafft. (2001). *Wayfinding*. http://www.ifi.uzh.ch/Ekrafft/papers/2001/wayfinding/html/node97.html

Elman, J. L. (1990). Finding structure in time. *Cognitive Science, 14*, 179–211. doi:10.1207/s15516709cog1402_1

Engelbrecht, A. P. (2001). A new pruning heuristic based on variance analysis of sensitivity information. *IEEE Transactions on Neural Networks, 12*(6), 1386–1399. doi:10.1109/72.963775

Estevez, P. A., Flores, R. J., & Perez, C. A. (2005). Color image segmentation using fuzzy min-max neural networks. In *Proceedings of IEEE International Joint Conference on Neural Networks,* (vol. 5, pp. 3052-3057).

Estevez, P. A., Perez, C. A., & Goles, E. (2003). Genetic input selection to a neural classifier for defect classification of radiata pine boards. *Forest Prod. Journal, 53*(7/8), 87–94.

Faber, J., & Giraldi, G. (1989). *Quantum models of artificial neural networks*. Retrieved from http://arquivosweb.lncc.br/pdfs/QNN-Review.pdf

Fausett, L. (1994). *Fundamentals of neural networks*. USA: Prentice Hall.

Freitas, F. D., De Souza, A. F., & de Almeida, A. R. (2009). Prediction-based portfolio optimization model using neural networks. *Neurocomputing, 72*(10-12), 2155–2170. doi:10.1016/j.neucom.2008.08.019

Gallinari, P. (1995). Training of modular neural net systems. In M. A, Arbib (Ed.), *The handbook of brain theory and neural networks* (pp. 582–585), Cambridge, MA: MIT Press.

Gerke, M., & Hoyer, H. (1997). Fuzzy backpropagation training of neural networks. In Reusch, B. (Ed.), *Computational intelligence theory and applications* (pp. 416–427). Berlin, Germany: Springer.

Ghosh, A., Pal, N. R., & Pal, S. K. (1993). Self-organization for object extraction using multilayer neural network and fuzziness measures. *IEEE Transactions on Fuzzy Systems, 1*(1), 54–68. doi:10.1109/TFUZZ.1993.390285

Ghosh, S., & Ghosh, A. (2002). A GA-fuzzy approach to evolve Hopfield type optimum networks for object extraction. In. *Proceedings of AFSS, 2002*, 444–449.

Goertzel, B. (1989). *Quantum neural networks*. Retrieved from http://goertzel/org/ben/quantnet.html

Goldberg, D. E. (1989). *Genetic algorithms: Search, optimization and machine learning*. New York, NY: Addison-Wesley.

Golub, G. H., Van, L., & Charles, F. (1996). *Matrix computations*. Johns Hopkins.

Gopathy, P., Nicolaos, B., & Karayiannis, N. B. (1997). Quantum neural networks are inherently fuzzy feedforward neural networks. *IEEE Transactions on Neural Networks, 8*(3), 679–693. doi:10.1109/72.572106

Goswami, J. C., & Chan, A. K. (1999). *Fundamentals of wavelets-Theory, algorithm, and applications*. Wiley Inter-Science.

Grossberg, S. (1976). Adaptive pattern classification and universal recoding: Parallel development and coding of neural feature detectors. *Biological Cybernetics*, *23*, 121–134. doi:10.1007/BF00344744

Grossberg, S. (n.d.). *Anticipatory brain dynamics in perception, cognition, and action*. Retrieved from http://www.cns.bu.edu/Profiles/Grossberg

Grover, L. K. (1998). Quantum computers can search rapidly by using almost any transformation. *Physical Review Letters*, *80*(19), 4329–4332. doi:10.1103/PhysRevLett.80.4329

Hagan, M. T., Demuth, H. B., & Beale, M. H. (1996). *Neural network design*. Boston, MA: PWS-Kent.

Hagan, M. T., & Menhaj, M. B. (1994). Training feedforward networks with the Marquardt algorithm. *IEEE Transactions on Neural Networks*, *5*(6), 989–993. doi:10.1109/72.329697

Hagiwara, M. (1993). Removal of hidden units and weights for backpropagation networks. In *Proceedings of International Joint Conference on Neural Networks*, *1*, 351-354.

Hahn, W. (1963). *Theory and application of Liapunov's direct method*. Englewood Cliffs, NJ: Prentice-Hall.

Hammer, B., Strickert, M., & Villmann, T. (2005). Supervised neural gas with general similarity measure. *Neural Processing Letters*, *21*(1), 21–44. doi:10.1007/s11063-004-3255-2

Harp, S. A., & Samad, T., & Guha. (1989). A. Designing application-specific neural networks using the genetic algorithm. *Advances in Neural Information Processing Systems*, *2*, 447–454.

Hassibi, B., & Stork, D. G. (1993). Second-order derivatives for network pruning: Optimal Brain Surgeon Advances. In Giles, C. L., Hanson, S. J., & Cowan, J. D. (Eds.), *Neural information processing systems*, *5* (pp. 164–171). San Mateo, CA: Morgan-Kaufmann.

Haykin, S. (1999). *Neural networks: A comprehensive foundation*. Upper Saddle River, NJ: Prentice Hall.

Hebb, D. O. (1949). *The organization of behavior*. New York: John Wiley.

Hecht-Nielsen, R. (1987). Counterpropagation networks. *Applied Optics*, *26*, 4979–4984. doi:10.1364/AO.26.004979

Ho, D. W. C., Zhang, P. A., & Xu, J. (2001). Fuzzy wavelet networks for function learning. *IEEE Transactions on Fuzzy Systems*, *9*, 200–211. doi:10.1109/91.917126

Hopfield, J. J. (1982). Neural networks and physical systems with emergent collective computational abilities. *Proceedings of the National Academy of Sciences of the United States of America*, *79*(8), 2554–2558. doi:10.1073/pnas.79.8.2554

Horikawa, S., Furuhashi, T., & Uchikawa, Y. (1992). On fuzzy modeling using fuzzy neural networks with back propagation algorithm. *IEEE Transactions on Neural Networks*, *3*, 801–806. doi:10.1109/72.159069

Huang, X., Jack, M., & Ariki, Y. (1990). *Hidden Markov models for speech recognition*. Edinburgh University Press.

Huang, Y. (2009). Advances in artificial neural networks – Methodological development and application. *Algorithms*, *2*, 973–1007. doi:10.3390/algor2030973

Hunt, K. J., Sbarbaro, D., Zbikowski, R., & Gawthrop, P. J. (1992). Neural networks for control system - A survey. *Automatica*, *28*, 1083–1112. doi:10.1016/0005-1098(92)90053-I

Iftekharuddin, K. M., Schechinger, T. D., & Jemili, K. (1995). Feature-based neural wavelet optical character recognition system. *Optical Engineering (Redondo Beach, Calif.)*, *34*(11), 3193–3199. doi:10.1117/12.213654

Jacobs, R. A. (1988). Increased rates of convergence through learning rate adaptation. *Neural Networks*, *1*, 295–307. doi:10.1016/0893-6080(88)90003-2

Jang, J. S. R. (1993). (1993). ANFIS: Adaptive-network-based fuzzy inference system. *IEEE Transactions on Systems, Man, and Cybernetics*, *23*, 665–685. doi:10.1109/21.256541

Jones, R. D., Lee, Y. C., Barnes, C. W., Flake, G. W., Lee, K., Lewis, P. S., & Qian, S. (1990). Function approximation and time series prediction with neural networks. In *Proceedings of the International Joint Conference on Neural Networks* (pp. 17-21).

Kaelbling, L. P., Littman, M. L., & Moore, A. W. (1996). Reinforcement learning: A survey. *Journal of Artificial Intelligence Research*, *4*, 237–285.

Karnin, E. D. (1990). A simple procedure for pruning backpropagation trained neural networks. *IEEE Transactions on Neural Networks*, *1*, 239–242. doi:10.1109/72.80236

Kasabov, N. K. Israel, & S. I., Woodford, B. J. (2000). Adaptive, evolving, hybrid connectionist systems for image pattern recognition. In S. K. Pal, A. Ghosh, & M. K. Kundu (Eds.), *Soft computing for image processing.* Heidelberg, Germany: Physica-Verlag.

Kerr, T. H. (1998). Critique of some neural network architectures and claims for control and estimation. *IEEE Transactions on Aerospace and Electronic Systems*, *34*(2), 406–419. doi:10.1109/7.670323

Kim, Y. H., & Lewis, F. L. (1999). Neural network output feedback control of robot manipulators. *IEEE Transactions on Robotics and Automation*, *15*(2), 301–309. doi:10.1109/70.760351

Kitano, H. (1990). Empirical studies on the speed of convergence of neural network training using genetic algorithms. In *Proceedings of the Eleventh International Conference on Artificial Intelligence* (pp. 789-795).

Kohonen, T. (1982). Self-organized formation of topologically correct feature maps. *Biological Cybernetics*, *43*, 59–69. doi:10.1007/BF00337288

Kohonen, T. (1988). *Self-organization and associative memory.* New York, NY: Springer-Verlag.

Kosko, B. (1988). Bidirectional associative memories. *IEEE Transactions on Systems, Man, and Cybernetics*, *18*(1), 49–60. doi:10.1109/21.87054

Kumar, S. (2004). *Neural networks: A classroom approach.* New Delhi, India: Tata McGraw-Hill.

Kwan, C., & Lewis, F. L. (2000). Robust back-stepping control of nonlinear systems using neural networks. *IEEE Transactions on Systems, Man, and Cybernetics. Part A, Systems and Humans*, *30*(6), 753–766. doi:10.1109/3468.895898

Leonard, J., & Kramer, M. A. (1990). Improvement of the backpropagation algorithm for training neural networks. *Computers & Chemical Engineering*, *14*(3), 337–341. doi:10.1016/0098-1354(90)87070-6

Li, F., & Tsien, J. Z. (2009). Clinical implications of basic research: Memory and the NMDA receptors. *The New England Journal of Medicine*, *361*(302).

Lin, J.-S., Cheng, K.-S., & Mao, C.-W. (1996). A fuzzy Hopfield neural network for medical image segmentation. *IEEE Transactions on Nuclear Science*, *43*(4), 2389–2398. doi:10.1109/23.531787

Liu, Z., Bai, Z., Shi, J., & Chen, H. (2007). Image segmentation by using discrete Tchebichef moments and quantum neural network. In *Proceedings of Third International Conference on Natural Computation (ICNC 2007)*.

Lukaszyk, S. (2004). A new concept of probability metric and its applications in approximation of scattered data sets. *Computational Mechanics, 33*, 299–3004. doi:10.1007/s00466-003-0532-2

MacQueen, J. B. (1967). Some methods for classification and analysis of multivariate observations. In *Proceedings of 5th Berkeley Symposium on Mathematical Statistics and Probability* (pp. 281-297).

Mallat, S. G. (1989). A theory for multiresolution signal decomposition: The wavelet representation. *IEEE Transactions on Pattern Analysis and Machine Intelligence, 11*(7), 674–693. doi:10.1109/34.192463

Mandic, D., & Chambers, J. (2001). *Recurrent neural networks for prediction: Learning algorithms, architectures and stability*. New York, NY: John Wiley & Sons. doi:10.1002/047084535X

Martinetz, T., Berkovich, S., & Schulten, K. (1993). Neural-gas network for vector quantization and its application to time-series prediction. *IEEE Transactions on Neural Networks, 4*(4), 558–569. doi:10.1109/72.238311

Matthews, G. G. (1991). *Cellular physiology of nerve and muscle*. Boston, MA: Blackwell Scientific Publications.

McCulloch, W. S., & Pitts, W. H. (1943). A logical calculus of the ideas immanent in nervous activity. *The Bulletin of Mathematical Biophysics, 5*, 115–133. doi:10.1007/BF02478259

Medin, D. L., & Schaffer, M. M. (1978). Context theory of classification learning. *Psychological Review, 85*, 207–238. doi:10.1037/0033-295X.85.3.207

Menneer, T., & Narayanan, A. (1995). *Quantum-inspired neural networks*. Technical report R329. Department of Computer Science, University of Exeter, UK.

Meyer, Y. (1993). *Wavelets: Algorithms and applications*. Philadelphia, PA: SIAM.

Miller, G. F., & Todd, P. M. (1990). Exploring adaptive agency in theory and methods for simulating the evolution of learning. In *Connectionist models*. Morgan Kaufmann.

Miller, G. F., Todd, P. M., & Hegde, S. (1989). Designing neural networks using genetic algorithms. In *Proceedings of the Third International Conference on Genetic Algorithms* (pp. 379-384), Arlington, VA: Morgan Kaufmann.

Moein, S., Monadjemi, S. A., & Moallem, P. (2008). A novel fuzzy-neural based medical diagnosis system. *World Academy of Science, Engineering and Technology, 37*.

Mozer, M. C., & Smolensky, P. (1989). Skeletonization: A technique for trimming the fat from a network via relevance assessment. In D. S. Touretzky (Ed.), *Advances in neural information processing systems, 1*, 107-115, San Mateo, CA: Morgan Kaufmann.

Muhammed, H. H. (2002). A new unsupervised fuzzy clustering algorithm (FC-WINN) using the new weighted incremental neural network. In *Proceedings of WINN 2002*.

Murphy, G. L., & Medin, D. L. (1985). The role of theories in conceptual coherence. *Psychological Review, 92*, 289–316. doi:10.1037/0033-295X.92.3.289

Niranjan, M., & Fallside, F. (1990). Neural networks and radial basis functions in classifying static speech patterns. *Computer Speech & Language, 4*, 275–289. doi:10.1016/0885-2308(90)90009-U

Nosofsky, R. M., & Palmeri, T. J. (1998). A rule-plus-exception model for classifying objects in continuous-dimension spaces. *Psychonomic Bulletin & Review, 5*(3), 345–369. doi:10.3758/BF03208813

Nosofsky, R. M., & Zaki, S. R. (2002). Exemplar and prototype models revisited: Response strategies, selective attention, and stimulus generalization. *Journal of Experimental Psychology. Learning, Memory, and Cognition, 28*(5), 924–940. doi:10.1037/0278-7393.28.5.924

Nossek, J. A., & Roska, T. (1993). Special issue on cellular neural networks. *IEEE Transactions on Circuits and Systems, 40*(3).

Oliker, S., Furst, M., & Maimon, O. (1992). A distributed genetic algorithm for neural network design and training. *Complex Systems, 6,* 459–477.

Opitz, D. W., & Shavlik, J. W. (1994). Using genetic search to refine knowledge-based neural networks. In W. Cohen, & H. Hirsh (Eds.), *Machine learning: Proceedings of the Eleventh International Conference.* San Fransisco, CA: Morgan Kaufmann.

Pal, S. K., & Ghosh, A. (1996). Neuro-fuzzy computing for image processing and pattern recognition. *International Journal of Systems Science, 27*(12), 1179–1193. doi:10.1080/00207729608929325

Pan, L., Zheng, H., & Nahavandi, S. (2003). The application of rough set and Kohonen network to feature selection for object extraction. *In Proceedings of the Second International Conference on Machine Learning and Cybernetics* (pp. 1185-1189).

Paul, V. Y., & Haykin, S. (2001). *Regularized radial basis function networks: Theory and applications.* John Wiley.

Pawlak, Z. (1982). Rough sets. *International Journal of Computer and Information Sciences, 11,* 341–356. doi:10.1007/BF01001956

Peters, J. F., Han, L., & Ramanna, S. (2001). Rough neural computing in signal analysis. *Computational Intelligence, 17*(3), 493–513. doi:10.1111/0824-7935.00160

Peters, J. F., Skowron, A., Han, L., & Ramanna, S. (2000). Towards rough neural computing based on rough membership functions: Theory and application. In *RSCTC (Vol. 2005,* pp. 611–618). LNAI. doi:10.1007/3-540-45554-X_77

Pfister, M. (1995). *Hybrid learning algorithms for neural networks.* PhD Thesis, Free University, Berlin.

Pfister, M., & Rojas, R. (1993). Speeding-up backpropagation – A comparison of orthogonal techniques. *In Proceedings of International Joint Conference on Neural Networks* (pp. 517–523), Japan.

Phung, S. L., & Bouzerdoum, A. (2007). A pyramidal neural network for visual pattern recognition. *IEEE Transactions on Neural Networks, 18*(2), 329–343. doi:10.1109/TNN.2006.884677

Poggio, T., & Girosi, F. (1990). Networks for approximation and learning. *Proceedings of the IEEE, 78*(9), 1484–1487. doi:10.1109/5.58326

Ponnapalli, P. V. S., Ho, K. C., & Thomson, M. (1999). A formal selection and pruning algorithm for feedforward artificial neural network optimization. *IEEE Transactions on Neural Networks, 10*(4), 964–968. doi:10.1109/72.774273

Prechelt, L. (1997). Connection pruning with static and adaptive pruning schedules. *Neurocomputing, 16*(1), 49–61. doi:10.1016/S0925-2312(96)00054-9

Reed, R. (1993). Pruning algorithms - A survey. *IEEE Transactions on Neural Networks, 4*(5), 740–747. doi:10.1109/72.248452

Reichert, H. (1990). *Neurobiologie.* Stuttgart, Germany: Georg Thieme.

Riedmiller, M., & Braun, H. (1993). A direct adaptive method for faster backpropagation learning: The rprop algorithm. In *Proceedings of IEEE International Conference on Neural Networks* (pp. 586-591), San Francisco.

Rojas, R. (1996). *Neural networks: A systematic introduction*. Berlin, Germany: Springer-Verlag.

Rosenblatt, F. (1958). The perceptron: A probabilistic model for information storage and organization in the brain. *Psychological Review, 65*, 386–408. doi:10.1037/h0042519

Ruck, D. W., Rogers, S. K., & Kabrisky, M. (1990). Feature selection using a multilayer perceptron. *Neural Network Computing, 2*(2), 40–48.

Rumelhart, D. E., Hinton, G. E., & Williams, R. J. (1986). Learning internal representations by error propagation. In Rumelhart, D. E., & McClelland, J. L. (Eds.), *Parallel distributed processing: Explorations in the microstructures of cognition* (*Vol. I*, pp. 318–362). Cambridge, MA: MIT Press.

Russo, F. (1999). Hybrid neuro-fuzzy filter for impulse noise removal. *Pattern Recognition, 32*(11), 1843–1855. doi:10.1016/S0031-3203(99)00009-6

Russo, F. (2000). Image filtering using evolutionary neural fuzzy systems. In *Soft computing for image processing* (pp. 23-43). S. K. Pal, A. Ghosh, M. K. Kundu (Eds.), *Proceedings of IEEE International Conference on Industrial Technology Vol. II* (pp. 335-340). Physica-Verlag, Heidelberg.

Salomon, R. (1992). Verbesserung konnektionistischer Lernverfahren. *die nach der Gradientenmethode arbeiten*, PhD Thesis, Technical University of Berlin.

Sanger, T. D. (1994). Neural network learning control of robot manipulators using gradually increasing task difficulty. *IEEE Transactions on Robotics and Automation, 10*, 323–333. doi:10.1109/70.294207

Sanner, R. M., & Slotine, J. J. E. (1992). Gaussian networks for direct adaptive control. *IEEE Transactions on Neural Networks, 3*, 837–863. doi:10.1109/72.165588

Scales, L. E. (1985). *Introduction to Non-linear optimization*. New York, NY: Springer-Verlag.

Sengupta, S. (1995). A comparative study of neural network and regression analysis as modeling tools. In *Proceedings of the Twenty-Seventh Southeastern Symposium on System Theory* (pp. 202-205).

Shanno, D. F. (1990). Recent advances in numerical techniques for large-scale optimization. In S. Miller, & Werbos (Eds.), *Neural networks for control*. Cambridge, MA: MIT Press.

Shashidhara, H. L., Lohani, S., & Gadre, V. M. (2000). Function learning wavelet neural networks. In *Proceedings of IEEE International Conference on Industrial Technology Vol. II* (pp. 335-340).

Shor, P. W. (1997). Polynomial-time algorithms for prime factorization and discrete logarithms on a quantum computer. *SIAM Journal on Computing, 26*(5), 1484–1509. doi:10.1137/S0097539795293172

Sietsma, J., & Dow, R. J. F. (1991). Creating artificial neural networks that generalize. *Neural Networks, 4*, 67–79. doi:10.1016/0893-6080(91)90033-2

Silva, F., & Almeida, L. (1990). Speeding-up backpropagation. In Eckmiller, R. (Ed.), *Advanced neural computers* (pp. 151–156). Amsterdam, The Netherlands: North-Holland.

Simpson, P. K. (1993). Fuzzy min-max neural networks: Part 2-Clustering. *IEEE Transactions on Fuzzy Sets, 1*, 32–45. doi:10.1109/TFUZZ.1993.390282

Sklansky, J., & Vriesenga, M. (1996). Genetic selection and neural modeling of piecewise-linear classifiers. *International Journal of Pattern Recognition and Artificial Intelligence, 10*(5), 587–612. doi:10.1142/S0218001496000360

Smith, J. D., & Minda, J. P. (1998). Prototypes, sage, exemplars and thyme. In *Proceedings of 90th Annual Meeting of the Southern Society for Philosophy and Psychology*, New Orleans, LA. Minda, J. P., & Smith, J. D. (1997). Prototypes in category learning. In *Proceedings of the 38th Annual Meeting of the Psychonomic Society*, Philadelphia, PA.

Snyman, J. A. (2005). *Practical mathematical optimization: An introduction to basic optimization theory and classical and new gradient-based algorithms*. New York, NY: Springer Publishing.

Somervuo, P., & Kohonen, T. (2004). *Self-organizing maps and learning vector quantization for feature sequences*. Netherlands: Kluwer Academic Publishers.

Steane, A. M., & Rieffel, E. G. (2000). Beyond bits: The future of quantum information processing. *IEEE Computers, 33*(1), 38–45. doi:10.1109/2.816267

Steppe, J. M., Bauer, K. W., & Rogers, S. K. (1996). Integrated feature and architecture selection. *IEEE Transactions on Neural Networks, 7*, 1007–1014. doi:10.1109/72.508942

Steward, O. (1989). *Principles of cellular, molecular, and developmental neuroscience*. New York, NY: Springer-Verlag. doi:10.1007/978-1-4612-3540-8

Thompson, R. (1990). *Das Gehirn: Von der Nervenzelle zur Verhaltenssteuerung*. Heidelberg, Germany: Spektrum der Wissenschaft.

Tzeng, Y. C., & Chen, K. S. (1998). A fuzzy neural network to SAR image classification. *IEEE Transactions on Geoscience and Remote Sensing, 36*(1), 301–307. doi:10.1109/36.655339

Vapnik, V., Golowich, S., & Smola, A. (1997). Support vector method for function approximation, regression estimation, and signal processing. In Mozer, M., Jordan, M., & Petsche, T. (Eds.), *Advances in neural information processing systems 9* (pp. 281–287). Cambridge, MA: MIT Press.

Vapnik, V. N. (1995). *The nature of statistical learning theory*. London, UK: Springer-Verlag.

Vapnik, V. N. (1998). *Statistical learning theory*. New York, NY: Wiley.

Ventura, D., & Martinez, T. (1998). Quantum associative memory with exponential capacity. In *Proceedings of the International Joint Conference on Neural Networks* (pp.509-513).

Villmann, T., Hammer, B., Schleif, F.-M., & Geweniger, T. (2005). Fuzzy labeled neural GAS for fuzzy classification. In *Proceedings of the Workshop on Self-Organizing Maps WSOM* (pp. 283-290).

Walter, J., & Ritter, H. (1995). Local PSOMs and Chebyshev PSOMs improving the parameterized self-organizing maps. In F. Fogelman-Soulie (Ed.), *Proceedings of International Conference on Artificial Neural Networks*.

Wang, X. G., Tang, Z., Tamura, H., Ishii, M., & Sun, W. D. (2004). An improved backpropagation algorithm to avoid the local minima problem. *Neurocomputing, 56*, 455–460. doi:10.1016/j.neucom.2003.08.006

Weymaere, N., & Martens, J. P. (1994). On the initialization and optimization of multilayer perceptrons. *IEEE Transactions on Neural Networks, 5*, 738–751. doi:10.1109/72.317726

White, D., & Ligomenides, P. (1993). GANNet: A genetic algorithm for optimizing topology and weights in neural network design. In J. Mira, J. Cabestany, & A. Prieto (Eds.), *New Trends in neural computation* In *Proceedings of International Workshop on Artificial Neural Networks* (pp. 332-327). Berlin, Germany: Springer-Verlag.

Whitley, D., & Bogart, C. (1990). The evolution of connectivity: Pruning neural networks using genetic algorithms. In *Proceedings of International Joint Conference on Neural Networks, 1*, 134-137.

Wikipedia. (n.d.). *Hopfield net*. Retrieved from www.wikipedia.org/wiki/Hopfield_net

Wikipedia. (n.d.). *NMDA receptor*. Retrieved from www.wikipedia.org/wiki/NMDA_receptor

Wikipedia. (n.d.). *Radial base function*. Retrieved from www.wikipedia.org/wiki/Radial_basis_function

Wikipedia. (n.d.). *Radial basis function network*. Retrieved from www.wikipedia.org/wiki/Radial_basis_function_network

Williams, C. P., & Clearwater, S. H. (1998). *Explorations in quantum computing*. New York, NY: Springer-Verlag.

Yu, X., Loh, N. K., & Miller, W. C. (1993). A new acceleration technique for the backpropagation algorithm. In *Proceedings of IEEE International Conference on Neural Networks, Vol. III* (pp. 1157-1161), San Diego, CA.

Zadeh, L. A. (1965). Fuzzy sets. *Information and Control, 8*, 338–353. doi:10.1016/S0019-9958(65)90241-X

Zaknich, A. (2003). *Neural networks for intelligent signal processing*. World Scientific.

Zamparelli, M. (1997). Genetically trained cellular neural networks. *Neural Networks, 10*(6), 1143–1151. doi:10.1016/S0893-6080(96)00128-1

Zeng, X., & Chen, X.-W. (2005). SMO-based pruning methods for sparse least squares support vector machines. *IEEE Transactions on Neural Networks, 16*(6), 1541–1546. doi:10.1109/TNN.2005.852239

Zhou, G., & Si, J. (1999). Subset-based training and pruning of sigmoid neural networks. *Neural Networks, 12*(1), 79–89. doi:10.1016/S0893-6080(98)00105-1

Zimmermann, H. G., Neuneier, R., & Grothmann, R. (2001). Modeling of dynamical systems by error correction neural networks. In Soofi, A., & Cao, L. (Eds.), *Modeling and forecasting financial data: Techniques of nonlinear dynamics*. Kluwer Academic Pub. doi:10.1007/978-1-4615-0931-8_12

Zurada, J. M., Malinowski, A., & Cloete, I. (1994). Sensitivity analysis for minimization of input data dimension for feedforward neural network. In *Proceedings of IEEE International Symposium on Circuits and Systems*.

Zurada, J. M., Malinowski, A., & Usui, S. (1997). Perturbation method for deleting redundant inputs of perceptron networks. *Neurocomputing, 14*(2), 177–193. doi:10.1016/S0925-2312(96)00031-8

## ADDITIONAL READING

Chong, E. K. P., & Zak, S. H. (1996). *An Introduction to Optimization*. New York: Wiley.

Egmont-Petersen, M., de Ridder, D., & Handels, H. (2002). Image processing with neural networks— a review. *Pattern Recognition, 35*, 2279–2301. doi:10.1016/S0031-3203(01)00178-9

Faber, J., & Giraldi, G. Quantum models of artificial neural networks. Retrieved from http://arquivosweb.lncc.br/pdfs/QNN-Review.pdf

Fausett, L. (1994). *Fundamentals of Neural Networks*. USA: Prentice Hall.

Goertzel, B. Quantum Neural Networks. http://goertzel/org/ben/quantnet.html Buhmann, M. D. (2003). *Radial Basis Functions: Theory and Implementations*. Cambridge University Press.

Goldberg, D. E. (1989). *Genetic Algorithms: Search, Optimization and Machine Learning*. New York: Addison-Wesley.

Goswami, J. C., & Chan, A. K. (1999). *Fundamentals of Wavelets-theory, Algorithm, and Applications*. Wiley Inter-Science.

Hagan, M. T., Demuth, H. B., & Beale, M. H. (1996). *Neural Network Design*. Boston, MA: PWS-Kent.

Haykin, S. (1999). *Neural Networks: A Comprehensive Foundation*. Upper Saddle River, NJ: Prentice Hall.

Hopfield, J. J. (1982). Neural networks and physical systems with emergent collective computational abilities. (National Academy of Sciences: Washington, DC, USA.). *Proceedings of the National Academy of Sciences of the United States of America, 79*(8), 2554–2558. doi:10.1073/pnas.79.8.2554

Huang, Y. (2009). Advances in Artificial Neural Networks–Methodological Development and Application. *Algorithms, 2*, 973–1007. doi:10.3390/algor2030973

Kohonen, T. (1988). *Self-Organization and Associative Memory*. New York: Springer-Verlag.

Meyer, Y. (1993). *Wavelets: Algorithms and Applications*. Philadelphia: SIAM.

Pal, S. K., & Ghosh, A. (1996). Neuro-fuzzy computing for image processing and pattern recognition. *International Journal of Systems Science, 27*(12), 1179–1193. doi:10.1080/00207729608929325

Pawlak, Z. (1982). Rough sets. *International Journal of Computer and Information Sciences, 11*, 341–356. doi:10.1007/BF01001956

Rojas, R. (1996). *Neural Networks: A Systematic Introduction*. Berlin: Springer-Verlag.

Vapnik, V. N. (1995). *The Nature of Statistical Learning Theory*. London: Springer-Verlag.

www.wikipedia.org/wiki/Hopfield_net

www.wikipedia.org/wiki/Radial_basis_function

www.wikipedia.org/wiki/Radial_basis_function_network

Zadeh, L. A. (1965). Fuzzy sets. *Information and Control, 8*, 338–353. doi:10.1016/S0019-9958(65)90241-X

## KEY TERMS AND DEFINITIONS

**Artificial Neural Network:** A simulated model of the biological neural network to mimic the functions of the human nervous system.

**Backpropagation:** An iterative algorithm to adjust the interlayer interconnection weights of an artificial neural network architecture based on the minimization of the network errors with time.

**Biological Neuron:** The basic unit of a human nerve cell comprising a cell body, dendrites, axon and synapses.

**Fuzzy Set:** A soft computing tool to explain the ambiguity, vagueness and uncertainty in real world knowledge bases.

**Genetic Algorithm:** A heuristic search methodology for achieving an optimum solution to combinatorial problems.

**Multilayer Perceptron:** A multiple layered artificial neural network model capable of classifying nonlinear datasets.

**Perceptron:** The basic model of an artificial neural network comprising of a single input layer and a single output layer.

**Quantum Neural Networks:** Quantum computing inspired efficient and faster neural network architectures.

**Rough Set:** A soft computing tool to describe imprecise data based on approximations.

**Self-Organizing Feature Map:** A topology preserving artificial neural network architecture capable of learning through self-supervision of incident input features.

**Supervised Learning:** An artificial neural network learning paradigm using a training set of input-output pairs and their relationships in presence of an external supervisor.

**Unsupervised Learning:** An artificial neural network learning paradigm where the network adapts to the incident inputs and its features.

# Chapter 25

# A New Optimization Approach to Clustering Fuzzy Data for Type-2 Fuzzy System Modeling

**Mohammad Hossein Fazel Zarandi**
*Amirkabir University of Technology, Iran*

**Milad Avazbeigi**
*European Centre for Soft Computing, Spain*

## ABSTRACT

*This chapter presents a new optimization method for clustering fuzzy data to generate Type-2 fuzzy system models. For this purpose, first, a new distance measure for calculating the (dis)similarity between fuzzy data is proposed. Then, based on the proposed distance measure, Fuzzy c-Mean (FCM) clustering algorithm is modified. Next, Xie-Beni cluster validity index is modified to be able to valuate Type-2 fuzzy clustering approach. In this index, all operations are fuzzy and the minimization method is fuzzy ranking with Hamming distance. The proposed Type-2 fuzzy clustering method is used for development of indirect approach to Type-2 fuzzy modeling, where the rules are extracted from clustering fuzzy numbers (Zadeh, 1965). Then, the Type-2 fuzzy system is tuned by an inference algorithm for optimization of the main parameters of Type-2 parametric system. In this case, the parameters are: Schweizer and Sklar t-Norm and s-Norm, α-cut of rule-bases, combination of FATI and FITA inference approaches, and Yager parametric defuzzification. Finally, the proposed Type-2 fuzzy system model is applied in prediction of the steel additives in steelmaking process. It is shown that, the proposed Type-2 fuzzy system model is superior in comparison with multiple regressions and Type-1 fuzzy system model, in terms of the minimization the effect of uncertainty in the rule-base fuzzy system models an error reduction.*

## INTRODUCTION

Clustering methods have been used extensively in computer vision and pattern recognition. In recent years, fuzzy clustering methods have gained a lot of attentions because of their advantageous over crisp clustering in that the total commitment of a vector to a given class is not mandatory i.e. an instance could be a member of more than one class at the same time. Also, fuzzy clustering methods have shown their capability to detect not only volume clusters, but also clusters which are actually thin shells i.e. curves and surfaces.

DOI: 10.4018/978-1-61350-429-1.ch025

Most analytic fuzzy clustering approaches are derived from the fuzzy C-means (FCM) algorithm (Celikyilmaz & Turksen, 2007). The FCM uses the probabilistic constraint that the membership of a data point across classes sums to 1. The constraint was used to generate the memberships update equations for an iterative algorithm. However, the memberships resulted from FCM and its variations do not always correspond to the intuitive concept of belonging or compatibility. Moreover, these algorithms usually do not produce good results in confront of noisy data. Melek et al. (2005) summarizes the main problems of classic FCM as:

- In order to get the optimal partitions, initial locations of the clusters' centers should be assigned. Different choices of initial clusters' centers lead to different clusters and The FCM algorithm always converges to local optima.
- There is no well structure, scientific solution for the choice of the weight exponent (m).
- The number of clusters is an argument of FCM and must be known before running FCM. Actually, this is an optimization problem that should be solved before clustering.

The main goal of this research is to present a systematic fuzzy system modeling based on a modified Fuzzy *c*-Mean algorithm that tries to address the mentioned problems of the FCM. For this purpose, a new distance measure is defined for measuring the distance between fuzzy points. The procedure of the proposed fuzzy system modeling approach is as follows:

- Feature Selection.
- Implementation of Type-2 fuzzy clustering algorithm for generation of Type-2 fuzzy membership functions (Castillo O. & Melin P. 2008; Wu, D.& Mendel, J. M., 2007;).

- Modification of Xie-Beni (1991) cluster validity index to optimize the weighting exponent of data ($m\square$) and the number of clusters (c). In order to choose the cluster validity index, some researches have evaluated many cluster validity indexes and Xie-Beni has shown the best performance among them base on the experimental results (Celikyilmaz and Burhan Turksen, 2008; Wu and Mendel, 2009; Weina and Yunjie, 2007).
- Assignment of the most suitable membership functions of the output variable by using of Neural Networks.
- Projection of the output space onto the input spaces to select the most effective input variables.
- Assignment of the most suitable membership functions of the input variables by using Neural Networks.
- Tuning the system by using inference algorithm.

## FUZZY CLUSTER ANALYSIS

In general, the aim of cluster analysis is to partition a given set of data or objects into clusters. The objective of a clustering approach is to minimize the compactness of data within the clusters as well as separation of the clusters. The most popular method of fuzzy clustering is Fuzzy c-Mean (FCM), proposed by Bezdek (1981):

$$\min_{(\mathbf{U},\mathbf{V})}\left\{J_m(\mathbf{U},\mathbf{V}) = \sum_{i=1}^{c}\sum_{k=1}^{n} u_{ik}^m D_{ik}^2\right\} \qquad (1)$$

$$\sum_{i=1}^{c} u_{ik} = 1 \ , \forall k \qquad (2)$$

$$D_{ik}^2 = \left\|\mathbf{x}_k - \mathbf{v}_i\right\|_{\mathbf{A}}^2 \qquad (3)$$

$$\left\| \mathbf{x} \right\|_{\mathbf{A}} = \sqrt{\left\langle \mathbf{x}, \mathbf{x} \right\rangle_{\mathbf{A}}} = \sqrt{\mathbf{x}^T \mathbf{A} \mathbf{x}} \qquad (4)$$

It should be mentioned that in (1) the distance $(D_{ik})$ between $x_k$ and $v_i$ is calculated crisply. Moreover, $m$ is a crisp number. Thus, $u_{ik}$ is crisp.

Our goal is to modify FCM algorithm in such a way that FCM could be applied for fuzzy type-2 numbers. By extending $X$ to fuzzy number $\tilde{X}$ and $V$ to fuzzy number $\tilde{V}$, all $u_{ik}$s have membership functions, themselves. Therefore, the elements in $U_t$ matrix are fuzzy numbers. In other words, by obtaining fuzzy membership values, Type-2 fuzzy clusters could be constructed and for this purpose a suitable fuzzy distance measure should be defined.

## FUZZY SIMILARITY MEASURE

In literature, scholars usually use distance for measuring (dis)similarity among entities. Classic distance between two fuzzy numbers is as follows. Assume $\tilde{A}$ and $\tilde{B}$ are two fuzzy numbers with the related membership functions $u_{\tilde{A}}(x)$ and $u_{\tilde{B}}(y)$. The subtraction of $\tilde{A}$ and $\tilde{B}$ can be calculated as [4]:

$$\forall z \in R \qquad u_{\tilde{A}-\tilde{B}}(z) = \sup_{z=x-y} \min[u_{\tilde{A}}(x), \ u_{\tilde{B}}(y)] \qquad (5)$$

The α-cuts of $\tilde{A}$ and $\tilde{B}$, *i.e.*, $^\alpha\tilde{A}$ and $^\alpha\tilde{B}$, are represented as follows:

$$^\alpha\tilde{A} = [\,^{\alpha-}\tilde{A}\,,\,^{\alpha+}\tilde{A}\,] \quad \text{and} \quad ^\alpha\tilde{B} = [\,^{\alpha-}\tilde{B}\,,\,^{\alpha+}\tilde{B}\,]$$
$$\Rightarrow {}^\alpha(\tilde{A} - \tilde{B}) = [\,^{\alpha-}\tilde{A}\,,\,^{\alpha+}\tilde{A}\,] - [\,^{\alpha-}\tilde{B}\,,\,^{\alpha+}\tilde{B}\,]$$
$$\Rightarrow {}^\alpha(\tilde{A} - \tilde{B}) = [\,^{\alpha-}\tilde{A} - {}^{\alpha+}\tilde{B},\ ^{\alpha+}\tilde{A} - {}^{\alpha-}\tilde{B}\,]$$
$$(6)$$

It should be noted that the distance between two fuzzy numbers should be a fuzzy number. This research presents a new method for calculating the distance between two fuzzy numbers. Assume that there are two fuzzy numbers $\tilde{A}$ and $\tilde{B}$. The distance between these two fuzzy numbers can be defined in Box 1 (equation 7), where $^{\alpha+}\tilde{A}$ is the right hand side of interval corresponding to α-cut of $\tilde{A}$ and $^{\alpha-}\tilde{A}$ is the left hand side of interval corresponding to α-cut of $\tilde{A}$. For obtaining the suitable distance, the α-cuts of equation 7 must be calculated. The proposed fuzzy distance has the following advantages:

- The distance measure produces fuzzy numbers.
- The support of fuzzy distance is positive.
- Distance measure space is convex.

This definition is used in Equation 3 for computing the distance of the centers from each data point. The algorithm terminates when the cluster centers do not change significantly after a few iterations. The criterion for the similarity is calculating the following distance: $\left\| \tilde{V}_t - \tilde{V}_{t-1} \right\| < \varepsilon$.

*Box 1.*

$$^\alpha\tilde{d}(\tilde{A}, \tilde{B}) = \begin{cases} \left[ 0, \max\left( \left| ^{\alpha-}\tilde{A} - {}^{\alpha+}\tilde{B} \right|, \left| ^{\alpha+}\tilde{A} - {}^{\alpha-}\tilde{B} \right| \right) \right] & if \ \tilde{A} \cap \tilde{B} \neq \varnothing \\ \left[ \min\left( \left| ^{\alpha-}\tilde{A} - {}^{\alpha+}\tilde{B} \right|, \left| ^{\alpha+}\tilde{A} - {}^{\alpha-}\tilde{B} \right| \right), \max\left( \left| ^{\alpha-}\tilde{A} - {}^{\alpha+}\tilde{B} \right|, \left| ^{\alpha+}\tilde{A} - {}^{\alpha-}\tilde{B} \right| \right) \right] & if \ \tilde{A} \cap \tilde{B} = \varnothing \end{cases}$$
$$(7)$$

## THE MODIFIED FCM WITH FUZZY NUMBERS

This section presents a modified FCM when the data are fuzzy numbers. First, it is mandatory to define an objective function with fuzzy numbers instead of crisp ones. Iteratively, this function is optimized to obtain final cluster centers and membership functions. For defining such an objective function the $\alpha$-cuts of fuzzy numbers should be defined to let us carry out the calculations. In general, any $\alpha$-cut of a fuzzy number $\tilde{x}_i$, $\forall \tilde{x}_i \in \tilde{X}$ can be defined as follows:

$$
{}^{\alpha}\tilde{x}_i = [{}^{\alpha-}\tilde{x}_i, {}^{\alpha+}\tilde{x}_i]
$$
$$
for \quad i = 1, \ 2, \ ...., \ n \tag{8}
$$

where $\tilde{X}$ is the set of data. The fuzzy partition space ($M_{fc}$) for $\alpha$-cuts is in equation 9, Box 2.

As Bezdek (1981) states, the objective function of FCM could be defined as:

$$
J_{fc}(M,U,V)
$$
$$
= \sum_{i=1}^{n}\sum_{j=1}^{c}(u_{ij})^m d^2(x_i, v_j) \tag{10}
$$

Generalizing (10) for fuzzy numbers results in the following equation:

$$
\tilde{J}_{fc}(M,\tilde{U},\tilde{V})
$$
$$
= \sum_{i=1}^{n}\sum_{j=1}^{c}(\tilde{u}_{ij})^m \tilde{d}^2(\tilde{x}_i, \tilde{v}_j) \tag{11}
$$

where $M$ is the partition space, $\tilde{U}$ is matrix of fuzzy memberships, $\tilde{V}$ is vector of fuzzy cluster centers, $\tilde{x}_i$ is $i$-th fuzzy data, $\tilde{v}_j$ is $j$-th fuzzy cluster center and $\tilde{u}_{ij}$ is membership of the $i$-th data in the $j$-th cluster. To be able to use (11) for clustering fuzzy numbers, it is necessary to transfer the fuzzy numbers into their related $\alpha$-cuts. Substituting $\alpha$-cuts of fuzzy numbers into (11) results in:

$$
{}^{\alpha}\tilde{J}_{fc}(M, {}^{\alpha}\tilde{U}, {}^{\alpha}\tilde{V})
$$
$$
= \sum_{i=1}^{n}\sum_{j=1}^{c}({}^{\alpha}\tilde{u}_{ij})^m \tilde{d}^2({}^{\alpha}\tilde{x}_i, {}^{\alpha}\tilde{v}_j) \ , \forall \alpha \in [0,1] \tag{12}
$$

Using the definition of $\tilde{d}$ in (7), (12) could be written as the equation in Box 3.

$J$ could be simplified as the equation in Box 4.

Since ${}^{\alpha-}u_{ij} > 0$, ${}^{\alpha+}u_{ij} > 0$ and interval of ${}^{\alpha}\tilde{d}$ are positive, $J$ could be rewritten as the equation in Box 5.

And using the law of associativity, the final objective function is in equation 13, Box 6.

*Box 2.*

$$
M_{fc} = \left\{ \begin{array}{l} {}^{\alpha}\tilde{u}_{ij} \in [0, \ 1] \\ \forall i,j \quad \exists \varepsilon > 0 \ ; \quad \sum_{i=1}^{c} {}^{\alpha}\tilde{u}_{ij} = [1-\varepsilon \quad 1+\varepsilon] \ ; \ 0 < \sum_{j=1}^{n} {}^{\alpha-}\tilde{u}_{ij} \ ; \sum_{j=1}^{n} {}^{\alpha+}\tilde{u}_{ij} < n \end{array} \right\} \tag{9}
$$

*Box 3.*

$$
{}^{\alpha}\tilde{J}_{fc}(M, {}^{\alpha}\tilde{U}, {}^{\alpha}\tilde{V}) = \left\{ \begin{array}{ll} \sum_{i=1}^{n}\sum_{j=1}^{c}\left[{}^{\alpha-}\tilde{u}_{ij} \ , \ {}^{\alpha+}\tilde{u}_{ij}\right] \cdot \left[0 \ , \ \left(\max\left(\left|{}^{\alpha-}\tilde{x}_i - {}^{\alpha+}\tilde{v}_j\right|, \left|{}^{\alpha-}\tilde{x}_i - {}^{\alpha+}\tilde{v}_j\right|\right)\right)\right] & if \ \tilde{v}_j \cap \tilde{x}_i \neq \varphi \\ \sum_{i=1}^{n}\sum_{j=1}^{c}\left[{}^{\alpha-}\tilde{u}_{ij} \ , \ {}^{\alpha+}\tilde{u}_{ij}\right] \cdot \left[\left(\min\left(\left|{}^{\alpha-}\tilde{x}_i - {}^{\alpha+}\tilde{v}_j\right|, \left|{}^{\alpha-}\tilde{x}_i - {}^{\alpha+}\tilde{v}_j\right|\right)\right) \ , \ \left(\max\left(\left|{}^{\alpha-}\tilde{x}_i - {}^{\alpha+}\tilde{v}_j\right|, \left|{}^{\alpha-}\tilde{x}_i - {}^{\alpha+}\tilde{v}_j\right|\right)\right)\right] & if \ \tilde{v}_j \cap \tilde{x}_i = \varphi \end{array} \right.
$$

*Box 4.*

$$
{}^{\alpha}\tilde{J}_{fc}(M, {}^{\alpha}\tilde{U}, {}^{\alpha}\tilde{V}) = \sum_{i=1}^{n}\sum_{j=1}^{c}\left[\left[{}^{\alpha-}\tilde{u}_{ij}^{m}, {}^{\alpha+}\tilde{u}_{ij}^{m}\right]\cdot\left[\left(0 \ OR \ \min\left(\left|{}^{\alpha-}\tilde{x}_{i} - {}^{\alpha+}\tilde{v}_{j}\right|, \left|{}^{\alpha+}\tilde{x}_{i} - {}^{\alpha-}\tilde{v}_{j}\right|\right)\right) , \left(\max\left(\left|{}^{\alpha-}\tilde{x}_{i} - {}^{\alpha+}\tilde{v}_{j}\right|, \left|{}^{\alpha+}\tilde{x}_{i} - {}^{\alpha-}\tilde{v}_{j}\right|\right)\right) \right]\right]
$$

*Box 5.*

$$
{}^{\alpha}\tilde{J}_{fc}(M, {}^{\alpha}\tilde{U}, {}^{\alpha}\tilde{V}) = \sum_{i=1}^{n}\sum_{j=1}^{c}\left[\left(0 \ OR \ \min\left(\left|{}^{\alpha-}\tilde{x}_{i} - {}^{\alpha+}\tilde{v}_{j}\right|, \left|{}^{\alpha+}\tilde{x}_{i} - {}^{\alpha-}\tilde{v}_{j}\right|\right)\cdot {}^{\alpha-}\tilde{u}_{ij}^{m}\right) , \left(\max\left(\left|{}^{\alpha-}\tilde{x}_{i} - {}^{\alpha+}\tilde{v}_{j}\right|, \left|{}^{\alpha+}\tilde{x}_{i} - {}^{\alpha-}\tilde{v}_{j}\right|\right)\cdot {}^{\alpha+}\tilde{u}_{ij}^{m}\right) \right]
$$

*Box 6.*

$$
{}^{\alpha}\tilde{J}_{fc}(M, {}^{\alpha}\tilde{U}, {}^{\alpha}\tilde{V}) = \left[\left[\sum_{i=1}^{n}\sum_{\substack{j=1 \\ \tilde{x}\cap\tilde{v}\neq\varnothing}}^{c}\min\left(\left|{}^{\alpha-}\tilde{x}_{i} - {}^{\alpha+}\tilde{v}_{j}\right|, \left|{}^{\alpha+}\tilde{x}_{i} - {}^{\alpha-}\tilde{v}_{j}\right|\right)\cdot {}^{\alpha-}\tilde{u}_{ij}^{m}\right], \left[\sum_{i=1}^{n}\sum_{j=1}^{c}\max\left(\left|{}^{\alpha-}\tilde{x}_{i} - {}^{\alpha+}\tilde{v}_{j}\right|, \left|{}^{\alpha+}\tilde{x}_{i} - {}^{\alpha-}\tilde{v}_{j}\right|\right)\cdot {}^{\alpha+}\tilde{u}_{ij}^{m}\right]\right]
$$

$$(13)$$

The domain of $\tilde{u}_{ij}$ is primary grade of membership functions and the amplitude of $\tilde{u}_{ij}$ is secondary grade of membership functions in Type-2 fuzzy set. Type-2 fuzzy sets would be the results and $\tilde{U}$ can be represented as:

$$
\tilde{U} = \begin{bmatrix} \tilde{u}_{11} & \tilde{u}_{12} & \cdots & \tilde{u}_{1n} \\ \tilde{u}_{21} & \tilde{u}_{22} & \cdots & \tilde{u}_{2n} \\ & & & \\ \tilde{u}_{c1} & \tilde{u}_{c2} & & \tilde{u}_{cn} \end{bmatrix}
$$

$$(14)$$

**Theorem:** The objective function (13) will be minimized for all clusters in $\tilde{X}$ :

If

$$
\min\left(\left|{}^{\alpha-}\tilde{x}_{i} - {}^{\alpha+}\tilde{v}_{k}\right|, \left|{}^{\alpha+}\tilde{x}_{i} - {}^{\alpha-}\tilde{v}_{k}\right|\right) = \left|{}^{\alpha-}\tilde{x}_{i} - {}^{\alpha+}\tilde{v}_{k}\right|
$$

$$(15)$$

Then,

$$
{}^{\alpha-}\tilde{u}_{ik} = \cfrac{1}{\displaystyle\sum_{\substack{j=1 \\ \tilde{x}_{i}\cap\tilde{v}_{j}\neq\varnothing}}^{c}\cfrac{1}{\left(\cfrac{\left|{}^{\alpha-}\tilde{x}_{i} - {}^{\alpha+}\tilde{v}_{k}\right|}{\left|{}^{\alpha-}\tilde{x}_{i} - {}^{\alpha+}\tilde{v}_{j}\right|}\right)^{\frac{2}{m-1}}}}
$$

$$(16)$$

and

$$
{}^{\alpha+}\tilde{u}_{ik} = \cfrac{1}{\displaystyle\sum_{j=1}^{c}\cfrac{1}{\left(\cfrac{\left|{}^{\alpha+}\tilde{x}_{i} - {}^{\alpha-}\tilde{v}_{k}\right|}{\left|{}^{\alpha+}\tilde{x}_{i} - {}^{\alpha-}\tilde{v}_{j}\right|}\right)^{\frac{2}{m-1}}}}
$$

$$(17)$$

If

$$
\min\left(\left|{}^{\alpha-}\tilde{x}_{i} - {}^{\alpha+}\tilde{v}_{k}\right|, \left|{}^{\alpha+}\tilde{x}_{i} - {}^{\alpha-}\tilde{v}_{k}\right|\right) = \left|{}^{\alpha+}\tilde{x}_{i} - {}^{\alpha-}\tilde{v}_{k}\right|
$$

$$(18)$$

Then

$$^{\alpha-}\tilde{u}_{ik} = \frac{1}{\displaystyle\sum_{\substack{j=1 \\ \tilde{x}_i \cap \tilde{v}_j \neq \varnothing}}^{c} \frac{1}{\left(\frac{\left|{}^{\alpha+}\tilde{x}_i - {}^{\alpha-}\tilde{v}_k\right|}{\left|{}^{\alpha+}\tilde{x}_i - {}^{\alpha-}\tilde{v}_j\right|}\right)^{\frac{2}{m-1}}}} \tag{19}$$

And

$$^{\alpha+}\tilde{u}_{ik} = \frac{1}{\displaystyle\sum_{j=1}^{c} \frac{1}{\left(\frac{\left|{}^{\alpha-}\tilde{x}_i - {}^{\alpha+}\tilde{v}_k\right|}{\left|{}^{\alpha-}\tilde{x}_i - {}^{\alpha+}\tilde{v}_j\right|}\right)^{\frac{2}{m-1}}}} \tag{20}$$

Using this theorem, the following Type-2 FCM algorithm is proposed:

**Step 1:** Initiation of the algorithm: Unlabeled fuzzy object data $\tilde{X} = \{\tilde{x}_1, \tilde{x}_2, \ldots, \tilde{x}_n\}$ , $\tilde{x}_i$ is a fuzzy number for $i = 1,2,\ldots,n$

**Step 2:** Choose $c$ such that $1<c<n$; $m>1$; $T=$ iteration limit; $0<\varepsilon=$ termination criterion; Initial fuzzy Vector $\tilde{V}_0$ (initial fuzzy cluster centers) $\tilde{V}_0 = \{\tilde{v}_{01}, \tilde{v}_{02}, \cdots, \tilde{v}_{0c},\}$.

**Step 3:** For $t$=1 to $T$ Calculate $^{\alpha}\tilde{U}_t$ with $^{\alpha}\tilde{V}_t$ $^{\alpha}\tilde{u}_{ij}$ as:

$$If \min\left(\left|{}^{\alpha-}\tilde{x}_i - {}^{\alpha+}\tilde{v}_k\right|, \left|{}^{\alpha+}\tilde{x}_i - {}^{\alpha-}\tilde{v}_k\right|\right) = \left|{}^{\alpha-}\tilde{x}_i - {}^{\alpha+}\tilde{v}_k\right|$$

then

$$^{\alpha-}\tilde{u}_{ik} = \frac{1-\varepsilon}{\displaystyle\sum_{\substack{j=1 \\ \tilde{x}_i \cap \tilde{v}_j \neq \varnothing}}^{c} \frac{1}{\left(\frac{\left|{}^{\alpha-}\tilde{x}_i - {}^{\alpha+}\tilde{v}_k\right|}{\left|{}^{\alpha-}\tilde{x}_i - {}^{\alpha+}\tilde{v}_j\right|}\right)^{\frac{2}{m-1}}}} \tag{21}$$

$$and \, ^{\alpha+}\tilde{u}_{ik} = \frac{1+\varepsilon}{\displaystyle\sum_{j=1}^{c} \frac{1}{\left(\frac{\left|{}^{\alpha+}\tilde{x}_i - {}^{\alpha-}\tilde{v}_k\right|}{\left|{}^{\alpha+}\tilde{x}_i - {}^{\alpha-}\tilde{v}_j\right|}\right)^{\frac{2}{m-1}}}} \tag{22}$$

else if

$$\min\left(\left|{}^{\alpha-}\tilde{x}_i - {}^{\alpha+}\tilde{v}_k\right|, \left|{}^{\alpha+}\tilde{x}_i - {}^{\alpha-}\tilde{v}_k\right|\right) = \left|{}^{\alpha+}\tilde{x}_i - {}^{\alpha-}\tilde{v}_k\right|$$

then,

$$^{\alpha-}\tilde{u}_{ik} = \frac{1-\varepsilon}{\displaystyle\sum_{\substack{j=1 \\ \tilde{x}_i \cap \tilde{v}_j \neq \varnothing}}^{c} \frac{1}{\left(\frac{\left|{}^{\alpha+}\tilde{x}_i - {}^{\alpha-}\tilde{v}_k\right|}{\left|{}^{\alpha+}\tilde{x}_i - {}^{\alpha-}\tilde{v}_j\right|}\right)^{\frac{2}{m-1}}}} \tag{23}$$

And

$$^{\alpha+}\tilde{u}_{ik} = \frac{1+\varepsilon}{\displaystyle\sum_{j=1}^{c} \frac{1}{\left(\frac{\left|{}^{\alpha-}\tilde{x}_i - {}^{\alpha+}\tilde{v}_k\right|}{\left|{}^{\alpha-}\tilde{x}_i - {}^{\alpha+}\tilde{v}_j\right|}\right)^{\frac{2}{m-1}}}} \tag{24}$$

Calculate $\tilde{V}_t$ with $\tilde{U}_t$ as:

$$^{\alpha}\tilde{V}_i = \frac{\displaystyle\sum_{i=1:c}\left[\sum_{k=1:N} ({}^{\alpha}\tilde{u}_{i,k})^m \cdot {}^{\alpha}\tilde{v}_i\right]}{\displaystyle\sum_{i=1:c}\left(\sum_{k=1:N} ({}^{\alpha}\tilde{u}_{i,k})^m\right)} \quad \forall \alpha \in [0,1], \tag{25}$$

$$If, E_t = \left\| defuz(\tilde{V}_{t-1}) - defuz(\tilde{V}_t)\right\| \leq \varepsilon \tag{26}$$

Stop
Else Next $t$

*Box 7.*

$$Lim_{m' \to 1^+} \tilde{I}_{XB} = Lim_{m' \to 1^+} \frac{\sum_{i=1}^{n} \sum_{j=1}^{c} \tilde{u}_{ij}^{m} \tilde{d}^2(\tilde{x}_i, \tilde{v}_j)}{n(\min_{\substack{fuzzy\ ranking \\ i \neq j}} \{\tilde{d}^2(\tilde{v}_i, \tilde{v}_j)\})} = I_{XB}(U, V, X) \tag{29}$$

**Step 4:** Use Prototypes $\tilde{V}_f$ or fuzzy labels $\tilde{U}_f$.

## CLUSTER VALIDITY INDEX

This section tries to extend Xie and Beni (1991) cluster validity index such that it could be used for clustering fuzzy numbers. The Xie-Beni cluster validity index ($I_{XB}$) is defined as:

$$I_{XB} = \frac{\sum_{i=1}^{n} \sum_{j=1}^{c} u_{ij}^{m} d^2(x_i, v_j)}{n(\min_{i \neq j} \{d^2(v_i, v_j)\})} \tag{27}$$

Xie and Beni introduced this index with the compactness (ratio of the total variation) of ($U, V$) and the separation of the vectors $V$. The modified Xie-Beni index is as follows:

$$\tilde{I}_{XB} = \frac{\sum_{i=1}^{n} \sum_{j=1}^{c} \tilde{u}_{ij}^{m} \tilde{d}^2(\tilde{x}_i, \tilde{v}_j)}{n(\min_{i \neq j}^{fuzzy\,ranking} \{\tilde{d}^2(\tilde{v}_i, \tilde{v}_j)\})} \tag{28}$$

In (28) since distances are now fuzzy, all operations must be fuzzy and minimization is carried out by the fuzzy ranking with Hamming-distance. Since the data are fuzzy numbers, we have a degree of fuzziness shown by $m'$ that is different from the degree of fuzziness of clustering ($m$). Studying the behavior of (28) in extremes values of $m'$ (shown by $m$) could be interesting. There exist two extremes for $m'$, in the first extreme, the degree of fuzziness ($m'$) is very close to one. In this case, the behavior of $\tilde{I}_{XB}$ is very similar to the behavior of $I_{XB}$. Thus, the Type-2 fuzzy FCM moves to Type-1 fuzzy FCM in this case (Box 7, equation 29).

In the other extreme, the behavior of $\tilde{I}_{XB}$ is as follows when $m'$ moves to infinity (Box 8, equation 30).

*Box 8.*

$$Lim_{m' \to +\infty} {}^{\alpha}\tilde{I}_{XB} = Lim_{m' \to +\infty} \frac{\sum_{i=1}^{n} \sum_{j=1}^{c} {}^{\alpha}\tilde{u}_{ij}^{m} \tilde{d}^2({}^{\alpha}\tilde{x}_i, {}^{\alpha}\tilde{v}_j)}{n(\min_{\substack{fuzzy\ ranking \\ i \neq j}} \{\tilde{d}^2({}^{\alpha}\tilde{v}_i, {}^{\alpha}\tilde{v}_j)\})}$$

$$Lim_{m' \to +\infty} {}^{\alpha}\tilde{I}_{XB} = Lim_{m' \to +\infty} \frac{\left[ \sum_{i=1}^{n} \sum_{\substack{j=1 \\ \tilde{x} \cap \tilde{v} \neq \varnothing}}^{c} \min\left( \left| {}^{\alpha-}\tilde{x}_i - {}^{\alpha+}\tilde{v}_j \right|, \left| {}^{\alpha+}\tilde{x}_i - {}^{\alpha-}\tilde{v}_j \right| \right) . {}^{\alpha-}\tilde{u}_{ij}^{m}, \sum_{i=1}^{n} \sum_{j=1}^{c} \max\left( \left| {}^{\alpha-}\tilde{x}_i - {}^{\alpha+}\tilde{v}_j \right|, \left| {}^{\alpha+}\tilde{x}_i - {}^{\alpha-}\tilde{v}_j \right| \right) . {}^{\alpha+}\tilde{u}_{ij}^{m} \right]}{n(\min_{\substack{fuzzy\ ranking \\ i \neq j}} \{\tilde{d}^2({}^{\alpha}\tilde{v}_i, {}^{\alpha}\tilde{v}_j)\})}$$

$$\tag{30}$$

*Figure 1. The behavior of $m'$ when it moves to infinity*

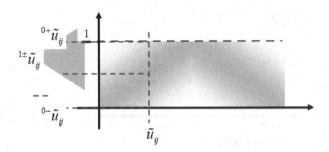

In this case, the worst case is when $^{0+}\tilde{u}_{ij} \to 1$ and $^{0-}\tilde{u}_{ij} \to 0$ (As shown is Figure 1).

Thus, the defuzzification of $\tilde{u}_{ij}$ is:

$$defuz(\tilde{u}_{ij}) = \frac{1}{c} \quad \forall i = 1,...,n \ \& \ j = 1,...,c \tag{31}$$

and

$$\tilde{v}_j = \tilde{v}_k \quad \forall k = 1,...,c \ \& \ j = 1,...,c \tag{32}$$

Therefore, the equation in Box 9.

Therefore, the behavior of $\tilde{I}_{XB}$ for large values of $m'$ is not predictable. From above calculations, it could be concluded that these extremes do not produce good results. Obviously increasing $m'$, results in decreasing the index for the same cluster number. It is also clear that finding the appropriate value for $m'$ is an optimization problem

and its optimal value along the $c$ will result in minimization of objective function of the fuzzy clustering which is the final goal of the clustering.

Next, we use the results of Type-2 fuzzy cluster analysis for Type-2 fuzzy system modeling. In general, two main problems of indirect approach to fuzzy modeling are: structure identification (determination of the number of rules) and parameter identification (determination of the most suitable membership functions for inputs and output(s) of a system). The next steps of the proposed Type-2 fuzzy system modeling are as follows:

1. Variable selection for the rules: In this paper, we implement Fukuyama-Sugeno method of variable selection (Fukuyama and Sugeno, 1988) (the variable selection algorithm).
2. Fuzzification of inputs and output(s)
3. Determination of the membership functions of the output(s): We have used Neural Network toolbox of MATLAB software.

*Box 9.*

$$Lim_{m'\to+\infty} \ ^{\alpha}\tilde{I}_{XB} = Lim_{m'\to+\infty} \frac{\left[\sum_{i=1}^{n}\sum_{\substack{j=1 \\ \tilde{x}\cap\tilde{v}\neq\varnothing}}^{c} \min\left(\left|^{\alpha-}\tilde{x}_i - ^{\alpha+}\tilde{v}_j\right|, \left|^{\alpha+}\tilde{x}_i - ^{\alpha-}\tilde{v}_j\right|\right).0 \ , \sum_{i=1}^{n}\sum_{j=1}^{c}\max\left(\left|^{\alpha-}\tilde{x}_i - ^{\alpha+}\tilde{v}_j\right|, \left|^{\alpha+}\tilde{x}_i - ^{\alpha-}\tilde{v}_j\right|\right).1\right]}{n.0}$$

$$\Rightarrow Lim_{m'\to+\infty} \ ^{\alpha}\tilde{I}_{XB} = Lim_{m'\to+\infty} \frac{\left[0 \ , \sum_{i=1}^{n}\sum_{j=1}^{c}\max\left(\left|^{\alpha-}\tilde{x}_i - ^{\alpha+}\tilde{v}_j\right|, \left|^{\alpha+}\tilde{x}_i - ^{\alpha-}\tilde{v}_j\right|\right)\right]}{0} = \frac{0}{0} \ or \ \infty$$

4. Determination of the most critical input variables: The output space is projected onto the input spaces to select the most critical inputs.
5. Assignment of the inputs membership functions: The membership functions of inputs are assigned by estimation using Neural Network toolbox of MATLAB software.
6. Tuning the system: Finally, the system is tuned by optimization of the parameters of $t$-norm, $s$-norm, defuzzifcation and combination of FATI (First-Aggregate-Then-Infer) and FITA (First-Infer-Then-Aggregate).

## IMPLEMENTATION

The proposed approach is tested by using a steel plant data. Implementing the Type-2 FCM ap-

proach, we obtain a fuzzy model with 12 rules. The rule base is shown in Figure 2.

After obtaining the mode, the model's parameters should be tuned. Here, we use Schweizer and Sklar T-Norm and S-Norm operators ($p$, $q$), α-cut of rule base (α), Yager diffuzification method ($\beta$), and parameter $\gamma$ for combination of FATI and FITA. Optimization process is performed according to the following constraints:

$$0 \leq p \leq 1$$
$$0 \leq \alpha \leq 1$$
$$1 \leq \gamma \leq \infty$$
$$0 \leq q \leq 1$$
$$1 \leq \beta \leq \infty$$

Using the optimization toolbox of MATLAB, the optimal values of $p, q, \alpha, \beta$ and $\gamma$ are as follows:

p=0.4, q=0.8, α=0.4, β=3, γ=2.3

*Figure 2. Second type-2 fuzzy rule base*

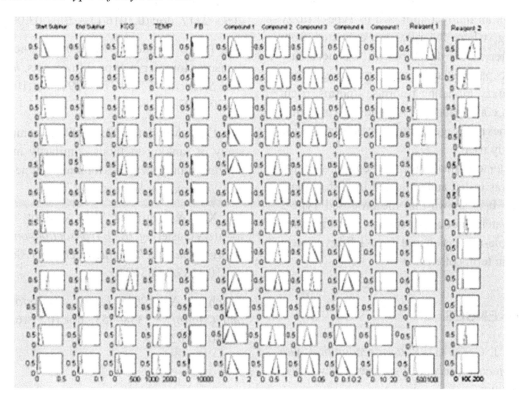

*Table 1. Comparison of models*

| Modeling Method | Error |
|---|---|
| The error of multiple regression | 0.061229 |
| The error of type-1 fuzzy system | 0.05129 |
| The error of type-2 fuzzy system | 0.05116 |

The results of multiple regressions, fuzzy type-1 model (Mamdani method) and the fuzzy Type-2 method are shown on Table 1. The following results show that the error of the proposed type-2 fuzzy models is less than the other methods.

## CONCLUSION

In this research, first a new distance measure for calculating the (dis)similarity between fuzzy data is proposed. Then, the fuzzy *c*-Mean clustering is modified base on the proposed distance measure. Xie-Beni validity index is also extended to be used for type-2 clustering approach. Finally, the proposed Type-2 fuzzy clustering method is used in an indirect approach to Type-2 fuzzy modeling, where the rules are extracted from data. After model development, it is necessary to tune its parameters by an inference algorithm. In our fuzzy modeling t-norms, s-norms, α-cut concepts, combination of FATI and FITA inference approaches and Yager parametric defuzzification are mainly used.

In order to evaluate the proposed approach, the model was tested and validated by a steel plant data set. It is shown that the proposed Type-2 fuzzy system model is superior in comparison to multiple-regression and Type-1 fuzzy system models in terms of error.

## REFERENCES

Bezdek, J. C. (1981). *Pattern recognition with fuzzy objective function algorithms*. New York, NY: Plenum.

Castillo, O., & Melin, P. (2008). *Type-2 fuzzy logic theory and applications*. Berlin, Germany: Springer-Verlag.

Celikyilmaz, A., & Burhan Turksen, I. (2007). Fuzzy functions with support vector machines. *Information Science, 177*, 5163–5177. doi:10.1016/j.ins.2007.06.022

Celikyilmaz, A., & Burhan Turksen, I. (2008). Validation criteria for enhanced fuzzy clustering. *Pattern Recognition, 29*, 97–108. doi:10.1016/j.patrec.2007.08.017

Melek, W. W., Goldenberg, A. A., & Emami, M. R. (2005). A fuzzy noise-rejection data partitioning algorithm. *International Journal of Approximate Reasoning, 38*, 1–17. doi:10.1016/j.ijar.2004.03.002

Mendel, J. M. (2007). Type-2 fuzzy sets and systems: An overview. *IEEE Computational Intelligence Magazine, 2*, 20–29.

Weina, W., & Yunjie, Z. (2007). On fuzzy cluster validity indices. *Fuzzy Sets and Systems, 158*, 2095–2117. doi:10.1016/j.fss.2007.03.004

Wu, D., & Mendel, J. M. (2007). Uncertainty measures for interval type-2 fuzzy sets. *Information Sciences, 177*, 5378–5393. doi:10.1016/j.ins.2007.07.012

Wu, D., & Mendel, J. M. (2009). A comparative study of ranking methods, similarity measures and uncertainty measures for interval type-2 fuzzy sets. *Information Sciences, 177*(23).

Xie, X. L., & Benni, G. (1991). A validity measure for fuzzy clustering. *IEEE Transactions on Pattern Analysis and Machine Intelligence, 11*, 841–847. doi:10.1109/34.85677

Zadeh, L. A. (1965). Fuzzy sets. *Information and Control, 8*, 338–353. doi:10.1016/S0019-9958(65)90241-X

# Chapter 26
# Estimation of MIMO Wireless Channels Using Artificial Neural Networks

**Kandarpa Kumar Sarma**
*Indian Institute of Technology, India*

**Abhijit Mitra**
*Indian Institute of Technology, India*

## ABSTRACT

*Artificial Neural Network (ANN) is a non-parametric statistical tool which can be used for a host of pattern classification and prediction problems. It has excelled in diverse areas of application ranging from character recognition to financial problems. One of these areas, which have ample of scope of application of the ANN, is wireless communication. Especially, in segments like Multi-Input Multi-Output (MIMO) wireless channels ANNs have seldom been used for problems like channel estimation. Very few reported work exists in this regard. This work is related to the application of ANN for estimation of a MIMO channel of a wireless communication set-up. As Orthogonal Frequency Division Multiplexing (OFDM) is becoming an option to tackle increased demands of higher data rates by the modern generation mobile communication networks, a MIMO-OFDM system assisted by an ANN based channel estimation can offer better quality of service (QoS) and higher spectral efficiency.*

## 1. INTRODUCTION

The proliferation of mobile communication networks over the last few years have congested the available spectrum, raised the levels of intersymbol interference (ISI) and have threatened to degrade quality of service (QoS) thereby necessitating the

search for innovative solutions to increase overall efficiency (Bolcskei & Zurich, 2006). Additionally there is a constant demand for higher bandwidth, increased data rates, lower cost, greater coverage etc for which the mobile networks are creating congestion in the available spectrum. In such a situation Multiple-Input Multiple-Output (MIMO) wireless technology seems to be able to meet these demands by offering increased spectral efficiency.

DOI: 10.4018/978-1-61350-429-1.ch026

MIMO architectures are useful for combined transmit receive diversity. When used in parallel mode of transmission, MIMO systems offer high data rates in a narrow bandwidth. MIMO systems, characterized by multiple antenna elements at the transmitter and receiver, have demonstrated the potential for increased capacity in rich multipath environments.

OFDM is gradually emerging as the chosen modulation technique for wireless communications nowadays. It is being adopted as one of the alternatives to meet the demands of high data rates by present day mobile communication networks. OFDM uses non-overlapping adjacent channel to increase spectral efficiency and allows multiple carriers be used to transmit different symbols with spectral overlap while ensuring co-existence of nearby signals due to orthogonality (Bolcskei & Zurich, 2006) to (Jiang & Hanzo, 2007).

The combination MIMO-OFDM together provides greater spatial multiplexing gain, and improved link reliability due to antenna diversity. This is because MIMO channel becomes frequency selective for high data rate transmission and OFDM can transform such frequency selective channels into a set of parallel frequency flat MIMO channels. Together the combination reduces receiver design complexity. Also OFDM is effective in dealing with multipath fading and ISI (Yang, 2005). Yet channel estimation remains a challenging issue for MIMO-OFDM systems.

Two common practices of channel estimation in MIMO - OFDM systems are pilot-based channel estimation and blind channel estimation. Pilot-based estimation techniques use least-squares (LS), minimum mean-square error (MMSE) and linear minimum mean square error (LMMSE) estimators. The pilot - based channel estimation, by requiring pilot symbol bits to be inserted as training sequence along with OFDM blocks, causes waste of bandwidth. Blind estimation techniques don't require training sequences but are extremely computationally intensive (Colieri et al., 2002) (Gacanin, Takaoka, & Adachi, 2005).

Innovative means are being formulated to tackle channel estimation and improve performance of mobile systems.

One of the viable means of better channel estimation is the use of soft-computing tools like the Artificial Neural Network (ANN)s (Jiang & Hanzo, 2007). An ANN can be used to provide an estimate of the channel which may help to mitigate some of the deficiencies of multi-user transmission. The ANN can be trained to make it robust enough to deal with multiple channel types and improve Bit Error Rate (BER)s. It can also be configured for applications like noise cancellation and equalization for a host of digital modulation schemes used in wireless communication. The work is related to an ANN based channel estimation of a MIMO system under Rayleigh and Rician multipath fading environment transmitting data using OFDM. The work is also extended to noise cancellation and equalization for digital modulation schemes like BPSk and QPSK in multipath fading environment. Rayleigh multipath fading is a common occurrence where the signal suffers multiple reflections due to high rise structures while Rician multipath fading is observed in situations where the LOS component is prominent. The work considers the use of an ANN to tackle a Rayleigh and Rician multipath faded channel to estimate the channel coefficients. The advantage of the schemes is that no pilot symbol bits are required to be inserted with the MIMO-OFDM transmission which can contribute towards preserving bandwidth and increasing spectral efficiency. The work also has the provision to use the complete learning ability of the ANNs for enhancing performance of a MIMO-OFDM transmission over multipath faded channels. The computational requirements are also not as stringent as blind estimation techniques. The work can also be extended to symbol recovery and user detection in the MIMO-OFDM framework. Some of the related works in MIMO-OFDM and relevant areas are (Bolcskei & Zurich, 2006) to (Ling & Xianda, 2007).

The work also explores the possibility to develop two architectures for dealing with time-varying patterns of input data especially relevant for wireless channels. Since, the results derived from the ANN based MIMO channel estimate, doesn't consider the time varying nature of wireless channel, the ANN configurations are varied and two modified architectures proposed. The modified forms are multi layer perceptron (MLP) s with temporal characteristics. The connecting weights between the neurons of the MLP are replaced by ARMA (Auto Regressive Moving Average) links. These are updated during the training stage with the aim to reach the desired goal.

The work is intended for slow fading wireless channels for applications with in indoor networks.

# 2. CHARACTERISTICS OF MULTIPATH CHANNEL

Wireless communication utilizes modulation of electromagnetic (radio) waves with a carrier frequency varying from a few hundred megahertz to several gigahertz depending on the system. Therefore, the behavior of the wireless channel is a function of the radio propagation effects of the environment. In such an environment the following may happen (Rappaport, 2004) (Proakis, 2001):

Multiple delayed receptions of the transmitted signals due to the reflections of buildings, hills, cars and other obstacles, etc.

Absence of a line-of-sight (LOS) path and prominence of non-LOS (NLOS) components.

Varying attenuation, time delay, phase shift etc in each path.

Constructive and destructive addition of the constituent paths due to multiple phase shifts resulting in fluctuations in the signal strength.

These factors act together to give rise to a phenomenon known as fading. The stochastic nature observed in wireless channels can be described by the Rayleigh and Rician fading which represent the absence and presence of a LOS

component respectively. A generalized model is often represented by Nakagami faded channel (Rappaport, 2004).

## 2.1 Statistical Models for Multipath Fading Channels

Several multipath models have been suggested to explain the observed statistical nature of a wireless channel. Clarke suggested a model where the statistical characteristics of the electro-magnetic fields of the received signal at the mobile handset are deduced from scattering. The model assumes a fixed transmitter and a vertically polarized antenna. The field incident on the mobile antenna is assumed to comprise of N azimuthal plane waves with arbitrary carrier phases, arbitrary azimuthal angles of arrival and each wave having equal average amplitude. The average amplitude assumption is based on the fact that in absence of a direct line-of-sight path, the scattered components arriving at a receiver will experience similar attenuation over small-scale distances (Rappaport, 2004).

The vertically polarized plane waves arriving at the mobile handset have E and H field components which based on the analysis by Rice can be expressed in an in-phase and quadrature form as

$$
\begin{aligned}
E_z(t) &= T_c(t)\cos(2\pi f_c t) \\
&- T_s(t)\sin(2\pi f_c t)
\end{aligned}
\tag{1}
$$

where

$$
T_c(t) = E_0 \sum_{n=1}^{N} C_n \cos(2\pi f_n t + \varphi_n)
\tag{2}
$$

and

$$
T_s(t) = E_0 \sum_{n=1}^{N} C_n \sin(2\pi f_n t + \varphi_n)
\tag{3}
$$

*Figure 1. Clark-Gans fading model using QAM and RF-Doppler Filter (Rappaport, 2004)*

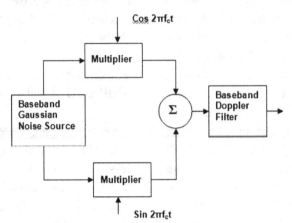

The first approach to model multipath fading channels suggested by Clark and Gans is shown in Figure 1.

The second approach uses a baseband Doppler Filter in the in-phase and quadrature fading branches generated by two independent Gaussian Noise Sources is represented by Figure 2.

Smith modified the above approaches and instead adopted a frequency domain representation to model the fading channel (Rappaport, 2004). Several Rayleigh fading simulators maybe used together with variable gains and time delays to produce frequency selective fading effects so common in wireless channels. Both flat and frequency selective fading conditions maybe simu-

lated (Figure 3) depending upon gain and time delay settings.

Suppose at the receiver, there are two path signals, sin(t) and sin(t −π). Therefore,

$$\sin(t) + \sin(t - \pi) = 0 \qquad (4)$$

Consider the transmission of the baseband signal

$$s_b(t) = \mathrm{Re}\{s(t)e^{j2\pi f_c t}\} \qquad (5)$$

where s(t) is the equivalent low-pass signal (also called as "complex envelope") and $f_c$ is the carrier frequency. Assuming that the channel consists of

*Figure 2. Clark-Gans fading model using QAM and Baseband-Doppler Filter (Rappaport, 2004)*

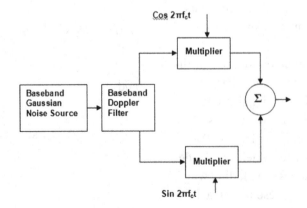

*Figure 3. Simulating frequency selective effects (Rappaport, 2004)*

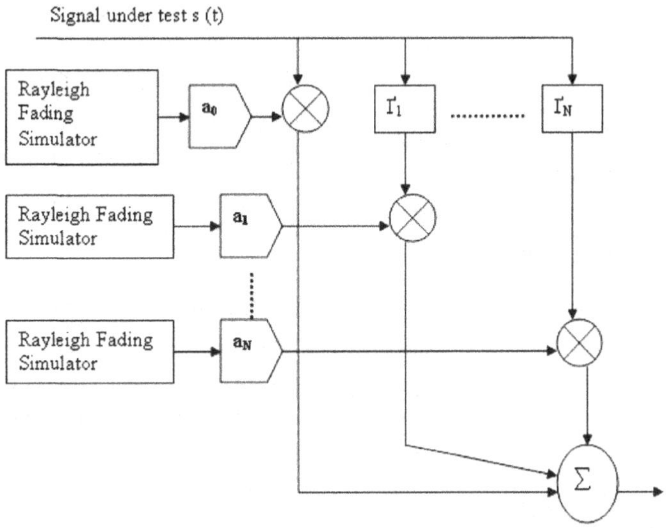

multiple paths, the received band-pass signal and its low-pass equivalent can be modeled as

$$r_b(t) = \text{Re}\{r(t)e^{j2\pi f_c t}\} \qquad (6)$$

with

$$r(t) = \sum \rho_k(t)e^{j\varphi_k(t)}s(t - \tau_k(t)) + \eta(t) \qquad (7)$$

where

$\rho_k(t) : attenuation\ of\ the\ k^{th}\ path$

$\varphi_k(t) : phase-shift\ of\ the\ k^{th}\ path$

$\varphi_k(t) = 2\pi f_k t - 2\pi(f_c + f_k)\tau_k(t)$

$f_k(t) : Doppler\ frequency\ of\ the\ k^{th}\ path$

$\tau_k(t) : Delay\ of\ the\ k^{th}\ path$

in

$$\varphi_k(t) = 2\pi f_k t - 2\pi(f_c + f_k)\tau_k(t)$$

The first term results from the Doppler shift. The second term is the phase shift caused by the delay $\tau_k(t)$. The various delayed paths overlap and cause ISI. Different frequency components of the transmitted signal experience different fading known as frequency-selective fading. Delay spread arises from broadband transmission also creates frequency-selective fading. When the receiver and transmitter are in relative motion with constant speed, the received signal is subjected to a constant frequency shift leading to Doppler spread and produces time-selective fading. It also creates the largest of the frequency shifts of the various paths. Coherent time is defined as the inverse of Doppler spread and used as a measure of the signal duration at which time-selectivity becomes relevant.

## 2.2 Rayleigh Multipath Fading Channels

A large part of the NLOS nature of multipath channel is modeled by the Rayleigh fading. The received signal can be modeled as

$$r(t) = \alpha(t)s(t) + \eta(t) \qquad (8)$$

where s(t) is the signal,

$$\alpha(t) = x(t) + jy(t) = a(t)e^{j\varphi(t)} \qquad (9)$$

is a zero-mean complex Gaussian. Denoting x and y as samples taken from x(t) and y(t) where x: $\aleph(0, \sigma^2)$ and y: $\aleph(0, \sigma^2)$. Then $\alpha$ is described by a zero mean complex Gaussian random variable

$$f(x,y) = \frac{1}{2\pi\sigma^2} \exp(-\frac{x^2 + y^2}{2\sigma^2}) \qquad (10)$$

Fading envelop (amplitude), $a = \sqrt{x^2 + y^2}$

Fading phase, $\varphi = \arctan\left(\dfrac{y}{x}\right)$.

Let x = a cosφ and y = a sinφ.

Using transformation formula between random variable pairs (x, y) and (a, φ)

$$f_{a,\varphi}(a,\varphi) = \left| J(a,\varphi) \right|$$
$$\times f_{x,y}(x,y) \Big|_{x=a\cos\varphi} \Big|_{y=a\sin\varphi} \qquad (11)$$

where J(.) is the Jacobian of the transformation.

From the above Rayleigh distribution maybe given as

$$f_a(a) = \int\limits_0^{2\pi} f_{a,\varphi}(a,\varphi)d\varphi$$
$$= \frac{a}{\sigma^2} \exp(-\frac{a^2}{2\sigma^2}) \qquad (12)$$

This is known as Rayleigh fading and is typically encountered in land-mobile channels in urban areas where there are many obstacles like high-rise structures and other obstructions which make LOS paths rare. Multipath channel modeled by Rayleigh fading can be simulated using the Clarke-Gans model (Rappaport, 2004) assuming mobility of a receiver handset. Such a simulation

is necessary to generate the data set required to train the ANNs for channel estimation.

## 2.3 Rician Multipath Fading Channels

The variation in signal characteristics observed in wireless channels where a large LOS component is present due to absence of high rise structures is modeled by the Rician fading. If a line-of-sight (LOS) path is present (or one path which dominates the rest), the Gaussian approximation usually preferred needs to be reconsidered. Without loss of generality, let the LOS path be assumed to be the first path.

$$\alpha = \sum_{k=1}^{N} \rho e^{j\theta_k} = \rho_1 e^{j\theta_1} + \sum_{k=2}^{N} \rho e^{j\theta_k}$$
$$= x_1 + jy_1 + \tilde{x} + j\tilde{y} \qquad (13)$$

$$\alpha = x_1 + j\tilde{x}(y_1 + \tilde{y}) \qquad (14)$$

Assuming $x_1$ and $y_1$ as fixed, $\alpha$ can be modeled as a non-zero mean complex Gaussian. Let these be assigned the values $\mu_x$ and $\mu_y$ respectively so that x: $\aleph(\mu_x, \sigma^2)$ and y: $\aleph(\mu_y, \sigma^2)$. Thus,

$$f_{x,y}(x,y)$$
$$= \frac{1}{2\pi\sigma^2} \exp[-\frac{(x-\mu_x)^2 + (y-\mu_y)^2}{2\sigma^2}] \qquad (15)$$

The pdfs for a and φ ie. $f_a$(a) and $f_\varphi$(φ) maybe found as below:

Let

x = a cos φ and

y = a sin φ.

Using transformation formula between random variable pairs (x, y) and (a, φ)

$$f_{a,\varphi}(a,\varphi) = \left|J(a,\varphi)\right| \\ \times f_{x,y}(x,y)\Big|_{x=a\cos\varphi}\Big|_{y=a\sin\varphi}$$

(16)

It can be finally written as

$$f_a(a) = \frac{a}{\sigma^2}\exp(-\frac{a^2+s^2}{2\sigma^2})I_0(\frac{as}{\sigma^2})$$

(17)

with the zero-order modified Bessel's function of the first kind is given as

$$I_0(x) = \frac{1}{2\pi}\int_0^{2\pi}\exp(-x\cos\theta)d\theta$$

(18)

This is known as Rician fading and is typically encountered in land mobile channels in areas with less high rise structures and in satellite channels where a direct component is more probable. The Rician parameter maybe defined as the ratio of power in the LOS and scattered components given as

$$K = \frac{s^2}{2\sigma^2}$$

(19)

Rician fading channels nearly approach Rayleigh Fading channel behaviour when there is no LOS component. Rician fading channels similarly generate Dirac impulse and show no fading when LOS component dominates. A conceptual implementation of the Rician Fading can be carried out by using the considerations given in (Rappaport, 2004) (Proakis, 2001).

## 3. MIMO CHANNEL CAPACITY AND MODELLING FADING CHARACTERISTICS

Information theory enunciated by Claude Shannon (1948) showed that by more intelligent coding of the information, communication can be done at a strictly positive rate but at the same time with as small an error probability as desired (Ogawa et al., 2003). Channel modeling of MIMO-OFDM systems involve the study of capacity limits of a MIMO-channel (Figure 4) compared to a SIMO

*Figure 4. Capacity of a MIMO system with increase in Tx-Rx pairs*

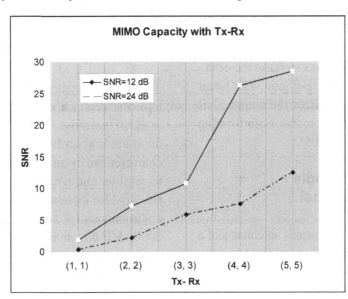

(Single Input Multiple Output) and MISO (Multiple Input Single Output) channel (Collados & Gorokhov, 2005).

## 3.1 Single Input Multiple Output (Simo) Channel

A SIMO channel with one transmit antenna and L receive antennas can be defined as

$$y_l[m] = h_l x[m] + w_l[m]$$
$$with \ l = 1, 2, 3, .....L$$

(20)

where $h_t$ is the fixed complex channel gain from the transmit antenna to the L-[th] receive antenna, and $w_1[m]$ with $C\,N\,(0, N0)$ is additive Gaussian noise independent across antennas. Here channel transfer function coefficients are $h = [h_1, h_2, h_3, ....... h_L]^t$. The output y may also be expressed as

$$\tilde{y}[m] = h * y[m]$$

(21)

If P is the average energy per transmit symbol, the capacity of this channel is therefore

$$C = \log(1 + \frac{P \|h\|^2}{N_0})$$
$$bits \ / \ s \ / \ Hz$$

(22)

Multiple receive antennas increase the effective SNR and provide a power gain. The linear combining (eq. 22) maximizes the output SNR and is sometimes called receive beamforming (Collados & Gorokhov, 2005).

## 3.2 Multiple Input Single Output (MISO) Channel

A MISO channel with L transmit antennas and a single receive antenna can be expressed as

$$y[m] = h * x[m] + w[m]$$
$$bits \ / \ s \ / \ Hz$$

(23)

where $h = [h_1, h_2, h_3, ........h_L]^t$ are the channel coefficients and hl is the (fixed) channel gain from transmit antenna l to the receive antenna. There is a total power constraint of P across the transmit antennas, the capacity of the MISO channel is given by eq. (22).

Intuitively, the transmission strategy maximizes the received SNR by having the received signals from the various transmit antennas add up in-phase (coherently) and by allocating more power to the transmit antenna with the better gain. This strategy, aligning the transmit signal in the direction of the transmit antenna array pattern, is called transmit beamforming. Through beamforming, the MISO channel is converted into a scalar AWGN channel and thus any code which is optimal for the AWGN channel can be used directly. In both the SIMO and the MISO examples the benefit from having multiple antennas is a power gain. To get a gain in degrees of freedom, multiple transmit and receive antennas are required - a setup supported

by MIMO. Both transmitter and receiver side diversity gain helps in generating high data rates in MIMO systems- a fact used as an advantage in MIMO-OFDM systems.

## 3.3 Modeling a MIMO System

MIMO architectures are useful for combined transmit receive diversity. When used in parallel mode of transmission, MIMO systems offer high data rates in a narrow bandwidth. MIMO systems, characterized by multiple antenna elements at the transmitter and receiver, have demonstrated the potential for increased capacity in rich multipath environments (Wang, Zhengdao, & Giannakis, 2000). MIMOs approach is to transmit and receive two or more data streams through a single radio channel. This means the system can deliver two

*Figure 5. MIMO scheme*

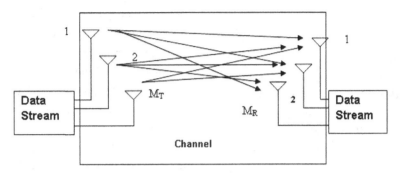

or more times the data rate per channel (Bocquet, Hayashi, & Sajau, 2004). By allowing for simultaneous transmission of multiple data streams (Figure 5), MIMO multiplies wireless data capacity without using additional frequency spectrum. Peak throughput in MIMO systems increases by a factor equal to the number of signal streams transmitted in the radio channel. Because there are multiple signals, each of which is transmitted from a different radio and antenna, MIMO signals are sometimes called multidimensional signals. Conventional radio signals are referred to as one-dimensional signals because they only transmit one data stream over the radio channel even if multiple antennas are used (Hijazi, 2006).

A *m x n* linear MIMO system with outputs $y_1$, $y_2$, … $y_n$ and inputs $x_1, x_2, x_3,.. x_m$ can be expressed as (Rappaport, 2004)

$$y_1 = f_1(x_1, x_2, ....x_n)$$
$$y_2 = f_2(x_1, x_2, ....x_n)$$
$$...$$
$$y_n = f_n(x_1, x_2, ....x_n)$$

where f(.) represents a transformation function at the receiver end. The MIMO channel input-output relationship maybe written as (Wang, Zhengdao, & Giannakis, 2000):

$$x_n = H_n(s_n) + v(n)$$

where $x$ is an Mx1 vector with $x_i(n)$, i=1, 2, ….M as the elements; *s(n)* is an N x 1 vector of the input symbols; *v(n)* is an additive noise vector; *H(n)* is an M x N channel matrix with elements $H_{ij}(n)$, i=1, 2, ….M, j=1, 2, ….N denoting the transfer function between the j[th] transmit and i[th] receive antenna.

Unlike traditional means of increasing throughput, MIMO systems do not increase bandwidth in order to increase throughput. They simply exploit the spatial dimension by increasing the number of unique spatial paths between the transmitter and receiver. However, to ensure that the channel matrix is invertible, MIMO systems require an environment rich in multipath. This has significant ramifications as it suggests that operators can provide broadband services within the current spectrum. Staying at the current carrier frequencies implies that (Bocquet, Hayashi, & Sajau, 2004):

- Signals can propagate further thus reducing the cost of overall network deployment and
- RF subsystems can be built using today's well understood and inexpensive processes.

## 3.4 Performance Gains in a MIMO Channel

The capacity of an $n_t$ x $n_r$ i.i.d. Rayleigh fading MIMO channel H with receiver channel side information (CSI) is:

$$C_{nn}(SNR) = E[\log \det (I_{nt} + \frac{SNR}{n_t} HH^*)]$$

$$(24)$$

At high SNR, the capacity is approximately equal (up to an additive constant) to high SNR, the capacity is approximately equal (up to an additive constant) to $n_{min} log (SNR)$ bits/s/Hz.

At low SNR, the capacity is approximately equal to $n_r SNRlog_2 e$ bits / s / Hz, so only a receive beamforming gain is realized. In an n x n MIMO channel, the capacity increases linearly with n over the entire SNR range. With channel knowledge at the transmitter, an additional $n_t$ / $n_r$-fold transmit beamforming gain can be realized with an additional power gain from temporal spatial water-filling at low SNR (Collados & Gorokhov, 2005).

### 3.5 MIMO Channel Models

Accurate modeling of MIMO channels is an important prerequisite for MIMO system design, simulation, and deployment. Especially analytical MIMO channel models that describe the impulse response (or equivalently the transfer function) of the channel between the elements of the antenna arrays at both link ends by providing analytical expressions for the channel matrix are very popular for developing MIMO algorithms in general. Most popular examples include the Kronecker model, the Weichselberger model and the virtual channel representation. The Kronecker model became popular because of its simple analytic treatment. However, the main drawback of this model is that it forces both link ends to be separable, irrespective of whether the channel supports this or not.

The idea of Weichselberger was to relax the separability restriction of the Kronecker model and to allow for any arbitrary coupling between the transmit and receive eigen base, i.e. to model the correlation properties at the receiver and transmitter jointly. The Weichselberger model parameters are the eigen basis of receive and transmit correlation matrices and a coupling matrix.

In contrast to the two prior models, the virtual channel representation (VCR) models the MIMO channel in the beam space instead of the eigen space. In particular, the eigenvectors are replaced by fixed and predefined steering vectors. The VCR can be easily interpreted. Its angular resolution, and hence accuracy, depends on the actual antenna configuration. Its accuracy increases with the number of antennas, as angular bins become smaller. The model is fully specified by the coupling matrix. Note that there still exists one degree of freedom in choosing the first direction of the unitary transmit/receive matrices (Proakis, 2001).

## 4. BASIC CONSIDERATIONS OF MIMO-OFDM SYSTEM

Orthogonal Frequency Division Multiplex(ing (OFDM) is becoming the chosen modulation technique for wireless communications. It is being adopted as one of the alternatives to meet the demands of high data rates by present day mobile communication networks. As data rates increase, channels become frequency selective which produces ISI. One solution though is the use of equalizers but beyond a certain limit, equalizer design is a complex issue. In such a backdrop multi-carrier modulation turned out to be an alternative. It required that the available spectrum be segmented into sub-bands for which fading over each sub-channel became flat thus eliminating the problem of ISI. The drawback that was found turned out to be poor spectral efficiency. The viable option then emerged was the OFDM which uses non-overlapping adjacent channel to increase spectral efficiency. The nearby channel are separated by half their two sided bandwidth allowing upto 50% adjacent channel overlap which allowed an increase in use of the available bandwidth. It also allowed multiple carrier be used to transmit different symbols with spectral overlap while ensuring co-existence of nearby signals due to orthogonality.

Hence, OFDM appeared as the option that could be used to provide large data rates with sufficient robustness to radio channel impairments (Bolcskei & Zurich, 2006), (Jiang & Hanzo, 2007).

In an OFDM scheme (Figure 6), a large number of orthogonal, overlapping, narrow band sub-channels or sub-carriers, transmitted in parallel, divide the available transmission bandwidth. The separation of the sub-carriers is theoretically minimal such that there is a very compact spectral utilization. The attraction of OFDM is mainly due to how the system handles the multipath interference at the receiver. Multipath generates two effects: frequency selective fading and ISI. The "flatness" perceived by a narrow-band channel overcomes the former, and modulating at a very low symbol rate, which makes the symbols much longer than the channel impulse response, diminishes the latter. Using powerful error correcting codes together with time and frequency interleaving yields even more robustness against frequency selective fading, and the insertion of an extra guard interval between consecutive OFDM symbols can reduce the effects of ISI even more. Thus, an equalizer in the receiver is not necessary.

There are two main drawbacks with OFDM, the large dynamic range of the signal (also referred as peak-to average [PAR] ratio) and its sensitivity to frequency errors (Bolcskei & Zurich, 2006), (Jiang & Hanzo, 2007).

MIMO architectures are useful for combined transmit receive diversity. When used in parallel mode of transmission, MIMO systems offer high data rates in a narrow bandwidth. MIMO systems, characterized by multiple antenna elements at the transmitter and receiver, have demonstrated the potential for increased capacity in rich multipath environments (Ling & Xianda, 2007). By allowing for simultaneous transmission of multiple data streams (Figure 5), MIMO multiplies wireless data capacity without using additional frequency spectrum.

MIMO-OFDM combines OFDM and MIMO techniques thereby achieving spectral efficiency and increased throughput. A MIMO-OFDM system transmits independent OFDM modulated data from multiple antennas simultaneously. At the receiver, after OFDM demodulation, MIMO decoding on each of the sub-channels extracts the data from all the transmit antennas on all the sub-channels (Ling & Xianda, 2007).

*Figure 6. OFDM transmit-receive system with associated channel*

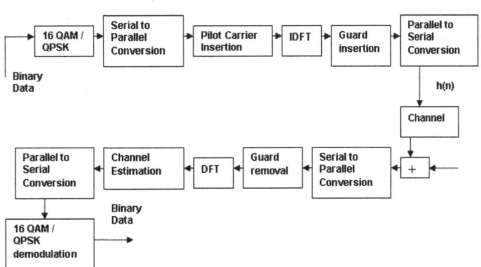

Electromagnetic waves propagating from the transmitter's antenna arrive at the receiver's antenna via different paths. It can lead to secondary reflections as well. Mathematically, the time variant channel impulse response of a multipath channel corresponds to (Hanzo et al., 2003):

$$h(t,\tau) - \sum_{g=0}^{N_p-1} \alpha_g(t,\tau)\exp(j(2\pi f_c \tau_g(t)$$
$$+\phi(t,\tau)))\delta(\tau - \tau_g(t)) \quad (25)$$

where $N_p$ is the number of multipath components, $\alpha_g(t,\tau)$ is the amplitude component and $\tau_g(t)$ is the excess delay component caused by the $g^{th}$ multipath component at time t and $\delta$ is the delta function. The term $j(2\pi f_c \tau_g(t) + \phi(t,\tau))$ represents the phase offset on the $g^{th}$ multipath component at time t. If the wireless channel is assumed to be slowly varying, its impulse response becomes time-invariant for several OFDM symbol durations. And the resulting channel impulse response model corresponds to (Hanzo, Choi, & Munster, 2004):

$$h(t,\tau) = \sum_{g=0}^{N_p-1} \alpha_g(t,\tau)\exp(j\phi_g)\delta(\tau - \tau_g(t))$$
$$(26)$$

where $\alpha_g(t,\tau)$ and $\phi_g$ is net attenuation and phase shift for each path. To model the multipath channel, the autocorrelation function of the channel impulse response which is defined for wide-sense stationary channels can be defined as:

$$r_h(\Delta t, \tau_1, \tau_2) = E\{h(t,\tau_1)h*(t-\Delta t, \tau_2)\} \quad (27)$$

$$r_h(\Delta t, \tau_1, \tau_2) = r_h(\Delta t, \tau_1)\delta(\tau_1 - \tau_2) \quad (28)$$

where E{} is the expectation operator; and * is the conjugate operator. For $\Delta t = 0$, the corresponding autocorrelation function, $r_h(.)$, is defined as the multipath intensity profile of the channel. Since $r_h(.)$ yields the average power of the spectrum for delay values of $\tau$, the rms delay spread, $\tau_{rms}$, which is the largest value of $\tau$ where the multipath intensity profile exhibits a significant response (Rajan, 2007).

Delay spreads in the time domain can be mapped to frequency correlation in the frequency domain (Hanzo, Choi, & Munster, 2004) via the spaced-time spaced-frequency correlation function. The spaced-time spaced-frequency correlation function is given by

$$r_h(\Delta t, \Delta f)$$
$$= E\{h(t,f)h*(t-\Delta t, f-\Delta f)\} \quad (29)$$

$$r_h(\Delta t, \tau_1, \tau_2)$$
$$= FT_{r\to\Delta f}r_h(\Delta t, \Delta f = 0) \quad (30)$$

where $FT_{r\to\Delta f}$ is the Fourier transform operation transforming delay, $\tau$, to frequency $\Delta f$ and $r_h(\Delta t, \Delta f)$ is the spaced-time spaced-frequency correlation function. The spaced time spaced-frequency correlation function shows that correlation due to multiple paths translates to correlation in frequency. The variation of the multipath channel with time can be captured using the spaced-time spaced-frequency correlation function given in eq. 29. Specifically, the correlation in time is related to Doppler spectrum $S_H(f_d)$ which is given by

$$S_H(f_d, \Delta f = 0)$$
$$= FT_{r\to\Delta f}r_h(\Delta t, \Delta f = 0) \quad (31)$$

where $f_d$ is the Doppler frequency. Similar to the spaced-time spaced-frequency correlation function, the Doppler power spectrum can be used to find a quantity known as the Doppler spread, $B_D$. The inverse of Doppler spread is used to calculate the coherence time, $(\Delta t)_c$ which is the amount of time for which the channel is assumed to be significantly static. Usually in OFDM systems, a carrier spacing of $\Delta f = 1/Ts$ to be much smaller than channel's coherence bandwidth. This choice guarantees each sub-carrier flat fading.

## 4.1 MIMO OFDM Detection Scheme

Two broad methods maybe adopted for MIMO-OFDMA detection. These methods are based on zero forcing (ZF) and the minimum mean square error (MMSE) criteria (Ozcelik, Czink, & Bonek, 2006).

**ZF Detector**: In a ZF linear detector, the received signal vector is multiplied with a filter matrix which is a pseudo inverse of the channel response.

$$\mathbf{G} = (\mathbf{H}^H \mathbf{H})^{-1} . \mathbf{H}^H \tag{32}$$

where $\mathbf{H}$ is a diagonal matrix where the diagonal quantities are the amplitudes of the h vector components defined in Section 3.3..

**MMSE Detector:** The MMSE detector minimizes the mean square error between the actually transmitted symbols and the output of the linear detector which is defined by:

$$\mathbf{G} = (\alpha . \mathbf{I}_{Nr} + \mathbf{H}^H)^{-1} . \mathbf{H}^H \tag{33}$$

where $\alpha = \dfrac{1}{SNR}$.

## 5. LITERATURE SURVEY

Some of the notable works on MIMO - OFDMA systems included in the bibliography between (Bolcskei & Zurich, 2006) to (Haykin, 2003) are as below.

H. Bolcskei and E. Zurich (Bolcskei & Zurich, 2006) have provided a perspective on the MIMO - OFDMA system as a means of providing greater bandwidth to wireless communication. H. Sampath, S. Talwar, J. Tellado, V. Erceg and A. Paulraj (Sampath et al., 2002) have provided a detailed account of the MIMO - OFDM system as the means of broadband service to be offered by 4G mobile communication. A similar treatment is provided by H. Yang in (Yang, 2005). M. Jiang and L. Hanzo (Jiang & Hanzo, 2007) offers an extensive description of different dimensions of MIMO - OFDM, contributors to the development process, possibilities, a detailed account of the technological complexity and solutions. The work provides an insight into the use of innovative channel estimation techniques using ANN. The paper also provides a review of the existing MIMO - OFDM systems, discusses their limitations and examines the use of Genetic Algorithms (GAs) as a tool to handle large numbers of users. Several works that discuss about different possibilities offered by MIMO - OFDMA systems are (Wang, Zhengdao, & Giannakis, 2000) to (Bercovich, 2004) and (MIMO, n.d.), (Dhillon, 2006), (Gupta, Mazumdar, & Patranobisc, 2002), (Bocquet, Hayashi, & Sajau, 2004) and (Hijazi, 2006).

A method of MIMO channel estimation and equalization is provided by Z. Ling and Z. Xianda (Ling & Xianda, 2007). The work shows the use of neural networks and Kalman filter to improve the estimation performance of the channel equalizer.

An insight into deriving a measure for ascertaining the acceptability of a MIMO channel using three different models namely- the narrowband Kronecker model, Weichselberger model and virtual channel representation (VCR) has been published by H. Ozcelik, N. Czink and E. Bonek (Ozcelik, Czink, & Bonek, 2006).

When OFDM is employed in a MIMO system another dimension, viz frequency, is available for coding along with the space and time dimensions. Codes that exploit space, time and frequency are known as Space-Time-Frequency Codes (STFCs). A work on these aspects is available due to S. Rajan (Rajan, 2007). The basic consideration on Multi-carrier Based Multiple Access Techniques is provided by M. I. Rahman (Rahman, 2004). The mathematical foundation of the MIMO-OFDM Wireless Systems is offered by H. Bolcskei (Bolcskei, 2006). The works provides a mathematical account of the spectral efficiency and link reliability MIMO – OFDM as part of future wireless communications systems. Y. Ogawa, K. Nishio, T. Nishimura and T. Ohgane (Ogawa et al., 2003) proposed a new signal detection for space division multiplexing in a MIMO - OFDM system for high data rate transmission.

M. Collados and A. Gorokhov provide a system with antenna selection to deal with MIMO - OFDM WLAN Systems (Collados & Gorokhov, 2005).

MIMO channel selection has multiple problems. One of them is the sub-channel selection. W. Ping, L. Li-hua, Z. Ping have shown that an improved SVD-based MIMO can fully cancel the inter sub-channel interferences by reconstructing the transmitter- receiver system matrix on interferences analysis is provided (Ping, Lhua, & Ping, 2007).

# 6 MOTIVATION

The present work is carried out with the following objectives:

- to use artificial neural network (ann)s for mimo channel estimation to explore if better ber values can be achieved compared to traditional estimation methods,
- to use the frame-work developed for mimo-ofdm system for ofdm symbol detection and thereby explore if enhanced spectral efficiency of mimo-ofdm systems can be achieved,
- to extend the framework for noise cancellation and equalization in mimo systems

using modulation schemes like bpsk and qpsk and
- to incorporate other soft-computational techniques like fuzzy-neural and hybrid (soft-computational and adaptive filtering) techniques to explore if better ber values in mimo systems configured for high data rate communication can be achieved.

# 7 NECESSITY OF ANN BASED METHODS

Statistical methods of modeling and estimation of MIMO channels are useful and proved their worth. But with increase in transmission rates and system complexity, the possibility always exists to explore other means for such applications. ANNs are non-parametric prediction tools and have the ability to adapt to a given environment (Jiang & Hanzo, 2007). Moreover, ANNs for their capacity to learn can exploit transmitter side information (TSI), channel side information (CSI) and receiver side information (RSI) better than the statistical techniques (Jiang & Hanzo, 2007). This is a major advantage which can be exploited to simply reception and receiver design despite using higher data rate techniques like MIMO-OFDM. Other probable advantages of such schemes are Application of the complete learning ability of the ANN for controlling precision, Discarding of pilot symbol bits for MIMO-OFDM transmission, which provides bandwidth preservation thereby increasing spectral efficiency and Combined channel estimation and symbol recovery in MIMO-OFDM transmission.

## 7.1 Prediction And Classification Using Artificial Neural Network (Ann)S

Accuracy of a prediction and estimation process depends to a large extent on a higher value of proper classification. ANNs have been one of the preferred classifiers for their ability to provide optimal solution to a wide class of arbitrary classification problems (Haykin, 2003). Multi Layered Perceptron (MLP)s trained with (error) Back Propagation (BP) in particular has found wide spread acceptance in several classification, recognition and estimation applications (Haykin, 2003).

## 7.2 Multi Layered Perceptron (MIP) Based Learning

The fundamental unit of the ANN is the Mc-Culloch-Pitts Neuron (1943). A neuron with the ability to learn is a perceptron. MLP contains several perceptrons grouped in layers. The MLP is the product of several researchers: Frank Rosenblatt (1958), H. D. Block (1962) and M. L. Minsky with S. A. Papart (1988). Backpropagation, the training algorithm, was discovered independently by several researchers (Rumelhart et. al.(1986) and also McClelland and Rumelhart (1988)).

A simple perceptron is a single McCulloch-Pitts neuron trained by the perceptron algorithm is given as:

$$O_x = g([w][x] + b) \tag{34}$$

where [x] is the input vector, [w] is the associated weight vector, b is the bias value and g(x) is then activation function.

Such a setup, namely the perceptron will be able to classify only linearly separable data. A multilayer perceptron (MLP), in contrast, consists of several layers of neurons. The equation for output in a MLP with one hidden layer is given as:

$$O_x = \sum_{i=1}^{N} \beta_i g([w]_i.[x] + b_i) \tag{35}$$

where $\beta_i$ is the bias value, $w_i$ weight value between the $i^{th}$ hidden neuron. Such a set-up maybe depicted as in Figure 7. The process of adjusting the weights and biases of a perceptron or MLP is known as *training*. The perceptron algorithm (for training simple perceptrons consists of comparing the output of the perceptron with an associated target value. The most common training algorithm for MLPs is error backpropagation (BP). This algorithm entails a back propagation of the error correction through each neuron in the network.

## 7.3 APPLICATION OF ERROR BACKPROPAGATION FOR MLP TRAINING

The MLP is trained using (error) Back Propagation (BP) depending upon which the connecting weights between the layers are updated. This adaptive updating of the MLP is continued till

*Figure 7. Multi layer perceptron*

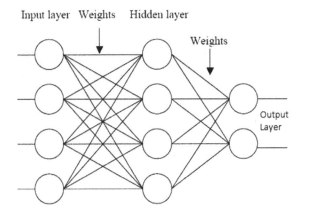

the performance goal is met. Training the MLP is done in two broad passes -one a forward pass and the other a backward calculation with error determination and connecting weight updating in between. Batch training method is adopted as it accelerates the speed of training and the rate of convergence of the MSE to the desired value (Haykin, 2003) (Figure 7).

The steps are as below:

- **Initialization**: First we weight matrix **W** with random values between [-1, 1] if a tan-sigmoid function is used as an activation function and between [0, 1] if log-sigmoid function is used as activation function. **W** is a matrix of $C$ x $P$ where $P$ is the length of the feature vector used for each of the $C$ classes.

- **Presentation of training samples**: Let the input be $p_m = [p_{m1}; p_{m2} \cdots\cdots p_{mL}]$. The desired output is $d_m = [d_{m1,} d_{m2} \cdots\cdots d_{mL}]$. The values of the hidden nodes are:

$$net^h_{mj} = \sum_{i=1}^{L} w^h_{ji} p^{mi} + \varphi^h_j \qquad (36)$$

We obtain the output from the hidden layer as:

$$o^h_{mj} = f^h_j(net^h_{mj}) \qquad (37)$$

where

$$f(x) = \frac{1}{e^x} \qquad (38)$$

or

$$f(x) = \frac{e^x - e^{-x}}{e^x + e^{-x}} \qquad (39)$$

depending upon the choice of the activation function. The values of the output node can be obtained as:

$$o^o_{mk} = f^o_k\left(net^h_{mj}\right) \qquad (40)$$

- **Forward Computation**: We can compute the errors as

$$e_{jn} = d_{jn} - o_{jn} \qquad (41)$$

The mean square error (MSE) is calculated as:

$$MSE = \frac{\sum_{j=1}^{M} \sum_{n=1}^{L} e^2_{jn}}{2M} \qquad (42)$$

Error terms for the output layer are:

$$\delta^o_{mk} = o^o_{mk}\left(1 - o^o_{mk}\right)e_{mn} \qquad (43)$$

Error terms for the hidden layer:

$$\delta^h_{mk} = o^o_{mk}\left(1 - o^o_{mk}\right)\sum \delta^o_{mj} w^o_{jk} \qquad (44)$$

- **Weight Update:**

Between the output and hidden layers

$$w^o_{kj}(t+1) = w^o_{kj}(t) + \eta\delta^o_{mk} o_{mj} \qquad (45)$$

where η is the learning rate. For faster convergence a momentum term (α) maybe added as:

$$w^o_{kj}(t+1) = w^o_{kj}(t) + \eta\delta^o_{mk} o_{mj} \\ +\alpha\left(w^o_{kj}(t+1) - w_{kj}\right) \qquad (46)$$

Between the hidden layer and input layer:

$$w_{kj}^{h}(t+1) = w_{kj}^{h}(t) + \eta\delta_{mj}^{h}p_i \\ +\alpha\left(w_{ji}^{o}(t+1) - w_{ji}\right) \tag{47}$$

A momentum term maybe added as:

$$w_{kj}^{h}(t+1) = w_{kj}^{h}(t) + \eta\delta_{mj}^{h}p_i \\ +\alpha\left(w_{ji}^{o}(t+1) - w_{ji}\right) \tag{48}$$

One cycle through the complete training set forms one epoch. The above is repeated till MSE meets the performance criteria. While repeating the above the number of epoch elapsed is counted.

A few of the methods used for MLP training includes:

- Gradient Descent (GDBP),
- Gradient Descent with Momentum BP (GDMBP),
- Gradient Descent with Adaptive Learning Rate BP (GDALRBP).

**Gradient Descent (GDBP):** In this back-propagation method the training will continue as long as the network has its weight, net input, and transfer functions generate derivative functions. Backpropagation is used to calculate derivatives of performance with respect to the weight and bias variables. Each variable is adjusted according to gradient descent. The training will be stop if the maximum number of epochs (repetitions) is reached, the maximum amount of time has been exceeded, or performance has been minimized to the goal.

**Gradient Descent with Momentum BP (GD-MBP):** In this method backpropagation is used to calculate derivatives of performance with respect to the weight and bias variables. Each variable is adjusted according to gradient descent with momentum a specific value and it depends on the previously changed weight or bias passing with every epochs with a given learning rate.

**Gradient Descent with Momentum and Adaptive Learning Rate BP (GDMALRBP):** This method is used to train any network as long as its weight, net input, and transfer functions have derivative functions. Each variable is adjusted according to gradient descent with momentum constant, and also depends upon previously changed weights. For each epoch, the performance decreases toward the goal, then the learning rate is increased by a specific factor. If performance increases by more than the specified factor, the learning rate is adjusted and the change, which increased the performance, is not made.

Here, while MSE approaches the convergence goal, training of the MLPs suffer if:

Corr ($p_{m,i}$ (j); $p_{m,i}$ (j + 1)) = high and
Corr ($p_{m,i}$ (j); $p_{m,i+1}$ (j)) = high.

This is due to the requirements of the (error) Back Propagation Algorithm.

## 7.4 Application of Artificial Neural Network (Ann)S for Channel Estimation of Mimo - Ofdm Systems

The application of the Artificial Neural Network (ANN) considers two aspects. The first is the training of the Multi Layer Perceptron (MLP)s- a class of feed-forward ANNs. The second stage is to test the trained ANN under varied condition to check its robustness under a range of channel conditions. To train the ANN the setup shown in Figure 7 is utilized.

Here the received signal is given as

$$s = x * H + n \tag{49}$$

where * is a convolution operation of the MIMO-OFDM signal **x** and the channel matrix **H** while **n** is the additive Gaussian white noise. Training an

*Table 1. Parameters used for generating the OFDM signal*

| Case | Parameter | Specification |
|:---:|:---:|:---:|
| 1 | Baseband modulation | 16-QAM, BPSK |
| 2 | FFT length | 1024 |
| 3 | Number of carriers | 128 |
| 4 | Cyclic Prefix | 16 |

ANN by back-propagation involves three stages: the feed-forward of the input training pattern, the back-propagation of the associated error and adjustment of the weights. Here the output of the ANN is the signal $s_N$ which is compared with the received signal $s$. Here the estimation can be carried out using $s_N/x$ assuming that AWGN $n$ is known or can be ignored. But if AWGN plays a significant role which is usually the case, channel estimation can be performed by a trained ANN. The channel matrix is determined as per the considerations described under Section 2.2. It offers the ANN to be familiar with separate approaches of channel estimation. Here the output of the ANN is the signal $s_N$ which is compared with the received signal $s$ and an error matrix $e$ generated such that

$$e = s - s_N \qquad (50)$$

where $s_N$ is the signal generated by the ANN such that

$$s_N = x * H_N + n \qquad (51)$$

At the trained state $e \rightarrow 0$ such that $s_N \rightarrow s$.

The training is carried out by using signal inputs from the transmitter section. The signal inputs used for ANN training are the ones used for transmission through the MIMO channel as well. These symbols are OFDM signals generated using the parameters given in Table 1.

The signal symbols generated and the channel matrix obtained from simulation are convolved to produce the training sequence.

This signal symbol and channel coefficient combined sample used for training helps the ANN to act as a combined channel estimator and OFDM symbol recovery system. The greatest strength of an ANN is that it can tackle any estimation problem despite the presence of irregularities. Thus, the trained ANN though receives stimulations from the transmitter side (Figure 8), in practice it is designed to handle received signals and thereby perform channel estimation (Figure 9). The received signal given by Eq. 27 contains irregularities in the channel due to multipath fading and a large component of AWGN.

Training continues till e approaches the desired goal. Several configurations of the MLP can be utilized for training. The ANN configurations used have one input layer, one hidden layer and one output layer. A single hidden layered MLP is found to be computationally efficient for the work as 2-hidden layered or a 3-hidden layered MLPs are found to be showing no significant performance improvement at the cost of slowing down training.

The choices of the length of the hidden layers have been fixed by not following any definite reasoning but by using trial and error method. For this case several sizes of the hidden layer have been considered. Table 2 shows the performance obtained during training by varying the size of the hidden layer.

The case where the size of the hidden layer taken to be 1.5 times to that of the input layer is found to be computationally efficient. Its MSE

*Figure 8. Training ANN for estimation of channel*

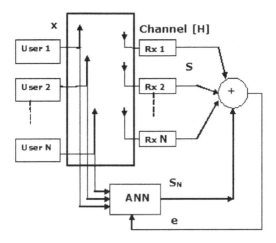

*Figure 9. Configuration of ANN to determine performance of training under test condition*

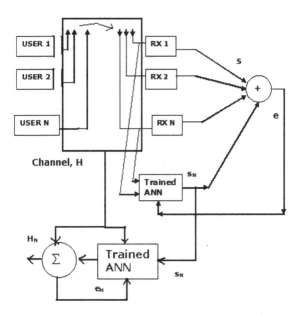

convergence rate (Table 3) and learning ability is found to be superior to the rest of the cases.

Hence, the size of the hidden layer of the ANNs considered is 1.5 times to that of the input layer. The size of the input layer depends upon the length of the input vector and the output layer represents the number of parameters. Noise free and noised data were used for the training. In this case a 4 x 4 Tx-Rx configuration is considered for which

the input and output layers of the ANN will have four neurons each.

The selection of the activation functions of the input, hidden and output layers plays another important part in the performance of the system. A common practice can be to use a similar type of activation function in all layers. But certain combinations and alterations of activation function types carried out during training provide certain different directions and show a way to attain better

*Table 2. Performance variation after 1000 epochs during training of an ANN with variation of size of the hidden layer*

| Case | Size of hidden layer (x input layer) | MSE Attained | Precision attained in % |
|------|--------------------------------------|--------------|-------------------------|
| 1 | 0.75 | $1.2 \times 10^{-3}$ | 87.1 |
| 2 | 1.0 | $0.56 \times 10^{-3}$ | 87.8 |
| 3 | 1.25 | $0.8 \times 10^{-4}$ | 87.1 |
| 4 | 1.5 | $0.3 \times 10^{-4}$ | 90.1 |
| 5 | 1.75 | $0.6 \times 10^{-4}$ | 89.2 |
| 6 | 2 | $0.7 \times 10^{-4}$ | 89.8 |

*Table 3. Effect on average MSE convergence after 1000 epochs with variation of activation functions at input, hidden and output layers*

| Case | Input layer | Hidden Layer | Output Layer | MSE x $10^{-4}$ |
|------|-------------|--------------|--------------|------------------|
| 1 | log-sigmoid | log-sigmoid | log-sigmoid | 1.45 |
| 2 | tan-sigmoid | tan-sigmoid | tan-sigmoid | 1.32 |
| 3 | tan-sigmoid | log-sigmoid | tan-sigmoid | 1.01 |
| 4 | log-sigmoid | tan-sigmoid | log-sigmoid | 1.08 |
| 5 | log-sigmoid | log-sigmoid | tan-sigmoid | 1.15 |
| 6 | log-sigmoid | tan-sigmoid | log-sigmoid | 1.19 |

performance. Two types of MLP configurations are considered- the first type constituted by a set of similar activation functions in all layers of the ANNs and the other with a varied combination of activation functions in different layers. Both these two configurations are trained with Gradient Descent with Momentum and Adaptive Learning Rate Back Propagation (GDMALBP) algorithm as a measure of training performance standardization. Other training methods that are also used to configure the ANN are Gradient Descent Back Propagation (GDBP), Gradient Descent with Momentum Back Propagation (GDMBP) and Gradient Descent with Adaptive Learning Rate Back Propagation (GDALBP).

In this case a 4 x 4 Tx-Rx configuration is considered for which the input and output layers of the ANN will have four neurons each. The back-propagation algorithm used for training often suffers from more than one problems leading to

difficulties in mean square error (MSE) convergence. Hence, varied AWGN considerations are used in the OFDM signal to make the correlation between adjacent samples of the training data as low as possible. The training continues till the MSE convergence attains the desired goal and the accuracy of generating the channel matrix by the ANN reaches the required precision level. After the training is over, inputs from the receiver end are fed to the ANN so as to provide a correct estimate of the channel and thereby increase the reception quality of the receiver. In such a case a block diagram as shown in Figure 9 is used. The ANNs are tested with four separate data sets of channel matrices generated with varying AWGN values for both the channel models and for four different training conditions. For testing the effectiveness of the trained ANN, the setup shown in Figure 9 is utilized.

*Table 4. Parameters used for simulating channel using Clarke-Gans model*

| Sl Num | Parameter | Value |
|:---:|:---:|:---:|
| 1 | Freq., $f_c$ | 900MHz |
| 2 | $\omega_c$ | $2\pi f_c$ |
| 3 | Mobile Speed, V | 3 kmph |
| 4 | No. of paths | 8 |
| 5 | Wavelength, $\lambda$ | $3\times10^8$ / fc |
| 6 | Doppler shift, $f_m$ | V / $\lambda$ |
| 7 | Sampling Freq., $f_s$ | $8 \times$ fm |
| 8 | No of samples, N | 10000 |
| 9 | Paths | 16 |
| 10 | Sampling Period, Ts | $1/t_s$ |

## 8 EXPERIMENTAL RESULTS AND DISCUSSION

For a generic discrete time multipath fading channel used in MIMO-OFDM system simulated using the Clarke and Gans model (Figures 1 and 2). These characteristics have been simulated for a pass-band of 0.2 ghz to 8 ghz to represent a frequency range suitable for mobile communication.

The channels have been assumed to have a flat-response pass band. With such an assumption, Butterworth filter characteristics have been used to generate a matrix of the coefficients of four channels. Four channels have been used to avoid complications to begin with which can be extended further. The experiment however can include equi-ripple behavior in the channel response- a condition which will offer greater variation in pattern for the ANN to deal with. The experiments carried out have restricted the domain to flat-band response of four channels and has laid stress on deriving the framework of ANN based channel estimation. Another set of characteristics of the channel model developed using the Clarke-Gans formulation considers the parameters as given in Table 4. The OFDM signals generated for the work has a center frequency at 100 MHz. The parameters shown in Table 4 are used to generate the OFDM signal and the results are as in Figure 10.

## 8.1 Performance of the MIMO Channel

MIMO is an important means to use the available bandwidth effectively. Unlike traditional means of increasing throughput, MIMO systems do not increase bandwidth in order to increase throughput. They simply exploit the spatial dimension by increasing the number of unique spatial paths between the transmitter and receiver.

This is shown by the plot shown in Figure 11. The application of MIMO-principles increases the effective utilization of the channels. Table 5 shows that compared to a (1, 1) Tx-Rx block a (5, 5) achieves over 40 times more capacity utilization.

## 8.2 ANN Based Channel Estimation

The training of the ANN for the channel estimation considers four ANN training methods to ascertain the best configuration for testing. Tables 6 and 7 shows data sets used to train an ANN for four different path delays and four different frequency selective paths of Rayleigh and Rician faded channels generated using Clarke-Gans model (Rappaport, 2004).

*Figure 10. Multipath fading channel simulated using Clarke and Gans model*

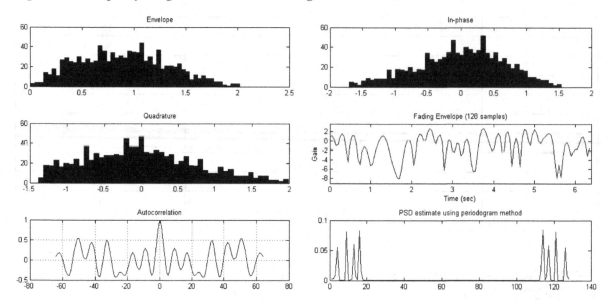

The size of the data involved in the training is not very large, hence a careful selection of training sessions is an important criterion to prevent over training of the ANN and thereby ensure optimum performance. If the ANN is over-trained it will fail to generalize instead will start to memorize. The number of training epochs required therefore is limited to a few hundreds only. The performance achieved during these epochs is noted. The ANN training considers the MSE convergence and precision generated in channel estimation and the BER calculation. If the MSE

*Figure 11. Improvement in capacity utilization by MIMO-channels*

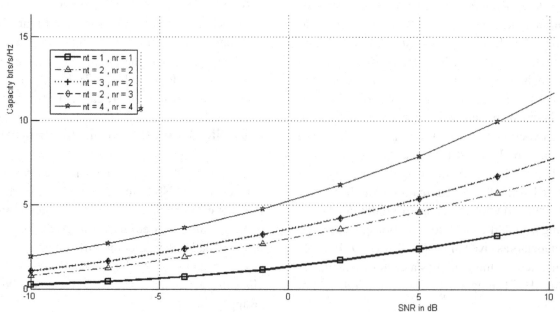

*Table 5. Capacity (b/s/Hz) achieved by MIMO-channels*

| Tx -Rx | SNR=12 dB | SNR=24 dB |
|--------|-----------|-----------|
| (1, 1) | 0.3 | 1.8 |
| (2, 2) | 2.2 | 7.2 |
| (3, 3) | 5.8 | 10.8 |
| (4, 4) | 7.5 | 26.2 |
| (5, 5) | 12.5 | 28.5 |

has converged to the fixed target value, the precision levels and the associated BER values are calculated. If the values fall within the desired levels, the training is extended to include more number of samples which represent varying channel conditions. The iterations are confined to only to a few hundreds during which a minimum MSE convergence of 0.006 x $10^{-2}$ has been attained using the GDALRMBP training method. The ANN trained by following these considerations is taken for performing the channel estimation. After the training is over, the ANNs are tested with four separate data sets of channel matrices

generated with varying AWGN values for both the channel models and for four different training conditions. The MSE values attained during training is shown in the Table 8. The iterations are confined to only 400 during which a minimum MSE convergence of 0.006 x $10^{-2}$ has been attained using the GDMALRBP training method. The MSE values by other training methods too are comparable. Table 8 shows that the 1-hidden layered MLP trained with GDMALRBP attains the best MSE convergence after 400 iterations.

The GDMALRBP based training to the ANN generates the best performance. The highest precision performance attained is around 92.5%. The ANN trained by following these considerations is taken for performing the channel estimation. The performance of the ANN during training has also been observed by measuring the success rate in estimating the channel coefficients. The greatest strength of the ANN in such application is related to the opportunity that the ANN provides in extending the performance domain by adopting better configuration and allowing increased num-

*Table 6. Truncated data set used to train an ANN for four different path delays and four different frequency-selective paths of a Rayleigh faded channel*

| Case | 1 | 2 | 3 | 4 |
|------|---|---|---|---|
| Delays | $1 \times 10^{-5}$ | $1.5 \times 10^{-5}$ | $2 \times 10^{-5}$ | $2.5 \times 10^{-5}$ |
| Path gain 1 | 0.467 | 0.353 | 0.555 | 0.036 |
| Path gain 2 | 0.281 | 0.031 | 0.815 | 0.732 |
| Path gain 3 | 0.367 | 0.893 | 0.462 | 0.381 |
| Path gain 4 | 0.212 | 0.691 | 0.021 | 0.811 |

*Table 7. Truncated data set used to train an ANN for channel estimation under Rician fading*

| Case | 1 | 2 | 3 | 4 |
|------|---|---|---|---|
| Delays | $1 \times 10^{-5}$ | $1.5 \times 10^{-5}$ | $2 \times 10^{-5}$ | $2.5 \times 10^{-5}$ |
| Path gain 1 | 0.136 | 0.446 | 0.125 | 0.162 |
| Path gain 2 | 0.087 | 0.306 | 0.595 | 0.433 |
| Path gain 3 | 0.761 | 0.239 | 0.064 | 0.213 |
| Path gain 4 | 0.572 | 0.196 | 0.351 | 0.087 |

*Table 8. Precision performance in % of channel estimation during training by a 1-hidden layered MLP trained with four different training methods with a learning rate of 0.4*

| Sessions | Precision % for different training methods | | | |
|----------|-------|--------|---------|-----------|
|          | GDBP  | GDMBP  | GDALBP  | GDMALRBP  |
| 1000     | 76.1  | 79.3   | 83.3    | 84.2      |
| 2000     | 77.9  | 81.2   | 84.2    | 85.7      |
| 3000     | 79.1  | 82.3   | 86.6    | 89.4      |
| 4000     | 81.9  | 84.4   | 88.6    | 92.5      |

ber of sessions to continue the learning till the desired performance levels are attained. The learning patterns and thereby performance of ANN varies with training method. Faster the learning, greater is the chance of the ANN falling a local trap where the convergence curve oscillates around a local minima. No such problems have been observed in the present case with all the four training methods.

The sample size considered for training includes two different forms of Clarke-Gans channel model each generated using three different AWGN values viz.- 3dB, 5dB and 10dB for the generic, Rayleigh and Rician faded channels. This way six sample sets are obtained for a 4x4 MIMO-OFDM set-up for each of the channel types considered. The testing includes a range of signal conditions with SNR values ranging from 1 to 25 dB.

The testing carried out with inputs from the receiver side calculates channel coefficients and compares them to the theoretically generated values for a frequency range of 0.2Ghz to 8GHz.

For channel estimation under test condition the experiential set-up shown in Figure 11 is modified a bit so that the set-up itself is able to generate the channel coefficients. This set-up has another 1-hidden layered ANN where the ANN receives the simulated channel coefficients as the reference for training. The training is similarly carried out till the desired goal is attained. The trained ANN is intended to provide the estimate of the channels. This ANN generates the estimate of the channels after receiving inputs from the first ANN gener-

ated signal $s_N$. The set-up shown in Figure 9 can also be used for OFDM symbol recovery. It, as a result, removes the necessity of inserting training symbols for recovery of the OFDM symbols. Since the trained ANN has the ability to estimate the channel coefficients, it can use the knowledge of the channel in recovering the OFDM symbols. This is again used to reinforce the channel estimation process of the set-up. Thus the combined channel estimation and OFDM symbol recovery saves important bandwidth space by not requiring the training symbols unlike the case with carrier insertion OFDM systems.

Under 3dB AWGN the channel estimation attained is around 94.5%. The BER values attained are in the $10^{-6}$ range -a value comparable to the rates achieved by currently available maximum-likelihood (ML) and similar methods including GA-assisted channel estimation methods (Jiang & Hanzo, 2007). The BER values generated by a trained ANN for a Rayleigh multi-path fading channel and that for the Rician channel are shown by Figure 16. The BER values are calculated using the figure of merit $E_b / N_0$ where $E_b$ is the energy per bit and N0 noise spectral density.

Figure 18 shows the BER values generated by the coefficients estimated by a trained ANN for a Rayleigh multipath fading channel. The ANN with its ability to learn given patterns (Figure 12, Figure 13, Figure 14, and Figure 15) can also predict values which here are utilized for channel coefficient estimation associated with Rayleigh and Rician multipath fading (Figures 21 and 22).

Figure 17 shows a comparative plot between LS, MMSE and MLP based methods of BER value calculation related to MIMO- channel estimation. The MLP based method provides better results at the cost of more computational time. But the results derived above donot consider the time varying nature of the MIMO channel. Hence, certain modifications need to be carried out as described in the sections below.

## 9 TEMPORAL-MLP ARCHITECTURE FOR MIMO CHANNEL MODELING

MLPs capturing time - varying patterns of input data must have temporal characteristics (Cadini, Zio, & Pedroni, 2008), (Koskela et al., 2001), (Back et al., 2001) which can be developed by building memory into an ANN (Haykin, 2003).

There are two basic methods which can be used to introduce memory into an ANN. The first one is to introduce time delays in the ANN and to adjust parameters during learning phase. The second way is to use a feedback which can make the ANN recurrent. Recurrent networks use global feed-forward and local feedback sections (Haykin, 2003) combining the above two techniques. An ARMA-MLP contains ARMA- synaptic weights which are updated with changing epochs of the ANN. A basic ARMA model can be expressed as

$$
y[n] = \sum_{i-0}^{M} a_i[n]u[n-i]
$$
$$
+\sum_{i=0}^{N} b_i[n]y[n-i]
$$
(52)

where $a_i[n]$ and $b_i[n]$ are adjustable coefficients for the model. The motivation for using an ARMA adaptive filter is related to the fact that the set-up can be used to realize a variable impulse response with a small number of adjustable coefficients (Haykins, 2002). Two broad architectures can be developed with ARMA synapses. These are called

**ARMA MLP** which has the following subclasses:

- MA-MLP
- AR MLP

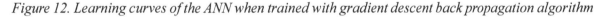

*Figure 12. Learning curves of the ANN when trained with gradient descent back propagation algorithm*

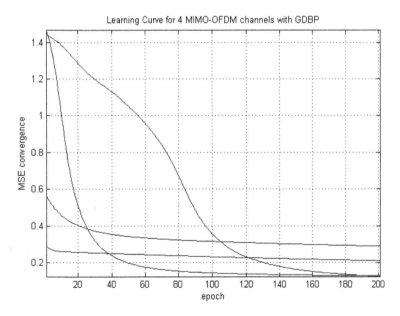

*Figure 13. Learning curves of the ANN when trained with gradient descent with momentum back propagation algorithm*

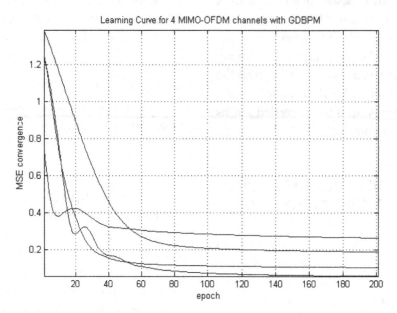

*Figure 14. Learning curves of the ANN when trained with gradient descent with adaptive learning rate back propagation algorithm*

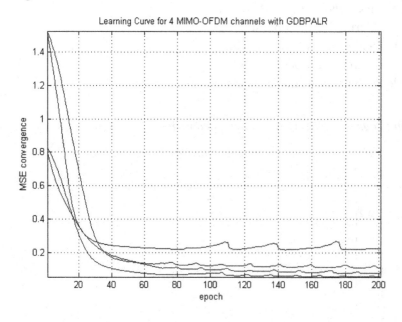

**Layered ARMA Perceptron Cluster (LAPC)** with variations of the synapses using MA and AR links.

## 9.1 ARMA MLP

The block diagram of the ARMA-MLP is shown in Figure 19. The $c_N(.)$'s represent the pre-trans-

*Figure 15. Learning curves of the ANN when trained with gradient descent with adaptive learning rate and momentum back propagation algorithm*

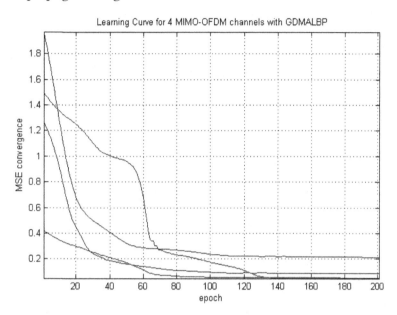

*Figure 16. BER values generated by a trained ANN for a Rayleigh and Rician multipath fading channel*

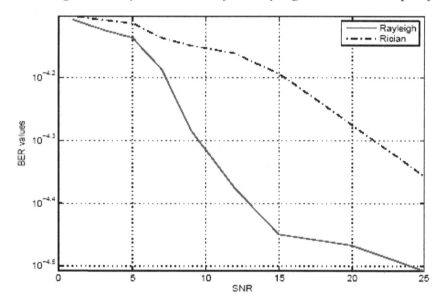

mission processing and amplifier gain while $g_N(.)$'s are activation functions associated with the ANN setup. The ANN set-up receives $x_N(.)$'s as inputs which are passed through $c_N(.)$ pre-transmission non-linear functions and activation functions linked with ARMA synapses $w_N(.)$. The response of the model at different stages can be expressed as below:

**At A**: The output can be expressed as

*Figure 17. BER values generated by LS, MMSE and MLP methods for different SNRs*

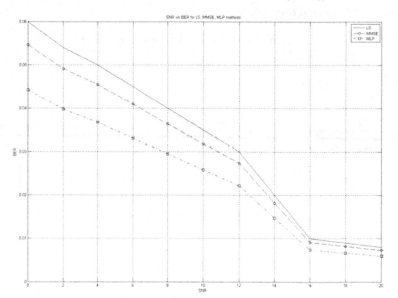

*Figure 18. Estimation of the BER values of four-path Rayleigh faded channels using ANN at test conditions*

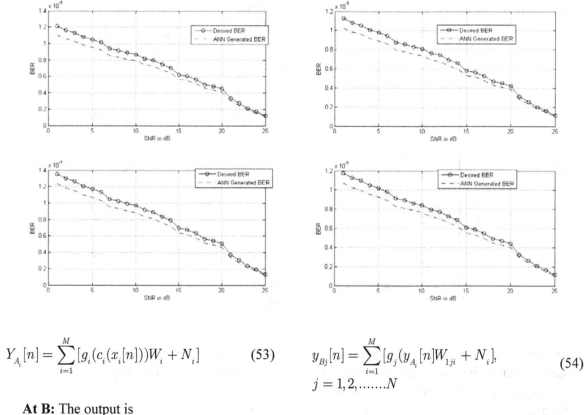

$$Y_{A_i}[n] = \sum_{i=1}^{M} [g_i(c_i(x_i[n]))W_i + N_i] \qquad (53)$$

$$y_{Bj}[n] = \sum_{i=1}^{M} [g_j(y_{A_i}[n]W_{1ji} + N_i], \qquad (54)$$
$$j = 1, 2, \dots\dots N$$

**At B:** The output is

**At C:** The output is

*Figure 19. ARMA MLP model*

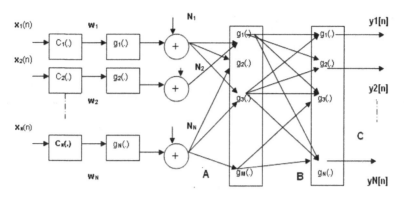

$$y_i[n] = \sum_{i=1}^{M} [g_j(y_{Bi}[n]W_{ji} + N_i],$$
$$j = 1, 2, \ldots\ldots N$$
(55)

where $w_N(.)$ are ARMA synapses.

**Error Calculation at point C:** Let $d_k[n]$ be the desired result and $y_k[n]$ be the actual result. The instantaneous performance criteria is defined as

$$\xi[n] = \frac{1}{2}\sum_{k=1}^{M}(d_k[n] - y_k[n])^2$$
(56)

The total error or cost function is given by summing the instantaneous error over all time T in the training sequence.

$$\xi_T = \sum_{n=0}^{T}\xi[n]$$
(57)

The ARMA synapses are updated following the gradient descent algorithm with variable learning rate and momentum term.

Here, the signal streams are handled by the MLP block and are made to operate in fixed duration time slots during which the ARMA synaptic links in the trained state help the system to capture the time-varying properties of the MIMO channel and derive the desired characteristics.

## 9.2. Layered ARMA Perceptron Cluster (LAPC)

The block diagram of the ARMA-MLP is shown in Figure 20. In this model, perceptron units are formed with ARMA filter synapse and configured to receive real and imaginary components of the input separately. The perceptron pairs train individually and contribute towards the generation of a global output at point C.

**At A:** The output is

$$y_{Ai}[n] = \sum_{i=1}^{M}\begin{bmatrix}g(x_{iR}(n)w_R[n] + N_i) \\ +g(x_{iI}(n)w_I[n] + N_i)\end{bmatrix}$$
(58)

**At B:** The output maybe expressed as

$$y_{Bj}[n] = \sum_{i=1}^{M}\begin{bmatrix}[g(x_{iR}(n)w_R[n] + N_i) \\ +g(x_{iI}(n)w_I[n] + N_i)]\end{bmatrix}W_i]W_{ji},$$
$$j = 1, 2, \ldots N$$
(59)

**At C:** The output expression becomes

$$y_{Ci}[n] = \sum_{i=1}^{M}\begin{bmatrix}g(y_{bj}(n)W_{Rp}[n]) \\ +g(y_{Bj}(n)W_{Ip}[n])\end{bmatrix},$$
$$j = 1, 2, \ldots N$$
(60)

*Figure 20. Layered ARMA Perceptron Cluster (LAPC) model*

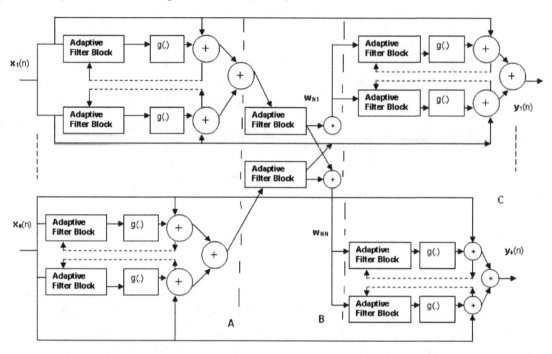

*Figure 21. Four path Rayleigh faded channel coefficients generated by a trained ANN during test conditions with AWGN of 3dB*

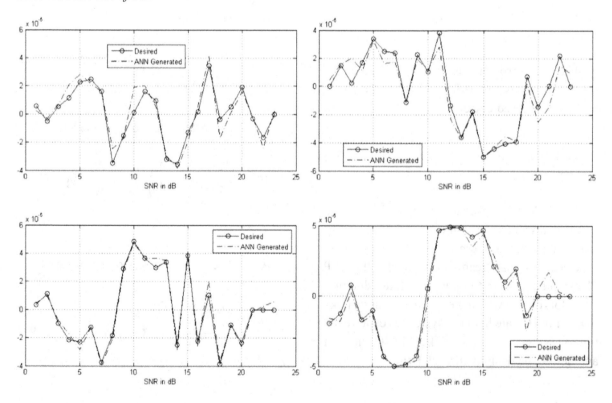

*Figure 22. Rician multipath fading channel coefficients generated by a trained ANN under test conditions*

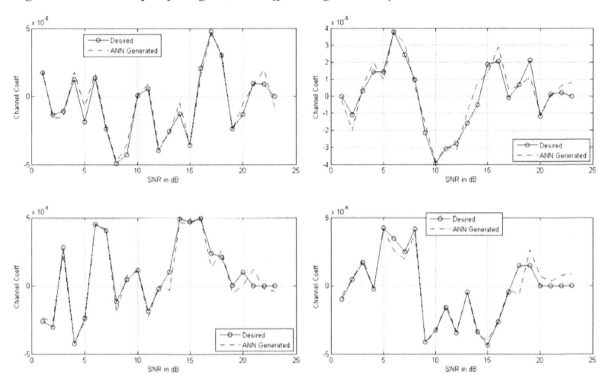

where $w_N(.)$ are ARMA synapses.

**Error Calculation at point A:** Let $d_k[n]$ be the desired result and $y_{Ak}[n]$ be the actual result. The instantaneous performance criteria is defined as

$$\xi_A[n] = \frac{1}{2}\sum_{k=1}^{M}\left(d_k[n]-y_{Ak}[n]\right)^2 \qquad (61)$$

The total error or cost function at point A is given by summing the instantaneous error over all time T in the training sequence.

$$\xi_A = \sum_{n=0}^{T}\xi_A[n] \qquad (62)$$

Similarly at point C, the error is calculated as

$$\xi_C[n] = \frac{1}{2}\sum_{k=1}^{M}\left(d_k[n]-y_{Ck}[n]\right)^2 \qquad (63)$$

The total error or cost function at point C is given by

$$\xi_C = \sum_{n=0}^{T}\xi_C[n] \qquad (64)$$

The LAPC is formed by unitary perceptron blocks which have the capacity to deal with time-varying signals due to the ARMA links provided to them. Each LAPC – perceptron deals with one signal stream at a time but all the constituent blocks handles all the signal streams simultaneously.

## 9.3 Gradient Computation for the Two Architectures

This weight changes can be adjusted by a simple gradient method:

$$W_{ikj}^{'l}[n+1]$$
$$= W_{ikj}^{'l}[n] + \nabla W_{ikj}^{'l}[n] \tag{65}$$

such that

$$\nabla W_{ikj}^{'l}[n] = -\eta \frac{\delta \xi[n]}{\delta W_{ikj}^{'l}[n]}$$
$$= -\eta \frac{\delta \xi[n]}{\delta x_k^{'l}[n]} * \frac{\delta x_k^{'l}[n]}{\delta W_{ikj}^{'l}[n]} \tag{66}$$

where $\eta$ is the learning rate. A secondary variable is defined as

$$\delta_k^{'l}[n] = -\frac{\delta \xi[n]}{\delta \xi_k^l[n]} \tag{67}$$

which is the gradient defined at time n. Then the instantaneous cost can be defined using an instantaneous gradient and an accumulation gradient.

## 1. Instantaneous Cost Using Instantaneous Gradient

$$\delta_k^l[n] = f'(x_k^{'l}[n]) \sum_{m=1}^{N+1} \delta_m^{l+1}[n+1] C_{km}^{l+1} W_{km}^{l+1} \tag{68}$$

where $C_{km}l+1$ is a synaptic gain updated as

$$C_i k^{'l}[n+1] = C_i k^{'l}[n] + \nabla C_i k^{'l}[n] \tag{69}$$

with

$$\nabla C_i k^{'l}[n] = -\eta \frac{\delta \xi[n]}{\delta C_{ik}^l[n]} \tag{70}$$

Another form is obtained if contributions of all elements are combined.

## 2. Instantaneous Cost-Accumulated Gradient

$$\delta_k^l[n] = f'(x_k^{'l}[n]) \sum_{m=1}^{N+1} \sum_{d=0}^{n_w} C_{km}^{l+1} W_{kmd}^{l+1} [q^{-d}] \delta_m^{l+1}[n]$$
$$= f'(x_k^{'l}[n]) \sum_{m=1}^{N+1} \sum_{d=0}^{n_w} C_{km}^{l+1} W_{kmd}^{l+1} \delta_m^{l+1}[n^{-d}]$$
$$= f'(x_k^{'l}[n]) \sum_{m=1}^{N+1} \sum_{d=0}^{n_w} C_{km}^{l+1} W_{kmd}^{l+1} [q^{-1}] \delta_m^{l+1}[n] \tag{71}$$

where $n_w$ is the order of ARMA block and N is the length of output layer. This is similar to algorithm proposed in (Cadini, Zio, & Pedroni, 2008), (Koskela et al., 2001), (Back et al., 2001). This final updating process may be expressed as

$$W_{ikj}^l[n+1] = W_{ikj}^l[n] + \eta \delta_k^l[n] C_{ik}^l Z_i^{l-1}(n-j) C_{ik}^l[n+1]$$
$$= C_{ik}^l[n] + \eta \delta_k^l[n] W_{ik}^l(q^{-1}) z_i^{l-1}(n) \tag{72}$$

## 3. Gradient Computation Using A Total Cost Function

The weight changes in eq.s 66 and 70 are modified as

$$\nabla W_{ikj}^l[n] = -\eta \frac{\delta \xi_T}{\delta W_{ikj}^l[n]} \tag{73}$$

and

$$\nabla C_{ik}^l[n] = -\eta \frac{\delta \xi_T}{\delta C_{ik}^l[n]} \tag{74}$$

Considering the output of the ANN to be $\mathbf{y}_N$ which when compared with the received signal $\mathbf{y}$ generates an error $\mathbf{e}$ such that

$$c = y - y_N \tag{75}$$

where

$$y_N = X * H_N + n \tag{76}$$

At the trained state $\mathbf{e}$ approaches $\mathbf{0}$ such that $\mathbf{y_N}$ approaches $\mathbf{y}$. By noting that as $\mathbf{y_N}$ approaches $\mathbf{y}$ the channel matrix generated by the trained ANN $\mathbf{H_N}$ approaches $\mathbf{H}$. The channel estimation can be carried out using

$$\frac{y_N}{X} \tag{77}$$

## 10 CONCLUSION

MIMO-OFDM is a solution for the up-coming mobile networks which constantly demands greater bandwidth and better quality of service. In all wireless based communication the channel is a highly volatile medium the behaviour of which is difficult to determine. As such channel estimation has been one of the areas which always offered ample of opportunity to experiment with innovative approaches to make receiver systems better. Application of ANNs for channel estimation is such an area which offers solutions to tackle the intricacies associated with the fluctuations observed in multipath propagation which is always the problem area in wireless communication.

This work offers insight into the application of ANN for channel estimation and shows its effectiveness. The results obtained show that more experiments are needed to fine tune the approach so as to make ANN an effective aid to strengthen traditional methods of channel estimation and make reception quality better in wireless based communication. The ANN with its ability to learn though helps in identifying channel properties and responses suffers from the fact that when the nearby samples have greater correlation the learn-

ing stops. As a result in all cases where adjacent samples are correlated ANN performance suffers. This situation can be observed in the multipath radio-channel with all the associated unpredictability. Then an ANN based channel estimator will find the situation quiet difficult to tackle. This is the often quoted problem of local minima. ANNs specially feed-forward networks- the types used in this work are the worst sufferers if proper care is not taken. Solutions however exist. One is to keep a constant vigil on the training carried out and the learning pattern which an ANN adopts.

A better approach is to device certain optimization methods. These can be in form of hybrid estimator- say a combination of ANNs and adaptive filters. Another approach can be a bank of ANNs, connected to an ANN intended to perform optimization. The output of each of the networks in the ANN-bank can be used by another ANN trained to optimize and select the best estimation offered by the ANNs forming the ANN-based estimator bank. Such approaches are likely to be adopted in subsequent stages of the work. the objective is to apply soft-computing tools to channel estimation as an aid to improve wireless-based communication.

This work also showed how MLPs can be modified to capture time-varying properties of input data. The ARMA-MLP and LAPC architectures proposed in this work are better suited to deal with time-varying properties of wireless channels transmitting data in MIMO-OFDM setups. The performance thus generated can be improved further by adopting recurrent neural networks which can be optimized better for real time signal processing.

## REFERENCES

Back, A., Wan, E. A., Lawrence, S., & Tsoi, A. C. (2001). *A unifying view of some training algorithms for multi layer perceptrons with FIR filter synapses.*

Bercovich, R. (2004). OFDM enhances the 3G high-speed data access. *Proc. GSPx 2004 Conf.*, Santa Clara, CA, USA.

Bocquet, W., Hayashi, K., & Sakai, H. (2004). A power allocation scheme for MIMO OFDM systems.

Bolcskei, H. (2006). *Principles of MIMO-OFDM wireless systems. Communication Technology Laboratory Swiss Federal Institute of Technology*. ETH.

Bolcskei, H., & Zurich, E. (August, 2006). MIMO - OFDMA wireless systems: Basics, perspectives, and challenges. *IEEE Wireless Communications*, (pp. 31-37).

Cadini, F., Zio, E., & Pedroni, N. (2008). *Validation of infinite impulse response multi layer perceptron for modelling nuclear dynamics*. Hindawi Publishing Corporation Science and Technology Installations.

Colieri, S., Ergen, M., Puri, A., & Bahai, A. (September, 2002). A study of channel estimation in OFDM systems. In *Proceedings of the IEEE 56th Vehicular Technology Conference*, vol. 2, (pp. 894-898).

Collados, M., & Gorokhov, A. (2005). Antenna selection for MIMO - OFDMWLAN systems. *International Journal of Wireless Information Networks, 12*(4). doi:10.1007/s10776-005-0007-9

Dhillon, G. (2006). MIMO tech for next-gen cellular systems. *Electronic Engineering Times- Asia, 1-15*, 1-2.

Gacanin, H., Takaoka, S., & Adachi, F. (September 2005). A study of channel estimation in OFDM systems. In *Proceedings of Pilot-Assisted Channel Estimation for OFDM / TDM with Frequency-Domain Equalization, Vehicular Technology Conference*, USA.

Gupta, A. Mazumdar, C., & Patranobisc, D. (2002). A distributed simulation technique for multiple input multiple output systems. *ISA: The Instrumentation, Systems, and Automation Society- ISA Transactions, 41*, 421 435.

Hanzo, L., Choi, B. J., & Munster, M. (2004, Nov.). A stroll along multi-carrier boulevard towards next-generation plaza - Space-time coded adaptive OFDM and MC-CDMA comparison. *IEEE Veh. Technol. Soc. Newslett., 51*, 10–19.

Hanzo, L., Yang, L. L., Kuan, E. L., & Yen, K. (2003). *Single- and multi-carrier DSCDMA: Multi-user detection, space-time spreading, synchronisation and standards*. Piscataway, NJ: IEEE Press/ Wiley. doi:10.1002/0470863110

Haykin, S. (2003). *Neural networks: A comprehensive foundation* (2nd ed.). New Delhi, India: Pearson Education.

Haykins, S. (2002). *Adaptive filter theory* (4th ed.). New Delhi, India: Pearson Education.

Hijazi, S. L. (2006). *Multiuser detection for multicarrier communication systems*. Manhattan, Kansas, USA: Department of Electrical and Computer Engineering, College of Engineering, Kansas State University.

Jiang, M., & Hanzo, L. (2007, July). Multiuser MIMO-OFDM for next-generation wireless systems. *Proceedings of the IEEE, 95*(7), 1430–1469. doi:10.1109/JPROC.2007.898869

Koffman, I., & Roman, V. (2002, Apr.). Broadband wireless access solutions based on OFDM access in IEEE 802.16. *IEEE Communications Magazine, 40*(4), 96–103. doi:10.1109/35.995857

Koskela, T., Lehtokangas, M., Saarinen, J., & Kashi, K. (2001). *Time series prediction with mult layer perceptron, FIR and elman neural networks*. Finland: Tampere University of Technology.

Ling, Z., & Xianda, Z. (2007, Dec.). MIMO channel estimation and equalization using three-layer neural networks with feedback. *Tsinghua Science and Technology*, *12*(6), 658–661. doi:10.1016/S1007-0214(07)70171-2

MIMO. (n.d.). *The non-engineer's introduction to MIMO and MIMO-OFDM*. Retrieved from http://www.mimo.ucla.edu

Ogawa, Y., Nishio, K., Nishimura, T., & Ohgane, T. (2003). A MIMO - OFDM system for high-speed transmission. *Proceedings of IEEE 58th Vehicular Technology Conference*, vol. 1, 6-9 Oct. 2003 (pp. 493-497).

Ozcelik, H., Czink, N., & Bonek, E. (2006). *What makes a good MIMO channel model? Institut fur Nachrichtentechnik und Hochfrequenztechnik, Technische Universitat Wien*. Vienna, Austria: IEEE VTC.

Ping, W., Lhua, L., & Ping, Z. (2007). Subchannel interference cancellation in SVP-based MIMO system. *Journal of China Universities of Posts and Telecommunications*, *14*(3).

Proakis, J. G. (2001). *Digital communications* (4th ed.). New York, N Y: McGraw-Hill Publication.

Rahman, M. I. (2004). *Basics about multi-carrier based multiple access techniques. Center for TeleInFrastruktur (CTiF)*. Aalborg University.

Rajan, B. S. (2007). *Space-time-frequency codes for MIMO-OFDM systems*. Department of Electrical Communication Engineering Indian Institute of Science Bangalore 560012, India.

Rappaport, T. S. (2004). *Wireless communications: Principles and practice*, 2nd edition. New Delhi, India: Pearson Education., Sampath, H., Talwar, S., Tellado, J., Erceg, V., & Paulraj, A. (2002). A fourth generation MIMO - OFDMA broadband wireless system: Design, performance and field trial results. *IEEE Communications Magazine*, *40*(9), 143-149.

Wang, W., Zhengdao, Z., & Giannakis, G. B. (2000, May). Wireless multicarrier communications. *IEEE Signal Processing Magazine*, 29–48. doi:10.1109/79.841722

Yang, H. (2005). A road to future broadband wireless access: MIMO-OFDM- based wireless access. *IEEE Communications Magazine*, *43*(1), 53–60. doi:10.1109/MCOM.2005.1381875

## KEY TERMS AND DEFINITIONS

**ANN:** It stands for Artificial Neural Network. It is an ensemble of computationally created neurons with the capacity to learn and thereby show analogy to biological neurons which forms the basis of machine learning and human – like decision making.

**Channel:** Interface between the transmitter and the receiver.

**Estimation:** It is the process of predicting an unknown quantity with or without prior knowledge.

**MLP:** It is an acronym for Multi Layer Perceptron. It is an ANN formed by more than one layer of neurons designed to work as a supervised network and trained with back-propagation algorithm. It has been successfully used for a host of pattern recognition, prediction and optimization problem over the last few decades.

**Rayleigh:** It is a type of distribution applicable to channel variations having strong line of sight components.

**Rician:** This is statistical distribution that can be used to describe channel characteristics where a strong LOS component is absent.

**Wireless:** It is state where there is no physical link. It refers to a type of channel that has no physical contact between the transmitter and receiver.

# Chapter 27
# A Novel 3D Approach for Patient Schedule Using Multi-Agent Coordination

**E. Grace Mary Kanaga**
*Karunya University, India*

**M.L. Valarmathi**
*Government College of Technology, India*

**Preethi S.H. Darius**
*Karunya University, India*

## ABSTRACT

*This chapter presents a novel 3D approach for patient scheduling (3D-PS) using multi-agents. Here the 3Ds refers to the Distributed, Dynamic and Decentralized nature of the patient scheduling. As in many other scheduling problems, in the hospital domain, a major problem is the efficient allocation of resources to the patients. The resources here mean the doctor, diagnosing equipments, lab tests, et cetera. Commonly, patient scheduling is performed manually by human schedulers with no automated support. Human scheduling is not efficient, because the nature of the problem is very complex; it is inherently distributed, dynamic, and decentralized. Since agents are known to represent distributed environment well and also being capable of handling dynamism, an agent based approach is chosen. The objectives are to reduce patient waiting times, minimize the patient stay in the hospital, and to improve resource utilization in hospitals. The comparison of several agent-based approaches is also reviewed, and the auction-based approach is chosen. The complete multi-agent framework given in literature is adapted to suit the patient scheduling scenario. The patient scheduling system is implemented in the JADE platform where patients and resources are represented as agents. The chief performance metric is the weighted tardiness which has to be minimized in order to obtain an effective schedule.*

DOI: 10.4018/978-1-61350-429-1.ch027

*The experiment is carried out using constant number of resources and varying number of patients. The simulation results are presented and analyzed. 3D-PS produces up to 30% reduction in total weighted tardiness in a distributed environment, as compared to other traditional algorithms. A further enhancement to this approach aims to reduce the communication overhead by reducing the number of messages passed and hence resulting in a better coordination mechanism. This auction based mechanism aims to provide the basic framework for future enhancements on patient scheduling.*

## INTRODUCTION

The process of scheduling patients involves different resources like doctors, diagnostic units, labs etc. Each one in general belongs to different – relatively autonomous – organizational units. Each organizational unit has particular preference structures, which lead to conflicts of interests. These conflicts should be resolved in a fair manner at the same time giving more preference to the patient need. The problem of resolving different interests becomes worse by environmental influences. In today's healthcare systems, patient satisfaction is a prime factor in addition to providing quality care. Priority is assigned for the patients and hence the resulting waiting time for various patients is depending on the health condition of the patient. A plausible solution and thus the objective of this chapter is to reduce the waiting times of patients while taking into account the priority level of each patient.

A multi-agent based approach is proposed in this chapter where each patient and resource is represented by an agent. In this fast growing era of technologies the application areas of agents are so vast. In most of the cases a single agent may not be able to achieve the entire goal by itself. So in complex applications, applying Multi-Agent System (MAS) is more reasonable. In most of the cases multi-agent systems are used to address the problems that are too large for a centralized agent. MAS are systems of interacting intelligent actors, or agents, existing in some environments. As discussed by Katia & Sycara(1998) the characteristics of a MAS is that, each agent has incomplete information or capabilities for solving the problem and, thus, has a limited view point, there is no system global control, data are decentralized and computation is asynchronous. The notions of multi-agent defined by Jiming Liu et al (2002), is presented below:

**Definition:** A multi-agent system is a system that contains the following elements:

1. An environment, *E*, a space in which the agents live.
2. A set of reactive rules, *R*, governing the interaction between the agents and their environment. They are the laws of the agent universe.
3. A set of agents, $A = \{a1, a2,..., an\}$

An altered variation of the common market based auction mechanism is used as a coordination mechanism in the scheduling process where the good to be auctioned is the timeslot, the resource agent is the auctioneer and the patients are the bidders. Integer programming with lagrangean relaxation is the optimization technique deployed to find an optimal and feasible schedule for a given time horizon.

## PROBLEM DOMAIN

In order to gain an in-depth comprehension of patient scheduling problem the typical model of patients flow adapted in the heath care domain is presented in the Figure 1. From this model, it can be seen that the patient care in hospitals is an iterative process and the treatment plan of patients keeps on changing with respect to time.

*Figure 1. Model of patient care in health care domain*

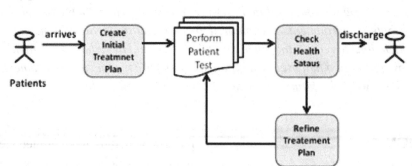

The healthcare domain is dynamic and distributed in nature as it involves various resources and departments and also the patient's health state changes unpredictably. To manage this situation the hospitals needs a better coordination among the hospital staff, resources and patients. The multiple constraints and goals like operation precedence, patient satisfaction, resource efficiency etc. to be achieved in minimal time makes this problem a complex one.

## Hospital Dynamics

In many modern hospitals, the hospitals are divided into many departments. This leads to a **distributed** structure where each department also has their own policies and preferences according to Vermeulen et al (2007) regarding the scheduling of their patients and allocation of the resources.

Some departments cater for the general needs of the hospital and other departments are highly specialized. Each department maintains a degree of independence and authority leading to a **decentralized** nature in hospitals.

Emergencies and complications result in a **dynamic** environment in a hospital. Emergencies are caused by an unpredictable arrival of patients requiring urgent care. Complications may arise during the course of treatment of a particular patient leads to unexpected delay and adjustments in the treatment plan. In some departments the influx of patients are stable and predictable such

as in orthopedics whereas in other departments such as surgical of neurosurgical the number of emergency cases and the patient dynamics are highly unpredictable (Decker & Li,1998).

## RELATED WORK

In the scheduling problem, a schedule has to be produced within a certain amount of time and all the agents involved have to agree with the produced schedule. Agents can reach an agreement by auctions, negotiation or argumentation or a combination of these techniques. Agents work together by task sharing or result sharing to achieve coordinated distributed problem solving (CDPS). The contract Net protocol is an example of a task-sharing protocol and agents often use some communication protocol such as FIPA for result-sharing. Agent coordination mechanisms include generalized partial global planning (GPGP), teamwork using joint intentions, cooperation without communication (coordination by mutual modeling) and also coordination via norms and social laws as stated by Michael Wooldridge (2009).

Auctions and negotiation are the coordination techniques that have been widely discussed in literature. In literature, the auction mechanism is usually used to produce a ranking of the tasks that result in a schedule. The negotiation approach is used during rescheduling an already existing schedule with the intention of improving the produced schedule. Auction-based scheduling has been proposed by Oueldhadj et al (2004), Lau et al (2007) and Liu et al (2004) for dynamic Job shop Scheduling (JSP) in the manufacturing domain. Dang & Frankovic (2002) have proposed it for operational planning and control. Furthermore, Mes et al (2007) and Jegou et al (2006) have proposed a similar approach for real-time transportation problems. Negotiation has been used in meeting scheduling as seen in BenHassine & Ho (2007) and Wainer et al (2007); Schedule adjustment in project management by Chen & Wang (2008) and also in the manufacturing domain by Wang et al (2008).

## Fields of Applications of Agents in Scheduling

Scheduling problems are found in a lot of application domains. Well known is the scheduling of production where manufacturing operations have to be assigned to limited resources like machines, but also other applications are important, e.g., the scheduling of airline crews, space missions, projects in different domains, clinical surgery, even timetabling and processor scheduling include scheduling problems.

## Agent-Assisted Scheduling in Education

Time-table scheduling, meeting scheduling, examination scheduling etc. are some of the complex NP hard problem involved in education domain. One such university course timetable scheduling is presented by Mihaela Oprea (2006).In the paper author has proposed a multi-agent based negotiation approach, which reduces the number of communication messages and improved the performance. Personalized software agents for meeting scheduling have the potential to reduce the daily cognitive load on computer users. Scheduling meetings can be a time consuming process requiring many email messages to be exchanged, and often existing meetings need to be moved to make room for new ones. Potentially, software agents can remove this burden entirely by communicating with each other to schedule meetings.

## Agent-Assisted Scheduling in Manufacturing Systems

The objective in a flexible manufacturing system is an optimal system resources scheduling. The production scheduling of such system may be resolved by a set of individual agents, which can work parallel and their coordination may bring a more effective way to find an optimal solution. An *agent based approach* allows representation of each object as responsible autonomous entities with own goals which models the inherently distributed environment of hospitals. The social abilities allow agents to interact with each other to reach their own goals that help realize adaptiveness and dynamism Chen and Wang (2008). Project scheduling in manufacturing units were discussed by Shen et al (2006).

## Agent-Assisted Scheduling in Business

Agent-assisted task allocation is used in many business applications such as airline reservation, cargo scheduling, consumer–buyer scenario etc. Rajdeep et al (2007) have been proposed market mechanisms in cases where the agents that are trying to sell the goods/resources (or provide services/ tasks) have a particular form of cost structure (consisting of a fixed overhead cost and a constant marginal cost) and finite production capacities (which are both privately known to them).

## Agent-Assisted Scheduling in Healthcare Domain

Scheduling is unavoidable and an integral part of hospital management. The systems developed for the hospital management are termed as Medical Information Systems. These systems include scheduling of personnel management, management of care units such as the Intensive Care Units (ICU's), management of Operating Rooms (OR's), management of laboratories and management of patient diagnoses and therapy and this has been discussed by Spyropoulos (2000).

The hospital scheduling problem is diverse and many papers have addressed different categories of the hospital scheduling problem and it is given in Figure 2. Some of the major problems addressed in literature are, patient/medical appointment scheduling (Vermeulen et al, 2007; Hans et al, 2008), specialized case of Surgical Case Scheduling (SCS) (Pham & Klinkert, 2008) / Operating Room(OR) scheduling (Becker et al, 2003), patient test scheduling in laboratories (Marinagi, 2000), and other specific scheduling for specific treatment plans such as scheduling for

treatment of radiotherapy (Kapamara et al, 2006). The problems specified can be solved using either a patient-centered approach or resource-centered approach.

## A NOVEL 3D PATIENT SCHEDULING

A novel 3D approach for patient scheduling using multi-agent coordination (3D-PS) is based on the Complete Multi-agent Framework (CMAF) in Liu et al (2007) and adapted for patient scheduling where each patient and resource is represented by an agent and combinatorial auction is used to produce a schedule. This framework employs a patient triggered auction where as CMAF is purely resource triggered to allocate resources to patients. A detailed system design is also given.

*Figure 2. Categories of hospital scheduling*

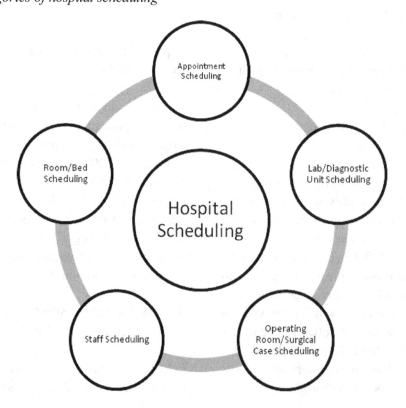

*Figure 3. Use case diagrams for 3D-PS*

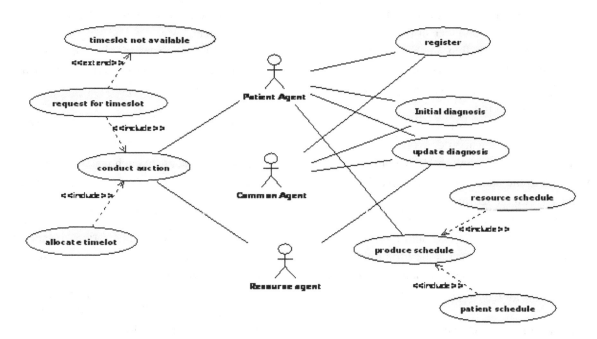

## 3D-PS Framework

A fully distributed framework proposed for patient scheduling problem is described using the use case diagram given in Figure 3.

In the use case diagram, there are 3 main actors, the Patient Agent (PA), Resource Agent (RA) and the Common Agent (CA). A brief description of each type of agent is given below:

**Common Agent (CA):** In our system, the common agent has multiple responsibilities. The common agent corresponds to the physical entity that registers a patient or resource to the system and maintains the patients and resources registered in the system. It is also responsible in some cases for prescribing an initial treatment plan for a patient.

**Patient Agent (PA):** The patient agents represent individually each instance of the patient entity. Multiple agents are used to represent each patient $PA_1, PA_2, ..., PA_n$. Patient agents are also bidders in the auction process. Both inpatients and outpatients are represented by a Patient Agent (PA). The patient agent is diagnosed and prescribed a treatment plan. This treatment plan is subject to constant disruption and changes due to the dynamics of the patient scheduling environment. Reasons include a change of treatment due to results obtained from a prior task or the improvement or deterioration of the patient's health condition. The treatment plan may span many departments in a hospital if each of the tasks involved needs a different resource. It is also subject to precedence constraints which task $i$ need to be performed before task $j$ can be carried out. Such constraints create a 'route' or 'flow' for a patient through the various resources involved.

**Resource Agent (RA):** The resource agent represents the various non-sharable resources in the hospital such as X-Rays, CT Scans, Lab tests, and also specialists and other physicians. Again, multiple agents are employed to represent each resource $RA_1, RA_2, ...RA_m$. Resource agents are subject to various machine constraints imposed by the physical limitations as well as organizational policies and goal. Each resource agent has multiple timeslots of a specified duration. These timeslots are integer values and will be allocated to the winning task in a patient agent. Resource agent acts as the auctioneer in the auction process of patient scheduling. Each resource agents consists of the logic necessary to calculate price, evaluate bid and perform price adjustment, and finally to select a bid.

The patient agents and resource agents then participate in an auction in order to obtain a schedule for both parties. If the timeslot is available, it is allocated to the patient agent. ACL (Agent Communication Language) messages such as CFP (Call for Proposal) and PROPOSE/REFUSE messages are passed between the PA's and RA's in order to arrive at an optimal schedule for a given time horizon. The final output is the optimal feasible schedule for patients and resources.

## Problem Formulation for the 3D-PS Framework

A patient scheduling problem is a scheduling environment in the hospital domain where a set of $n$ patients (or jobs) $J = \{J_1, ..., J_n\}$ have to be scheduled on a set of $m$ resources $R = \{R_1, ..., R_n\}$. Each patient $J_i$ is composed of a set of sequential tasks (operations). $O_{ik}$, $i = 1, ..., n_i$, $n_i \leq m$, where $i$ is the index of the patient, and $k$ is the index of the task or the operation. Processing time of task $j$ of patient $i$ is denoted by $p_{ij}$. Patients can have any number of tasks and sequences of using resources. The problem constraints of patient scheduling include the following:

- Operation constraints to ensure that at any particular time slot only one operation of the same patient can be performed.
- Operational temporal precedence constraints, i.e., a task (preliminary lab test) must be finished before the next task (consultation with the doctor) of the patient can be started.

- Resource capacity constraints, i.e., at any point of time, a resource can process only one patient.
- Arrival time constraints, i.e., the first task of the patient can be started only after the arrival time $at_i$ of the patient $J_i$

A solution of the patient scheduling problem is a feasible schedule, which assigns a start time $st_{ij}$ and an end time $et_{ij}$ to each task $O_{ij}$ that satisfies all the aforesaid constraints. Hospitals are interested in optimizing a schedule according to the objective functions that reflects patient satisfaction and resource utilization. Hence in this thesis, as mentioned in the previous chapters, the weighted tardiness (lateness) is used as the objective function. The Integer Programming formulation for the novel 3D-patient scheduling problem is modeled as follows.

The objective function minimizes total weighted waiting time given by

$$\sum_{i=1}^{Nc} \sum_{t=t_c}^{t_c+L} w_i T_i X_{iO_it} \qquad (1)$$

This objective is subject to the following constraints:

*Constraint 1:* Operation constraints to ensure that at any particular time slot only one operation of the same patient can be completed.

$$\sum_{t=t_c}^{t_c+L} X_{ijt} = 1, \forall i, j \qquad (2)$$

*Constraint 2:* Task Precedence constraints of two tasks.

$$\sum_{t=t_c}^{t_c+L} t X_{ijt} + p_{ij+1} \leq \sum_{t=t_c}^{t_c+L} t X_{i,j+1,t}, \forall i, j \qquad (3)$$

*Constraint 3:* Resource capacity constraints to ensure that the capacity of the resource is not violated in each timeslot.

$$\sum_{i=1}^{Nc}\sum_{j=K_i}^{O_i}X_{ijt}Y_{ijm}$$
$$+\sum_{i=1}^{Nc}\sum_{j=K_i}^{O_i}\sum_{t'=L+1}^{\min\{L,t+p_{ij}-1\}}\times X_{ijt'}Y_{ijm}\le 1,\forall m,t$$

$$(4)$$

*Constraint 4:* Patient release date constraints to ensure that the first task cannot be completed before the patient has been in the hospital for at least the time equal to the processing of the first task.

$$\sum_{t=t_c}^{t_c+L}tX_{ijt}\ge p_{i1}+r_i,\forall i \qquad (5)$$

where,

$i = 1,...Nc$ Total number of patients.

$j = 1,...O_i$ Total number of tasks.

$m=1, M_c$ Total number of resources.

$t = t_c,...t_c + L$ Time horizon.

$K_i$ Total number of unprocessed tasks.

$\lambda_{mt}$ Price of the timeslot $t$ in resource $m$.

$p_{ij}$ Processing time of task $j$ of patient $i$.

$r_i$ Arrival time of patient $i$.

$d_i$ Due time of patient $i$.

$C_i$ Completion time of task $O_i$.

$T_i=max(0,C_i-d_i)$ The tardiness (waiting time) of patient $i$.

$w_i$ Weight based on priority assigned to patient $i$.

$tavail_i=t_1,t_2,...$ Availability of patient $i$,

$X_{ijt} \in \{0,1\}, \forall i,j,t$ Integer variable equals 1 if task (i,j) is completed at time t.

$Y_{ijm} \in \{0,1\}, \forall i,j,m$ Integer variable equals 1 if task (i,j) is processed on resource m.

The above problem formulation is for a centralized approach. Lagrangean relaxation of the resource constraints is done to decompose the problem into patient level and resource level sub problems in order to solve the problem in a *distributed* environment.

## 3D-PS Auction Based Scheduling Mechanism

The scheduling mechanism is auction based and each resource and each patient is an agent. Each resource agent is an auctioneer and each patient agent is a bidder. Patient agent requests for a combination of timeslots from resource agents leading to a combinatorial auction. The fully distributed algorithm is partly adapted from (Czap &M. Becker, 2003).

**Step 1:** Registration of Patient

Upon Patient's arrival the patient is registered by the Common Agent. The initial set of tasks and any precedence constrained are also recorded. Each task requires a particular resource for a given time period. The patient availability times, given by the set of Timeslots requested, $TS_{req_i} t_1, t_2...$ are also recorded.

In the case where the patients request is not met due to the resource not being available at the requested timeslot, the auction becomes resource triggered where the patient waits for Call For Proposals (CFP) from the resource. The procedure is given in Steps 10 and 11.

**Step 2:** Construction of Bids by Patient Agents

After the Patient registration is complete, a local schedule for each patient that minimized total weighted waiting time is created subject to the constraints given in addition to the patient availability constraints and patient preference.

The patient agents look up the prices of the required timeslots in various resources, $\lambda_{mt}$ and constructs bids. The bids consist of the required timeslots for the duration of the task's processing time and the value of the bid given by $\{[X_{ijt} - p_{ij}, X_{ijt}], P_{\lambda_i}\}$.

**Step 3:** Calculation of price by the resource agent.

If the timeslot requested is not taken, initial price is calculated, as the sum of weighted waiting time of all the patients in the feasible schedule. Patient agents are then inquired with the new cost. This is the upper bound of the auction at iteration r.

$$UB^r = \min\{UB^{r-1}, |V(P(\lambda_{feasible}^r)|\} \tag{6}$$

**Step 4:** Updation of bids by patient agent

With the prices $\lambda_{mt}$, patient agents again compute and submit bid in the auction. $\{[X_{ijt} - p_{ij}, X_{ijt}], P_{\lambda_i}\}$.

**Step 5:** Updation of its prices by the resource agent for the patient agents who submitted bids.

The lower bound of the auction is the value of the total weighted waiting time of the infeasible schedule.

$$LB^r = \max\{LB^{r-1}, |V(P_D(\lambda^r)|\},$$

where

$$P_D = \sum_{i=1}^{N_c} V(P_{\lambda_i}) - \sum_{t=t_c}^{t_c+L} \lambda_{mt} \tag{7}$$

**Step 6:** Checking for Stopping Criterion

If $UB^r - LB^r < \square(\square > 0,\ \alpha^r \approx 0, r > \max$ *Iterations*), go to step 9, else go to step 7.

**Step 7:** Calculation of Price Adjustment by the resource agent.

A sub gradient search (SG) in the context of lagrangean relaxation is a particular version of combinatorial auction as given in Pooja Dewan and Sanjay Joshi (2002).

$$SG_t^r = \left\{ \sum_{i=1}^{N_c} \sum_{j=K_i}^{O_i} X_{ijt} + \sum_{i=1}^{N_c} \sum_{j=K_i}^{O_i} \sum_{t'=t+1}^{\min\{L,t+p_{ij}-1\}} X_{ijt'} - 1 \right\} \tag{8}$$

The step size for the auction is also calculated.

$$S^r = \frac{\alpha^r.(UB^r - LB^r)}{\sum_{t_c+L}^{t_c+L} (SG_t^r)^2} \tag{9}$$

The new prices are calculated as follows,

$$(F_s)\lambda_t^{r+1} = \max\{0, \lambda_t^r + S^r.SG_t^r\} \tag{10}$$

Now, the new prices are announced to all the patient agents who requested the resource.

**Step 8:** Incrementing the iteration counter

$r = r + 1$; Go to step 4.

**Step 9:** Evaluate the bids

Announce the patient agent with $Min\{X_{ijt} - p_{ij}\}$ as the winner.
Assign the timeslots

$$\begin{bmatrix} Min\{X_{ijt} - p_{ij}, t + X_{ijt} - p_{ij}\}, \\ Min\{X_{ijt} - p_{ij}, t + X_{ijt} - p_{ij}\} + p_{ij} \end{bmatrix}$$

to the winner patient agent.

Resource-oriented – If resource is not available and patient needs the resource.

**Step 10:** Sending explicit request to resource

The patient agent sends an explicit request to the resource to indicate the need for the resource at any time the resource becomes available.

**Step 11:** Triggering of auction by resource agent when timeslot becomes available.

When the resource agent becomes available, it looks up the list of pending patient agents, and invites bids for the timeslot from the patient agents. Go to Step 2.

## IMPLEMENTATION

The proposed system is implemented in the JADE platform. JADE (Java Agent DEvelopment Framework) Fabio Bellifemine et al (2007) is a software framework fully implemented in Java language. It simplifies the implementation of multi-agent systems through a middle-ware that complies with the FIPA specifications. The agent platform can be distributed across machines (which need not share the same OS) and the configuration can be controlled via a remote GUI. The Novel 3D Patient Scheduling (3D-PS) is simulated in the JADE platform and results are discussed below

### Experimental Design

In order to evaluate the performance of the framework as compared to other frameworks or algorithms, standard JSP bench mark problems are used. These problems are available in various sizes. These problems are used to calculate the objective, which is the weighted tardiness (waiting time), based on the number of jobs, resources and operations, release date, due date and weight of the job and also its route through the machines. For comparison, the random 3x3 JSP (Kutanoglu and Wu. 1999), and Qi8x4 problem are used. The input for the 3x3 patient scheduling problem in accordance with 3x3 JSP bench mark problem is given in Table 1.

For 3x3 problem, 3 resources are considered. Say, *Resource 1:* Cardiologist, *Resource 2:* CT scan and Resource *3:* Blood Test. An assumption is made that the patients require these three resources in different orders for varying durations.

*Table 1. 3x3 JSP Bench mark problem*

| Patient | Arrival | Weight | Task Sequence | Processing Time (min) | | | Due Date |
|---|---|---|---|---|---|---|---|
| 1 | 3 | 4 | 1 2 3 | 3 | 1 | 6 | 10 |
| 2 | 6 | 6 | 3 2 1 | 3 | 7 | 1 | 10 |
| 3 | 9 | 2 | 1 3 2 | 2 | 4 | 4 | 12 |

The weight and the arrival times of the patients are taken similar to the values given by the bench mark problems. The processing time is the time required to complete a particular task in particular resource. Here the assumption is made that 1 time slot is equal to 10 minutes.

The dynamic release time is given by grouping patients together and giving an arbitrary arrival time 3, 6, 9, The due date is calculated using the following formula,

$$d_i = r_i + \left\lceil f \sum_{j=1}^{O_i} p_{ij} \right\rceil \qquad (11)$$

where $f$ is the due date tightness factor. In our simulations we have used $f=1.7$. Experimental inputs are generated for 3 patients, 10 patients, 15 patients and 20 patients. The performance evaluation and result analysis will be discussed in the following section.

## Results and Discussion

The auction-based multi-agent framework is implemented in the JADE multi-agent platform. The patient agents and resource agents in the database are first initialized. Patient interface and resource interface are developed showing the scheduling details for the individual patient and resource. At the end of the auction, optimal feasible schedules are produced for each patient agent and resource agent. Figure 4 shows the screen shot of patient agents placing bids for timeslots and allocation of resource after auction. Figure 5 displays the global optimal feasible schedule for 3x3 problem.

## Performance Evaluation

The performance of the multi-agent system is evaluated against the performance of traditional scheduling algorithms such as (First Come First Serve) FCFS, (Earliest Due Date first) EDD, (Longest Processing time first) LPT, (Shortest Processing time first) SPT, (Weighted Shortest

*Figure 4. Patient agents placing bids for timeslots and allocation of resource after auction*

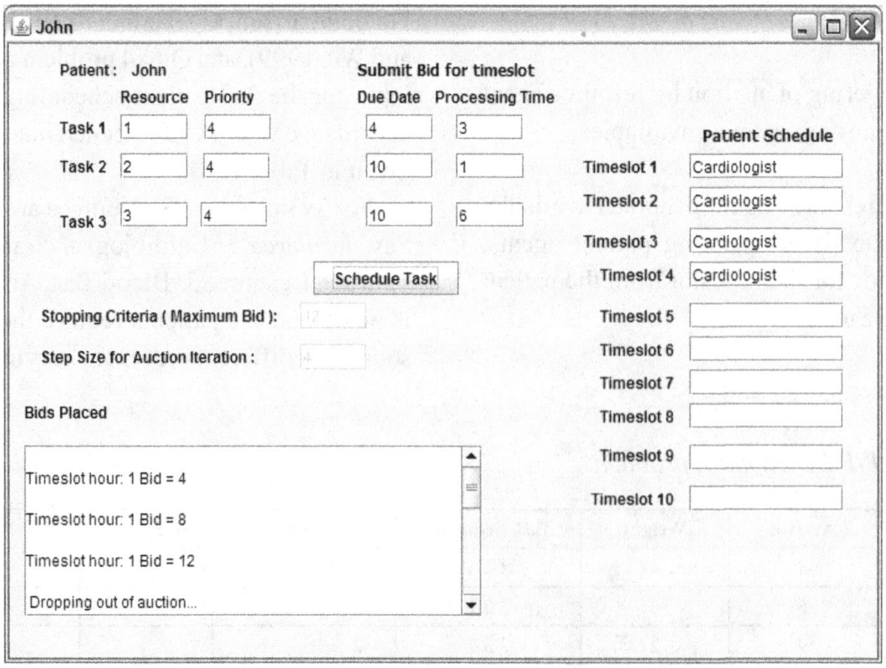

*Figure 5. The global optimal feasible schedule for 3x3 problem*

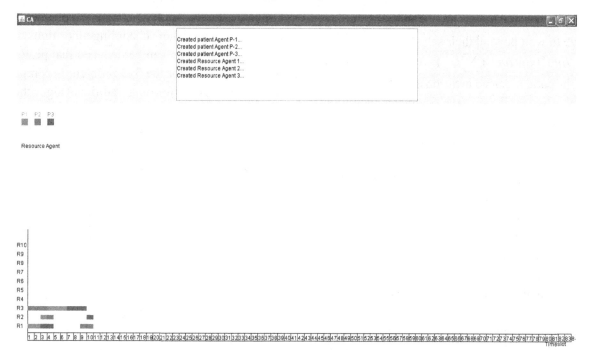

Processing Time first) WSPT and (Minimal Slack first) MS. LEKIN software is used to obtain the performance of these commonly used dispatching rules.

## Performance Metrics

The objective of patient scheduling problem is to minimize the patient waiting time and improve the resource utilization in the hospitals. The following performance metrics are useful in evaluating the patient scheduling problem. A good scheduling technique will effectively minimize the values of all these metrics.

*Total weighted Waiting Time* $\left( \sum w_j T_j \right)$ - chief metric used to evaluate the patient scheduling algorithm. It indicates whether the patient waiting time is minimized by also taking the priority of the patient into account. Below is an explanation of the calculation of the total weighted waiting time.

*Total weighted waiting time* is calculated using the formula

$$\sum_{i=1}^{n} w_i \times T_i \tag{12}$$

*Total Waiting Time* $\left( \sum T_j \right)$ - gives the overall total waiting time of all the patients.

*Maximum Waiting Time* $(T_{max})$- The metric is refers to the maximum lateness of all patients where for an individual patient it is a value equal to the completion time minus the due time. gives the worst case scenario of how long a patient might be delayed in the worst case.

*Makespan* $(C_{max})$ - The maximum completion time for all the patients. In terms of patient scheduling, it refers to the time the last patient checks out and the time all the tasks in their diagnosis is complete.

555

*Total number of Patients scheduled late* $(\sum U_j)$ - a good measure of how many patients have to wait beyond their scheduled time.

*Total flow time* $(\sum C_j)$ - Amount of time the all the patients spend in the hospital from the time they arrive until they have completed their treatment. For patient scheduling we want to minimize this metric to minimize the patient stay in the hospital.

*Total weighted flow time* $(\sum w_j C_j)$ - includes the priority of the patient when calculating the total flow time.

The results are compared against traditional scheduling algorithms based on the above said performance metrics. The coordination technique is also analyzed and discussed. The numerical results for 3x3 problem and Qi8x4 problem are presented in Tables 2 and 3 respectively. For the 3x3 problem, the results obtained for the 3D-PS

framework is identical to the WSPT results. In Qi8x4 problem, 3D-PS performs averagely as compared to the other scheduling algorithms.

From Figure 6 it can be deduced that performance of 3D-PS for the 3x3 problem is comparable to the best performing traditional algorithm which is MS.

Figure 6 (a) shows the different performance results obtained for the maximum waiting time, total waiting time, and total number of patients scheduled late, and total weighted waiting time from comparisons made against traditional scheduling algorithms. Fig. 6(b) shows the comparison of weighted waiting time for 3x3 and 8x4 problems. The maximum waiting time can be seen in Figure 7(a). We can deduce that the performance of 3D-PS is comparable to FCFS. Also we can see that MS and WSPT perform worst when number of patient is equal to 10. SPT produces the least number of patients scheduled late as seen

*Table 2. Comparison of performance metrics for 3x3 benchmark problem*

|  | Max Waiting time | Total Waiting Time | Total Weighted Waiting Time | Number of Late Patients |
|---|---|---|---|---|
| **FCFS** | 6 | 6 | 12 | 1 |
| **EDD** | 11 | 15 | 74 | 2 |
| **MS** | 4 | 7 | 74 | 2 |
| **LPT** | 4 | 7 | 22 | 2 |
| **WSPT** | 6 | 6 | 12 | 1 |
| **3D-PS** | 6 | 6 | 12 | 1 |

*Table 3. Comparison of performance metrics for Qi8x4 problem*

|  | Max Waiting time | Total Waiting Time | Total Weighted Waiting Time | Number of Late Patients |
|---|---|---|---|---|
| **FCFS** | 2 | 3 | 9 | 2 |
| **EDD** | 14 | 14 | 77 | 4 |
| **MS** | 10 | 30 | 136 | 5 |
| **SPT** | 24 | 46 | 218 | 3 |
| **LPT** | 11 | 30 | 77 | 4 |
| **WSPT** | 8 | 18 | 59 | 5 |
| **3D-PS** | 10 | 35 | 125 | 4 |

*Figure 6. (a) Comparison of Maximum Waiting time, Total Waiting time and Makespan with 3D-PS for 3x3 Problem, (b) Comparison of Weighted Waiting time of 3x3 and 8x4 benchmark problems.*

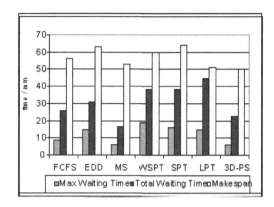 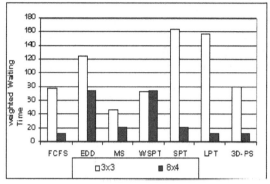

*Figure 7. Comparison of Dynamic Patient Scheduling for 3 resources and varying number of patients for (a) Maximum Waiting Time, (b) Total number of Patients Scheduled Late, (c) Makespan (d) Total Weighted Waiting Time.*

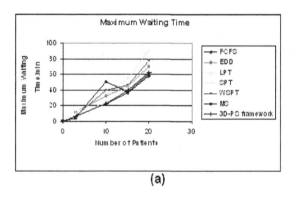 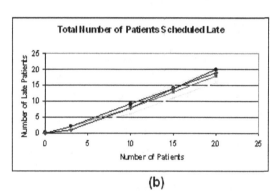

(a)      (b)

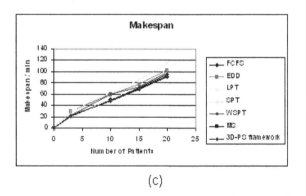 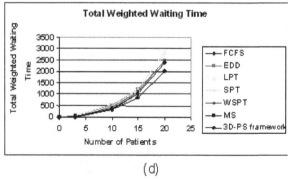

(c)      (d)

in Figure 7(b). It performs best and 3D-PS is comparable to EDD and performs slightly better than MS and FCFS. Figure 7(c) shows the comparison of makespan and it can be deduced that

3D-PS is very effective in reducing the makespan as the number of patients increase. In reducing the weighted waiting time as seen in Figure 7(d), 3D-PS performance is comparable to the best

*Table 4. Analysis of messages passed for a time horizon of 100 timeslots*

| ACL Messages | 3x3 | 3x10 | 3x15 | 3x20 |
|---|---|---|---|---|
| CFP | 837 | 2280 | 2850 | 3120 |
| PROPOSE/REFUSE | 837 | 2280 | 2850 | 3120 |
| ACCEPT/REJECT PROPOSAL | 12 | 61 | 126 | 246 |
| INFORM/FAILURE | 9 | 30 | 45 | 60 |
| Total | 1695 | 4651 | 5871 | 6546 |

performing traditional technique such as WSPT and MS. For 20 patients, the weighted waiting time of FCFS and 3D-PS is 2000 whereas in other algorithms it is 2500 to 2900 which a 20-30% increases in performance.

## Theoretical Analysis of the Efficiency of the Coordination Technique

The effectiveness of the scheduling technique can be evaluated by analyzing the number of messages passed. As given in Table 4, the total number of messages passed including CFP's, PROPOSE/REFUSE messages, ACCEPT_PROPOSAL/REJECT_PROPOSAL messages and INFORM/FAILURE messages during the course of the auctions is given by the formula

$$\sum_{1}^{a} \left( \sum_{1}^{r} 2n \right) + (n+1) \qquad (13)$$

where a is the number of auctions conducted during the timeslot $t = t_c..t_c+L$ and $1 \geq r \leq$ max *Iterations*.

Figure 8 shows the analysis of the number of messages passed during a period of 100 timeslots for up to 20 patients. This graph is extrapolated for 100 patients in Figure 9 and analyzed.

As the number of patients increase as seen in Figure 9, it can be observed that the number of message increases logarithmically. The logarithmic increase indicates that the framework is efficient because the growth is slow.

## FUTURE WORK AND RESEARCH DIRECTIONS

The future scope of the project work involves employing Genetic Algorithm (GA), Particle Swarm Optimization (PSO) and other heuristic approaches instead of the exact methods. Integer Linear Programming involves searching the

*Figure 8. Analysis of messages passed for up to 20 patients for 100 timeslots*

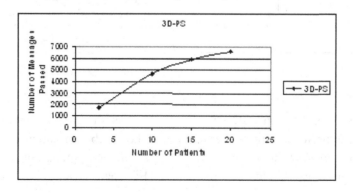

*Figure 9. Analysis of the number of messages passed during time horizon of 100*

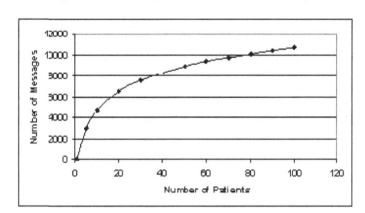

entire search space. Genetic algorithm can be applied to reduce this search space in distributed environment. Genetic algorithm has been proved to reduce computations time and also produce a fully improved solution as compared to other dispatching rules for dynamic scheduling as discussed by Mattfeld & Bierwirth C(2004), Other evolutionary techniques can also be researched such as simulated annealing (Krishna et al,1995) and ant-colony optimization as specified by Xiang & Lee (2008). Other bidding strategies can also be explored such as with Dutch auctions, Vickrey auctions (Reeves et al,2005).

## CONCLUSION

The Dynamic Multi-agent Patient Scheduling (3D-PS) framework is analyzed, designed and implemented. This framework is implemented in JADE agent platform. This agent-based solution is chosen because of the flexibility, robustness and adaptability of agents as compared to the traditional scheduling algorithms and also because agents work well in dynamic, distributed and decentralized environment. This framework has the ability to handle the dynamic nature of patient scheduling quite effectively. The patient scheduling domain is a highly dynamic domain and an effective solution will improve the quality of life of the society. A schedule that minimizes the patient waiting time may even aid in saving the person's life.

## REFERENCES

Becker, M., Navarro, M., Krempels, K. H., & Panchenko, A. (2003). *Agent based scheduling of operation theatres*. In EU-LAT eHealth Workshop on Agent Based Scheduling of Operation Theatres.

Bellifemine, F., Caire, G., & Greenwood, D. (2007). *Developing multi-agent system with JADE.* Wiley series.

Ben Hassine, A., & Ho, T. B. (2007). An agent-based approach to solve dynamic meeting scheduling problems with preferences. *Engineering Applications of Artificial Intelligence, 20*(6), 857–873. doi:10.1016/j.engappai.2006.10.004

Chen, Y. M., & Wang, S. C. (2008). An evolutionary compensatory negotiation model for distributed dynamic scheduling. *Applied Soft Computing, 8*(2), 1093–1104. doi:10.1016/j.asoc.2007.05.018

Czap, H., & Becker, M. (2003). Multi-agent systems and microeconomic theory: A negotiation approach to solve scheduling problems in high dynamic environments. In *Proceedings of the 36th Annual Hawaii International Conference on System Sciences*, (p. 8).

Dang, T.-T., & Frankovic, B. (2002). Agent based scheduling in production systems. *International Journal of Production Research*, *40*(15), 3669–3679. doi:10.1080/00207540210140022

Dash, R. K., Vytelingum, P., Rogers, A., David, E., & Jennings, N. R. (2007). Market-based task allocation mechanisms for limited-capacity suppliers. *IEEE Transactions on Systems Man and Cybernetics – Part A: Systems and*, *37*(3), 391–405. doi:10.1109/TSMCA.2007.893474

Decker, K., & Li, J. (1998). Coordinated hospital patient scheduling. *Third International Conference on Multi Agent Systems (ICMAS'98)*, (p. 104).

Dewan, P., & Joshi, S. (2002). Auction-based distributed scheduling in a dynamic job shop environment. *International Journal of Production Research*, *40*(5), 1173–1191. doi:10.1080/00207540110098445

Hans, E., Wullink, G., van Houdenhoven, M., & Kazemier, G. (2008). Robust surgery loading. *European Journal of Operational Research*, *185*(3), 1038–1050. doi:10.1016/j.ejor.2006.08.022

Jegou, D., Kim, D. W., Baptiste, P., & Lee, P. K. H. (2006). A contract net based intelligent agent system for solving the reactive hoist scheduling problem. *Expert Systems with Applications*, *30*(2), 156–167. doi:10.1016/j.eswa.2005.06.019

Kapamara, T., Sheibani, K., Hass, O. C. L., Reeves, C. R., & Petrovic, D. (2006). A review of scheduling problems in radiotherapy. In *Proceedings of 18th International Conference on Systems Engineering*, (pp. 207-211).

Krishna, K., Ganeshan, K., & Ram, D. J. (1995). Distributed simulated annealing algorithms for job shop scheduling. *IEEE Transactions on Systems, Man, and Cybernetics*, *25*(7), 1102. doi:10.1109/21.391290

Kutanoglu, E., & Wu, S. D. (1999). On combinatorial auction and Lagrangean relaxation for distributed resource scheduling. *IIE Transactions*, *31*(9). doi:10.1080/07408179908969883

LEKIN. (2001). *LEKIN*. The Stern School of Business, New York University, New York.

Liu, J., Jing, H., & Tang, Y. Y. (2002). Multi-agent oriented constraint satisfaction. *Artificial Intelligence*, *136*, 101–144. doi:10.1016/S0004-3702(01)00174-6

Marinagi, C. C., Spyropoulos, C. D., Papatheodorou, C., & Kokkotos, S. (2000). Continual planning and scheduling for managing patient tests in hospital laboratories. *Artificial Intelligence in Medicine*, *20*(2), 139–154. doi:10.1016/S0933-3657(00)00061-0

Mattfeld, D. C., & Bierwirth, C. (2004). An efficient genetic algorithm for job shop scheduling with tardiness objectives. *European Journal of Operational Research*, 616–630. doi:10.1016/S0377-2217(03)00016-X

Mes, M., Van der Heijden, M., & Van Harten, A. (2007). Comparison of agent-based scheduling to look-ahead heuristics for real-time transportation problems. *European Journal of Operational Research*, *181*(1), 59–75. doi:10.1016/j.ejor.2006.02.051

Oprea, M. (2006). Multi-agent system for university course timetable scheduling. In the *1st International Conference on Virtual Learning, ICVL*, (pp. 231-238).

Ouelhadj, D. (2004). Inter-agent cooperation and communication for agent-based robust dynamic scheduling in steel production. *Advanced Engineering Informatics*, *18*(3), 161–172. doi:10.1016/j.aei.2004.10.003

Pham, D.-N., & Klinkert, A. (2008). Surgical case scheduling as a generalized job shop scheduling problem. *European Journal of Operational Research*, *185*(3), 1011–1025. doi:10.1016/j. ejor.2006.03.059

Reeves, D. M., Wellman, M. P., & MacKie-Maso, J. K. (2005). Exploring bidding strategies for market-based scheduling. *Decision Support Systems*, *39*(1), 67–85. doi:10.1016/j.dss.2004.08.014

Shen, W., Wang, L., & Hao, Q. (2006). Agent-based distributed manufacturing process planning and scheduling: A state-of-the-art survey. *IEEE Trans. Systems, Man, and Cybernetics-Part C. Applications and Reviews*, *36*(4), 563–577.

Spyropoulos, C. D. (2000). AI planning and scheduling in the medical hospital environment. *Artificial Intelligence in Medicine*, *20*(2), 101–111. doi:10.1016/S0933-3657(00)00059-2

Sycara, K. P. (1998). *Multi-agent systems*. Publication of AAAI, 1998.

Trentesaux, D., Pesin, P., & Tahon, C. (2001). Comparison of constraint logic programming and distributed problem solving: A case study for inter-active, efficient, and practicable job-shop scheduling. *Computers & Industrial Engineering*, *29*, 187–211. doi:10.1016/S0360-8352(00)00078-4

Vermeulen, I., Bohte, S., Somefun, K., & La Poutré, H. (2007). Multi-agent pareto appointment exchanging in hospital patient scheduling. *Service Oriented Computing and Applications*, *1*(3), 185–196. doi:10.1007/s11761-007-0012-1

Wainer, J., Ferreira, P. R., & Constantino, E. R. (2007). Scheduling meetings through multi-agent negotiations. *Decision Support Systems*, *44*(1), 285–297. doi:10.1016/j.dss.2007.03.015

Wooldridge, M. (2009). *An introduction to multi agent systems* (2nd ed.). John Wiley and Sons.

Xiang, W., & Lee, H. P. (2008). Ant colony intelligence in multi-agent dynamic manufacturing scheduling. *Engineering Applications of Artificial Intelligence*, 73–84. doi:10.1016/j.engappai.2007.03.008

## ADDITIONAL READING

BenHassine, A., & Ho, T. B. (2007). An agent-based approach to solve dynamic meeting scheduling problems with preferences. *Engineering Applications of Artificial Intelligence*, *20*(6), 857–873. doi:10.1016/j.engappai.2006.10.004

Cheng, R., Gen, M., & Tsujimura, Y. (1996). A tutorial survey of job-shop scheduling problems using genetic algorithms, part I: Representation. *Computers & Industrial Engineering*, *30*, 983–987. doi:10.1016/0360-8352(96)00047-2

Durfee, E. H. (2001). Scaling up agent coordination strategies. *IEEE Computer*, *34*(7), 39–46. doi:10.1109/2.933502

Eren, T., & Guener, E. (2008). A bicriteria flow-shop scheduling with a learning effect. *Applied Mathematical Modelling*, (32): 1719–1733. doi:10.1016/j.apm.2007.06.009

Gen, M., Tsujimura, Y., & Kubota, E. (1994), "Solving job-shop scheduling problem using genetic algorithms," *Proceedings of the 16th International Conference on Computer and Industrial Engineering*, pp. 576-585.

Glover, F. (1989), "Tabu search - Part I," ORSA Journal on Computing, vol.1, no.3, pp. 190-206.

Jegou, D., Kim, D. W., Baptiste, P., & Lee, K. A. (2006). A contract net based intelligent agent system for solving the reactive hoist scheduling problem. *Expert Systems with Applications*, *30*(2), 156–167. doi:10.1016/j.eswa.2005.06.019

Jegou, D., Kim, D. W., Baptiste, P., & Lee, K. A. (2006). A contract net based intelligent agent system for solving the reactive hoist scheduling problem. *Expert Systems with Applications, 30*(2), 156–167. doi:10.1016/j.eswa.2005.06.019

Kennedy, J., & Eberhart, R. (1995), " Particle Swarm Optimization," *Proceedings of IEEE International Conference on Neural Networks*, vol.4, pp. 1942-1948.

Lau, H. C., Cheng, S. F., Leong, T. Y., Park, J. H., & Zhao, Z. (2007), "Multi-Period Combinatorial Auction Mechanism for Distributed Resource Allocation and Scheduling", in IEEE/WIC/ACM Int. Conf. on Intelligent Agent Technology, pp. 407-411

Liu, H., Abraham, A., & Wang, Z. (2009). A Multi-swarm Approach to Multi-objective Flexible Job-shop Scheduling Problems. *Fundamenta Informaticae, 95*, 1–25.

Liu, N. Abdelrahman. M.A,Ramaswamy. S (2004), "A multi-agent model for reactive job shop scheduling", In Proc. of the 36th Southeastern Symp. on System Theory, pp. 241-245.

Maik Günther and Volker Nissen (2010), "Particle Swarm Optimization and an Agent-Based Algorithm for a Problem of Staff Scheduling, " Applications of Evolutionary Computation LNCS vol. 6025/2010, pp. 451-461.

Malone, T. W., & Crowston, K. (1994). The interdisciplinary study of coordination. *ACM Computing Surveys, 26*(1), 87–119. doi:10.1145/174666.174668

Mehouuni, E., Sammadi, S., & Borne, P. (2004). Evolutionary Algorithms for Job Shop Scheduling. *International Journal on Applied Mathematical Sciences, 14*, 91–103.

Mes, M., van der Heijden, M., & van Harten, A. (2007). Comparison of agent-based scheduling to look-ahead heuristics for real-time transportation problems. *European Journal of Operational Research, 181*(1), 59–75. doi:10.1016/j.ejor.2006.02.051

Mosheiov, G. (2001). Scheduling problems with a learning effect. *European Journal of Operational Research, 132*(3), 687–693. doi:10.1016/S0377-2217(00)00175-2

Ouelhadj, D., Petrovic, S., Cowling, P. I., & Meisels, A. (2004). Inter-agent cooperation and communication for agent-based robust dynamic scheduling in steel production. *Advanced Engineering Informatics, 18*(3), 161–172. doi:10.1016/j.aei.2004.10.003

Patrick Beaumont and Brahim Chaib-draa (2007), "Multi-agent Coordination Techniques for Complex Environments: The Case of a Fleet of Combat Ships," IEEE Trans. on System Man and Cybernetics Part C Part C Applications And Reviews, vol. 37, no. 3, pp. 373–385.

Paulussen, T. O., Jennings, N. R., Decker, K. S., & Heinzl, A. (2003). "Distributed patient scheduling in hospital", proceedings of International Joint Conference. *Artificial Intelligence, 18*, 1224–1232.

Starkweather, T., Whitley, D., & Cookson, B. (1993), "A Genetic Algorithm for scheduling with resource consumption.," *Proceedings of the Joint German/US Conference on Operations Research in Production Planning and Control*, 567-583.

Tasgetiren, F. M, Mehmet Sevkli, Yun-Chia Liang, and Gunes Gencyilmaz (2004), "Particle Swarm Optimization Algorithm for Permutation Flowshop Sequencing Problem," *Proceedings of the International Workshop on Ant Colony Optimization and Swarm Intelligence*, LNCS 3172, pp.382-390.

Vakharia A. and Y. Chang (1990), "A simulated annealing approach to scheduling a manufacturing cell,"Naval Research Logistics, 37, pp- 559-577.

Villi Podgorelec and Peter Kotal, (December 1997) "Genetic Algorithm Based System for Patient Scheduling in Highly Constrained Situations," Journal of Medical Systems, Springer Netherlands, Volume 21, Number 6.

Wainer, J., Ferreira, P. R., & Constantino, E. R. (2007). Scheduling meetings through multi-agent negotiations. *Decision Support Systems*, *44*(1), 285–297. doi:10.1016/j.dss.2007.03.015

Zhixiong Liu. (2007), "Investigations of Particle Swarm Optimization for Job Shop Scheduling Problem," *Proceedings of the Third International Conference on Natural Computation*, vol.3, pp. 799-803.

## KEY TERMS AND DEFINITIONS

**Agent:** An agent is a computational system, situated in some environment that is capable of flexible, autonomous action in order to meet its design objectives, as defined by (Wooldridge 2009).

**Auction:** A public sale in which property or items of merchandise are sold to the highest bidder.

**Coordination:** Coordination is the process by which the inter-dependencies between the agent's activities are managed, as mentioned by Patrick Beaumont and Brahim Chaib-draa (2007).

**Multi-Agent System:** Multi-agent systems are systems of interacting intelligent actors, or agents, existing in some environments.

**Optimization:** Optimization refers to choosing the best element from some set of available alternatives.

**Scheduling:** A method used to schedule jobs for execution.

**Tardiness:** Lateness - occurring or done after the scheduled, expected, or usual time.

## Chapter 28

# A Fuzzy Approach to Disaster Modeling:
## Decision Making Support and Disaster Management Tool for Emergency Medical Rescue Services

**Jan Stoklasa**
*Palacky University in Olomouc, Czech Republic*

## ABSTRACT

*The decision making process of the Emergency Medical Rescue Services (EMRS) operations centre during disasters involves a significant amount of uncertainty. Decisions need to be made quickly, and no mistakes are tolerable, particularly in the case of disasters resulting in a large number of injured people. A multiphase linguistic fuzzy model is introduced to assist the operator during the initial phase of the medical disaster response. Based on uncertain input data, estimating the severity of the disaster, the number of injured people, and the amount of forces and resources needed to successfully deal with the situation is possible. The need for reinforcements is also considered. Fuzzy numbers, linguistic variables and fuzzy rule bases are applied to deal with the uncertainty. Outputs provided by the model (severity of the disaster, number of reinforcements needed etc.) are available both as fuzzy sets (for the purposes of disaster planning) and linguistic terms (for emergency call evaluation purposes).*

## INTRODUCTION

Disaster can be defined as an event threatening human life, health, property or environment, with an unusually extensive impact on the society. Such situations usually require a change of attitude and value system revision to be successfully dealt with.

For the purpose of this chapter only disasters that result in a large (significantly surpassing the usual) number of injured people with prevailing mechanical injuries will be considered. There are many disaster classifications. We can distinguish between man-made disasters (traffic accidents, industrial accidents etc.) and god-made (or natural) disasters, such as earthquakes, tsunamis etc.

DOI: 10.4018/978-1-61350-429-1.ch028

It makes sense to use this approach to disaster classification from the perspective of general disaster response. The case of medical rescue services response to disasters requires a different classification approach. A useful classification should be based on the prevailing type (source) of injuries. Among the typical types on injuries, mechanical injuries are the most frequent. We can also consider chemicals, radiation, biological agents or explosions to be possible sources of injuries. In this chapter, we focus on the mechanical type of injuries and all disasters resulting in this type of injuries.

Should such a life or health threatening event occur in our lives, we count on the Emergency Medical Rescue Services (EMRS) to provide us with assistance. Their forces are trained to be able to cope with almost any every-day health threatening event that might happen. But when a more serious event – disaster – occurs, classical problem solving strategies seize to work. EMRS staff needs to think and act differently, procedures they know and do well no longer suffice (Boer, 1999).

The amount of forces and resources needed to successfully cope with such situations may be difficult to determine or even to estimate. The key role in the rescue process is played by the EMRS operator, who evaluates the emergency call. Disasters occur quickly, suddenly and with an unusual impact on the environment and people. This implies that whatever decisions need to be made can not be postponed, and every mistake can result in damage to property or health or even in casualties. Moreover, people reporting these events to the EMRS Operations center may be affected by the disaster themselves. This can make their evaluation of the severity of the disaster inappropriate (both under and over-estimated).

In order to make the decision as correctly and quickly as possible, every available piece of information needs to be taken into consideration, regardless of its uncertainty. Decision making support in the form of a mathematical model can mean a substantial simplification of EMRS operator's work as well as a means of mistake elimination. And in this context mistakes can mean life losses.

The main purpose of this chapter is to show that linguistic fuzzy modeling can prove itself useful even in the context of medical disaster response, where mainly during the initial time period uncertainty is inevitable and has to be dealt with. The emergency call usually comprises rough information describing the event. The exact location, number of casualties, severity of injuries etc. is not available. We usually deal with guesses of the person that is reporting the disaster. This is however the only piece of information concerning the disaster itself and its impact (Stoklasa, 2009) that is available during the first minutes of disaster response. Decisions need to be made even in situations when there is lack of information, or the precision of data is low. We may even need to deal with contradictory information. Any tool that can help us use this kind of data effectively, to verify it somehow and to draw valid conclusions is most welcome. We need to speed up the decision making process and eliminate possible mistakes when lives are at stake. Fuzzy logic and linguistic fuzzy modeling may provide such a tool.

The stress under which the operators of EMRS operation centers work reaches critical levels during disasters. It is surprising that we still do not have available a sufficiently well working system for these purposes (at least in the Czech Republic) – not even now in the 21st century. The need for such a decision making support tool has been at least recognized during the last few years. This chapter describes how we deal with this challenge. Based on the practical experience of professional EMRS workers and operators, as well as hospital representatives and interviews with them, the linguistic fuzzy model described later in this chapter was developed.

## BACKGROUND

The use of operations research (OR) in disaster management is nothing new. According to Altay & Green (2006) there is an increasing need for OR study in disaster management. It is also true to say that some areas of disaster management need yet to be convinced that the use of OR may bring benefits. Wide use of mathematical programming in the context of disaster management is understandable. Statistics are another branch of OR that is widely used in disaster management (according to Altay & Green, 2006). Interesting applications of soft computing methods in connection with disaster management can be also found. Cret et al. (1993) use the fuzzy approach for earthquake damage estimation; seismic hazard analysis is considered by Dong, Chiang & Shah (1987). Applications to flood control are presented by Esogbue, Theologidu & Guo (1992) and some more general recommendations given in Esogbue (1996). It is interesting to see that similar approaches are applied in the field of medicine. Fuzzy rule bases help with medical diagnostics in the field of internal medicine (Rotshtein, 1999) and even to control drug infusion during anesthesia (Abbod & Linkens, 1998). Almost all the fields of medicine seem to profit (at least potentially) from the use of fuzzy logic (see Abbod et al. (2001) for more detailed information on the use of fuzzy methods in medicine). Disaster medicine however seems to resist this trend. We can find applications of fuzzy approach even in the form of a mobile Triage decision support (San Pedro et al., 2004) – a useful tool that helps hospital nurses perform injury severity classification, but the area of EMRS remains almost untouched by OR. This is surprising, as without functional and well working medical rescue services, there is usually nobody to be classified and treated in hospitals during disasters. This chapter describes an application of fuzzy methods on EMRS decision making process and provides a mathematical description of the disaster from the medical rescue services'

point of view. We reflect the specific needs of the EMRS (in the Czech Republic) and provide them with a custom made decision support tool.

The chain of medical care can be divided, according to Štětina (2000) and Boer (1999), into four phases. The first phase (omitted from the chain of medical care by some authors) comprises first aid activities performed by laymen directly at the disaster site before the arrival of the EMRS (including the emergency call). The second phase consists of professional first aid administration by medical rescue workers and doctors (still at the disaster site). The third phase can be described as the transportation phase – the main goal is to transport all the injured people from the disaster site to appropriate medical facilities (specialized hospitals etc.) within given time limits. After that the fourth phase follows, comprising all the medical care provided to the injured people by hospital staff. All these four phases are linked and problems in any of them can negatively influence the whole chain of medical care.

In some countries, the third part of the chain of medical care is not performed by the EMRS. As this model was developed mainly for the use by Czech EMRS, where patients need to be both treated and transported to hospitals by the emergency medical rescue services, the second and third phase will play an important role in the design of the model. We will try to determine the appropriate amount of forces and resources needed to enable the emergency medical rescue services to provide medical treatment to all people affected by the disaster and to transport them appropriate medical facilities. However the first phase (mainly the emergency call) and the fourth phase (mainly in terms of hospital treatment capacity (HTC) – the number of patients that can be treated per hour, for more details see Boer (1999)) – need to be reflected in the model.

During the construction of the model we realized, that all four phases of the chain of medical care should be reflected in any decision making support model for the previously described purpose. Only then we have a tool that can provide us with valuable information. In this chapter we present a mathematical model of the EMRS operator decision making process during disasters that result in a large number of mechanical injuries. The model uses linguistic variables, fuzzy rule bases and performs optimization tasks under fuzzy constraints in order to provide outputs useful in the decision making process. In the first phase it determines the capacity of a current EMRS center (number of patients that can be treated by available EMRS teams per hour). Then, based on the emergency call, it estimates the severity of the disaster (number of people affected by the disaster, number of people injured) in the second phase. In the third phase it determines which medical facilities need to be alerted to start preparations to receive patients. Finally the fourth phase provides the number of ambulances (EMRS teams) needed to successfully deal with the disaster and assesses the need for reinforcements. The model has to be able to deal with uncertainty in all these phases. Fuzzy set theory is used to meet this requirement and to allow the use of linguistic labels.

## PRELIMINARIES

Fundamentals of the fuzzy set theory (introduced by Zadeh (1965)) are described in detail, e.g., in Dubois & Prade (2000). Let $U$ be a nonempty set (the universe). A fuzzy set $A$ on $U$ is defined by the mapping $A: U \rightarrow [0,1]$. For each $x \in U$ the value $A(x)$ is called the membership degree of the element $x$ in the fuzzy set $A$ and $A(\cdot)$ is called the membership function of the fuzzy set $A$. The height of a fuzzy set $A$ is the real number $\mathrm{hgt}(A) = \sup_{x \in U}\{A(x)\}$. Other important concepts related to fuzzy sets are: (a) the kernel of $A$, $\mathrm{Ker}(A) = \{ x \in U | A(x) = 1\}$, (b) the support of $A$, $\mathrm{Supp}(A) = \{ x \in U | A(x) > 0\}$ and c) the $\alpha$-cut of $A$, $A_\alpha = \{ x \in U | A(x) \geq \alpha\}$, for $\alpha \in [0,1]$.

A function $T:[0,1]^2 \rightarrow [0,1]$ is called a triangular norm or t-norm if for all $\alpha, \beta, \gamma, \delta \in [0,1]$ it satisfies

the following four properties: (1) commutativity: $T(\alpha,\beta) = T(\beta,\alpha)$, (2) associativity: $T(\alpha,T(\beta,\gamma)) = T(T(\alpha,\beta),\gamma)$, (3) monotonicity: if $\alpha \leq \gamma$, $\beta \leq \delta$, then it holds that $T(\alpha,\beta) \leq T(\gamma,\delta)$, and (4) boundary condition: $T(\alpha,1) = \alpha$.

A function $S: [0,1]^2 \rightarrow [0,1]$ is called a triangular conorm or t-conorm if for all $\alpha, \beta, \gamma, \delta, \in [0,1]$ it satisfies the properties (1)–(3) from the previous definition and (4) the boundary condition: $S(\alpha,0) = \alpha$.

A function $N: [0,1,] \rightarrow [0,1]$ satisfying conditions: (a) $N(0) = 1$ and $N(1) = 0$, (b) $N$ is strictly decreasing, (c) $N$ is continuous and 4) $N(N(x)) = x$ for all $x \in [0,1]$ ($N$ is involutive), is called a strong negation. For the purposes of this paper we consider the following strong negation: $N(x) = 1-x$, where $x \in [0,1]$.

If $T(x,y) = N(S(N(x),N(y)))$ for all $x,y \in [0,1]$, we call $S$ the $N$-dual t-conorm to $T$. Triangular norms and conoroms are used to define the intersection and union of fuzzy sets respectively. Let $A$ and $B$ be fuzzy sets on $U$. The intersection of $A$ and $B$ is a fuzzy set $(A \cap_T B)$ on $U$ given by $(A \cap_T B)(x) = T(A(x),B(x))$ for all $x \in U$, where $T$ is a t-norm. The union of $A$ and $B$ on $U$ is a fuzzy set $\left(A \cup_S B\right)$ on $U$ given by

$$\left(A \cup_S B\right)(x) = S(A(x), B(x))$$

for all $x \in U$, where $S$ is a t-conorm $N$-dual to $T$, for more details see Dubois & Prade (2000). Let $A$ be a fuzzy set on $U$ and $B$ be a fuzzy set on $V$. Then the Cartesian product of $A$ and $B$ is a fuzzy set $A \times_T B$ on $U \times V$ given by $(A \times_T B)(x,y) = T(A(x),B(y))$ for all $(x,y) \in U \times V$. See Dubois & Prade (2000) for more details on triangular norms and conorms. A binary fuzzy relation is any fuzzy set $P$ on $U \times V$.

In this paper we will use the minimum t-norm ($T(\alpha,\beta) = \min\{\alpha,\beta\}$, for all $\alpha,\beta \in [0,1]$) and the maximum t-conorm ($S(\alpha,\beta) = \max\{\alpha,\beta\}$, for all $\alpha,\beta \in [0,1]$). For the union, intersection and Cartesian product of fuzzy sets A and B based on this t-norm and t-conorm we use the following notation: $\left(A \cup B\right)$, $(A \cap B)$ and $(A \times B)$ respectively.

Let $P$ be a fuzzy relation on $U \times V$ and $Q$ be a fuzzy set on $V \times W$. The composition of these two fuzzy relations is a fuzzy set $P \circ Q$ on $U \times W$ with a membership function defined for all $(x,z) \in U \times W$ by the formula $(P \circ Q)(x,z) = \sup_{y \in V} \{\min\{P(x,y), Q(y,z)\}\}$.

Let $\mathbf{R}$ denote the set of all real numbers. Fuzzy set $C$ on $\mathbf{R}$ is called fuzzy number if it satisfies three conditions: (1) the kernel of $C$, Ker($C$), is a nonempty set, (2) the $\alpha$-cuts of $C$, $C_\alpha$, are closed intervals for all $\alpha \in (0,1]$, and (3) the support of $C$, Supp($C$), is bounded. The symbol $F_N(\mathbf{R})$ denotes the family of all fuzzy numbers on $\mathbf{R}$. If Supp($C$)$\subseteq [a,b]$, we call $C$ a fuzzy number on the interval $[a,b]$. The family of all fuzzy numbers on the interval $[a,b]$ will be denoted by $F_N([a,b])$.

Let $A_1, A_2, ..., A_n \in F_N([a,b])$, we say that $A_1, A_2, ..., A_n$ form a fuzzy scale on $[a,b]$ if these fuzzy numbers form a Ruspini fuzzy partition (see Ruspini, 1969 or Codara, D'Antona & Marra, 2009) on $[a,b]$ (i.e. $\sum_{i=1}^{n} A_i(x) = 1$, for all $x \in [a,b]$) and are numbered in accordance with their ordering.

The basics of linguistic fuzzy modelling were introduced by Zadeh (1975). A linguistic variable is the quintuple $(X, T(X), U, M, G)$ where $X$ is the name of the linguistic variable, $T(X)$ is the set of its linguistic values (linguistic terms), $U$ is the universe, $U = [a,b] \subseteq \mathbf{R}$, which the mathematical meanings (fuzzy numbers) of the linguistic terms are defined on, $G$ is a syntactic rule (grammar) for generating linguistic terms from $T(X)$ and $M$ is a semantic rule (meaning), that assigns to every linguistic term $\mathcal{A} \in T(X)$ its meaning $A = M(\mathcal{A})$ as a fuzzy number on $U$. Linguistic terms and fuzzy numbers representing their meanings will be distinguished in the text by different fonts (calligraphic letters for linguistic terms and standard capital letters for their respective meanings - fuzzy numbers on $U$).

The linguistic variable $(X, T(X), U, M, G)$, $T(X) = \{\mathcal{T}_1, \mathcal{T}_2, ..., \mathcal{T}_s\}$, $M\left(\mathcal{T}_p\right) = T_p$, $T_p \in F_N\left(U\right)$ for $p = 1,...,s$, defines a linguistic scale on $U$, if the fuzzy numbers $T_1, T_2, ..., T_s$ form a fuzzy scale on $U$.

Let $(X_j, T(X_j), U_j, M_j, G_j)$, $j = 1,...,m$, and $(Y, T(Y), V, M, G)$ be linguistic variables. Let $\mathcal{A}_{ij} \in T(X_j)$ and $M_j(\mathcal{A}_{ij}) = A_{ij} \in F_N(U_j)$, $i = 1,...,n$, $j = 1,...,m$. Let $\mathcal{B}_i \in T(Y)$ and $M(\mathcal{B}_i) = B_i \in F_N(V)$, $i = 1,...,n$. Then the following scheme is called a linguistically defined function (a base of fuzzy rules, see Zadeh (1975)):

If $X_1$ is $\mathcal{A}_{11}$ and ... and $X_m$ is $\mathcal{A}_{1m}$ then $Y$ is $\mathcal{B}_1$.

If $X_1$ is $\mathcal{A}_{21}$ and ... and $X_m$ is $\mathcal{A}_{2m}$ then $Y$ is $\mathcal{B}_2$.

........................................................

If $X_1$ is $\mathcal{A}_{n1}$ and ... and $X_m$ is $\mathcal{A}_{nm}$ then $Y$ is $\mathcal{B}_n$.

$$(1)$$

The process of calculating an output for current input values by means of such a rule base is called approximate reasoning (or fuzzy inference). In the model we use approximate reasoning mechanisms based on Takagi & Sugeno's fuzzy inference (Takagi & Sugeno, 1985) and Generalized Sugeno fuzzy inference (for more details see Sugeno & Yasukawa (1993) or Talašová (2003)).

Let us have the base of fuzzy rules defined previously. Let us have an observation in the form of $X_1$ is $\mathcal{A}_1$' and ... and $X_m$ is $\mathcal{A}_m$'. Then by entering these observed values into the linguistically defined function, we get the output

$$B^S = \left(\sum_{i=1}^{n} h_i B_i\right) / \left(\sum_{i=1}^{n} h_i\right), \text{ where}$$

$$h_i = \min\left\{\mathrm{hgt}\left(A_{i1} \cap A_i'\right), ...,\right.$$

$\mathrm{hgt}\left(A_{im} \cap A_m'\right)\Big\}$. For the classical Sugeno's fuzzy inference, $B_i$ is a real number for all $i=1,...,n$. If we use the generalized Sugeno's fuzzy inference introduced by Talašová (2003), $B_i$ is a fuzzy number for all $i=1,...,n$.

Mamdani & Asilian (1975) introduced another approach to fuzzy inference. Let us consider the rule base (1). Each rule is modeled by the fuzzy relation

$$R_i = A_{i1} \times_T A_{i2} \times_T ... \times_T A_{im} \times_T B_i, \, i=1,...,n$$

The whole rule base is represented by the union of all these fuzzy relations $R = \bigcup_{i=1}^{n} R_i$. Let $(A_1', A_2', ..., A_m')$ be an m-tuple of fuzzy inputs. The output $B^M$ is then calculated as

$$B^M = (A_1' \times_T A_2' \times_T ... \times_T A_m') \circ R.$$

Mamdani & Asilian's approach (1975) preserves information regarding the uncertainty of input values. This is important particularly when the inputs are highly uncertain. On the other hand, the output of Mamdani's fuzzy model is usually not a fuzzy number. To interpret the Mamdani output linguistically may prove problematic. The center of gravity method is usually used to defuzzify the Mamdani & Asilian's output $B^M$. This way we get a crisp output

$$b^M = \int_{y \in V} B^M(y) \cdot y \, dy \, / \int_{y \in V} B^M(y) \, dy).$$

The asymmetry of fuzzy numbers can negatively influence the output of the defuzzification process and thus reduce the interpretation possibilities of such an output. A proper linguistic approximation of $B^M$ may, on the other hand, be too uncertain to provide the desired amount of information. The generalized Sugeno inference (Talašová, 2003 or Sugeno & Yasukawa, 1993) provides fuzzy numbers as outputs (if the inputs are fuzzy numbers) which makes the output $B^S$ easier to interpret linguistically. Partial loss of information concerning the uncertainty of input

values is compensated by easier interpretability of the output. As linguistic terms (linguistic approximations of $B^S$) are easier to interpret for the EMRS operators than general fuzzy set outputs, we use the Sugeno's fuzzy inference (Takagi & Sugeno, 1985) and the generalized Sugeno's fuzzy inference (Talašová, 2003) in the model.

## PROBLEM SPECIFICATION

A decision making support for the EMRS Operations Center can be considered beneficial, if it (1) is able to process any input data (uncertain or precise), (2) provides an estimation of the number of people moderately and severely wounded, (3) determines to which medical facilities should the injured people be transported (4) is able to assess the sufficiency of any provincial EMRS center's forces and resources and (5) performs these operations in real-time.

The relatively low frequency rate of disasters limits the amount of data available to construct the mathematical model. Some parts of the model therefore need to be based on expert and professional medical rescue worker's experience. The model has to be able to communicate with the EMRS operator in an easy to understand way. Outputs must be "intuitively clear" to the operator. A linguistic form of outputs is therefore preferred. A multiphase mathematical model designed to meet these requirements will be described.

In the whole chapter we consider only disasters resulting in mechanical injuries (which is the case of many traffic accidents, but also earthquakes etc.). There is not enough experience and data available for other sources of injuries, such as chemicals, radiation, explosions, fire, biological agents etc. to develop similar model. This fact should be addressed in future research.

## MATHEMATICAL MODEL

To be able to deal with the uncertainty of input data and to model the expert-based knowledge of some parts of this problem, the tools of fuzzy mathematics described above are used. Namely fuzzy sets, fuzzy numbers, linguistic scales and linguistic fuzzy models are the basis of the described solution. For a more detailed explanation see Talašová (2003) or Dubois & Prade (2000). The fuzzy number $\alpha$- degree upper bound had to be defined as a new way of fuzzy and crisp number comparison in order to meet the model requirements.

### Phase 1: Rescue Capacity Determination

One of the key pieces of information we are interested in at the moment any disaster occurs (resulting in many injured people) is the amount of people we are able to provide care to within a time unit (hour). Such quantity is, according to Boer (1999), called the Medical Rescue Capacity (*MRC*).

Each EMRS center has a certain number of medical rescue teams on duty. There does not necessarily have to be a doctor in all these teams. Let us assume that teams have 2 to 4 members and that each team can be treating no more than one patient at a time. We can assume that only teams with doctors will be taking care of seriously injured people and both teams with and without doctors will take care of people with moderate injuries. People that are just slightly injured do not interest us now, as during disasters all the forces and resources of EMRS need to concentrate on people that are unable to transport themselves to the hospital.

We consider two categories of injured people: seriously injured (T1 – for "triage group 1") and moderately injured (T2). T1 and T2 patients differ mainly in the time needed to treat them so that they are able to withstand the transport to hospital

– T1 patients need more treatment and therefore more time (Boer (1999) suggests a method of mean treatment time determination). We also have many different teams with different experience and skills. The *MRC* should therefore be determined for each team separately and of course we need to distinguish between the *MRC* for T1 patients and the MRC for T2 patients.

We consider the team quality (*TQ*), its time on duty (*ToD*) and the weather at the disaster site (*WE*) to be the most important factors influencing the actual medical rescue capacity of each team. Each of these variables is represented by a linguistic scale in the model. We use linear membership functions to define the meanings of the respective linguistic terms on the respective universes (example for *TQ* can be seen in Figure 1).

As the relationship among these three factors and the resulting *MRC* can only be described linguistically (based on interviews with experienced rescue workers – no other information is available at this time) both inputs (*TQ,ToD,WE*) and output of this phase (*MRC*) are modeled by linguistic scales. The relationship is then described by a fuzzy rule base consisting of 48 rules such as:

*"If TQ is average and ToD is short and WE is ideal, the MRC is average."*

We use the generalized Sugeno approximate reasoning mechanism (Talašová, 2003) to obtain results for any combination of inputs. Thus we get a fuzzy number describing the current *MRC* for a particular team. The use of linguistic variables allows us to have a single rule base for *MRC* determination for the case of T1 and T2 patients, thus simplifying the model significantly. We can use the same linguistic terms for team quality description, only their meanings (fuzzy numbers assigned to them) will differ. For T1, we have the universe [0,4] (in terms of patients treated per hour) and for T2 we have the universe [0,6] again in terms

*Figure 1. Differences in the meanings of linguistic terms for team quality description for T1 and T2 patients*

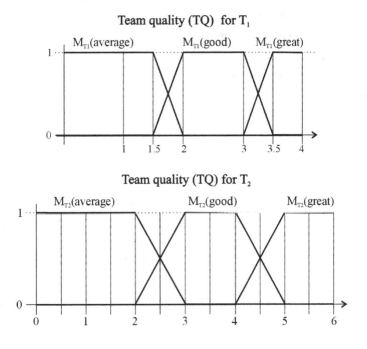

of patients treated per hour. For the differences in meanings of the linguistic terms see Figure 1.

The fuzzy approach also allows users to input *TQ* in linguistic terms (using the predefined linguistic variable for team quality description) as well as in precise numbers (supposing a team quality evaluation mechanism is available).

The exact time of duty is easy to obtain and input as a precise number. To assess the weather quality (*WE*), we define an evaluation function (a membership function of a fuzzy set that describes conditions appropriate for the rescue operation) for each of the three important weather characteristics – temperature (*t*), wind strength (*w*) and rainfall (*r*). These evaluation functions map the real weather characteristics values into the closed interval [0,1] (see Figure 2) and using the extension principle (see Dubois & Prade, 2000) they

*Figure 2. Evaluation function for one of the important weather characteristics – wind. Evaluation is determined for a fuzzy (uncertain) input as a fuzzy number using the extension principle.*

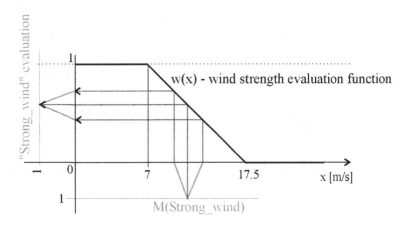

also map the fuzzy sets describing the estimates of current weather characteristics (defined on the universe of the respective weather characteristics) into fuzzy sets on [0,1]. The resulting evaluation 1 means our complete satisfaction and evaluation 0 our complete dissatisfaction or even dangerousness of the weather. The overall weather quality evaluation is then computed by aggregating the above mentioned important weather characteristics evaluations (*T* for temperature, *W* for wind strength and *R* for rainfall) using a fuzzified geometric mean:

$$(F)\left(T \cdot W \cdot R\right)^{\frac{1}{3}}(y) = \sup\{\inf\{T(x_1), W(x_2), R(x_3)\} \mid y = (x_1 \cdot x_2 \cdot x_3)^{\frac{1}{3}}; x_1, x_2, x_3 \in [0,1]\}$$

(2)

The geometric mean (its fuzzification) was chosen because of its suitable properties: 1) if any of the values is completely dissatisfactory, then the weather evaluation is 0 (completely dissatisfactory), 2) if any of the weather characteristics evaluations is low, the overall weather evaluation will be lowered accordingly (only weather with all evaluations really close to 1 will be evaluated as satisfactory), 3) it is easy enough to use and to be understood by laymen.

The output of the first rule base, that describes the relationship between the inputs (*TQ, ToD, WE*) and output (*MRC*) is the medical rescue capacity for a current team (*MRC*). The time of day (*TDy*) can also be taken into account in order to model reaction time prolonging, fatigue and drowsiness of the staff. For this purpose a second fuzzy rule base is defined to determine how to correct the *MRC* according to the time of the day. There are 4 linguistic fuzzy rules available for this purpose and classical Sugeno approximate reasoning is applied (Sugeno & Yasukawa, 1993):

- *If TDy is night, then the correction is 1.*
- *If TDy is morning, then the correction is 0.*

- *If TDy is afternoon, then the correction is 0.3.*
- *If TDy is evening, then the correction is 0.6.*

The result of this rule base is shifting the *MRC* lower or leaving it unchanged. *TDy* was left out of the first rule base to maintain simplicity of the model and to preserve the information concerning potential (maximal) *MRC* for the purposes of disaster planning.

Applying this process on every team on duty and adding up the resulting fuzzy numbers we get the total *MRC* (*TMRC*) for a particular provincial EMRS center: $TMRC = \sum_{i=1}^{t} MRC_i$, where *t* is the number of teams available at this center. An average *MRC* (*AMRC*) is easy to determine as well: $AMRC = \sum_{i=1}^{t} MRC_i / t$. Fuzzy number arithmetic used to carry out the calculations is based on interval arithmetic (see Dubois & Prade, 2000).

As the location of the disaster is not known in advance, some calculations can be done no sooner than the emergency call is answered (particularly those requiring specific weather data from the disaster site). To obtain the results of phase one – the *MRC* for each team and the *TMRC* and *AMRC* – we need to consider all the data concerning the conditions at the disaster site and its location from the emergency call (precise or not). We can supply additional data from other sources if possible (e.g. weather conditions data from meteorological stations). Outputs of phase 1 are therefore highly relevant for the emergency medical rescue services decision making, for they reflect much of the disasters context.

## Phase 2: Severity of the Disaster Determination

This part of the model is partly dependent on the data obtained during the emergency call and partly on the so called common knowledge. Both these things have to be combined to derive an output that really provides a decision making support. The disaster has to be described using all the data available, regardless of the uncertainty. We need to assess the disaster severity – to be able to estimate the number of people injured. It is even more important to determine how many people belong to T1 group and how many to T2.

First we define a linguistic variable describing the disaster severity with the set of linguistic terms {*small traffic accident, medium traffic accident, serious traffic accident, small disaster, medium disaster and serious disaster*}, their respective meanings being fuzzy numbers on the interval [0;10000]. These fuzzy numbers should be defined with respect to the needs of the EMRS and disaster management of the country our model will be used in. Thus the EMRS operator gets a means of roughly describing the disaster (linguistically),

when almost no other information is available. We also allow the operator to input exact numbers of injured people (in case the precise number is available), as well as his guesses in the form of fuzzy numbers (a way of customizing/refining the meanings of the previously mentioned predefined linguistic terms).

However the largest benefit of our proposed fuzzy approach in this phase is the possibility to input linguistic terms (Figure 3). We predefine the meanings of such terms as a "full car", "small group of people", "full train wagon", "small basic school" as fuzzy numbers. The information from an emergency call: "A car crashed into a small group of people and then collided with a bus" can then be inputted by simply choosing the buttons "bus", "small group of people" and "car" on a touch screen in the EMRS operations centre. The computer can add up the meanings of these linguis-

*Figure 3. Examples of the meanings of some predefined linguistic terms describing the basic units of possible disasters in terms of the amount of people affected by the disaster*

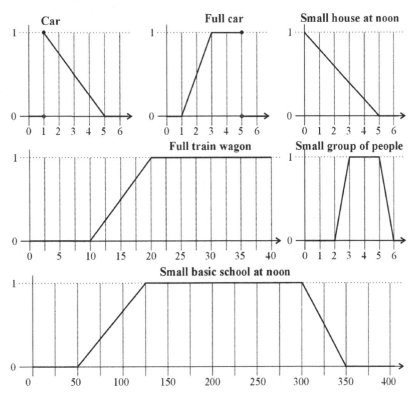

tic terms and thus give the operator the expected amount of people affected by the disaster (*AFF*) again as a fuzzy number or in linguistic terms.

When mechanical injuries prevail (which is the case of most disasters), the relative amount of severely wounded is about 10% and the relative amount of moderate injuries is about 20% (Boer, 1999). To estimate how many people have been injured, we define two fuzzy numbers – *M*("about 10%") and *M*("about 20%"). The kernels of these fuzzy numbers will be 0.1 and 0.2 respectively and their supports (0,0.2) and (0.1,0.3) respectively. Using fuzzy number arithmetic (Talašová, 2003, Dubois & Prade, 2000) we can obtain the estimate of the amount of both severely injured (*NT1*, where *NT1=AFF·M*("about 10%")) and moderately injured (*NT2*, where *NT2=AFF·M*("about 20%")) people as fuzzy numbers.

## Phase 3: Determination of Medical Facilities Involved

At this point we know how many patients we are able to treat per hour and how many of them we

can expect at the disaster site. Since the location of the disaster is known, we also know how far the nearest hospitals are and what their treatment capacity (*HTC* – number of patients that can receive appropriate treatment per hour, should be a piece of information available in advance) is. We need to consider time limitations – for the severely injured must be treated in appropriate medical facilities within an hour and moderately injured within 6 hours (Boer, 1999; Stoklasa, 2009).

Let us consider two types of hospitals: regular hospitals (*H*) and specialized hospitals with emergency departments (*SH*). We suppose that T1 patients can be treated only in specialized hospitals and we need to transport them there within one hour (so called "golden hour" – see Boer (1999) or Stoklasa (2009)). T2 patients can be treated either in regular or in specialized hospitals and we have 6 hours to transport them there (so called Friedrich's time). Figure 4 shows the situation. Let $I = \{1, 2, ..., n\}$ be the set of indices of all the hospitals close to the disaster site (indexed according to the distance from the disaster site, index 1 meaning the hospital closest to the disaster site). The last index n is dependent on the time

*Figure 4. Determining which medical facilities will be involved. (DS=disaster site, HTC=hospital treatment capacities)*

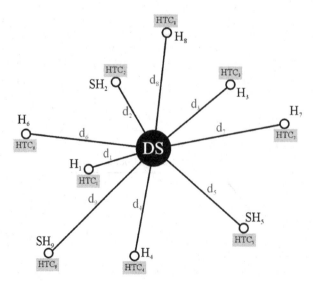

limits we set for the transport of the patients to medical facilities. Let us denote $I_{SH}$ the set of indices of all specialized hospitals, $I_{SH} \subseteq I$, $I_{SH} = \{i_1, i_2, ..., i_r\}$ and $I_H$ the set of indices of all regular hospitals, $I_H \subseteq I$, $I_H = \{j_1, j_2, ..., j_s\}$. It holds that $I_{SH} \cup I_H = I$ and $I_{SH} \cap I_H = \varnothing$. Conditions that need to be fulfilled are as follows.

We need to employ so many specialized hospitals, so that all the T1 patients can receive appropriate care within the first hour

$$\sum_{i \in I_{SH}} HTC_i \geq NT1 \qquad (3)$$

For this purpose we suppose that no T2 patients will be transported within the first hour.

We need to employ so many regular and specialized hospitals, so that all the T2 patients can receive appropriate care within the following five hours

$$\sum_{i \in I_{SH}} HTC_i + \sum_{j \in I_H} HTC_j \geq \frac{NT2}{5} \qquad (4)$$

As the sums of hospital treatment capacities are real numbers, whereas $NT1$ and $NT2$ are fuzzy numbers, we need to define the meaning of the symbol "$\geq$". For this purpose we introduce the fuzzy number $\alpha$- degree upper bound.

**Definition 1.** Let $h$ be a real number on $[a,b]$ and $A$ be a fuzzy number with a non-zero membership function on $[a,b]$ and zero membership function outside this interval. Then we say that $h$ is the $\alpha$- *degree upper bound for the fuzzy number* $A$, $\alpha \in [0,1]$, if and only if

$$\alpha = \frac{\int_a^h A(t)dt}{\int_a^b A(t)dt} \qquad (5)$$

Definition 1 describes how to compare a fuzzy number with a crisp one. Parameter $\alpha$ describes the amount of uncertainty we are willing to tolerate. If $\alpha$ is set to 1, we need $h$ to be larger or equal than the largest number from Supp($A$), in other words we do not tolerate any uncertainty ($h$ has to be larger or equal than any value with a non-zero membership degree to $A$). For a fixed $\alpha$ the condition (3) is fulfilled if and only if $\sum_{i \in I_{SH}} HTC_i$ is a $\beta$- degree upper bound of $NT1$, and $\beta \geq \alpha$. By choosing $\alpha$ we can influence the degree of satisfaction of the constraints. According to $(1-\alpha)$ (the degree to which the total $HTC$ of all the hospitals can be exceeded) we determine to which hospitals the injured people need to be transported to receive appropriate care. If we choose $\alpha = 1$, we employ as many hospitals as it is needed to provide care to the maximum estimated number of injured people (for T1 category it is the supremum of Supp($NT1$). We try to determine the least amount of $SH$ hospitals so that the condition (3) is fulfilled for a given $\alpha$. This way we get the set of all employed specialized hospitals in the first hour $I_{SH_1} = \left\{ i_1, i_2, ..., i_{r_1} \right\}$. We do the same for the condition (4), but this time for any type of hospitals – $H$ and $SH$.

## Phase 4: Estimation of the Amount of Forces and Resources Needed

Once we know which hospitals need to be alerted to start preparing themselves to receive patients, the number of ambulances needed to transport the patients to the hospitals has to be determined. Let us for the i-th employed hospital $i=1, 2, ..., n$, define

$$trav_i = \frac{v}{2 \cdot d_i}, \qquad (6)$$

where $v$ is the supposed average traveling speed of ambulances (say 50 km/h) and $d_i$ is the distance from the i-th hospital (regular or specialized) to the disaster site. $Trav_i$ then describes the number of journeys from the disaster site to the hospital and back that a single ambulance traveling at an average speed of 50 km/h is able to make within one hour. Let us for now consider the first hour of the disaster response (and therefore only the transportation of T1 patients to $SH$). Let us denote $x_i$ the number of ambulances needed to transport patients to the i-th specialized hospital. The following conditions need to be fulfilled.

1. The total number of ambulances should be as low as possible

$$\sum_{k=1}^{r_1} x_{i_k} \rightarrow \min \qquad (7)$$

2. All T1 patients need to be transported to hospitals

$$\sum_{k=1}^{r_1} trav_{i_k} \cdot x_{i_k} \geq NT1 \qquad (8)$$

3. We do not allow any of the hospital treatment capacities to be exceeded

$$trav_{i_k} \cdot x_{i_k} \leq HTC_{i_k}, \qquad k = 1, 2, ..., r_1 \qquad (9)$$

As can be easily seen, we have a fuzzy linear programming problem to solve. Condition (8) has a fuzzy number constraint $NT1$. We can again use the fuzzy number α- degree upper bound to deal with this condition.

We have devised a heuristic algorithm based partially on the α- degree fuzzy number upper bound to determine how many ambulances will be needed to successfully cope with the situation. The previous selection of involved medical facilities was performed in a way that can be exploited now. We still consider just the T1 category of injuries. T2 category can be treated analogously. If we take all the hospitals with in-

dices belonging into $I_{SH_1} = \left\{ i_1, i_2, ..., i_{r_1} \right\}$, we have enough hospital treatment capacity to treat all the T1 patients within the first hour. This is ensured by the hospital selection process introduced earlier in this chapter. The minimum number of ambulances needed to transport all the T1 patients ($NT1$ in total) to these hospitals remains to be determined. The main idea of our heuristic approach is to start with the hospital closest to the disaster site (just a reminder - for T1 patients we need only specialized hospitals) and determine the minimum number of ambulances needed to fill this hospital's treatment capacity within one hour and then continue the same with the second closest hospital. Such a number is now easy to obtain for the i-th hospital,

$$i \in I_{SH_1} - \left\{ i_{r_1} \right\} = \left\{ i_1, i_2, ..., i_{r_1-1} \right\},$$

as $x_i = HTC_i / trav_i$. For calculations involving T1 patients we may round $trav_i$, for if the fractional part of $trav_i$ is greater or equal to 0.5, we can assume that the ambulance will manage to transport the last patient to the hospital within the time limit (in this case we round $trav_i$ up), while if the fractional part of $trav_i$ is less than 0.5, the last patient will not arrive in the hospital in time (so we round $trav_i$ down in this case).

We shall round up the resulting $x_i$ to the closest positive integer (to avoid confusions during the decision making process). However doing so we risk exceeding the hospital treatment capacity of the particular hospital (should all $x_i$ ambulances transport patients for the whole hour) by $trav_i$ -1 in the worst case. This is in our opinion a low price to pay for a simpler computation.

The treatment capacity of the most remote hospital might not be fully exploited. To determine the number of ambulances needed to transport patients to this hospital $x_{i_{r_1}}$, we first add up all the previously determined numbers of ambulances needed $\sum_{k=1}^{r_1-1} x_{i_k}$ . We choose an $\alpha$ and set $x_{i_{r_1}} = 1$ . We then increase $x_{i_{r_1}}$ by 1, until

$$\sum_{k=1}^{r_1} trav_{i_k} \cdot x_{i_k} \geq NT1 ,$$

in other words until $\sum_{k=1}^{r_1} trav_{i_k} \cdot x_{i_k}$ is a $\beta$- degree upper bound of $NT1$, and $\beta \geq \alpha$. The total amount of ambulances needed is then $AMB = \sum_{k=1}^{r_1} x_{i_k}$ .

Knowing the number of ambulances needed to transport patients away from the disaster site is however not yet sufficient to be able to assess if the current (provincial) EMRS center has enough forces and resources to deal with the disaster. In order to do so, we need to determine how many teams will be needed at the disaster site to provide care to all the severely injured within the first hour (phases 1 and 2) first.

We expect $NT1$ severely injured people at the disaster site (output of phase 2) and we can determine the average medical rescue capacity ($AMRC$) as $TMRC/N$, where $N$ is the number of teams used to compute $TMRC$ (output of phase 1). $TMRC$ is a sum of fuzzy numbers. Generalized Sugeno deduction is used to determine current medical rescue capacities. The output of this process for each team – the current $MRC$ – is a

weighted average of fuzzy numbers and therefore a fuzzy number. It can be easily seen that the average medical rescue capacity will be a fuzzy number. If we divide $NT1$ by $AMRC$, we obtain the amount of EMRS teams needed at the disaster site as a fuzzy number (let us denote this fuzzy number $TEAMS$).

Once we know the required amount of forces and resources needed both at the disaster site and to transport patients to hospitals, we can compare it with the amount that is available at the current provincial EMRS centre. We can assume that a provincial EMRS center can handle the situation without any assistance from other EMRS centers, if ($TEAMS + AMB$) $\leq$ *Number of teams available*. We can again use the fuzzy number $\alpha$- degree upper bound to interpret the symbol $\leq$. Should the resources of a current provincial EMRS center prove insufficient, we can linguistically approximate the fuzzy number ($TEAMS + AMB$) - *Number of teams available* using the linguistic variable "Reinforcements", its linguistic terms being for example "closest provincial EMRS units", "whole country EMRS stations", "surrounding countries EMRS stations", etc. (Figure 5). The meanings of these linguistic terms need to be set up according to the real numbers of reinforcements available.

Similarly we can run the whole procedure for the moderately injured people. This way an easy to understand piece of information concerning

*Figure 5. Meanings of the linguistic terms of the linguistic variable "Reinforcements"*

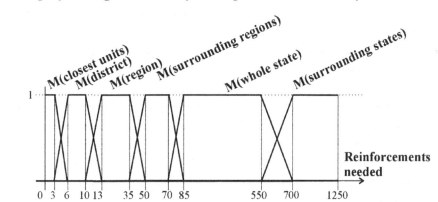

the need of reinforcements is available to the EMRS operator.

## NUMERICAL EXAMPLE

Let us consider the following situation. It is September, we are in the Czech Republic at 10:30. An emergency call is registered by an EMRS operator: "*A train collided with a bridge construction. All 10 wagons! I am in XZ.*" This is all the information we have. How serious is the event? How many people are injured? How many ambulances should we send? Do we have enough sources and resources?

Let us suppose we have 7 teams with a doctor (all considered "good") and 14 teams without a doctor (7 considered "good" and 7 considered "great") available. Let us suppose that it is 17°C, the wind is 2 m/s and it is not raining at the disaster site and this information is available to us.

Let us consider the following hospital structure near the disaster site ($SH$ = specialized hospitals capable of treating T1 and T2, $H$ = ordinary hospitals, capable of treating T2):

- $H_1 d$ = 5km $HTC$ = 5
- $SH_2 d$ = 10 km $HTC$ = 20
- $SH_3 d$ = 15km $HTC$ = 15
- $H_4 d$ = 15 km $HTC$ = 10
- $H_5 d$ = 20km $HTC$ = 10
- $SH_6 d$ = 25 km $HTC$ = 30,

where $d$ is the distance between the current hospital and the disaster site, $HTC$ is the hospital treatment capacity of the respective hospital (number of people the hospital is able to treat per hour). We also consider the ambulances to be moving at the average speed of 50 km/h.

Operator has to put into the model two facts: "10 full train wagons" are involved and that the disaster site is XZ. The model then provides the following outputs (only the most important ones for the decision are listed).

1. 39 ambulances are needed during the first hour (25 to transport patients to hospitals, 14 teams to provide care at the disaster site)
2. 11 ambulances will be needed during the following 5 hours (7 to transport patients to hospitals, 4 to provide care at the disaster site)
3. "You need reinforcements for the first hour. Mobilise the region!"

Outputs provided by the model are easily interpretable. It is still the operator who has to decide, what to do. He can now compare his or her guess (for he/she has no time for anything more sophisticated than guesses) with the output of the model and then act. More outputs are available from the model – estimated number of injured people, distribution of ambulances (patients) among the hospitals etc.

## FUTURE RESEARCH DIRECTIONS

Until now not much attention has been paid to the decision making processes of the medical rescue services and the uncertainty they involve. If the first decisions are wrong or late, we can not expect the whole system to work well. This is one of the reasons why this model has been developed – to show the importance of first decisions and the role of the vagueness that is carried through the decision making process.

During the work on the model, we encountered some problems that may be addressed in the future. The first one is the lack of experience and even information concerning disasters and disaster procedures thanks to the relatively low frequency of disaster appearance. Further on no EMRS quality assessment tool was found in the Czech Republic, although the rescue capacity of each team is an important piece of information both for the disaster response and planning, even for EMRS management.

We also realized that a functional data exchange system for the EMRS, medical facilities and other rescue services would simplify the decision making process significantly, by reducing the uncertainty of some data by confirming them from multiple sources and by sharing the decision making process outputs in real time with all the units involved in the disaster response.

## CONCLUSION

The model described above was designed primarily as a decision making support for the EMRS operators, should a disaster resulting in a large number of casualties occur. The main advantage of the proposed model and the mathematical tools used is the ability to accept and also provide linguistic values and this way deal with uncertainty. The model estimates the current total medical rescue capacity (number of people treated per hour) for a current provincial EMRS centre. Based on the emergency call it estimates the severity of the disaster and then determines which hospitals will be included into the rescue process and the number of ambulances needed. The number of ambulances needed is then compared with the number of forces and resources available and the required number of reinforcements is suggested in linguistic terms. At present we are gathering more data to field-test the model and to adapt it to the needs of the disaster response system in the Czech Republic.

The use of this model can not substitute the human factor completely – EMRS operators still play the key role in the disaster response. This model is intended to provide information to compare the EMRS operator's opinion with, this way eliminating mistakes and speeding up the decision making process. The second field of use for this model is disaster planning. The model provides insights into EMRS activity during disasters, describing this activity in an easy to understand way. Many potential disaster scenarios can be explored using the model and the need of sources and resources can be determined. This way an optimal distribution of EMRS centers and resource stores can be determined.

In such situations as the first minutes of the disaster response, when little information is available and the uncertainty level is high, the above mentioned approach can provide useful results. A model that is able to deal with uncertainty when the uncertainty is inherent to the situation modeled is most appreciated for it can help us identify the blind spots within the system. Once we know how uncertain the decisions may be, we can start working on measures to reduce the level of uncertainty.

## REFERENCES

Abbod, M. F., & Linkens, D. A. (1998). Anaesthesia monitoring and control using fuzzy logic fusion. *J. Biomed. Eng. – Appl. Basis Commun. Special Issue on Control Methods in Anaesthesia*, *10*(4), 225–235.

Abbod, M. F., von Keyserlingk, D. G., Linkens, D. A., & Mahfouf, M. (2001). Survey of utilisation of fuzzy technology in medicine and health-care. *Fuzzy Sets and Systems*, *120*, 331–349. doi:10.1016/S0165-0114(99)00148-7

Altay, N., & Green, W. G. III. (2006). OR/MS research in disaster operations management. *European Journal of Operational Research*, *175*, 475–493. doi:10.1016/j.ejor.2005.05.016

Boer, J. D. (1999). *Order in chaos*. Amsterdam, The Netherlands: Free University Hospital.

Codara, P., D'Antona, O. M., & Marra, V. (2009). An analysis of Ruspini partitions in Gödel logic. *International Journal of Approximate Reasoning*, *50*, 825–836. doi:10.1016/j.ijar.2009.02.007

Cret, L., Yamazaki, F., Nagata, S., & Katayama, T. (1993). Earthquake damage estimation and decision-analysis for emergency shutoff of city gas network using fuzzy set theory. *Structural Safety*, *12*(1), 1–19. doi:10.1016/0167-4730(93)90015-S

Dong, W. M., Chiang, W. L., & Shah, H. C. (1987). Fuzzy information processing in seismic hazard analysis and decision making. *Soil Dynamics and Earthquake Engineering*, *6*(4), 220–226. doi:10.1016/0267-7261(87)90003-0

Dubois, D., & Prade, H. (2000). *Fundamentals of fuzzy sets*. Boston, MA: Kluwer Academic Publishers.

Esogbue, A. O. (1996). Fuzzy sets modeling and optimization for disaster control systems planning. *Fuzzy Sets and Systems*, *81*(1), 169–183. doi:10.1016/0165-0114(95)00248-0

Esogbue, A. O., Theologidu, M., & Guo, K. J. (1992). On the application of fuzzy sets theory to the optimal flood control problem arising in water resources systems. *Fuzzy Sets and Systems*, *48*(2), 155–172. doi:10.1016/0165-0114(92)90330-7

Mamdani, E. H., & Assilian, S. (1975). An experiment in linguistic synthesis with a fuzzy logic controller. *Int. J. Man-machine Studies*, *7*, 1–13. doi:10.1016/S0020-7373(75)80002-2

Rotshtein, A. (1999). Design and tuning of fuzzy rule-based systems for medical diagnosis. In Teodorescu, H. N., Kandel, A., & Jain, L. C. (Eds.), *Fuzzy and neuro-fuzzy systems in medicine*. Boca Raton, FL: CRC Press.

Ruspini, E. (1969). A new approach to clustering. *Information and Control*, *15*, 22–32. doi:10.1016/S0019-9958(69)90591-9

San Pedro, J., Burstein, F., Churilov, L., Wassertheil, J., & Cao, P. (2004). Mobile decision support system for triage in emergency departments. *Decision Support in Uncertain and Complex World: The IFIP TC8/WG8.3 International Conference*, (pp. 714-723).

Štětina, J. (Ed.). (2000). *Disaster medicine*. Praha, Czech Republic: Grada Publishing. (in Czech)

Stoklasa, J. (2009). *Classical and fuzzy models for efficiency assessment* (in Czech). Unpublished Master's thesis, Palacky University, Olomouc, Czech Republic

Sugeno, M., & Yasukawa, T. (1993). A fuzzy-logic-based approach to qualitative modeling. *IEEE Transactions on Fuzzy Systems*, *1*(1), 7–31. doi:10.1109/TFUZZ.1993.390281

Takagi, T., & Sugeno, M. (1985). Fuzzy identification of systems and its application to modeling and control. *IEEE Transactions on Systems, Man, and Cybernetics*, *1*(15), 116–132.

Talašová, J. (2003). *Fuzzy methods of multiple-criteria evaluation and decision making*. Olomouc, Czech Republic: VUP. (in Czech)

Zadeh, L. A. (1965). Fuzzy sets. *Information and Control*, *8*, 338–353. doi:10.1016/S0019-9958(65)90241-X

Zadeh, L. A. (1975). The concept of linguistic variable and its application to approximate reasoning. *Information Sciences, 8*, 199-249; 301-357; *9*, 43-80.

## ADDITIONAL READING

Altay, N., & Green, W. G. III OR/MS research in disaster operations management. (2006). *European Journal of Operational Research*, *16*(175), 475-493. doi:10.1016/j.ejor.2005.05.016

Avouris, N. M. (1995). Cooperating knowledge-based systems for environmental decision support. *Knowledge-Based Systems*, *1*(8), 39–54. doi:10.1016/0950-7051(94)00289-U

Avouris, N. M., & Finotti, S. (1993). User interface design to expert systems based on hierarchical spatial representations. *Expert Systems with Applications*, *2*(6), 109–118. doi:10.1016/0957-4174(93)90001-M

Chongfu, H. (1996). Fuzzy risk assessment of urban natural hazards. *Fuzzy Sets and Systems*, *2*(83), 271–282. doi:10.1016/0165-0114(95)00382-7

Gray, J. (1981). Characteristic patterns of and variations in community response to acute chemical emergencies. *Journal of Hazardous Materials*, *4*(4), 357–365. doi:10.1016/0304-3894(81)87006-9

Guohua, Ch. & Xinmei, Zhang. (2009). Fuzzy-based methodology for performance assessment of emergency planning and its application. *Journal of Loss Prevention in the Process Industries*, *2*(22), 125–132.

Hogan, D. E., & Burstein, J. L. (Eds.). (2007). *Disaster medicine*. Philadelphia: Lippincott Williams & Wilkins.

Huang, Ch., & Inoue, H. (2007). Soft risk maps of natural disasters and their applications to decision-making. *Information Sciences*, *7*(177), 1583–1592. doi:10.1016/j.ins.2006.07.033

Jiuh-Biing, S. (2007). An emergency logistics distribution approach for quick response to urgent relief demand in disasters. *Transportation Research Part E, Logistics and Transportation Review*, *6*(43), 687–709.

Karimi, I. & Hüllermeier, E. (2007). Risk assessment system of natural hazards: A new approach based on fuzzy probability. *Fuzzy Sets and Systems*, *9*(158), 987–999. doi:10.1016/j.fss.2006.12.013

Lillibridge, S. L., Noji, K. & Burkle, F. M. Jr. (1993). Disaster assessment: The emergency health evaluation of a population affected by a disaster. *Annals of Emergency Medicine*, *11*(22), 1715–1720. doi:10.1016/S0196-0644(05)81311-3

Masár, O., Štorek, J., Brenner, M., Turečková, H., Sysel, D., & Belejová, H. (2010). *Selected chapters from disaster medicine*. Bratislava: Faculty of Medicine, Komenský University in Bratislava. (in Czech)

McCaughrin, W. C., & Mattammal, M. (2003). Perfect storm: Organizational management of patient care under natural disaster conditions. *Journal of Healthcare Management*, (48): 295–308.

Pokorný, J., & Štorek, J. (2003). Aktuelle Entwicklungen im tschechischen Rettungsdienst. Beericht anslässlich der ersten Koferenz zu den Terroranschlägen des 11.September 2001. *Notfall&Rettungsmedizin*, *2*(6), 107–108.

Rosenthal, U., & Kouzmin, A. (1997). Crises and crisis management: Toward comprehensive government decision making. *Journal of Public Administration Research and Theory: J-PART*, *2*(7), 277–304.

Quelch, J., & Cameron, I. T. (1994). Uncertainty representation and propagation in quantified risk assessment using fuzzy sets. *Journal of Loss Prevention in the Process Industries*, *6*(7), 463–473. doi:10.1016/0950-4230(94)80004-9

Son, J., Aziz, Z., & Pena-Mora, Z. (2007). Supporting disaster response and recovery through improved situation awareness. *Structural Survey*, *5*(26), 411–425. doi:10.1108/02630800810922757

Stoklasa, J., & Štorek, J. (2008). *Disaster Medicine – first aid principles. (in Czech, study materials)*. Opava, Mathematical Institute in Opava, Silesian University in Opava.

Štorek, J. (2001). Traumatological planning model of a emergency medical rescue services centre. (in Czech). *Urgentní medicína*, 4(4), 6-8.

Štorek, J. (2004) Disaster management of the hospital care provider. (in Czech). *Urgentní medicína*, 2(7), 4 – 9.

Štorek, J. (2005) Public health and National security system – preparedness of the department to face disasters and crisis situations – documentation area. (in Czech). *Urgentní medicína*, 1(8), 4-6.

Tufekci, S. (1995). An integrated emergency management decision support system for hurricane emergencies. *Safety Science*, 1(20), 39–48. doi:10.1016/0925-7535(94)00065-B

Wallace, W. A. & De Balogh, F. (1985). Decision support systems for disaster management. *Public Administration Review,* Special issue: Emergency Management: A Challenge for Public Administration (45), 134-146.

Yang, L., Jones, B. F., & Yang, S.-H. (2007). A fuzzy multi-objective programming for optimization of fire station locations through genetic algorithms. *European Journal of Operational Research*, 2(181), 903. doi:10.1016/j.ejor.2006.07.003

Yang, L., Prasanna, R., & King, M. (2009). On-site information system design for emergency first responders. *Journal of Information Technology Theory and Application*, 1(10), 5–27.

Zerger, A., & Smith, D. I. (2003). Impediments to using GIS for real-time disaster decision support. *Computers, Environment and Urban Systems*, 2(27), 123–141. doi:10.1016/S0198-9715(01)00021-7

## KEY TERMS AND DEFINITIONS

**Decision Making Support:** A tool to help the decision maker achieve the desired decision by eliminating possible mistakes, carrying out some difficult computations and speeding up the process.

**Disaster:** An unexpected and devastating event with unusual impact on health, lives and/or property of people or the environment.

**Emergency Medical Rescue Services:** A component of the disaster response system, whose task it is (in the Czech Republic) to provide medical care to those people that are injured during the disaster and to transport them into proper medical facilities to receive further care.

**Fuzzy Number α-Degree Upper Bound:** A way of comparing a fuzzy number with a real number introduced in this chapter.

**Linguistic Fuzzy Modeling:** A two level mathematical modeling tool, with the first level described linguistically (using linguistic terms, linguistically defined functions) intended to mediate the communication between the model and the user of the model and the second level dealing with the meanings of these linguistic terms (using fuzzy sets, fuzzy numbers and approximate reasoning), computations are carried out within the second level and the outputs then linguistically approximated – this way transferred into the first level.

**Linguistic Scale:** A linguistic variable with a special structure of the meanings of its linguistic terms, such that the belonging of each element of the universal set is divided completely among the fuzzy numbers representing the meanings of the linguistic terms. For each element of the universal set the sum of the degrees of membership of this element to all the fuzzy numbers is equal to one.

**Uncertainty:** The lack of precise or desired information.

# Chapter 29
# Fuzzy Cognitive Map Reasoning Mechanism for Handling Uncertainty and Missing Data:
## Application in Medical Diagnosis

**Elpiniki I. Papageorgiou**
*Technological Educational Institute of Lamia, Greece*

## ABSTRACT

*In this study, the fuzzy causal map inference mechanisms are analyzed for decision making tasks and a comparative analysis is performed to handle with the uncertainty in the problem of pulmonary risk prediction. Fuzzy Cognitive Mapping (FCM) is a causal graphical representation including nodes, determining the most relevant factors of a complex system, and links between these nodes determining the relationships between those factors. It represents knowledge in a symbolic manner and relates states, processes, policies, events, values, and inputs in an analogous manner. In the proposed work, a modified inference mechanism for FCM approach, which handles uncertainty and missing data, is presented and compared with the common fuzzy causal graph reasoning process for a medical diagnosis problem. Through this study, we overcome the problem of missing data and/or incomplete knowledge, especially for the cases where there is no any information about a concept-state or the knowledge of some concepts is insufficient. By this way, the rescaled inference process is proved more reliable, yielding more exact and natural inference results than traditional FCMs. A number of different scenarios for medical diagnosis concentrated on the pulmonary infections are elaborated to demonstrate the functioning of the rescaled FCM inference mechanism.*

## INTRODUCTION

FCMs are able to capture and imitate human behavior by describing, developing and representing models. Their aim is to mimic the reasoning process of the human. They are graphical representation tools proposed by Kosko to represent the causal relationship between concepts and analyze inference patterns (Kosko, 1986, 1992). FCMs include nodes determining the most relevant factors of a complex system and links between these nodes determining the relationships between

DOI: 10.4018/978-1-61350-429-1.ch029

those factors (Rodriguez-Repiso, 2005). The graph structure of FCMs allows for static analysis, while its execution model allows for dynamic analysis of the modeled system (Froelich et al., 2009). FCMs are convenient to handle issues of knowledge representation and reasoning, which are essential to intelligent systems (Kosko, 1992). This modeling technique comes with a number of desirable properties, such as abstraction, flexibility, adaptability, and fuzzy reasoning (Banerjee, 2008; Wei et al., 2009).

The core task of a decision support system (DSS) is decision analysis. Real-life problems are mostly unstructured in nature, which makes it difficult to apply algorithmic methods based on mathematical models to the process of decision analysis. Decision makers often find it difficult to cope with significant real-world systems. These systems are usually characterized by a number of concepts or facts interrelated in complex ways (Hudson, 2006). They are often dynamic ie, they evolve through a series of interactions among related concepts. Feedback plays a prominent role among them by propagating causal influences in complicated pathways. Formulating a quantitative mathematical model for such a system may be difficult or impossible due to lack of numerical data, its unstructured nature, and dependence on inexact or "fuzzy" verbal expressions.

FCMs are knowledge-based systems which represent knowledge in a symbolic manner. Compared either expert system or neural networks, it has several desirable properties, such as it is relatively easy to use for representing structured knowledge, and the inference can be computed by numeric matrix operation. FCMs are appropriate to explicit the knowledge which has been accumulated for years on the operation of a complex system (Stylios & Georgopoulos, 2008). They provide a qualitative and semi-quantitative tool for representing and analyzing such systems with the goal of aiding decision making.

Basically, the inference mechanism (engine) is a computer program that attempt to infer or derive a deep insights or answers from the knowledge base. Typically, expert systems analyze the knowledge base in the inference mechanism which is designated to simulate human like expertise and reason for problem solving in a certain domain. As such, expert system could explain the reasoning process and handle levels of confidence and uncertainty, which straight algorithms do not do (Sordo et al., 2008). In this study we are modeling our proposed soft computing components as an adaptive inference mechanism for the decision support process. The FCM inference mechanism is an important issue for FCM operation which significantly improves the functionality and effectiveness of the approach.

FCMs are popular for their simplicity and transparency while being successful in a variety of applications (Aguilar 2003). Examples of specific applications include political developments (Taber, 1991), support for strategic problem formulation and decision analysis (Eden & Ackermann, 1993), electrical circuits (Styblinski & Meyer, 1988), knowledge bases construction (Silva, 1995), computing and decision sciences (Craiger et al. 1996; Schneider et al. 1998; Liu and Satur, 1999; Konar & Chakraborty, 2005; Osei-Bryson, 2004; Papageorgiou et al. 2006b; Stach et al. 2007, Yaman and Polat, 2009), urban design support (Xirogiannis & Glykas, 2004), relationship management in airline services (Kang, Lee, & Choi, 2004), web-mining inference amplification (Lee et al., 2002), agriculture and ecological sciences (Mendoza & Prabhu, 2006; Ozesmi & Ozesmi, 2004), engineering analysis (Pelαez & Bowles, 1996; Lee, et al., 2004), and medical diagnosis and decision support (Georgopoulos, Malandraki, & Stylios, 2003; Papageorgiou et al., 2006a, Yue He 2008, Papageorgiou et al., 2003, 2006, Georgopoulos and Stylios 2007, Stylios et al. 2008, Froelich and Wakulicz-Deja, 2009). In medical diagnosis, FCM based decision methodologies include an integrated structure for treatment planning management in radiotherapy (Papageorgiou et al, 2003), a model for specific language impairment (Stylios et al., 2008), models for bladder and brain tumor characterization (Papageorgiou et al., 2006, 2008), an approach for the pneumonia severity assessment (Papageorgiou et al., 2009a), and a model for the management of urinary tract infections (Papageorgiou et al., 2009b).

A preliminary trial to propose a model based on FCMs for assessing pulmonary infections has been presented in Papageorgiou et al. (2009a). In this chapter, an extensive and enhanced version of the proposed approach for predicting risk of pneumonia using a modified inference mechanism for FCMs and comparing its predictive capabilities with the common FCM process is presented. The FCM technique is introduced as a flexible and easy to use approach in modeling the causality inherent in medical knowledge and giving a front-end decision about the risk of pulmonary infections. This is an alternative approach to consider the missing data and uncertainty management, especially when the disease has multiple symptoms based on the idea that the FCMs are suitable to model complex systems and to make decisions easily and efficiently.

The main goal of this work is to present a modified FCM inference mechanism which is able to handle with missing data and incomplete knowledge, and compare its prediction and decision making capabilities with the traditional FCM reasoning process proposed by Kosko. Both of the fuzzy causal graph inference mechanisms are implemented to predict the risk of pulmonary infection in medical diagnosis. A comparative analysis was performed to show the effectiveness of the rescaled FCM inference algorithm as it takes under consideration the cases where there is missing data for the system and no any knowledge available for a number of concepts.

# FUZZY COGNITIVE MAPS

## 2.1 Overview

A fuzzy cognitive map consists of a set of state variables (nodes/concepts) linked together by interaction strengths that take linguistic fuzzy values which after defuzzification process can vary from -1 to 1. The interaction strengths indicate the degree to which one variable (node) influences another. A FCM represents state variables (concepts) and their interactions as fuzzy sets where a particular variable can take on partial membership or partial activation (Kosko 1986). In the context of models of community structure, the activation level of concept can loosely be defined as relative abundance scaled on the interval [0,1] or can represent membership in a fuzzy set describing linguistic measures of relative abundance (e.g. low, average, high). At a same manner, the interaction strengths are used to represent either 'expert opinion', semi-quantitative or quantitative data on the relative degree to which one concept influences another. The advantage of FCMs is that they are flexible and transparent knowledge representation tools, they are relatively easy to construct and parameterize and are capable of handling the dynamic effects on the feedback structure of a system. In addition, FCMs can also incorporate non-biological information such as the degree of human disturbance or management decisions. Once constructed, a FCM is then conducted numerically to find the equilibrium value of variables ($V_i$), given any fixed boundary conditions (e.g. sustained press of a variable) and the matrix of interaction strengths $E_{ij}$.

According to (Papageorgiou et al., 2003), the directional influences in FCM are presented as all-or-none relationships i.e. FCM provide qualitative as oppose to quantitative information about relationships. In Figure 1, a simple FCM (graph) representation is illustrated which has five generic vertices ($C_1$ to $C_5$) and the weighted arcs (edges) showing the relationships between

*Figure 1. Representing a simple fuzzy cognitive map*

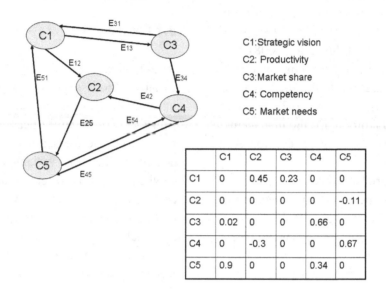

C1: Strategic vision
C2: Productivity
C3: Market share
C4: Competency
C5: Market needs

|     | C1   | C2   | C3   | C4   | C5    |
|-----|------|------|------|------|-------|
| C1  | 0    | 0.45 | 0.23 | 0    | 0     |
| C2  | 0    | 0    | 0    | 0    | -0.11 |
| C3  | 0.02 | 0    | 0    | 0.66 | 0     |
| C4  | 0    | -0.3 | 0    | 0    | 0.67  |
| C5  | 0.9  | 0    | 0    | 0.34 | 0     |

concepts. In this simple fuzzy cognitive map, the relation between two vertices is determined by taking a value in interval [-1, 1]. While -1 corresponds to the strongest negative, +1 corresponds to the strongest positive one. The other values express different levels of influence. This model can be presented by a square matrix called adjacency matrix.

Experts developed an FCM or a mental model manually based on their knowledge in related area. At first, they identify key domain aspects or concepts (Table 1). Secondly, each expert identifies the causal relationships among these concepts and estimates causal relationships strengths. This achieved digraph (FCM) shows not only the components and their relationships but also the strengths (Figure 1).

A comparison of different transformation functions for FCMs was carried out in a recent paper by Tsadiras (Tsadiras, 2008). Figure 2 shows a sample simulation of the model from Figure 1.

The simulation was carried out with the use of logistic transformation function; see formula (3), which is the most commonly used function (Bueno & Salmeron, 2009).

All type of information has numerical values. FCM allows us to perform qualitative simulations and experiment with a dynamic model. This type of analysis allows investigating "what-if" scenarios by performing simulations of a given model from different initial state vectors. Simulations offer description of dynamic behavior of the system that can be used to support decision making or predictions about its future states (Stylios & Groumpos, 2004).

## 2.2 Common FCM Inference Mechanism

According to the FCM construction process by an expert, a user can perform dynamic analysis of the model using FCM inference mechanism (as adopted by Kosko, 1992). The FCM based on the performed simulations is used to draw conclusions as to the dynamic behavior of the system. Simulation boils down to calculating system states over successive iterations. The degree of activation of all concepts is usually limited to [0,1] and describe the system state (Kosko, 1986). When a given concept is not present in the system at a

*Table 1. Factor and selector concepts coding pulmonary infection*

| Concepts | Description of concepts | Type of values |
|---|---|---|
| C1: Dyspnea | Dyspnea is a subjective experience of breathing discomfort that is comprised of qualitatively distinct sensations that vary in intesity.<br>According to the NYHA classification four discrete values have been assigned describing four progressively more serious states of dyspnea. In this approach four fuzzy values have been considered | Four fuzzy values ("no dyspnea", "less serious", moderate serious, serious dyspnea state) |
| C2: Cough | Cough is a deep inspiration folowed by a strong expiration against a closed glottis, which then opens with an expulsive flow of air, followed by a restorative inspiration. It is a defense mechanism against respiratory infections and can be productive or nonproductive, depending on whether sputum is produced or not. | Three fuzzy values ("no cough" (0-0.15), "non-productive" (0-0.3), "productive" (0.4-1)) |
| C3: Rigor/chills | Rigor is the involuntary shaking occurring during a high fever. It is part of an immune response and increase the set point for body temperature in the hypothalamus. The increased set point causes the body temperature to rise (pyrexia), but also makes the patient feel cold-chills until the new set point is reached. | Two discrete values ("no" (0), "yes" (1)) |
| C4: Fever | Fever is a frequent medical sign that describes an increase in internal body temperature to levels above normal. Usually the initial presentation is acute and it is accompanied by chills in 'typical' pneumonia rather than the gradual onset of "atypical" pneumonia Hypothermia can also be present in a small group of patient and indicates serious infection and worse prognosis. | Six Fuzzy values ("hypothermia" (34-36), "no fever" (36-38.4), "low" (38.5-38.9), "moderate" (38.9-39.5), "high" (39.5-40.9), "hyperpyrexia" (>41)) |
| C5: Loss of appetite | Loss of appetite is the decreased sensation of appetite, leading to loss of weight if the symptom prolong | Two discrete values ("no" (0), "yes" (1)) |
| C6: Debility | Debility is a non specific symptom of pneumonia refereed to the altered general well-being. According to the NYHA classification there are four discrete values describing four progressively more serious states of debility. | Four fuzzy values ("no" (1), "small" (2), "moderate" (3), "large" (4)) |
| C7: Pleuritic pain | Pleuritic pain is the result of acute inflammation of the pleural surfaces that covers lungs. It is restricted and tends to be distributed along the intercostals nerve zones. The pain perceived while the patient is breathing quietly, it is typically worsened by taking a deep breath, and coughing or sneezing causes intense distress | Two discrete values ("no" (0), "yes" (1)) |
| C8: Heamoptysis | Hemoptysis or haemoptysis is the expectoration (coughing up) of blood or of blood-stained sputum from the respiratory tract. The severity depends on the extent (small < 20ml/24h to massive >200-600ml/24h and life threatening) | Two discrete values ("no" (0), "yes" (1)) |
| C9:Oxygen requirement | There are four different states describing four progressively more serious states of oxygen requirement: no need of oxygen, the need of applying nasal kanula (~ 2-4lt oxygen) or Ventury mask (~ 4-15lt oxygen), NIMV (non invasive mechanical ventilation) and MV (mechanical ventilation) | Four fuzzy values ("no" (0), "low" (2-4lt), "medium" (4-15lt), "high" (mechanical ventilation, MV)) |
| C10: Tachypnea | Tachypnea (or "tachypnoea") is defined as the increase of respiratory rate of > 16 for men and 19 breaths for women breaths per minute. Respiratory rate > 30 breaths per minute is associated with worse prognosis and possible need of MV. | Four fuzzy values ("normal" (12-24), "moderate" (25-38), "severe" (35-49), "very severe" (>50)) |

*continued on following page*

*Table 1. Continued*

| Concepts | Description of concepts | Type of values |
|---|---|---|
| C11: Acoustic characteristics | Bronchial breath sounds produced when the lung parenhyma is consolidated and the airway leading to this region is parent. It is loud, high-pitched, tubular or whistling. Bronchophony mean that spoken sounds are transmitted with increased intensity and pitch through consolidated lung. | Two discrete values- "no" (0), "yes" (1) |
| C12:GCS | Glasgow Coma Scale (GCS) is a neurological scale which aims to give a reliable, objective way of recording the conscious state of a person, for initial as well as continuing assessment. A patient is assessed against the criteria of the scale, and the resulting points give a patient score between 3 (indicating deep unconsciousness) and 15 for alert individual. | Three fuzzy values: ("severe" ($\leq$ 8), "moderate" (9-12), "minor" ($\geq$ 13)) |
| C13:Systolic Blood Pressure | Blood pressure is a measurement of the force applied to the walls of the arteries during cardiac cycle The pressure is determined by the force and amount of blood pumped, and the size and flexibility of the arteries. The top number is the systolic blood pressure reading. It represents the maximum pressure exerted when the heart contract. | Seven fuzzy values ("hypotension" (<90), "optimal" (<120), "normal" (<130), "high-normal" (130-139), "grade-1 hypertension" (140 – 159), "grade-2 hypertension" (160-179), "grade-3 hypertension" (>=180)) |
| C14: Diastolic blood pressure | The bottom number is the diastolic blood pressure reading. It represents the pressure in the arteries when the heart is at rest | Seven fuzzy values ("hypotension" (<60), "optimal" (<80), "normal" (<85), "high-normal" (85-89), "grade-1 hypertension" (90-99), "grade-2 hypertension" (100-109), "grade-3 hypertension" (>=110)) |
| C15: Tachycardia | Tachycardia is the increased heart rate greater than 100 beats per minute. It is indicator of the haemodynamic situation of individual and often associated with fever. Pulse should increase by 10 beats per minute per degree Celsius of temperature elevation | Four fuzzy values ("low" (<80), "normal" (90-110), "moderately severe" (110-140), "severe" (>140)) |
| C16:Radiologic evidence of pneumonia | Alveolar infiltrate: localized in segment, lobe, nodular or diffuse Interstitial infiltrate; Nodular, reticular, septal, linear pattern. | Two discrete ("no" (0), "yes" (1)) |
| C17: Radiologic evidence of complicated pneumonia | Their presence indicates serious infection worse prognosis and possible need for more aggressive therapeutic techniques. Such complications are: atelectasis, pleural effusion, lung abscess, empyema, ARDS et. other | Two discrete values- "no" (0), "yes" (1) |
| C18: pH | It is an indicator that reflects the effectiveness of mechanism for regulating the acid-base status of the organism. It can be calculated by arterial blood gas analysis. | Three fuzzy values ("acidosis" (<7.35), "normal" (7.35-7.45), "alkalosis" (>7.45)) |
| C19:$pO_2$ | The partial pressure of oxygen in the arterial blood is an early indicator of respiratory failure. Low values of $pO_2$ demand oxygen therapy $pO_2 = 102 - 0,33 \times age$ (mmHg) | Two fuzzy value ("normal" (70-100), "hypoxia" (<70)) |
| C20: $pCO_2$ | The partial pressure of carbon dioxide is also an indicator of respiratory failure. High values of $pO_2$ demonstrate hypoventilation and possible need for NIMV or MV. | Three fuzzy values ("normal" (35-45mmHg) "hypocapnia" (<35 mmHg) "hypercapnia" (>45mmHg)) |
| C21: $sO_2$% | Oxygen saturation (sO2%) is the fraction of the hemoglobin molecules in a blood sample that are saturated with oxygen at a given partial pressure of oxygen. Normal saturation is 95%-100%.It is an easy and practical way to detect respiratory failure using pulse oximetry. | Two fuzzy values ("normal" (>95), "hypoxia" (<95)) |

*continued on following page*

*Table 1. Continued*

| Concepts | Description of concepts | Type of values |
|---|---|---|
| C22: WBC | White blood cells.Marked leukocytosis(>10x10³/µl)with leftward shift(increased absolute number of neutrophils> 7,710³/µl) is more often seen in bacterial pneumonia caused by Streptococcus pneumoniae, Haemophillus influenzae rather than normal number or leukopenia (<1000/µl) which is usual in atypical and viral pneumonia | Three fuzzy values ("leukopenia" (<1000), "normal" (4.3-10×10³), "leukocytosis" (>10×10³)) |
| C23: Immunocompromise | Immunodeficiency is a condition of altered mechanical and cellular defense mechanism of organism. As a result of that is the inability to fight infection. An immunocompromised person may be particularly vulnerable to opportunistic infections Also in immunocompromised patients the signs and symptoms of pulmonary infection may be muted and overshadowed by nonspecific complaints. Such conditions are:HIV infection, organ transplantation, neoplasms, corticosteroides, chemotherapeutics etc. | Two fuzzy values (presence, absence) |
| C24: Comorbidities | Comorbidities include conditions and diseases of individual associated with increased rate of pneumonia. Most frequently they are: COPD, bronchiectasis, asthma, congestive heart disease, diabetes, renal and liver disease etc) | Two discrete values (presence=1, absence=0) |
| C25: Age | Patient age is a serious factor for assessment severity of pneumonia according to CURB-65 scale. Age >65 is connected with greater mortality. Also due to the lack of specific symptoms the diagnosis of pneumonia is frequently delayed in the elderly. | Three fuzzy ("young" (1-30), "middle aged" (31-65), "old" (66-100)) |
| C26 (Out_C): Decision Concept | Risk of the pulmonary infection | Five fuzzy values ("very low", "low", "moderate", "high", "very high") |

*Figure 2. Sample FCM simulation of the model from Figure 1*

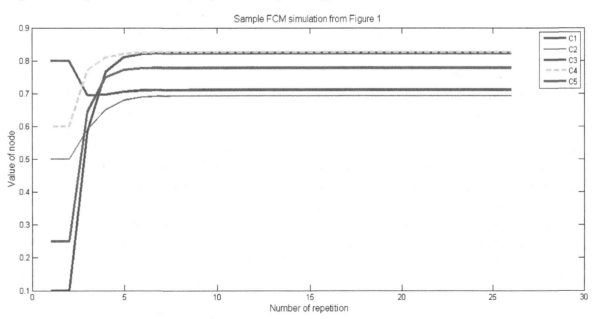

particular iteration then its value is zero, whereas a given concept is present to its maximum degree then its value is one. Other values correspond to intermediate levels of activation. The activation level of each concept depends on its value at the initial iteration as well as on the preceding values of all concepts that exert influence on it through non-zero relationships. The simulation requires knowledge of an initial state vector in order to determine successive states of the model, which is carried out using the following expression (Kosko, 1986, Aguilar, 2005):

$$V = f(V + V \times E) \qquad (1)$$

where the state vector $V$ is passed repeatedly through the FCM connection matrix $E$ and through the multiplication $V$ by $E$, the result is transformed and produced.

An FCM state vector at any point in time gives a snapshot of events (concepts) in the scenario being modeled.

$$V_i(k+1) = f((V_i(k) + \sum_{\substack{j \neq i \\ j=1}}^{N} V_j(k) \cdot E_{ji}) \qquad (2)$$

where $V_i(t)$ is the value of concept $Ci$ at step $k$, $V_j(t)$ is the value of concept $Cj$ at step k, $Eji$ is the weight of the interconnection from concept $Cj$ to concept $Ci$ and $f$ is the threshold function that squashes the result of the multiplication in the interval [0, 1]. This equation indicates that a FCM is free to interact; at every step of interaction every concept has a new value. Several formulas can be used as threshold function (Bueno and Salmeron, 2009), and as the interval of concept is bivalent (i.e., the concepts belong to the interval [0, 1]), we propose the function $f(x)$:

$$f(x)=1/(1+\exp(-mx)) \qquad (3)$$

where $m$ is a real positive number and $x$ is the value $V_i(t)$ on the equilibrium point. In this work we use $m=5$, because this value showed best results in previous works (Miao & Liu, 2000).

A concept is turned on or activated by making its vector element 1. New state vectors showing the effect of the activated concept are computed using method of successive substitution, i.e., by iteratively multiplying the previous state vector by the relational matrix using standard matrix multiplication $V^k = V^{k-1} + V^{k-1} \cdot E$. The eqs (1) or (2) indicate that a FCM is free to interact; at every step of interaction every concept has a new value. The simulation outcomes directly depend on the type of threshold (transformation) function. Discrete output functions lead the simulation into either hidden pattern (fixed-point attractor) or limit cycle. The former term refers to a scenario, in which the state vector is kept unchanged after a certain number of iterations. Limit cycle describes a situation, in which the system keeps cycling between certain states. When the transformation (threshold) function is continuous, the system may produce fixed-point attractor, limit cycle, and chaotic attractor, in which case different state vectors are computed in successive iterations.

The traditional FCM simulation algorithm (proposed by Kosko and expressed with eqs. (1)-(2)) consists of a number of steps gathered at follows and is used to simulate a process by giving the necessary decisions about it.

- **Step 1:** Definition of the initial vector $V$ that corresponds to the elements-concepts identified by experts' suggestions and available knowledge.
- **Step 2:** Multiply the initial vector $V$ and the matrix $E$ defined by experts by the eq. (1).
- **Step 3:** The resultant vector $V$ at time step $k$ is updating using eqs. (1)–(3).
- **Step 4:** This new vector $V^k$ is considered as an initial vector in the next iteration.

- **Step 5:** Steps 2–4 are repeated until $V^k - V^{k-1} \leq e = 0.001$ (where $e$ is a residua, describing the minimum error difference among the subsequent concepts) or $V^k = V^{k-1}$. Thus $V\_f = V^k$.

In each of the case study, an initial vector $V$ is assigned (consisting of $Vi$ values corresponding to each one concept $Ci$), representing the performed events at a given time of the process, and a final vector $V\_f$ is calculated at the steady state of the system, representing the last state that can be arrived at.

## 2.3 Modified FCM Inference Mechanism

A rescaled FCM inference algorithm, which updates the common FCM simulation process, has been deployed against to the inference mechanism suggested by Kosko, to avoid the conflicts emerge in cases where the initial values of concepts are 0 or 0.5 and especially for the cases where there is no any information about a concept-state or the expert (physician in our case study) doesn't know the initial state of the concept (patient symptom/observable), (Papageorgiou, 2010). By this way, the problem of insufficient initial knowledge about concept states from experts as well as the non discrimination between the values 0 and 0.5 overcame. Thus new rescaled inference process is more reliable, yielding more exact and natural inference results than traditional FCMs. The FCM network works with truth values in the range [-1,1] whereas the input/output should be truth values in the range [0,1]. This is perfectly feasible and all that is needed is a translation between the initial concept state -vector $V$ to the $2V$-1. This change to the concept vector can be implemented with the following mathematical equation:

$$V = f((2V - 1) + (2V - 1) \times E) \qquad (4)$$

Thus, a new simulation function has been determined, substituting the initial eq. (2), with the following equation:

$$V_i(k + 1) =$$
$$f((2V_i(k) - 1) + \sum_{\substack{j \neq i \\ j=1}}^{N} (2V_j(k) - 1) \cdot E_{ji}) \qquad (5)$$

Using the above inference algorithm, the final vector $V\_f$ is also obtained. The decision concepts of the final vector **V_f** are assessed and clarify the final decision of the specific decision support system, which gives in percentage the truth state of the decision value.

By this implementation change, we have solved the problem of missing data and/or incomplete knowledge for each input concept state. Furthermore, the problem with the initial zero values of concepts which through the threshold function, at second iteration step, take the value of 0.5, is also solved (Papageorgiou, 2011).

## FUZZY COGNITIVE MAP MODELING APPROACH TO ASSESS PULMONARY RISK

The prediction of risk in pulmonary infections is a complex process with enough parameters, factors and different conditions (Gennis et al., 1989; Hoare and Lim, 2006; Metlay et al., 1997; CDC Criteria for Defining Pneumonia). For the problem of pneumonia, a number of typical symptoms are associated including fever (80%) often accompanied by chills or hypothermia in a small group of patients, altered general well-being and respiratory symptoms such as cough (90%), expectoration (66%), dyspnea-shortness of breath (66%), pleuritic pain-a sharp or stabbing pain, experienced during deep breaths or coughs (50%), and hemoptysis-expectoration of blood (15%). The initial presentation is frequently acute, with an intense and unique chill. Productive cough is present and the expectoration is purulent or bloody. Pleuritic pain may be present.

Physical examination reveals typical findings of pulmonary consolidation- bronchial breath sounds, bronchophony, crackles, increased fremitus, dullness during percussion, tachypnea-increased respiratory rate, tachycardia-high heart rate (pulse should increase by 10 beats per minute per degree Celsius of temperature elevation) or a low oxygen saturation, which is the amount of oxygen in the blood as indicated by either pulse oximetry or blood gas analysis. In elderly and immunocompromised patients, the signs and symptoms of pulmonary infection may be muted and overshadowed by nonspecific complaints. If pneumonia is suspected on the basis of a patient's symptoms and findings from physical examination, further investigations are needed to confirm the diagnosis. Laboratory studies should be performed that include blood cell counts, serum glucose, transaminases, urea, creatinine and electrolyte measurements. From these lab tests only the white blood cells (WBC) have been considered as the most important one to increase mainly the risk of infection (CDC criteria for defining pneumonia). These data provide a logical basis for evaluation the risk of infection and the need for intensive care (Langer et al., 1994; Hoare and Lim, 2006).

Three physicians-experts, two physicians from the General Hospital of Lamia, and one from the University General Hospital of Patras, Greece, were pooled to define the number and type of parameters-factors affecting the problem of pulmonary infection (Papageorgiou et al. 2009a). These parameters (concepts) are listed in Table 1 and are well documented in bibliography. The 26 concepts are the factor and selector concepts representing the main variables that physicians in ICU usually take into consideration in assigning the existent and the grade of the infection. For this application, concept values take either two, three, four or five possible discrete or fuzzy values, as shown in Table 1. The Decision Concept (Out-

C) represents the risk of pulmonary infection in percentage and takes *five fuzzy values (very low, low, moderate, high, very high)* (Papageorgiou et al., 2009a).

After the description of FCM concepts, the design of FCM model continues with the determination of fuzzy sets. There are two different ways to define fuzzy sets for each one concept variable: (a) to define linguistic values based on variable behavior (through historical data where it's possible to determine the number and the shape of the sets); (b) or to define linguistic values based on experts' knowledge into a range between zero and one. In this section, the corresponding fuzzy sets for each variable of the model have been defined with a brief interpretation of experts' knowledge and literature review.

Examples of fuzzy membership functions for the input variables of dyspnea, fever, systolic pressure and white blood cells are illustrated in Figure 3 (a,b,c). Also, the decision concept (Out-C) is prescribed in Figure 3 (d). The construction of the whole model and the computations for each one of the inference mechanisms were carried out using subroutines implemented in Matlab programming language version R2008a.

After the determination of fuzzy sets, each expert was asked to define the degree of influence among the concepts and to describe their interrelationship using an IF—THEN rule, assuming the following statement where Ci and Cj are all the ordered pair of concepts:

```
IF a {no, very small, small, medium,
large, very large} change occurs in
the value of concept Ci THEN a {no,
very small, small, medium, large,
very large} change in value of con-
cept Cj is caused. THUS the influ-
ence of concept Ci on concept Cj is
T(influence).
```

The term set *T(influence)* is suggested to comprise thirteen variables. Using thirteen lin-

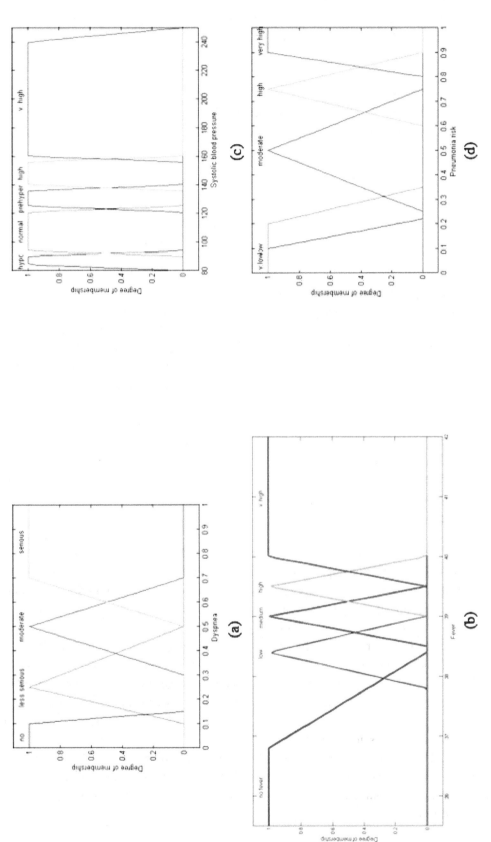

*Figure 3. Membership functions corresponding to the linguistic variables describing the (a) dyspena (b) fever (c) systolic blood pressure, and (d) the decision concept DC for pneumonia risk*

*Figure 4. Defuzzification of linguistic weights. A numerical weight is produced.*

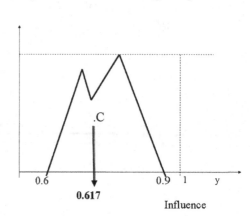

guistic variables, an expert can describe in detail the influence of one concept on another and can discern between different degrees of influence. The thirteen variables used here are:

```
T(influence) = {negatively very very
strong, negatively very strong, nega-
tively strong negatively medium, neg-
atively weak, negatively very weak,
zero, positively very weak, positive-
ly weak, positively medium, positive-
ly strong, positively very strong,
positively very very strong}.
```

Then, experts inferred a linguistic weight to describe the cause and effect relationship between every pair of concepts. To illustrate how numerical values of weights are produced, the three experts' suggestions on how to indicate the interconnection between concepts C22 (number of white blood cells) and Out-C (risk of pulmonary infection) are shown below:

**1st expert:**

IF a small change occurs in the value of concept C22, THEN a medium change in value of concept DC is caused.

Infer: The influence from C22 to DC is **positive medium**.

**2nd expert:**

IF a small change occurs in the value of concept C22, THEN a large change in value of concept DC is caused.

Infer: The influence from C22 to DC is **positive strong**.

**3rd expert:**

IF a very small change occurs in the value of concept C22, THEN a large change in value of concept DC is caused.

Infer: The influence from C22 to DC is **positive very strong**.

These linguistic variables (medium, positive strong and positive very strong) are summed and an overall linguistic weight is produced, which with the defuzzification method of CoG is transformed into the numerical value of $E_{22\text{-Out}} = 0.617$ (see Figure 4).

The 26 identified concepts (Table 1) keep relations with each other, in order to characterize the process of predicting the risk of pulmonary infectious diseases and to provide a first front-end decision tool about the prediction of pulmonary infection.

Figure 5 illustrates the FCM model for predicting the risk of pulmonary infection with the assigned numerical values of weights.

*Figure 5. The FCM model for assessing the risk of pulmonary infection*

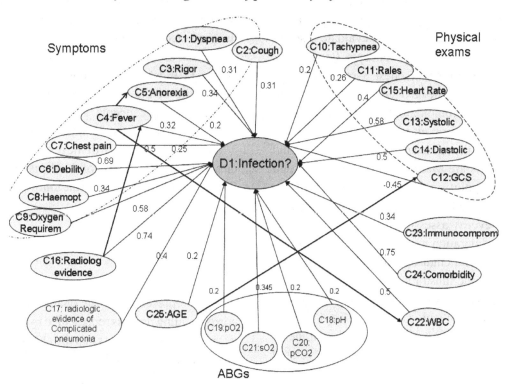

*Figure 6. Hierarchical structure for final decision about antibiotic treatment using FCMs*

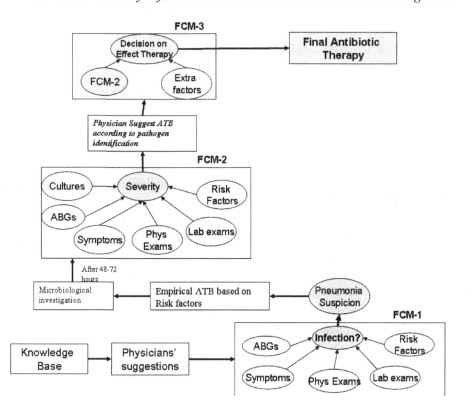

The proposed method based on FCMs for predicting pulmonary infection provides a framework within which physicians evaluate a series of traditional diagnostic concepts (symptoms, signs, laboratory tests, chest x-rays, risk and other factors). At the next step, further examinations about microbiological cultures and laboratory tests are important to be investigated. After 48-72 hours, the related results form cultures and antibiograms are available to the physician and in this time point, a second module, called FCM-2, is constructed to simulate the process for pulmonary severity assessment. This module takes under consideration more laboratory exams and microbiological cultures. The FCM-2 tool, with a more specific illustration depicted in Figure 6, is based on the main concepts described in FCM-1 module and on new concepts defined by new measurements and exams of cultures, pathogens, urinary antigen tests as well as any other related observables. The decision of this module is the severity degree of pneumonia. The module namely FCM-3, is considered as an extension of FCM-2 where more available factors (observables, examinations) might be considered according to new investigations and microbiological results adding antibiotic resistances. The produced FCM-3 module reaches a decision about the effectiveness of the overall therapy and the optimum use of antibiotics. This tool is under investigation and will be presented in a future work after clinical evaluation.

## RESULTS AND DISCUSSION

After construction of FCM tool for assessing the severity risk of pneumonia, a number of scenarios are introduced and the decision making capabilities of the inference techniques are presented by simulating these scenarios. Specifically, fifteen (15) decision making cases on pneumonia risk assessment have been derived from a randomly selected set of anonymous patients. The decision

making capabilities of the technique was presented by simulating these patient cases and estimating the predicted outcomes.

In each of the patient cases, we have an initial vector $V$, illustrating the presented events at a given time of the process which constitute the initial activated concepts, and a final vector $V\_f$, representing the last state that can be arrived at.

For the interpretation of the results, an average only for the output value of the decision concept DC is computed according to the following criteria:

$$R(x) \begin{cases} 0, x \leq 0.5 \\ \dfrac{x - 0.5}{0.5} \times 100\%, 0.5 < x \leq 1 \end{cases} \quad (6)$$

where 0 represents that the characteristic of the corresponding process represented by the concept x is null, and 1 represents that the characteristic of the process represented by the concept is present at 100%. For the specific approach, the function $R(x)$ gives the severity degree of pulmonary infection in percentage. When $R$(value of DC)=1, then the severity degree is 100%. The final value of DC applying this criterion is denoted by DC\_f. This criterion can be modified according with the expert judgment.

### 5.1 Simulations

First Scenario

Table 2 presents the description, observables, relevant medical information and discussion of results for the first scenario.

The initial concept vector for first inference mechanism (IM-1) is described at follows:

*V1_1*=[0  0  0  0.7  1  0  0  0  0  0
0  0  0  0.7  0  1  0  0  0  0
0.3  1  0  0  0]

*Table 2. Presentation of first scenario*

| Description | An immunocompromized adult 38 year old patient is suffering from high fever and loss of appetite, high systolic pressure and the radiological examination indicated localized evidence. Furthermore, after examinations, a small number of WBC was observed. |
|---|---|
| Observables | Immunocompromised patient ($V_{23}=1$)<br>Fever – High ($V_4=0.7$)<br>Loss of appetite ($V_5=1$)<br>Systolic blood pressure- high ($V_{13}=0.7$)<br>Radiological examination-localized evidence ($V_{16}=1$)<br>Number of WBCs- small ($V_{22}=0.3$) |
| Relevant medical information and expectations | Medically, we have a serious condition with known symptoms and important examination results which obviously bring on very high risk of pulmonary infection. |
| Result discussion | The result (Figures 6-7) clearly states that the above symptoms and examinations contribute to a high to very high risk of pulmonary severity. |

*Table 3. First scenario- Final concept state vectors for common and rescaled inference mechanisms (IM-1 and IM-2)*

| Steady state using **IM-1** | C1 | C2 | C3 | C4 | C5 | C6 | C7 | C8 | C9 | C10 | C11 | C12 | C13 |
|---|---|---|---|---|---|---|---|---|---|---|---|---|---|
| | 0.7233 | 0 | 0 | 0.7830 | 0.7226 | 0 | 0 | 0 | 0 | 0 | 0 | 0 | 0 |
| | C14 | C15 | C16 | C17 | C18 | C19 | C20 | C21 | C22 | C23 | C24 | C25 | C26 |
| | 0.7 | 0.7226 | 1 | 0 | 0 | 0 | 0.7926 | 0 | 0.4 | 1 | 0 | 0 | 0.9735 |
| Steady state using **IM-2** | C1 | C2 | C3 | C4 | C5 | C6 | C7 | C8 | C9 | C10 | C11 | C12 | C13 |
| | 0.5431 | 0.5 | 0.5 | 0.7185 | 0.5648 | 0.5 | 0.5 | 0.5 | 0.5 | 0.5 | 0.5 | 0.5 | 0.5 |
| | C14 | C15 | C16 | C17 | C18 | C19 | C20 | C21 | C22 | C23 | C24 | C25 | C26 |
| | 0.7 | 0.5648 | 1 | 0.5 | 0.5 | 0.5 | 0.6445 | 0.5 | 0.4 | 1 | 0.5 | 0.5 | 0.8963 |

*Figure 7. System convergence for the first case study using FCM IM-1*

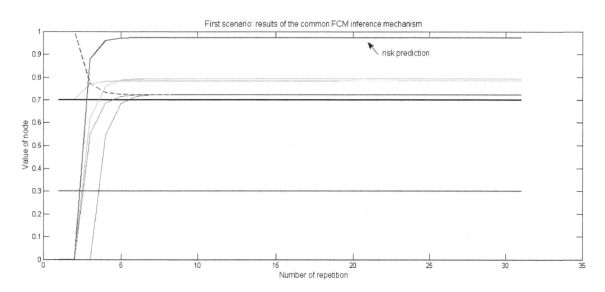

*Figure 8. System convergence for the first case study using FCM IM-2*

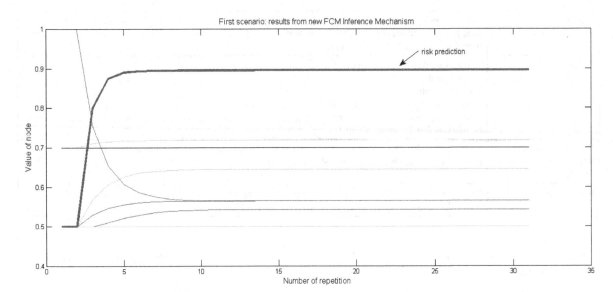

The initial concept vector for second inference mechanism (IM-2) is described at follows:

**V1_2**=[0.5   0.5   0.5   0.7   1   0.5   0.5
0.5   0.5   0.5   0.5   0.5   0.5   0.7
0.5   1   0.5   0.5   0.5   0.5   0.5   0.3
1   0.5   0.5   0.5].

It is considered that in cases where there is no initial information and/or data for some of the FCM concepts, the initial value of these concepts is assigned to 0.5 instead of 0 in the case of IM-1.

After using FCM IM-1, proposed by Kosko and described in section 2.2, the system converges in a steady state with the final concept state vector to be presented in Table 3. Furthermore the same Table illustrates the calculated concept state vector for FCM IM-2.

Figure 7 illustrates the subsequent values of calculated concepts after 30 steps.

The final value of decision concept is V1_f(26)=0.9710, which following the above criterion (DC=R(0.9710)) corresponds to the 91.34% of risk, thus means that the risk of infec-

*Table 4. Presentation of second scenario*

| Description | An old patient, with altered mental status, is suffering from high oxygen requirements. Furthermore, after examinations, a normal number of WBC was observed. |
| --- | --- |
| Observables | Old patient ($V_{25}$=0.8)<br>Altered mental status ($V_{12}$=0.4)<br>Oxygen requirements - high ($V_9$=0.8)<br>Number of leukocytes-WBC -- normal ($V_{22}$=0). |
| Relevant medical information and expectations | Medically we have a less serious condition with few symptoms and normal examination results which obviously bring on moderate risk of pulmonary infection. |
| Result discussion | The result clearly states that the above symptoms and examinations contribute to a moderate risk of pulmonary severity. |

*Table 5. Second scenario -Calculated concept values after thirty iterations for common and rescaled inference mechanisms (IM-1 and IM-2)*

| Steady state using **IM-1** | C1 | C2 | C3 | C4 | C5 | C6 | C7 | C8 | C9 | C10 | C11 | C12 | C13 |
|---|---|---|---|---|---|---|---|---|---|---|---|---|---|
| | 0 | 0 | 0 | 0 | 0 | 0 | 0 | 0.8 | 0 | 0 | 0.4 | 0.5596 | 0 |
| | C14 | C15 | C16 | C17 | C18 | C19 | C20 | C21 | C22 | C23 | C24 | C25 | C26 |
| | 0 | 0 | 0 | 0 | 0 | 0 | 0 | 0 | 0 | 0 | 0 | 0.8 | 0.8203 |
| steady stete using **IM-2** | C1 | C2 | C3 | C4 | C5 | C6 | C7 | C8 | C9 | C10 | C11 | C12 | C13 |
| | 0.5 | 0.5 | 0.5 | 0.5 | 0.5 | 0.5 | 0.5 | 0.8 | 0.5 | 0.2 | 0.4213 | 0.5 | 0.5 |
| | C14 | C15 | C16 | C17 | C18 | C19 | C20 | C21 | C22 | C23 | C24 | C25 | C26 |
| | 0.5 | 0.5 | 0.5 | 0.5 | 0.5 | 0.5 | 0.5 | 0.5 | 0.5 | 0.5 | 0.5 | 0.8 | 0.6778 |

tion is very high according to the related fuzzy regions, initially prescribed.

The final value of calculated DC using IM-2 is 0.8963, which means that a very high risk of infection (89.63%) is predicted. Figure 8 illustrates the subsequent values of calculated concepts after thirty iterations. Both inference mechanisms gave a very high risk of infection. This is in compliance with the physicians' opinions.

## Second Scenario

Table 4 gathers the states of the second scenario giving the relevant medical information, expectations and results.

The initial concept state for first IM-1 is described on the following vector:

$V2\_1 = [0 \ 0 \ 0 \ 0 \ 0 \ 0 \ 0 \ 0.8 \ 0 \ 0 \ 0.4 \ 0 \ 0 \ 0$
$0 \ 0 \ 0 \ 0 \ 0 \ 0 \ 0 \ 0 \ 0 \ 0 \ 0 \ 0.8 \ 0]$

The initial concept state for second IM-2 is described on the following vector:

$V2\_2 = [0.5 \ 0.5 \ 0.5 \ 0.5 \ 0.5 \ 0.5 \ 0.5 \ 0.8$
$0.5 \ 0.5 \ 0.4 \ 0.5 \ 0.5 \ 0.5 \ 0.5 \ 0.5 \ 0.5$
$0.5 \ 0.5 \ 0.5 \ 0.5 \ 0.5 \ 0.5 \ 0.5 \ 0.8 \ 0.5 \ ]$

Implementing both inference mechanisms, the steady states of concepts values were derived. Table 5 gathers the calculated concept states for the IM-1 and new rescaled IM-2 for the second scenario after a number of 12 iterations for IM-1 and 18 iterations for IM-2.

The final value of decision concept is V2_f(26)=0.8203, and following the above crite-

*Table 6. Presentation of third scenario*

| Description | A 48 year old patient with good mental status is suffering from chest pain, weak tachypnea and moderate fever. Furthermore, after examinations, a large number of WBC was observed. |
|---|---|
| Observables | Mental status – good ($V_{12}$=0.8)<br>Chest pain – v.high ($V_7$=1)<br>Tachypnea ($V_{10}$=0.3)<br>Fever – moderate ($V_4$=0.3)<br>Large number of WBC ($V_{22}$=0.8) |
| Relevant medical information and expectations | This relevant medical information has also an expectation for low or moderate pulmonary risk. The referred symptoms obviously bring on low or moderate risk of pulmonary infection. |
| Result discussion | The result clearly states that the above symptoms and examination results contribute to a low to moderate risk of pulmonary severity. |

rion, corresponds to the 64.06% of risk, thus means that the risk of pulmonary infection is moderate according to the related fuzzy regions in concept description.

The final value of decision concept Out-C calculated by IM-2 is 0.6778, which means that the risk is 67.78%, corresponding to a moderate risk of infection. Using both inference mechanisms a high infection risk was predicted which is in compliance with the physicians' opinions.

## Third Scenario

Table 6 gathers the states of the forth scenario giving the relevant medical information, expectations and results. This relevant medical information has also an expectation for low to moderate pulmonary risk.

The initial concept vector for this scenario is:

**V4** = [0 0 0 0.3 0 0 1 0 0 0.3 0 0.8 0 0 0 0 0 0 0 0 0.8 0 0 0.5 0];

After the FCM simulation process described in previous five steps the system converges in a steady state with the final concept vector to be:

**V4_f** = [0.7176 0 0 0.3000 0.6845 0 1.0000 0 0 0.3000 0 0.5983 0 0.6845 0 0 0 0 0.7163 0 0.8000 0 0 0.5000 0.9254]

Final value of output concept is V_f(26)=0.9254, which following the above criterion R(x) correspond to the 86,07% of risk, thus means that the risk of pulmonary infection is high according to the related fuzzy regions. Table 7 gathers the activation levels of concepts for the new rescaled inference mechanism and the calculated concept state at equilibrium point after a number of iterations.

The final value of calculated DC using IM-2 is 0.3502, which means that a low to moderate risk of infection is predicted. Through the common inference mechanism a high risk was predicted. The IM-2 gives a result which clearly agrees with the physicians' suggestions. Figure 9 illustrates the subsequent values of calculated concepts after 30 steps.

Fifteen representative scenarios (see in Table 8) were considered to assess the process of predicting risk of pulmonary infection, and the results were evaluated by physicians-experts.

## 5.2 Discussion of Results

The two FCM inference mechanisms were evaluated in fifteen patient cases. Table 8 gathers the examined fifteen patient cases, considering the physicians' suggestions as the "gold" standard for the evaluation analysis. The success rates for each one FCM inference mechanism have been assessed; 60% and 80% for the IM-1 and IM-2 respectively. The FCM IM-2 gives better discrimination results and shows its superior-

*Table 7. Forth scenario - Initial and final concept values for IM-2*

| Initial activation level using IM-2 | C1 | C2 | C3 | C4 | C5 | C6 | C7 | C8 | C9 | C10 | C11 | C12 | C13 |
|---|---|---|---|---|---|---|---|---|---|---|---|---|---|
| | 0.5 | 0.5 | 0.5 | 0.3 | 0.5 | 0.5 | 1 | 0.5 | 0.2 | 0.3 | 0.5 | 0.8 | 0.5 |
| | C14 | C15 | C16 | C17 | C18 | C19 | C20 | C21 | C22 | C23 | C24 | C25 | C26 |
| | 0.5 | 0.5 | 0.5 | 0.5 | 0.5 | 0.5 | 0.5 | 0.5 | 0.8 | 0.5 | 0.5 | 0.5 | 0.5 |
| Steady state using IM-2 | C1 | C2 | C3 | C4 | C5 | C6 | C7 | C8 | C9 | C10 | C11 | C12 | C13 |
| | 0.4602 | 0.5 | 0.5 | 0.3 | 0.4406 | 0.5 | 1 | 0.5 | 0.2 | 0.3 | 0.5 | 0.8 | 0.5 |
| | C14 | C15 | C16 | C17 | C18 | C19 | C20 | C21 | C22 | C23 | C24 | C25 | C26 |
| | 0.5 | 0.4406 | 0.5 | 0.5 | 0.5 | 0.5 | 0.3666 | 0.5 | 0.8 | 0.5 | 0.5 | 0.5 | 0.3502 |

*Figure 9. Variation of concepts values of the FCM tool for the third case study using IM-2*

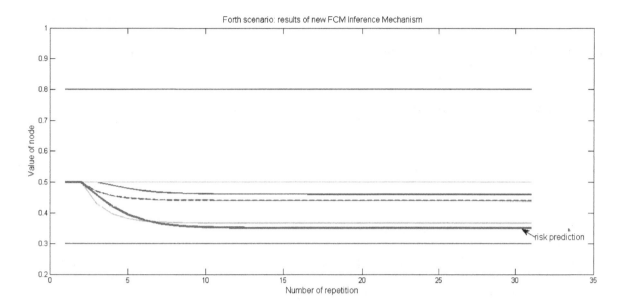

ity in the cases where there is missing data and incomplete knowledge from physicians and/or in the cases where there is no knowledge available for concepts which are activated initially. Thus, it gives a front-end decision about the degree of risk, providing similar results to those obtained with physicians' intuition. Of course, more trials and clinical experiences are needed for a large number of real patient cases in order to confirm or improve this result. Future work will be directed towards this direction.

The strongest point of the methodology is the insight it can provide on the role of key feedbacks in the system. These feedbacks can remain hidden and can be uncovered by applying a tool such FCM. Also, FCM represents a system in a form that corresponds closely to the way humans perceive it. Therefore, the model is easily understandable, even by a non-technical audience and each parameter has a perceivable meaning. The model can be easily altered to incorporate new phenomena, and if its behavior is different than expected, it is usually easy to find which factor should be modified and how. In this sense, a FCM

is a dynamic modeling tool in which the resolution of the system representation can be increased by applying further mapping. The resulting fuzzy model was used to analyze, simulate, test the influence of parameters and predict the behavior of the system.

## FUTURE RESEARCH DIRECTIONS

In future work, this FCM tool will be enhanced by other knowledge schemes to assess the risk and the severity of infectious diseases. The FCM approach will be strengthened by using knowledge from clinical data through data mining techniques. This knowledge will be inserted into the FCM tool that is initially constructed by experts to enhance its structure and functionality. Towards this direction, knowledge extraction methods, data mining and rule-based knowledge elicitation techniques will be investigated to gather more information in an automatic approach without the deficiencies coming from the experts opinions.

*Table 8. Evaluation of 15 representative scenarios with both inference mechanisms*

| a/a | Patient case | FCM IM-1 | FCM IM-2 | Physicians' evaluation |
|-----|-------------|----------|----------|------------------------|
| 1 | Immunocompromized adult 38 year old patient with high fever, loss of appetite, high systolic pressure, the radiological examination indicated localized evidence, small number of WBC. | Very high | Very high | Very high |
| 2 | Old patient, with altered mental status, suffers from high oxygen requirements, but the WBC was normal. | moderate | moderate | moderate |
| 3 | Middle age patient, with good mental status, with very low oxygen requirements, large number of leukocytes-WBC, and moderate fever. | high | Low to moderate | Low to moderate |
| 4 | 48 year old patient with good mental status, chest pain, weak tachypnea, moderate fever, large number of WBC. | high | Low to moderate | Low to moderate |
| 5 | patient with fever and all other symptoms to be zero | high | Very low | Very low |
| 6 | Young patient with chest pain and tachypnea (unknown information for other symptoms) | moderate | moderate | moderate |
| 7 | Young patient with chest pain and tachypnea and no other symptoms (this means other symptoms take zero values) | high | high | high |
| 8 | Young patient presents high cough, high pressure, high number of WBCs, and localized acoustic characteristics | high | high | high |
| 9 | Young patient with localized acoustic characteristics, high cough, high pressure, high number of WBCs, and no other symptoms | high | low | Moderate to high |
| 10 | Patient with dyspnea, high diastolic pressure, with rigor and plevritic pain, with no radiologic evidence of pneumonia and normal pH, and $pO_2$ | moderate | moderate | moderate |
| 11 | Patient with dyspnea, high diastolic pressure, with rigor and plevritic pain, with no radiologic evidence of pneumonia, normal pH, and $pO_2$, and no other symptoms | High | moderate | low |
| 12 | 52 year old patient, with no dyspnea, no cough, moderate diastolic pressure, with no rigor and no plevritic pain, with normal sO2 and presence of comorbidities, normal pH and pO2 | High | Very low | low |
| 13 | Young patient with fever and high systolic pressure and no other symptoms | High | low | low |
| 14 | Young patient with fever and large number of WBCs and unknown information for other observables and examination results | high | high | Moderate to high |
| 15 | Patient with dyspnea, no other knowledge for symptoms and missing data for examinations | low | low | low |

Success rates: FCM IM-1, 9/15=**60%**, FCM IM2 12/15=**80%**

## CONCLUSION

In this paper, the Fuzzy Cognitive Map modeling technique with a rescaled inference mechanism for making predictions in pulmonary infections was proposed, as an alternative knowledge-based system inheriting the advantages of simplicity and easiness of use. FCM provides a tool for capturing the system's behavior from available information and handles with missing data and incomplete knowledge. The main idea of this work was to model and predict efficiently the risk of pulmonary infections, considering the uncertainty and missing data. This research goal was achieved by using a modified inference mechanism for FCMs.

Throughout the rescaled inference mechanism, the insufficient knowledge in medical tasks, as well as the missing data that emerged in most of the complex medical cases, may be copied with sufficiency. By this way, the rescaled inference process is more reliable than conventional FCMs as it has been proved from the proposed medical problem. The updated inference equation has been emerged an important issue for FCM simulation which significantly improves the functionality and effectiveness of the approach.

## ACKNOWLEDGMENT

The DebugIT project (http://www.debugit.eu/) is receiving funding from the European Community's Seventh Framework Programme under grant agreement n° FP7–217139, which is gratefully acknowledged. The information in this document reflects solely the views of the authors and no guarantee or warranty is given that it is fit for any particular purpose. Also, the author wants to thank the three medical doctors, namely G. Karagianni, D. Sfyras and N. Papandrianos, who gave their useful knowledge and suggestions for the construction and evaluation of FCM model for pulmonary risk prediction.

## REFERENCES

Aguilar, J. (2003). A dynamic fuzzy-cognitive-map approach based on random neural networks. *International Journal of Computational Cognition*, *1*(4), 91–107.

Alizadeh, S., & Ghazanfari, M. (2009). Learning FCM by chaotic simulated annealing. *Chaos, Solitons, and Fractals*, *41*(3), 1182–1190. doi:10.1016/j.chaos.2008.04.058

Axelrod, R. (1976). *Structure of decision–The cognitive maps of political elites*. Princeton, NJ: Princeton University Press.

Banerjee, G. (2008). Adaptive fuzzy cognitive maps vs neutrosophic cognitive maps: Decision support tool for knowledge based institutions. *Journal of Scientific and Industrial Research*, *67*(9), 665–673.

Bueno, S., & Salmeron, J. L. (2009). Benchmarking main activation functions in fuzzy cognitive maps. *Expert Systems with Applications*, *36*(3), 5221–5229. doi:10.1016/j.eswa.2008.06.072

CDC. (n.d.). *Criteria for defining nosocomial pneumonia*. Retrieved from http://www.cdc.com/

Chen, H., Fuller, S. S., & Friedman, C. P. (Eds.). (2005). *Medical informatics: Knowledge management and data mining in biomedicine. Integrated Series in Information Systems*. Springer.

Craiger, J. P., Weiss, R. J., Goodman, D. F., & Butler, A. A. (1996). Simulating organizational behavior with fuzzy cognitive maps. *Int J Comp Intell Organ*, *1*, 120–133.

Eden, C., & Ackermann, F. (1993). Evaluating strategy-Its role within the context of strategic control. *The Journal of the Operational Research Society*, *44*, 76–88.

Froelich, W., & Wakulicz-Deja, A. (2007). Learning fuzzy cognitive maps from the Web for the stock market decision support system. *Advances in Soft Computing, 43*, 106–111. doi:10.1007/978-3-540-72575-6_17

Froelich, W., & Wakulicz-Deja, P. (2009). A predictive capabilities of adaptive and evolutionary fuzzy cognitive maps - A comparative study. In Nguyen, N. T., & Szczerbicki, E. (Eds.), *Intel. Sys. for Know. Management, SCI 252* (pp. 153–174). Berlin, Germany: Springer Verlag. doi:10.1007/978-3-642-04170-9_7

Gennis, P., Gallagher, J., Falvo, C., Baker, S., & Than, W. (1989). Clinical criteria for the detection of pneumonia in adults: Guidelines for ordering chest roentgenograms in the emergency department. *The Journal of Emergency Medicine, 7*(3), 263–268. doi:10.1016/0736-4679(89)90358-2

Georgopoulos, V., & Stylios, C. D. (2005). Augmented fuzzy cognitive maps supplemented with case base reasoning for advanced medical decision support. In Nikravesh, M., Zadeh, L. A., & Kacprzyk, J. (Eds.), *Soft computing for information processing and analysis enhancing the power of the Information Technology, Studies in fuzziness and soft computing* (pp. 391–405). Springer-Verlag. doi:10.1007/3-540-32365-1_17

Georgopoulos, V. C., Malandraki, G. A., & Stylios, C. D. (2003). A fuzzy cognitive map approach to differential diagnosis of specific language impairment. *Artificial Intelligence in Medicine, 29*(3), 261–278. doi:10.1016/S0933-3657(02)00076-3

Hoare, Z., & Lim, W. S. (2006). Pneumonia: update on diagnosis and management. *BMJ (Clinical Research Ed.), 332*, 1077–1079. Retrieved from http://www.bmj.com/cgi/content/full/332/7549/1077. doi:10.1136/bmj.332.7549.1077

Hudson, D. L. (2006). Medical expert systems. In *Encyclopedia of biomedical engineering*. John Wiley and Sons. doi:10.1002/9780471740360.ebs0751

Khan, M. S., & Khor, S. W. (2004). A framework for fuzzy rule-based cognitive maps. *Lecture Notes in Artificial Intelligence, 3157*, 454–463.

Konar, A., & Chakraborty, U. K. (2005). Reasoning and unsupervised learning in a fuzzy cognitive map. *Information Sciences, 170*(2-4), 419–441. doi:10.1016/j.ins.2004.03.012

Kosko, B. (1986). Fuzzy cognitive maps. *International Journal of Man-Machine Studies, 24*(1), 65–75. doi:10.1016/S0020-7373(86)80040-2

Kosko, B. (Ed.). (1992). *Neural networks and fuzzy systems*. Englewood Cliffs, NJ: Prentice-Hall.

Koulouriotis, D. E., Diakoulakis, I. E., Emiris, D. M., Antonidakis, E. N., & Kaliakatsos, I. A. (2003). Efficiently modeling and controlling complex dynamic systems using evolutionary fuzzy cognitive maps (invited paper). *International Journal of Computational Cognition, 1*(2), 41–65.

Langer, M., Pifferi, S., & Peta, M. (1994). Diagnosis of bacterial infection in the ICU: General principles. *Intensive Care Medicine, 20*(4), 1432–1238. doi:10.1007/BF01713977

Lee, K. C., Kim, J. S., Chung, N. H., & Kwon, S. J. (2002). Fuzzy cognitive map approach to web mining inference amplification. *Expert Systems with Applications, 22*, 197–211. doi:10.1016/S0957-4174(01)00054-9

Lee, S., Kim, B. G., & Lee, K. (2004). Fuzzy cognitive map-based approach to evaluate EDI performance: A test of causal model. *Expert Systems with Applications, 27*(2), 287–299. doi:10.1016/j.eswa.2004.02.003

Liu, Z. Q., & Satur, R. (1999). Contextual fuzzy cognitive map for decision support in geographic information systems. *IEEE Transactions on Fuzzy Systems, 7*, 495–507. doi:10.1109/91.797975

Mendoza, G. A., & Prabhu, R. (2006). Participatory modeling and analysis for sustainable forest management: Overview of soft system dynamics models and applications. *Forest Policy and Economics, 9*(2), 179–196. doi:10.1016/j.forpol.2005.06.006

Metlay, J. P., Kapoor, W. N., & Fine, M. J. (1997). Does this patient have community- acquired pneumonia? Diagnosing pneumonia by history and physical examination. *Journal of the American Medical Association, 278*(17), 1440–1445. doi:10.1001/jama.278.17.1440

Miao, Y., & Liu, Z. Q. (2000). On causal inference in fuzzy cognitive maps. *IEEE Transactions on Fuzzy Systems, 8*, 107–119. doi:10.1109/91.824780

Osei-Bryson, K. (2004). Generating consistent subjective estimates of the magnitudes of causal relationships in fuzzy cognitive maps. *Computers & Operations Research, 31*(8), 1165–1175. doi:10.1016/S0305-0548(03)00070-4

Ozesmi, U., & Ozesmi, S. L. (2004). Ecological models based on people's knowledge: A multi-step fuzzy cognitive mapping approach. *Ecological Modelling, 176*(1–2), 43–64. doi:10.1016/j.ecolmodel.2003.10.027

Papageorgiou, E. I. (2011). A new methodology for decisions in medical informatics using fuzzy cognitive maps based on fuzzy rule-extraction techniques. *Applied Soft Computing, 11*, 500–513. doi:10.1016/j.asoc.2009.12.010

Papageorgiou, E. I., & Groumpos, P. P. (2005). A new hybrid learning algorithm for fuzzy cognitive maps learning. *Applied Soft Computing, 5*, 409–431. doi:10.1016/j.asoc.2004.08.008

Papageorgiou, E. I., & Groumpos, P. P. (2005). A weight adaptation method for fine-tuning fuzzy cognitive map causal links. *Soft Computing Journal, 9*, 846-857. Springer Verlag. DOI 10.10007

Papageorgiou, E. I., Papadimitriou, C., & Karkanis, S. (2009b). Management of uncomplicated urinary tract infections using fuzzy cognitive maps. *Proc. IEEE Int. Conference on Information Technology in Biomedicine (ITAB)*. doi:10.1109/ITAB.2009.5394374

Papageorgiou, E. I., Papandrianos, N. I., Karagianni, G., Kyriazopoulos, G., & Sfyras, D. (2009). Fuzzy cognitive map model for assessing pulmonary infections. *Proc. IEEE Int. Conf on Fuzzy Systems, FUZZ-IEEE 2009*, art. no. 5277254, (pp. 2094-2099).

Papageorgiou, E. I., Papandrianos, N. I., Karagianni, G., & Sfyras, D. (2009a). Fuzzy cognitive map based approach for assessing pulmonary infections. In J. Rauch, et al. (Eds.), *Proc 18th International Symposium on Methodologies for Intelligent Systems, ISMIS 2009, Lecture Notes in Computer Science, LNAI 5722*, (pp. 109–118). Berlin, Germany: Springer-Verlag.

Papageorgiou, E. I., Parsopoulos, K. E., Stylios, C. D., Groumpos, P. P., & Vrahatis, M. N. (2005). Fuzzy cognitive maps learning using particle swarm optimization. *International Journal of Intelligent Information Systems, 25*(1), 95–121. doi:10.1007/s10844-005-0864-9

Papageorgiou, E. I., Spyridonos, P., Glotsos, D., Stylios, C. D., Ravazoula, P., Nikiforidis, G., & Groumpos, P. P. (2008). Brain tumour characterization using the soft computing technique of fuzzy cognitive maps. *Applied Soft Computing, 8*, 820–828. doi:10.1016/j.asoc.2007.06.006

Papageorgiou, E. I., Spyridonos, P., Ravazoula, P., Stylios, C. D., Groumpos, P. P., & Nikiforidis, G. (2006a). Advanced soft computing diagnosis method for tumor grading. *Artificial Intelligence in Medicine*, *36*, 59–70. doi:10.1016/j.artmed.2005.04.001

Papageorgiou, E. I., Stylios, C. D., & Groumpos, P. (2003). An integrated two level hierarchical decision making system based on fuzzy cognitive maps (FCMs). *IEEE Transactions on Bio-Medical Engineering*, *50*(12), 1326–1339. doi:10.1109/TBME.2003.819845

Papageorgiou, E. I., Stylios, C. D., & Groumpos, P. P. (2004). Active Hebbian learning to train fuzzy cognitive maps. *International Journal of Approximate Reasoning*, *37*, 219–249. doi:10.1016/j.ijar.2004.01.001

Papageorgiou, E. I., Stylios, C. D., & Groumpos, P. P. (2006). A combined fuzzy cognitive map and decision trees model for medical decision making. *Proc 28th IEEE EMBS Annual Intern. Conference in Medicine and Biology Society, EMBS 2006*, (pp. 6117-6120). 30 Aug.-3 Sept, New York, USA.

Papageorgiou, E. I., Stylios, C. D., & Groumpos, P. P. (2007). Novel architecture for supporting medical decision making of different data types based on fuzzy cognitive map framework. *Proc. 28th IEEE EMBS Annual Intern. Conference in Medicine and Biology Society*, EMBS 2007, 21-23 August, Lyon, France, 2007.

Pearl, J. (Ed.). (2000). *Causality, models reasoning and inference*. Cambridge, UK: Cambridge University Press.

Rodriguez-Repiso, L., Setchi, R., & Salmeron, J. (2007). Modelling IT projects success with fuzzy cognitive maps. *Expert Systems with Applications*, *32*, 543–559. doi:10.1016/j.eswa.2006.01.032

Schneider, M., Kandel, A., & Chew, G. (1998). Automatic construction of FCMs. *Fuzzy Sets and Systems*, *93*, 161–172. doi:10.1016/S0165-0114(96)00218-7

Silva, C. (1995). *Fuzzy cognitive maps over possible worlds*. In 4th IEEE International Conference on Fuzzy Systems, Japan.

Sordo, M., Vaidya, S., & Jain, L. C. (2008). An introduction to computational intelligence in healthcare: New directions. *Studies in Computational Intelligence*, *107*, 1–26. doi:10.1007/978-3-540-77662-8_1

Stach, W., Kurgan, L., & Petrycz, W. (2007). A framework for a novel scalable FCM learning method. *Proc 2007 Symposium on Human-Centric Computing and Data Processing* (HCDP07), February 21 - 23, (pp. 13-14). Canada.

Styblinski, M. A., & Meyer, B. D. (1988). Fuzzy cognitive maps, signal flow graphs, and qualitative circuit analysis. *Proc. 2nd IEEE Internat. Conf. on Neural Networks (ICNN-87), vol II*, (pp. 549-556).

Stylios, C. D., & Georgopoulos, V. C. (2008). Fuzzy cognitive maps structure for medical decision support systems. *Studies in Fuzziness and Soft Computing*, *218*, 151–174. doi:10.1007/978-3-540-73185-6_7

Stylios, C. D., Georgopoulos, V. C., Malandraki, G. A., & Chouliara, S. (2008). Fuzzy cognitive map architectures for medical decision support systems. *Applied Soft Computing*, *8*(3), 1243–1251. doi:10.1016/j.asoc.2007.02.022

Taber, R. (1991). Knowledge processing with fuzzy cognitive maps. *Expert Systems with Applications*, *2*, 83–87. doi:10.1016/0957-4174(91)90136-3

Tsadiras, A. K. (2008). Comparing the inference capabilities of binary, trivalent and sigmoid fuzzy cognitive maps. *Information Sciences*, *178*(20), 3880–3894. doi:10.1016/j.ins.2008.05.015

Tsadiras, A. K., Kouskouvelis, I., & Margaritis, K. G. (2001). Making political decisions using fuzzy cognitive maps: The FYROM crisis. *Proc 8th Panhellenic Conference on Informatics, 2*, (pp. 501–510).

Vascák, J., & Rutrich, M. (2008). Path planning in dynamic environment using fuzzy cognitive maps. *SAMI 2008, 6th International Symposium on Applied Machine Intelligence and Informatics, IEEE*, (pp. 5-9).

Wei, Z., Baowen, S., & Yanchun, Z. (2009). Design of inference model based on activation for fuzzy cognitive map. *2009 International Workshop on Intelligent Systems and Applications, ISA 2009*, art. no. 5072819, 2009.

Xirogiannis, G., & Glykas, M. (2004). Fuzzy cognitive maps in business analysis and performance-driven change. *IEEE Transactions on Engineering Management, 51*(3), 334–351. doi:10.1109/TEM.2004.830861

Yaman, D., & Polat, S. (2009). A fuzzy cognitive map approach for effect based operations: An illustrative case. *Information Sciences, 179*, 382–403. doi:10.1016/j.ins.2008.10.013

Yue, H. (2008). Application study in decision support using fuzzy cognitive map. In Lovrek, I., Howlett, R. J., & Jain, L. C. (Eds.), *KES 2008, Part II, LNAI 5178* (pp. 324–331). Berlin, Germany: Springer-Verlag.

## ADDITIONAL READING

Adlassnig, K. P. (1986). Fuzzy Set Theory in Medical Diagnosis. *IEEE Trans SMC, 16*(2), 260–265.

Berner, E. S. (2007). *Clinical Decision Support Systems: Theory and Practice*. Springer. doi:10.1007/978-0-387-38319-4

Chen, H., Fuller, S. S., & Friedman, C. P. (2005). *Medical Informatics: Knowledge Management and Data Mining in Biomedicine, Integrated Series in Information Systems*. Springer Verlag.

Glykas, M. (Ed.). (2010). *Fuzzy Cognitive Maps*, Studies in Fuzziness and Soft Computing, Vol. 247, 1st edition July 2010, Springer Verlag Berlin Heidelberg.

Haas, O. C. L., & Burnham, K. J. (Eds.). (2008). *Intelligent and adaptive Systems in medicine*, (Series in Medical Physics and Biomedical Engineering), Taylor & Francis, 1st edition (March 19, 2008).

Hunt, D. L., Haynes, R. B., Hanna, S. E., & Smith, K. (1998). Effects of computer-based clinical decision support systems on physician performance and patient outcomes: a systematic review. *Journal of the American Medical Association, 280*, 1339–1346. doi:10.1001/jama.280.15.1339

John, R. I., & Innocent, P. R. (2005). Modeling uncertainty in clinical diagnosis using fuzzy logic. *IEEE Trans on Systems, Man and Cybernetics. Part B-Cybernetics, 35*(6), 1340–1350. doi:10.1109/TSMCB.2005.855588

Papageorgiou, E. I. (2010). A Novel approach on constructed dynamic Fuzzy Cognitive Maps using fuzzified decision trees and knowledge-extraction techniques. In Glykas, M. (Ed.), *Fuzzy Cognitive Maps* (pp. 43–70). Springer Verlag Berlin Heidelberg. doi:10.1007/978-3-642-03220-2_3

Pearl, J. (1997). *Probabilistic Reasoning in Intelligent Systems: Networks of Plausible Inference*. Morgan Kaufmann.

Pearl, J. (2000). *Causality, Models Reasoning and Inference*. Cambridge University Press.

Yardimci, A. (2009). Soft Computing in Medicine *Applied Soft Computing, 9*(3), 1029–1043. doi:10.1016/j.asoc.2009.02.003

# KEY TERMS AND DEFINITIONS

**Causal Model:** an abstract model that uses cause and effect logic.

**Cognitive Map:** is a directed graph, consists of nodes and edges among them. It models of how a system operates. The map is based on defined variables (nodes) and the directed causal relationships (edges) between these variables. These variables can represent events, states, factors, policies, symptoms, decisions etc.

**FCM Model:** a model which attempts to simulate the abstract FCM model of a particular system.

**Fuzzy Cognitive Map:** is a cognitive map in which the edges take fuzzy causal values corresponding to fuzzy membership functions such as low, medium and high. The fuzzy causal edges take real values in [-1,1].

**Graph:** Graph is a mathematical structure used to model pair wise relations between objects from a certain collection. A "graph" in this context refers to a collection of vertices or 'nodes' and a collection of edges that connect pairs of vertices. A graph may be undirected, meaning that there is no distinction between the two vertices associated with each edge, or its edges may be directed from one vertex to another.

**Inference Mechanism:** a computer program that attempt to infer or derive a deep insights or answers from the knowledge base.

**Pulmonary Infection (or pneumonia):** is an inflammatory condition of the lung. Its infection occurs when normal lung or systemic defense mechanisms are impaired.

# Chapter 30
# On the Use of Fuzzy Logic in Electronic Marketplaces

**Kostas Kolomvatsos**
*National and Kapodistrian University of Athens, Greece*

**Stathes Hadjiefthymiades**
*National and Kapodistrian University of Athens, Greece*

## ABSTRACT

*Today, there is a large number of product providers in the Web. Electronic Marketplaces (EMs) enable entities to negotiate and trade products. Usually, intelligent agents assume the responsibility of representing buyers or sellers in EMs. However, uncertainty about the characteristics and intentions of the negotiating entities is present in these scenarios. Fuzzy Logic (FL) theory presents a lot of advantages when used in environments where entities have limited or no knowledge about their peers. Hence, entities can rely on a FL knowledge base that determines the appropriate action on every possible state. FL can be used in offers, trust, or time constraints definition or when an agent should decide during the negotiation process. The autonomic nature of agents in combination with FL leads to more efficient systems. In this chapter, the authors provide a critical review on the adoption of FL in marketplace systems and present their proposal for the buyer side. Moreover, the authors describe techniques for building FL systems focusing on clustering techniques. The aim is to show the importance of FL adoption in such settings.*

## INTRODUCTION

Nowadays, it is known that users acting in the Web are in front of a huge amount of resources. Users are able to search, find and utilize a large amount of pieces of information and other products. However, searching for products among of millions of pages is a very tedious, non-scalable task for

human capabilities. An automated approach for product-finding in the Web is a sound strategy. Intelligent autonomous software components, such as agents, appear to be the appropriate solution to this problem. An Intelligent Agent (IA) is a software or hardware component capable of acting in order to accomplish the tasks delegated by its user (Nwana, 1996). Intelligent agents integrate Artificial Intelligence (AI), which means that they are capable of learning the preferences and the

DOI: 10.4018/978-1-61350-429-1.ch030

characteristics of their owners, thus, increasing their efficiency. Agents can learn the behavior of their owners as well as their environment in order to choose their course of action. They can undertake the responsibility of finding products in the Web with the minimum intervention from their users.

These software components can act in Electronic Markets (EMs) where entities, not known in advance, can negotiate on the trade of products. Web marketing models typically involve payment for the acquisition of products. Providers require specific returns in exchange for goods. Usually, there are groups of market members such as: the consumers or buyers or customers, the providers or sellers and members that are in the middle between buyers and sellers helping them in their tasks. Buyers aim to buy products while sellers offer a number of specific products. Middle entities deal with administration or mediation tasks. The combination of the discussed technologies yields a lot of advantages to the product acquisition and delivery processes.

However, limited information is present concerning the characteristics of entities participating in EMs. A buyer or a seller agent cannot be sure for the intentions as well as the characteristics of their trading peers. In such settings, we need a technique that efficiently treats the incomplete information. Fuzzy Logic (FL) theory can provide significant advantages for the definition of the knowledge base (KB) of these autonomous components when acting in EMs. FL is a precise system of reasoning, deduction and computation in which the objects of discourse and analysis are associated with information which is, or is allowed to be, imprecise, uncertain, incomplete, unreliable, partially true or partially possible (Zadeh, 1965). FL deals with incomplete information and helps at representing the knowledge of the agents involved in an EM in order to automatically take decisions during a certain interaction. Such knowledge base is an efficient mechanism that determines the buyer

or seller decision at every step of the negotiation process or the definition of critical parameters.

In this chapter, we provide a critical review on the use of the FL in every part of the interaction process between buyers and sellers or other intermediate entities. Mainly, the FL is used in:

- the proposal definition at the buyer or at the seller side. In such cases, there are a number of offers that are issued during the negotiation process. Usually, a Bargaining Game (BG) (Fudeberg & Tirole, 1991) is used to model such interaction. The BG involves a set of alternating offers and the two entities have to agree upon the price of a product.
- The trust level calculation or other security issues. FL can prove very advantageous in cases where autonomous entities need an efficient trust mechanism. Specific fuzzy models have been created for the calculation of the trust level of each entity with increased efficiency.
- the interaction deadline calculation. To the best of our knowledge, in the majority of the models found in the literature, there is no model or mechanism for the negotiation deadline calculation. A reasoning mechanism that is based on the FL adapted to the entities or products characteristics can be very advantageous. This way, each entity can dynamically calculate the deadline for which it will participate in the negotiation process.
- the decision process of each entity. This is the most important aspect of FL use in this setting. Entities can have a FL KB that will determine the action taken on every state of the world. This knowledge base is used at every step of the interaction process and it will be fed by crisp values representing each state of world, resulting the appropriate action. For example, in a BG, at every round, there is uncertainty about

the behaviour of the opponent due to the limited knowledge available. The seller does not know either the buyer's deadline or the next proposal and, thus, cannot know if the current proposal is the last one or not. Furthermore, it cannot know if the upcoming proposal is better than the previous one. Hence, the critical questions that every player has to answer are: the opponent should defect at the current round or not? the opponent will propose a better offer or not? Concerning the first question, if the answer is positive, the player probably prefers to accept the current proposal rather than risk a conflict (the disagreement case) in the next round. Otherwise, the player probably prefers to reject the current proposal and propose a new one with the understanding that the opponent may accept it or make a better proposal. From our point of view, FL seems to be the best option for handling this uncertainty in the decision process. Through fuzzy inference rules, we can add a level of intelligence in the decision process.

In this chapter, our main objective is to describe the advantages that the FL yields to the EM entities. We present relevant efforts found in the literature as well as our research in the specific domain. We describe models for the definition of important parameters for every entity as well as the decision process in these highly dynamic environments.

The rest of the chapter is organized as follows. The 'Background' Section discusses the related work found in the EM-FL literature. Moreover, in this Section we briefly describe previous research efforts in the domains of EMs and the adoption of FL in EMs. The following Section discusses how the FL can be used in EMs by describing existing models. We focus on the issues described above and give some examples. The 'Methodologies for Building Fuzzy Systems' Section describes methodologies used for the creation of fuzzy systems. Finally, we describe some future directions in this domain and conclude the chapter.

## BACKGROUND

## Electronic Marketplaces

An Electronic Marketplace (EM) is a virtual environment where entities, probably geographically distributed and not known a priori, may cooperate in order to achieve their goals (Bakos, 1998). The main goal is the exchanged of products for specific returns. Additionally, we can define Information Markets (IMs), (Ge & Rothenberger, 2007; Laufmann, 1994) that are virtual places involving a set of entities trying to negotiate and exchange information products. Information goods include but are not limited to images, videos, music, source code, electronic articles, etc. There are several differences between IMs and classic electronic markets. First of all, the economics of information production indicate that the production of the first copy may be more expensive than the cost of the creation of additional copies (Rose, 1999). Moreover, information products may lose their value and become stale more easily than other product types. Hence, providers may wish to sell these products as soon as possible, probably by decreasing their prices. Finally, information products are always available to buyers in contrast to other products. For example, a seller, which negotiates DVD writers, can run out of products when demand exceeds the offer.

In general, the owners of the commodities want to sell them to every interested member of the community. On the other hand, there is a demand for these products and a group of entities is willing to pay in order to obtain them. EMs are characterized by their dynamic nature (i.e., the number and the behavior of the involved entities). Such markets are considered as open markets. The number of buyers and sellers could change over time, thus, changing the basic characteristics of the market (e.g., product demand or supply). For example, an increased number of buyers leads to an increased demand for products. This situation adds an increased load to the side of sellers and, surely, the administrators of the market. Moreover, a variation in the number of sellers may cause problems in product delivery because fewer sellers should handle the whole number of buyers.

Moreover, markets should define mechanisms for the manipulation of other critical issues such as seller advertisements, buyer/seller registration, information searching and trust establishment. For this reason, a common communication protocol should be used. Mechanisms for error handling should also be defined. For example, if a provider fails to provide its products, steps should be taken in order to have the specific information source excluded from current negotiations.

The entities participating in the market can be represented by intelligent agents to capitalize on their features. For example, users may pose money, time and product type limitations to their agents and wait for their results. On the other side, agents could represent product sources in the market while being capable of handling many clients simultaneously. Agent technology offers a lot of advantages. We have already mentioned that the current form of the Web is not appealing for end users due to the huge amount of product sources. A user should spend time and effort to search and retrieve products. Agents are capable of searching in numerous sources in order to satisfy their owners. Users are free to engage in other tasks while their agents undertake the assigned tasks. Concerning the roles of entities participating in the market, we can discern the following:

- *The buyers or customers or consumers.* Buyers are users that search products and are, usually, represented by an agent. Each buyer has a different valuation for every product (Aron et al., 2006). The valuation is very important because it shows how much the buyer is willing to pay for each product. The buyer is not willing to pay more than the valuation.

- *The sellers or providers.* Sellers are entities that have some goods in their property and sell them to potential customers. Sellers have a specific production cost and, in the majority of cases, they are not willing to sell products below this value. The cost is an indication of the lowest price.

- *The middle members.* Middle members of a market aim to facilitate buyers and sellers in their interaction process (Lin et al., 2006). Numerous taxonomies for middle entities have been proposed (Klusch, 2001). Matchmakers and brokers are two types of middle entities. Matchmakers can return the actual address of a seller according to the buyer needs. On the other hand, brokers can undertake the responsibility to find a return the appropriate product to the buyer according to its needs. Usually, there is a service fee for the services provided by the middle entities.

## Fuzzy Logic

*Fuzzy Logic (FL)* was introduced in 1965 by L. Zadeh (Zadeh, 1965). FL is a multi valued logic that allows values to be defined between conventional evaluations. FL is a convenient and efficient way to map an input space to an output space. It is appropriate for uncertain or incomplete information handling at the decision making phase. FL principles express human expert knowledge and facilitate the automated interpretation of the results. A basic concept in FL is *fuzzy sets*. In contrast to crisp sets used in mathematics, fuzzy sets are sets where elements have a specific membership degree. FL allows the gradual assessment of the membership of each element that belongs to a set. Membership values belong to the interval between 0 and 1. *Membership functions* yield the membership value of a variable. The membership function of a fuzzy set indicates the degree of truth for a specific variable. Examples of functions are linear functions such as triangular or trapezoidal functions, however, gaussian, sigmoid or other type of functions can be used for membership functions. A list of membership functions can be found in (Engelbrecht, 2007).

A fuzzy logic controller F is a non-linear mapping between n inputs $u_i \in U_p$, $i = 1, ..., n$ and $m$ outputs $y_i \in Y_p$, $i = 1, ..., m$. The architecture of such a controller is depicted in Figure 1. The inputs are crisp, i.e., they are real numbers (not fuzzy sets). The ordinary sets $U_i$ and $Y_i$ are called universes of discourse - domains - for $u_i$ and $y_i$, respectively. The F represents a three step process: a) the *fuzzification* step transforms the input values into a normalized fuzzy subset, b) using the *fuzzy rule base* an inference takes place for the output value, and, c) the *defuzzification* process converts the fuzzy conclusions into the crisp outputs. For the defuzzification process, a number of methods are used. The most known is the *Center-of-Gravity (COG)* methodology. In this case, the output value is calculated as:

$$output = \frac{\sum_{i=1}^{N} \mu_j(u_i) \cdot u_i}{\sum_{i=1}^{N} \mu_j(u_i)} \qquad (1)$$

where $N$ is the number of variables and $\mu_j$ depicts the membership function of the inputs. The rea-

soning process in the controller F involves a set of fuzzy rules. To specify rules for the rule base, an expert can use either linguistic or arithmetic descriptions for both $u_i$ and $y_i$. Fuzzy rules are used for inference based on the crisp input data as mentioned above. Hence, the mapping of the inputs to the outputs of a fuzzy logic system is characterized by a set of *condition - action* rules.

The form of each rule is as follows:

$R_j$: If $in_{1(j)}$ is $A_{1(j)}$ AND $in_{2(j)}$ is $A_{2(j)}$ AND ... AND $in_{n(j)}$ is $A_{n(j)}$ Then $out_{1(j)}$ is $B_{1(j)}$ ... AND $out_{m(j)}$ is $B_{m(j)}$

where $in_{i(j)}$ are the input variables, $out_{i(j)}$ are the output variables, $A_{i(j)}$ and $B_{i(j)}$ are the fuzzy sets representing the $j^{th}$ value for the input and for the output variable $i$ respectively. There are two main inference models: The *Assilian - Mamdani* (Mamdani & Assilian, 1975) and the *Takagi – Sugeno* (Takagi & Sugeno, 1985) model types. In the Assilian – Mamdani model input and output values are linguistic values while in the Takagi – Sugeno inference type, outputs are linear combinations of inputs.

FL can enhance the interaction between entities searching for products in an open and highly dynamic environment like the Web. FL deals with incomplete or uncertain information and helps in representing the knowledge of interacting entities in open environments. This knowledge is necessary for entities in order to have the opportunity to decide important parameters of their behavior.

*Figure 1. A FL controller architecture*

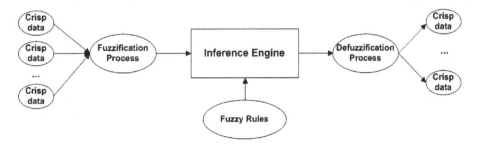

Such parameters include the time allowed for purchase, the decision at every step of the interaction process, the proposal to the opponent, etc.

FL provides a number of advantages when used in real applications. We can list these advantages as follows:

- FL is very simple to use. Developers can describe the desired system by using simple '*If-Then*' rules. This simple solution requires less time for developing intelligent systems. As discussed in the following Sections, the developer can either manually define the rule base or can rely upon automatic techniques that increase efficiency.

- FL can utilize the experience of experts. The definition or management of a fuzzy rule base can take into account the experience of the developer. This experience is reflected on the number and the type of fuzzy rules or even on the membership functions used in the fuzzification or defuzzification processes.

- FL is very easy to understand. The model of a fuzzy controller is very simple and is based on linguistic terms. This makes it more comprehensible by developers. Moreover, the mathematics used in FL systems are very simple.

- FL can handle uncertain or incomplete data. This is the common case for a user acting in dynamic environments. There is no way to have full information about the characteristics or even more the intentions of entities representing other users in the Web. This makes FL the most appropriate tool for such scenarios.

- FL systems do not need any training process. It is an important characteristic that saves time in building a system. In other cases (supervised or unsupervised techniques, neural networks, etc) training is an initial step before the system starts to work in real situations. However, in training

there are two main problems: a) the data used for training, and, b) the time required for training. Training data should reflect reality in order to result to a fine-grained system, while time is very critical in some cases. For example, in buying process, it is not efficient to spend a lot of time for training and it is not possible to have data reflecting all the scenarios that a buyer could face in a purchase interaction.

## Previous Work

In the literature one can find very interesting articles focusing on virtual marketplaces. In this sub-section, we shortly describe some of the related research efforts. In the rest of our chapter, we discuss the most important of them in more detail. In (Collins et al., 1998), a collection of domain-specific markets is discussed. Every market includes a number of services (e.g., administration services for identity verification, reliability). Buyers and sellers are represented by agents.

Information marketplaces are studied in (Ge & Rothenberger, 2007; Laufmann, 1994). In (Ge & Rothenberger, 2007), the authors describe a business model for information trading based on a reverse auction approach. A price ranking and selection process is presented. Finally, they list a number of existing information intermediaries. In (Laufmann, 1994), authors study Cooperative Information Systems (CIS) where some entities can exchange information components. An IM is described consisting of a number of information and services components.

Intelligent agents in electronic marketplaces are discussed in (Barbosa & Silva, 2001). In the presented architecture, there are three types of agents: buyers, sellers and intermediary agents. Agents reflect the needs of their owners. An intermediary agent coordinates buyers and sellers w.r.t. issues like security and payments.

MAGMA (Tsvetovatyy, 1997) is an agent-based market architecture for products. It supports manual and automatic negotiation. Administration services are defined (e.g., product storage and payment mechanisms). MAGMA includes an advertisement server where product descriptions are matched against buyer needs, a "bank" that handles payments and trader agents for buying, selling or negotiating prices. A relay server handles all inter-agent message exchanges.

Kasbah (Chavez & Maes, 1996) is an online multiagent system where agents represent users in a marketplace (either buyers or sellers). Agents communicate with a single marketplace agent in order to conclude their transactions. The strategy of each agent is based on the values of specific parameters such as initial/lowest/highest acceptable price and date. After matching buying and selling agents, the negotiation protocol indicates that buyers offer prices to sellers and vice versa up to the defined deadlines. If an offer is rejected the rejecting agent is asked to issue a counter proposal. Three types of entities can be discerned: anxious, cool-headed, and frugal, depicting three different functions (linear, quadratic and cubic) for tuning their proposals over time. The proposed functions are either concave or linear. Users have a large degree of involvement in the transactions as they can change the strategy at every point of the interaction and need to approve the final agreement.

In (Lin et al., 2006), and (Wang et al., 2006), the authors adopt FL in agent systems. More specifically, the authors in (Lin et al., 2006) present a sequential bargaining technique based on FL for the estimation of acceptable prices of parties trying to form joint ventures of companies. In (Wang et al., 2006), the authors present the rationale of an intelligent fuzzy-based, agent negotiation process in e-commerce. The inference rules and the decision strategies are described along with the relevant implementation.

In (Carbo et al., 2003), the authors present an automated negotiation model, which adopts FL for the formulation of offers. Three alternative schemes are proposed for calculating counter-offers. The first model deals with crisp values while in the second model fuzzy sets-based representation is adopted. In the third model, they adopt fuzzy linguistic terms in order to describe the negotiated attributes of products i.e., price and quality. For each negotiation, a deadline of ten (10) counter-offers was defined.

In (Raeesy et al., 2007), a fuzzy-model for intelligent agent negotiations is presented. Authors investigate negotiations dealing with fuzzy values to represent offers on both sides of the negotiation. They use a protocol that allows both fuzzy and crisp prices to be proposed. The discussed model involves parameters like deadline, minimum / maximum acceptable reservation prices. The presented results assume that such characteristics are common knowledge between the two parties. In our model, this limiting assumption is not adopted.

In (Kolomvatsos & Hadjiefthymiades, 2008) and (Kolomvatsos et al., 2008), authors present a bargaining scenario for agents participating in IMs. In the former paper, the direct interaction between buyers and sellers is studied. This interaction involves a set of alternating offers for a specific product. Authors describe a mathematical model for the seller's deadline calculation and present their results. In the latter paper, authors extend the previously reported work and describe a fuzzy model for the deadline calculation. This model is based on a set of fuzzy rules defined according to experts' knowledge for the discussed scenario.

## FUZZY LOGIC IN E-MARKETS

FL can provide a lot of advantages in EMs. The most important reason is that FL is very efficient in those cases where there is limited or no information about various parameters of an interaction process. This is the most common case in real environments. The adoption of FL in E-commerce applications is reported in many articles including ours. In the majority of cases a reasoning mechanism based on FL is described. This reasoning mechanism provides the necessary decision mechanism for various parameters of an interaction process for the entities that utilize it. Mainly, FL is used: (a) for the definition of the players' proposals, (b) for the calculation of trust level, (c) for the definition of time constraints for each player, or (d) in the final decision process. This review is complemented by our research key findings in the discussed domain.

## Offer Definition

In a trading interaction process, the most common case is the exchange of a number of proposals between the participating entities. For example, a BG may model such interaction. Usually, BGs involve a number of alternating offers. Each participant has the opportunity to propose its own price to the opponent. Every entity aims to challenge the opponent to accept its offer trying to maximize its profit. In this process, FL can be used to formulate the offer issued by a certain entity.

In (Raeesy et al. 2007), a fuzzy model for agents negotiation is presented. The authors investigate negotiations for a single issue with fuzzy values. Two agents with opposite goals are competing in order to conclude the product purchase. Agents are capable of sending crisp and fuzzy offers to the opponent. The fuzzy values are defined by a set of triangular membership functions. These offers are proposed at every step of the interaction process in a sequential order. Agents utilize fuzzy numbers in order to formulate their offers, however, they have the opportunity to switch to crisp values when they are confident that they will not lose the negotiation. This way, there is an adaptation to the interaction process characteristics.

In (Carbo et al. 2003), the authors propose the adoption of fuzzy sets to express the counter-offer of the buyer in a trading process. Every product attribute has an associated fuzzy set and it is used to challenge the seller to improve the offer. Specific weights and thresholds are used in the model and based on them the buyer decides on the conclusion of the interaction process. There are two alternatives for buyers: The first is a piece wise definition of a trapezium over dominion of fictitious values. The preferences of buyers affect the shape and the position of the trapezium. The second alternative uses two linguistic labels per attribute. One of them represents the fuzzy set and the other represents a linguistic modifier that changes the gradient of the trapezium sides. Results show an maximum percentage of agreements (fuzzy set case) equal to 86% and minimum number of steps to reach an agreement equal to 1.79.

## Trust and Security Issues

One of the most important issues in open and dynamic environments is trust. In real applications, there is a difficulty to trust everyone in a market. A buyer should be sure about the seller with which it interacts. Moreover, it should be sure for the quality of the product as well as that the seller will deliver the product. On the other side, the seller should be confident that the buyer will conclude the transaction without problems. This is very important when products are information pieces. This stands because in such cases the transaction concludes in real time successive steps. Hence, agents should have a mechanism in order to be able to decide the trust level of each entity in the market. Such mechanisms mainly rely upon the personal experiences as well as upon market refferals. *Refferal* is the opinion that others have about an entity. FL can also be used in this research field. Usually, a FL system is built in order to result the final trust level of an entity based on a number of parameters.

In (Carbo et al., 2005), authors study the adoption of fuzzy logic in a social network of agents. Agenst in a multiagent system utilize fuzzy referrals in order to be able to formulate a fuzzy opinion about other agents. Through this process, they are capable of interacting with only trusted entities in a very dynamic environment. The opinion about an agent is calculated by a combination of a fuzzy refferal and fuzzy opinion. Also, the relationship with the source of the refferal acts as weight.

$$m = \frac{m + S(o_i, e_i)}{2} \tag{2}$$

where $m$ is the memory or remembrance of the agent, $S$ declares the similarity between the final opinion about an agent and the direct experience with the specific agent, $o_i$ is the opinion for agent $i$ and $e_i$ is the personal experience we have for agent $i$. The final opinion about an agent is calculated based on the fuzzy sets. The system that authors developed is named *AFRAS*.

FL is also used in (Schmidt et al. 2007) for the calculation of the trust level of agents interacting on behalf of their owners. A framework for trust evaluation based on the integration of post interaction processes and credibility assesments is presented. Each agent has a specific trustworthiness level that belongs to a range $[T_{min}, T_{max}]$. This value is named *Weighted Trustworthiness Value (WTV)*. Each trustworthiness value is scaled to the range [0..5] and is weighted by its timeliness within the time spot collection using an exponential function. The *Opinion Weight (OW)* is an attribute that is used when multiple timeslots and trustworthiness values are present. Such scenario involves multiple interactions between agents. Finally, the *Agent Credibility (AC)* is an attribute that shows the credibility of an agent and could be based on trustworthiness reviews or past ineractions or opinion reviews. Actually, the credibilty is the capability of an agent to deliver a correct opinion within a specific context. If no credibilty exists a neutral value (equal to 2.5 – the middle of the region [0..5]) is assigned to the attribute. Concerning the FL system, three triangular fuzzy sets are defined for each variable: WTV, OW, and AC. Fuzzy rules are based on linguistic values following the Mamdani model. This way, the fuzzy

system receives values for the input paramaters (WTV, OW, and AC) and accordingly results the final value of the trustworthiness for each agent.

The trust evaluation system built in (Zhang & Guo, 2009) is based on an hierarchy reflecting the affecting factors: *factors of technology, factors of website*, and *factors of customers*. Each of them includes three other hierarchical factors. The first kind of factors involves security and payment mechanisms as well as availability of the transaction system. The second kind implicates the website brand image, the product quality and the seller's after sale service. Finally, the third kind of factors contains the consumption psychology, the experience for online transactions and recommedations of other customers. Five fuzzy sets are defined for linguistic variables corresponding to basic system parameters. Moreover, different weights for each hierarchical factor are defined in order to make the system more efficient. The values of hierarchical factors are fed to the fuzzy system and this way the final trust value is extracted. Customers need to judge the final value in order to be consistent to their intentions.

## Time Constraints Definition

In a trading interaction process there are time limitations for the participating entities. Buyers should be involved in the process for limited time as they may have a lot of objective to accomplish. Sellers have their own deadlines. They cannot also wait for ever as a number of buyers waits for purchases. Moreover, waiting for a long time means that they spend time and resources in a meaningless process as they do not know if the transaction will be concluded successfully.

The authors in (Kolomvatsos & Hadjiefthymiades, 2008; Kolomvatsos et al., 2008) present a model for the calculation of the deadline for a seller agent that acts in an EM. They describe a BG between buyers and sellers and give the basic parameters that govern the process. Every seller at every round of the BG issues an offer to the buyer. Its aim is to challenge the buyer to accept the proposal in order to obtain some profit. The seller can deliver products to interested parties more than once. The proposals that the seller addresses to buyers are based on a pricing function. This pricing function takes into account the product characteristics as well as the number of the current round. The seller can sell popular products in smaller prices because it gains from the increased number of clients interested in such products. For example, if a product has a production cost equal to 5 monetary units (MU) then it is more convenient to sell it with a profit of 2 MU to 100 clients than to sell it with a profit of 20 MU to 10 clients. In the first case the product price is 7 MU and it is more challenging than in the second case where the price is 25 MU. A high price in the majority of cases repulses buyers. Hence, a pricing function is defined as follows:

$$p_s(x) = \frac{\varepsilon}{x^{q+1}} + c, \qquad x = 1,2,.... \qquad (3)$$

where $\varepsilon$ is the profit, $c$ is the production cost, $x$ indexes the seller round (i.e. x=2 implies the second proposal at the third round of the BG) and $q$ is the Zipfian popularity measure (probability of reference) (Zipf, 1949). A large q indicates that the product is very popular and can be sold in smaller prices according to seller policy. However, another pricing function can be defined. The seller can produce prices using the following pricing function:

$$p_s^t = c + \varepsilon \cdot (1 - t \cdot T_s^{-1})^k \qquad (4)$$

where $c$ is the seller cost, $\varepsilon$ is the profit, $t$ is the current number of the proposal, $T_s$ is the seller deadline and $k$ defines its policy. The function defined in (4) is very similar to the (3), however it cannot be adapted to the product characteristics.

Based on the first pricing policy of the seller and by analyzing the specific pricing function,

we understand that the pricing function tends to cost line without intersecting it. The reason is that the seller does want to sell its products in prices below the production cost. Hence, we can determine a time instance beyond which all subsequent proposals change marginally. If the buyer has not accepted the seller proposals up to this point, probably its policy is to wait for better offers or its offers acceptance. The time $T_s$ shows the deadline of the seller and represents from which time instance it is not profitable for the seller to continue proposing prices. In order to have such time point the following relation should stand:

$$\lim_{t \to \infty} \left| \frac{-\varepsilon \cdot (q+1)}{T_s^{q+2}} \right| = 0 \qquad (5)$$

and consequently:

$$T_s \approx (\alpha \cdot \varepsilon \cdot (q+1))^{\frac{1}{q+2}} \qquad (6)$$

where $\alpha$ shows how much closer to the zero the (6) could be. Factor $\alpha$ reflects the patience of the seller. A high value of $\alpha$ means that the seller is a very patient player who can wait for its offers acceptance and when $\alpha$ is small means that the seller wants to conclude the BG as soon as possible.

Extending the previous mentioned research, a FL system is proposed in (Kolomvatsos et al., 2008) for the calculation of the factor $\alpha$ and the seller deadline respectively (Figure 2). FL rule base implicates the product characteristics which are the profit $\varepsilon$ and the popularity measure $q$. Hence, at every BG the system has the capability to adapt on the different product characteristics.

The authors define a Mamdani FL system and follow a Multiple-Input-Single-Output approach for each FL rule. Figure 3 depicts the regions in which every linguistic value for $q$ corresponds. Concerning the profit $\varepsilon$, five linguistic values are defined.

*Figure 2. FL controller for the deadline calculation*

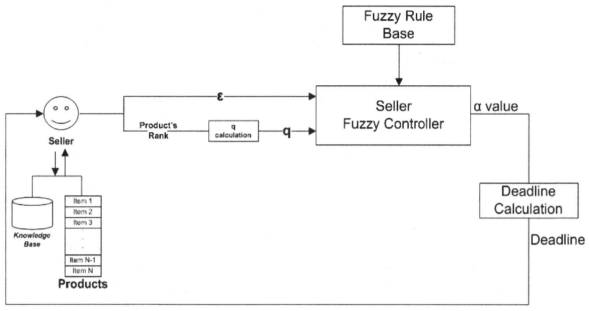

Finally for the output, factor $\alpha$, the authors also define five linguistic values. Based on the specified fuzzy rule base, the seller acts under the following rationale:

1. When the product is not popular it stays as long as it can in order to secure its profit. In such cases, there are not a lot of clients interested in these products. Consequently, the output value for $\alpha$ will be large enough close to the top value.

2. When the product is very popular the seller can reduce more quickly its prices and this way to challenge the buyer to accept the proposals. In such cases the factor $\alpha$ is a small number close to 0.

*Figure 3. Cache popularity rank regions*

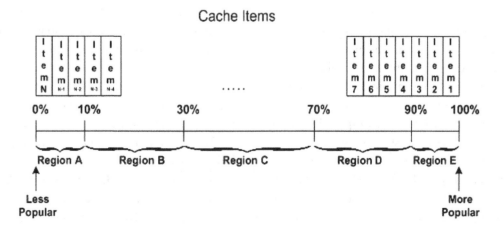

## Decision Process

Probably, it is the most important field where FL can be used. When entities participate in an interaction process should decide their line of actions according to the environment characteristics. For example, in a BG process, at every round the buyer or the seller should decide the acceptance or the rejection of a proposal according to the offer proposed by the opponent, the time remaining for the process, the product characteristics, etc. However, this should be done by using limited information or even more no information about the opponent's characteristics. In these cases a FL system may be it is the most appropriate tool for decision making. Such a system is characterized by its simplicity, comparing to other possible solutions, as well as its efficiency as it is adapted to the developers needs. Furthermore, a FL system can be used either on the buyer or on the seller side.

A fuzzy expert system is responsible to evaluate the proposals made by sellers or buyers. The system is responsible to accept the incoming offers, evaluate them and result the final conclusion. In (Al-Ashmaway et al., 2007), fuzzy reasoning implicates two parameters: the price of the product and its quality. When the FL system accepts the two values it fuzzifies them by using fuzzy sets with two terms: low and high. The same membership functions are applied for both, price and quality. Four fuzzy rules are responsible to result the final decision. Additionally, a counter offer generation model is presented. The counter offer generation model is based on tactics and strategies.

FL can also be used in reasoning about other basic parameters such as opponent's beliefs. In (Yu et al., 2007), a fuzzy constraint directed approach is adopted for modelling the opponent's beliefs in an interaction process. The proposed learning methodology includes: strategy identification, instance matching and adaptive interaction. For strategy identification, fuzzy concession values are adopted to cluster proximate paradigms and this way avoiding the problem of slow convergence.

Each agent can alter concession values after each negotiation round observing a specific fuzzy probability constraint. The conclusion of the opponent strategy is extracted when the set of fuzzy concession values matches one of the regularities of meta strategies within a specific threshold of the fuzzy probability constraint. The fuzzy instance matching involves the extraction of appoximate instances with similar beliefs from historical instances. The matching process employs the least square error methodology for matching the current negotiation instance with historical instances. Finally, a number of constraints are defined for agents adaptation when negotiating. Agents have the opportunity to choose if they will be selfish, fair or impatient for an agreement. For each of these cases specific constraints define the behavior of the agent. A detailed algortihm for opponent learnign is descibed and analyzed.

The model presented in (Zuo & Sun 2009) is consisted of three parts: offer evaluation, bargaining agreement and concession strategy. The first part is responsible to evaluate the proposal of the opponent in each round of the interaction process. It calculates the *Aggregated Satisfaction Value (ASV)* of each offer and accordingly results if the proposal should be acceptable or not. For this, fuzzy sets are used for two variables: price and quality. The module of bargaining agreement is responsible to make a decision about the offer proposed by the opponent. The decision is based on the ASV calculated in the previous step. Specific threlolds are used for the decision process. Finally, the module of concession offer results a counter offer based on a strategy. Three concession strategies are adopted: greedy, calm, and anxious. This way, the agent is able to cacluate and propose a counter offer to the opponent trying to gain as much profit as it can.

Negotiation tactics can be represented as fuzzy rules in many cases. In (Cheng et al. 2005), a number of fuzzy rules are used for the tactics definition of an agent when receiving offers sent by the opponent. The interaction process is studied

*Figure 4. Fuzzy logic system for the buyer*

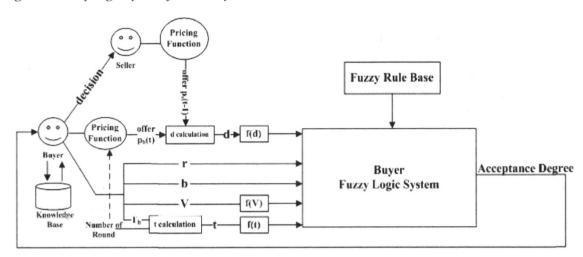

by the supplier side and triangular rmembership functions are defined on the universe of weight. In fuzzy rules, two factors are important: the difference between the respective offers and a tolerance rate of concession. There are 9 rules indicating the behavior of the player. In the inference system, multiple rules are active at the same time with different firing strengths. The firing strength of each rule is calculated by a '*fuzzy and*' operator to the condition of each rule.

In this field, our proposal is to define a specific FL controller for entities participating in a BG. In this point, we propose a FL controller for the buyer side. In a BG, participants propose at every round a price for the negotiated product. Entities accept an offer if it is higher (lower) than the production cost (product's valuation). Moreover, if the participants believe that their deadline or their opponent's deadline expires in the current or the next round they accept the offer in order to conclude the BG without conflict.

The buyer uses a reasoning mechanism in order to decide if it will accept or reject the seller's offer. For this, the FL system presented in Figure 4 is utilized. The FL system is responsible for defining the buyer's reaction to the seller's proposals. The *Acceptance Degree (AD)* indicates when the

buyer should accept the seller's offer and relies on the following parameters:

- The *relevance factor* ($r$), which shows to which extend the product corresponds to the buyer's needs,
- The absolute value of the *price difference* ($d$) between the seller's proposal and the upcoming buyer's offer,
- The *belief* ($b$) about the expiration of the seller's deadline,
- The *time difference* ($t$) between the current time of the BG and the buyer's deadline, and,
- The buyer's *valuation* ($V$) about the product.

The buyer maintains a knowledge base (KB) with the necessary information for the determination of the above described parameters. At every interaction round, the buyer receives the proposal of the seller and calculates the values of each parameter. These values are used by the FL system in order to determine the value of the *AD*. *AD* is the basis for the buyer's decision, which is announced to the seller. Specific linguistic expressions of the values for the parameters $r$, $d$, $b$, $t$, $V$ and *AD* are defined. Three values for fuzzy sets are defined: *low*, *medium*, and *high*. Specifically, a fuzzy value of *low* indicates that, the specific parameter of the product has low values close to the lowest. A value of *medium* denotes that, the specific parameter has middle values and a value of *high* refers to the fact that, the parameter has large value close to the highest. For a more fine-grained resolution of the fuzzy linguistic values for some of the parameters, we use the linguistic modifier very; $very(\mu(...)) = \mu(...)^2$. For example, very low $r$ denotes that the product is not relevant with the buyer's goals and very high $r$ denotes that, the product has the highest relevance with the buyer's goals. The values of each parameter are in the interval [0, 1] (for those are not in the [0..1] region we use sigmoid transformation functions in order to have values in the specified region – see Figure 4 - $f(d)$, $f(V)$, and $f(t)$).

In a set of experiments, we can see that the proposed FL system is very profitable for the buyer. The buyer starts to propose prices in the BG from a very low price and as the BG evolves it increases its offers in order to challenge the seller to accept it. For this, we define a *Coverage Factor* (CF) which depicts how much closer to the first price proposed by the buyer, the agreement price is. Hence, we take:

$$CF = \frac{Valuation - Agreement}{Valuation - First\_Price} \qquad (7)$$

where *Valuation* is the buyer's valuation about the product, *First_Price* is the buyer's first proposed price and *Agreement* is the agreement price at the end of the BG. Of course, the CF is estimated when the final result of the BG is an agreement. When CF=1 means that the product is sold in price equal to the buyer's first price which the ideal case where the buyer buys the product at the lowest price. The CF shows how much pressure the buyer drilled to the seller during the BG.

We have applied our FL model on the reasoning process of the buyer. At every round of the BG,

the buyer defuzzifies the AD value and decides either to accept or to reject the proposed offer. In Table 1, we can see that the average CF is equal to 0.821. This means that the average agreement price is very close to the first proposed price. Due to this reason, the FL mechanism is proved as very efficient and profitable in the buyer side. However, the same FL system can also be profitable for the seller.

In Figure 5, we compare a simple BG (without using the FL mechanism) with the FL system concerning the average seller profit. We can see that the FL system leads to higher average seller profit when agreement is the final result of each BG. Also, in the FL case the profit increases as the buyer valuation increases while in the simple BG case remains at low levels. The increased seller profit is extracted by the increased number of agreements while the buyer valuation takes large values. Furthermore, in the simple BG case, each of the players does not have any efficient reasoning mechanism that indicates when it is profitable for the player to conclude the transaction and this way each player continues the BG till the end of the deadline. In the FL case, the fuzzy rules used indicate when probably the opponent will defect and if it is profitable for the player result the acceptance of the offer. It should be noted that in our experiments the seller profit is randomly chosen between 1 and 20 MUs.

*Table 1. Results for different values of buyer's valuation*

| Buyer's Valuation (max value) | Coverage Factor (CF) |
|---|---|
| 5 | 0.837 |
| 20 | 0.702 |
| 50 | 0.771 |
| 80 | 0.829 |
| 100 | 0.844 |
| 150 | 0.874 |
| 200 | 0.891 |

*Figure 5. Average seller profit for different buyer valuation values*

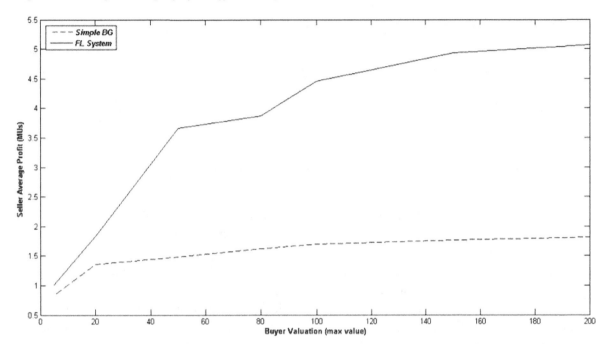

In (Faratin et al., 1998), authors examine a large set of tactics and they define the intrinsic benefit of the agent participating in a negotiation process. In their results, they examine two cases concerning the deadline of players: (a) short term deadlines, and, (b) long term deadlines. Long term deadlines are randomly chosen between 30 and 60 ticks of discrete clock while short term deadlines are randomly chosen between 2 and 10 clock ticks.

In order to have a more objective view on the buyer utility from each interaction, we also adopt the rationale described in (Faratin et al., 1998) and we define the buyer intrinsic utility as follows:

$$U_{\text{int } r}^{B} = \min\left(1, \left(\frac{\max_{price} - Agreement}{\max_{price} - \min_{price}}\right)^{\frac{1}{\beta}}\right)$$

where, in our model, $max_{price}$ is buyer's valuation, $min_{price}$ is the buyer's first price and *Agreement* is the agreement price. The parameter $\beta$ determines the convexity of the utility function and we con-

sider it as equal to 1 (it is also consider equal to 1 in (Faratin et al., 1998)). We compare our results, concerning the buyer intrinsic utility with the results taken by (Faratin et al., 1998). In Table 2, we can see that our approach achieves high values for the buyer intrinsic utility. For short term deadlines the maximum intrinsic value is equal to 0.97 while the minimum is equal to 0.41. In (Faratin et al., 1998), for short term deadlines, the maximum value is equal to 0.35 while the minimum is equal to 0.1. The same conclusion stands for the long term deadlines scenario. In our case, we take 0.99 and 0.79 for the maximum and the minimum value while in (Faratin et al., 1998) they are equal to approximately 0.65 and 0.1 respectively. In our model, we can discern that even for small buyer valuation values (this restricts the agreement zone of the interaction process) the average intrinsic utility is at high levels. This means that the usage of the FL in the decision process of the buyer seems to be very effective and profitable when used in the purchase interactions.

*Table 2. Results for the buyer intrinsic utility*

| Buyer's Valuation (max value) | Short Term Deadlines | Long Term Deadlines |
|:---:|:---:|:---:|
| 5 | 0.41 | 0.79 |
| 20 | 0.70 | 0.90 |
| 50 | 0.88 | 0.96 |
| 80 | 0.91 | 0.98 |
| 100 | 0.94 | 0.97 |
| 150 | 0.96 | 0.98 |
| 200 | 0.97 | 0.99 |

## METHODOLOGIES FOR BUILDING FUZZY SYSTEMS

In this Section, we descibe and analyze methods to develop FL systems that are used in E-commerce applications. In a FL system the most important issue is the definition of the membership functions and the fuzzy rule base. An efficient FL rule base will consist of the knowledge base of each entity. The fuzzy parameters can be defined either manually or by using an automatic technique.

### Manual Definition of Fuzzy Parameters

The manual definition of a FL system requires a lot of time and experience in the developer side. The developer should define the membership functions in a way that depicts real situations. The shape of membership functions is very important as the developer should cover all the aspects of a marketplace scenario. In this process, the experience of the developer plays an important role. This experience is depicted on the shape and the place of membership functions as well as in the fuzzy rule base. The fuzzy rule base should be efficient depicting an productive behavior in a real marketplaces. However, it concerns a difficult task requiring a lot of time due to the reason that should cover all the aspects of the behavior of an agent.

### Automatic Definition of Fuzzy Parameters

In contrast to the manual definition of basic parameters of a FL system, there are some methodologies for the automatic definition of a FL system. These methods are usually based on a set of data – mostly simple arithmetic data – which depict the behavior of an entity in a real marketplace. These techniques do not require experience and a large amount of time in the developer side, however, they implicate a number of algorithms. Two main categories of tools / algorithms can be used for the automatic generation of a FL system: (a) Clustering techniques, and, (b) Artificial Intelligence (AI) techniques. In AI, we can meet neural networks as well as genetic algorithms. In this Section we focus on the clustering algorithms due to their simplicity and we shortly describe the rest of the categories.

### Clustering Techniques

In this Section, we shortly describe some of the most known algorithms and discuss the methodology for rules extraction. *K-means*, *Fuzzy C-means*, *Subtractive*, and *Nearest Neighborhood Clustering (NNC)* algorithms are some of the most known methods for clustering. Furthermore, except from unsupervised learning techniques, there are two intuitive approaches so as to construct fuzzy rules directly from input data. Such techniques differ from clustering algorithms. In clustering there are several steps of execution which try to optimize metrics such as a cost function. *Learning From Examples (LFE)* is an easy algorithm for constructing fuzzy rule bases. The algorithm relies on the knowledge of the membership functions. A template of membership functions is provided to the system for every dimension, distinguishing which dimensions needs more precision from others. *Modified Learning From Examples (MLFE)* is a generalization of *LFE*. In *MLFE*, we don't need to make estimations about dimensions and it does not need to have previous knowledge about the membership functions.

## K-Means Clustering

The K-means clustering algorithm (Hartigan & Wong, 1979) is a simple algorithm that determines data clusters which minimize a cost function. The cost function is:

$$J = \sum_{i=1}^{c} J_i = \sum_{i=1}^{c} \left( \sum_{k, x_k \in G_i} \left\| x_k - c_i \right\| \right) \tag{8}$$

where $c$ is the number of clusters, $G_i$ is the i-th group, $x_k$ is the k-th vector in group $J_i$, and $\| \ \|$ represent the Euclidean distance between $x_k$ and the cluster center $c_i$. The partitioned groups are defined by using a membership matrix depicted by the variable U. Each element $u_{ij}$ of this matrix is equal to 1 if the specific j-th data point $x_j$ belongs to cluster $I$, and 0 otherwise. The element $u_{ij}$ can be derived as follows:

$$u_{ij} = \begin{cases} 1, & \text{if } \left\| x_j - c_i \right\|^2 \leq \left\| x_j - c_k \right\|^2 \ \text{for each } k \neq i \\ 0, & \text{otherwise} \end{cases} \tag{9}$$

which means that $x_j$ belongs to group $I$, if the $c_i$ is the closest of all centers. Hence, the optimal center that minimizes equation (3) is:

$$c_i = \frac{1}{|G_i|} \cdot \sum_{k, x_k \in G_i} x_k \tag{10}$$

with:

$$|G_i| = \sum_{j=1}^{n} u_{ij} \tag{11}$$

## Fuzzy C-Means (FCM) Clustering

In Fuzzy C-Means algorithm (Dunn, 1973; Bezdek, 1981), a point could belong to more than one clusters. The algorithm is based on the minimization of the following function:

$$J_k = \sum_{i=1}^{M} \sum_{j=1}^{C} u_{ij}^k \left\| x_i - c_j \right\|^2 \tag{12}$$

where $M$ is the number of data points, $C$ is the number of cluster centers, $1 \leq k \leq \infty$, $u_{ij}$ is the membership degree of the $x_i$ in the cluster $j$, $x_i$ is the i[th] measured data, and $c_j$ is the center of each cluster. The membership degree is calculated by:

$$u_{ij} = \left( \sum_{m=1}^{C} \left( \frac{\left\| x_i - c_j \right\|}{\left\| x_i - c_m \right\|} \right)^{\frac{2}{k-1}} \right)^{-1} \tag{13}$$

with

$$c_j = \frac{\sum_{i=1}^{M} u_{ij}^k \cdot x_i}{\sum_{i=1}^{M} u_{ij}^k} \tag{14}$$

## Subtractive Clustering

In Subtractive clustering (Jang et al., 1997) every data point is rescaled to [0, 1]. For each of them, a potential degree $P_i$ is defined according to its location to all other points. This potential depends on the Euclidean distance between the examined point and all other points. The point with the higher potential becomes the first cluster center and all the potentials for the other points are recalculated. The point with the highest potential becomes the next cluster center. The distance of the new candidate cluster center with all the previously defined cluster centers should fulfil a specific distance condition defined by the algorithm and ensures that cluster centers will have a minimum distance between them. If this condition is true then the point becomes the next cluster center or else it is rejected and its potential is set to 0. The potential degree for each point is calculated by:

$$P_j = \sum_{i=1}^{N} e^{-a \cdot ||x_i - x_j||^2} \tag{15}$$

where

$$a = \frac{\gamma}{r_\alpha} \tag{16}$$

and $x$ is the data point, $N$ is the number of points, $\gamma$ is a variable and $r_\alpha$ is the cluster radius.

## Nearest Neighborhood Clustering (NNC)

The NNC algorithm assigns each point to its nearest neighbor that is clustered if the distance is sufficiently small (Passino & Yurkovich, 1998). NNC can be seen as an agglomerative single link clustering technique. At first, the algorithm starts considering each sample as a singleton cluster and at each stage of the process the closest pair of clusters are merged. After *N-1* steps a unique cluster is created through the merged sub-clusters. This process defines a hierarchical tree which can be cut at any level resulting to the desired number of clusters. The most important decision in the discussed process is the desired distance between clusters.

## Extracting Fuzzy Rules from Clusters

Clusters, created by the above described algorithms, consist of the main stage to the construction of fuzzy rules that will be the knowledge base of the buyer. Apart from the selected algorithm it is considered that every cluster corresponds to a fuzzy rule. For example, if $x * (x_1^*, x_2^*, ..., x_n^*)$ is a cluster center, then the equivalent fuzzy rule is:

$$IF \; x_1 \; is \; x_1^* \; AND \; x_2 \; is \; x_2^* \; ... \; AND \; x_{n-1} \; is \; x_{n-1}^* \; THEN \; x_n \; is \; x_n^*$$

This means that every dimension is also a fuzzy variable. The next step is to find the shape of membership functions for every fuzzy variable for every fuzzy rule. For this purpose, the most common technique is the projection of membership values of data points (belonging to a cluster) in each dimension. However, projection differs in every algorithm.

In FCM, every point belongs to several clusters. So, it has different membership degrees less than 1. The center of each cluster is laid in an area with membership degree $\approx 1$. We can approximate this projection by a truncated Gaussian function. Applying this methodology for every cluster, we are able to create the fuzzy rule base. In K-means, the process is different. Due to the fact that every point belongs to a cluster exclusively, a projection will have the form of a crisp set. We have to turn the orthogonal graphic representation into a Gaussian function. This approach results to the loss of data, but it is essential for the fuzzy rule base. In Subtractive clustering, each cluster is thought as a fuzzy rule. The degree of rule is given from the following equation:

$$\mu_i = e^{-a \cdot ||x - c_i||^2} \tag{17}$$

where $x$ is an input data applied to a fuzzy rule, $c_i$ is $i^{th}$ cluster center, $\mu_i$ is the membership degree of $i^{th}$ rule, and a is given by (16). Finally, in NNC, we can derive fuzzy rules from clusters using a distance parameter between clusters depicted by $e_f$. Every cluster is considered as a fuzzy rule and the membership functions are Gaussian functions whose dissemination is a constant depicted by $\sigma$.

## Learning from Examples (LFE) & Modified Learning from Examples (MLFE)

Both methodologies (Passino & Yurkovich, 1998) do not belong to the clustering algorithms. In LFE technique, we construct fuzzy rules not only from an input set of data points but also from linguistic information. In this algorithm a template for every membership function is defined and accordingly based on an iterative process each data point is examined in order to create a new fuzzy rule. Moreover, a point can belong to an existing fuzzy rule. A point has a number of dimensions. For each dimension, we consider the point coordinate in order to compute a value (the membership degree) for all the membership functions and we choose the maximum one. As a result a data point creates a fuzzy rule because we have chosen for every membership variable (in the antecedent or the consequent part) the "most appropriate" membership function. On the other hand, it is possible that a point can create an existing fuzzy rule (with the same antecedent part). In this case, no further addition is done at the existing rule base.

MLFE works in a similar way. However, the most significant difference with the LFE is that MLFE tries on its own to compute the membership functions, without an input template for guiding the rule base construction. Initially, MLFE considers the first data point as if represents a fuzzy rule. Continuing the execution, it applies the next data point to the existing rule base. There, the difference between the result of the rule base and the

value of the last coordinate (it is thought as the consequent part) is examined if it is smaller than the distance threshold $e_f$. If so, no new rule is added, otherwise, a new rule is derived by estimating the membership functions in order to enter the rule without distorting the previous rule base.

LFE is an easy to implement technique especially when the template of possible membership functions is defined for every dimension. It is a good practice to run first the FCM so as to get the truncated Gaussians functions and accordingly to apply the LFE algorithm. The problem in LFE is that we do not know beforehand which dimension membership functions are narrow and which are not. The results from FCM will give us a general aspect of the input data points. In MLFE there is a significant detail. The points must have unique coordinates. If not so, an assumption is made for the value of the dissimilarity measure.

## AI Techniques

AI techniques usually involve the usage of neural networks and genetic algorithms. FL theory provides efficient inference mechanisms in cases where incomplete knowledge is present while AI theory deals with learning, adaptation, fault tolerance, etc. The combination of these two theories can provide a lot of advantages in FL systems creation.

Neuro-Fuzzy systems are FL systems which are based on neural network for the definition of basic parameters of the system. The network can be viewed as a three layer feed forward network and it is trained through asset of data in order to produce the final membership functions and rules. For this a specific learning algorithm is used. Fuzzy sets in such systems are depicted by weights in the network. The learning algorithm is responsible to define the final weights of the network. Hence, the first layer represents the input parameters, the middle layer represents the fuzzy rules and the third layer represents the output parameters. Some of the most known neuro-fuzzy systems are:

1.  ANFIS (Kasabov & Qun Song, 1999)
2.  FALCON (Lin & Lee, 1991)
3.  GARIC (Bherenji & Khedkar, 1992)
4.  NEFCON (Nauck & Kruse, 1997)
5.  FINEST (Tano et al., 1996)
6.  FUN (Sulzberger et al., 1993)
7.  EFuNN (Kasabov & Qun Song, 1999)

The main advantage of neuro-fuzzy systems is that we can find suitable membership functions taking advantage of the black box behaviour of neural network. The learning mechanism based on data given by experts provides a problem-specific behaviour of the system that can be adapted in real situations. More details in neuro-fuzzy systems can be found in (Lin & Lee, 1996; Nauck et al., 1997) as well as in the above referenced research efforts. Due to space limitations, we cannot give a detailed description of these systems.

Genetic alorithms can be used for learning the rules of a FL system. A common approach in research efforts using genetic algorithms is the consideration of parameters identification concerning memebrship functions constrained by a fixed rule structure (Angelov & Buswell, 2003). The rule structure is predefined. In (Lim et al., 1996), a fuzzy rules learning model is presented. The model is based on genetic algorithms. A set of linguistic variables for inputs and outputs is given as well as the number of fuzzy rules. In the first step of the process, a random population of chromosomes is created. Every chromosome depicts a fuzzy rule set. A specific fitness function is used in order to to evaluate the fitness of each chromosome in the population. A number of fuzzy rules are randomly distributed in the produced string. Every resulted crhomosome contains the same number of rules.

In (Chiang et al., 1996), authors propose the usage of genetic algorithms and reinforcement learning techniques for the automatic definition of the FL rule base. The proposed FL controller has the capability to learn its own control rules instead of using experts' knowledge. This provides efficiency in the functionality of the controller. The main parts of the controller are: the *Action Evaluation Network (AEN)* responsible to advise the controller during its actions, the *Action Generation Network (AGN)* responsible to result the appropriate controler action. A fitness mechanism is used in the main controller concenring the genetic algorithms.

## FUTURE RESEARCH DIRECTIONS

FL can be proved very important when used in electronic marketplaces. A number of research efforts utilize FL in various parts of an interaction process. Future trends indicate that a large amount of systems will incorporate FL in order to represent human thinking in various domains and of course in E-Commerce. FL could be used in combination with other techniques such as neural networks, genetic algorithms, reinforcement learning algorithms, etc. This way, developers have the opportunity to take advantage by the combination of FL with AI techniques. The power of FL is the efficient decision making when incomplete knowledge is present while AI techniques can provide a lot of advantages such as learning, fault tolerance, etc. This way, developers have the opportunity to create efficient E-Commerce systems adapted to each environment characteristics.

Furthermore, some work should be done in the definition of FL systems that will fully support the decision making process of entities. These mechanisms could result the appropriate action that entities should take at every state of the world. Rule bases and membership functions could convey the experience of market developers either by the manual or by the automatic definition of the FL system characteristics. Also, the experience of each entity when acting in markets should be incorporated in the FL mechanism in order to result the most efficient system.

Finally, due to the uncertainty in the Web, more fine – grained and simple trust mechanisms should be proposed. Trust is very important especially in cases where there is a large amount of entities interacting with in a market. However, a trust mechanism should be simple and efficient in order to save time in the purchase process. The usage of FL in trust calculation mechanisms should be more intensive in order to lead to more productive systems.

## CONCLUSION

In this chapter, we try to analytically present the parts of a marketplace scenario where FL can be used providing a number of advantages. We focus on the behavior of entities participating on such places and we describe how FL could be used in such cases. Usually, there is an interaction process between competitive entities that try to fulfill their goals. The entities want to profit in a purchase interaction based on products characteristics. In this interaction process, FL plays an important role as it can be used in: (a) proposal definition, (b) trust level calculation, (c) time constraints definition, and, (d) decision making. The usage of FL is very beneficial because entities can rely upon a efficient mechanism in cases where no knowledge is present about the characteristics of the opponents. In the decision making field, we present our proposal for a FL system used by agents when interacting in a BG process. We describe our model and we give numerical results for our experiments.

Furthermore, we describe methodologies for building FL systems. Apart from the manual definition of basic parameters of a FL system, there are a number of techniques for the automatic definition of these parameters. We mainly focus on the clustering techniques as their usage is very simple, however, we provide short information about neuro – fuzzy systems and genetic algorithms. The combination of FL and AI techniques could be broadly used in future applications as by using them we can combine the efficiency of the

FL with the adaptation to real situations provided by the AI methodologies.

## REFERENCES

Al-Ashmaway, W. H., El-Sisi, A. B., Nassan, H. M., & Ismail, N. A. (2007). Bilateral agent negotiation for e-commerce based on fuzzy logic. In *Proceedings of the International Conference on Computer Engineering & Systems (ICCES '07)*, November 27-29, Cairo, Egypt, (pp. 64-69).

Angelov, P. P., & Buswell, R. A. (2003). Automatic generation of fuzzy rule–based models from data by genetic algorithms. (Elsevier.). *Information Sciences*, *150*, 17–31. doi:10.1016/S0020-0255(02)00367-5

Arapoglou, R., Kolomvatsos, K., & Hadjiefthymiades, S. (2010). Buyer agent decision process based on automatic fuzzy rules generation methods. In *Proceedings of the 2010 IEEE World Congress on Computational Intelligence (WCCI 2010), FUZZ-IEEE*, July 18th – 23rd, Barcelona, Spain, (pp. 856-863).

Aron, R., Sundararajan, A., & Viswanathan, S. (2006). Intelligent agents in electronic markets for information goods: Customization, preference and pricing. *Decision Support Systems*, *41*(4), 764–786. doi:10.1016/j.dss.2004.10.007

Bakos, Y. (1998). The emerging role of electronic marketplaces on the Internet. *Communications of the ACM*, *41*(8), 35–42. doi:10.1145/280324.280330

Barbosa, G. P., & Silva, Q. B. (2001). *An electronic marketplace architecture based on technology of intelligent agents and knowledge* (pp. 39–60). Lecture Notes in Computer Science E-Commerce Agents, Marketplace Solutions, Security Issues, and Supply and Demand.

Bezdek, J. C. (1981). *Pattern recognition with fuzzy objective function algoritms*. New York, NY: Plenum Press.

Bherenji, H. R., & Khedkar, P. (1992). Learning and tuning fuzzy logic controllers through reinforcements. *IEEE Transactions on Neural Networks, 3*, 724–740. doi:10.1109/72.159061

Carbo, J., Molina, J. M., & Davila, J. (2003). Reaching agreements through fuzzy counteroffers. In *Proc. of the International Conference in Web Engineering,* Oviedo, Spain, July 14-18.

Carbo, J., Molina, J. M., & Davila, J. (2005). Fuzzy referral based cooperation in social networks of agents. *AI Communications, 18*(1), 1–13.

Chavez, A., & Maes, P. (1996). Kasbah: An agent marketplace for buying and selling goods. In *Proc. of the 1st International Conference on the Practical Application of Intelligent Agents and Multi-Agent Technology (PAAM '96),* London, UK.

Cheng, C. B., Chan, H. C. C., & Lin, C. C. (2005). Buyer-supplier negotiation by fuzzy logic based agents. In *Proceedings of the 3rd International Conference on Information Technology and Applications (ICITA '05),* Sydney, Australia, (pp. 137–142).

Chiang, C. K., Chung, H. Y., & Lin, J. J. (1996). A self-learning fuzzy logic controller using genetic algorithms with reinforcements. *IEEE Transactions on Fuzzy Systems, 5*, 460–467. doi:10.1109/91.618280

Collins, J., Jamison, S., Mobasher, B., & Gini, M. (1998). A market architecture for multi-agent contracting. In *Proceedings of the 2nd International Conference on Autonomous Agents,* New York, (pp. 285-292).

Dunn, J. C. (1973). A fuzzy relative of the ISODATA process and its use in detecting compact well-separated clusters. *Journal of Cybernetics, 3*, 32–57. doi:10.1080/01969727308546046

Engelbrecht, A. P. (2007). *Computational intelligence: An introduction* (2nd ed.). Wiley.

Faratin, P., Sierra, C., & Jennings, N. (1998). Negotiation decision functions for autonomous agents. *International Journal of Autonomous and Robotics Systems, 24*(3-4), 159–182. doi:10.1016/S0921-8890(98)00029-3

Fudeberg, D., & Tirole, J. (1991). *Game theory.* Cambridge, MA: MIT Press.

Ge, W., Rothenberger, M., & Chen, E. (2007). A model for an electronic information marketplace. *Australasian Journal of Information Systems, 13*(1).

Hartigan, J. A., & Wong, M. A. (1979). A k-means clustering algorithm. *Applied Statistics, 28*, 100–108. doi:10.2307/2346830

Jang, J. S. R., Sun, C. T., & Mizutani, E. (1997). *Neuro-fuzzy and soft computing – A computational approach to learning and machine intelligence.* Prentice Hall.

Kasabov, N., & Song, Q. (1999). *Dynamic evolving fuzzy neural networks with 'm-out-of-n' activation nodes for on-line adaptive systems.* Technical Report TR99/04, Department of Information Science, University of Otago.

Klusch, M. (2001). Information agent technology for the Internet: A survey. *Data & Knowledge Engineering, 36*(3), 337–372. doi:10.1016/S0169-023X(00)00049-5

Kolomvatsos, K., Anagnostopoulos, C., & Hadjiefthymiades, S. (2008). On the use of fuzzy logic in a seller bargaining game. In *Proc. of the 32nd Annual IEEE International Computer Software and Applications Conference (COMPSAC 2008),* July 28th - August 1st, Turku, Finland, (pp. 184-191).

Kolomvatsos, K., & Hadjiefthymiades, S. (2008). Implicit deadline calculation for seller agent bargaining in information marketplaces. In *Proceedings of the 2nd International Conference on Complex, Intelligent and Software Intensive Systems (CISIS 2008),* March 4th-7th, Barcelona, Spain, (pp. 184-190).

Kolomvatsos, K., & Hadjiefthymiades, S. (2009). Automatic fuzzy rules generation for the deadline calculation of a seller agent. In *the Proc. of the 9th International Symposium on Autonomous Decentralized Systems (ISADS 2009)*, Athens, Greece, March 23-25, (pp. 429-434).

Laufmann, S. (1994). The information marketplace: The challenge of information commerce. In *Proceedings of the 2nd International Conference on Cooperative Information Systems*, (pp. 147-157).

Lim, M. H., Rahardja, S., & Gwee, B. H. (1996). A GA paradigm for learning fuzzy rules. *Fuzzy Sets and Systems, 82*, 177–186. doi:10.1016/0165-0114(95)00254-5

Lin, C. L., Lo, W., & Yan, M. R. (2006). Bargaining strategies for construction joint ventures by fuzzy logic. In *Proceedings of the 9th Joint Conference on Information Sciences*, October 8-11, Taiwan.

Lin, C. T., & Lee, C. C. (1996). *Neural fuzzy systems. A neuro-fuzzy synergism to intelligent systems*. New York, NY: Prentice Hall.

Lin, C. T., & Lee, C. S. G. (1991). Neural network based fuzzy logic control and decision system. *IEEE Transactions on Computers, 40*(12), 1320–1336. doi:10.1109/12.106218

Mamdani, E. H., & Assilian, S. (1975). An experiment in linguistic synthesis with a fuzzy logic controller. *International Journal of Man-Machine Studies, 7*, 1–13. doi:10.1016/S0020-7373(75)80002-2

Nauck, D., Klawonn, F., & Kruse, R. (1997). *Foundations of neuro-fuzzy systems*. Chichester, UK: Wiley.

Nauck, D., & Kruse, R. (1997). Neuro-fuzzy systems for function approximation. In *Proceedings of the 4th International Workshop on Fuzzy-Neuro Systems*.

Nwana, H. S. (1996). Software agents: An overview. *The Knowledge Engineering Review, 11*(2), 205–244. doi:10.1017/S026988890000789X

Passino, K., & Yurkovich, S. (1998). *Fuzzy control*. Menlo Park, CA: Addison Wesley Longman.

Raeesy, Z., Brzostwoski, J., & Kowalczyk, R. (2007). Towards a fuzzy-based model for human-like multi-agent negotiation. In *Proc. of the 2007 IEEE/WIC/ACM International Conference on Intelligent Agent Technology*, November 2-5, Silicon Valley, USA, (pp. 515-519).

Rose, F. (1999). *The economics, concept, and design of information intermediaries*. Heidelberg, Germany: Physika-Verlag.

Schmidt, S., Steele, R., Dillon, T., & Chang, E. (2007). Fuzzy trust evaluation and credibility development in multi-agent systems. *Applied Soft Computing, 7*, 492–505. doi:10.1016/j.asoc.2006.11.002

Sulzberger, S. M., Tschicholg-Gurman, N. N., & Vestli, S. J. (1993). FUN: Optimization of fuzzy rule based systems using neural networks. In *Proceedings of IEEE Conference on Neural Networks*, San Francisco, USA, (pp. 312-316).

Takagi, T., & Sugeno, M. (1985). Fuzzy identification of systems and its application to modeling and control. *IEEE Transactions on Systems, Man, and Cybernetics, 15*(1), 116–132.

Tano, S., Oyama, T., & Arnould, T. (1996). Deep combination of fuzzy inference and neural network in fuzzy inference. *Fuzzy Sets and Systems, 82*(2), 151–160. doi:10.1016/0165-0114(95)00251-0

Tsvetovatyy, M., Gini, M., Mobasher, M., & Wieckowski, Z. (1997). MAGMA: An agent-based virtual market for electronic commerce. *Applied Artificial Intelligence, 11*(6), 501–523. doi:10.1080/088395197118046

Wang, X., Shen, X., & Georganas, N. D. (2006). A fuzzy logic based intelligent negotiation agent (FINA) in e-commerce. In *Proceedings of the IEEE Canadian Conference on Electrical and Computer Engineering,* Ottawa, ON, Canada.

Yu, T. J., Lai, R., Lin, M. W., & Kao, B. R. (2007). Modeling opponent's beliefs via fuzzy constraint–directed approach in agent negotiation. In *Proceedings of the 3rd International Conference on Advanced Intelligent Computing Theories and Applications,* August 2007, Qingdao, China, (pp. 167-178).

Zadeh, L. A. (1965). Fuzzy sets. *Information and Control, 8*(3), 338–353. doi:10.1016/S0019-9958(65)90241-X

Zhang, J., & Guo, X. (2009). Trust evaluation model based on fuzzy logic for C2C e-commerce. In *Proceedings of the International Symposium on Information Engineering and Electronic Commerce (IEEC '09),* May 16–17, Ternopil, Ukraine, (pp. 403-407).

Zipf, G. K. (1949). *Human behavior and the principle of least effort.* Cambridge, MA: Addison-Wesley.

Zuo, B. H., & Sun, Y. (2009). Fuzzy logic to support bilateral agent negotiation in e-commerce. In *Proceedings of the International Conference on Artificial Intelligence and Computational Intelligence,* November 7 – 8, Shanghai, China, (pp. 179-183).

## KEY TERMS AND DEFINITIONS

**Bargaining Game:** the bargaining process between entities that involve a set of alternating offers for the purchase of a product or a service.

**Buyers:** users that search products and are, usually, represented by an agent.

**Electronic Markets:** places where entities, not known in advance, can negotiate on the trade of products.

**Fuzzy Logic:** is a precise system of reasoning, deduction and computation in which the objects of discourse and analysis are associated with information which is, or is allowed to be, imprecise, uncertain, incomplete, unreliable, partially true or partially possible.

**Intelligent Agents:** is a software or hardware component capable of acting in order to accomplish the tasks delegated by its user.

**Negotiation:** the interaction process between entities in order to agree upon the exchange of a product or a service.

**Sellers:** are entities that have some goods in their property and sell them to potential customers.

# Chapter 31
# A Neuro–Fuzzy Expert System Trained by Particle Swarm Optimization for Stock Price Prediction

**Mohammad Hossein Fazel Zarandi**
*Amirkabir University of Technology, Iran*

**Milad Avazbeigi**
*European Centre for Soft Computing, Spain*

**Meysam Alizadeh**
*University of Maryland, USA*

## ABSTRACT

*In today's competitive markets, prediction of financial variables has become a critical issue. Especially in stock market analysis where a wrong prediction may result in a big loss in terms of time and money, having a robust prediction is a crucial issue. To model the chaotic, noisy, and evolving behavior of stock market data, new powerful methods should be developed. Soft Computing methods have shown a great confidence in such environments where there are many uncertain factors. Also it has been observed through many experiments that the hybridization of different soft computing techniques such as fuzzy logic, neural networks, and meta-heuristics usually results in better results than simply using one method. This chapter presents an adaptive neuro-fuzzy inference system (ANFIS), trained by the particle swarm optimization (PSO) algorithm for stock price prediction. Instead of previous works that have emphasized on gradient base or least square (LS) methods for training the neural network, four different strategies of PSO are implemented: gbest, lbest-a, lbest-b, and Euclidean. In the proposed fuzzy rule based system some technical and fundamental indexes are applied as input variables. In order to generate membership functions (MFs), a robust noise rejection clustering algorithm is developed. The proposed neuro-fuzzy model is applied for an automotive part-making manufactory in an Asia stock market. The results show the superiority of the proposed model in comparison with the available models in terms of error minimization, robustness, and flexibility.*

DOI: 10.4018/978-1-61350-429-1.ch031

## INTRODUCTION

In today's competitive markets, prediction of financial variables has become a critical issue. Especially in stock market analysis where a wrong prediction may result in a big loss in terms of time and money having a robust prediction is a crucial thing. For predicting stocks' return/price and making buy/sell decisions in stock market people generally use two types of analysis including security analysis and portfolio analysis (selection). The security analysis itself can be divided into two categories as technical analysis and fundamental analysis.

In technical analysis, all the information about the stocks is hidden in the prices and trading volumes. Thus, an investment policy based on technical analysis is a policy for predicting future stock prices by studying the historical prices and volumes' data. On the other hand, fundamental analysis lies in information about macroeconomic variables, company's performance and related industries in order to predict the future stock price direction. Finally, portfolio selection is concerned with selecting a combination of securities among portfolios containing large numbers of securities to reach the investment goal (Li & Xu, 2009).

Recent advances in soft computing offer many tools and techniques for forecasting noisy environments like stock markets and capturing the nonlinear behavior of these environments (Atsalakis & Valavanis, 2008). Also, artificial neural networks (ANNs) have been used for this purpose for a long time (Kim & Han, 1998; Aiken & Bsat, 1999; Chi, Chen, and Cheng, 1999; Lee, 2001; Wah & Qian, 2002). However these models have their own limitations due to the noise and complex dimensionality of stock price data. Besides, the size of data set and the input variables may also interfere with each other. Therefore, the result of these models and methods may not be very persuasive.

Fuzzy system modeling is a powerful tool for stock market analysis. Wang (2002) presents a data mart to reduce the size of stock data by combining fuzzification techniques with the grey theory to develop a fuzzy grey prediction as one of predicting functions to predict the possible answers immediately. Fazel Zarandi et al. (2009) proposed an interval type-2 fuzzy rule based system for stock price prediction. Their proposed type-2 fuzzy model applies both the technical and fundamental indexes as the input variables. In this work an indirect approach is used to fuzzy system modeling by implementing the modified cluster validity index for determining the number of rules in fuzzy clustering. Jilani and Burney (2008) presented a simple time-variant fuzzy time series forecasting method. They have proposed a fuzzy metric to use the frequency-density-based partitioning. The proposed fuzzy metric also uses a trend predictor to calculate the forecast. Chang and Liu (2008) introduced a fuzzy system based on Takagi-Sugeno-Kang (TSK) for prediction of stock price. Chu et al. (2009) presents a new time-series model for stock index forecasting using dual factors to improve the forecasting accuracy of fuzzy time-series models.

At the computational level, a fuzzy system can be observed as a layered structure (network) similar to artificial neural networks of the Radial Basis Function (RBF) type (Jang & Sun, 1993). For parameters optimization in a fuzzy system, gradient-descent training algorithms can be employed. Hence, this approach is usually referred to as neuro-fuzzy modeling (Brown & Harris, 1994; Jang, 1993).

In recent years, neuro-fuzzy systems have frequently been used for stock price prediction. These approaches are to use quantitative inputs like technical indices and qualitative factors such as political effects. Kuo, Chen, and Hwang (2001) fuzzy neural network trained with a genetic algorithm to measure the qualitative effects on stock price. They applied their system to the Taiwan stock market. Aiken and Bsat (1999) used a Fuzzy Neural Network (FNN) trained by a genetic algorithm (GA) to forecast three-month US

Treasury Bill rates. They concluded that a neural network (NN) can be used to accurately predict these rates. Thammano (1999) used a neuro-fuzzy model to predict future values of Thailand's largest government-owned bank. The inputs of the model are the closing prices for the current and prior three months, and the profitability ratios. The output of the model was the stock prices for the following three months. He concluded that the neuro-fuzzy architecture is able to recognize the general characteristics of the stock market faster and more accurately than the basic back propagation algorithm. It could also predict investment opportunities during the economic crisis when statistical approaches were not able to deliver satisfactory results. Pokropinska and Scherer (2008) present an application of neuro-fuzzy systems to support trading decisions. Atsalakis and Valavanis (2008) surveyed articles that have applied neural networks and neuro-fuzzy models to predict stock market values.

The aim of this chapter is to develop a neuro-fuzzy modeling algorithm for stock price prediction problem that is able to:

- Choose the optimal number of rules, fuzzy sets and weighting exponent,
- Generate a fuzzy rule base from numerical data,
- Tune the parameters of fuzzy membership functions,
- Enhance the robustness of the system.

To achieve these objectives, an adaptive neuro-fuzzy inference system is proposed by incorporating a robust fuzzy noise-rejection clustering algorithm and a hybrid learning method which is based on Particle Swarm Optimization (PSO). In order to create the neuro-fuzzy model, ANFIS (Jang, 1993) is used. To enhance the robustness of the model, method of Melek, Goldenberg and Emami (2005) is used with some modifications.

The rest of the chapter is organized as follows. First, ANFIS and PSO basic concepts are reviewed.

This section also explains other variations of PSO. Then the proposed neuro-fuzzy model is presented. The model is applied for some real world cases to show the performance of the model. Finally, conclusions and future works are presented.

## BACKGROUND

This section reviews the concepts and structures of ANFIS and PSO which are used in this research.

## ANFIS STRUCTURE

The TSK is a fuzzy system with crisp functions in consequents that is more useful for complex applications (Alcala et al. 2000). TSK systems are widely used in the form of a neuro-fuzzy system called ANFIS.

An ANFIS is a fuzzy inference system that can be trained to model input/output data. ANFIS combines neural network and fuzzy modeling to tune its parameters to learn the input/output relationships hidden in the data set. By combining these two intelligent approaches, it is possible to use the capability of both fuzzy reasoning and network calculation (Teshnehlab, Shoorehdeli, and Sedigh, 2008). When regarding fuzzy systems as types of neural networks, the role of membership functions in determining decision surfaces forms is highlighted instead of accuracies in modeling vagueness or uncertainty associated with particular linguistic terms (Atsalakis & Valavanis, 2008). The rule-based representation of neuro-fuzzy systems offers transparency.

For simplicity, we assume that the fuzzy inference system has two inputs x and y and one output z. The equivalent ANFIS architecture (Type-3 ANFIS) is illustrated in Figure 1. The node functions in the same layer are from the same function family. In such architecture, the first layer implements a fuzzification, the second layer executes the T-norm of the antecedent part of the fuzzy rules, the third layer normalizes the membership functions (MFs), the fourth layer calculates the consequent parameters and finally the last layer computes the overall output as the summation of all incoming signals. The feed forward equations of the considered ANFIS are as follows:

$$w_i = \mu_{A_i}(x) \times \mu_{B_i}(x) \tag{1}$$

$$\bar{w}_i = \frac{w_i}{w_1 + w_2}, \quad i = 1, 2. \tag{2}$$

$$\begin{cases} f_1 = p_1 x + q_1 y + r_1 z \\ f_2 = p_2 x + q_2 y + r_2 z \end{cases} \tag{3}$$

$$f = \frac{w_1 f_1 + w_2 f_2}{w_1 + w_2} = \bar{w}_1 f_1 + \bar{w}_2 f_2 \tag{4}$$

where, x is the input to node i, $\mu_{A_i}(x)$ is the node i node function, $A_i$ is the linguistic label associated with node functions, $w_i$ is the firing strength of ith rule, $w_i$ is the ratio of ith rule's firing strength to the sum of all rules' firing strength, $\{p_i, q_i, r_i\}$ is the parameter set, and $f_i$ is the consequent value. Note that the network's output y is nonlinear in the weights $w$. The training of a multilayered neural network is thus a nonlinear optimization problem to which various methods can be applied (Babuska & Verbruggen, 2003).

## LEARNING ALGORITHMS

The neuro-fuzzy inference system is optimized by adapting the antecedent parameters and consequent parameters so that a specified objective function (usually a difference between the model output and the actual output) is minimized. Many methods have been proposed for learning rules and obtaining an optimal set of them. Mascioli, Varazi,

and Martinelli (1997) have proposed merging of Min-Max and ANFIS model to obtain neuro-fuzzy network and determine the optimal set of fuzzy rules. Jang and Mizutani (1996) have presented application of Lavenberg-Marquardt method that is a nonlinear least-squares technique for training neural networks. Kumar and Garg (2004) used Kohonen's map to training. Later, Tang, Quek, and Ng (2005) proposed a hybrid system combining a Fuzzy Inference System and Genetic Algorithms to tune the parameters of Takagi-Sugeno-Kang fuzzy neural network.

Jang (1993) proposed four methods to update the parameters of ANFIS:

1. Gradient decent only: all parameters are updated by the gradient descent.
2. Gradient decent only and one pass of Least Square Error (LSE): the LSE is applied only once at the very beginning to get the initial values of the consequent parameters and then the gradient decent takes over to update all parameters.
3. Gradient decent only and LSE: this is the hybrid learning which is introduced by the author.
4. Sequential LSE: using extended Kalman filter algorithm to update all parameters.

These methods update antecedent parameters by using Gradient Descent (GD) or Kalman filtering. Complexity of these methods grows exponentially when the network grows. Chen (1999) compared several popular training algorithms in tuning parameters of ANFIS membership functions (MFs).

## PARTICLE SWARM OPTIMIZATION (PSO)

PSO is one of the most powerful swarm intelligence-based optimization techniques, which was introduced by Kennedy and Eberhart (1995). PSO

*Figure 1. The equivalent ANFIS structure*

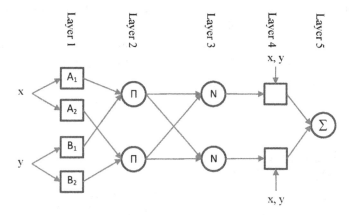

is inspired from the swarming behavior of animals and human social behavior. This algorithm is a zero-order, non-calculus-based method (no gradients are needed) that can solve discontinuous, multimodal and non-convex problems. Furthermore, it includes some probabilistic features in the motion of particles.

During the last decade many studies have focused on PSO and almost all of them have confirmed the capabilities of this newly proposed optimization (Parsopoulos & Vrahatis, 2002; Parsopoulos & Vrahatis, 2004; Scutte et al. 2004; Tan, 2007) and it has been applied to a variety of problems such as constrained optimization problems, min-max problems, multiobjective optimization problems and dynamic tracking (Shi, 2004). Besides, some papers have tried to improve the original PSO by introducing new features to the original PSO such as variable inertia coefficient, constriction factor (Parsopoulos & Vrahatis, 2002), maximum velocity limit, parallel optimization (Scutte et al. 2004), deflection, repulsion, stretching (Parsopoulos & Vrahatis, 2004), mutation (Tan, 2007), neighborhood and so on (Shi, 2004).

PSO is a population-based algorithm that exploits a population of individuals to probe promising region of the search space. In this context, the population is called swarm and the individuals

are called particles. Each particle moves with an adaptable velocity within the search space and retains in its memory the best position it has ever encountered. Each of them also knows about the best position of its neighbors ever reached. The concept of neighborhood, here is a general concept in the sense that a particle may be neighbor with all other particles (gbest topology) or some of them. The general principles for the PSO algorithm are stated as follows:

Suppose that the search space is n-dimensional, then the $i^{th}$ particle can be represented by a *n*-dimensional vector $x_i$, and velocity $v_i = [v_{i1}, v_{i2}, ..., v_{in}]^T$, where $i = 1, 2, ..., N$ and $N$ is the size of population. In PSO, particle $i$ remembers the best position it visited so far, referred to as $P_i = [p_{i1}, p_{i2}, ..., p_{in}]^T$ and the best position of the best particle in its neighborhood is referred as $L = [l_1, l_2, ..., l_n]^T$.

Each particle $i$ adjusts its position in next iteration $t+1$ with respect to Eqs. (5) and (6) (Parsopoulos & Vrahatis, 2004):

$$v_i(t+1) = \omega(t)V_i(t) + c_1r_1(P_i(t) - X_i(t)) + c_2r_2(P_i(t) - X_i(t)) \tag{5}$$

$$X_i(t+1) = X_i(t) + \chi V_i(t+1) \tag{6}$$

where, $c_1$ and $c_2$ are positive constants, $r_1$ and $r_2$ are two random variables in the range [0, 1], and $\omega(t)$ is the inertia coefficient which gradually decreases linearly from 0.95 in the first iteration to 0.4 and $\chi$ is the constriction factor which is used to limit velocity. In our experiments, it is set to 1 and has no effect.

## DESIGNING A SYSTEMATIC NEURO-FUZZY EXPERT SYSTEM

A mathematical definition of stock price prediction problem can be provided as follows:

Suppose there is *ND*, which stands for Number of Data, historical data vectors that are obtained from the subjects available and each data is associated with *NV* number of features, such as *demand index*, *moving average*, *price channel*, etc. Let $X_1, X_2, ..., X_{NV}$ be *NV* fuzzy linguistic variables in the universe of discourse $U_1, U_2, ..., U_{NV}$ and *Y* be a fuzzy linguistic variable in the universe of discourse *V*. Let $X_k = [x_{k,1}, ..., x_{k,NV}]$ denote the input data vector of the *k*th sample, where, $k = 1, 2, ..., ND$ and $y_k$ is the output. Let *R* be a fuzzy relation in $U_1 \times U_2 \times ... \times U_{NV} \times V$.

The two basic steps in fuzzy systems modeling are *system (structure) identification* and *fuzzy reasoning*. In system identification stage, the significant input variables are determined and then fuzzy if–then rules are generated and the parameters of the model such as the number of clusters, the level of fuzziness, the operators to be used in the reasoning are determined. Finally in *fuzzy reasoning,* the obtained system is used to infer new knowledge using new data (Kilic, Uncu, and Turksen, 2007). In fuzzy system modeling, the relationships between variables are represented by means of *if-then* rules with imprecise predicates. In this case, the advantage of using a neuro-fuzzy model is the possibility to interpret the obtained result, which is not possible with black-box structures such as neural networks (Babuska &

Verbruggen, 2003). The proposed methodology for fuzzy systems modeling has the following steps:

1. Fuzzy clustering of the output,
2. Input selection,
3. Input membership assignment,
4. Tuning the parameters of membership function of input and output variables,
5. Inference.

## FUZZY CLUSTERING OF THE OUTPUT

In order to determine the number of rules of the initial ANFIS, we propose a robust noise-rejection fuzzy clustering algorithm for clustering the output space. Our approach is based on the Melek, Goldenberg, and Emami (2005). They proposed a systematic methodology to find the number of clusters, selection of the weighting exponent, selection of the initial cluster centers, finding the noisy data and calculation of the membership matrix. We follow the above steps and modify some parts of them as follows:

Initially, the number of clusters should be determined. Therefore, a validity index proposed by Kim et al. (2004) and modified by Fazel Zarandi et al. (2009) is used. The number of clusters (C) is the C that minimizes the following value:

$$V_{FNT}(U, V : X) = \frac{2}{c(c-1)} \sum_{p \neq q}^{c} S_{rel}(A_p, A_q)$$

(7)

The optimal number of the clusters is obtained by minimizing $V_{FNT}(U, V; X)$ over the range of $c$ values $(2, ..., c_{max})$ where $S_{rel}(A_p, A_q)$ is the relative similarity between two fuzzy sets $A_p$ and $A_q$ and is defined as:

$$S_{rel}(A_p, A_q) = \sum_{i=1}^{n} S_{rel}(x_j : A_p, A_q)h(x_j)$$

(8)

where,

$$h(x_j) = -\sum_{p=1}^{c} u_{A_p}(x_j) \log(u_{A_p}(x_j)) \qquad (9)$$

and $S_{rel}(x_j : A_p, A_q)$ is the relative similarity between two fuzzy sets $A_p$ and $A_q$ at $x_j$ which is defined as:

$$S_{rel}(x_j : A_p, A_q) = \frac{f(x_j : A_p \cap A_q)}{f(x_j : A_p \cap A_q) + f(x_j : A_p - A_q) + f(x_j : A_q - A_p)} \qquad (10)$$

Here, $h(x_j)$ is the entropy of datum $x_j$ and $u_{A_p}(x_j)$ is the membership value with which $x_j$ belongs to the cluster $A_p$.

For the selection of the weighting exponent ($m$), Emami, Turksen, and Goldenberg (1998) suggested to choose it far from it's both extremes so as to ensure that the cluster validity index shows the optimum number of fuzzy clusters. Sugeno and Yasukawa (1993) defined a fuzzy total scatter matrix as follows:

$$s_T = \sum_{k=1}^{N} (\sum_{i=1}^{c} (u_{ik})^m)(x_k - \overline{v})(x_k - \overline{v})^T \qquad (11)$$

The trace of the $s_T$ decreases monotonically from a constant value $z$ to zero as $m$ varies from one to infinity. For clustering, a convenient value for $m$ is that which gives a value for trace $(s_T)$ equal to $z/2$ (Emami, Turksen, and Goldenberg, 1998). The constant value $z$ is defined as:

$$z = trace(\sum_{k=1}^{N} [(x_k - \frac{1}{N}\sum_{k=1}^{N} x_k)(x_k - \frac{1}{N}\sum_{k=1}^{N} x_k)^T]) \qquad (12)$$

For the selection of initial cluster centers, Melek, Goldenberg, and Emami (2005) suggested to use an agglomerative hierarchical clustering algorithm (AHC) as the initial clustering tool.

Then, by defining a matrix of dissimilarities, the AHC merges into two or more of these clusters. The process is repeated to form a sequence of nested clustering in which the number of clusters decreases gradually until the minimum required number of cluster is obtained. Obviously, this method is crisp and is not suitable for accommodation of fuzzy logic concepts. Hence, to create initial cluster centers, we used a modified version of Gustafson-Kessel (GK) clustering algorithm introduced by (Babuska, Van Der Veen, and Kaymak, 2002). This clustering method does not change the performance of the GK algorithm but guarantees the capability of clustering any data set. Next, in order to find the data points that are "too far" from all cluster centers, we propose the following index for each data point $x_j$:

$$MW_j = \frac{\sum_{i=1}^{c} (u_{ij})^m \|x_j - v_i\|_A}{\sum_{i=1}^{c} (u_{ij})^m} \qquad (13)$$

where, $j = 1, 2, \dots, N$, $c$ is the number of clusters, $N$ is the number of data, $u_{ij}$ is the membership of datum $j$ in cluster $i$th, and $m$ is the degree of fuzziness. The index $MW_j$ is weighted average of the distance of the data point $x_j$ to all cluster centers. We use Mahalanobis distance norm in the above index. The noise is identified through the data points that have large values of $MW_j$ and, therefore, a threshold $\Omega$ is assigned to trim these outliers from the data set. After choosing the $\Omega$, we compute:

$$z = \frac{\eta_n}{N} \qquad (14)$$

where, $\eta_n$ is the number of noise points and N is the number of data. The percentage of inliers data can be calculated as:

$$\hat{z} = (1 - z) \qquad (15)$$

After identifying the percentage of inliers data, we should compute the corresponding chi-square data distribution value ($\chi^2$). Then, we calculate the cutoff distance:

$$u_{FC_{cut}}{}^2 = v_i \chi^2 \qquad (16)$$

where, $v_i$ is a resolution parameter, which depends on the number of clusters. Now, by knowing the cutoff distance, the optimum number of clusters, the weighting exponent, and the initial cluster centers, we use the NPCM clustering algorithm which is proposed by Krishnapuram (1994).

## INPUT SELECTION

The performance of non-linear identification techniques is often determined by the appropriateness of the selected input variables and the corresponding time lags. High correlation coefficients between candidate input variables in addition to a non-linear relation with the output signal induce the need for an appropriate input selection methodology (Maertens, Baerdemaeker, and Babuska, 2006).

Feature extraction, feature selection, and feature weighting are three different schools of thought used in order to find the significant input variables or the significance of input variables. The feature extraction transforms the coordinate system in order to improve a determined goal; whereas feature selection only reduces the dimensionality. Feature weighting is the generalized form of feature selection (Uncu & Turksen, 2007).

In this research, for feature selection, the Sugeno and Yasukawa (1993) method is used. They proposed a combinatorial approach in which all possible combinations of input candidates are considered. For each combination, they built two fuzzy models based on two separated sets of data and calculated a performance index called "Regularity Criterion" (RC) based on a method

of group data handling in an attempt to cause data independence in model formation after choosing input variables' combination, which has the minimum value of the performance index.

## INPUT MEMBERSHIP ASSIGNMENT

After clustering the output space, there are different methods to construct the fuzzy rule base. Sugeno and Yasukawa (1993) suggested determining the input membership degrees by projecting the output fuzzy clusters onto input space. Fazel Zarandi (1998) proposes another algorithm based on the optimization of a classifier function. Kilic et al. (2004) discussed the drawbacks of the Sugeno's method and introduced a modified approach. In the modified approach, after partitioning of the output space, the output clusters are projected onto $N$ dimensional input space, where $N$ is the number of variables.

In this research, we projects the output clusters onto the input space and construct our rule base.

## TUNING THE PARAMETERS OF MEMBERSHIP FUNCTION OF INPUT AND OUTPUT VARIABLES

In this section, the PSO is employed for training the ANFIS parameters. The ANFIS has two kinds of parameters that need to be trained: the antecedent parameters and the consequent parameters. Gaussian membership functions (GMFs) are located in the antecedent and consequent part:

$$\mu_{A_i}(x) = \exp\left\{-\left[\left(\frac{x - c_i}{a_i}\right)^2\right]^{b_i}\right\} \qquad (17)$$

Gaussian membership function has three parameters including $a_i$ that is the variance, $b_i$ that is the crossover slop and $c_i$ as the center of MFs.

For implementing the Particle Swarm Optimization tool, we used the Matlab® toolbox named psotb-beta-0.3 available at (http://downloads. sourceforge.net/psotoolbox/psotb-beta-0.3.zip), debugged it, and made some revisions on it. The toolbox itself contained the *gbest* and *lbset (ring)* topologies. The ability of Euclidean neighborhood calculation was added. Four neighborhood types are described as follows:

1. **gbest.** This method does not use any neighborhood topology. It considers all of the particles as neighbors to each other.
2. **lbest-a.** This method is a social topology, which is mostly known as ring lattice. In this method at the initiating phase each particle is associated with two particles and they will be considered as its neighbors throughout the run.
3. **lbest-b.** In this method each particle is randomly associated with $n/2$ particles at initiating phase where $n$ is the total number of the particles. It is actually implemented in order to demonstrate the effect of the degree of connectivity on the PSO.
4. **Euclidean.** In this method at each iteration a fixed radius is considered for all particles and the particles that lie within the circle surrounding each particle are considered as its neighbors. This radius is dynamically calculated over different iterations and is based on the maximum of distances between the particles.

## APPLICATION OF THE PROPOSED NEURO-FUZZY EXPERT SYSTEM MODEL FOR STOCK PRICE PREDICTION

In this section, we present a neuro-fuzzy expert system model for analysis of stock price of automotive part-making manufacturing shares from an Asian Stock Exchange. The candidate variables of the system in the form of input and output are shown in Table 1 and the stock close price is the only output. The development steps of the neuro-fuzzy MISO (Multiple Input Single Output) model are as follows:

1. For variable selection, the Sugeno and Yasukawa (1993) method is used. So, we begin with a fuzzy model with one input. We generate 24 models; one model for every input is developed and the RC of each model is calculated. The variable that makes the model with the minimum value of RC is selected. The procedure is repeated until the value of RC increases. The result is shown in Figure 2. As a result, typical price is selected at the first step, Price channel (bottom) at the second step, Price change at the third step, Momentum at the fourth step, Range at the fifth step and Moving Average MACD at the sixth step. At the seventh step, all of the values of RC for the seventh input are bigger than the minimal RC at the sixth step. So the search is terminated at this stage.

2. Robust fuzzy noise-rejection clustering algorithm is implemented to cluster the output space of the automotive part-making manufactory. As shown in Figure 3, the suitable weight exponent is selected as m=3.5. Then, the cluster validity index based on similarity measure ($V_{FNT}$) is implemented to determine the most suitable number of clusters or rules ($c$).

As shown in Figure 4, the best number of clusters based on this cluster validity index is obtained by the minimum value of the index that corresponds to 5 clusters.

3. The output space is projected onto the input spaces to select the most critical inputs and the membership functions of input and output are assigned based on estimation. It is

*Table 1. Variables of the system*

| Variable name | Variable description | Variable |
|---|---|---|
| Date | It is the day of trading | - |
| Volume | It shows how many money transact in trading | - |
| Value | It shows how much money transact in trading | - |
| Number of trading | It shows the number of transactions | - |
| Open price | It shows the open price which is most of the time is equal to last day close price | - |
| Maximum price | It shows the maximum price of stock in trade day | - |
| Minimum price | It shows the minimum price of stock in trade day | - |
| Typical price | It is average of max price, min price, and close price | Average {min price, max price, close price} |
| Price change | It is the difference between today close and the last day | $Change_i = day_i\ Price - day_{i-1}\ Price$ |
| Number of buyers | It shows the number of buyers | - |
| Moving average convergence divergence (MACD) | It uses two different exponential smoothing moving average lines and helps us determining price trends | MACD = exponential smoothing average 12 days (weeks) - exponential smoothing average 26 days (weeks) |
| Moving average MACD (MA-MACD) | It uses exponential smoothing moving average line in contrast to MACD | MA-MACD = exponential smoothing average 9 days (weeks) |
| Positive directional movement index (DI+) | It shows power of up moving trend | If DI+ > DI- then you should buy else you should sell |
| Negative directional movement index (DI-) | It shows power of down moving trend | |
| Moving average (MA) | It is sum of single period close prices dividend on numbers of periods | $MA(n) = \dfrac{\sum_{i=1}^{n} close\ prices\ of\ period(i)}{n}$ |
| Price channel (top) | It is maximum of price in last four week period | Max{close price of last four week} |
| Price channel (bottom) | It is minimum of price in last four week period | Min{close price of last four week} |
| Range (R) | It is the range of price in one specific day | Range = Maximum Price - Minimum Price |
| Price per earning per share (P/E) | It shows the payback period or its inversion shows the stock rate of return | $\dfrac{P}{E} = \dfrac{PRICE}{EPS}$ |
| Price and volume trend (PVT) | It relates price and volume in the stock market | $PVT = PVT_{prev} + volume \times \dfrac{close_{tdag} - close_{prev}}{lose_{prev}}$ |
| Stochastic oscillator | It compares a stock's closing price to its price range over a given period of time | $Stochastic\ Oscillator = 100 \times \dfrac{close - min}{max - min}$ |

*continued on following page*

*Table 1. Continued*

| Variable name | Variable description | Variable |
|---|---|---|
| Accumulation/Distribution index (AccDist) | adds or subtracts each day's volume in proportion to where the close is between the day's high and low | $AccDist = AccDist_{prev} + volume \times CLV$ $$CLV = 100 \times \frac{(close - min) - (max(-close))}{max - min}$$ |
| Momentum | It shows the difference between today's closing price and the close N days ago | $Momentum = close_{today} - close_{N\,days\,ago}$ |
| Rate of change (ROC) | It shows the difference between today's closing price and the close N days ago as a fraction | |
| Close price | It is the close price of the day | - |

*Figure 2. Behavior of RC in proposed model*

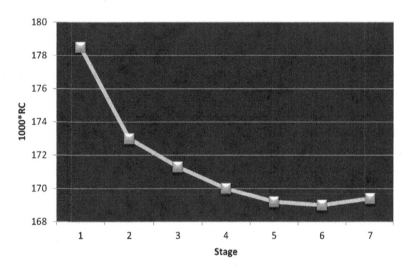

*Figure 3. Selection of level of fuzziness of the fuzzy clustering algorithm for the automative part-making manufactory*

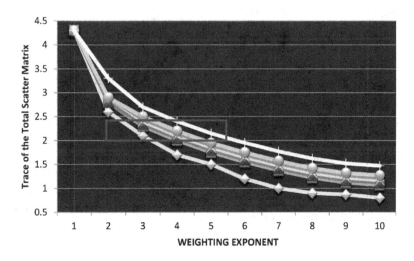

*Figure 4. Identification of the optimum number of clusters for the automative part-making manufactory*

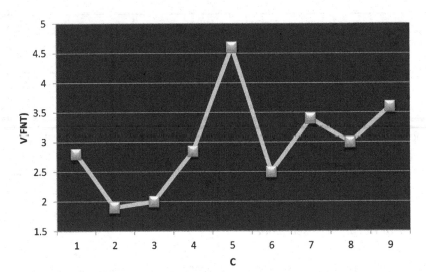

assumed that inputs and output membership functions are Gaussian.

4. For tuning the membership function parameters, instead of using the conventional gradient descent method, four different strategies of PSO are implemented and the results are compared. In our experiments, $c_1$ and $c_2$ which denote the cognitive and social parameters in equation 5, similar to Kennedy and Eberhart (1995) work are set to $c_1 = 2$, $c_2 = 2$ and $r_1$, $r_2$ are random real numbers which are drawn from the uniformly distributed interval $[0, 1]$. Figure 5 and Figure 6 illustrate the developed rule-based before and after tuning by the *gbest* strategy of PSO respectively.

In this research 643 data points have been selected where 442 data points are used for training and the rest for testing the model.

We run the algorithm with swarm sizes of 10, 20, 50, 100, 200 and 500. The termination criteria are the maximum of iterations and the minimum of performance which are set to 1000 and 1E-10 respectively. The results are shown in Table 2. In order to compare the performance of different models, RMSE (root mean square error) is used which is equal to

$$= \sqrt{\frac{1}{N} \sum_{i=1}^{N} (y_i - y_i^2)^2} \, .$$

The results show that the connectivity degree of the particles in the swarm can play an important role in the performance of the PSO.

Furthermore, the best average result of the above models is compared with the results of the following models:

## MULTIPLE REGRESSIONS

We have used the regression analysis with Matlab®. The regression equation is:

$$y = 0.9787 \, x_1 + 0.0457 \, x_2 + 0.0205 \, x_3 + 0.0015 \, x_4 - 0.0569 \, x_5 + 0.0007 \, x_6$$

After finding a linear method for showing the relationship between these 6 parameters, we must look at the residual plots to examine the formula.

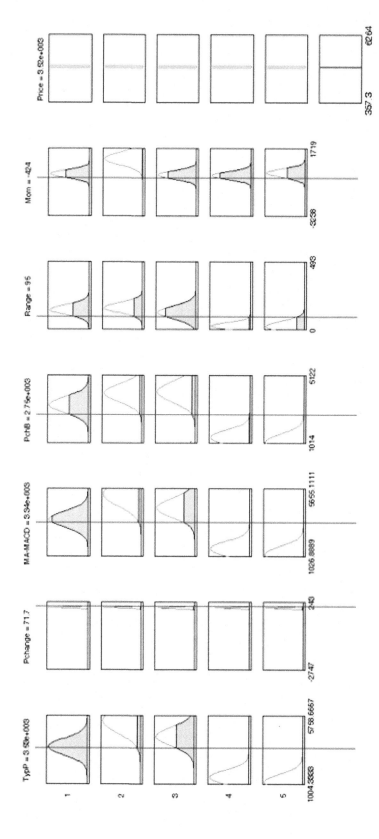

*Figure 5. Fuzzy rule base of automotive part-making manufactory before tuning*

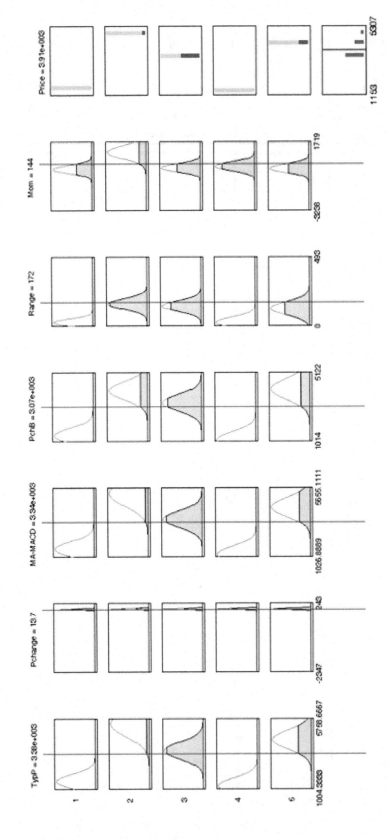

*Figure 6. Fuzzy rule base of automotive part-making manufactory after tuning*

*Table 2. Comparison between different PSO strategies in tuning of the ANFIS*

| Method | Train RMSE | | | Test RMSE | | |
|---|---|---|---|---|---|---|
| | average | min | max | average | Min | Max |
| PSO – 1 (gbest) | 5.2224 | 5.0928 | 7.6558 | 14.8625 | 2.8432 | 130.3827 |
| PSO – 2 (lbest-a) | 32.1178 | 27.3233 | 36.6337 | 29.4746 | 9.0790 | 44.7551 |
| PSO – 3 (lbest-b) | 37.5273 | 29.5896 | 41.9650 | 39.0826 | 17.4506 | 45.2403 |
| PSO – 4 (Euclidean) | 35.2386 | 32.5846 | 38.3189 | 40.2153 | 32.5259 | 53.8539 |

Base on the results, the linear formula gives a better estimation.

## SUGENO-YASUKAWA APPROACH

By using Sugeno software a fuzzy model is developed with four rules, five inputs and one output. The inputs are Typical price, Price Channel (bottom), Price Changes, Momentum, Range and Moving Average MACD and the output is portfolio return. We use Mamdani inference system with min–max operators and centroid defuzzification method.

## ANFIS

We have used the conventional ANFIS method with Matlab®. A correspond adaptive network has six inputs and one output. Other options are defaults of Matlab®. Table 3 shows the average results for five runs obtained with the training and test data sets for the proposed neuro-fuzzy model with that of Sugeno and Yasukawa (1993), multiple regression and ANFIS approach. The

tests were carried out for a maximum iteration number fixed in 500 epochs.

## CONCLUSION AND FUTURE WORKS

In this chapter, a new neuro-fuzzy expert system for stock price prediction is presented. In this system, an indirect approach to neuro-fuzzy system modeling is applied by implementing a modified robust noise-rejection data partitioning algorithm in fuzzy clustering. Then, Sugeno and Yasukawa method is used to select the most relevant, effective variables for the fuzzy rule-base system. In this method, to generate the membership values of input values, the output is projected onto the input spaces. Finally, the membership functions of inputs and output are tuned by particle swarm optimization algorithm. For tuning the membership functions of the rules, four different variations of particle swarm optimization are implemented and their results are compared to select the best strategy.

Proposed solutions are compared with some other models in the literature including Sugeno-Yasukawa approach, ANFIS and Multiple Regres-

*Table 3. Comparison between different models applying in stockprice prediction*

| Method | Number of Rules | RMSE | |
|---|---|---|---|
| | | Training | testing |
| ANFIS | 5 | 5.3162 | 15.3921 |
| Multiple Regression | - | 53.1844 | 24.3282 |
| Sugeno-Yasukawa Approach | 4 | 31.4128 | 21.0892 |
| PSO – 1 (gbest) | 5 | 5.2224 | 14.8625 |

sion. Finally, the proposed system is applied for stock price prediction in an Asian stock market. The proposed system shows that it presents better results than some other available models in the literature in terms of robustness, flexibility and error minimization.

Since, the presented method is a hybrid method, for future works the combination of other different methods such as Bayesian networks and Super Vector Machines could be considered. Also, recently multiple classifier systems such as artificial neural networks ensembles have attracted a lot of attention in the area of prediction because of their robust performance. Setup of an ensemble including some fuzzy neural networks tuned by different meta-heuristics could be a good research topic.

# REFERENCES

Aiken, M., & Bsat, M. (1999). Forecasting market trends with neural networks. *Information Systems Management*, *16*(4), 42–48. doi:10.1201/1078/4 3189.16.4.19990901/31202.6

Alcala, R., Casillas, J., Cordon, O., & Herrera, F. (2000). *Learning TSK rule-based system from approximate ones by mean of MOGUL methodology*. Unpublished doctoral dissertation, Granada University, Spain.

Atsalakis, G. S., & Valavanis, K. P. (in press). Surveying stock market forecasting techniques – Part II: Soft computing methods. *Expert Systems with Applications*.

Babuška, R., Van der Veen, P. J., & Kaymak, U. (2002). *Improved covariance estimation for Gustafson-Kessel Clustering*. Paper presented at IEEE International Conference on Fuzzy Systems, Honolulu, HI, USA, (pp. 1081-1085).

Babuška, R., & Verbruggen, H. (2003). Neuro-fuzzy methods for nonlinear system identification. *Annual Reviews in Control*, *27*, 73–85. doi:10.1016/S1367-5788(03)00009-9

Brown, M., & Harris, C. (1994). *Neuro-fuzzy adaptive modeling and control*. New York, NY: Prentice-Hall.

Chang, P. C., & Liu, C. H. (2008). A TSK type fuzzy rule based system for stock price prediction. *Expert Systems with Applications*, *34*, 135–144. doi:10.1016/j.eswa.2006.08.020

Chen, M. S. (1999). *A Comparative study of learning methods in tuning parameters of fuzzy membership functions*. Paper presented at IEEE SMC '99 Conference, Tokyo, Japan, (pp. 40-44).

Chi, S. C., Chen, H. P., & Cheng, C. H. (1999). *A forecasting approach for stock index future using Grey theory and neural networks*. Paper presented at IEEE International Joint Conference on Neural Networks, Washington, DC, USA, vol. 6, (pp. 3850-3855).

Chu, H. H., Chen, T. L., Cheng, C. H., & Huang, C. C. (2009). Fuzzy dual-factor time-series for stock index forecasting. *Expert Systems with Applications*, *36*, 165–171. doi:10.1016/j. eswa.2007.09.037

Emami, M. R., Turksen, I. B., & Goldenberg, A. A. (1998). Development of a systematic methodology of fuzzy logic modeling. *IEEE Transactions on Fuzzy Systems*, *6*(3), 346–361. doi:10.1109/91.705501

Fazel Zarandi, M. H. (1998). *Aggregate system analysis for prediction of tardiness and mixed zones of continuous casting with fuzzy methodology*. Doctoral dissertation, University of Toronto.

Fazel Zarandi, M. H., Rezaee, B., Turksen, I. B., & Neshat, E. (2009). A type-2 fuzzy rule-based expert system model for stock price analysis. *Expert Systems with Applications*, *36*, 139–154. doi:10.1016/j.eswa.2007.09.034

Jang, J.-S. R. (1993). ANFIS: Adaptive-network-based fuzzy inference systems. *IEEE Transactions on Systems, Man, and Cybernetics*, *23*(3), 665–685. doi:10.1109/21.256541

Jang, J.-S. R., & Mizutani, E. (1996). *Levenberg-Marquardt method for ANFIS learning*. Paper presented at Biennial Conference of the North American Fuzzy Information Processing Society, (pp. 87 -91).

Jang, J.-S. R., & Sun, C.-T. (1993). Functional equivalence between radial basis function networks and fuzzy inference systems. *IEEE Transactions on Neural Networks*, *4*(1), 156–159. doi:10.1109/72.182710

Jilani, T. A., & Burney, S. M. A. (2008). A refined fuzzy time series model for stock market forecasting. *Physica A*, *387*, 2857–2862. doi:10.1016/j.physa.2008.01.099

Kennedy, J., & Eberhart, R. C. (1995). *Particle swarm optimization*. Paper presented at IEEE int. Conf. Neural Networks, Perth, Australia, vol. IV, (pp. 1942-1948).

Kilic, K., Sproule, B., Turksen, I. B., & Naranjo, C. (2004). Pharmacokinetic application of fuzzy structure identification and reasoning. *Information Sciences*, *162*, 121–137. doi:10.1016/j.ins.2004.03.005

Kilic, K., Uncu, O., & Turksen, I. B. (2007). Comparison of different strategies of utilizing fuzzy clustering in structure identification. *Information Sciences*, *177*, 5153–5162. doi:10.1016/j.ins.2007.06.030

Kim, K., & Han, I. (1998). *Extracting trading rules from the multiple classifiers and technical indicators in stock market*. Paper presented at KMIS'98 International Conference.

Kim, Y. I., Kim, D. W., Lee, D., & Lee, K. H. (2004). A cluster validation index for GK cluster analysis based on relative degree of sharing. *Information Sciences*, *168*, 225–242. doi:10.1016/j.ins.2004.02.006

Krishnapuram, R. (1994). *Generation of membership functions via possibilistic clustering*. Paper presented at IEEE International Conference on Fuzzy Systems, 2, (pp. 902-908).

Kumar, M., & Garg, D. P. (2004). *Intelligent learning of fuzzy logic controllers via neural network and genetic algorithm*. Paper presented at JUSFA 2004 Japan – USA Symposium on Flexible Automation Denver, Colorado, (pp. 19-21).

Kuo, R. J., Chen, C. H., & Hwang, Y. C. (2001). An intelligent stock trading decision support system through integration of genetic algorithm based fuzzy neural network and artificial neural network. *Fuzzy Sets and Systems*, *118*, 21–24. doi:10.1016/S0165-0114(98)00399-6

Lee, J. W. (2001). *Stock price prediction using reinforcement learning*. Paper presented at IEEE International Joint Conference on Neural Networks, 1, (pp. 690–695).

Li, J., & Xu, J. (2009). A novel portfolio selection model in a hybrid uncertain environment. *Omega*, *37*, 439–449. doi:10.1016/j.omega.2007.06.002

Maertens, K., De Baerdemaeker, J., & Babuška, R. (2006). Genetic polynomial regression as input selection algorithm for non-linear identification. *Soft Computing*, *10*, 785–795. doi:10.1007/s00500-005-0008-8

Mascioli, F. M., Varazi, G. M., & Martinelli, G. (1997). *Constructive algorithm for neuro-fuzzy networks*. Paper presented at the Sixth IEEE International Conference Fuzzy Systems, Spain, Vol. 1, (pp. 459- 464).

Melek, W. W., Goldenberg, A. A., & Emami, M. R. (2005). A fuzzy noise-rejection data partitioning algorithm. *International Journal of Approximate Reasoning*, *38*, 1–17. doi:10.1016/j.ijar.2004.03.002

Parasopoulos, K. E., & Vrahatis, M. N. (2004). On the computation of all global minimizers through particle swarm optimization. *IEEE Transactions on Evolutionary Computation, 8*(3).

Parsopoulos, K. E., & Vrahatis, M. N. (2002). Particle swarm optimization method for constrained optimization problems. In Sincak, P., Vascak, J., Kvasnicka, V., & Pospichal, J. (Eds.), *Intelligent technologies--Theory and application: New trends in intelligent technologies- Frontiers in artificial intelligence and applications* (Vol. 76, pp. 214–220). IOS Press.

Pokropinska, A., & Scherer, R. (2008). Financial prediction with neuro-fuzzy systems. In Rutkowski, L. (Eds.), *Artificial intelligence and soft computing* (pp. 1120–1126). Springer-Verlag.

Scutte, J. F., Reinbolt, J. A., Fregly, B. J., Haftka, R. T., & George, A. D. (2004). Parallel global optimization with the particle swarm algorithm. *International Journal for Numerical Methods in Engineering, 61,* 2296–2315. doi:10.1002/nme.1149

Shi, Y. (2004). *Particle swarm optimization.* IEEE Neural Networks Society.

Sugeno, M., & Yasukawa, T. (1993). A fuzzy logic based approach to qualitative modeling. *IEEE Transactions on Fuzzy Systems, 1,* 7–31. doi:10.1109/TFUZZ.1993.390281

Tan, R. R. (2007). Hybrid evolutionary computation for the development of pollution prevention and control strategies. *Journal of Cleaner Production, 15,* 902–906. doi:10.1016/j.jclepro.2006.01.011

Tang, A. M., Quek, C., & Ng, G. S. (2005). GA-TSKfnn: Parameters tuning of fuzzy neural network using genetic algorithms. *Expert Systems with Applications, 29,* 769–781. doi:10.1016/j.eswa.2005.06.001

Teshnehlab, M., Aliyari Shoorehdeli, M., & Sedigh, A. K. (2008). *Novel hybrid learning for tuning ANFIS parameters as an identifiers using fuzzy PSO.* Paper presented at IEEE International Conference on Networking, Sensing and Control, Sanya, China, (pp. 111-116).

Thammano, A. (1999). Neuro-fuzzy model for stock market prediction. In C. H. Dagli, A. L. Buczak, J. Ghosh, M. J. Embrechts, O. Ersoy (1999). *Smart engineering system design: Neural networks, fuzzy logic, evolutionary programming, data mining, and complex systems.* Paper presented at the Artificial Neural Networks in Engineering Conference (ANNIE '99), (pp. 587–591). New York, NY: ASME Press.

Uncu, O., & Turksen, I. B. (2007). A novel feature selection approach: Combining feature wrappers and filters. *Information Sciences, 177,* 449–466. doi:10.1016/j.ins.2006.03.022

Wah, B. W., & Qian, M. (2002). *Constrained formulations and algorithms for stock price predictions using recurrent FIR neural networks.* Paper presented at Eighteenth National Conference on Artificial Intelligence, (pp. 211–216).

Wang, Y.-F. (2002). Predicting stock price using fuzzy grey prediction system. *Expert Systems with Applications, 22,* 33–39. doi:10.1016/S0957-4174(01)00047-1

# Chapter 32
# Hand Tremor Prediction and Classification Using Electromyogram Signals to Control Neuro–Motor Instability

**Koushik Bakshi**
*Jadavpur University, India*

**Sourav Chandra**
*Jadavpur University, India*

**Amit Konar**
*Jadavpur University, India.*

**D.N. Tibarewala**
*Jadavpur University, India*

## ABSTRACT

*This chapter provides a prototype design of a hand tremor compensator/controller to reduce the effect of the tremor to an external device/ apparatus, such as a magnetic pen for the patients suffering from Parkinson and similar diseases. It would also be effective for busy surgeons suffering from hand tremor due to muscle fatigue. Main emphasis in this chapter is given on the prediction of the tremor signal from the discrete samples of electromyogram data and tremor. The predicted signal is inverted in sign and added to the main tremor signal through a specially designed magnetic actuator carrying the external device, such as a magnetically driven pen or surgical instrument. Two different prediction algorithms, one based on neural nets and the other based on Kalman Filter have been designed, tested, and validated for the proposed application. A prototype model of the complete system was developed on an embedded platform. Further development on the basic model would be appropriate for field applications in controlling tremors of the subjects suffering from Parkinson and the like diseases.*

DOI: 10.4018/978-1-61350-429-1.ch032

# INTRODUCTION

McCarthy coined the name Artificial Intelligence (AI) in the famous 1956 Darmouth conference (Konar, 2000). Since its foundation the subject of AI has evolved through many phases. The early research in AI was confined in toy problems; but with the passage of time, AI has gradually been enriched with new theories, which found interesting applications in different spheres of human life and civilization.

Machine learning is one of the fundamental areas of research of the modern AI. Late 1980's has seen significant contribution of research in machine learning. The main stream research in machine learning gradually merged with statistical learning and pattern recognition algorithms over the last two decades.

People suffering from Parkinson's and the like diseases face difficulty in performing common tasks, such as writing, taking food etc. because of uncontrolled shaking of their hands and body parts. This chapter provides an interesting solution to this problem using the principles and techniques of AI and pattern recognition.

Hand motion control has always been an area of interest of the modern bio-mimetic robotics, bio-robotics and smart rehabilitation engineering. Hand motion in a sense can be classified into many types of actions depending upon their appearance. Origin of different type of movements also varies extensively, but grossly the movements are always classified into two types, intended or desired motion and other is tremor. One novel approach to control hand tremor is to predict the amplitude of the tremor around the principal plane of vibration, and add the predicted signal to the original tremor signal to reduce or nullify its effect.

The performance of the tremor compensation system mainly depends on the quality of prediction of tremor signal. Prediction of the compensatory signal at time t in general is considered as a linear combination of its n previous samples at time (t-T), (t-2T), ……..(t-nT), where T is the sampling interval. Thus apparently, the compensatory signal can be predicted from the last n previous samples of the tremor signal. Any standard linear prediction algorithm can be employed to estimate the compensatory signal from its previous n samples. Alternatively, a supervised neural learning algorithm can also be used to aid the linear estimation process.

Measurement of the tremor signal thus indeed is a fundamental step for the prediction process. An accelerometer is a device that senses acceleration and produces an output according to the linear displacement, it experiences. Thus measurement of tremor signal can be performed by an accelerometer. Recent research however demonstrate that Electromyogram (EMG), which is a simultaneous manifestation of neural control signal over muscle fibers (Wolf et al., 1996; De Luca et al., 1997; Haig et al., 1996; Pullman et al., 2000; Rechtien et al., 1999) is also a good source for tremor prediction (Lippold et al., 1970; Fox et al., 1970; Cameron et al., 1998; Widjaja et al., 2003; Veluvolu et al., 2007). In this chapter, we employed both accelerometer and the EMG signal for prediction of tremor signal.

Controlling the movement of an external device, such as a magnetic pen for people suffering from Parkinson's like diseases, is the primary problem addressed in this chapter. This needs an actuator to control the motion of the pen. We design magnetic actuator and a specialized device holder which can be controlled by a changing magnetic field in the desired direction of motion of the pen.

Finally realization of the complete tremor control system on an embedded platform would be an added problem to be undertaken here. The input of the embedded system would be the digitized previous n samples of EMG and tremor signals. The output of the embedded system would be the compensatory tremor signal, which would be transferred to the actuator through an actuator circuit.

The objective of this study is two fold. First, we examine the viability of the proposed tremor compensatory system. Second, we study the relative performance of both neural net based and Extended Kalman Filter based tremor compensation and realize the better one on the embedded platform.

Next section provides a brief overview on previous approaches to tremor compensation. Then we present the biological motivation of EMG-Tremor correlation and a brief outline of the design aspects. Neural net and Kalman Filter based compensation is also discussed in the following section. After that development of an embedded system is covered and experiment and performance analysis is given. Lastly conclusions are listed in the final section.

## PREVIEW OF LITERATURE

Remarkable progression on tremor compensation has been noticed in the research realm of biomedical engineering (Riviere et al., 1998). However most of these are about intriguing the physiological understanding of origin, effect on body system, and efficacy of different drugs on the compensation problem. The existing literatures hardly utilized AI, Pattern recognition technique to control tremor, especially in real time. The proposed work thus is unique and original as it considers tremor compensation/control in real time. History of research on tremor compensation can be broadly categorized into three main heads.

### Clinical and Physiological Study of Tremor

Research on clinical and physiological studies aimed at identifying the source of tremor signal, and designing appropriate clinical strategy, such as administration of drug or therapy, to relive patients from tremor. Some of the useful works in this regard include (Meara et al., 2000; Stiles et al., 1967; Elble et al., 1978; Hagbarth et al., 1979; Duval et al., 2003; McAuley et al., 2000; Timmer et al., 1993; Ramana et al., 2009; Kuzma

et al., 1965; Tourtellotte et al., 1965 ; Bishop et al., 1948; Robson et al., 1959; Sutton and Herrota, 1967; Smirnov et al., 2008; Boshes et al., 1968; Xinpu et al., 2008).

## Tremor Compensating Schemes Using AI and Machine Learning

The second category of the tremor compensation research (Nagayama et al., 1997; Riviere et al., 1997a; Riviere et al.,1997b) particularly deals with designing several learning algorithm and prediction algorithm. Some of the research work employed supervised neural network for tremor compensation. Later on some interesting research work on recurrent neural network are noted. Lastly Extended Kalman Filter (EKF) has also been used for some of the very interesting application (Singhal et al., 1989) giving very good accuracy to the prediction of the tremor.

## Tremor Compensating Devices & Hardware

Lastly researchers have focused on the tremor compensatory devices and different other aspects of them. They designed different actuators, considered the structural frameworks of different hardware, considering the acquisition of EMG signals and accelerometric signal, analog to digital conversion, then microcontrollers, digital to analog converters, actuator devices (Wei Tech Ang et al., 2003; Kexin et al., 2008).

## BIOLOGICAL BASIS OF CONSIDERING EMG SIGNALS FOR TREMOR COMPENSATION

Intended movement of our body part is a manifestation of simultaneous complex chemical, electrical and mechanical activity. It is a complex and precise control maneuver of nervous system, musculoskeletal system and associated sensory receptor. On the other hand, tremor basically originates because of the lack of synchronization in the control mechanism for this precise movements involving Central Nervous system (CNS, mainly brain), Peripheral Nervous System along with the musculo-skeletal systems.

The control signal first initiates in the Brain and propagates through specific nerve fiber to activate particular muscle actuator under controlled intervention of spinal cord. The process of voluntary muscle contraction is initiated by an alpha motor neuron (part of Autonomic Nervous System). A successful excitatory nerve impulse is transmitted to the muscle through the release of neurotransmitter molecule, which carries neural information between the nerve and muscle at neuromuscular junction. Figure 1 offers an idea of muscle control through a feedback system via the brain, the spinal cord and neuro-motors. This structure along with some other systems in the human body, control all those critical and precise sequencing of different processes and act basically as the main controller.

This signal then activates the excitation-contraction processes in the muscle system. The process will continue until stimulation of the muscle ceases. Spinal cord, associated nerve fibers and muscle actuator forms a stretch reflex arc.

The CNS excites the muscle and controls the force generated by the muscle by an automatic selection of appropriate motor units and their firing rates. As a consequence, the muscle generates a special pulse trains, informally called surface EMG (SEMG). EMG signal in fact refers to an electric potential field generated by the depolarization of the outer muscle-fiber membrane.

How tremor is generated from the muscle? Is it a regular phenomenon or a special circumstance? This would be clear simply from the pulses generated by the CNS and the response of the muscle in turn to this. Figure 2 demonstrates that during the first 2 cycles the response of the muscle is in tune with the source CNS activation, but in the third and the fourth cycle the time delays in muscle response are longer, which causes a non-uniform oscillation of the body part controlled by the muscle. Informally, the root cause of tremor

*Figure 1. (a) Showing the control of CNS and spinal nervous system on musculoskeletal system through motor unit and motor neurons, called alpha neurons, (b) Schematic representation of the motor Unit and the muscle fiber and activation phenomenon*

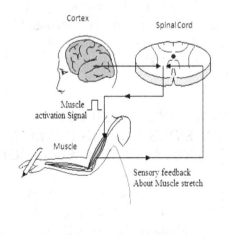

(a)　　　　　　　　　　(b)

*Figure 2. Absence of synchronization between the muscle activation signal and the muscle feedback response (inhibition signal)*

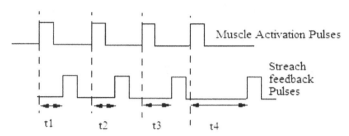

is lack of synchronization between the muscle activation input and muscle feedback response.

An interesting experiment to establish a good correlation between the SEMG and tremor is undertaken in our research laboratory at Jadavpur University. The details of the experiments go beyond the scope of the work. We just briefly point out the interesting results, which we would use throughout the rest of this chapter. We mount an accelerometer on the wrist and the SEMG sensor on a specific muscle on the forearm. The hand was shaken randomly, representing pseudo tremor, and the SEMG and the tremor were recorded. An analysis of the results of the muscle movement and SEMG indicates that there is a good correlation between the two sets of temporal data. The result is also evident from Figure 3.

One important issue that needs to be added here is that the researchers so far presumed that the tremor data and EMG are stationary, which however is not correct. This can be verified from a specialized plot often used to check the stationary nature of the signal. This is called a Quantile-Quantile (Q-Q) plot. The Q-Q plot given in Figure 4 reveals that both the SEMG and the tremor are non-stationary. Our approach of analysis thus would be different from the methods introduced by previous researchers. The details of the principle of tremor compensation from these two signals would be undertaken in the next section.

## PRINCIPLES AND FUNCTIONAL ARCHITECTURE OF THE TREMOR PREDICTION SYSTEM

It's apparent from section III that tremor signal has a good correlation with the EMG signal. Since tremor signal peaks appear after an average delay of 20ms of the EMG peaks, the EMG signal can be used to predict the tremor. Sometimes for low amplitude tremors, the peaks in EMG cannot be easily be detected. This motivated us to use EMG and tremor signal itself to predict tremor at time t. We here consider that the current tremor sample at time t is a linear combination of previous tremor samples and previous/current EMG samples. Linear adaptive filters/ neural algorithm can be used for the estimation of the coefficients of the EMG/ tremor samples in the present context. After the tremor signal at time t is predicted, we add the anti-phase of this predicted tremor signal to the actual tremor, through an actuator, thereby reducing the tremor amplitude. The above principle is schematically given in Figure 5.

The functional architecture of the tremor prediction /control system is given in Figure 6. Different units employed in this scheme can be described as follows.

An accelerometer is mounted on the palm to measure the tremor signal, while the EMG sensor placed on the arm gives a measure of the muscle movements. The analog EMG and tremor signal are passed through proper band pass filters and amplifiers, and then they are digitized by analog

*Figure 3. (a) the EMG, (b) the tremor, and (c) the combined plot of the EMG and the tremor to demonstrate correlation between them*

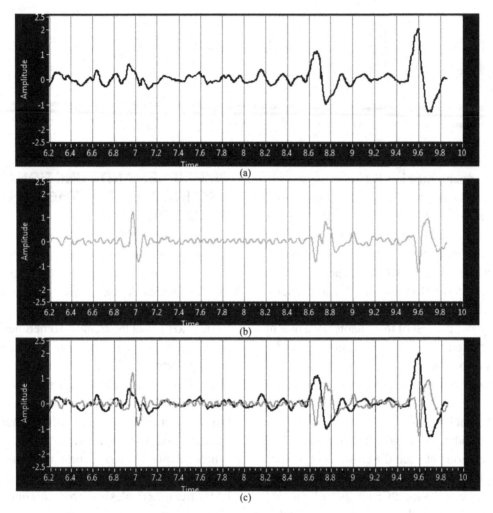

*Figure 4. (a): QQ plot of EMG signal. (b): QQ plot of the tremor signal.*

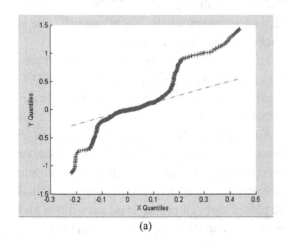
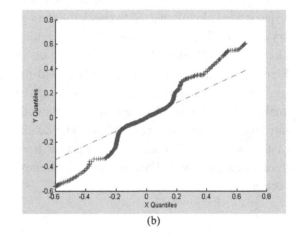

*Figure 5. The principle of tremor control*

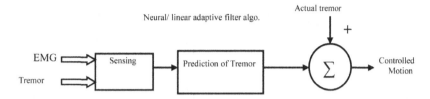

*Figure 6. Block diagram of Kalman based approach for fore-hand tremor estimation and compensation*

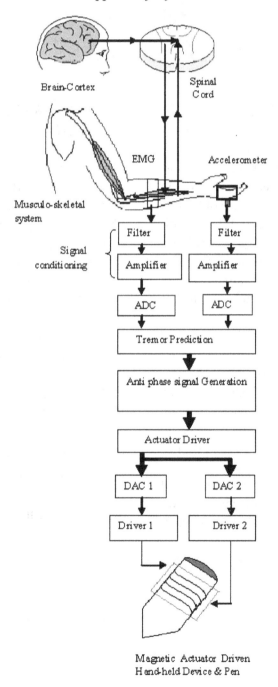

*Figure 7. Schematics of the driver circuit and the apparatus holder, actuator*

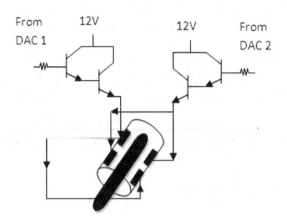

to digital converters (ADC). The digitized EMG and tremor data are fed to a computer for prediction of the current amplitude and sign of the tremor signal. An anti-phase signal generator just inverts the sign of the predicted tremor. The sign bit of the anti-phase signal selects one of the two digital to analog converters (DAC). If the anti-phase signal is positive, DAC1 is selected else DAC2 is selected. The magnitude part of the predicted tremor is then passed through the selected DAC and driver to ultimately transfer the signal to the actuator.

It may be added here that the actuator is a magnetically driven holder type of system to accommodate it to pen or like apparatus. The pen, for example, floats inside the cylindrical cage containing four magnetic pole pieces (Figure 7). Each transistorized driver circuit selects to diagonal pole pieces to control motion of the pen in the desired direction.

The most important module in the functional architecture is the tremor prediction unit. We would address tremor prediction by neural/digital filter algorithm in the next section.

## TREMOR PREDICTION BY NEURAL NET

The neural prediction algorithm includes a Radial Basis Function (RBF) layer followed by a Time Delayed Back Propagation neural network (TDBPNN). Tremor signal has been classified into nine classes depending on the type of movements. The tremor signal within a class is averaged (Figure 8 & 9) and the averaged sample values for each class are used to classify the cluster center of the RBF neurons.

The RBF layer has thus nine neurons. These neurons then select one of the nine TDBPNNs for the prediction of the tremor signal. The integration of the RBF layers and the TDBPNNs are shown in the following Figure 10 (a) and (b).

Let $\vec{P}$ be the input vector of $(1 \times 500)$ dimension, representing 500 samples of an unknown tremor signal. Let $\vec{C}_j$, j=1 to 9 be the 500 dimensional cluster center for 9 RBF neurons. The output of the RBF neuron j is given by

$$Output(j) = \exp(-\parallel \vec{P} - \vec{C}_j \parallel) \qquad (1)$$

When $\vec{C}_j \approx \vec{P}$, Output (j) approaches 1.

*Figure 8. Obtaining average of sample values from the EMG resulting in similar type of tremor. Nine tremor types were used, each type was recorded for ten times with 500 samples and average was taken to compute redial basis center.*

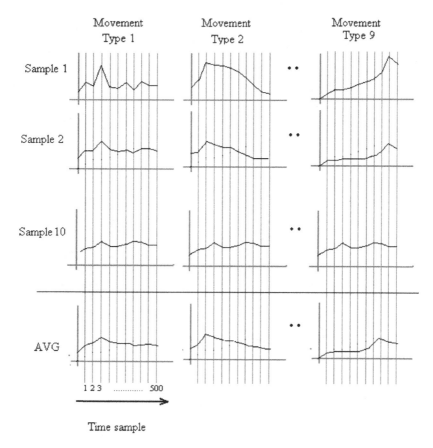

*Figure 9. Showing the cluster center for each RBF neuron*

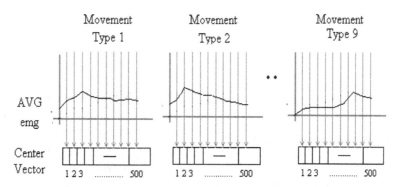

Thus an RBF having j out of 9 neurons in the RBF layer yields an output closest to 1. This neuron is one of 9 TDBPNNs. Each TDBPNN is pre-trained with signals under a single tremor class.

The schematic architecture of RBF-TDBPNN is given in the Figure 10 (a). In Figure 10 (b), the RBF layer is shown separately.

*Figure 10. (a) Structure of kernalised RBF network used for tremor classification & compensation, (b) schematic showing the RBF layer*

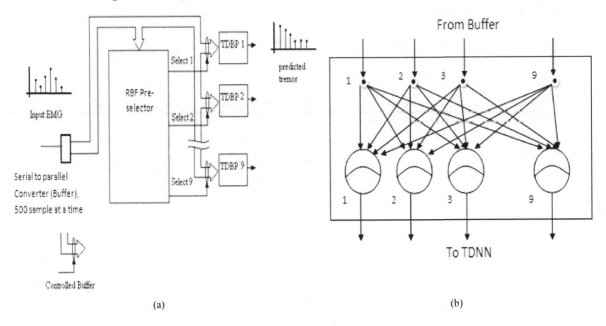

(a)　　　　　　　　　　　　　(b)

Let the output of the TDBPNN module be $y_j$ (n), then

$$y_j(n) = \varphi(\sum W(m) \cdot x(n-m) + b_j) \qquad (2)$$

where $W(m)$ is the weight to time sampled input x (n-m), $b_j$ is the bias term and $\varphi(.)$ is an sigmoid type activation function.

Let $d_j(n)$ be the desired signal of TDBPNN j at time n. Then the root mean squire error is given by

$$e_j(n) = \frac{1}{2}(d_j(n) - y_j(n))^2 . \qquad (3)$$

A cost function J is now defined as follows

$$J = \sum_{\forall n} e_j(n) = \frac{1}{2}\sum_{\forall n}(d_j(n) - y_j(n))^2. \qquad (4)$$

The weights $W_m$ Can be evaluated by steepest descent learning approach

$$W(m) = W(m-1) - \eta \frac{\partial J}{\partial W(m)}, \qquad (5)$$

where

$$\frac{\partial J}{\partial W(m)} = (-\frac{1}{2} \cdot 2)(d_j(n) - y_j(n)) \cdot \frac{\partial y_j(n)}{\partial \varphi} \frac{\partial \varphi}{\partial W(m)}$$

$$= -(d_j(n) - y_j(n)) \cdot y_j(n) \cdot (1 - y_j(n)) \cdot x(n-m), \qquad (6)$$

and $\Box$, the learning rate is in (0,1).

Each TDBPNN is trained with EMG signal corresponding to the respective class as include, and tremor signal of the same class as the output. Both the tremor and EMG signals are sampled at 1kHz frequency, and averages over the sample from the same class are taken for both EMG and tremor signal (Figure 8 and 9). Thus each TDB-PNN has 500 inputs and 500 hundred outputs, and the steepest descent learning rule is used to adopt weight till convergence in weight is noticed. The training is done offline. During the application phase, an unknown input EMG signal is mapped to the predicted samples using the TDBPNN.

## TREMOR PREDICTION BY EXTENDED KALMAN FILTER

Kalman filter employs a linear recurrent equation for state estimation from a given set of measurements of a plant. It attempts to minimize estimation error (noise) and measurement error (noise), so as to improve the prediction gradually with new measurement inputs in discrete time steps. Several formulations of the Kalman filter are prevalent in the literature (Bishop, G.W.). The main advantage of Kalman filter over existing Least Square algorithms lies in the phenomena that the filter does not require all the time-staggered measurements together, but allows correction in estimation by sequential submission of measurements. This particular feature of Kalman filter made it appropriate for real time estimation. The Extended Kalman Filter (EKF) is generally used for prediction of the estimator of a non-linear plant. The nonlinear dynamics and measurement equations of the plant are first linearized using Taylor's series, so that the resulting equations can subsequently be used to predict the estimator vector by EKF. A brief review of discrete Kalman filter is introduced here.

Let the state $\mathbf{X}_k$ of a Process is to be estimated. The dynamics of the process is governed by the linear stochastic difference equation such that $\mathbf{X} \in \mathbf{R}^n$, where R is the set of real numbers and 'n'.

$$\mathbf{X}_k = \mathbf{A}\mathbf{X}_{k-1} + \mathbf{B}\mathbf{U}_{k-1} + \mathbf{W}_{k-1} \qquad (7)$$

This equation (7) is called the **Process Equation**. Here

$\mathbf{W} \equiv$ random variable, representing the process noise; white and Gaussian in nature with normal probability distribution.

$\mathbf{A} \equiv \mathbf{(n\ x\ n)}$; transition matrix which relates the state at the previous time step $\mathbf{(k-1)}$ to the state at the current step $\mathbf{k}$, along with a driving function $\mathbf{U}$ and process noise $\mathbf{W}_k$.

$\mathbf{U} \equiv \mathbf{optional}$ control input to the state $\mathbf{X}_k$; $\mathbf{U} \in \mathbf{R}^l$

$\mathbf{B} \equiv \mathbf{(n\ x\ l)}$; matrix which relates the optional control input $\mathbf{U}$ to the state $\mathbf{X}_k$.

Then when the system state is measured with some kind of sensors or transducers, the measurement $\mathbf{Z}$ is **expressed** as

$$\mathbf{Z}_k = \mathbf{H}\mathbf{X}_k + \mathbf{V}_k \qquad (8)$$

Where,

$$\mathbf{Z} \equiv \mathbf{Z} \in \mathbf{R}^m$$

$\mathbf{H} \equiv \mathbf{(m\ x\ n)}$; matrix which relates the state $\mathbf{X}$ to the measurement $\mathbf{Z}_k$

$\mathbf{V} \equiv$ random variable, representing the measurement noise, white and Gaussian in nature with normal probability distribution.

$\mathbf{W}, \mathbf{V}$ are assumed to be independent of each other. So, according to the assumption,

$$p(\mathbf{W}) \approx N(\mathbf{0}, \mathbf{Q}) \qquad (9)$$

$$p(\mathbf{V}) \approx N(\mathbf{0}, \mathbf{R}) \qquad (10)$$

Here $\mathbf{Q}$ and $\mathbf{R}$ are corresponding **Noise Covariance Matrices**. These two noise covariance matrices might change with each time instance or measurement iteration, but for simplicity of understanding and implementation they are considered as constant and invariant. The matrices $\mathbf{A}$, $\mathbf{B}$ and $\mathbf{H}$ might change with each time iteration or measurement, but it is also assumed to be constant.

Now again, let $\tilde{\mathbf{X}}_K$ be our *a priori* state estimate at instance $\mathbf{k}$ given the knowledge of the process prior to step $\mathbf{k}$, and $\hat{\mathbf{X}}_K \in \mathbf{R}^n$ be our *a posteriori* state estimate at step $\mathbf{k}$ given measurement $Z_k$. Then *a priori* and *a posteriori* estimate errors come as

$$\tilde{e}_k \equiv X_k - \tilde{X}_k \tag{11}$$

$$\hat{e}_k \equiv X_k - \hat{X}_k \tag{12}$$

and the *a priori* estimate error covariance is,

$$\tilde{P}_k = E[\tilde{e}_k \tilde{e}_k^T] \tag{13}$$

The *a posteriori* estimate error covariance is

$$\hat{P}_k = E[\hat{e}_k \hat{e}_k^T] \tag{14}$$

Kalman Filter equations are derived as an *a posteriori* state estimate $\hat{X}_K$ which is a linear combination of an *a priori* estimate $\tilde{X}_K$ and a weighted difference between an actual measurement $Z_K$ and a measurement prediction $H\tilde{X}_K$ as shown below in (15).

$$\hat{X}_K = \tilde{X}_K + K(Z_K - H\tilde{X}_K) \tag{15}$$

The difference $(Z_K - H\tilde{X}_K)$ in (15) is called the **Measurement Innovation**, or the **Residual.** This innovation term indicates the difference between the predicted measurement and the actual measurement.

The matrix **K (m x n)** in (15) is chosen to be the **Kalman Gain** that minimizes the *a posteriori* error covariance (14). This optimization is accomplished by first substituting (15) into the above definition for $e_k$, substituting that into (14), performing the indicated expectations, taking the derivative of the trace of the result with respect to **K**, setting that result equal to zero, and then solving for **K**. One form of the resulting **K** that minimizes (14) is given by

$$K_K = \tilde{P}_K H^T (HP_K H^T + R)^{-1} \tag{16}$$

This Kalman Filter Gain is then used to compute *a posteriori* error covariance matrix and *a posteriori state* estimate as already described.

## The Algorithm for Discrete Kalman Filtering

The algorithm for the Kalman filter falls into two steps: prediction state and corrector state. It can be summarized for each iteration as below.

## Step 1: Prediction of State of the System and Error Covariance-- A Priori Estimates

Predictor equations are also called time update equations as it updates the state. It projects the state and covariance estimates forward from time step $(k - 1)$ to step **k.** Initial conditions for these estimates are determined from its previous condition of the same parameters.

$$\tilde{X}_K = A \hat{X}_{K-1} + BU_K$$

$$\tilde{P}_K = A\hat{P}_{K-1}A^T + Q$$

## Step 2: Correction of a Priori Estimates-- A Posteriori Estimate Determination

The measurement update equations are responsible for correction through the feedback—i.e. for incorporating a new measurement into the *a priori* estimate to obtain an improved *a posteriori* estimate. First step here is to calculate Kalman gain and measurement data as feedback control. Then generation of an *a posteriori* state estimate by incorporating linearly Kalman gain, the measurement and the *a priori* state estimates from the previous step. The final step is to obtain an *a*

*Table 1. Parameters of EKF in the context of tremor prediction*

---

*Let,*

$Y_K$ = Measurement Vector at instance k $\equiv Z_K$

$V_k$ = Measurement noise vector at time instance k

H = System Matrix

$W_k$ = Process Noise Vector at instance k

$EP_k$ = Expected/ Projected Error Co-variance matrix at instance k $\equiv \tilde{P}_K$

$K_k$ = Kalman Filter Gain at instance k

$ET_k$ = Expected/ Projected tremor at instance k $\equiv \tilde{X}_K$

$CT_k$ = Corrected/ a posterior tremor at instance k $\equiv \hat{X}_K$

$CP_k$ = Corrected Eorror Covariance at instance k $\equiv \hat{P}_K$

$T_k$ = Tremor (signal at instance k) $\equiv X_K$

$E_k$ = EMG (signal at instance k) $\equiv U_K$

A, B = Real symetric matrices, or transition matrices with definte dimension as required.

[Value of these two transition matrices depends on the present states of the allied variables]

R = Variance Matrix of process noise $W_k$

Q = vaiance matrix of measurment noise $V_k$

---

*posteriori* error covariance estimate. The corresponding steps are formulated mathematically as

$$\mathbf{K_K} = \tilde{\mathbf{P}}_K \mathbf{H}^T (\mathbf{H}\tilde{\mathbf{P}}_K \mathbf{H}^T + \mathbf{R})^{-1}$$

$$\hat{\mathbf{X}}_K = \tilde{\mathbf{X}}_K + \mathbf{K}_K(\mathbf{Z}_K - \mathbf{H}\tilde{\mathbf{X}}_K)$$

$$\hat{\mathbf{P}}_K = (\mathbf{I} - \mathbf{K}_K\mathbf{H})\tilde{\mathbf{P}}_K$$

Thus the final estimation algorithm resembles that of a *predictor-corrector* algorithm for solving numerical problems.

We now define the parameters of EKF in the context of tremor prediction (Table 1). Corresponding terms as mentioned in Kalman Filter are also included in the right side for better readability.

So for tremor prediction, the process equation and the measurement equation are respectively as

$$\mathbf{T_K} = \mathbf{f}\left(\mathbf{T_{K-i}}, \mathbf{E_K}, \mathbf{W}\right) \text{ for i=1,2,3 (k-1).} \quad (17)$$

$$\mathbf{Z_K} = \mathbf{f}\left(\mathbf{T_K}, \mathbf{V}\right) \text{ for k=1,2} \quad (18)$$

These two equations are taken in EKF in a linearised version and the basic flowchart of EKF for tremor prediction is given in the following figure (Figure 11).

## Filter Parameters and Tuning

It is indeed important to note that the the measurement variable and estimator are of one dimensional as presented in this article. Thus the vector-matrix equations are transformed to algebraic equation.

*Figure 11. The flowchart of EKF for tremor prediction. It is submitted with tremor signal with $T_{k-1}$ and EMG samples $E_k$. The loop is iterated until the modulus of element of $K_k$ is less than a predefined positive constant $\square$. The EKF returns estimated tremor signal $CT_k$.*

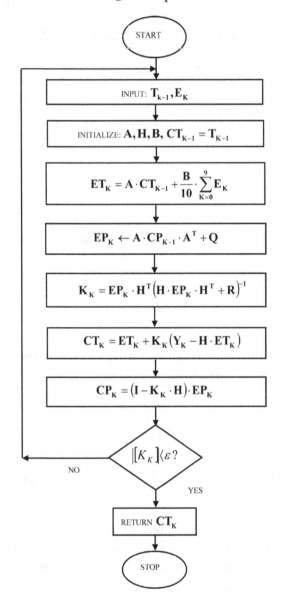

values are taken as input. Then according to the difference equations 17 and 18 and values of those samples, A, B and H are initialized. Then the corrected tremor's value initialization is done with previous tremor samples. The measurement noise covariance is measured prior to execution of the filter algorithm. The measurement error covariance is generally assigned by taking some off-line sample measurements and calculating the variance of the measurement noise.

The determination of the process noise covariance is difficult as the dynamics of the underlying system is not known. Here a random variable is assigned to satisfy the process equation offline. Superior filter performance (statistically speaking) can be obtained by tuning the filter parameters. The tuning can be performed off-line, frequently with the help of another Kalman filter in a process, termed as system identification.

In another approach, we have tried to initialize scalar parameters A, B and H randomly and then use the Least Square Optimization technique for the resulting error to get the optimized value of those parameters. For this the value range are used as between -10 to +10, which is also what we have seen in our first approach. Then with these random values, we have started the Kalman filter algorithm and got the final estimate of tremor. The resulting error squares between the estimated value and the actual value are taken for hundred samples and stored. Then minimum of theses error square is searched for and the corresponding value for the parameters is taken as the optimizing solution for their value. The pseudocode for the above algorithm can be presented as in Box 1.

This method also showed quite a good response for the estimation process, which is displayed later.

Now, often the measurement error and process noise does not remain constant. It changes dynamically during filter operation. The Kalman filter and more precisely the Kalman Gain take care of it to adjust to different dynamics of the system itself.

However, for convenience, we would prefer to use the same EKF equations without any change in structure.

In the actual implementation of the filter, first the tremor sample value and EMG sample

*Algorithm 1.*

```
Pseudocode for A, B, H Determination

    Begin
        Err-Sq-Sum (i)=0 for all i;
          for i=1 to 50;
            for k=1 to 100;
              initialize A_i, B_i, H_i randomly between -10 to +10;
              run Kalman filter algorithm (as indicated in Figure 11.);
              compute error square, ES(k)= (CT_k - T_k)²;
              Err-Sq-Sum(i)= Err-Sq-Sum(i) + ES(k);
            end for ;
          end for;
         if   Err-Sq-Sum(i) < = Err-Sq-Sum(j)   for all i, j =1 to 50
        then A= A_i, B=B_i, H=H_i ;
        End;
```

## EMBEDDED REALIZATION OF THE TREMOR CONTROLLER

The complete architecture of the tremor controller is realized into prototype platform. First it is realized on a laptop with additional boards for sensor, actuator, ADC, & DAC, and analog boards for amplifier filter and driver circuit once the prototype model get acceptable performance we realize system on PIC microcontroller platform with PC interface. A brief outline to the second prototype model is given in the Figure 12. Here the PIC boards include the PIC processor, Universal Asynchronous Receiver Transmitter (UART), and two ADCs. The PIC board receives the EMG and the tremor signal, Samples and digitizes it in ADC of PIC processor and sends them to the PC through an RS 232 serial interface. The PC predicts the tremor signal by EKF, inverts it, and returns the same to the PIC board.

The PIC processor now acts as Pulse with modulator (PWM). The on-time of the pulses is proportional to the positive of the pwm signal. When the PWM signal is negative, the off time of the output square wave is proportional to the

magnitude of the predicted signal. Thus for a given frequency of the output, the pulse width of the output signal is modulated based on the sign and the magnitude of the predicted tremor. The modulated signal is passed through a low pass filter (LPF), and amplified the driver separates the positive and the negative half of the LPF output, and submits the positive and the negative halves to two diagonal coils of the magnetic actuator system (Figure 12 and 13).

## EXPERIMENTS AND RESULTS

After the Hardware and software realization of the overall system was complete we went for the experimentation with real tremor signal. A real human subject was used here in this present context to measure the tremor signal generated from the forearm muscle that causes the upper limb wrist tremor (as we have focused to wrist tremor) on the hand. We have wrapped the EMG sensors at the proper forearm muscle (with the help of anatomy specialist) near the elbow (Figure 14), and also the accelerometer in the palm region

*Figure 12. Schematics showing the overall integration of different system parts and PIC based embedded system to form the final compensatory device*

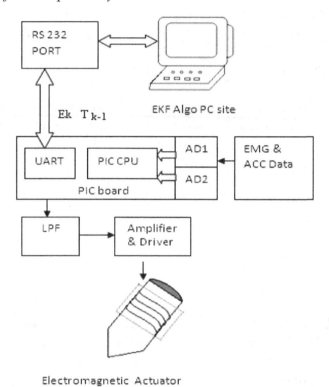

*Figure 13. (a) Schematics of the four pole magnetic actuator driven holding device, (b) the fabricated prototype*

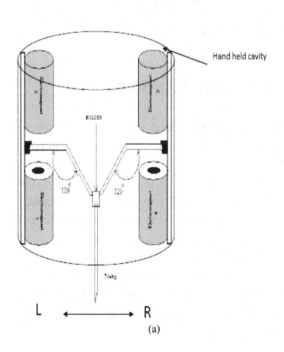

(a)  (b)

*Figure 14. Showing experimental set up for tremor prediction*

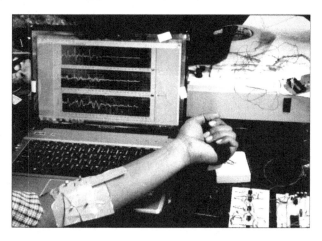

of the human subject. Because of hand tremor, the accelerometer generates electrical signal, the magnitude of which is proportional to the tremor (on that specific direction) and the EMG signal which is generated by the muscle which is also measured by the EMG sensors. Both the signals are then transferred to ADC and the rest of the hardware is utilized as discussed previously.

In Figure 14, we note three waveforms on the screen. Top waveform represents EMG The second one refers to the accelerometer signal and the third one is the predicted tremor signal. Actually we predicted the tremor signal by two ways as already discussed; one is neural network and the second one by Extended Kalman Filtering. To make sense how the performance of the process can be compared we just considered the plot of the EMG signal, the tremor signal and the predicted tremor signal. It is noted that the predicted tremor signal in this figure is almost similar with the real tremor signal but there exists a high frequency noise around the main contour of the tremor signal. High frequency noise can be filtered and we can get rid of this easily by low pass filter that was realized in a hardware circuit before the power amplification. To study the performance of the overall system we made a regression analysis, the regression analysis evaluates the predicted tremor signal with the actual tremor

signal and we fitted it by a straight line plot we found that the most of the point of the predicted tremor verses the real tremor signal falls on or around the regression line (Figure 15). And the root Mean Square error of the regression we found is very small of the order 0.00042.

When the same thing was realized with extended Kalman Filter we got slightly different result and we found that the EKF provides root mean squire error much less that of the neural net. In our actual realization in the hybrid PIC platform we implemented the Kalman Filter system (Figure 16).

## CONCLUSION

The stipulation of this idea of hand held tremor compensation device was obsessed by the demand of separate cluster of society that differs from the general mass, in needs & application. A Parkinson's disease patient needs a usual daily life with freedom from hand tremor. Aged Medical Surgeon demands a more accurate tooltip holder that gives the power of precise surgical abilities. A Business Executive needs to stabilize his handheld laser pointer in time of his projected demonstration For all these & similar type of requirements, the custom made handheld tremor compensation

*Figure 15. (a) Input EMG, (b) Actual tremor, (c) Predicted tremor, (d) Regression analysis*

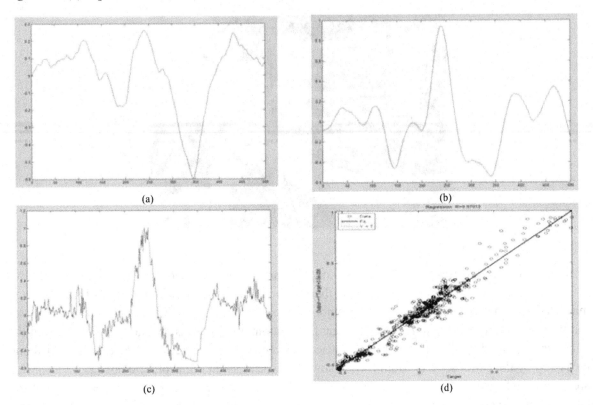

*Figure 16. (a) Input EMG, (b) Actual tremor, (c) Predicted tremor*

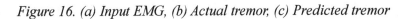

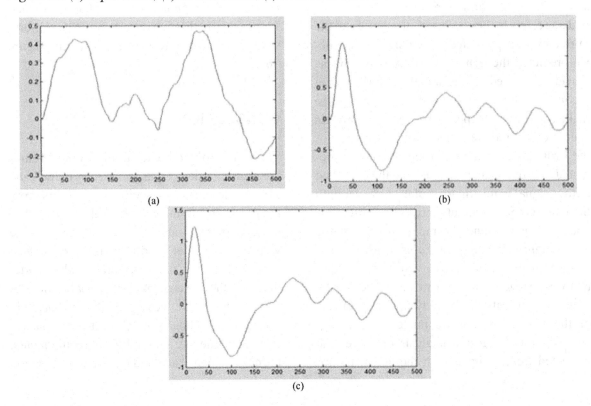

device as reported here should proved to be an appropriate aid.

Realization of conventional engineering approaches in the area of hand tremor compensation was been a constant effort of this study. Hand tremor compensation research domain is not a compact & distinct scientific area. It demands a continuous & profound attachment of Biological Science, Fundamentals of Mechanics and a paramount conjunction of Applied Electronics as well. As a domain of engineering application, foremost intensions of this study was to find out a custom made device starting from the mechanical (accelerometric) and electrophysiological (SEMG) sensing to Actuator design & drive it through a structured novel intelligent embedded algorithm.

The footprints of the previous studies show that few works have been done to predict the tremor from the EMG. All the previous work in a brief with advancement and the way it has evolved has been reported comprehensively. A thorough improvisation of biological aspect of tremor generation was also demanded by this study. Technical feasibility can be only assessed after a proper attachment of the biomedical origin of tremor that has been documented. The whole set up depends upon these fundamental improvisations. In one area, the Artificial Neural Net is used to predict the tremor. The conventional architecture performance was not up to the mark, a smart hybrid karnelised RBF Time delayed ANN is proposed and implemented in MATLAB platform. It reflects a promising improvement. A hardwired version of this network is likely to work. The signals were processed in LABVIEW for study purpose, primarily revealed two important facts. Firstly, there is a time lag between the EMG and consecutive tremor. The second is the morphological similarity among the accelerometer signal and the first derivative of the EMG. A further study in this area can open a new domain of research involving rotational limb movements and surface electromyographic signal satisfactorily in real-time, but it needs to be developed.

## REFERENCES

Ang, W. T., Khosla, P. K., & Riviere, C. N. (2003). Design of all-accelerometer inertial measurement unit for tremor sensing in hand-held microsurgical instrument. *Proceedings of the 2003 IEEE international Conference on Robotics & Automation,* Taipei, Taixao, September 14-19.

Basmajian, J. V., & De Luca, C. (1985). *Muscles alive: Their functions revealed by electromyography.* Williams & Wilkins.

Bishop, G. W., Clare, M. H., & Price, J. (1948). Patterns of tremor in normal and pathological conditions. *Journal of Applied Physiology, 1,* 123–147.

Boshes, B., Herota, T., & Klein, K. (1968). Further observations in tremor mechanisms in Parkinsonism. *Transactions of the American Neurological Association, 1,* 158–162.

Christian, D., Sadikot, A. F., & Panisset, M. (2003). The detection of tremor during slow alternating movements performed by patients with early Parkinson's disease. [Springer-Verlag.]. *Experimental Brain Research, 154,* 395–398.

David, A. (1985). *Biomechanics IX (Vol. 1).* Human Kinetics Publishers.

Dirgo, C. (2008). *Tremor.* Onyx Books.

Elble, R. J., & Randall, J. E. (1978). Mechanistic components of normal hand tremor. *Electroencephalography and Clinical Neurophysiology, 44,* 72–82. doi:10.1016/0013-4694(78)90106-2

Findley, L. J. (1994). *Handbook of tremor disorders.* M. Dekker.

Fox, J. R., & Randall, J. E. (1970). Relationship between forearm tremor and the biceps electromyogram. *Journal of Applied Physiology, 29.*

George, W. B. (2004). *Neurology in clinical practice: Principles of diagnosis and management.* Taylor & Francis.

Grewal, M. S., & Andrews, A. P. (2008). *Kalman filtering: Theory and practice using Matlab*. New Jersey: John Wiley & Sons. Inc.

Hagbarth, K. E., & Young, R. R. (1979). Participation of the stretch reflex in human physiological tremor. *Brain, 102,* 509–526. doi:10.1093/brain/102.3.509

Haig, A. J., Geblum, J. B., Rechtien, J. J., & Gitter, A. J. (1996). Technology assessment: The use of surface EMG in the diagnosis and treatment of nerve and muscle disorders. *Muscle & Nerve,* 392–395. doi:10.1002/(SICI)1097-4598(199603)19:3<392::AID-MUS21>3.0.CO;2-T

Hallett, M. (2003). *Movement disorders*. Elsevier Health Sciences.

Haykin, S. (1999). *Neural networks: A comprehensive foundation*. New Delhi, India: Prentice Hall.

Herota, T. (1967). The variation of hand tremor with force in healthy subjects. *The Journal of Physiology, 191,* 699–711.

Itaru, N., & Yosnino, T. (1997). An analysis of the chaotic transition of odel muscle tremor mechanism obtained by artificial neural network, *Journal of Neuroscience Methods*.

Jankovic, J. (2009). Movement disorders. *Issue of Neurologic Clinics*. Saunders.

Jankovic, J., & Tolosa, E. (2007). *Parkinson's disease and movement disorders*. Lippincott Williams & Wilkins.

Kuzma, J. W., Tourtellotte, W. W., & Remington, R. D. (1965). Quantitative clinical neurological testing. *Journal of Chronic Diseases, 18*.

Lippold, O. C. J. (1970). Oscillations in the stretch reflex are and the origin of the rhythmical component of physiological tremor. *Journal of Physiology*. (London).

Luca, D. (1997). The use of surface electromyography in biomechanics. *Journal of Applied Biomechanics, 13,* 135–163.

Marsden, D. C., & Stanley, F. (1982). *Movement disorders*. Butterworth Scientific.

Mazidi, M. A., McKinlay, R., & Causey, D. (2008). *PIC microcontroller*. New Delhi, India: Pearson Education.

McAuley, J. H., & Marsden, C. D. (2000). Physiological and pathological tremors and rhythmic central motor control. (Oxford University Press.). *Brain, 123*(8), 1545–1567. doi:10.1093/brain/123.8.1545

Meara, J., & Koller, W. C. (2000). *Parkinson's disease and Parkinsonism in the elderly*. The press syndicate of the University of Cambridge.

Nordin, M., & Frankel, V. H. (2001). *Basic biomechanics of the musculoskeletal system*. Lippincott Williams & Wilkins.

Plumb, M., & Bain, P. (2007). *Essential tremor: The facts*. Oxford University Press.

Pullman, S. L., Goodin, D. S., Marquinez, A. I., Tabbal, S., & Rubin, M. (2000). Clinical utility of surface EMG. *Report of the Therapeutics And Technology Assessment Subcommittee of the American Academy of Neurology, 55*.

Rechtien, J., Gelblum, B., Haig, A., & Gitter, A. (1999). Technology review: Dynamic electromyography in gait and motion analysis. *Muscle & Nerve, 22*(Suppl), S233–S238.

Riviere, C. N., & Khosla, P. K. (1997b). Augmenting the human-machine interface: Improving manual accuracy. *Proceedings of the IEEE International Conference on Robotics and Automation,* Albuquerque, New Mexico, 20-25 April.

Riviere, C. N., Reich, S. G., & Thakor, N. V. (1997a). Adaptive Fourier modeling for quantification of tremor. *Journal of Neuroscience Methods*, *74*(1), 77–87. doi:10.1016/S0165-0270(97)02263-2

Riviere, C. N., Scott, R., & Thakor, N. V. (1998). Adaptive canceling of physiological tremor for improved precision in microsurgery. *IEEE Transactions on Bio-Medical Engineering*, *45*(7). doi:10.1109/10.686791

Robson, J. G. (1959). The effect of loading upon the frequency of muscle tremor. *The Journal of Physiology*, 149.

Singhal, S., & Wu, L. (1989). Training multilayer perceptrons with the extended Kalman algorithm. In Touretzky, D. S. (Ed.), *Advances in neural information processing systems, 1* (pp. 133–140). Los Altos, CA: Morgan Kauffman.

Smirnov, D. A., Barnikol, U. B., Barnikol, T. T., Bezruchko, B. P., Hauptmann, C., Bührle, C., … Tass, P. A. (2008). The generation of Parkinsonian tremor as revealed by directional coupling analysis. *IOP, July*.

Stergiou, N. (2004). *Innovative analyses of human movement*. Human Kinetics.

Stiles, R. N., & Randall, J. E. (1967). Mechanical factors in human tremor frequency. *Journal of Applied Physiology*, *23*(3), 324–330.

Sutton, G. G., & Sykes, K. (1967). The effect of withdrawal of visual presentation of errors upon the frequency spectrum of tremor in a manual task. *The Journal of Physiology*, *190*, 281–283.

Timmer, J., Gantert, C., Deuschl, G., & Honerkamp, J. (1993). Characteristics of hand tremor time series. (Springer-Verlag.). *Biological Cybernetics*, 70.

Tourtellotte, W. W. (1965). Quantitative clinical neurological testing. *Annals of the New York Academy of Sciences*, *122*, 480–505. doi:10.1111/j.1749-6632.1965.tb20231.x

Veluvolu, K. C., Tan, U. X., Latt, W. T., & Shee, C. Y. (2007). Bandlimited multiple Fourier linear combiner for real-time tremor compensation. *Proceedings of the 29th Annual International Conference of the IEEE EMBS*, Cité Internationale, Lyon, France August 23-26.

Vinjamuri, R., Crammond, D. J., & Kondziolka, D. (2009). Extraction of sources of tremor in hand movements of patients with movement disorders. *IEEE Transactions on Information Technology in Biomedicine*, 13.

Widjaja, F., Shee, C. Y., Latt, W. T., Au, W. L., Poignet, P., & Ang, W. T. (2003). Kalman filtering of accelerometer and electromyography (EMG) data in pathological tremor sensing system. *Proceedings of the 2003 IEEE International Conference on Robotics & Automation*, Taipei, Taixao.

Wolf, W. (1996). The EMG as a window to the brain: Signal processing tools to enhance the view. In Gath, I., & Inbar, G. (Eds.), *Advances in processing and pattern analysis of biological signals* (pp. 339–356). New York, NY: Plenum Press.

Xing, K., Xu, Q., He, J., Wang, Y., Zhongwei, L., & Huang, Z. (2008). A wearable device for repetitive hand therapy. *Proceedings of the 2nd Biennial IEEE/RAS-EMBS International Conference on Biomedical Robotics and Biomechatronics*, Scottsdale, AZ, USA.

Xinpu, C., & Xiangyang, Z. (2008). A novel spectral analysis method of EMG feature extraction for wrist motions recognition. In *Proceedings of 2nd Biennial IEEE/RAS-EMBS International Conference on Biomedical Robotics and Biomechatronics*, Scottsdale, AZ, USA.

# KEY TERMS AND DEFINITIONS

**Electromyogram:** Electrical signals of muscle fiber, in microvolt to millivolt range. EMG originates due to activation of the muscle fibers by nerve stimulus in human body.

**Embedded System:** An embedded system is a computer system designed to perform one or a few dedicated functions often with real-time computing constraints. It is embedded as part of a complete device often including hardware and mechanical parts.

**Kalman Filter:** The Kalman Filter (KF) is an algorithm which provides a recursive solution to an estimation process.

**Parkinson's Disease:** A progressive nervous disease occurring most often after the age of 50, associated with the destruction of brain cells and characterized by muscular tremor, slowing of movement, partial facial paralysis, peculiarity of gait and posture, and weakness.

**Radial Basis Neural Network Switched Back Propagation Neural Network:** This is a two stage neural net. The first stage acts as a switching section depending on some criterion and fires the appropriate Back Propagation Neural Network, attached in the next section of the neural net.

**Tremor:** Unwanted vibration of human body parts due to pathological conditions and fatigue.

## APPENDIX: FURTHER READINGS

Principle of EMG (or SEMG) signal and tremor generation always remained the interest of the biologists since the beginning. There are numerous literatures available where the biological basis of understanding these two phenomena are explained (Tourtellotte et al., 1965; Bishop et al., 1948). Basmajian (1985) demonstrated the basics of the muscle movement and the manifestation of its electrical signal, the EMG. The recent contributions of Hallett (2003), Stergiou (2004), Nordin and Frankel (2001)Marsden and Stanley (1982), Dirgo (2008), Plumb and Bain (2007), Jankovic and Tolosa (2007), and Jankovic (2009) introduces the engineering approach of understanding the same problem from a system analysis point of view and this has lead to novel research findings.

Different approaches of tremor compensation are discussed in Wei Tech Ang et al. (2003), Riviere et al. (1997a,b), and Kexin et al. (2008). A methodical reading of these materials would aid the readers to develop a clear understanding of different tremor compensation approaches and henceforth new ideas of better tremor management and different methodologies can take its shape.

Neural network (RBF TDBPNN) and Kalman filtering has been used here, as the main framework of the algorithm for tremor prediction and classification. An introduction to this is available in (Konar, 2005). RBF TDBPNN has never been used before in tremor compensation. Haykins (1997) provides a comprehensive account on TDBPNN and RBF neural net structures. Kalman filtering has been quite extensively used in almost every sphere of engineering problems where an estimation of the process state is required. It does not only give an estimation of the state of the system, along with its processing it provides high ratio of noise cancellation with respect to other processing algorithms. Reading Grewal et al. (2008) gives a detailed account of Kalman filtering technique.

Mazidi et al. (2008) introduces the application of embedded processor and particularly PIC microcontroller.

# Compilation of References

Abbod, M. F., & Linkens, D. A. (1998). Anaesthesia monitoring and control using fuzzy logic fusion. *J. Biomed. Eng. – Appl. Basis Commun. Special Issue on Control Methods in Anaesthesia, 10*(4), 225–235.

Abbod, M. F., von Keyserlingk, D. G., Linkens, D. A., & Mahfouf, M. (2001). Survey of utilisation of fuzzy technology in medicine and healthcare. *Fuzzy Sets and Systems, 120,* 331–349. doi:10.1016/S0165-0114(99)00148-7

Abd-Almaged, W., Smith, W., & Ramadan, S. (2003). Kernel snakes: Non-parametric active contour models. In *Proceedings of IEEE International Conference on Systems, Man, and Cybernetics* (vol. 1, pp. 240-244).

Abraham, A. (2004). Meta-learning evolutionary artificial neural networks. *Neurocomputing, 56c,* 1–38. doi:10.1016/S0925-2312(03)00369-2

Ackley, D. H., Hinton, G. E., & Sejnowski, T. J. (1985). A learning algorithm for Boltzmann machines. *Cognitive Science, 9,* 147–169. doi:10.1207/s15516709cog0901_7

Adrian. (n.d.). *Paper.* Retrieved from www-users.cs.york.ac.uk/~adrian/Papers/Others/OSEE01.pdf

Agarwal, A. (1997). A systematic classification of neural-network-based control. *IEEE Control Systems Magazine, 17*(2), 75–93. doi:10.1109/37.581297

Aggarwal, K. K., Singh, Y., Kaur, A., & Malhotra, R. (2007). *Application of artificial neural network for predicting fault proneness models.* International Conference on Information Systems, Technology and. Management (ICISTM 2007), March 12-13, New Delhi, India.

Aggarwal, K. K., Singh, Y., Kaur, A., & Malhotra, R. (2008). *Empirical analysis for investigating the effect of object-oriented metrics on fault proneness: A replicated case study. Software Process Improvement and Practice.* Wiley.

Aguilar, J. (2003). A dynamic fuzzy-cognitive-map approach based on random neural networks. *International Journal of Computational Cognition, 1*(4), 91–107.

Ahonen, T., Hadid, A., & Pietikainen, M. (2004). Face recognition with local binary patterns. European Conference on Computer Vision, (pp. 469-481).

Ahonen, T., Hadid, A., & Pietikainen, M. (2006). Face descriptor with local binary patterns: Application to face recognition. *IEEE Transactions on Pattern Analysis and Machine Intelligence, 28*(12), 2037–2041. doi:10.1109/TPAMI.2006.244

Aiken, M., & Bsat, M. (1999). Forecasting market trends with neural networks. *Information Systems Management, 16*(4), 42–48. doi:10.1201/1078/43189.16.4.19990901/31202.6

Al-Ashmaway, W. H., El-Sisi, A. B., Nassan, H. M., & Ismail, N. A. (2007). Bilateral agent negotiation for e-commerce based on fuzzy logic. In *Proceedings of the International Conference on Computer Engineering & Systems (ICCES '07),* November 27-29, Cairo, Egypt, (pp. 64-69).

Alcala, R., Casillas, J., Cordon, O., & Herrera, F. (2000). *Learning TSK rule-based system from approximate ones by mean of MOGUL methodology.* Unpublished doctoral dissertation, Granada University, Spain.

Alfredo. (n.d.). *Website*. Retrieved from www.cannes. itam.mx/Alfredo/English/Nslbook/MitPress/Publications/157_170.CH08.pdf

Alizadeh, S., & Ghazanfari, M. (2009). Learning FCM by chaotic simulated annealing. *Chaos, Solitons, and Fractals, 41*(3), 1182–1190. doi:10.1016/j.chaos.2008.04.058

Almeida, L. B., & Silva, F. (1991). Speeding-up backpropagation by data orthonormalization. *Artificial Neural Networks, 2*, 56–149.

Altay, N., & Green, W. G. III. (2006). OR/MS research in disaster operations management. *European Journal of Operational Research, 175*, 475–493. doi:10.1016/j. ejor.2005.05.016

Aluz, N., Gokberk, B., & Akarun, L. (2008). 3D face recognition system for expression and occlusion invariance. *2nd Intl. Conf. on Biometrics: Theory, Applications, and Systems,* (pp. 1-7).

Amit, Y., & Geman, D. (1997). Shape quantization and recognition with randomized trees. *Neural Computation, 9*, 1545–1588. doi:10.1162/neco.1997.9.7.1545

An, S., Ma, X., & Li, R. S. Y. (2009). *Face detection and recognition with SURF for human-robot interaction.* Paper presented at the International Conference on Automation and Logistics, Shenyang, China.

Anderson, A. J. (1982). *Handbook of statistics.* Amsterdam, The Netherlands: North Holland.

Anderson, J. A., Silverstein, J. W., Ritz, S. A., & Jones, R. S. (1977). Distinctive features, categorical perception, probability learning: Some applications of a neural model. *Psychological Review, 84*, 413–451. doi:10.1037/0033-295X.84.5.413

Andreopoulos, A., & Tsotsos, J. (2009). A theory of active object localization. In *The Proceedings of the International Conference on Computer Vision, Poster Session.*

Ang, W. T., Khosla, P. K., & Riviere, C. N. (2003). Design of all-accelerometer inertial measurement unit for tremor sensing in hand-held microsurgical instrument. *Proceedings of the 2003 IEEE international Conference on Robotics & Automation,* Taipei, Taixao, September 14-19.

Angelov, P. P., & Buswell, R. A. (2003). Automatic generation of fuzzy rule–based models from data by genetic algorithms. (Elsevier.). *Information Sciences, 150*, 17–31. doi:10.1016/S0020-0255(02)00367-5

Anoraganingrum, D. (1999). Cell segmentation with median filter and mathematical morphology operations. In *Proceedings of International Conference on Image Analysis and Processing,* (pp. 1043-1046).

Arapoglou, R., Kolomvatsos, K., & Hadjiefthymiades, S. (2010). Buyer agent decision process based on automatic fuzzy rules generation methods. In *Proceedings of the 2010 IEEE World Congress on Computational Intelligence (WCCI 2010), FUZZ-IEEE,* July 18th – 23rd, Barcelona, Spain, (pp. 856-863).

Armangué, X., & Salvi, J. (2003). Overall view regarding fundamental matrix estimation. *Image and Vision Computing, 21*(2), 205–220. doi:10.1016/S0262-8856(02)00154-3

Aron, R., Sundararajan, A., & Viswanathan, S. (2006). Intelligent agents in electronic markets for information goods: Customization, preference and pricing. *Decision Support Systems, 41*(4), 764–786. doi:10.1016/j. dss.2004.10.007

ART. (n.d.). *Website*. Retrieved from http://www.learnartificialneuralnetworks.com/art.html

Arvis, V., Debain, C., Berducat, M., & Benassi, A. (2004). Generalization of the cooccurrence matrix for colour image: Application to colour texture classification. *Image Analysis & Stereology, 23*, 63–72. doi:10.5566/ias. v23.p63-72

Atanassov, K. (1999). *Intuitionistic fuzzy sets: Theory and applications.* Berlin, Germany: Springer Physica-Verlag.

Atsalakis, G. S., & Valavanis, K. P. (in press). Surveying stock market forecasting techniques – Part II: Soft computing methods. *Expert Systems with Applications.*

Auwatanamongkol, S. (2007). Inexact graph matching using a genetic algorithm for image recognition. *Pattern Recognition Letters, 28*, 1428–1437. doi:10.1016/j. patrec.2007.02.013

Axelrod, R. (1976). *Structure of decision–The cognitive maps of political elites.* Princeton, NJ: Princeton University Press.

Babuška, R., Van der Veen, P. J., & Kaymak, U. (2002). *Improved covariance estimation for Gustafson-Kessel Clustering*. Paper presented at IEEE International Conference on Fuzzy Systems, Honolulu, HI, USA, (pp. 1081-1085).

Babuška, R., & Verbruggen, H. (2003). Neuro-fuzzy methods for nonlinear system identification. *Annual Reviews in Control, 27*, 73–85. doi:10.1016/S1367-5788(03)00009-9

Back, A., Wan, E. A., Lawrence, S., & Tsoi, A. C. (2001). *A unifying view of some training algorithms for multi layer perceptrons with FIR filter synapses.*

Bahlmann, C., Heidemann, G., & Ritter, H. (1999). Artificial neural networks for automated quality control of textile seams. *Pattern Recognition, 32*(6), 1049–1060. doi:10.1016/S0031-3203(98)00128-9

Bakos, Y. (1998). The emerging role of electronic marketplaces on the Internet. *Communications of the ACM, 41*(8), 35–42. doi:10.1145/280324.280330

Balakrishnan, S. N., & Weil, R. D. (1996). Neurocontrol: A literature survey. *Mathematical Modeling and Computing, 23*, 101–117. doi:10.1016/0895-7177(95)00221-9

Banerjee, G. (2008). Adaptive fuzzy cognitive maps vs neutrosophic cognitive maps: Decision support tool for knowledge based institutions. *Journal of Scientific and Industrial Research, 67*(9), 665–673.

Banerjee, M., & Kundu, M. K. (2006). Content-based image retrieval using wavelet packets and fuzzy spatial relations. *ICVGIP 2006. LNCS, 4338*, 861–871.

Banerjee, M., & Kundu, M. K. (2008). Handling of impreciseness in gray level corner detection using fuzzy set theoretic approach. *Applied Soft Computing, 8*(4), 1680–1691. doi:10.1016/j.asoc.2007.09.001

Barambones, O., & Etxebarria, V. (2002). Robust neural control for robotic manipulators. *Automatica, 38*, 235–242. doi:10.1016/S0005-1098(01)00191-1

Barbosa, G. P., & Silva, Q. B. (2001). *An electronic marketplace architecture based on technology of intelligent agents and knowledge* (pp. 39–60). Lecture Notes in Computer Science E-Commerce Agents, Marketplace Solutions, Security Issues, and Supply and Demand.

Bartlett, H., Lades, M., & Sejnowski, T. J. (1998). Independent component representations for face recognition. In. *Proceedings of the SPIE: Conference on Human Vision and Electronic Imaging, 3299*, 528–539.

Bartoli, A., & Lapreste, J.-T. (2008). Triangulation for points on lines. *Image and Vision Computing, 26*(2), 315–324. doi:10.1016/j.imavis.2007.06.003

Basak, J., & Pal, S. (2005). Theoretical quantification of shape distortion in fuzzy Hough transform. *Fuzzy Sets and Systems, 154*, 227–250. doi:10.1016/j.fss.2005.02.014

Bashyal, S., & Venayagamoorthy, G. K. (2008). Recognition of facial expressions using Gabor wavelets and learning vector quantization. *International Journal of Engineering applications of Artificial Intelligence, 21*, 1056-1064.

Basmajian, J. V., & Deluca, C. J. (1985). *Muscles alive: Their functions revealed by electromyography* (5th ed.). Baltimore, MD: Williams & Wilkins.

Batista, J. P. (2005). A real-time driver visual attention monitoring system. *Iberian Conference on Pattern Recognition and Image Analysis, 3522*, (pp. 200-208).

Baudat, B., & Anouar, A. (2000). Generalized discriminant analysis using kernel approach. *Neural Computation*, 2385–2404. doi:10.1162/089976600300014980

Baumberg, A. (2000). Reliable feature matching across widely separated views. In *Proceedings of the IEEE Computer Society Conference on Computer Vision and Pattern Recognition*, (pp. 774-781). Hilton Head, USA.

Bay, H., Ess, A., Tuytelaars, T., & Van Gool, L. (2008). Speeded-up robust features (surf). *International Journal of Computer Vision and Image Understanding, 110*(3), 346–359. doi:10.1016/j.cviu.2007.09.014

Bebčáková, I., & Talašová, J. (2010). Fuzzified Choquet integral: A way to model interacting criteria in decision making. *Proceedings of the 28th International Conference on Mathematical Methods in Economics*, (vol. 1, pp. 30 – 35). ISBN 978-80-7394-218-2

Bebčáková, I., Talašová, J., & Pavlačka, O. (2010). Fuzzification of Choquet integral and its application in multiple criteria decision making. *Neural Network World, 20*, 125–137.

Becker, M., Navarro, M., Krempels, K. H., & Panchenko, A. (2003). *Agent based scheduling of operation theatres*. In EU-LAT eHealth Workshop on Agent Based Scheduling of Operation Theatres.

Belhumeur, P., Hespanha, J., & Kriegman, D. (1997). Eigen Faces vs. Fisherfaces: Recognition using class specific linear projection. *IEEE Trans. on PAMI*, *19*(7), 711–720. doi:10.1109/34.598228

Bell, A. J., & Sejnowski, T. J. (1995). An information-maximization approach to blind separation and blind deconvolution. *Neural Computation*, *7*(6), 1129–1159. doi:10.1162/neco.1995.7.6.1129

Bell, A. J., & Sejnowski, T. J. (1997). The independent components of natural scenes are edge filters. *Vision Research*, *37*(23), 3327–3338. doi:10.1016/S0042-6989(97)00121-1

Bellifemine, F., Caire, G., & Greenwood, D. (2007). *Developing multi-agent system with JADE*. Wiley series.

Bellman, R. E., & Zadeh, L. A. (1970). Decision-making in fuzzy environment. *Management Science*, *17*(4), 141–164. doi:10.1287/mnsc.17.4.B141

Belue, L. M., & Bauer, K. W. (1995). Determining input features for multilayer perceptrons. *Neurocomputing*, *7*, 111–121. doi:10.1016/0925-2312(94)E0053-T

Ben Hassine, A., & Ho, T. B. (2007). An agent-based approach to solve dynamic meeting scheduling problems with preferences. *Engineering Applications of Artificial Intelligence*, *20*(6), 857–873. doi:10.1016/j.engappai.2006.10.004

Bengoetzea, E., Larranaga, P., Bloch, I., Perchant, A., & Boeres, C. (2002). Inexact graph matching by means of estimation of distribution algorithms. *Pattern Recognition*, *35*(12), 2867–2880. doi:10.1016/S0031-3203(01)00232-1

Benvenuto, F., & Marani, A. (2000). Neural networks for environmental problems: Data quality control and air pollution nowcasting. *International Journal of Global Nest.*, *2*(3), 281–292.

Bercovich, R. (2004). OFDM enhances the 3G high-speed data access. *Proc. GSPx 2004 Conf.*, Santa Clara, CA, USA.

Berman, G. P., Doolen, G. D., Mainieri, R., & Tsifrinovich, V. I. (1998). *Introduction to quantum computers*. London, U. K.: World Scientific. doi:10.1142/9789812384775

Bernard, S., Heutte, L., & Adam, S. (2007). Using random forests for handwritten digit recognition. *Ninth International Conference on Document Analysis and Recognition*, 23-26 September, (pp. 1043-1047).

Besl, P. J., & Jain, R. C. (1985). Three-dimensional object recognition. *Computing Surveys*, *17*(1), 75–145. doi:10.1145/4078.4081

Betser, A., Vela, P., & Tannenbaum, A. (2004). Automatic tracking of flying vehicles using geodesic snakes and Kalman filtering. In *Proceedings of IEEE Conference on Decision and Control* (vol. 2, pp. 14-17).

Beyer, W. H. (1987). *CRC standard mathematical tables* (28th ed., p. 127). Boca Raton, FL: CRC Press.

Bezdek, J. C. (1973). *Fuzzy mathematics in pattern classification*, Ph.D. Thesis, Unpublished doctoral dissertation, Applied Mathematics Center, Cornell University, Ithaca.

Bezdek, J. C. (1981). *Pattern recognition with fuzzy objective function algoritms*. New York, NY: Plenum Press.

Bhattacharyya, S., Dutta, P., & DuttaMajumder, D. (2007b). A parallel self-organizing neural network (SONN) based color object extractor using MUSIG activation function with CONSENT. In D. Chakraborty, S. Nanda, & D. DuttaMajumder (Eds.), *Fuzzy logic and its application in technology and management* (pp. 206-213). New Delhi, India: Narosa Publishing House.

Bhattacharyya, S., Dutta, P., & Maulik, U. (2007c). Binary object extraction using bi-directional self-organizing neural network (BDSONN) architecture with fuzzy context sensitive thresholding. *International Journal of Pattern Analysis and Applications*, 345-360.

Bhattacharyya, S., Dutta, P., Maulik, U., & Nandi, P. K. (2007a). Multilevel activation functions for true color image segmentation using a self supervised parallel self organizing neural network (PSONN) architecture: A comparative study. *International Journal of Computer Science*, *2*(1), 09-21.

Bhattacharyya, S., & Dutta, P. (2006b). Designing pruned neighborhood neural networks for object extraction from noisy background. *International Journal of Foundations of Computing and Decision Sciences, 31*(2), 105–134.

Bhattacharyya, S., Dutta, P., & Maulik, U. (2008a). Self organizing neural network (SONN) based gray scale object extractor with a Multilevel Sigmoidal (MUSIG) activation function. *International Journal of Foundations of Computing and Decision Sciences, 33*(2), 46–50.

Bhattacharyya, S., Dutta, P., Maulik, U., & Nandi, P. K. (2006a). A self supervised bi-directional neural network (BDSONN) architecture for object extraction guided by beta activation function and adaptive fuzzy context sensitive thresholding. *International Journal of Intelligent Systems and Technologies, 1*(4), 345–365.

Bhattacharyya, S., Maulik, U., & Bandyopadhyay, S. (in press). Soft computing and its applications. In Dai, Y., Chakraborty, B., & Shi, M. (Eds.), *Kansei engineering and soft computing: Theory and practice*. Hershey, PA: IGI Global.

Bhattacharyya, S., Maulik, U., & Dutta, P. (2008b). A pruning algorithm for efficient image segmentation with neighborhood neural networks. *IAENG International Journal of Computer Science, 35*(2), 191–200.

Bhattacharyya, S., Maulik, U., & Dutta, P. (2010). Multilevel image segmentation with adaptive image context based thresholding. *International Journal of Applied Soft Computing, 11*, 946–962. doi:10.1016/j.asoc.2010.01.015

Bherenji, H. R., & Khedkar, P. (1992). Learning and tuning fuzzy logic controllers through reinforcements. *IEEE Transactions on Neural Networks, 3*, 724–740. doi:10.1109/72.159061

Bhowmik, P., Das, S., Halder, A., Chakraborty, A., Konar, A., & Janarthanan, R. (2009). *Emotion classifier from stimulated EEG signals by support vector machine.* 5th National Conference on Innovation in Information and Communication Technology", NCIICT, 2009, September 25 - 26, Coimbatore, India.

Bhowmik, P., Das, S., Nandi, D., Chakraborty, A., Konar, A., & Nagar, A. K. (2010). *Electroencephalographic signal based clustering of stimulated emotion using Duffing Oscillator.* The 3rd International Multi-Conference on Engineering and Technological Innovation", IMETI 2010, June 29th - July 2nd, Orlando, Florida, USA.

Bhowmik, P., Das, S., Nandi, D., Chakraborty, A., Konar, A., & Nagar, A. K. (2010a). Emotion clustering from stimulated electroencephalographic signals using Duffing Oscillator. *The International Journal of Computers in Healthcare, 1*(1), 66–85. doi:10.1504/IJCIH.2010.034131

Bickmore, T. W., & Picard, R. W. (2005). Establishing and maintaining long-term human-computer relationships. *ACM Transactions on Computer-Human Interaction, 12*(2), 293–327. doi:10.1145/1067860.1067867

Binford, T. O. (1981). Inferring surfaces from images. *Artificial Intelligence, 17*, 205–244. doi:10.1016/0004-3702(81)90025-4

Bishop, C. M. (1995). *Neural networks for pattern recognition*. Oxford, UK: Oxford University Press.

Bishop, G. W., Clare, M. H., & Price, J. (1948). Patterns of tremor in normal and pathological conditions. *Journal of Applied Physiology, 1*, 123–147.

Biswas, B., Mukherjee, A. K., & Konar, A. (1995). Matching of digital images using fuzzy logic. *AMSE Publication, 35*(2), 7–11.

Bi, W., Wang, X. G., Tang, Z., & Tamura, H. (2005). Avoiding the local minima problem in backpropagation algorithm with modified error function. *IEICE Trans. Fundam. Electron. Commun. Comput. Sci. E (Norwalk, Conn.), 88-A*, 3645–3653.

Bjorkman, M., & Kragic, D. (2004) Combination of foveal and peripheral vision for object recognition and pose estimation. In *Proceedings of the IEEE International Conference on Robotics and Automation,* (pp. 5135-5140).

Black, M. T., & Yacoob, Y. (1997). Recognizing facial expressions in image sequences using local parameterized models of image motion. *International Journal of Computer Vision, 25*, 23–48. doi:10.1023/A:1007977618277

Blake, A., & Isard, M. (1998). *Active contour*. Secausus, NJ: Springer-Verlag New York.

Bock, H. H., & Diday, E. (2000). *Analysis of symbolic data*. Springer Verlag.

Bocquet, W., Hayashi, K., & Sakai, H. (2004). A power allocation scheme for MIMO OFDM systems.

Boer, J. D. (1999). *Order in chaos*. Amsterdam, The Netherlands: Free University Hospital.

Bolcskei, H., & Zurich, E. (August, 2006). MIMO - OFDMA wireless systems: Basics, perspectives, and challenges. *IEEE Wireless Communications*, (pp. 31-37).

Bolcskei, H. (2006). *Principles of MIMO-OFDM wireless systems. Communication Technology Laboratory Swiss Federal Institute of Technology*. ETH.

Bonatto, C., Gallas, J. A. C., & Ueda, Y. (2008). Chaotic phase similarities and recurrences in a damped-driven Duffing oscillator. *Physical Review E: Statistical, Nonlinear, and Soft Matter Physics*, 77, 026217.doi:10.1103/PhysRevE.77.026217

Bookstein, L. (1996). Landmark methods for forms without landmarks: Morphometrics of group differences in outline shape. *Medical Image Analysis*, 1(3), 225–243. doi:10.1016/S1361-8415(97)85012-8

Bookstein, L. (1997). *Morphometric tools for landmark data: Geometry and biology*. Cambridge, UK: Cambridge Univ. Press.

Borges, A. P., Ribeiro, R., Avila, B. C., Enembreck, F., & Scalabrin, E. E. (2009). A learning agent to help drive vehicles. In *Proceedings of the International Conference on Computer Supported Cooperative Work in Design*, (pp. 282-287).

Bors, A. G., & Pitas, I. (1998). Optical flow estimation and moving object segmentation based on median radial basis function network. *IEEE Transactions on Image Processing*, 7(5), 693–702. doi:10.1109/83.668026

Boshes, B., Herota, T., & Klein, K. (1968). Further observations in tremor mechanisms in Parkinsonism. *Transactions of the American Neurological Association*, 1, 158–162.

Bouguet, J. Y. (2008). *Camera calibration toolbox for Matlab*. Retrieved from http://www.vision.caltech.edu/bouguetj/calibdoc/

Bouguet, J.-Y. (2000) *Pyramidal implementation of the Lucas Kanade feature tracker: Description of the algorithm*. Technical Report, Intel Corporation, Microprocessor Research Labs, OpenCV documentation.

Bouguila, N., & Ziou, D. (2004). *Improving content based image retrieval systems using finite multinomial dirichlet mixture*. In IEEE Workshop on Machine Learning for Signal Processing, 2004.

Box, G. E. P., & Jenkins, G. M. (1970). *Time series analysis, forecasting and control*. CA: Holden Day.

Boyd, S., El Ghaoui, L., Feron, E., & Balakrishnan, V. (1994). *Linear matrix inequalities in system and control theory*. SIAM. doi:10.1137/1.9781611970777

Bradski, G. R., & Kaehler, A. (2008). *Learning OpenCV* (1st ed.). Sebastopol, CA: O'Reilly Media, Inc.

Brave, S., & Nass, C. (2002). Emotion in human–computer interaction. In Sears, A., & Jacko, J. A. (Eds.), *The human computer interaction handbook: Fundamentals, evolving technologies and emerging applications* (pp. 81–96). Hillsdale, NJ: L. Erlbaum Associates Inc.

Breiman, L. (2001). Random forests. *Machine Learning*, 45, 5–32. doi:10.1023/A:1010933404324

Broomhead, D. S., & Lowe, D. (1988). Multivariable functional interpolation and adaptive networks. *Complex Systems*, 2, 321–355.

Brown, A. (1991). *Nerve cells and nervous systems*. Berlin, Germany: Springer-Verlag.

Brown, M., & Harris, C. (1994). *Neuro-fuzzy adaptive modeling and control*. New York, NY: Prentice-Hall.

Brox, T., Rousson, M., Deriche, R., & Weickert, J. (2003). Unsupervised segmentation incorporating colour, texture, and motion. In *Computer analysis of images and patterns*, (LNCS 2756, pp. 353-360).

Brunelli, R., & Poggio, T. (1993). Face recognition features versus templates. *IEEE Transactions on Pattern Analysis and Machine Intelligence*, 15(10), 1042–1052. doi:10.1109/34.254061

Bueno, S., & Salmeron, J. L. (2009). Benchmarking main activation functions in fuzzy cognitive maps. *Expert Systems with Applications*, 36(3), 5221–5229. doi:10.1016/j.eswa.2008.06.072

Buhmann, M. D. (2003). *Radial basis functions: Theory and implementations*. Cambridge University Press. doi:10.1017/CBO9780511543241

Burges, C. J. C. (1996). *Simplified support vector decision rule*. IEEE International Conference on Machine Learning.

Burges, C. J. C. (1998). A tutorial on support vector machines for pattern recognition. *Data Mining and Knowledge Discovery, 2*, 121–167. doi:10.1023/A:1009715923555

Busso, C., Deng, Z., Yildirim, S., Bulut, M., Lee, C. M., & Kazemzadeh, A. … Narayanan, S. (2004). *Analysis of emotion recognition using facial expressions, speech and multimodal information*. ICMI'04, State College, Pennsylvania, USA.

Busso, C., & Narayanan, S. (2007). Interaction between speech and facial gestures in emotional utterances: A single subject study. *IEEE Trans. Audio. Speech and Language Processing, 15*(8), 2331–2347. doi:10.1109/TASL.2007.905145

Butler, D., Sridharan, S., & Chandran, V. (2002). Chromatic colour spaces for skin detection using GMMs. *Inter. Conf. on Acoustics, Speech, and Signal Processing, 4*, (pp. 3620-3623).

Byrod, M., Josephson, K., & Astrom, K. (2007). Fast optimal three view triangulation. In *Asian Conference on Computer Vision, LNCS 4844*, Tokyo, Japan, (pp. 549-559).

Cadini, F., Zio, E., & Pedroni, N. (2008). *Validation of infinite impulse response multi layer perceptron for modelling nuclear dynamics*. Hindawi Publishing Corporation Science and Technology Installations.

Canny, J. F. (1986). A computational approach to edge detection. *IEEE Transactions on Pattern Analysis and Machine Intelligence, 8*(6), 679–698. doi:10.1109/TPAMI.1986.4767851

Cao, X., & Foroosh, H. (2004). Camera calibration without metric information using 1D objects. In *International Conference on Image Processing, 2*, (pp. 1349–1352).

Carbo, J., Molina, J. M., & Davila, J. (2003). Reaching agreements through fuzzy counter-offers. In *Proc. of the International Conference in Web Engineering*, Oviedo, Spain, July 14-18.

Carbo, J., Molina, J. M., & Davila, J. (2005). Fuzzy referral based cooperation in social networks of agents. *AI Communications, 18*(1), 1–13.

Carlsson, C., & Fullér, R. (1996). Fuzzy multiple criteria decision making: recent developments. *Fuzzy Sets and Systems - Special Issue on Fuzzy Multiple Criteria Decision Making, 78*(2), 139-153.

Carpenter, G. A., & Grossberg, S. (1987a). A massively parallel architecture for a self-organizing neural pattern recognition machine. *Computer Vision Graphics and Image Processing, 37*, 54–115. doi:10.1016/S0734-189X(87)80014-2

Carpenter, G. A., & Grossberg, S. (1987b). ART2: Self-organization of stable category recognition codes for analog input patterns. *Applied Optics, 26*, 4919–4930. doi:10.1364/AO.26.004919

Carpenter, G. A., & Grossberg, S. (1990). ART 3: Hierarchical search using chemical transmitters in self-organizing pattern recognition architectures. *Neural Networks, 3*, 129–152. doi:10.1016/0893-6080(90)90085-Y

Carpenter, G. A., & Grossberg, S. (2003). Adaptive resonance theory (ART). In Arbib, M. A. (Ed.), *The handbook of brain theory and neural networks* (pp. 79–82). Cambridge, MA: MIT Press.

Carpenter, G. A., Grossberg, S., Markuzon, N., Reynolds, J. H., & Rosen, D. B. (1992). Fuzzy ARTMAP: A neural network architecture for incremental supervised learning of analog multidimensional maps. *IEEE Transactions on Neural Networks, 3*, 698–713. doi:10.1109/72.159059

Carpenter, G. A., Grossberg, S., & Reynolds, J. H. (1991b). ARTMAP: Supervised real-time learning and classification of nonstationary data by a self-organizing neural network. *Neural Networks, 4*, 565–588. doi:10.1016/0893-6080(91)90012-T

Carpenter, G. A., Grossberg, S., & Rosen, D. B. (1991a). ART 2-A: An adaptive resonance algorithm for rapid category learning and recognition. *Neural Networks, 4*, 493–504. doi:10.1016/0893-6080(91)90045-7

Carpenter, G. A., Grossberg, S., & Rosen, D. B. (1991c). Fuzzy ART: Fast stable learning and categorization of analog patterns by an adaptive resonance system. *Neural Networks, 4*, 759–771. doi:10.1016/0893-6080(91)90056-B

Casdagli, M. (1989). Nonlinear prediction of chaotic time series. *Physica D. Nonlinear Phenomena, 35*, 335–356. doi:10.1016/0167-2789(89)90074-2

Castellano, G., Kessous, L., & Caridakis, G. (2007). Multimodal emotion recognition from expressive faces, body gestures and speech. In F. de Rosis, & R. Cowie (Eds.), *Proc. of the Doctoral Consortium of 2nd International Conference on Affective Computing and Intelligent Interaction*, Lisbon.

Castellano, G. (1997). An iterative pruning algorithm for feedforward neural networks. *IEEE Transactions on Neural Networks, 8*(3), 519–537. doi:10.1109/72.572092

Castillo, O., & Melin, P. (2008). *Type-2 fuzzy logic theory and applications*. Berlin, Germany: Springer-Verlag.

Castillo, O., Melin, P., Alanis, A., Montiel, O., & Sepulveda, R. (2010). Optimization of interval type-2 fuzzy logic controllers using evolutionary algorithms. *Soft Computing-A Fusion of Foundations. Methodologies and Applications, 1*, 1–16.

CAVIAR. (2005). *CAVIAR: Context aware vision using image-based active recognition*. Retrieved from http://homepages.inf.ed.ac.uk/rbf/CAVIAR/

CDC. (n.d.). *Criteria for defining nosocomial pneumonia*. Retrieved from http://www.cdc.com/

Celikyilmaz, A., & Burhan Turksen, I. (2007). Fuzzy functions with support vector machines. *Information Science, 177*, 5163–5177. doi:10.1016/j.ins.2007.06.022

Celikyilmaz, A., & Burhan Turksen, I. (2008). Validation criteria for enhanced fuzzy clustering. *Pattern Recognition, 29*, 97–108. doi:10.1016/j.patrec.2007.08.017

Cesar, R. M., Bengoetzea, E., Bloch, I., & Larranaga, P. (2005). Inexact graph matching for model-based recognition: Evaluation and comparison of optimization problems. *Pattern Recognition, 38*(11), 2099–2113. doi:10.1016/j.patcog.2005.05.007

Cha, I., & Kassam, S. A. (1996). RBFN restoration of nonlinearly degraded images. *IEEE Transactions on Image Processing, 5*(6), 964–975. doi:10.1109/83.503912

Chai, D., & Bouzerdoum, A. (2000). A Bayesian approach to skin color classification in YCbCr color space. *Proceedings, TENCON, 2*, 421–424.

Chakraborty, A., Bhowmik, P., Das, S., Halder, A., Konar, A., & Nagar, A. K. (2009c). *Correlation between stimulated emotion extracted from EEG*. 2009 IEEE International Conference on Systems, Man, and Cybernetics, IEEE SMC 2009, October 11 - 14, San Antonio, Texas, USA.

Chakraborty, A., Ghosh, M., Acharya, A., Konar, A., & Nagar, A. (2009b). A recurrent neural dynamics for parameter estimation of mixed emotions from facial expressions of the subject. *Proc. of the Int. Joint Conf. on Neural Networks*, Atlanta.

Chakraborty, A., & Konar, A. (2009). *Emotional intelligence: A cybernetic approach*. Heidelberg, Germany: Springer.

Chakraborty, A., Konar, A., Chakraborty, U. K., & Chatterjee, A. (2009a). Emotion recognition from facial expressions and its control using fuzzy logic. *IEEE Transactions on Systems, Man, and Cybernetics. Part A, Systems and Humans, 39*(4), 726–743. doi:10.1109/TSMCA.2009.2014645

Chakroborty, A. (2005). *Cognitive cybernetics – A study of the behavioral models of human interaction*. Unpublished doctoral dissertation, Jadavpur University, India.

Chamberlin, G. J., & Chamberlin, D. G. (1980). *Colour: Its measurement, computation and application*. London, UK: Heyden & Son.

Chan, A. D. C., Englehart, K., Hudgins, B., & Lovely, D. F. (2002). A multi-expert speech recognition system using acoustic and myoelectric signals. *24th Annual Conference and the Annual Fall Meeting of the Biomedical Engineering Society. Ottawa, Canada, (*vol. 1, pp. 72-73).

Chan, A. D. C., & Englehart, K. B. (2005). Continuous myoelectric control for powered prostheses using hidden Markov models. *IEEE Transactions on Bio-Medical Engineering, 52*(1), 121–124. doi:10.1109/TBME.2004.836492

Chang, C. C., & Lin, C. J. (2001). *LIBSVM – A library for support vector machines*. Retrieved from http://www.cse.ntu.edu.tw/~cjlin/libsvm/

Chang, S. F., Eleftheriadis, A., & Mcclintock, R. (1998). Next generation content representation, creation and searching for new media and application in education. *IEEE Proc.*, 1998.

Chang, N. S., & Fu, K. S. (1980). *Image query by pictorial–example*. IEEE Trans Software.

Chang, P. C., & Liu, C. H. (2008). A TSK type fuzzy rule based system for stock price prediction. *Expert Systems with Applications, 34*, 135–144. doi:10.1016/j.eswa.2006.08.020

Chapelle, O., Schölkopf, B., & Zien, A. (2006). *Semi-supervised learning*. Cambridge, MA: MIT Press.

Charalambous, C. (1992). Conjugate gradient algorithm for efficient training of artificial neural networks. *Proceedings of the IEEE, 139*(3), 301–310.

Chaudhary, B. B., & Majumdar, D. D. (1993). *Two tone image processing and recognition*. India: Wiley Eastern Ltd.

Chaudhuri, B. B., & Pal, U. (1997). An OCR system to read two Indian language scripts: Bangla and Devnagari (Hindi). In *International Conference on Document Analysis and Recognition*, (pp. 1011-1015). Ulm, Germany.

Chaumette, F., & Hutchinson, S. (2006). Visual servo control, part I: Basic approaches. *IEEE Robotics & Automation Magazine, 13*(4), 82–90. doi:10.1109/MRA.2006.250573

Chaumette, F., & Hutchinson, S. (2007). Visual servo control, part II: Advanced approaches. *IEEE Robotics & Automation Magazine, 14*(1), 109–118. doi:10.1109/MRA.2007.339609

Chauvin, Y., & Rumelhart, D. E. (1995). *Backpropagation: Theory, architectures, and applications*. Hillsdale, NJ: L. Erlbaum Associates Inc.

Chavez, A., & Maes, P. (1996). Kasbah: An agent marketplace for buying and selling goods. In *Proc. of the 1st International Conference on the Practical Application of Intelligent Agents and Multi-Agent Technology (PAAM '96)*, London, UK.

Chen, G. Y., & Kegl, B. (2005). *Invariant pattern recognition using dual-tree complex wavelets and Fourier features*. IVCNZ 2005, Image and Vision Computing, New Zealand, 28-29 Nov. 2005.

Chen, L. S., Tao, H., Huang, T. S., Miyasato, T., & Natakatsu, R. (1998). Emotion recognition from audiovisual information. In *Proc. IEEE Workshop on Multimedia Signal Processing*, (pp. 83-88).

Chen, M. S. (1999). *A Comparative study of learning methods in tuning parameters of fuzzy membership functions*. Paper presented at IEEE SMC '99 Conference, Tokyo, Japan, (pp. 40-44).

Chen, Y., Biddeli, K., Sun, A., Relue, P. A., & Johonson, D. J. (1999). An automatic cell counting method for optical images. In *Proceedings of the First Joint BMES/EMBS Conference, Atlantic*, (p. 819).

Chen, C., & Chiang, S.-P. (1997). Detection of human faces in colour images. *IEE Proceedings. Vision Image and Signal Processing, 144*, 384–388. doi:10.1049/ip-vis:19971414

Cheng, C. B., Chan, H. C. C., & Lin, C. C. (2005). Buyer-supplier negotiation by fuzzy logic based agents. In *Proceedings of the 3rd International Conference on Information Technology and Applications (ICITA '05)*, Sydney, Australia, (pp. 137–142).

Chen, G. Y., & Bui, T. D. (1999). Invariant Fourier wavelet descriptor for pattern recognition. *Pattern Recognition, 32*(7), 1083–1088. doi:10.1016/S0031-3203(98)00148-4

Chengjun, L. (2004). Gabor based kernel PCA with fractional power polynomial models for face recognition. *IEEE Transactions on Pattern Recognition and Machine Intelligence, 26*(5), 572–581. doi:10.1109/TPAMI.2004.1273927

Chen, H., Fuller, S. S., & Friedman, C. P. (Eds.). (2005). *Medical informatics: Knowledge management and data mining in biomedicine. Integrated Series in Information Systems*. Springer.

Chen, P. H., Lin, C. J., & Scholkopf, B. (2005). A tutorial on v-support vector machines. *Applied Stochastic Models in Business and Industry, 21*, 111–136. doi:10.1002/asmb.537

Chen, Q., Sun, Q.-S., Heng, P.-A., & Xia, D.-S. (2008). Parametric active contours for object tracking based on matching degree image of object contour points. *Pattern Recognition Letters, 29*(2), 126–141. doi:10.1016/j.patrec.2007.09.009

Chen, Q., & Weigand, W. A. (1994). Dynamic optimization of nonlinear processes by combining neural net model with UDMC. *AIChE Journal. American Institute of Chemical Engineers, 40*, 1488–1497. doi:10.1002/aic.690400908

Chen, S., Cowan, C. F. N., & Grant, P. M. (1991). Orthogonal least squares learning algorithm for radial basis function networks. *IEEE Transactions on Neural Networks*, *2*(2), 302–309. doi:10.1109/72.80341

Chen, T. (2001). Audiovisual speech processing. *IEEE Signal Processing Magazine*, *18*(9).

Chen, Y. M., & Wang, S. C. (2008). An evolutionary compensatory negotiation model for distributed dynamic scheduling. *Applied Soft Computing*, *8*(2), 1093–1104. doi:10.1016/j.asoc.2007.05.018

Cheron, G., Draye, J. P., Bourgeios, M., & Libert, G. (1996). A dynamic neural network identification of electromyography and arm trajectory relationship during complex movements. *IEEE Transactions on Bio-Medical Engineering*, *43*(5), 552–558. doi:10.1109/10.488803

Chesi, G. (2009a). Camera displacement via constrained minimization of the algebraic error. *IEEE Transactions on Pattern Analysis and Machine Intelligence*, *31*(2), 370–375. doi:10.1109/TPAMI.2008.198

Chesi, G. (2009b). Visual servoing path-planning via homogeneous forms and LMI optimizations. *IEEE Transactions on Robotics*, *25*(2), 281–291. doi:10.1109/TRO.2009.2014131

Chesi, G., Garulli, A., Tesi, A., & Vicino, A. (2009). *Homogeneous polynomial forms for robustness analysis of uncertain systems*. Springer.

Chesi, G., Garulli, A., Vicino, A., & Cipolla, R. (2002). Estimating the fundamental matrix via constrained least-squares: A convex approach. *IEEE Transactions on Pattern Analysis and Machine Intelligence*, *24*(3), 397–401. doi:10.1109/34.990139

Chesi, G., & Hashimoto, K. (Eds.). (2010). *Visual serving via advanced numerical methods*. Springer.

Chesi, G., & Hung, Y. S. (2007). Image noise induced errors in camera positioning. *IEEE Transactions on Pattern Analysis and Machine Intelligence*, *29*(8), 1476–1480. doi:10.1109/TPAMI.2007.70723

Cheung, K.-H., You, J., Kong, W.-K., & D., Z. (2004). A study of aggregated 2D Gabor features on appearance-based face recognition. *Proceedings of Image and Graphics*, (pp. 310-313).

Chi, S. C., Chen, H. P., & Cheng, C. H. (1999). *A forecasting approach for stock index future using Grey theory and neural networks*. Paper presented at IEEE International Joint Conference on Neural Networks, Washington, DC, USA, vol. 6, (pp. 3850-3855).

Chiang, C. K., Chung, H. Y., & Lin, J. J. (1996). A self-learning fuzzy logic controller using genetic algorithms with reinforcements. *IEEE Transactions on Fuzzy Systems*, *5*, 460–467. doi:10.1109/91.618280

Chidamber, S., & Kamerer, C. (1994). A metrics suite for object-oriented design. *IEEE Transactions on Software Engineering*, *20*(6), 476–493. doi:10.1109/32.295895

Choi, C., Baek, S. M., & Lee, S. (2008). Real-time 3D object pose estimation and tracking for natural landmark based visual servo. In *Proceedings of the IEEE/RSJ International Conference on Intelligent Robots and Systems*, (pp. 3983-3989). Nice, France.

Chong, C. W., Raveendran, P., & Mukundan, R. (2003). A comparative analysis of algorithms for fast computation of Zernike moments. *Pattern Recognition*, *36*(3), 731–742. doi:10.1016/S0031-3203(02)00091-2

Choquet, G. (1953). Theory of capacities. *Ann. Inst. Fourier*, *5*, 131–295. doi:10.5802/aif.53

Christian, D., Sadikot, A. F., & Panisset, M. (2003). The detection of tremor during slow alternating movements performed by patients with early Parkinson's disease. [Springer-Verlag.]. *Experimental Brain Research*, *154*, 395–398.

Chua, W., & Yang, L. (1988a). Cellular networks: Theory. *IEEE Transactions on Circuits and Systems*, *35*(10), 1257–1272. doi:10.1109/31.7600

Chua, W., & Yang, L. (1988b). Cellular networks: Applications. *IEEE Transactions on Circuits and Systems*, *35*(10), 1273–1290. doi:10.1109/31.7601

Chu, H. H., Chen, T. L., Cheng, C. H., & Huang, C. C. (2009). Fuzzy dual-factor time-series for stock index forecasting. *Expert Systems with Applications*, *36*, 165–171. doi:10.1016/j.eswa.2007.09.037

Cibas, T., Souli, F. F., Gallinari, P., & Raudys, S. (1996). Variable selection with neural networks. *Neurocomputing*, *12*, 223–248. doi:10.1016/0925-2312(95)00121-2

Cichocki, A., & Amari, S.-I. (2002). *Adaptive blind signal and image processing: Learning algorithms and applications.* John Wiley \& Sons, Inc.

Cichosz1, J., & Ślot, K. (2007). Emotion recognition in speech signal using emotion extracting binary decision trees. In R. Cowie & F. Rosis (Chairs), *Affective Computing and Intelligent Interfaces-ACII.* Doctoral Consortium.

Cipolla, R., & Pentland, A. P. (1998). *Computer vision for human-machine interaction.* Cambridge, UK: Cambridge University Press.

Codara, P., D'Antona, O. M., & Marra, V. (2009). An analysis of Ruspini partitions in Gödel logic. *International Journal of Approximate Reasoning, 50*, 825–836. doi:10.1016/j.ijar.2009.02.007

Cohen, I. (2000). *Facial expression recognition from video sequences.* MS Thesis, Unpublished doctoral dissertation, Dept. of Electrical Engg., Univ. of Illinois at Urbana-Champaign.

Cohen, I., Garg, A., & Huang, T. S. (2000a). Emotion recognition using facial multilevel HMM. In. *Proc. Of NIPS Workshop on Affective Computing,* Colorado.

Cohen, I., Sebe, N., Garg, A., Chen, L. S., & Huang, T. S. (2003). Facial expression recognition from video sequences: Temporal and static modeling. *Computer Vision and Image Understanding, 91*(1-2), 160–187. doi:10.1016/S1077-3142(03)00081-X

Colieri, S., Ergen, M., Puri, A., & Bahai, A. (September, 2002). A study of channel estimation in OFDM systems. In *Proceedings of the IEEE 56th Vehicular Technology Conference,* vol. 2, (pp. 894-898).

Collados, M., & Gorokhov, A. (2005). Antenna selection for MIMO-OFDM WLAN systems. *International Journal of Wireless Information Networks, 12*(4). doi:10.1007/s10776-005-0007-9

Collins, J., Jamison, S., Mobasher, B., & Gini, M. (1998). A market architecture for multi-agent contracting. In *Proceedings of the 2nd International Conference on Autonomous Agents,* New York, (pp. 285-292).

Colombo, A., Cusano, C., & Schettini, R. (2006). Detection and restoration of occlusions for 3D face recognition. *Proc. of IEEE Intl. Conf. on Multimedia & Expo (ICME),* (pp. 1541-1546).

Colombo, A., Cusano, C., & Schettini, R. (2009). Gappy PCA classification for occlusion tolerant 3D face detection. *Journal of Mathematical Imaging and Vision, 35*(5), 193–207. doi:10.1007/s10851-009-0165-y

Comon, P. (1994). Independent component analysis: A new concept? *Signal Processing, 36*(3), 287–314. doi:10.1016/0165-1684(94)90029-9

Conati, C. (2002). Probabilistic assessment of user's emotions in educational games. *J. of Applied Artificial Intelligence. Special Issue on Merging Cognition and Affect in HCI, 16*(7-8), 555–575.

Congedo, G., Dimauro, G., Impedovo, S., & Pirlo, G. (1995). A structural method with local refining for handwritten character recognition. In *International Conference on Document Analysis and Recognition,* (pp. 853-856). Montreal, Canada.

Connel, S. D., Sinha, R. M. K., & Jain, A. K. (2000). Recognition of un-constrained on-line Devnagari characters. In *International Conference on Pattern Recognition ICPR,* (pp. 2368-2371). Barcelona, Spain.

Cootes, T. F., Edwards, G. J., & Taylor, C. J. (1998). Active appearance models. In *Proceedings of European Conference on Computer Vision (ECCV),* vol. 2, (pp. 484-498). Springer Verlag.

Cootes, T. F., Walker, K. N., & Taylor, C. J. (2000). View-based Active appearance models. In *Proceedings of International Conference on Automatic Face and Gesture Recognition (FG),* (pp. 227-232). IEEE CS Press.

Cootes, T. F., & Lanitis, A. (2004). *Statistical models of appearance for computer vision. Technical Report.* University of Manchester.

Cootes, T. F., Taylor, C. J., Cooper, D. H., & Graham, J. (1995). Active shape models - Their training and application. *Computer Vision and Image Understanding, 61*(1), 38–59. doi:10.1006/cviu.1995.1004

Cordelia, S., Mohr, R., & Bauckhage, C. (2000). Evaluation of interest point detectors. *International Journal of Computer Vision, 37*(2), 151–172. doi:10.1023/A:1008199403446

Corrêa, F. R., Deccó, C. C. G., & Okamoto, J., Jr. (2003). *Obtaining range information with an omnidirectional vision system.* In XVII Congresso Brasileiro de Engenharia Mecânica.

Correction Neural Networks*Modeling and forecasting financial data, techniques of nonlinear dynamics* (Soofi, A., & Cao, L., Eds.). Kluwer Academic Press.

Correia, P. L., & Pereira, F. (2002). Objective evaluation of video segmentation quality. *IEEE Transactions on Image Processing, 12*(2), 186–200. doi:10.1109/TIP.2002.807355

Cortes, C., & Vapnik, V. (1995). Support-vector networks. *Machine Learning,* 273–297. doi:10.1007/BF00994018

Cowie, R., Douglas-Cowie, E., Tsapatsoulis, N., Votsis, G., Kollias, S., Fellenz, W., & Taylor, J. G. (2001). Emotion recognition in human-computer interaction. *IEEE Signal Processing Magazine, 18*(1), 32–80. doi:10.1109/79.911197

Craiger, J. P., Weiss, R. J., Goodman, D. F., & Butler, A. A. (1996). Simulating organizational behavior with fuzzy cognitive maps. *Int J Comp Intell Organ, 1,* 120–133.

Cret, L., Yamazaki, F., Nagata, S., & Katayama, T. (1993). Earthquake damage estimation and decision-analysis for emergency shutoff of city gas network using fuzzy set theory. *Structural Safety, 12*(1), 1–19. doi:10.1016/0167-4730(93)90015-S

Cristea, P., Tuduce, R., & Cristea, A. (2000). Time series prediction with wavelet neural networks. In []. Belgrade.]. *Proceedings of IEEE Neural Network Applications in Electrical Engineering, 25-27,* 5–10.

Cristianini, N., & Taylor, J. S. (2000). *An introduction to support vector machines and other kernel-based learning methods.* New York, NY: Cambridge University Press.

Cui, J., et al. (2004). An iris image synthesis method based on PCA and super-resolution. *Int. Conf. on Pattern Recognition,* (pp. 471-474).

Cun, Y. L., & Bengio, Y. (1995). Convolutional networks for images, speech, and time series. In Arbib, M. A. (Ed.), *The handbook of brain theory and neural networks* (pp. 255–258). Cambridge, MA: MIT Press.

Cun, Y. L., Denker, J. S., & Solla, S. A. (1990). Optimal brain damage. In Touretzky, D. S. (Ed.), *Advances in neural information processing systems, 2* (pp. 598–605). San Mateo, CA: Morgan Kaufmann.

Cybenko, G. (1989). Approximation by superposition of a sigmoidal function. *Mathematics of Control, Signals, and Systems, 2,* 303–314. doi:10.1007/BF02551274

Czap, H., & Becker, M. (2003). Multi-agent systems and microeconomic theory: A negotiation approach to solve scheduling problems in high dynamic environments. In *Proceedings of the 36th Annual Hawaii International Conference on System Sciences,* (p. 8).

Dalal, N., & Triggs, B. (2005). Histograms of oriented gradients for human detection. *IEEE Int. Conf. on Computer Vision and Pattern Recognition,* (pp. 886-893).

Dambreville, S., Rathi, Y., & Tannenbaum, A. (2006). Tracking deformable objects with unscented Kalman filtering and geometric active contours. In *Proceedings of American Control Conference* (vol. 1, pp. 14-16).

Dang, T.-T., & Frankovic, B. (2002). Agent based scheduling in production systems. *International Journal of Production Research, 40*(15), 3669–3679. doi:10.1080/00207540210140022

Das, S., Bhowmik, P., Halder, A., & Chakraborty, A. Konar, & A., Nagar, A. K. (2010). *Emotion recognition from facial expression and electroencephalographic signals using vector quantization and support vector machines.* 2010 World Congress in Computer Science, Computer Engineering, and Applied Computing, WORLDCOMP 2010, July 12 - 15, Las Vegas, Nevada, USA.

Das, S., Halder, A., Bhowmik, P., & Chakraborty, A. Konar, & Janarthanan, R. (2009a). *A support vector machine classifier of emotion from voice and facial expression data.* World Congress on Nature & Biologically Inspired Computing, NaBIC 2009, December 09-11, Coimbatore, India.

Das, S., Halder, A., Bhowmik, P., Chakraborty, A., Konar, A., & Nagar, A. K. (2009). *Voice and facial expression based classification of emotion using linear support vector machine.* Development in eSystems Engineering Conference, DeSE ' 09, December 14 - 16, Abu Dhabi, UAE.

Dash, R. K., Vytelingum, P., Rogers, A., David, E., & Jennings, N. R. (2007). Market-based task allocation mechanisms for limited-capacity suppliers. *IEEE Transactions on Systems Man and Cybernetics – Part A: Systems and, 37*(3), 391–405. doi:10.1109/TSMCA.2007.893474

Datcu, D., & Rothkrantz, L. (2008b). Automatic bimodal emotion recognition system based on fusion of facial expressions and emotion extraction from speech. *Proceedings of the IEEE Face and Gesture Conference FG2008.*

Datcu, D., & Rothkrantz, L. (2008a). Semantic audiovisual data fusion for automatic emotion recognition. ( []. EUROSIS-ETI, Porto.]. *Euromedia, 2008*, 58–65.

Daubechies, I. (1988). Orthonormal bases of compactly supported wavelets. *Communications on Pure and Applied Mathematics, 41*, 909–996. doi:10.1002/cpa.3160410705

Daugman, J. (2004). How iris recognition works. *IEEE Trans. on Circuits and Systems for Video Technology, 14*(1), 21–30. doi:10.1109/TCSVT.2003.818350

Daugman, J. (2006). Probing the uniqueness and randomness of iris codes: Results from 200 billion iris pair comparisons. *Proceedings of the IEEE, 94*(11), 1927–1935. doi:10.1109/JPROC.2006.884092

Daugman, J. (2007). New methods in iris recognition. *IEEE Trans. on Systems. Man and Cybernetics B, 37*(5), 1167–1175. doi:10.1109/TSMCB.2007.903540

Daugman, J. G. (1988). Complete discrete 2-D Gabor transforms by neural networks for image analysis and compression. *IEEE Transactions on Pattern Analysis and Machine Intelligence, 36*, 1169–1179.

David, A. (1985). *Biomechanics IX (Vol. 1)*. Human Kinetics Publishers.

Davies, J. R., Coggeshall, S. V., Jones, R. D., & Schutzer, D. (1995). Intelligent security systems. In Freedman, S. R., Flein, A. R., & Lederma, J. (Eds.), *Artificial intelligence in the capital markets*. Chicago, IL: Irwin.

Daw-Tung, L., & Chen-Ming, Y. (2004). Real-time eye detection using face circle fitting and dark-pixel filtering. *IEEE International Conference on Multimedia and Expo, 2*, (pp. 1167-1170).

de França, J. A., & Stemmer, M. R., de M. França, M. B., & Alves, E. G. (2010). Revisiting Zhang's 1D calibration algorithm. *Pattern Recognition, 43*(3), 1180–1187. doi:10.1016/j.patcog.2009.08.001

de Kruif, B. J., & de Vries, T. J. (2003). Pruning error minimization in least squares support vector machines. *IEEE Transactions on Neural Networks, 14*(3), 696–702. doi:10.1109/TNN.2003.810597

de Oliveira, W. R. (2009). Quantum RAM based neural networks. In *Proceedings of European Symposium on Artificial Neural Networks - Advances in Computational Intelligence and Learning* (pp. 331-336).

de Oliveira, W. R., et al. (2008). Quantum logical neural networks. In *Proceedings of 10th Brazilian Symposium on Neural Networks SBRN '08* (pp. 147-152).

Debevec, P. E., & Malik, J. (1997). Recovering high dynamic range radiance maps from photographs. In *Proceedings of the 24th Annual Conference on Computer Graphics and Interactive Techniques* (pp. 369-378).

Decker, K., & Li, J. (1998). Coordinated hospital patient scheduling. *Third International Conference on Multi Agent Systems (ICMAS'98)*, (p. 104).

De, S., Bhattacharyya, S., & Dutta, P. (2009). Multilevel image segmentation using OptiMUSIG activation function with fixed and variable thresholding: A comparative study. In Mehnen, J., Koppen, M., Saad, A., & Tiwari, A. (Eds.), *Applications of soft computing: From theory to praxis, advances in intelligent and soft computing* (pp. 53–62). Berlin: Springer-Verlag. doi:10.1007/978-3-540-89619-7_6

De, S., Bhattacharyya, S., & Dutta, P. (2010). Efficient gray level image segmentation using an optimized MUSIG (OptiMUSIG) activation function. *International Journal of Parallel, Emergent and Distributed Systems*, 1-39.

Deschenes, S., Sheng, Y., & Chevrette, P. C. (1998). Three-dimensional object recognition from two-dimensional images using wavelet transforms and neural networks. *Optical Engineering (Redondo Beach, Calif.), 37*(3), 763–770.

DeSmet, M., Franses, R., & Gool, L. V. (2006). A generalized EM approach for 3D model based face recognition under occlusions. *CVPR, 2*, 1423–1430.

Devijver, P. A., & Kittler, J. (1982). *Pattern classification: A statistical approach*. Prentice-Hall.

Dewan, P., & Joshi, S. (2002). Auction-based distributed scheduling in a dynamic job shop environment. *International Journal of Production Research*, 40(5), 1173–1191. doi:10.1080/00207540110098445

Dhillon, G. (2006). MIMO tech for next-gen cellular systems. *Electronic Engineering Times-Asia, 1-15*, 1-2.

Dietterich, T. (1998). Approximate statistical tests for comparing supervised classification learning algorithms. *Neural Computation, 10*, 1895–1924. doi:10.1162/089976698300017197

Dikkers, H. J., Spaans, M. A., Datcu, D., Novak, M., & Rothkrantz, L. (2004). Facial recognition system for driver vigilance monitoring. In *Proceedings of the IEEE International Conference on System, Man and Cybernetics,* (pp. 3787-3792).

Dimberg, U., & Karlsson, B. (1997). Facial reactions to different emotionally relevant stimuli. *Scandinavian Journal of Psychology*, 38.

Dingledine, R., Borges, K., Bowie, D., & Traynelis, S. F. (1999). The glutamate receptor ion channels. *Pharmacological Reviews, 51*(1), 7–61.

Dirgo, C. (2008). *Tremor*. Onyx Books.

Djuwari, D., Kumar, D. K., Naik, G. R., Arjunan, S. P., & Palaniswami, M. (2006). Limitations and applications of ICA for surface electromyogram. *Electromyography and Clinical Neurophysiology, 46*(5), 295–309.

Dodd, N. (1990). Optimization of network structure using genetic techniques. In *Proceedings of IEEE International Joint Conference on Neural Networks, 3*, 965-970.

Doerschuk, P., Gustafon, D., & Willsky, A. (1983). Upper extremity limb function discrimination using EMG signal analysis. *IEEE Transactions on Biomedical Engineering, BME-30*(1), 18-29.

Donato, G., Bartlett, M. S., Hager, J. C., Ekman, P., & Sejnowski, T. J. (1999). Classifying facial action. *IEEE Transactions on Pattern Analysis and Machine Intelligence, 21*, 974–989. doi:10.1109/34.799905

Dong, W. M., Chiang, W. L., & Shah, H. C. (1987). Fuzzy information processing in seismic hazard analysis and decision making. *Soil Dynamics and Earthquake Engineering, 6*(4), 220–226. doi:10.1016/0267-7261(87)90003-0

Dornaika, F., & Chung, R. (2001). An algebraic approach to camera self-calibration. *Computer Vision and Image Understanding, 83*(3), 195–215. doi:10.1006/cviu.2001.0925

Dryden, I. L., & Mardia, K. V. (1998). *Statistical shape analysis*. John Wiley and Sons.

Dubois, D., & Prade, H. (2000). *Fundamentals of fuzzy sets*. Boston, MA: Kluwer Academic Publishers.

Dubois, D., & Prade, H. (Eds.). (2000). *Fundamentals of fuzzy sets. The handbook of fuzzy sets series*. Boston, MA: Kluwer Academic Publishers.

Duda, R. O., Hart, P. E., & Stork, D. G. (2001). *Pattern classification*. Singapore: Wiley International.

Duda, R. O., Hart, P. E., & Stork, D. G. (2002). *Pattern classification*. New York, NY: John Wiley and Sons.

Dunn, J. C. (1973). A fuzzy relative of the ISO-DATA process and its use in detecting compact well-separated clusters. *Journal of Cybernetics, 3*, 32–57. doi:10.1080/01969727308546046

Dutta, R., Joshi, D., Lee, J., & Nang, J. (2005). Image retrieval: Ideas, influences and trends of new age. *Proceedings of 7th ACM SIGMM International Workshop on Multimedia Retrieval Information*, November 10-11, 2005, Singapure.

Du, Y., Ives, R. W., & Etter, D. M. (2004). Iris recognition: A chapter on biometrics. In *The electrical engineering handbook*. Boca Raton, FL: CRC Press.

Eden, C., & Ackermann, F. (1993). Evaluating strategy-Its role within the context of strategic control. *The Journal of the Operational Research Society, 44*, 76–88.

Egmont-Petersen, M., de Ridder, D., & Handels, H. (2002). Image processing with neural networks—A review. *Pattern Recognition, 35*, 2279–2301. doi:10.1016/S0031-3203(01)00178-9

Ekman, P., & Friesen, W. V. (1975). *Unmasking the face: A guide to recognizing emotions from facial clues*. Englewood Cliffs, NJ: Prentice-Hall.

Ekman, P., & Friesen, W. V. (1978). *The facial action coding system: A technique for the measurement of facial movement.* San Francisco, CA: Consulting Psychologists Press.

Ekrafft. (2001). *Wayfinding.* http://www.ifi.uzh.ch/Ekrafft/papers/2001/wayfinding/html/node97.html

Ekvall, S., Kragic, D., & Hoffmann, F. (2005). Object recognition and pose estimation using color cooccurrence histograms and geometric modeling. *International Journal of Image and Vision Computing, 23*(11), 943–955. doi:10.1016/j.imavis.2005.05.006

Elble, R. J., & Randall, J. E. (1978). Mechanistic components of normal hand tremor. *Electroencephalography and Clinical Neurophysiology, 44,* 72–82. doi:10.1016/0013-4694(78)90106-2

Elman, J. L. (1990). Finding structure in time. *Cognitive Science, 14,* 179–211. doi:10.1207/s15516709cog1402_1

Emami, M. R., Turksen, I. B., & Goldenberg, A. A. (1998). Development of a systematic methodology of fuzzy logic modeling. *IEEE Transactions on Fuzzy Systems, 6*(3), 346–361. doi:10.1109/91.705501

Engelbrecht, A. P. (2001). A new pruning heuristic based on variance analysis of sensitivity information. *IEEE Transactions on Neural Networks, 12*(6), 1386–1399. doi:10.1109/72.963775

Engelbrecht, A. P. (2007). *Computational intelligence: An introduction* (2nd ed.). Wiley.

Englehart, K., & Hudgins, B. (2003). A robust, real-time control scheme for multifunction myoelectric control. *IEEE Transactions onBiomedical Engineering, 50*(7), 848-854.

Esogbue, A. O. (1996). Fuzzy sets modeling and optimization for disaster control systems planning. *Fuzzy Sets and Systems, 81*(1), 169–183. doi:10.1016/0165-0114(95)00248-0

Esogbue, A. O., Theologidu, M., & Guo, K. J. (1992). On the application of fuzzy sets theory to the optimal flood control problem arising in water resources systems. *Fuzzy Sets and Systems, 48*(2), 155–172. doi:10.1016/0165-0114(92)90330-7

Essa, I. A., & Pentland, A. P. (1997). Coding, analysis, interpretation and recognition of facial expressions. *IEEE Transactions on Pattern Analysis and Machine Intelligence, 19,* 757–763. doi:10.1109/34.598232

Estevez, P. A., Flores, R. J., & Perez, C. A. (2005). Color image segmentation using fuzzy min-max neural networks. In *Proceedings of IEEE International Joint Conference on Neural Networks,* (vol. 5, pp. 3052-3057).

Estevez, P. A., Perez, C. A., & Goles, E. (2003). Genetic input selection to a neural classifier for defect classification of radiata pine boards. *Forest Prod. Journal, 53*(7/8), 87–94.

Etemad, K., & Chellappa, R. (1997). Discriminant analysis for recognition of human face images. *Journal of the Optical Society of America, 14,* 1724–1733. doi:10.1364/JOSAA.14.001724

Everingham, M., & Zisserman, A. (2006). *Regression and classification approaches to eye localization in face images.* Int. Conf. on Automatic Face and Gesture Recognition.

Faber, J., & Giraldi, G. (1989). *Quantum models of artificial neural networks.* Retrieved from http://arquivosweb.lncc.br/pdfs/QNN-Review.pdf

Fang, J. L., & Chen, S. (2006). A simplification to support vector machine for the second training. IEEE *International Conference on Artificial Reality and Telexistence,* (pp. 73-78).

Faratin, P., Sierra, C., & Jennings, N. (1998). Negotiation decision functions for autonomous agents. *International Journal of Autonomous and Robotics Systems, 24*(3-4), 159–182. doi:10.1016/S0921-8890(98)00029-3

Farkas, L. G. (1994). *Anthropometry of the head and face.* New York, NY: Raven Press.

Farry, K. A., & Walker, I. D. (1993). *Myoelectric tele-operation of a complex robotic hand.* Paper presented at the IEEE International Conference on Robotics and Automation.

Fatemizadeh, E., Lucas, C., & Soltanian-Zadeh, H. (2003). Automatic landmark extraction from image data using modified growing neural gas network. *IEEE Transactions on Information Technology in Biomedicine, 7,* 77–85. doi:10.1109/TITB.2003.808501

Faugeras, O., & Luong, Q.-T. (2001). *The geometry of multiple images*. Cambridge, MA: MIT Press.

Fausett, L. (1994). *Fundamentals of neural networks*. USA: Prentice Hall.

Favata, J. T., Srikantan, G., & Srihari, S. N. (1994). Hand-printed character/digit recognition using a multiple feature/resolution philosophy. In *International Workshop in Frontiers of Handwriting Recognition*, (pp. 57-66), Taipei, Taiwan.

Fazel Zarandi, M. H. (1998). *Aggregate system analysis for prediction of tardiness and mixed zones of continuous casting with fuzzy methodology*. Doctoral dissertation, University of Toronto.

Fazel Zarandi, M. H., Rezaee, B., Turksen, I. B., & Neshat, E. (2009). A type-2 fuzzy rule-based expert system model for stock price analysis. *Expert Systems with Applications*, *36*, 139–154. doi:10.1016/j.eswa.2007.09.034

Fellenz, W. A., Taylor, J. G., Cowie, R., Douglas-Cowie, E., Piat, F., & Kollias, S. … Apolloni, B. (2000). On emotion recognition of faces and of speech using neural networks, fuzzy logic and the ASSESS systems. In *Proc. IEEE -INNS-ENNS Int. Joint Conf. Neural Netw*, (pp. 93–98).

Feng, G. C., & Yuan, P. C. (1998). Various projection function and its application to eye detection for human face recognition. *Pattern Recognition Letters*, *19*(9), 899–906. doi:10.1016/S0167-8655(98)00065-8

Fernandez-Dols, J. M., Wallbotl, H., & Sanchez, F. (1991). Emotion category accessibility and the decoding of emotion from facial expression and context. *Journal of Nonverbal Behavior*, *15*, 107–123. doi:10.1007/BF00998266

Field, D. J. (1987). Relations between the statistics of natural images and the response properties of cortical cells. *Journal of the Optical Society of America*, *4*(12), 2379–2394. doi:10.1364/JOSAA.4.002379

Findley, L. J. (1994). *Handbook of tremor disorders*. M. Dekker.

Fischler, M., & Wolf, H. C. (1994). Locating perceptually salient points on planar curves. *IEEE Transactions on Pattern Analysis and Machine Intelligence*, *16*(2), 113–129. doi:10.1109/34.273737

Fisher, R. A. (1936). The use of multiple measurements in taxonomic problems. *Annals of Eugenics*, *7*, 179–188. doi:10.1111/j.1469-1809.1936.tb02137.x

Flom, L., & Safir, A. (1987). *Iris recognition system*. (U.S. Patent 4,641,349).

Förstner, W., & Gülch, E. (1987). A fast operator for detection and precise location of istinct points, corners and centers of circular features. In *Proc. Intercommission Conf. Photogrammetric Data*, Interlaken, Switzerland, (pp. 281-305).

Forsyth, D., & Ponce, J. (2003). *Computer vision: A modern approach*. Upper Saddle River, NJ: Prentice Hall.

Fourer, R., Gray, D. M., & Kernighan, B. W. (2002). *AMPL: A modeling language for mathematical programming*. Duxbury Press.

Fox, J. R., & Randall, J. E. (1970). Relationship between forearm tremor and the biceps electromyogram. *Journal of Applied Physiology*, *29*.

Freedman, D., Pisani, R., & Purves, R. (1997). *Statistics* (3rd ed.). New York, NY: Norton College Books.

Freeman, H., & Davis, L. S. (1977). A corner-finding algorithm for chain-coded curves. *IEEE Transactions on Computers*, *C-26*, 297–303. doi:10.1109/TC.1977.1674825

Freitas, F. D., De Souza, A. F., & de Almeida, A. R. (2009). Prediction-based portfolio optimization model using neural networks. *Neurocomputing*, *72*(10-12), 2155–2170. doi:10.1016/j.neucom.2008.08.019

Freund, Y., & Schapire, R. E. (1995). Experiments with a new boosting algorithm. The Thirteenth International Conference on Machine Learning, (pp. 148-156).

Fridlund, A. J., & Cacioppo, J. T. (1986). Guidelines for human electromyographic research. *Journal of Psychophysiology*, *23*(4), 567–589.

Fridlund, A. J., & Cacioppo, J. T. (1986). Guidelines for human electromyographic research. *Psychophysiology*, *23*(5), 567–589. doi:10.1111/j.1469-8986.1986.tb00676.x

Froelich, W., & Wakulicz-Deja, A. (2007). Learning fuzzy cognitive maps from the Web for the stock market decision support system. *Advances in Soft Computing*, *43*, 106–111. doi:10.1007/978-3-540-72575-6_17

Froelich, W., & Wakulicz-Deja, P. (2009). A predictive capabilities of adaptive and evolutionary fuzzy cognitive maps - A comparative study. In Nguyen, N. T., & Szczerbicki, E. (Eds.), *Intel. Sys. for Know. Management, SCI 252* (pp. 153–174). Berlin, Germany: Springer Verlag. doi:10.1007/978-3-642-04170-9_7

Fudeberg, D., & Tirole, J. (1991). *Game theory*. Cambridge, MA: MIT Press.

Fujisawa, Y., Meng, S., Wakabayashi, T., & Kimura, F. (2002). Handwritten numeral recognition using gradient and curvature of gray images. *Pattern Recognition, 5*(10), 2051–2059.

Fukunaga, K. (1990). *Introduction to statistical pattern recognition*. New York, NY: Academic Press.

Fürst, K. (2010). Applying fuzzy models in rating systems. *Neural Network World, 20*, 113–124.

Fu, Y., Guo, G., & Huang, T. S. (2010). Age synthesis and estimation via faces: A survey. *IEEE Transactions on Pattern Analysis and Machine Intelligence, 32*(11), 1955–1976. doi:10.1109/TPAMI.2010.36

Gacanin, H., Takaoka, S., & Adachi, F. (September 2005). A study of channel estimation in OFDM systems. In *Proceedings of Pilot-Assisted Channel Estimation for OFDM / TDM with Frequency-Domain Equalization, Vehicular Technology Conference*, USA.

Gallinari, P. (1995). Training of modular neural net systems. In M. A, Arbib (Ed.), *The handbook of brain theory and neural networks* (pp. 582–585), Cambridge, MA: MIT Press.

Gall, R. B. J., & Seidel, H. P. (2006). *Robust pose estimation with 3D textured models*. Lecture Notes in Computer Science.

Ganis, M. D., Wilson, C. L., & Blue, J. L. (1998). Neural network based systems for hand-print OCR applications. *Transactions on Image Processing, 7*(8), 1097–1112. doi:10.1109/83.704304

Gao, Y., Leung, M. K. H., Hui, S. C., & Tananda, M. W. (2003). Facial expression recognition from line-based caricatures. *IEEE Transactions on Systems, Man, and Cybernetics. Part A, Systems and Humans, 33*(3), 407–412. doi:10.1109/TSMCA.2003.817057

Gaspar, J., Decc'o, C., Okamoto, J., Jr., & Santos-Victor, J. (2002). In *Constant resolution omnidirectional cameras*. In III Workshop on Omnidirectinal Vision.

Ge, W., Rothenberger, M., & Chen, E. (2007). A model for an electronic information marketplace. *Australasian Journal of Information Systems, 13*(1).

Geng, X., Zhou, Z., & Smith-Miles, K. (2007). Automatic age estimation based on facial aging patterns. *IEEE Transactions on Pattern Analysis and Machine Intelligence, 29*(12), 2234–2240. doi:10.1109/TPAMI.2007.70733

Gennis, P., Gallagher, J., Falvo, C., Baker, S., & Than, W. (1989). Clinical criteria for the detection of pneumonia in adults: Guidelines for ordering chest roentgenograms in the emergency department. *The Journal of Emergency Medicine, 7*(3), 263–268. doi:10.1016/0736-4679(89)90358-2

Gentile, J. E., Ratha, N., & Connell, J. (2009, September). *SLIC: Short length iris code*. International Conference on Biometrics: Theory, Applications and Systems, Washington, DC.

George, W. B. (2004). *Neurology in clinical practice: Principles of diagnosis and management*. Taylor & Francis.

Georgopoulos, V. C., Malandraki, G. A., & Stylios, C. D. (2003). A fuzzy cognitive map approach to differential diagnosis of specific language impairment. *Artificial Intelligence in Medicine, 29*(3), 261–278. doi:10.1016/S0933-3657(02)00076-3

Georgopoulos, V., & Stylios, C. D. (2005). Augmented fuzzy cognitive maps supplemented with case base reasoning for advanced medical decision support. In Nikravesh, M., Zadeh, L. A., & Kacprzyk, J. (Eds.), *Soft computing for information processing and analysis enhancing the power of the Information Technology, Studies in fuzziness and soft computing* (pp. 391–405). Springer-Verlag. doi:10.1007/3-540-32365-1_17

Gerke, M., & Hoyer, H. (1997). Fuzzy backpropagation training of neural networks. In Reusch, B. (Ed.), *Computational intelligence theory and applications* (pp. 416–427). Berlin, Germany: Springer.

Ghosh, A., Pal, N. R., & Pal, S. K. (1993). Self-organization for object extraction using multilayer neural network and fuzziness measures. *IEEE Transactions on Fuzzy Systems, 1*(1), 54–68. doi:10.1109/TFUZZ.1993.390285

Ghosh, S., & Ghosh, A. (2002). A GA-fuzzy approach to evolve Hopfield type optimum networks for object extraction. In. *Proceedings of AFSS, 2002*, 444–449.

Giraldi, G. A., Rodrigues, P. S., Kitani, E. C., Sato, J. R., & Thomaz, C. E. (2008). Statistical learning approaches for discriminant features selection. *Journal of the Brazilian Computer Society, 14*(2), 7–22. doi:10.1007/BF03192556

Glover, J., Rus, D., & Roy, N. (2008). Probabilistic models of object geometry for grasp planning. *Robotics: Science and Systems IV Conference*, held in 2008 at the Swiss Federal Institute of Technology in Zurich, (pp. 278-285).

Glover, J., Rus, D., Roy, N., & Gordon, G. (2006). Robust models of object geometry. In *Proceedings of the IROS Workshop on From Sensors to Human Spatial Concepts*, Beijing, China.

Goertzel, B. (1989). *Quantum neural networks*. Retrieved from http://goertzel/org/ben/quantnet.html

Goldberg, D. E. (1989). *Genetic algorithms: Search, optimization and machine learning*. New York, NY: Addison-Wesley.

Goleman, D. (1995). *Emotional intelligence*. New York, NY: Bantam.

Golub, G. H., & Van Loan, C. F. (1996). *Matrix computations*. The Johns University Press.

Golub, G. H., Van, L., & Charles, F. (1996). *Matrix computations*. Johns Hopkins.

Gomathi, V., Ramar, K., & Jeevakumar, A. Santhiyaku. (2010). A neuro fuzzy approach for facial expression recognition using LBP histograms. *International Journal of Computer Theory and Engineering, 2*(2), 1793–8201.

Gonzalez, C. G., & Woods, R. E. (2001). *Digital image processing*. Upper Saddle River, NJ: Prentice Hall.

Gonzalez, R. C., & Woods, R. E. (2002). *Digital image processing* (2nd ed.). Pearson Education.

Gonzalez, R. C., & Woods, R. E. (2003). *Digital image processing*. India: Pearson Education.

Gool, L. V., Dewaele, P., & Oosterlinck, A. (1985). Texture analysis anno 1983. *Computer Vision Graphics and Image Processing, 29*, 336–357. doi:10.1016/0734-189X(85)90130-6

Gopathy, P., Nicolaos, B., & Karayiannis, N. B. (1997). Quantum neural networks are inherently fuzzy feedforward neural networks. *IEEE Transactions on Neural Networks, 8*(3), 679–693. doi:10.1109/72.572106

Gordon, R. N. (1990). *The structure of emotions: Investigations in cognitive philosophy*. Cambridge, UK: Cambridge Studies in Philosophy, Cambridge University Press.

Goswami, J. C., & Chan, A. K. (1999). *Fundamentals of wavelets-Theory, algorithm, and applications*. Wiley Inter-Science.

Gourier, N., Hall, D., & Crowley, J. L. (2004). *Facial features detection robust to pose, Illumination and identity* Paper presented at the IEEE International Conference on Systems, Man and Cybernetics.

Grabisch, M., & Labreuche, C. (2010). A decade of application of the Choquet and Sugeno integrals in multicriteria decision making. *Annals of Operations Research, 175*, 247–286. doi:10.1007/s10479-009-0655-8

Grassi Junior, V., & Okamoto Junior, J. (2000). Development of an omnidirectional vision system. *Journal of the Brazilian Society of Mechanical Sciences and Engineering, 28*(1), 58–68. doi:10.1590/S1678-58782006000100007

Graupe, D., & Cline, W. (1975). Functional separation of EMG signals via ARMA identification methods for prosthesis control purposes. *IEEE Transactions on Systems, Man, and Cybernetics, 5*, 252–259.

Greene, J. D., Sommerville, R. B., Nystrom, L. E., Darley, J. M., & Cohen, J. D. (2001). An fMRI investigation of emotional engagement in moral judgment. *Science, 293*(5537), 2105–2108. doi:10.1126/science.1062872

Grewal, M. S., & Andrews, A. P. (2008). *Kalman filtering: Theory and practice using Matlab*. New Jersey: John Wiley & Sons. Inc.

Grimson, W. E. L. (1990). *Object recognition by computer: The role of geometric constraints* (p. 33). Cambridge, MA: MIT Press.

Grossberg, S. (n.d.). *Anticipatory brain dynamics in perception, cognition, and action*. Retrieved from http://www.cns.bu.edu/Profiles/Grossberg

Grossberg, S. (1976). Adaptive pattern classification and universal recoding: Parallel development and coding of neural feature detectors. *Biological Cybernetics, 23,* 121–134. doi:10.1007/BF00344744

Grover, L. K. (1998). Quantum computers can search rapidly by using almost any transformation. *Physical Review Letters, 80*(19), 4329–4332. doi:10.1103/PhysRevLett.80.4329

Guo, L., Ma, Y., Cukic, B., & Singh, H. (2004). Robust prediction of fault proneness by random forests. In *Proceedings of the 15th International Symposium on Software Reliability Engineering* (ISSRE'04), (pp. 417–428).

Gupta, A. Mazumdar, C., & Patranobisc, D. (2002). A distributed simulation technique for multiple input multiple output systems. *ISA: The Instrumentation, Systems, and Automation Society- ISA Transactions, 41,* 421 435.

Gutierrez-Osuna, R. (2001). *Lecture 13: Validation.* Wright State University. Retrieved September 2007 from http://research.cs.tamu.edu/prism/lectures

Haag, A., Goronzy, S., Schaich, P., & Williams, J. (2004). *Emotion recognition using bio-sensors: First steps towards an automatic system, (LNCS 3068).* Berlin, Germany: Springer.

Haddadnia, J., Ahmadi, M., & Faez, K. (2003). An efficient feature extraction method with Pseudo-Zernike moment in RBF neural network-based human face recognition system. *EURASIP Journal on Applied Signal Processing,* (9): 890–901. doi:10.1155/S1110865703305128

Hafed, Z. M., & Levine, M. D. (2001). Face recognition using the discrete cosine transforms. *International Journal of Computer Vision, 43*(3), 167–188. doi:10.1023/A:1011183429707

Hagan, M. T., Demuth, H. B., & Beale, M. H. (1996). *Neural network design.* Boston, MA: PWS-Kent.

Hagan, M. T., & Menhaj, M. B. (1994). Training feedforward networks with the Marquardt algorithm. *IEEE Transactions on Neural Networks, 5*(6), 989–993. doi:10.1109/72.329697

Hagbarth, K. E., & Young, R. R. (1979). Participation of the stretch reflex in human physiological tremor. *Brain, 102,* 509–526. doi:10.1093/brain/102.3.509

Hagiwara, M. (1993). Removal of hidden units and weights for backpropagation networks. In *Proceedings of International Joint Conference on Neural Networks, 1,* 351-354.

Hagras, H. (2004). A type-2 fuzzy logic controller for autonomous mobile robots. In *Proceeding of IEEE FUZZ Conference,* Budapest, Hungary.

Hahn, W. (1963). *Theory and application of Liapunov's direct method.* Englewood Cliffs, NJ: Prentice-Hall.

Haig, A. J., Geblum, J. B., Rechtien, J. J., & Gitter, A. J. (1996). Technology assessment: The use of surface EMG in the diagnosis and treatment of nerve and muscle disorders. *Muscle & Nerve,* 392–395. doi:10.1002/(SICI)1097-4598(199603)19:3<392::AID-MUS21>3.0.CO;2-T

Hair, J., Anderson, R., & Tatham, W. (2006). *Black multivariate data analysis.* Pearson Education.

Hall, M. (2000). Correlation-based feature selection for discrete and numeric class machine learning. In *Proceedings of the 17th International Conference on Machine Learning,* (pp. 359–366).

Hallett, M. (2003). *Movement disorders.* Elsevier Health Sciences.

Halstead, M. (1977). *Elements of software science.* Elsevier.

Hamdy, A., Elmahdy, M., & Elsabrouty, M. (2007). Face detection using PCA and skin-tone extraction for drowsy driver application. *5th International Conference on Information & Communications Technology,* (pp. 135-137).

Hameed, I. A. (2009). Simplified architecture of a type-2 fuzzy controller using embedded type-1 fuzzy controllers and its application to a greenhouse climate control system. *Proceedings of the Institution of Mechanical Engineers. Part I, Journal of Systems and Control Engineering, 233*(5), 619–631. doi:10.1243/09596518JSCE708

Hammarstedt, P., Sturm, P., & Heyden, A. (2005). Closed-form solutions and degenerate cases for camera calibration with one-dimensional objects. In *Proceedings of X IEEE International Conference on Computer Vision.*

Hammer, B., Strickert, M., & Villmann, T. (2005). Supervised neural gas with general similarity measure. *Neural Processing Letters, 21*(1), 21–44. doi:10.1007/s11063-004-3255-2

Hammoud, R. I., Witt, G., Dufour, R., Wilhelm, A., & Newman, T. (2008). On driver eye closure recognition for commercial vehicles. *Proceedings of SAE Commercial Vehicles Engineering Congress and Exhibition,* Chicago, IL, USA.

Han, Y., Koike, H., Wang, B., & Idesawa, M. (2010). Recognition of objects in various situations from two dimensional images. *IEEE International Conference on Image Processing Theory, Tool and Applications* (IPTA'10), (pp. 405-410).

Hanley, J., & McNeil, B. J. (1982). The meaning and use of the area under a receiver operating characteristic (ROC) curve. *Radiology, 143,* 29–36.

Hans, E., Wullink, G., van Houdenhoven, M., & Kazemier, G. (2008). Robust surgery loading. *European Journal of Operational Research, 185*(3), 1038–1050. doi:10.1016/j.ejor.2006.08.022

Han, Y., Wang, B., Idesawa, M., & Shimai, H. (2010). Recognition of multiple configurations of objects with limited data. *Pattern Recognition, 43,* 1467–1475. doi:10.1016/j.patcog.2009.09.028

Hanzo, L., Choi, B. J., & Munster, M. (2004, Nov.). A stroll along multi-carrier boulevard towards next-generation plaza - Space-time coded adaptive OFDM and MC-CDMA comparison. *IEEE Veh. Technol. Soc. Newslett., 51,* 10–19.

Hanzo, L., Yang, L. L., Kuan, E. L., & Yen, K. (2003). *Single- and multi-carrier DSCDMA: Multi-user detection, space-time spreading, synchronisation and standards.* Piscataway, NJ: IEEE Press/ Wiley. doi:10.1002/0470863110

Hao, F., Daugman, J., & Zielinski, P. (2008). A fast search algorithm for a large fuzzy database. *IEEE Transactions on Information Forensics and Security, 3*(2), 203–212. doi:10.1109/TIFS.2008.920726

Haralick, R. M. (1979). Statistical and structural approaches to texture. *Proceedings of the IEEE, 67*(5), 786–804. doi:10.1109/PROC.1979.11328

Harp, S. A., & Samad, T., & Guha. (1989). A. Designing application-specific neural networks using the genetic algorithm. *Advances in Neural Information Processing Systems, 2,* 447–454.

Harris, C., & Stephens, M. (1988). A combined corner and edge detection. In *Proceedings of the Fourth Alvey Vision Conference* (pp. 147-151). Manchester, UK.

Harris, K. S. (1970). Physiological measures of speech movements: EMG and fiberoptic studies. *ASHA Reports, 5,* 271–282.

Harrison, R., Counsell, S. J., & Nithi, R. V. (1998). An evaluation of MOOD set of object-oriented software metrics. *IEEE Transactions on Software Engineering, 24*(6), 491–496. doi:10.1109/32.689404

Hartigan, J. A., & Wong, M. A. (1979). A k-means clustering algorithm. *Applied Statistics, 28,* 100–108. doi:10.2307/2346830

Hartley, L., Horberry, T., & Mabbott, N. (2000). *Review of fatigue detection and prediction technologies*: Institute for Research in Safety and Transport, Murdoch University, Western Australia and Gerald Krueger - Krueger Ergonomics Consultants, Virginia, USA.

Hartley, R., & Schaffalitzky, F. (2004). L-infinity minimization in geometric reconstruction problems. In *IEEE Conference on Computer Vision and Pattern Recognition,* Washington, USA, (pp. 504-509).

Hartley, R., & Seo, Y. (2008). Verifying global minima for L2 minimization problems. In *IEEE Conference on Computer Vision and Pattern Recognition,* Anchorage, USA, (pp. 1-8).

Hartley, R. (1997a). In defence of the eight point algorithm. *IEEE Transactions on Pattern Analysis and Machine Intelligence, 19*(6), 580–593. doi:10.1109/34.601246

Hartley, R. (1997b). Self-calibration of stationary cameras. *International Journal of Computer Vision, 22*(1), 5–23. doi:10.1023/A:1007957826135

Hartley, R., & Sturm, P. (1997). Triangulation. *Computer Vision and Image Understanding, 68*(2), 146–157. doi:10.1006/cviu.1997.0547

Hartley, R., & Zisserman, A. (2000). *Multiple view geometry in computer vision.* Cambridge University Press.

Hartley, R., & Zisserman, A. (2000). *Multiple view in computer vision*. Cambridge University Press.

Hassibi, B., & Stork, D. G. (1993). Second-order derivatives for network pruning: Optimal Brain Surgeon Advances. In Giles, C. L., Hanson, S. J., & Cowan, J. D. (Eds.), *Neural information processing systems, 5* (pp. 164–171). San Mateo, CA: Morgan-Kaufmann.

Haykin, S. (1999). *Neural networks: A comprehensive foundation*. New Delhi, India: Prentice Hall.

Haykin, S. (2003). *Neural networks: A comprehensive foundation* (2nd ed.). New Delhi, India: Pearson Education.

Haykins, S. (1999). *Neural networks and learning machines*. Upper Saddle River, NJ: Prentice-Hall.

Haykins, S. (2002). *Adaptive filter theory* (4th ed.). New Delhi, India: Pearson Education.

Hebb, D. O. (1949). *The organization of behavior*. New York: John Wiley.

Hecht-Nielsen, R. (1987). Counterpropagation networks. *Applied Optics, 26*, 4979–4984. doi:10.1364/AO.26.004979

Heikkilä, J. (2000). Geometric camera calibration using circular control points. *IEEE Transactions on Pattern Analysis and Machine Intelligence, 22*(10), 1066–1076. doi:10.1109/34.879788

He, K., Zhou, J., Song, Y., & Qiao, Q. (2004). Multiresolution eye location from image. *Proceedings of Signal Processing, 2*, 901–905.

Hermens, H. (1999). *European recommendations for surface electromyography: Results of the Seniam Project (SENIAM)*. Roessingh Research and Development.

Hernandez, O. J., & Kleiman, M. S. (2005). Face recognition using multispectral random field texture models, color content, and biometric features. *Proceedings of Applied Imagery and Pattern Recognition Workshop*, (p. 209).

Herota, T. (1967). The variation of hand tremor with force in healthy subjects. *The Journal of Physiology, 191*, 699–711.

Hewavitharana, S., & Fernando, H. C. (2002). A two stage classification approach to Tamil handwriting recognition. *Tamil Internet*, 118–124.

Hijazi, S. L. (2006). *Multiuser detection for multicarrier communication systems*. Manhattan, Kansas, USA: Department of Electrical and Computer Engineering, College of Engineering, Kansas State University.

Hines, W. W., & Montgomery, D. C. (1990). *Probability and statistics in engineering and management science* (3rd ed.). John Wiley and Sons.

Hiremath, P. S., & Humnabad Iranna, Y. (December 2005). Color image segmentation based on clustering method for esophageal cancer detection in endoscopic images. In *Proceedings of the International Conference on Cognition and Recognition (ICCR-2005)*, Mysore, Karnataka, India, (pp. 705-710). Allied Publishers Pvt. Ltd.

Hiremath, P. S., & Humnabad Iranna, Y. (December 2006a). Automated cell nuclei segmentation and classification of squamous cell carcinoma from microscopic images of esophagus tissue. In *Proceedings of IEEE 14th International Conference on Advanced Computing and Communication (ADCOM-2006)*, NITK, Surathkal, Karnataka, India, IEEE, (pp. 211-216).

Hiremath, P. S., & Humnabad Iranna, Y. (December 2006c). Automatic identification of abnormal region (esophageal cancer) of esophagus from endoscopic images using textural features. In *Proceedings of the IEEE 1st International Conference on Signal and Image Processing (ICSIP-2006)*, BVB, Hubli, Karnataka, India, (pp. 295-299). Macmillan India Ltd.

Hiremath, P. S., Dhandra, B. V., Humnabad Iranna, Y., Hegadi, R., & Rajput, G. G. (2003). Detection of esophageal cancer (necrosis) in endoscopic images using color image segmentation. In *Proceedings of the Second National Conference on Document Analysis and Recognition (NCDAR-2003)*, PES, Mandya, Karnataka, India, (pp. 417-422).

Hiremath, P. S., Humnabad Iranna, Y., Dhandra, B. V., & Rajput, G. G. (December 2003). On the comparison of color image segmentation algorithms with reference to the detection of esophagus cancer (necrosis). In *Proceedings of the Fifth International Conference on Advances in Pattern Recognition (ICAPR-2003)*, ISI, Kolkata, India, (pp. 223-226). Allied Publishers Pvt. Ltd.

Hiremath, P. S., & Humnabad Iranna, Y. (2005, August). Automated detection of esophageal cancer (necrosis) in endoscopic images using color image segmentation. *Global Engineering, Science, and Technology Society. International Transactions on Computer Science and Engineering, 16*(1), 107–118.

Hiremath, P. S., & Humnabad Iranna, Y. (2006b, December). Automatic detection of abnormal regions in endoscopic images of esophagus using a skin color model. *ICGST International Journal on Artificial Intelligence and Machine Learning, 6*(4), 53–57.

Hiremath, P. S., Humnabad Iranna, Y., & Pujari, J. D. (2007). Classification of squamous cell carcinoma based on color and textural features in microscopic images of esophagus tissues. *International Journal of Computer Science, 3*(7), 566–573.

Hiremath, P. S., & Prabhakar, C. J. (2006). Acquiring non linear subspace for face recognition using symbolic kernel PCA method. *Journal of Symbolic Data Analysis, 4*, 15–26.

Hiremath, P. S., & Prabhakar, C. J. (2008a). Extraction and recognition of non linear interval type features using symbolic KDA algorithm with application to face recognition. [Hindawi Publishing Corporation.]. *Research Letters in Signal Processing, 2*, 1–5.

Hiremath, P. S., & Prabhakar, C. J. (2008b). Symbolic factorial discriminant analysis for illumination invariant face recognition. [World Scientific Publisher.]. *International Journal of Pattern Recognition and Artificial Intelligence, 22*(3), 371–387. doi:10.1142/S021800140800634X

Hiremath, P. S., & Prabhakar, C. J. (2009). Symbolic kernel Fisher discriminant method with a new RBF kernel function for face recognition. *International Journal of Machine Graphics and Vision, 18*(4), 383–404.

Hoare, Z., & Lim, W. S. (2006). Pneumonia: update on diagnosis and management. *BMJ (Clinical Research Ed.), 332*, 1077–1079. Retrieved from http://www.bmj.com/cgi/content/full/332/7549/1077. doi:10.1136/bmj.332.7549.1077

Ho, D. W. C., Zhang, P. A., & Xu, J. (2001). Fuzzy wavelet networks for function learning. *IEEE Transactions on Fuzzy Systems, 9*, 200–211. doi:10.1109/91.917126

Hoffman, D. D., & Richards, W. A. (1984). Parts of recognition. *Cognition, 18*, 65–96. doi:10.1016/0010-0277(84)90022-2

Holeček, P., & Talašová, J. (2010). FuzzME: A new software for multiple-criteria fuzzy evaluation. *Acta Universitatis Matthiae Belii, series Mathematics, 16*(2010), 35–51

Hon, H.-P., Yunmei, C., Huafeng, L., & Pengcheng, S. (2005). Level set active contours on unstructured point cloud. In *Proceedings of IEEE International Conference on Computer Vision and Pattern Recognition* (vol. 2, pp. 20-25).

Hopfield, J. J. (1982). Neural networks and physical systems with emergent collective computational abilities. [National Academy of Sciences: Washington, DC, USA.]. *Proceedings of the National Academy of Sciences of the United States of America, 79*(8), 2554–2558. doi:10.1073/pnas.79.8.2554

Horikawa, S., Furuhashi, T., & Uchikawa, Y. (1992). On fuzzy modeling using fuzzy neural networks with back propagation algorithm. *IEEE Transactions on Neural Networks, 3*, 801–806. doi:10.1109/72.159069

Horlings, R., Datcu, D., & Othkrantz, I. J. M. (2008). Emotion recognition using brain activity. In *Proc. of Int. Conf. on Computer Systems and Technologies – CompSysTech*, (pp. 1-6).

Hosny, K. M. (2007). Exact Legendre moment computation for gray level images. *Pattern Recognition, 40*(12), 3597–3705. doi:10.1016/j.patcog.2007.04.014

Hou, C., Ai, H. Z., & Lao, S. H. (2007). Multiview pedestrian detection based on vector boosting. *The 8th Asian Conference on Computer Vision*, (pp. 210-219).

Hsu, R. L., Abdel-Mottaleb, M., & Jain, A. K. (2002). Face detection in color images. *IEEE Transactions on Pattern Analysis and Machine Intelligence, 24*(5), 696–706. doi:10.1109/34.1000242

Huang, X., Jack, M., & Ariki, Y. (1990). *Hidden Markov models for speech recognition*. Edinburgh University Press.

Huang, Y. (2009). Advances in artificial neural networks – Methodological development and application. *Algorithms, 2*, 973–1007. doi:10.3390/algor2030973

Huang, Y., Luo, S., & Chen, E. (2002). *An efficient iris recognition system* (pp. 450–454). Machine Learning and Cybernetics.

Hudgins, B., Parker, P., & Scott, R. N. (1993). A new strategy for multifunction myoelectric control. *IEEE Transactions on Bio-Medical Engineering, 40*(1), 82–94. doi:10.1109/10.204774

Hudson, D. L. (2006). Medical expert systems. In *Encyclopedia of biomedical engineering*. John Wiley and Sons. doi:10.1002/9780471740360.ebs0751

Hu, M. K. (1962). Visual pattern recognition by moment invariants. *I.R.E. Transactions on Information Theory, 8,* 179–187. doi:10.1109/TIT.1962.1057692

Hu, M., Ping, X., & Ding, Y. (2004). *Automated cell nucleus segmentation using improved snake* (pp. 2737–2740). ICIP.

Humnabad, I. (September 2007). *A study on the medical image analysis using digital image processing techniques*. Gulbarga University, Gulbarga, Karnataka State, India.

Hung, Y. S., & Tang, W. K. (2006). Projective reconstruction from multiple views with minimization of 2D reprojection error. *International Journal of Computer Vision, 66*(3), 305–317. doi:10.1007/s11263-005-3675-0

Hunt, K. J., Sbarbaro, D., Zbikowski, R., & Gawthrop, P. J. (1992). Neural networks for control system - A survey. *Automatica, 28,* 1083–1112. doi:10.1016/0005-1098(92)90053-I

Husler, G., & Ritter, D. (1999). Feature-based object recognition and localization in 3D-space, using a single video image. *International Journal of Computer Vision and Image Understanding, 73*(1), 64–81. doi:10.1006/cviu.1998.0704

Hutton, T. J., Buxton, B. F., Hammond, P., & Potts, H. W. W. (2003). Estimating average growth trajectories in shape-space using Kernel smoothing. *IEEE Transactions on Medical Imaging, 22*(6), 747–753. doi:10.1109/TMI.2003.814784

Hwang, B. W., & Lee, S. W. (2003). Reconstruction of partially damaged face images based on a morphable face model. *IEEE Transactions on Pattern Analysis and Machine Intelligence, 25*(3), 365–372. doi:10.1109/TPAMI.2003.1182099

Hyvärinen, A., Karhunen, J., & Oja, E. (2001). *Independent component analysis*. Wiley-Interscience. doi:10.1002/0471221317

Iftekharuddin, K. M., Schechinger, T. D., & Jemili, K. (1995). Feature-based neural wavelet optical character recognition system. *Optical Engineering (Redondo Beach, Calif.), 34*(11), 3193–3199. doi:10.1117/12.213654

ILOG, Inc. (1998). *CPLEX 6.0 documentation supplement.*

Intel. (2006). *Open source computer vision library*. Retrieved from http://www.intel.com/research/mrl/research/opencv/

Itaru, N., & Yosnino, T. (1997). An analysis of the chaotic transition of ode1 muscle tremor mechanism obtained by artificial neural network, *Journal of Neuroscience Methods.*

Ives, R. W., Guidry, A. J., & Etter, D. M. (2004). *Iris recognition using histogram analysis* (pp. 562–566). Signals, Systems and Computers.

Izumitani, K., Mikami, T., & Inoue, K. (1984). A model of expression grade for face graphs using fuzzy integral. *Syst. Control, 28*(10), 590–596.

Jacobs, R. A. (1988). Increased rates of convergence through learning rate adaptation. *Neural Networks, 1,* 295–307. doi:10.1016/0893-6080(88)90003-2

Jacquey, F., Comby, F., & Strauss, O. (2008). Fuzzy Edge detection for omnidirectional images. *Fuzzy Sets and Systems, 159,* 1991–2010. doi:10.1016/j.fss.2008.02.022

Jain, A. K., Duin, R. P. W., & Mao, J. (2000). Statistical pattern recognition: A review. *IEEE Transactions on Pattern Analysis and Machine Intelligence, 22*(1), 4–37. doi:10.1109/34.824819

Jain, A. K., Duin, R. P. W., & Mao, J. (2000). Statistical pattern recognition: A review. *Transactions on Pattern Analysis and Machine Intelligence, 2*(1), 4–35. doi:10.1109/34.824819

Jamshidnejad, A., & Jamshidined, A. (2009). *Facial emotion recognition for human computer interaction using a fuzzy model in the e-business*. IEEE Conference on Innovative Technologies in Intelligent Systems and Industrial Applications (CITISIA 2009) Monash University, Sunway campus, Malaysia.

Jang, J.-S. R., & Mizutani, E. (1996). *Levenberg-Marquardt method for ANFIS learning*. Paper presented at Biennial Conference of the North American Fuzzy Information Processing Society, (pp. 87 -91).

Jang, J. S. R. (1993). (1993). ANFIS: Adaptive-network-based fuzzy inference system. *IEEE Transactions on Systems, Man, and Cybernetics*, *23*, 665–685. doi:10.1109/21.256541

Jang, J. S. R., Sun, C. T., & Mizutani, E. (1997). *Neuro-fuzzy and soft computing – A computational approach to learning and machine intelligence*. Prentice Hall.

Jang, J.-S. R. (1993). ANFIS: Adaptive-network-based fuzzy inference systems. *IEEE Transactions on Systems, Man, and Cybernetics*, *23*(3), 665–685. doi:10.1109/21.256541

Jang, J.-S. R., & Sun, C.-T. (1993). Functional equivalence between radial basis function networks and fuzzy inference systems. *IEEE Transactions on Neural Networks*, *4*(1), 156–159. doi:10.1109/72.182710

Jankovic, J. (2009). Movement disorders. *Issue of Neurologic Clinics*. Saunders.

Jankovic, J., & Tolosa, E. (2007). *Parkinson's disease and movement disorders*. Lippincott Williams & Wilkins.

Jayadeva, R. K., & Khemchandani, R. (2007). TWIN support vector machines for pattern classification. *IEEE Transactions on Pattern Analysis and Machine Intelligence*, *29*(5), 905–910. doi:10.1109/TPAMI.2007.1068

jedit. (n.d.). *Website*. Retrieved from http://sourceforge.net/projects/jedit/

Jee, H., Lee, K., & Pan, S. (2004). Eye and face detection using SVM. *Conference on Intelligent Sensors, Sensor Networks and Information*, (pp. 577-580).

Jegou, D., Kim, D. W., Baptiste, P., & Lee, P. K. H. (2006). A contract net based intelligent agent system for solving the reactive hoist scheduling problem. *Expert Systems with Applications*, *30*(2), 156–167. doi:10.1016/j.eswa.2005.06.019

Jia, H. J., & Martinez, A. M. (2009). *Support vector machines in face recognition with occlusion*. IEEE International Conference on Computer Vision and Pattern Recognition.

Jianbo, S., & Tomasi, C. (1994) Good features to track. In *Proceedings of the International Conference on Computer Vision and Pattern Recognition*, (pp. 593-600).

Jiang, J., Alwan, A., Keating, P., Auer, E. T., Jr., & Bernstein, L. E. (2002). On the relationship between face movements, tongue movements, and speech acoustics. *EURASIP Journal on Applied Signal Processing: Special Issue on Joint Audio-Visual Speech Processing*, 1174-1188.

Jiang, M., & Hanzo, L. (2007, July). Multiuser MIMO-OFDM for next-generation wireless systems. *Proceedings of the IEEE*, *95*(7), 1430–1469. doi:10.1109/JPROC.2007.898869

Jilani, T. A., & Burney, S. M. A. (2008). A refined fuzzy time series model for stock market forecasting. *Physica A*, *387*, 2857–2862. doi:10.1016/j.physa.2008.01.099

Jin, L., Junhong, X., Wang, C., Lulu, Z., Hong, Y., & Hong, L. (2006). Contour segmentation algorithm of multi-scale GVF snake. In *Proceedings of IEEE International Conference on Mechatronics and Automation* (pp. 537-542).

Ji, Q., & Yang, X. (2002). Real-time eye, gaze, and face pose tracking for monitoring driver vigilance. *Real-Time Imaging*, *8*, 357–377. doi:10.1006/rtim.2002.0279

Johnson, R. A., & Wichern, D. W. (1998). *Applied multivariate statistical analysis*. New Jersey: Prentice Hall.

Johnstone, T., van Reekum, C. M., Oakes, T. R., & Davidson, R. J. (2006). The voice of emotion: An FMRI study of neural responses to angry and happy vocal expressions. *Social Cognitive and Affective Neuroscience*, *1*(3), 242–249. doi:10.1093/scan/nsl027

Jones, M. J., & Viola, P. (2003). *Face recognition using boosted local features*. IEEE International Conference on Computer Vision.

Jones, R. D., Lee, Y. C., Barnes, C. W., Flake, G. W., Lee, K., Lewis, P. S., & Qian, S. (1990). Function approximation and time series prediction with neural networks. In *Proceedings of the International Joint Conference on Neural Networks* (pp. 17-21).

Jones, J., & Palmer, L. (1987). An evaluation of the two dimensional gabor filter model of simple receptive fields in cat striate cortex. *Journal of Neural Networks*, *58*(6), 1233–1258.

Jorge, F., Carvalho, S., Manuel, J., & Tavares, R. S. (2007). Eye detection using a deformable template in static images. *VIPimage - I ECCOMAS Thematic Conference on Computational Vision and Medical Image Processing*, (pp. 209-215).

Joshi, N., Sita, G., Ramakrishnan, G., Deepu, V., & Madhavnath, S. (2005). Machine recognition of online handwritten Devnagari characters. In *International Conference on Document Analysis and Recognition*, (pp. 1156-1160). Seoul, South Korea.

Ju, P., Kaelbling, L. P., & Singer, Y. (2000). *State-based classification of finger gestures from electromyographic signals.* Paper presented at the Seventeenth International Conference on Machine Learning.

Jun, L., Shunyi, Z., Ye, X., & Yanfei, S. (2007), Identifying Skype traffic by random forest. *International Conference on Wireless Communications, Networking and Mobile Computing*, 21-25 September, (pp. 2841–2844).

Jung, T.-P., Makeig, S., Lee, T.-W., McKeown, M., Brown, G., Bell, A., et al. (2000). *Independent component analysis of biomedical signals.* Paper presented at the International Workshop on Independent Component Analysis and Signal Separation.

Jung, T. P., Makeig, S., Humphries, C., Lee, T. W., McKeown, M. J., & Iragui, V. (2000). Removing electroencephalographic artifacts by blind source separation. *Psychophysiology*, *37*(2), 163–178. doi:10.1111/1469-8986.3720163

Kadir, T., & Brady, M. (2001). Saliency, scale and image description. *International Journal of Computer Vision*, *45*(2), 83–105. doi:10.1023/A:1012460413855

Kaelbling, L. P., Littman, M. L., & Moore, A. W. (1996). Reinforcement learning: A survey. *Journal of Artificial Intelligence Research*, *4*, 237–285.

Kan, C., & Srinath, M. D. (2002). Invariant character recognition with Zernike and orthogonal Fourier-Mellin moments. *Pattern Recognition*, *35*(1), 143–154. doi:10.1016/S0031-3203(00)00179-5

Kang, D. J., Kim, J. Y., & Kweon, I. S. (2001). A stabilized snake constraint for tracking object boundaries. In *Proceedings of IEEE International Symposium on Industrial Electronics* (vol. 1, pp. 672-677).

Kang, S. B., Uyttendaele, M., Winder, S., & Szeliski, R. (2003). High dynamic range video. *ACM Transactions on Graphics*, *22*(3), 319–325. doi:10.1145/882262.882270

Kapamara, T., Sheibani, K., Hass, O. C. L., Reeves, C. R., & Petrovic, D. (2006). A review of scheduling problems in radiotherapy. In Proceedings of 18th International Conference on Systems Engineering, (pp. 207-211).

Karakasis, E. G., Papakostas, G. A., & Koulouriotis, D. E. (submitted). *Translation, scale and rotation dual Hahn moment invariants.*

Karkanis, S. A., Iakovidis, D. K., Maroulis, D. E., Karras, D. A., & Tzivars, M. (2003, September). Computer-aided tumor detection in endoscopic video using color wavelet features. *IEEE Transactions on Information Technology in Biomedicine*, *7*(3), 141–152. doi:10.1109/TITB.2003.813794

Karmakar, G., & Dooley, L. (2002). A generic fuzzy rule based in image segmentation algorithm. *Pattern Recognition Letters*, *23*, 1215–1227. doi:10.1016/S0167-8655(02)00069-7

Karnik, N. N., & Mendel, J. M. (1999). Applications of type-2 fuzzy logic systems to forecasting of time-series. *Information Sciences*, *120*, 89–111. doi:10.1016/S0020-0255(99)00067-5

Karnik, N. N., & Mendel, J. M. (2001). Centroid of a type-2 fuzzy set. *Information Sciences*, *132*(6), 195–220. doi:10.1016/S0020-0255(01)00069-X

Karnin, E. D. (1990). A simple procedure for pruning back-propagation trained neural networks. *IEEE Transactions on Neural Networks*, *1*, 239–242. doi:10.1109/72.80236

Kasabov, N. K. Israel, & S. I., Woodford, B. J. (2000). Adaptive, evolving, hybrid connectionist systems for image pattern recognition. In S. K. Pal, A. Ghosh, & M. K. Kundu (Eds.), *Soft computing for image processing.* Heidelberg, Germany: Physica-Verlag.

Kasabov, N., & Song, Q. (1999). *Dynamic evolving fuzzy neural networks with 'm-out-of-n' activation nodes for on-line adaptive systems.* Technical Report TR99/04, Department of Information Science, University of Otago.

Kass, M., Witkin, A., & Terzopoulos, D. (1987). Snakes: active contour models. *International Journal of Computer Vision*, *1*(4), 321–331. doi:10.1007/BF00133570

Kawaguchi, T., & Rizon, M. (2004). *An algorithm for real time eye detection in face images*. IEEE International Conference on Pattern Recognition.

Kawakami, F., Morishima, S., Yamada, H., & Harashima, H. (1994). Construction of 3-D emotion space using neural network. *Proc. of the 3rd International Conference on Fuzzy Logic, Neural Nets and Soft Computing*, Iizuka, (pp. 309-310).

Ke, Q., & Kanade, T. (2006). Uncertainty models in quasiconvex optimization for geometric reconstruction. In *IEEE Conference on Computer Vision and Pattern Recognition*, New York, USA, (pp. 1199-1205).

Ke, Y., & Sukthankar, R. (2004). PCA-SIFT: A more distinctive representation for local image descriptors. In *Proceedings of the IEEE Conference on Computer Vision and Pattern Recognition*, (pp. 506-513).

Keerthi, S. S., & Shevade, S. K. (2003). SMO algorithm for least squares SVM. *IEEE International Joint Conference on Neural Networks, 3*, 2088–2093.

Kendall, D. G. (1984). Shape manifolds, Procrustean metrics, and complex projectivespaces. *Bulletin of the London Mathematical Society, 16*, 81–121. doi:10.1112/blms/16.2.81

Kendall, D. G., Barden, D., Carne, T. K., & Le, H. (1999). *Shape and shape theory*. John Wiley and Sons Inc.

Kennedy, J., & Eberhart, R. C. (1995). *Particle swarm optimization*. Paper presented at IEEE int. Conf. Neural Networks, Perth, Australia, vol. IV, (pp. 1942-1948).

Kepenekci, B., Tek, F. B., & Akar, G. B. (2002). Occluded face recognition based on Gabor wavelets. *Proc. of Intl. Conf. on Image Processing*, vol. 1, (pp. 293-296).

Kerbyson, D. J., & Atherton, T. J. (1995). *Circle detection using hough transform filter*. International Conference on Image Processing and Its Application.

Kerr, T. H. (1998). Critique of some neural network architectures and claims for control and estimation. *IEEE Transactions on Aerospace and Electronic Systems, 34*(2), 406–419. doi:10.1109/7.670323

Khac, C. N., Park, J. H., & Jung, H.-Y. (2009). Face detection using variance based Haar-Like features and SVM. *World Academy of Science. Engineering and Technology, 60*, 165–168.

Khairosfaizal, W. M. K. W. M., & Nor'aini, A. J. (2009). Eyes detection in facial images using circular hough transform. *IEEE Conference on Signal Processing and Its Application*, (pp. 238-242).

Khan, M. S., & Khor, S. W. (2004). A framework for fuzzy rule-based cognitive maps. *Lecture Notes in Artificial Intelligence, 3157*, 454–463.

Khoshgaftaar, T. M., Allen, E. D., Hudepohl, J. P., & Aud, S. J. (1997). Application of neural networks to software quality modeling of a very large telecommunications system. *IEEE Transactions on Neural Networks, 8*(4), 902–909. doi:10.1109/72.595888

Khoshgoftaar, T., Allen, E., & Deng, J. (2002). Using regression trees to classify fault-prone software modules. *IEEE Transactions on Reliability, 51*(4), 455–462. doi:10.1109/TR.2002.804488

Kilian, M., Mitra, N., & Pottmann H. (2007). *Geometric modeling in shape space*. ACM SIGGRAPH 2007.

Kilic, K., Sproule, B., Turksen, I. B., & Naranjo, C. (2004). Pharmacokinetic application of fuzzy structure identification and reasoning. *Information Sciences, 162*, 121–137. doi:10.1016/j.ins.2004.03.005

Kilic, K., Uncu, O., & Turksen, I. B. (2007). Comparison of different strategies of utilizing fuzzy clustering in structure identification. *Information Sciences, 177*, 5153–5162. doi:10.1016/j.ins.2007.06.030

Kim, D., & Dahyot, R. (2008). *Face components detection using SURF descriptors and SVMs*. Paper presented at the International Machine Vision and Image Processing Conferenc.

Kim, I., Liu, C., & Kim, J. (1997). Stroke-guided pixel matching for handwritten Chinese character recognition, *In International Conference on Document Analysis and Recognition*, (pp.665-686). Bangalore, India.

Kim, K., & Han, I. (1998). *Extracting trading rules from the multiple classifiers and technical indicators in stock market*. Paper presented at KMIS'98 International Conference.

Kim, S.-H., Alattar, A., & Jang, J. W. (2006). A snake-based segmentation algorithm for objects with boundary concavities in stereo images. In *Proceedings of International Conference on Computational Intelligence and Security* (vol. 1, pp. 645-650).

Kim, W., Hong, S.-G., & Lee, J.-J. (1999). An active contour model using image flow for tracking a moving object. In *Proceedings of IEEE/RSJ International Conference on Intelligent Robots and Systems* (vol. 1, pp. 216-221).

Kim, C., & Hwang, J.-K. (2002). Fast and automatic video object segmentation and tracking for content-based applications. *IEEE Transactions on Circuits and Systems for Video Technology*, 12(2), 122–129. doi:10.1109/76.988659

Kim, D., Lee, W., & Kweon, I. (2004). Automatic edge detection using 3x3 ideal binary pixel patterns and fuzzy-based edge thresholding. *Pattern Recognition Letters*, 25, 101–106. doi:10.1016/j.patrec.2003.09.010

Kim, H.-J., & Kim, W.-Y. (2008). Eye detection in facial images using Zernike moments with SVM. *ETRI Journal*, 30(2), 335–337. doi:10.4218/etrij.08.0207.0150

Kim, I., & Kim, J. (2003). Statistical character structure modeling and its application to handwritten Chinese character recognition. *Transactions on Pattern Analysis and Machine Intelligence*, 25(11), 1422–1436. doi:10.1109/TPAMI.2003.1240117

Kim, J. (2007). Bimodal emotion recognition using speech and physiological changes. In Grimm, M., & Kroschel, K. (Eds.), *Robust speech recognition and understanding* (p. 460). Vienna, Austria.

Kim, J., & Andre, E. (2008). Emotion recognition based on physiological changes in music listening. *IEEE Transactions on Pattern Analysis and Machine Intelligence*, 30(12), 2067–2083. doi:10.1109/TPAMI.2008.26

Kim, Y. H., & Lewis, F. L. (1999). Neural network output feedback control of robot manipulators. *IEEE Transactions on Robotics and Automation*, 15(2), 301–309. doi:10.1109/70.760351

Kim, Y. I., Kim, D. W., Lee, D., & Lee, K. H. (2004). A cluster validation index for GK cluster analysis based on relative degree of sharing. *Information Sciences*, 168, 225–242. doi:10.1016/j.ins.2004.02.006

Kingsbury, N. G. (1999). Shift invariant properties of the dual-tree complex wavelet transform. *Proc. IEEE ICASSP '99*, Phoenix, AZ, March 1999.

Kingsbury, N. G. (2000). A dual-tree complex wavelet transform with improved orthogonality and symmetry properties. *Proc. IEEE ICIP*, Vancouver, Sept.11-13, 2000.

Kingsbury, N. G. (2005). The dual-tree complex wavelet transform- A coherent framework for multiscale signal and image processing. *IEEE Signal Processing Magazine*, (Nov): 2005.

Kirby, M., & Sirovich, L. (1990). Application of the Karhunen-Loeve procedure for the characterization of human faces. *IEEE Transactions on Pattern Analysis and Machine Intelligence*, 12(1), 103–108. doi:10.1109/34.41390

Kitani, E. C., Thomaz, C. E., & Gillies, D. F. (2006). A statistical discriminant model for face interpretation and reconstruction. In *Proceedings of Brazilian Symposium on Computer Graphics and Image Processing (SIBGRAPI)*, (pp. 247-254). IEEE CS Press.

Kitano, H. (1990). Empirical studies on the speed of convergence of neural network training using genetic algorithms. In *Proceedings of the Eleventh International Conference on Artificial Intelligence* (pp. 789-795).

Kitchen, L., & Rosenfeld, A. (1982). Gray-level corner detection. *Pattern Recognition Letters*, 1, 95–102. doi:10.1016/0167-8655(82)90020-4

Klir, G. J., & Yuan, B. (1995). *Fuzzy sets and fuzzy logic: Theory and applications*. NJ: Prentice-Hall.

Klusch, M. (2001). Information agent technology for the Internet: A survey. *Data & Knowledge Engineering*, 36(3), 337–372. doi:10.1016/S0169-023X(00)00049-5

Kobayashi H., & Hara, F. (1993). The recognition of basic facial expressions by neural network. *Trans. on the society of Instrument and Control Engineers*, 29(1), 112-118.

Kobayashi, H., & Hara, F. (1993a). Recognition of mixed facial expressions by neural network. *Trans. Jpn. Soc. Mech. Eng. (C)*, 59(567), 184–189.

Kobayashi, H., & Hara, F. (1993b). Measurement of the strength of six basic facial expressions by neural network. *Trans. Jpn. Soc. Mech. Eng. (C)*, 59(567), 177–183.

Koffman, I., & Roman, V. (2002, Apr.). Broadband wireless access solutions based on OFDM access in IEEE 802.16. *IEEE Communications Magazine*, 40(4), 96–103. doi:10.1109/35.995857

Kohonen, T. (1982). Self-organized formation of topologically correct feature maps. *Biological Cybernetics*, *43*, 59–69. doi:10.1007/BF00337288

Kohonen, T. (1988). *Self-organization and associative memory*. New York, NY: Springer-Verlag.

Koike, Y., & Kawato, M. (1996). Human interface using surface electromyography signals. *Electronics and Communications in Japan (Part III Fundamental Electronic Science)*, *79*(9), 15–22. doi:10.1002/ecjc.4430790902

Kojima, Y., Fujii, T., & Tanimoto, M. (2005). New multiple camera calibration method for a large number of cameras. In *Proceedings of VIII Videometrics Conference*.

Kollias, S., & Karpouzis, K. (2005). Multimodal emotion recognition and expressivity analysis. *IEEE International Conference on Multimedia and Expo, ICME*, (pp. 779–783).

Kolomvatsos, K., & Hadjiefthymiades, S. (2008). Implicit deadline calculation for seller agent bargaining in information marketplaces. In *Proceedings of the 2nd International Conference on Complex, Intelligent and Software Intensive Systems (CISIS 2008)*, March 4th-7th, Barcelona, Spain, (pp. 184-190).

Kolomvatsos, K., & Hadjiefthymiades, S. (2009). Automatic fuzzy rules generation for the deadline calculation of a seller agent. In *the Proc. of the 9th International Symposium on Autonomous Decentralized Systems (ISADS 2009)*, Athens, Greece, March 23-25, (pp. 429-434).

Kolomvatsos, K., Anagnostopoulos, C., & Hadjiefthymiades, S. (2008). On the use of fuzzy logic in a seller bargaining game. In *Proc. of the 32nd Annual IEEE International Computer Software and Applications Conference (COMPSAC 2008)*, July 28th - August 1st, Turku, Finland, (pp. 184-191).

Kompalli, S., Nayak, S., Setlur, S., & Govindaraju, V. (2005). Challenges in OCR of Devnagari documents. In *International Conference on Document Analysis and Recognition*, (pp. 327-331). Seoul, South Korea.

Konar, A. (2005). *Computational intelligence: Principles, techniques and applications*. Heidelberg, Germany: Springer.

Konar, A., & Chakraborty, U. K. (2005). Reasoning and unsupervised learning in a fuzzy cognitive map. *Information Sciences*, *170*(2-4), 419–441. doi:10.1016/j.ins.2004.03.012

Koru, A., & Liu, H. (2005). Building effective defect-prediction models in practice. *IEEE Software*, 23–29. doi:10.1109/MS.2005.149

Koru, A., & Tian, J. (2003). An empirical comparison and characterization of high defect and high complexity modules. *Journal of Systems and Software*, *67*, 153–163. doi:10.1016/S0164-1212(02)00126-7

Koskela, T., Lehtokangas, M., Saarlnen, J., & Kashi, K. (2001). *Time series prediction with mult layer perceptron, FIR and elman neural networks*. Finland: Tampere University of Technology.

Kosko, B. (1986). Fuzzy cognitive maps. *International Journal of Man-Machine Studies*, *24*(1), 65–75. doi:10.1016/S0020-7373(86)80040-2

Kosko, B. (1988). Bidirectional associative memories. *IEEE Transactions on Systems, Man, and Cybernetics*, *18*(1), 49–60. doi:10.1109/21.87054

Kosko, B. (1993). *Fuzzy thinking: The new science of fuzzy logic*. New York, NY: Hyperion.

Kosko, B. (Ed.). (1992). *Neural networks and fuzzy systems*. Englewood Cliffs, NJ: Prentice-Hall.

Koulouriotis, D. E., Diakoulakis, I. E., Emiris, D. M., Antonidakis, E. N., & Kaliakatsos, I. A. (2003). Efficiently modeling and controlling complex dynamic systems using evolutionary fuzzy cognitive maps (invited paper). *International Journal of Computational Cognition*, *1*(2), 41–65.

Kouskouridas, R., Badekas, E., & Gasteratos, A. (2010). (in press). Evaluation of two-parts algorithms for objects' depth estimation. *IET Computer Vision*.

Kragic, D., & Christensen, H. I. (2003). Confluence of parameters in model-based tracking. In *Proceedings of the IEEE International Conference on Robotics and Automation*, Taipei, Taiwan.

Kragic, D., Bjorkman, M., Christensen, H., & Eklundh, J. (2005). Vision for robotic object manipulation in domestic settings. *International Journal of Robotics and Autonomous Systems*, *52*(1), 85–100. doi:10.1016/j.robot.2005.03.011

Kramer, A. F., Sirevaag, E. J., & Braune, R. (1987). A psycho-physiological assessment of operator workload during simulated flight missions. *Human Factors, 29*(2), 145–160.

Krishna, K., Ganeshan, K., & Ram, D. J. (1995). Distributed simulated annealing algorithms for job shop scheduling. *IEEE Transactions on Systems, Man, and Cybernetics, 25*(7), 1102. doi:10.1109/21.391290

Krishnapuram, R. (1994). *Generation of membership functions via possibilistic clustering.* Paper presented at IEEE International Conference on Fuzzy Systems, 2, (pp. 902-908).

Kulkarni, A. D. (1994). *Artificial neural network for image understanding.* Van Nostrand Reinhold.

Kumar, M., & Garg, D. P. (2004). *Intelligent learning of fuzzy logic controllers via neural network and genetic algorithm.* Paper presented at JUSFA 2004 Japan – USA Symposium on Flexible Automation Denver, Colorado, (pp. 19-21).

Kumar, S., Kumar, D. K., Alemu, M., & Burry, M. (2004). EMG based voice recognition. *Intelligent Sensors, Sensor Networks and Information Processing Conference,* (pp. 593-597).

Kumar, S. (2004). *Neural networks: A classroom approach.* New Delhi, India: Tata McGraw-Hill.

Kuo, B. C. (1985). *Automatic control systems.* John Wiley & Sons Inc.

Kuo, R. J., Chen, C. H., & Hwang, Y. C. (2001). An intelligent stock trading decision support system through integration of genetic algorithm based fuzzy neural network and artificial neural network. *Fuzzy Sets and Systems, 118,* 21–24. doi:10.1016/S0165-0114(98)00399-6

Kutanoglu, E., & Wu, S. D. (1999). On combinatorial auction and Lagrangean relaxation for distributed resource scheduling. *IIE Transactions, 31*(9). doi:10.1080/07408179908969883

Kuzma, J. W., Tourtellotte, W. W., & Remington, R. D. (1965). Quantitative clinical neurological testing. *Journal of Chronic Diseases,* 18.

Kwan, C., & Lewis, F. L. (2000). Robust backstepping control of nonlinear systems using neural networks. *IEEE Transactions on Systems, Man, and Cybernetics. Part A, Systems and Humans, 30*(6), 753–766. doi:10.1109/3468.895898

Lai, Y. J., & Hwang, C. L. (1994). *Multiple objective decision making.* Berlin, Germany: Springer - Verlag.

Lamard, M., Cazuguel, G., Quelled, G., Bekri, L., Roux, C., & Cochener, B. (2007). Content based image retrieval based on wavelet transform coefficients distribution. In *Proceedings of the 29th Annual International Conference of the IEEE EMBS Cité International,* Lyon, France August 23-26, 2007.

Lam, K. M., & Yan, H. (1996). Locating and extracting the eye in human face images. *Pattern Recognition, 29*(5), 771–779. doi:10.1016/0031-3203(95)00119-0

Langer, M., Pifferi, S., & Peta, M. (1994). Diagnosis of bacterial infection in the ICU: General principles. *Intensive Care Medicine, 20*(4), 1432–1238. doi:10.1007/BF01713977

Lanitis, A. (2004). Person identification from heavily occluded face images. *Proc. of the 2004 ACM Symposium on Applied Computing* (pp. 5-9).

Lanitis, A., Taylor, C. J., & Cootes, T. F. (1997). Automatic interpretation and coding of face images using flexible models. *IEEE Transactions on Pattern Analysis and Machine Intelligence, 19*(7), 743–756. doi:10.1109/34.598231

Lanitis, A., Taylor, C. J., & Cootes, T. F. (2002). Toward automatic simulation of ageing effects on face images. *IEEE Transactions on Pattern Analysis and Machine Intelligence, 24*(4), 442–455. doi:10.1109/34.993553

Lapatki, B. G., Stegeman, D. F., & Jonas, I. E. (2003). A surface EMG electrode for the simultaneous observation of multiple facial muscles. *Journal of Neuroscience Methods, 123*(2), 117–128. doi:10.1016/S0165-0270(02)00323-0

Laufmann, S. (1994). The information marketplace: The challenge of information commerce. In *Proceedings of the 2nd International Conference on Cooperative Information Systems,* (pp. 147-157).

Lazebnik, S., & Ponce, J. (2005). A sparse texture representation using local affine regions. *IEEE Transactions on Pattern Analysis and Machine Intelligence*, *27*(8), 1265–1278. doi:10.1109/TPAMI.2005.151

Lee, J. W. (2001). *Stock price prediction using reinforcement learning*. Paper presented at IEEE International Joint Conference on Neural Networks, 1, (pp. 690–695).

Lee, Y. J., & Mangasarian, O. L. (2001). *RSVM: Reduced support vector machines*. The First SIAM International Conference on Data Mining.

Lee, K. C., Kim, J. S., Chung, N. H., & Kwon, S. J. (2002). Fuzzy cognitive map approach to web mining inference amplification. *Expert Systems with Applications*, *22*, 197–211. doi:10.1016/S0957-4174(01)00054-9

Lee, S., Kim, B. G., & Lee, K. (2004). Fuzzy cognitive map-based approach to evaluate EDI performance: A test of causal model. *Expert Systems with Applications*, *27*(2), 287–299. doi:10.1016/j.eswa.2004.02.003

Lee, S.-W., Kang, J., Shin, J., & Paik, J. (2007). Hierarchical active shape model with motion prediction for real-time tracking of non-rigid objects. *IET Computer Vision*, *1*(1), 17–24. doi:10.1049/iet-cvi:20045243

Lee, T.-W. (1998). *Independent component analysis: Theory and applications*. Kluwer Academic Publishers.

LEKIN. (2001). *LEKIN*. The Stern School of Business, New York University, New York.

Lenskiy, A., & Lee, J.-S. (2010). Face and iris detection algorithm based on SURF and circular Hough transform. *Signal Processing, The institute of Electronics Engineers of Korea, 47*(5).

Lenskiy, A. A., & Lee, J.-S. (2010). Machine learning algorithms for visual navigation of unmanned ground vehicles. In Igelnik, B. (Ed.), *Computational modeling and simulation of intellect: Current state and future perspectives*. Hershey, PA: IGI Global.

Lenz, R., & Tsai, R. (1988). Techniques for calibration of the scale factor and image center for high accuracy 3-d machine vision metrology. *IEEE Transactions on Pattern Analysis and Machine Intelligence*, *10*(5), 713–720. doi:10.1109/34.6781

Leonard, J., & Kramer, M. A. (1990). Improvement of the backpropagation algorithm for training neural networks. *Computers & Chemical Engineering*, *14*(3), 337–341. doi:10.1016/0098-1354(90)87070-6

Lepetit, V., & Fua, P. (2006). Keypoint recognition using randomized trees. *IEEE Transactions on Pattern Analysis and Machine Intelligence*, *28*(9), 1465–1479. doi:10.1109/TPAMI.2006.188

Levenberg, K. (1944). A method for the solution of certain non-linear problems in least squares. *Quarterly of Applied Mathematics*, 164–168.

Liang, L., & Looney, C. (2003). Competitive edge detection. *Applied Soft Computing*, *3*, 123–137. doi:10.1016/S1568-4946(03)00008-5

Liang, Q., & Mendel, J. M. (2000a). Equalization of non-linear time-varying channels using type-2 fuzzy adaptive filters. *IEEE Transactions on Fuzzy Systems*, *8*, 551–563. doi:10.1109/91.873578

Liang, Q., & Mendel, J. M. (2000b). Interval type-2 fuzzy logic systems: Theory and design. *IEEE Transactions on Fuzzy Systems*, *8*(5), 535–550. doi:10.1109/91.873577

Liang, Q., & Mendel, J. M. (2001). MPEG VBR video traffic modeling and classification using fuzzy techniques. *IEEE Transactions on Fuzzy Systems*, *9*(1), 183–193. doi:10.1109/91.917124

Liao, S. X., & Pawlak, M. (1996). On image analysis by moments. *IEEE Transactions on Pattern Analysis and Machine Intelligence*, *18*(3), 254–266. doi:10.1109/34.485554

Li, F., & Tsien, J. Z. (2009). Clinical implications of basic research: Memory and the NMDA receptors. *The New England Journal of Medicine*, *361*(302).

Li, J., & Xu, J. (2009). A novel portfolio selection model in a hybrid uncertain environment. *Omega*, *37*, 439–449. doi:10.1016/j.omega.2007.06.002

Li, L. (1999). Corner detection and interpretation on planar curves using fuzzy reasoning. *IEEE Transactions on Pattern Analysis and Machine Intelligence*, *21*(11), 1204–1210. doi:10.1109/34.809113

Li, L., & Chen, J. (2006). Emotion recognition using physiological signals. In Pan, Z. (Eds.), *ICAT 2006, LNCS 4282* (pp. 437–446). Berlin, Germany: Springer-Verlag.

Lim, M. H., Rahardja, S., & Gwee, B. H. (1996). A GA paradigm for learning fuzzy rules. *Fuzzy Sets and Systems, 82,* 177–186. doi:10.1016/0165-0114(95)00254-5

Lin, C. L., Lo, W., & Yan, M. R. (2006). Bargaining strategies for construction joint ventures by fuzzy logic. In *Proceedings of the 9th Joint Conference on Information Sciences,* October 8-11, Taiwan.

Lin, Y. P., Wang, C.-H., Jung, T.-P., Wu, T. L., Jeng, S. K., Duann, J.-R., & Chen, J. H. (2010). EEG based emotion recognition in music listening. *IEEE Trans. on Biomedical Engg., 57*(7).

Lin, C. T., & Lee, C. C. (1996). *Neural fuzzy systems. A neuro-fuzzy synergism to intelligent systems.* New York, NY: Prentice Hall.

Lin, C. T., & Lee, C. S. G. (1991). Neural network based fuzzy logic control and decision system. *IEEE Transactions on Computers, 40*(12), 1320–1336. doi:10.1109/12.106218

Lindeberg, T. (1994). Scale-space theory: A basic tool for analyzing structures at different scales. *International Journal of Applied Statistics, 21*(2), 414–431.

Lingras, P. (1996). Rough neural networks. In *Proceedings of the 6th International Conference on* Liu, Z., Bai, Z., Shi, J., & Chen, H. (2007). Image segmentation by using discrete Tchebichef moments and quantum neural network. In *Proceedings of Third International Conference on Natural Computation (ICNC 2007).*

Ling, Z., & Xianda, Z. (2007, Dec.). MIMO channel estimation and equalization using three-layer neural networks with feedback. *Tsinghua Science and Technology, 12*(6), 658–661. doi:10.1016/S1007-0214(07)70171-2

Lin, J.-S., Cheng, K.-S., & Mao, C.-W. (1996). A fuzzy Hopfield neural network for medical image segmentation. *IEEE Transactions on Nuclear Science, 43*(4), 2389–2398. doi:10.1109/23.531787

Lin, K. M., & Lin, C. J. (2003). A study on reduced support vector machine. *IEEE Transactions on Neural Networks, 14*(6), 1449–1559. doi:10.1109/TNN.2003.820828

Lippold, O. C. J. (1970). Oscillations in the stretch reflex are and the origin of the rhythmical component of physiological tremor. *Journal of Physiology.* (London).

Lisetti, C. L., & Schiano, D. J. (2000). Automatic facial expression interpretation: Where human-computer interaction, artificial intelligence and cognitive science intersect. *Pragmatics and Cognition. (Special Issue on Facial Information Processing: A Multidisciplinary Perspective), 8*(1), 185-235.

Liu, X., Bowyer, K. W., & Flynn, P. J. (2005). Experiments with an Improved Iris Segmentation Algorithm. *Workshop on Automatic Identification Advanced Technologies,* (pp. 118-123).

Liu, C. (2007). The Bayes decision rule induced similarity measures. *IEEE Transactions on Pattern Analysis and Machine Intelligence, 29*(6), 1116–1117. doi:10.1109/TPAMI.2007.1063

Liu, C. J. (2003). A Bayesian discriminating features method for face detection. *IEEE Transactions on Pattern Analysis and Machine Intelligence, 25*(6), 725–740. doi:10.1109/TPAMI.2003.1201822

Liu, C., & Wechsler, H. (2000). Evolutionary pursuit and its appliction to face recognition. *IEEE Transactions on Pattern Analysis and Machine Intelligence, 22*(6), 570–582. doi:10.1109/34.862196

Liu, C., & Wechsler, H. (2000). Robust coding schemes for indexing and retrieval from large face databases. *IEEE Transactions on Image Processing, 9*(1), 132–137. doi:10.1109/83.817604

Liu, C., & Wechsler, H. (2002). Gabor feature based classification using the enhanced \textsc{F}isher linear discriminant model for face recognition. *IEEE Transactions on Image Processing, 11*(4), 467–476. doi:10.1109/TIP.2002.999679

Liu, C., & Yang, J. (2009). ICA color space for pattern recognition. *IEEE Transactions on Neural Networks, 20*(2), 248–257. doi:10.1109/TNN.2008.2005495

Liu, J., Jing, H., & Tang, Y. Y. (2002). Multi-agent oriented constraint satisfaction. *Artificial Intelligence, 136,* 101–144. doi:10.1016/S0004-3702(01)00174-6

Liu, Z. Q., & Satur, R. (1999). Contextual fuzzy cognitive map for decision support in geographic information systems. *IEEE Transactions on Fuzzy Systems*, *7*, 495–507. doi:10.1109/91.797975

Li, X., & Ji, Q. (2005). Active affective state detection and user assistance with dynamic Bayesian networks. *IEEE Transactions on Systems, Man, and Cybernetics. Part A, Systems and Humans*, *35*(1), 93–105. doi:10.1109/TSMCA.2004.838454

Lopresti, D., & Wilfong, G. (2001). Applications of graph probing to Web document analysis. In *International Workshop on Web Document Analysis*, (pp. 51-54). Seattle, USA.

Loupias, E., & Sebe, E. (2000). Wavelet-based salient points: Applications to image retrieval using color and texture features. In *Advances in Visual Information Systems, Proceedings of the 4th International Conference, VISUAL 2000*, (pp. 223–232).

Lowe, D. G. (1999). Object recognition from local scale-invariant features. *Proceedings of the International Conference on Computer Vision*, *1*, (pp. 1150-1157).

Lowe, D. G. (1985). *Perceptual organization and visual recognition*. USA: Kluwer Academic Publishers.

Lowe, D. G. (2004). Distinctive image features from scale-invariant keypoints. *International Journal of Computer Vision*, *60*(2), 91–110. doi:10.1023/B:VISI.0000029664.99615.94

Lu, F., & Hartley, R. (2007). A fast optimal algorithm for l2 triangulation. In *Asian Conference on Computer Vision. Tokyo, Japan, LNCS 4844*, (pp. 279-288).

Luca, D. (1997). The use of surface electromyography in biomechanics. *Journal of Applied Biomechanics*, *13*, 135–163.

Lukaszyk, S. (2004). A new concept of probability metric and its applications in approximation of scattered data sets. *Computational Mechanics*, *33*, 299–3004. doi:10.1007/s00466-003-0532-2

Luo, B., & Hancock, E. R. (2001). Structural graph matching using the EM algorithm and singular value decomposition. *Transactions on Pattern Analysis and Machine Intelligence*, *23*(10), 1120–1136. doi:10.1109/34.954602

Lutz, J., Joachim, V., Frauke, M., Kai, L., & Karl, T. K. (1996). Facial EMG responses to auditory stimuli. *International Journal of Psychophysiology*, 22.

Lyons, M. J., Akamatsu, S., Kamachi, M., & Gyoba, J. (1998). Coding facial expressions with Gabor wavelets. *Proceedings of the 3rd IEEE International Conference on Automatic Face and Gesture Recognition* (pp. 200-205). Nara, Japan.

Lyons, M. J., Budynek, J., & Akamatsu, S. (1999). Automatic classification of single facial images. *IEEE Transactions on Pattern Analysis and Machine Intelligence*, *21*(12), 1357–1362. doi:10.1109/34.817413

Mackey, M. C., & Glass, L. (1977). Oscillation and chaos in physiological control systems. *Science*, *197*, 287–289. doi:10.1126/science.267326

MacQueen, J. B. (1967). Some methods for classification and analysis of multivariate observations. In *Proceedings of 5th Berkeley Symposium on Mathematical Statistics and Probability* (pp. 281-297).

Maertens, K., De Baerdemaeker, J., & Babuška, R. (2006). Genetic polynomial regression as input selection algorithm for non-linear identification. *Soft Computing*, *10*, 785–795. doi:10.1007/s00500-005-0008-8

Mai, F., Hung, Y. S., & Chesi, G. (2010). Projective reconstruction of ellipses from multiple images. *Pattern Recognition*, *43*(3), 545–556. doi:10.1016/j.patcog.2009.07.003

Majumdar, A. (2007). Bangla basic character recognition using digital curvelet transform. *Journal of Pattern Recognition Research*, *2*(1), 99–107.

Makeig, S., Bell, A., Jung, T., & Sejnowski, T. (1996). *Independent component analysis of electroencephalographic data*. Paper presented at the Advances in Neural Information Processing Systems.

Ma, L., Tan, T., Wang, Y., & Zhang, D. (2004). Efficient iris recognition by characterizing key local variations. *IEEE Transactions on Image Processing*, *13*(6), 739–750. doi:10.1109/TIP.2004.827237

Malik, L., Deshpande, P. S., & Bhagat, S. (2006). Character recognition using relationship between connected segments and neural network. *Transaction on Computers*, *5*(1), 229–234.

Mallat, S. G. (1989). A theory for multiresolution signal decomposition: The wavelet representation. *IEEE Transactions on Pattern Analysis and Machine Intelligence, 11*(7), 674–693. doi:10.1109/34.192463

Mamdani, E. H., & Assilian, S. (1975). An experiment in linguistic synthesis with a fuzzy logic controller. *International Journal of Man-Machine Studies, 7*, 1–13. doi:10.1016/S0020-7373(75)80002-2

Manabe, H., Hiraiwa, A., & Sugimura, T. (2003). Unvoiced speech recognition using EMG - Mime speech recognition. *ACM Conference on Human Factors in Computing Systems,* Ft. Lauderdale, Florida, USA, (pp. 794-795).

Mandic, D., & Chambers, J. (2001). *Recurrent neural networks for prediction: Learning algorithms, architectures and stability.* New York, NY: John Wiley & Sons. doi:10.1002/047084535X

Marinagi, C. C., Spyropoulos, C. D., Papatheodorou, C., & Kokkotos, S. (2000). Continual planning and scheduling for managing patient tests in hospital laboratories. *Artificial Intelligence in Medicine, 20*(2), 139–154. doi:10.1016/S0933-3657(00)00061-0

Marquardt, D. (1963). *Ab algorithm for least squares estimation of nonlinear paramteres.* Paper presented at the SIAM.

Marquardt, D. W. (1963). An algorithm for least-squares estimation of nonlinear parameters. *Journal of the Society for Industrial and Applied Mathematics, 11*(2), 431–441. doi:10.1137/0111030

Marsden, D. C., & Stanley, F. (1982). *Movement disorders.* Butterworth Scientific.

Martinetz, T., Berkovich, S., & Schulten, K. (1993). Neural-gas network for vector quantization and its application to time-series prediction. *IEEE Transactions on Neural Networks, 4*(4), 558–569. doi:10.1109/72.238311

Martinez, A. M. (2002). Recognizing imprecisely localized, partially occluded, and expression variant faces from a single sample per class. *IEEE Transactions on Pattern Analysis and Machine Intelligence, 24*(6), 748–763. doi:10.1109/TPAMI.2002.1008382

Martin, P., Refregier, Ph., Galland, F., & Guerault, F. (2006). Nonparametric statistical snake based on the minimum stochastic complexity. *IEEE Transactions on Image Processing, 15*(9), 2762–2770. doi:10.1109/TIP.2006.877317

Mascioli, F. M., Varazi, G. M., & Martinelli, G. (1997). *Constructive algorithm for neuro-fuzzy networks.* Paper presented at the Sixth IEEE International Conference Fuzzy Systems, Spain, Vol. 1, (pp. 459- 464).

Mase, K. (1991). Recognition of facial expression from optical flow. *Proc. IEICE Trans., Special Issue Coput. Vis. And Its Applications, 74*(10), 3474-3483.

Masek, L. (2003). *Recognition of human iris patterns for biometric identification.* The University of Western Australia. Retrieved from www.csse.uwa.edu.au/~pk/studentprojects/libor

Matas, J., Chum, O., Urban, M., & Pajdla, T. (2004). Robust wide-baseline stereo from maximally stable extremal regions. *International Journal of Image and Vision Computing, 22*(10), 761–767. doi:10.1016/j.imavis.2004.02.006

Mattfeld, D. C., & Bierwirth, C. (2004). An efficient genetic algorithm for job shop scheduling with tardiness objectives. *European Journal of Operational Research,* 616–630. doi:10.1016/S0377-2217(03)00016-X

Matthews, G. G. (1991). *Cellular physiology of nerve and muscle.* Boston, MA: Blackwell Scientific Publications.

May, S., Droeschel, D., Holz, D., Wiesen, C., Birlinghoven, S., & Fuchs, S. (2008). 3D pose estimation and mapping with time-of-flight cameras. *In Proceedings of the International Conference on Intelligent Robots and Systems (IROS), 3D Mapping Workshop,* Nice, France.

Maybank, S., & Faugeras, O. (1992). A theory of self-calibration of a moving camera. *International Journal of Computer Vision, 8*(2), 123–151. doi:10.1007/BF00127171

Mazidi, M. A., McKinlay, R., & Causey, D. (2008). *PIC microcontroller.* New Delhi, India: Pearson Education.

McAuley, J. H., & Marsden, C. D. (2000). Physiological and pathological tremors and rhythmic central motor control. (Oxford University Press.). *Brain, 123*(8), 1545–1567. doi:10.1093/brain/123.8.1545

McCabe, T. A. (1976). Complexity measure. *IEEE Transactions on Software Engineering*, 2(4), 308–320. doi:10.1109/TSE.1976.233837

McCulloch, W. S., & Pitts, W. H. (1943). A logical calculus of the ideas immanent in nervous activity. *The Bulletin of Mathematical Biophysics*, 5, 115–133. doi:10.1007/BF02478259

McGilloway, S., Cowie, R., Cowie, E. D., Gielen, S., Westerdijk, M., & Stroeve, S. (2000). Approaching automatic recognition of emotion from voice: A rough benchmark. In *Speech and Emotion*, (pp. 207-212).

McKeown, M. (2000). Cortical activation related to arm-movement combinations. *Muscle & Nerve*, 23(S9), S19–S25. doi:10.1002/1097-4598(2000)999:9<::AID-MUS5>3.0.CO;2-L

McKeown, M. J., & Radtke, R. (2001). Phasic and tonic coupling between EEG and EMG demonstrated with independent component analysis. *Journal of Clinical Neurophysiology: Official Publication of the American Electroencephalographic Society*, 18(1), 45–57. doi:10.1097/00004691-200101000-00009

MDP. (2006). *Website*. Retrieved from http://sarpresults.ivv.nasa.gov/ViewResearch/107.jsp

Meara, J., & Koller, W. C. (2000). *Parkinson's disease and Parkinsonism in the elderly*. The press syndicate of the University of Cambridge.

Medin, D. L., & Schaffer, M. M. (1978). Context theory of classification learning. *Psychological Review*, 85, 207–238. doi:10.1037/0033-295X.85.3.207

Melek, W. W., Goldenberg, A. A., & Emami, M. R. (2005). A fuzzy noise-rejection data partitioning algorithm. *International Journal of Approximate Reasoning*, 38, 1–17. doi:10.1016/j.ijar.2004.03.002

Mendel, J. (2007). Type-2 fuzzy sets and systems: An overview. *Computational Intelligence Magazine, IEEE*, 2(1), 20–29. doi:10.1109/MCI.2007.380672

Mendel, J. M. (2001). *Uncertain rule-based fuzzy logic systems: Introduction and new directions*. Upper Saddle River, NJ: Prentice-Hall.

Mendel, J. M. (2007). Type-2 fuzzy sets and systems: An overview. *IEEE Computational Intelligence Magazine*, 2, 20–29.

Mendel, J. M., & John, R. I. (2002). Type-2 fuzzy sets made simple. *IEEE Transactions on Fuzzy Systems*, 10(2), 117–127. doi:10.1109/91.995115

Mendel, J. M., John, R. I., & Liu, F. (2006). Interval type-2 fuzzy logic systems made simple. *IEEE Transactions on Fuzzy Systems*, 14(6), 808–821. doi:10.1109/TFUZZ.2006.879986

Mendonça, P. R. S., & Cipolla, R. (1999). A simple technique for self-calibration. In *IEEE Conference on Computer Vision and Pattern Recognition*, (pp. 1500–1505).

Mendoza, G. A., & Prabhu, R. (2006). Participatory modeling and analysis for sustainable forest management: Overview of soft system dynamics models and applications. *Forest Policy and Economics*, 9(2), 179–196. doi:10.1016/j.forpol.2005.06.006

Menneer, T., & Narayanan, A. (1995). *Quantum-inspired neural networks*. Technical report R329. Department of Computer Science, University of Exeter, UK.

Mes, M., Van der Heijden, M., & Van Harten, A. (2007). Comparison of agent-based scheduling to look-ahead heuristics for real-time transportation problems. *European Journal of Operational Research*, 181(1), 59–75. doi:10.1016/j.ejor.2006.02.051

Metlay, J. P., Kapoor, W. N., & Fine, M. J. (1997). Does this patient have community-acquired pneumonia? Diagnosing pneumonia by history and physical examination. *Journal of the American Medical Association*, 278(17), 1440–1445. doi:10.1001/jama.278.17.1440

Meyer, Y. (1993). *Wavelets: Algorithms and applications*. Philadelphia, PA: SIAM.

Miao, Y., & Liu, Z. Q. (2000). On causal inference in fuzzy cognitive maps. *IEEE Transactions on Fuzzy Systems*, 8, 107–119. doi:10.1109/91.824780

Mika, S., Ratsch, G., Weston, J., Scholkopf, B., & Mullers, K. R. (1999). Fisher discriminant analysis with kernels. *Proceedings of IEEE International Workshop on Neural Networks for Signal Processing*, (pp. 41-48).

Mika, S., Ratsch, G., & Muller, K. R. (2001). A mathematical programming approach to the kernel Fisher Algorithm. *Advances in Neural Information Processing Systems, 13*, 591–597.

Mikolajczyk, K., & Schmid, C. (2004). Scale & affine invariant interest point detectors. *International Journal of Computer Vision, 60*(1), 63–86. doi:10.1023/B:VISI.0000027790.02288.f2

Mikolajczyk, K., & Schmid, C. (2005). A performance evaluation of local descriptors. *IEEE Transactions on Pattern Analysis and Machine Intelligence, 27*(10), 1615–1630. doi:10.1109/TPAMI.2005.188

Mikolajczyk, K., Tuytelaars, T., Schmid, C., Zisserman, A., Matas, J., & Schaffalitzky, F. (2005). A comparison of affine region detectors. *International Journal of Computer Vision, 65*(1-2), 43–72. doi:10.1007/s11263-005-3848-x

Miller, G. F., Todd, P. M., & Hegde, S. (1989). Designing neural networks using genetic algorithms. In *Proceedings of the Third International Conference on Genetic Algorithms* (pp. 379-384), Arlington, VA: Morgan Kaufmann.

Miller, G. F., & Todd, P. M. (1990). Exploring adaptive agency in theory and methods for simulating the evolution of learning. In *Connectionist models*. Morgan Kaufmann.

MIMO. (n.d.). *The non-engineer's introduction to MIMO and MIMO-OFDM*. Retrieved from http://www.mimo.ucla.edu

Mitsunaga, T., & Nayar, S. K. (2000). High dynamic range imaging: Spatially varying pixel exposures. In. *Proceedings of the IEEE Computer Vision and Pattern Recognition, 1*, 472–479. doi:10.1109/CVPR.2000.855857

Moein, S., Monadjemi, S. A., & Moallem, P. (2008). A novel fuzzy-neural based medical diagnosis system. *World Academy of Science, Engineering and Technology, 37*.

Moghaddam, B. (1999). Principal manifolds and probabilistic subspaces for visual recognition. In *Proceedings of International Conference on Computer Vision*, (pp. 1131-1136).

Moghaddam, B. (2002). Principal manifolds and probabilistic subspaces for visual recognition. *IEEE Transactions on Pattern Analysis and Machine Intelligence, 24*(6), 780–788. doi:10.1109/TPAMI.2002.1008384

Moghaddam, B., & Pentland, A. (1997). Probabilistic visual learning for object representation. *IEEE Transactions on Pattern Analysis and Machine Intelligence, 19*(7), 696–710. doi:10.1109/34.598227

Mohan, H. (1994). *Textbook of pathology* (2nd ed., pp. 148–151). Delhi, India: P.L. Printers, Rana Pratap Bagh.

Mokhtarian, F., & Mohanna, F. (2006). Performance evaluation of corner detectors using consistency and accuracy measures. *Computer Vision and Image Understanding, 102*(1), 81–94. doi:10.1016/j.cviu.2005.11.001

Moon, J. M., & Joo, L. H. (1995). A combined method on the handwritten character recognition. In *International Conference on Document Analysis and Recognition* (pp. 112–115). Montreal, Canada.

Moravec, H. (1997). Towards automatic visual obstacle avoidance. In *Proceedings of the 5th International Joint Conference on Artificial Intelligence*, (p. 584).

Moriyama, T., Kanade, T., Xiao, J., & Cohn, J. F. (2006). Meticulously detailed eye region model and its application to analysis of facial images. *IEEE Transactions on Pattern Analysis and Machine Intelligence, 28*(5), 738–752. doi:10.1109/TPAMI.2006.98

Morse, S., & Wrightpp, M. (1991). Speech recognition using myoelectric signals with neural network. *Annual International Conference of the IEEE Engineering in Medicine and Biology Society*, (vol. 13, no. 4, pp. 1977-178).

Motwani, R., Motwani, M., & Harris, F. (2004). Eye detection using wavelets and ANN. *Proceedings of GSPx*.

Mozer, M. C., & Smolensky, P. (1989). Skeletonization: A technique for trimming the fat from a network via relevance assessment. In D. S. Touretzky (Ed.), *Advances in neural information processing systems, 1*, 107-115, San Mateo, CA: Morgan Kaufmann.

Muhammed, H. H. (2002). A new unsupervised fuzzy clustering algorithm (FC-WINN) using the new weighted incremental neural network. In *Proceedings of WINN 2002*.

Mukherji, P., & Rege, P. P. (2006). A survey of techniques for optical character recognition of handwritten documents with reference to Devnagari script. In *International Conference on Signal and Image Processing* (pp. 178-184). Hubli, India.

Mukherji, P., & Rege, P. P. (2007). Stroke analysis of handwritten Devnagari characters. In *Proceedings of International Conference on circuit, System, Electronics, Control and Signal Processing,* (pp. 843 - 848). Cairo, Egypt.

Mukherji, P., & Rege, P. P. (2008). Feature dependent adaptive zoning based "Devnagari" handwritten character recognition. In *International Conference on Cognition and Recognition,* (pp. 141-146). Mandya, India.

Mukherji, P., & Rege, P. P. (2008). Fuzzy stroke analysis of 'Devnagari' handwritten characters. *World Scientific Engineering Academy and Society (WSEAS)'s Trans. on Computers, 7*(5), 351–362.

Mukherji, P., Gapchup, V. B., & Rege, P. P. (2006). Feature extraction of 'Devnagari' characters using sub-bands of binary wavelet transform. In *Proceedings of Recent Trends in Information Systems,* (pp. 176-179). Kolkata, India.

Mukherji, P., Rege, P. P., & Pradhan, L. K. (2006). Analytical verification system for handwritten 'Devnagari' script. In *International Conference on Visualization, Imaging and Image Processing,* (pp. 237-242). Palma de Mallorca, Spain.

Mukherji, P., Thipsay, A., & Sethuraman, S. (2008). Multi-discriminant analysis of 'Devanagri' numerals for postal automation. In *International Conference on Signal Processing, Communications and Networking,* (pp. 482 - 487). Chennai, India.

Mukherji, P., & Rege, P. P. (2009). Shape feature and fuzzy logic based offline 'Devnagari' handwritten optical character recognition. *Journal of Pattern Recognition Research, 4*, 52–68.

Mukherji, P., & Rege, P. P. (2010). Hierarchical attributed relational graph based 'Devnagari' character recognition. *International Journal of Information Processing, 4*(3), 22–33.

Mukundan, R., Ong, S. H., & Lee, P. A. (2001). Image analysis by Tchebichef moments. *IEEE Transactions on Image Processing, 10*(9), 1357–1364. doi:10.1109/83.941859

Mukundan, R., & Ramakrishnan, K. R. (1998). *Moment functions in image analysis*. Singapore: World Scientific Publisher. doi:10.1142/9789812816092

Muldoon, T. J., Anandasabapathy, S., Maru, D. D., & Richards-Kortum, R. (2008, October). High-resolution imaging in Barrett's Esophagus: A novel, low-cost endoscopic microscope. *Gastrointestinal Endoscopy, 68*(4), 737–744. doi:10.1016/j.gie.2008.05.018

Murphy, G. L., & Medin, D. L. (1985). The role of theories in conceptual coherence. *Psychological Review, 92*, 289–316. doi:10.1037/0033-295X.92.3.289

Murugappan, M., Nagarjana, R., & Sazali, Y. (2009a). *Appraising human emotions using time frequency analysis based EEG alpha band features*. 2009 Conference on Innovative Technologies in Intelligent Systems and Industrial Applications (CITISIA 2009), Monash University, Sunway campus, Malaysia, 25th & 26th July 2009.

Murugappan, M., Juhari, M. R. B. M., Nagarajan, R., & Yaacob, S. (2009). An investigation on visual and audio-visual stimulus based emotion recognition using EEG. *International Journal of Medical Engineering and Informatics, 1*(3), 342–356. doi:10.1504/IJMEI.2009.022645

Murugappan, M., Nagarjana, R., & Sazali, Y. (2010). Classification of human emotion from EEG using discrete wavelet transform. *Journal of Biomedical Science and Engineering, 3*(4), 390–396. doi:10.4236/jbise.2010.34054

Naik, A. M., & Rege, P. P. (2006). Structural approach in recognition of handwritten Devnagari script. In *Symposium at Government College of Engineering,* (pp. 177-180). Aurangabad, India.

Naik, G., Kumar, D., & Palaniswami, M. (2008). *Multi run ICA and surface EMG based signal processing system for recognising hand gestures*. Paper presented at the Computer and Information Technology, 2008. CIT 2008. 8th IEEE International Conference on.

Naik, G., Kumar, D., Singh, V., & Palaniswami, M. (2006). *Hand gestures for HCI using ICA of EMG*. Paper presented at the VisHCI '06: The HCSNet workshop on Use of Vision in Human-Computer Interaction.

Naik, G., Kumar, D., Weghorn, H., & Palaniswami, M. (2007). *Subtle hand gesture identification for HCI using temporal decorrelation source separation BSS of surface EMG*. Paper presented at the 9th Biennial Conference of the Australian Pattern Recognition Society on Digital Image Computing Techniques and Applications (DICTA 2007), Glenelg, Australia.

709

Nakamura, H., Yoshida, M., Kotani, M., Akazawa, K., & Moritani, T. (2004). The application of independent component analysis to the multi-channel surface electromyographic signals for separation of motor unit action potential trains: Part I-Measuring techniques. *Journal of Electromyography and Kinesiology: Official Journal of the International Society of Electrophysiological Kinesiology, 14*(4), 423–432.

Nakano, H., & Saito, T. (2004). Grouping synchronization in a pulse-coupled network of chaotic spiking oscillators. *IEEE Transactions on Neural Networks, 15*(5), 1018–1026.doi:10.1109/TNN.2004.832807

NASA. (2004). *Metrics data repository*. Retrieved from www.mdp.ivv.nasa.gov

Naseem, I., & Deriche, M. (2005). Robust human face detection in complex color images. *IEEE International Conference on Image Processing, 2*, (pp. 338-341).

Nauck, D., & Kruse, R. (1997). Neuro-fuzzy systems for function approximation. In *Proceedings of the 4th International Workshop on Fuzzy-Neuro Systems*.

Nauck, D., Klawonn, F., & Kruse, R. (1997). *Foundations of neuro-fuzzy systems*. Chichester, UK: Wiley.

Nene, S. A., Nayar, S. K., & Murase, H. (1996). *Columbia Object Image Library* (COIL-20). Technical Report No. CUCS-006-96.

Neubeck, A., & Van Gool, L. (2006). Efficient nonmaximum suppression. In *Proceedings of the International Conference on Pattern Recognition*, (pp. 850-855).

Nguyen, M. H., Perez, J., & Frade, F. D. L. T. (2008). *Facial feature detection with optimal pixel reduction SVM*. IEEE International Conference on Automatic Face and Gesture.

Niblack, W., & Barber, R. (1994). The QBIC project: Querying images by content using color, texture, shape. In *Proc. SPIE Storage & Retrieval for Images & Video Database*, Feb 1994.

Niranjan, M., & Fallside, F. (1990). Neural networks and radial basis functions in classifying static speech patterns. *Computer Speech & Language, 4*, 275–289. doi:10.1016/0885-2308(90)90009-U

Nishikawa, D., Yu, W., Yokoi, H., & Kakazu, Y. (1999). *Emg prosthetic hand controller discriminating ten motions using real time learning method*. Paper presented at the IEEE/RSJ international conference on intelligent robots and systems.

Nishimura, H., & Tsutsumi, M. (2001). Off-line handwritten character recognition using integrated 1-D HMMs based on feature extraction filters. In *International Conference on Document Analysis and Recognition* (pp. 417-421). Seattle, USA.

Nister, D., & Stewenius, H. (2006). Scalable recognition with a vocabulary tree. In *Proceedings of the IEEE International Conference on Computer Vision and Pattern Recognition*. (pp. 2161-2168). New York, USA.

Nordin, M., & Frankel, V. H. (2001). *Basic biomechanics of the musculoskeletal system*. Lippincott Williams & Wilkins.

Nosofsky, R. M., & Palmeri, T. J. (1998). A rule-plus-exception model for classifying objects in continuous-dimension spaces. *Psychonomic Bulletin & Review, 5*(3), 345–369. doi:10.3758/BF03208813

Nosofsky, R. M., & Zaki, S. R. (2002). Exemplar and prototype models revisited: Response strategies, selective attention, and stimulus generalization. *Journal of Experimental Psychology. Learning, Memory, and Cognition, 28*(5), 924–940. doi:10.1037/0278-7393.28.5.924

Nossek, J. A., & Roska, T. (1993). Special issue on cellular neural networks. *IEEE Transactions on Circuits and Systems, 40*(3).

Nwana, H. S. (1996). Software agents: An overview. *The Knowledge Engineering Review, 11*(2), 205–244. doi:10.1017/S026988890000789X

Ogata, K. (1990). *Modern control engineering*. Englewood Cliffs, NJ: Prentice-Hall.

Ogawa, Y., Nishio, K., Nishimura, T., & Ohgane, T. (2003). A MIMO - OFDM system for high-speed transmission. *Proceedings of IEEE 58th Vehicular Technology Conference*, vol. 1, 6-9 Oct. 2003 (pp. 493-497).

Oh, H. J., Lee, K. M., & Lee, S. U. (2008). Occlusion invariant face recognition using selective local non-negative matrix factorization basis images. *Image and Vision Computing, 26*(11), 1515–1523. doi:10.1016/j.imavis.2008.04.016

Olabarriaga, S. D., Snel, J. G., Botha, C. P., & Belleman, R. G. (2007, January). Intergrated support for medical image analysis methods: From development to clinical application. *IEEE Transactions on Information Technology in Biomedicine, 11*(1), 47–57. doi:10.1109/TITB.2006.874929

Oliker, S., Furst, M., & Maimon, O. (1992). A distributed genetic algorithm for neural network design and training. *Complex Systems, 6*, 459–477.

Oota, K., & Sobin, L. H. (1977). *Histological typing of gastric and oeophageal tumours* (pp. 33–35). Geneva, Switzerland: World Health Organization.

Opitz, D. W., & Shavlik, J. W. (1994). Using genetic search to refine knowledge-based neural networks. In W. Cohen, & H. Hirsh (Eds.), *Machine learning: Proceedings of the Eleventh International Conference*. San Fransisco, CA: Morgan Kaufmann.

Oprea, M. (2006). Multi-agent system for university course timetable scheduling. In the *1st International Conference on Virtual Learning, ICVL*, (pp. 231-238).

Orazio, T. D., Guaragnellab, C., Leoa, M., & Distantea, A. (2004). A new algorithm for ball recognition using circle Hough transform and neural classifier. *Pattern Recognition, 37*, 393–408. doi:10.1016/S0031-3203(03)00228-0

Osei-Bryson, K. (2004). Generating consistent subjective estimates of the magnitudes of causal relationships in fuzzy cognitive maps. *Computers & Operations Research, 31*(8), 1165–1175. doi:10.1016/S0305-0548(03)00070-4

Osuna, E., Freund, R., & Girosi, F. (1997). *Training support vector machines: An application to face detection*. IEEE International Conference on Computer Vision and Pattern Recognition.

Ott, E. (2002). *Chaos in dynamical systems* (2nd ed.). Cambridge University Press.

Ouelhadj, D. (2004). Inter-agent cooperation and communication for agent-based robust dynamic scheduling in steel production. *Advanced Engineering Informatics, 18*(3), 161–172. doi:10.1016/j.aei.2004.10.003

Oweiss, K. G. (2010). *Statistical signal processing for neuro- science and neurotechnology*. Burlington, VT: Academic Press, Elsevier.

Ozcelik, H., Czink, N., & Bonek, E. (2006). *What makes a good MIMO channel model? Institut fur Nachrichtentechnik und Hochfrequenztechnik, Technische Universitat Wien*. Vienna, Austria: IEEE VTC.

Ozertem, U., & Erdogmus, D. (2007). Nonparametric snakes. *IEEE Transactions on Image Processing, 16*(9), 2361–2368. doi:10.1109/TIP.2007.902335

Ozesmi, U., & Ozesmi, S. L. (2004). Ecological models based on people's knowledge: A multi-step fuzzy cognitive mapping approach. *Ecological Modelling, 176*(1–2), 43–64. doi:10.1016/j.ecolmodel.2003.10.027

Pabboju, S., & Reddy, A. V. G. (2009). A novel approach for content-based image indexing and retrieval system using global and region features. *International Journal of Computer Science and Network Security, 9*(2).

Pal, U., Sharma, N., Wakabayashi, T., & Kimura, F. (2007). Off- line handwritten character recognition of Devnagari script. In *International Conference on Document Analysis and Recognition*, (pp. 496-500). Brazil.

Pal, S. K., & Ghosh, A. (1996). Neuro-fuzzy computing for image processing and pattern recognition. *International Journal of Systems Science, 27*(12), 1179–1193. doi:10.1080/00207729608929325

Pal, S. K., Ghosh, A., & Kundu, M. K. (2000). *Soft computing for image processing* (pp. 44–78). Physica-Verlag.

Pal, S. K., & Pal, A. (2002). *Pattern recognition: From classical to modern approaches*. World Scientific Pub Co Inc.

Pan, L., Zheng, H., & Nahavandi, S. (2003). The application of rough set and Kohonen network to feature selection for object extraction. *In Proceedings of the Second International Conference on Machine Learning and Cybernetics* (pp. 1185-1189).

Papadopoulos, A. N., & Manolopoulos, Y. (1999). Structure-based similarity search with graph histograms. In *International Workshop on Database & Expert System Application,* (pp. 174–178).

Papageorgiou, C. P., Oren, M., & Poggio, T. (1998). *A general framework for object detection*. IEEE International Conference on Computer Vision.

Papageorgiou, E. I., & Groumpos, P. P. (2005). A weight adaptation method for fine-tuning fuzzy cognitive map causal links. *Soft Computing Journal, 9,* 846-857. Springer Verlag. DOI 10.10007

Papageorgiou, E. I., Papadimitriou, C., & Karkanis, S. (2009b). Management of uncomplicated urinary tract infections using fuzzy cognitive maps. *Proc. IEEE Int. Conference on Information Technology in Biomedicine (ITAB).* doi:10.1109/ITAB.2009.5394374

Papageorgiou, E. I., Papandrianos, N. I., Karagianni, G., & Sfyras, D. (2009a). Fuzzy cognitive map based approach for assessing pulmonary infections. In J. Rauch, et al. (Eds.), *Proc 18th International Symposium on Methodologies for Intelligent Systems, ISMIS 2009, Lecture Notes in Computer Science, LNAI* 5722, (pp. 109–118). Berlin, Germany: Springer-Verlag.

Papageorgiou, E. I., Papandrianos, N. I., Karagianni, G., Kyriazopoulos, G., & Sfyras, D. (2009). Fuzzy cognitive map model for assessing pulmonary infections. *Proc. IEEE Int. Conf on Fuzzy Systems, FUZZ-IEEE 2009,* art. no. 5277254, (pp. 2094-2099).

Papageorgiou, E. I., Stylios, C. D., & Groumpos, P. P. (2006). A combined fuzzy cognitive map and decision trees model for medical decision making. *Proc 28th IEEE EMBS Annual Intern. Conference in Medicine and Biology Society, EMBS 2006,* (pp. 6117-6120). 30 Aug.-3 Sept, New York, USA.

Papageorgiou, E. I., Stylios, C. D., & Groumpos, P. P. (2007). Novel architecture for supporting medical decision making of different data types based on fuzzy cognitive map framework. *Proc. 28th IEEE EMBS Annual Intern. Conference in Medicine and Biology Society,* EMBS 2007, 21-23 August, Lyon, France, 2007.

Papageorgiou, E. I. (2011). A new methodology for decisions in medical informatics using fuzzy cognitive maps based on fuzzy rule-extraction techniques. *Applied Soft Computing, 11,* 500–513. doi:10.1016/j.asoc.2009.12.010

Papageorgiou, E. I., & Groumpos, P. P. (2005). A new hybrid learning algorithm for fuzzy cognitive maps learning. *Applied Soft Computing, 5,* 409–431. doi:10.1016/j.asoc.2004.08.008

Papageorgiou, E. I., Parsopoulos, K. E., Stylios, C. D., Groumpos, P. P., & Vrahatis, M. N. (2005). Fuzzy cognitive maps learning using particle swarm optimization. *International Journal of Intelligent Information Systems, 25*(1), 95–121. doi:10.1007/s10844-005-0864-9

Papageorgiou, E. I., Spyridonos, P., Glotsos, D., Stylios, C. D., Ravazoula, P., Nikiforidis, G., & Groumpos, P. P. (2008). Brain tumour characterization using the soft computing technique of fuzzy cognitive maps. *Applied Soft Computing, 8,* 820–828. doi:10.1016/j.asoc.2007.06.006

Papageorgiou, E. I., Spyridonos, P., Ravazoula, P., Stylios, C. D., Groumpos, P. P., & Nikiforidis, G. (2006a). Advanced soft computing diagnosis method for tumor grading. *Artificial Intelligence in Medicine, 36,* 59–70. doi:10.1016/j.artmed.2005.04.001

Papageorgiou, E. I., Stylios, C. D., & Groumpos, P. (2003). An integrated two-level hierarchical decision making system based on fuzzy cognitive maps (FCMs). *IEEE Transactions on Bio-Medical Engineering, 50*(12), 1326–1339. doi:10.1109/TBME.2003.819845

Papageorgiou, E. I., Stylios, C. D., & Groumpos, P. P. (2004). Active Hebbian learning to train fuzzy cognitive maps. *International Journal of Approximate Reasoning, 37,* 219–249. doi:10.1016/j.ijar.2004.01.001

Papakostas, G. A., Boutalis, Y. S., Karras, D. A., & Mertzios, B. G. (2007a). A new class of Zernike moments for computer vision applications. *Information Sciences, 177*(13), 2802–2819. doi:10.1016/j.ins.2007.01.010

Papakostas, G. A., Boutalis, Y. S., Karras, D. A., & Mertzios, B. G. (2007b). Fast numerically stable computation of orthogonal Fourier-Mellin moments. *IET Computer Vision, 1*(1), 11–16. doi:10.1049/iet-cvi:20060130

Papakostas, G. A., Boutalis, Y. S., Karras, D. A., & Mertzios, B. G. (2010b). Efficient computation of Zernike and Pseudo-Zernike moments for pattern classification applications. *Pattern Recognition and Image Analysis, 20*(1), 56–64. doi:10.1134/S1054661810010050

Papakostas, G. A., Karakasis, E. G., & Koulouriotis, D. E. (2008). Efficient and accurate computation of geometric moments on gray-scale images. *Pattern Recognition, 41*(6), 1895–1904. doi:10.1016/j.patcog.2007.11.015

Papakostas, G. A., Karakasis, E. G., & Koulouriotis, D. E. (2010a). Accurate and speedy computation of image Legendre moments for computer vision applications. *Image and Vision Computing, 28*(3), 414–423. doi:10.1016/j.imavis.2009.06.011

Papakostas, G. A., Karakasis, E. G., & Koulouriotis, D. E. (2010e). Novel moment invariants for improved classification performance in computer vision applications. *Pattern Recognition, 43*(1), 58–68. doi:10.1016/j.patcog.2009.05.008

Papakostas, G. A., Karras, D. A., Mertzios, B. G., & Boutalis, Y. S. (2005). An efficient feature extraction methodology for computer vision applications using wavelet compressed Zernike moments. *ICGST International Journal on Graphics, Vision and Image Processing. Special Issue: Wavelets and Their Applications, SI1*, 5–15.

Papakostas, G. A., Koulouriotis, D. E., & Karakasis, E. G. (2009). A unified methodology for efficient computation of discrete orthogonal image moments. *Information Sciences, 179*(20), 3619–3633. doi:10.1016/j.ins.2009.06.033

Papakostas, G. A., Koulouriotis, D. E., & Karakasis, E. G. (2010c). Computation strategies of orthogonal image moments: a comparative study. *Applied Mathematics and Computation, 216*(1), 1–17. doi:10.1016/j.amc.2010.01.051

Papakostas, G., Karras, D. A., Boutalis, Y., & Mertzios, B. G. (2010d). Efficient computation of moment descriptors. In Karras, D. A. (Ed.), *Recent advances in applied signals, systems and image processing (Series: Signals and communication technology)*. Springer.

Parasopoulos, K. E., & Vrahatis, M. N. (2004). On the computation of all global minimizers through particle swarm optimization. *IEEE Transactions on Evolutionary Computation, 8*(3).

Park, H. W., Schoeflin, T., & Kim, Y. (2001). Active contour model with gradient directional information: Directional snake. *IEEE Transactions on Circuits and Systems for Video Technology, 11*(2), 252–256. doi:10.1109/76.905991

Park, J. S., Oh, Y. H., Ahn, S. C., & Lee, S. W. (2005). Glasses removal from facial image using recursive error compensation. *IEEE Transactions on Pattern Analysis and Machine Intelligence, 27*(5), 805–811. doi:10.1109/TPAMI.2005.103

Park, U., Tong, Y., & Jain, A. K. (2010). Age-invariant face recognition. *IEEE Transactions on Pattern Analysis and Machine Intelligence, 32*(5), 947–954. doi:10.1109/TPAMI.2010.14

Parsons, T. W. (1986). *Voice and speech processing* (1st ed.). New York, NY: McGraw-Hill.

Parsopoulos, K. E., & Vrahatis, M. N. (2002). Particle swarm optimization method for constrained optimization problems. In Sincak, P., Vascak, J., Kvasnicka, V., & Pospichal, J. (Eds.), *Intelligent technologies--Theory and application: New trends in intelligent technologies-Frontiers in artificial intelligence and applications* (*Vol. 76*, pp. 214–220). IOS Press.

Passino, K., & Yurkovich, S. (1998). *Fuzzy control*. Menlo Park, CA: Addison Wesley Longman.

Paul, V. Y., & Haykin, S. (2001). *Regularized radial basis function networks: Theory and applications*. John Wiley.

Pavlačka, O. (2007). *Fuzzy methods of decision making (in Czech)*. PhD thesis, Faculty of Science, Palacký Univerzity, Olomouc

Pavlačka, O. (2010) *Definition of the Choquet integral with respect to fuzzified fuzzy measure*. Retrieved August 15, 2010, from http://aix-slx.upol.cz/~pavlacka/fuzzy_choquet.pdf

Pavlačka, O., & Talašová, J. (2006). The fuzzy weighted average operation in decision making models. In L. Lukáš (Ed.), *Proceedings of the 24th International Conference Mathematical Methods in Economics,* 13th - 15th September 2006, Plzeň (pp. 419–426).

Pavlačka, O., & Talašová, J. (2007). Application of the fuzzy weighted average of fuzzy numbers in decision-making models. In M. Štěpnička, V. Novák, & U. Bodenhofer (Eds.), *New Dimensions in Fuzzy Logic and related technologies, Proceedings of the 5th EUSFLAT Conference,* Ostrava, Czech Republic, September 11-14 2007 (pp. 455–462).

Pavlačka, O., & Talašová, J. (2010). Fuzzy vectors as a tool for modeling uncertain multidimensional quantities. *Fuzzy Sets and Systems, 161*, 1585–1603. doi:10.1016/j.fss.2009.12.008

Pavlovic, V., Sharma, R., & Huang, T. (1997). Visual interpretation of hand gestures for human-computer interaction: A review. *IEEE Transactions on Pattern Analysis and Machine Intelligence, 19*(7), 677–695. doi:10.1109/34.598226

Pawlak, Z. (1982). Rough sets. *International Journal of Computer and Information Sciences, 11*, 341–356. doi:10.1007/BF01001956

Pearl, J. (Ed.). (2000). *Causality, models reasoning and inference*. Cambridge, UK: Cambridge University Press.

Pedrycx, W., & de Oliveria, J. V. (2008). A development of fuzzy encoding and decoding through fuzzy clustering. *IEEE Trans. Instrumentation and Measurements, 57*(4), 829–837. doi:10.1109/TIM.2007.913809

Peleg, D., Braiman, E., Yom-Tov, E., & Inbar, G. (2002). Classification of finger activation for use in a robotic prosthesis arm. *IEEE Transactions on Neural Systems and Rehabilitation Engineering: A Publication of the IEEE Engineering in Medicine and Biology Society, 10*(4), 290-293.

Penev, P. S., & Sirovich, L. (2000). The global dimensionality of face space. In *Proceedings of IEEE International Conference on Face and Gesture Recognition,* (pp. 264-270), Grenoble, France.

Peng, E., & Li, L. (2010). Camera calibration using one-dimensional information and its applications in both controlled and uncontrolled environments. *Pattern Recognition, 43*(3), 1188–1198. doi:10.1016/j.patcog.2009.08.003

Peterfreund, N. (1999). Robust tracking of position and velocity with Kalman snakes. *IEEE Transactions on Pattern Analysis and Machine Intelligence, 21*(6), 564–569. doi:10.1109/34.771328

Peters, J. F., Han, L., & Ramanna, S. (2001). Rough neural computing in signal analysis. *Computational Intelligence, 17*(3), 493–513. doi:10.1111/0824-7935.00160

Peters, J. F., Skowron, A., Han, L., & Ramanna, S. (2000). Towards rough neural computing based on rough membership functions: Theory and application. In *RSCTC* (*Vol. 2005*, pp. 611–618). LNAI. doi:10.1007/3-540-45554-X_77

Petrantonakis, P. C., & Hadjileontiadis, L. J. (2010). Emotion recognition from brain signals using hybrid adaptive filtering and higher order crossings analysis. *IEEE Transactions on Affective Computing*. IEEE computer Society Digital Library. Retrieved from http://doi.ieeecomputersociety.org/10.1109/T-AFFC.2010.7

Petrushin, V. A. (2000). *Emotion recognition in speech signal: experimental study, development, and application* (*Vol. 2*, pp. 222–225). ICSLP.

Pfister, M. (1995). *Hybrid learning algorithms for neural networks*. PhD Thesis, Free University, Berlin.

Pfister, M., & Rojas, R. (1993). Speeding-up back-propagation – A comparison of orthogonal techniques. *In Proceedings of International Joint Conference on Neural Networks* (pp. 517–523), Japan.

Pham, D.-N., & Klinkert, A. (2008). Surgical case scheduling as a generalized job shop scheduling problem. *European Journal of Operational Research, 185*(3), 1011–1025. doi:10.1016/j.ejor.2006.03.059

Phil, C., & Christos, G. (2005). *A fast skin region detector*. ESC Division Research.

Philips, P. J., Wechsler, H., Huang, J., & Rauss, P. (1998). The FERET database and evaluation procedure for face recognition algorithms. *Image and Vision Computing, 16*(5), 295–306. doi:10.1016/S0262-8856(97)00070-X

Phillips, P. J. (2006). *FRGC and ICE Workshop*. Tech. Report. National Institute of Standards and Technology.

Phillips, P. J., Flynn, P. J., & Scruggs, T. (2005). *Overview of the face recognition grand challenge*. IEEE Int. Conf. on Computer Vision and Pattern Recognition.

Phillips, P. J., Moon, H., Rizvi, S. A., & Rauss, P. J. (2000). The FERET evaluation methodology for face recognition algorithms. *IEEE Transactions on Pattern Analysis and Machine Intelligence, 22*(10), 1090–1104. doi:10.1109/34.879790

Phung, S. L., & Bouzerdoum, A. (2007). A pyramidal neural network for visual pattern recognition. *IEEE Transactions on Neural Networks, 18*(2), 329–343. doi:10.1109/TNN.2006.884677

Picard, R. (1997). *Affective computing.* Cambridge, MA: MIT Press.

Picard, R. W., Vyzas, E., & Healy, J. (2001). Toward machine emotional intelligence: Analysis of affective psychological states. *IEEE Transactions on Pattern Analysis and Machine Intelligence, 23*(10), 1175–1191. doi:10.1109/34.954607

PICS. (n.d.). *The psychological image collection at Stirling.* Retrieved from http://pics.psych.stir.ac.uk/

Ping, W., Lhua, L., & Ping, Z. (2007). Subchannel interference cancellation in SVP-based MIMO system. *Journal of China Universities of Posts and Telecommunications, 14*(3).

Pitts, D., Cullen, A., & Dayhew-Barker, P. (1980). *Determination of ocular threshold levels for infrared radiation cataractogenesis.* (NIOSH research report, DHHS publication ; no. (NIOSH) 80-121, DHHS publication - no. (NIOSH) 80-121).

Pitts, W., & McCulloch, W. S. (1949). How we know universals: The perception of auditory and visual forms. *The Bulletin of Mathematical Biophysics, 9,* 127–147. doi:10.1007/BF02478291

Plamondon, R., & Srihari, S. N. (2000). On-line and off-line handwriting recognition: A comprehensive survey. *Transactions on Pattern Analysis and Machine Intelligence, 22*(1), 63–84. doi:10.1109/34.824821

Plumb, M., & Bain, P. (2007). *Essential tremor: The facts.* Oxford University Press.

Poggio, T., & Girosi, F. (1990). Networks for approximation and learning. *Proceedings of the IEEE, 78*(9), 1484–1487. doi:10.1109/5.58326

Pokropinska, A., & Scherer, R. (2008). Financial prediction with neuro-fuzzy systems. In Rutkowski, L. (Eds.), *Artificial intelligence and soft computing* (pp. 1120–1126). Springer-Verlag.

Ponnapalli, P. V. S., Ho, K. C., & Thomson, M. (1999). A formal selection and pruning algorithm for feedforward artificial neural network optimization. *IEEE Transactions on Neural Networks, 10*(4), 964–968. doi:10.1109/72.774273

Prechelt, L. (1997). Connection pruning with static and adaptive pruning schedules. *Neurocomputing, 16*(1), 49–61. doi:10.1016/S0925-2312(96)00054-9

Proakis, J. G. (2001). *Digital communications* (4th ed.). New York, N Y: McGraw-Hill Publication.

Prokis, J. G., & Manolakis, D. G. (2009). Digital signal processing: Principles, algorithms & applications, 4th ed.

Promise. (n.d.). *Promise data repository.* Retrieved from http://promisedata.org/repository/

Pullman, S. L., Goodin, D. S., Marquinez, A. I., Tabbal, S., & Rubin, M. (2000). Clinical utility of surface EMG. *Report of the Therapeutics And Technology Assessment Subcommittee of the American Academy of Neurology, 55.*

Qi, F., Li, Q., Luo, Y., & Hu, D. (2007a). Camera calibration with one-dimensional objects moving under gravity. *Pattern Recognition, 40*(1), 343–345. doi:10.1016/j.patcog.2006.06.029

Qi, F., Li, Q., Luo, Y., & Hu, D. (2007b). Constraints on general motions for camera calibration with one-dimensional objects. *Pattern Recognition, 40*(6), 1785–1792. doi:10.1016/j.patcog.2006.11.001

Qiu, H., & Hancock, E. R. (2006). Graph matching and clustering using spectral partitions. *Pattern Recognition, 39*(1), 22–34. doi:10.1016/j.patcog.2005.06.014

Quek, F., Mcneill, D., Bryll, R., Duncan, S., Ma, X.-F., & Kirbas, C. (2002). Multimodal human discourse: Gesture and speech. *ACM Transactions on Computer-Human Interaction, 9*(3), 171–193. doi:10.1145/568513.568514

Quinney, D. (1985). *An introduction to the numerical solution of differential equation.* Hertforshire, UK: Research Studies.

Raeesy, Z., Brzostwoski, J., & Kowalczyk, R. (2007). Towards a fuzzy-based model for human-like multiagent negotiation. In *Proc. of the 2007 IEEE/WIC/ACM International Conference on Intelligent Agent Technology,* November 2-5, Silicon Valley, USA, (pp. 515-519).

Rahman, M. I. (2004). *Basics about multi-carrier based multiple access techniques. Center for TeleInFrastruktur (CTiF)*. Aalborg University.

Rajan, B. S. (2007). *Space-time-frequency codes for MIMO-OFDM systems.* Department of Electrical Communication Engineering Indian Institute of Science Bangalore 560012, India.

Ramanathan, N., & Chellapa, R. (2006). Modeling age progression in young faces. In *Proceedings of the Conference on Computer Vision and Pattern Recognition (CVPR)*, (pp. 387-394). IEEE CS Press.

Ramík, J., & Perzina, R. (2010). A method for solving fuzzy multicriteria decision problems with dependent criteria. *Fuzzy Optimization and Decision Making, 9*(2), 123–141. doi:10.1007/s10700-010-9078-x

Rani, P., Sarkar, N., & Adams, J. (2007). Anxiety-based affective communication for implicit human-machine interaction. *Advanced Engineering Informatics, 21*(3), 323–334.doi:10.1016/j.aei.2006.11.009

Rani, P., Sarkar, N., Smith, C., & Kirby, L. (2004). Anxiety detecting robotic systems— Towards implicit human-robot collaboration. *Robotica, 22*(1), 83–93.doi:10.1017/S0263574703005319

Rao, C. R. (1948). The utilization of multiple measurements in problems of biological classification. *Journal of the Royal Statistical Society. Series B. Methodological, 10*, 159–203.

Rappaport, T. S. (2004). *Wireless communications: Principles and practice*, 2nd edition. New Delhi, India: Pearson Education., Sampath, H., Talwar, S., Tellado, J., Erceg, V., & Paulraj, A. (2002). A fourth generation MIMO - OFDMA broadband wireless system: Design, performance and field trial results. *IEEE Communications Magazine, 40*(9), 143-149.

Rattarangsi, A., & Chin, R. T. (1992). Scale-based detection of corners of planar curves. *IEEE Transactions on Pattern Analysis and Machine Intelligence, 14*(4), 430–449. doi:10.1109/34.126805

Rechtien, J., Gelblum, B., Haig, A., & Gitter, A. (1999). Technology review: Dynamic electromyography in gait and motion analysis. *Muscle & Nerve, 22*(Suppl), S233–S238.

Reed, R. (1993). Pruning algorithms - A survey. *IEEE Transactions on Neural Networks, 4*(5), 740–747. doi:10.1109/72.248452

Reed, T. R., & du Buf, J. (1993). A review of recent texture segmentation and feature extraction techniques. *Computer Vision. Graphics and Image Processing: Image Understanding, 57*, 359–372. doi:10.1006/cviu.1993.1024

Reeves, D. M., Wellman, M. P., & MacKie-Maso, J. K. (2005). Exploring bidding strategies for market-based scheduling. *Decision Support Systems, 39*(1), 67–85. doi:10.1016/j.dss.2004.08.014

Refai, H., Li, L., Kent Teague, T., & Naukam, R. (September 2003). Automatic count of hepatocytes in microscopic images. In *Proceedings of International Conference on Image Processing, ICIP-2003*, (pp. 1101-1104).

Rehg, J., & Kanade, T. (1993). *DigitEyes: Vision-based human hand tracking.*

Reichert, H. (1990). *Neurobiologie*. Stuttgart, Germany: Georg Thieme.

Riedmiller, M., & Braun, H. (1993). *A direct adaptive method for faster backpropagation learning the RPROP algorithm.* Paper presented at the IEEE International Conference on Neural Networks (ICNN).

Rippon, G. (2006). Electroencephalography. In Senior, C., Russell, T., & Gazzaniga, M. S. (Eds.), *Methods in mind*. Cambridge, MA: MIT Press.

Riviere, C. N., & Khosla, P. K. (1997b). Augmenting the human-machine interface: Improving manual accuracy. *Proceedings of the IEEE International Conference on Robotics and Automation*, Albuquerque, New Mexico, 20-25 April.

Riviere, C. N., Reich, S. G., & Thakor, N. V. (1997a). Adaptive Fourier modeling for quantification of tremor. *Journal of Neuroscience Methods, 74*(1), 77–87. doi:10.1016/S0165-0270(97)02263-2

Riviere, C. N., Scott, R., & Thakor, N. V. (1998). Adaptive canceling of physiological tremor for improved precision in microsurgery. *IEEE Transactions on Bio-Medical Engineering, 45*(7). doi:10.1109/10.686791

Robson, J. G. (1959). The effect of loading upon the frequency of muscle tremor. *The Journal of Physiology, 149*.

Rocha, J., & Pavlidis, T. (1994). A shape analysis model with application to character recognition system. *Transactions on Pattern Analysis and Machine Intelligence, 16*(4), 393–404. doi:10.1109/34.277592

Rodriguez-Repiso, L., Setchi, R., & Salmeron, J. (2007). Modelling IT projects success with fuzzy cognitive maps. *Expert Systems with Applications, 32*, 543–559. doi:10.1016/j.eswa.2006.01.032

Rojas, R. (1996). *Neural networks: A systematic introduction.* Berlin, Germany: Springer-Verlag.

Rolfes, S., & Rendas, J. (2004). Statistical snakes: Robust tracking of benthic contours under varying background. In *Proceedings of IEEE/RSJ International Conference on Intelligent Robots and Systems* (vol. 3, pp. 3056-3061).

Romberg, J., Choi, H., Baraniuk, R., & Kingsbury, N. G. (2000). Multiscale classification using complex wavelets. *Proc. IEEE ICIP*, Vancouver, Sept. 11-13, 2000.

Romdhani, S., Torr, B., Scholkopf, B., & Blake, A. (2001). *Computationally efficient face detection.* IEEE International Conference on Computer Vision.

Rommelfanger, H. (1988). *Fuzzy decision support system.* Berlin, Germany: Springer - Verlag.

Rong-Ben, W., Ke-You, G., Shu-Ming, S., & Jiang-Wei, C. (2003). A monitoring method of driver fatigue behavior based on machine vision. *Intelligent Vehicles Symposium*, (pp. 110-113).

Rose, F. (1999). *The economics, concept, and design of information intermediaries.* Heidelberg, Germany: Physika-Verlag.

Rosenblatt, F. (1958). The perceptron: A probabilistic model for information storage and organization in the brain. *Psychological Review, 65*, 386–408. doi:10.1037/h0042519

Rosenblum, M., Yacoob, Y., & Davis, L. (1996). Human expression recognition from motion using a radial basis function network architecture. *IEEE Transactions on Neural Networks, 7*, 1121–1138.doi:10.1109/72.536309

Rosenfeld, A., & Johnston, E. (1973). Angle detection on digital curves. *IEEE Transactions on Computers, C-22*, 858–875. doi:10.1109/TC.1973.5009188

Rosten, E., & Drummond, T. (2006). *Machine learning for high-speed corner detection* (pp. 395–430). Lecture Notes in Computer Science.

Rosten, E., Porter, R., & Drummond, T. (2010). Faster and better: A machine learning approach to corner detection. *IEEE Transactions on Pattern Analysis and Machine Learning, 32*(1), 105–119. doi:10.1109/TPAMI.2008.275

Rothe, I., Susse, H., & Voss, K. (1996). The method of normalization to determine invariants. *IEEE Transactions on Pattern Analysis and Machine Intelligence, 18*(4), 366–376. doi:10.1109/34.491618

Rother, C. (2003). *Multi-view reconstruction and camera recovery using a real or virtual reference plane.* PhD thesis, Royal Institute of Technology, Stockholm, Sweden.

Rothganger, F., Lazebnik, S., & Ponce, J. (2006). 3D object modeling and recognition from photographs and image sequences. In *Proceedings toward Category-Level Object Recognition* (pp. 105-126).

Rotshtein, A. (1999). Design and tuning of fuzzy rule-based systems for medical diagnosis. In Teodorescu, H. N., Kandel, A., & Jain, L. C. (Eds.), *Fuzzy and neuro-fuzzy systems in medicine.* Boca Raton, FL: CRC Press.

Rowley, H. A., Baluja, S., & Kanade, T. (2004). Neural network-based face detection. *IEEE Transactions on Pattern Analysis and Machine Intelligence, 20*, 23–38. doi:10.1109/34.655647

Ruck, D. W., Rogers, S. K., & Kabrisky, M. (1990). Feature selection using a multilayer perceptron. *Neural Network Computing, 2*(2), 40–48.

Rumelhart, D. E., Hinton, G. E., & Williams, R. J. (1986). Learning internal representations by error propagation. In Rumelhart, D. E., & McClelland, J. L. (Eds.), *Parallel distributed processing: Explorations in the microstructures of cognition (Vol. 1*, pp. 318–362). Cambridge, MA: MIT Press.

Rurainsky, J., & Eisert, P. (2004). *Eye center localization using adaptive templates.* IEEE Conference on Computer Vision and Pattern Recognition.

Ruspini, E. (1969). A new approach to clustering. *Information and Control, 15*, 22–32. doi:10.1016/S0019-9958(69)90591-9

Russo, F. (2000). Image filtering using evolutionary neural fuzzy systems. In *Soft computing for image processing* (pp. 23-43). S. K. Pal, A. Ghosh, M. K. Kundu (Eds.), *Proceedings of IEEE International Conference on Industrial Technology Vol. II* (pp. 335-340). Physica-Verlag, Heidelberg.

Russo, F. (1999). FIRE operators for image processing. *Fuzzy Sets and Systems, 103*, 265–275. doi:10.1016/S0165-0114(98)00226-7

Russo, F. (1999). Hybrid neuro-fuzzy filter for impulse noise removal. *Pattern Recognition, 32*(11), 1843–1855. doi:10.1016/S0031-3203(99)00009-6

Russo, F. (2004). Impulse noise cancellation in image data using a two-output nonlinear filter. *Measurement, 36*(3-4), 205–213. doi:10.1016/j.measurement.2004.09.002

Ryoo, H. S. (2006). Pattern classification by concurrently determined piecewise linear and convex discriminant functions. *Computers & Industrial Engineering, 51*(1), 79–89. doi:10.1016/j.cie.2006.06.015

Ryoo, H. S., & Sahinidis, N. V. (2001). Analysis of bounds for multilinear functions. *Journal of Global Optimization, 19*(4), 403–424. doi:10.1023/A:1011295715398

Saengdeejing, A., Qu, Z. H., Chaeroenlap, N., & Jin, Y. F. (2003). 2-D shape recognition using recursive landmark determination and fuzzy ART network learning. *Neural Processing Letters, 18*, 81–95. doi:10.1023/A:1026261202044

Sahbi, H., & Boujemaa, N. (2000). *From coarse to fine skin and face detection*. Paper presented at the Proceedings of 8th ACM International Conference on Multimedia.

Salomon, R. (1992). Verbesserung konnektionistischer Lernverfahren. *die nach der Gradientenmethode arbeiten*, PhD Thesis, Technical University of Berlin.

Salvi, J., Armangu'e, X., & Batlle, J. (2002). A comparative review of camera calibrating methods with accuracy evaluation. *Pattern Recognition, 35*(7), 1617–1635. doi:10.1016/S0031-3203(01)00126-1

Samaria, F., & Harter, A. C. (1994). Parameterisation of a stochastic model for human face identification. In *Proceedings of the 2nd IEEE Workshop on Applications of Computer Vision* (pp. 138–142). Sarasota, FL, USA.

San Pedro, J., Burstein, F., Churilov, L., Wassertheil, J., & Cao, P. (2004). Mobile decision support system for triage in emergency departments. *Decision Support in Uncertain and Complex World: The IFIP TC8/WG8.3 International Conference,* (pp. 714-723).

Sandhu, R., Dambreville, S., Yezzi, A., & Tannenbaum, A. (2009). Non-rigid 2D-3D pose estimation and 2D image segmentation. In *Proceedings of the IEEE Conference on Computer Vision and Pattern Recognition* (pp. 786-793). Miami, USA.

Sanger, T. D. (1994). Neural network learning control of robot manipulators using gradually increasing task difficulty. *IEEE Transactions on Robotics and Automation, 10*, 323–333. doi:10.1109/70.294207

Sanner, R. M., & Slotine, J. J. E. (1992). Gaussian networks for direct adaptive control. *IEEE Transactions on Neural Networks, 3*, 837–863. doi:10.1109/72.165588

Sarfraz, M. S., Hellwich, O., Yilmaz, U., Bellmann, A., Rodehorst, V., & Erten, E. (2008). Head pose estimation in face recognition across pose scenarios. In *International Conference on Computer Vision Theory and Applications* (pp. 235-242). Funchal, Portugal.

Sato, J. R., Fujita, A., Thomaz, C. E., Morais-Martin, M. G., Mourao-Miranda, J., Brammer, M. J., & Junior, E. A. (2009). Evaluating SVM and MLDA in the extraction of discriminant regions for mental state prediction. *NeuroImage, 46*(1), 105–114. doi:10.1016/j.neuroimage.2009.01.032

Sato, J. R., Thomaz, C. E., Cardoso, E. F., Fujita, A., Morais-Martin, M. G., & Junior, E. A. (2008). Hyperplane navigation: A method to set individual scores in fMRI group datasets. *NeuroImage, 42*(4), 1473–1480. doi:10.1016/j.neuroimage.2008.06.024

Scales, L. E. (1985). *Introduction to Non-linear optimization*. New York, NY: Springer-Verlag.

Scandrett, C. M., Solomon, C. J., & Gibson, S. J. (2006a). Towards a semi-automatic method for the statistically rigorous ageing of the human face. *IEE Proceedings. Vision Image and Signal Processing, 153*(5), 639–649. doi:10.1049/ip-vis:20050027

Scandrett, C. M., Solomon, C. J., & Gibson, S. J. (2006b). A person-specific, rigorous aging model of the human face. *Pattern Recognition Letters*, *27*, 1776–1787. doi:10.1016/j.patrec.2006.02.007

Schaffalitzky, F., & Zisserman, A. (2002). *Multi-view matching for unordered image sets, or How do I organize my holiday snaps?* (pp. 414–431). Lecture Notes in Computer Science.

Scheirer, J., Fernadez, R., Klein, J., & Picard, R. (2002). Frustrating the user on purpose: A step toward building an affective computer. *Interacting with Computers*, *14*(2), 93–118.

Schlenzig, J., Hunter, E., & Jain, R. (1994). *Vision based hand gesture interpretation using recursive estimation.* Paper presented at the 1994 Conference Record of the Twenty-Eighth Asilomar Conference on Signals, Systems and Computers.

Schmid, C., & Mohr, R. (1997). Local grayvalue invariants for image retrieval. *IEEE Transactions on Pattern Analysis and Machine Intelligence*, *19*(5), 530–535. doi:10.1109/34.589215

Schmidt, S., Steele, R., Dillon, T., & Chang, E. (2007). Fuzzy trust evaluation and credibility development in multi-agent systems. *Applied Soft Computing*, *7*, 492–505. doi:10.1016/j.asoc.2006.11.002

Schneider, F., Grodd, W., Gur, R. E., Klose, U., Alavi, A., & Gur, R. C. (1997). PET and fMRI in the study of emotion. *Psychiatry Research: Neuroimaging*, *68*(2-3), 174–175.doi:10.1016/S0925-4927(97)81569-7

Schneider, M., Kandel, A., & Chew, G. (1998). Automatic construction of FCMs. *Fuzzy Sets and Systems*, *93*, 161–172. doi:10.1016/S0165-0114(96)00218-7

Scholkopf, B. (1999). Input space versus feature space in kernel-based methods. *IEEE Transactions on Neural Networks*, *10*(5), 1000–1017. doi:10.1109/72.788641

Scholkopf, B., & Smola, A. J. (2002). *Learning with kernels: Support vector machines, regularization, optimization, and beyond.* Cambridge, MA: MIT Press.

Scholkopf, B., Smola, A., & Muller, K. (1998). Nonlinear component analysis as a kernel Eigenvalue problem. *Neural Computation*, *10*, 1299–1319. doi:10.1162/089976698300017467

Scitools. (n.d.). *Website*. Retrieved from http://www.scitools.com/index.php

Scutte, J. F., Reinbolt, J. A., Fregly, B. J., Haftka, R. T., & George, A. D. (2004). Parallel global optimization with the particle swarm algorithm. *International Journal for Numerical Methods in Engineering*, *61*, 2296–2315. doi:10.1002/nme.1149

Sebe, N., & Lew, M. S. (2002). Emotion recognition using a Cauchy naïve Bayes classifier. In *Proc. Int. Conf. Pattern Recognition* (pp. 17-20).

Sengupta, S. (1995). A comparative study of neural network and regression analysis as modeling tools. In *Proceedings of the Twenty-Seventh Southeastern Symposium on System Theory* (pp. 202-205).

Seow, M.-J., Valaparla, D., & Asari, V. K. (2003). Neural network based skin color model for face detection. *Proceedings of Applied Imagery Pattern Recognition Workshop*, (pp. 141-145).

Sethi, I. K., & Chatterjee, B. (1977). Machine recognition of constrained hand-printed Devnagari. *Pattern Recognition*, *9*(2), 69–75. doi:10.1016/0031-3203(77)90017-6

Shanno, D. F. (1990). Recent advances in numerical techniques for large-scale optimization. In S. Miller, & Werbos (Eds.), *Neural networks for control.* Cambridge, MA: MIT Press.

Sharifi, M., Fathy, M., & Mahmoudi, M. T. (2002). A classified and comparative study of edge detection algorithms. In *Proceedings of International Conference on Information Technology: Coding and Computing* (pp. 117-120).

Sharma, N., Pal, U., Kimura, F., & Pal, S. (2006). Recognition of off-line handwritten Devnagari Characters using quadratic classifier. In *Indian Conference on Computer Vision Graphics and Image Processing*, (pp. 805-816). Madurai, India.

Shashidhara, H. L., Lohani, S., & Gadre, V. M. (2000). Function learning wavelet neural networks. In *Proceedings of IEEE International Conference on Industrial Technology Vol. II* (pp. 335-340).

Shen, W., Wang, L., & Hao, Q. (2006). Agent-based distributed manufacturing process planning and scheduling: A state-of-the-art survey. *IEEE Trans. Systems, Man, and Cybernetics-Part C. Applications and Reviews*, *36*(4), 563–577.

Sherrod, P. (2003). *DTreg predictive modeling software.*

Shih, S., Hung, Y., & Lin, W. (1996). *Accuracy analysis on the estimation of camera parameters for active vision systems.* Technical Report TR-IIS-96-006, Institute of Information Science, Taipei, Taiwan.

Shi, Y. (2004). *Particle swarm optimization.* IEEE Neural Networks Society.

Shi, Y., Eberhart, R., & Chen, Y. (1999). Implementation of evolutionary fuzzy systems. *IEEE Transactions on Fuzzy Systems*, 7(5), 109–119. doi:10.1109/91.755393

Shor, P. W. (1997). Polynomial-time algorithms for prime factorization and discrete logarithms on a quantum computer. *SIAM Journal on Computing*, 26(5), 1484–1509. doi:10.1137/S0097539795293172

Shuo, C., & Liu, C. (2010, September). *Eye detection using color information and a new efficient SVM.* International Conference on Biometrics Theory, Applications and Systems, Washington, DC.

Sietsma, J., & Dow, R. J. F. (1991). Creating artificial neural networks that generalize. *Neural Networks*, 4, 67–79. doi:10.1016/0893-6080(91)90033-2

Silva, C. (1995). *Fuzzy cognitive maps over possible worlds.* In 4th IEEE International Conference on Fuzzy Systems, Japan.

Silva, F., & Almeida, L. (1990). Speeding-up back-propagation. In Eckmiller, R. (Ed.), *Advanced neural computers* (pp. 151–156). Amsterdam, The Netherlands: North-Holland.

Simpson, A. M., Stone, M. A., & Glasberg, B. R. (1990). Spectral enhancement to improve the intelligibility of speech in noise for hearing-impaired listeners. *Acta Oto-Laryngologica. Supplementum*, 469, 101–107.

Simpson, P. K. (1993). Fuzzy min-max neural networks: Part 2-Clustering. *IEEE Transactions on Fuzzy Sets*, 1, 32–45. doi:10.1109/TFUZZ.1993.390282

Singh, S. (2010). *Investigations in evolution of type-1 and type-2 fuzzy systems.* Unpublished doctoral dissertation, Maharshi Dayanand University, Rohtak, India.

Singh, S., Saini, J. S., Khosla, A. (2010). A MATLAB based versatile toolbox for generalized fuzzy system design automation. *Applied Soft Computing* (Elsevier).

Singhal, S., & Wu, L. (1989). Training multilayer perceptrons with the extended Kalman algorithm. In Touretzky, D. S. (Ed.), *Advances in neural information processing systems, 1* (pp. 133–140). Los Altos, CA: Morgan Kauffman.

Sinha, R. M. K., & Mahabala, H. N. (1979). A complete OCR for printed Hindi text in Devnagari script. In *International Conference on Document Analysis and Recognition*, (pp. 800-804). Seattle, US.

Sinha, R. M. K., & Mahabala, H. N. (1979). Machine recognition of Devnagari script. *Transactions on Systems. Man and Cybernetics*, 9(8), 435–441. doi:10.1109/TSMC.1979.4310256

Sirovich, L., & Kirby, M. (1987). Low-dimensional procedure for the characterization of human face. *Journal of the Optical Society of America*, 4, 519–524. doi:10.1364/JOSAA.4.000519

Sivic, J., & Zisserman, A. (2003). Video Google: A text retrieval approach to object matching in videos. In *Proceedings of the Ninth IEEE International Conference on Computer Vision* (pp. 1470-1477). Nice, France.

Sklansky, J., & Vriesenga, M. (1996). Genetic selection and neural modeling of piecewise-linear classifiers. *International Journal of Pattern Recognition and Artificial Intelligence*, 10(5), 587–612. doi:10.1142/S0218001496000360

Small, C. G. (1996). *The statistical theory of shape. Springer series in statistics.* New York, NY: Springer-Verlag Inc.

Smeulders, A. W. M., Worring, M., Santini, S., Gupta, A., & Jain, R. (2000). Content-based image retrieval at the end of the early years. *IEEE Transactions on Pattern Analysis and Machine Intelligence*, 22(12), 1349–1380. doi:10.1109/34.895972

Smirnov, D. A., Barnikol, U. B., Barnikol, T. T., Bezruchko, B. P., Hauptmann, C., Bührle, C., … Tass, P. A. (2008). The generation of Parkinsonian tremor as revealed by directional coupling analysis. *IOP, July.*

Smith, J. D., & Minda, J. P. (1998). Prototypes, sage, exemplars and thyme. In *Proceedings of 90th Annual Meeting of the Southern Society for Philosophy and Psychology*, New Orleans, LA. Minda, J. P., & Smith, J. D. (1997). Prototypes in category learning. In *Proceedings of the 38th Annual Meeting of the Psychonomic Society*, Philadelphia, PA.

Smith, J. R., & Chang, S. F. (1996). Tools and techniques for image color retrieval. In *Proc. IEEE Int. Conf. Acoust, Speech and Signal Proc.*, May 1996.

Smith, S., & Brady, M. (1997). A new approach to low level image processing. *International Journal of Computer Vision, 23*(1), 45–78. doi:10.1023/A:1007963824710

Snyman, J. A. (2005). *Practical mathematical optimization: An introduction to basic optimization theory and classical and new gradient-based algorithms*. New York, NY: Springer Publishing.

Soman, K. P., Loganathan, R., & Ajay, V. (2009). *Machine learning with SVM and other kernel methods*. New Delhi, India: PHI Learning Private Limited, Connaught Circus.

Somervuo, P., & Kohonen, T. (2004). *Self-organizing maps and learning vector quantization for feature sequences*. Netherlands: Kluwer Academic Publishers.

Sordo, M., Vaidya, S., & Jain, L. C. (2008). An introduction to computational intelligence in healthcare: New directions. *Studies in Computational Intelligence, 107*, 1–26. doi:10.1007/978-3-540-77662-8_1

Spath, H. (1980). *Cluster analysis – Algorithms for data reduction and classification of objects*. West Sussex, UK: Ellis Horwood Limited.

Sprengelmeyer, R., Rausch, M., Eysel, U. T., & Przuntek, H. (1998). *Neural structures associated with recognition of facial expressions of basic emotions*. The Royal Society.

Spyropoulos, C. D. (2000). AI planning and scheduling in the medical hospital environment. *Artificial Intelligence in Medicine, 20*(2), 101–111. doi:10.1016/S0933-3657(00)00059-2

Srihari, S. N., Hong, T., & Srikantan, G. (1997). Machine-printed Japanese document recognition. *Pattern Recognition, 30*(8), 1301–1313. doi:10.1016/S0031-3203(96)00168-9

Stach, W., Kurgan, L., & Petrycz, W. (2007). A framework for a novel scalable FCM learning method. *Proc 2007 Symposium on Human-Centric Computing and Data Processing* (HCDP07), February 21-23, (pp. 13-14). Canada.

Steane, A. M., & Rieffel, E. G. (2000). Beyond bits: The future of quantum information processing. *IEEE Computers, 33*(1), 38–45. doi:10.1109/2.816267

Steppe, J. M., Bauer, K. W., & Rogers, S. K. (1996). Integrated feature and architecture selection. *IEEE Transactions on Neural Networks, 7*, 1007–1014. doi:10.1109/72.508942

Stergiou, N. (2004). *Innovative analyses of human movement*. Human Kinetics.

Štětina, J. (Ed.). (2000). *Disaster medicine*. Praha, Czech Republic: Grada Publishing. (in Czech)

Steward, O. (1989). *Principles of cellular, molecular, and developmental neuroscience*. New York, NY: Springer-Verlag. doi:10.1007/978-1-4612-3540-8

Stewenius, H., Schaffalitzky, F., & Nister, D. (2005). How hard is 3-view triangulation really? In *International Conference on Computer Vision*, Beijing, China, (pp. 686-693).

Stiles, R. N., & Randall, J. E. (1967). Mechanical factors in human tremor frequency. *Journal of Applied Physiology, 23*(3), 324–330.

Stoklasa, J. (2009). *Classical and fuzzy models for efficiency assessment* (in Czech). Unpublished Master's thesis, Palacky University, Olomouc, Czech Republic

Stone, M. (1974). Cross-validatory choice and assessment of statistical predictions. *Journal of the Royal Statistical Society. Series A (General), 36*, 111–147.

Stone, M. A., & Moore, B. C. (1992). Spectral feature enhancement for people with sensorineural hearing impairment: effects on speech intelligibility and quality. *Journal of Rehabilitation Research and Development, 29*(2), 39–56. doi:10.1682/JRRD.1992.04.0039

Stork, D. G., Duda, R. O., & Hart, P. E. (2000). *Pattern classification*. Wiley, John, and Sons.

Streit, M., Brinkmever, J., Wolwer, W., & Gaebel, W. (2003). EEG brain mapping in Schizophrenic patients and healthy subjects during facial emotion recognition. *Schizophrenia Research*, *61*(1), 121.doi:10.1016/S0920-9964(02)00301-8

Sturm, P. F., & Maybank, S. J. (1999). On plane-based camera calibration: A general algorithm, singularities, applications. In *IEEE Conference on Computer Vision and Pattern Recognition*, (pp. 432–437).

Sturm, P. F., & Triggs, B. (1996). A factorization based algorithm for multi-image projective structure and motion. In *IV European Conference on Computer Vision, volume 2*, (pp. 709–720). London, UK: Springer-Verlag.

Styblinski, M. A., & Meyer, B. D. (1988). Fuzzy cognitive maps, signal flow graphs, and qualitative circuit analysis. *Proc. 2nd IEEE Internat. Conf. on Neural Networks (ICNN-87), vol II*, (pp. 549-556).

Stylios, C. D., & Georgopoulos, V. C. (2008). Fuzzy cognitive maps structure for medical decision support systems. *Studies in Fuzziness and Soft Computing*, *218*, 151–174. doi:10.1007/978-3-540-73185-6_7

Stylios, C. D., Georgopoulos, V. C., Malandraki, G. A., & Chouliara, S. (2008). Fuzzy cognitive map architectures for medical decision support systems. *Applied Soft Computing*, *8*(3), 1243–1251. doi:10.1016/j.asoc.2007.02.022

Suematsu, N., Ishida, Y., Hayashi, A., & Kanbara, T. (2004). Region-based image retrieval using wavelet transform. In *Transactions on Image Processing*, 2004.

Sugeno, M. (1985). An introductory survey on fuzzy control. *Information Sciences*, *36*, 59–83. doi:10.1016/0020-0255(85)90026-X

Sugeno, M., & Yasukawa, T. (1993). A fuzzy logic based approach to qualitative modeling. *IEEE Transactions on Fuzzy Systems*, *1*, 7–31. doi:10.1109/TFUZZ.1993.390281

Sulzberger, S. M., Tschicholg-Gurman, N. N., & Vestli, S. J. (1993). FUN: Optimization of fuzzy rule based systems using neural networks. In *Proceedings of IEEE Conference on Neural Networks*, San Francisco, USA, (pp. 312-316).

Sumi, Y., Ishiyama, Y., & Tomita, F. (2007). Robot-vision architecture for real-time 6-dof object localization. *International Journal of Computer Vision and Image Understanding*, *105*(3), 218–230. doi:10.1016/j.cviu.2006.11.003

Sumi, Y., Kawai, Y., Yoshimi, T., & Tomita, F. (2002). 3D object recognition in cluttered environments using segment-based stereo vision. *International Journal of Computer Vision*, *46*(1), 5–23. doi:10.1023/A:1013240031067

Sung, K. K., & Poggio, T. (1997). Example-based learning for view-based human face detection. *IEEE Transactions on Pattern Analysis and Machine Intelligence*, *20*(1), 39–51. doi:10.1109/34.655648

Sun, S., Haynor, D.-R., & Kim, Y. (2003). Semiautomatic video object segmentation using V Snakes. *IEEE Transactions on Circuits and Systems for Video Technology*, *13*(1), 75–82. doi:10.1109/TCSVT.2002.808089

Sural, S., & Das, P. K. (2001). Recognition of an Indian script using multilayer perceptrons and fuzzy features. In *International Conference on Document Analysis and Recognition*, (pp. 1120-1124). Seattle, USA.

Sutton, G. G., & Sykes, K. (1967). The effect of withdrawal of visual presentation of errors upon the frequency spectrum of tremor in a manual task. *The Journal of Physiology*, *190*, 281–283.

Swets, D. L., & Weng, J. J. (1996). Using discriminant eigenfeatures for image retrieval. *IEEE Transactions on Pattern Analysis and Machine Intelligence*, *18*(8), 831–836. doi:10.1109/34.531802

Swets, D., & Weng, J. (1996). Using discriminants eigenfeatures for image retrieval. *IEEE Transactions on Pattern Analysis and Machine Intelligence*, *18*(8), 831–836. doi:10.1109/34.531802

Sycara, K. P. (1998). *Multi-agent systems*. Publication of AAAI, 1998.

Taber, R. (1991). Knowledge processing with fuzzy cognitive maps. *Expert Systems with Applications*, *2*, 83–87. doi:10.1016/0957-4174(91)90136-3

Takagi, T., & Sugeno, M. (1985). Fuzzy identification of systems and its application to modeling and control. *IEEE Transactions on Systems, Man, and Cybernetics*, *1*(15), 116–132.

Takahashi, K. (2004). *Remarks on emotion recognition from bio-potential signals.* 2nd International Conference on Autonomous Robots and Agents. December 13-15, Palmerston North, New Zealand.

Talašová, J., & Bebčáková, I. (2008). Fuzzification of aggregation operators based on Choquet integral. *Aplimat - Journal of Applied Mathematics, 1*(1), 463–474. ISSN 1337-6365

Talašová, J., & Stoklasa, J. (2010). Fuzzy approach to academic staff performance evaluation. *Proceedings of the 28th International Conference on Mathematical Methods in Economics 2010*, September 2010, České Budějovice, Czech Republic, (pp. 621-626). ISBN 978-80-7394-218-2

Talašová, J. (2000). NEFRIT - Multicriteria decision making based on fuzzy approach. *Central European Journal of Operations Research, 8*(4), 297–319.

Talašová, J. (2003). *Fuzzy methods of multiple-criteria evaluation and decision making.* Olomouc, Czech Republic: VUP. (in Czech)

Tan, C.-Q., & Chen, X.-H. (2010). Intuitionistic fuzzy Choquet integral operator for multi-criteria decision making. *Expert Systems with Applications, 37*(1), 149–157. doi:10.1016/j.eswa.2009.05.005

Tang, A. M., Quek, C., & Ng, G. S. (2005). GA-TSKfnn: Parameters tuning of fuzzy neural network using genetic algorithms. *Expert Systems with Applications, 29*, 769–781. doi:10.1016/j.eswa.2005.06.001

Tano, S., Oyama, T., & Arnould, T. (1996). Deep combination of fuzzy inference and neural network in fuzzy inference. *Fuzzy Sets and Systems, 82*(2), 151–160. doi:10.1016/0165-0114(95)00251-0

Tan, R. R. (2007). Hybrid evolutionary computation for the development of pollution prevention and control strategies. *Journal of Cleaner Production, 15*, 902–906. doi:10.1016/j.jclepro.2006.01.011

Tariq, U., Jamal, H., Shahid, M. Z. J., & Malik, M. U. (2004). Face detection in color images, a robust and fast statistical approach. *Proceedings of INMIC*, (pp. 73-78).

Tarres, F., Rama, A., & Torres, L. (2005). A novel method for face recognition under partial occlusion or facial expression variations. In *Proc. ELMAR*, (pp. 163-166).

Taylor, J. S., & Cristianini, N. (2000). *Support vector machines and other kernel-based learning methods.* Cambridge University Press.

Teague, M. (1980). Image analysis via the general theory of moments. *Journal of the Optical Society of America, 70*, 920–930. doi:10.1364/JOSA.70.000920

Teh, C. H., & Chin, R. T. (1988). On image analysis by the methods of moments. *IEEE Transactions on Pattern Analysis and Machine Intelligence, 10*(4), 496–513. doi:10.1109/34.3913

Teh, C., & Chin, R. T. (1989). On the detection of dominant points on digital curves. *IEEE Transactions on Pattern Analysis and Machine Intelligence, 11*(8), 859–872. doi:10.1109/34.31447

Tenore, F., Ramos, A., Fahmy, A., Acharya, S., Etienne-Cummings, R., & Thakor, N. (2007). *Towards the control of individual fingers of a prosthetic hand using surface EMG signals.* Paper presented at the IEEE Engineering in Medicine and Biology Society. IEEE Engineering in Medicine and Biology Society.

Terzopoulus, D., & Waters, K. (1993). Analysis and synthesis of facial image sequences using physical and anatomical models. *IEEE Transactions on Pattern Analysis and Machine Intelligence, 15*, 569–579. doi:10.1109/34.216726

Teshnehlab, M., Aliyari Shoorehdeli, M., & Sedigh, A. K. (2008). *Novel hybrid learning for tuning ANFIS parameters as an identifiers using fuzzy PSO.* Paper presented at IEEE International Conference on Networking, Sensing and Control, Sanya, China, (pp. 111-116).

Thammano, A. (1999). Neuro-fuzzy model for stock market prediction. In C. H. Dagli, A. L. Buczak, J. Ghosh, M. J. Embrechts, O. Ersoy (1999). *Smart engineering system design: Neural networks, fuzzy logic, evolutionary programming, data mining, and complex systems.* Paper presented at the Artificial Neural Networks in Engineering Conference (ANNIE '99), (pp. 587–591). New York, NY: ASME Press.

Thomas, A., Ferrari, V., Leibe, B., Tuytelaars, T., & Van Gool, L. (2009). Shape-from-recognition: Recognition enables meta-data transfer. *International Journal of Computer Vision and Image Understanding, 113*(12), 1222–1234. doi:10.1016/j.cviu.2009.03.010

Thomaz, C. E. (2004). *Maximum entropy covariance estimate for statistical pattern recognition.* Unpublished doctoral thesis, Department of Computing, Imperial College, London, UK.

Thomaz, C. E., Amaral, V., Giraldi, G. A., Kitani, E. C., Sato, J. R., & Gillies, D. F. (2009). A multi-linear discriminant analysis of 2D frontal face images. In *Proceedings of Brazilian Symposium on Computer Graphics and Image Processing (SIBGRAPI),* (pp. 216-223). IEEE CS Press.

Thomaz, C. E., Boardman, J. P., Counsell, S., Hill, D. L. G., Hajnal, J. V., & Edwards, A. D. (2007). A multivariate statistical analysis of the developing human brain in preterm infants. *Image and Vision Computing, 25*(6), 981–994. doi:10.1016/j.imavis.2006.07.011

Thomaz, C. E., Gillies, D. F., & Feitosa, R. Q. (2004). A new covariance estimate for Bayesian classifiers in biometric recognition. *IEEE Transactions on Circuits and Systems for Video Technology, 14*(2), 214–223. doi:10.1109/TCSVT.2003.821984

Thomaz, C. E., Kitani, E. C., & Gillies, D. F. (2006). A maximum uncertainty LDA-based approach for limited sample size problems - With application to face recognition. *Journal of the Brazilian Computer Society, 12*(2), 7–18. doi:10.1007/BF03192391

Thompson, R. (1990). *Das Gehirn: Von der Nervenzelle zur Verhaltenssteuerung.* Heidelberg, Germany: Spektrum der Wissenschaft.

Thornton, J., Savvides, M., & Vijayakumar, B. V. K. (2007). A Bayesian approach to deformed pattern matching of iris images. *Transactions on Pattern Analysis and Machine Intelligence, 29*(4), 596–606. doi:10.1109/TPAMI.2007.1006

Tian, Y., Kanade, & T., Cohn, J. (2001). Recognizing action units for facial expression analysis. *IEEE Transactions on Pattern Analysis and Machine Intelligence, 23*(2), 97–116. doi:10.1109/34.908962

Timmer, J., Gantert, C., Deuschl, G., & Honerkamp, J. (1993). Characteristics of hand tremor time series. (Springer-Verlag.). *Biological Cybernetics, 70.*

Ting, C.-C., Yu, J.-S., Tzeng, J.-S., & Wang, J.-H. (2006). Improved snake model for fast image segmentation. In *Proceedings of International Joint Conference on Neural Networks* (pp. 3936-3941).

Tipping, M. E., & Bishop, C. M. (1997). *Probabilistic principal component analysis.* Technical Report NCRG/97/010, Aston University.

Tisse, C., Martin, L., Torres, L., & Robert, M. (2002). *Person identification technique using human iris recognition* (pp. 294–299). Proc. Vision Interface.

Tizhoosh, H. (2003). Fast and robust fuzzy edge detection. In Nachtegael, M. (Ed.), *Fuzzy filters for image processing.* Berlin, Germany: Springer.

Torra, V., & Narukawa, Y. (2007). *Modelling decisions.* Berlin, Germany: Springer-Verlag. doi:10.1007/978-3-540-73729-2

Tourtellotte, W. W. (1965). Quantitative clinical neurological testing. *Annals of the New York Academy of Sciences, 122,* 480–505. doi:10.1111/j.1749-6632.1965.tb20231.x

Trentesaux, D., Pesin, P., & Tahon, C. (2001). Comparison of constraint logic programming and distributed problem solving: A case study for interactive, efficient, and practicable job-shop scheduling. *Computers & Industrial Engineering, 29,* 187–211. doi:10.1016/S0360-8352(00)00078-4

Trier, O. D., Jain, A. K., & Taxt, T. (1996). Feature extraction methods for character recognition: A survey. *Pattern Recognition, 29*(4), 641–662. doi:10.1016/0031-3203(95)00118-2

Triesch, J., & von der Malsburg, C. (1996). Robust classification of hand postures against complex backgrounds. In *Proceedings of the 2nd International Conference on Automatic Face and Gesture Recognition* (pp. 170-175). Killington, Vermont, USA.

Triggs, B. (1998). Autocalibration from planar scenes. In *V European Conference on Computer Vision,* (pp. 89–105).

Tsadiras, A. K., Kouskouvelis, I., & Margaritis, K. G. (2001). Making political decisions using fuzzy cognitive maps: The FYROM crisis. *Proc 8th Panhellenic Conference on Informatics, 2,* (pp. 501–510).

Tsadiras, A. K. (2008). Comparing the inference capabilities of binary, trivalent and sigmoid fuzzy cognitive maps. *Information Sciences, 178*(20), 3880–3894. doi:10.1016/j.ins.2008.05.015

Tsai, R. Y. (1987). A versatile camera calibration technique for high-accuracy 3D machine vision metrology using off-the-shelf cameras and lenses. *IEEE Journal on Robotics and Automation, RA-3*(4), 323–344. doi:10.1109/JRA.1987.1087109

Tsai, V. J. D. (2006, June). A comparative study on shadow compensation of color aerial images in invariant color models. *IEEE Transactions on Geoscience and Remote Sensing, 24*(6), 1661–1671. doi:10.1109/TGRS.2006.869980

Tse, E., Shen, S., Greenberg, S., & Forlines, C. (2006). Enabling interaction with single user applications through speech and gestures on a multi-user tabletop. *AVI '06, May 23-26, 2006, Venezia, Italy*, (pp. 336-343).

Tsvetovatyy, M., Gini, M., Mobasher, M., & Wieckowski, Z. (1997). MAGMA: An agent-based virtual market for electronic commerce. *Applied Artificial Intelligence, 11*(6), 501–523. doi:10.1080/088395197118046

Turk, M., & Pentland, A. (1991). Eigenfaces for recognition. *Journal of Cognitive Neuroscience, 3*(1), 71–86. doi:10.1162/jocn.1991.3.1.71

Tzeng, Y. C., & Chen, K. S. (1998). A fuzzy neural network to SAR image classification. *IEEE Transactions on Geoscience and Remote Sensing, 36*(1), 301–307. doi:10.1109/36.655339

Ueki, N., Morishima, S., & Harashima, H. (1994). Expression analysis/synthesis system based on emotion space constructed by multilayered neural network. *Systems and Computers in Japan, 25*(13), 95–103.

Ullman, S. (1996). *High-level vision*. Cambridge, MA: MIT Press.

Uncu, O., & Turksen, I. B. (2007). A novel feature selection approach: Combining feature wrappers and filters. *Information Sciences, 177*, 449–466. doi:10.1016/j.ins.2006.03.022

Ursula, H., Pierre, P., & Sylvie, B. (1998). Facial reactions to emotional facial expressions: Affect or cognition? *Cognition and Emotion, 12*(4).

Uwechue, O. A., & Pandya, S. A. (1997). *Human face recognition using third-order synthetic neural networks*. Boston, MA: Kluwer Academic publishers.

Vaish, V., Levoy, M., Szeliski, R., Zitnick, C., & Kang, S. (2006). Reconstructing occluded surfaces using synthetic apertures: Stereo, focus and robust measures. In *Proceedings of the International Conference on Pattern Recognition*.

Van Gestel, T., Suykens, J. A. K., De Brabanter, J., De Moor, B., & Vandewalle, J. (2001). Least squares support vector machine regression for discriminant analysis. *Proc. International Joint INNS-IEEE Conf. Neural Networks (INNS2001)*, (pp. 2445-2450). New York, NY: Wiley.

Van Gool, J., Moons, T., & Ungureanu, D. (1996). Affine/photometric invariants for planar intensity patterns. In *Proceedings of the European Conference on Computer Vision* (pp. 642-651). Cambridge, UK.

Vanger, P., Honlinger, R., & Haykin, H. (1995). Applications of synergetic in decoding facial expressions of emotions. *Proc. of Int. Workshop on Automatic face and Gesture recognition*, Zurich, (pp. 24-29).

Vapnik, V. N. (1995). *The nature of statistical learning theory*. London, UK: Springer-Verlag.

Vapnik, V. N. (1998). *Statistical learning theory*. New York, NY: Wiley.

Vapnik, V., Golowich, S., & Smola, A. (1997). Support vector method for function approximation, regression estimation, and signal processing. In Mozer, M., Jordan, M., & Petsche, T. (Eds.), *Advances in neural information processing systems 9* (pp. 281–287). Cambridge, MA: MIT Press.

Várkonyi-Kóczy, A. (2008). Fuzzy logic supported corner detection. *Journal of Intelligent & Fuzzy Systems, 19*, 41–50.

Vascák, J., & Rutrich, M. (2008). Path planning in dynamic environment using fuzzy cognitive maps. *SAMI 2008, 6th International Symposium on Applied Machine Intelligence and Informatics, IEEE*, (pp. 5-9).

Vasilakos, A., & Pedrycz, W. (2006). *Ambient intelligence, wireless networking and ubiquitous computing*. Norwood, MA: Artech House.

Vasilescu, M. A. O., & Terzopoulos, D. (2003). Multilinear subspace analysis of image ensembles. In *Proceedings of IEEE Computer Vision and Pattern Recognition*, (pp. 93-99). Madison, WI.

Veldhuizen, I. J., Gaillard, A. W., & de Vries, J. (2003). The influence of mental fatigue on facial EMG activity during a simulated workday. *Journal of Biological Psychology*, *63*(1), 59–78. doi:10.1016/S0301-0511(03)00025-5

Veluvolu, K. C., Tan, U. X., Latt, W. T., & Shee, C. Y. (2007). Bandlimited multiple Fourier linear combiner for real-time tremor compensation. *Proceedings of the 29th Annual International Conference of the IEEE EMBS*, Cité Internationale, Lyon, France August 23-26.

Ventura, D., & Martinez, T. (1998). Quantum associative memory with exponential capacity. In *Proceedings of the International Joint Conference on Neural Networks* (pp.509-513).

Verma, A., Liu, C., & Jia, J. (2011). New color SIFT descriptors for image classification with applications to biometrics. *International Journal of Biometrics*, *3*(1), 56–75. doi:10.1504/IJBM.2011.037714

Vermeulen, I., Bohte, S., Somefun, K., & La Poutré, H. (2007). Multi-agent pareto appointment exchanging in hospital patient scheduling. *Service Oriented Computing and Applications*, *1*(3), 185–196. doi:10.1007/s11761-007-0012-1

Villmann, T., Hammer, B., Schleif, F.-M., & Geweniger, T. (2005). Fuzzy labeled neural GAS for fuzzy classification. In *Proceedings of the Workshop on Self-Organizing Maps WSOM* (pp. 283-290).

Vinjamuri, R., Crammond, D. J., & Kondziolka, D. (2009). Extraction of sources of tremor in hand movements of patients with movement disorders. *IEEE Transactions on Information Technology in Biomedicine*, 13.

Viola, P., & Jones, M. (2001). Rapid object detection using a boosted cascade of simple features. In *Proceedings of IEEE Computer Society Conference on Computer Vision and Pattern Recognition* (pp. 511-518).

Von Altrock, C. (1996). *Fuzzy logic and neurofuzzy applications in business and finance*. New Jersey: Prentice Hall.

Wah, B. W., & Qian, M. (2002). *Constrained formulations and algorithms for stock price predictions using recurrent FIR neural networks*. Paper presented at Eighteenth National Conference on Artificial Intelligence, (pp. 211–216).

Wainer, J., Ferreira, P. R., & Constantino, E. R. (2007). Scheduling meetings through multi-agent negotiations. *Decision Support Systems*, *44*(1), 285–297. doi:10.1016/j.dss.2007.03.015

Walter, J., & Ritter, H. (1995). Local PSOMs and Chebyshev PSOMs improving the parameterized self-organizing maps. In F. Fogelman-Soulie (Ed.), *Proceedings of International Conference on Artificial Neural Networks*.

Wang, L., Wu, F. C., & Hu, Z. Y. (2007). Multi-camera calibration with one-dimensional object under general motions. In *IEEE 11th International Conference on Computer Vision*, (pp. 1–7). Rio de Janeiro, Brazil.

Wang, P., & Ji, Q. (2005). *Learning discriminating features for multi-view face and eye detection*. IEEE Int. Conf. on Computer Vision and Pattern Recognition.

Wang, P., Green, M. B., Ji, Q., & Wayman, J. (2005). Automatic eye detection and its validation. *IEEE International Conference on Computer Vision and Pattern Recognition*, (pp. 164–172).

Wang, P., Krishnan, S. M., Kugean, C., & Tjoa, M. P. (October 2001). Classification of endoscopic images based on texture and neural network. In *Proceedings of the 23rd Annual EMBS International Conference*, (pp. 3691-3695).

Wang, X., Shen, X., & Georganas, N. D. (2006). A fuzzy logic based intelligent negotiation agent (FINA) in e-commerce. In *Proceedings of the IEEE Canadian Conference on Electrical and Computer Engineering*, Ottawa, ON, Canada.

Wang, X., Yang, Y., & Huang, K. (2006). Combining discrete orthogonal moments and DHMMS for off-line handwritten Chinese character recognition. In *International Conference on Cognitive Informatics* (pp. 788-793). Beijing, China.

Wang, G., & Wang, S. (2006). Recursive computation of Tchebichef moment and its inverse transform. *Pattern Recognition*, *39*(1), 47–56. doi:10.1016/j.patcog.2005.05.015

Wang, P., & Ji, Q. (2007). Multi-view face and eye detection using discriminant features. *Computer Vision and Image Understanding*, *105*(2), 99–111. doi:10.1016/j.cviu.2006.08.008

Wang, S. S., Chen, P. C., & Lin, W. G. (1994). Invariant pattern recognition by moment Fourier descriptor. *Pattern Recognition*, *27*(12), 1735–1742. doi:10.1016/0031-3203(94)90090-6

Wang, W., Zhengdao, Z., & Giannakis, G. B. (2000, May). Wireless multicarrier communications. *IEEE Signal Processing Magazine*, 29–48. doi:10.1109/79.841722

Wang, X. G., Tang, Z., Tamura, H., Ishii, M., & Sun, W. D. (2004). An improved backpropagation algorithm to avoid the local minima problem. *Neurocomputing*, *56*, 455–460. doi:10.1016/j.neucom.2003.08.006

Wang, Y.-F. (2002). Predicting stock price using fuzzy grey prediction system. *Expert Systems with Applications*, *22*, 33–39. doi:10.1016/S0957-4174(01)00047-1

Weber, M. (n.d.). *Caltech face database*. Retrieved from http://www.vision.caltech.edu/html-files/archive.html

Wee, C. Y., & Paramesran, R. (2007). On the computational aspects of Zernike moments. *Image and Vision Computing*, *25*(6), 967–980. doi:10.1016/j.imavis.2006.07.010

Wei, Z., Baowen, S., & Yanchun, Z. (2009). Design of inference model based on activation for fuzzy cognitive map. *2009 International Workshop on Intelligent Systems and Applications, ISA 2009*, art. no. 5072819, 2009.

Weina, W., & Yunjie, Z. (2007). On fuzzy cluster validity indices. *Fuzzy Sets and Systems*, *158*, 2095–2117. doi:10.1016/j.fss.2007.03.004

Weka. (n.d.). *Website*. Retrieved from http://www.cs.waikato.ac.nz/ml/weka/

Weymaere, N., & Martens, J. P. (1994). On the initialization and optimization of multilayer perceptrons. *IEEE Transactions on Neural Networks*, *5*, 738–751. doi:10.1109/72.317726

Wheeler, K. R., & Jorgensen, C. C. (2003). Gestures as input: Neuroelectric joysticks and keyboards. *Pervasive Computing, IEEE*, *2*(2), 56–61. doi:10.1109/MPRV.2003.1203754

White, D., & Ligomenides, P. (1993). GANNet: A genetic algorithm for optimizing topology and weights in neural network design. In J. Mira, J. Cabestany, & A. Prieto (Eds.), *New Trends in neural computation* In *Proceedings of International Workshop on Artificial Neural Networks* (pp. 332-327). Berlin, Germany: Springer-Verlag.

Whitley, D., & Bogart, C. (1990). The evolution of connectivity: Pruning neural networks using genetic algorithms. In *Proceedings of International Joint Conference on Neural Networks, 1*, 134-137.

Widjaja, F., Shee, C. Y., Latt, W. T., Au, W. L., Poignet, P., & Ang, W. T. (2003). Kalman filtering of accelerometer and electromyography (EMG) data in pathological tremor sensing system. Proceedings of *the 2003 IEEE International Conference on Robotics & Automation*, Taipei, Taixao.

Wikipedia. (n.d.). *Hopfield net*. Retrieved from www.wikipedia.org/wiki/Hopfield_net

Wikipedia. (n.d.). *NMDA receptor*. Retrieved from www.wikipedia.org/wiki/NMDA_receptor

Wikipedia. (n.d.). *Radial base function*. Retrieved from www.wikipedia.org/wiki/Radial_basis_function

Wildes, R. (1997). Iris recognition: An emerging biometric technology. *Proceedings of the IEEE*, *85*(9), 1348–1363. doi:10.1109/5.628669

Williams, C. P., & Clearwater, S. H. (1998). *Explorations in quantum computing*. New York, NY: Springer-Verlag.

Wiskott, L., Fellous, J. M., Kruger, N., & Malsburg, C. V. D. (1999). Face recognition by elastic bunch graph matching. In Jain, L. C. (Eds.), *Intelligent biometric techniques in fingerprint and face recognition* (pp. 355–396). CRC Press. doi:10.1109/34.598235

Witten, I., & Frank, E. (2005). *Data mining: Practical machine learning tools and techniques* (2nd ed.). San Francisco, CA: Morgan Kaufmann.

Wohlert, A. B., & Goffman, L. (1994). Human perioral muscle activation patterns. *Journal of Speech and Hearing Research*, *37*, 1032–1040.

Wolf, W. (1996). The EMG as a window to the brain: Signal processing tools to enhance the view. In Gath, I., & Inbar, G. (Eds.), *Advances in processing and pattern analysis of biological signals* (pp. 339–356). New York, NY: Plenum Press.

Wong, B., & Spetsakis, M. (2000). Scene reconstruction and robot navigation using dynamic fields. *International Journal of Autonomous Robots*, *8*(1), 71–86. doi:10.1023/A:1008992902895

Wooldridge, M. (2009). *An introduction to multi agent systems* (2nd ed.). John Wiley and Sons.

Wu, C., Fraundorfer, F., Frahm, J., & Pollefeys, M. (2008). 3D model search and pose estimation from single images using VIP features. In *Proceedings of IEEE Computer Society Conference on Computer Vision and Pattern Recognition Workshops*, (pp. 1-8).

Wu, D., & Mendel, J. M. (2007). Uncertainty measures for interval type-2 fuzzy sets. *Information Sciences, 177*, 5378–5393. doi:10.1016/j.ins.2007.07.012

Wu, D., & Mendel, J. M. (2009). A comparative study of ranking methods, similarity measures and uncertainty measures for interval type-2 fuzzy sets. *Information Sciences, 177*(23).

Wu, F., Hu, Z., & Zhu, H. (2005). Camera calibration with moving one-dimensional objects. *Pattern Recognition, 40*(1), 755–765. doi:10.1016/j.patcog.2004.11.005

Wu, J. X., & Zhou, Z. H. (2003). Efficient face candidates selector for face recognition. *Pattern Recognition, 36*(5), 1175–1186. doi:10.1016/S0031-3203(02)00165-6

Xiang, W., & Lee, H. P. (2008). Ant colony intelligence in multi-agent dynamic manufacturing scheduling. *Engineering Applications of Artificial Intelligence*, 73–84. doi:10.1016/j.engappai.2007.03.008

Xie, X. L., & Benni, G. (1991). A validity measure for fuzzy clustering. *IEEE Transactions on Pattern Analysis and Machine Intelligence, 11*, 841–847. doi:10.1109/34.85677

Xie, X., Sudhakar, R., & Zhuang, H. (1994). On improving eye feature extraction using deformable templates. *Pattern Recognition, 27*(8), 791–799. doi:10.1016/0031-3203(94)90164-3

Xing, K., Xu, Q., He, J., Wang, Y., Zhongwei, L., & Huang, Z. (2008). A wearable device for repetitive hand therapy. *Proceedings of the 2nd Biennial IEEE/RAS-EMBS International Conference on Biomedical Robotics and Biomechatronics*, Scottsdale, AZ, USA.

Xinpu, C., & Xiangyang, Z. (2008). A novel spectral analysis method of EMG feature extraction for wrist motions recognition. In *Proceedings of 2nd Biennial IEEE/RAS-EMBS International Conference on Biomedical Robotics and Biomechatronics*, Scottsdale, AZ, USA.

Xirogiannis, G., & Glykas, M. (2004). Fuzzy cognitive maps in business analysis and performance-driven change. *IEEE Transactions on Engineering Management, 51*(3), 334–351. doi:10.1109/TEM.2004.830861

Xu, L. Zhuge, & Z., Yang, J. (2004). Artificial emotion and its recognition, modeling and applications: An overview. In. *Proc. of the 5th World Congress on Intelligent Control and Automation*, Hangzhou. P.R. China.

Xu, C., & Prince, J. L. (1998). Snakes, shape, and gradient vector flow. *IEEE Transactions on Image Processing, 7*(3), 359–369. doi:10.1109/83.661186

Xu, N., Ahuja, N., & Bansal, R. (2007). Object segmentation using graph cuts based active contours. *Computer Vision and Image Understanding, 107*(3), 210–224. doi:10.1016/j.cviu.2006.11.004

Yacoob, Y., & Davis, L. (1996). Recognizing human facial expression from long image sequences using optical flow. *IEEE Transactions on Pattern Analysis and Machine Intelligence, 16*, 636–642. doi:10.1109/34.506414

Yager, R. R. (1988). On ordered weighted averaging aggregation operators in multicriteria decision making. *IEEE Transactions on Systems, Man, and Cybernetics, 3*(1), 183–190. doi:10.1109/21.87068

Yamada, H. (1993). Visual information for categorizing facial expression of emotion. *Applied Cognitive Psychology, 7*, 257–270. doi:10.1002/acp.2350070309

Yaman, D., & Polat, S. (2009). A fuzzy cognitive map approach for effect based operations: An illustrative case. *Information Sciences, 179*, 382–403. doi:10.1016/j.ins.2008.10.013

Yang, M. H. (2002). Kernel eigenfaces vs. kernel fisherfaces: Face recognition using kernel methods. *Proceedings of the Fifth IEEE International Conference on Automatic Face and Gesture Recognition*, (pp. 215-220).

Yang, M. H., Ahuja, N., & Kriegman, D. (2000). Face recognition using kernel eigenfaces. *Proceedings of IEEE International Conference on Image Processing, 1*, (pp. 37-40).

Yang, H. (2005). A road to future broadband wireless access: MIMO-OFDM- based wireless access. *IEEE Communications Magazine, 43*(1), 53–60. doi:10.1109/MCOM.2005.1381875

Yang, J., Liu, C., & Zhang, L. (2010). Color space normalization: Enhancing the discriminating power of color spaces for face recognition. *Pattern Recognition, 43*(4), 1454–1466. doi:10.1016/j.patcog.2009.11.014

Yap, P. T., Paramesran, R., & Ong, S. H. (2003). Image analysis by Krawtchouk moments. *IEEE Transactions on Image Processing, 12*(11), 1367–1377. doi:10.1109/TIP.2003.818019

You, H.-J., Shin, D.-K., Kim, D.-H., Kim, H.-S., & Park, S.-H. (2003). A rotation invariant image retrieval with local features. *International Journal of Control, Automation, and Systems, 1*(3), 332–338.

Yu, T. J., Lai, R., Lin, M. W., & Kao, B. R. (2007). Modeling opponent's beliefs via fuzzy constraint–directed approach in agent negotiation. In *Proceedings of the 3rd International Conference on Advanced Intelligent Computing Theories and Applications,* August 2007, Qingdao, China, (pp. 167-178).

Yu, X., Loh, N. K., & Miller, W. C. (1993). A new acceleration technique for the backpropagation algorithm. In *Proceedings of IEEE International Conference on Neural Networks, Vol. III* (pp. 1157-1161), San Diego, CA.

Yua, D., Hu, Q., & Wua, C. (2007). Uncertainty measures for fuzzy relations and their applications. *Applied Soft Computing, 7*(3), 1135–1143. doi:10.1016/j.asoc.2006.10.004

Yuan, Y., & Li, Y. (2008). Study on EEG time series based on Duffing equation. *International Conference on BioMedical Engineering and Informatics, BMEI,* vol. 2, (pp. 516-519).

Yue, H. (2008). Application study in decision support using fuzzy cognitive map. In Lovrek, I., Howlett, R. J., & Jain, L. C. (Eds.), *KES 2008, Part II, LNAI 5178* (pp. 324–331). Berlin, Germany: Springer-Verlag.

Yu, H., & Yang, J. (2001). A Direct LDA algorithm for high dimensional data with application to face recognition. *Pattern Recognition, 34*(7), 2067–2070. doi:10.1016/S0031-3203(00)00162-X

Yüksel, M. (2007). Edge detection in noisy images by fuzzy processing. *International Journal of Electronics and Communications, 61,* 82–89. doi:10.1016/j.aeue.2006.02.006

Zadeh, L. A. (1975). The concept of linguistic variable and its application to approximate reasoning. *Information Sciences, 8,* 199-249; 301-357; *9,* 43-80.

Zadeh, L. A. (1965). Fuzzy sets. *Information and Control, 8*(3), 338–353. doi:10.1016/S0019-9958(65)90241-X

Zadeh, L. A. (1975). The concept of a linguistic variable and its application to approximate reasoning - 1. *Information Sciences, 8,* 199–249. doi:10.1016/0020-0255(75)90036-5

Zaknich, A. (2003). *Neural networks for intelligent signal processing.* World Scientific.

Zamparelli, M. (1997). Genetically trained cellular neural networks. *Neural Networks, 10*(6), 1143–1151. doi:10.1016/S0893-6080(96)00128-1

Zemková, B., & Talašová, J. (2010). Application of fuzzy sets in human resources management. *Proceedings of the 28th International Conference Mathematical Methods in Economics,* 8th – 10th September 2010, České Budějovice, (pp. 682 – 687). ISBN 978-80-7394-218-2

Zeng, X., & Chen, X.-W. (2005). SMO-based pruning methods for sparse least squares support vector machines. *IEEE Transactions on Neural Networks, 16*(6), 1541–1546. doi:10.1109/TNN.2005.852239

Zeng, Z., Fu, Y., Roisman, G. I., Wen, Z., Hu, Y., & Huang, T. S. (2006). Spontaneous emotional facial expression detection. *J. of Multimedia, 1*(5), 1–8.

Zernike, F. (1934). Beugungstheorie des Schneidenverfahrens und seiner verbesserten Form, der Phasenkonstrastmethode. *Physica, 1,* 689–701. doi:10.1016/S0031-8914(34)80259-5

Zhang, J., & Guo, X. (2009). Trust evaluation model based on fuzzy logic for C2C e-commerce. In *Proceedings of the International Symposium on Information Engineering and Electronic Commerce (IEEC '09),* May 16 – 17, Ternopil, Ukraine, (pp. 403-407).

Zhang, J., McMillan, L., Yu, J., & Hill, U. (2006) Robust tracking and stereo matching under variable illumination. In *Proceedings of the International Conference on Pattern Recognition.*

Zhang, J., Zhang, X., & Krim, H. (1998). Invariant object recognition by shape space analysis. ICIP 98, (vol.3 pp. 581-585).

Zhang, X. M., & Zhan, H. Y. (2006). *An illumination independent eye detection algorithm.* IEEE International Conference on Pattern Recognition.

Zhang, D., & Lu, G. (2001). Segmentation of moving objects in image sequence: A review. *International Journal of Circuits, Systems, and Signal Processing, 20*(2), 143–189. doi:10.1007/BF01201137

Zhang, J., Zhang, X., Krim, H., & Walter, G. G. (2003). Object representation and recognition in shape spaces. *Pattern Recognition, 36,* 1143–1154. doi:10.1016/S0031-3203(02)00226-1

Zhang, Q., & Lee, M. (2009). Analysis of positive and negative emotions in natural scene using brain activity and GIST. *Neurocomputing, 72,* 1302–1306. doi:10.1016/j.neucom.2008.11.007

Zhang, Z. (1994). Iterative point matching for registration of free-form curves and surfaces. *International Journal of Computer Vision, 7*(3), 119–152. doi:10.1007/BF01427149

Zhang, Z. (2000). A flexible new technique for camera calibration. *IEEE Transactions on Pattern Analysis and Machine Intelligence, 22*(11), 1330–1334. doi:10.1109/34.888718

Zhang, Z. (2004). Camera calibration with one-dimensional objects. *IEEE Transactions on Pattern Analysis and Machine Intelligence, 26*(7), 892–899. doi:10.1109/TPAMI.2004.21

Zhao, S., & Grigat, R.-R. (2006). Robust eye detection under active infrared illumination. *In Proceedings of the 18th International Conference on Pattern Recognition (ICPR 2006),* (pp. 481-484).

Zhao, W., Chellappa, R., & Krishnaswamy, A. (1998). Discriminant analysis of principal components for face recognition. In *Proceedings of International Conference on Automatic Face and Gesture Recognition,* (pp. 336-341).

Zhao, L., & Yang, Y. H. (1999). Theoretical analysis of illumination in PCA based vision systems. *Pattern Recognition, 32,* 547–564. doi:10.1016/S0031-3203(98)00119-8

Zhao, W., Chellappa, R., & Phillips, P. (1999). *Subspace linear discriminant analysis for face recognition. Technical Report, CS-TR4009.* University of Maryland.

Zhao, W., Chellappa, R., Phillips, P. J., & Rosenfeld, A. (2003). Face recognition: A literature survey. *ACM Computing Surveys, 35*(4), 399–458. doi:10.1145/954339.954342

Zhao, Z., & Liu, Y. (2008). New multi-camera calibration algorithm based on 1D objects. *Journal of Zhejiang University Science A, 9*(6), 799–806. doi:10.1631/jzus.A071573

Zheng, Z., Wang, H., & Teoh, E. (1999). Analysis of gray level corner detection. *Pattern Recognition Letters, 20*(2), 149–162. doi:10.1016/S0167-8655(98)00134-2

Zhou, G., & Si, J. (1999). Subset-based training and pruning of sigmoid neural networks. *Neural Networks, 12*(1), 79–89. doi:10.1016/S0893-6080(98)00105-1

Zhou, Z. H., & Geng, X. (2004). Projection function for eye detection. *Pattern Recognition, 37*(5), 1049–1056. doi:10.1016/j.patcog.2003.09.006

Zhu, Q., Avidan, S., Yeh, M. C., & Cheng, K. T. (2006). *Fast human detection using a cascaded of histogram of oriented gradients.* IEEE International Conference on Computer Vision and Pattern Recognition.

Zhu, H., Shu, H., Liang, J., Luo, L., & Coatrieux, J. L. (2007b). Image analysis by discrete orthogonal Racah moments. *Signal Processing, 87*(4), 687–708. doi:10.1016/j.sigpro.2006.07.007

Zhu, H., Shu, H., Xia, T., Luo, L., & Coatrieux, J. L. (2007c). Translation and scale invariants of Tchebichef moments. *Pattern Recognition, 40*(9), 2530–2542. doi:10.1016/j.patcog.2006.12.003

Zhu, H., Shu, H., Zhou, J., Luo, L., & Coatrieux, J. L. (2007a). Image analysis by discrete orthogonal dual Hahn moments. *Pattern Recognition Letters, 28*(13), 1688–1704. doi:10.1016/j.patrec.2007.04.013

Zhu, Z. W., & Ji, Q. (2005). Robust real-time eye detection and tracking under variable lighting conditions and various face orientations. *Computer Vision and Image Understanding, 98*(1), 124–154. doi:10.1016/j.cviu.2004.07.012

Zimmermann, H. G., Neuneier, R., & Grothmann, R. (2001). Modeling of dynamical systems by error correction neural networks. In Soofi, A., & Cao, L. (Eds.), *Modeling and forecasting financial data: Techniques of nonlinear dynamics.* Kluwer Academic Pub. doi:10.1007/978-1-4615-0931-8_12

Zipf, G. K. (1949). *Human behavior and the principle of least effort.* Cambridge, MA: Addison-Wesley.

Zou, L., Chen, J., Zhang, J., & Dou, L. (2008). The comparison of two typical corner detection algorithms. *Second International Symposium on Intelligent Information Technology Application.* ISBN 978-0-7695-3497

Zuo, B. H., & Sun, Y. (2009). Fuzzy logic to support bilateral agent negotiation in e-commerce. In *Proceedings of the International Conference on Artificial Intelligence and Computational Intelligence,* November 7 – 8, Shanghai, China, (pp. 179-183).

Zurada, J. M., Malinowski, A., & Cloete, I. (1994). Sensitivity analysis for minimization of input data dimension for feedforward neural network. In *Proceedings of IEEE International Symposium on Circuits and Systems.*

Zurada, J. M., Malinowski, A., & Usui, S. (1997). Perturbation method for deleting redundant inputs of perceptron networks. *Neurocomputing, 14*(2), 177–193. doi:10.1016/S0925-2312(96)00031-8

Zwicker, M., Vetro, A., Yea, S., Matusik, W., Pfister, H., & Durand, F. (2007). Resampling, antialiasing, and compression in multiview 3-D displays. *IEEE Signal Processing Magazine, 24*(6), 88 96. doi:10.1109/MSP.2007.905708

# About the Contributors

**Vijay Kumar Mago** received PhD in Computer Science from Panjab University, India in 2010. In January 2011, he joined The Modelling of Complex Social Systems (MoCSSy) program, The IRMACS Centre, Simon Fraser University, Canada as postdoctoral fellow. His research interests include decision making in multi-agent environment, probabilistic networks, neural networks, and fuzzy logic based expert systems. He has served on the program committees of many international conferences and workshops. He is also associated with various international journals as reviewer and as an associate editor with *Journal of Intelligent Systems*.

**Nitin Bhatia** received his Graduation in Computer Applications in 2001, from Guru Nanak Dev University, India. He is currently working towards his PhD from Punjabi University, India. He is also working as Assistant Professor in the Department of Computer Science, DAV College, India. He has fifteen research papers to his credit and has published in *Pattern Recognition* journal and various ACM and IEEE supported conferences. His areas of interest are pattern recognition, computer vision, and fuzzy logic. He is associated with various international journals as reviewer.

\* \* \*

**Meysam Alizadeh** is now a graduate research assistant in Information Science and Technology at the University of Pittsburgh. He entered Amirkabir University of Technology in 2003, finished his B.S. in 2007 and his M.S in 2009 both in Industrial Engineering. In 2007, he began working in the area of neuro-fuzzy systems and their applications on stock market data under the supervision of Prof. Dr. Mohammad Hossein Fazel Zarandi who is a Professor at the Department of Industrial Engineering of Amirkabir University of Technology. He continued his collaboration with Prof. Fazel until 2009 in soft computing related areas when he finished his M.S., and in that year he left Iran to begin his Ph.D. Program at the University of Pittsburgh.

**Vagner Do Amaral** is currently a technical trainee of FAPESP and a M.Sc student at the Department of Electrical Engineering of Centro Universitario da FEI, São Paulo, Brazil. In 2006, he received his Information Technology degree from Termomecanica Technology College, São Paulo, Brazil. He has worked for six years as a system analyst in industry and periodically presented lectures at academic events. His general interests are in computer vision, pattern recognition and machine learning, with application particularly in face recognition problems.

**Sridhar Arjunan**, PhD'09, M.E'02, B.E'00. He received his B.E degree in Electronics communication from University of Madras, India in 2000, M.E degree in Communication systems from Madurai Kamaraj University, India in 2002, and his PhD in Biomedical signal processing in 2009 from RMIT University, Melbourne in 2009. He is currently a post doctoral research fellow with Bio signals Lab at RMIT University. He is a reviewer of *IEEE Transactions on Neural Systems and Rehabilitation Engineering* and *Journal of Medical and Biological Engineering*. He is a life member of ISTE and member of IEEE. His major research interests include biomedical signal processing, rehabilitation study, and human computer interface applications.

**Milad Avazbeigi** is a graduate student from the Department of Industrial Engineering at Amirkabir University Technology, Tehran, Iran. He finished his B.S. in 2007 and his M.S in 2010 both in Industrial Engineering. Since 2006, he has been working on the development and implementation of various aspects of soft computing and intelligent data analysis techniques such as fuzzy systems, neural network, evolutionary systems, and uncertainty theory under supervision of Prof. Dr. Mohammad Hossein Fazel Zarandi who is a Professor at the Department of Industrial Engineering of Amirkabir University of Technology. He was awarded by a scholarship for his M.S. in Amirkabir Univeristy of Technology and honored the title of a distinguished graduate by the university in 2010. In 2010, he was awarded with a grant from European Centre for Soft Computing under a one-year Master's program. He is currently doing his research in the field of "Intelligent data analysis of sensory data" under the supervision of Dr. Enrique Ruspiniin European Centre for Soft Computing.

**T. Ravindra Babu** has been working as Principal Researcher, E-Comm. Research Laboratories, Education and Research Group, Infosys for the last 2 years. He heads a team of researchers working in the area of Image Processing and Pattern Recognition. He had earlier served ISRO for over 24 years as Scientist. He did his Ph.D. and M.Sc.(Engg) from Department of Computer Science and Automation, Indian Institute of Science, Bangalore under the guidance of Prof. M. Narasimha Murty. Dr. T. Ravindra Babu was awarded Seshgiri Kaikini medal for best M.Sc.(Engg) Thesis in the Division of Electrical Sciences, Indian Institute of Science. The areas of his interest include image processing, biometrics, pattern recognition, data mining, evolutionary algorithms, large data clustering and classification; and spacecraft orbital dynamics. He has a number of international journal/conference publications and book-chapters to his credit in the above areas.

**Koushik Bakshi** has obtained his M.E. from the Department of Biomedical Engineering, Jadavpur University, Kolkata-700032, India. His major research interests lie in biomedical engineering with special emphasis on the domain of cognitive science and human-computer-interaction and biorobotics. He also takes keen interest to handle the classification and clustering problems. Currently, he is working under Prof. Amit Konar. In his leisure hours, he likes to listen to music or watch films.

**Siddhartha Bhattacharyya** did his Bachelor's in Physics, Bachelor's in Optics and Optoelectronics and Master's in Optics and Optoelectronics from University of Calcutta, India in 1995, 1998, and 2000, respectively. He completed PhD in Computer Science and Engineering from Jadavpur University, India in 2008. He is currently an Associate Professor in Information Technology of RCC Institute of Information Technology, Kolkata, India. He was a Lecturer in Computer Science and Information Technology of University Institute of Technology, The University of Burdwan, India from 2005-2011. Prior to this, he was a Lecturer in Information Technology of Kalyani Government Engineering College, India from 2001-2005. He is a co-author of a book and more than 60 research publications. He was the member of the Young Researchers' Committee of the WSC 2008 Online World Conference on Soft Computing in Industrial Applications. He was the convener of the AICTE-IEEE National Conference on Computing and Communication Systems (CoCoSys-09) in 2009. He has been the member of the organizing and technical program committees of several conferences. He is the section editor of *International Journal of Pattern Recognition Research*. He is the member of the editorial board of *International Journal of Engineering, Science and Technology* and the member of the editorial advisory board of *HETC Journal of Computer Engineering and Applications*. His research interests include soft computing, pattern recognition, and quantum computing. Dr. Bhattacharyya is a member of IEEE, IRSS, and IAENG. He is a life member of OSI and ISTE, India.

**Maria Bernadete De Morais França** received the BS degree in Electrical Engineering from the Universidade Federal de Campina Grande (UFCG), Brazil, in 1996, the MS degree in Electrical Engineering from the UFCG, Brazil, in 1998. Nowadays, she is Professor at the Electrical Engineering Department from the Universidade Estadual de Londrina.

**Pavel Bhowmik** received the B.E. degree from Department of Electronics and Telecommunication Engineering, Jadavpur University, Kolkata-700032, India. His principal research interests lie in artificial intelligence, especially evolutionary algorithms, image processing, pattern recognition, cognitive science, and human-computer-interaction. Currently, he is working under Prof. Amit Konar. Solving puzzles, collecting stamps, and watching movies at leisure hours are some of his hobbies.

**Aruna Chakraborty** received the M.A. degree in Cognitive Science and the Ph.D. degree on Emotional Intelligence and Human–Computer Interactions from Jadavpur University, Calcutta-700032, India, in 2000 and 2005, respectively. She is currently an Assistant Professor with the Department of Computer Science and Engineering, St. Thomas' College of Engineering and Technology, Calcutta. She is also a Visiting Faculty with Jadavpur University, Calcutta-700032, India, where she offers graduate-level courses on intelligent automation and robotics, and cognitive science. She, with her teacher A. Konar, has written a book on Emotional Intelligence: A Cybernetic Approach, which has appeared from Springer, Heidelberg, 2009. She serves as an Editor to the *International Journal of Artificial Intelligence and Soft Computing*, Inderscience, UK. Her current research interest includes artificial intelligence, emotion modeling, and their applications in next-generation human–machine interactive systems. She is a nature lover, and she loves music and painting.

**Sourav Chandra** has obtained his M.E. from the Department of Biomedical Engineering, Jadavpur University, Kolkata-700032, India. His principal research interests lie in biomedical engineering, particularly in the field of cognitive science and human-computer-interaction and biorobotics. He also takes strong interest to handle the neuro-motor instability. Currently, he is working under Prof. Amit Konar. In his leisure hours, he likes to listen to music and read story books.

**Shuo Chen** received the M.S. degree in Computer Science from Hangzhou Dianzi University, Hangzhou, China, in 2007. He is currently a Ph.D. student in the Department of Computer Science at New Jersey Institute of Technology. His research interests include computer vision, pattern recognition, object detection, biometrics, machine learning, and support vector machine. His present work focuses on eye detection, the development of simplified support vector machines, and the design of novel discriminatory features for biometrics.

**Graziano Chesi** received the Laurea in Information Engineering from the University of Florence in 1997 and the Ph.D. in Systems Engineering from the University of Bologna in 2001. He was with the Department of Information Engineering of the University of Siena during 2000-2006 and then he joined the Department of Electrical and Electronic Engineering of the University of Hong Kong. He served/is serving as Associate Editor for *Automatica, BMC Research Notes, the European Journal of Control,* and the *IEEE Transactions on Automatic Control.* Also, he served/is serving as Guest Editor of the *Special Issues on Positive Polynomials in Control, Systems Biology,* and *Visual Servoing* for various journals. He is the Founder and Chair of the Technical Committee on Systems with Uncertainty of the IEEE Control Systems Society. He is author of the book "Homogeneous Polynomial Forms for Robustness Analysis of Uncertain Systems" (Springer, 2009) and editor of the book "Visual Servoing via Advanced Numerical Methods" (Springer, 2010). He is first author in more than 100 technical publications.

**Erik Cuevas** received the B.S. degree with distinction in Electronics and Communications Engineering from the University of Guadalajara, Mexico in 1995, the M.Sc. degree in Industrial Electronics from ITESO, Mexico in 2000, and the Ph.D. degree from Freie Universität Berlin, Germany in 2005. From 2001 he was awarded a scholarship from the German Service for Academic Interchange (DAAD) as full-time researcher. Since 2006 he has been with University of Guadalajara, where he is currently a full-time Professor in the Department of Computer Science. From 2008, he is a member of the Mexican National Research System (SNI). His research interest includes computer vision and artificial intelligence.

**Chethan S.A. Danivas** presently works at Infosys Limited as a Principal in the Education & Research Group and contributes to research in the field of pattern recognition. He is one of the key members of the group that is performing research in the area of face recognition using advanced techniques in image processing and pattern recognition. He has completed Master of Science in Computer Science from University of Texas at Arlington, Texas, USA. He has more than 13 years of experience in software industry in various domains including medical, banking, telecom, and industrial automation. Most of his experience is in product development. His current areas of interest include pattern recognition, image processing, computer system security, databases, and algorithms.

**Sauvik Das** is currently a final year BE student of Electronics and Telecommunication Engineering Department, Jadavpur University, Kolkata-700032, India. His principal research interests lie in artificial intelligence, especially pattern recognition, cognitive science, and human-computer-interaction. Currently, he is working under Prof. Amit Konar. In his leisure hours, he likes to listen to music or watch films. He also likes to solve puzzles and riddles.

**José Alexandre De França** received the BS degree in Electrical Engineering from the Universidade Federal de Campina Grande (UFCG), Brazil, in 1995, the MS degree in Electrical Engineering from the UFCG, in 1997, the PhD degree in Electrical Engineering from the Universidade Federal de Santa Catarina, Brazil, in 2005. Nowadays, he is Professor and coordinator of the Master's degree course in Electrical Engineering at the Universidade Estadual de Londrina.

**Karakassis G. Evaggelos** received the diploma in Production Management Engineering. He is currently pursuing the Ph.D. degree in the Department of Production Management Engineering, Democritus University of Thrace in Greece. His research interest includes robotics, image processing, and computational intelligence.

**Antonios Gasteratos** is an Assistant Professor of Mechatronics and Artificial Vision at the DPME. He teaches the courses of Robotics, Automatic Control Systems, Measurements Technology, and Electronics. He holds a Diploma and a Ph.D. from the Department of Electrical and Computer Engineering, DUTH, Greece, 1994 and 1999, respectively. During 1999-2000 he was a Post-Doc Fellow at the Laboratory of Integrated Advanced Robotics (LIRA-Lab), DIST, University of Genoa, Italy. He has served as a reviewer to numerous of scientific journals and international conferences. He is the Greek Associate High Level Group (HLG) Delegate at EUREKA initiative. His research interests are mainly in mechatronics and in robot vision. He has published one textbook, 3 book chapters, and more than 90 scientific papers. He is a member of the IEEE, IAPR, ECCAI, EURASIP, and the Technical Chamber of Greece (TEE). Dr. Gasteratos is a member of EURON, euCognition and I*PROMS European networks. He organized the International Conference on Computer Vision Systems (ICVS 2008).

**Duncan Fyfe Gillies** graduated from Cambridge University with a degree in Engineering Science in 1971. He worked for three years as a Control Engineer in industry, before returning to full time study and obtaining an M.Sc. Degree in Computing from Birkbeck College London and a Ph.D. in the area of Artificial Intelligence from Queen Mary College. After teaching for six years at the Polytechnic of the South Bank, he moved to the Department of Computing at Imperial College in October 1983 where he is currently Professor of Biomedical Data Analysis. He has worked in the areas of Computer Graphics and Vision, and their applications in the medical field, and in Probabilistic Inference methods, particularly Bayesian networks and classifiers.

**Gilson Antonio Giraldi** received his B.Sc. degree in Mathematics from Pontifical Catholic University of Campinas, Sao Paulo, Brazil, M.Sc. in Applied Mathematics from State University of Campinas, Sao Paulo, Brazil, and Ph.D. degree in Computer Graphics from Federal University of Rio de Janeiro, Rio de Janeiro, Brazil, in 1986, 1993, and 2000, respectively. Since 2000 he has been with the National Laboratory for Scientific Computing, Petropolis, Brazil, where he is responsible for academic research projects in the area of image segmentation, data visualization, and fluid animation. More recently, he has worked on the application of SVM in Medical Image Analysis and on new ranking methods for principal component and discriminant analyses.

**Stathes Hadjiefthymiades** received his B.Sc., M.Sc., and Ph.D. degrees in Informatics from the Dept. of Informatics and Telecommunications, University of Athens (UoA). He also received a Joint Engineering-Economics M.Sc. from the National Technical University of Athens. In 1992 he joined the Greek consulting firm Advanced Services Group. In 1995 he joined the Communication Networks

Laboratory (CNL) of UoA. During the period 2001–2002, he served as a visiting Assistant Professor at the University of Aegean, Dept. of Information and Communication Systems Engineering. On the summer of 2002 he joined the faculty of the Hellenic Open University, Patras, Greece, as an Assistant Professor. Since December 2003, he is in the faculty of the Dept. of Informatics and Telecommunications, University of Athens, where he is presently an Assistant Professor. He has participated in numerous EU & national projects. His research interests are in the areas of Web engineering, mobile/pervasive computing and networked multimedia. He has contributed to over 100 publications in these areas. Since 2004 he co-ordinates the Pervasive Computing Research Group of CNL.

**Anisha Halder** received the B. Tech degree in Electronics and Communication Engineering from Haldia Institute of Technology, Midnapore-721657, India, and M.E. degree from Electronics and Telecommunication Engineering Department, Jadavpur University, Kolkata-700032, India in 2007 and 2009, respectively. Currently, she is pursuing her Ph.D. degree under Prof. Amit Konar, dept. of ETCE, Jadavpur University, India. Her principal research interests lie in artificial intelligence, especially pattern recognition, cognitive science, and human-computer-interaction.

**Yuexing Han** received his B.S. degree from Department of Mathematics, Mudanjiang Normal University, China, in 1998, M.S. degree from Department of Applied Mathematics, Dalian University of Technology, China, in 2003, and Ph.D degree from Graduate School of Information Systems, the University of Electro-Communications, Japan, in 2011. Now he is a postdoctor of Intelligent Systems Research Institute, National Institute of Advanced Industrial Science and Technology, Japan. His research interests include image processing, curve and surface modeling, computer vision, object recognition and robot vision. He is a member of Information Processing Society of Japan (IPSJ).

**Preethi Sheba Hepsiba** has completed her M.E. (CSE) in Karunya University, India. She had previously completed her BIT (Hons) in UNITEN, Malaysia. Currently, she is working as a Lecturer in MVJ College of Engineering in Bangalore, India. Her area of interest includes software agents, distributed systems, et cetera.

**P.S. Hiremath**, Professor and Chairman, Department of P. G. Studies and Research in Computer Science, Gulbarga University, Gulbarga-585106, Karnataka, INDIA. He has obtained M.Sc. degree in 1973 and Ph.D. degree in 1978 in Applied Mathematics from Karnatak University, Dharwad. He had been in the Faculty of Mathematics and Computer Science of various institutions in India, namely, National Institute of Technology, Surathkal (1977-79), Coimbatore Institute of Technology, Coimbatore (1979-80), National Institute of Technology, Tiruchinapalli (1980-86), Karnatak University, Dharwad (1986-1993) and has been presently working as Professor of Computer Science in Gulbarga University, Gulbarga (1993 onwards). His research areas of interest are computational fluid dynamics, optimization techniques, image processing, and pattern recognition. He has published 125 research papers in peer reviewed international journals and proceedings of international conferences.

**Pavel Holeček**, after graduating from Computer Science at the Palacký University in Olomouc in 2008, went on to study Applied Mathematics at the same university. His field of interest and also the topic of his upcoming doctoral thesis are fuzzy methods of multiple criteria evaluation. He has developed the

FuzzME software and cooperated in applying it to practical problems, e.g. the soft-fact rating problem described in this chapter. Based on the needs that had arisen from these applications, he also developed several new algorithms, e.g. a new inference method. Currently, he is working on an Information System for the academic staff performance evaluation.

**Y. S. Hung** received his B.Sc. (Eng) in Electrical Engineering and B.Sc. in Mathematics, both from the University of Hong Kong, and his M.Phil. and Ph.D. degrees from the University of Cambridge. He has worked at the University of Cambridge and the University of Surrey before he joined the University of Hong Kong, where he is now a Professor at the Department of Electrical and Electronic Engineering. He has authored and co-authored over 180 publications in books, journals, and conferences. His research interests include control systems, robotics, computer vision, and biomedical engineering.

**Masanori Idesawa** got his B.S degree from Yokohama National University, Japan, in 1968 and PhD of Engineering from Graduate School of the University of Tokyo, Japan, in 1973. He was with the Institute of Physical and Chemical Research (Riken), Information Science Laboratory, Japan from 1973 to 1993. He was a Professor of the Graduate School of Information Systems, University of Electro-Communications. Currently he is a Professor Emeritus and belongs to the UEC Museum of Communications. His primary research includes human interface, human vision system, visual illusion, optical sensors, robotic sensors, 3D measuring system, and mechatronics. He is a member of SPIE, IEEE, JSAP, JSME, IPSJ, SICE, INNS, JNNS, and RSJ.

**Y. Humnabad Iranna**, System Analyst, University Computer Centre, Gulbarga University, Gulbarga - 585106, Karnataka, India. He has obtained M.Sc. degree in 1989 in Physics, PGDCA degree in 1990, MCA degree in 2002, M.Phil degree in Computer Science in 2003, and Ph.D. degree in Computer Science in 2007. He had been in the Faculty of Computer Science in various institutions namely, Karnatak Arts, Science and Commerce College, Bidar, Karnataka State, India (1991-1993), Sharanabasaveshwar Science College, Gulbarga, Karnataka State, India (1993-1994), and has been presently working as System Analyst in Gulbarga University, Gulbarga (1994 onwards). His research areas of interest are image processing and pattern recognition.

**E. Grace Mary Kanaga** received her Bachelor of Engineering degree in Computer Science and Engineering in 1997 from Madras University and her Master of Technology degree with Distinction in Computer Science and Engineering from Vellore Institute of Technology, India in 2002. She started her career as Lecturer in Priyadharshini Engineering College in the year 1997. After six months she joined as a Lecturer in Ramakrishna Engineering College in 1998. She is working in Karunya University, Coimbatore, India since 2002 and currently working as an Assistant Professor (SG) in the Department of Computer Science and Engineering and pursuing her research work in the area of software agents. She has guided number of UG and PG projects. She has published number of papers in national and international conferences and in international journals.

**Arun Khosla** is presently working as Associate Professor in the Department of Electronics and Communication Engineering, Dr. B R Ambedkar National Institute of Technology, Jalandhar. India. His areas of interest are fuzzy modeling, biologically inspired computing, and high performance computing. He is a reviewer for various IEEE and other national and international conferences and journals. He also serves on the editorial board of *International Journal of Swarm Intelligence Research*. He has conducted a number of tutorials in the domain of soft computing at various national & international conferences.

**Mamta Khosla** is presently working as Associate Professor in the Department of Electronics and Communication Engineering, National Institute of Technology, Jalandhar. India. Her areas of interest are digital design and realization of intelligent systems. She received her Bachelor of Technology from National Institute of Technology, Kurukshetra, Haryana (India) with specialization in Electronics & Communication Engineering and Master of Technology from Punjab Technical University, Jalandhar with distinction in Electronics & Communication Engineering. Her name has been inscribed in Academic Roll of Honour of Guru Harkrishan Educational Society, Chandigarh for securing first position in Punjab Technical University, Jalandhar in Master of Technology.

**Edson Caoru Kitani** is an Assistant Professor at FATEC, Santo Andre, Sao Paulo, Brazil, and head of the Machine Design Engineering Department at Mahle. He received his undergraduate degree in Industrial Automation Engineering Technology from Centro Universitario de Santo Andre in 2003, and the professional degree in Fine Mechanics from Universidade Sao Judas Tadeu in 2005. In 2007, he obtained his M.Sc. degree in Electrical Engineering from Centro Universitario da FEI, Sao Paulo, Brazil. Currently, he is a Ph.D. student in Neurocomputing at University of Sao Paulo, Sao Paulo, Brazil. His research area and general interests are in artificial neural networks, neuroscience, computational intelligence, statistical pattern recognition, and machine learning.

**Hideki Koike** received his BS degree in Mechanical Engineering from the University of Tokyo, Japan, in 1986. He got his MS and Dr. of Eng., degrees in Information Engineering from the University of Tokyo in 1988 and 1991, respectively. Now, he is a Professor at the Graduate School of Information Systems, University of Electro-Communications, Tokyo, Japan. His research interests include information visualization and vision-based human-computer interaction. He is a member of the IEEE/CS and ACM.

**Kostas Kolomvatsos** received his B.Sc. in Informatics from the Department of Informatics at the Athens University of Economics and Business in 1995 and his M.Sc. in Computer Science - New Technologies in Informatics and Telecommunications from the Department of Informatics and Telecommunications at the National and Kapodistrian University of Athens (UoA) in 2005. He is now a Ph.D. candidate in the National and Kapodistrian University of Athens – Department of Informatics and Telecommunications under the supervision of Assistant Professor Stathes Hadjiefthymiades. His research interests are in the areas of Semantic Web technologies, ontological engineering, agent technologies, and pervasive computing.

**Amit Konar** obtained his B.E. degree from Bengal Engineering and Science University, Howrah, India, in 1983 and the M.E.Tel.E., M.Phil., and Ph.D. (Engineering) from Jadavpur University, in 1985, 1988, and 1994, respectively. He is a Professor in the Electronics and Tele-communication Engineering Department, Jadavpur University. He has around 300 publications in international journal and conference proceedings. He is the author of seven books, including two most popular texts: Artificial Intelligence and Soft Computing, from CRC Press in 2000 and Computational Intelligence: Principles, Techniques and

Applications from Springer in 2005. His research areas include the study of computational intelligence algorithms and their applications to the complete domain of electrical engineering, computer science and cognitive science. He received the All India Council for Technical Education-accredited 1997–2000 Career Award for Young Teachers. Dr. Konar serves as the Editor-in-Chief of the *International Journal of Artificial Intelligence and Soft Computing* from Inderscience, U.K., and he is also the member of the editorial board of 5 other international journals. Furthermore he is serving the editorial board of *IEEE Trans. on Systems, Man, and Cybernetics* as an Associate Editor.

**Dimitrios E. Koulouriotis** received his PhD in Intelligent Systems from Department of Production and Management Engineering, Technical University of Crete, Greece, in 2001. He received the Diploma in Electrical and Computer Engineering at the Democritus University of Thrace and the M.S. in Electronic and Computer Engineering at the Technical University of Crete, in 1993 and 1996, respectively. He is currently in the Department of Production and Management Engineering, Democritus University of Thrace, as an Associate Professor. His research interests include computational intelligence, machine learning, and pattern recognition and their applications in vision, image, and signal processing, robotics, and production engineering. He has published over 150 research papers, and he served as reviewer in numerous conferences and journals.

**Rigas Kouskouridas** received the Diploma degree from the Democritus University of Thrace, Xanthi, Greece, in 2006. He is currently working towards the Ph.D. degree with the Laboratory of Robotics and Automation, Department of Production and Management Engineering, Democritus University of Thrace. His areas of interest include object recognition, machine learning, multi camera systems, and robotics. He is involved in several national (Greek) and international (European) research projects in the field of machine vision systems. Mr. Kouskouridas is a member of the IEEE, euCognition II, the Technical Chamber of Greece (TEE), and the National Union of Production and Management Engineers.

**Dinesh Kant Kumar** received the BE degree in Electrical Engineering from the Indian Institute of Technology (IIT) Madras, India, in 1982, and the PhD degree from IIT, Delhi, India, in 1990. He has worked in the engineering industry for over ten years in various capacities. Since 1996, he has been an Academic with RMIT University, Melbourne, Australia. His research interests include iterative signal processing, computer vision, and intelligent systems for application such as biometrics, human computer interface, and helping the disabled. He is an Associate Editor for *IEEE Transactions on Neural Systems and Rehabilitation Engineering*.

**Dong-Kyu Lee** was born in Seoul, Korea, in 1984. He received the B.S. degree in electronic engineering from Sogang University in 2010. Currently he is working toward the M.S. degree in electronic engineering from Sogang University. He is a Student Member of the IEEE. His current research interests are computer vision, image processing, and image enhancement.

**Jong-Soo Lee** received his BS in Electrical Engineering in 1973 from Seoul National University, Korea and his M.Eng in 1981 and Ph.D. in 1985 from Virginia Polytechnic Institute and State University, USA. He is currently working in the area of multimedia at the University of Ulsan, Korea.

**Artem A. Lenskiy** received the BS degree in Computer and Information Science and the MS degree in Digital Signal Processing and Data Mining from Novosibirsk State Technical University (NSTU), Russia. He received the PhD degree in Electrical Engineering from University of Ulsan, Korea in 2010. Prior coming to Korea in 2005, he was a Lecturer and a head of IT laboratory at NSTU. His current research interests include computer vision, machine learning algorithms, and self-similar random processes.

**Chengjun Liu** received the PhD from George Mason University in 1999, and he is presently an Associate Professor of Computer Science and the Director of the Face Recognition and Video Processing Lab at New Jersey Institute of Technology. His research interests are in pattern recognition (face/iris recognition, colour image feature extraction and classification, classifier fusion), machine learning (statistical learning, Kernel methods, innovative Kernel functions/models, similarity measures), computer vision (object/face detection, video processing), image processing (image search and retrieval, image category classification, new colour spaces, gabor image representation), and security (biometrics).

**Abhijit Mitra** received the Ph.D. degree from IIT Kharagpur in 2004. Since 2004, he has been with the Department of ECE, IIT Guwahati as a faculty member where he is presently an Associate Professor. His areas of interest include adaptive signal processing and wireless communication, with a special emphasis on low power realization of these. He has around 100 journal and conference publications in these fields including a book on Mobile Communication. In the year 2008, he received the URSI Young Scientist Award (Chicago, USA) as well as was elected as an Associate of the Indian Academy of Sciences. In the year 2010, apart from being elected as a Fellow of IETE (India) and a Senior Member of IEEE (USA), he also received the prestigious IETE N V Gadadhar Memorial Gold Medal for his outstanding contribution in low power mobile communication. Dr. Mitra serves as an Associate Editor of the 'Recent Patents in Electrical Engineering' (Bentham Science, USA) since 2007.

**Prachi Mukherji** is working as Professor with the Department of Electronics and Telecommunication, Smt. Kashibai Navale College of Engineering, Pune, India. She received her B.E. from Madhav institute of Technology and Science, Gwalior and M.Tech. from MACT(NIT) Bhopal in 1994. She completed her PhD in Optical Character Recognition of Devnagari Script under Pune University.

**Ivo Müller** is Senior Lecturer at the Palacký University Faculty of Science, Olomouc, Czech Republic. He received his education at Charles University in Prague in the areas of probability and statistics, psychology, and translatology. His mathematical interests cover multivariate statistics, robust and nonparametric methods. Recently he has joined forces with his colleagues to tackle both theoretical and practical problems in multiple-criteria evaluation and decision making via fuzzy methods.

**Ganesh R. Naik** received B.E. degree in Electronics and Communication Engineering from the University of Mysore, Mysore, India, in 1997, M.E. degree in Communication and Information Engineering from Griffith University, Brisbane, Australia, in 2002, and Ph.D. degree in the area of Digital Signal Processing from RMIT University, Melbourne, Australia, in 2009. He is currently an academician and researcher at RMIT University. As an early career researcher, he has authored more than 60 papers in peer reviewed journals, conferences, and book chapters over the last five years. His research interests include pattern recognition, blind source separation techniques, audio signal processing, biosignal processing, and human–computer interface. Dr. Naik was the Chair for the IEEE Computer Society CIT08 Conference, Sydney and a member of the organising committee for IEEE BRC2011 conference, Vitoria, Brazil. He is a recipient of the Baden–Württemberg Scholarship from the University of Berufsakademie, Stuttgart, Germany (2006–2007).

**Rodrigo Henrique Cunha Palácios** received the BS degree in Computer Engineering from the Universidade Norte do Paraná, Brazil, in 2002, the MS degree in Electrical Engineering from the Universidade Estadual de Londrina (UEL), Brazil, in 2010. Nowadays, he is Professor at the Computer Engineering Department from the Universidade Tecnológica Federal do Paraná (UTFPR), Campus Cornélio Procópio.

**Elpiniki Papageorgiou** received her B.Sc. degree in Physics in 1997 from the University of Patras, Greece. In July 2000, she received her M.Sc. degree in Medical Physics with honors from the University of Patras and in September 2004 her Ph.D. degree in Computer Science from the Dept. of Electrical and Computer Engineering, from the same University. She is Lecturer at the Dept. of Informatics and Computer Technology of the Technological Education Institute of Lamia, Greece, and adjunct Assistant Professor at Dept. of Informatics with applications in Biomedicine at the University of Central Greece. She has been actively involved in several research projects, European, and National R&D, related with the development of new methodologies based on soft computing and artificial intelligence techniques for complex diagnostic and decision support systems in medicine and engineering. She is author and co-author of more than 70 journals, conference papers, and book chapters, and she has more than 285 citations from independent researchers. She is also a reviewer in many international journals. Her research interests include expert systems, fuzzy cognitive maps, soft computing methods, decision support systems, artificial intelligent algorithms, machine learning, and data mining algorithms.

**George A. Papakostas** received the diploma of Electrical and Computer in Engineering in 1999 and the M.Sc. and PhD Degree in Electrical and Computer Engineering (in Feature Extraction and Pattern Recognition) in 2002 and 2007, respectively, from Democritus University of Thrace (DUTH) in Greece. He is the author of 45 publications in international scientific journals, conferences, and book chapters. His research interests are focused in the field of pattern recognition, computer vision, robotics, neural networks, computational intelligence, feature extraction, optimisation, and signal and image processing. Dr. Papakostas served as reviewer in numerous conferences and journals, and he is a member of several scientific groups.

**Rae-Hong Park** was born in Seoul, Korea, in 1954. He received the B.S. and M.S. degrees in Electronics Engineering from Seoul National University, Seoul, Korea, in 1976 and 1979, respectively, and the M.S. and Ph.D. degrees in Electrical Engineering from Stanford University, Stanford, CA, in 1981 and 1984, respectively. In 1984, he joined the faculty of the Department of Electronic Engineering, School of Engineering, Sogang University, Seoul, Korea, where he is currently a Professor. In 1990, he spent his sabbatical year as a Visiting Associate Professor with the Computer Vision Laboratory, University of Maryland at College Park. Dr. Park was the recipient of a 1990 Post-Doctoral Fellowship (KOSEF), the 1987 Academic Award (KITE), and the 2000 Haedong Paper Award (IEEK), the 1997 First Sogang Academic Award, and the 1999 Professor Achievement Excellence Award presented by Sogang University. He is a Senior Member of the IEEE. His current research interests are computer vision, video communication, and pattern recognition.

**Sung Hee Park** received the B.S. degree in Electrical Engineering from Seoul National University in 2007, and his M.S. degree in Electrical Engineering from Stanford University in 2010. He is currently a PhD student in Computer Graphics Laboratory at Stanford University. His current research interest includes computational photography, image processing, and developing an open source camera platform for computational photography.

**Marco Pérez-Cisneros** received the B.S. degree with distinction in Electronics and Communications Engineering from the University of Guadalajara, Mexico in 1995, the M.Sc. degree in Industrial Electronics from ITESO University, Mexico in 2000, and the Ph.D. degree from the Control Systems Centre, UMIST, Manchester, UK in 2004. Since 2005 he has been with University of Guadalajara, where he is currently a Professor and Head of Department of Computer Science. Since 2007 he has spent yearly spells at the University of Manchester as an invited honorary Professor. He is a member of the Mexican National Research System (SNI) from 2007. His current research interest includes robotics and computer vision in particular visual servoing applications on humanoid walking control.

**C.J. Prabhakar** is an Assistant Professor, Department of Studies in Computer Science, Kuvempu University, Shankaraghatta-577451, Karnataka, India. He has obtained M.Sc., degree in Mathematics from Kuvempu University, in 1998 and the M.Tech. degree in Computer Science from University of Mysore, in 2001. He has received the Ph.D. degree in Computer Science in the year 2009 from Department of Computer Science, Gulbarga University, India. His research interests include 3D reconstruction, stereo vision, and face recognition.

**Rakesh Kumar Sarin** was born on September 5, 1955 in New Delhi, India. He did his BSc (Engg) ECE, from NIT–Kurukshetra in 1978, ME (ECE) from IIT-Roorkee in 1980 and PhD from A F Ioffe Physico Technical Institute-St Petersburg (Russia) in 1987. He has interests in semiconductors, optoelectronics, microelectronics/VLSI, microwaves, and RF and has published papers in these areas. He had worked at IIT-Kharagpur and at SAMEER in India and at University of Sheffield in the UK, after completing his PhD. Presently he is a Professor in the Department of Electronics and Communication Engineering and also Dean (Academic Programmes) at NIT-Jalandhar. He has contributed to the engineering education and educational management in the region of his Institute. He has been instrumental in introducing new courses in the field of electronics at the Institute and also took the initiative of starting M Tech and PhD programmes in the ECE Department of the Institute. Dr. Sarin is coordinator of VLSI Project -SMDP II- at NIT Jalandhar. He is member of IEEE and Fellow of IETE.

**Marcelo Ricardo Stemmer** received the BS degree in Electrical Engineering from the Universidade Federal de Santa Catarina (UFSC), Brazil, in1982, the MS degree in Electrical Engineering from the same university in 1985, and the PhD degree in Industrial Automation from WZL/RWTH-Aachen, Germany, in 1991. Nowadays, he is a Professor and leader of the Intelligent Industrial Systems research group at the Automation and Systems Department from the Universidade Federal de Santa Catarina.

**Jan Stoklasa** studied Applied Mathematics in Disaster Management at Silesian University in Opava, Applied Mathematics in Economy at Palacky University in Olomouc, and currently is studying Applied Mathematics (in a Ph.D. programme) and Psychology at Palacky University in Olomouc. His professional interests include applications of mathematics in disaster management, focused mainly on the medical rescue services. Other areas of interest and research focus include multiple criteria decision making and evaluation, fuzzy modelling, and applications of fuzzy methods in medicine and psychology. He also conducts research concerning application of mathematics in human resources management.

**Priti P. Rege** received her B.E (Bachelor in Engineering) with distinction in 1983 and M.E degree with Gold medal in 1985, both from Devi Ahilya University of Indore, India. She received her Doctoral degree from Pune University, India. She is a Professor at College of Engineering, Pune. Currently, she is also working as Dean of Student Affairs at the same Institute. She has authored/co-authored over 70 research publications in peer-reviewed journals and conference proceedings. Her research interests include digital watermarking, texture analysis, optical character recognition, document enhancement, and 3-D volume rendering. She has contributed in research projects funded by government and industries.

**Kandarpa Kumar Sarma** received the M.Tech. degree from IIT Guwahati in 2005. Presently, he is a research scholar at the Department of ECE, IIT Guwahati as well as serves Gauhati University as an Assistant Professor. His areas of interest include document image analysis, pattern recognition, artificial neural networks, and their application in mobile communication. He is a member of IEEE (USA) and IETE (India) and he has published 2 books in the area of practical electronic circuit design and mathematical concepts with Matlab.

**João Ricardo Sato** obtained his undergraduate, M.Sc. and Ph.D. degrees in Statistics from the Institute of Mathematics and Statistics, University of Sao Paulo, Brazil. Since 2009 he has been a Lecturer and researcher at the Center of Mathematics, Computation and Cognition, Universidade Federal do ABC, Brazil. His main research is focused on interdisciplinary fields such as quantitative methods in neuroscience, computational neuroscience, econometrics, biological signals processing, and biostatistics.

**Deepak Sharma** received his Master's in Electronics & Communication Engg. from M.M.University, Mullana (Ambala), India in 2009 and his Bachelor's degree in Electronics & Instrumentation Engg. from Kurukshetra University, Kurukshetra, India in 2005. At present he is Lecturer in the Department of Electronics & Instrumentation Engg., M.M. University, Mullana, Ambala, India. His research interests include signal processing and image processing.

**Satvir Singh** was born on Dec 7, 1975. He received his Bachelor of Technology from Dr B R Ambedkar National Institute of Technology, Jalandhar, Punjab (India) with specialization in Electronics & Communication Engineering in 1998 and Master of Engineering from Delhi College of Engineering, Delhi (India) with distinction in Electronics & Communication Engineering in 2000. He is life member of Indian Society of Technical Education, New Delhi and Institution of Electronics and Telecommunication Engineers, New Delhi. His teaching experience as Assistant Professor is nearly 10 years. Presently, he is Head of Department, Electronics & Communication Engineering, SBS College of Engineering & Technology, Ferozepur (Punjab) India. His fields of special interest include swarm intelligence, type-1 and type-2 fuzzy logic systems, and their applications.

**H.P. Sinha** received his Bachelor's degree in Electronics & Communication Engg. from Ranchi University, India in 1965, Master's in Electronics & Communication Engg. from IIT, Roorkee, India in 1974 and Ph.D. (Bio-Medical Engg.) from Bihar University in 1986. He has teaching experience of more than 34 years at under Graduate and Post Graduate Level, both in India and abroad. At present he is Associate Director of M.M. Engg. College and Professor and Head in the Department of Electronics & Communication Engg, M.M. University, Mullana, Ambala, India. He has worked as Director, School of Technology, KIIT University, Bhubaneshwar and Programme Director & Executive Secretary of Indian Society for Technical Education, New Delhi. He is the member of many professional societies, i.e. Institutions of Electronics & Tele Communication Engineers, Institutions of Engineers (India) & Indian Society for Technical Education. His research interests include bio-medicine and communication. He has a number of international journal and conference publications to his credit. He has guided many M.Tech. theses, and students are also pursuing Ph.D. under his guidance.

**S. V. Subrahmanya** did his M. Tech from IIT Kharagpur. Currently he is working at Infosys Limited as Vice-President, Research Fellow and Head of E-Commerce Research Lab, Education and Research Group. He has authored more than 20 papers that are published in journals, international conferences, and book-chapters. He co-authored 3 books, titled, "Web Services," published by Tata McGraw-Hill (2004), "J2EE Architecture," published by Tata McGraw-Hill (2005), and "Enterprise Architecture," published by Wiley (2006). He was one granted patent from US PTO. His areas of interest include software architecture, mathematical modelling, and data and information management.

**Jana Talašová** is Associate Professor of Applied Mathematics at Faculty of Science of Palacký University in Olomouc, Czech Republic. In research she focuses on the theory and methods of multiple-criteria evaluation, and on fuzzy sets and their applications. She has developed an original theoretical concept of fuzzy evaluation, which serves as a basis for a system of fuzzy methods intended to solve a wide range of problems in multiple-criteria evaluation. She has participated in development of several software packages designed for decision-making support (support to innovation management in engineering industry, support to decision making for credit granting in banking industry). Lately she has specialized in developing mathematical models of evaluation in the area of university management (the model of performance evaluation of academic staff, the model of output evaluation of creative work at Faculties of Fine Arts).

**Carlos Eduardo Thomaz** is an Associate Professor at the Department of Electrical Engineering, Centro Universitario da FEI, Sao Paulo, Brazil. In 1993, he received his B.Sc. degree in Electronic Engineering from Pontifical Catholic University of Rio de Janeiro (PUC-RJ), Rio de Janeiro, Brazil. After working for six years in industry, he obtained the M.Sc. degree in Electrical Engineering from PUC-RJ in 1999. In October 2000, he joined the Department of Computing at Imperial College London where he obtained the Ph.D. degree in Statistical Pattern Recognition in 2004. He was a Research Associate at the Department of Computing, Imperial College London, from December 2003 to January 2005 working in the UK EPSRC e-science project called Information eXtraction from Images (IXI). His general interests are in computer vision, statistical pattern recognition, medical image computing, and machine learning, whereas his specific research interests are in limited-sample-size problems in pattern recognition.

**D.N. Tibarewala** is presently a Professor of Biomedical Engineering and Director in the School of Bioscience & Engineering at Jadavpur University, Kolkata, India. Born in December 1951, he did his B.Sc. (Honours) in 1971, and B. Tech (Applied Physics) in 1974 from the Calcutta University, India. He obtained his Ph.D. (Tech) degree of the same University in 1980. Having professional, academic, and research experience of more than 30 years, Dr. Tibarewala has contributed about 100 research papers in the areas of rehabilitation technology, biomedical instrumentation, and related branches of biomedical engineering.

**Moin Uddin** is currently serving as Pro Vice-Chancellor of Delhi Technological University, Delhi. Prior to this he was Director of Dr. B R Ambedkar National Institute of Technology, Jalandhar. He has over thirty years of teaching and research experience. Twelve research scholars have completed their PhD under his guidance and seven more are pursuing the same. He has designed the computer engineering curriculum of many international and national universities and is on expert panel of various universities and institutions. He is Senior Member, IEEE and life member, ISTE national society and member, board of studies of many institutions. He has completed several projects under Ministry of Human Resource Development and All India Council for Technical Education, Govt. of India.

**M. L. Valarmathi** received the B.E degree from Madurai Kamraj University and M.E degree from Bharathiar University, Tamilnadu, India in 1983 and 1990, respectively, and PhD degree from the Bharathiar University, Coimbatore, India, in 2007. She is currently Assistant Professor, in the Department of Computer Science & Engineering, Government College of Technology, Coimbatore, Tamilnadu, India. Before joining Government College of Technology, Professor Valarmathi has been a Lecturer in Allagappa Chettiyar College of Technology, Karaikudi, Tamilnadu, India. Her research interests include theory and practical issues of building distributed systems, Internet computing and security, mobile computing, performance evaluation and fault tolerant computing, image processing, and optimization techniques. She is a member of the ISTE. Professor Valarmathi has published more than 30 papers in refereed international journals and refereed international conferences proceedings.

**Abhishek Verma** received the Master of Computer Applications (MCA) Degree from Bangalore University, Bangalore, India, in 2003, and the MS in Computer Science from New Jersey Institute of Technology, NJ, USA, in 2006. He is currently working towards the PhD Degree in Computer Science at New Jersey Institute of Technology. His research interests include object and scene classification, pattern recognition, content-based image retrieval systems, image processing, and iris recognition.

**Ekta Walia** received her Bachelor's degree in Computer Science from Kurukshetra University, India in 1995 and Master's in Computer Applications, as well as Ph.D. (Computer Science) from Punjabi University, Patiala, India in 1998 and 2006, respectively. She started her professional career as a Software Consultant with DCM Data Systems, New Delhi where she was actively involved in development of database applications like medical transcription system and scheduling system. Later, she served as Lecturer and Senior Lecturer in the National Institute of Technical Teachers Training and Research (NITTTR), Chandigarh, India for approximately 7 years. Later she worked as Reader in the Department of Computer Science, Punjabi University, Patiala, India. At present she is Professor and Head in the Department of Information Technology, M.M. University, Mullana, Ambala, India. Her academic achievements include University Gold medal in Graduation as well as in Post Graduation. She is the author of two textbooks.

Her research interests include computer graphics, databases, and image processing. She has a number of international journal and conference publications to her credit. She was sponsored by DST to attend an IEEE sponsored conference held at University of London in 2006. She has guided many M.Tech. theses, and students are also pursuing Ph.D. under her guidance. She is reviewer of a reputed annual international conference of Europe.

**Bing Wang** got her Ph.D degree from Department of Applied Mathematics, Dalian University of Technology, China, in 2006. She worked as a Postdoc in Sungkyunkwan University, Korean, from 2006 to 2007. She also joined Aihara Complexity Modelling Project, JST as a Postdoc during 2007~2009. Now she is doing research under the support of JSPS Fellows. Her present research is about epidemic spread of networks. Her research interests also include complex system, network robustness, community detection algorithm on networks, and image processing.

**Hans Weghorn** is currently the Head of Mechatronics department in the BW Cooperative State University, Stuttgart, Germany. For the past 10 years, he has also been the head of different examination boards. He was also the Head of Department in Information Technology for the past 8 years. He is involved in various on-going international research exchange programs. His expertise is based on a Physics study for which he has been awarded a Ph.D. He has several years of experience in telecommunications industry in various leading positions.

**Sang-Myoung Ye** was born in Seoul, Korea, in 1980. He received the B.S. and M.S. degrees in Electronic Engineering from Sogang University, Seoul, Korea, in 2006 and 2008, respectively. He is currently working in Visual Display division, Samsung Electronics Co., Ltd. His current research interests are computer vision, LED back light unit in LED TV, and future TV.

**Daniel Zaldivar** received the B.S. degree with distinction in Electronics and Communications Engineering from the University of Guadalajara, Mexico in 1995, the M.Sc. degree in Industrial Electronics from ITESO, Mexico in 2000, and the Ph.D. degree from Freie Universität Berlin, Germany in 2005. From 2001 he was awarded a scholarship from the German Service for Academic Interchange (DAAD) as full-time researcher. Since 2006 he has been with University of Guadalajara, where he is currently a Professor in the Department of Computer Science. Since 2008, he has been a member of the Mexican National Research System (SNI). His current research interest includes biped robots design, humanoid walking control, and artificial vision.

**Mohammad Hossein Fazel Zarandi** is a Professor at Department of Industrial Engineering of Amirkabir University of Technology, Tehran, Iran, and a member of Knowledge-Information Systems Lab of University of Toronto, Toronto, Ontario, Canada. His main research interests focus on intelligent Information Systems, soft computing, computational intelligent, fuzzy sets and systems, multi-agent systems, networks, meta-heuristics, and optimization. Professor Fazel Zarandi has lots of books, scientific papers, and technical reports in the above areas, most of them are accessible on the Web. He has taught several courses in Fuzzy Systems Engineering, Decision Support Systems, Management Information Systems, Artificial Intelligence and Expert Systems, Systems Analysis and Design, Scheduling, Neural Networks, Simulations, and Production Planning and Control, in several universities in Iran and North America.

# Index

# T

# U

# V

# W

# Z